Short Story Criticism

Guide to Gale Literary Criticism Series

For criticism on	Consult these Gale series
Authors now living or who died after December 31, 1959	*CONTEMPORARY LITERARY CRITICISM (CLC)*
Authors who died between 1900 and 1959	*TWENTIETH-CENTURY LITERARY CRITICISM (TCLC)*
Authors who died between 1800 and 1899	*NINETEENTH-CENTURY LITERATURE CRITICISM (NCLC)*
Authors who died between 1400 and 1799	*LITERATURE CRITICISM FROM 1400 TO 1800 (LC)* *SHAKESPEAREAN CRITICISM (SC)*
Authors who died before 1400	*CLASSICAL AND MEDIEVAL LITERATURE CRITICISM (CMLC)*
Black writers of the past two hundred years	*BLACK LITERATURE CRITICISM (BLC)*
Authors of books for children and young adults	*CHILDREN'S LITERATURE REVIEW (CLR)*
Dramatists	*DRAMA CRITICISM (DC)*
Hispanic writers of the late nineteenth and twentieth centuries	*HISPANIC LITERATURE CRITICISM (HLC)*
Native North American writers and orators of the eighteenth, nineteenth, and twentieth centuries	*NATIVE NORTH AMERICAN LITERATURE (NNAL)*
Poets	*POETRY CRITICISM (PC)*
Short story writers	*SHORT STORY CRITICISM (SSC)*
Major authors from the Renaissance to the present	*WORLD LITERATURE CRITICISM, 1500 TO THE PRESENT (WLC)*

Volume 22

Short Story Criticism

Excerpts from Criticism of the
Works of Short Fiction Writers

Margaret Haerens, Editor

Jeff Hill
Drew Kalasky
Julie Karmazin
Marie Rose Napierkowski
Mary K. Ruby
Christine Slovey
Lawrence J. Trudeau
Associate Editors

GALE

DETROIT · NEW YORK · TORONTO · LONDON

STAFF

Margaret Haerens, *Editor*

Jeff Hill, Drew Kalasky, Mary K. Ruby,
Christine Slovey, Lawrence J. Trudeau,
Associate Editors

Debra A. Wells, *Assistant Editor*

Marlene S. Hurst, *Permissions Manager*
Margaret A. Chamberlain, Maria Franklin, *Permissions Specialists*

Susan Brohman, Diane Cooper, Michele Lonoconus, Maureen Puhl,
Shalice Shah, Kimberly F. Smilay, Barbara A. Wallace, *Permissions Associates*

Sarah Chesney, Edna Hedblad, Margaret McAvoy-Amato, Tyra Y. Phillips,
Lori Schoenenberger, Rita Velazquez, *Permissions Assistants*

Victoria B. Cariappa, *Research Manager*

Julia C. Daniel, Tamara C. Nott, Michele P. Pica, Tracie A. Richardson,
Norma Sawaya, Cheryl L. Warnock, *Research Associates*

Mary Beth Trimper, *Production Director*
Deborah L. Milliken, *Production Assistant*

C. J. Jonik, *Desktop Publisher*
Randy Bassett, *Image Database Supervisor*
Robert Duncan, *Scanner Operator*
Pamela Hayes, *Photography Coordinator*

Margaret Haerens, Jeff Hill, Drew Kalasky, Michael L. Lablanc,
Christine Slovey, Lawrence J. Trudeau, *Desktop Typesetters*

Library of Congress Catalog Card Number 88-641014
ISBN 0-7876-0754-1
ISSN 0895-9439

Printed in the United States of America
10 9 8 7 6 5 4 3 2 1

Contents

Preface   vii

Acknowledgments   xi

Preface

A Comprehensive Information Source
on World Short Fiction

*S*hort Story Criticism (SSC) presents significant passages from criticism of the world's greatest short story writers and provides supplementary biographical and bibliographical materials to guide the interested reader to a greater understanding of the authors of short fiction. This series was developed in response to suggestions from librarians serving high school, college, and public library patrons, who had noted a considerable number of requests for critical material on short story writers. Although major short story writers are covered in such Gale series as *Contemporary Literary Criticism (CLC), Twentieth-Century Literary Criticism (TCLC), Nineteenth-Century Literature Criticism (NCLC),* and *Literature Criticism from 1400 to 1800 (LC),* librarians perceived the need for a series devoted solely to writers of the short story genre.

Coverage

SSC is designed to serve as an introduction to major short story writers of all eras and nationalities. Since these authors have inspired a great deal of relevant critical material, *SSC* is necessarily selective, and the editors have chosen the most important published criticism to aid readers and students in their research.

Approximately eight to ten authors are included in each volume, and each entry presents a historical survey of the critical response to that author's work. The length of an entry is intended to reflect the amount of critical attention the author has received from critics writing in English and from foreign critics in translation. Every attempt has been made to identify and include excerpts from the most significant essays on each author's work. In order to provide these important critical pieces, the editors sometimes reprint essays that have appeared elsewhere in Gale's Literary Criticism Series. Such duplication, however, never exceeds twenty percent of an *SSC* volume.

Organization

An *SSC* author entry consists of the following elements:

- The **Author Heading** cites the name under which the author most commonly wrote, followed by birth and death dates. If the author wrote consistently under a pseudonym, the pseudonym will be listed in the author heading and the author's actual name given in parentheses on the first line of the biographical and critical introduction.

- The **Biographical and Critical Introduction** contains background information designed to introduce a reader to the author and the critical debates surrounding his or her work.

- A **Portrait of the Author** is included when available. Many entries also contain illustrations of materials pertinent to an author's career, including holographs of manuscript pages, title pages, dust jackets, letters, or representations of important people, places, and events in the author's life.

- The list of **Principal Works** is chronological by date of first publication and lists the most important works by the author. The first section comprises short story collections, novellas, and novella collections. The second section gives information on other major works by the author. For foreign authors, the editors have provided original foreign-language publication information and have selected what are considered the best and most complete English-language editions of their works.

- **Criticism** is arranged chronologically in each author entry to provide a useful perspective on changes in critical evaluation over the years. All short story, novella, and collection titles by the author featured in the entry are printed in boldface type to enable a reader to ascertain without difficulty the works discussed. Also for purposes of easier identification, the critic's name and the publication date of the essay are given at the beginning of each piece of criticism. Unsigned criticism is preceded by the title of the journal in which it appeared.

- Critical essays are prefaced with **Explanatory Notes** as an additional aid to students and readers using *SSC*. An explanatory note may provide useful information of several types, including: the reputation of the critic, the intent or scope of the critical essay, and the orientation of the criticism (biographical, psychoanalytic, structuralist, etc.).

- A complete **Bibliographical Citation,** designed to help the interested reader locate the original essay or book, precedes each piece of criticism.

- The **Further Reading List** appearing at the end of each author entry suggests additional materials on the author. In some cases it includes essays for which the editors could not obtain reprint rights. Boxed material following the further reading list provides references to other biographical and critical sources on the author in series published by Gale.

Beginning with volume six, *SSC* contains two additional features designed to enhance the reader's understanding of short fiction writers and their works:

- Each *SSC* entry now includes, when available, **Comments by the Author** that illuminate his or her own works or the short story genre in general. These statements are set within boxes or bold rules to distinguish them from the criticism.

- A **Select Bibliography of General Sources on Short Fiction** is included as an appendix. This listing of materials for further research provides readers with a selection of the best available general studies of the short story genre.

Other Features

A **Cumulative Author Index** lists all the authors who have appeared in *SSC, CLC, TCLC, NCLC, LC,* and *Classical and Medieval Literature Criticism (CMLC),* as well as cross-references to other Gale series. Users will welcome this cumulated index as a useful tool for locating an author within the Literary Criticism Series.

A **Cumulative Nationality Index** lists all authors featured in *SSC* by nationality, followed by the number of the *SSC* volume in which their entry appears.

A **Cumulative Title Index** lists in alphabetical order all short story, novella, and collection titles contained in the *SSC* series. Titles of short story collections, separately published novellas, and novella collections are printed in italics, while titles of individual short stories are printed in roman type with quotation marks. Each title is followed by the author's name and corresponding volume and page numbers where commentary on the work is located. English-language translations of original foreign-language titles are cross-referenced to the foreign titles so that all references to discussion of a work are combined in one listing.

Citing *Short Story Criticism*

When writing papers, students who quote directly from any volume in the Literary Criticism Series may use the following general forms to footnote reprinted criticism. The first example pertains to material drawn from periodicals, the second to material reprinted from books:

[1]Henry James, Jr., "Honoré de Balzac," *The Galaxy 20* (December 1875), 814-36; excerpted and reprinted in *Short Story Criticism,* Vol. 5, ed. Thomas Votteler (Detroit: Gale Research, 1990), pp. 8-11.

[2]F. R. Leavis, *D. H. Lawrence: Novelist* (Alfred A. Knopf, 1956); excerpted and reprinted in *Short Story Criticism,* Vol. 4, ed. Thomas Votteler (Detroit: Gale Research, 1990), pp. 202-06.

Comments

Readers who wish to suggest authors to appear in future volumes, or who have other suggestions, are invited to contact the editors by writing to Gale Research Inc., Literary Criticism Division, 835 Penobscot Building, Detroit, MI 48226-4094.

Acknowledgments

The editors wish to thank the copyright holders of the excerpted criticism included in this volume and the permissions managers of many book and magazine publishing companies for assisting us in securing reprint rights. We are also grateful to the staffs of the Detroit Public Library, the Library of Congress, the University of Detroit Mercy Library, Wayne State University Purdy/Kresge Library Complex, and the University of Michigan Libraries for making their resources available to us. Following is a list of the copyright holders who have granted us permission to reprint material in this volume of *SSC*. Every effort has been made to trace copyright, but if omissions have been made, please let us know.

COPYRIGHTED EXCERPTS IN *SSC*, VOLUME 22, WERE REPRINTED FROM THE FOLLOWING PERIODICALS:

American Bar Association, v. 58, February, 1972. Reprinted by permission of the publisher.—*American Literary Realism 1870-1910*, v. 7, Autumn, 1974. Copyright © 1974 by the Department of English, The University of Texas at Arlington. Reprinted by permission of the permission.—*American Literature*, v. XLIII, January, 1972. Copyright © 1972 Duke University Press, Durham, NC. Reprinted by permission of the publisher.—*The Atlantic Monthly*, v. 237, April, 1976 for a review of "The Winthrop Covenant" by Richard Todd. Copyright 1976 by The Atlantic Monthly Company Boston, MA. Reprinted by permission of the author.—*Canadian Journal of Italian Studies*, v. 12, 1989. Copyright 1989, Stelio Cro. Both reprinted by permission of the publisher.—*Chicago Tribune—Books*, January 1, 1995. © copyrighted 1995, Chicago Tribune Company. All rights reserved. Used with permission.—*Chinese Culture*, v. V, March, 1964. Reprinted by permission of the publisher.—*The Christian Science Monitor*, August 20, 1970. © 1970 The Christian Science Publishing Society. All rights reserved. Reprinted by permission from The Christian Science Monitor.—*The Commonweal*, v. LXXI, October 2, 1959. Copyright © 1959, renewed 1987 by Commonweal Publishing Co., Inc. Reprinted by permission of Commonweal Foundation.—*Commonweal*, v. LXXXVI, June 16, 1967. Copyright © 1967 Commonweal Publishing Co., Inc. Reprinted by permission of Commonweal Foundation.—*Critique: Studies in Modern Fiction*, v. VII, Winter, 1964-65; v. XV, 1973. Copyright © 1964, 1973 Helen Dwight Reid Educational Foundation. Renewed 1992. Both reprinted with permission of the Helen Dwight Reid Educational Foundation, published by Heldref Publications, 1319 18th Street, N. W., Washington, DC 20036-1802.—*The Dutch Quarterly Review of Anglo-American Letters*, v. 18, 1988. Both reprinted by permission of the publisher.—*The Emory University Quarterly*, v. 18, Summer, 1962. Copyright © 1962 by The Emory University Quarterly. Reprinted by permission of the publisher.—*The Georgia Review*, v. XLV, Winter, 1991. Copyright, 1991, by the University of Georgia. Reprinted by permission of the publisher.—*German Life & Letters*, v. XXXI, January, 1978. Reprinted by permission of the publisher.—*Kirkus Reviews*, v. LII, January 1, 1984. Copyright © 1984 The Kirkus Service, Inc. All rights reserved.—*The Los Angeles Times Book Review*, February 2, 1992. Copyright, 1992, Los Angeles Times. Reprinted by permission of the publisher.—*The Markham Review*, v. 3, October, 1972. Reprinted by permission of the publisher.—*The Mississippi Quarterly*, v. 25, Winter, 1971-72. Copyright 1972 Mississippi State University. Reprinted by permission of the publisher.—*Monatshefte*, v. LVI, April-May, 1964. Copyright © 1964, renewed 1992 by the Board of Regents of the University of Wisconsin System. Reprinted by permission of The University of Wisconsin System.—*The New Republic*, v. 141, September 28, 1959. © 1959, renewed 1987 by The New Republic, Inc. Reprinted by permission of The New Republic.—*The New Statesman*, v. XXV, May 9, 1925. Copyright 1925 The Statesman Publishing Co. Ltd. Reprinted by permission of the publisher.—*New York Herald Tribune Books*, v. 12, November 3, 1935. Copyright 1935, renewed 1963, The Washington Post./January 6, 1935; May 21, 1939. Copyright 1935, 1939, New York Herald Tribune Inc. All rights reserved. All reprinted by permission.—*The New York Review of Books*, July 18, 1974. Copyright © 1974 Nyrev, Inc. Reprinted with permission from The New York Review of Books.—*The New York Times Book Review*, September 16, 1923; October 12, 1930; September 9, 1934; October 27, 1935; May 14, 1939; May 16, 1954; August 18, 1963; October 11, 1970; May 24, 1987; July 7, 1991; July 4, 1993; December 4, 1994. Copyright © 1970, 1987, 1991, 1993/copyright © 1923, renewed 1951; 1930, renewed 1958; 1934, renewed 1962; 1935, renewed 1963; 1954, renewed 1982; 1963, renewed 1991 by The New York Times Company. All reprinted by permission of the publisher.—*Oral Tradition*, v. 2, January, 1987. Reprinted by permission of the

PHOTOGRAPHS AND ILLUSTRATIONS APPEARING IN *SSC*, VOLUME 22, WERE RECEIVED FROM THE FOLLOWING SOURCES:

Louis Auchincloss
1917–

American short story writer, novelist, essayist, literary critic and lawyer.

INTRODUCTION

Closely associated with the literary and social traditions of old New York, Auchincloss is widely regarded as the heir to novelists Henry James and Edith Wharton. His short stories and novels depict in ironic detail the moral and ethical implications of the actions of Wall Street lawyers and executives at work and at play; as a lawyer and member of a prominent family himself, he knows his subject intimately. Credited with furthering the tradition of the novel of manners in contemporary American fiction, Auchincloss is also the author of respected literary criticism both on American writers and William Shakespeare.

Biographical Information

Auchincloss was born in Lawrence, New York, and raised in Manhattan and on Long Island. His father, a lawyer, and his mother, whose literary tendencies he inherited, were of upper crust New York society, which allowed him to observe firsthand the people whose ways would find their way into his fiction. He attended prep school at Groton, a world that provided the basis for his novel *The Rector of Justin*, published many years later in 1964, and Yale University, where he wrote his first novel. Failing to interest a publisher in his book, he left Yale abruptly and enrolled at the University of Virginia Law School, where he wrote for the law review. In 1941, he joined Sullivan and Cromwell, a well-connected Wall Street firm that he left twice, once to serve in the U.S. Navy as an intelligence and gunnery officer during World War II, and once to devote several years, from 1951 to 1954, to his writing, during which time he also underwent psychoanalysis. Satisfied that he could both practice law and write fiction, he returned to his trusts and estates practice, this time at Hawkins, Delafield and Wood, and there remained until his retirement in 1986. Auchincloss serves as president of the Museum of New York and is a member of the National Institute of Arts and Letters and the New York Bar Association. He was awarded honorary degrees by New York University in 1974, Pace University in 1979, and the University of the South in 1986; he currently teaches at New York University.

Major Works of Short Fiction

Auchincloss's short story collections depict New York blue-blood society during its heyday and twilight. Often

focusing on high-powered lawyers and their families and firms, he relates tales about social status, ambition, codes of behavior, and office politics. His first collection, *The Injustice Collectors*, is unified by themes, containing stories of wronged and wrongheaded individuals. In *The Romantic Egoists*, a collection containing "The Great World and Timothy Colt," the stories are narrated by one character, Peter Westcott. *Powers of Attorney* evinces Auchincloss's use of the law firm as a framing device, an approach he employed again ten years later in *The Partners*, a collection of stories linked by the recurring character Beeky Ehninger, a law firm partner from the old school. Spanning lives of two generations of characters, *Second Chance* is an experiment with a shortened form of the novel of manners. *The Winthrop Covenant* and *The Book Class* are both family sagas, the first depicting the historic Puritan John Winthrop and his descendants (of whom Auchincloss is one), and the latter portraying the strong, literary-minded women of Auchincloss's mother's generation. *The Book Class*, too, is narrated by a single character, likely modeled on Auchincloss. The novels he wrote during the late 1950s and 1960s, *The Rector of Justin*, *The House of Five Talents,* and *Portrait in Brownstone*, remain, however, some of his most famous and well-regarded works, chronicling, as do the stories, the general decline of the ruling WASP class from their glory days at the turn of the century.

Critical Reception

Auchincloss's critics fall mainly into two camps: those who regard the world he describes as too narrow in scope for substantive fiction and those who, like novelist Gore Vidal, believe that much can be learned from an insightful rendering of the elite of Wall Street. Defenders argue that his characters achieve psychological complexity despite the similarity of their problems, and his plot-driven writing is significantly enhanced by his experimentation with a variety of narrative forms. One area of agreement among commentators is that he is a true novelist of manners and may, in fact, have taken this particular literary form to new heights. Auchincloss's career spans five decades, and his staying power is an indication of his popularity.

PRINCIPAL WORKS

Short Fiction

The Injustice Collectors 1950
The Romantic Egoists 1954
Powers of Attorney 1963
Tales of Manhattan 1967
Second Chance: Tales of Two Generations 1970
The Partners 1974
The Winthrop Covenant 1976
Narcissa and Other Fables 1983
The Book Class 1984
Skinny Island 1987
False Gods 1992
Three Lives (novellas) 1993
The Collected Stories 1994

Other Major Works

*The Great World and Timothy Colt (novel) 1956
The House of Five Talents (novel) 1960
Reflections of a Jacobite (criticism) 1961
Edith Wharton (criticism) 1962
Portrait in Brownstone (novel) 1962
The Rector of Justin (novel) 1964
The Embezzler (novel) 1966
Motiveless Malignity (criticism) 1969
A Writer's Capital (autobiography) 1974
Reading Henry James (essay) 1975
Diary of a Yuppie (novel) 1986

*Based on a short story of the same name published in *The Romantic Egoists.*

CRITICISM

Sara Henderson Hay (essay date 1950)

SOURCE: "Seekers of Hurt," in *The Saturday Review of Literature,* Vol. XXXIII, No. 41, October 14, 1950, pp. 37-8.

[Hay was an American poet and critic. In the following review, she discusses characterization in The Injustice Collectors *and praises Auchincloss for his "excellent portrait studies."]*

The title of **The Injustice Collectors** derives from Dr. Edmund Bergler's "The Battle of the Conscience," where the phrase is used to describe neurotics who continually and unconsciously construct situations in which they are disappointed or mistreated. In his foreword Mr. Auchincloss says:

> I do not purport to use the term in Dr. Bergler's exact medical sense, but in a wider sense to describe people who are looking for injustice, even in a friendly world, because they suffer from a hidden need to feel that this world has wronged them. Turning the idea over, one begins to speculate if punishment and injustice are not always more sought after than seeking, not only for such a reason as self pity, but for other reasons. . . . Is not the neurotic or the maladjusted or the unconventional or even the saint in some fashion the magnet which attracts the very disaster that he may appear to be seeking to avoid?

This is the theme which Mr. Auchincloss engages in his collection of short stories. The injustice collectors who move through these pages are not the underprivileged, the social outcasts, or those loosely termed unfortunates; the milieu of which he writes is that of wealth and leisure and caste; these are nice people, often charming people, stuffy people, expensively provincial people of Anchor Harbor, Maine; of Park Avenue and Long Island and Florida and the Riviera in winter. His stories are the more subtly penetrating because they are not melodramatic nor dismally sordid; the neurotics, the maladjusted, the self-punishers who in these eight excellent portrait studies work out their own destruction and defeat seldom realize that they are either destroyed or defeated. Mr. Auchincloss points no moral, nor suggests any alternatives for his characters. He is not concerned with analyzing the reasons why they behave as they do; he contents himself with symptoms rather than causes.

He is wonderfully adept at showing the conflicts between personalities; at exposing the tyrannies, the dominations, the iron fingers in the velvet gloves of courtesy and social convention and family relationships; he can draw a devastating picture in a few brief lines:

> George, without being attractive, or handsome, or witty; being indeed the very reverse of these things, could nonetheless fill me with a sense of confusion and self doubt by the very firmness of his own self righteousness and the very blatancy of his affectation

of a friendly homespun tolerance that undermined opposition to his dogma. . . .

The story **"Maude"** is one of the most effective in the book. "All Maude's life it had seemed to her that she was like a dried-up spring at the edge of which her devoted relatives and friends used to gather hopefully in the expectation that at least a faint trickle would appear. . . ." Maude so resented what she conceived of as the obligation to feel and be like other people that she negated and denied her own honest reactions, finding in her frustration of herself both justification and penance, taking an unconscious satisfaction, even, when her lover's death prevented the emotional release which she desired but did not want to desire. This story is a penetrating and expert portrayal of a neurotic refusal to meet life, of a clinging to a fancied independence which was in fact only a fear of emotional involvement.

In **"The Ambassadress"** he tells the story of Tony, the dilettante who believes himself a rebel against conventions, which he really clings to, almost convincing himself in his thrashing about to escape the domination of his sister that he actually wants to cut the bond between them, settling at last with a kind of relief into Edith's pattern for his life, an end to which he has been inevitably and irresistibly directing himself.

In these and the six other stories in the collection Mr. Auchincloss explores some of the various paths of defeat which people can unconsciously pursue. His style is fluent, cultivated, urbane. In spite of the inherent tragedy in the situations and the people involved, there is much that is deftly humorous. He has wit and irony; he has also a real understanding of and pity for the seekers of their own hurt.

The Injustice Collectors is the work of an extremely skilful and observant writer. These are not clinical case histories, but with the device of fiction Mr. Auchincloss puts his finger on fact.

James Stern (essay date 1954)

SOURCE: A review of *The Romantic Egoists,* in *The New York Times Book Review,* May 16, 1954, p. 4.

[*Stern was an Irish short story writer and critic. Here, he discusses* The Romantic Egoists, *admiring the book's innovative design and skilled characterization.*]

[*The Romantic Egoists*] reveals Louis Auchincloss as a writer of unusual brilliance. In it he combines a Henry Jamesian knowledge of upper-class New York society with an economy of style, an alertness of eye, an artful disarming modesty reminiscent of the stories of Christopher Isherwood. Mr. Auchincloss, however, does not carry a camera; he sees, or rather sees through people, with the piercing lens of an X-ray. Peter Westcott, the "I" of *The Romantic Egoists,* is a young man in whose company, one

feels, even silence might not be sufficiently discreet, discretion not always the better part of valor.

The Romantic Egoists is neither a novel nor, in the conventional sense, a collection of stories. It is rather a reflection in an octagonal mirror. This ingenious device involves eight dramatic episodes in the lives of eight friends. It enables us to watch the bewildered, conforming yet obstinately loyal schoolboy of **"Billy and the Gargoyles"** grow up into the 33-year-old novelist who travels to Venice to visit, "partly out of curiosity and partly out of affection," a dried-up recluse of a cousin. He proceeds to write about this cousin a story which Mr. Auchincloss, infected no doubt with his narrator's devastating affection, calls **"The Gem-like Flame."** This portrait, incidentally, would have had the full approval of the author of "The Beast in the Jungle."

In the second reflection in the mirror, Peter Westcott is seen in the company of a colossally rich contemporary—an episode in which he observes that "royalty and great wealth . . . are on their best behavior in a day of militant democracy." It was the forthright behavior of Arleus Kane in a political situation, and the hypocritical conduct on the part of his spiteful friend Phoenix, that taught Peter Westcott a lesson—a lesson he was to learn again later when he became involved with a confirmed non-combatant in Naval Intelligence during the war. In each case Westcott was to detect in other people's characters traits he recognized in his own and which he realized he could not "stand to live with for any length of time."

As a psychological study of an idealistic young man faced with the problem of immense wealth and of the effect that wealth has on his friends' attitude toward him, **"The Fortune of Arleus Kane"** would be a masterly piece of writing in any book. In *The Romantic Egoists* some readers may feel that for sheer characterization and the art of story-telling it is overshadowed by the long episode entitled **"The Great World and Timothy Colt."**

Here Peter Westcott is shown acting as principal assistant to the most promising clerk in a New York law firm. As a personal friend of the Colts, the narrator describes how the democratic, happily married Timothy loses, by blind ambition, the affection of his colleagues and friends; how, on his acquisition of power, he sheds his democratic principles and all but wrecks his marriage. This may sound like a familiar story, the tale of a man who made a pact with the devil, but I doubt very much if it has been, even could be, more brilliantly, more terrifyingly told.

Granville Hicks (essay date 1963)

SOURCE: "Fiction Brief of a Law Factory," in *Saturday Review,* New York, Vol. XLVI, No. 33, August 17, 1963, pp. 15-16.

[*Hicks was an American literary critic whose famous study* The Great Tradition: An Interpretation of American Literature since the Civil War *(1933) established him as the foremost advocate of Marxist critical thought in Depression-era America. Throughout the 1930s, he argued for a more socially engaged brand of literature and severely criticized such writers as Henry James, Mark Twain, and Edith Wharton, whom he believed failed to confront the realities of their society and, instead, took refuge in their own work. After 1939, Hicks sharply denounced communist ideology, which he called a "hopelessly narrow way of judging literature," and in his later years adopted a less ideological posture in critical matters. In the following review, Hicks comments on the authenticity of Auchincloss's stories in* Powers of Attorney.]

During the past sixteen years Louis Auchincloss has published twelve books, most of them fiction. This is not a bad record in itself, and it is the more impressive because during this entire period Auchincloss has been a practicing lawyer with a Wall Street firm. Law, according to a statement by his publisher, "is still a nine to five job with him, while fiction writing is a five and after job." He makes good use of his leisure hours.

He also, it is clear, makes good use of his business hours as a source of material. He knows the people who work in downtown New York, how they make their money and how they spend it. He is, indeed, an authority on whatever survives as an upper class in America, and he is one of the few contemporary writers who can be described as a novelist of manners.

In the twelve stories that make up *Powers of Attorney* Auchincloss has drawn directly on his legal experience. At least one character in every story is connected with the firm of Tower, Tilney & Webb. This firm, with seventy lawyers and a staff of over 100, occupies "two great gleaming floors in a new glass cube at 65 Wall Street, with modern paintings and a marble spiral staircase and a reception hall paneled in white and gold." Clitus Tilney, the senior partner, knows that the firm is sometimes described as a "law factory," but he does not mind, for he is convinced of the value of efficiency. He is not only "the finest security lawyer in New York"; he is a remarkably competent administrator. His influence makes itself felt in several of the stories.

Some of the stories have only a slight connection with Tower, Tilney & Webb. In **"The Single Reader,"** for instance, a somewhat Jamesian story about a man who keeps a diary, the protagonist is one of the partners, but he could be anyone. Again, in **"The Ambassador from Wall Street,"** the central figure is an old lady who dominates the social life of a Maine island resort. Her lawyer, who brings the story to a climax, is the Webb of Tower, Tilney & Webb, but there is no necessary connection.

On the other hand, the office is the background of several of the stories, and several hinge on details of legal strategy. In the first story, **"Power in Trust,"** Clitus Tilney is matched against Francis Hyde, a partner whom he has always found barely tolerable and whom he now resolves to force out of the firm. It is by way of an ingenious

---

Angus Wilson calls Auchincloss a talented snob:

The Romantic Egoists has a strict social framework and a convinced social standpoint. . . . I find the creed most distasteful. Mr. Auchincloss is an arrogant neo-aristocrat and his convictions make him, I think, cocksure, lacking in compassion, and, on occasion, deficient in good taste. Nevertheless, he is a very clever and subtle student of human social behaviour in the widest sense and one is led from one story to another by the unity of mood and viewpoint to a very rewarding total effect which goes far deeper than any subtle momentary flash or exact recapture of evanescent sensibility.

Angus Wilson, "Short Story Changes," in Spectator, *Vol. 193, No. 6588, October 1, 1954.*

---

device that Tilney wins the battle. In **"The Power of Appointment"** an old-timer, who distrusts himself and has all his life been afraid of making a fatal error, does blunder, but his mistake has no serious consequences, and he realizes that all the time he has been only a figurehead.

Office politics on a lower level is the theme of **"The Revenges of Mrs. Abercrombie."** A veteran secretary with a privileged position, Mrs. A. is demoted in the last year before her retirement. Learning that she is to be given a present at the Christmas party, she prepares a speech that criticizes by implication the firm and especially Clitus Tilney. The speech, however, becomes a fiasco when she has an attack of hiccups, and what happens thereafter changes her mind about Tilney.

Auchincloss describes his characters sharply. Here, for instance, is Waldron P. Webb, the firm's principal trial lawyer:

> Litigation, indeed, was more than Webb's profession; it was his catharsis. He was one of those unhappy men who always wake up angry. He was angered by the sparrows outside his bedroom window in Bronxville, by the migraines of his long-suffering wife, by the socialism in the newspaper, the slowness of the subway, the wait for the elevator, the too casual greeting of the receptionist. It was only the great morning pile on his desk of motions, attachments, injunctions that restored his calm. Sitting back in his red plush armchair under the dark lithograph of an orating Daniel Webster, facing his secretary and two chief law clerks, he would open the day with a rattling dictation of letters and memoranda. Gradually, as he talked and telephoned, as he stamped again and again on the hydra-headed serpent of presumption that daily struck anew at his clients with the forked tongues of legal subterfuge, as he defeated motion with countermotion, question with accusation, commitment with revocation, the earlier irritations of the morning subsided, the Santa Claus

began to predominate over the Scrooge, and Waldron P. Webb assumed his midday look of benevolent, if rather formidable cheer.

This is the introduction to a comic, or at any rate ironic, story about divorce. There is much variety in the stories. **"The Mavericks"** is a complicated story about a casual affair and a great romance. **"The Deductible Yacht,"** on the other hand, relates a simple tale about an income tax lawyer who is stricken by conscience. The last story tells how Clitus Tilney is offered the presidency of his alma mater, and is tempted, for he sees this as a noble way of rounding out his career. He is surprised by his wife's opposition, but in time he comes to recognize her wisdom.

Auchincloss entitled a collection of his essays *Reflections of a Jacobite,* and it is true that he is something of a conservative, in the sense that he accepts the world as he finds it, believing that, though it has its evils, any change would probably be for the worse. He has the kind of irony that often accompanies a mild conservatism. In the last story, for instance, Tilney is naïvely pleased by the offer of the college presidency until he learns why the offer was made. In **"Deductible Yacht,"** the young income tax lawyer who makes a gallant gesture accomplishes absolutely nothing by it. In **"The 'True Story' of Lavinia Todd,"** Chambers Todd decides that he does not want a divorce after his wife's account of the failure of their marriage has made her famous.

Always one has the feeling that Auchincloss knows what he is talking about. He is careful not to bury his readers under heaps of legal terminology; he never shows off; but he does use his knowledge of the law to good effect. The little world of Tower, Tilney & Webb seems real and alive, and full of what Hardy called "life's little ironies." Auchincloss is perhaps not so good a short story writer as he is a novelist, but he can tell an effective and engaging tale.

Maxwell Geismar   (essay date 1963)

SOURCE: "Life at 65 Wall Street," in *The New York Times Book Review,* August 18, 1963, p. 4.

[*Geismar was one of America's most prominent historical and social critics and the author of a multi-volume history of the American novel from 1860 to 1940. Though he often openly confessed that literature is more than historical documentation, Geismar's own critical method suggests that social patterns and the weight of history, more than any other phenomenon, affect the shape and content of all art. In the following review of* Powers of Attorney, *Geismar describes Auchincloss as a technician in the style of J. D. Marquand and John O'Hara. The critic also finds that the stories are a "very literate and polished kind of entertainment."*]

Louis Auchincloss has a neat talent for light fiction. A disciple of Edith Wharton and of Henry James, he deals with the remnants—saving or otherwise—of that "Old New York society" which has had to face the debased standards of the modern age. Mr. Auchincloss frankly admires wealth, social position, good breeding. In [*Powers of Attorney,* a] collection of a dozen tales about the law firm of Tower, Tilney & Webb, the minority groups—the Irish, the Jews, and the rest—still have a hard time of it. But they are given a fair chance, and sometimes one of them makes it.

Makes what? Mr. Auchincloss is also a firm believer in success. To become a partner of this law firm, a disciple of Clitus Tilney himself, is still the fervent desire of all these ambitious young lawyers; even though Mr. Auchincloss, rather like J. P. Marquand and John O'Hara, shows the penalties and perils of success, the moral burdens of the upper classes, the slightly sour taste of social and financial leadership. The remarkable thing is, of course, that within this rather narrow intellectual framework, these stories are still so entertaining and readable. Mr. Auchincloss is a good technician; he *believes* in the literary world he is creating; and he succeeds, at least momentarily, in casting his spell over us.

Thus Clitus Tilney himself, though he runs a modern and efficient "law factory" at 65 Wall Street, still retains the old-fashioned virtues of the legal profession. When one of his more cynical partners, Francis Hyde, takes on a dubious case of what amounts to financial blackmail, Hyde must go. (Though I must admit I had a certain sympathy for this erring partner, drunken realist that he is.) In the same law firm, the Midwestern Jake Platt, on the verge of becoming a partner, has a nightmare vision that Barry Schlide—the brilliant but obsequious, cheap and uncultivated tax expert—will cut him out. Jake resorts to some very dubious tactics himself before he realizes that Clitus Tilney would never really permit this, and that Barry Schlide is too smart to expect a partnership. Yet Clitus is just as fair to Barry as he is to Jake; he emerges as the stern and righteous, but just and merciful father-image whose legal "sons" can never quite match his own moral fiber.

In a curious way, too, Mr. Auchincloss makes Clitus Tilney an appealing hero who is quite human; that is the real achievement of *Powers of Attorney.* There is the rather touching tale of Rutherford Tower, the ineffectual and terrified nephew of "the great chancellor." There is the entertaining story of another tax expert in this modern law firm which is so closely involved with big business—Morris Madison, whose secret diary has become more important to him than his work, acquaintances or the woman he loves. The best chronicle here is that of the tough cynical Harry Reilley, who has a dreadful little affair with the pathetic and opportunist Doris Marsh, and then falls in love with Clitus Tilney's own daughter.

Well, that has a happy ending too; things always manage to work out not too unpleasantly in this upper-class orbit of fictional fantasy. But in this story Mr. Auchincloss is moving very close to the "real world" of the law, of business, of the Social Register, of love, of human character and relations which the purpose of his writing is usually to transform. Nevertheless, as a very literate and polished kind of entertainment, I can't quarrel with *Powers of Attorney*. In fact, I enjoyed it.

Patricia Kane (essay date 1964-1965)

SOURCE: "Lawyers at the Top: The Fiction of Louis Auchincloss," in *Critique: Studies in Modern Fiction,* Vol. VII, No. 2, Winter, 1964-65, pp. 36-46.

[*In this excerpt, Kane compares Auchincloss's treatment of lawyers with those of other American writers.*]

A pat declaration of faith in mankind and the bar is among the inevitable platitudes of lawyers' public speeches, according to a Louis Auchincloss lawyer. Just as the character only amuses himself with wistful and whimsical thoughts about delivering any but the expected oration, Louis Auchincloss' fiction only hints a doubt about the rightness of the world created and maintained by Wall Street law firms.

The cautious and correct lawyers of Auchincloss are not the hierophants that Alexis de Tocqueville once found American lawyers to be. They are practicing a well-known profession, not participating in a mystery—to paraphrase Oliver Wendell Holmes, Jr. Master of occult learning, knowledgeable about securities, trusts, taxes, and estates, they devote themselves, not to an abstraction called law or justice, but to their firms, their own careers, and their clients.

Mr. Auchincloss could tender impeccable credentials as an interpreter of this downtown world; he is a partner in a Wall Street law firm of twenty partners whose practice is largely in estates and tax law. Although as a novelist he admittedly lacks the stature of a Henry James, he is a facile writer who presents with dispatch and lucidity an insider's view of a world nearly as bizarre for most readers as Samarkand. Many American novelists have written about lawyers, but no writer of consequence has written with such authority of the distinctively twentieth-century climate of finance in legal practice.

Auchincloss writes about downtown not just because it is the world he knows and can report, but because its hierarchy admirably suits a literary form that attracts him. In an essay called "The Novel of Manners Today" [published in *Reflections of a Jacobite,* 1961], Auchincloss remarks, in an unconscious echo of Hawthorne's preface to *The Marble Faun,* that while as a citizen he has no nostalgia for the old ways, as a novelist his eyes might "light up at the first glimpse of social injustice" because a novel of manners loses significance in a classless society. While Auchincloss locates nothing that could be called social injustice, he does find a stratified society in huge Wall Street law firms, an attendant snobbishness about other firms engaged in other kinds of practice, and a perspective from which to view the rich, both old and new.

Auchincloss' fiction differs in several particulars from that of others who have portrayed lawyers. He brings to the structured world that he knows intimately no Populist prejudice against city lawyers, no nostalgia for the less organized life of a small-town practitioner, and almost no interest in courtroom advocacy. While he takes for granted the necessity of the Wall Street world, he brings to his fiction a quality of detachment, even of irony, that produces readable novels, which contain comic and witty moments. He does not satirize lawyers, however, as did James G. Baldwin in *Flush Times in Alabama and Mississippi* or Mark Twain in *Roughing It.* Auchincloss' lawyers are neither the uneducated swindlers nor the pompous buffoons of those frontier tales. Nor are they secular priests in the style of a lawyer created by William Faulkner in such works as *Requiem for a Nun* or by William Dean Howells in *The Leatherwood God.* Certainly not the contemptible pawns of financiers found in Theodore Dreiser's *The Titan,* neither are they saviors of civilization in the pattern of the judge in James Fenimore Cooper's *The Pioneers.*

Auchincloss' lawyers have as clients those with money and power. They have no sense of calling or responsibility to society as distinct from their clients. Expending no energy serving or preserving law, they look for loopholes in the statutes that will help their clients' prosperity. Unlike the sanctimonious lawyers of James Gould Cozzens' *By Love Possessed,* they seldom delude themselves or others by pretending that they have other dedications. Indeed they may see their role as contributing to the general welfare in that they work out the relationship between government and industry and have [as Auchincloss writes in *The Great World and Timothy Colt,* 1956] a "glory" as "architects of society." If they have any literary antecedent, it is Cooper's ideal lawyer who allied himself with the agrarian aristocracy of that day. In temperament they are not unlike the New York lawyer in Cooper's *The Ways of the Hour* who was so governed by his sense of decorum that he deigned to employ an emotional appeal to a jury, but their sense of decorum would necessitate rejecting as pretentious and undescriptive Cooper's choice of *votaries* as an appellation for lawyers.

Auchincloss' lawyers of a given position in a firm not only resemble each other sufficiently to make possible generalizations about them, they have few qualities that one could call distinctively those of a lawyer. They are virtually interchangeable with their counterparts in the trust department of a bank [as reflected in Auchincloss's fiction, including *Venus in Sparta* and *Portrait in Brownstone*]. If, as seems likely, this interchangeability—unremarked by Auchincloss—accurately reflects reality rather than the novelist's inability to imagine more than one kind of character, it reveals on another level the union of finance and law shown in the stories. Despite the details of the law of trusts, estates, taxation, and the like, and although the moral crisis for a character may turn on a decision within the maze of such law, Auchincloss does not convey a clear association between character and occupation. Indeed he has disclaimed a connection in a remark about the protagonist of *The Great World and Tim-*

othy Colt: "He is not a man who finds it hard to be honest in a New York firm because of his milieu." Auchincloss' lawyers are less men of the law, which for good or ill the lawyers in most novels by American writers are, than they are men of the world of finance who specialize in the law of finance.

In the legal establishment of the world of finance a writer of Auchincloss' perceptions can find many elements to make the novel of manners a viable form. The structure of the firm contains clear gradations. Any suggestions of a more fluid organization, such as an open door to the senior partner's office, does not camouflage for those in the group what the lines are. Among the ingredients of such a firm and its members are conventions, prescribed amenities, definable manners, exclusiveness, and pride. Toward outsiders the expected responses range from scorn for the "uptown bar" and its divorce practice to courtesy toward clients, whatever one's personal feelings or however gross and insulting the client. In chronicling the adventures of members of this society, Auchincloss' tone often resembles that of high comedy although it also has something in common with that of Faulkner's comic tales. Auchincloss avoids the vice that he deplores in "most novels that deal with society": they "take on some of the meretricious gaudiness that it is their avowed purpose to deplore," and their "authors become guilty of the snobbishness and triviality of which they accuse their characters" (*Jacobite*). Not an apologist for the manners he observes, neither is Auchincloss a reformer. His analysis evokes laughter more likely to be thoughtful than derisive because he finds moral values to reside within the conventions and disciplines of the class-like organization of a law firm.

At the top of a Wall Street firm resides the eminence of a senior partner. In an Auchincloss novel the senior partner is not only successful and respected, he is likely to be a talented and well-mannered man, satisfied with the world he has helped to create. But unlike Faulkner's Gavin Stevens, he would not become a district attorney, defend an unsavory murderess, or devote himself to stemming the rise of a clan of plutocrats. Nor would he enter a courtroom to establish truth and solve a murder as does Mark Twain's Pudd'nhead Wilson. His occasional courtroom appearance is undertaken only in behalf of a valued client and friend. His demeanor there might be more suitable to "a legal discussion over an after-dinner brandy than an argument in court," and his treatment of the opposing lawyer reflect "the good manners of a clubman to a fellow member's guest who is misbehaving himself" (*Egoists*).

A senior partner rarely questions that a life devoted to manipulating power and aiding the rich fulfills and discharges his lawyer's function. For example, without a qualm he might assign such other responsibilities as membership on legal committees to a member of the firm who is a poor lawyer. Something like a civil liberties case seems to be unthinkable. If a senior partner feels any lack in his legal life, it is his sense that something of the "greater glory" of the profession has disappeared since the time that a man like Joseph H. Choate could persuade the Supreme Court that the income tax is unconstitutional

(*Egoists*). That a lawyer who served business and argued a financial matter should represent glory identifies their ambition and values. The portrait of Daniel Webster on the wall is only interior decoration.

The senior partner can be as ruthless in his devotion to the firm as any arbiter of the standards of a class. The head of the firm portrayed in *Powers of Attorney* is shrewd at picking men who will be assets to the firm and brutal about those who lack "the personality for our kind of firm." When he is morally outraged at a partner's taking the wrong sort of case, he serves the firm at some personal risk in order to purge the offending partner. He violates legal ethics and counsels the opposing party, with the hoped-for result that the partner loses and resigns from the firm. The more cautious senior portrayed in *A Law for the Lion* waits to ask an offending partner to leave until he is assured of the continuing business of the firm's wealthiest client. The younger partner has displayed the "crudest possible taste" in bringing a scandalous divorce action against his wife. Although the victim is the niece of the senior partner, so long as he feels that the firm cannot weather the loss of the partner, he subordinates any family or personal feeling. The senior partner in an Auchincloss novel is not a rigid man of principle, but most of them have mastered the knack of compromise without losing their sense of integrity. In the privacy of his home one might occasionally call his firm "Shyster, Beagle and Shyster" after the firm in a Marx brothers movie (*Powers of Attorney*), but he would not indulge whims when a serious matter is at stake. For him the firm usually has the majesty and priority that Faulkner's Gavin Stevens accords justice.

The other partners resemble the senior in most particulars, but they are sometimes lesser men in talent or ethics. Some incompetents remain in their jobs because of family connections or long association with the firm. One such person (in *Powers of Attorney*), theoretically the authority on property law, devotes his life to studying Plantaganant law. In his reverence for principles of law removed from the facts of present practice he resembles the "new judge" in *Adventures of Huckleberry Finn* who awards custody of Huck to his drunken father because of the legal principle that families should not be separated. Auchincloss' tone is gentler than Twain's, and his lawyer does no actual harm, but the comic portraits are of similar mentalities.

An able partner may lack ethics. One, whose manners "verge on the greasy" (*The Great World and Timothy Colt*), counsels an associate to be expedient when it means being unfaithful as an estate trustee, then rewards him with a partnership. Still another abuses his position on a Bar Association committee to serve a client. When an associate questions its rightness, he hotly declares that if he is fortunate enough to secure a big company as a client, a "good lawyer eats, lives and breathes for his clients" (*Powers of Attorney*). He differs only in degree from the lawyers in Dreiser's *The Titan* who buy, influence, or blackmail city councils and state legislatures to further the ends of the financier who employs them.

Below the partners are the associates, the bright young men, most of whom led their classes at the best law schools, who yearn to move up. They are expected to move with ease in the world of the rich, not to be what Auchincloss describes in another connection as "wide-eyed Scott Fitzgeralds, bareheaded before the refracted gleam of gold" (*The Romantic Egoists*). An associate's pride in his present status and his expectation of success stem from the kind of law he practices. For example, when one is asked by his son about being a mouthpiece, he stuffily and peevishly retorts that he does not argue in court and is "not that kind of lawyer" (*Colt*). Most associates work hard to improve their position, but some lack the requisites for promotion, and occasionally a rebel may leave voluntarily. Those who continue the climb work in the approved section of the firm, usually securities rather than litigation or real estate, under the direction of the senior partner. Auchincloss describes their devotion to the senior, with characteristic mild irony, as like that of "acolytes at an altar" as they move "silently to and fro with absorbed, preoccupied faces, conscious only of their high priest and his ministrations" (*Colt*).

Upward progress has its pitfalls. One tale of particular pithiness introduces a young associate who sometimes feels like a "captive Athenian scholar in the court of a Macedonian king" (*Powers*). The associate, Bayard Kip, claims a social position superior even to that of most downtown lawyers. His family has lost its wealth, but it confidently identifies itself with the small group of families that were considered Manhattan society in the eighteenth century. Bayard Kip is assigned the tax work for Inka Dahduh, "the son of an Armenian rug peddler," who looks to Kip like "a conquering Tartar" and represents "the incarnation of the destroying spirit that had laid low the poor old shabby, genteel past." Kip tries to salvage his self-esteem by boasting that the tax returns that he prepares for Dahduh honestly disclose the facts.

Kip's refuge fails, and he assumes another moral stance. When he must spend a weekend on Dahduh's yacht, he looks at the visitor's log at first from idle curiosity, then with the realization that his client has used the yacht rarely for the business purposes reported on the income tax forms. Kip decides that even at the risk of his partnership he will refuse to sign Dahduh's tax forms. As a Kip he will make a gesture of repudiation of "the whole wretched age," just as his ancestors had resisted Astors and Fisks.

Kip insists on his gesture with unexpected results. The partner in charge of the tax department brusquely asks why he cannot simply take the word of an important client. Kip remains adamant, and to his chagrin the client is unruffled and immediately insists that the yacht not be claimed as a business expense. Thus when Kip is shortly thereafter made a partner, he feels that his principles are vindicated and his success a result of integrity.

But Kip has more to learn. He discovers that the client had intended to sell the yacht anyway and consequently acquired without cost what one of Kip's friends calls "the lifetime devotion of a brilliant young tax lawyer of unim-

peachable respectability." In the face of this intelligence, Kip concludes that his "simple philosophy" is inadequate: "One tried to fight wrong, and the enemy turned up after the bout in even richer ermine. Perhaps the lesson of it all was that the *appearances* of honor and scrupulousness, of dignity and aristocratic distinction, were, after all, the only things that could be preserved." Kip learns from his defeat in success something of the complex fabric of the practice of law in a Wall Street firm and, not unhappily, salvages what he can. He thinks about restoring an Upjohn-designed house, a suitable pre-occupation for one who has just discovered that appearances suffice for the pride in status that has replaced pride in class. One feels confident that one day he will be a senior partner.

In the tale of the deductible yacht, Auchincloss displays his forte, the comedy of manners. His special awareness of the nuances of position, social and business, flavors the story. He manages without shifting from the perspective of Kip's thoughts and experiences to project a slightly ironic but not hostile account of the code of a member of the old aristocracy and the protocol of a Wall Street law firm. Juxtaposed is the shrewd conduct of the wheeler-dealer who, having no restraint of manners, can manipulate those who do and achieve for himself some appearance of honor. Kip's defeat has the pathos that Auchincloss notes "has a bigger place than tragedy in the study of manners" (*Jacobite*). The comic effect of the double twist in Kip's adventures is not unworthy of comparison with a Faulkner tall tale, such as the incident in *The Hamlet* in which the innocent victims injured by a runaway horse first testify so as to establish that the man willing to compensate them is not responsible for their damages, then are awarded as damages the dead body of the horse.

Kip's story involves a character rarely seen in Auchincloss' fiction, a government-employed lawyer. Although he appears only briefly, he vigorously questions the sanctity of lawyers' serving financiers. He asks Kip if it ever occurs to him that there is "something wrong with a country whose best brains are spent in attacking and defending the shenanigans of an old trickster like Inka Dahduh?" Such a viewpoint rarely appears in an Auchincloss novel. Equally rare are lawyers who have served in government and discuss affairs of state rather than finance, such as one, briefly seen in another story (*Colt*), who seems to be modeled on a man like Dean Acheson or Adlai Stevenson. The existence of this urbane, knowledgeable, socially sought-after aristocrat who has once been an assistant secretary of state threatens a Wall Street lawyer sufficiently to make him forget himself at a party and speak rudely and boorishly. . . .

Auchincloss exposes with the same precision lawyers who enforce or follow understood principles of behavior and those who become indiscreet violators. In short, he is not over-awed by lawyers. This attitude informs his perceptive study of Edith Wharton, in which he dissects her typical male character, a "well-born, leisurely bachelor lawyer, with means just adequate for a life of elegant solitude" [*Edith Wharton*]. He insists on the accuracy of her portraits, saying of the lawyer in *The Age of Innocence* that "the reader who doubts that such a type existed has only to turn the pages of the voluminous diary of George Templeton Strong." Auchincloss' judgment has the authority of his having edited a portion of Strong's diary, which is published in *Reflections of a Jacobite*. Further, the lawyers in Mrs. Wharton's fiction are not unlike some in his own.

Auchincloss' refusal to be awed by lawyers combines with his admiration for them to produce his characteristic tone of detachment. A delightful example is the mocking, yet loving, look at a hero in the moment when he comes into the clubhouse after playing golf and sees a partner and several associates sitting in the bar:

> As Tilney paused now, . . . his sweater and flannels a reproach to their urban darkness, . . . there was in Tilney's gaze, unconcealed by his perfunctory grin, some of the sternness of Abraham contemplating Sodom. . . . To his surprise and indignation he found himself surveyed as if he were something quaint and ridiculous, a sort of vaudeville character, vaguely suggestive of Edwardian sports and fatuity. . . . (*Powers*)

The humor of this passage lacks the bite of a Faulkner tale [*The Town*] in which a sardonic friend says of the lawyer hero that he misses the point entirely because "if it aint complicated it dont matter whether it works or not because . . . it aint right." But both writers mock as friends.

Despite the rueful awareness of Auchincloss' heroes that life in "green goods" (the insider's terms for securities practice) in a downtown firm is not paradise, and despite their attraction to occasional mavericks who make them briefly dissatisfied with their lot, they content themselves with a secure life that is familiar and respected. Although even a senior partner can be tempted at the thought of life as a college president, when he discovers that the offer is a ruse engineered by an ambitious younger partner, he can return with real pleasure to "weighing the chances of winning a directed verdict" in a securities case, laughing at his dream of being "whimsical and philosophical, entrancing his disciples under the crab-apple trees," and insisting that "all is for the best in the best of all possible worlds" (*Powers*). The character and Mr. Auchincloss know how platitudinous that last phrase is, but platitude or not, they believe in mankind and the bar.

Leon Edel   (essay date 1967)

SOURCE: "High Polish," in *The Washington Post Book Week*, April 9, 1967, p. 14.

[*An American critic and biographer, Edel is a highly acclaimed authority on the life and work of Henry James. His five-volume biography* Henry James *(1953-73) is considered the definitive life and brought Edel critical praise for his research and interpretive skill. In the following review of* Tales of Manhattan, *Edel praises the skill, the "insights" and "delicate subtleties" of Auchincloss's stories, yet the reviewer also complains of a "certain thinness" in the author's work.*]

Louis Auchincloss continues to tell his tales of Manhattan as an endless Arabian Nights entertainment. This is his fourth collection, and his earlier volumes, *The Injustice Collectors, The Romantic Egoists,* and *Powers of Attorney,* long ago demonstrated his ease and skill in the short story. It is perhaps his characteristic form: for his novels are also constructed on a short-story principle, as in *The Embezzler,* in which he told the same story from three different angles. In *Tales of Manhattan* he begins with five episodes told by an expert in an art auction firm; then he has four linked tales about (and by) the members of a law firm. He adds a final group called "The Matrons," in which we see various society women, both generous and predatory, in the social world of New York.

His skill, in spite of his rapid and abundant production, has grown. He has acquired great smoothness in spinning his stories, and his varnished situations are suffused with psychological truth and moral power. Readers of this volume will discover in it a fascinating tale about an art collector specializing in paintings of famous children who have met violent ends, like the little princes in the tower. With dramatic flair, the narrator reveals this man's constant turning to his own psychic "death" when he was young, his lost childhood. The same kind of subtle anecdote is told in **"The Senior Partner's Ghosts,"** in which the partner, trying to write the life of his predecessor, discovers he can't get his words out without sounding like his subject. When he wants to set down eulogy, he records rascality. He is "possessed," as in the old medieval tales, and for all his high morality he has unwillingly embodied within himself all the venality and crookedness of his former chief.

In such tales Auchincloss combines with his narrative skills a documented knowledge of society; he knows it in depth and he has an uncommon grasp of the dynamics of power, social and financial. A whole phase of enterprise and psychological history is embodied in his tale of Louis Degener and Eric Temple, members of a law firm: Temple's recurrent rebellion and self-assertion against the rigidities and traditions of his class and profession, and Degener's constant discovery of the ideal compromise for him which advances the firm, satisfies the rebellion, and gives Temple more power. Degener in a sense becomes Temple's evil genius, taking the edge off his self-assertion yet making a pragmatic virtue of it. This is one of Auchincloss' ironic-moral tales, and it is matched by that of **"The Money Juggler,"** a less finely written narrative, in which three socialite graduates of the Columbia Law School gossip about the money-and-success madness of one of their socially—and racially—"inferior" classmates. They describe his dizzy climb and fall with cool contempt, only to be reminded that each one of them aided and abetted the careerist in destroying the very values they pretend to cherish. This is Auchincloss' favorite theme.

The metaphor for the entire Auchinclossian society is to be found in his touching tale of **"The Landmarker,"** in which a declining cookie pusher, Chauncey Lefferts, devoted to New York society and to the city's landmarks, begins to recognize in the disappearing city his own impending disappearance, "the very precariousness of surviving beauty, was analogous to his own threadbare elegance. What was he but a sober, four-story brownstone facade, with Gothic arches and an iron grille, such as one might find in Hicks Street or over at Brooklyn Heights." This story, like the others, has its further ironic twist, in Lefferts' final recognition that the very landmarks he loves are often destroyed by his own class, discarded as he has been socially discarded.

To reduce these tales to a brief sentence or two, however, does not suggest their insights and their delicate subtleties. Nevertheless, with a writer of such gifts, we ask ourselves why Auchincloss' work gives an impression of a certain thinness, of being in two dimensions. In part this may derive from the fact that he writes in the margin of his law practice; in part it may also come from his apparent need to produce a book a year, as he has done now for more than a decade. He might reply that this is what Anthony Trollope did, and perhaps we can find an answer in the example of that novelist. Trollope wrote his quota of words by the clock each morning before going to his job at the Post Office. However, he wrote as if he had all the time in the world to explore the society he knew so well; his characters have growth and development. With Auchincloss we are rushed along, in a kind of restless creation; the narrative leaves the reader—and the characters—little time for reflection and the sense of being in time and in space; we do not get a chance to live through the experience; it is over before we attain full awareness of it.

This is true of his novels as well as his tales. We never get a sense of "felt life." It is in this, I believe, that Auchincloss makes his compromise with excellence; this is the deeper flaw in his extraordinary virtuosity.

Martin Tucker (essay date 1967)

SOURCE: A review of *Tales of Manhattan*, in *Commonweal*, Vol. LXXXVI, No. 13, June 16, 1967, pp. 372-73.

[*Tucker is an American educator and critic. In the following review, he discusses Auchincloss's narrative technique in* Tales of Manhattan *and finds that the author's frequent use of passive observers to relate stories robs the works of passion.*]

The dominant impression a reader is likely to get from Louis Auchincloss' *Tales of Manhattan* is that the rich worry more about money than the poor. When threatened, they scratch and claw—some like tigers, some like kittens—but very few question the struggle in any terms but moneyed triumphs. Most of Auchincloss' characters reserve their moral complexities for questions of what things to buy with their money.

Such a theme is no more restrictive a representation of human nature than Dreiser's emphasis on the bitch-god-dess of success in American society. Dreiser's characters bumbled and groped their way; Auchincloss' characters elegantly knife a man with a Renaissance stiletto. Among the rich in fiction, Henry James and Edith Wharton's people seem no less aware of money and manners than Auchincloss'. But Dreiser and James and Wharton did not fashion their characters in *objets d'art* as Auchincloss does in this newest book, a collection of stories and one playlet held together by the common theme and milieu of the rich and the near-mighty. In *Tales of Manhattan* the passion of Auchincloss' people does not carry much urgency, and their convictions all seem part of a crafty puppeteer show.

Certainly the raw material is present. One story concerns a man who has surrendered to his dream to build the most beautiful house in America. He spends almost his entire fortune to create this esthetic paradise, and then finds that his wife and children will not move into it with him, and that he has almost no money left to run it in the fashion it deserves. Another story concerns the machinations by which a junior partner evicts a doddering senior partner from the firm. An even more potentially sensational situation lies in the playlet, **"The Club Bedroom,"** in which a mother admits to herself that her daughter is a tramp, and her only son a homosexual. She stands before a portrait of her dowager mother-in-law and accuses her of evading the responsibilities that have led to such a shambles of the family tradition.

The situations then are as much raw material for passion as anything found in Dreiser's working-class figures or Henry James' desperately moral characters. In Auchincloss, however, the passion does not hold. I suspect one of the reasons is his increasing use of a technique he displayed brilliantly—but not successfully—in *The Rector of Justin.* In that novel a schoolmaster and his life were dissected by the many people who knew him, and the reader came to know him through their voices: the man himself rarely spoke. In this collection of stories, every piece is told by an observer, who is in most cases passive.

Auchincloss divides his book into three sections. The first reveals the characters of several people as the narrator (an antique dealer) discovers them. The second concerns a composite biography of a law firm which various partners in the firm are writing: each revealing himself as he discusses the others. The last section, "The Matrons," deals with several old ladies who are studied by their acquaintances. Auchincloss' attraction to the oddball, the sensitive or artistic member of a society that allows eccentricity but not passionate criticism, runs through all the stories. What happens is that the oddball—the man who built his dream castle, the erratic lawyer who sacrificed his wife's reputation for the joy of political slugging, the painter who drew erotic fantasies with his parents in mind—becomes a case study for a compassionate conservative reluctant to break his own ties. The attraction of the wayward impulsive romantic is real enough, but the stately narration of events produces more passivity than passion. The choice of the narrator, particularly in the second section, is also mystifying sometimes. Why does Auchincloss choose one man as narrator above another? All people are interesting, of course, and what one man has to say about another is the stuff of literature. But Auchincloss' choice of narrator does not create a profundity of illumination, it merely creates a clever diversionary tactic from the real stuff he should be shaping.

Auchincloss' technique is not a new one. In fact, the point of view technique has already taken on an academic air. Certainly that academic tone—even dehumanizing would not be too strong a word—characterizes this latest work. It is a pity, because all the virtues of Auchincloss—precision, elegance, wit of style—are not allowed to add up to more than decoration.

Nora Sayre　(essay date 1967)

SOURCE: "Lampshades," in *The Reporter,* Vol. 37, No. 1, July 13, 1967, pp. 60-1.

[*Sayre is a Bermudan-born writer and critic. Here, she uses a review of* Tales of Manhattan *to address two "perplexities" that appear in much of Auchincloss's work: the "drab and stunted" nature of his narrators and the "double views" that he provides of his main characters. The critic concludes that these elements ultimately hurt Auchincloss's fiction and result in a lack of variety.*]

In a period which savages the tangible past, landmark preservation becomes an emotional necessity. It is not surprising that even a defective lampshade should be cherished. Louis Auchincloss's catalogues of Tiffany glass, parental portraits by Sargent, club lunches, debuts at Sherry's, façades by Richard Morris Hunt and Louis Sullivan no doubt answer a craving for civilization, a nostalgia for something slightly senior to the Green Hornet. Hence anyone who cares about an earlier America is apt to feel ungrateful on recoiling from his fiction. But one rebels at Auchincloss's own treatment of landmarks: "In Washington one dined with Henry Adams and Bessie Lodge; in Boston with Mrs. 'Jack'; in London with Ottoline Morrell and 'Emerald,' or else drove down to Rye to see poor old Henry James. In Paris, there was 'Dear Edith,' in Rapallo 'Max'; in Florence 'BB.'" Even though the tone is supposed to be ironic, the best names curdle at this treatment.

By depicting an age of infinite tassels, social prejudice, and little else, Auchincloss has done the past a disservice. In fact, he has preserved the lampshade without the bulb. His characters have none of the violence and few of the valid dilemmas bestowed by Edith Wharton and Henry James. Some of his readers even blame his flaws on the dead writers, conferring a double death. But Mrs. Wharton hated the social system that shattered her characters, whereas Auchincloss seems to share the code of his personae. This is faintly mysterious, since he has criticized Proust (and others) for being "obsessed" with social position, adding that the authors of novels about society can "become guilty of the snobbishness and triviality of which

they accuse their characters." Moreover, his good essay "The Novel of Manners Today" reproves John O'Hara for stressing that "the most important thing about any character is the social niche in which he was born." Both remarks might come from churlish descriptions of Auchincloss's own work.

The perplexity of his attitude may be a stepchild of James's "operative irony"; the possibility of implying "the case rich and edifying where the actuality is pretentious and vain." (In a preface, James explained that projecting foolish characters could highlight "the superior case.") Auchincloss's ambiguities take two forms, and both seem deliberate. First, he nearly always chooses drab and stunted narrators: old women, musty bachelors, timid young men. These naturally have a walleyed view of society, or of his recurrent protagonists: the domineering fathers, disappointing sons, large, insensitive daughters, and the plain, mistreated mothers. There are also the raucous fiancées who have ferocious ambitions for their future husbands, and the intelligent upstarts with "no family" who nonetheless thrive professionally. His most sensual women are usually rapacious social hedonists: "More than ever she was like a doll in an expensive dress." Whether the narrators idolize or deplore these characters, their intonation is inevitably prim or censorious.

Auchincloss sometimes means these commentators to be laughable. But since their prejudices dominate almost all of his work, they fail as a satirical chorus, and it sounds as though the author were luxuriating behind their views. Unhorrified by clichés, he feeds them to all his characters: "My first instinct was to shoot you down like a dog." Or: "He then proceeded to drink his way through Harvard to an early grave." When the whole cast speaks or thinks in this style, it's hard to feel that the author has separated himself from their mentality. Elsewhere, he has labeled the hero of Mrs. Wharton's *The Glimpses of the Moon* "an unmitigated cad."

Some of Auchincloss's narrators confess that they would like to be "peacocks," but he firmly maintains them as wrens. Admittedly, it's daring to permit a narrator of *The Rector of Justin* to announce on page 1: "Not that my life has been an exciting one. On the contrary, it has been very dull." In contrast, how swiftly Mrs. Wharton could make a character intriguing: on page 1 of *The House of Mirth,* Lily Bart has "an air of irresolution which might . . . be the mask of a very definite purpose." Hence one can immediately believe that "it was characteristic of her that she always roused speculation."

While Auchincloss's characters don't excite the same speculation, he is deft at plotting. One may not care why Geraldine Brevoort leapt out of a window or why Guy Prime indulged in embezzlement, yet one is curious about the process and solution of the total scheme. He does provide what publishers wistfully call "pull," and his particular public is probably plot-starved.

The second perplexity stems from Auchincloss's pleasure in giving double views of his leading characters. Each may or may not be morally monstrous. Ida, the diffident heroine of *Portrait in Brownstone,* triumphantly arranges a possibly crippling marriage for her adored son; the Rector of Justin paralyzes many lives; Guy, of *The Embezzler,* is defended in the first half (by himself) and degraded by two sequential narratives. Auchincloss meticulously reports all aspects. His primary theme is that people can direct and govern each other's lives: he shows them devising careers, preventing or concocting marriages, and controlling one another's money. Cruelty—through such tyranny, rather than verbal cruelty—is one of his preoccupations. Hence one wants very much to know whether he considers that his dislikable protagonists are "justified" in their ruthlessness—or unforgivable, or even tolerable, or whether they were partially misunderstood by their era. Auchincloss constructs each moral dilemma skillfully, and then abandons the problem.

It would be easy to pronounce all his people abominable. But he doesn't intend that: so much space is spent on their defense. However, their most odious social values usually prevail—if only to punish them. Hence the impression that those who perpetuate their money and position are superior. A social columnist remarks, "Nobody who really counts gives a hoot about family any more." Perhaps the reason is that anyone who "really counts" in an Auchincloss novel already has copious "family." Thus, the ambiguities hang on Auchincloss's concealed point of view—instead of his characters' complexities. One doesn't ask for glaring conclusions. But since this novelist focuses on morality, his deviousness is frustrating.

The inmates of *Tales of Manhattan* concentrate on unveiling the sins of others. Most of the accused are decedents, not decadents. The iniquities of the dead are revealed through written memoirs, notebooks, or conversations with elderly descendants—another opportunity for peevish narration. It's a detective-story technique: many of the stories start with a mystery, which is amiable to unravel but usually disappointing when solved. The characters usually betrayed or abused one another for financial reasons, but some indulged in psychological revenge—such as a Bostonian painter who sketched his parents in "frankly pornographic" positions. The first section is narrated by a gallery auctioneer who tries to re-create personalities by studying their collections (a pleasing device); the second groups some parched lawyers' opinions of one another; the third concerns "The Matrons," a glimpse of female comptrollers which seems to suggest that money is corrupting for women.

One story has a touching validity that the rest lack: in **"The Landmarker,"** an aged bachelor relives the past by revisiting New York's antique buildings; when his favorite is about to be demolished, he has a stroke. He recovers to find it gone. Here, Auchincloss expresses a loss that is perhaps more acute for New Yorkers than for any other city's inhabitants. Since he knows Manhattan's oldest bones so well, and since his material is delectable, it's a pity that his natives are an incapacious, whispery cluster—who, in fact, "count" only in the Social Register or in slices of cash, or by possessing "Henry Adams's own copy of

---

Auchincloss on artistic representation of society:

I have no desire to return to a New York where servants slept in unheated cubicles on the top of drafty brownstones, with an evening off every second week, and where W. A. Croffut, in his public eulogy of the Vanderbilt family, could describe the old Commodore as "puffed with divine greed." But every writer has two points of view about the society in which he lives: that of a citizen and that of an artist. The latter is concerned only with the suitability of society as material for his art. Just as a liberal journalist may secretly rejoice at the rise of a Senator McCarthy because of the opportunity which it affords him to write brilliant and scathing denunciations of demagogues, so will the eye of the novelist of manners light up at the first glimpse of social injustice. For his books must depend for their life blood on contrast and are bound to lose both significance and popularity in a classless society.

Louis Auchincloss in Reflections of a Jacobite, *The Riverside Press, 1961.*

Democracy" and "Abraham Lincoln's bookmark." Their insignificance stimulates the memory that Sybille Bedford's *A Legacy* is probably the only modern novel descended from Henry James, and their bigotry can serve as an incentive to read Edith Wharton, who is (finally) rolling out of the trough. She can match all of Auchincloss's draperies, although his characters can't answer the variety of hers.

Carolyn F. Ruffin   (essay date 1970)

SOURCE: A review of *Second Chance: Tales of Two Generations,* in *The Christian Science Monitor,* August 20, 1970, p. 13.

[*In the following review, Ruffin discusses the puritanical nature of the characters in* Second Chance.]

The Puritans are always with us.

They are particularly with American literary men, even today. It's as though they didn't get in enough licks against the irreverent scribes of this world during the last century, haunting Hawthorne and shooting up out of the deep to disturb Melville.

Now they are after Louis Auchincloss.

Apparently in this collection of some new, some previously published, short stories [*Second Chance: Tales of Two Generations*], he set out to write about New Yorkers of that notorious generation. He confronts them with their own hypocrisy and weakness, and gives them the chance to decide whether or not it's too late to change.

They place high value on respectability, rectitude, and taste. They have worked, hard to attain their present status in society and in their professions. And while these pro- fessions may coincidentally be lucrative, they are not oc- cupations associated directly with rank materialism. Among the callings are law, publishing, curating in a history museum, collecting valuable editions of great literature, etc.

When these characters' respectability is questioned, they fall back on that good old debit-credit approach to moral- ity which sees Providence as the great Auditor in the sky. As long as their own bookkeeping appears impeceable, they are sure they will be treated justly.

They expect this justice to come from a Deity, who, as one character describes him, is "white, Anglo-Saxon, gen- teel," and Protestant. (Genteel after the tradition of Jonathan Edwards's divinity.)

And they know that His Justice is precise and predictable. For instance, if one's cherished wife sleeps around, it is because Heaven is punishing one for seeking pleasure in this world. It could have nothing to do with the fact that a man has failed to understand or communicate with his spouse.

What is most Puritan about these characters is their dilem- ma. Despite then outward confidence that they are among the chosen, inwardly they have a growing fear that they are among the damned.

For these Puritans the handwriting on the wall is the graf- fiti of a younger generation. (That's the reason for the collection's subtitle.) The youthful message is familiar: Cut the hypocrisy, practice law for the underprivileged; marry for love, not some grand design; communicate. There's more to morality than balancing your own books.

Mr. Auchincloss has done a fascinating study of the var- ious ways people react when the moving finger is put on them. Some of the stories are a little too neat and precise. And unless the plot is thoroughly thickened, his even- tempered, gentlemanly prose gets a little transparent and unconvincing.

However, four of the tales—two of which have appeared before in magazines—are particularly masterful. They are **"Black Shylock," "The Sacrifice," "The Collector,"** and **"The Prison Window."**

"The Prison Window" exudes the same brooding super- natural mood conjured by Shirley Jackson in such short stories as "The Lottery."

In all of the stories Mr. Auchincloss sustains a carefully created but subtle tension. He lets his character build a convincing case for his own rectitude which lasts at times until the final sequence. Yet even while this case is being argued, circumstances and other people's needs intrude upon the Puritan, unsettling his well-structured world.

Then in the last paragraph, with the mildest kind of irony, Auchincloss exposes his character's self-deception as in **"The Collector."** Or with a brutal accusation the author may bring the speaker to his knees, as in **"Black Shylock."**

The effect of both techniques is similar. The absolute blacks and whites of Puritan justice get shaded into the gray of ambivalence and uncertainty. The good and the bad are more likely to end up here or hereafter in a kind of pur- gatory of bewilderment than among the well-cataloged blisses of heaven or tortures of hell.

The finale of **"The Sacrifice"** is an example.

A justice finds in the brutal murder of his young grandson a purging of his own hatred of the frustrated, violent el- ement in his city. His wife, her hope and will to live almost destroyed by the tragedy, cannot forgive her hus- band's reaction. She loses all love and respect for him.

The justice concludes the story with this:

> But this, the nightmare, had been only a nightmare. *He* had survived. For what he had discovered was that his love for Mary Ellen did not, after all, depend on her love for him. It existed of and by itself, and it might survive all her scoffing, all her cruelty, even all her hate. He would look after Mary Ellen, and this love now proven so tough, so durable, so oddly independent, might expand indefinitely to take in . . . the whole of the big dirty world. . . .

The saving grace of Mr. Auchincloss's collection is that Puritans from whatever era make good drama. And his Puritans grapple with those hard to get at sins—prejudice and neglect of others.

Despite rumors to the contrary, there are enough of us left who haven't shook the Puritans to guarantee that Mr. Auchincloss's New Yorkers will find soul brothers.

Brom Weber (essay date 1970)

SOURCE: A review of *Second Chance: Tales of Two Generations,* in *The Saturday Review,* New York, Vol. LIII, No. 35, August 29, 1970, pp. 24-25.

[*Weber is an American educator and critic, who has published extensively on the poet Hart Crane. In the fol- lowing review, he discusses psychological and sociolog- ical identity as it is explored by Auchincloss in* Second Chance.]

Louis Auchincloss is an urbane, ironic, and experienced chronicler of the doings of our Anglo-Saxon, genteel wealthy in New York, familiar with their values, their modes of behavior and organization, and the extent to which they encounter and react to phenomena from the world outside their offices, apartments, and suburban es- tates. The stories in **Second Chance,** Auchincloss tells us on its jacket, have been designed as an exploration of "the identity crisis among the middle-aged and elderly in this city and its suburbs in the immediate present. They are concerned with the bewilderment in people from forty to ninety at finding themselves living in a world in which there is no general agreement not only as to what is a good life, but as to what is an amusing one."

As usual, Auchincloss's fictional reports are interesting as literature, informative as social observation. They illuminate not only the upper strata of Manhattan and Long Island, but also those of Philadelphia, Chicago, and elsewhere, even though details vary. Consequently, the generally negative import of *Second Chance*—that there is little likelihood of one for most of the book's characters—will arouse disquietude in more than a few communities.

The majority of the stories deal with individuals who, after contemplating or launching a new life on the sea of emotional or social possibility, forgo their adventure or conclude it by foundering badly. Defeat occurs most often because of indecision about the propriety or desirability of a new life. The individual then recedes into his habitual pattern despite its inadequacies. Frequently, nonheroic reactions such as lethargy and fear of novelty are concealed behind transparently irrelevant moral excuses.

In several stories, however, a character recognizes quite clearly that a projected change is either meretricious or incapable of realization. These particular fictions reach beyond mere depiction of the travail of a social class that sometimes senses it is obsolescent and corrupt or is accused of being so. In these stories Auchincloss by implication prescribes values and attitudes which, in his judgment, justify the survival of those guided by them.

In both types of story, strangely enough in view of Auchincloss's intention to probe an "identity crisis," there is no intermingling of social classes. Messages of discord or change from without are generally delivered by children or grandchildren rather than by interlopers. When the latter do appear—Jews in **"Second Chance"** and **"Suttee,"** an Italian immigrant's son in **"The Prince and the Pauper"**—they turn out to be incorporated members of the Establishment. Furthermore, young family emissaries of alien concepts are not particularly effective champions of the "socialism" and "liberalism" they urge upon their elders. As the tough old grandfather in **"The Double Gap"** keeps reminding the grandson who has rejected the family law firm's ethos in favor of action "in the ghettos, the slums, the poor rural areas, the starving parts of the world":

> I'm glad that I've made you [financially] independent so you won't be compelled, like your breadwinner friends, to go to work for a firm in whose "mystique" you cannot believe.

Since the problem of identity is not merely psychological but sociological as well, the social insularity of almost all the characters in these stories prevents them from developing a significant segment of whatever identities they possess or might create. Indeed, the relegation to offstage of the social conflict and turmoil so prevalent in our time establishes a dreamlike pall around the characters that

hampers any genuine search for their identities.

The fictionist of manners may, if he wishes, flesh out the being and world of a character by concentrating upon personal depth rather than social breadth. Henry James, for example, so complicated and intensified the emotional, physical, and intellectual experience of his characters that in his pages a paralyzed, isolated creature will appear to be electrically charged, connected by hot wires to a myriad invisible yet tangible people, his social existence taking form quite miraculously.

Just that kind of rich creation is to be found in **"Black Shylock,"** the initial and also most successful story in *Second Chance*. Powerfully, dramatically, Auchincloss shows that perversity of spirit raised to high art may produce apocalyptic revelation, yet is essentially socially delusive and personally non-sustaining. This fictional argument against pure negation and for moral responsibility achieves its victory because the central character is permitted to develop his paranoid fantasies without visible restraint on the part of his creator.

There are, of course, other good stories in *Second Chance,* but none achieves the strength and magic pervading "**Black Shylock.**" One admires Auchincloss's delicate wit, firm language, knowledge of contemporary events and catchwords, and admirable distaste for vulgarity and mendacity. Yet all too often he does not put his gifts to full use, seemingly hesitant to risk marring the polish of his fiction by exposing it to unknown strains. In this he may well be one of his own characters, still not aware of the range of his own identity.

The concluding story in this collection, **"The Sacrifice,"** suggests that the end of the search for identity is to be found in a willingness to abandon the search. Judge Platt discovers, to his horror, that he hates the violators of "law and order." Recognizing that hatred, like rudeness and murder, is a human phenomenon, he frees himself of human ties and thus can experience the love inherent in the "peace of God." *Second Chance,* then, appears to be saying that spiritual transcendence is all that remains for its characters.

The answer is much too simple, as simple as the belief that the absence of "general agreement" is a phenomenon of the 1970s. It may well be that the exclusiveness, the naïveté, the complacency, and the inertia of the twentieth-century heirs of the genteel tradition have rendered them irreversibly anachronistic. Perhaps they are fated to vanish wholly. Auchincloss's authority is such that one hesitates to reject his conclusion. He probably has good sociological support for it. Nevertheless, not having plumbed the regenerative powers of his characters sufficiently in these stories, he has not established his conclusion's validity artistically.

James Tuttleton (essay date 1972)

SOURCE: "Louis Auchincloss: The Image of Lost Elegance and Virtue," in *American Literature,* Vol. XLIII, No. 4, January, 1972, pp. 616-32.

[*Tuttleton is an American educator and critic whose books include* The Novel of Manners in America *(1972). In the following excerpt, he compares Auchincloss's fiction to that of Henry James and maintains that Auchincloss's writing is as much a departure from James's work as it is influenced by it. The critic also comments on the subject matter of Auchincloss's fiction and its relationship to issues of class. Tuttleton argues that Auchincloss effectively depicts affluent New York society and that critics shouldn't dismiss his work merely because of his well-to-do characters.*]

> The simplest truths are the most consoling: one of them is that New York will always have a past, together with writers consumed with nostalgia for lost days. Henry James and Mrs. Wharton—even Washington Irving—looked back at things that were gone, and we have become accustomed to look back at these writers who are also gone, in this way obtaining a doubled effect of remoteness, looking down a corridor of mirrors endlessly reflecting the image of lost elegance and virtue. The past, however, need not be distant nor the authors dead.
>
> —Gouverneur Paulding

Louis Auchincloss most nearly resembles Henry James in the emphasis he gives to the moral issues that grow out of the social lives of the very rich in New York City. And because he has described himself as a "Jacobite," many reviewers have concluded that it is therefore enough to describe him as merely an imitator of the Master. Auchincloss most differs from James, though, in the informed analysis he is able to give to the nice problems of ethics in the legal profession—a command of the world of Wall Street brokers and bankers which James himself sorely regretted not having. Auchincloss calls himself a Jacobite because so much of his lifetime's reading has been "over the shoulder of Henry James." To read the fiction of Proust, Trollope, Meredith, Thackeray, George Eliot, and Mrs. Wharton in the light of the criticism, fiction, and letters of James, Auchincloss has observed, is to be exposed to the full range of possibility for the novel of manners, "to be conducted through the literature of [James's] time, English, American, French and Russian, by a kindly guide of infinitely good manners, who is also infinitely discerning, tasteful and conscientious." James, for Auchincloss, has always been a "starting point," a "common denominator" [*Reflections of a Jacobite*]. But Auchincloss has always, once started, gone his own way—often qualifying and contesting, as well as enlarging, the social insights of the nineteenth-century novelist of manners.

The world brought to life in his novels is the nineteenth- and twentieth-century life of the metropolitan rich in New York City—particularly the lives of the lawyers, bankers, trust officers, corporation executives, and their wives and daughters. As a lawyer, Auchincloss knows them in their Park Avenue apartments and in their Wall Street offices. He sees the glitter and glamour of their world, its arrogant materialism and its unexpected generosities. He knows the rigidity of its conventions—just how far they can be bent, at what point they break, just when convention may break

a character. He understands what happens to the idealistic men and the unfulfilled women of this world. And he is able to tell their stories with unusual sympathy. Rarely has Auchincloss ventured from this small but exclusive world, because it is the world he knows best. For this "narrowness," I suppose, it is possible to criticize him. But if he does not write panoramic novels of the U.S.A., great fluid puddings encompassing the whole of the American scene, it is because he has learned from Henry James the lesson James tried to teach Mrs. Wharton: that she *must* be "tethered in native pastures, even if it reduces her to a backyard in New York" [*The Letters of Henry James,* ed. Percy Lubbock, 1920; I, 396]. The New York *haut monde* is Louis Auchincloss's backyard. His ten novels are his Austenean two inches of carefully carved ivory.. . . . .

In semipolitical literary criticism there are sometimes objections to the kind of people Auchincloss writes about. It is sometimes said, for example, that the world of New York society people is somehow not as interesting as that of share-croppers, boxers, or big-game hunters. Granville Hicks [in *Saturday Review* XLIX (February 5, 1966)] has confessed this bias in remarking that "to many people, myself included, an Italian boy who robs a poor Jew is a more challenging subject than an upperclass New Yorker who misappropriates funds, and a bewildered intellectual in search of wholeness of spirit belongs more truly to our times than the aged headmaster of a fashionable preparatory school."

But there is no necessary reason why this claim should be true. *The Assistant* and *Herzog* may be better novels than *The Embezzler* and *The Rector of Justin*. But their superiority has nothing to do with the subject matter or the "relevance" of these books—it has only to do with the greater artistry by which the novels of Malamud and Bellow are brought to life. In justifying the attention Auchincloss gives to people like Guy Prime, Augusta Millinder, Ida Trask, and Frank Prescott, I find it instructive to remember Auchincloss's observation on the universality of Tolstoy's art [in *Reflections of a Jacobite*]: "What he understands is that if a human being is described completely, his class makes little difference. He becomes a human being on the printed page, and other humans, of whatever class, can recognize themselves in his portrait. The lesson of Tolstoy is precisely how little of life, not how much, the artist needs."

His view of Proust also casts light on Auchincloss's choice of subject. In arguing that there has never been "so brilliant or so comprehensive a study of the social world" as that found in Proust, Auchincloss observes:

> To him the differences between class and class are superficial. Snobbishness reigns on all levels, so why does it matter which level one selects to study? Why not, indeed, pick the highest level, particularly if one's own snobbishness is thus gratified? Society in Proust parades before us, having to represent not a segment of mankind, but something closer to mankind itself. It is the very boldness of Proust's assumption that his universe is *the* universe . . . that gives to his distorted picture a certain universal validity. It is his faith that

a sufficiently careful study of each part will reveal the whole, that the analysis of a dinner party can be as illuminating as the analysis of a war. It is his glory that he very nearly convinces us.

Without drawing the parallel too closely, I submit that Auchincloss too sees that the differences between classes are superficial and that there is therefore no adequate reason why one should not deal with headmasters and lawyers, bankers and brokers, if they permit the kind of social analysis that illuminates our essential human predicament. The problem implicit in his choice is that of making is believe that this universe is—if not *the* universe—at least a *believable* universe, and describing his characters so fully and convincingly that we do not care about the class they belong to. It is Auchincloss's difficulty that, as good as some of his novels are, he does not always so convince us. But the limitation is one of his talent, not of his material.

It is, in fact, a mistake to think about Auchincloss's characters as belonging to a distinct "class." He does not believe that the United States is a classless society. But he does recognize that it is not possible for the contemporary American novelist of manners to write the kind of social fiction produced by Howells, Wharton, and James. The increasing democratization of the United States, he argues in *Reflections of a Jacobite,* has resulted in a rearrangement of social attitudes, so that today "snobbishness is more between groups than classes, more between cliques than between rich and poor." Surely there is a difference, he remarks, "between the feelings of the man who has not been asked to dinner and those of the man who has been thrown down the front stairs."

Most of these "groups," however (labor-capital, East-West, North-South, young-old, workers-intelligentsia), do not provide much social conflict for the would-be novelist of manners. "It is my simple thesis," Auchincloss has argued, "that the failure more generally to produce this kind of novel is not attributable to the decadence or escapism of mid-twentieth century writers, but rather to the increasingly classless nature of our society which does not lend itself to this kind of delineation. I do not mean that we are any duller than the Victorians, but simply that the most exciting and significant aspects of our civilization are no longer to be found in the distance and hostility between the social strata." Consequently, he has turned increasingly toward the inward world of his characters in order to explore why, in this cliqueish, classless society, people hang onto their snobbishness in the ways they do.

The divided career of Louis Auchincloss as lawyer/novelist and his indifference to "sociological" explanations of evil have led other critics to attack his social and moral criticism as fakery and to claim that he is captivated by the very social prejudices which are his subject. Robert M. Adams, for example, has ridiculed Auchincloss for writing, "like a latter-day Trollope, a pseudo-critique of commercialism which collapses docilely as soon as one perceives it is being launched from a platform provided by commercialism itself." The assumption on which this statement is based—that the novelist must stand outside the society he seeks to criticize before his criticism can be authentic—is arrant nonsense. Auchincloss may be a conservative opposed to Old and New Left radicalism. But this fact in itself does not invalidate his insider's criticism of the limitations—moral and social—of the world he describes. There is certainly adequate rational, theological, and moral justification for the claim that evil arises from selfish, snobbish and dissipated people as well as from economic or sociological causes.

No politician, Auchincloss takes society, for literature, more or less as he finds it. But he is not guilty of what Edith Wharton called [in *A Background Glance,* 1934] "the tendency not infrequent in novelists of manners—Balzac and Thackeray among them—to be dazzled by contact with the very society they satirize." He is fascinated by the world he portrays: he loves the details of an estate settlement as much as Thackeray loved the stylish little supper parties of Mrs. Rawdon Crawley; he is as fascinated by the complexities of a corporation merger as Proust was by the intricacies of precedence; and he is as delighted by the eccentricities of the rich as Balzac was by the spectacle of miserly greed. But if Auchincloss loves his world, he is not taken in by it. Conscious of the moral and social incongruities between his world and the world, say, of Malamud, he is as disturbed as any reader of the *Partisan Review* that no matter how painstakingly Proust "underlines the dullness, the selfishness, and the fatuity of the Guermantes set, they remain to the end still invested with much of the glamour in which his imagination clothed them" [*Reflections of a Jacobite*].

But Auchincloss has no wish to idealize or glamorize his "aristocracy," or to claim for it, nostalgically, an elegance or virtue inconsistent with the known facts of New York City social history. Nor is he "hankering after any good old days." He has asked whether anyone *would* wish to return to "a New York where [in *Reflections of a Jacobite*] servants slept in unheated cubicles on the top of drafty brownstones, with an evening off every second week. . . ." His love for the elegance and virtue of this affluent world is the love of an artist for his material, which is quite another thing from his feeling for it as a man. Every writer, he has observed, has two points of view about "the society in which he lives: that of a citizen and that of an artist. The latter is concerned only with the suitability of society as material for his art. Just as a liberal journalist may secretly rejoice at the rise of a Senator McCarthy because of the opportunity which it affords him to write brilliant and scathing denunciations of demagogues, so will the eye of the novelist of manners light up at the first glimpse of social injustice. For his books must depend for their life blood on contrast and are bound to lose both significance and popularity in a classless society." Our awareness of this distinction between society as experienced and society as transformed in fiction ought to discourage us from condemning, as reactionary, the novelist who insists on exploring inequities and ambiguities from the inside of the social mechanism. Auchincloss's virtue is that he brings alive the New York City life of Henry James and Mrs. Wharton by showing us that, however elegant or virtuous it may seem, it is nei-ther very distant nor dead.

G. Edward White (essay date 1972)

SOURCE: "Human Dimensions of Wall Street Fiction," in *American Bar Association,* Vol. 58, No. 2, February, 1972, pp. 175-80.

[*White is an author and legal scholar. In the following article, he discusses the themes of bureaucratization, class consciousness, ethics, and contemporary Wall Street legal practices as they are treated in Auchincloss's fiction.*]

During the past four decades much has been written on the public image of large New York City law firms. The "Wall Street" firms, as they have come to be called, have been denounced as capitalist predators, hailed as responsible intermediaries between corporations and the public, seen as bureaucratic structures in an increasingly specialized and hierarchical world and viewed as the last bastions of nineteenth century individualism. In most of these accounts, far less attention has been paid to what the Wall Street lawyer does than to what he symbolizes. Although a survey of the literature on Wall Street firms may give some insight into the changing impressions those institutions have made upon the public mind, it yields little understanding of the effect of Wall Street practice upon the individuals who engage in it.

There has been one notable exception to this generalization: the novels and short stories of Wall Street practitioner Louis Auchincloss. Beginning in 1953, Auchincloss has produced novels—*A Law for the Lion* (1953) and *The Great World and Timothy Colt* (1956)—and four collections of short stories—*The Romantic Egoist* (1954), *Powers of Attorney* (1963), *Tales of Manhattan* (1967) and *Second Chance: Tales of Two Generations* (1970)—about the working lives of Wall Street lawyers. The information about Wall Street practice contained in these books has been subordinated, of course, to Auchincloss's major novelistic purposes; it is arguably less "reliable" or "authentic" than a similar nonfictional account might be. Nonetheless it provides a basis for understanding the human dimensions of Wall Street practice missing in other accounts. Through Auchincloss's fiction one gets a sense of how, in a myriad diverse ways, it feels to work for a large New York City law firm.

I propose to concentrate on four themes of Auchincloss's Wall Street fiction: bureaucraticization, class consciousness, professional ethics and the contemporary critique of Wall Street practice by young lawyers. The first three of these are described by Smigel [in *The Wall Street Lawyer,* 1964] and Carlin [in *The Lawyers Ethics,* 1967] as central to an understanding of large-firm law practice; the fourth is a matter of much interest for prospective Wall Street practitioners and the firms that interview them. The themes by no means exhaust the material pertaining to Wall Street life in Auchincloss's fiction, and they should not be regarded as, in their totality, serving to define the Wall Street lawyer's universe. They are, however, pervasive and pressing aspects of the world of contemporary Wall Street firms.

Nonfictional accounts of the history of large New York City firms during the twentieth century stress the change in size and structure of the firm unit and a consequent change in the character of law practice. In the early twentieth century, the ancestors of the present Wall Street firms were relatively small in size with a general practice that included anything from litigation to probate work. With rapid developments in technology and the consequent growth of large-size specialized business enterprises, they took on a new appearance. Firms grew in size, became more specialized and compartmentalized, drew an increasing percentage of their business from corporate work and assumed the characteristics of large-scale hierarchical organizations. Of particular importance for the members of those firms was the apparent clash between a mode of their professional heritage—the "free", independent general practitioner—and the increasingly specialized and constrained character of their own practice. The tensions produced by this clash are at the heart of Auchincloss's treatment of bureaucratization.

In developing the bureaucratization and other themes, Auchincloss stresses the interaction of two levels of human response. The first level is the subscription by most of a firm's lawyers, and especially by those holding internal positions of power, to a general professional stance on a particular issue, such as bureaucratization. The second is the emergence of tensions and contradictions in that stance and the reaction to them by individual firm members.

The general professional stance on bureaucratization views it as a necessary but lamentable phenomenon. The change is necessary, as Sheridan Dale, one of the principal characters in *The Great World and Timothy Colt,* put it, because "when you get up to eighty-six lawyers with an overhead of a million a year . . . you're a big business, and you ought to act like one". Another senior partner, Clitus Tilney of *Powers of Attorney,* "knew what disorganization did to overhead". For "every sixty minutes dedicated to the law" Tilney "had to devote twenty to administration". Lloyd Deneger, Dale's and Tilney's counterpart in *Tales of Manhattan,* was able to attribute "the splendid position that [his firm] occupied in the field of corporation law" to the fact that its internal atmosphere resembled "a huge, bright, humming legal machine" far more than "a gentleman's chaos of prima donnas in high white collars at rolltop desks".

But the change is also lamentable: the acceptance of increased organization is continually accompanied by a professed adherence to an older, more informal way of practicing law. Tilney was conscious of "the fashion among [Wall Street] lawyers to affect an aversion to administrative detail, to boast that their own firms were totally disorganized, that they practiced law in a bookish, informal atmosphere, suggestive of Victorian lithographs of county

Auchincloss and his wife at a party given by Truman Capote.

solicitors seated at rolltop desks and listening with wise smiles to the problems of youth and beauty". Some senior partners made serious attempts to approximate the older style. Dale's predecessor, Henry Knox, despised "administrative problems", which he considered "beneath him", and described his firm as "a group of gentlemen loosely associated by a common enthusiasm for the practice of law".

Auchincloss's lawyers and staff members attempt to shape their working lives in response to the ambiguities in their stance toward bureaucratization in two notable ways: through "teamwork" and through the presence of status gradations within the firm.

"Teamwork" for Auchincloss is a concept limned with ironies, some of them savage. The modern Wall Street firm requires a fair amount of co-operation among individuals who are competing with one another for positions of internal power: influence among one's partners or partnerships themselves. Henry Knox's image of law practice implied only a cursory degree of co-operation among gentlemen loosely associated by a common enthusiasm for the law; the complexity of the real-life modern law office

necessitates far more interdependence among its members. But interdependence, in a firm staffed by individuals in direct competition with one another for a small number of lucrative positions, faces powerful currents of resistance.

Auchincloss's lawyers resolve this difficulty by defining "teamwork" in anarchistic terms. A "team man" is not one who butters up his superiors or champions the joys of group labor, but rather one who is willing to devote the bulk of his time and energy to producing work that reflects craftsmanship of a superior quality. The firm benefits from this product but recognizes it to be primarily the result of high personal standards and strong ambitions for power and success in the individual lawyer. Auchincloss's lawyers expect their office mates to be primarily concerned with their own ambitions and achievements, even at their colleagues' expense. It is no shock to Clitus Tilney to discover that Chambers Todd, one of his partners, had attempted to entice him to take a college presidency because Todd wanted Tilney's senior partnership. Nor is it surprising to Horace Mason, an associate in *Powers of Attorney,* to learn that coassociate Jake Platt snoops in his personal files; he cheerfully confesses to Platt that he has snooped in Platt's.

A second way in which the Auchincloss characters resolve the difficulties inherent in superimposing an individualistic professional model on a large interdependent business organization is the creation and maintenance of informal status gradations. The primary purpose of these gradations is to create a set of specialized identities for the lawyers. An associate working in the corporate department need not see himself in the context of the entire firm but merely in terms of those in his immediate area. He is located at a point in the vertical arrangement of the firm, and he may find solace, as did one of the characters in *Tales of Manhattan,* in its "orderly, hierarchical atmosphere . . . where one knew precisely at all times what was expected of one and where one rose from tier to tier pretty much in proportion to one's efforts". He may also take comfort in his horizontal location: the "corporate men" in *The Great World and Timothy Colt* "looked down on everything" outside their department. Departments have their own personalities. In *Powers of Attorney* a partner in estates sees the corporate department as made up of "bright, intolerant younger men who had been on the *Harvard Law Review*"; a head of litigation in *A Law for the Lion* is "not sure" that one of the younger associates "wouldn't turn out to be too tweedy, too social for the discipline and dedication of the litigation group".

Not all associates enjoy their locations. A contemporary of Timmy Colt finds the estates department a "morgue" and feels that he "might as well be an undertaker". A young man in real estate in *Powers of Attorney* is conscious that working in his department "was like climbing the stairs in a department store while alongside one an escalator carried the other customers smoothly and rapidly to the landing". Some of Auchincloss's lawyers are constrained by their roles. Sylvester Brooks of *Powers of Attorney* can function only in his wholly ceremonial role as the "perfectly charming and worldly-wise old gentleman" and "supreme arbiter of wills"; his "job was a form, an ingenious face saver, conceived by a benevolent senior partner to keep an old body occupied". Rutherford Tower, a nephew of his firm's founder in the same collection, had been made a partner "for only three reasons: because of his name, because of his relatives, and because he was there".

In other cases, however, a man's personality blends so smoothly with his working role that the two become indistinguishable. Waldron Webb, the senior litigator of Clitus Tilney's firm, "was one of these unhappy men who always wake up angry. He was angered by the sparrows outside his bedroom window in Bronxville, by the migraines of his long-suffering wife, by the socialism in the newspaper, the slowness of the subway, the wait for the elevator, the too casual greeting of the receptionist. It was only the great morning pile on his desk of motions, attachments and injunctions that restored his calm. . . . Litigation, indeed, was more than Webb's profession; it was his catharsis." Harry Hamilton, Webb's counterpart in *A Law for the Lion,* was able to "play without rival his chosen role of enfant terrible" in the "sober and mild atmosphere" of his firm. He surrounded himself with a "little clique of admirers who aped his cynicism, his heavy humor, his

extravagant passion for baseball, and who every evening at six were to be found ambling after him down the corridor on their way to dinner at the same waterfront restaurant".

Other status gradations exist in Auchincloss's firms. Managing clerks, secretaries and women lawyers are set apart by their lack of mobility and the regimented quality of their working lives. In general, status gradations serve as devices through which Auchincloss's practitioners, by limiting the number of persons whose approval is necessary for their professional development, can deepen their sense of autonomy. Although the vertical and horizontal subdivisions of the offices serve as constraints, they also breed a kind of independence by fostering the creation of a plethora of small subfirms, each a microcosm of an older style of law practice, within the large, impersonal whole. One of Auchincloss's characters in *Powers of Attorney* recalls that the senior partner responsible for establishing in his firm an "elaborate [system of] etiquette" that publicized and reinforced status differences among the employees was remembered by his colleagues as the last of "the great individualist lawyers".

Auchincloss's treatment of the theme of social class runs counter to the traditional identification of Wall Street firms as apologists for an upper-class way of life. In Auchincloss's hands class consciousness becomes a two-edged concept. Sheridan Dale's success with his upper-class clientele, for example, comes from the fact that he is not one of them. Dale's mentor, Cyrus Sheffield, had seen in the "unprepossessing young man from Fordham the future confidant of his rich widows and old maids". Rather than delegating this business "to attenuated young men of better family than brains", Sheffield "had the wits to perceive . . . that affluent ladies from east of Central Park, distrustful of anyone from their own world as for that very reason too soft, would eagerly embrace, in their business affairs a champion from the great murky outside city which they felt to threaten them—that they would prefer to fight, like ancient Romans, barbarians with barbarians".

Alongside a general inclination among members of Wall Street firms toward upper-class life styles, Auchincloss places a sense of the relative insignificance of those styles in forging a successful law practice. Clitus Tilney may wear "aristocratically" unpressed tweeds, cover the walls of his brownstone with Hudson River School landscapes and pour "very cold dry martinis into chilled silver mugs", but he has a "habit of checking the firm's books to see if Rutherford [Tower]'s 'Social Register practice', as he slightlingly called it, paid off". At one point in Jake Platt's agonizing over his potential partnership, he is disconcerted by an associate's remark that "this firm is properly concerned with its reputation of being a bit on the social side. Having Barry [Schilde] [a Jewish competitor of Platt's] as a partner might balance things out."

Auchincloss's portrait of the pervasive yet limited influence of upper-class life styles among Wall Street firms suggests that it is one thing to determine that firms are aware of class characteristics among their personnel but quite another to assess the importance of those character-istics. On one occasion Professor Detlev Vagts of Harvard Law School expressed surprise [in *Harvard Law Review,* 1964] at Auchincloss's emphasis on "sartorial matters and the Social Register", things he felt "made little difference" to Wall Street lawyers. In making that comment Vagts unintentionally captured the essence of Auchincloss's view of Wall Street class consciousness—matters such as dress and club membership receive a great deal of emphasis and are seen as making very little difference.

Auchincloss's lawyers profess a strict adherence to high ethical standards and voice their allegiance to the Can-ons of Professional Ethics. A senior partner of *Tales of Manhattan,* his successor recalls, "always insisted that the Code of Professional Ethics should be . . . strictly interpreted. . . . He never held a share of stock in a corporation that he represented. He would not even allow the firm's telephone number to appear on our letterhead, and it was only with the greatest difficulty that we per-suaded him to enter it in the directory."

But this public stance does not prevent them from not following their principles when, as one from the same collection puts it, "they stand in the way of old and valued clients". In fact, Auchincloss appears to suggest, the pres-ence of a high-powered clientele may increase the pres-sures on Wall Street lawyers to behave in unethical ways. "If you ever have the good fortune to secure a big com-pany as your client," Chambers Todd informs a subordi-nate on one occasion, "you will learn that the word 'un-biased' has no further meaning for you. . . . A good law-yer eats, lives and breathes for his clients." Clitus Tilney wistfully acknowledges the truth of Todd's remark: "I wish we could return to the old days of great integrity. . . . Before we were captured by the corporations. Before we became simple mouth-pieces."

An extended treatment of the effect of clients upon ethical issues appears in *The Great World and Timothy Colt.* Timmy Colt, the protagonist, is confronted with an ethical question involving the management of a trust.

One of Colt's clients, George Emlen, the nephew of the surviving senior partner in Colt's firm, suggests, upon the maturation of an Emlen family trust, that he take the stock of a small family company that leases textile patents as his third of the trust principal, allowing his two sisters, the other beneficiaries, to divide the cash and marketable securities. The book value of the company stock is worth less than one third of the total trust holdings.

Colt becomes suspicious of George's motives, and he resolves to check his firm's files that pertain to the activ-ities and plans of the Emlen company and of Holcombe textiles, a giant company on whose board of directors George sits. He finally finds a Holcombe memorandum of new business in which the company declares its intention to increase the production of a new kind of washable summer suit and to acquire a series of patents to that end. The Emlen company holds three of the patents. George's scheme becomes clear: he intends to make the Emlen

patents available to Holcombe for a reasonable sum in return for Holcombe's eventually steering some business toward one of his textile mills.

Colt then communicates George's scheme to his cotrustee, Florence Emlen, George's mother. But Mrs. Emlen, a fig-urehead who simply signs releases and distribution pa-pers, fails to grasp the implications of Colt's remarks and turns to George in her confusion. Colt then capitulates, and on hearing from one of George's sisters that they are most anxious to have the distribution made, resolves not to oppose it. Still troubled, however, by "his own depre-cated conscience", he confides in Ellen Shallcross, the stepdaughter of his senior partner, with whom he has been having an affair during his separation from his wife. At-tempting to save Colt from his dilemma, Ellen tells one of the Emlen sisters the details of George's scheme, only to find that the trust distribution has already been made.

Ellen's information stimulates one of the Emlen sisters to hire a lawyer and sue for a compulsory accounting of the trust, alleging that the trust distribution releases the sisters signed were invalid as fraudulently obtained. Colt's first resolve is to perjure himself at trial, since he is certain that none of the adversary parties can prove that he knew of any arrangement between George Emlen and Holcombe which would have made the Emlen company shares worth more than their book value. But at the last minute Colt takes the stand and simply tells the truth: that he investi-gated the Emlen-Holcombe files, learned of the patents and concealed this information from the Emlen sisters, thus facilitating an unequal distribution of trust assets and consequently neglecting his responsibilities as trustee.

Confessing that "the case is unprecedented in my experi-ence", the judge refers the matter to the Grievance Com-mittee of The Association of the Bar of the City of New York. Ultimately, Colt learns that the committee probably will not disbar him, since Canon 11 of the New York City Code of Professional Ethics confines abuses "dealing with trust property" to those instances where the lawyer abused his fiduciary position "for his personal benefit or gain". "I'm told", Colt informs his wife, "the committee may regard it as a quixotic breach of trust and only censure me. But it's not going to make it any easier to get a job."

In this example Auchincloss seems to be suggesting that the world of Wall Street practice is an especially difficult one for those, such as Colt, who are "governed by their consciences". At every stage in the Emlen trust proceed-ing Colt's desire to arrive at a fair and straightforward distribution of the assets runs up against pressures from his clients or his senior partner. Ultimately he is faced with the choice of either deliberately violating his trust or losing his place as junior manager of the Emlen family fortunes. When he temporarily chooses the latter, this choice fills him with such self-hate that he subsequently jeopardizes his career in Wall Street practice.

The Timothy Colts are the casualties of the prevailing stance toward professional ethics in Auchincloss's Wall Street. Those who survive are those who adhere to the dictum of Gerald Hunt, senior partner of the principal firm in *A Law for the Lion*. Hunt, Auchincloss notes, "was too much a man of the world to find in the application of broad moral rules to individual problems anything but the crudest possible taste". Hunt "professed many principles himself; few people, indeed, professed more", but "to premise one's conduct on their absolute relation to reality, well, that was being childish". Translated into law office terms, Hunt's dictum suggests that a successful practitioner keeps his sense of ethical outrage in the perspective of his clients' interests. To do otherwise is not to live in the world.

Are the major themes of Auchincloss still central to an understanding of Wall Street life? Do the dynamics of bureaucratization, class consciousness and professional ethics still serve as a means of defining the character of professional life for the Wall Street lawyer? Or have those issues been altered by the recent concern among young lawyers for the ways in which large private law firms respond to the presence of minority groups, the problems of poverty and the demands of consumer interests? Has, for example, the specter of the "organization man" become outdated, the WASP upper-class success model been replaced, the multileveled ethical philosophy of a Gerald Hunt been dismissed as hypocrisy? Some of these questions are tentatively addressed by Auchincloss in **"The Double Gap"**, a story in his recent work, ***Second Chance: Tales of Two Generations***.

"The Double Gap" involves an extended dialogue between Albert Ellsworth, senior partner of Carter & Ellsworth, and his grandson, Philip Kyles, concerning the latter's decision not to work for Ellsworth's firm on his graduation from law school. Ellsworth presents an "apologia" for the prevailing professional stance with regard to bureaucratization, class consciousness and questions of professional ethics. Kyles, in his turn, offers a critique of Ellsworth's position and emphasizes what he judges to be the central concerns facing a prospective Wall Street lawyer in the 1970s.

Early in the conversation Ellsworth states that his "greatest concern over the last thirty years" has been "the increase in size of our office". His chief dilemma, as managing partner, has been "to preserve the individualist spirit and the moral standards of the old-time practitioner" in the face of "the fantastic business regulations exacted by modern socialism". To achieve this he has reached out to the spirit of the firm's founder, Elihu Cowden Carter, the individualist lawyer incarnate. Ellsworth, sensing the contrast between his own "drab way" and the "color and inspiration" of his firm's founder, "deliberately set out to create the legend of Elihu Cowden Carter as a religion and a creed to hold [his] office together".

This classic approach to the problem of bureaucracy is ridiculed by Kyles, who finds Carter's French furniture, which Ellsworth had moved from the founder's office to the firm's reception hall, "pompous", Carter's writings "windy", and Carter himself "a brilliant ham actor who persuaded a credulous public to accept the hatchet man of a big, bullying corporation as a, legal philosopher and statesman". In keeping Carter's spirit alive, Ellsworth has revealed himself, in his grandson's opinion, as "a magnificent old cynic" who "can't admit it", a trait "my generation can never understand".

Class consciousness also enters the dialogue. Ellsworth recalls the time "a journalist . . . came to interview me about a book that he wanted to write on the big New York law firms". The interviewer, "was frankly cynical about what he expected to find", Ellsworth notes, "nepotism, old school ties, inter-firm back scratching. I told him that none of the big firms could long survive those things, that character and brains were their indispensable stock in trade. I invited him to use a desk in our office and to open all files that were not privileged. After three months he wrote a piece that justified me." At another point Ellsworth refers to his "great . . . inhibitions about his social inferiority", that marked his courtship of Kyles's grandmother, whom Ellsworth saw as marked by "impulses of generosity" that "reached out to . . . the servants, the hard-working clerks in the office, the poor of her charities, the world itself".

Kyles sees some of these issues rather differently. He remembers his grandmother as one who "could no more love the people in the slums than she could love the members of her own family" and who "tried", in his opinion, "to cover the desert of a heart dried up by a psychic shame with the flowers of charity". Kyles feels that "the gap seems to be narrowing between the big corporations and their lawyers and the Mafia and theirs"; he wants to "benefit [his] fellow men directly, in the ghettoes, the slums, the poor rural areas, the starving parts of the world".

In matters of professional ethics, as well, Ellsworth's attitudes approximate the prevailing attitude of Auchincloss's Wall Street. His "game", as Kyles terms it, is "to be at once the greatest and most ethical member of the whole wide bar". He believes, like one of his peers from another story in ***Second Chance,*** that "a law firm is something much more than its clients' problems", that lawyers "must be dedicated to something higher than the client, something higher than mere monetary reward". Yet on occasion he adopts Gerald Hunt's view of the relationship of principles to specific situations, especially those involving important clients. He confesses to Kyles that he looked the other way when the Great American Fruit Company, a major client of his firm, bribed courts in Dutch Honduras, accepting that practice "as a *sine qua non* to doing business in Central America", and that he allowed the firm "to try and win a case before a judge whom I knew had been fixed" without resigning.

Ellsworth's attitude is described by Kyles as a "compensating game of ethical canons which has the function, at least in the minds of your generation, of raising the lawyer to a higher moral plane than that of his client". For Kyles, this "game" is simply a rationalization for the fact that "clients' best interests" are "the be-all and end-all" of his grandfather's peers' "professional lives". "I want to bust . . . the 'establishment,'" Kyles tells Ellsworth, "you want to romanticize it. Neither of us can bear it as it is."

Auchincloss appears to suggest in **"The Double Gap"** that, although the themes of bureaucratization, class consciousness and professional ethics may remain central to Wall Street practice in the coming generation, the prevailing responses to those themes among lawyers may be altered. If the respective professional stances combine to form, as Kyles asserts, a "mystique" in which Wall Street practitioners wrap themselves, the capacity of that mystique to survive appears questionable. Kyles informs his grandfather that "those of us who have to earn our bread may go to work for firms like yours, but they won't buy the 'mystique'".

Should this phenomenon occur in great enough numbers or permeate not only the lower but the upper levels of Wall Street firms, the professional world that Auchincloss's characters strive to understand may well become new, and even brave.

Though *The Partners* is a collection of tales rather than a novel, it has novelistic unity; and it proves that the novel of manners is far from passé: when it is well done, it not only winds up on the best-seller list but provokes the attention of the literary establishment as well.

—*James Tuttleton, a review of* A Writer's Capital, *in* Sewanee Review, *Vol. LXXXII, No. 3, Summer, 1974.*

Gore Vidal (essay date 1974)

SOURCE: "Real Class," in *The New York Review of Books*, Vol. XXI, No. 12, July 18, 1974, pp. 10-15.

[*The author of such works as* Visit to a Small Planet *(1956),* Myra Breckenridge *(1968),* Burr *(1973), and* Lincoln *(1984), Vidal is an American author particularly noted for his historical novels and iconoclastic essays. In his work he examines the plight of modern humanity as it exists in a valueless world and amid the world's corrupt institutions. Vidal's work in all genres is marked by urbane wit and brilliant technique. Here, he takes issue with other critics, especially Granville Hicks, who complain that Auchincloss's subject matter is too limited. Vidal counters that Auchincloss's characters are drawn from the "ruling class of the United States" and that his focus on this group is unique and valuable, though it has caused many critics and educators to ignore his work. Commenting specifically about* The Partners, *Vidal notes several flaws and virtues that he believes are typical of Auchincloss's work.*]

"What a dull and dreary trade is that of critic," wrote Diderot. "It is so difficult to create a thing, even a mediocre thing; it is so easy to detect mediocrity." Either the great philosophe was deliberately exaggerating or else Americans have always lived in an entirely different continuum from Europe. For us the making of mediocre things is the rule while the ability to detect mediocrity or anything else is rare. A century ago, E. L. Godkin wrote in *The Nation*: "The great mischief has always been that whenever our reviewers deviate from the usual and popular course of panegyric, they start from and end in personality, so that the public mind is almost sure to connect unfavorable criticism with personal animosity.

Don't knock, boost! was the cry of Warren Harding. To which the corolary was plain: anyone who knocks is a bad person with a grudge. As a result, the American has always reacted to the setting of standards rather the way Count Dracula responds to a clove of garlic or a crucifix. Since we are essentially a nation of hustlers rather than makers, any attempt to set limits or goals, rules or standards, is to attack a system of free enterprise where not only does the sucker not deserve that even break but the honest man is simply the one whose cheating goes undetected. Worse, to say that one English sentence might be better made than another is to be a snob, a subverter of the democracy, a Know-Nothing enemy of the late arrivals to our shores and its difficult language.

I doubt if E. L. Godkin would find the American bookchat scene any better today than it was when he and his literary editor Wendell Phillips Garrison did their best to create if not common readers uncommon reviewers. Panegyric is rarer today than it was in the last century but personality is still everything, as the Sunday *New York Times Book Review* demonstrates each week: who can ever forget the *Times*'s gorgeous tribute not to the book by Mr. Saul Bellow under review but to its author's admittedly unusual physical beauty? What matters is not if a book is good or bad (who, after all, would know the difference?) but whether or not the author is a good person or a bad person. It is an article of faith among us that only a good person can write a good book; certainly, a bad person will only write bad books (the continuing Ezra Pound debate is full of fine examples of this popular wisdom).

But then moralizing is as natural to the American bookchat writer as it is to the rest of our countrymen—a sort of national tic. Naturally, there are fashions in goodness owing to changes in the Climate of Opinion (current forecast: Chomsky occluded, low pressure over the black experience, small Stravinsky-Craft warnings). Also, since Godkin's time, the American university has come into its terrible own. Departments of English now produce by what appears to be parthenogenesis novels intended only for the classroom; my favorite demonstrated that the universe is—what else?—the university. Occasionally a university novel (or U-novel) will be read by the general (and dwindling) public for the novel; and sometimes a novel written for that same public (P-novel) will be absorbed into Academe, but more and more the division between the two realms grows and soon what is written to be taught in class will stay there and what is written to be read outside will stay there, too. On that day the kingdom of prose will end, with an exegesis.

Meanwhile, bookchat, both P and U, buzzes on like some deranged bumblebee with a taste for ragweed; its store of bitter honey periodically collected and offered the public (?) in books with titles like *Literary Horizons: A Quarter Century of American Fiction* by Granville Hicks, one of the most venerable bees in the business, a nice old thing who likes just about everything that's "serious" but tends to worry more about the authors than their books. Will X develop? Get past the hurdle of The Second Novel (everyone has One Novel in him, the First) or will fashion destroy him? Drink? Finally, does he deserve to be memorialized in *Literary Horizons*? Mr. Hicks's list of approved novelists contains one black, one Catholic, one Southern Wasp, and six Jews. That is the standard mix for the Seventies. The Fifties mix would have been six Southern Wasps, one Jew, no black, etc.

For those who find puzzling the high favor enjoyed by the Jewish novelist in today's bookchat land, I recommend Mr. Alfred Kazin's powerful introduction to *The Commentary Reader,* "The Jew as Modern American Writer." Mr. Kazin tells us, with pardonable pride, that not only are Jews "the mental elite of the power age" but "definitely it was now [1966] the thing to be Jewish." As a result, to be a Jew in America is the serious subject for a P or even U novel, while to be a Wasp is to be away from the creative center; the born Catholic (as opposed to a convert like Flannery O'Connor) is thought at best cute (if Irish), at worst silly (if drunken Irish). In the permissive Sixties, Negroes were allowed to pass themselves off as blacks and their books were highly praised for a time but then there was all that trouble in the schools and what with one thing or another the black writers faded away except for James Baldwin, Mr. Hicks's token nigger. Yet even Mr. Hicks is worried about Mr. Baldwin. Does he *really* belong on the List? Is it perhaps time for his "funeral service" as a writer? Or will he make one final titanic effort and get it all together and write The Novel?

Like Bouvard, like Pecuchet, like every current bookchatterer, Hicks thinks that there really is something somewhere called The Novel which undergoes periodic and progressive change (for the better—this is America!) through Experiments by Great Masters. Consequently the Task of the Critic is to make up Lists of Contenders, and place his bets accordingly. Not for Mr. Hicks Brigid Brophy's truism: there is no such thing as The Novel, only novels.

At any given moment the subject or the matter of American fiction is limited by the prevailing moral prejudices and assumptions of the residents in bookchat land. U-novels must always be predictably experimental (I reserve for another occasion a scrutiny of those interesting cacti) while the respectable P-novel is always naturalistic, usually urban, often Jewish, always middle-class, and of course, deeply, sincerely heterosexual.

Conscious of what the matter of fiction *ought* to be, Mr. Hicks somewhat nervously puts Louis Auchincloss on his list. On the one hand, Auchincloss deals entirely with the American scene, writes in a comfortably conventional manner, and is one of the few intellectuals who writes popular novels. On the other hand, despite virtues, Auchincloss is not much thought of in either the P or the U world and Mr. Hicks is forced to buzz uneasily: "Although I have read and reviewed most of Louis Auchincloss's work in the past twelve years, I hesitated about including him in this volume." So the original Debrett must have felt when first called upon to include the Irish peerage. "Certainly he has not been one of the movers and shakers of the postwar period." As opposed, presumably, to Reynolds Price, Wright Morris, Herbert Gold, Bernard Malamud, and the other powerhouses on Mr. Hicks's list. Actually, only two or three of Mr. Hicks's writers could be said to have made any contribution at all to world literature. But that is a matter of taste. After all, what, Pontius, *is* literature?

Mr. Hicks returns worriedly to the *matter* of fiction. Apparently Auchincloss "has written for the most part about 'good' society, the well-to-do and the well-bred. And he has written about them with authority. What bothers me is not that he writes about this little world but that he seems to be aware of no other. Although he is conscious of its faults, he never questions its values in any serious way." This is fascinating. I have read all of Auchincloss's novels and I cannot recall one that did not in a most serious way question the values of his "little world." Little world!

It is a fascinating tribute to the cunning of our rulers and to the density of our intellectuals (bookchat division, anyway) that the world Auchincloss writes about, the domain of Wall Street bankers and lawyers and stockbrokers, is thought to be irrelevant, a faded and fading genteel-gentile enclave when, in actual fact, this little world comprises the altogether too vigorous and self-renewing ruling class of the United States—an oligarchy that is in firm control of the Chase Manhattan Bank, American foreign policy, and the decision-making processes of both divisions of the Property Party; also, most "relevantly," Auchincloss's characters set up and administer these various foundations that subsidize those universities where academics may serenely and dully dwell like so many frogs who think their pond the ocean (the universe is the university again).

Of all our novelists, Auchincloss is the only one who tells us how our rulers behave in their banks and their boardrooms, their law offices and their clubs. Yet such is the vastness of our society and the remoteness of academics and bookchatterers from actual power that those who should be most in this writer's debt have no idea what a useful service he renders us by revealing and, in some ways, by betraying his class. But then how can the doings of a banker who is white and gentile and rich be *relevant* when everyone knows that the only meaningful American experience is to be Jewish, lower-middle-class, and academic? Or (in Mr. Hicks's words), "As I said a while ago and was scolded for saying, the characteristic hero of our time is a misfit." Call me Granville.

Ignorance of the real world is not a new thing in our literary life. After the Second World War, a young critic made a splash with a book that attributed the poverty of American fiction to the lack of a class system—a vulgar variation on Henry James's somewhat similar but usually misunderstood observations about American life. This particular writer came from a small town in the Midwest; from school, he had gone into the service and from there into a university. Since he himself had never seen any sign of a class system, he decided that the United States was a truly egalitarian society. It should be noted that one of the charms of the American arrangement is that a citizen can go through a lifetime and never know his true station or who the rulers are.

Of course our writers know that there are rich people hidden away somewhere (in the columns of Suzy, in the novels of Louis Auchincloss) but since the Depression, the owners of the country have played it cool, kept out of sight, consumed inconspicuously. Finally, no less a P (now P-U) writer than that lifelong little friend of the rich Ernest Hemingway felt obliged to reassure us that the rich are really just folks. For the P-writer the ruling class does not exist as a subject for fiction if only because the rulers are not to be found in his real world of desperate suburbs. The U-writer knows about the Harkness plan—but then what is a harkness? Something to do with horse racing? While the names that the foundations bear do not suggest to him our actual rulers—only their stewards in the bureaucracy of philanthropy: the last stronghold of the great immutable fortunes.

The serious P-writer knows that he must reflect the world he lives in: the quotidian of the average man. To look outside that world is to be untrue and, very possibly, undemocratic. To write about the actual movers and shakers of the world we live in (assuming that they exist of course) is to travel in fantasy land. As a result, novels to do with politics, the past, manners, are as irrelevant to the serious P-writer as the breathy commercial fictions of all the Irvingses—so unlike the higher relevancies of all the Normans.

In a society where matters of importance are invariably euphemized (how can an antipersonnel weapon actually kill?) a writer like Louis Auchincloss who writes about the way money is made and spent is going to have a very hard time being taken seriously. For one thing, it is now generally believed in bookchat land that the old rich families haven't existed since the time of Edith Wharton while the new-rich are better suited for journalistic exposés than for a treatment in the serious P or U novel. It is true that an indiscriminate reading public enjoys reading Auchincloss because, unlike the well-educated, they suspect that the rich are always with us and probably up to no good. But since the much-heralded death of the Wasp establishment, the matter of Auchincloss's fiction simply cannot be considered important.

This is too bad. After all, he is a good novelist, and a superb short-story writer. More important, he has made a brave effort to create his own literary tradition—a private oasis in the cactus land of American letters. He has written about Shakespeare's penchant for motiveless malignity (a peculiarly American theme), about Henry James, about

our women writers as the custodians and caretakers of the values of that dour European tribe which originally killed the Indians and settled the continent.

Mr. Hicks with his eerie gift for misunderstanding what a writer is writing about thinks that Auchincloss is proudly showing off his class while bemoaning its eclipse by later arrivals. Actually, the eye that Auchincloss casts on his own class is a cold one and he is more tortured than complacent when he records in book after book the collapse of the Puritan ethical system and its replacement by—as far as those of us now living can tell—nothing. As for the ruling class being replaced by later arrivals, he knows (though they, apparently, do not) that regardless of the considerable stir the newcomers have made in the peripheral worlds of the universities, showbiz, and bookchat, they have made almost no impact at all on the actual power structure of the country.

Auchincloss deals with the movers and shakers of the American empire partly because they are the people he knows best and partly, I suspect, because he cannot figure them out to his own satisfaction. Were they better or worse in the last century? What is good, what is bad in business? And business (money) is what our ruling class has always been about; this is particularly obvious now that the evangelical Christian style of the last century has been abandoned by all but the most dull of our rulers' employees (read any speech by the current president to savor what was once the very sound of Carnegie, of Gould, and of Rockefeller).

Finally, most unfashionably, Auchincloss writes best in the third person; his kind of revelation demands a certain obliqueness, a moral complexity which cannot be rendered in the confessional tone that marks so much of current American fiction good and bad. He plays God with his characters, and despite the old-fashionedness of his literary method he is an unusually compelling narrator, telling us things that we don't know about people we don't often meet in novels—what other novelist went to school with Bill and McGenghis Bundy? Now, abruptly, he ceases to play God. The third person becomes first person as he describes in *A Writer's Capital* the world and the family that produced him, a world and family not supposed either by their own standards or by those of book-chatland to produce an artist of any kind.

I must here confess to an interest. From the time I was ten until I was sixteen years old my stepfather was Hugh D. Auchincloss, recently saluted by a society chronicler as "the first gentleman of the United States"—to the enormous pleasure and true amazement of the family. The Auchinclosses resemble the fictional Primes in *The Embezzler,* a family that over the years has become extraordinarily distinguished for no discernible reason or, as Louis puts it, "There was never an Auchincloss fortune . . . each generation of Auchincloss men either made or married its own money."

Plainly, even sharply, Louis chronicles the family's history from their arrival in America (1803) to the present day.

He is realistic about the family's pretensions though he does not seem to be aware of the constant chorus of criticism their innumerable in-laws used to (still do?) indulge in. I can recall various quasi-humorous rebellions on the part of the in-laws (once led by Wilmarth Lewis) at the annual clan gathering in New York. What the in-laws could never understand was the source of the family's self-esteem. After all, what had they ever *done?* And didn't they come to America a bit late by true "aristocratic" standards? And hadn't they been peddlers back in Scotland who had then gone into *dry goods* in New York? And what was so great about making blue jeans? Besides, weren't they all a bit too dark? What about "those grave, watery eyes over huge aquiline noses"? And wasn't there a rumor that they had Italian blood and when you come right down to it didn't they look (this was only whispered at Bailey's Beach, muttered in the men's room of the Knickerbocker) *Jewish?*

In the various peregrinations of the branch of the family that I was attached to (I almost wrote "assigned to": sooner or later the Auchinclosses pick up one of everything, including the chicest of the presidents), I never came across Louis, who was, in any case, eight years older than I. Right after the war when I was told that a Louis Auchincloss had written a novel, I said: Not possible. No Auchincloss could write a book. Banking and law, power and money—that was their category.

From reading Louis's memoir I gather that that was rather his own view of the matter. He had a good deal to overcome and this is reflected in the curiously tense tone of his narrative. He had the bad luck, for a writer, to come from a happy family, and there is no leveler as great as a family's love. Hatred of one parent or the other can make an Ivan the Terrible or a Hemingway; the protective love, however, of two devoted parents can absolutely destroy him. This seems to have been particularly true in the case of Louis's mother. For one thing she knew a good deal about literature (unlike every other American writer's mother) and so hoped that he would not turn out to be second-rate, and wretched.

From the beginning, Louis was a writer: word-minded, gossip-prone, book-devouring. In other words, a sissy by the standards of the continuing heterosexual dictatorship that has so perfectly perverted in one way or another just about every male in the country. The sensitive, plump, small boy like Louis has a particularly grim time of it but, happily, as the memoir shows, he was able eventually to come to grips with himself and society in a way that many of the other sensitive, plump boys never could. A somber constant of just about every American literary gathering is the drunk, soft, aging writer who bobs and weaves and jabs pathetically at real and imagined enemies, happy in his ginny madness that he is demonstrating for all the world to see his manliness.

By loving both parents more or less equally, Auchincloss saw through the manly world of law and finance; saw what it did to his father who suffered, at one point, a nervous breakdown. Not illogically, "I came to think of

women as a privileged happy lot. With the right to sit home all day on sofas and telephone, and of men as poor slaves doomed to go downtown and do dull, soul-breaking things to support their families." As for Wall Street, "never shall I forget the horror inspired in me by those narrow dark streets and those tall sooty towers. . . ." The story of Auchincloss's life is how he reconciled the world of father with that of mother; how he became a lawyer and a novelist; how the practice of law nourished his art and, presumably, the other way around, though I'm not so sure that I would want such a good novelist creating a trust for me.

Groton, Yale, Virginia Law School, the Navy during World War II, then a Manhattan law firm, psychoanalysis, marriage, children, two dozen books. Now from the vantage point of middle age, the author looks back at himself and our time, holding the mirror this way and that, wondering why, all in all, he lacked the talent early on for being happy, for being himself. With characteristic modesty, he underplays his own struggle to reconcile two worlds, not to mention the duality of his own nature. Yet I suspect that having made himself a writer, he must have found demoralizing the fact that the sort of writing he was interested in doing was, simply, not acceptable to the serious U or even the serious P-chatterers.

The literary line to which he belongs was never vigorous in the United States—as demonstrated by its master Henry James's wise removal to England. Edith Wharton remained an American; yet to this day she is regarded as no more than pale James. Since Mrs. Wharton, the novel of manners has been pretty much in the hands of commercialites. But of the lot neither the insider Marquand nor the outsider O'Hara is taken seriously in U-land while in P-land they were particularly downgraded after the war when bookchat was no longer written by newspapermen who were given books to review because they were not good enough to write about games but by young men and women who had gone to universities where the modern tradition (sic) was entirely exotic: Joyce and Lawrence, Proust and Kafka were solemnly presented to them as the models worth honoring or emulating. It is true that right after the war James made a comeback, but only as an elaborate maker of patterns: *what* Maisie knew was not so important as her way of telling what she knew.

The early Fifties was not a good time for a writer like Louis Auchincloss. But it could have been worse: at least he did not have to apologize for his class because, pre-Camelot, no American writer had a clue who or what an Auchincloss was. Yet even then his novels never much interested his fellow writers or those who chatted them up because he did not appear to deal with anything that really mattered, like the recent war, or being Jewish/academic/middle-class/heterosexual in a world of ballcutters. No one was prepared for dry ironic novels about the ruling class— not even those social scientists who are forever searching for the actual bill of sale for the United States.

Auchincloss himself was no help. He refused to advertise himself. If the bookchatterers had no idea what Sullivan and Cromwell was he wasn't going to tell them: he just showed the firm in action. He also knew, from the beginning, what he was doing: "I can truly say that I was never 'disillusioned' by society. I was perfectly clear from the beginning that I was interested in the story of money: how it was made, inherited, lost, spent." Not since Dreiser has an American writer had so much to tell us about the role of money in our lives. In fascinating detail, he shows how generations of lawyers have kept intact the great fortunes of the last century. With Pharaonic single-mindedness they have filled the American social landscape with pyramids of tax-exempt money, for the eternal glory of Rockefeller, Ford, et al. As a result, every American's life has been affected by the people Auchincloss writes so well about.

I cannot recall where or when I first met Louis. He lists me among a dozen writers he met twenty years ago at the Greenwich Village flat of the amiable Vance Bourjaily and his wife. I do recall the curiosity I had about him: how on earth was he going to be both a lawyer and a writer (a question entirely subjective: how could I write what I did and be an effective politician? Answer: forget it). I can't remember how he answered the question or if he did. I was amused by the reaction of other writers to him. They knew—particularly the wives or girlfriends—that there was something "social" about him but that was neither a plus nor a minus in the Eisenhower era. Earlier it would have been a considerable handicap. In my first years as a writer, I was often pleased to be identified with the protagonist of *The City and the Pillar*—a male prostitute. After all, that was a *real* identity, I thought, sharing the collective innocence.

Louis moved through these affairs with considerable charm and he exaggerates when he writes: "The fact that I was a Wall Street lawyer, a registered Republican, and a social registrite was quite enough for half the people at any one party to cross me off as a kind of duckbill platypus not to be taken seriously." Rather wistfully, he observes: "I am sure I had read more books by more of the guests at any one party than anyone else." I am sure that he had. But then it has always been true that in the United States the people who ought to read books write them. Poor Louis who *knew* French and American literature, who "kept up" with what was going on, now found himself in a literary society of illiterate young play-actors; overexcited by the publicity surrounding Hemingway and Fitzgerald, they decided to imitate these "old masters." At least a dozen were playing Hemingway—several grizzled survivors still are. Fitzgerald, Thomas Wolfe, Faulkner were also popular archetypes. No one was himself—but then selves are hard to come by in America. So, in a way, Louis was indeed like a platypus in that farmyard of imitation roosters. After all, he didn't resemble any famous writer we had ever heard of. He was simply himself, and so odd man out to the young counterfeiters.

Since then, Auchincloss has learned (through psychoanalysis, he tells us) that "a man's background is largely of his own creating." Yet pondering the response to this discovery as expressed in his work, he writes,

American critics still place a great emphasis on the fact of background on character, and by background they mean something absolute which is the same for all those in the foreground. Furthermore, they tend to assume that the effect of any class privilege in a background must be deleterious to a character and that the author has introduced such a background only to explain the harm done. Now the truth is that the background to most of my characters has been selected simply because it is a familiar one to me and is hence more available as a model. . . . I cannot but surmise that the stubborn refusal on the part of many critics to see this is evidence of a resentment on their part against the rich, a resentment sometimes carried to the point of denying that a rich man can be a valid subject for fiction. . . . Such a point of view would have been, of course, ridiculous in the eighteenth or nineteenth centuries when the great bulk of the characters of fiction came from the upper or upper middle class. Critics did not resent Anna Karenina or Colonel Newcome.

Louis Auchincloss's latest book, **The Partners,** is a collection of related short stories set in a New York law firm. A merger has been proposed between the demure firm of the partners and a larger, flashier firm. Old values (but are they really values?) combat new forces. Invariably those who do the right self-sacrificing thing end up echoing Mrs. Lee in Henry Adams's *Democracy:* "The bitterest part of all this horrid story is that nine out of ten of your countrymen would say I have made a mistake."

The author's virtues are well displayed: almost alone among our writers he is able to show in a convincing way men at work—men at work discreetly managing the nation's money, selecting its governors, creating the American empire. Present, too, are his vices. Narrative is sometimes forced too rapidly, causing characters to etiolate while the profound literariness of the author keeps leaking into the oddest characters. I am sure that not even the most civilized of these Wall Street types is given to quoting *King Lear* and Saint-Simon quite as often as their author has him do. Also, there are the stagy bits of writing that recur from book to book—hands are always "flung up" by Auchincloss characters; something I have never seen done in real life west of Naples.

One small advance: in each of Auchincloss's previous books sooner or later the author's Jacobite fascination with the theater intrudes and, when it does, I know with terrible foreboding that I shall presently see upon the page that somber ugly word "scrim." I am happy to report that in **The Partners** there is no scrim, only the author's elegant proscenium arch framing our proud, savage rulers as they go single-mindedly about their principal task: the preserving of fortunes that ought to be broken up.

Richard Todd (essay date 1976)

SOURCE: A review of *The Winthrop Covenant,* in *The Atlantic Monthly,* Vol. 237, No. 4, April, 1976, p. 112.

[*In the following review of* The Winthrop Covenant, *Todd comments on the moral situations Auchincloss presents and the author's focus on Puritan values and behavior.*]

Wonderful money. It is such interesting stuff, and yet current fiction pays so little attention to it. American novelists love to *talk* about money, as everyone who has seen two of them together has noticed. But these days they don't write about it very often or very well. I can think of just one contemporary American writer who has made a career of observing wealth: Louis Auchincloss. . . .

He has slowly attracted a sizable audience, though he has few friends in the critical Establishment. Perhaps the warmest praise he has received came from his distinguished distant cousin Gore Vidal, in an essay in *The New York Review of Books*. Vidal remarked approvingly on Auchincloss' frank fascination with money, and said, "of all our novelists Auchincloss is the only one who tells us how our rulers behave in their boardrooms, their law offices, their clubs. . . . Almost alone among our writers he is able to show in a convincing way men at work . . . discreetly managing the nation's money, selecting its governors, creating the American empire."

Auchincloss is a relentlessly old-fashioned novelist, as even many of his titles make plain (*The Great World and Timothy Colt; Pursuit of the Prodigal*). His novels suffer from artificiality of plot and manner. I suspect, though, that unlike most writers, he's probably more embarrassing at the moment than he will be in the future. He is, at a minimum, an entertaining correspondent from an underreported country, the country of the rich.

His new book, **The Winthrop Covenant,** aims higher. It's an effort to examine the philosophical underpinnings of the American upper class.

It consists of nine short stories, all related, as Auchincloss says in a preface, to "the rise and fall of the Puritan ethic." "By Puritan ethic I mean that preoccupying sense, found in certain individuals, of a mission, presumably divinely inspired, toward their fellow men." This headmasterly tone is typical of Auchincloss. But this definition is also a bit wry. The "preoccupying sense" of Auchincloss' characters is more often than not a ruinous obsession.

The movement of the book is a long climb up the Winthrop family tree, beginning with Governor John Winthrop and General Wait Still Winthrop, a judge at the Salem witch trials. The rest of the branches are fictive—three centuries of representative patrician types, ending with a portrait of a CIA old-boy.

These stories are uneven; some of them suffer from being more nearly outlines for novels. And there is the difficulty of Auchincloss' rarefied diction. His seventeenth-century figures often sound more contemporary than his contemporaries. Consider these eloquent snippets of post-coital recrimination (c. 1950):

"At least I shall have given you the satisfaction of making a cuckold of a man you deeply envy and can never possibly equal." . . . "I suggest that you sought my chamber only to revenge yourself on John."

But manners interest Auchincloss less than morals in this book. **The Winthrop Covenant** matters mostly as an extended act of brooding on a central strain in American character. Auchincloss' Puritans brood a great deal themselves. Although they are afflicted with a sense of mission, they are hardly altruistic; the greatest efforts go toward self-justification. In an early story, Wait Still Winthrop, at the end of his life, anguishes over having sent a Salem witch to death, only to find a moral loophole that excuses him from guilt. His imaginary descendant, the CIA official, uses his inherited gift for indignant wrath to shame his son out of draft evasion; meanwhile the man is lying to the public about American warfare in Southeast Asia. The mildest of the Winthrops, a prep school chaplain, is told by a more worldly figure: "For you, the drama is all within you." It might be said of all these characters.

For Auchincloss, Puritanism is an exquisite mix of arrogance and guilt—arrogance breeding guilt, and guilt doting on its own niceties to the point of renewed arrogance. The contradictions were there from the start. The doctrine of grace, central to Puritan theology, might have been devised by R. D. Laing as a model for the creation of schizophrenics. Some are saved and there is nothing anyone can do about it: to be a member of the elect is to feel both helpless and omnipotent. **The Winthrop Covenant** implies that those Americans with the clearest claim to aristocracy have always been profoundly confused about the meaning of their presumed superiority.

Louis Auchincloss with Vincent Piket (interview date 1985-1987)

SOURCE: An interview with Louis Auchincloss, in *The Dutch Quarterly Review of Anglo-American Letters,* Vol. 18, No. 1, 1988, pp. 20-37.

[*In this excerpt from an interview conducted between October 1985 and July 1987, Auchincloss discusses various subjects related to his work, including characterization and the evolution of his career. The author also comments on his relationship with other writers and his opinion of contemporary society and the world of letters.*]

[Piket]: *You have written that most of a writer's characters are just himself "wearing different funny hats".*

[Auchincloss]: That seems true to me. Basically you have no one else to write about other than yourself, no other source than yourself. Who else do you know, I mean truly know? It's a banal but true thing that we are all islands, with very little knowledge, deep down, of other people. If we read that Napoleon was banned to Elba, then of course we only have ourselves as a source to imagine how bad and terrible that sentence must have been. We can't imagine Napoleon's feelings. So even if a writer chooses a model for a character, he is still writing his own perception of that model, which means that he is making that model into a reflection of himself.

Would you agree that there was a direct influence of the psycho-analysis you underwent in 1952-1953 on your writing? Your novels of the later 1950s, The Great World and Timothy Colt, Venus in Sparta *and* Pursuit of the Prodigal *are markedly different from the novels of the years before psycho-analysis.*

Yes, I would agree that I enlarged my field. But I don't know the exact extent of the influence. I think it is impossible or at least very difficult for a writer to say what has influenced him. But I'm sure that psycho-analysis helped me. It made me realize fears of my own. I was aware that with *Timothy Colt* I started writing about male main characters rather than female ones. Still, it was not a conscious decision. I recall a friend of mine saying, "The hero of *Pursuit of the Prodigal* is the first real man in your fiction", and my thinking that was so, that he was a very male male. I also think that without the analysis I would never have written a book like *The Rector of Justin,* touching on a school not modeled on Groton but in its atmosphere and influence not dissimilar from Groton. The anger which that book created among the Groton family would have been nerveracking for me before. Now I had much more confidence in myself and I didn't care. . . .

The stories in **Second Chance: Tales of Two Generations** *[1970] typically deal with attempts at revitalization and rejuvenation after disillusionment and disappointment. Were you aware of that? Would you say that the theme applied to this period of your career?*

No, I think that was a way of putting them together, I had been looking rather desperately for a common denominator for the book of short stories, but it was hard to find, and I rather pushed that.

Why did you decide to write your autobiography A Writer's Capital *in this period?*

Well, because John Irwin, the editor of the University of Minnesota Press, suggested that I either write—I remember the letter, it seems silly—a biography of myself or of Mary McCarthy. So I picked myself. Then I became intrigued with the idea, because it seemed to me rather conceited to write an autobiography, but as long as somebody else asked for it I felt it was all right. I also thought that the University Press having asked for it gave it a dignity which it wouldn't have if I wrote it of my own accord. The only one I really worried about was my brother John, I thought that he would think it was terrible to go into mother and father the way I did. I rather quaked about that, and then I would think it was written for a University Press, and that this would give it a sanction and a dignity. I could say, "After all, the University Press wants it." But when I sent John the book he loved it. He said, "I can't imagine why you thought I'd object to that."

He said, "Of course you wouldn't have written it if mother and father were alive, but I have no objections to your doing it now." The family all liked it, I had no trouble with that.

In A Writer's Capital *you suggest that your "writer's capital" is constituted by your boyhood and young manhood, roughly the period from 1930 to 1950. Would you say that this period in American social history interests you more than any other period?*

The 1930s, yes, I think there's always some period in life that you regard as the "real world", maybe it's when you first mature in some ways. There's a book out called *New York in the Thirties* and looking at its pictures I keep thinking, "That's New York, that's New York". The Thirties seem to me a more real world than the Twenties or than any of the decades since. I think it's when one first becomes aware of the world as an adult. I think that the development of one's basic interests and one's ways of viewing the world are most often settled much earlier than the age of thirty, sometimes even as early as the age of ten. Certainly people change little after their teens, at least I feel I have and feel that I have taken the Thirties with me. I have used that period a great deal in my fiction, more than any other period.

In the final story of the 1974 story collection, **The Partners,** *your character Beeky resolves to leave the large law firm of which he has been senior partner and to form a smaller, "crazy new law firm". After the many years of adhering to the role of the responsible and moral head of the firm, he is determined to have as much fun as his partners have had all the time. Would you say that the period in your writing career from 1974 onwards reflects a similar attempt at a new direction?*

No, I don't think so. The idea of Beeky having his own firm was just a kind of fantasy. It wasn't based on any kind of reality and I'd never heard of anybody doing anything quite like that. I just liked the idea that somebody might. I liked Beeky's character. He was a little bit like a former senior partner that I knew and of whom I was very fond, but only a little bit. But I don't see a relation between Beeky's state of mind and his resolution and my own at that time. Certainly no conscious relation.

How then would you characterize the last ten years of your career? That you have become very eclectic in your subjects and forms is indicated particularly by the many historical novels and stories that you've written recently.

Yes, I dropped limitations. It was like Flaubert going from *Madame Bovary* to the wildness of *Salammbô.* I had always kept away from the past because it seemed to me that since I lacked the personal knowledge of it, I had no right to it. I thought my view was too limited for it. When I started out as a writer I wrote not only about things and events I knew and people I knew, but people that I could imagine myself being, and events that I could imagine happening to myself. Almost every character in my earlier fiction I was able to imagine myself being.

But gradually I began to wonder why I should be bound in this way, and this caused me to drop a number of limitations. I used some history in *The Rector of Justin,* but I studied for it: I read two books about Dr Jowett before I used one little scene with him in it. The history of *The House of the Five Talents,* I felt, was so close to the present that I could barely regard it as history. The same goes for *Watchfires. The Cat and the King* and *Exit Lady Masham* are my first truly historical novels, dealing with an era which is completely removed from my own experience, as to a certain degree the short stories of **The Winthrop Covenant** had been. I very much enjoyed doing those historical novels, and once I found that the water was all right I decided to stay in it for a while. Still, I look upon my historical novels very much as *tours de force,* as tests of the imagination, as tricks. However much I enjoyed doing those books, they do not constitute the most important part of my work.

So I have expanded my field to the past, even though I have stayed in my small area in the present. Which in effect means that I have made an escape, an escape from the responsibility of dealing with one's own time (which is not to mean that it is always the writer's task to write about his own time). I like what Mary McCarthy once wrote. She wrote that the novel was essentially a thing of the past, for instance the nineteenth century, because it pretends to deal with a world that makes sense. There is something in that. The point is that the twentieth century does not make sense. It is rather hard to present this world of intercommunication and lack of communication in a novel. It is perhaps therefore that the novel has come to be more and more introspective.

Why did you put so much autobiography into **The Book Class***?*

Well, there is as much in the main character of *Honorable Men,* and you can't imagine characters more different than he and the character in **The Book Class.** But the most important reason for putting those elements in is that I have them at hand. There's no other reason. Why invent a law school if you have one? And, for young men of certain means Yale and Virginia law school are natural choices.

The story of "The Country Cousin" pops up several times throughout your career.

I have been concerned with that story for a long time. First in **The Injustice Collectors,** in 1950, where it appeared as **"The Unholy Three"**. Before that a manuscript of the story had got lost, but I managed to recreate it. I later did a one-act play of it, and also a three-act play, which I was dissatisfied with and threw out. And finally I wrote the novel. People, I think my mother, used to ask me, "Why do you come back to that story? It's ridiculous". It is, but I love that theme. I used to know a lady acquaintance of my parents, who was an old maid and I use the term advisedly, with lesbian streaks—although then it wasn't called that: in those days lesbians were said to have a "Boston marriage". She had a musical ear, went to the opera a lot. She showed me tickets for 54 performances of "Tristan" which she had been to, which must have been about as many as there had been in New York at that time. She was a noisy, art-loving, heavy-breathing woman; I liked her, and went to the opera with her several times. My parents didn't like her, because she drank too much. So she wasn't invited to their parties because she was no "addition". She was a model for the elderly lady in the story.

The novel as such is to some extent a mystery to me. It has a complicated plot, especially in the second part. Probably there is too much plot, and I seem to be losing my hold of the theme in the second part. The theme, or rather the real story of the book is the episode of the night club. I think I'm through with that story by now. . . .

Do you plan and outline a novel with great care before starting it?

Yes. I have the book wholly outlined before I start. I find it impossible to work otherwise. But, of course, there are often many changes. For instance, *Watchfires* ended in my original draft right after the Civil War, even though it had the same epilogue it has now. I found the jump in time too big and decided to extend the story and add the wife's part about the suffrage question as well as the son's part, the part about his job in Grand Central. Some novels I was able to write in a more straight way, *The Embezzler* is one of those.

Sometimes I have a terrible desire to revise my work. I think all writers have, even though they don't do it, like myself. Except James. But the debate is still going on whether he improved his work by his revisions. One novel which I should like to revise is *The Embezzler:* the novel would be more exciting if I had made the dramatic contrast between the individual viewpoints greater. Sybil in *Sybil* should in the end not have gone back to her husband. She goes back to him because she thinks that there is only one love in one's life; but she is too intelligent to think that. One of the editors at Houghton Mifflin suggested that she should have married her cousin and I think he was right. In *A Law for the Lion,* the little plot in the end, where the young lawyer marries the reserved girl is sheer muck. I find the book embarrassing, I can't look at it. In *Watchfires,* the part about the suffragette movement is anachronistic, as some of the critics were right to suggest. That is to say, it is not unhistoric, and it is possible to document all of the events, but the atmosphere is 1970ish. The ending of *Honorable Men* is too kaleidoscopic and too quick; it's too tied. The main character of *Diary of a Yuppie* is too literary, even for the novelist manqué that he is. I'm happy about *The House of Five Talents.* I'm fairly happy about *Portrait in Brownstone.* I would leave *The Great World and Timothy Colt* alone. I would suppress *The Dark Lady. The Country Cousin* is much too overplotted. I would leave my short stories alone; I think of **"The Wagnerians"** [in **Tales of Manhattan**] as my best short story. *A World of Profit* is as good as it can be. *I Come as a Thief* doesn't come across. I would leave the historical novels alone, they are little *tours de force.* **The**

Book Class is all right. I would suppress *The Indifferent Children*.

At the moment I'm going very slowly with the stories that I'm writing now [published as *Skinny Island*]. I always have this impatience with what I have on my desk. I always have the desire to go on to the next thing. But right now I'm paying careful attention to the stories.

A few months ago I had all my early stories and other contributions to *The Grotonian, The Yale Literary Magazine* and the *Virginia Law Review* bound and so I reread them. And it occurred to me that the most striking thing about them is that they show no promise whatsoever! Of course, there are always people saying, "No promise? Naturally, why should there be any promise if there is no talent?", but to my mind they contain no promise that their author would even be a published author in later days. The pieces are perfectly terrible, and yet unmistakably by me. You wouldn't think that after so many decades they could pain me, but they do. I suppose they're really painful because I feel there's so much in them that is still there in me. If I could really put them into the past altogether, then I wouldn't mind so much. But I don't quite have that feeling. In some ways I feel I haven't changed at all, which makes it quite unbearable to read them. The first story that I can read without a feeling that it is perfectly awful is **"Maud"**, which appeared in *The Atlantic* in 1949.

If you look at post-war American fiction, where would you place yourself as a writer?

Oh, I don't know. That's for other people to say.

With whom do feel you have much in common?

You mean who writes most the way I do?

Yes.

Well, I don't know really if anybody does. I think Hortense Calisher really writes somewhat my way. Obviously Marquand and I had a good deal in common, but he's no longer with us. I suppose the character most like me is Anthony Powell in England. I read all of *A Dance to the Music of Time,* and I'm always finding that I don't like it quite as much as I think I'm going to, but I like it nonetheless. But I think Anthony Powell is by far the closest of anybody writing to what I do.

Are you happy being called a novelist of manners?

I don't really know, because I don't exactly know what the term means. James Tuttleton includes Henry James in the category, and if one does that—even though there is justification for it in James's earlier novels, but certainly not in *The Golden Bowl*—one might as well include me. So I think the term is rather vague. Often the term is associated with good manners, the novel of good manners or even artificial manners. One might then think of Jane Austen. But personally, when I think of the novel of manners I do not necessarily think of "good manners". I would think of Sinclair Lewis's *Babbit,* which decribes the manners of a whole community, or of Trollope's *The Way We Live Now.*

You're also often included among the present-day WASP writers, whom Joan Didion once described as "homeless": "The white, Protestant writer in America is . . . homeless—as absent from the world of his fathers as he is 'different' within the world of letters." Would you agree with that?

I don't feel that at all. I feel I have a very definite niche. In fact, I feel at home in many places.

In your novelistic methods and styles you largely adhere to the principles of realism. Doesn't the modernist and postmodernist critique of realism bother you at all?

No it doesn't bother me. I think it is nonsense to say that in a particular era you can write in only one particular way. I think there is always room for all styles and methods of composition, and I don't see, for instance, why it would be impossible to write a novel of letters in the 1980s, or an epic narrative for that matter. Each writer should be free to choose a style which suits him best. I am tolerant in these matters. I am irritated by any theory which dictates what the right style is at a particular time in history. And about modernism or postmodernism: that seems to me a thing of the 1960s-1970s. Besides, many writers have nothing to do with postmodernism. Joan Didion, for instance, writes straight narrative. Hortense Calisher does so, too. Saul Bellow might have written the way he does in the early 1900s. He happens to do it in these times and is much applauded for it. But if, say, a WASP writer does the same thing he is rejected. That may sound bitter but it's true. William Gaddis, whom I am reading now [*Recognitions*] and whom I much admire, does the same as me: he changes point of view, goes in and out of his characters, and is in flavour still like Trollope. I think Gaddis catches the spirit of our times perhaps best of our present-day novelists. The latest heresy in literary criticism is the idea that has emerged during the surge of feminism in the past years, the idea that the fiction by women is different from that by men, *per se.*

Critics have objected that the world which I write about is small. Well, New York City is big enough for me. A man like William Faulkner wrote about a small town down south and gets away with it. Great novels have been written about so-called irrelevant subjects and settings. I notice a continuing resentment in this country over any aspect of class distinction, even though Americans are obsessed with class. If I send one of my characters to a private boarding school in the Northeast I get criticized for parochialness, even though during the first half of this century particularly the boarding school was the equivalent of the orindary high school to the entire Northeast managerial class. And I would say that it has continued to be that to this day. But as soon as you *write* about a boarding school in a novel you get criticized for narrowness.

Are you in any way interested in contemporary critical theory?

No, not really. Whenever I write a critical piece about a certain book my starting-point is never theory, but rather my own impressions or ideas of that book.

Do you meet many fellow writers?

I have been meeting more of them since my retirement from the law in 1986. In my legal life, and my life in New York cultural institutions I didn't meet any writers. My schedule was too busy for it, and I was working office hours. You know, many writers like to stay up late and when some time ago one of them invited me for a party beginning eleven o'clock p.m. I simply couldn't accept. That's when I go to bed.

Things were different when I didn't practice; I would meet Phillip Roth and Jean Stafford and stay up and talk all night. I was on friendly terms with quite a number of writers then. Hortense Calisher was rather a friend—I always liked her very much. Vance and Tina Bourjaily were good friends. So was Gore Vidal. Norman Mailer I saw, but he wasn't a friend. We were just too different to be friends, and also I couldn't keep up with his sort of life. No, Jean Stafford was the only first-class writer who was a close friend. I was thrilled by knowing her. I had never known a first-class writer well, and I was flattered by her kindness even though she may have been more interested in my background than in myself. We remained friends until her disintegration, when her alcoholism made friendship more and more pointless.

My life changed with my marriage in 1957, and when shortly afterwards I became a partner in the firm. Then the artist type of life became totally out of keeping with my life as a lawyer. But as my retirement approached I had more time for literary activities, for lectures and so. Not long ago I went on a trip to Russia with a number of other writers under the cultural treaty between the United States and the Soviet Union. I loved it. I loved talking to them, to Charles Fulller, William Gass, William Gaddis, Arthur Miller, Jerome Lawrence. And I realized what I had missed. But I guess you pay a price for everything.

Some time ago you were invited to serve as a judge in a contest in creative writing. You declined because, as you wrote to the organizers, you found that you lacked "the necessary criteria to judge the fiction of young writers"; these criteria you defined as "the necessary scope and sympathy".

Yes, I do not read enough young writers for that. I only read well-known authors. Not because I lack sympathy, or because of a hostility on my part to young writers, but because I lack the time. Also I almost always read for a purpose, for an essay or for a book.

I find that my tastes have hardly changed over the years. My Groton education was almost entirely in English and French literature. And to the present day I keep on reread-ing the English nineteenth-century novelists, the Brontës, Thackeray, Trollope, as well as their French counterparts, the Goncourts, Proust, Flaubert, and Balzac to a lesser extent. I am still devoted to the French neo-classical dramatists, Racine and Corneille. I revisit Racine constantly; here is the copy of his collected works that I bought in 1935, when I was an undergraduate. And of course I read Shakespeare, who remains a great inspiration.

It wasn't until Yale that I came to American fiction. I don't remember reading any American fiction at all at Groton; I was very, very heavily nurtured in English nine-teenth-century fiction. I never read any Edith Wharton and Henry James before I went to Yale, I even think I didn't read *Moby Dick* and *The Scarlet Letter* until I went to Yale. There also I discovered James under the influ-ence of my late friend Jack Woods. I read Edith Wharton, and others, Dreiser, Fitzgerald, Hemingway, Lewis, Faulkner. Although I remember not liking Faulkner when I was at Yale. I came to Faulkner later. And of course Thomas Wolfe, whom we all read frantically.

To what extent do you share the view of Chip Benedict, the main character of Honorable Men, *that since the beginning of this century there has been a general de-cline of culture, art, and morals?*

Chip is a very extreme case. He is suffering from a moral compulsion which makes him take extreme views. I do not take so dim a view. But if you ask me whether moral standards have shown a decline, I would say yes. People have ceased to be shocked. There is a widespread, rather cynical acceptance of events. Think for instance of the Richard Whitney case in the 1930s, which created a tre-mendous excitement in New York and in the class Whit-ney belonged to. Nowadays that seems impossible. Nor do I think that the commercialization of art has had a great impact on art itself. It hasn't led to a considerable vulgar-ization. There has always been vulgar clack. And for those who care there has always been the right kind of art. Gen-erally, I don't think that the world changes very much. Henry Adams made the mistake of thinking that. Some of the at-titudes towards events change perhaps, but not the events themselves. Man can't be more corrupt than he is. Think of Commodore Vanderbilt who frankly admitted that he had bought the entire state legislature. That was last century, it would be impossible now. You could buy one or two indi-vidual judges, but not the entire legislative body.

I agree with Chip's feeling that the existence of nuclear weapons extinguishes the old-fashioned notion of human courage, honour, valour. Visiting Nagasaki in 1945 I felt that myself. I thought if someone's going to throw an atom bomb at you you're going to have to surrender, and you only have one alternative. If you've got one, you throw a bomb at him, then you both blow up, but you can't afford a war—it's either death or compromise, so it's kind of an end of valour. I did not foresee how long conven-tional warfare would go on. I would have been amazed if you had told me in 1945 that almost half a century later there would be an active war going on in the Gulf, and one in Afghanistan, in which no atomic weapons were used. I think that would have surprised everybody. I think we thought that they would proliferate faster than they have, I mean in other countries. They will.

Would you agree that your novels express a combination of a social, a moral and a psychological interest, together with a more straightforward delight in story-telling?

I think that's true. Morals and story-telling. I used to be more psychologically minded than I am today. I was more interested in self-destruction than I am today. Timothy Colt is a character, of course, who completely destroys his own career. I was fascinated that people did that, but I have exhausted most of that fascination. I certainly would not call the honourable man in *Honorable Men* a self-destructive character, although he has elements of it in him, but then everybody has elements of it. I also used to explore the idea that my wife finds fascinating, the idea that people create their own environments. But morals are certainly a persisting interest of mine. There are morals in all my books. The ethical question is always there. In 1986 I was given the New York State Governor's Arts Award, and they praised my work for its examination of "man's ongoing struggle to apply ethical values in everyday life". I am quite happy with that.

Christopher C. Dahl (essay date 1986)

SOURCE: "The Stories," in *Louis Auchincloss,* The Ungar Publishing Company, 1986, pp. 137-69.

[*In the following chapter from his book-length study of Auchincloss's work, Dahl provides an overview of the author's short fiction. The critic summarizes the short story collections, then analyzes several stories that he feels are representative of Auchincloss's most accomplished work in the short fiction genre.*]

Auchincloss's productivity as a writer of short stories rivals his output as a novelist. . . . Although his literary reputation will no doubt ultimately rest on his novels, he is an able practitioner of short fiction. Gore Vidal has called him "a superb short-story writer," and he has been praised for his "thoroughly disciplined technical skill and artistry" in William Peden's standard study of modern American short fiction. Occasionally Auchincloss's stories are overly contrived, and several of the longer ones seem outlines for novels, but at their best they are very good indeed. They display their author's psychological acuity and quick grasp of the ironies interwoven in complex human relationships. They achieve their effects—often pathetic as well as ironical—with admirable ease and economy of means, and in several of the stories that depict contemporary manners, an almost uncanny prescience accompanies Auchincloss's usual versimilitude of detail.

When they have been published separately, Auchincloss's stories have appeared almost exclusively in general-circulation magazines. None have appeared in the "little" magazines, and, though Auchincloss has published three stories in *The New Yorker* and several in *Harper's* and *The Atlantic,* most of his work has made its way into magazines that cater to an even broader popular audience, magazines ranging from the old *Saturday Evening Post* to *McCall's, Cosmopolitan,* and *Playboy.* In an age of shrinking markets for short fiction, Auchincloss has been fairly successful as a short-story writer, though he has achieved nothing on the scale of the commercial success of such earlier writers as John Marquand or even Edith Wharton. . . .

Anyone who considers Auchincloss's short stories, however, encounters much the same paradox that is raised by the novels. Because the stories are not self-consciously difficult on the surface, they appeal to a popular audience. Yet, at the same time, they are marked by a profound literariness. While they meet the expectations of the average reader much more completely and easily than many stories published in, say, *The New Yorker,* they are frequently allusive and sometimes depend for their full effect upon knowledge of particular literary antecedents. Plot is also much more important in a typical Auchincloss story than in the stories of such writers as John Cheever and John Updike, both of whom share Auchincloss's interest in contemporary manners, but whose stories are often vignettes or brief impressionistic sketches. Auchincloss's stories, in contrast, often deal with events that develop over many years, and they may rely upon unexpected twists in plot or ironic conclusions. Almost always, they fulfill our conventional expectations for narrative, for a "good story."

> More than most other short-story writers, Auchincloss has attempted to construct unified collections of stories. All his collections have coherent rationales—either a unifying theme or a set of recurring characters. In some cases Auchincloss's quest for unity has led to a literary form that mediates between the usual collection of unrelated stories and the novel.
>
> —*Christopher C. Dahl*

Though the publications in which his stories have been published tell us much about Auchincloss's fiction, their wide appeal should not be overemphasized. Auchincloss has never aimed for a particular magazine audience. He has never been influenced by contracts with a magazine publisher, like Wharton and Marquand, nor has he been exclusively associated with a single journal, like Updike or Cheever. Indeed, almost half of Auchincloss's stories were first published as parts of collections rather than in periodicals.

Within the obvious limits imposed by their author's choice of social milieu and geographic location, Auchincloss's stories display a good deal of variety, and his interests as a story writer have changed as his career has developed over the years. As in his early novels, Auchincloss is often interested in the weak—failures or misfits who nonetheless possess peculiar strength despite their awkwardness or oddity. Though the settings of the earlier stories are always richly realized and authentically portrayed, Auchincloss's primary focus is upon the psychology of his characters. Throughout his career, he has been interested in the figure of the artist; like Henry James he frequently depicts writers, artists, or people who spend their lives acquiring works of art. Even though several collections are set in law firms, that has not limited him from pursuing extralegal interests in many of the stories involving lawyers. The more recent stories, especially those written since the late 1960s, have often tended to deal with social change in the worlds they portray. With his sardonic wit and elegant eye, Auchincloss has always been a fine chronicler of his times. Some of his keenest commentaries on contemporary life are contained in his stories.

The Collections

More than most other short-story writers, Auchincloss has attempted to construct unified collections of stories. All his collections have coherent rationales—either a unifying theme or a set of recurring characters. In some cases Auchincloss's quest for unity has led to a literary form that mediates between the usual collection of unrelated stories and the novel. Indeed, several reviewers have mistakenly referred to two of his collections, *The Partners* and *The Winthrop Covenant,* as novels, and one of his recent novels, *The Book Class* (1984), comes close to being a collection of short stories. Since all the collections are so carefully planned, it is useful to describe each one briefly.

The first volume of stories, *The Injustice Collectors,* published in 1950, takes its title from a term coined by the psychoanalyst Edmund Bergler. Injustice collectors, as Auchincloss explains the term, are "people who are looking for injustice, even in a friendly world, because they suffer from a hidden need to feel that this world has wronged them." Each story focuses upon one such collector—the girl who destroys her chances of marriage to the most eligible young man in the Maine summer resort by unleashing her impossible parents in a nasty dispute with the boy's father, for example, or the LST commander who ruins his career by his inability to accept assistance from his executive officer in his first attempt to bring his ship alongside a larger supply ship. The characters and settings are typical of Auchincloss's early work: shy girls and matrons in New York society, expatriate Americans in Paris, eccentrics in Maine resort towns. Each story is related with precision and dry humor, often by a first-person narrator who is himself the subject of Auchincloss's ironic scrutiny. Because of its craftsmanship, *The Injustice Collectors* remains in many respects Auchincloss's finest collection.

The Romantic Egoists (1954) depicts a similar group of outsiders, many of whom also display the same self-destructive tendencies. Though the outsiders in *The Romantic Egoists* share a self-preoccupation that is romantic in its intensity, the collection is unified not so much by a common theme as by the use of a single first-person narrator, Peter Westcott, whose responses to the cruder, but more vital characters he observes often shape the individual stories. F. Scott Fitzgerald adopted an almost identical title, "The Romantic Egotists," for the original version of his first novel, *This Side of Paradise,* and Peter Westcott is Fitzgeraldian in his sympathy and urbanity. The characters and situations depicted in the collection are more varied than those in *The Injustice Collectors.* In addition to **"The Great World and Timothy Colt,"** which Auchincloss reworked and expanded into the novel of the same title, there is another law-firm story, as well as a fine story about prep-school life, **"Billy and the Gargoyles,"** two stories about life in the U.S. Navy, a Fitzgeraldian study of a rich schoolmate, a sketch of an elegant divorcée transformed by her boorish second husband, and a powerful story about a middle-aged American in Venice, **"The Gemlike Flame."** Even in *The Romantic Egoists* there are hints of the unifying techniques that characterize the more tightly integrated collections that follow. Auchincloss repeats characters and settings. Lorna Treadway, the elegant divorcee in one story, appears again as a minor character in **"The Great World and Timothy Colt."** The first two stories in the collection deal with overlapping events from Peter Westcott's prep-school days.

Auchincloss's next collection, *Powers of Attorney,* published in 1963, makes full use of interlocking characters and situations. All the stories involve the partners and employees of the Wall Street law firm of Tower, Tilney & Webb. Rather than producing boring homogeneity, this unifying device yields a broad panorama of characters from secretaries to senior partners. Several of the stories portray weak or pathetic characters—the old partner who is so irrelevant to the firm that no one even blames him for a costly mistake in a will that he has officially approved, or the nostalgic executive secretary at a farewell reception who delivers a tipsy speech punctuated by her own hiccups—while others portray the hard-driving litigators and managing partners in the firm.

At the center of the collection is Clitus Tilney, the head of the firm, and the man who has transformed Tower, Tilney into a modern, highly efficient corporate organization. Tilney is not above forcing a rival representing the older, less organized style of legal practice out of the firm by giving secret advice to the other side in a lawsuit brought by the rival. Although Tilney's conduct is unethical, Auchincloss does not sit in judgment. He does not see the senior partner as radically evil, and in the final story in the collection, **"The Crowning Offer,"** he celebrates Tilney's innate pleasure in practicing law. As in *A Law for the Lion* and *The Great World and Timothy Colt,* Auchincloss stresses the bureaucratization of legal practice and the ways in which modern Wall Street firms have become subservient to their largest corporate clients. Although every story involves a member or employee of the firm, several stories diverge from law-firm life per se to describe the personal dilemmas of wives or clients.

In *Tales of Manhattan* (1967), Auchincloss again uses the device of interconnected stories. In this volume, however, the tales are grouped in three separate sets. The first section, "Memories of an Auctioneer," includes five stories told in the first person by Roger Jordan, the vice-president of a leading auction gallery. The final story in the section, **"The Money Juggler,"** which Auchincloss later expanded into the novel *A World of Profit,* recounts four friends' memories of their college classmate, a shady businessman whose tactics they deplore, but from whose activities they have all profited. In each of the preceding stories, items offered for sale by Roger's gallery lead him into interesting quests that reveal the personalities or lives of their owners.

The second group of stories in the volume, "Arnold & Degener," is another law-firm series. Each story is cast as a chapter in the firm's history written by a specific partner. Here the very act of telling becomes an act of appropriation as each writer attempts to impose his own image on the firm, to assert his dominance over his subject, or to express long-concealed anger or jealousy. As in *The Rector of Justin,* which immediately preceded this collection, and in *The House of the Prophet,* published twelve years later, writing biography becomes an attempt to assert personal power as well as a search for the true pattern of events.

The final section, entitled "The Matrons," contains three stories and a one-act play. At the center of each work is the sort of upper-class woman well beyond middle age for whom Auchincloss seems to have special sympathy and affection. Two of the stories depict figures from the turn-of-the-century New York described in *The House of Five Talents.* One is an aged "extra man," somewhat like the protagonist in Edith Wharton's "After Holbein," who is taken under the powerful wing of his wealthy hostess. The other is a gentle alcoholic who becomes for a brief time manager of the Metropolitan Opera House, whose experiences are recalled by his elderly niece who knew him in her girlhood. Another story is a study of the relations between a "perfect," noninterfering mother and her daughters on the occasion of her seventieth birthday.

The relation between a mother and her grown daughter generates the action of Auchincloss's slightly Ibsenesque play, *The Club Bedroom,* which was performed at the A.P.A. Theatre in December 1967 and televised on the New York educational channel. Influenced by the popular monologues of Ruth Draper, the play is Auchincloss's only stage production. It does not seem out of place in *Tales of Manhattan,* for the events of the plot build to an ironic climax reminiscent of the endings of several of the stories. In the final scene, Mrs. Ruggles, the genteel but impecunious protagonist whose dwindling resources help support her daughter's affair with a married man, is denied her one small hope for the remaining years of her life—a permanent room in the fashionable ladies club to which she belongs. The only person who might conceivably have a grudge against her, the wife of the man with whom her daughter is involved, happens ironically to be chairwoman of the committee that must approve requests for rooms in the club.

Auchincloss's fifth collection, *Second Chance: Tales of Two Generations,* was published in 1970. Although not all the stories are equally successful, *Second Chance* is arguably Auchincloss's best collection of stories of manners. As the subtitle suggests, many of the stories deal in some way with the so-called generation gap, a source of much painful discussion in the late 1960s. Auchincloss is concerned not only with the relationships between parents and children but also with the connections between grandparents and grandchildren, old people and young, contemporary figures and their historical antecedents; and he is interested as well in different "generations" of behavior within the lives of individuals. In the fine title story of the volume, for example, a middle-aged business man abandons the assumptions of his own generation and lives out the "new morality" of the young. *Second Chance* is decidedly Auchincloss's most topical collection. **"The Cathedral Builder"** was obviously suggested by the decision of the Episcopal Diocese of New York during the late 1960s to abandon plans to finish the construction of the Cathedral of St. John the Divine, and other stories in the collection involve a black English teacher at a private school and the takeover of a publishing house by a large conglomerate.

In *The Partners* (1974), perhaps his most popular collection, Auchincloss returns to the technique of interlocking stories involving members of a large Wall Street law firm. *The Partners* is also his most highly unified collection. The central character, Beekman ("Beeky") Ehninger, a senior partner in the firm of Shepard, Putney & Cox, appears in all but two of the fourteen stories and is thus far more fully developed than Auchincloss's usual protagonists. In contrast to Clitus Tilney, the aggressive, self-confident senior partner in *Powers of Attorney,* Beeky is a conciliator and negotiator who often doubts himself. Married, like Michael Farish in *Venus in Sparta,* to an older woman who has been divorced, he is troubled by a milder and nondebilitating version of Michael's sexual insecurity. As in the previous law-firm collections, Auchincloss provides a number of incisive views of human relationships in large corporate firms. Though several stories are satiric or critical, the collection as a whole comes around—in the final story especially—to a wry but genial endorsement of the special desire of some men to practice law in firms. Having negotiated the merger of Shepard, Putney & Cox with a larger firm headed by an old prep-school rival of his, Beeky decides to retire. He makes the decision at a party, in a kind of comic epiphany: he will retire from the firm only to set up "a crazy new law firm" composed entirely of "duplicates," the redundant lawyers who must be dropped from the two firms because of the merger. At the end of the story, Beeky goes to bed happily, clutching this new "fierce little resolution." In all the stories in which he appears, Beeky's great gifts are his gregariousness, loyalty, and fellow-feeling; he is, above all, a man who shares the love Auchincloss's own father felt for his law firm as a human institution.

The Winthrop Covenant, Auchincloss's seventh collection, grew out of the American Bicentennial in 1976. It is an attempt to explore one strand in the American character—"the rise and fall of the Puritan ethic in New England and New York"—as displayed in the lives of members of a single family, the Winthrops. Written especially for this volume, the nine stories cover the years from 1630 to 1975. Though Auchincloss does not fully achieve his ambitious historical aim, the collection contains several fine stories, such as **"The Arbiter"** and **"In the Beauty of the Lilies,"** set in those particular periods of American history in which Auchincloss is most at home. . . .

In his . . . collection, **Narcissa and Other Fables** (1983), Auchincloss returns to the looser organization found in his earliest collections. Though none of the stories are fables in the conventional sense of the term, each deals in some way with a favorite Auchincloss theme: the moral confusion that arises when older values lose their legitimacy and are not replaced by anything even remotely satisfactory. As a sort of coda, there are twelve **"Sketches of the Seventies"**—a new genre for Auchincloss but one well suited to his sensibility. None of the sketches is longer than a page or so, but each captures a moment in which the ironies or shortcomings of fashionable life in the 1970s are revealed. The range of settings, situations, and types of stories in the volume—from sketches to long stories, from a tale about an elegant expatriate in Florence in the 1920s to a wry first-person narrative by the victim of a corporate takeover in the 1970s—reminds one of the variety that Auchincloss is capable of and attests to his continuing vitality as a short-story writer.

Because of their sheer numbers, it is impossible to analyze all, or even a significant fraction, of Auchincloss's stories in detail here. The rest of this chapter, however, will suggest the variety and range of the stories as well as some of Auchincloss's artistry by considering a sampling of his work: two strong early stories; a series of stories on a single theme, writers and writing; and several recent tales in which Auchincloss offers keen commentary on the changing manners of the last two decades.

"GREG'S PEG"

Most of the early stories tend to be more obviously polished performances than the more relaxed stories in some of the later volumes, and two of them, **"Greg's Peg"** and **"The Gemlike Flame,"** are especially powerful and carefully crafted. The former story, published in **The Injustice Collectors,** depicts the improbable rise to social prominence of a thirty-five-year-old innocent, Gregory Bakewell, who is taken up by the members of the fast set at a Maine summer resort. The tale is told by the middle-aged headmaster of a boarding school who befriends Greg and urges him to make something of himself. In a carefully controlled narrative, Auchincloss sketches the strange rise and fall of Greg, while at the same time revealing the enigmatic character of the narrator.

Greg is an unprepossessing, even grotesque character, "an oddly shaped and odd-looking person, wide in the hips and narrow in the shoulders," whose "face, very white and round and smooth, had, somewhat inconsistently, the uncertain dignity of a thin aquiline nose and large, owl-like eyes." Dressed in white flannels and a red blazer—garb seldom seen outside a schoolboy's sixth-form graduation ceremony—Greg is "a guileless child" who still lives with his widowed mother. Having been educated by private tutors, he has never left home or really done anything with his life. Thus he presents a challenge to the headmaster, who takes him mountain-climbing and advises him to spend the winter away from his mother so that he can "learn to think." Though Greg seems deaf to the narrator's appeals, he does respond in his own way. Over the next three summers, he carries out an elaborate campaign to make himself a social leader in the resort community. Beginning at the bridge table with his mother's elderly friends, Greg gradually comes to meet their children and grandchildren and is finally adopted by the hard-drinking, sophisticated set in the resort. In showing Greg's social progress, Auchincloss provides a succinct anatomy of the various generations and groups in an old-line summer resort.

Greg becomes a "character" in Anchor Harbor, and thus immune to criticism, but his new role as "one of the respected citizens of the summer colony" does not really represent an advance for him. Though "his spotless white panama was to be seen bobbing on the bench of judges at the children's swimming meet," and he has become a sponsor for the summer theater and outdoor concerts, his winning costume at the annual fancy dress ball reveals his true nature: twice in a row, he goes dressed as a baby. Greg starts to drink too much, and, as his mother realizes, his frenetic new life is killing him. The climax of the story occurs when, for the last time, Greg does the little drunken dance that gives the story its title. The narrator, who has carefully avoided seeing "Greg's peg" before, observes his actions at the tennis club dance with fascination and horror:

> His eyes were closed, and his long hair, disarrayed, was streaked down over his sweating face. His mouth, half open, emitted little snorts as his feet capered about in a preposterous jig that could only be described as an abortive effort at tap dancing. His arms moved back and forth as if he were striding along; his head was thrown back; his body shimmied from side to side. It was not really a dance at all; it was a contortion, a writhing. It looked more as if he were moving in a doped sleep or twitching at the end of a gallows. The lump of pallid softness that was his body seemed to be responding for the first time to his consciousness; it was only thus, after all, that the creature could use it. (*Injustice Collectors*)

Greg's macabre dance is cut short by some rowdy visitors who hoist him on their shoulders in mock triumph and throw him into the swimming pool. The young visitors are put to rout by Greg's indignant friends, who fish him out of the pool, but he is never the same again. He seems to realize that even the admirers who applauded him and called for his dance that summer were really on the side of the young men. Rather than become a social leader, he has turned into a pet or mascot. The Bakewells do not return to Anchor Harbor the next summer, and two years later the narrator learns that Greg has died in Cape Cod, where he is remembered dimly, if at all, as "a strange, pallid individual" carrying a market-basket for his mother.

Like the characters in the other stories of **The Injustice Collectors,** Greg is impelled to seek out his own humiliation. Part of the effect of the story comes from the pathos and oddity of his situation. Yet Auchincloss carefully avoids the predictable psychologizing that a character like Greg might evoke. Rather than the conventional domineering mother one might expect, Mrs. Bakewell turns out to be a brisk, efficient woman who does not pressure her son to stay at home and who recognizes far more clearly than the narrator the evil and destructiveness of the frivolous society Greg has entered. Indeed, she is both a comic figure, as she announces to the headmaster that she has read his books and disapproves of them, and a moral voice in the story, when she questions his belief in heightened awareness as the ultimate goal in life.

It is Auchincloss's expert handling of the narrator, however, that gives **"Greg's Peg"** its distinctive interest. Though honest and perceptive, the headmaster also has a gloomy, misanthropic side. When he first meets Greg, he is still recovering from the death of his wife. He takes pleasure in coming to Anchor Harbor, a place not unlike Bar Harbor, Maine, in the early fall after most of the summer people have gone. His headmasterly desire to improve Greg's character leads, ironically, to Greg's downfall, and his partial complicity in the downfall gives the story its bleak edge. After he finds that Greg has never heard of him or his wife, the headmaster finds himself "oddly determined to imprint my ego on the empty face of all he took for granted." For him Greg is "a perfect *tabula rasa,*" and he eagerly seizes the "responsibility of writing the first line." His grand miscalculation is to presume that the blank surface that Greg presents is capable of being inscribed with any sort of definite message. Greg remains, throughout, the "lump of pallid softness" that is revealed in his little dance, incapable of being shaped by the headmaster's version of muscular Christianity.

When the headmaster finds out what his advice has wrought, he angrily abandons his protégé. A couple of times thereafter, and especially as he watches the grotesque little dance, he thinks he glimpses an appeal for rescue in Greg's eyes, but he is uncertain and takes no action. When Mrs. Bakewell suggests that he save Greg, he points out that "people don't *save* people at Anchor Harbor." The headmaster is of course not directly responsible for Greg's downfall—he could not, after all, have predicted Greg's elaborate campaign for social self-advancement. But the vehemence with which he rejects Greg's overtures for continued friendship and the impassive tone in which he relates the story suggest puzzling depths in his character. One shares the narrator's uneasy interest in Greg's fate, while Auchincloss skillfully leads one to ask uncomfortable questions about the narrator's

own role. Though it might initially seem merely a story about an eccentric in the fashionable setting of an old summer resort, **"Greg's Peg"** is an elegantly unsettling examination of a perceptive but flawed individual who intervenes in someone else's life without fully knowing his own motives.

"The Gemlike Flame," first published in *New World Writing* for 1953, and reprinted in **The Romantic Egoists,** is a brilliantly developed portrait of another lonely figure. The story depicts Clarence McClintock, an American expatriate in Venice, at a crucial and revealing moment in his life. Like **"Greg's Peg,"** the story, in its sympathy and focused intensity, is a good example of Auchincloss's early style at its best.

Clarence McClintock is seen through the eyes of his cousin Peter Westcott, the young novelist who appears in all the stories in **The Romantic Egoists**. Peter is an ideal narrator, a sympathetic observer who knows Clarence's past but is objective and honest about his own responses. He encounters Clarence—a sort of legend in his family, "personally distinguished and prematurely bizarre"—on a visit to Venice. Emotionally scarred by a domineering mother who waged a bitter custody battle for him when he was a child, Clarence had come to Italy many years before "to admire it and be left alone." Since he had never bothered to make any friends in Venice during all this time, Clarence clings to Peter as an embodiment of a past that remains very real to him. When Peter is beginning to feel trapped, he introduces his cousin to Neddy Bane, a charming but feckless college classmate who has left his wife and now dabbles in painting. Inevitably, their relationship is broken up by Clarence's mother, who arrives in Venice for an elaborate masked ball that represents everything the serious and almost ascetic Clarence abhors. "Quite remorseless in her pursuit of pleasure," his mother in effect steals Neddy away. At the end of the story, having desperately tried to keep his friend away from the ball, Clarence catches sight of Neddy in a silly costume kneeling at the feet of his mother, and he stalks off alone into the night.

Early in the story Clarence warns Peter that he "burns with a hard gemlike flame." The phrase, from the Conclusion to Walter Pater's *Studies in the History of the Renaissance,* points to the heart of the story: Clarence's unexpected intensity as revealed in perhaps his only serious relationship with another human being. Practically everyone except Peter—and especially Clarence's mother—is eager to see his friendship with Neddy as a tawdry homosexual affair, but Clarence regards it, ironically, as an ideal love and his own highest contribution to Art, insofar as he supplies the order and discipline Neddy needs to paint. That Neddy is a totally unworthy object of devotion ultimately means very little, for Clarence has found "a love that I've looked for all my life." Even Peter has difficulty understanding that there is something ineffable in his love, "a quality in his feelings that was over and above what is called sublimation, a quality that made of it something higher than—." Peter's sentence breaks off as he realizes how hopeless the task of explaining that "something higher" would be, and the story proceeds to the final scene, in which Clarence turns away to guard the gemlike flame alone: "Should not true flame-tenders, the people like himself, enjoy in solitude the special compensations of their devotion?" he seems to ask. Clarence continues to walk resolutely away from the scene of the ball, as described in the strong final image of the story, "away from the lighted palace and the gondolas that swarmed about it like carp."

"The Gemlike Flame" is a fine story not because of the exotic, Jamesian situation of wealthy Americans abroad, but because Auchincloss refuses to cheat the reader of the complexity of Clarence's feelings, even though he offers no alternative to the psychological explanation that comes to Peter's mind. Despite the abundance of specific detail, the power of the story comes from the absolute economy of its essentials. In *A Writer's Capital,* Auchincloss recalls his extreme pleasure when Norman Mailer told him at a party that he would not mind having written the story himself. Though Mailer's sensibility and interests are radically different from Auchincloss's, he was right to admire this story.

STORIES ON WRITERS AND WRITING

Peter Westcott's presence in all the stories of *The Romantic Egoists* is only a suggestion of the prominence of writers and the act of writing in Auchincloss's stories. No fewer than ten stories are directly concerned with writing fiction, biography, or autobiography, and the essential situations and characters in another half dozen stories are drawn from previous works of literature. Several of the latter stories are explicit homages to James or Wharton. Given Auchincloss's admiration for James, this persistent interest in art and the artist as a theme for short fiction is hardly surprising. What is distinctive, however, is Auchincloss's repeated attention to the effects of all sorts of writing on not only authors but other people as well. The stories about writers and writing, which come from all periods of his career, are among his most characteristic and effective.

In Auchincloss's fiction, the activity of writing is invariably more than a simple recording of events or a form of creative expression. Writing may well be a mode of communication or self-revelation, but at the same time it may also be an act of aggression, a defense mechanism, or a means of appropriating, and thereby controlling, someone else's life. This sense of writing-as-appropriation, as has been suggested, is particularly prevalent in some of the law-firm stories (as well as in the biography-novels, *The Rector of Justin* and *The House of the Prophet*). One of the "Arnold & Degener" stories in *Tales of Manhattan* raises the issue in a striking, though comic fashion.

In "The Senior Partner's Ghosts," Sylvaner Price decides to write the biography of Guthrie Arnold, founder of Arnold & Degener and his mentor. Though he appears to others as "a man of no accessories, no appendages, no stray bits or loose ends," Price fancies himself a romantic

a la Victor Hugo. Unlike the usual law-firm history, his biography will be a work of art, a vivid evocation of Arnold's true personality. As Price sits down to dictate portions of his book, horrible revelations of cutthroat buccaneering practices on Arnold's part tumble out of his mouth. Shortly thereafter, as if possessed by "the evil genius of Guthrie Arnold," Price makes a speech at a meeting of the firm urging his partners to take business away from a rival firm whose senior corporate expert is dying of cancer, and a few days later he finds himself involuntarily tearing up a page from the will of a deceased client. After the latter episode, Price suffers a stroke and is hospitalized. His partners make him consult a psychiatrist, who assures him that his visions are merely the result of long-suppressed guilt. After one more disquieting excursion into sensational biography, Price gives up private composition and free association and dictates an ordinary, boring firm history in the presence of his censorious secretary. Though the new biography kills off any humanity in its subject, "what did it matter, so long as there was peace?"

On one level, "The Senior Partner's Ghosts" offers a humorous explanation for the dullness of many official histories of law firms. At the same time it also points up the disparity between the respectable front of the large corporate law firm and the aggressive activities of some of its partners. Even if Sylvaner Price's memories of Guthrie Arnold are the product of an overheated imagination as the psychiatrist suggests, they describe plausible instances of dubious professional conduct—behavior no doubt occasionally encountered by the lawyers who first read the story in *The Virginia Law Review.*

More generally, the story is a study of an ordinary, seemingly bloodless professional man who cherishes a secret romantic streak in his nature. Price is silently pleased, for example, to learn that a young partner's wife has compared him to King Philip II at the Escorial. The comic denouement of the story suggests how difficult it is for a man like Price to escape the bounds of the professional persona he has assiduously cultivated for forty years. Perhaps the psychiatrist is right: in Price's mind, only his godlike mentor Guthrie Arnold is permitted to get away with expressing the romantic side of his nature. Yet, like several other psychiatric opinions in Auchincloss's fiction, this diagnosis, though correct in its way, seems reductive. Sylvaner Price creates his own hero and a myth of the firm, which he can control, but the hidden power of the subconscious mind is more difficult to contain. Though its tone is fanciful rather than portentous, "The Senior Partner's Ghosts" reminds us of the dangerous power of the writer's imagination. It is not a major story, but it illustrates Auchincloss's masterful skill in balancing a number of disparate elements in a single story without capsizing what is admittedly a light vessel.

In two other law-firm stories, both from *Powers of Attorney,* Auchincloss further explores the uneasy connection between writing and human relationships. For Morris Madison, the tax attorney in "The Single Reader," writing fulfills some of the same secret desires that it reflected in the mind of Sylvaner Price. Madison, however, is not troubled by "ghosts" as Price was. Over a period of thirty years he fills more than fifty morocco-bound volumes of his diary with carefully polished and often bitingly satiric entries. As the years go by, the diary takes over his life. He rearranges all the engagements outside the office in order to provide the best possible raw material for the diary and even leaves money in his will for its posthumous publication. When he shows a few representative volumes to the woman he wishes to marry—the "single reader" of the title—she recoils in horror, not because the diary is bad (it is brilliant), but because she fears becoming a human sacrifice to its insatiable appetite.

In **"The 'True Story' of Lavinia Todd,"** writing is not only self-expression but also a rueful emblem for failed communication and the inconspicuous self of the writer. Mrs. Todd, a middle-aged woman who is deserted by her husband, pours out the story of her betrayal in a long account that is accepted for publication in a woman's magazine. Rather than offend her husband, the candid story of their marriage and his callous behavior seems to bring him back to her side. He invites her out for dinner, praises the story, and asks for a reconciliation. She discovers, however, that he has never read the story and has only praised her work because his colleagues and several powerful clients have expressed their admiration. The "true" Lavinia Todd remains unread, and the art of the story, which has merely mirrored life, is once again mirrored in her own life.

The stories in which Auchincloss borrows situations or characters from previous authors may strike contemporary readers as overly derivative. This is not the case at all. Somewhat like the early films of François Truffaut, the best of these stories are *hommages,* or tributes, to Auchincloss's masters, James and Wharton. A good example of this type of tribute in its simplest form is **"The Evolution of Lorna Treadway."** This slickly written tale from *The Romantic Egoists* involves a sophisticated divorcée who marries a boorish Texas oilman and adopts all his values, becoming vulgar and trivial herself as she throws large parties to advance her husband's business career. While the narrator of the story talks with the husband, he momentarily plays with a Jamesian conclusion for his tale. "How neat it would have been," he thinks, if the oilman "had become with marriage the suave, accomplished man of the world, if he and Lorna, in other words, had changed places," so that people would pity him for being tied down to the giddy, unsophisticated "bride of his earlier and poorer days." But, of course, "that would have been strictly fiction." Though the pliant heroine might have come out of an Edith Wharton story such as "The Other Two," Auchincloss's story remains firmly anchored in the sharply defined reality of the fashionable world it describes.

In **"The Diner Out,"** from *The Partners,* Auchincloss takes the basic situation of Wharton's "After Holbein" and grafts it onto a story about an aging attorney, Burrill Hume, who faces the bleak prospect of retirement from practice. The grafting is not quite successful—and per-

haps few if any of the young attorneys who first read the story in *Juris Doctor* would have caught the allusion. But the final lines, in which Hume recognizes his approaching death, acquire added resonance by their direct reference to the ending of Wharton's story, in which the senile, dying protagonist, leaving a dinner party given by an even more senile old lady, takes a "step forward, to where a moment before the pavement had been—and where now there was nothing." Auchincloss has transmuted Wharton's mordant comedy into sympathetic humor tinged by pathos.

Auchincloss renders his most elaborate and subtle tribute to Henry James in **"The Ambassadress."** In this story from *The Injustice Collectors,* he reenvisions the main characters of James's late novel *The Ambassadors* from the perspective of Chad Newsome, the young man who must be rescued from the clutches of Europe, rather than through the consciousness of Lambert Strether, the middle-aged protagonist and rescuer in the novel. Auchincloss's central character and narrator, Tony Rives, is a somewhat older Chad Newsome endowed with a good deal of Lambert Strether's sensibility. The rescue mission in the story is carried out by Tony's older sister Edith MacLean, who parallels Sarah Pocock in James's version, but who also reflects some aspects of Strether's experience. Edith not only manages to bring her brother home but also gets him to marry her husband's niece—something her counterpart in the novel had been ordered to do but does not accomplish. In Auchincloss's ironic version of the tale, Edith's triumph is even greater, for it also includes taking away Gwladys Kane, the older woman to whom Tony had been attached, and making her one of her own friends. Edith's deepening relationship with Gwladys excludes Tony, which throws him into renewed acquaintance with the niece and eventually leads to his marriage. Strether's respect for the older woman in the novel (Madame de Vionnet) is transformed in Auchincloss's story into something that appears to be an instance of successful social manipulation by a powerful woman. And yet, in the concluding scene of the story, which takes place at his wedding, Tony still does not know whether his sister consciously plotted to draw Gwladys away from him or things merely worked out to her advantage by a lucky coincidence.

"The Ambassadress" is not merely a witty reworking of a Jamesian situation but a finely articulated tale of complex relationships in a closely knit group of people. As might be expected in a short story rather than a novel, Tony is a more limited character than Strether. In Tony's appreciation of his expatriate life, one finds none of Strether's luminous vision of European culture. Tony's reeducation, unlike Strether's, teaches him the power of strong family ties, which can even reach across the Atlantic. Tony returns to New York to be married, not with Strether's sense of renunciation and all it entails, but with a sense of how life is determined—albeit for the best—by forces we do not understand. Auchincloss is finally more interested in the complex psychological dynamics at work in a given situation than in James's theme of enlightenment and renunciation. The result is more realistic; though not so richly

Auchincloss at home.

resonant, nonetheless subtle: a sharper, brisker story, but still a work worthy of the master.

The three stories that focus directly upon professional writers, **"The Question of the Existence of Waring Stohl," "The Novelist of Manners,"** and **"The Arbiter,"** show the aggressive or hostile impulses in writers who make use of people around them as material for their art. Auchincloss, a writer who himself draws much of the material for his fiction from life, shows a decided tendency to stress this exploitive side of the artist. In the earliest of the three tales, **"The Question of the Existence of Waring Stohl,"** reprinted in *Tales of Manhattan,* a distinguished professor of English befriends one of his students, a young novelist with very little talent and an obnoxious personality. No one understands why he goes out of his way to cultivate the young man's acquaintance until the novelist dies and leaves him his unpublished journal. The journal becomes the central piece of evidence in the professor's last and greatest work: a literary history in which the young writer becomes the embodiment of the superficiality and vacuousness of his era, a "non-author" whose novel is called a "non-book." The professor wins a Pulitzer prize, and the young novelist receives a negative

sort of immortality. In **"The Arbiter,"** one of the stories in *The Winthrop Covenant,* the novelist Ada Guest bases one of the characters in her best novel, "a sterile dilettante, who is trying to hide his business failure in a drawing room success," on her long-time friend Adam Winthrop, and she seems likely to make similar use of her husband later. Though Auchincloss's primary interest in this fine story is the relationship that develops between the two men, Ada shows the same voracity in using material from life for her art.

Why this strange voracity in appropriating other people's lives? For the novelist of manners, as for the historian or journalist, it may be inevitable. Discussing class distinctions in an essay on Marquand and O'Hara, Auchincloss has observed that the novelist of manners "has two points of view about the society in which he lives: that of a citizen and that of an artist, The latter is concerned only with the suitability of society as material for his art. Just as a liberal journalist may secretly rejoice at the rise of a Senator McCarthy because of the opportunity it affords him to write brilliant and scathing denunciations of demogogues, so will the eye of the novelist of manners light up at the first glimpse of social injustice." So too, within the limits of human decency or the libel laws, the novelist of manners may exploit the human material he finds around him, often in a seemingly amoral fashion.

"The Novelist of Manners" looks most directly at this exploitive tendency and suggests it may also be a weapon for striking back when the author is wounded. Published in *The Partners,* the story describes the relationship between a young lawyer and the novelist Dana Clyde. It is at once an interesting psychological study and an oblique defense of the novel of manners in the late twentieth century. The hero of the story, Leslie Carter, a junior partner in Shepard, Putney & Cox, has been sent abroad to take charge of the firm's Paris office. A frustrated novelist who unsuccessfully tried to write his own *Great Gatsby* in college, he eagerly makes his way into French society, much like the young Proust. He is delighted to find that his firm must represent Dana Clyde, whose society novels he has admired since college, in a libel suit brought by someone maligned in his latest book. After the suit is settled, he attaches himself to Clyde as a kind of disciple, urging him to write "the last great novel of manners of the western world"—the great work he himself could never write. His life takes on new meaning, for he now has a mission: "to save Dana Clyde and make him compose his masterpiece."

When, however, after some urging, Clyde retires to a hillside in Malaga to write the great book, he mysteriously breaks off all connection with the younger man. The reason for the break is revealed only when Leslie reads the manuscript of the new novel. One of the main characters is a wickedly satiric potrait of himself as an absurd young lawyer who becomes the fifth husband of the novel's heroine, but who proves impotent on his wedding night and commits suicide. On his return to Paris, Clyde avoids Leslie entirely, and Leslie must seek an explanation for the malevolence of the portrait from the novelist's wife. Quite aware of what might happen all along, Mrs. Clyde had tried to warn Leslie, but he would not listen. Instead, his badgering has forced Clyde to recognize that he is an irrevocably second-rate writer. As Leslie admits, the new novel is "Dana Clyde at his best," but it is hardly the "last great novel of manners" he had predicted. In creating the character of the young lawyer, Clyde has gotten revenge against Leslie for destroying the saving illusion on which he has operated for many years—the idea that, if only he had worked harder, he could have written another *Madame Bovary.* At the end of the story Leslie recognizes that he has been a fool. The novel of manners "*does* still have a function," he says, "if only to prove to a poor thing like Leslie Carter that he doesn't want to write one any more."

Considered as a whole, the story recalls a pattern found in several of James's stories, in which a second-rate artist is protected by a wife who clearly sees her husband's lack of genius and the complication and interest of the plot arise from the entry of some third person who upsets the equilibrium achieved by the couple. In Auchincloss's variation of the pattern, however, Leslie is innocent of any intention to denigrate Dana Clyde's work. After having been at-

tacked in the novel, he learns several lessons. He recognizes the folly of his own hidden aspirations to be a novelist and the ridiculousness of trying to live out those aspirations in someone else's career, and he is presumably a bit wiser about rushing in to meddle in someone else's life. Under Auchincloss's scrutiny, a seemingly casual relationship turns out to have multiple, ramifying effects.

Viewed in its biographical and historical context, however, **"The Novelist of Manners"** gains further interest. The story takes place in 1972, in a period when, as Dana Clyde is well aware, the novel of manners is in eclipse. "Oh, I have a following yet, I grant," he says to Leslie. "There are plenty of old girls and boys who still take me to the hospital for their hysterectomies and prostates. But the trend is against me. The young don't read me. The literary establishment scorns me." Clyde's plaint is heard frequently in Auchincloss's writings of the late 1960s and 1970s: "I have always dealt with the great world. The top of the heap. How people climbed up and what they found when they got there. That was perfectly valid when the bright young people were ambitious for money and social position. But now they don't care for such things. They care about stopping wars and saving the environment and cleaning up the ghettos. And they're right too. When the world's going to pieces, who has time to talk about good form and good taste?" Leslie suspects that Clyde's endorsement of social activism is not quite sincere, but the general question remains valid and pertains to Auchincloss's work as well.

Though much of the passage sounds as though it might fit Auchincloss himself, James Tuttleton is right to maintain that Dana Clyde is not Auchincloss. As is true of many of his characters, there are elements of Auchincloss in Clyde, but there are also details from Auchincloss's personal history in Leslie Carter as well. Like Leslie, Auchincloss was impelled on his way to law school by the failure of a novel he had written in his last year at college. Though Dana Clyde is not Auchincloss, it is nevertheless correct to see the story in the context of Auchincloss's own work and the tradition of the novel of manners in the 1970s. As usual, Auchincloss keeps his claims for what he and others like him are doing quite modest and somewhat sardonic. Leslie's final words about the function of the novel of manners do not constitute a ringing general defense. But, as the story itself suggests, this sort of fiction is certain to endure in some form. Wherever human folly displays itself in faulty behavior, there is a need for the novel of manners, and, whether or not it is in current critical favor, fiction that evokes a particular time and place always seems to find an audience.

Obviously, however, even the most faithful rendering of the manners and customs of a given era will not necessarily yield great art. In a story from his most recent collection, Auchincloss carefully distinguishes between life and art and takes a more sanguine view of the writer in his role as an artist. Worthington Whitson, the absurd Mauve Decade dandy who is the protagonist in **"The Artistic Personality,"** has, like the characters in the other stories,

CHRONICLES OF OUR TIME

been wronged by a novelist, Alistair Temple. But Auchincloss varies the pattern. Rather than exploiting Whitson as a character in his fiction, Temple had staged an elaborate drama in real life that led to Whitson's downfall as "the acknowledged *arbiter elegantarium* of Fifth Avenue and Newport" at the end of the nineteenth century. The reader sees Temple obliquely, through Whitson's indignant remarks almost twenty-five years later in a conversation with Bernard Berenson, who admires one of Temple's novels and wants to know more about him.

As he questions Whitson about Temple, Berenson speculates about the artistic personality. Temple had cleverly engineered a situation in which the prominent hostess with whom Whitson was allied was tempted, against Whitson's advice, into attending a ball given by an unacceptable new family. This event effectively destroyed Whitson's authority as a social arbiter and put an end to his grandiose scheme to set standards for entry into New York society. For Whitson, Temple's actions represent betrayal—a betrayal all the more perfidious because the novelist arranged the episode deliberately "to divert himself by creating a drama in New York society." But for Berenson his actions are those of an artist. "You mean he constructed a scenario for his own inspiration? He modeled a plot out of real life? And then never used it?" he asks. "Perhaps," he suggests to Whitson, "you provided the scaffolding, my friend, which he had later to remove" when he wrote his greatest novel. Berenson toys with Whitson throughout the dialogue, however, and when the absurd Whitson decides at the end of the story that perhaps he can claim some renown for having helped a great novelist, Berenson laughingly rejects his own speculation.

In the course of the conversation one learns that Temple not only has played a clever trick on Whitson but that he himself was the most ardent of social climbers, in no way removed from the society he set out to satirize. Temple's actions and his character in life finally do not matter, for according to Berenson one "must distinguish . . . between an artist's individual personality and his artistic one." In the light of his masterpiece, Temple's personal failings are irrelevant: "The artistic personality is the creator. And that is something totally detached from the vulgar appetites, from greed, from Mammon, from snobbishness and social ambition. Alistair Temple the man may have been everything you think. But Alistair Temple the artist had not the smallest ounce of worldliness. Of that I am convinced." Though there is much else going on in the story—in his conversation with Whitson, for example, Berenson himself may be constructing a "scenario" not unlike Temple—Auchincloss provides, in the distinction between the two personalities, a final line of defense for all the voracious novelists in his fiction. Though it is presented in a complicated, oblique fashion and hedged about by ironies and qualifications, Auchincloss's view of the writer in **"The Artistic Personality"** is essentially Romantic. Art, especially great art, works in a mysterious way its wonders to perform; by some unfathomable process, the work of art, if it is worthy, transcends its creator. Like Henry James, Auchincloss accepts only the highest view of the writer's art.

"But why is the artist whose subject is society any better than that society?" Whitson asks Berenson in the story just discussed. "Because he must see it in a different light. He illuminates it," Berenson replies. At their best, Auchincloss's stories about contemporary life do indeed manage to illuminate society and thereby illuminate the lives of everyone.

Since the beginning of his career as a writer, Auchincloss has kept careful watch on what was going on in the various worlds he has inhabited. In his first novel, *The Indifferent Children,* he captures the essential futility of the military bureaucracy, and in *The Great World and Timothy Colt* he presents a definitive account of life among young associates in the large corporate law firms during the early 1950s. Because of their smaller scope, however, the short stories have provided him with an especially useful medium for observing particular changes in business, society, and the professions. Indeed, in the last decade and a half, as his novels have tended to be increasingly concerned with the past, Auchincloss's keenest observations in contemporary life have most often been found in his stories.

In the stories in his four most recent collections, published from 1970 to 1983, Auchincloss notes many of the changes in sex roles, relations between generations, and behavior at the office witnessed in the 1960s and 1970s. Sometimes, as in **"The Marriage Contract,"** published in *The Partners* (1974), Auchincloss simply looks at the enduring problems of marriage as they are manifested in a new situation. Marcus and Felicia Currier are both lawyers, representatives of the sort of two-career couple that was becoming more common in the early seventies. The stresses on their marriage come from new sources—managing two careers, including a temporary move to another city by Felicia, competing for professional success, and simultaneously raising two children—but the fundamental conflict for control between Marc and Felicia is not radically different from the conflicts between husbands and wives that one encounters in the novels Auchincloss wrote in the 1950s.

At times, however, from his basically conservative perspective Auchincloss can be amazingly prescient about trends in American society. **"The Double Gap,"** which appeared in 1970, for instance, nicely predicts the disillusionment and grim professionalism that set in during the early 1980s among those who had been the idealistic young people of the sixties. Cast in the form of a series of memos between a young law student and his grandfather, who is the senior partner in a large law firm, the story vividly states the case for both sides of the debate between generations during the era of the "generation gap." Neither advocate persuades the other, but, after the grandson has refused for the last time his grandfather's offer to join his firm and has totally rejected his justification for practicing corporate law, the grandfather writes one more memo. Warning his grandson that in his zeal for representing the downtrodden he too may become "a one-client man" not unlike a dishonest former member of his firm, he wishes him good luck.

> I'm glad that I've made you independent so you won't be compelled, like your breadwinner friends, to go to work for a firm in whose "mystique" you cannot believe. I am convinced, sincerely convinced, that you will do big things. I am only disappointed that you will not be doing them with me. And I cannot help but wonder a bit, when you and your contemporaries have scraped all the gilt off the statue of life (gilt which I call passion and you call sentimentality), whether you will not be a bit disappointed at the dull gray skeleton that you find beneath. (*Second Chance*)

By the end of the decade in which this story appeared, not only had the idealists of the sixties come face to face with the dull gray skeleton, but their younger brothers and sisters were rushing cynically into law and medical school without even the passion that justified the grandfather's career.

Though **"The Marriage Contract"** and **"The Double Gap"** accurately illustrate Auchincloss's responses to social change, neither represents his short fiction at its best. Another story of the 1970s, **"Second Chance"** is richer, more finely wrought, and characteristic of its author's unique strengths. In this, the title story of Auchincloss's 1970 collection, Gilbert Van Ness divorces his wife of more than twenty years, takes an entirely new job, and marries a younger woman—a common enough occurrence in recent years and a topic of much discussion when the story appeared. Auchincloss approaches this central situation from a fresh perspective, however. We see Gilbert's midlife transformation through the eyes of his brother-in-law Joe, who has known him since college and who handles the divorce for the family. Before he leaves his first wife, Gilbert seems a failure, "a Confederate officer returning to his ruined plantation after Appomattox." After the divorce he becomes an almost instant success in a flashy Madison Avenue advertising agency, quickly rising to president and ultimately marrying the daughter of the founder. Joe is blamed by his wife's family, the Kilpatricks, for letting his old friend off with a one-time financial settlement rather than a percentage of Gilbert's future earnings.

The central drama in the story is not Gilbert's amazing luck but rather his more stable brother-in-law's uneasy response to his success, which Auchincloss depicts with great subtlety and tact. When the Kilpatricks start complaining about the settlement, Joe finds that he would rather have them believe that he was swayed by his longtime friendship than that Gilbert's "stronger personality had put it over my weaker one. Or that I had been dazzled—even envious—at the prospect of his liberty." Later in the story Gilbert accuses him of fearing the idea that one can "start again and win" and argues that his moral indignation is merely a convenient way of avoiding an opportunity to change his own life. "You hate me because I remind you in your indolence that you could do it, too. That it's *not* too late." It is this "demon of the second chance" that Joe must confront in himself.

After he gets home from the party at which he talked to Gilbert, he carefully considers his indictment. He is reasonably certain that it is not valid, but a small doubt remains. When he attends an impressive dinner party at Gilbert's apartment, he is almost convinced again that Gilbert has been right all along—until he notices a very small detail. Gilbert hands a fork to his butler without even pausing in conversation. Obviously there was a speck on it, but the fact that the butler knows just what to do with the fork reveals "the enormous amount of domestic machinery that must have been hid behind that simple gesture." Rather than being the free soul that he claims to be, Gilbert is a fraud. "I had exorcised the demon of the second chance," Joe comments at the end of the story. "I had saved my marriage, not from dissolution, but from the cloying idea that I wanted its dissolution. Or that I had wanted to be like Gilbert. Or that I had thought it might be unmanly *not* to be like Gilbert. Now he could go on handing spotted spoons to his butler for eternity. I simply did not care."

That the major psychological insight of the story should turn upon this small detail of manners is thoroughly characteristic of Auchincloss's approach. The lawyer-protagonist is also typical of Auchincloss's reserved and invariably decent heroes; both his dilemma and its resolution seem fitting. Yet, in spite of the rather specialized elements present in **"Second Chance,"** the story describes and offers surprisingly immediate and generally accessible commentary upon an ordinary experience shared by many men of the protagonist's age. In addition to this, Joe is expertly placed in the context of his marriage and his relations with his wife's family. We are given just the right amount of psychological and social background, and Auchincloss's tone, faintly ironic but generally sympathetic, achieves sufficient distance to permit us to see the humor in the narrator's situation. In **"Second Chance"** and in several other stories like it, we see what makes Auchincloss's short fiction entertaining and valuable.

Peter Cameron (essay date 1987)

SOURCE: A review of *Skinny Island: More Tales of Manhattan,* in *The New York Times Book Review,* May 24, 1987, p. 5.

[*Cameron is an American short story writer and critic whose short fiction collection* One Way or Another *(1986) earned him recognition as a skilled and highly promising young author. In the following review, he argues that some of Auchincloss's stories in* Skinny Island *are less successful than others, but asserts that the collection is "first and foremost elegant fiction."*]

Louis Auchincloss's 30th book of fiction, **Skinny Island,** is a collection of stories about man versus high society. The center of this world is Fifth Avenue and 57th Street, and except for an occasional meeting on Wall Street, a season in Newport, Bar Harbor or Narragansett, a semester at a prep school, and a moment or two on the Avenue

Foch, these stories are all set like vertebrae on the expensive backbone of Manhattan. Fifth Avenue is a street where a character "knew all the houses by the names of their owners and kept a mental list of those in which he dined." The St. Regis is where one moves into "a delicious little suite" when one gets tired of the brownstone on East 73d.

The stories begin in 1875 and conclude in the 1980's, and thus we see how both the idle rich and the short story have evolved over the last century. We move from the Washington Square of Henry James (**"A Diary of Old New York"**), to the Fifth Avenue mansions of Edith Wharton (**"The Wedding Guest"**), yet this journey through literary Gotham stalls on the commuter trains of John Cheever. The later stories—from the 40's on—all read similarly, and the feeling of moving onward is missed. It is ironic that the concluding stories—the ones set in this decade—seem the least specifically grounded in time and place.

Two themes are prevalent. Either a character wants to behave in a way that polite society deems unsuitable, or society insists on changing in ways that an individual cannot abide. In **"A Diary of Old New York,"** Adrian Peltz, an aging widower, is forced to realize that what he assumes is morality everyone else believes is either wishful thinking or lunacy. His refusal to admit a lying, cheating real estate developer into his men's club is his undoing. In **"The Wedding Guest,"** Griswold Norrie's insistence on inviting his vaguely licentious step-grandmother to his perfect wedding appears to ruin what had promised to be a perfect marraige.

Morality is not the only conflict in these privileged lives: art, religion and money are all potential pitfalls and the ease with which Mr. Auchincloss introduces these larger issues into his crafted narratives is admirable. The best stories turn on politics and sex. **"America First,"** set on the eve of World War II, finds Elaine Wagstaff returning to New York from her beloved, but no longer safe, Paris. In New York she finds her allegiance divided between Suzannah, her deadbeat, long-suffering daughter, who is working on a campaign to keep America out of the war ("America First") and her old friends, who, with their ties to Europe, are pressing for the United States to enter the war. Elaine pledges herself to America First and reconciles with Suzannah, only to realize that the cause is not only the wrong one for her, but that it, and its adherents, are dreary, selfish and parochial.

She defects and joins the hedonistic Europeans—"She had almost forgotten what it was like to be among people who cared so intensely for appearances, for things. Dining at Erica's apartment . . . was like swimming in a translucent Caribbean cove amid brilliantly colored fish over a sand as smooth as a rich carpet. It made Suzannah's world seem like the hustle and bustle of a Coney Island beach covered with bulbous women and white-limbed men in lumpy black bathing suits."

The widowed and wealthy Frances Hamill in **"No Friend Like a New Friend"** also abandons family and appearances in pursuit of a good time. After her husband's death,

she takes up with an aging, pathetic, yet companionable homosexual, despite how it "looks" to everyone else. When Frances announces, "Looks? Why should I care about looks?" her lifelong friend replies, "I thought we both did. I thought it was important how we appeared to the world . . . I thought you and I believed that our outward selves should reflect, as far as possible, the things we stand for." All this refined behavior in the midst of scandal can get a little monotonous, so one especially appreciates the moments when characters forget their manners.

The citizens of Mr. Auchincloss's island don't have to work for a living. "Darling, if you're too proud to live on my money—*our* money, as I've always regarded it—if you insist on wasting your life in a family business that hardly pays the cook, then that must be *your* problem. *I'm* going to Paris." Their days, over the course of a hundred years, vary little. The men stop in at their offices on the way to their clubs, while the women sit on committees and lunch. They rendezvous at the opera.

The stories in *Skinny Island* are slight, but they're svelte. In a matter of pages Mr. Auchincloss can set up a whole life, richly and accurately. Yet some of these lives seem less deserving of his talent than others—there are stories here whose characters and actions seem negligible and anemic when compared to their juicier counterparts. If there is a sameness to the lives of these characters, the narrator moves through this limited gallery generously and expertly. There is nothing anthropological in Mr. Auchincloss's approach, however. Happily, *Skinny Island* is more than a record of how the other half lived, and continues to live. It is first and foremost elegant fiction—a century of vicarious pleasures.

M. O'Sullivan (essay date 1988)

SOURCE: "Postlapsarians: Louis Auchincloss's *The Winthrop Covenant*," in *The Dutch Quarterly Review of Anglo-American Letters*, Vol. 18, No. 1, 1988, pp. 38-45.

[*In the following essay, O'Sullivan analyzes biblical allusions in* The Winthrop Covenant. *The critic notes that the collection initially compares America to an idyllic Garden of Eden, but eventually develops a more complex view wherein characters must deal with an imperfect land and their own sense of mission.*]

In *The Winthrop Covenant,* his collection of stories examining the rise and fall of the Puritan ethic in New York and New England, Louis Auchincloss examines the movement from public to private redemption in the world of the privileged. Although Auchincloss, almost inevitably, begins by introducing imagery that reflects the traditional view of the American as a prelapsarian Adam and his country as a fresh Eden, he goes beyond these images in his nine stories to bring the tale nearer completion with true and false prophets, a proto-feminist trinity, and even a new gospel with its false—and possibly true—messiahs. In the ironic wit of his delicately poised prose, Auchincloss traces the difficulties of characters who confuse their own search for salvation with their attempts to become saviours.

Auchincloss's first story, **"The Covenant"**, establishes the terms of his theme, the "preoccupying sense, found in certain individuals, of a mission, presumably divinely inspired, toward their fellow men" [as stated in his foreword to *The Winthrop Covenant*]. The story focuses on William and Anne Hutchinson's alienation from the old world, their decision to join John Winthrop's colony in the new one, and their subsequent problems with the authorities of the new colony and with each other. William and Anne are never quite in agreement on the matter of the covenant. William's problems stem from a lack of conviction that he is among the elect, a fear that never seems to affect the other characters in the story. His solution is to envision a new covenant for the new world, a covenant that would provide "a fresh start for everybody". Where the founders of the Bay Colony proposed an ideal site for the working out of the old covenant, restricting participation as far as possible to the elect, William seeks to escape that covenant into a new one. Both visions, of course, were to prove inadequate.

William's illusions might never have happened had he remembered the time when his grandmother had quietly challenged her husband's theology and received a blow for her presumption: "And William thus dimly derived this early lesson: that there were two forces in the world, authority and the resistance which authority generated". Authority reappears in the story in the fixed, sinister gleam of Queen Elizabeth, the hard little light of John Winthrop, and even the earnestly limited vision of Anne. At every point that humanity asserts itself, as when the Bay Colony ministers try to strengthen the colonists' confidence in their labours by skirting the debate between work and grace, an authoritarian figure demands the reassertion of the rule of principle and force. William finally acknowledges his illusion by voluntarily joining his wife in her exile in Rhode Island, while understanding that she is moving inexorably towards martyrdom. Only as a martyr can she fulfill her mission. Perhaps realizing that the new garden had always been an illusion, at the end of the story William sits, cared for by his married daughter who visits, ironically, from Providence, starting out to sea, to the past, to the old world.

Auchincloss's next story is, appropriately, **"The Fall"**, a letter from a young clergyman about his deathbed interview with Major General Wait Still Winthrop, one of the Salem witch trial judges. In the course of attempting a confession, General Winthrop can only complain about the pride of those he tried. Complaint easily metamorphoses into justification:

> "But every man in that first settlement knew that he lived under a divine light as bright as any that shone in Europe. Brighter even. It was that shared spirit that saved the Bay Colony from wolves and Indians, from frost and hunger. We were *united,* Mr. Leigh! And because our union had no king or pope to protect it,

it was vital that we should learn to maintain that consensus. It was not easy. We were soon threatened by separatists. The witch Hutchinson was the first. Then came the Quakers. But the community was never threatened as perilously as in 1692. God alone knows the full extent of the deviltries with which our colony then seethed. But when the accused in Salem were given the chance to help the magistrates to reassert the indispensable cohesion of a colony in covenant with God, they refused. By God, I say they deserved their deaths! They had denied their Puritan heritage!"

The fall is confirmed in the general's eyes by the witches' refusal to repent and in our eyes by his refusal. In one case a force for disruption is inadequately dealt with; in the other the delusion of a new covenant and its corollary, the conviction by the covenanted of their right to enforce it, overcome deathbed reservations.

Wait Still Winthrop's granddaughter becomes the central figure in the third story, **"The Martyr"**, an account by a young French tutor of a family's attempt to escape its fate. A young European sent to the wilderness for the indiscretion of socializing with the philosophes offers an ideal vehicle for Auchincloss's examination of the Winthrops' preoccupation with duty. Rebecca Bayard, the Winthrop, fears that her children, Katrina and Sylvester, may suffer for the sins of their great-grandfather and thus encourages them to become just like their father, the rather mindless, visceral Patroon of Bayardwick on the Hudson River. With the aid of the tutor, Rebecca attempts to help a man she believes to be a slave accused of arson to escape. Unfortunately, Katrina betrays the attempt and the man is caught and hanged. Only then does Bayard tell Rebecca that the man who died was a free man whom "Sylvester had bribed . . . to take the part because he wanted you, Rebecca, to believe that you had saved a man's life. He told me he had to exorcise the Winthrop curse". Although she attempts to establish a messianic role for herself—the tutor rather superfluously notes to Sylvester, "Your mother wishes to take on her own shoulders all the sins of the world"—the myth she finally recreates is an older one, that of Orestes. Having set the Winthrop's furies to work, Rebecca sends the tutor home: "I hope you will forget all about the bleak new world in that sunny land". She dies and neither child marries, perhaps to avoid passing on the family's guilt. Bayard, however, passes through all this apparently oblivious to the world of guilt and memory which overwhelms his wife and children.

The Paris to which the tutor returns becomes, at the beginning of the nineteenth century, the setting of **"The Diplomat"**. Samuel Shaw Russell, a young diplomat, is the first Winthrop to reject the family mission, to refuse to see himself "as another link in that chain of special human obligation which began in Boston in 1630". Russell can only arrive at this position after resolving two conflicts. The first is with his image of his father, the bearer of the sacred name, Everett Winthrop Russell, who believed that

> God viewed with especial favor his domain in the northern New World. He professed to see signs of

divine partiality in our successful escape from ancient tyranny, in our preservation from cold winters and Indians, in our deliverance from the German mercenaries of George III. God manifested His will through individuals, divinely selected, whose impact upon history was undoubted. Where, he would ask, would Massachusetts have been without our ancestor John Winthrop?

Russell's second conflict is with the wily Talleyrand's old-world criticism of the new land: "'There is something in your air that . . . well, that I grasp only with difficulty. It is a kind of repudiation, not exactly of the past, but of all that I, at least, find most important in this vale of tears. The *douceur de vivre*—we might put it that way. Americans are not strong on *douceurs*. You believe more in morals. You even seem to believe that morals began with you'." His father's position falls after the young man envisions himself a great bird of prey soaring over the American continent. The somewhat secular mysticism of this vision gives him a "sense of human powerlessness" which establishes him as an outsider in both the game of diplomacy and the mission of the family.

Winthrop self-righteousness reasserts itself forcefully in the next two stories. The first, **"In the Beauty of the Lilies Christ Was Born Across the Sea"**, fulfills the promise implicit in its orphic title. Winthrop Ward, whose flights of imagination combine casual anti-Black, anti-Semitic, and anti-Irish prejudices with violently sexual fantasies, organizes the economic interests of New York against the lover of his cousin's (and partner's) wife. Ward is so preoccupied with playing his roles—overtly as an arbiter of behaviour and covertly as a hero—that even his language takes the flavour of melodramatic nineteenth-century prose: "'She has not submitted to the lewd embracements of that fiend'." In the next story, **"The Arbiter"**, Adam Winthrop, a more comfortably established guide to the mores and morals of New York than his predecessor, tries to discourage the novelist wife of a friend from travelling to Paris. He insists that her genius can only develop at home. Both Winthrops oppose movement towards self-fulfillment by women they admire. And both base their opposition on an aversion to passion. When Annie Ward points out to her cousin that she has learned from works like *Jane Eyre, The Scarlet Letter* and *Phedre* that "passion is the whole thing in this world", Winthrop Ward reacts by staring at her, "sobered by the enormity of her misconstruction. 'But those books and plays all point out the pitfalls of illicit love'." In a similar outburst, Ada Guest, Adam Winthrop's protege, points out her newly found understanding about him and his fellow members of her salon: "You are dry, Adam, all of you! Dry with the dust of New York, derivative rather than inspired, clever rather than forceful. . . . The old Puritan fire has gone out." But where nothing challenges Adam's condemnation—even Bob Guest, Ada's husband, returns alone from Paris to rejoin Adam's circle—Winthrop Ward suffers the anguish of a perceptive wife who recognizes and criticizes both his public and private roles. Her suggestion that his reality relies as much on fantasy as his dreams leads him to the story's penultimate prayer. In asking God's forgive-

ness for any carnal thoughts, he offers a Winthrop extenuation, "My conduct has been correct, even if my heart has been sinful."

Auchincloss's pair of arbiters are followed by a pair of Winthrops who turn inward. The first, Danny Buck, refuses to take a public role in judging his friend and superior, the headmaster of Farmingdale Academy, Titus Larsen. After the chairman of the board of trustees asks Danny to keep a journal to see if Larsen has become incapable of governing, Danny finds that this diary, from which the story receives its title, **"The Mystic Journal"**, soon begins to fill with fantasies of jealousy and resentment, fantasies which he must repudiate. Although Danny recognizes that his journal is a false gospel and burns it, he suggests to the chairman of the board that its very existence might, in some magical way, have actually helped Larsen. But the chairman sees something else, the traditional Winthrop sense of self-righteousness and the Puritan ethic manifesting themselves in a purely private way:

> "What concerns you is not the capacity or incapacity of Titus Larsen to be headmaster, but the moral capacity or incapacity of Daniel Buck to judge him. The drama for you is all in you. You are happy now, obviously. Why? Because it has been decided that Titus Larsen is qualified to continue in Farmingdale? No. Because it has been decided that Danny Buck was almost a sinner and has now ceased to be! What does it matter, I ask you, what happens to a million schools and headmasters so long as Danny Buck saves his own soul?"

The next story, **"The Triplets"**, continues this transferral of the Winthrop sense of mission from the external world to the internal one. The central character is Natica Seligman, daughter of the Winthrop triplets, three sisters who act in unison with their children. The triplets, who exist for the most part outside the story, function as an indivisible but impotent trinity. While they counsel Natica to "love and let love"—a strange Winthropian injunction— they cannot help her penetrate the privacies of a husband who has decided to leave a successful public career for teaching. As with most Winthrops, Natica must sort out her relationship with her family before she can resolve her problems with her husband. To help her, the triplets' greatest admirer and closest friend tries to define the ambiguous nature of the current Winthrop role:

> "The triplets are so manifestly the fine flower of a great tradition. Who dares to challenge them? They have combined their great ancestor's passionate mission to save the world with all that is beautiful and luxurious in the world to be saved. We may suspect, at least down here in benighted New York, that the mission is defunct and that its lovely ministers are frauds—or let us say illusions—but what have we that is better?"

A bit later, sensing that he might have been too negative in his assessment, he suggests they retain an important function for society as the "masks our civilization wears." Only when Natica discovers that her husband suffers from a debilitating disease, however, can she seek redemption in his illness. When he rebuffs her, she resolves to explore a new dimension of the family's tradition:

> She would give up the mask, at any rate, even if that was all she had left from the Winthrops. Without it she might expose herself as a cipher to the world. But perhaps to be a cipher was better than to be a pose. So long as the tablet was blank, there was no reason to assume that one could not write on it. At any rate, she would have given up the mission, or the burden of seeming to have one. From henceforth the mission would be only to herself.

As her words reveal, the need for a mission remains; her only hope for individual salvation lies in imposing its demands on herself rather than others.

Auchincloss's last story, **"The Penultimate Puritan"**, a long letter from a mother to her son resisting the Vietnam war in Stockholm, returns explicitly to the biblical theme in its opening sentence: "Here beginneth the first chapter of the gospel according to Althea Stevens Gardiner . . . ." The story concentrates on the relationship between Althea Stevens and John Winthrop Gardiner, seen from the perspective of a deserted wife whose husband abandoned her for a little "chit of a girl." Althea, sets the tone for her epistle with the comment:

> You will remember from your sacred studies at Farmingdale that in the first century Christians believed that Christ would come again to judge the world in only a few years time. They also believed that this second and final coming would be preceded by a false one, that of an antichrist, who would spread fire and destruction along with his false doctrine. Your generation believes only in the false coming. You see the future as terminated by a hypocrite with a hydrogen bomb. Your father sees only the bomb.

It takes Althea some time after her marriage to realize that John needed an antichrist even more than a Christ: when Hitler fails to offer a sustained evil, communism becomes an adequate substitute as John joins the CIA. After the Vietnam War leads to a rupture between father and son, with the father supporting clandestine activity while demanding of his son strict adherence to traditional values, Althea raises the inevitable question of Winthrop spouses and gets the inevitable response:

> "And what is [your faith] based on? Do you even believe in God?"

> "My faith is in *me*."

But just as the father's self-righteousness motivates him, the son, Jock's, self-righteousness forces him into deserting from the army and condemning his father and country. His mother sees accurately the source of his protest, a source consonant with that projection of the ego implicit in the covenant: "You and I, Jock, want to tear down the Establishment because we loathe and resent it—not because we give a damn about the great unwashed." His act of protest, the flight to Europe from a postlapsarian garden of Eden, merely reverses the original progress and aligns him as firmly with the other Adamic figures in the stories, as does his ironic surname, Gardiner.

If John is the penultimate Puritan and Jock the ultimate one, where is the saviour, the figure who might either fulfill the Winthrop mission or establish a new covenant? There is a comic possibility in Althea's dowdy, dreaming daughter Christine "with her rosy view of an imminent socialist future." But the story dismisses Christine so fully that it is hard to think of her as more than a naive innocent who has translated the Winthrop legacy into a vague desire to do good for the world. If Jock can be seen as the Baptist, then the true messiah might be his as yet unborn stepbrother, the child John's lover bears. That child offers the possibility of extending his father's mandate against the forces of darkness or of emerging as the first truly spontaneous symbol of love in a far from spontaneous clan.

Auchincloss's tale is not finished, as, of course, it cannot be. In fact, it serves as but a chapter in his writings, for all of his works deal, directly or indirectly, with the preoccupying sense of mission. Despite Gore Vidal's observation that he "plays God with his characters" [in *The New York Review of Books* XXI, No. 12 (July 18, 1974)], however, he does so no more than most other novelists. And, as Vidal has also noted, as a member of the class he portrays, Auchincloss shares the temptations, illusions, and frustrations of their postlapsarian state. Defining and redefining that state has become his preoccupying mission, a mission which is, appropriately, more Promethean than messianic.

David Parsell (essay date 1988)

SOURCE: "The Novel as Omnibus: Auchincloss's Collected Short Fiction," in *Louis Auchincloss*, Twayne Publishers, 1988, pp. 84-95.

[*In this chapter from his book on Auchincloss's work, Parsell discusses the author's short story collections, commenting on the manner in which they experiment with long and short forms.*]

Although deservedly best known for his novels, Auchincloss since the later 1940s has earned acclaim also as a writer of incisive, memorable short stories. In his first two published collections, **The Injustice Collectors** (1950) and **The Romantic Egoists** (1954), the stories are thematically linked; in certain subsequent collections, such as **Powers of Attorney** (1963), **Tales of Manhattan** (1967), **The Partners** (1974), the collected stories are linked through recurrent characters as well. In those volumes Auchincloss appears to be attempting a fusion of short and long fiction with stories that can be read either individually or in sequence, offering the double satisfactions of the short story and the novel. **The Partners** in fact, was originally advertised and published as a novel, although it is little different in form and structure from the earlier **Powers of At-**

Auchincloss's writing process:

[Auchincloss]: I found that writing took a bit of adjusting—essentially to be able to use little scratches of time to do it. Lots of writers have to have whole days or nights to get ready to write; they like to be by a fire, with absolute quiet, with their slippers on and a pipe or something, and then they're ready to go. They can't believe you can use five minutes here, ten minutes there, fifteen minutes at another time. Yet it's only a question of training to learn that trick. If they *had* to do it that way, they'd be able to, the real writers, that is. I can pick up in the middle of a sentence and then go on. I wrote at night; sometimes I wrote at the office and then practiced law at home. My wife and I never went away on weekends. I wouldn't recommend that anyone else try this method, but it worked for me. And it did for Trollope. I don't mean to compare myself to Trollope, but it was said that he made a habit of writing from nine to noon, and if he finished a novel at a quarter to twelve, he'd start another. Unfortunately, he put that all into his autobiography, which killed his reputation for decades because people wanted to think of writing as suffering.

[Plimpton]: *Do you think you'd write better if you did suffer?*

No. And I don't think most writers do, either. I think Shakespeare got drunk after he finished *King Lear*. That he had a ball writing it.

Do you get drunk after you finish one of your books?

No, I don't. I'm a very regular person.

> *Louis Auchincloss and George Plimpton in an*
> *interview in* Paris Review, *Vol. 36, No. 132,*
> *Fall, 1994.*

---

torney. *The Winthrop Covenant* (1976) attempts a family saga of sorts through a chronological series of short fictions; *Narcissa and Other Fables* (1983) is basically a traditional collection of shorter pieces, some of them very short indeed. In *The Book Class*, published the following year as a novel, Auchincloss again combines the conventions of short and long fiction, although rather less successfully than in *Powers of Attorney* or *The Partners*: Although episodic in form, *The Book Class* has the outward structure of a novel, demanding that it be read from start to finish, not piecemeal; at the same time, the action remains too loosely plotted to deliver the satisfactions normally expected of the novel. Notwithstanding, *The Book Class* remains noteworthy as an example of his continued experimentation with the fusion of long and short fictional forms.

THE INJUSTICE COLLECTORS AND THE ROMANTIC EGOISTS

Auchincloss's early short stories are generally incisive, well-crafted character sketches with crisp, self-expository dialogue. His proclivity, reflected in the titles of his first two collections, is toward conspicuous if less than deviant behavior set against the generally well ordered social background featured in the novels. In a preface to *The Injustice Collectors* Auchincloss attributes his choice of title to the psychiatrist Edmund Bergler, acknowledging that his own use of the term extends well beyond the limits of Bergler's strict medical definition:

> I do not purport to use the term in Dr. Bergler's exact medical sense, but in a wider sense to describe people who are looking for injustice, even in a friendly world, because they suffer from a hidden need to feel that the world has wronged them. . . . That a character's undoing or rejection may be the result of his own course of action is hardly surprising, but it may be significant that he has chosen, not only the course but also the result to which it leads.

The characters surveyed in *The Injustice Collectors* are a varied and generally interesting lot. Maud Spreddon, the title character of **"Maud,"** is an early prototype of the intelligent, restless Auchincloss woman; ill at ease in her lawyer father's household, Maud will break her engagement to Halsted Nicholas, her father's partner and a long-time family friend, presumably because she doubts her fitness for marriage. Later, during World War II, she will meet Halsted by chance in London and agree to marry him at last. After Halsted's death in battle two days later, Maud decides to keep their renewed acquaintance a secret from her family: "She did not tell her parents or even Sammy that she had seen Halsted again before his death, or what had passed between them. Such a tale would have made her a worthy object of the pity she had so despised herself for seeking. It was her sorrow, and Halsted would have admired her for facing it alone."

In **"The Miracle,"** which opens the collection, a well-born but self-made tycoon schemes successfully to keep his cherished only son from marrying a somewhat older spinster. **"The Fall of a Sparrow"** recalls the author's naval service during World War II. **"Finish, Good Lady,"** narrated in the first person by a middle-aged nurse-companion, recalls stresses in the family of one of her elderly patients. **"Greg's Peg,"** told by a prep-school headmaster, revisits the oddly futile life of one Gregory Bakewell, a summer acquaintance, who clung to his indifferent, eccentric mother until his own death in early middle age. On balance, the stories in Auchincloss's first collection are polished and thoughtful, told from a variety of viewpoints; it was not until *The Romantic Egoists* that the author would adumbrate both the form and the style of his later collections, closing the perceived distance between short and long fiction.

Like the "injustice collectors," the "romantic egoists" featured in the second collection differ slightly from the supposed norm. Egoists, not egotists, they tend toward self-absorption, with impossible dreams and ambitions. Perhaps the strongest and most representative tale included in *The Romantic Egoists* is **"The Great World and Timothy Colt,"** in effect a preliminary study toward the novel of the same name in which the title character's obsession is already quite fully developed.

Without exception, the eight stories comprising *The Romantic Egoists* are told by the lawyer Peter Westcott, a semi-autobiographical persona similar to O'Hara's James Malloy. The facts of Westcott's life, however, remain secondary to his observations, and when Westcott functions within the various narratives he is of interest mainly as a foil or interlocutor. He tells the story of Timmy Colt from the point of view of a younger associate in Timmy's law firm, privy to Timmy's thoughts and decisions; in **"Wally,"** set in Panama during the war, he recalls the amusing, if faintly pathetic efforts of a fellow officer named Wallingford, a graduate of Cornell University's hotel school, to obtain a transfer to hotel duty. **"Billy and the Gargoyles"** recalls Westcott's prep-school days, in particular the misadventures of a less adaptable cousin. **"The Legends of Henry Everett"** contrasts appearance with reality in the life and career of the octogenarian senior partner of Westcott's law firm. **"The Fortune of Arleus Kane,"** although it deals with a familiar Auchincloss theme, is perhaps a bit simplistic in its portrayal of a young attorney continually hampered in courtship, career, marriage, and politics by the burden of his family's wealth. Nearly one-fourth of the volume, however, is devoted to Auchincloss's original telling of the Timmy Colt story, stopping short of the turnabout and eventual disgrace recorded in the novel. Taken together, the eight stories almost constitute a novel, or a portion of one, except that none of Westcott's diverse acquaintances appear to be acquainted with each other. Significantly, the viewpoint character of Westcott, although satisfactory, would never again appear in Auchincloss's fiction, either long or short. His next volume of collected stories, published nearly a decade later, would be narrated throughout in the third person, yet would resemble even more closely a novel thanks to the prevalence of shared and recurrent characters.

POWERS OF ATTORNEY AND THE PARTNERS

Although published just over a decade apart, *Powers of Attorney* and *The Partners* are basically similar in tone, content, and subject matter, as well as in accomplishment, regardless of the fact that the earlier volume was initially marketed as a collection of stories and the second as a novel. Both volumes deal episodically with the problems and personalities of a large, "modern" Wall Street law firm, known as Tower, Tilney, and Webb in *Powers of Attorney,* as Shepard, Putney, and Cox in *The Partners*. In each volume the exposition centers around a responsible, middle-aged partner charged with guiding his colleagues through transitions in the legal profession: Clitus Tilney of Tower, Tilney, and Webb carries the designation of senior partner, while Beekman "Beeky" Ehninger of Shepard, Putney, and Cox holds the somewhat less prestigious title of managing partner. Typically, each firm has at least one eccentric elderly partner, several youngish "drones," and a number of ambitious young associates both with and without Ivy League degrees. Some of the latter are female. To a greater degree than in the novels,

Auchincloss's presentation is here tinged with a heavy irony that often approaches broad humor:

> Webb stared in fascination at the beautiful, promiscuous, near-naked quartet, with their host of beautiful, near-naked children. Who would have believed that a scant eighteen months before they had been engaged in no fewer than six bitter lawsuits? And now, with children tumbling over each other and over them (children who hardly knew, perhaps, which adult was a parent and which a step-parent), laughing and sipping gin, making jokes—oh, agony to think of!—of their "little men downtown" who had taken their squabbles with such amusing, passionate seriousness, they might have been the foreground in an advertisement for an exotic foreign car, so congenial, so gay, so pearly-toothed did they all appear. "Rabbits," he muttered angrily to his partner as they turned back to the club house. "They're nothing but rabbits. People like that don't deserve the time the courts waste over them. They should do their breeding without sanction of law!" (**"From Bed and Board,"** *Powers of Attorney*)

In both volumes, Auchincloss's approach to character often recalls the incisive portraits of the seventeenth-century French satirist Jean de la Bruyère, whose work Auchincloss knows well. Unlike the Frenchman, however, Auchincloss most frequently manages the delineation of character through the sustained portrayal of behavior. The spineless but petulant Rutherford Tower, a partner in Tower, Tilney, and Webb by sheer force of nepotism, dreams of revenge against his stronger partners and believes that he has found the means when an elegant old gentleman enlists his help in writing a will; too late, Rutherford will learn that the old man was a true eccentric, with dozens of worthless wills scattered across the Eastern seaboard. Morris Madison, another Tilney partner, deserted by his socialite wife early in his successful career as a tax specialist, has since devoted all of his spare time to a diary of social observation inspired by the Duc de Saint-Simon. Some twenty-five years later Madison will contemplate remarriage to the widowed Aurelia Starr, carefully selected as **"The Single Reader"** of the story's title; by that time, however, Madison's obsession has all but consumed him, enough so to send the poor woman fleeing for dear life. Ronny Simmonds, a junior associate in Shepard, Putney, and Cox, has seen service in Vietnam and is still considering his options when he is nearly trapped into loveless marriage by the machinations of a female senior partner and her divorced daughter, possibly a nymphomaniac. In **"The Novelist of Manners,"** perhaps the most memorable episode included in *The Partners,* Auchincloss turns his ironic wit not only upon the law but also upon the writer's craft, with observations as incisive as any to be found in such nonfiction volumes as *A Writer's Capital* and *Life, Law and Letters.*

Set in France, **"The Novelist of Manners"** recounts a clash of wills between one Dana Clyde, a decidedly "popular" novelist known for his lurid portrayals of the "jet set," and Leslie Carter, a junior partner who, as head of the firm's Paris office, has been engaged to defend Clyde against a libel action from an offended "shyster" lawyer.

Young Carter, an impassioned francophile with some unresolved literary aspirations, quickly befriends the prosperous middle-aged writer and urges him to attempt, away from his fast cars and high-living friends, the true literary masterpiece of his career. When the long-awaited volume is at last ready to appear, with galley proofs mailed to Carter in his capacity as Clyde's attorney, Carter notes with some surprise that the novel is little different from the usual Clyde standard, certainly no better; although well aware of Clyde's tendency to use real-life models, especially among lawyers, Carter is nonetheless stung to discover himself in the character of Gregory Blake, an attorney who marries a glamorous woman who is his client in a divorce case only to kill himself on the wedding night, having discovered his own impotence. It is Clyde's wife Xenia who will explain to a bewildered Carter both the nature and the extent of his transgressions:

> "But is it a great novel? Is it that last great novel of manners of the western world?"

> "It is not."

> "You say that very positively. Didn't you assure him it would be?"

> "I was a fatuous ass. I was Gregory Blake."

> "I'm afraid you were worse than that, Leslie. You badgered Dana into writing that book. You never stopped to think it might hurt him. Well, it did. It hurt him terribly. That's why he can't forgive you."

> "But I never meant it to hurt him!"

> "Of course you didn't. You're not a sadist. But it still did. You see, Dana had a secret fantasy. He liked to think of himself as a genius, but a genius manqué. He liked to tell himself that if it hadn't been for his love of the good life—the *douceur de vivre,* as he always called it—he might have been another Flaubert. "Ah, if only I could work as he worked," he used to say. Well, he worked at Malaga, he really did. And you see what he produced. He sees it, too. He can no longer kid himself that he could ever have written *Madame Bovary.* So he took his revenge."

Apart from its finely honed satire of "life, law and letters," **"The Novelist of Manners"** is notable also for the implied view of the convention reflected in its title. By implication, the novel of manners has long since been deserted by such "serious" practitioners as Auchincloss and his predecessors, leaving the field to slick, prolific craftsmen like the fictional Dana Clyde. The reading public, denied the talents even of O'Hara and Marquand, is thus increasingly dependent for its knowledge of society upon the commercial product most commonly peddled in supermarkets and at airport newsstands.

Ironically, the mere existence of such volumes as *Powers of Attorney* and *The Partners* suggests a viable direction for future would-be novelists of manners: Combining the incisiveness of the short story, particularly as practiced by O'Hara in his later years, with the unifying vision peculiar to the novel, Auchincloss's hybrid ventures provide rich and satisfying reading, even as their episodic structure might make them suitable fare for such casual readers as the airline passenger. Unfortunately, Auchincloss's experiments in combining two genres have yielded distinctly uneven results, with *Powers of Attorney* and *The Partners* emerging as the most successful such efforts to date.

TALES OF MANHATTAN AND SECOND CHANCE

Between *Powers of Attorney* and *The Partners* Auchincloss further enhanced his reputation as a writer of short fiction with two collections that, although less unified than the two volumes just cited, consist of tales related to one another by common elements of theme and structure. Published soon after the author's most successful novels, both *Tales of Manhattan* (1967), and *Second Chance* (1970) helped sustain Auchincloss's reputation as a keen observer of manners and morals.

Divided into three approximately equal subgroups, each containing closely interrelated pieces, *Tales of Manhattan* contains some of his strongest, most memorable writing, particularly in the fictional memoirs of the auctioneer Roger Jordan. An avid student of human nature with the instincts of a sleuth, Jordan delves beneath the polished surface of the social and artistic world to reveal the darker side of collectors and artists alike: **"Stirling's Folly"** uncovers, beneath the remnants of a distinguished collection, a long-buried intrigue of self-indulgence, arson, and betrayal; in **"The Moon and Six Guineas"** Jordan discovers incontrovertible evidence that a group of near-pornographic sketches, thought to represent painter John Howland's licentious senility, are in fact juvenilia portraying the artist's stiff, straitlaced parents in positions of amorous abandon. In **"Collector of Innocents"** Jordan deals perceptively and, in the end, diplomatically with an aging clubman once committed to canvas as a happy, carefree child. The two remaining Jordan stories, however, reach beyond the art world into territory even more familiar to readers of the author's longer fiction. **"The Question of the Existence of Waring Stohl"** recalls the world of letters as seen in *Sybil* and *Pursuit of the Prodigal,* while **"The Money Juggler"** clearly adumbrates the plot, theme, and characters of Auchincloss's subsequent novel, *A World of Profit.*

"The Question of the Existence of Waring Stohl," among the more incisive and ironic of Auchincloss's short stories, cleverly reverses the perceived roles of predator and victim. At first, it appears even to the perceptive Roger Jordan that the brash literary upstart Waring Stohl is taking unfair advantage of the genteel, dilettantish professor and critic, Nathaniel Streebe. Stohl, however, knows himself to be in precarious health and suggests to an astonished Jordan that the situation is indeed quite the opposite: Streebe is the true opportunist, now pressuring Stohl to write and publish a second novel. Soon after Stohl's early death, Streebe will further enhance his own reputation with an edition of the younger man's unpublished journals, complete with commentary, bearing the same title as the Auchincloss short story.

In **"The Money Juggler"** Auchincloss presents his basic outline for *A World of Profit,* including such supporting characters as the writer Hilary Knowles and the attorney John Grau. In the shorter version all the male principals are portrayed as members of Jordan's Columbia University graduating class of 1940; the title character, prototypical of Jay Livingston, is here known as Lester Gordon, having traded his original surname of Kinsky for that of some maternal relatives originally known as Ginsberg. Although *A World of Profit* remains, on balance, among the author's weaker novels, it is nonetheless more successful as fiction than **"The Money Juggler,"** in which the limitations of the shorter form force a substitution of crammed narration for the dialogue and action later portrayed in the novel.

The second group of stories, entitled "Arnold and Degener, One Chase Manhattan Plaza," surveys territory similar to that covered in *Powers of Attorney,* later to be revisited in *The Partners*; the main difference, from a technical point of view, is that the characters here speak for themselves, having been asked by the senior partner to contribute to a history of their firm. "The Matrons," comprising the final section, includes Auchincloss's only published play, *The Club Bedroom,* later successfully televised with Ruth White cast in the main role of Mrs. Ruggles.

Second Chance, subtitled *Tales of Two Generations,* combines in most of its component tales the intense irony of *Tales of Manhattan* with a strong sense of society in transition. **"The Prince and the Pauper,"** [is] perhaps the most masterful and memorable of the stories . . . ; the title tale, previously unpublished, is notable for its double-edged portrayal of two middle-aged men whose wives happen to be sisters. Gilbert Van Ness, after two decades of subjugation to his wife's large, close-knit family, emerges from psychoanalysis with a fierce determination to start over again, changing both wives and careers. His former brother-in-law, known only as Joe, is alternately fascinated and repelled as he observes—and records—Gilbert's successful if ruthless rise to power. Among the other notable stories in *Second Chance* are **"The Cathedral Builder,"** describing the obsession of a miserly nonagenarian lawyer, and **"The Sacrifice,"** in which an aging jurist contemplates the prevalence and consequences of violence. Notable for its polished prose as well as for its varied insights, *Second Chance* compares favorably with such earlier collections as *The Injustice Collectors* and *The Romantic Egoists,* even as it lacks the added "novelistic" dimension found in *Powers of Attorney* and *The Partners*.

THE WINTHROP COVENANT AND THE BOOK CLASS

In *The Winthrop Covenant* Auchincloss attempted yet another sort of fusion between long and short fiction with a series of episodes purporting to show the Puritan ethic as formed and deformed from colonial times through the narrative present. Centering more or less upon the arche-

typal Winthrop family, rich in clergymen, lawyers, and diplomats, the various component stories are decidedly uneven in tone and quality, yielding an overall result considerably less successful than *Powers of Attorney* or *The Partners*. Curiously, however, Auchincloss continued to value *The Winthrop Covenant* among his favorite works and would, during the following decade, develop two of its episodes into full-length novels: *Watchfires* (1982) owes much to the story **"In the Beauty of the Lilies Christ Was Born Across the Sea"**; similarly, **"The Penultimate Puritan"** contains, in germ, most of the plot and characters of *Honorable Men* (1985), although the characters have different names. A third episode, **"The Mystic Journal,"** harks back to *The Rector of Justin* in its evocation of a private school for boys during the early years of the twentieth century. The remaining tales, although hardly negligible, do little to enhance the author's already estimable reputation as a master of both long and short fiction.

Although published and presented as a novel, *The Book Class* (1984) remains more closely linked, in theme and structure, to Auchincloss's short stories than to his earlier novels. Like *The Winthrop Covenant,* it represents still another effort to call into question the presumed boundaries between long and short fiction.

More anecdotal than episodic in structure, *The Book Class* represents the efforts of the narrator, Christopher Gates, to understand, and indeed to explain, the often obscure lives of his mother and her friends, founding members of the "book class." The class itself, stopping always short of true education or enlightenment, exemplifies the peculiar paradox that Christopher sees in the women's now-vanished life-style: Neither feminist nor feminine, the New York society matrons born around 1890 nonetheless exercised considerable power among their families and friends. Their power, however, was often exercised in secret, and it is Christopher's chosen task to afford his readers a peek behind the scenes rendered even more vivid by his singular personal perspective. Having intervened, unsuccessfully, as a youth to prevent his mother's implication in a 1936 financial scandal similar to that described in *The Embezzler,* Chris developed not long thereafter a true vocation for meddling; throughout the action recalled, the narrator himself often figures as participant as well as observer.

Cast in the form of a memoir, *The Book Class* lacks the structure normally expected of the novel and is nearly devoid of plot. Following the drift of his own memories and argument, Chris moves from one member of the book class to another, even back again, pausing to ruminate on such questions as viewpoint and narrative voice: In the case of Justine Bannard, for example, Chris Gates can only speculate on how Justine must have contrived to keep her marriage intact after learning from young Chris that it was threatened. Published by itself, as a self-contained unit, the Justine Bannard chapter would be a typical, even distinguished Auchincloss short story; so also would Christopher's recollections of Georgia Bristed, whose activities helped to convict one of his former classmates for treason. Unfortunately, such episodes—or anecdotes—remain trapped within the apparent framework of a novel, which demands that they be read consecutively, and together. On balance, however, *The Book Class* is in all likelihood a more successful effort than *The Winthrop Convenant,* despite—or perhaps due to—its less ambitious scope.

NARCISSA AND OTHER FABLES

Just as he continued, throughout the 1970s and well into the 1980s, to write conventionally plotted novels, so also did Auchincloss continue to write conventional short stories. *Narcissa and Other Fables,* published during 1983, is a conventional story collection, including some items initially appearing elsewhere and others published for the first time. If there is a common element among the stories it is the author's keen sense of irony, here honed and polished to a fine satirical edge. In **"Charade"** the well-derived but impoverished bluestocking Madge Dyett, retrieved from Auchincloss's long-discarded first novelistic effort, engages in delicate "mind-games" with a rich couple seeking a wife for their blatantly homosexual son, a most reluctant law student; in **"Equitable Awards,"** . . . a would-be divorcee in early middle age finds herself caught between the expectations of two generations without having truly belonged to either. There is, to be sure, a fabulistic cast to many of the tales, as to much good short fiction, but the designation "fable" applies most specifically to the very short fictions appearing at the end of the volume as **"Sketches of the Nineteen Seventies,"** originally published in *New York* magazine as **"Stories of Death and Society."** Never more than one and one-half pages in length, the fabulistic **"Sketches"** most resemble rather grim jokes, easily retold, well summarized in the representative titles **"Sic-transit"** and **"Do You Know This Man?"** In the former the octogenarian heiress of several generations of bankers, invited out of respect, strolls unrecognized through a gathering of young executives, the original bank having since undergone several mergers; the woman is deferred to by reason of her regal bearing, although no one present seems to know who she is. In the latter "fable" an aspirant benefactor seeks immortality through his art collection, only to have his will so construed that he is soon forgotten.

Other notable stories in the collection include the title tale, in which a rich dilettante is expected to pay for her strange compulsion to pose in the nude, and **"Marley's Chain,"** set in Virginia, in which a retired bachelor diplomat reconsiders the option of marriage. Perhaps typically those stories, like **"Charade"** and many anecdotes in *The Book Class,* are set during the 1930s, the period of the author's richest recollections. Less typical, and somewhat less successful, is **"The Cup of Coffee,"** a broad farce dealing with office politics in a contemporary setting; although humorous, the story is hampered by the flatness and implausibility of the principal characters. **"The Seagull,"** couched in epistolary form, presents the nearly implausible apologia of an Episcopal priest who has conceived the scope of his "ministry" to include adultery. On balance, however, the collection ranks in style and quality with such earlier efforts as *The Injustice Collectors* and

Tales of Manhattan, showing that the author has not lost his singular talent for deft exposition in the shorter form.

Taken together, Auchincloss's collected short fictions compose a not inconsiderable body of work. As social observation, they are perhaps as remarkable as those of O'Hara, although fewer in number and somewhat narrower in scope. As an ironist in the short story form, Auchincloss is perhaps outshone only by John Updike, whose frequent experiments with form, style, and voice are even bolder, with frequently remarkable effect. Auchincloss's principal contribution, however, appears to be in his frequent pressure against the boundaries that appear to separate the short story from the novel; perhaps future prose writers would do well to follow his example.

Anne Bernays (essay date 1992)

SOURCE: "Downtown Deities," in *The Los Angeles Times Book Review,* February 2, 1992, p. 2.

[*Bernays is an American author and educator. In the following review of* False Gods, *she declares that Auchincloss's "language, world view and subject matter seem to be in a time warp," and that the author's dated style results in unrealistic characters.*]

Reading Louis Auchincloss is a little like watching one of those engaging Victorian scenes in the window of a pricey department store at Christmastime, with elegantly dressed, animated doll figures executing a domestic choreography. In *False Gods,* Auchincloss's 32nd book of fiction, the author once again proves that he understands the nuances of what we used to call "moral dilemma" in a way no other American writer does. For him, the deadly serious moral dilemma is all—plot and theme, text and subtext.

Each of the six stories in *False Gods* takes place chiefly in New York, Auchincloss's special turf, and focuses on one of six Greek gods got up in more or less modern dress. Thus **"Hermes, God of the Self-Made Man"** is about Maurice Leonard, a Jew whose father changed his name and who manages to thrive in pre-World War II WASP society. When Maurice falls for Dorothy, her powerful father makes him the following offer: "I like you, and if you will go away today and stay away from Dorothy, I'll give you a boost when the right time comes." The pact consummated, Maurice goes to work for a Gentile law firm. Twisting fate delivers Dorothy into his arms; she becomes more Jewish than he, and, to Maurice's distress, their son wants to change the family name once again—this time back to its original form.

In a story entitled **"Polyhymnia, Muse of Sacred Song."** a Catholic society woman suffers over her daughter's engagement to a Protestant; she is overjoyed when the daughter is killed, because her soul has been saved. In the same story a great deal is made of a wealthy dilettante's so-called "heretical" novel—which the author eventually destroys in order to preserve his standing in the community.

In **"Hephaestus, God of Newfangled Things,"** the story turns on the spiritual miseries suffered by a late-marrying architect. His new wife persuades him to abandon artistic integrity by designing "modern" houses rather than sticking to his particular—and not very popular—style. His mother compounds his despair by reminding him that artists "could do anything they liked with their lives, so long as the art always came first."

"Athene, Goddess of the Brave" is about a man who has made some questionable moral decisions as a youth, and is shamed for life after he saves himself from drowning in a marine disaster by getting into a lifeboat dressed in a woman's fur coat and hat filched from an empty stateroom. This is a story that begs out loud to be treated humorously, but even here, Auchincloss does not forsake the high serious mode that characterizes both his voice and its limitations.

All the stories in this collection draw the reader close to people who seem to be battling their own psyches over matters that—viewed objectively and with contemporary eyes—don't have all that much moral voltage. Auchincloss performs the verbal equivalent of a visual artist who turns out pictures indistinguishable from those of a 19th-Century painter. All the people in the paintings wear "period" dress and behave with 19th-Century decorum; they are faithful imitations without contemporary gloss or comment.

Auchincloss's language, world view and subject matter seem to be in a time warp—so much so that he often sounds like a parody of Henry James or Edith Wharton, as in the following description: "Heloise was not so much beautiful as exquisite. Her blond hair and wide opaque eyes and pale luminous skin might have evoked a sense of serenity had they not been balanced by her darting gestures and the vivid mobility of her facial expression, which announced the accomplished *maitresse de maison*, and by the low musical voice that constituted so perfect an instrument for her fine intelligence."

But there's a difference between writing about people who live by obsolete codes and writing in their emotional and verbal idiom. What Auchincloss delivers is an exact imitation rather than an inflected narrative—as if he were unaware of that most useful of contemporary takes on experience: irony. So the figures in Auchincloss's well-crafted stories seem more like archaic dolls performing an archaic dance than they do real men and women with urgent emotional business to transact.

Bruce Bawer (essay date 1994)

SOURCE: A review of *The Collected Stories of Louis Auchincloss,* in *The New York Times Book Review,* December 4, 1994, p. 62.

[*Bawer is an American author who has served as literary critic for* The New Criterion *and whose published works include* Diminishing Fictions: Essays on the Modern American Novel *(1988). In the following excerpt, Bawer praises Auchincloss's* Collected Stories, *Asserting that the book's depiction of "upper-crust New York WASPs" chronicles one of "the most significant social changes of recent decades." Bawer also argues that Auchincloss's fiction will outlast that of many of his contemporaries.*]

Forty-seven years and 50 books after he published his first novel, *The Indifferent Children,* Louis Auchincloss has yet to receive his full due. Academic critics and editors of anthologies have almost completely ignored him; so have the bestowers of literary awards. (Of all his books, only the splendid 1964 best seller *The Rector of Justin* has been nominated for major prizes.)

Why is this? The complaints are remarkably consistent: Mr. Auchincloss focuses on too tiny a sliver of human society—namely, the world of upper-crust New York WASP's, especially white-shoe Wall Street lawyers (of which he is one)—and treats his material in an old-fashioned manner that is overly derivative of Edith Wharton and Henry James. But these charges are outrageously unfair.

Yes, Mr. Auchincloss's social-register characters and stately prose often bring Wharton and James to mind; for some of us, that is not an unpleasant experience. Unfortunately for Mr. Auchincloss, he lives in a time when the protagonists of literary fiction tend to be middle- or lower-class, when the rich and powerful (in the form of movie stars and self-made tycoons) are found mostly in Jackie Collins-style potboilers, when both popular culture and serious fiction have propagated the notion that Ivy League Episcopalian types are emotionless snobs.

These days the general public, though fascinated by the superficial trappings of privilege, seems to have little interest in the deeper truths with which Mr. Auchincloss is passionately concerned—with, that is, the beliefs, principles, hypocrisies, prejudices and assorted strengths and defects of character that typify the American WASP civilization that produced what was for a long time the country's undisputed ruling class. Mr. Auchincloss may concentrate on a limited milieu, but it is a milieu whose impact on American society has been immense and whose decline in influence has been intimately connected to some of the most significant social changes of recent decades. It is a milieu, one might add, that Mr. Auchincloss knows intimately, and of which he is at once a sincere eulogist and a trenchant critic.

Few of Mr. Auchincloss's books demonstrate this fact as surely as ***The Collected Stories of Louis Auchincloss*** . . . [which] shows some of Mr. Auchincloss's best work in his strongest genre. Several of the earliest stories here—there are 19 in all, the oldest dating back to the late 1940's—view Mr. Auchincloss's little world through the eyes of characters who inhabit it but who are, in some way, outsiders. Both **"Greg's Peg"** and **"The Single Reader,"** for example, are about friendless bachelors: one finds his niche as the local buffoon in a summer beach town; the other keeps a voluminous diary about the elite circles in which he moves, observing everything but never really participating. Mr. Auchincloss shows off his sense of humor in **"The Colonel's Foundation,"** an eminently anthologizable little tale about a misfit lawyer who foolishly leaps at an apparent opportunity that his wiser colleagues would flatly reject, and in **"The Mavericks,"** wherein an Irish-American lawyer's bluntness wins him the affection of his boss's unconventional daughter.

The theme of not belonging figures pivotally in the book's two most impressive stories, both of which were first collected in *The Romantic Egoists* (1954). **"The Gem-like Flame"** brilliantly delineates the complex, ambiguous relationship between Clarence, a reclusive American esthete in Venice, and Neddy, a male artist who becomes his protége and (as Clarence puts it) the object of his "pure love." The situation strongly recalls James's novel *Roderick Hudson*; the narrator's description of Clarence as Neddy's "preceptor," furthermore, seems calculated to stir memories of James's story "The Pupil," in which that word occurs repeatedly.

"Billy and the Gargoyles" relates the quietly disturbing experience of Billy, a popular boarding-school boy who is mercilessly harassed when he violates the unwritten student code by befriending a "new kid." That new kid, who serves as narrator, recalls how a bully named George Neale initiated Billy's harassment and notes ironically that while he shared Billy's distress, he couldn't share his "attitude of superiority" toward the tormentors, "for I believed, superstitiously, in all the things that he sneered at. I believed, as George believed, in the system, the hazing, in the whole grim division of the school world into those who 'belonged' and those who didn't." The story's picture of that brutal school "system" amounts, by extension, to a cogent critique of the grown-up system of blue-blood society, with its careful drawing of lines between those who belong and those who don't.

Many of Mr. Auchincloss's later stories, composed in the twilight of that system, contemplate the good and bad aspects of its passing. In **"The Prince and the Pauper,"** a highborn lawyer drinks himself into obloquy while a worthy, lowborn colleague graduates into the country club set; in **"The Prison Window,"** a museum curator's love of beautiful 18th-century objects d'art is clouded by the introduction into her gallery of a rusty prison window, symbolizing the plebeian suffering that made possible these aristocratic pleasures.

Several of Mr. Auchincloss's stories of recent decades reflect at once a sad acknowledgment of yesterday's inequities and a disdain for today's culture, in which, as a character complains in **"The Fabbri Tape,"** opposition to ethnic and racial discrimination is "the only moral value we have left." It is also a culture in which, as the protagonist of a story entitled **"The Novelist of Manners"** ruefully observes, authors who follow in the footsteps of James and Wharton are doomed to be seen as anachronistic.

This collection asks some weighty questions. What happens to non-WASP's when they achieve ascendancy in a culture founded by WASP's and historically dominated by their rituals, manners and values? What happens to the WASP's? What happens to the culture, for better and worse? The answers to these questions are important to our understanding of ourselves and our times, but the questions themselves are politically incorrect; they concern social facts that we're supposed to pretend nowadays not to notice. Among the things for which readers should be grateful to Mr. Auchincloss are his refusal to adhere to this or any other fashion and the independence and high artistry with which he has, over his prolific decades, persevered in constructing unfaddish novels and stories about unfaddish people. If there is any justice, Mr. Auchincloss's *Collected Stories* will continue to be read when the work of the trendier talents of our day has long been forgotten.

FURTHER READING

Biography

Gelderman, Carol. *Louis Auchincloss: A Writer's Life.* New York: Crown Publishers, Inc., 1993, 287 p.
> A good introduction to the man and his works. Gelderman offers a highly detailed chronological and anecdotal account of Auchincloss's life, and refers to his literary output without extensive literary analysis.

Piket, Vincent. *Louis Auchincloss: The Growth of a Novelist.* New York: St. Martin's Press, 1991, 258 p.
> Chronological view of Auchincloss's works, with reference to biographical details that shed light on his literary career.

Criticism

Dahl, Christopher C. *Louis Auchincloss.* New York: The Ungar Publishing Company, 1986, 276 p.
> Overview of Auchincloss's works. Dahl analyzes Auchincloss's major fiction primarily through character analysis.

Milne, Gordon. "Louis Auchincloss." In *The Sense of Society: A History of the American Novel of Manners*, pp. 236-53. London and Cranbury: Associated University Presses, 1977.
> Offers a comprehensive overview of the novel of manners as adapted by Auchincloss.

Parsell, David B. *Louis Auchincloss.* Boston: G. K. Hall & Company, 1988, 121 p.
> Discusses Auchincloss's works in the context of the American literary tradition and his own awareness of his place within that framework.

Plimpton, George. "Louis Auchincloss: The Art of Fiction." *Paris Review* 36, No. 132 (Fall 1994): 73-94.
> Auchincloss speaks about his own and others' writing, as well as the literary life.

Additional coverage of Auchincloss's life and career is contained in the following sources published by Gale Research: *Contemporary Authors*, Vols. 1-4 (rev. ed.); *Contemporary Authors New Revision Series*, Vols. 6, 29; *Contemporary Literary Criticism*, Vols. 4, 6, 9, 18, 45; *Dictionary of Literary Biography*, Vol. 2; *Dictionary of Literary Biography Yearbook*, 1980; and *Major 20th-Century Writers*.

John Galsworthy
1867–1933

(Also wrote under the pseudonym John Sinjohn) English short fiction writer, novelist, dramatist, poet, and essayist.

INTRODUCTION

A prolific author who worked in many genres, Galsworthy is most widely recognized as a chronicler of English bourgeois society during the early twentieth century. His most acclaimed work, *The Forsyte Saga,* is a trilogy of novels and two short stories, featuring Soames Forsyte, a prosperous and materialistic solicitor. A passionate humanist, Galsworthy criticized social injustice in Victorian society and exalted nature, beauty, and love. His style was noted for its charm, delicacy, and descriptive detail.

Biographical Information

Galsworthy was born on a family estate in Kingston Hill, Surrey, near London. His mother was a descendant of provincial squires, while his father was of Devonshire yeoman stock. His father was a successful solicitor who had financial interests in mining companies in Canada and Russia, and who later served as the model for Old Jolyon Forsyte in *The Forsyte Saga.* At the age of nine, Galsworthy was sent to a boarding school and later to the prestigious Harrow School in London, where he excelled in athletics. In 1886 he enrolled at Oxford to study law, graduating with second degree honors in 1889. The following year he was admitted to the bar. For a short while he worked at his father's legal firm but showed little interest in the law. He left for Canada in 1891 to inspect his family's mining interests and traveled extensively thereafter. In 1893, while aboard the *Torrens,* he befriended the first mate, Joseph Conrad, who was working on his first novel. Conrad would later become an important source of encouragement in Galsworthy's writing career. When Galsworthy returned to London in 1894, he had his own legal chambers but heard only one case. Within a short time, he gave up his chambers and spent the next few years reading and writing assiduously. Galsworthy was interested in writing about the plight of the working class, and he spent many hours roaming the impoverished neighborhoods of London. Ada Galsworthy, a married cousin with whom he became romantically involved, encouraged him to pursue a writing career, and her unhappiness with her failed marriage inspired many of his stories. In 1905 John and Ada Galsworthy were married. In 1897 he published his first collection of short stories, *From the Four Winds,* under the pseudonym John Sinjohn. Shortly thereafter he wrote two novels and another book of short stories called *A Man of Devon.* In 1917 Galsworthy was offered a knighthood, which he declined, arguing that it was not fitting for a writer; he later accepted the Order of Merit for

his literary achievements. For twelve years he served as the first president of PEN, the international writers' organization. In December 1932, just a month before his death, he was awarded the Nobel Prize in literature.

Major Works of Short Fiction

Galsworthy's short fiction exhibits similar themes to those of his novels, challenging upper-class Victorian standards. Though he himself was born to a wealthy family, Galsworthy espoused a liberal philosophy, opposing rigid doctrines of morality and religion. He believed that justice depended on the individual and on faith in humanity. He wrote about social justice, poverty, and old age, as well as love, beauty, and nature. Some of his stories are passionate tales of romance, such as "A Man of Devon" and "The Apple Tree," both of which take place in the Devonshire countryside. The former features the relationship between a young girl, Paisance, and the man she falls in love with, Zachary Pearse. Tragically, Paisance, as she watches her love sail away on a voyage that she was forbidden by her grandfather to join, trips and falls from the edge of a cliff to her death. In "The Apple Tree," a man returns after twenty-six years to Devon, where he had deserted a relationship with a farm girl in order to pursue a wife of greater social status. The story focuses on the remorse that he feels about his past choice as well as the guilt that he experiences upon discovering that the farm girl had committed suicide soon after he had left many years ago. Sanford Sternlicht called "The Apple Tree" Galsworthy's "most finely crafted, most symbolic, and most poetic tale." Other stories are character portraits or mood pieces such as "Spindleberries." He created his visions in minute detail, imbuing a strong sense of atmosphere and character. In general, Galsworthy's stories tend to center more on characters and their environment rather than plot. In many of his stories, Galsworthy empathizes with characters who are unappreciated by society for their kindness and humanity. Those who are depicted as most admirable are individuals who recognize goodness and beauty in others. For instance, in *The Forsyte Saga,* Irene leaves her husband, Soames, for Young Jolyon because Soames considers her his property and merely lusts for her, whereas Young Jolyon loves Irene and worships her beauty. In the idyllic "Indian Summer of Forsyte," first published in *Five Tales,* Old Jolyon, an epicurean, dies as he sips an exquisite wine, as if from excess of delight. *A Modern Comedy,* on the other hand, denounces the post-World War I generation for their aimlessness and restlessness. Commentators have noted that while Galsworthy satirized the wealthy in his early works, he presented a more sympathetic view of the Forsytes in his later works, especially those collected in *A Modern Comedy.* Collectively, *On Forsyte 'Change, The Forsyte Saga,* and *A Modern Comedy* have been referred to as "The Forsyte Chronicles."

Critical Reception

Galsworthy's earliest work showed the influence of Conrad, though Galsworthy insisted he was influenced most by Ivan Sergeevich Turgenev and Guy de Maupassant. His writings have also been compared to those of Rudyard Kipling, Charles Dickens, and Katherine Mansfield. Galsworthy's talents were first widely recognized in 1906 upon the publication of his novel *The Man of Property* and his first play, *The Silver Box.* The novel introduced his famous Forsyte family, through whom he satirized Victorian society. Galsworthy finally achieved international acclaim when *The Man of Property* was republished in 1922 as part of *The Forsyte Saga,* along with two of his most famous stories, "Indian Summer of a Forsyte" and *Awakening.* Galsworthy was widely regarded as a compassionate humanist whose work evinced sensitivity, sincerity, and charm. Many believe that he successfully captured the spirit of his age. Yet, while some consider him a critic of the upper class, others assert that he admired it, especially later in his life. Some of his contemporaries, especially experimental modernists, disdained his work. Virginia Woolf, for instance, considered him a "stuffed shirt" and found him guilty of the same behavior and attitudes to which he objected in his writing. His style was variously faulted as overly sentimental and melodramatic or too analytical and pessimistic. His plays in particular were often criticized as social propaganda lacking dramatic intensity.

However, many critics agree that as his style evolved it became less rigid and more subtle. Galsworthy's earlier style showed similarities to French naturalism, shifting later to a more deliberate use of symbolism and mythology.

PRINCIPAL WORKS

Short Fiction

From the Four Winds [as John Sinjohn] 1897
A Man of Devon [as John Sinjohn] 1901
A Commentary (essays and sketches) 1908
A Motley (short stories, sketches, and essays) 1910
The Little Man, and Other Satires (short stories, satires, and sketches) 1915
Five Tales 1918
*Awakening (short story) 1920
Tatterdemalion 1920
The Forsyte Saga (novels and short stories) 1922
Captures 1923
The Works of John Galsworthy. 30 vols. (novels, dramas, essays, poetry, and short stories) 1923-36
Caravan: The Assembled Tales of John Galsworthy 1925
†Two Forsyte Interludes: A Silent Wooing; Passers By 1927
A Modern Comedy (novels and short stories) 1929
On Forsyte 'Change 1930
‡Forsytes, Pendyces, and Others 1935

Other Major Works

Jocelyn [as John Sinjohn] (novel) 1898
Villa Rubein [as John Sinjohn] (novel) 1900
The Island Pharisees (novel) 1904
*The Man of Property (novel) 1906
The Silver Box (drama) 1906
The Country House (novel) 1907
Joy (drama) 1907
Fraternity (novel) 1909
Strife (drama) 1909
Justice (drama) 1910
The Little Dream (drama) 1911
The Patrician (novel) 1911
The Eldest Son (drama) 1912
The Inn of Tranquillity: Studies and Essays (essays) 1912
Moods, Songs & Doggerels (poetry) 1912
The Pigeon (drama) 1912
The Dark Flower (novel) 1913
The Fugitive (drama) 1913
The Mob (drama) 1914
The Freelands (novel) 1915
A Sheaf (essays) 1916
Beyond (novel) 1917
Addresses in America (essays) 1919
Another Sheaf (essays) 1919
The Burning Spear (essays) 1919
Saint's Progress (novel) 1919
*In Chancery (novel) 1920

The Skin Game (drama) 1920
The Bells of Peace (poetry) 1921
*To Let (novel) 1921
Loyalties (drama) 1922
Abracadabra, and Other Satires (essays) 1924
Old English (drama) 1924
†*The White Monkey* (novel) 1924
Escape (drama) 1926
†*The Silver Spoon* (novel) 1926
Verses New and Old (poetry) 1926
Castles in Spain (essays) 1927
†*Swan Song* (novel) 1928
‡*Maid in Waiting* (novel) 1931
Candelabra: Selected Essays and Addresses (essays) 1932
‡*Flowering Wilderness* (novel) 1932
‡*Over the River* (novel) 1933; also published as *One More River,* 1933
The Collected Poems of John Galsworthy (poetry) 1934
End of the Chapter (novels) 1934

*These works and the short story "Indian Summer of a Forsyte" from *Five Tales* (1918) were published as *The Forsyte Saga* in 1922.

†These works were published as *A Modern Comedy* in 1929.

‡These works were published as *End of the Chapter* in 1934.

CRITICISM

Joseph Conrad (letter date 1901)

SOURCE: A letter to John Galsworthy in 1901, *The Life and Letters of John Galsworthy,* by H. V. Marrot, Charles Scribner's Sons, 1936, pp. 129-30.

[*Conrad was born and raised in Poland and later resided in England. A major novelist, he is considered an innovator of novel structure as well as one of the finest stylists of modern English literature. In the following letter, originally written in 1901, he critiques* A Man of Devon *and suggests that Galsworthy should regard his characters with more skepticism.*]

11*th Nov.* 1901.

DEAREST JACK,—I didn't write about the book before, first because Jess had it—and she reads slowly—and then I had at last some proofs of mine—a whole batch—which it took me several days to correct. Nevertheless I've read the book twice—watching the effect of it impersonally during the second reading—trying to ponder upon its reception by the public and discover the grounds of general success—or the reverse.

There is a certain caution of touch which will militate against popularity. After all, to please the public (if one isn't a sugary imbecile or an inflated fraud) one must handle one's subject intimately. Mere intimacy with the subject won't do. And conviction is found (for others, not for the author) only in certain contradictions and irrelevancies to the general conception of character (or characters) and of the subject. Say what you like the man lives in his eccentricities (so called) alone. They give a vigour to his personality which mere consistency can never do. One must explore deep and believe the incredible to find the few particles of truth floating in an ocean of insignificance. And before all one must divest oneself of every particle of respect for one's characters. You are really most profound and attain the greatest art in handling the people you do not respect. For instance the minor characters in [*Villa Rubein*]. And in this volume I am bound to recognize that Forsythe (*sic*) is the best. I recognize this with a certain reluctance because indubitably there is more beauty (and more felicity of style too) in the [**Man of Devon**]. The story of the mine shows best your strength and your weakness. There is hardly a word I would have changed; there are things in it I would give a pound of my flesh to have written. Honestly—there are; and your mine manager remains unconvincing because he is too confoundingly perfect in his very imperfections. The fact is you want more scepticism at the very foundation of your work. Scepticism, the tonic of minds, the tonic of life, the agent of truth—the way of art and salvation. In a book you should love the idea and be scrupulously faithful to your conception of life. There lies the honour of the writer, not in the fidelity to his personages. You must never allow them to decoy you out of yourself. As against your people you must preserve an attitude of perfect indifference—the part of creative power. A creator must be indifferent; because directly the "Fiat" has issued from his lips there are the creatures made in his image that'll try to drag him down from his eminence—and belittle him by their worship. Your attitude to them should be purely intellectual, more independent, freer, less rigorous than it is. You seem for their sake to hug your conceptions of right and wrong too closely. There is exquisite atmosphere in your tales. What they want now is more air.

You may wonder why I write you these generalities. But first of all in the matters of technique, where your advance has been phenomenal and which has almost (if not quite) reached the point of crystallization, we have talked so much and so variously that I could tell you now nothing that you have not heard already. And secondly, these considerations are not so general as they look. They are even particular in as much that they have been inspired by the examination of your work as a whole. I have looked into all the volumes; and this—put briefly, imperfectly, and obscurely—is what they suggested to me.

That the man who has written once the **Four Winds** has written now the **M of D** volume is a source of infinite gratification to me. It vindicates my insight, my opinion, my judgment—and it satisfies my affection for you—in whom I believed and am believing. Because that is the point: I *am* believing. You've gone now beyond the point where I could be of any use to you otherwise than just by my belief. It is if anything firmer than ever before—whether my remarks above find their way to your conviction or not. You may disagree with what I said here but in our main convictions we are at one.

The New York Times Saturday Review   (essay date 1910)

SOURCE: A review of *A Motley,* in *The New York Times Saturday Review,* Vol. XV, No. 88, September 17, 1910, pp. 505-06.

[*In the following review, the critic offers a favorable assessment of* A Motley.]

John Galsworthy is one of the few really significant figures in the literary world to-day. It is difficult to understand the attitude of those who dismiss him with the slightly condescending dictum, "Oh, yes—Galsworthy. He's the Socialist and propagandist, isn't he?"

Socialist he may be, but he is too much the artist to be a mere propagandist. As a man of thought and imagination he reflects the ultra-modern temper—the new humanitarianism, which is concerned less with theories and formulae than with the actualities of life. The volume [*A Motley*] of short stories, studies, and impressions just published is doubly interesting, for, apart from its intrinsic value, it is a striking revelation of the personality of the writer. As in the plays *Strike* and *The Silver Box* and the novel *Fraternity,* one finds here the presentation of life, and modern problems concretely treated. If Mr. Galsworthy cherishes any solution of these problems he does not give utterance to it. Seemingly, he is content to write of what he sees and feels, not despairing of Utopia, yet not overconfident of its coming.

The book opens with "A Portrait"—a study, slightly in the eighteenth century manner, of a man of no particular importance in this hurrying world. It is detailed, leisurely and suavely written. One notes in it what may be quoted as an expression of the author's own views.

It is a kindly study, on the whole, and in contrast to the second, "A Fisher of Men." In this is a certain irony, a reflected bitterness, which still, in its own way, does not lack an emotional appeal. "The Prisoner" is a short sketch, impressionistic, plainly mirroring a protest against the penal system (which is undergoing reform in England to-day as a direct result of the author's play, entitled *Justice*), though no direct word of protest appears. "Courage," again, is impressionistic—a poverty-stricken little barber does his duty, as he sees it. He assumes the burden of a woman and her seven children, saying: "Life is hard! What would you have? I knew her husband. Could I leave her to the streets?"

"The Meeting" and "A Parting" are a little depressing. There is always sorrow, even to the mere looker-on, in the parting of those who love; and, after all, there may be sadness to the looker-on in the first meeting—but is it always wise to ignore the brightness of to-day for the grayness of to-morrow? "The Pack" is a study of the psychology of the crowd.

> It's only when men run in packs that they lose their sense of decency. * * * Individual man—I'm not speaking of savages—is more given to generosity than meanness, rarely brutal, inclines in fact to be a gentleman. It's when you add three or four more to him that his sense of decency, his sense of personal responsibility, his private standards, go by the board. I am not at all sure that he does not become the victim of a certain infectious fever. Something physical takes place, I am sure. * * * Single man is not an angel; collective man is a bit of a brute.

"Joy of Life," "Bel Colore" and "A Pilgrimage" are brief impressions, notable chiefly for their vivid but fleeting glimpses of children. There is grimness in the stories "A Miller of Dee" and "The Neighbors"—sordid tragedy, if tragedy may ever be sordid. "The Japanese Quince" is a curious little sketch. Two respectable, stolid business men are lured into a square by the subtle odor of an exotic tree. There is no denouement, but the impression is as clear as a cameo. There is humor in "The Cadjer." But what one receives is, in the main, a conviction of the writer's art and of his intense desire to set forth plainly and effectively the case of those who cannot speak for themselves; the sense of an imagination readily touched, and a mentality essentially masculine. Some of the stories are commonplace as to theme, but each is vivified by a passionate sympathy with life in its every manifestation.

Peculiarly enough, here is a writer of whom one cannot say that he is the disciple of this master or that. Doubtless Mr. Galsworthy has absorbed much from the French writers of short stories, yet his method, no less than his matter, is strongly individual. *A Motley* is stimulating both to imagination and to thought; and it touches very close to the heart of to-day.

Sheila Kaye-Smith   (essay date 1916)

SOURCE: An excerpt from *John Galsworthy,* H. Holt and Company, 1916, pp. 86-99.

[*Kaye-Smith was an English novelist, short story writer, and critic best known for her portrayals of the land, people, and history of Sussex, England. In the following excerpt, she analyzes short stories by Galsworthy, comparing them to a few of his essays and poems.*]

Villa Rubein and four short stories under the title of *A Man of Devon* were published anonymously. All early efforts, they are not on a line with Galsworthy's later work, but they have about them a certain beauty and individuality which makes them worth considering. Perhaps their chief characteristic is delicacy: they are water-colours, in many ways exquisitely conceived and shaded, but perhaps a trifle pale and washed out, a trifle—it must be owned—uninteresting.

Villa Rubein, describing with much sensitive charm the life of a half-Austrian household, is full of tenderness, but lacking somehow in grip. The characters are more attractive than most of Galsworthy's—in fact, in no work of his do we meet such a uniformly charming group of people. They are sketched, even the less pleasing, with an entire absence of bitterness, and the heroine, Christian, and her little half-German sister are delightful in their freshness and grave sweetness. Miss Naylor and old Nic Treffry are also drawn with a loving and convincing hand. The book seems to have been written in a mellow mood which passed with it. Yet we pay for any absence of bitterness, propaganda or pessimism, by a corresponding lack of force. It must be confessed that Galsworthy is most effective when he is most gloomy, most penetrating when he is most bitter, most humorous when he is most satirical.

The short stories call for no special comment except **"The Salvation of a Forsyte,"** where we meet for the first time Swithin Forsyte, later to figure in *The Man of Property*. We are introduced to an early adventure of his, which is treated with some technical skill and an impressive irony. The tale has grip, and is not far off French excellence of craft. The other stories are too long for their themes, which, if not actually thin in themselves, are dragged out in the telling.

Of very different stuff are the four volumes of sketches— *A Commentary, A Motley, The Inn of Tranquillity,* and *The Little Man*. In these, except, perhaps, in the last, we have some of Galsworthy's best work, much of it equal, in its different way, to the finest of the plays and novels.

A Commentary deals chiefly with the life of the very poor, showing the intimacy of the author's knowledge, and the depths of his sympathy. Some of the sketches are indictments of the social order which favours those who have money and tramples those who have none. *Justice,* for instance, is a fresh exposure of the oft-exposed inequality of the divorce laws where rich and poor are concerned. **"A Mother"** is a piteous revelation of those depths of horror and humiliation which form the daily life of many. Continually, in the plays and in the novels, Galsworthy reveals the utter brutishness of some of these submerged ones. He never attempts to enforce his social ethics by glorification of those he champions. Such men as Hughes, in *Fraternity,* or the husband, in **"A Mother,"** are absolutely of the lowest stuff and, it would seem, unworthy of a hand to help them out of the mud in which they roll. But here lies the subtlety of the reproach—it is the social system with its cruelties and stupidities which is responsible for this. There is something more forceful than all the sufferings of the deserving in this grim picture of utter degradation, the depths of bestialism into which mismanaged civilisation can grind divine souls.

In other of the sketches we are shown the opposite side of the picture—the selfishness of the prosperous, their lack of ideals and imagination. Now Galsworthy becomes bitter; with a steely hardness he describes the comfortable life of the upper middle classes, of the fashionable and wealthy. The bias of *A Commentary* is obvious throughout, and throughout propaganda takes the first place. The fragments are held together by the central idea, which is

the exposure—ironic, indignant, embittered, infinitely pitying—of the inequalities between the poor and the rich. True, there is atmosphere, style, a sense of character; but in *A Commentary* the artist takes second place.

A Motley is, as the title implies, a collection linked up by no central view-point. Character sketches, episodes of the streets and of the fields, reflections on life, art, manners, anything, and all widely different in style and length, crowd together between the covers, without any definite scheme. They show extraordinary powers of observation and intuition, and at the same time a certain lack of grip, which is always the first of Galsworthy's weaknesses to come to light in a failing situation. Some of the sketches are too slight, over-fined. On the other hand, some have true poetry and true pathos in their conception. The style is more polished, the pleading less special, the knowledge less embittered than in *A Commentary*. Particularly successful is **"A Fisher of Men,"** in which Galsworthy is at his best, giving us a sympathetic and tragic picture of a type with which we know he has little sympathy—there is no bitterness here, just pathos. **"Once More"** is a study of lower-class life slightly recalling **"A Mother,"** but here again is far more tenderness, due partly, no doubt, to the wistfulness of youth that creeps into the story. Then there are sketches of life and the furtive love of the London parks; no one has realised more poignantly than Galsworthy all the tragedy of hidden meetings and hidden partings with which our public places are filled.

The Inn of Tranquillity is also a mixed collection, and in it we see far more of Galsworthy the poet and the artist than of Galsworthy the social reformer. There are in the book fragments of sheer beauty which would be hard to beat anywhere in modern prose. Take, for instance, the painting of dawn in "Wind in the Rocks.":

> That god came slowly, stalking across far over our heads from top to top; then, of a sudden, his flame-white form was seen standing in a gap of the valley walls; the trees flung themselves along the ground before him, and censers of pine gum began swinging in the dark aisles, releasing their perfumed steam. Throughout these happy ravines where no man lives, he shows himself naked and unashamed, the colour of pale honey; on his golden hair such shining as one has not elsewhere seen; his eyes like old wine on fire. And already he had swept his hand across the invisible strings, for there had arisen the music of uncurling leaves and flitting things.

Take also just this sentence from "A Novelist's Allegory": "those pallid gleams . . . remain suspended like a handful of daffodils held up against the black stuffs of secrecy."

Galsworthy allows himself to play with words, blend them, contrast them, savour their sweet sound and the roll and suck of them under the tongue . . . he becomes a poet in prose. But it is not only words that make his poetry. He seizes aspects of beauty and gives them to us palpitating, fresh from their capture, a poet's prey. Such is "Riding in Mist," a consummate study of the misty moor, damp, sweet, and dangerous. There is, too, a wonderful sense of locality in "That Old-Time Place"—it throbs with atmosphere.

But we have many studies besides of words and place. There is "Memories," in which Galsworthy uses his real understanding of dog-nature, faithful and true. There is "The Grand Jury," in which he shows the fullness of his sympathy for the human dog, the bottom dog, so generally and necessarily ignored by laws which are inevitably made for the upper layer of humanity. We have, too, some illuminating comments on the world of letters. In "About Censorship" there is fine irony, and in "Some Platitudes Concerning the Drama" plenty of illumination. Indeed, in this article we are given a plain enough statement of the rules which evidently govern Galsworthy's own work. For instance: "A good plot is that sure edifice which slowly rises out of the interplay of circumstance on temperament and temperament on circumstance, within the enclosing atmosphere of an idea." There could be no clearer definition of the plan governing *Strife* and *The Silver Box*. The pronouncement on dramatic dialogue, too, applies admirably to much of Galsworthy's own achievement:

> The art of writing true dramatic dialogue is an austere art, denying itself all license, grudging every sentence devoted to the mere machinery of the play, suppressing all jokes and epigrams severed from character, relying for fun and pathos on the fun and tears of life. From start to finish good dialogue is hand-made, like good lace; clear, of fine texture, furthering with each thread the harmony and strength of a design to which all must be subordinated.

In his last book of sketches—*The Little Man and Other Satires*—Galsworthy has made a deliberate sacrifice of beauty. He has left the luminous Italian backgrounds of *The Inn of Tranquillity,* the rustling English twilights of *A Motley,* for the midnight lamp on his study table. This is why, perhaps, **The Little Man** depresses me. Galsworthy has not stood the tests—he has grown bitter. His satire is more akin to that of Swift than Samuel Butler, but without Swift's redeeming largeness, his tumbling restlessness. Galsworthy's bitterness is the well-bred bitterness of the pessimist at afternoon tea; Swift is the pessimist in the tavern, raging round and breaking pots.

However, an author's point of view is not a fair subject for criticism, any more than the shape of his head; he probably cannot help it. But it may be deplored.

The most striking thing about the book itself is the subdivision titled **"Studies in Extravagance."** Here we have some remorseless, if only partial, truth—the fierce glow of the searchlight, more concentrated though more limited than the wide shining of the sun. We have **"The Writer," "The Housewife," "The Plain Man,"** etc., all pierced through to their most startling worst. Galsworthy will make no concessions—he will not show us a single motherly redeeming virtue in that woman of schemes and covert horribleness whom he presents as a possible variety of British matron. So too with his Writer—those flickers of

amiable naivety which occasionally humanise the writers most of us know are shut out from this portrait of an ape playing with the ABC. It is clever, fierce, vindictive, and partly true.

There are some gentler sketches in the book—for instance, the name-piece, in which we have a really witty and typical picture of an American, with his God's own gift of admiring good deeds he will not do himself. There is also *Abracadabra,* in which the satire is fundamentally tender, and with little significant bitterness—though in time one comes to resent Galsworthy's inalienable idea that every woman is ill-used in marriage. There is also such genuine wit, terseness, and point in "Hall Marked" that one can afford to skip the humours of the parson's trousers. **"Ultima Thule"** is more in *The Motley* and **Commentary** vein. We are glad to meet the old man who could tame cats and bullfinches. But why sigh over him so much? He was happy and to be envied, even though he lived in a back room on a few farthings. This misplaced pity is becoming irritating in Galsworthy. His earlier works—*Strife, The Man of Property*—are innocent of it, but lately it has grown to be a habit with him. He cannot resist the temptation to weep over everyone whose clothes are not quite as good as his own.

Galsworthy allows himself to play with words, blend them, contrast them, savour their sweet sound and the roll and suck of them under the tongue . . . he becomes a poet in prose.

—Sheila Kaye-Smith

It is scarcely surprising that a writer with Galsworthy's sense of words and atmosphere should have written a book of verse—the only surprise is that his solitary experiment in poetry should not have been more successful. When we remember the exquisite prose of his plays, novels and sketches, the admirable description, the sense of atmosphere, not forgetting also the genuine poetry of much of **The Little Dream,** we are surprised not to find in *Moods, Songs and Doggerels,* anything of permanent quality, or worthy to stand beside his other work. There are some delightful songs of the country, of Devon, one or two little fragrant snatches, like puffs of breeze. But the more ambitious pieces, the *Moods,* are for the most part wanting in inspiration. They are just prose, and not nearly such fine prose as we have a right to expect from Galsworthy. One or two stand out as poetry, and these are mostly studies in atmosphere, such as "Street Lamps":

> Lamps, lamps! Lamps ev'rywhere!
> You wistful, gay, and burning eyes,
> You stars low-driven from the skies
> Down on the rainy air.
>
> You merchant eyes, that never tire
> Of spying out our little ways;

Of summing up our little days
In ledgerings of fire—

Inscrutable your nightly glance,
Your lighting and your snuffing out,
Your flicker through the windy rout,
Guiding this mazy dance.

O watchful, troubled gaze of gold,
Protecting us upon our beats—
You piteous glamour of the streets,
Youthless, and never old!

The Times Literary Supplement   (essay date 1918)

SOURCE: "Mr. Galsworthy's Tales," in *The Times Literary Supplement,* No. 864, August 8, 1918, p. 371.

[*Below, the critic lauds* Five Tales.]

Mr. Galsworthy's work, on a small scale or a big, has the quality of greatness. It is largely planned and stately built. There is dignity in its substance and in its form. It is not showy; it is not brilliant; it is not even clever. It is as free from that cocksureness which is the attitude of much modern writing as it is from the tip-and-run sensation which his younger contemporaries mistake for feeling, and from the "carrying-on" which it was a fault of his predecessors to mistake for sensitiveness. You may dig deep into what he gives you, and the deeper you dig the richer you find the store to be. And his prose reveals his nature. It never shows off. It moves with dignity, but so quietly that at times you are tempted to declare it sluggish or even commonplace, until, when the tale is finished, you realize how apt an expression it has given to the quality of the mind that made it. The secret of this greatness may be partly shyness. It has taken Mr. Galsworthy some time to reveal himself. For years he seemed to be afraid of his own convictions and his own feelings. Little by little he has burned through the obstruction; but he is still rather shy, and the shyness saves him from exaggeration and display. But behind it lies a bigger and nobler quality—the habit of reverence. He reverences life, and nature, and men. He brushes nothing aside; he "turns" nothing impatiently "down." A mind that has this quality goes on developing and enriching itself. It may do its finest work when the man is an old man.

That Mr. Galsworthy is still shy is proved by his abiding preference for the ironic method. "Life calls the tune—we dance," he reminds us on his title-page. Life called such a tune to Keith Darrant, that eminent and respectable barrister, [**"The First and the Last"**], that he found himself accessory after the fact to a murder, and the cause that an innocent man was hanged. We know that this is not what he wants to tell us. The point behind this woeful exhibition of respectability tricked and tortured is the contrasted happiness of Keith Darrant's brother, the murderer, the drunkard, who loved a woman of the streets and died happy in her dying arms. Life called such a tune to

Frank Ashurst [in **"The Apple Tree"**], that he left a passionate farm-girl to kill herself for love of him, while he ran away and hid in marriage with a dull young lady who embodied for him just then respectability and good form and whatever is seemly and safe. Again, the point behind the tale is the beauty of that moonlit, apple-blossom idyll in a Devon farm; and very beautifully it is told. But still, Mr. Galsworthy is shy of telling it for its own sake. We do not mean that he loads the dice against love, but the bent of his mind is such that he shrinks from showing love triumphant. He must, as it were, apologize for it by holding it against the "real" world of convention and class and property. He is still a little afraid of his own tenderness, his own passion for beauty and good will. He must show us by his irony what we should like to find him showing for once in its naked beauty, unashamed.

In two of these tales he "lets himself go," nerved by his admiration of power, and adopts the direct, not the ironic, method. They are both tales of old men—old men very unlike each other, though in youth they were friends. One is Sylvanus Heythorp, paralysed, lonely, beset by creditors, but still fighting, in a mawkish world that he despises, for his independence, his dinner, and his own way [in **"A Stoic"**]. A noble old fellow this, for all his materialism; a noble old bear, harried by curs, and defiantly dying just before they can pull him down. The other is our old friend (for a friend he has seemed ever since *The Man of Property*) Jolyon Forsyte, now in his "Indian summer." No one who cares for craftsmanship in letters can fail to enjoy the difference between Mr. Galsworthy's method of rapping out the rough tune of old Heythorp and his method of lingering over, "pressing out" the sweetness of Uncle Jolyon's last days, sunset-lit with his love of beauty, especially as it calls to him in the eyes and hair and movement of tragic Irene Heron. "What is it makes us love, and makes us die? I must go to bed." We know, or thought we knew, this masterful old fellow, this Forsyte; but to meet him here with his little granddaughter, his dog, and Irene is to hear a strange music of love and death. Mr. Galsworthy is not here shy of his subject.

You may dig deep into what Galsworthy gives you, and the deeper you dig the richer you find the store to be.

—*The Times Literary Supplement*

The most subtle and te most subtly balanced of all these five tales is that called **"The Juryman."** It seems obvious enough, this contrast (very characteristic of Mr. Galsworthy) between the wretched little Welsh conscript, who had tried to kill himself because he could not longer bear separation from his wife, and the sleek, prosperous, uxorious stockbroker who is one of the jurymen at his trial. A few years ago, we fancy, Mr. Galsworthy would have stopped short at the contrast. He can go beyond it now to the mystery of life. His irony plays about Mr. Bosengate's self-satisfaction; but before we have done with Mr. Bosengate he too is caught in the mystery.

> Curious thing—life! Curious world! Curious forces in it—making one do the opposite of what one wished; always—always making one do the opposite, it seemed! The furtive light from that creeping moon was getting hold of things down there, stealing in among the boughs of the trees. "There's something ironical," he thought, "which walks about. Things don't come off as you think they will. I meant, I tried—but one doesn't change like that all of a sudden, it seems. Fact is life's too big a thing for one!"

The story is short, but it is also great; and it speaks even more clearly than the other four of a mind in which sternness is matched with tenderness, imagination with sound sense; a mind which dreams out upon the vision without being blind to the fact.

Louise Maunsell Field   (essay date 1920)

SOURCE: "Mr. Galsworthy in War and Peace," in *The New York Times Review of Books,* March 28, 1920, p. 139.

[*Below, Field commends Galsworthy's attention to beauty in* Tatterdemalion.]

If one were to try to sum up in a single word that for which John Galsworthy stands, both in the matter of expression and of creed, it would seem inevitable that the word should be "beauty." Beauty of expression, in the style whose exquisite finish is flowerlike in its all but flawless perfection, yet resembles a hot-house flower in that it is no untrained thing, but at once natural and carefully, skilfully cultivated. Beauty, too, as a creed, expressed in many different books, yet never—to our recollection, at least—so briefly and completely as in the sketch or essay, whichever you may choose to call it, that closes the first section of this volume, **"A Green Hill Far Away."** There, with the war a thing of the past and peace a blessed fact the author declares, "There are not enough lovers of beauty among men," and that until there shall be "more lovers of beauty in proportion to those who are indifferent to beauty," wars will not cease. No matter what other sterling qualities men may possess; so long as they lack this one they are, and will remain, fighting animals.

The book is divided into two sections, "Of War-Time" and "Of Peace-Time," titles which quite sufficiently explain themselves. And in war, however ugly it may be in many of its aspects, beauty is not always lacking, nor the expression of a beautiful spirit. The reader will have to go far to find, even in Mr. Galsworthy's own works, anything lovelier or more gently, poignantly appealing than the tale which opens the volume—the story of the aristocratic old English lady who became **"The Grey Angel"** of a French hospital. Told with the utmost simplicity, and that quiet, unerring choice of diction which is the hall-mark of a master, this tale of a rare, brave spirit encased in a frail, outworn body is one of those few which are to be read, and read again, and remembered always. To say that it is the best not only of the section but of the volume, is not to belittle the rest but merely to give this one its due meed of praise.

> If one were to try to sum up in a single word that for which John Galsworthy stands, both in the matter of expression and of creed, it would seem inevitable that the word should be "beauty."
>
> —*Louise Maunsell Field*

Perhaps the tale which in some ways approaches **"The Grey Angel"** the most nearly is the very different **"Cafard,"** the story of a French soldier who had in his brain "the little black beetle which gnaws and eats and destroys all hope and heaven in a man"—"Cafard," they call it. Jean Liotard, lying solitary out upon the grass, and due to appear next day before the authorities who would probably send him back to the Front, told himself that there was "no pity, no God," in the world, but only despair, and "the preying of creatures the one on the other." So he thought he believed, until there came to him—no heavenly vision, but a wretched little black dog. **"The Muffled Ship"** and **"A Green Hill Far Away"** are alike in being impressions, reflections of a mood, imagination bringing into contrast with the actual that which is at once its antithesis and its complement. Following the great homecoming ship, the ship of life, the ship of those who have returned, comes slowly creeping the "Muffled Ship" of the grey yearning dead, who will never return any more.

SOLDIERS IN HOSPITALS

Among the other of the fifteen tales and sketches in this section "Of War-Time," several have to do with stray soldiers in the hospitals. There was Gray, who had been a Belgian glass blower, and who, released from a German prison after twenty months because of a half paralyzed tongue—"The boches * * * had put him and two others against a wall and shot those other two"—drifted into a French hospital. At first he wanted to work for France; but soon he asked "only to rest." And then there were the two amusingly different chums, Poirot and Bidan, whose fate was happier than that of Gray. A couple of tales have to do with Germans long resident in England and married to English wives, but not naturalized, men with whose troubles the author sympathizes deeply—more perhaps than the reader will, especially in the case of Holsteig, who had lived twenty years in England and married a Scotch-woman, but was quite ready to have his son join the German army. And the son would have gone to join the forces of the Kaiser, had he been able to get to Germany. **"The Peace Meeting,"** on the other hand, is an excellent bit of irony which will be enjoyed by all but the pacifists.

If the first section has its **"Green Hill Far Away,"** the second contains the no less exquisite **"Buttercup Night."** It is practically impossible to give any real idea of the sheer loveliness of the descriptions of this night of "frozen beauty," when the moonlight "caught on the dewy buttercups; and across this ghostly radiance the shadows of the yew-trees fell in dense black bars." But curious as it may seem, it is in this second part "Of Peace-Time" that one finds the two tales, which of all those the volume contains, have in them the most of horror—**"Manna,"** and **"The Nightmare Child."** The story of starving, half-insane clergyman is powerful and very dreadful, but no more dreadful than the story the kindly country doctor tells of the poor girl who was one of those creatures "one simply dare not take notice of, however sorry one may be for them," a story both pitiful and dreadful in its utter hopelessness. There was not, and never would or could be, the shadow of a chance for Em'leen. In this, the narrative differs greatly from that other story of the countryside, **"A Strange Thing,"** the tale of two women, one resembling "a young apple tree with the Spring sun on its blossom," while the other was as incongruous, there amid the beauty of that wonderful Spring day, as the old discarded boot was with the ferns and wild plants among which it had fallen.

CYNICAL AND IDYLLIC

For, like the first part of the volume, the second contains contrasts sharp as black and white—the cynical, dramatic **"Two Looks,"** for instance, and the charming, idyllic **"Fairyland"**—and because of this it is difficult, if not impossible, to write of the volume as a whole. Indeed, its very title explains how exceedingly varied is its content. But unalike as these tales and sketches are in many ways, they resemble one another in this—that always there is the intense feeling for beauty, the power of divination which penetrates beneath the surface-seeming of the men and women who appear in them, the sure and delicate craftsmanship that enables Mr. Galsworthy to show the reader the thing as he sees it, or so much of it, at least, as the reader is capable of being shown. Among the artists in literature of the present day—and they are not so few as some would like to imagine—those are rare who can safely challenge comparison with the John Galsworthy of *Tatterdemalion.*

The Nation (essay date 1920)

SOURCE: "Beauty and the Beast," in *The Nation,* Vol. CX, No. 2859, April 17, 1920, p. 522.

[*In the following review of* Tatterdemalion, *the critic declares some of Galsworthy's stories "among the best of our time," yet notes limitations of his literary style.*]

There is a moving little essay in Mr. Galsworthy's new volume which he calls **"A Green Hill Far Away."** It is a breath of relief and thanksgiving at the coming of peace. It was written in 1918, and as he permits an untroubled

spirit to blend once more with his beloved English countryside, he says "There is Peace again and the souls of men fresh murdered are not flying into our lungs with every breath we draw." Now it is 1920 and such souls are still flying, for hunger is a more cruel murderer than the sword and the sword itself is far from idle. And one wonders whether this wise and truly lofty soul still believes—for this is the central note of the collection—that the world is full of war and hate because "there are not enough lovers of beauty among men." "It all," he continues, "comes back to that. Not enough who want the green hill far away—who naturally hate disharmony and the greed, ugliness, restlessness, cruelty, which are its parents and children." Alas, in 1914 there was Paris, a city that loved beauty, and there was Vienna, whose many, many poets sought only after the green hills and temples of the soul. The love of beauty lingered in Florence and it had come to a new birth in Munich. And men in all those cities that had loved beauty exchanged it for wrath and saw in war and nationalistic passion another, fiercer, and more burning beauty, and poets of all peoples—Brooke and Seeger and Heymel—are rotting somewhere in the old battlefields. Perhaps they loved beauty too much and truth too little. The passions and the myths have an intense beauty of their own until the time of the dreadful harvest. Thought and resistance are cold and solitary.

In Mr. Galsworthy emotion has always been a little stronger than reflection. His very excess of restraint bears witness to that. But his passion for beauty burns with a very steady flame in the fine story **"Spindleberries,"** though even here it is tempered in expression by that "gentillesse" of Chaucer which Mr. Galsworthy recalls to us by his motto and has so carefully cultivated within himself. The war came and, because it wrenched him from his absorption in beauty, stirred him to thought. He himself could not identify his vision of beauty with the crimson of carnage, or fling himself wholly back into the ardors of the tribe. Hence in 1917 he wrote **"Cafard"** with far-reaching implications that touch both Barbusse and Latzko, and during that year and the next, **"Defeat"** and **"The Bright Side,"** and finally, in 1919, **"The Dog It Was Who Died."** And these stories—already dismissed or scoffed at by the red-blooded press—illustrate how those years found his other passion for justice more real and useful in a world of horror than his passion for beauty. **"Defeat,"** the earliest of the stories, makes the fact very clear. For in this account of a German street walker in London he rises to those ultimate perceptions that seek humanity beyond the tribe, see the same qualities and reactions in all tribes, and thus by dispassionate observation and thought reach the only possible haven of peace—a haven of the mind rather than of the heart.

On the side of art *Tatterdemalion* illustrates the Galsworthian qualities which are quite familiar by this time: a mellowness that never degenerates into softness (unless for a moment in **"The Grey Angel"** in this very collection); a virile tenderness of tone; an unobtrusive ease in the progression of the narrative; a diction which is always adequate, often beautiful, but which will not or cannot exploit all its own full resources of either beauty or strength through some inflexibility of inner modulation. Not that his prose-rhythm is monotonous. Its range is small like that of a beautiful and cultivated voice dwelling on a few notes and unconscious of the worlds of sound beyond. Some of the short stories here are, with these definite qualities and their defects, among the best of our time. In addition to those named, especially **"Spindleberries,"** there is **"Expectations,"** which, with its robuster undertone and pleasant edge of irony, shows that Mr. Galsworthy, were he to be but a shadow less conscious of the necessity of "gentillesse," could oftener exhibit the unbreathed-on grain of life.

The Times Literary Supplement   (essay date 1922)

SOURCE: A review of *The Forsyte Saga,* in *The Times Literary Supplement,* No. 1066, June 22, 1922, p. 411.

[*In the following review, the critic praises Galsworthy's ability to create familiar and sympathetic characters in* The Forsyte Saga.]

At various times Mr. Galsworthy has written three novels and two short stories about the same family. The last of the novels brings the chronicle down to the year 1920. It is therefore closed, at least for some time, and Mr. Galsworthy has taken the opportunity of grouping all these works within one cover. He has also, and, we cannot help thinking, unluckily, taken the opportunity of presenting all these works as if they were one work. So regarded, they make, at least at first sight, a very imposing whole. It is a volume of over eleven hundred pages. It contains more characters (and real, recognizable characters) than can easily be counted. It covers thirty-four years. It is a sort of English *War and Peace.* Only it is not. The device of calling novels "books" and short stories "interludes" does not make one work out of five or give unity and symmetry to what obviously was not composed or even imagined as a whole. And perhaps the title given to the collection is a trifle unfortunate. Mr. Galsworthy says:—

> *The Forsyte Saga* was the title originally destined for the part of it which is called *The Man of Property*; and to adopt it for the collected chronicles of the Forsyte family has indulged the Forsytean tenacity which is in all of us. The word saga might be objected to on the ground that it connotes the heroic and that there is little of heroism in these pages. But it is used with a suitable irony; and, after all, this long tale, though it may deal with folk in frock coats, furbelows, and a gilt-edged period, is not devoid of the essential heat of conflict. Discounting for the gigantic stature and blood-thirstiness of old days, as they have come down to us in fairy-tale and legend, the folk of the old sagas were Forsytes, assuredly, in their possessive instincts, and as little proof against the inroads of beauty and passion as Swithin, Soames, or even young Jolyon. And if heroic figures, in days that never were, seem to startle out from their surroundings in fashion unbecoming to a Forsyte of the Victorian era, we may be sure that tribal instinct was even then the prime force, and that "family" and the sense of home

and property counted as they do to this day, for all the recent efforts to "talk them out."

"Days that never were"! That is precisely the point. Mr. Galsworthy is a realist, not in any vulgar sense, but in a true sense; his people exist and move on the same plane as ourselves. The people of the Sagas do not. And the word "Saga" is used to describe a work of literary art. Whether the real people whose projections we have in the Sagas were like the Forsytes—that is, like ourselves—is immaterial. This is not "suitable irony," for Mr. Galsworthy apparently does not intend any satirical contrast between the Forsytes and the heroes. It is merely a little joke; and to put a little joke on the title-page of so large a book is surely rather a mistake.

It has been worth while drawing attention to these two small points, because they do stand somewhat hinderingly on the threshold of what is undoubtedly the most considerable part of Mr. Galsworthy's work. When they are disposed of, it is possible to see how considerable a thing in itself has been the creation of the Forsyte family. Mr. Galsworthy obligingly affixes a genealogical table to this edition which serves a certain purpose in that when we look at it we find it to be unnecessary. We know the Forsyte family as well as our own; indeed, while we are in the book it *is* our own family, we ourselves are Forsytes, and do not need to be reminded of the various relationships of our uncles and aunts and cousins. How Mr. Galsworthy manages to produce this effect it is by no means easy to say. He does not exhaustively tell us everything about the Forsytes. He swoops down on them on three occasions, narrates three episodes in their collective existence, and yet somehow he does convey to us the sense he himself must have very strongly of their continuous life.

Galsworthy does not exhaustively tell us everything about the Forsytes. He swoops down on them on three occasions, narrates three episodes in their collective existence, and yet somehow he does convey to us the sense he himself must have very strongly of their continuous life.

—*The Times Literary Supplement*

And he has achieved this without making his work merely a transcript from reality. "This long tale," he says, "is no scientific study of a period; it is rather an intimate incarnation of the disturbance that Beauty effects in the lives of men." Here, again, one cannot help quarrelling a little with the author's own explanation. This seems to us to ascribe altogether too much importance, both particularly and symbolically, to Irene Heron, who wrecked June Forsyte's marriage, brought about the death of Philip Bosinney, ran away from Soames Forsyte, and was eventually divorced by him with "Young Jolyon" Forsyte for co-respondent. It is to her that Mr. Galsworthy refers as "a concretion of disturbing Beauty impinging on a possessive world." But surely the beauty with which Mr. Galsworthy makes these chronicles something better than a transcript from life is not isolated in Irene; it is in his own attitude, in his own delighted awareness of the life of the persons he has recorded or created. Irene is beautiful, true enough, and sometimes a sense of her mysterious power starts out of the pages of the book, though, as Mr. Galsworthy points out, she is "never . . . present, except through the senses of other characters." But there is beauty, too, in the understanding of old Swithin, in the just appreciation of the unloved Soames, cursed by being too sensitive and yet not sensitive enough. Indeed, Mr. Galsworthy's greatest successes are always with conventionally "unsympathetic" characters. Give him a fine old gentleman like Old Jolyon, or a knight-errant like Young Jolyon, and he can do little more than express his liking and approval. The effect these characters have on the reader depends on what they are in themselves. But give him a character whom it is in the conventions to condemn or to deride, and he is at his best. Then the effect on the reader is of that subtle and often impressive sort which springs precisely from the relation between author and character.

> He stood at the sideboard in a white waistcoat with large gold and onyx buttons, watching his valet screw the necks of three champagne bottles deeper into ice pails. Between the points of his stand-up collar which—though it hurt him to move—he would on no account have had altered, the pale flesh of his underchin remained immovable. His eyes roved from bottle to bottle. He was debating, and he argued like this:— "Jolyon drinks a glass, perhaps two, he's so careful of himself. James, he can't take his wine nowadays. Nicholas—" Fanny and he would swill water, he shouldn't wonder! Soames didn't count, these young nephews—Soames was thirty-eight—couldn't drink! But Bosinney? Encountering in the name of this stranger something outside the range of his philosophy, Swithin paused. A misgiving arose within him! It was impossible to tell! June was only a girl, in love, too! Emily (Mrs. James) liked a good glass of champagne. It was too dry for Juley, poor old soul, she had no palate. As to Hatty Chessman! The thought of this old friend caused a cloud of thought to obscure the perfect glassiness of his eyes. He shouldn't wonder if she drank half a bottle!

> . . . He himself might drink a good deal, for, thanks to that p—prescription of Blight's, he found himself extremely well, and he had been careful to take no lunch. He had not felt so well for weeks. Puffing out his lower lip, he gave his last instructions:—

> "Adolf, the least touch of the West India when you come to the ham."

This is like one of those pictures in which mean or indifferent objects are made to seem beautiful by the light in which they stand. This quality in Mr. Galsworthy's work is of a variable, come-and-go order. Sometimes his austere, impartial love of his characters as they are—for in

this sense he, if no one else, loves Soames the unlovable—passes over into bias and favouritism. Old Jolyon, for example, begins as a much less fine, much more *borné* character than he afterwards becomes; and this is not due to development in him, for he is eighty when we first meet him. But though it is intermittent, it is the dominating and peculiar quality in Mr. Galsworthy's work, this dry, cool, and yet golden light which from time to time he is able to shed on his characters and their interactions.

The Times Literary Supplement   (essay date 1923)

SOURCE: A review of *Captures,* in *The Times Literary Supplement,* No. 1130, September 13, 1923, p. 602.

[*In the following mixed review, the critic maintains that the stories comprising* Captures *possess the characteristic beauty of Galsworthy's writing, but lack incisiveness and intensity.*]

Mr. Galsworthy's sixteen new stories, here collected [in] *Captures,* are neither unworthy of him nor yet on a level with his best work. They are characteristic. But one feels that in writing them he allowed himself a certain relaxation: they are deficient not in truth but in intensity. He has always surveyed life with the cool and ironic detachment which is the natural refuge of the man who feels acutely. In *The Forsyte Sage* his detachment was a desperately maintained pose, more dreadful and moving than could have been the least restrained partisanship. But here the detachment is rather that of a certain fatigue. The outlines of his persons are not less true, but they are less incisive. Rupert K. Vaness was a hedonist—"Life moved round him with a certain noiseless ease or stood still at a perfect temperature like the air in a conservatory round a choice blossom which a draught might shrivel." But he was still "the sort of man of whom one could never say with safety whether he was revolving round a beautiful young woman or whether the beautiful young woman was revolving round him." He was fifty-five when he concerned himself with Miss Monroy, and expounded to her his philosophy of life. She had a keen enough wit to take it literally:—

> "Your philosophy is that of faun and nymph. But can you play the part?"

> "Only let me try." Those words had each a fevered ring that in imagination I could see Vaness all flushed, his fine eyes shining, his well-kept hands trembling, his lips a little protruded.

> Then came a laugh, high, gay, sweet.

> "Very well then; catch me!" I heard a swish of skirt against the shrubs, the sounds of flight; an astonished gasp from Vaness, and the heavy thud, thud of his feet following on the path through the azalea maze. I hoped fervently that they would not suddenly come running past and see me sitting there. My straining ears caught

another laugh far off, a panting sound, a muttered oath, a far-away coo-ee! And then, staggering, winded, pale with heat and with vexation, Vaness appeared, caught sight of me and stood a moment—baff! Sweat was running down his face, his hand was clutching at his side, his stomach heaved—a hunter beaten and undignified.

This is the coolness of acquiescence; and one's consciousness of it is only increased when Mr. Galsworthy ends by remarking that he "was sorry—very sorry, at that moment, for Rupert K. Vaness." The addition would once have been unnecessary; and Mr. Galsworthy has never been the man to underline where underlining is not needed.

Galsworthy has always surveyed life with the cool and ironic detachment which is the natural refuge of the man who feels acutely.

—The Times Literary Supplement

There is a similar coolness in all these pieces. In one, two farmers quarrel and one of them as a result suffers the loss of his son. In another a good soldier suffers every undeserved misfortune until at last he is driving a taxi about the streets of London. In a third a man emerges from a term of penal servitude, morally undeserved, hardened so as to be sufficient to himself and impervious to all other persons. In a fourth ["**Had a Horse**"] an inferior bookie, who knows nothing of horses save their form on paper, accidentally acquires one and cannot bear that it should be run otherwise than to win. In all these Mr. Galsworthy records with all his old exquisite sympathy, with all of his old discernment of what is fine and beautiful in the gross characters whose grossness he used to hate. The grace, the sympathy, the economy are still there: the fervour, visible only in the immense restraint which kept it from unseemly displays, is gone. Has Mr. Galsworthy despaired of shaming the Forsytes—he never wished to destroy them, he loved them too much—out of their evil courses in the world? These tales are, we say again, characteristic; and there is always a certain beauty in the fatigue and relaxation of a warm passion. Possibly Mr. Galsworthy is entering into the Indian Summer of his art. At all events his readers, though they may find here something that is a little perplexing, will find nothing that can dissatisfy them.

The New York Times Book Review (essay date 1923)

SOURCE: A review of *Captures,* in *The New York Times Book Review,* September 16, 1923, p. 11.

[*In the review below, the critic compares Galsworthy's stories in* Captures *with the game of cricket, asserting that they both contain a "code of gentility."*]

Reading another Galsworthy short stories, essays or poems book, whether a novel, plays, is like following a team, or a sportsman, in a familiar game, and seeing the supported colors come to the defeat of a gentleman. It is again Galsworthy's code of gentility, of "cricket," against a more material, coarse-fibred world that is revealed in his latest collection of short stories, *Captures*.

Reference to games in connection with Galsworthy is not to be construed as convicting that fine artist of triviality; it is rather a recognition of a quality held in common—that "inner pluck" which is perhaps the most engaging attribute of the Anglo-Saxon, at work or at play.

It is a world, Galsworthy would seem to be saying, scarcely worth the trouble of carrying on one's back. His characters play at life earnestly and gallantly, with no hope of winning. Persons in Galsworthy's books are developed with that swift selectiveness of his and groomed for their bit of drama—an encounter with some individual or some brute force which is "not quite cricket." The cricketers go down to be frustrated, in a sense, and to have living made intolerable, by the very scrupulousness with which they observe their inbred code. They have not even the satisfaction of being defeated according to the "game."

Galsworthy seldom makes his confession of faith explicit. It is an undercurrent to the statement of his conflicts and becomes apparent by implication in his resolutions. In "**A Hedonist,**" however, there occurs:

> The microbe of fatalism, already present in the brains of artists before the war, had been considerably-enlarged by that depressing occurrence. Could a civilization basing itself on the production of material advantages do anything but insure the desire for more and more material advantages? * * * The war had seemed to me to show that mankind was too combative an animal ever to recognize that the good of all was the good of one. The coarse-fibred, pugnacious and self-seeking would, I had become sure, always carry too many guns for the refined and kindly. * * * The simple heroism of mankind, disclosed or rather accentuated by the war, seemed to afford no hope; it was so exploitable by the rhinoceri and tigers of high life. * * * Success, power, wealth—those aims of profiteers and Premiers, pedagogues and pandemoniacs, of all, in fact, who could not see God in a dewdrop, hear Him in distant goat bells and scent Him in a pepper tree—had always appeared to me akin to dry rot.

Most of the stories in *Captures,* as the above quotation would indicate, introduce the World War as Galsworthy's latest instance of the refusal or the inability of the lower orders to play cricket. He subscribes to the amazed discovery of the British Army officer of years' experience in the colonies: "It is not a gentleman's war."

It might appear that Galsworthy had been discovered by this reviewer in the clutches of a fixed idea. Nothing could less closely approximate an actual intention to convey the infinite possibilities which Galsworthy has found in the relationship which he exploits. He enriches it with profound observation of its social and intimate significances. He is never arguing for or against—"cricket," or anything else. Galsworthy, if he has nothing else, possesses the sweet reasonableness of the judicial temperament. At times his plays, in particular, take on the complexion of the argument of opposing counsel in a trial at law; his fiction has the more seasoned, mellow aspect of the Court's summation. He is too much the tactician, even if he were not also the philosopher, to indulge in villains, completely black, for his tragic futilities. Whatever desperate thing happens to his cricketers, it is no one's fault. Or it is left to the reader to find, to answer his overwhelming questions.

To a man so saturated with the hereditary stereotype of gallantry and Spartan courage, it is inevitable that the major impulse of drama should derive out of the opposition of cricket to non-cricket. Galsworthy, however, is also fascinated by the war between the ascetic ideal and the warm rush of instinctive fulfillment of life. The first story, **"A Feud,"** combines both themes unfolded against a background of a rural English village. The story has dimension and atmosphere. The reader is made aware, in a clarified essential development of a fully realized situation, of landmarks in the progress of the feud which are not consciously apprehended by the participants themselves. The love affair of the young heir and the dubious farm girl is handled with a deft sympathy that extracts from it all its pathos and all its irony.

Galsworthy may not carry you all the way in the story of the Cockney bookie who **"Had a Horse,"** and was brought for the first time in his cringing life into close contact with the thoroughbred. It is unimportant whether you believe that sniveling Jimmie captured something from the horse and ever afterward had a little stiffening of the spine in him. The story is an interesting restatement of Galsworthy's obsession in another absorbing form.

"The Man Who Kept His Form" is perhaps the purest example of "cricket." The closing tableau of the leading figure—"symbol of that lost cause, gentility"—is not only a scathing indictment of the muddling by the British Government of the after-war employment problem; it is a justification of Galsworthy. Erect and uncomplaining, proud to the last, taking his reverses without bitterness, you have in this hero the consummation of playing the game.

A suggestion of Algernon Blackwood is discernible in **"Timber,"** the story of the profiteer who sold his ancestral wood at a huge profit to the Government, and the revenge of the trees upon him for his treachery. Blackwood would have given the yarn a mystical fervor and a terrifying animation of accumulated animosity. Galsworthy has traced the psychological disintegration of his grasping gentleman with a sure touch. It is a little too suave to be horrible, and a little too remote to be tangible. Galsworthy is betrayed, as he seldom is, into losing an individual for the sake of an idea. It is as if he preferred to stew the profiteer in his own juice to giving a poignant immediacy to the downfall of a gross person, who yet has an individuality.

On the whole, this new volume deserves to stand beside the rest of Galsworthy's sensitive, questioning criticisms of the life we live.

L. P. Hartley   (essay date 1925)

SOURCE: A review of *Caravan,* in *The Bookman,* Vol. 68, No. 404, May, 1925, pp. 114-15.

[*Author of the acclaimed novel trilogy* Eustace and Hilda *(1944-47), Hartley was an English novelist and short story writer whose fiction is unified by the theme of the search for individuality and meaning in the post-Christian era. A literary critic as well, Hartley contributed reviews for many years to the* Saturday Review, Time and Tide, *the* Spectator, *and other periodicals. In the following review, he describes the stories in* Caravan *as inventive, indignant, and at times sentimental.*]

An exhausted and pitiable caravan, this of Mr. Galsworthy's, composed of the maimed, the halt and the blind, the victims of circumstance, the victims of themselves—depressed, unsuccessful, down-at-heel, under-dogs nearly all of them. There are fifty-six stories in [*Caravan*], and nearly a thousand pages; in nearly every story, on nearly every page, the most we see of Happiness is her heels vanishing round a corner. Moments of elation occur and, more rarely, moments of ecstasy; but they are the brief summits of a sharply-declining curve. The caravan catches the sunlight for a second before it plunges into the shadows.

Pathos rather than tragedy is the note of Mr. Galsworthy's tales. He is for ever pitying somebody, and the shorter the story the more pity he contrives to squeeze into it. He manages to engage our sympathy for the most unpromising characters; hard, worldly, merciless as they are, we shed a tear for them simply because they are afflicted with those qualities; we sympathise with them for being so unsympathetic. It is due to Mr. Galsworthy to say that scarcely ever can we resist his humanitarianism, even when (as is not often the case) he preaches it too openly and writes what is perilously near "sob-stuff." He has so much invention and resource, he draws his instances from so far afield, he is familiar with so many modes of living, that his stories escape monotony. Even though, emotionally, the destination may vary little, the route is always different, and Mr. Galsworthy has a chameleon-like power of identifying himself with his surroundings. He is a countryman in the country; a townsman in the town; in the directors' board-room or the flower-seller's attic he seems equally at home. Thus if his impressions sometimes lack unexpectedness and the charm of freshness, they have a maturity and a reliability which wear better in the end. No contemporary writer can show the same versatility: Mr. Arnold Bennett and Mr. Eden Phillpotts have as many forms of art at their command, but when they leave their beaten track they become explorers and make lucky shots, hit or miss; whereas Mr. Galsworthy would always be indigenous, whether his scene were laid at the equator or the pole.

The stories are grouped in couples, an early one beside a late one, and linked loosely by some common quality of mood. They cover about a quarter of a century; and it is perhaps not fanciful to say that in the earlier pieces Turgenev's influence is uppermost, in the later, Conrad's. Both those writers, of course, preferred to tell their stories indirectly, and from a distance: Conrad because the interposition of an intermediate consciousness gave a depth and flavour and colour; Turgenev because his art demanded a stillness and coherence which could scarcely be achieved by a direct narration of events. When Mr. Galsworthy summons up remembrance of things past, he also makes the flight of time subserve the ends of art, but his medium imposes its own colours, and they are almost invariably autumnal. Time, for him, is not Time the abstraction, but Time with the scythe, Time the destroyer, the subtle thief of youth. He mounts the historian's pinnacle, not to make an impartial survey but to cry *"Quantum mutatus!"*—and the change is usually for the worse; not merely change, but change and decay. He relates the stories of two men, in one instance a crossing-sweeper, in the other a shoemaker. Already shadows hang over both: the crossing-sweeper, though moderately affluent, has before him the alternative of the workhouse or the river; the shoemaker, still prosperous, is beginning to suffer from the competition of machine-made goods. Business or pleasure removes the narrator from the scene; in time he returns to find his friends a little older, a little poorer, a little nearer the breaking-point. Again, after doing all in his power to relieve them, he goes away, returning once more to find the process of mortification a degree or two advanced. And with the fourth or fifth visit of the wanderer they are dead, and their place knows them no more. These are two of the cruder examples of Mr. Galsworthy's almost morbid sense of mortality; in many of the stories it is present only as a flavour of exquisite subtlety. But they show his limitation as a short-story writer; his conception of people as always looking before and after and pining for what is not, instead of living in the present and for the present, which is an instinct of equal strength.

Mr. Galsworthy is an emotionalist always, a sentimentalist sometimes, a partisan never.

—L. P. Hartley

These considerations do not affect Mr. Galsworthy as an artist, for an artist has the right to put upon life whatever interpretation he chooses or his temperament dictates. And it would be particularly unfair and misleading to try to fix a label on work which has, in its subject-matter and its handling, as much diversity and vitality as any that is being written to-day. Many of the stories in *Caravan,* especially the longer ones, are models of what stories ought to be: delicately written, conscientious, well worked out, amusing, exciting, moving. But the most impressive are those in which the emotion is most restrained or most diffused. Mr. Galsworthy is an emotionalist always, a sentimentalist sometimes, a partisan never. It is this admirable aloofness that sometimes betrays him into sentimentality, as does also the conviction, so common in fine natures, that anyone who is unfortunate and at odds with society is therefore in the right. He appears to resent injustice, but it is suffering that he really minds; he is capable of moral indignation, but he vents it upon systems, not upon individuals. Universally charitable, he will not accept the hard doctrine of personal responsibility, and that is the reason his characters so seldom attain tragic proportions; they are more sinned against than sinning, and the tragic expiation is for them an irrelevance, a meaningless addition to their sufferings. *Tout comprendre, c'est tout pardonner.* He assumes the world to be harsher in its judgments than it really is. Of a street-walker he writes: "Women of her profession are not supposed to have redeeming points." But is this really the case? What modern writer of serious fiction would dare to bring a prostitute into his pages and not endow her with all the virtues, except one, which he would be reluctant to consider a virtue?

P. C. Kennedy   (essay date 1925)

SOURCE: A review of *Caravan,* in *The New Statesman,* Vol. XXV, No. 628, May 9, 1925, p. 106.

[*In the following review, Kennedy offers a generally positive review of Galsworthy's* Caravan *but contends that "a golden mediocrity honeys and mitigates all his achievement."*]

But two birds haunt the heights of Parnassus—not, as some have fabled, the eagle and the dove, but the phœnix and the ibis: the phœnix, lonely in eminence:

> that self-begotten bird,
> In the Arabian woods imbost,
> That no second knows nor third;

and the ibis, which, as everybody remembers, is safest in the middle. There is a paradox about each of them. By the phœnix one does not mean a single literal supremacy, such as might be claimed for Shakespeare: one means the supreme quality which, wherever it is met, stands out as lord and beacon of its kind. One meets it more often in Shakespeare than anywhere else, of course; but it is to be found in lesser folk, and in odd corners. It is known by indubitable physical signs: the pit of the stomach gives, the backbone dissolves, tears come into the eyes, and one exclaims publicly in a clear voice (or privately in the heart): "By Heaven, this is the goods!" By these signs is the phœnix recognised in many places. There is one phœnix, but there are several thousand phœnixes; and that is the paradox. The paradox of the ibis is different, and reminds one of Aristotle's argument about virtue. Virtue is a mean between two extremes, and yet to be virtuous is to take an extreme course: just so, the ibis is in a sense mediocre, missing the raptures as well as the depths, and yet this very adherence to the mean may prove an art so admirable in its adequacy as to rise, to shine, to soar, to have a supremacy all its own.

Mr. Galsworthy's muse is the chief ibis of our day. A golden mediocrity honeys and mitigates all his achievement. His theme is the middle-class, his range the middle register: the brutality of his method is nicely balanced with its sentimentality, so that his characters often appear (as Mr. Beerbohm pointed out in an unkind parody) futile: he excels in description of those two essentially middle-class occupations, board-meetings and meals; nobody ever less resembled Sir Andrew Aguecheek, yet it is impossible to read his works without recalling the wise knight's epigram—who, when he was asked: "Does not our life consist of the four elements?" replied: "Faith, so they say; but I think it rather consists of eating and drinking." Even here the paradox runs. The Forsytes as a family resemble that hero described by Mr. Barry Pain: "He does everything well. He does himself well." They do themselves *too* well; yet Soames, their representative and core, is almost excessively moderate. There is nothing remarkable about Soames; he is the very embodiment of what Mr. Galsworthy calls "Forsyte tenacity," yet he can neither hold what is his or get what he wants; he is at once a failure and a success, a scapegoat and a conqueror. But he will occupy a permanent place in the great gallery of British portraits, with Falstaff and Squire Western and Mr. Wardle and Mr. Polly.

This being so, it follows that Mr. Galsworthy is not merely an artist, but, with all his limitations, a great artist: one of the few living novelists who have added something to the corpus of the indestructible. His collected tales, called *Caravan,* will scarcely rival *The Forsyte Saga* in importance; but they contain some first-rate stuff. Perhaps the two best stories in the collection are **"A Stoic"** and **"Had a Horse."** The former is an epic of oysters and sweetbreads and cutlets, champagne and sherry and old brandy; the latter is equine; and, in the British middle-class hierarchy of idealisms, horse-flesh comes next to beef and mutton. Both stories are first-rate, because in both, whether through the grossness or through the meanness, the pure light of human personality, the unquenched lamp of human heroism, shines. Futile? No, no: that Beerbohm arrow, though sharp and piercing, was fledged with injustice: there is a notable though not a large proportion of Galsworthian characters who escape futility. But it must be admitted that some of the short ironic sketches in this book are comparative failures.

A special interest should be taken in the first story, which appeared, I believe, in *Villa Rubein* in 1900—thus preceding by six years the publication of *A Man of Property.* It is called **"Salvation of a Forsyte,"** and its topic is an old one: the topic of Browning's

> Alas,
> We loved, sir—used to meet:
> How sad and bad and mad it was—
> But then, how it was sweet!

Swithin is on his death-bed, and he remembers. Now it is a firm convention, rooted like most conventions in the realities of human nature, that old gentlemen on their death-beds remember the romance of their youth. Passion, like faith and sanctity, is an error only when present: it is always found correct by the audit of time. Some men, indeed, do not wait for the death-bed. There used to be a figure very popular on the London stage—it was enacted with the perfection of virtuosity by George Alexander—the elderly though still attractive fellow, the friend of the family, who lectured the young ones for their good and yet let the audience know that he had been a dog too in his day. He wore the white flower of a blameless life in his buttonhole and a crown of wild oats in his hair—thus making the best of both worlds. Then there is that happy and lovely book, *Young April,* by Agnes and Egerton Castle, in which the hero's brief love-affair is so thrilling that he must surely hold a life-time of subsequent respectability to be but light payment for it. Mr. Galsworthy, as usual, is in the middle: he allows himself neither the false sentiment of the one type nor the pure romance of the other; Swithin, at thirty-eight, when he met and loved Rozsi in Salzburg, was bothered all the time by doubts and hesitations. Perhaps she was making a fool of him! Perhaps she was trying to trap him into marriage! And anyway she was a foreigner. A foreigner! But her image returns after forty years to trouble him. "Aloud, in his sleep, Swithin muttered: 'I've missed it.'" When he woke, he could not remember what it was that he had lost.

> Struggling on his pillows, he clutched the wine-glass. His lips touched the wine. "This isn't the 'Heidseck!'" he thought angrily, and before the reality of that displeasure all the dim vision passed away. But as he bent to drink, something snapped, and, with a sigh, Swithin Forsyte died above the bubbles. . . .

A beautiful death, and characteristic of its author. His irony lends originality. In the volume as a whole, the hits exceed the misses by a considerable proportion; and the many sides of Mr. Galsworthy's talent are revealed to one purpose. The ibis whets its silver wings.

The Times Literary Supplement   (essay date 1930)

SOURCE: A review of *On Forsyte 'Change,* No. 1497, October 9, 1930, p. 804.

[*Below, the critic presents a favorable assessment of* On Forsyte 'Change.]

Mr. Galsworthy gives us with unneeded apologies his volume of "apocryphal Forsyte tales," (***On Forsyte 'Change***), fragments that stop the remaining chinks in the history of the clan between 1821 and 1918. Time has moved on while Mr. Galsworthy has been writing these annals, and more and more his Forsytes, who began by being very much of a joke, have acquired the dignity of history; they are no longer mere individuals or a mere family, they are a whole social order and a lost one.

The consciousness, or subconsciousness, of this in the author's mind gives a unity to these detached pieces; for nearly each one of them shows the time-spirit gnawing away some timber of the splendidly upholstered Forsyte mansion. Amid the insecure chaos of post-War England the survivors of the great Victorian Forsytes stand like grey monoliths covered with unintelligible maxims of prudence and morality, in the same way as in their heyday the relics of the Georgian Forsytes encumbered their drawing-rooms with the rugged or fantastic outlines of a ruder and more reckless age. Just as in the first episode of this collection young Jolyon fingers with amused perplexity the paste shoe-buckles that old "Superior Dosset" Forsyte used to wear with his knee-breeches, while Aunt Ann recalls the harsh integrity of his builder's creed: just as later on the "Dromios" (Giles and Jesse Hayman) pause in the lounge of the Brighton Hotel to comment with laconic pity on the ornate and slumbering figure of "Four-in-Hand Forsyte" (Uncle Swithin) while he dreams of the days of "Lord Melbourne, the Cider Cellars and the Pavilion": so in the last episode Soames Forsyte is eyed askance by the Armistice mob as he stands listening to the maroons blowing into air the last scraps of his world. And in between that prologue haunted by the ghost of "Superior Dosset" and this epilogue that relegates Soames to the shades we are shown some of the stages and signposts of the change. We learn how Aunt Juley dared to introduce a dog into Timothy's household: how Mrs. Nicholas Forsyte actually gained independence and an allowance of her own: how poor old James when he bought the Hondekoeter as a bargain at the picture auction had to bow to the judgment of the younger members of the clan and hide the huge glistening canvas of cocks and hens in the boxroom—*although it was a bargain:* how Eustace Forsyte, jammed among a proletarian crowd in the Tube during an air-raid, perceived that there was a people and couldn't deny that the people were human.

In all these stories you are led to smile at the old Forsytes, but the laugh is not always against them. They reveal in such tales as **"Hester's Little Tour," "Aunt Juley's Courtship," "Midsummer Madness"** and the wistfully lovely **"Cry of Peacock"** that they are of our clay, with ordinary passions and, men and women alike, capable—even in 1845 or 1880—of trampling on their Prayer-books or throwing their caps over the mill. Behind their stucco façades and brass doorknobs they are not all the time shrinking from life, but considering how to dominate it. How Napoleonic is the march whereby Roger Forsyte extricates his daughter Francie from her entanglement with the "fourpenny foreigner" who played the fiddle! And Mr. Galsworthy loyally points the moral. Francie opined that her father would "have a fit" when he learned of her engagement.

> There . . . she went wrong in her psychology, incapable, like all the young Forsytes, of appreciating exactly the quality which had made the fortunes of all the old Forsytes. In a word, they had fits over small matters, but never over large. When stark reality stared them in the face they met it with the stare of a still starker reality.

This profound verdict on the caste he has described so often and so lovingly, despite his castigation of it, throws light on that beautiful last chapter to which one is drawn back again as one reads it. For this quintessential Forsytism is concentrated in Soames as he faces in old age the strain of the War. With his stubborn Victorian distaste for the whole idea of England in a European conflict, and his tenacity in maintaining that she must yet see the thing through; with his hatred of the vapouring and the panics, and his inarticulate furious patriotism—there he stands, the epitome of a generation. We leave him on Armistice morning under the dome of St. Paul's.

> He went because it was big and old and empty, and English, and because it reminded him. He walked up the aisle and stood looking at the roof of the dome. Christopher Wren! Good old English name! Good old quiet English stones and bones! No more sudden death, no more bombs, no more drowning ships, no more poor young devils taken from home and killed! Peace!

Farewell, forgotten sentry over old treasure-chests!

Percy Hutchison (essay date 1930)

SOURCE: "New Tales of the Forsyte Clan," in *The New York Times Book Review,* October 12, 1930, p. 1.

[*In the following laudatory review of* On Forsyte 'Change, *Hutchison commends the insightful and familiar nature of the stories in the collection.*]

The nineteen stories in John Galsworthy's new volume are so many episodes, farcical, grave, satirical, as the case may be, in the lives of that Forsyte clan the history of which has for so long been the major occupation of England's distinguished novelist. No doubt there are persons who have never heard of the Forystes, but with these the present writer refuses to converse. He merely informs them that in *On Forsyte 'Change* they will find a collection of some of the very best short stories they have encountered in recent years, varied of mood and perfect in execution. And that they had best, after reading them, familiarize themselves with the book's background, namely, the history of the Forsytes, as contained in *The Forsyte Saga* and *A Modern Comedy*. By so doing not only will they find that the present stories suddenly enrich and broaden and grow immensely more humane, but they will become acquainted with a family they have always known and yet never quite known.

If evidence were lacking (as evidence is not) of the reality of the scores of persons that walk in and out of the Forsyte pages, from *The Man of Property* to *Swan Song,* the appearance of *On Forsyte 'Change* would convince the most skeptical. For in doing these addenda—or whatever one wishes to call the stories of the book—Mr. Galsworthy gives ample proof that, although he had buried the greatest of the clan, namely, Soames, not only could he not part company with the people he had created, but, and more significant, they refused to part company with him! It makes one realize why the Forsyte novels appeared one after another, six of them, over a period of years. Every individual lived, moved, had his corporeal and spiritual (and sometimes less than spiritual) existence as truly as the flesh and blood members of one's immediate family and group of friends. And, astounding robots of a writer's imagination, once set in motion, they took life into their own hands and reduced their originator to the rank of amanuensis. Yet there was a limitation to their activities. John Galsworthy was master of their fate to the extent that it was his to say what of their chronicle should go between any set of covers. One sees now how much he left out—Aunt Juley's courtship, the reduction to vassalage of "Nicholas-Rex" by his gently spoken wife, June's first lame duck, young Jolyon's escapades at Cambridge. In the march of the major narrative these little side affairs could not find place. Mr. Galsworthy either wrote them and put them aside, or he did not write them out; they stayed in his memory; and now, with others, they come together to fill in the picture.

The first story, **"The Buckles of Superior Dosset,"** is the least impressive. And the reason is clear. In going back to Dorsetshire and the founding of the family, Galsworthy, in his chronicle, was interested solely in indicating how deep in the soil the roots of the Forsytes penetrated. The present story, if it accomplishes anything, makes more insistent that idea, but it contributes not a great deal more except, perhaps, further evidence as to Forsyte honesty and solidity.

The reviewer may not dwell on each separate piece. The second is a delicately ironic fragment (the year is 1860, but the irony is of all dates) in which Young Jo is taken by his father to the British Museum to see the Egyptian mummies. And dad, half asleep over his cigar, remembers going back to Dorset to find a railway running where his mother's grave had been and her bones scattered none knew where. And suddenly the youngster makes him see that that is just what had been done to the Egyptians.

"Hester's Little Tour" is next; just such a frightened half-moment of romance as must have come to thousands of the Victorian maidens who were the spinster aunts of the present generation. And this is followed by **"Timothy's Narrow Squeak,"** as it came to be called on Forsyte 'Change. Timothy was one of the major persons of the chronicle, and with this story the preset collection acquires the reality missed by its predecessors. Timothy lived with Galsworthy as the others did not. The "narrow squeak" (in 1850) was when Timothy wrote a proposal of marriage to a young woman, but refrained from handing her the letter when he saw her driving alone with a man in a hansom cab. It is impossible to stop over each vignette. But **"Revolt at Roger's"** is a charming story of children—it has to do with the Francie and Eustace—as sensitive a reading of the child mind and heart as one may wish to find. And **"Dog of Timothy's"** is such a whimsical account of an ingratiating stray as could come only from such a lover of dogs as John Galsworthy. It is the laughing complement to the dog's death so movingly done in the *Saga*. And it is shrinking Aunt Juley who beards

her tyrannical brother and insists that the homeless canine shall remain. Galsworthy, in these sly contributions to the Forsyte history, takes especial delight in giving the subdued middle-century females a fling at rebellion. And the very furtiveness of his sallies in this direction makes the wit more relishable. The all but complete omission of Irene from the collection suggest that Galsworthy feared he might disturb the delicacy of his earlier handiwork if he added thereto. Yet in the handful of pages of **"The Peacock Cry,"** when Soames parts with his dignity to stand outside Irene's window two weeks before their marriage, one is brought to a fuller realization of the possible depth of Victorian passion (and passion for possession) than even the chronicle conveyed. The tragedy of Soames, however much he brought it on himself, is become more poignant, more deserving of sympathy.

> Blotted against the lamp-post he stayed unmoving, aching for a sight of her. With his coat he blotted the whiteness of his shirtfront, took off his hat and crushed it to him. Now he was any stray early idler with cheek against lamp-post and no face visible, any returning reveler.

In **"Francie's Fourpenny Foreigner,"** an Italian violinist whom Francie for the moment thinks of marrying, is a passage which throws light on the whole Forsyte history. It is not impossible that the author, when first he planned his work, jotted it down in rough form as a guide. If so, then the double trilogy to which the full narrative grew is cumulative evidence of a psychological reading never deviated from. Francie, knowing well the disapproval of her father, writes her mother of her intention, adding that "she was going to sleep at her studio till father had got over the fit he would certainly have."

> There again she went wrong in her psychology [writes Galsworthy], incapable, like all the young Forsytes, of appreciating exactly the quality which had made the fortunes of all the old Forsytes. In a word, they had fits over small matters, but never over large. When stark reality stared them in the face they met it with a stare of a still starker reality.

The two war pieces, **"A Forsyte Encounters the People"** and **"Soames and the Flag,"** the latter the most truly masterly of them all, are of Galsworthy's best. The passage just quoted, besides its function in the story in which it appears, is also a sort of beam flashed ahead on these two pieces. Perhaps the stark reality of the war could not be met, even by a Forsyte, with a reality more stark; but it was met with a stare that did not waver. Both pieces go deep; and both make the reader appreciative of something in human beings he may not always have recognized. It will be the guess of many that John Galsworthy, now that he has come down so far in the gossip on Forsyte 'Change, will again put his ear to the ground and listen to what they say of Fleur, and Mont, and Jon, and, of course, of Soames in his later days. The record will be eagerly awaited. To the readers of the *Saga* and the *Comedy* they who people the pages have ever been as real as for their creator. It is pleasure unalloyed whenever they walk.

John and Ada Galsworthy, circa 1930.

Percy Hutchison   (essay date 1935)

SOURCE: "Fragments and Remainders of Galsworthy's Writing," in *The New York Times Book Review,* October 27, 1935, p. 2.

[*Below, Hutchison provides a generally positive review of the stories included in* Forstyes, Pendyces, and Others.]

Perhaps the striking thing about this collection of crumbs from the abundant board set by John Galsworthy is the proof of the degree to which this paramount delineator of persons and manners lived with and among the characters of his creation. Few authors, we fancy, ever dwelt with a single family for so many years as Mr. Galsworthy dwelt with the Forsyte clan.

Take only the year 1906, when Soames, who was to live in the novelist's pages for twenty years, made his first bow in *The Man of Property.* Nearly contemporaneous was *The Country House,* not primarily concerned with Forsytes. Yet, Mr. Galsworthy could not get this under way without their assistance. On the third page of four subsequently deleted introductory chapters we meet James Forsyte, and soon we find ourselves also in the company

of his brother George, and of both Old and Young Jolyon. With these excised pages, grouped under the title **"Danaë"** (Danaë Bellew, née Thornworthy), Mrs. Galsworthy opens her anthology from the unpublished sheets left by her husband. Those who feel that *The Country House* is also among his distinguished works will wish to see this omitted beginning.

Following this fragmentary group come eight short stories never before published, with the exception of **"The Doldrums,"** which appeared in the not generally available volume, *From the Four Winds.* Aside from the fact that the mate in the story is none other than Joseph Conrad, who was first officer of the sailing ship *Torrens,* on which, when a young barrister, Galsworthy made a voyage, the story is a remarkably moving sea tale. It is somewhat marred by Galsworthy's attempt to reproduce phonetically the foreign accent which was doubtless Conrad's at at that date, otherwise the brief picture of the opium-ridden ship's doctor dying miserably "because the breeze came too late" is probably just as fine a thing, inherently, as Conrad himself could have made it at the time. The date of **"The Doldrums"** is 1896. All the other pieces, with one exception, were written between 1922 and 1927.

"Water" is the first of these tales, and unquestionably the most subtle of them. Henry Cursitor, who writes publicity for the Rangoon Wayside Waterworks Trust, headquarters London, is so much a born promoter that when it is evident that the R. W. W. W. T. is going on the rocks, not from the water under it but because of the water within, he follows the pipe-dream of an Australian who would develop for irrigation a subterranean river in the torrid bush. Too late Cursitor discovers it a pipe-dream—when he finds his guide floating off on a wreath of opium smoke. But on his return the Londoner falls in with a man who wants to develop Basque copper. So off he gets at Gibraltar to follow another dream.

"Told by the Schoolmaster" is as pathetic a tale of the war as one is likely to meet, and also as original. The story is developed with mastery. It is a tale of patriotism, love and intense ignorance in a losing conflict with the harsh, if necessary, justice of wartime discipline.

We are glad to have seen these short stories, each and all. If they add nothing to the stature of John Galsworthy, they take nothing away, albeit none is quite up to the high standard of those he preserved in the omnibus volume *Caravan*. Unfortunately, not so much is to be said for the remainder of the book.

To be sure, all that Mr. Galsworthy had to say about authors and their works is pertinent; often of more than ordinary critical value. But most of his comments are to be found elsewhere. Of course, the merit of an inclusion here lies in the fact that Mrs. Galsworthy has brought together those most important, thus giving a fairly comprehensive view of his critical range and an insight into this novelist's attitude toward literature. What he has to say of Dickens, Tolstoy and Hudson is the most arresting.

The third part is made up of four unpublished dramatic fragments.

Isabel Paterson   (essay date 1935)

SOURCE: A review of *Forsytes, Pendyces and Others,* in *New York Herald Tribune Books,* November 3, 1935, p. 12.

[*In the review below, Paterson terms the stories in* Forsytes, Pendyces and Others *"incisive analyses of the middle-class temperament."*]

Several of the items included in this final miscellany from the pen of John Galsworthy come under the head of unfinished business, including two plays never completed. There are also two more "dramatic pieces," one a "cut" from "Escape," the other a one-act squib. A number of short stories, all rather slight, a fantasy, a few prefaces and speeches, graceful compliments to fellow authors: and several chapters entitled "Danae," originally written as the beginning of *The Country House,* but discarded at the time, make up the lot. Their main interest is associational.

One of the short stories, "The Doldrums," rescued from a volume long since out of print, was written in 1896, and contains in fiction form a souvenir of Galsworthy's first meeting with Joseph Conrad, when Galsworthy was a passenger aboard a ship on which Conrad was first officer, and both unknown to fame.

It is interesting to note what a strong impression Conrad made. Though in this short story he appears only as a commentator, one feels that nevertheless it was written about him. He is the most striking character, with his "brown, almond-shaped Slav eyes, the eyes of a man who has been many times to the edge of the world and looking over," the "cynical and mournful curve" of his mouth, his pointed beard, his accent, all somehow expressive of the cast of his mind. To a young man who saw, or thought he saw, a terrifying apparition, Galsworthy makes this fictional character drawn from Conrad say: "You are not to be pitied, you know, you are to be envied: a man does not often see these things." This is a curious confirmation, perhaps an anticipation, of Conrad's definition of his purpose as a writer, "to make you see."

The short story is otherwise insignificant. The "Danae" chapters contain some of Galsworthy's incisive analyses of the middle-class temperament, in which he excelled. This is specifically the second generation of the middle class, the sons of the men who had sufficient character and initiative, to get on in the world. The fathers may not have had very lofty aims, but they had decision and bold minds within the scope of their desires. The sons became either mild "liberals," or cagey bachelors about town, or sober householders, taking refuge in their family life as behind barricades, from the temptations of the world, the flesh and the devil. They were essentially timid souls. Here are perfect examples of the first two types: and they reveal themselves most fully in their attitude toward Danae Bellow, a careless feminine hedonist.

Gregory Vigil, the endowed idealist, "respected" Danae; he respected her far too much to pay her bills when she hinted she was hard up. He thought of her as "his good angel, keeping him from himself," that is, by sentimentalizing about her he dodged any dangers from other women. Giving her money would have "sullied his high conception of her." In fact, giving her anything whatever would have injured his delicate sensibilities. He just hung around, mooning over her.

George Forsyte, the man about town, was worried by Danae's attraction for him because "to George, born and bred to commercialism, this passion for a married woman, coming not in his first youth, was charged with the countless doubts and fears that hover around passion in a fundamentally commercial mind. . . . Was it worth it?—for a woman that you couldn't make out, that had something in her that beat you altogether? George's reason told him, No. He was putting his money on the wrong horse, and with all his might he tried to hedge his bets."

Galsworthy had his own sentimentalities, and his work was a little too "timely" to outlast his time long, but for the low-down on his own class, he should always be a valuable reference source. He had no mercy on those comfortable, cautious men he knew so well, the "men of property."

P. C. Gupta   (essay date 1963)

SOURCE: "The Short Stories of Galsworthy and Other Studies," in *The Art of Galsworthy and Other Studies,* Vidyarthi Granthagar, 1963, pp. 53-60.

[*In the following excerpt, Gupta provides a thematic analysis of Galsworthy's short stories, concluding that his body of work is "truly impressive in its range and compass."*]

Galsworthy wrote a large number of short stories of various lengths, some like **"A Stoic"** or **"Salvation of a Forsyte,"** almost novelettes, others mere skits like **"Nightmare Child,"** **"Strange Things,"** **"Expectations,"** or **"A Woman."** These are an organic part of his work as a writer of fiction and "help to fill in and round out" the corners in his work. They are, like the Interludes in the Forsyte Chronicles, pendents or "cameos" serving as essential ornaments in his work.

These stories follow the same technique of brooding, introspective writing which characterises the novels. It is as though his work, representing life such as he knows it, has been cut into various lengths, and some of it has been labelled as "novels", and some as "short stories". The essential temperament behind them, the mood, the craftsmanship are the same.

Fifty-six of these stories have been assembled together in *Caravan*. There are still others like *On Forsyte 'Change* and *Forsytes, Pendyces* etc. to be added to these. This by itself is impressive in volume and range, but when one remembers the intensity of perception behind this work, its sheer quality of excellence and the fact that novelettes and snippets from the chronicles of Forsytes or Ferrand only fill in the crevices and serve to round off the edges in his great epic work, one cannot help wondering at his mastery as the supreme chronicler of our times.

These short stories deal with some of the most basic things in life—love, hate, beauty, ugliness, war, hunger. They present to us a vast panorama of life, representing various cross-sections of life—rich, old men who on the basis of their gilt-edged securities, their "safe six percent, dream" of beauty; variations on the theme of Old Jolyon dying as he watches beauty step across the lawn towards him, or Soames brooding over his old masters or Fleur; down and outs who have foundered and touched rock-bottom; daughters of joy, the love of lad and his lass, lonely dogs eating their hearts out; all sorts and conditions of men and women enacting the passionate, forbidding drama of life, mostly ending in death and defeat. There is a haunting sense of beauty brooding over this sad, tragic world and the refrain seems to be: how beautiful the world is, but also how cruel!

Some of the best short stories of Galsworthy are portraits of old men, sometimes old women as in **"The Grey Angel."** Galsworthy finds old age beautiful, mellow and wistful, a rare vintage which has only improved its quality with the passage of time. It is well-known that the inspiration behind these portraits was his father, a wonderful old man who filled Galsworthy's heart with awe, reverence and affection.

One of the finest of these stories is **"A Stoic."** It has been dramatised and filmed as *Old English.* Heythorp has a shrewd business head, functions as a strong chairman at Boards of Directors' and Shareholders' meetings. He devotes himself to pleasure and the excitement of beauty, particularly as represented in the younger generation. Ultimately, he falls a martyr to his ideal—love and beauty.

All these qualities are found in quintessence in **"A Portrait,"** an abstract, generalised version of his father's character. He is presented at the age of eighty, possessing balance, poise, money; a well-ordered life and no edges or sharp corners. The story of his life is summed up in its movement through eighty years' span from conservative liberalism to liberal conservatism!

Other portraits of the same kind are to be found in **"A Man of Devon,"** **"A Knight"** and the **"Juryman."** These are eccentric people, crusty and case-hardened. Galsworthy pierces the shell and tries to get behind their defences. The nearest approach to a villain in these short stories is Ventnor, the lawyer, in **"A Stoic."** Even he has much of the human being in him, though he behaves like a cad and a blackguard. Usually, Galsworthy analysing human character, finds much excuse for men as they are, though rarely for man's existence on earth.

Galsworthy has painted an equally large number of portraits of down-and-outs, men who have seen the yawning gulf below and stood on the edge of things. The finest of them are Gessler in **"Quality"**; Miles Ruding, "the man who kept his form"—an ex-gentleman, a war-veteran, reduced to taxi-driving; Caister, the jobless actor in **"The Broken Boot"**; the crossing sweeper in **"The Choice,"** the eccentric in **"Ultima Thule,"** the French barber in **"Courage,"** and many another. In these stories we see the accusing finger pointed at society which has no use for all this talent, goodness, nobility, this overflowing human energy, and allows it to go waste. We seem to see the chasm opening at our feet, ready to swallow all and everything. In stories like **"Compensation,"** **"Conscience"** or **"Once More"** the bottom seems to have been touched!

The two worlds are presented by Galsworthy with superb skill and mastery. In *Fraternity* he placed them close together, side by side and studied their contrasts. But in these stories, they exist apart, in isolation from each other, strips cut from life and presented to us without comment. He seems to put special emphasis on the rich, human quality of the material, indifferent seemingly to the source from which he draws it. Wealth or destitution, what does it matter?—he seems to say. All that matters is the rich, overflowing quality of life. And this he offers to us, with both hands, in abundance and plenty.

He glanced back at the past of these lives, prosaic and uninspring today, and discovered passionate drama, haunting undertones of romance in the background. Who could have imagined, for instance, that Swithin Forsyte concealed behind that stiff, heavy, slow-moving exterior, a story of exotic adventure, participation in revolutionary intrigues and romance, exciting and deeply moving? And yet, such was the strange experience of his youth; also that of Aunt Ann. The veil is lifted for a moment and behind the drab mask of Forsyteism we find warm, palpitating human hearts.

There are among these stories, sketches of life with hardly any movement in them. Also, there are tales of rich and thrilling adventure. Such is **"A Man of Devon"** which behind the quiet and somnolent beauty of the Devon country presents a tale of wild love, hate and adventure such as the Elizabethans might have applauded at the Globe Theatre. It is as though the spirit of Drake and his sea-dogs lives on and moves once again through Zachary.

In **"The Apple Tree," "Stroke of Lightning," "The First and the Last"** and other stories wild passion and drama have been unfolded. Writing of love, his most common theme, Galsworthy writes with an intensity and verve unequalled in other stories by him. Love is a wild passion-flower, blooming where it will and leaving men strangely helpless under its influence. In **"Stroke of Lightning"** it strikes down its victims suddenly like a flash of lightning in the desert.

The objects of these amours are often girls, loose and immoral in the social sense. Galsworthy brings out the innate nobility of human nature behind all these illicit and shabby adventures. One of the finest of such portraits is in **"The First and the Last,"** regarded by many as the best of Galsworthy's stories. In **"The Apple Tree," "Solution of a Forsyte"** and some other of his stories love offers itself without counting the cost or any wordly calculations. In these stories, Galsworthy's soul cast away its shell of respectability and expressed itself in the manner of the French naturalists, Flaubert, Maupassant or Dumas younger.

There is a haunting sense of beauty brooding over Galsworthy's sad, tragic world and the refrain seems to be: how beautiful the world is, but also how cruel!

—P. C. Gupta

Along with the themes of social justice and love, another preoccupation of Galsworthy is beauty. He writes with extreme sensitiveness of the beauty of the earth and sky, particularly the countryside, of flowers and the stars, the great heart of nature breathing all-unawares and moving human hearts, startling them out of their self-possession. He speaks of "the true Devon country-hills, hollows, hedge-banks, lanes dipping down into the earth, or going up like the sides of houses, coppices, cornfields, and little-streams wherever there's a place for one . . . the downs along the cliff, all gorse and ferns . . ." [*Caravan*, **"The Apple Tree"**]; of

> the quick chatter of the little bright trout-stream, the dazzle of the butter-cup, the rocks of the old "wild men"; the calling of the cuckoos and yaffles, the hooting of the owls; and the red moon peeping out of the velvet dark at the living whiteness of the blossom . . . a sort of atmosphere as of some old walled-in English garden, with pinks, and cornflowers, and roses, and scents of lavender and lilac cool and fair, untouched, almost holy . . ."

In **"Spindleberries"** while this beauty of earth is described with a sense of wonder, almost breathless, it is suggested that it is a blasphemy to dream of ever being able to depict it through colour and brush. All that one can do is to stand in reverence and admire it. One can never capture it through pen or paint.

> Beauty, by starlight and sunlight and moonlight, in the fields and woods, on the hill-tops, and by riverside . . . Flowers, and the flight of birds, and the ripple of the wind, and all the shifting play of light and colour which made a man despair when he wanted to use them.

A number of these stories were written under the shadow of the First World-War. They have an ache behind them, a dislike of all forms of cheap, tawdry Jingoism. He writes about the victims of mass-hysteria worked up by the press, pacifists, German war-internees, their families. The pack is on the trail and the victims at bay. Galsworthy returns to his pet theme that the individual left to himself is harmless enough; it is only when he gets together in a pack that he becomes dangerous. This is the theme of a small skit, **"The Pack,"** which reminds one of his full-length play on the same subject, *The Mob*. He opens this story with the following words:

> "It's only," said H., "when men run in packs that they lose their sense of decency. At least that's my experience. Individual man—I'm not speaking of savages—is more given to generosity than meanness, rarely brutal, inclines in fact to be a gentleman. It's when you add three or four more to him that his sense of decency, his sense of personal responsibility, his private standards, go by the board . . ."

These short stories of Galsworthy cover a wide range in technique and quality. He specializes in portraits, stories of slow, imperceptible movement of life, almost studies of still-life, like **"Spindleberries,"** but there are also stories of wild passion and drama, like **"The Man of Devon"** or **"The First and the Last."** There are stories with only character in them, as **"A Portrait,"** or only incident or atmosphere in them as **"The Black Godmother"** or **"Spin-**

dleberries." There are also stories perfectly rounded in form, with plot, character and setting, an onward rush and movement in them. They are, like **"The Apple Tree"** or **"The First and the Last,"** some of his best work.

Galsworthy's peculiar gift as a writer is to convey a vivid impression of life in its gentle, onward flow like that of a river in open, flat country. His technique may best be studied in a story like **"A Stoic,"** where the thoughts and movements of Heythorp have been captured and reproduced in all their life-like quality. Heythorp attends a meeting with the Board of Directors, walks home, bathes, broods, dines, sleeps, ultimately triumphing over his debtors and killing himself deliberately with drink, balking them of victory, setting at naught the instructions of his doctor. Heythorp's whole life is passed in review, as he sits brooding in a chair:

> Alone again, he had browsed, developing the idea which had come to him.
>
> Though, to dwell in the heart of shipping, Sylvanus Heythorp had lived at Liverpool twenty years, he was from the Eastern Countries, of a family so old that it professed to despise the Conquest. Each of its generations occupied nearly twice as long as those of less tenacious men . . . Born in the early twenties of the nineteenth century, Sylvanus Heythorp, after an education broken by escapades both at school and college, had fetched up in that simple London of the late forties, where claret, opera, and eight per cent for your money ruled a cheery roost. Made partner in his shipping firm well before he was thirty, he had sailed with a wet sheet and a flowing tide; dancers, claret, clicquot, and picket, a cab with a tiger; some travel— all that delicious early-Victorian consciousness of nothing save a golden time. It was all so full and mellow that he was forty before he had his only love affair of any depth. . . .

> [*Caravan,* "A Stoic"]

Thus stroke by stroke, the portrait grows, with infinite deft touches. The whole procession of life passes through the consciousness and is transferred to the paper with care and skill, reminicent of a landscape or portrait painter. The sharp, crisp strokes, small, infinite almost in number—and impression is piled on impression. Finally, the picture emerges, complete, life-like, moving in its deep human content and quality.

There are other occasions, when the torrent rushes forth as in a flood, with no dykes to contain it. The whole story of English society, Victorian, post-Victorian, war-years and post-War is thus presented as a grand old pageant before us. A hundred characters, carved out from all sections of society, pass before us and haunt the memory for ever afterwards. It is an elaborate canvas which is ultimately put before us after including all these brief, intimate studies. The effect of the whole is truly impressive in its range and compass.

Discussing the art of the short story in the Foreword to *Caravan* Galsworthy writes:

If the writer of the short tale submit himself to the discipline demanded by the crisp and clear expression of his genuine fancies and his genuine moods, he has submitted to quite enough.

As the untaught spider spins his delicate rose-window and assures it against wind and rain by sheer adjustment—not a thread too many or too few—so let us writers of short tales try to spin out of our own instinct and vision the round and threaded marvel. If in it we catch some hopeful editor and hold him to ransom—all the better for us; but if we don't we have none the less fulfilled our being, and that is our real end in life.

The writing of Galsworthy is a marvel of delicate adjustments, economy and restraint in expression—a model of crisp and clear expression, "not a thread too many or too few". It is no less certain that through these stories, he has "fulfilled his being" and served his "real end in life," because he has successfully held in his joined hands the flowing waters of life and offered them to the reader for a brief, fleeting moment which, however, remains with him a warm, palpitating memory for ever.

J. Henry Smit   (essay date 1966)

SOURCE: An excerpt from *The Short Stories of John Galsworthy,* Haskell House, 1966, pp. 43-6, 56-60, 143-46.

[*Below, Smit explores stylistic aspects of certain stories by Galsworthy and discusses his contributions to the development of the short story genre.*]

Stories belonging to the older school were more or less rounded off, had a beginning, contained dramatic action, and ended at a definite point, in a word contained plot.

With the earlier fiction we are well aware that the events narrated are over and done with. The first paragraphs rouse our curiosity, and from that moment the plot progresses with a singleness of purpose to the conclusion. The shapeless short story of the present age is a far different matter. Modern writers, especially the followers of Tchehov,

> have tried to effect an illusion of present time, to produce a feeling of immediacy.

> Using every device of artifice to generate an atmosphere of the real they have attempted to seduce the reader with a vivid sense of intimacy. Time and place grow up around the reader just as they surround the characters throughout the sequences of reading or action (Derek Stanford, "Elements of Modern Fiction," in *Modern Reading* 12).

Life because of its innumerable aspects seems blurred and devoid of all form. As experience is continuous writers of the modern school depict only a segment of existence and style it "a slice of life."

This concentration on the living minute—this desire to create the very texture of the moment in hand has been suggestively termed "Actualism" by the American critic Carl Grabo.

Galsworthy cannot be regarded as an exponent of the Actualist school. It seems that he wanted to prevent certain critics from calling him old-fashioned when he gave a quotation from Don Quixote as the motto to his collection of short stories **Captures**: "Soft and fair, Gentleman, never look for birds of this year in the nests of the last."

It is as he wanted to say: "Do not look for new wine in old bottles. Expect no modernity."

As the leader in *The Times* put it on Galsworthy's death, he did not have "any particular tricks, any discomforting theories about style or method." We have already seen that Galsworthy knew and highly appreciated the short stories of Tchehov and Katherine Mansfield. In contradistinction to numbers of writers who thought that the modern method was easy, he realised that is was very difficult.

[In] *Candelabra* we read:

> Writers may think they have just to put down faithfully the daily run of feeling and event, and they will have a story as marvellous as those of Tchehov. Alas! things are not made "marvellous" by being called so, or there would be a good many "marvellous" things to-day. It is much harder for a Westerner than for a Russian to dispense with architecture in the building of a tale, but a good many Western writers now appear to think otherwise.
>
> I don't wish to convey the impression of insensibility to the efforts and achievements of our "new" fiction; which has so out-Tchehoved Tchehov that it doesn't know its own father. Very able and earnest writers are genuinely endeavouring with astounding skill to render life in its kaleidoscopic and vibrational aspects; they are imbued too with a kind of pitiful and ironic fatalism which seems to them new perhaps, but which is eminently Tchehovian, and can be found also in the work of many other writers whom they affect to have outgrown. There is that which is genuinely new in the style and methods of some of these adventuring new fictionists, but I do not think there is anything new in their philosophy of life.
>
> They have thrown over story and character, or rather the set and dramatic ways of depicting story and character; but they are no more philosophically emancipated than their forebears, Turgenev, De Maupassant, Flaubert, Henry James, Meredith, Hardy, France, Conrad.
>
> . . . . .

There are but few short stories by Galsworthy written in the modern undramatic manner.

"The Japanese Quince" is one of them. Some people find the story difficult to understand, see no point in it.

One reader who wrote to Galsworthy that she did not know what to make of the story received the following reply.

> Dear Madam,
>
> **"The Japanese Quince"** attempts to convey the feeling that comes to all of us—even the most unlikely—in the spring. It also attempts to produce in the reader the sort of uneasy feeling that now and then we run up against ourselves. It also is a satire on the profound dislike which most of us have of exhibiting the feelings which Nature produces in us, when those feelings are for one quite primitive and genuine. And there are other aspects. No wonder it puzzled you—when I come to think of it.
>
> Yours very truly,
> John Galsworthy.

The story which was intended to express a certain mood begins and ends "in medias res"; it presents us with, to use the expression again, a slice of life. The initial sentence shows us Mr. Nilson opening the window of his dressing-room. Thinking that the peculiar sensation he experienced might be indigestion he decided to take a stroll in the Gardens.

The bushes budding in the sunshine emanated a faint sweet lemony scent. A blackbird burst into song.

There was the bird perched on a little tree.

> He stood staring curiously at this tree, recognising it for that which he had noticed from his window. It was covered with young blossoms, pink and white, and little bright green leaves both round and spiky; and on all this blossom and these leaves the sunlight glistened. Mr. Nilson smiled; the little tree was so alive and pretty! And instead of passing on, he stayed there smiling at the tree. "Morning like this!" he thought: "and here I am the only person in the Square who has the —— to come out and ——!"

But he had no sooner conceived this thought than he saw quite near him a man with his hands behind him, who was also staring up and smiling at the little tree. Rather taken aback, Mr. Nilson ceased to smile, and looked furtively at the stranger. It was his next-door neighbour, Mr. Tandram, well known in the city, who had occupied the adjoining house for some five years.

The two gentlemen exchanged some trivial remarks, and once more gazed up at the blossom.

And the little tree, as if appreciating their attention, quivered and glowed. From a distance the blackbird gave a loud, clear call.

Mr. Nilson dropped his eyes. It struck him suddenly that Mr. Tandram looked a little foolish; and, as if he had seen himself, he said: "I must be going in. Good morning!"

When Mr. Nilson had reached the door of his house he cast another look at the tree.

"The sound of a cough or sigh attracted his attention. There, in the shadow of his French window, stood Mr. Tandram, also looking forth across the Gardens at the little quince tree." And then the story ends: "Unaccountably upset, Mr. Nilson turned abruptly into the house, and opened his morning paper."

. . . . .

In *Caravan* this short story is coupled with **"The Broken Boot,"** a little tragi-comedy on a theme which Galsworthy repeatedly treated viz. the irony of life.

A down and out actor meets a rich friend who treats him to a grand dinner. With great bravado he manages to hide his split boot, the symbol of his poverty from his friend's eyes. The actor sits in the restaurant till the waiter asks leave to clear the table.

"Certainly—I'm going."

Some young women who have recognised him, look up. "Elegant, with faint smile, he passed them close, so that they could not see, managing—his broken boot."

. . . . .

We are not told if the actor's luck took a turn, whether happier times ever came for him. The story ends here in the middle of things, its author has given us a slice of the poor actor's life.

"The Bright Side," a very touching story, ends with the words with which the heroic cockney woman tries to console her husband as he returns home, grey and bent, broken by his long internment.

"Once More" has a very similar ending.

After one of his escapades the young husband of a flower-girl comes home, frozen and starved. The flower-seller had been furious at the thought of him spending his money with some woman about town.

> She could have seized and twisted back his head. In fancy she was already doing this, putting her eyes close to his, setting her teeth in his forehead—so vividly that she had the taste of blood in her mouth.

But when she saw him, a poor helpless creature "she pulled his head down on her breast, and with all her strength clutched him to her. And as the fire died, she still held him there, rocking him and sobbing, and once more trying to give him of the warmth of her little body."

Other stories giving segments of life and ending in medias res are **"Late 299," "The Juryman"** and **"Manna"**. . . .

. . . . .

Michael Joseph [in his *Short Story Writing for Profit*, 1923] states that the plot is the skeleton of the story and quotes Gilbert Frankau where he says that before a short story-writer begins he must have a clear idea of his tale.

> A complete visualization of the story he means to tell, of the characters who play their part in it and of the local colour in which those characters play their part, is absolutely necessary. A writer must be able to see in his mind's eye the whole story. It must be as visible to him as the wood of his writing-desk or the walls of his study.

When discussing the climax in the short story Joseph points out that some authors prefer to write their endings first, which plan has the merit of fixing the desired final impression and of enabling the writer to balance the remainder of the story. An artistically perfect short story must be well balanced; and the balance of a story undoubtedly hinges on the climax.

Now Leon Schalit [in his *John Galsworthy: A Survey*, 1929] states that the creative procedure of Galsworthy was entirely unconscious, almost occult one might say.

In Mr. Schalit's survey it says:

> Galsworthy does no preliminary work, never prepares a scenario to a play, or a plan, or a summary to a short story or novel. . . . He never knows in advance how he is going to end. . . . The end is there when inspiration ceases. He believes that the whole imaginative process is far more subconscious than conscious, at least in his own case. This disposes of the contention of many critics, that this or that of Galsworthy's works is constructed, a pure matter of intellect.

W. H. Hudson (An introduction to the *Study of Literature*) mentions that the great novelists Scott, Thackeray and Trollope, did not have any distinct plan when they commenced a new work.

They left the story to unfold itself as it went along. Galsworthy told of a similar proceeding when he delivered the Romanes Lecture in the Sheldonian Theatre at Oxford, taking for his subject *The Creation of Character in Literature*.

After first treating of biography and of drama he came to discuss the novel and said:

> The vitality and freedom of character creation derives, as a rule, from the subconscious mind instinctively supplying the conscious mind with the material it requires. In attempting an illustration of that process you must forgive my being personal for a moment. I sink into my morning chair, a blotter on my knee, the last words or deed of some character in ink before my eyes, a pen in my hand, a pipe in my mouth, and nothing in my head. I sit, I don't intend; I don't expect; I don't even hope. I read over the last pages. Gradually my mind seems to leave the chair, and be where my character is acting or speaking, leg raised, waiting to

come down, lips opened ready to say something. Suddenly, my pen jots down a movement or remark, another, another, and goes on doing this, haltingly, perhaps, for an hour or two. When the result is read through it surprises one by seeming to come out of what went before, and by ministering to some sort of possible future.

Galsworthy was thinking more especially of his novels when he spoke these words but the fact remains that his personal friend Leon Schalit wrote that Galsworthy never prepared a plan or a summary for a short story.

There must have been exceptions to this rule.

In certain instances Galsworthy must have had an idea, if not the certainty, of how a tale was going to end.

Although Galsworthy hardly ever (never?) wrote out a synopsis for a tale beforehand it cannot be denied that the best of his short stories, especially those called "long-short", show the plot of a well-built play with a careful exposition, development, crisis and resolution.

—J. Henry Smit

When Mr. Joseph said that some writers preferred to write the ending of the story first he undoubtedly had in mind the so-called surprise-ending, stories with what Galsworthy labelled "sting in the tail" (Foreword to *Caravan*).

Galsworthy did not favour this kind. There are but two examples viz. **"Acme"** and **"Blackmail."**

In the surprise-ending story the climax, dénouement and conclusion are identical. The effect is gained by keeping the reader in the dark (or at least in suspense) until the end of the story.

The "point" of the story is given in the last line and the story has evidently been written to illustrate it. It must be deemed an impossibility to begin a tale of this type without knowing how it is going to end. The same would seem to apply to the after-dinner stories and expanded anecdotes, as everything depends on and leads up to the surprising "sting in the tail."

"The Patriot," for example, is the sort of good story Galsworthy picked up at a gathering of lawyers as worth treasuring, and casting into a shapely form.

"Had a Horse" is a joke which by Galsworthy's love of horses and racing was made into a long-short story. He evidently so loved the telling of it that it grew under his pen and fingers to an almost inordinate proportion for an anecdote. Galsworthy, however, must have known all along how the joke would end.

In the cases where they are not reminiscences pure and simple, the stories which have a so-called loose plot will have been started without Galsworthy knowing where they would lead him.

The story is composed of a number of detached incidents having little or no connection among themselves. The unity of the narrative does not depend on the action but on the person of the story-teller who binds the scattered elements together.

"Quality" and **"The Man Who Kept His Form"** both open with an early memory of the writer's schoolboy days. In the latter story the name chosen for the hero, that of Bartlet (Mrs. Galsworthy's maiden name) and the records kept at Galsworthy's former college prove that at any rate part of **"The Man Who Kept His Form"** is autobiographical. As in the stories **"The Choice"** and **"Ultima Thule,"** both with an "underdog" as hero, seven meetings, seven episodes are described.

Galsworthy summons up remembrances of things past and makes the flight of time subserve the ends of art.

Time for him is Time with the scythe, Time the destroyer, the thief of youth.

He relates the stories of his friends—in **"The Choice"** of a crossing-sweeper, in **"Quality"** of a shoemaker.

When the story begins shadows already hang over both; the crossing-sweeper has before him the alternative of the workhouse or the river; the shoemaker, still prosperous, is beginning to suffer from the competition of machine-made goods.

Business or pleasure removes the narrator from the scene; in time he returns to find his friends a little older, a little poorer, a little nearer the breaking-point. Again, after doing all in his power to relieve them, he goes away, returning once more to find the process of mortification a degree or two advanced. And with the wanderer's seventh visit they are dead, and their place knows them no more.

The oldest story of this type is **"A Knight,"** (1900). **"Courage"** followed in 1904. Other examples are **"A Strange Thing," "The Nightmare Child," "Compensation"** and **"The Dog It Was That Died."**

Although Galsworthy hardly ever (never?) wrote out a synopsis for a tale beforehand it cannot be denied that the best of his short stories, especially those called "long-short", show the plot of a well-built play with a careful exposition, development, crisis and resolution.

The exposition is the most important part in Galsworthy's stories. His interest is primarily in the characters and in the surroundings of which they form part. Both are depicted at great length. Indeed, in **"The Neighbours"** the exposition takes up three quarters of the story. Once the scene has been set, the action soon leads to the crisis that is sometimes only just hinted at. Thus in **"The Neighbours,"** Galsworthy instead of the murder describes the glamorous heat of the sense-bewitching night.

The plot-idea develops from character and environment. It is clear that Galsworthy preferred this development of plot from character to the development of character from plot. He did not provide his readers with stories containing plenty of action and incident, in which stories character is of secondary importance.

. . . . .

The short story provides little or no scope for the development of character, which was not the strong point of Galsworthy the novelist. Many of his tales are just intensely dramatic situations. Miss Sheila Kaye-Smith found fault with this fact in Galsworthy's novels.

She said: "He likes to take a situation, examine it from characteristic and conflicting points of view, and show the effect it has on different lives, but he never attempts to develop it, to start a chain of events from it, mould characters by it."

This is not the place to go into Miss Kaye-Smith's criticism that Galsworthy left his characters at the close of a novel much as we knew them at the beginning. In a tale at any rate the unfolding of a situation, with its effects on character and corresponding reactions provides us with the singleness of purpose, with the totality of impression, which is one of the characteristics of the short story.

Many a reviewer praised the crude and sensational plots in Galsworthy's **From the Four Winds,** the book which he ordered to be destroyed, as nobody should be allowed to read his "first sins."

In his "Platitudes Concerning Drama" Galsworthy wrote:

> The demand for a good plot, not unfrequently heard, commonly signifies: "Tickle my sensations by stuffing the play with arbitrary adventures, so that I need not be troubled to take the characters seriously. Set the person of the play to action, regardless of time, sequence, atmosphere, and probability!"

There is no reason why—mutatis mutandis—one should not read "short story" instead of "the play" in this quotation. The idea remains the same.

The conclusion of all this is that Galsworthy's tales show no particular inventiveness of plot. To use Mr. E. J. O'Brien's terminology and division, they are character-type stories rather than plot-stories. . . .

. . . . .

In the early stages of novel-writing there is little or no description to be found. No attempt is made to give a realistic reproduction of things actually seen, there are no references to the faces, figures and dress of the characters, there is no painting of their homes and surroundings.

Sir Thomas Malory in his *Morte d'Arthur* is satisfied with the bare statement that a certain knight was riding through a wood, and then passes on at once to the adventure that he met with there.

This paucity of description remains throughout the stretch of many years. Thus we find no descriptive passages at all in Defoe's novels. After Sir Walter Scott, however, most writers have taken great pains to give their readers a clear image of the characters and a detailed picture of their surroundings.

This fidelity of representation, the insistence upon details called *realism,* we also find in Galsworty's writings.

Whenever a new personage appears Galsworthy gives a full description of his features and figure—in the case of a minor character a clever thumb-nail sketch is given.

As the story goes on many little traits are added to the initial description and the reader is constantly reminded of the character's physiognomy and characteristics, but all these details are given *indirectly.*

When once the characters have been introduced to us by the author they are further only shown us via the eyes of others—the description is now indirect.

Megan, the country-girl in **"The Apple Tree,"** will serve as a good example.

We see her first as she is outlined against the sky, carrying a basket; the sky is visible through the crook of her arm.

> The wind, blowing her dark frieze skirt against her legs, lifted her battered peacock tam-o'-shanter; her greyish blouse was worn and old, her shoes were split, her little hands rough and red, her neck browned. Her dark hair waved untidy across her broad forehead, her face was short, her upper lip short, showing a glint of teeth, her brows were straight and dark, her lashes long and dark, her nose straight; but her eyes were the wonder—dewy as if opened for the first time that day.

In the evening Garton, one of the two walkers who have met the lass Megan, descants on the Celts and on "the exquisite refinement and emotional capacity of that Welsh girl."

Ashurst, Garton's friend, does not listen, thinking, as he is of the girl's face. "It had been exactly like looking at a flower, or some other pretty sight in Nature."

Garton suggests going to the kitchen in order to see some more of her. If Galsworthy gives us a full description of the characters when they are introduced, he does the same with every new scene. Galsworthy depicts the kitchen for us, a white-washed room with rafters, to which smoked hams are attached. There are flower-pots on the window-sill, and guns hanging on nails, queer mugs, china and pewter, and portraits of Queen Victoria. A long, narrow table of plain wood is set with bowls and spoons, under a string of high-hung onions. Two sheepdogs and three cats lie here and there. The men are gathered round the recessed fireplace. The women are preparing the meal.

Seeing them about to eat, the two friends withdraw.

They are sorry to leave the "colour in the kitchen, the warmth, the scents". Their being together for days on end has made them rather moody.

Garton's remarks about Megan irritate Ashton. In his irritation he throws up the window and leans out. The description that follows of the dusk is very true, natural and convincing.

Galsworthy makes use of the device he so often employs of not only telling us what his characters see but also what they hear, feel and smell, he describes all their sensations.

In the gathering dusk Ashurst sees everything dim and bluish, the apple-trees are but a blurred wilderness. The air smells of woodsmoke from the kitchen fire. From the stable comes the snuffle and stamp of a feeding horse. As the young man holds out his hand, he can feel the dew on the upturned palm. Suddenly he hears Megan putting her cousins to bed overhead. After a skirmish of giggles and gurgles, a soft slap, a laugh so low and pretty that it makes him shiver, silence reigns.

The next impression the reader gets of Megan is from a conversation Ashurst carries on with her. We see her then only from his point of view.

He is so full of the girl that he cannot help telling an old farm-labourer how she had put a poultice on his hurt leg.

"She'm a gude maid wi' the flowers. There's folks zeem to know the healin' in things."

Ashurst smiles. "Wi' the flowers!" A flower herself.

The next persons to augment our knowledge of Megan are the two little boys at the farm. They tell Ashurst how a gipsy bogle sits on a rock in the trout-stream at the back of the farm.

"Megan zays 'e zets there. . . . . .

"D'yu think 'e might want to take me away? Megan's feared of 'e."

"Has she seen him?"

"No. She's not afeared o' yu."

"I should think not. Why should she be?"

"She zays a prayer for yu."

"How do you know that, you little rascal?"

"When I was asleep," she said: "God bless us all, an' Mr. Ashes. I yeard 'er whisperin'."

The spring is working in Ashurst's blood. Every now and then "with the sensation a cat must feel when it purs" he becomes conscious of Megan's eyes—those dew-grey eyes—fixed on him with a sort of lingering soft look.

Then one Sunday in the orchard under the pink clusters of the apple blossom he comes upon her, standing there quite still, very pretty, with her fine, dark hair, blown loose about her face, and her eyes cast down.

Yielding to a swift impulse, he kisses Megan's forehead. Then he is frightened—she goes so pale, closing her eyes, so that the long, dark lashes lie on her pale cheeks. One moment he is proud at having captured "this pretty, trustful, dewy-eyed thing." The next he thinks of what the world would say. He sees her aunt's shrewd face hardening, the gipsy-like cousins coarsely mocking and distrustful. And the village pub!—the gossiping matrons he passes on his walk; and then—his own friends—Garton's smile—so ironical and knowing! Disgusting! When she has been deserted the girl comes to Torquay to look for him. Ashurst sees her there on the sea front.

> Megan—Megan herself! was walking on the far pathway, in her old skirt and jacket and her tam-o'-shanter, looking up into the faces of the passers-by. . . . moving, not with her free country steps, but wavering, lost-looking, pitiful—like some little dog which has missed its master and does not know whether to run on, to run back—where to run.

Ashurst begins to follow the little sad figure, but almost at once checks himself.

> The little spot of faded colour, her tam-o'-shanter cap, wavered on in front of him; she was looking up into every face, and at the house windows. Had any man ever such a cruel moment to go through?

He has begun to love an aristocratic girl who radiates an atmosphere as of some old walled-in English garden, with pinks, and corn-flowers, and roses, and scents of lavender and lilac, an atmosphere of healthy, happy English homes.

> To go back to the farm and love Megan out in the woods, among the rocks, with everything around wild and fitting—that, he knew, was impossible, utterly. To transplant her to a great town, to keep, in some little flat or rooms, one who belonged so wholly to Nature—the poet in him shrank from it.

What Galsworthy wrote concerning Irene in the preface to **The Forsyte Saga** also applies here. The figure of Megan is never present except through the senses of other characters.

Megan is mostly seen through the eyes of Ashurst who notices her every movement and change of colour. The image thus gradually obtained is so life-like that one visualizes the pathetic figure and commiserates with her as she wanders along the front, watching for her lover; Megan in her delicate chastity and her despairing search.

Beauty cast her veil over Megan's death as she did over Ophelia's in *Hamlet*.

> 'Er was lyin' on 'er face in the watter. There was a plant o' goldie-cups growin' out o' the stone just above 'er 'ead. An' when I come to luke at 'er face, 'twas luvly, butiful, so calm's a baby's—wonderful butiful et was.—'T was June then, but she'd a-found a little bit of appleblossom left over somewheres, and stuck et in 'er air.

To Galsworthy the eye verily was the mirror of the soul. When Ashurst had surprised Megan, had accidentally seen her pretty act of devotion as she kissed his pillow at the hollow made by his head the night before, the girl

> put her hands up to her cheeks, but her eyes seemed to look right into him. He had never before realised the depth and purity and touching faithfulness in those dewbright eyes . . .

Ashurst, who is somewhat of a dreamer, has large remote grey eyes which sometimes fill with meaning and become almost beautiful. Megan's shrewd aunt has a quick, dark eye, like a mother wild-duck's, and something of the same snaky turn about her neck.

The farm-hand Joe is jealous of Ashurst.

His blue eyes with their flaxen lashes—they look like those of a young and angry bull—stare fixedly at his rival.

The lame farm-labourer's eyes have the upward look which prolonged suffering often brings.

In a single sentence Galsworthy makes the eyes convey the emotional significance of a whole character.

Old Heythorp, **"A Stoic,"** looks at his secretary.

> Only from those eyes could one appreciate the strength of life yet flowing underground in that well-nigh helpless carcase—deep-coloured little blue wells, tiny, jovial, round windows.

The convict's eyes (**"The Prisoner"**) are incarnate tragedy—all those eternities of solitude and silence he had lived through, all the eternities he had still to live through before they buried him in the grave-yard outside, are staring out of them.

Galsworthy knew the art of compressing much significance in a few words. Very often a single exclamation, a look, a smile or some other little gesture reveals as in a flash the whole history or typical traits of a character.

A little detail symbolizes all that has gone before, condenses the events of a long period of time.

"The Workers" contains a striking example.

> . . . there passed between his whitish eyes and the grey eyes of his wife one of those looks which people who have long lived together give each other. It had no obvious gleam of affection, but just the matter-of-fact mutual faith of two creatures who from year's end to year's end can never be out of arm's length of one another.

Other examples are:

> All those months of hatred looked out of their eyes, and their hands twitched convulsively. (**"A Feud"**)

> Whole centuries of antagonism glared out of their eyes (**"A Reversion to Type"**)

> Sometimes she rubbed her fingers on his hand, without speaking. It was a summary of their lives together (**"A Man of Devon"**)

Galsworthy often showed the inner significance of a gesture, of a look. Two recruiting officers have done their best among a crowd of farm-labourers.

> Hackneyed words, jests, the touch of flattery changing swiftly to chaff—all the customary performance, hollow and pathetic; and then the two figures re-emerged, their hands clenched, their eyes shifting here and there, their lips drawn back in fixed smiles. They had failed and were trying to hide it. (**"The Recruit"**)

Galsworthy painted his *dramatis personae* at the outset of his stories, he began by giving us portraits, but every time they re-appeared on the scene he referred again to their features or to their carriage and frequently added a little trait. He clearly visualized the people that throng his books but never forgot that if the readers were to retain these pictures reference must continually be made to their outward appearance.

It has already been pointed out that this is done indirectly. The author does not intrude himself, the references are, as it were, inserted, casually. Everything, the painting of the character's exterior, the gestures betraying what goes on beneath it, contributes towards the reader obtaining a lifelike image and true conception of the person depicted.

Galsworthy did not overlook the fact that environment is an important factor in life. The girl Megan is as much the product of her surroundings as Zachary Pearse, the man of Devon, is of his. The country they live in, their farms and kitchens are realistically described.

The importance Galsworthy attaches to soil, descent and surroundings is best seen in **"The Neighbours"** where description forms three quarters of the story.

First the landscape is depicted, a patch of moorland with a pagan spirit stealing forth through the wan gorse, gliding round the stems of the lonely, gibbet-like fir trees which peep out amongst the reeds of the white marsh.

The two cottages are then described and in the third place their inhabitants.

> They were all four above the average height, and all four as straight as darts. The innkeeper, Sandford, was a massive man, stolid, grave, light-eyed with big fair moustaches, who might have stepped straight out of some Norseman's galley. Leman was lean and lathy, a regular Celt, with an amiable, shadowy, humorous face. The two women were as different as the men. Mrs. Sandford's fair, almost transparent cheeks coloured easily, her eyes were grey, her hair pale brown; Mrs. Leman's hair was of a lustreless jet-black, her eyes the colour of a peaty stream, and her cheeks had the close creamy texture of old ivory.

Sandford—"that blond, ashy-looking Teuton" was feared—no one quite knew why.

> To see this black-haired woman, with her stoical, alluring face, (Mrs. Leman) come out for a breath of air, and stand in the sunlight, her baby in her arms, was to have looked on a very woman of the Britons. In conquering races the men, they say, are superior to the women; in conquered races, the women to the men. . . . No one ever saw a word pass between her and Sandford. It was almost as if the old racial feelings of this borderland were pursuing in these two their unending conflict. For there they lived, side by side under the long, thatched roof, this great primitive, invading male, and that black-haired, lithe-limbed woman of older race, avoiding each other, never speaking.

The bewitching paleness of the glamorous night hides the murder from the reader's eyes. The remainder of the story, the end, consists of Leman's, the lean and lathy Celt's confession.

In the country the simple, unspoiled people live nearer to nature; they bear the imprint of their surroundings.

In the town man has lost contact with the soil and has become sophisticated.

Instead of being a product of their surroundings it is they who print their personalities on the furnishing and decoration of their houses. The apartments of a towndweller mirror the character of their inhabitant.

> There are rooms which refuse to give away their owners, and rooms which seem to say: "They really are like this." Of such was Rosamund Larne's—a sort of permanent confession, seeming to remark to anyone who entered: "Her taste? Well, you can see—cheerful and exuberant: her habits—yes, she sits here all the morning in a dressing-gown, smoking cigarettes and dropping ink; kindly observe my carpet. Notice the piano—it has a look of coming and going, according to the exchequer. This very deep-cushioned sofa is permanent, however; the water-colours on the walls are safe, too—they're

by herself. Mark the scent of mimosa—she likes flowers, and likes them strong. No clock, of course. Examine the bureau—she is obviously always ringing for "the drumstick," and saying: "Where's this, Ellen, and where's that? You naughty gairl, you've been tidying." Cast an eye on that pile of manuscript—she has evidently a genius for composition; it flows off her pen—like Shakespeare, she never blots a line. See how she's had the electric light put in, instead of that horrid gas; but try and turn either of them on—you can't; last quarter isn't paid, of course; and she uses an oil lamp, you can tell that by the ceiling. (**"A Stoic"**)

In **"The Indian Summer of a Forsyte"** Irene's tasteful rooms and Old Jolyon's treasures and pictures are described.

Keith Darrant's study with its rich furnishings, the leather-bound volumes and oak-panelled walls reflect the successful solicitor.

The opening sentences of **"The First and the Last"** evince Galsworthy's love of description. The delineation of Darrant's study might have come from the pen of Oscar Wilde who revelled in depicting luxurious interiors. The first six sentences contain some twenty references to colour. The green shade of the reading-lamp lets fall a dapple of light over the Turkey carpet and over the deep blue and gold of the coffee service on the little old stool with its Oriental embroidery.

> In red Turkish slippers and his old brown velvet coat, he was well suited to that framing of glow and darkness. A painter would have seized avidly on his clear-cut, yellowish face, with its black eyebrows twisting up over eyes—grey or brown, one could hardly tell, and its dark grizzling hair still plentiful, in spite of those daily hours of wig. . . .

. . . . .

Although the history of the short story may be traced back to the birth of civilisation, the development of the short story proper is a comparatively late one. Indeed, as a conscious expression of art its history begins little more than a hundred years ago with the American authors Irving, Hawthorne and Poe. In England Kipling was unquestionably the leader of the older generation of short story writers; among the great exponents of the 20th century English short story rank authors as Katherine Mansfield, Ethel Colburn Mayne, Stacy Aumonier and A. E. Coppard. John Galsworthy is also a master of the short story but in surveys of its history his name is frequently overlooked. Galsworthy is primarily regarded as a novelist and a dramatist. His novels and dramas have all been subjected to various studies but his short stories have so far been comparatively neglected.

What may be the reason that, for instance Evelyn M. Albright in her excellent study *The Short Story* gives no attention to John Galsworthy?

> It will be for posterity to decide if, and through which of his works, Galsworthy shall live on in the annals of literature.

Although his fame and popularity have already greatly waned in Great Britain, it seems safe to state that owing to the stimulus Galsworthy gave to the early 20th century drama he will be remembered as also for the "fashion" he set in writing family chronicles.

Did Galsworthy contribute to the development of the modern short story?

Undoubtedly he exerted influence but this was not of the same importance as his leadership in other literary spheres. . . . Galsworthy has given us some splendid examples of the short story, that he has enriched the world's literature with unforgettable tales as **"Indian Summer of a Forsyte"** and **"The Apple Tree."**

He had his own style; all his writings exude the special Galsworthy flavour, but he was not an innovator and did not stimulate a certain school or set a new mode of short story writing.

Kipling influenced Galsworthy's very first literary efforts, the short stories contained in **From the Four Winds** (1897).

In 1920 Galsworthy had all the remaining copies of this volume "his first sins" destroyed.

Of far greater moment than the influence of Kipling on Galsworthy's first immature attempts was the lasting influence of Tchehov, Turgenev and de Maupassant.

To Turgenev and de Maupassant Galsworthy "served that spiritual and technical apprenticeship which every young writer serves, guided by some deep kinship in spirit to one or other of the old past-masters of his craft" (*Castles in Spain*).

"Turgenev possessed my mind and soul at about the age of thirty" (**Forsytes, Pendyces and Others**).

Ward complains that it is a great pity that we cannot be ourselves, that our minds must be a patchwork of a thousand and one other minds.

> Though we travel the world over, we inevitably become composite creatures, intellectual mosaics made up of pieces gathered here, gathered there.

Like everybody else Galsworthy also underwent some influences but the resulting pattern of his "intellectual mosaics" was something entirely individual. The circumstances of his life, his education, his surroundings, friends and last but not least his wife made Galsworthy into what he was; all the influences were blended into something specifically his own. Could anyone else have written the splendid **Five Tales**? And is it at all impossible that these stories will probably be wider read by later generations than for instance the Forsyte series?

Galsworthy's short stories reveal more of Galsworthy the artist and the man than his other works do. Most of his

dramas are too much bound up with the sociological problems of his time to be of lasting interest and will very likely be forgotten. His short stories may prove to be of lasting value, and assure Galsworthy a place among the immortal names of English literature.

One of the reasons for the present popularity of the short story is that in the stress and rush of modern times people have not leisure enough nor the peace of mind to read lengthy novels. Man has grown impatient of those "great still books" (as Tennyson called them), over which readers were glad to linger in more leisurely ages.

Very few people will in years to come find time to read the complete history of the Forsyte family as given by Galsworthy in **The Forsyte Saga** and subsequent trilogies.

To become acquainted with the Forsytes the reader may, however, turn to the short stories in **On Forsyte 'Change** and get an excellent idea of Galsworthy the chronicler.

For Galsworthy's expressions of lyrical beauty he will read **"Indian Summer of a Forsyte"** and **"The Apple Tree,"** both captivating prose poems and probably the best pieces of all Galsworthy's writings. The concise form of the short story, with few characters and a simple uncomplicated plot, permits of perfection. In the novel on a large scale, with its various plots, its profusion and multicolours, in the drama with its elaborate construction, a writer can rarely approach the ideal. It may be that true perfection is only attainable in this shorter form, in the short story, of the brief lyrical poem or song.

Arthur Waugh once stated that for some not altogether inexplicable reason short story writing seemed to be generally alien to the English literary temperament.

> For the very qualities which constitute the essence of the short story—restraint, austerity, selection, the prevailing and controlling moral idea—for these the typically impetuous and fecund English temperament has neither the time nor the disposition. The short story is an essay in discipline and interruption, in which everything depends upon construction, the delicate choice and arrangement of effects, the gradual development and revelation of the idea—in short, upon artistry and soul. And it is a plain fact that the average English novelist cannot take his art seriously enough to master the methods of elimination and production essential to the writing of a satisfactory short story.

Curiously enough all the characteristics necessary for the perfect short story writer as enumerated by Arthur Waugh are found in Galsworthy. The restraint, the austerity, the moral idea, the self-discipline, the delicate choice and arrangement of effects, the artistry and the soul—they are all there.

"Indian Summer of a Forsyte" and **"The Apple Tree"** also contain ample proof that the criticism of those who maintain that Galsworthy had no poetical feeling is unfounded. Throughout his literary career Galsworthy was a subject for arguments—he was called cynically impartial and indifferent, bloodless and inhuman; he was regarded as a relentless, insidious special pleader, sentimental, narrow and biased, as a great artist, with the breadth and depth of vision that only the great can attain, as an honest but not very clear-sighted purveyor of fictions of the second class.

It is impossible that Galsworthy can have been all these very diverse beings. Now it is in his short stories that Galsworthy can be studied to the greatest advantage. In them we find his whole personality revealed and it is there that we can find the material to refute unfounded criticism.

There are many veins in Galsworthy's temperament. Passionless reflections on all the pros and cons of a case; the thoroughness and objectivity of the lawyer, sometimes carried to excess; the impulse to justice in the best sense of the word, and curiously mixed with it a great compassion for all who are weaker, or scurvily treated by man or nature.

The application of the term sentimentality to Galsworthy's works and life implies merely a lack of near acquaintance with either one or the other; . . . Galsworthy was not a dry and aloof man devoid of any humour.

We saw that in a subtle way Galsworthy imparts atmosphere to his short stories by stating what his senses undergo. Sight, touch, hearing, taste and especially smell are the means by which Galsworthy obtained that sensation of reality. He had a special genius for suggesting the spirit of passion. Over many short stories there is a strange brooding sense of a summer evening, an atmosphere of the passionate perfumed dusk which blots out the figures of the lovers, even as they hide their love from the eyes of the world.

In his short stories Galsworthy attained what Conrad referred to in the preface to *The Nigger of the "Narcissus"*:

> To arrest, for the space of a breath, the hands busy about the work of the earth, and compel men entranced by the sight of distant goals to glance for a moment at the surrounding vision of form and colour, of sunshine and shadows; to make them pause for a look, for a sigh, for a smile—such is the aim, difficult and evanescent, and reserved only for a very few to achieve. But sometimes, by the deserving and the fortunate, even that task is accomplished. And when it is accomplished—behold—all the truth of life is there: a moment of vision, a sigh, a smile—and the return to an eternal rest.

Roger Ramsey   **(essay date 1971)**

SOURCE: "Another Way of Looking at a Blackbird," in *Research Studies*, Vol. 39, No. 2, June, 1971, pp. 152-54.

[*In the following essay, Ramsey analyzes the role of the blackbird in "The Japanese Quince," concluding that "the reader is left with the pathos of life missed, life here*

understood as dark, mysterious, dangerous, not quite proper."]

Laurence Perrine's brief analysis of John Galsworthy's **"The Japanese Quince"** seems to have begun and ended all consideration of that very short story. In Perrine's view, the two characters, Mr. Nilson and Mr. Tandram, "are clearly meant to be representative of a social class," the ordered and measured life style of the British upper crust as it is reflected in several images, especially the cuckoo clock [*Literature: Structure, Sound, and Sense*, 1970]. The quince tree itself is "a radiant symbol for beauty, joy, life, growth, freedom, ecstasy" [Perrine, assisted by Margaret Morton Blum, *Instructor's Manual for Literature: Structural, Sound, and Sense*, 1970]. The men confront the tree but fail to respond adequately to it, thus missing out on a great part of life. The story is therefore static, almost inert, and the other "symbol," the blackbird who sings in the tree, "functions simply as part of the tree symbol."

But there is another way of looking at this blackbird and consequently at the action of the story. In the first paragraph, Mr. Nilson, from whose point of view the story is related, cannot judge the value difference between the tree and the temperature; both serve only to make it a comfortable day. At the close of the story, however, the quince "seemed more living than a tree." A dramatic change in Mr. Nilson's perceptions has indeed taken place; this is the action.

Mr. Nilson does not notice the blackbird until he is down in the courtyard; in fact, it is the blackbird's song which draws his attention to the "little tree, in the heart of whose branches the bird was perched." As Mr. Nilson admires the tree, Mr. Tandram suddenly appears. Without a word from Galsworthy, the blackbird disappears. Mr. Nilson looks "furtively at the stranger," and later he is "visited somehow by the feeling that he had been caught out." The two men have the same physical characteristics. All of this is mysterious to the reader, but to the prosaic Mr. Nilson it is merely awkward. Ill at ease, he offers a greeting as he passes Mr. Tandram and seems anxious to quit the tree, the courtyard, and the stranger.

To his surprise, Mr. Tandram detains him by responding heartily and engaging him in conversation. The exchange is superbly modulated by Galsworthy, at once oblique, vacuous, and indicative. Mr. Nilson finds himself picking up Mr. Tandram's informality and affability. When Mr. Tandram drops a "g" ("Quite a feelin'"), Mr. Nilson responds with "It was a blackbird singin'." When Mr. Tandram looks at Mr. Nilson "in an almost friendly way," Mr. Nilson responds by thinking to himself, "Nice fellow, this, I rather like him." Together they gaze at the tree, which quivers and glows as if acknowledging them.

The influence which Mr. Tandram seems to have on Mr. Nilson is abruptly truncated when "from a distance the blackbird gave a loud, clear call." Mr. Tandram immediately appears foolish to Mr. Nilson. They separate. As Mr. Nilson reaches the top step of his house, he pauses and notes the tree and the blackbird. "The blackbird had returned to it, and was chanting out his heart." Whose heart? The possessive pronoun is ambiguous. It likely refers to the bird, although it has not anywhere before been identified as male. It surely refers to Mr. Nilson, who has abandoned the "tree of life" but can now hear his own heart's call clearly.

The bird at the heart of the branches of the tree can then be identified with the unusual feeling Mr. Nilson has "just under his fifth rib." Its song is a plea for attention and a call to life, just as the bird literally directed his attention to the Japanese quince. Of course, Mr. Nilson ultimately rejects the call; it is a call to the darker places of the heart for which he finds no place in his regulated world. As Herbert J. Muller said long ago about Galsworthy's characters, "They do not come really to grips with life, they never know it profoundly" [*Modern Fiction: A Study of Values,* 1937]. It is also to be noted that Galsworthy never describes the bird's song as joyous; Perrine assumes this when he defines it as "the expression of lyric ecstasy" [Perrine and Blum]. Although Mr. Nilson rejects the call, he can no longer ignore it; he has been tempted.

As indicated earlier, Mr. Tandram has also tempted Mr. Nilson, drawing him very near to a meaningful human relationship. At this point it would appear that the blackbird and Mr. Tandram and the empty feeling in Mr. Nilson's heart are all one. They call Mr. Nilson to life. The parallels are clearly indicated when the reader notes two devices: the word heart applied to the blackbird's position in the tree and to Mr. Nilson's feeling of emptiness; the disappearance of the bird when Mr. Tandram appears and its reappearance when he leaves. A further, less obvious device is the use of the color black.

The darkness of the heart's recesses, the bird's blackness, and the black frock coat worn by Mr. Tandram imply the world of unknowns. Blackness may suggest nothingness, in the sense which Robert Martin Adams suggests: "Nothing is frequently what we do not know or cannot imagine" [*Nil: Episodes in the Literary Conquest of Void during the Nineteenth Century,* 1966]. It might suggest a destructive principle or element, in the manner of Conrad. (Dare one relate **"The Japanese Quince"** to "The Secret Sharer" which appeared in 1912, two years after Galsworthy's story?) Darkness might even suggest evil, as it has since *Beowulf.* Perhaps any enticement out of his routinely proper world would appear to Mr. Nilson as evil. In any case, the reader is not likely to honor Perrine's dictum: "There is no symbolic significance in its being black" [Perrine and Blum].

Finally, the reader is left with the pathos of life missed, life here understood as dark, mysterious, dangerous, not quite proper. As the bird chants out "his" heart, both Mr. Nilson and Mr. Tandram sigh. The failure to immerse himself in this "destructive element" makes Mr. Nilson almost nostalgic. As Muller says of Galsworthy, "His melancholy is a gentle melancholy, quite lacking in wild, strange, rebellious moments." The dark place of his heart continues to sing, to call, while Mr. Nilson returns to his morning paper, to an 8:30 breakfast, and to that other, safer bird song—the cuckoo clock.

Carol Gesner   (essay date 1972)

SOURCE: "Galsworthy's *Apple Tree* and the Longus Tradition," in *Studies in the Twentieth Century,* No. 9, Spring, 1972, pp. 83-8.

[*Gesner is a Panamanian-born American educator and critic. In the following essay, she determines the influence of classical Greek and Renaissance literature on Galsworthy's short story "The Apple Tree."*]

Galsworthy leaves his reader in little doubt of his intention to cast a Greek mood over his finest short story, **"The Apple Tree."** As the story opens, the dominant Greek chord is introduced. Ashurst, the leading character, is alone near a country roadside reading of the Cyprian (Aphrodite) in Murray's translation of the *Hippolytus* of Euripides, and meditating on the unachievable elysium of "the Apple Tree, the singing, and the gold," the elysium which may be perceived for brief moments of a human life, but which in reality may never be captured and held except in art. This reading announces the major theme of the story: the inexorable power and vengence of Aphrodite, and the helplessness of man to control his emotions and order his life against the will of the goddess. When the story has closed, the reader infers that the Cyprian's balm and bale underlay all of the action, all of the passion, all of the tragedy, which has been unfolded. He is assured of the correctness of his conclusion by the quotation of lines from the *Hippolytus* which serve as a restatement of the theme and, by repetition of the initial reference to the *Hippolytus* and to the Cyprian, bring the story to a closed circle, a device which is a common feature in the Greek novel. [The critic provides examples of Greek novels in a footnote: the *Chaereas and Callirhoe* of Chariton, the *Ephesiaca* of Xenophon of Ephesus, and *Daphnis and Chloe* of Longus.]

Pastoral details and allusions to Greek literature amplify the Greek mood: As Ashurst reads and muses on the Cyprian and the fleeting moments of beauty which taunt us, never to be captured " . . . as the face of Pan, which looks round the corner of a rock, vanishes at your stare," he recognizes the location as the scene of a major experience of his youth and he recalls the episode with Megan. At once we plunge into the past, into the pastoral setting of farm and farmhouse, brook and meadow, which was Megan's home. Here Ashurst is received with traditional pastoral offerings of cream, cakes, and cider, bathes in the stream, and thinks of Theocritus. A few days after he has joined the farm family Ashurst is in love with Megan and musing on the golden age in the garden of Hesperides, the fauns, the dryads, and the nymphs which dwell under the apple tree. When the story shifts from the rapture of love with Megan— Ashurst has been reading the *Odyssey* before their first assignation—to the cool propriety of Stella, we find that Stella is described as a "young Diana." In the second movement when Ashurst, already under the spell of Stella, sees Megan once more he wants her again "with a horrible intensity, as the faun wants the nymph."

Quite as Greek as these details and the theme is the plot structure. The overall parallel with the *Hippolytus* is immediately obvious: Hippolytus flouts the Cyprian

> . . . and seeks no woman's kiss
> But great Apollo's sister, Artemis,
> He holds of all most high.
>   [Europedes, trans. by Gilbert Marray, 1915]

The tragic consequences—the suicide of Phaedra and the death of Hippolytus—are the Cyprian's revenge. Similarly, when Ashurst denies his passion for Megan and turns to the cool arms of Stella, the "young Diana" (Artemis), he too has flouted the dictates of the Cyprian. Megan's suicide and his own mediocre marriage (" . . . he has learned not to be a philosopher in the bosom of his family") are the revenge of the goddess. Similarly obvious is the traditional argument over the relative advantages of town and country living found frequently in the classical pastoral. This is supplied by the strong contrast in the pastoral and urban episodes.

More obscure is the traditional Greek character of the pastoral scenes between Ashurst and Megan, the details of which can be traced to *Daphnis and Chloe,* a second or third century pastoral romance attributed to Longus, a romance which embodies in prose all of the pastoral traditions and moods which Moschus, Theocritus, and Bion embody in poetry. The essentials of the *Daphnis and Chloe* plot have been recognized as the source of the chief elements of a plot which evolved as traditional pastoral material during the Renaissance, and was used by Sidney in the *Arcadia;* by Spenser in Book VI of *The Faerie Queene;* by Shakespeare in *As You Like It, The Winter's Tale,* and *Cymbeline;* as well as by a host of lesser writers [Edwin Greenlaw, "Shakespeare's Pastorals," *Studies in Philology,* Vol. XIII, 1916. The same plot has also been related to *The Tempest* by Carol Gesner, "*The Tempest* as Pastoral Romance," *The Shakespeare Quarterly,* Vol. X, 1959]. From a study of these Renaissance sources, Edwin Greenlaw delineated what he described as a composite pastoral plot derived ultimately from Longus:

> 1) A child of unknown parentage, usually a girl, is brought up by shepherds or country folk. As a variant, she may be living among them in seclusion, her parentage a secret. Her superiority to her fellows is obvious.

> 2) A lover, who may be a foundling or a man of high birth in guise of a shepherd or a forester, is introduced.

> 3) The love story is complicated by a rival shepherd, usually a rude, bumbling, or cowardly person who serves as a contrast and foil to the hero.

> 4) Melodramatic incidents—the attack of a lion or a bear, etc.—give the hero opportunity to prove his prowess.

> 5) A captivity episode is introduced. The heroine is abducted; the hero comes to the rescue.

> 6) It finally develops that the heroine is of high birth and may marry the hero.

It is easy to see that in **"The Apple Tree"** Galsworthy has turned this ancient stock situation to good advantage, utilizing the traditional Greek plot, but at the same time modifying it to suit twentieth-century realities. First, Megan fills the role of the beautiful girl of shadowy origin living humbly among rude country folk, her obvious superiority unmistakable. In line with twentieth-century realism, Galsworthy could not make aristocratic parents suddenly materialize to lift her to the social rank of her lover. Instead, he sets her apart in a way that will convince the modern reader: She is related to the farm family, simple Devonshire folk, only by marriage. She originated in Wales; thus she is "a daughter of the bards," lovely and sensitive, a Celtic spirit imprisoned in the rudeness of a Devon farm. "Her shoes were split, her hands rough; but— what was it? Was it really her Celtic blood, . . . she was a lady born, a jewel," her lover muses.

The highborn lover who comes to disturb the pastoral calm of the twentieth-century heroine is Ashurst, the scholarly college man of poetic tastes and independent income in whom people found "a certain lordliness." Unlike his Renaissance counterpart, he can not in our century wear a disguise, but he appears in the informal gear of a hiker, not his conventional upper-class dress. This corresponds roughly to the garb of a shepherd or a forester conventionally worn by the pastoral lover.

The traditional rival shepherd, the rude bumpkin who loses to the courtly manners of the stranger, is supplied in the person of Megan's cousin Joe "in his soiled brown velvet-cards, muddy gaiters, and blue shirt; red-armed, the sun turning his hair from tow to flax; . . . ashamed not to be slow and heavy-dwelling on each leg." His inarticulate love is expressed by the traditional sexual attack on the maid, which is repulsed by the hero, giving him opportunity to prove that his superiority is physical as well as social and intellectual. Although Joe is certainly a foil to Frank, the reader never thinks of him as a rival, and were he dropped from the story the plot would be virtually unaltered. His presence and the episode of the attack can be explained as a convention of the pastoral tradition.

Twentieth-century realism demanded the omission of the last three stock points: thus no wild beasts attack the lovers; Megan is not held in captivity; and since no amount of magic can turn overnight a beautiful peasant girl into a lady of gentle rank, Galsworthy realistically, if tragically, does not let the lovers wed.

Other plot elements raise the question of whether Galsworthy's model was the source plot, *Daphnis and Chloe,* or the Renaissance adaptations. Of first importance is the matter of supernatural direction, an element which Greenlaw has not recognized in the Renaissance versions. Eros deliberately instigates the love of Daphnis and Chloe, and

Photograph of Galsworthy taken by H. G. Wells in 1898.

Pan and the nymphs assist his work and in motivating and manipulating other plot details. Similarly, the tragic love of Ashurst and Megan is attributed to the Cyprian, Venus-Aphrodite. "Was it just Love seeking a victim!" The role of Pan and the nymphs in *Daphnis and Chloe* is filled in **"The Apple Tree"** by the gipsy bogle, a local spirit described as hairy and fiddle-playing, thus as Pan-like in effect. Megan and her family firmly believe in the bogle and fear his appearance as a forecast of death. Similarly, Daphnis and Chloe have a deep fear of Pan, but the fear relates more to his awesome power than to a specific superstition. Further, the *Daphnis and Chloe* plot also features an elderly, philosophic shepherd who observes the youthful lovers with understanding sympathy. Frequently he guides or comments on their affairs. In **"The Apple Tree"** the elderly, lame workman fills this role. He tells Ashurst of Megan's unusual abilities with flowers and animals and of her tender and sensitive nature. He observes the ripening love and Megan's dejection at the loss of Ashurst. The old workman seems to have been the only one on the farm who understood what happened. It is his sensitive observation that interprets to Ashurst Megan's last days and death. The philosophic shepherd, Philetas, of *Daphnis and Chloe* has a close relative in Galsworthy's lame workman. His vestigial relatives in the Renaissance plots—such intellectual char-

acters as Jacques in *As You Like It* and Philisides of the *Arcadia*—have departed too far from Longus for us to consider them in relation to the Galsworthy story. But here the problem takes another turn in the character of Ashurst.

In the Renaissance plot the lover may be a foundling or a man of high birth in guise of a shepherd, but in the more obvious examples, the *Arcadia, The Winter's Tale, The Faerie Queene,* we find young men of courtly sophistication playing the hero's role—men of Ashurst stamp. But Daphnis, the progenitor of them all, although in the end he proves to have aristocratic parents, is in every way characterized as childish and naive; especially is his role as lover.

It would seem then that Longus as well as Euripides has cast his shadow on **"The Apple Tree,"** and his shade might well be called double, strong and clear in its classical outline and somewhat present in its Renaissance manifestation.

Catherine Dupré (essay date 1976)

SOURCE: "Sinjohn becomes Galsworthy," in *John Galsworthy: A Biography,* Coward, McCann & Geoghegan, 1976, pp. 66-71.

[*Dupré is an English novelist and biographer. In the following excerpt, she investigates the satirical nature of the short stories in* The Man of Devon.]

[It is in his] collection of stories, published under the title **The Man of Devon** in September 1901, that Galsworthy claims to have really found the satirical vein within himself. 'I owe Swithin much, for he first released the satirist in me, and is moreover, the only one of my characters whom I killed before I gave him life, for it is in the *Man of Property* that Swithin Forsyte more memorably lives' [Preface to the Manaton edition, Vol. IV].

Galsworthy's friend and biographer, R. H. Mottram, sees this story, **'The Salvation of Swithin Forsyte'**, as the real turning point in its author's career, and one of the most biographically significant that he ever wrote. I doubt if many modern readers would share this view; they would perhaps see Swithin Forsyte's greatest merit in his refusal to die, in his insistence on remaining instead lurking somewhere in his creator's mind, a fantasy of the future, a premonition of the great genealogy of Forsytes that was to come.

The Swithin Forsyte of the short story *does* die, but as he lies on his death bed his mind wanders into the past and relives an incident that is utterly uncharacteristic of him, or anything else in his life. At that moment, had he not run away from the experience, the whole course of his life would have been different from what it was, he himself would have become a different person. As a young man travelling in Salzburg, he comes across a strange group of

Hungarian exiles in a *bierhalle,* becomes involved in their quarrels, and falls passionately in love with the daughter of one of them, a young girl called Rozsi. He is tempted to marry her, but convention and prudence deter him. 'They meant him to marry her! And the horrid idea was strengthened by his own middle-class reverence for marriage . . . he was afraid of the other way—too primitive.' 'He set to thinking what such a marriage meant. In the first place it meant ridicule, in the second place ridicule, in the third place ridicule. She would eat chicken bones with her fingers . . .'

The choice is all too clear, to take this beautiful vision, to make it his own, this chance that has come to him, that will redeem his life from its dreary course, or to flee from it. He chooses the latter. But as he dies he is revisited by the ghost of Rozsi, who reproaches him for his cowardice.

'I could show you things,' she says.

'Where are you?' gasped Swithin; 'What's the matter? I'm lost.' . . . Suddenly aloud in his sleep, Swithin muttered, 'I've missed something.'

Again fingers touched his brow; again Rozsi's eyes were looking at him from the wall. 'What is it?' he asked, 'Can't I get out of here and come with you? I'm choking.' 'What is it,' he thought; 'what have I lost?' And slowly his mind began to travel over his investments . . . What is it? Things he had never seen, was never meant to see—sacrifice, chivalry, love, fidelity, beauty and strange adventure—things remote, that you couldn't see with your eyes—had they come to haunt him?

Galsworthy later revised this story and cut out most of Swithin's final dream, to the great loss of the story. When it was reissued in 1909 with *The Villa Rubein,* a very different version appeared entitled now **'Salvation of a Forsyte'**.

It is an allegorical tale, though the characters bear no sort of resemblance to Ada and John. Yet Ada was John's Rozsi; she was the chance which fortune sent him, the chance to break away from convention and to make this vision of beauty and all that it brought with it his own—in his case the world of imagination and writing. But both Swithin and John made the mistake of assuming that life contains only one such moment, failing to see that the gift of living lies in the ability to remain ever open and receptive to all the experiences that may come.

This story is perhaps the first example of what Galsworthy came to refer to as his 'negative method' of writing: in telling the story of Swithin Forsyte and his terrible death-bed realization that his life, now so nearly over, has in fact never been lived, Galsworthy is telling us the opposite of his own story. He did take his chance, his Ada, and from the struggles of *Jocelyn* we know that there were moments when, like Swithin, he had felt like jumping into his carriage and 'Flying back along the road faster than he had come, with pale face and eyes blank'.

Conrad had much to do with the publication of *The Man of Devon*. 'I've written to Blackwood,' he wrote, 'mainly for the purpose of insinuating amongst other matters that a quick decision as to your story would be welcome.' His negotiations were successful and the book was published by Blackwood in September 1901. Upon its publication Conrad wrote a most interesting letter to Galsworthy; the letter is dated 11 November 1901.

> There is a certain caution of touch which will militate against popularity. After all, to please the public (if one isn't a sugary imbecile or an inflated fraud) one must handle one's subject intimately. Mere intimacy with the subject won't do. And conviction is found (for others, not for the author) only in certain contradictions and irrelevancies to the general conception of character (or characters) and of the subject. Say what you like the man lives in his eccentricities (so called) alone. They give a vigour to his personality which mere consistency can never do. One must explore deep and believe the incredible to find the few particles of truth floating in an ocean of insignificance. And before all one must divest oneself of every particle of respect for one's characters. You are really most profound and attain the greatest art in handling the people you do not respect. For instance the minor character in *V.R.* And in this volume I am bound to recognize that Forsythe [sic] is the best. I recognize this with a certain reluctance because indubitably there is more beauty (and more felicity of style too) in the *M of D*.

Written at this early date this piece of criticism is astonishingly perceptive. Conrad points to a danger that is already apparent in Galsworthy's writing, that of shying away from what was most personal, 'a certain caution of touch'. Where Conrad was wrong, of course, was in suggesting that this element in his friend's writing would militate against popularity. Galsworthy was to know a success in his lifetime that none of his English contemporaries were to approach, though after his death it was this very impersonality that was to doom his work for many years to almost complete obscurity.

It is interesting, too, that Conrad should have praised his handling of the 'people you do not respect'; the negative method was already beginning to work, making a convincing case for Swithin, as it was, to a far greater extent, to make for Soames a few years later.

As Conrad says, **'The Man of Devon',** the title story of the book, is a far more beautiful and poetic piece of writing than **'The Salvation of Swithin Forsyte'**; it is a strange, almost whimsical story written in the first person as a series of letters. The heroine, Pasiance, is an extraordinary character; she has a wild savageness that is reminiscent of Emily Brontë's Cathy Earnshaw. Like Cathy, she is a child of her particular countryside; she knows nothing of the life of the town or the civilized world. In fact in this story Galsworthy sees his beloved Devon rather as the Brontës saw Yorkshire, or Hardy, Dorset; the countryside becomes another character in the story, a force that determines the lives of the people who live in it. Thus it contains within itself elements of tragedy that may ulti-

When on 31 January 1933 John Galsworthy died, he was indisputably the head of his profession. A month previously he had been awarded the Nobel Prize for Literature. After refusing a knighthood years earlier, he had in 1929 been made a member of the Order of Merit, the most prized of all the rewards in the gift of the Sovereign. He had been almost for twelve years the first President of the Founding Centre of International PEN, the organization that brought together writers from all parts of the world. . . . It was only natural that a Memorial Service should be held for him in Westminster Abbey. John Galsworthy represented English Literature to a multitude of people. Yet Virginia Woolf, the leading novelist of the Bloomsbury Set, recorded in her diary her thankfulness that 'that stuffed shirt' had died.

Mrs Woolf was not alone, not even eccentric, in expressing antipathy towards Galsworthy. It was a feeling that was shared by many in the early 1930s. His success, his attitude to life, the very fact that he was naturally regarded as the head of their profession was taken as a natural affront by some writers, particularly those who were growing in influence at the time. It was not the way he said it that annoyed them but what he said. During the 1930s his popularity declined sharply. It is natural that any author should go into a 'twilight' period for some years after his death, but in Galsworthy's case the twilight deepened into dark night, so much so that in the three standard works on the English novel written in the 1950s he gets no more than a passing mention, usually in a list of names of the also-rans.

David Holloway, in John Galsworthy, *International Profiles, 1968.*

mately destroy its own, as in the end it does Pasiance, who throws herself over the cliff because she believes her lover, Zachary Pearse, has deserted her:

Fancy took me to the cliff where she had fallen. I found the point of rock where the cascade of ivy flows down the cliff; the ledge on which she had climbed was a little to my right—a mad place. It showed plainly what wild emotions must have been driving her! Behind was a half-cut cornfield with a fringe of poppies, and swarms of harvest insects creeping and flying; in the uncut corn a landrail kept up a continual charring. The sky was blue to the very horizon, and the sea wonderful, under that black wild cliff stained here and there with red. There are no brassy, east-coast skies here; but always sleepy, soft-shaped clouds, full of subtle stir and change. Passages of Zachary Pearse's letter kept rising to my lips. After all he's the man that his native place, and life, and blood have made him.

With the possible exception of the story 'The Apple Tree' and a few very minor pieces, 'The Man of Devon' is unlike anything else that Galsworthy wrote; there is no element of satire here, no wish to reform or criticize; it is a tale of simple but passionate people set in the Devonshire countryside. Galsworthy is experimenting at this stage, seeking out his true métier, and it is interesting that two stories as different as 'The Man of Devon' and 'The Salvation of Swithin Forsyte' should appear in the same volume. But having found the satirist in himself, he is not easily going to reject his new weapon. Pasiance is the more beautiful character, but Swithin is the more powerful; the choice is made and Swithin Forsyte, in more than name, is to be the first child of Galsworthy's pen.

James Gindin (essay date 1987)

SOURCE: "'I'm Not Such a Fool as I Seem'," in *John Galsworthy's Life and Art: An Alien's Fortress,* Macmillan, 1987, pp. 114-52.

[*Gindin is an American educator and critic. In the following excerpt, he surveys the plots and major themes of Galsworthy's short stories.*]

Galsworthy's first published fiction is difficult to take "seriously". Several of the stories in *From the Four Winds* centre around the character of Dick Denver, a vagabond adventurer, in Canada or the West Indies, who seems derived from a boys' weekly. One story, **"The Spirit of the Karroo"**, recognizes the growing antagonism between the English and the Boers in South Africa, equating the English with generosity toward the natives and the Boers with an evil and cruelty finally avenged by the native spirit. Only a few years later, in another South African story, **"On the Veldt"**, published in the *Outlook,* 30 December 1899, Galsworthy's version of the conflict between Englishman and Boer is no longer a simple struggle between good and evil. In the later story, neither Englishman nor Boer can understand the value in the simple black man who will not sell his soul for material advantage. The 1897 stories, however, all rely on cultural stereotypes in spite of the range of the geographical settings. The one most talked about in the reviews, and most connected with Kipling, the first story in the volume, **"The Running Amok of Synge Sahib"**, has white men in the Fiji Islands on a hot tropical night telling stories. In the Conradian manner of narration within narration, like several of the other stories, one narrator tells of a half-black doctor who ran "amok" and held a knife over the speaker's baby, concluding that a buried strain of savagery exists within even apparently acculturated natives. In other stories, like **"Tally Ho Budmâsh"**, about a lost and incompetent Indian boy on the London Underground, the stereotypes are comic. More individually revealing than the use of cultural stereotypes, which Galsworthy questioned and abandoned within a few years, is the strain of noble character that runs through the stories. Doubtless the most unconvincing story in the volume is **"The Capitulation of Jean Jacques"**, in which some escaped convicts in a French colony kidnap the colonial governor's four-year-old daughter, but return her unharmed when she becomes ill. Equally noble, the governor allows them to escape. In this melodramatically-written tale in a dark and exotic setting, all the characters talk alike, as if they were brought up within the same English conventions of polite consideration. The story that [Ford Madox] Ford and [Joseph] Conrad picked to admire most, **"According to his Lights"**, is written with more restraint and less melodrama, but is also dependent on a noble gesture, a criminal returning money and securities to the uncle he intended to rob when he sees how feeble the old uncle is.

Galsworthy clearly was embarrassed by this volume of stories within a very short time. He never reprinted any of them, and he soon dropped the title from his list of publications. In the one copy he kept, he apparently, at some later time, went through the stories crossing out all the excess words. He excised a great many. After his death, Ada republished only one of the stories, **"The Doldrums"**, in the volume *Forsytes, Pendyces, and Others,* of occasional and hitherto unpublished pieces that she put together. As she explained in her preface, the story "gives true and striking portraits of Conrad . . . and of the narrator, Galsworthy. . . . Neither had then any intention of taking Literature as a profession." The story takes place on a ship caught in the hot, sticky, tropical doldrums. At night, a group of Englishmen are on deck telling stories, joined by the mate with dark, almond-shaped "Slav" eyes. Several interior stories illustrate points of national difference, such as Chinese from European. Later, the doctor, a rather Chekhovian character, is found dead, perhaps an overdose of opium, perhaps just the heat. The mate draws the themes together, explaining that the cause of death can't be entirely known, that national identities can't be entirely assimilated, and that there is a time between life and death, between identities, that is a twilight, a calm and unidentifiable state, like the doldrums. Although somewhat derivative and overwritten, the story does hold together imagistically and is probably the only one in the volume that justifies reprinting.

Another characteristic visible in a number of the stories in *From the Four Winds* is an attitude of chivalry, of giving up or denying the self in order to protect the woman. Even the vagabond Dick Denver can be noble and self-sacrificing when a woman is involved, making his renunciation sound like a triumph. The last story in the volume, called **"The Demi-Gods"**, can be read as a melodramatically falsified version of Galsworthy taking Ada away from his cousin Arthur, and the story has been praised as "the only story that really comes to life . . . in the collection" [Catherine Dupé, *John Galsworthy,* 1976]. In this story, the love affair is hopeless, prevented by the cruelty of prior marriage and circumstance. But the situation itself is left so vague and the emotions are so repetitiously and heavily elaborated that it reads like an endless litany of pain and self-denial. More effective, although apparently never published, is another story, written at about the same time by "John Sinjohn", entitled **"Passing"**. In **"Passing"** (a title Galsworthy used later for a 1914 essay, totally unconnected), an observer overhears one sailor telling another the story of a man confronting his unfaithful wife. When she admits the

infidelity, he throws her and her child out on the streets. The lover cannot help since he is off with his regiment. The layers of distance, the narrator thrice removed from his subject, palliate the effect of the story, but the prose is quicker, more spare, more controlled than any of the prose in *From the Four Winds*.

In his later recollections, Galsworthy viewed the stories much more as derivative literary exercises than as first approaches to his themes of chivalry or renunciation. An account of *From the Four Winds* and what happened to it provides almost the only light interlude in the 1932 Nobel Prize acceptance speech:

> From the title of that story [the first written], **"Dick Denver's Idea"**, you can tell how much of it can be traced to the inspiration of Bret Harte and how much to the influence of Rudyard Kipling. For nearly two years that tale and its successors exhausted my literary afflatus, and my experience was not unlike that of the experimenting aviators of a decade back, who were always trying to leave the ground and always coming back to the ground with the greater regret. And yet— my conscience not having yet been born—I was more proud of the vile little body which bound those nine tales under the title of *From the Four Winds* than I was of any of its successors. In 1920, possessed by the desire to prevent anyone else from reading that dreadful little book, I wrote to the publisher. He had twenty copies left. Since they had no value he parted from them with I know not what alacrity. Tempted three years later by my bibliographer, I sold them to the firm of which he was a member for a hundred pounds. In the boom which followed they fetched perhaps two thousand pounds. Twenty copies of my first and worst book fetched one hundred pounds apiece! Dear God, is there anything more absurd than the values of first editions? [H. V. Marrot, *The Life and Letters of John Galsworthy,* 1935]

. . . . .

During 1899 and 1900, while finishing *Villa Rubein,* Galsworthy was also working on a number of long short stories. He continued the work during the early part of 1901, and by that summer thought that four of them were ready for publication in a volume. In the 1921 preface to *Villa Rubein,* he remarks that in these stories, especially in those entitled **"A Knight"** and **"Salvation of a Forsyte"**, he first began to achieve a little of "that union of seer with thing seen" he had been working toward for five years. Nevertheless, he had more trouble getting the volume published than he had had with *Villa Rubein.* Duckworth, citing the novel's poor sales, refused. [Joseph] Conrad volunteered to help, and, early in August 1901, began a correspondence with Blackwoods. After several letters back and forth, requests for revision and cuts in length, four of the stories were published by Blackwoods as *A Man of Devon* in the autumn of 1901. Unlike the earlier work, each of these four stories is "written", each establishing a tone and a point of view which is consistently worked out and encompasses all the elements in the story. In the first, the title story, dedicated to his father, a young narrator from London, staying at a farm in Devon, tells, through letters, the story of a young girl's rebellion from her grandfather which leads eventually to her death. The narrator is always the outsider, sometimes comically as in his drinking whisky when everyone else drinks local wine or brandy and in his meticulous diagram of the rooms in the farmhouse, the placement of which enable him to hear the girl's tears. The outsider leads the reader slowly into the territory of the story, providing full descriptions of the lush farm, the changing weather, and the thick Devon land- and seascapes, and concentrating, like some of Conrad's ambivalent narrators, on a gradual immersion in the strange world. The narrator concentrates on the "feelings" he sees, the constant emotional conflict between the old man's "fierce tenderness" and the young girl's "restless, chafing", fond, and sometimes irresponsible temperament. The girl, Paisance, falls in love with Zachary Pearse, the adventurous and irresponsible son of a local seacaptain, who develops a scheme to grow rich by practising piracy on the Moroccan coast. Pearse defines his manhood as freedom, although the narrator sees him as a brutal opportunist with "no ideals, no principles". Paisance sees Pearse's kind of freedom as embodying the kind of God she is looking for: "Grandfather's God is simply awful. When I'm playing the fiddle, I can *feel* God; but grandfather's is such a stuffy God—you know what I mean: the sea, the wind, the trees, colours too—they make one *feel*." Prevented from sailing with Pearse by her grandfather and thinking of suicide, Paisance trips on the ledge of a cliff while watching Pearse's departing ship and falls to her accidental death.

The second story in the volume, written with crisper severity, is dedicated to his mother and called **"A Knight"**. A young narrator, at Monte Carlo in the 1890s, sees a rather old, trim, shabby, ex-military gentleman walking his dog near the casino every day. They begin to talk and the narrator learns that the gentleman, an American, had fought with Garibaldi for Italian freedom in 1860 and in the American Civil War. The narrator is rather surprised when, at a concert with the old gentleman, seeing a whorish-looking woman stared at and hearing a whispered "the brazen baggage", the military man fulminates:

> The hue and Cry! Comtemptible! How I hate it! . . . There are people to be found who object to vivisecting animals; but the vivisection of a woman, who minds that? . . . That her fellow-women should make an outcast of her? That we, who are *men,* should make a prey of her? . . . It is *we* who make them what they are.

This apparently random incident develops into the theme of the story, for, when the military man overhears two young Frenchmen casually insult a woman as "déclassé", he challenges the speaker to a duel and is killed. Later, the narrator discovers that the old gentleman was so protective of women, so much the "Don Quixote", because he was still defending his mysterious and unfaithful young wife, long since dead; looking at the old man's will, his careful protection of what little he had, the narrator recognizes him as "a knight". Done succinctly, the perspective of the story, presenting the "knight" as simultaneously outmoded, ludicrous and admirable, balances satire and pathos.

The third story in the volume, dedicated to Hubert Galsworthy, is called **"Salvation of a Forsyte"** and is the first of Galsworthy's works to introduce the Forsyte family, as well as the model for the later expansions of the Saga into the past that comprises *On Forsyte 'Change*. The story concerns Swithin, one of the Forsyte twin brothers, as he is dying in London in 1891, an old bachelor thinking back to his one journey to the Continent in 1850, "the only one of my characters", as Galsworthy said in his 1921 preface, "whom I killed before I gave him life". Remembering his trip with his twin James and a friend, Swithin recalls the time in Salzburg when he, siding automatically with the underdog, had defended a Hungarian in a fight in a café. Drawn into the life of a colony of Hungarians, nationalists and former freedom-fighters defeated in the aftermath of the continental uprisings of 1848, and having fallen in love with a vivacious and unpredictable Hungarian girl, Swithin decided to stay in Salzburg. He and the girl, Roszi, made love, and he lived more in terms of emotions and passions than he ever had in England. Awakening one morning to discover that the whole group, for political reasons, had hastened back to Hungary, Swithin followed, divided between attraction, fear, and shame for, as a middle-class Englishman, part of him was still distressed that "I've given myself away." Although he caught up with the family and was welcomed, he was unable to commit himself to the new life he saw, left and returned to join his twin. More than forty years later, his last words, spoken aloud in his revery, are "I've missed it." Developed slowly, with a careful analysis of Swithin's conflict and long imaginatively detailed descriptions of central Europe in the middle of the nineteenth century, the story is a convincing depiction of Forsyte self-denial that, for the most part, does not sink in its own nostalgia. The final and slightest story in *A Man of Devon* is **"The Silence"**, dedicated to his sister Mabel. Through a series of narrators within narrators, travellers and company directors, the story emerges of a manager in the remote part of an unnamed colony who runs his mine efficiently and profitably, manages strikes and native rebellions successfully, but kills himself when finally forced to report what has been going on. The final words of the report echo a theme frequent in Conrad's fiction, the ambivalently seen defeat of civilisation by the encroaching forest of darkness and silence. **"The Silence"** is, however, tame Conrad, and, although the story contains a number of sharply effective images, like the suburban villa of the company director near London described "as if the whole thing had been fastened to an anchor sunk beneath the pink cabbages of the drawing-room carpet", the theme here restricts any sense of experience too simply and rigidly, and the evocative richness of Conrad's kind of primeval darkness is never developed.

The four stories contain a number of elements that anticipate *The Man of Property*. Some of these are simply names, like Treffry and Forsyte, or classifications of character like the scene in which James' interest in "cures", in what other people think, in wills and in profit play against Swithin's characteristic focus on good food, elegant equipages of horse and carriage, and champagne. Galsworthy was also, in these stories, working toward some of the principal themes of *The Man of Property*. The fascination with emotional intensity that has Galsworthy almost seem to be visibly debating with himself in having Paisance think of suicide before tripping accidentally anticipates something of the more carefully developed treatment of the self-destructiveness of extreme emotion in Bosinney's death in *The Man of Property*. The theme of the nature of women, the questioning of what would be in our contemporary psychological terms the polarity between the madonna and the whore, is central to two of the stories. The theme, seen dramatically and from the outside, is the focus of **"A Knight"**. And the same question, the same scepticism that any woman can be relegated to a category like madonna or whore, is seen internally in Swithin's recollected debates with himself in **"Salvation of a Forsyte"**. Part of Swithin is the stereotype of his representation of family and society. When he realizes that Roszi and her family might have expected him to marry her, he is appalled: "Considering that she had already yielded, it would be all the more monstrous." Yet he dies knowing that this internalized attitude has led him to miss everything that matters. A few other, much slighter, stories written at about the same time, **"A Woman"** (1900) and **"The Miller of Dee"** (1903), demonstrate Galsworthy's growing sympathy for the woman labelled as social outcast and his interest in the complicated nature of the female, almost invariably more direct and more unconventional than the male.

John Sinjohn's *A Man of Devon* received as many notices and reviews as had *From the Four Winds*. Most of them were mildly favourable, and reviewers were beginning to pay Galsworthy the compliment of seeing him within a fictional tradition, as a modern Thackeray or a more laborious version of Emily Brontë. The most extended favourable review and probably the first instance of unequivocal public appreciation of Galsworthy by someone he did not know appeared in the *Graphic*. The reviewer thought all four of the stories "exceptionally worthy":

> All are tragic: but the tragedy is of the only right, that is to say, of the inevitable kind. Now and then Mr Sinjohn is to be suspected of having borrowed Mr Henry James's spectacles, and of seeing in a glance or a trick of habit more than such things can ever really mean, without attempting to say what it is he sees. But, after all, this is an extreme consequence of his insight into the infinite pathos of little things, and never blinds him to the import of the great ones [Marrot, *Galsworthy*].

Commentators since have generally followed the point of view that Ralph Mottram later suggested in calling the volume "Jack's true starting point". Mottram, in claiming particular "importance" for **"Salvation of a Forsyte"**, acknowledged the introduction of the family on which much of Galsworthy's reputation and "the social history of England rests"; he argued that this is the first example of Galsworthy's "exposition of the base of all genuine tragedy . . . the time factor that brings and withdraws opportunity"; he praised the treatment of Salzburg and of the "poor, proud, incomprehensible Magyar characters". Yet,

for Mottram, all these qualities were far less than the fact that "in this story as in no other that he wrote we can trace vividly by a sort of reflection what happened to Jack between 1895 and 1905, what part Ada played, fatefully, in his life, and what therefore survived indelibly moulded, to be the Ada and John Galsworthy of history" [R. H. Mottram, *For Some We Loved*]. The attitudes and perspectives of **"A Knight"** and **"A Man of Devon"** can, however, be read just as closely as can **"Salvation of a Forsyte"** to a "reflection of what happened to Jack between 1895 and 1905". "What happened" certainly concerned Ada centrally, but, in its objections to chauvinistic judgements, narrow codes of morality and imperialism, it concerned society, politics and more understanding of human nature as well.

Comment among Galsworthy's literary friends and contemporaries at the time showed more interest in and judicious appraisal of all four stories. Conrad, as administrator of the organization to help Jack Galsworthy become a writer, sent an early draft of **"A Knight"** (then called **"A Cosmopolitan"**) to Ford for his opinion and a version of **"A Man of Devon"** to Edward Garnett for his. Always smoothly flattering, Conrad wrote to Mabel, who had apparently written thanking him for his help to her brother,

> That I have detected the existence of that talent when in the nature of things it could not but be very obvious I shall always remember with pride, but in all conscience I must disclaim the credit you give me of being of help to him. One needs to be a very exceptional person to be of real use to his fellowmen. I've certainly talked, but had I never existed someone else would have found the same things to say—though not with the same loving care for his promise. That much I may admit without self-deception.

Conrad did, however, manage to inject something of his candid assessment: "I am afraid he can never look forward to other than limited appreciation. That he shall have it I feel certain—and even the other kind is possible too" [Letter, September 5, 1900, in Marrot]. Acting still as intermediary, Conrad reported to Galsworthy that Garnett had appreciated **"A Man of Devon"** "much more than is his nature to show to the author himself", although he had a few minor reservations about the "lack of some illustrative detail" in the characterization of Zachary Pearse [Letter, undated (probably September, 1900) in Marrot]. Garnett soon wrote Galsworthy a long letter, the first in a series of many over the next ten years, in which he went through the manuscript almost page by page, expressing agreement or disagreement with the fictional strategy, encouraging and giving advice for improvement. Garnett began his letter by saying that both he and his wife liked the story, thought it done with "no faltering, no falsity" and felt "the subtle changes of mood and emotion". He then went on to pick out passages in which he felt Galsworthy "overpleased with the picturesque", too inclined toward the *romantic* and too literal to be convincing about the motives of Zachary Pearse, suggesting that development of the natures of both Pearse and his mate was sacrificed to an excessive articulation of the writer's attitude

[September 25, 1900, in *Letters,* Garnett]. Less than a month later, Garnett wrote a similarly detailed letter about **"A Knight"**, praising that story as "quite successful, indeed *too* successful" because, although the old military man is done perfectly, the surviving letter from his wife that the narrator reads ought to add a "shock" of something that the old man was not himself aware of. This is the first of a number of examples of Garnett trying to make Galsworthy more dramatic, sometimes even melodramatic, than he was.

Ford's opinions were less likely to concern plot or drama, more likely to concentrate on images and references that expressed qualities in the texture of Galsworthy's fiction. He praised **"Salvation of a Forsyte"** as "far and away the best thing you have done" with "more grip, more force, and more reticence" [Letter to Galsworthy, in Marrot]. Ford thought the characterization of Swithin "finely ground glass", although at other points the story suffered from Galsworthy's "charm". On this occasion, the most astute and penetrating criticism of the volume of stories came, finally, from Conrad himself. After publication and after his wife had read the volume, Conrad read each story a second time and, without the slightly patronizing tone of the commentary on *Jocelyn* that "to invent depths is not art either", he tried to summarize what he thought of Galsworthy's achievements and possibilities:

> There is a certain caution of touch which will militate against popularity. After all, to please the public (if one isn't a sugary imbecile or an inflated fraud) one must handle one's subject intimately. . . . You are really most profound and attain the greatest art in handling the people you do not respect. . . . The fact is you want more scepticism at the very foundation of your work. Scepticism, the tonic of minds, the tonic of life, the agent of truth—the way of art and salvation. In a book you should love the idea and be scrupulously faithful to your conception of life. There lies the honour of the writer, not in the fidelity to his personages. You must never allow them to decoy you out of yourself. As against your people you must preserve an attitude of perfect indifference—the part of creative power. . . . Your attitude to them should be purely intellectual, more independent, freer, less rigorous than it is. You seem for their sake to hug your conceptions of right and wrong too closely. There is exquisite atmosphere in your tales. What they want now is more air. [November 11, 1901, in Marrot]

Toward the end of the long letter, Conrad particularly praised *A Man of Devon,* concluding that "You've gone now beyond the point where I could be of any use to you otherwise than just by my belief." Conrad did not always follow the implications of that conclusion, but, from late 1901 on, in his letters to Galsworthy, a new kind of respect is sometimes visible in addition to the old affection. . . .

Five Tales, for the most part avoiding both banality and melodrama, shows a variety of themes and contains Galsworthy's best writing since *The Freelands.* Each story, following his precepts about the form, is carefully shaped and represents a balance of character, drama and what he called "atmosphere". The first of the tales, **"The First and the Last"**, concerns a man who, in sudden rage, kills his mistress' brutal and cruel husband and then is so consumed with guilt, both for the killing and for the fact that someone else is convicted of the crime, that he kills himself. The story, however, is not dependent on the familiar Galsworthy theme of excessive guilt, but, rather, on the effective and understated irony of the difference between the guilty man and his brother, a respectable lawyer who had been trying to save him and who burns the suicide's confession in order to keep his own career spotless. The contrast between brothers implicitly questions and explores connections between guilt and responsibility that Galsworthy had not reached in his earlier similar fiction. **"A Stoic"**, written in 1916, describes the final days of the strong old chairman of the board, trying to arrange security for the sexually appealing widow and children of his indigent illegitimate son, preferring those descendants to his legitimate ones, a dull, banal son and a dried-up, respectable daughter. The contrast and its thematic implications are familiar for Galsworthy, but the treatment of a number of businessmen's differing motives, the extensive description of the old sybarite's last elegant dinner, and a series of historical descriptions, embedded in his musings about the past, are all done with a clarity, conviction and compression that Galsworthy had not fully managed earlier. For example:

> Born in the early twenties of the nineteenth century, Sylvanus Heythorp, after an education broken by escapades both at school and at college, had fetched up in that simple London of the late forties, where claret, opera, and eight per cent. for your money ruled a cheery roost. Made partner in his shipping firm well before he was thirty, he had sailed with a wet sheet and a flowing tide; dancers, claret, Cliquot, and piquet; a cab with a tiger; some travel—all that delicious early-Victorian consciousness of nothing save a golden time. It was all so full and mellow that he was forty before he had his only love affair of any depth—with the daughter of one of his clerks, a *liaison* so awkward as to necessitate a sedulous concealment.

Galsworthy was beginning to fashion a prose of imagistic compression for the details of ordinary life and social history. Both of these first two stories became plays, **"The First and the Last"** a short one with the same title, and **"A Stoic"** the full-length play "Old English." In each case, however, the play, while sharpening the dramatic implications of the contrast in character, eliminates the complexity of character's motives, and Galsworthy's sense of action in those instances has not the resonance of his prose at its best. Both **"A Stoic"** and the next tale, **"The Apple Tree"**, in which a man, after twenty-six years, returns to the site of his brief love for a Devon farm girl, complicate and play with uses of the frequent Galsworthy term "chivalry". "Chivalry" can suggest sensitivity, sometimes appearing in places and characters unexpected, or it can be rescue, from a variety of motives, or it can mean abandonment, a world well lost for love. Although always connecting the term with a man's sexual feeling for a woman, the varieties of usage, in context, suggest a growing capacity to treat varieties of sexual and emotional experience without resorting to the cosmic as a repository for human passion. **"The Apple Tree"** also uses effectively the Devon landscape that is simultaneously particular, vibrant and a convincing metaphorical statement about the characters' emotions. The story, however, does end in melodrama. Having carefully shown the principal character's guilty desertion of the love of the Devon farm girl and his conscious choice for a wife of the contrasting familiar "atmosphere as of some old walled-in English garden, with pinks, and corn-flowers, and roses, and scents of lavender and lilac—cool and fair, untouched, almost holy—all that he had been brought up to feel was clean and good", the story ends with his discovery that the Devon girl had committed suicide shortly after he left. The ending wrenches the tale out of balance, emphasizes the guilt and self-punishment at the expense of the complexity and flawed humanity of the choice so carefully developed through most of the story. The fourth tale, **"The Juryman"**, the shortest and slightest of the five, which had been widely noticed when it appeared in magazines in both England and America in September 1917, is an effective and understated contrast between the life of the respectable and prosperous juryman with the cool wife of whom he is proud and the life of the neurasthenic soldier he judges who is on trial for desertion because, unable to bear separation from his wife, he tried to kill himself. To his surprise, the juryman is moved by the soldier's emotion and argues for acquittal. When he later tries to explain to his wife his newly conscious emotions and sympathies, his fuller understanding of the varieties of "chivalry", she, in a brilliantly conveyed conclusion, submits good-humouredly and indifferently to their usual act of sex. As in the other stories, familiar Galsworthy themes are given more compressed, psychologically complex and deeper treatment.

The last of the stories in *Five Tales* is the famous continuation of the Forsytes, left off more than a decade earlier, entitled **"Indian Summer of a Forsyte"**. Galsworthy wrote the long story, about 18,000 words, in London in April and May of 1917, just after he returned from France. He soon wrote to Charles Scribner to substitute the story for **"Defeat"**, an earlier undistinguished story about a proud and cynical German prostitute in London during the war, in the impending edition of *Five Tales* [Letter, July 17, 1917]. Taking place about four years after the end of *The Man of Property,* **"Indian Summer of a Forsyte"** switches away from the novel's conclusion in which Irene had been left enclosed in Soames' house in Montpelier Square, as if permanently imprisoned. The story reveals that she left the next day, at first wandering and desolate, eventually recovering to live independently as a music teacher in Chelsea. During the story, she wanders back to Robin Hill, the country house Soames had built for her and that Old Jolyon had later bought to live in with the son with whom he was reunited and all his grandchildren. Irene and Old Jolyon meet, while Young Jolyon, his wife, and June are away travelling in Spain for months, and they see each other several times a week, at Robin Hill, where Irene gives music lessons to Holly, and in London, where they go to the opera together, until Old Jolyon dies on a hot

summer day waiting for Irene's last visit. Not only do the implications of the plot change, but the characters are also expanded. Old Jolyon is less a symbol of benevolent orthodoxy and patriarchy than an old man with a particular set of tastes and convictions that both express his own sense of art and beauty and reflect something about his historical generation. In showing Irene Robin Hill, which Young Jolyon had decorated in "pearl-grey and silver", Old Jolyon thinks of the difference between himself and his son:

> He would have had gold himself; more lively and solid. But Jo had French tastes, and it had come out shadowy like that, with an effect as of the fume of cigarettes the chap was always smoking, broken here and there by a little blaze of blue or crimson colour. It was not his dream! Mentally he had hung this space with those gold-framed masterpieces of still and stiller life which he had bought in days when quantity was precious.

Old Jolyon is, however, open-minded and willing to move some distance toward the tastes of the new age, as he is willing to move some distance toward emotions in revolt from Victorian property and propriety:

> By the cigars they smoke, and the composers they love, ye shall know the texture of men's souls. Old Jolyon could not bear a strong cigar or Wagner's music. He loved Beethoven and Mozart, Handel and Glück, and Schumann, and, for some occult reason, the operas of Meyerbeer; but of late years he had been seduced by Chopin, just as in painting he had succumbed to Botticelli. In yielding to these tastes he had been conscious of divergence from the standard of the Golden Age. Their poetry was not that of Milton and Byron and Tennyson; of Raphael and Titian; Mozart and Beethoven. It was, as it were, behind a veil; their poetry hit no one in the face, but slipped its fingers under the ribs and turned and twisted, and melted up the heart.

Similarly, Irene, dressed always in "pearl-grey", is no longer simply the vague symbol for beauty. She is a hard-working music teacher, a charitable sponsor of women bearing illegitimate children, a conscious philo-Semite (in contrast with Old Jolyon's Victorian feelings that Jews are "strange, and doubtful"), and a woman sensitive to the way emotions from the past linger in the present. In short, both Old Jolyon and Irene are given social and personal identities. They are not, as they sometimes seemed to be in the earlier novel, Irene more than Old Jolyon, simply counters for approbation or satire, and they become, through the tangible imagery of their tastes and opinions, more complicated and searching historical representations.

Irene and Old Jolyon are also able to talk with one another, to face the implications of the past and recognize what is possible for the present. Irene can talk of what Bosinney was and thought and represented for her; Old Jolyon, even as he approaches death, can recognize his own jealousy of Bosinney. For Galsworthy, the reconciliation between the loved woman and the father, a reconciliation that never occurred in reality and that takes place when the central character and surrogate for the author, the son, is not even there, is a necessary element for any sense of unified experience. The father is so strong and so worshipped that he must be appeased; the woman is so venerated and so different that she must be brought into the central focus of social history. That the son is still passive in his absence, still withdrawn while others create the reconciliation for him, gives the tale something of an aura of sentimental wish-fulfilment. And this incipient sentimentality is compounded by all the repeated images of and references to Old Joylon's impending death. Yet the sentimentality, unlike that in some of Galsworthy's earlier fiction, is never made cosmic or "spiritual", and it does not destroy the fabric of historical and personal connection between the characters. Although still needing more hardness, activity and compression, **"Indian Summer of a Forsyte"** begins Galsworthy's full artistic transposition of his past into detailed historical myth.

Five Tales, dedicated to André Chevrillon, generated an enthusiastic reception. The American edition, for example, was reprinted three times in less than a year. Reviews, although limited in number because of the limited space in 1918 publications, were uniformly favourable. A number praised the volume for the omission of old Galsworthy faults, exaggerated "sexuality" and "socialism" ["Mr. Galsworthy's Old Men," *Saturday Review,* August 17, 1918]. Others praised Galsworthy's irony, sympathy and, above all, his "art", one critic, appreciating the stories as different combinations of "passion" and "ironic method", described the whole volume as an example of his artistic growth. For the first time in more than a decade, a Galsworthy volume seemed to excite numbers of literate readers individually, becoming the subject of frequent recommendations from one person to another. The young Protean intellectual Harold Laski (1893-1950), in his correspondence with Justice Oliver Wendell Holmes, praised the volume's "exquisite sensitiveness", and recommended that the Justice read it [May 6, 1918, in *Holmes-Laski Letters,* Vol. 1]. William Lyon Phelps thought his earlier faith in Galsworthy, tried for years, completely restored, and he continued to maintain that **"Indian Summer of a Forsyte"** was the most moving and effective fiction Galsworthy ever wrote. Other friends were equally unequivocal, like Conrad, reading the volume before publication: "Dearest Jack—The only thing that can be said of the stories without the slightest qualification is that they ARE. I mean that they *are* from the first line to the last" [Letter, October 21, 1917, in Marrot]. He went on to praise each story individually. Archer particularly liked **"Indian Summer of a Forsyte"** and **"A Stoic"**:

> Where *do* you get your power of drawing old age? I think you must have been an octogenarian in your last incarnation, and have some trailing clouds of memory with you from the experience. I wonder what old man you were? It would be interesting to read the obituary column of *The Times* on the day of your birth. For you must have been an Englishman and a man of property, whose death would be sure to go into *The Times.* [August 7, 1918, in Marrot]

Florence Hardy wrote to Ada because she wanted to say how much both she and her husband loved the volume:

> It was a joy to read it aloud to him. I read it to myself first. He made me read it very carefully and slowly 'because,' he said, 'it's Galsworthy.'

> Upon the whole he liked best **"The Apple Tree"** because of its poetry. I preferred **"Indian Summer of a Forsyte"** and **"A Stoic"** because of the two wonderful old men. Jolyon Forsyte is a most beautiful character, and now I can read *The Man of Property* without a terrible feeling of despair [August 13, 1918, in Marrot].

Hardy himself wrote to Galsworthy about the volume twice, the first time to thank the author and report that his wife was reading the volume first so that he had, as yet, no chance to respond. The second letter, including a poem he had just written, combined high praise with his own direct and personal kind of response. He appreciated the portraits of the old men particularly, despite the fact that he did not "usually like old men" in fiction, perhaps because "I am one myself".

Sanford Sternlicht (essay date 1987)

SOURCE: "The Short-Story Writer," in *John Galsworthy,* Twayne Publishers, 1987, pp. 87-100.

[*Sternlicht is an American educator, critic, and poet. In the following excerpt, he traces the development in Galsworthy's short fiction from the earlier influence of French naturalism to a greater use of symbolism and references to classical mythology.*]

John Galsworthy considered the long short story to be "one of the best of all forms of fiction; it is the magic vehicle for atmospheric drama. In this form the writer . . . comes nearest to the poet, the painter, the musician. The tale rises, swells and closes, like some movement of a symphony" [Leon Schalit, *John Galsworthy: A Survey,* 1929]. The shorter story was a quick-flashing effort "over almost before form is thought of." Galsworthy wrote long short stories, short stories, and sketches, fairly brief descriptions of individuals representing a type or class of people, or personifying an idea, an ideal, or a value. The sketches are carryovers from Victorian literature, with a long ancestry back to the Renaissance writers and even to the ancient Romans and Greeks, but little seen by the time Galsworthy was writing his.

The main preoccupations of Galsworthy's short fiction are love, beauty, the glory of nature, social justice, hatred, old age, the poor, and care for animals. Few of his stories present high adventure. More are either mood pieces or stories of passions in conflict. As his storytelling art developed, he moved away from the French naturalism in vogue at the end of the nineteenth century and wrote stories incorporating careful use of symbols and classical myths.

Galsworthy published fourteen volumes of stories and sketches, two of which, *Two Forsyte Interludes* (1927) and *On Forsyte 'Change* (1930), are part of the chronicles. The fifteenth volume of stories, selected by Ada Galsworthy and titled *Forsytes, Pendyces, and Others,* was published posthumously in 1935. Some of Galsworthy's stories, like **"The Apple Tree,"** are among his most famous works, regularly anthologized and often a part of the curriculum in English-speaking schools the world over.

Galsworthy began as a short-story writer. *From the Four Winds* (1897) brought him some forty reviews, mostly favorable, and convinced him that he could indeed be a writer. Yet, in his 1932 Nobel Prize address, near the end of his life, he would call this collection of nine stories, imitative of Rudyard Kipling and Bret Harte, "that dreadful little book" [R. H. Mottram, *For Some We Loved,* 1956]. Galsworthy never revised that first collection or allowed it to be republished. In fact, twenty-five years after it was published he bought up the few remaining unsold copies to keep them out of circulation. Still, it was with the short story that he chose to begin his apprenticeship in writing. Galsworthy's major story and sketch collections are *A Man of Devon* (1901), *A Commentary* (1908), *A Motley* (1910), *The Little Man* (1915), *Five Tales* (1918), *Tatterdemalion* (1920), and *Captures* (1923). *Abracadabra* (1924) is a reprint of the last five stories in *The Little Man. Caravan: The Assembled Tales* (1925) is an anthology containing all of Galsworthy's notable long short stories, with the date of writing affixed to each piece, thus providing the best single volume opportunity to understand the development, scope, and achievement of the author as a writer of short fiction. *Satires* (1927) does much the same thing for Galsworthy's short short fiction and sketches, essentially reprinting *A Commentary* and the "Studies of Extravagance" section of *The Little Man.*

A MAN OF DEVON (1901)

Galsworthy's fourth book, the last written under a pseudonym, is, like his first, a collection of stories. *A Man of Devon* contains four long pieces: **"A Man of Devon,"** **"The Salvation of Swithin Forsyte,"** **"The Silence,"** and **"A Knight."** The title piece, set in the author's ancestral home shire, is an adventure tale of wild love and hate in a lovely countryside. A beautiful farmer's daughter is distracted from her young swain by a gun-running, buccaneering sailor. Finally, she is so upset that she jumps to her death from a cliff. Galsworthy uses the time-honored, if very old-fashioned, epistolary form, which harkens back to Samuel Richardson. The letters are written by a visitor who happens to witness the events. The story is extremely hard to read because of Galsworthy's strained and unsuccessful attempt to write dialect. Moreover, the work is so imitative of Thomas Hardy that it accidentally approaches parody.

By far the best and only memorable story in *A Man of Devon* is **"The Salvation of Swithin Forsyte,"** the first story in what would eventually be "The Forsyte Chronicles." The story is the initial indication of great talent in

Galsworthy. In it, Old Swithin Forsyte, a rich man, company director, and a bachelor, is dying alone. He dreams of an adventure he had as a young man, fifty years before, in which while traveling in Europe he met and fell in love with a young working-class girl. Tempted to marry her, he finally realized that it would not do. She would never be acceptable to his family and class, and so, by giving her up he "saved" himself at the last moment. The story, rich in irony, portrays one of Galsworthy's fine old men who "die without seeing sacrifices, chivalry, love, fidelity, beauty, and strange adventure." In other words, Swithin dies without having lived. Rich living is no substitute for an engaged life. The unloved leave life like bubbles breaking in the air. Galsworthy is almost cruel in his depiction of the epicurean bachelor's death. Swithin dies drinking champagne: "'It isn't Heidseck!' he though angrily. . . . 'But as he bent to drink again something snapped, and, with a sigh, Swithin Forsyte died over the bubbles." And in the end the reader feels both pity and scorn for the old man.

"The Silence" is the Joseph Conrad-like story of a mining engineer's suicide overseas, worn down by a job that forces him to send men to their deaths in deep, unsafe shafts; by the terrible silence of the jungle around him; and by the implacable incomprehension of his masters at company headquarters in London. Once more, an observer, also an engineer, sees, learns, and reveals how far men may be driven even against their nature by those who have power. In the end, after learning of suffering and death, the owners merely remark: "Business is Business! Isn't it?"

Set in Monte Carlo, **"A Knight"** is the romantic story of an old soldier of fortune who, like the hero of Arthur Conan Doyle's *The Exploits of Brigadier Gerard* (1896), enjoys recounting his past battles and adventures to the narrator. Many years ago, at forty-five, he fell in love with an eighteen-year-old girl, married her, and lost her to a young man. She died leaving a child that is not his but whom the old soldier struggles to support. He is a man, nevertheless, who deeply respects women, and when a woman's reputation is traduced in his presence, he provokes a duel, which he then uses to end his life of heartbroken misery. In this piece, Galsworthy shows his admiration for those men who gallantly act to protect and serve the opposite sex regardless of the cost to themselves.

In *A Man of Devon,* Galsworthy struggled to find a personal voice as a short-story writer. In three of the four stories he used someone else's. In **"The Salvation of Swithin Forsyte"** he found his own.

A COMMENTARY (1908)

A Commentary is a book of twenty short, satirical sketches in which Galsworthy presents contemporary problems and the realities of life in an industrial society to an audience of readers not much given to thinking about the poor, the unemployed, the aged, and the powerless. Galsworthy indicts the economic system of Edwardian England, and asks, "What will we do about it?"

A crippled old man whose job is to warn the public of the danger of a steam roller points out the evils of society as an introduction to the commentary provided in the sketches. **"A Lost Dog"** shows how an unemployed man can come to think of himself as an animal. **"Demos"** portrays a brutal man who cannot accept that his wife has left him for good reasons: "I'm 'er 'usband, an I mean to 'ave er, alive or dead."

In **"Old Age,"** a seventy-one-year-old painter, out of work, with no food or blankets, and his equally old wife refuse to go into a workhouse for the poor. **"The Careful Man"** satirizes a politician afraid that social change will take place too quickly. **"Facts"** satirizes the literal-minded. **"Fear"** depicts the terror of an unemployed and dying consumptive who is no longer able to support his family. In **"Fashion,"** Galsworthy attacks insensitive rich women, as he would do in the novel *Fraternity*. Fashion is allegorized as an elegant lady: "You pass, glittering . . . and the eyes of the hollow-chested work girls on the pavement fix on you a thousand eager looks. . . . They do not know that you are as dead as snow around a crater."

"Sport" depicts the harassment of a prostitute. **"Money"** points out the idolatrous worship of wealth. **"Progress"** shows that modern inventions do not serve the progress of humanity. Other pieces show the barriers middle-class society erects to protect itself from those aspiring to rise out of poverty. In **"Justice"** the author argues, as he does on the stage, that there is one law for the rich and another for the poor. **"Mother"** and **"Child"** depict the effect of poverty on the helpless. But at the end, **"Hope"** somewhat sentimentally indicates that optimism can survive even in an old cripple, if courage endures.

As always, Galsworthy's heart is in the right place. However well-meaning, the viewpoint is still that of a rich reformer venturing from his club to observe and deplore. The sketches are frank, uncomplicated, and only a little self-conscious, but they lack individuality. That is their fatal weakness. One at a time they have some impact. All together they cancel each other out.

A MOTLEY (1910)

A Motley is a collection of twenty-eight stories, studies, and impressions written between 1899 and 1910, many of which first appeared in such periodicals as the *English Review, Nation, Englishwoman,* and *Westminster Gazette*. The book opens with a sketch that is obviously a portrait of, and a homage to, the author's solicitor father at age eighty. **"A Portrait"** had not been previously published. Galsworthy saved it for a place of honor in this collection. His painting of his deceased father is most tender and loving. The author also seems to be intending to show the source of his own convictions and carings, for the unnamed old gentleman believed that "money was . . . the symbol of a well-spent, well-ordered life." He had "never been a sportsman—not being in the way of hunting . . . preferring to spend such time as he might have had for shooting, in communing with his beloved mountains." His "love of beauty was a sensuous, warm glow, secretly sep-

arating him from the majority of his associates." The old man believed in equality, saw charity as a personal obligation, and loved cricket. Furthermore, he did not like the profession of law. Galsworthy was reminding himself that the apple does not fall far from the tree.

"A Fisher of Men" is a short story, a portrait, and a study all in one. In this piece Galsworthy depicts a country parson who feels that his congregation does not give him his due. His flock constantly diminished during his twenty years of pastoring, for he was small-minded: "His face had been set, too, against irreverence; no one . . . might come to his church in flannel trousers"; and he was stiff-necked and without compassion, always pointing out that "the fearful and unbelieving shall have their part in the lake which burneth fire and brimstone." He has no love or gentleness for his parishioners. Vexed near to madness by their rejection, he prays himself to death in a fierce rain by the seashore and they bury him beneath a paradoxically admonishing and forgiving inscription: "God is love." As usual, Galsworthy is hard on the established church and its purveyors of religion. Their intolerance of human drives and needs is not only counterproductive, it is a repressive source of human unhappiness. **"A Fisher of Men"** is one of Galsworthy's finest stories to the time he penned it, 1908. The parson is a tragic, Captain Ahab-like figure. The author's treatment of him is a skillful mix of invective, satire, and sharp characterization.

"The Prisoner" is a story full of compassion and pathos, in which Galsworthy shows the dehumanizing effect of long imprisonment. He argues that no crime committed by a human is equal to the crime done to that person by the state when it incarcerates him or her for tens of years or even life. Galsworthy's horror of imprisonment in small cells seems almost claustrophobic.

In truth Galsworthy was always content in being a middle-brow writer for a middle-brow audience.

—Sanford Sternlicht

In **"A Parting,"** the persona observes and comments on the farewell of a pair of lovers. It contrasts with the lightly ironic depiction of two lovers having their first secret meeting presented earlier in *A Motley* as **"The Meeting."** **"The Japanese Quince"** is a charming vignette in which a flowering exotic tree attracts two very conservative business men, who although next-door neighbors, have never spoken to each other. The tree brings them together, but alas, their inbred reticence prevents friendship for these mirror-image men, and they return to relating to life through their newspapers.

"The Consummation," a rare, lighter moment in Galsworthy's stories, is an amusing piece for any reader familiar with Galsworthy's life. An amiable man named Harrison is told at a railway station by a lady in whom he is interested: "Why don't you write? You are just the person!" This, of course, is what Ada had said to Galsworthy to get him started on a career. Harrison writes a collection of short stories that he can only get published by subsidizing it. It receives good reviews, however, and he is compared to Poe, de Maupassant, and Kipling. Harrison decides to write a novel, and a friend who is "a man of genius" undertakes to "help" him. As a result, the novel is less well received by the public but is admired by the "man of genius." Then a well-known critic decides to help him make "art" out of his work. Each new book is less well received by the public and more difficult to read, but to the critical eye his work is advancing. Finally, Harrison writes a novel that is truly great: "'I *have* done it at last. It *is good*, wonderfully good!' . . . He had indeed exhausted his public. It was *too* good— he could not read it himself! Returning to his cottage he placed the manuscript in the drawer. He never wrote another word." The man of genius is Joseph Conrad and the critic is Edward Garnett, and Galsworthy is getting even, good-naturedly, for the early somewhat insincere patronizing by the former and the school-mastering of the latter, both trying to make Galsworthy a "serious" writer. In truth Galsworthy was always content in being a middle-brow writer for a middle-brow audience.

"**Once More**" is a powerful and moving story of a young flower girl, resembling Mrs. Megan in the play *The Pigeon,* who, deserted by her young husband, attempts prostitution to support her child. In the end he returns, starving and frozen, and she takes him back into her arms to nurture him.

A Motley shows growth in narrative skills. Galsworthy was learning how to trim back the elaborate plots of *A Man of Devon* and expand on the acute economical character insights of *A Commentary.* Combining simple and believable plots with sharp observation and a less self-conscious prose style would result in the master storytelling evidenced in the later collections.

The Little Man (1915)

The Little Man contains a short play with the same title; a second entitled *Hall-Marked*; ten satiric sketches of such contemporary types as "**The Writer**," "**The Critic**," "**The Plain Man**," "**The Artist**," "**The Housewife**," and "**The Competitor**," generally shown as selfish, egotistical, competitive, and argumentative; and nine short stories of which "**The Voice of—**," "**A Simple Tale**," and "**Ultima Thule**" are the best known and most memorable.

"**The Voice of—**" takes place in a music hall where the program has become rather sordid, featuring a woman dancing indecorously. A voice is heard condemning the performance, and a strange light is seen on stage. The audience departs in terror and the theater staff are perplexed. The implication is that the voice of God has cried out against the profanation of female beauty. "**A Simple Tale**" uses Ferrand again to comment on how

the poor are neglected. In it a demented old man who thinks he is the Wandering Jew of ancient legend becomes more Christ-like as he endures suffering and neglect. Indirectly, it is also an attack on anti-Semitism.

The last piece in *The Little Man,* "**Ultima Thule**," is a touching story of an old musician who feeds stray cats and mends injured birds instead of feeding himself. He dies and his beloved bullfinch falls dead on his heart. The old man is a St. Francis of Assisi, and the story is one of Galsworthy's many tributes to humans who love and save animals. In death "his face, as white now, almost as his silvery head, had in the sunlight a radiance like that of a small, bright angel gone to sleep."

The Little Man is not a major part of Galsworthy's short fiction. In one or two stories, however, it foreshadows the achievements of *Five Tales* and *Captures.*

Five Tales (1918)

In *Five Tales* Galsworthy reaches the height of his ability as a writer of short stories. Two of these tales, "**A Stoic**" and "**The Apple Tree**," are his most anthologized stories. "**Indian Summer of a Forsyte**" not only serves as a bridge between *The Man of Property* and the rest of the *Saga,* it is the single most lyric moment in the entire chronicles. Although "**The First and the Last**" was begun just before the war, the five stories were a product of the First World War, but only the shortest, "**The Juryman**," deals with the conflict. Galsworthy used the writing of these long stories as a method of escaping from dismal reality into the happier world of the imagination, and in the case of "**The Apple Tree**," particularly, the world of love, beauty, and interpersonal passion.

"**The First and the Last**" is a melodramatic tale of passion, murder, and suicide, in which an eminent but ruthless attorney tries to conceal the crime of his weak but kindly younger brother. The latter has killed a brute who was forcing his attentions on the devoted young prostitute with whom the young man is having an affair. The older brother is motivated to help, not out of love, but out of a desire to protect his own reputation. Thus, when an innocent tramp is accused and sentenced to death, the attorney is delighted, and plans to send the lovers to Argentina. But the younger brother has too much integrity and compassion to allow someone else to die for his crime. The lovers choose suicide, leaving an exonerating note. But when the attorney finds the bodies, he destroys the note to save himself, even though it means an innocent man will die. Thus, the powerful older brother, first in the world, becomes last in the eyes of God, while the poor, lowly lovers have become first.

The story's ending is tragically ironic. The lovers' sacrifice has been for naught. In this world at least, the hard ones, without principles, triumph. Galsworthy turned this story into an effective one-act play. In both story and play he is especially skillful in delineating the character of Wanda, the Polish-born prostitute. She is a touching figure of female helplessness, a young woman who, despite being the victim of male exploitation and domination, maintains her great innate capacity for love, devotion, and abnegation.

"A Stoic" takes place in Liverpool in 1905. As with "The First and the Last" and also "The Apple Tree," Galsworthy turned the story into a play, in this case a three-act comedy called *Old English.* Again Galsworthy draws a vivid and memorable old man, Sylvanus Heythorp, an unscrupulous company director who lives life to the full. He is the father of an illegitimate son by a mistress who has died, and he has also fathered two legitimate children by an unloved wife, also deceased. For some years he has been a widower doting on the family of his illegitimate son, whom he loved most of all but who died young and impoverished.

Old Heythorp goes deeply into debt to support his lifestyle, and in order to obtain cash, he carries out an unlicensed transaction for a large commission. Trapped by a hating creditor trying to disgrace him just before death, the eighty-year-old Heythorp shows his disdain for his enemies and society by ending his life with a glorious dinner deliciously described by Galsworthy. He literally eats, drinks, and smokes himself into a happy sleep from which he does not awake. The author and the reader identify with the old bon vivant and his joie de vivre. He successfully defied society's conventions and got away with it.

"The Apple Tree" is the perennially favorite story of Galsworthy fans. Based on an old Dartmoor legend of a girl crossed in love who takes her own life, it is his most finely crafted, most symbolic, and most poetic tale [Catherine Dupré, *John Galsworthy,* 1976]. The title is from a line of Gilbert Murray's translation of Euripides' play *Hippolytus*: "The apple tree, the singing and the gold," a line Galsworthy uses to open and close the story.

The simple plot centers on the return of Frank Ashurst, a middle-aged man, to the place on the moorlands of Devonshire where, twenty-six years ago, as a twenty-three-year-old student, he met, made love to, proposed to, and abandoned a beautiful, seventeen-year-old Welsh farm girl named Megan. After recalling the memory, he learns that she drowned herself after he deserted her. Ashurst, his life turned to ashes by the revelation, believes that he has been punished by love for his traitorous ways: "'The Cyprian,' goddess of love [had] taken her revenge! And before his eyes, dim with tears, came Megan's face with the sprig of apple blossoms in her dark wet hair."

Galsworthy symbolically evokes memories of both the Garden of Eden, with its apple of temptation, and the Garden of the Hesperides, with its golden apples, the prizes for great efforts. Frank finds Megan beneath an apple tree in a garden. She is both an Aphrodite and an Eve. He rejects the goddess of love by mistaking her for the temptress, and by marrying Stella, a figure like the Artemis of *Hippolytus* and Diana, the goddess of chastity and the night. In doing so, and because he is prideful and unable to embrace the primordial patterns of life, Frank loses the garden for both of them. Megan dies, and he lives a sterile and conventional life. All that remains for him is the memory that once "he was not quite sane, thinking of that morning's kiss, and of tonight under the apple tree [where] fauns and dryads surely lived."

"The Juryman" is the story of Henry Bosengate, a successful businessman, who during the First World War is called upon to serve on a jury hearing the case of an army private who was so miserable away from his wife that he tried to kill himself. He is charged with attempting suicide and thus trying to deprive the king of a soldier. Bosengate finds his sympathy growing for the accused, and he argues successfully on his behalf with the other jurors. Returning home after the trial, he realizes how much he loves and needs his wife, Kate, whom he has taken for granted. He thinks:

> "We haven't been close—really close, you and I, so that we each understand what the other is feeling. It's all in that, you know; understanding—sympathy—it's priceless. When I saw that poor devil . . . sent back to his regiment to begin his sorrows all over again— wanting his wife, thinking and thinking of her just as you know I'd be thinking and wanting you, I thought what an awful outside sort of life we lead, never telling each other what we really think and feel, never being really close."

The sensitive tale proposes that there is a store of warmth and compassion in most people. One can learn from the misfortune and suffering of another that the time to cherish those one loves is now.

The beautiful "Indian Summer of a Forsyte," . . . is the last story in *Five Tales*. These long pieces, especially "The Apple Tree," "A Stoic" and "Indian Summer of a Forsyte," show Galsworthy's mastery of the genre. His short fiction could create that kind of resonance in a reader that causes him or her to go back to the piece again and again to find new meaning, as well as remembered beauty.

Tatterdemalion (1920)

The last of Galsworthy's war stories and the first of his stories written in the peace that followed appeared in *Tatterdemalion,* a "ragamuffin" of a collection. The book contains fifteen pieces in "Part I. Of War-time" and eight in "Part II. Of Peace-time." All are shorter than the stories in *Five Tales,* and they are not memorable, representing Galsworthy's lesser fictional efforts of the 1914-19 period. The stories are generally about the fate of the noncombatants on the home front in the war, the unsung sacrifice of some, and the unnecessary suffering of others at the hands of jingoists.

The first story, "The Grey Angel," is probably a companion piece to "Portrait" in *A Motley,* in that it seems to be a fictionalized and idealized sketch of his mother, who died in 1915. In it a valiant eighty-year-old English lady gives her all doing Red Cross work in France during the war. She thinks of everyone but herself, and although most of the gifts she brings the wounded French soldiers are useless to them, they appreciate the spirit of heartfelt giving. As she dies, she shows her inner peace, her indifference to death, and her concern for her children: "'My darlings—don't cry; smile!'"

"**Defeat**" tells of a German prostitute trapped in London during the war and, in order to survive, forced to service the very soldiers who are killing her countrymen in battle. Her life is, to Galsworthy, as terrible as any combatant's. In fact, the wounded young officer she picks up enjoys trench warfare: "It was great. We did laugh that morning. They got me much too soon, though—a swindle!" He had been cut down in a charge by four machine-gun bullets. Galsworthy was naive and out of touch in implying, as late as 1916, the date of the writing of the story, that most English soldiers were exhilarated by battle. The poor girl suffers terribly as she hears of an English victory and then tears up the money the soldier gave her. Alone, lying on the floor, she sings *Die Wacht am Rhein.*"

"**Flotsam and Jetsam**," "**Cafard**," and "**Bidan**" are stories about wounded French soldiers and stem from Galsworthy's hospital experience. "**The Recruit**" is about an undersized Dartmoor agricultural worker of little intelligence who tries to enlist but is rejected. He is deeply hurt, but of course, he survives the war while the brighter and stronger die by the millions. "**The Peace Meeting**" tells of an attempt to end the war that is frustrated by the very men it could save. In "**Heaven and Earth**" an old man sadly buries his dog, ironically noting that he could be sad for an animal's death and impervious to the war slaughter. In "**The Muffled Ship**" Canadian soldiers return home. "**Heritage**" tells of the service to crippled children and those who were air-raid victims. "**The Mother Stone**" implies that the First World War occurred because of the greed and power-seeking of colonial exploiters. "**The Bright Side**" and "**The Dog It Was That Died**" attack the British treatment of resident Germans, like Galsworthy's brother-in-law, during the war years, while "**Recorded**" is a soldier's sad farewell to his wife and babes. "**A Green Hill Far Away**" is a thanksgiving for peace.

"Part II. Of Peace-time" begins with an excellent tale, "**Spindleberries**," one of Galsworthy's finest short stories. It tells of two painters, cousins: a woman who gives up everything for beauty, and a man who is commercially successful and who is both disdainful and jealous of his relative. "Life! Alica! She had made a pretty mess of it, and yet who knew what secret raptures she had felt with her subtle lover, beauty, by starlight and sunlight and moonlight, in the fields and woods, on the hilltops, and by riverside! . . . Who could say that she had missed the prize of life?"

"**Expectations**" is a somewhat humorous story of a married couple inept in everything except keeping their relationship going. "**Manna**" is a biting tale of the travails of a stubborn clergyman, reminiscent of Reverend Pierson in *Saint's Progress*. "**Two Looks**" tells of the painful love of two women for the same dying old man. "**Fairyland**" is a very short but lovely countryside sketch. "**A Strange

Thing,**" "**The Nightmare Child,**" and "**Buttercup-night**" are village tales set in a place like Manaton on Dartmoor.

Tatterdemalion is a minor work. As much as anything it is a workbook for themes, ideas, and scenes in the novels and plays written during the same period. *Captures* comes much closer to the great skill in writing short fiction Galsworthy showed in *Five Tales*.

Captures (1923)

Captures contains sixteen short stories. The first, longest, and strongest is "**A Feud**." Another Dartmoor piece like "**The Apple Tree**," it is a village tragedy in which two men quarrel over the shooting of a dog, engage in a disastrous law suit, and cause the death of one litigant's son, who runs off to the war. In the end, the young man's contentious father, while trying to kill his enemy, hears the church bell tolling for his son's death, and "in Bowden something went out. He had not the heart to hate." It has taken the death of a loved one to bring peace to two troubled families. In "**A Feud**," Galsworthy again shows that he can write with success about rural, agricultural people. Of course in his home at Manaton he had direct daily contact with them. Galsworthy had less success depicting the proletariat and urban poor, for although he had great sympathy for them, he had almost no contact with them.

In "**Timber**," a baronet decides to sell his ancestral works to the government during the war to make great profit and appear patriotic at the same time. Walking in the woods in winter, he loses his way and freezes to death. The woods take revenge before their own demise. "**Santa Lucia**," "**Blackmail**," "**A Hedonist**," "**Stroke of Lightning**," and "**A Long-ago Affair**" are effective stories of sexual passion, longing, and jealousy concerning middle-aged spouses and lovers. "**The Broken Boot**" and "**The Man Who Kept His Form**" are sad pieces about men who struggle to live up to a code of honor and a way of life. In the former it is an impoverished actor and in the latter a gentleman, the dying "symbol of that lost cause, gentility."

"**Philanthropy**" and "**Acme**" are stories of writers who are surprised by the unexpected ways of their fellow humans. "**Salta pro Nobis (A Variation)**" is a version of the Mata Hari story: a dancer spy performs for the last time before being shot. "**Late—299**," like the play *Justice*, shows the devastating result of imprisonment. A doctor serves two years for performing an abortion on a woman to save her honor. Afterward, with anger and cynicism, he defies the world: "I am so human that I'll see the world damned before I'll take its pity. . . . Leave me alone. I am content." "**Conscience**" and "**Virtue**" show young men who act according to their conscience regardless of personal cost.

"**Had a Horse**," the last and second longest story in *Captures* tells of a nonentity of a bookmaker who obtains a racehorse as payment on a debt and for the first time actually sees such an animal. He comes to love the beauty of his beast, and his regard for his animal gives him pride and self-respect that lasts "for years betting on horses he never saw, underground like a rat, yet never again so accessible to the kicks of fortune, or so prone before the shafts of superiority." In this story Galsworthy enjoys showing his intimate and precise knowledge of the sport of kings.

In *Captures* Galsworthy once more approaches the level of excellence in short fiction first achieved in *Five Tales.* Galsworthy's post-World War I outlook, however, was different from that he espoused during fierce wartime. His fiction mellowed, grew more nostalgic, and showed a growing tolerance for human frailty.

From *A Man of Devon* through *Captures,* Galsworthy's short fiction paralleled his novels in subject and style. His ability as a novelist peaked first, before the First World War, with the social satires like *A Man of Property* and *The Country House.* The high-water mark of his short fiction came later, during the war, with *Five Tales.* When he continued the chronicles after the war, his interest in the short story declined.

Although produced by a master stylist, a skilled satirist, and a careful craftsman, Galsworthy's short fiction has several imperfections. For one, the author is often a blatant sentimentalist, particularly when it comes to portraying women or the poor. His women are almost always self-sacrificing sufferers like Wanda, the Polish prostitute in **"The First and the Last,"** May, the German prostitute in **"Defeat,"** or Megan in **"The Apple Tree."** They are invariably courageous in their travail, like Mrs. Holsteig in **"The Dog It Was That Died,"** the Scotswoman whose German-born husband and English-born son are interned in the war. When old, like the **"Grey Angel"** they are noble. Galsworthy's chivalric code seems to have made him incapable of villainizing a woman or granting her major human imperfections, at least within the confines of short fiction.

Also, Galsworthy's working-class men, like Tom in **"The Recruit"** and the private in **"The Juryman,"** are almost always humble hat-in-handers. They are primitively eloquent, but ultimately unconvincing in dialogue or dialect.

Other characters bathe in self-pity. Sometimes, particularly in the fine depiction of old men like Heythorp in **"A Stoic,"** there is "at times the breath of decadence" [Joseph J. Reilly, "John Galsworthy and His Short Stories," *The Catholic World* 123, 1926]. These men fear death less because of a natural terror of oblivion or concern for an afterlife, than because their already dulling senses will be forever extinguished.

Finally, Galsworthy's stories are unrelentingly serious. Humor is almost totally absent. An occasional lighter touch would have offered a contrast that could have exculpated the author from the charges of bleakness and unremitting pessimism.

Still, on balance, few of Galsworthy's contemporaries spoke out in short fiction against the injustice of life as successfully as he did. Nor did they match his broad vision of an often hypocritical society in transition from the seemingly stable Victorian era to the war-weary, cynical, anarchistic, and sexually emancipated world of the 1920s.

FURTHER READING

Bibliography

Stevens, Earl E., and Stevens, H. Ray. *John Galsworthy: An Annotated Bibliography of Writings about Him.* De Kalb: Northern Illinois University Press, 1980, 484 p.
> Comprehensive bibliography of primary and secondary sources.

Biography

Barker, Dudley. *The Man of Principle: A View of John Galsworthy.* London: Heinemann, 1963, 240 p.
> Examines the events that shaped Galsworthy's life and work.

Holloway, David. *John Galsworthy.* International Profiles, edited by Edward Stoner. London: Morgan-Grampian Books, 1968, 92 p.
> Brief introductory biography of Galsworthy. Includes photographs from productions of Galsworthy's plays and the 1967 BBC adaptation of *The Forsyte Saga.*

Marrot, H. V. *The Life and Letters of John Galsworthy.* New York: Charles Scribner's Sons, 1936, 819 p.
> Official biography of Galsworthy which includes correspondence and photographs.

Mottram, R. H. *John Galsworthy.* London: Longmans, Green & Co., 1953, 40 p.
> An overview of Galsworthy's life and work.

Sauter, Rudolf. *Galsworthy the Man: An Intimate Portrait.* London: Peter Owen, 1967, 176 p.
> Appreciative biography by Galsworthy's nephew.

Criticism

Dooley, D. J. "Character and Credibility in *The Forsyte Saga.*" *The Dalhousie Review* 50 (Autumn 1970): 373-77.
> Praises the BBC adaptation of *The Forsyte Saga.*

Fisher, John. *The World of the Forsytes.* London: Martin Secker & Warburg, 1976, 224 p.
> A discussion of the social and political climate in England between 1886 and 1926, a period that Fisher refers to as the "Forsyte Era."

Fréchet, Alec. *John Galsworthy: A Reassessment.* Translated by Denis Mahaffey. Totowa, N.J.: Barnes & Noble Books, 1982, 229 p.

A reevaluation of Galsworthy's life and writing in light of the renewed interest in the author during the 1960s.

Kaye-Smith, Sheila. *John Galsworthy*. New York: H. Holt and Company, 1916, 128 p.
Surveys Galsworthy's career and analyzes his writings.

McQuitty, Peter. "The Forsyte Chronicles: A Nineteenth-Century Liberal View of English History." *English Literature in Transition* 23, No. 2 (1980): 99-114.
Argues that Galsworthy did not attack Victorian standards—especially, the acquisition of property—in "The Forsyte Chronicles," but rather that he justified and embraced its ideals.

Wagenknecht, Edward. "Pity, Irony, and John Galsworthy." In his *Cavalcade of the English Novel: From Elizabeth to George VI*, pp. 477-93. New York: H. Holt and Company, 1954.
Surveys *The Forsyte Saga, A Modern Comedy,* and *End of the Chapter* and discusses literary influences on Galsworthy's work.

Wilson, Angus. "Galsworthy's *Forsyte Saga.*" In *Diversity and Depth in Fiction,* edited by Kerry McSweeney, pp. 149-52. New York: Viking Press, 1984.
A negative review of *The Forsyte Saga,* criticizing Galsworthy's technique, especially his character and plot development.

Additional coverage of Galsworthy's life and career is contained in the following sources published by Gale Research: *Contemporary Authors,* **Vols. 104, 141;** *Concise Dictionary of British Literary Biography 1890-1914*; *Dictionary of Literary Biography*; *DISCovering Authors*; *Twentieth-Century Literary Criticism,* **Vols. 1, 45; and** *World Literature Criticism,* **Vol. 2.**

Heinrich von Kleist
1777–1811

German short story writer, essayist, journalist, and dramatist.

INTRODUCTION

Unappreciated in his own time, Kleist posthumously received wide critical acclaim for his short prose. His eight short stories, or *Novellen*, originally published in two volumes in 1810-11, are considered comparable to the work of Giovanni Boccaccio and Johann Wolfgang von Goethe. In addition to his *Novellen*, Kleist wrote eight plays and many political essays. The extreme stylization and frank sexuality of his works shocked his contemporaries, denying him the acclaim he coveted; however, these same qualities have ensured continuing interest in his work today, and he is now particularly praised for his acute psychological insight and honest depictions of sexuality.

Biographical Information

Kleist was born in Frankfurt an der Oder on October 18, 1777, into a prominent military family that had produced eighteen Prussian generals. He was educated privately until the age of eleven, when he went to the French Gymnasium in Berlin. He joined the army at the age of fifteen and participated in the 1793 Rhine campaign against the French. Kleist broke with family tradition in 1799 when, disillusioned with military life, he resigned his commission to attend the University of Frankfurt. There he studied mathematics, science, and philosophy for one year while also serving as tutor to Wilhelmine von Zenge, the daughter of a family friend. The two became engaged and Kleist left the university for a job in the civil service. Soon, however, he resigned his position to embark alone on a journey through Europe. Scholars note the importance of this trip in Kleist's intellectual development; it was in his letters to Wilhelmine that he first expressed his desire to pursue a literary career. Another key event in Kleist's education was his 1801 reading of Immanuel Kant's *The Critique of Pure Reason* (1788). Kleist's rationalistic belief in human perfectibility and immortality was challenged by Kant's ideas on the inability of reason to discern the truth behind appearances, and he entered a period of despondency that scholars commonly call his "Kant crisis." Critics note that Kleist's reaction to Kant set the tone for the metaphysical background of his creative work, especially his *Novellen*. Kleist wrote all of his major works between 1804 and 1810 and, with the German economist Adam Muller, started the literary journal *Phöbus* as a vehicle for his stories. Lack of financial support caused the journal's early demise. In 1810, the first volume of Kleist's *Erzhälungen* (the collection of his *Novellen*), which includes *Michael Kohlhaas*, "Die Marquise von O . . ." ("The Marquise of

O . . ."), and "Das Erdbeben in Chili" ("The Earthquake in Chile"), was published. At this time he also started a political periodical, *Die Berliner Abendblätter*, in which he published anti-Napoleonic articles, but the paper was discontinued after six months due to a lack of popular support. Throughout his life, Kleist had expressed a wish to die and had frequently asked friends to commit suicide with him. In 1811, he befriended Henriette Vogel, an actress dying of cancer who agreed to a suicide pact. They traveled together to an inn near Potsdam, and on November 21, Kleist shot Vogel and then himself.

Major Works of Short Fiction

Kleist's eight *Novellen* were collected in the two-volume *Erzhälungen*: "Der Findling" ("The Foundling"); *Michael Kohlhaas*; "Das Bettelweib von Locarno" ("The Beggarwoman of Locarno"); "Der Zweikampf" ("The Duel"); "Die Marquise von O . . ." ("The Marquise of O . . ."); "Das Erdbeben in Chile" ("The Earthquake in Chile"); "Die Verlobung in St. Domingo" ("The Engagement in Santo Domingo"); and "Die Heilige Cäcilie" ("St. Cecilia, or The Power of Music"). These narratives form the body of Kleist's short fiction and are considered major contributions to the German *Novelle* genre. Kleist himself has been variously described as extremist, neurotic, and tense. There can be no doubt that his personality as well as his failure to find acceptance, fame, and meaning in life informed his work. Arthur A. Cohen wrote that Kleist "was always intent on an inversion of sensibility, on externalizing the riot of passions that he discerned within himself and, by extension, with everyone. He used himself continuously as his test case." Kleist's internal conflicts infuse his stories and are manifested in the paradoxical themes of his work. Seemingly normal characters are tested under suddenly extraordinary and chaotic circumstances: an earthquake in "The Earthquake in Chile," a racial uprising in "The Engagement in Santo Domingo." The play of opposites is central to "The Foundling," in which good and evil characters resemble each other and whose names are anagrams of each other. "St. Cecilia, or The Power of Music" features men bent on destruction at a church who are transformed into *Gloria*-singing acolytes. As Denys Dyer noted in his *The Stories of Kleist: A Critical Study*, these stories are "narrated in a prose style staggering in its originality and quite unique in German literature." The singularity of these *Novellen* prompted E. K. Bennett in his *A History of the German Novelle from Goethe to Thomas Mann* to describe the stories as having "significantly no framework." Bennett concluded that the deviation of Kleist's *Novellen* from the standards of the time served to widen acceptable *Novelle* parameters, "opening the genre to other themes and other treatment."

Critical Reception

Kleist's potential genius was acknowledged by such leading German literary figures as Goethe and Christoph Martin Wieland, though most considered Kleist's work eccentric and problematical. Since his death, speculation about the cause and meaning of Kleist's suicide has been an integral part of most interpretations of his works. Nineteenth-century critics searched the author's writings for evidence of mental illness, focusing on the extreme and eccentric nature of his characters. In the early twentieth century, scholars influenced by Arthur Schopenhauer and Friedrich Nietzsche regarded Kleist's suicide in a more positive light, elevating him as an example of Nietzsche's tragic artist. Others saw him, in the words of Julius Petersen, as the "classic of Expressionism," interpreting his works as a quest for philosophical certainty. In the later twentieth century, critics influenced by existentialist philosophy saw Kleist's suicide as a normal response to the tragic nature of human existence, and they praised his artistic obsession with the human struggle to make sense of an incomprehensible universe. It was not until Marxist critics expressed interest in the political and historical aspects of Kleist's works that literary interpretation was separated from biographical concerns. Many Marxist scholars believe that Kleist's primary concern was the relation of man to society under capitalism, though they debate whether he condoned middle-class values or supported a rebellion against authority. Despite such uncertainty, critics have praised Kleist's perception and honesty and have acknowledged the unique power of his prose narratives.

PRINCIPAL WORKS

Short Fiction

Erzhälungen [*Tales*] 2 vols. (short stories and novellas) 1810-11
The Marquise of O— and Other Stories (novellas; translated and with an introduction by Martin Greenberg, preface by Thomas Mann) 1960

Other Major Works

Die Familie Schroffenstein [*The Feud of the Schroffensteins*] (drama) 1804
*Amphitryon: Ein Lustspiel nach Molière [*Amphitryon: A Comedy*; adaptor; from the drama *Amphitryon* by Molière] (drama) 1807
*Penthesilea: Ein Trauerspiel (drama) 1808
Der zerbrochene Krug: Ein Lustspiel [*The Broken Jug: A Comedy*] (drama) 1808
Das Käthchen von Heilbronn oder Die Feuerprobe: Eins großes historisches Ritterschauspiel [*Kate of Heilbronn*] (drama) 1810
*Die Hermannsschlacht [*The Battle of Arminius*] (drama) 1821
*Prinz Friedrich von Homburg [*Prince Frederick of Homburg*] (drama) 1821

*This is the date of first publication rather than first performance.

CRITICISM

Donald H. Crosby (essay date 1964)

SOURCE: "Heinrich von Kleist's *Der Zweikampf*," in *Monatschefte*, Vol. LVI, No. 4, April-May, 1964, pp. 191-201.

[*In the following essay, Crosby examines the motifs, language, and origin of "Der Zweikampf."*]

Kleist's Novelle **"Der Zweikampf"** is customarily included last in collections of his stories and rarely draws the critical encomiums accorded, say, **Michael Kohlhaas** or **"Die Marquise von O. . . ."** Erich Schmidt [in the "Einleitung" to Kleist's *Erzählungen* in the *Werke*, ed. by Erich Schmidt and others, 1904-05], citing what he called the Novelle's "verblasene Reden" and "die wohlfeile Abrechnung zwischen Tugend unde Laster," thought **"Der Zweikampf"** symptomatic of a temporary flagging of Kleist's narrative skill. To these remarks must be added the strictures of commentators who are disturbed by what they perceive as a "zweiteilige Handlung" anomalous among Kleist's Novellen.

Such criticism has obscured the fact that the Novelle is nevertheless in its plot, character portrayal, and language a valuable repository of elements which are indisputably *echt Kleistisch.* Also, by the nature of its inception **"Der Zweikampf"** affords a fascinating glimpse into Kleist's workshop. Finally, a certain opacity surrounding the conclusion sets **"Der Zweikampf"** off from the earlier Novellen and has constantly called forth widely varying interpretations. To reconsider Kleist's literary intentions while examining the Novelle's genesis is the object of the present study.

In Kleist's ill-starred newspaper, *Die Berliner Abendblätter,* there appeared in February 1811 a short article entitled "Geschichte eines merkwürdigen Zweikampfes." The short piece was a retelling by Kleist of an actual trial by combat recorded by the fourteenth century French chronicler Jean Froissard. The story may be summarized briefly as follows: Hans Carouge, a knight and the vassal of the Count of Alenson, goes abroad on a business errand, leaving his castle in the charge of his devoted lady. During his absence, the castle is visited by Carouge's fellow vassal Jacob der Graue, who is secretly in love with his friend's wife. In the course of a tour conducted by the unsuspecting lady, the wayward knight seizes the opportunity to force her to his will. Unrepentant and apparently unconcerned by Lady Carouge's threat to report all to her husband, Jacob races his horse back to his own castle. When Carouge returns and hears of the outrage, he decides to seek legal redress from Jacob at the court of their common liege lord. Jacob is able to cast doubt on the credibility of the lady's complaint, however, by proving that he was away from his castle for only five and one-half hours. The count is unwilling to accept Lady Carouge's complaint in the face of the fact that Jacob would have had to cover a distance of 115 miles by horse within this time, a feat which would scarcely allow time for his unholy adventure at the castle. Denied legal satisfaction, Carouge agrees to participate with Jacob in a "Zweikampf," a trial by combat. With his own life as well as his wife's hanging in the balance, Carouge presses his attack on the false friend; and though wounded in the first exchange, Carouge ultimately lays the betrayer in the dust. His wife's veracity and honor upheld, Carouge is rewarded by the bounty of his king and the admiration of the lady herself, while the dishonored corpse of Jacob is burned by the executioner.

The question immediately arises as to why Kleist labeled this report "merkwürdig." After all, "right" triumphs, the aggrieved party is vindicated, and the slanderer pays for his trespass with his life. Nothing happens, in other words, which does not fit within the theological-judicial "ground-rules" of the medieval trial by combat. Most likely, it was the incidence of certain motifs in the historical record which first captured Kleist's attention and then stimulated his poetic fantasy. Some of these are quite obvious: the violence done to Carouge's wife aligns her directly with Kleist's Marquise von O. . . . and, more distantly, with Alkmene; with both these heroines, moreover, she shares an image of virtue wronged and falsely accused. The obstacles placed in the path of a clear-cut justice suggest similar legal stalemates in the *Prinz von Homburg,* **"Der Findling,"** and *Michael Kohlhaas.* The motif of *Vertrauen,* suggested by Carouge's faith in his wife, is one encoun-

tered throughout Kleist's own works; and the supposition that God intervenes directly in the affairs of man doubtless stimulated an intellect which had repeatedly come to grips with this very problem.

With such congenial motifs compressed within a colorful medieval framework, the main lines for Kleist's expansion of the historical vignette were clearly drawn. Yet the retention of even minor details attests to Kleist's narrative economy as well as to the impact which his source made upon him. In the chronicle, for example, the King postpones the combat so that he may be present to watch it. In the Novelle, the Emperor postpones the execution of Littegarde so that he can prolong his observation of the ailing Jacob, of whom he is suspicious. In the *Abendblätter* version the following line appears: "Die Kämpfer erschienen vom Kopf bis zu den Füßen gewaffnet"; in **"Der Zweikampf"** the combatants are described as being "von Kopf zu Fuß in schimmerndes Erz gerüstet." In the chronicle, Carouge approaches his wife at the combat site and reminds her that he is risking his life on the verity of her complaint against Jacob; in **"Der Zweikampf"** Littegarde is approached just before the start of the duel by Trota's mother, who implores her not to sacrifice her only son if Jacob's accusation is really true. In each case the champion is sent into battle with a ringing assurance from the lady, i. e., Carouge's wife: "Ihr könnt Euch auf die Gerechtigkeit Eurer Sache verlassen, und mit Zuversicht in den Kampf gehen"; and Littegarde: "Keine Schuld befleckt mein Gewissen; und ginge er ohne Helm und Harnisch in den Kampf, Gott und alle seine Engel beschirmen ihn!"

The style of the *Abendblätter* "Zweikampf" is scarcely recognizable as Kleist's, with short, uncomplicated sentences appearing in the place of the author's familiar *Langsatzstil.* Even the incidence of a favorite Kleistian word, "Schenkel," given as the location of Carouge's wound, is misleading, since the phrase is taken literally from Froissard (*navre en la cuisse*). The style of the Novelle, however, leaves no doubt as to the identity of its author. The very first sentence, though lacking the paradoxical impact of other Kleistian beginnings (cf. *Michael Kohlhaas,* **"Die Marquise von O. . .",** **"Das Erdbeben in Chile"** clearly bears Kleist's unmistakable stamp; no less than sixteen commas interrupt what is basically a long independent clause followed by an equally long dependent clause. Through the inclusion of four relative clauses, three adverbial and two appositive phrases we are apprised of the following: 1. the name and social rank of the man about to become a victim; 2. that he had recently legalized a clandestine liaison with a certain countess; 3. that the countess seemed to have been beneath his station; 4. that this attachment has provoked the enmity of his half-brother Jacob (now called "Der Rotbart"); 5. that he had obtained the legitimation of his natural son from the Emperor; 6. that the crime about to be perpetrated takes place on the night of Saint Remigius toward the end of the fourteenth century.

Like this motif-laden opening sentence, the language of **"Der Zweikampf"** is very much the poet's own, and since it has to serve a plot compounded of violence, mystery, puzzle, and paradox, the diction tends toward extremes. Striking, however, is the too-frequent repetition of certain phrases, a symptom of haste, one suspects, and a flaw which could easily have been corrected had Kleist lived to revise the work. Von Trota, we read, is "äußerst betroffen" over the Duke's death; the Chancellor is likewise "äußerst betroffen" to hear that the murder arrow came from Jacob's armory; the simple villagers are "äußerst bestürzt" to find Littegarde lying on the road; Littegarde is in turn "äußerst ermüdet" by the trip to the Trota castle; Trota is plunged into "äußerste Besorgnis" when he hears that Littegarde has refused all visitors to her dungeon. The rhetorical locution "Aber wer beschreibt . . ." is twice used to convey extremes of surprise and shock: when Trota finds the distraught Littegarde seeking shelter at his castle ("Aber wer beschreibt das Erstaunen . . ."); and when Littegarde discovers that Trota has come to visit her in the dungeon ("Aber wer beschreibt das Erstaunen . . ."). Extremes of anger are twice called forth in Littegarde's brothers; on both occasions they are described as "vor Wut schäumend." Typical Kleistian *Steigerung* is revealed by the sequence of similes used by Littegarde to underscore her innocence: "Wie die Brust eines neugebornen Kindes, wie das Gewissen eines aus der Beichte kommenden Menschen, wie die Leiche einer, in der Sakristei, unter der Einkleidung, verschiedenen Nonne."

Characteristically, the occurrence of images in Kleist's prose is much less frequent than in his dramas, where his command of *Bildersprache* is in constant and brilliant evidence. Such images as are found in **"Der Zweikampf"** remind the reader of related imagery in specific dramas and, again, typify Kleist's tendency to re-use words, phrases, and situations throughout his works. One cannot fail to recall the vivid storm-imagery of *Penthesilea* in the description of the combat between Jacob and Trota; "Jetzt wogte zwischen beiden Kämpfern der Streit, wie zwei Sturmwinde einander begegnen, wie zwei Gewitterwolken, ihre Blitze einander zusendend, sich treffen, und, ohne sich zu vermischen, unter dem Gekrach häufiger Donner, getürmt um einander herumschweben." Similarly, Trota's expression of joy and relief over Littgarde's reaffirmation of her innocence ("Der Tod schreckt mich nicht mehr, und die Ewigkeit, soeben noch wie ein Meer unabsehbaren Elends vor mir ausgebreitet, geht wieder, wie ein Reich voll tausend glänziger Sonnen, vor mir auf!") is both in diction and specific imagery reminiscent of Homburg's soliloquy: "Nun, O Unsterblichkeit, bist du ganz mein!" (*Homburg*). Finally, when the dying Jacob speaks of the wound which has felled his strength "wie der Sturmwind eine Eiche," he uses an image which had already served Kleist, in variant forms, from an early letter through *Die Familie Schroffenstein* to *Penthesilea*.

Like all of Kleist's Novellen, **"Der Zweikampf"** is memorable for the pervasive dynamism which animates the prose narrative. Never is this poet content with merely static description: everything—the characters, the public surrounding them, the phases of the day are, like the language itself, constantly in motion. Kleist's literary alchemy, practiced in this case on a short chronicle, may be

said to have transformed his sources into a full-dimensional "Schwester eines Dramas." As one of many examples, there is Kleist's description of Jacob's reception of the messenger who brings a letter from Breysach's widow, together with the incriminating murder-arrow, to his castle. There is no precedent for this incident in the source, and the sketchily-drawn Jacob the Grey of the chronicle has been "filled out," as it were, to a sanguine villain of some panache. "Der Graf, der eben mit einer Gesellschaft von Freunden bei der Tafel saß, stand, als der Ritter, mit der Botschaft der Herzogin, zu ihm eintrat, verbindlich von seinem Sessel auf; aber kaum, während die Freunde den feierlichen Mann, der sich nicht niederlassen wollte, betrachteten, hatte er in der Wölbung des Fensters den Brief überlesen: als er die Farbe wechselte, und die Papiere mit den Worten den Freunden übergab: 'Brüder, seht! welch eine schändlich Anklage, auf den Mord meines Bruders, wider mich zusammengeschmiedet worden ist!'" The passage is in no particular way striking or exceptional, yet it clearly illustrates how the "mind's eye" in which Kleist imagined the mimetic actions of characters shaped the contours of his prose. The initial tableau showing Jacob seated at the table is greatly animated by the presence of his friends; every description which follows recreates the interaction of characters on a stage. As the messenger enters, Jacob arises from his chair (always an indispensable prop in any Kleist work), and does so "verbindlich," thus establishing a mood which will shortly be contrasted. While Jacob retires to a window niche—the reader can easily imagine him crossing the stage—another bit of "stage business" must be provided for the messenger, and hence Kleist has him refuse a proffered seat at the table, a bearing which is consistent with Kleist's one-word characterization of the messenger, "feierlich." Jacob's change of color (either the Kleistian "Erröten" or "Erblassen" could be assumed here) supplies the dramatic contrast to the friendly reception of the messenger, and finally the sudden outburst in direct discourse which forms the emotional climax of the scene shatters the silence of the pantomime.

> Like all of Kleist's Novellen, "Der Zweikampf" is memorable for the pervasive dynamism which animates the prose narrative. Never is this poet content with merely static description: everything—the characters, the public surrounding them, the phases of the day are, like the language itself, constantly in motion.
>
> —*Donald H. Crosby*

With respect to both its style and its central problem, **"Der Zweikampf"** suggests comparison with **"Die Marquise von O. . . . ,"** a Novelle in which Kleist again combined an existential crisis with a paradox-mystery plot. In both Novellen, it is recalled, Kleist defers solution until after an apparently "airtight" case has been built up against the heroines. Also, both Littegarde and the Marquise are described in such terms (the former as "die unbescholtenste und makelloseste Frau des Landes," the latter as "eine Dame von vortrefflichem Ruf") and, indeed, comport themselves in such a way that the reader can hardly doubt their innocence. Yet the condition of the Marquise is undeniable, and Jacob's claim to having spent a night of love with Littegarde seems well-documented.

Both Novellen, too, are hobbled with improbabilities: in **"Der Zweikampf"** Jacob is duped into spending the all-important love night with Littegarde's scheming chambermaid Rosalie, all the while thinking that it was Littegarde who had succumbed to his charm. This century-old literary fiction is made all the harder to take by our knowledge that Rosalie had in fact been Jacob's paramour for a time; now we are asked to believe that this worldly man would be so carried away by the "Taumel des Vergnügens, in seinem Alter noch eine solche Eroberung gemacht zu haben," that his senses were blinded to a gross deception! Likewise, in the **"Marquise von O...."** we must believe that an intelligent widow, awakening from a faint, would be unaware of the fact that she had just been raped. In addition, we must close our eyes to the failure of the Marquise's family to guess the identity of the perpetrator, and to such bizarre spectacles as the pathological behavior of the father in the reconciliation scene and the unrelenting punishment imposed upon him by his wife. Such flaws are, of course, irreconcilable with a consistent realism, but they are characteristic rather than atypical in Kleist's *Novellen,* and additional examples could be adduced at length. As Walter Silz has recently written [in *Heinrich von Kleist: Studies in His Literary Character,* 1961]: "These realistically implausible factors deepen the impression that Kleist's work is that of a visionary who imposes an inner world on an outer, a stylist who uses the devices of realism, but not a realist in the true sense of the term."

Looking back at the chronicle, we note that actually five major germinal motifs were transplanted by Kleist into the richer soil of the Novelle: 1) the rape of Lady Carouge; 2) the motif of *Vertrauen,* evidenced by Carouge's faith in his wife; 3) the legal stalemate arising from Jacob's alibi; 4) the "first blood" drawn by the eventual loser of the duel; 5) the pious acceptance of the duel's outcome as a manifestation of God's will.

Kleist's reworking of his source material around these main motifs offers numerous insights into his creative process. The first alteration made by the poet, after substituting fictionalized names for the historical characters, was to change the motive crime from rape to murder by having Duke William struck down on the first page of the story. The Duke's murder served Kleist in two ways: the unsolved crime created a "Rahmen" for the central Littegarde plot, and the Duke's prompt exit made room for a new male protagonist of greater fictional potential. Kleist thus effectively added an air of mystery to the anecdote's "open and shut" case, and conjugal devotion was replaced with the tension of burgeoning romance.

The motif of physical rape, which perforce vanished when Kleist invented the Duke's murder, nevertheless survives vestigially in the assault on Littegarde's "good name," for Jacob's claim to have spent the murder night in Littegarde's bed chamber dishonors her in her own eyes as much as if he had actually violated her person. And Littegarde, though as a character she lacks the sharp "profile" of other Kleist heroines—one thinks of Penthesilea, the Marquise von O...., and Alkmene—is subjected to agonies of the spirit no less excruciating than those suffered by her fictional half-sisters. One might venture the claim that Littegarde, in her passivity, is in some ways the most tortured of Kleist's heroines. The Marquise von O.... whose predicament most closely resembles Littegarde's, has a certain "modern" sense of female emancipation which furthers a quick recovery after the agonized hour at her father's house; also she finds a mystical-religious solace in associating her situation—however inappropriately—with that of the Virgin Mary. Littegarde, however, finds herself defeated and condemned by just that agency in which her simple piety had placed its trust: the judgment of the Almighty. . . .

Sir Friedrich von Trota, as Littegarde's champion in the trial by combat, becomes the fictive surrogate for the outraged spouse of the anecdote, and his role in **"Der Zweikampf"** is greatly deepened. He of course functions as the masculine pole of the new romantic attraction added by Kleist, but more important he represents a bastion of the *Vertrauen* constantly pursued by Kleist's characters. In the *Abendblätter,* there is a trace of doubt detectable in Carouge's words to his wife just before the battle: "Madame, in Eurer Fehde, und auf Eure Versicherung schlage ich jetzt mein Leben in die Schanze, und fechte mit Jakob dem Grauen; niemand weiß besser als Ihr, ob meine Sache gut und gerecht ist." In **"Der Zweikampf,"** Trota's trust knows no such reservations. "Genug, meine teure Littegarde!" he cries, interrupting her narration of the unhappy events, "verliert kein Wort zur Verteidigung und Rechtfertigung Eurer Unschuld!" The Kleistian "Goldwaage der Empfindungen" has convinced him of the lady's innocence, and no further evidence is needed: "In meiner Brust spricht eine Stimme für Euch, weit lebhafter und überzeugender, als alle Versicherungen, ja selbst als alle Rechtgründe und Beweise, die Ihr vielleicht . . . vor dem Gericht zu Basel für Euch aufzubringen vermögt". Trota's greatest "Vertrauensprobe" however comes after his apparent defeat in the trial by combat. The *Faust*-like *Kerkerszene* in which Trota, still weak from his wounds and oblivious to the outraged protests of his mother and sisters, limps to Littegarde's cell to console the wretched woman—*in whom he still believes!*—supplies one of the most moving tableaus in Kleist's entire *Novellistik.*

In the source, Jacob's denial of the rape leads ultimately to the adjudication of Carouge's complaint by the Parliament at Paris, where "Das Tribunal" ordains a trial by combat as the only means for settling the dispute. That this legal stalemate must have had an immediate fascination for Kleist is clear from the prominence he gave to such proceedings in his own works; the "Fehmgericht" in

Kätchen von Heilbronn, the "Kriegsgericht" of the *Prinz von Homburg,* and the legal labyrinth of **Michael Kohlhaas** are only obvious examples. Jacob's simple time-space alibi reported in the chronicle, however, had to yield to a more elaborate defense in the fictionalized atmosphere of **"Der Zweikampf."** In the Novelle, Jacob insists that he spent the night of the crime in the boudoir of the noble Littegarde, and even produces an "eloquent object," a ring from the lady's finger, as proof of his conquest. The kernel of the alibis of both the historical and fictional Jacob thus remains the same: it is impossible for a man to be in two different places at the same time; but the "twist" Kleist gives to Jacob the Grey's tricky equestrian feat actually leads to the main problem of **"Der Zweikampf,"** Littegarde's quest for vindication. In addition, the fact that Jacob the Red-beard sincerely believes that he is telling the truth proves to be a fertile invention by Kleist; it raises the fictional villain several cuts above the crafty liar of the source, and at the same time beclouds the point at issue in the "Gottesurteil." Finally, when the end of the Novelle reveals the emptiness of Jacob's claim—he had of course been duped by the chambermaid—we see how the poet was able to develop a simple alibi into a favorite motif of "illusion versus reality."

The antithesis between *Wahn und Wirklichkeit* also figures prominently in the next motif expanded by Kleist, that of the wound suffered by the historical Carouge. In the *Abendblätter* we read only that it was sustained in the "Schenkel" and that Carouge, thanks to his "Wut und Geschicklichkeit," succeeded in defeating his adversary. In **"Der Zweikampf"** it is Jacob—and thus again the eventual "victor"—who is dealt the first wound, which (oddly enough!) Kleist transfers to the wrist joint, and which is described as being nothing more than a scratch. In keeping with his character, Jacob's conduct in the duel is portrayed as being uncourtly, even ignoble. When he is wounded, he momentarily breaks off the combat ("geschreckt"!) to assess the damage, an action which moves the spectators to grumbling, and when he does prevail over Trota, it is less through "anger and dexterity" than through unsportsmanlike conduct. The wound itself is quickly forgotten in the wake of events following Jacob's apparent victory in the duel, and ten pages (in the standard edition) pass before we hear of it again. Yet the wound, "unbedeutend" only "dem Anschein nach," has actually taken a hideous development, as Kleist unsparingly makes clear: "ein ätzender, der ganzen damaligen Heilkunst unbekannter Eiter fraß, auf eine krebsartige Weise, bis auf den Knochen herab im ganzen System seiner Hand um sich, dergestalt, daß man zum Entsetzen aller seiner Freunde genötigt gewesen war, ihm die ganze schadhafte Hand, und späterhin, da auch hierdurch dem Eiterfraß kein Ziel gesetzt ward, den Arm selbst abzunehmen . . . Die Ärzte, da sich sein ganzer Körper nach und nach in Eiterung und Fäulnis auflöste, erklärten, daß keine Rettung für ihn sei." Only at this point, then, do we become aware that an apparently trifling incident described ten pages back was actually the *Wendepunkt* of the Novelle; that Jacob had enjoyed the illusion, but not the reality of victory; and that the "Gottersurteil," as the dying Jacob's interpretation has it, was ultimately correct.

It is precisely because of the "delayed action" of the "Gottesurteil" that the role assigned to the Deity in **"Der Zweikampf"** has been the subject of numerous interpretations by Kleist scholars. No such diversity of interpretation could possibly be provoked by the source, where Carouge slays Jacob, is acclaimed the victor, and hastens his faithful Lady off to Mass. It is clear that God is unquestioningly recognized as the divine instrument of victory, and the infallibility of the trial by combat is upheld. The conclusion of the Novelle has fared quite differently, for Trota's apparent defeat and his miraculous recovery, coupled with the gruesome reversal of Jacob's fortunes, suggest a more equivocal attitude toward God on Kleist's part. Gerhard Fricke [in *Gefühl und Schicksal bei Heinrich Von Kleist,* 1929] saw Trota as a religious prophet of sorts, one who conquers God with God and creates "eine neue, dem Ewigen gemäßere Form." Lugowski [in *Wirklichkeit und Dictung,* 1936] described God in **"Der Zweikampf"** as a *Hilfskonstruktion,* and, interpreting the Novelle as an apotheosis of *Gefühl,* went even farther than Fricke: "Mit dem *'Zweikampf'* hat Kleist die letzte und höchste objektive Möglichkeit: Gott selbst zerschlagen."

Among more recent writers, Friedrich Koch [in his *Heinrich von Kleist,* 1958] regards the ordeal by combat as a clumsy institution, which impedes yet reveals God's will: "Aber Gott bedient sich dieser menschlich unvollkommenen Einrichtung, um in ihr und durch sie hindruch seine Gerechtigkeit offenbar werden zu lassen, nicht wie die Menschen denken, sondern frei nach seinem Ratschluß. So bleibt Gottes Gottheit bewahrt." At the other extreme is Walter Silz's categorical dismissal of any intrusion from *jenseits* in this tale: "The outcome . . . is a solution without god, in purely human terms. . . . God was not needed for the solution in this story, and nothing is adduced to prove that He is anything but a figment of men's minds."

Such learned disagreement underscores the point that the solution of **"Der Zweikampf"** is steeped in duality, a duality which is the last significant improvement Kleist made on his source. The author obviously does not insist that *we* believe that the delayed revelation of the true victor of the trial by combat is a manifestation, say, of God's mills "grinding slowly but exceedingly fine." There is no palpable miracle in **"Der Zweikampf"** to compare with the earthly visit of Saint Cecelia in **"Die heilige Cäcelia,"** and neither the "miraculous" recovery of Trota nor the progressive decay of Jacob need be classed as preternatural; like the appearance of the cranes in Schiller's "Kraniche des Ibykus" they can be explained away as mere coincidence. Yet belief in God and the mysterious workings of His ways is—for the *dramatis personae* of **"Der Zweikampf"**—an absolute historical and structural necessity.

Nowhere in the story is this made clearer than in Jacob's "deathbed" confession, in which he finally exonerates Littegarde from the charge he had erringly pressed against her: "[Sie ist] unschuldig . . . , wie es der Spruch des höchsten Gottes, an jenem verhängnisvollen Tage, vor den Augen aller versammelten Bürger von Basel entschieden hat! Denn er, von drei Wunden, jede tödlich, getroffen, blüht, wie ihr seht, in Kraft und Lebensfülle, indessen ein

Hieb von seiner Hand, der kaum die äußerlich Hülle meines Lebens zu berühren schien, . . . meine Kraft . . . gefällt hat."

Jacob's confession complements words spoken by Trota after his recovery, words which form the *Idee* of the Novelle: "Wo liegt die Verpflichtung der höchsten göttlichen Weisheit, die Wahrheit, im Augenblick der glaubensvollen Anrufung selbst, anzuzeigen und auszusprechen? . . . deine Unschuld wird, und wird durch den Zweikampf, den ich für dich gefochten, zum heitern, hellen Licht der Sonne gebracht werden. These lines are invariably cited (at least in part) by commentators on **"Der Zweikampf,"** and have been made to serve many points of view. Within the context of the Novelle itself, however, Trota's words do not destroy the notion of God's intervention in the trial by combat, but rather redefine God as a superior being who, in His wisdom, will speak the truth when it pleases Him and not necessarily mankind. Trota's words are those of a man ahead of his time, and this "new" interpretation of the working of the Deity is a first step toward the notion that man's fate is independent of a direct "Gottesurteil"; perhaps independent of God's will entirely. From this position, he indeed "might have gone further," as Silz suggests, to question the very existence of God, but he does not.

Toward its conclusion, then, the Novelle becomes pregnant with that atmosphere of change one finds evoked in Hebbel's plays. Only in such a context can sense be made of the closing paragraph, in which the Emperor amends the articles of the "geheiligten göttlichen Zweikampf" (as it is pointedly called) to include the phrase "if it be God's will" wherever the assumption exists, "daß die Schuld unmittelbar ans Tagelicht komme." That it is sheer presumption to expect God to adjudicate human quarrels, "unmittelbar" or any other way, does not and cannot occur to the Emperor, who unlike Trota is every inch a man of his time. The delayed action of the "Gottesurteil" in **"Der Zweikampf"** has merely driven a chink into what was previously a monolith of medieval dogma. Subsequent events will widen this chink until the monolith splits and falls, but all this, like the logical answer to Trota's question, lies in a future well beyond the temporal boundary of the Novelle.

Although any "ranking" of Kleist's Novellen will of necessity always be a subjective matter, it seems clear that **"Der Zweikampf"** need not shirk comparison with its companion pieces in the slim volume Kleist left to posterity. Bold in conception, unexcelled as an apotheosis of *Vertrauen,* **"Der Zweikampf"** deserves recognition as a thought-provoking amalgam of the medieval and the modern. Kleist's final Novelle is a fitting epitaph to his greatness.

Richard L. Johnson (essay date 1975)

SOURCE: "Kleist's *Erdbeben in Chili,*" in *Seminar,* Vol. XI, No. 1, February, 1975, pp. 33-45.

[*In the following essay, Johnson explores Kleist's preoccupation with morality, and focuses on its role in "Das Erdbeben in Chili."*]

Kleist subordinated knowledge to moral action. In some of his works understanding plays a central role, but only *after* a main character is able to act in a threatening situation. In **"Das Erdbeben von Chili"** Jeronimo and Josephe act with great resolve to save their child, but they die before knowledge is attained. Don Fernando does have time to reflect about the child he has lost and the child he has saved, but his knowledge at the end of the story is tentative at best. Kleist placed much more emphasis on Don Fernando's courageous actions in his struggle against the mob.

Kleist suggested in a letter to his publisher that his first volume of stories, including **Michael Kohlhaas, "Die Marquise von O. . . ,"** and **"Erdbeben,"** be called *Moralische Erzählungen.* Although the suggestion was not carried out, the intent is significant. It is surprising that few interpretations focus on the ethical aspects in these stories. Karl Otto Conrady has made a major contribution to Kleist scholarship by emphasizing moral action and the interaction of characters. . . . However he does not see that Kleist, by placing his characters into positions that require ethical responses, provides positive and negative examples of action. Conrady asserts: 'Es sind keine Vorbild-Modelle für menschliches Verhalten, die vorgeführt werden. Zwar leuchten unableitbare Festpunkte letzter Wahrheit in dem Versuchsspiel Kleistischer Erzählung auf: das Zusichselbstfinden und das Vertrauen zum Du, was beides zusammengehört. Aber der Erzähler selbst bleibt Fragender, ist suchender Erzähler.' In **"Erdbeben"** some actions are meant to display what an ethical person ought to do, and others what he ought not to do.

In his recent interpretation, 'Skepsis, Noblesse, Ironie: Formen des Als-ob in Kleists "Erdbeben" [in *Euphorion,* 63, 1969], Wolfgang Wittkowski discusses the ethical aspect in **"Erdbeben."** He states that the only secure foundation the author portrays is 'das Ethische, das Ethos der Noblesse, in dem das trügerische Als-ob unkritischer Erkenntnis von vornherein "aufgehoben," nämlich angeeignet und der höchsten Aufgabe, der moralischen Bewährung, dienstbar gemacht ist.' His concept of *Noblesse* cannot, however, be accepted here. Wittkowski describes ethical nobility as a state of being, a quality in a character which distinguishes him from others. As will be shown below, by 1801 Kleist had lost his faith that man could attain a state of being, whether through knowledge or virtue, which assured him of moral action when faced with a threatening event. This analysis deals first with the illusions and tragic errors of the main characters and then proceeds to their responses to the world of appearances.

There are three distinct sections of the story: the earthquake in Santiago and the flight from the city, the survivors' idyll in the country, and the tragic events at the church after their return. The violent deaths in the city in the first and last sections stand in stark contrast to the harmony which all experience in nature. Kleist's language reveals that the complete social unity of the middle section is beautiful but illusory. . . .

The influence of Rousseau here is clear and has often been stressed. However the 'als ob' and 'schien' indicate that the idyll in nature has limited validity. As Müller-Seidel has stated [in *Versehen und Erkennen*], Jeronimo's and Josephe's tragic decision to return to Santiago is a result of their failure to recognize the 'Als-Ob-Charakter dieser Welt'.

The most striking paradox of the story—that Josephe's religious impulse to thank God for her deliverance leads to her death—cannot be understood without reference to her misunderstanding of the events in the middle section. Jeronimo falls prey to illusion before Josephe, and, although she seems to recognize the potential danger of returning to the city, she obviously does not understand that the harmony in nature is temporary. The human spirit that unfolded 'wie eine schöne Blume' is a part of man, but the violence and hatred in the last section are no less human. The failure to interpret the world accurately occurs in every section of the story. After his escape from the city Jeronimo at first thanks God for his deliverance and then turns against him because Josephe has apparently died. The priest's statement that God was punishing the city for Jeronimo's and Josephe's sins is one of the most disastrous misunderstandings of the story. J. M. Ellis [in 'Kleist's "Das Erdbeben in Chili," *Publications of the English Goethe Society*, 32, 1962-63] has explained the role of interpretation in **"Erdbeben"** particularly well. The characters, even the narrator, go from one interpretation to another. But Ellis fails to see that accurate interpretation of events is possible and that Kleist placed even more emphasis on courageous action than on the problem of understanding.

Donna Elisabeth speaks out against returning to the city even before Josephe expresses her desire to go. It is important that both Jeronimo and Josephe were aware of the dangers in Santiago and had agreed twice not to return. Kleist drew attention to their decisions by placing them at the end of both the first and second sections. The lovers do not consider returning the first time because the experiences of cruel social conventions and personal betrayals are still fresh in their minds. Towards the end of the second section they have been so moved by the warm reception of Don Fernando and his group that their earlier experiences are nearly forgotten. Donna Elisabeth's warning should make a strong impression on Josephe who, on the previous day, was nearly executed by church officials. . . . Josephe's and Jeronimo's tragic error is understandable, but we must not assume that Kleist was portraying a world in which events are always inexplicable. Donna Elisabeth's statement and premonition are too well founded and too prominent in the story to be ignored.

Josephe and most of the other characters try unsuccessfully to interpret both human nature and divine will. Even before the second section she and Jeronimo 'waren sehr gerührt, wenn sie dachten, wie viel Elend über die Welt kommen mußte, *damit* sie glücklich würden!' (italics mine).

Their reaction is innocent enough, but the implication that others die so that they can be happy can be dangerous. Josephe's religious interpretation of the earthquake comes out clearly the next day while she is with Don Fernando's group: 'Josephe dünkte sich unter den Seligen. Ein Gefühl, das sie nicht unterdrücken konnte, nannte den verflossnen Tag, so viel Elend er auch über die Welt gebracht hatte, eine Wohltat, wie der Himmel noch keine über sie verhängt hatte.' Although she later states that God's power is inexplicable, she obviously feels that his will was manifested in the earthquake. She is favoured by God and therefore need not be concerned about the dangers in Santiago. Neither her interpretation nor the priest's that the earthquake was God's punishment can be accepted.

Kleist's works and letters reveal that he was nearly overwhelmed by man's fragile and often inadequate understanding of the world. During all of his adult life he was searching for meaning and a sense of direction. As a young man he hoped to attain happiness by fulfilling one of his most sacred duties, his moral education. All virtue is rewarded, all vice punished, for happiness is the impetus to virtue and virtue the path to happiness. Although he admitted that he did not fully understand the nature of virtue, he felt that the clarity of his moral vision had already increased so much that continued progress was assured. Kleist's assertions at this time are often so strident that we sense his deeper uncertainty, but he clearly wanted to believe that man could live according to moral precepts which lead to happiness. He decided to dedicate himself to science because virtue was an inevitable result of increased knowledge.

Later Kleist revealed in his letters to his fiancée a new model of virtue, Ludwig Brockes, but one who taught that 'Handeln ist besser als Wissen' (31 January 1801). Kleist moved away from knowledge to an ideal of moral action at least in part derived from Schiller's dramas. . . .

It seems that Kleist's Kant crisis, which occurred only two months after his ecstatic praise of Brockes, was prepared when he lost his faith in knowledge as the primary guide to virtue and happiness. The Kant crisis was so devastating not only because Kleist felt that man cannot perceive the real world as it is, but also because man must act virtuously in a world which is misleading. In his letters and creative works Kleist does not dwell on the problem of knowledge, but rather on the necessity of moral action even though it is difficult to avoid error: 'es liegt eine Schuld auf den Menschen, etwas Gutes zu tun, verstehe mich recht, ohne figürlich zu reden, schlechthin zu *tun*' (15 August 1801). His 'tatenlechzendes Herz' compelled him to desire much throughout his life: his own farm, a child, a great deed, an extraordinary literary work, a successful literary journal and newspaper, victory over the French, and finally a death arising out of devotion to the incurable Henriette Vogel. This impulse found its highest expression in his stories and dramas.

In confronting a threatening event a Kleistian hero must possess the inner strength to overcome the danger by affirming another character. If he acts in isolation or fails to act, he falls into despair; if his bond is strong enough, he acts resolutely and triumphs. Courageous action generally leads to the character's acceptance of an inscrutable God. Both the courage and the acceptance are the central ethical imperatives in Kleist's works. Paul Tillich's discussion of courage and religious acceptance in *The Courage to Be* and *The Dynamics of Faith* is particularly relevant here. His contrast between despair and courage reveals their ethical and religious significance. He sees the essence of faith in total acceptance of and submission to God.

Kleist's works and letters reveal that he was nearly overwhelmed by man's fragile and often inadequate understanding of the world. During all of his adult life he was searching for meaning and a sense of direction.

—Richard L. Johnson

There is practically no biographical evidence that Kleist was as religious as Tillich or even that he considered himself to be a Christian. His strong feelings against established religion come out clearly in **"Erdbeben."** The condemnation of Jeronimo's and Josephe's natural love by the church is portrayed as unjust, and their final brutal murder is a direct result of the priest's sermon. A profound distrust of all religious speculation is evident throughout the story. However, as was so common among Kleist's contemporaries, rejection of religious institutions was by no means a rejection of divine will or the religious impulse in man. Wittkowski asserts that Kleist enthroned, like Kant and Fichte, 'die autonome Moralität . . . als wahre Religion."

In the first paragraph of **"Erdbeben"** it is reported that Jeronimo has made several vain efforts to escape from prison and is now in despair: 'Doch der gefürchtete Tag erschien, und mit ihm in seiner Brust die Überzeugung von der völligen Hoffnungslosigkeit seiner Lage. Die Glocken, welche Josephen zum Richtplatze begleiteten, ertönten, und Verzweiflung bemächtigte sich seiner Seele.' He is unable to gain solace in her love for him or in faith that they might be united after death. Nothing exists for him but his own feeling of utter hopelessness. As he escapes from Santiago during the earthquake, he is too confused and occupied with himself to consider Josephe. He remains unaffected by the fortunes of those around him, even by the good example of others. After he is safe, his first feeling is the joy of living and the next, gratitude to God. He turns against God when he thinks Josephe may be dead. Although he inquires about her, he never returns to the place of execution. His isolation is so great that he is totally oblivious to the fate of the child.

Josephe's actions provide a strong contrast to his. Although she is about to be executed, she experiences no despair. When the earthquake begins, she is at first terri-

fied and starts to run towards the nearest gate. . . . Her progress through the city is even more strikingly different from Jeronimo's. . . . *He* is overpowered by his own distress, but *she* goes on 'durch das Entsetzen gestärkt.' Josephe's love for the child, her strength and purpose in the face of the ruins where Jeronimo had been, prove that she is 'mutig.' After she is safe, her first thoughts are not of herself, but of Jeronimo. She fears that he is dead, but, instead of turning against God, she prays to him for Jeronimo's soul. Josephe acts with courage and continues to demonstrate love and devotion, in spite of the destruction she sees around her. Surely Kleist intended her actions to serve as a model, a corrective to Jeronimo's in the mind of the reader.

In the idyllic setting of the second section no one is called upon to respond to danger. The survivors do, however, recall the courageous acts required in their escape from Santiago. . . . The people are bound not merely by their sorrows and the subsequent joy of deliverance, but also by the experience of these acts: 'nicht einer war, für den nicht an diesem Tage etwas Rührendes geschehen wäre, oder der nicht selbst etwas Großmütiges getan hätte.' Josephe's affirmative action in the first section and the 'ungeheure Taten' reported here prepare the reader for the resolve and self-sacrifice displayed in the last section.

The scene within and just outside the church in the last section is filled with chance occurrences and rapid changes in the fortunes of the heroes. When Josephe's child goes to Don Fernando, the crowd believes that he is the father, and the cries 'Steinigt sie. Steinigt sie!' come from the whole congregation. Jeronimo identifies himself to save Don Fernando, and when a friend of Don Fernando appears, it seems that they will all escape. The cobbler points out Josephe to the crowd, but they reach the front of the church unharmed. 'The reader is almost dizzy after this succession of changes of fortune; they are so many, so entirely fortuitous, and so serious in their eventual consequences, that it seems we should never be able to make any sense of this bewildering sequence' [Ellis].

And yet, although the events change rapidly, the courage of Jeronimo, Josephe, and Don Fernando remain constant throughout the scene. Jeronimo, who could not face Josephe's execution, is now able to save Don Fernando's life by calling attention to himself. He is killed, but only after his courageous act. By saving Don Fernando's life, he has made his own child's survival possible. Josephe, when she sees that Don Fernando and the two children are about to be overcome by the mob, cries out: ' "hier mordet mich, ihr blutdürstenden Tiger!" und stürzte sich freiwilling unter sie.' Although Jeronimo and Josephe die, their lives are not without meaning and consequence. Their child is saved because both parents were willing to sacrifice their lives for him and the others. They are not entirely successful, for Don Fernando's child and Donna Constanze are ruthlessly murdered; but no one can doubt the importance of their actions.

After the death of the lovers Don Fernando is the only character who is able to stand up against the mob. He is, in Kleist's words, 'dieser göttliche Held.' The source of his courageous acts is in part his sense of responsibility for the others. He fought to protect not only Jeronimo, Josephe, and their child, but also Donna Constanze and his own child. But when Kleist calls him the divine hero, he suggests that he could not act as he did without being in harmony with God. In his final defence, with his sword fighting against the 'satanische Rotte,' he is strikingly similar to the archangel Michael. When his only child is murdered, he does not turn against God. Even though he experiences great pain, he demonstrates his acceptance of his fate by turning his eyes to heaven. Unlike the priest Don Fernando does not find anyone guilty for the events which he has experienced; and unlike Jeronimo shortly after the earthquake he does not inveigh against 'das Wesen, das über den Wolken waltet.'

The intimate relation between moral action and divine inscrutability is suggested in one of Kleist's letters to his friend Rühle von Lilienstern:

> Es kann kein böser Geist sein, der an der Spitze der Welt steht; es ist ein bloß unbegriffener! Lächeln wir nicht auch, wenn die Kinder weinen? Denke nur, diese unendliche Fortdauer! Myriaden von Zeiträumen, jedweder ein Leben, und für jedweden eine Erscheinung, wie diese Welt! Wie doch das kleine Sternchen heißen mag, das man auf dem Sirius, wenn der Himmel klar ist, sieht? Und dieses ganze ungeheure Firmament nur ein Stäubchen gegen die Unendlichkeit! O Rühle, sage mir, ist dies ein Traum? Zwischen je zwei Lindenblättern, wenn wir abends auf dem Rücken liegen, eine Aussicht, an Ahndungen reicher, als Gedanken fassen, und Worte sagen können. Komm, laß uns etwas Gutes tun, und dabei sterben! Einen der Millionen Tode, die wir schon gestorben sind, und noch sterben werden. Es ist, als ob wir aus einem Zimmer in das andere gehen. (31 August 1806)

He could see that we must act morally even though we shall never comprehend divine will. Moreover his acceptance of death is clarified: as long as we can do something good, we can die with the conviction that we are merely passing into another room. Jeronimo's death as a result of his efforts to save the others is incomparably more significant than if he had hanged himself in prison. The exultation Kleist experienced in preparation for his suicide was undoubtedly because he felt that he was dying for someone. The intention is clear even though Henriette Vogel had not been very important in his life. His death was in a way a fulfillment of his desire to affirm another person totally.

Don Fernando is not beyond error. Donna Elisabeth and his wife, Donna Elvire, warn him of the dangers of the city, but he does not wish to be deterred. Kleist suggests that Don Fernando fails to listen to them because he has already agreed to accompany Josephe to the city. The safety of the whole party may be less important to him than fulfilling his role as gentleman: 'Don Fernando stieg eine Röte des Unwillens ins Gesicht; er antwortete: es wäre gut! Donna Elvire möchte sich beruhigen; und führte seine Dame weiter.' This decision to ignore well founded warn-

ings may explain in part his reluctance to discuss the events at the church with his wife. The tragic error of Josephe, Jeronimo, and Don Fernando leads to the death of the lovers, Don Fernando's child Juan, and Donna Constanze. According to Wittkowski the decision to go to Santiago is a positive, noble disregard of possible dangers. 'Die Noblesse entfaltet sich umso reiner, je entschiedener sie die Gefahren ignoriert.' The inner strength of Kleist's heroes is not purer or more decisive because of ignorance, but rather in spite of it. It seems unlikely that Kleist would have the completely innocent Juan and Donna Constanze die, if he intended to portray the decision to go to Santiago as an expression of nobility of soul.

Kleist realized that individual actions—no matter how important they may be—are no more than moments in our lives. Even a cursory reading of his works reveals that these moments are central in his conception of the world, but he did not indicate that illusion and error could be overcome forever by courageous acts. Don Fernando cares about Philipp, the child of the lovers, and seems reconciled to the loss of his own child: 'wenn Don Fernando Philippen mit Juan verglich, und wie er beide erworben hatte, so war es ihm fast, als müßt er sich freuen.' However the 'fast' and the subjunctive express a degree of ambiguity that many scholars have failed to consider. [In *Das Bild in der Dichtung* 2, Marburg, 1939], Hermann Pongs asserts that Philipp's deliverance is 'ein untrügliches Zeichen einer höheren Ordnung.' A God who decides to allow the death of the innocent Juan but to save the innocent Philipp is certainly enigmatic. [In *Heinrich von Kleist: Studies in His Works and Literary Character*, Philadelphia, 1961], Walter Silz rightly criticizes optimistic interpretations of the events in **"Erdbeben,"** but he fails to recognize the importance of the main characters' actions: 'The surviving child is not a symbol of the triumph of love over death and evil; it is an example of the fortuitousness of existence in an incomprehensive world.' In Kleist's world the divine is generally manifested in human actions, not in events. In **"Erdbeben"** the two major occurrences of 'göttlich' refer to heroic affirmation. The survivors relate their experiences of the earthquake and speak of 'Beispiele . . . von Selbstverleugnung und der göttlichen Aufopferung.' The description of Don Fernando as 'der göttliche Held' is even more striking. The earthquake is no more than a natural phenomenon, but courageous actions express divine will.

Many of Kleist's characters in the stories and plays provide examples of moral action. The instances of failure to affirm others are the other side of the same coin, examples of how *not* to act in a threatening situation. When Homburg sees his open grave, he despairs and is willing to renounce everything to live, including his love for Natalie. The Kurfürstin recognizes his error and tells him he must display 'Mut' and 'Fassung.' In act IV, and even more clearly in act V, he finds the inner strength he needs because his faith in himself, the Kurfürst, and Natalie is regained. The Marquise von O, Friedrich von Trota in **"Der Zweikampf,"** Alkmene and Amphitryon, the lovers in *Schroffenstein*—all experience great conflict, even despair, but they are able to act for others.

Kleist was not merely 'auf der Suche nach Möglichkeiten menschlichen Verhaltens.' Unfortunately so many in his time and in ours have failed to see the ethical imperatives that Kleist portrayed in a number of his works. It is apparent that *Homburg* was not produced in Berlin during Kleist's lifetime because the inflexible, shortsighted Prussian court saw only cowardice and disgrace in Homburg. Although Kleist experienced quite deeply the despair man faces in a confusing world, he continued to believe that we are able to overcome threatening events as long as we have a significant bond to others. No one could deny that despair, error, and destruction form an integral part of **"Erdbeben."** Kleist's conception of the world revealed in the story was tragic, but he also demonstrated that courageous action and acceptance of an inscrutable God are both possible and significant expressions of man.

Robert E. Helbling (essay date 1975)

SOURCE: "The Foundling," "The Duel," "The Beggarwoman of Cocarno" and "St. Cecilia, or the Power of Music," in *The Major Works of Heinrich von Kleist*, New Directions Books, 1975, pp. 114-17, 152-59, 249-51.

[*Helbling is a Swiss-born American educator and critic. In the essay below, he analyzes the theme of artifice in "The Foundling," the anguish inherent in "St. Cecilia, or the Power of Music," and "The Beggarwoman of Locarno," and ambiguous aspects of "The Duel,"*]

"The Foundling"

It has been surmised that this *Novelle* is one of Kleist's earlier works, conceived sometime in 1805-6, and that it underwent considerable revision before it was finally published in volume two of his *Erzählungen* (1811). But it is equally plausible that he wrote it specifically for the purpose of amplifying the contents of the second tome, for which he apparently accepted a publishing contract before he had composed all of the requisite stories. In any case, **"The Foundling"** [**"Der Findling"**] has a plot that lends it a particular distinction among Kleist's works. It does not revolve around a character whose purity of feeling is subjected to severe, even cruel tests. At least none of the three principals is drawn from that angle of perception. Entrapped in an infernal rondo of events, they are rather shown to be inwardly tainted as though infected by a radical evil.

Piachi, a prosperous old merchant living in Rome at the time of the Renaissance, lost his young son during a plague. In his stead he adopted Nicolo, the very same boy who had infected his own son but, thanks to Piachi's care, recovered from the disease. He showers Nicolo with kindness as though he were his own son, rears him in his business, and makes him sole heir to his estate. Elvire, Piachi's young second wife, seemingly attached to her aging husband, pines away for the love of Colino, a young nobleman who had saved her life years before, and had subsequently died from an injury received in the attempt.

Nicolo bears a striking resemblance to the dead Colino. Unscrupulous, he knows how to take advantage of this coincidence and contrives to seduce his benefactor's wife. Caught in the attempt, he has the impudence to invoke his right of legal ownership to Piachi's estate and sends the old man packing, while Elvire, weak in health, dies from the shock of her experience. Piachi, seething with rage, crushes the usurper's skull in a scuffle and calmly surrenders to the authorities. Condemned to hang, he steadfastly refuses absolution, insisting that he wants to pursue his revenge against Nicolo in the deepest pit of hell.

The story goes through several cycles of irony and contains the usual Kleistian motifs of misjudgment, misuse of trust, and chance happenings. The orphan boy Nicolo, infected by the plague, moves Piachi to Christian charity, for which he must pay with his own son's life. And he adopts the orphan only to be brought to ruin by him. At the end the story takes an unexpected new turn when Piachi, not content with having snuffed out Nicolo's life, declares his intent to torture him further in a Dantesque inferno.

All three characters misjudge each other and thus help conjure up calamity. At one point, Elvire literally mistakes Nicolo for the ghost of Colino. Nicolo misinterprets Elvire's devotion to a man long since dead as a sign of her availability. Piachi gauges his adoptive son's character wrongly, although there is enough evidence that Nicolo is unworthy of his trust, and he also seems to underestimate, largely by ignoring them, Elvire's feelings for her departed lover. A diabolic streak of distorted character traits and specious feelings pervades the story from the start. Piachi's wooing of Elvire is done in a businesslike manner. Elvire's nostalgic attachment to her dead lover has a sickly element in it. Nicolo's callousness is alluded to early in the story when, instead of sharing Piachi's sorrow over the death of his son, he cracks open nuts and eats them with relish. As he grows older, he reveals himself more and more to be the parasite and sensualist he is. Caught in a maelstrom of inauthentic feelings, the three must destroy each other. The chance happenings which impel the action forward are but an expression of the dark forces that fix the course of their destinies. It is by coincidence that Nicolo chooses the Genoese costume to go to a ball in which he surprises Elvire, who then is struck for the first time by his astonishing resemblance to the dead Colino. Again as if by chance, Nicolo discovers that his first name is, mysteriously, an anagram of Colino. And Piachi happens to come home earlier than usual just as Nicolo is attempting to seduce the fainting Elvire.

Thematically, this intriguing *Novelle* cannot easily be assigned a proper place within the corpus of Kleist's works. It occupies its own unique position since it does not dwell much on the usual Kleistian theme of foiled inner certainties causing a tragic reorientation of the protagonist in a world of inescapable realities, although this theme could conceivably be read into Piachi's inner experience. In **"The Foundling,"** Kleist seems rather preoccupied with the preponderance of evil in the world manifesting itself in crass self-interest or counterfeit emotions. The logographic play with the two names "Colino" and "Nicolo" and the masquerade which so impresses Elvire suggest that Nicolo is the counterfeit of Colino. In their striking resemblance there is also a hint of the terrifying proximity of good and evil in the world. If Nicolo is the obverse of Colino, his impudence is a travesty of the dead man's courage, his lecherousness a parody of Colino's capacity for love. The most significant element in the story, however, is the enormity of Piachi's wrath, which takes on metaphysical dimensions:

> "I don't want to be saved, I want to go down to the lowest pit of hell. I want to find Nicolo again, who won't be in heaven, and take up my revenge again, which I could only satisfy partly here!" And with these words he climbed the ladder and told the hangman to do his duty.

Ultimately, it is directed at evil *per se* rather than an evildoer. Piachi embodies Kleist's outrage—by proxy, to be sure—toward the prevalence of egotism, sham feelings, and abuse of trust in the world. What cannot be set aright can only be trampled under foot. No redeeming force can be detected in the *Novelle*. Even Elvire's love for her dead hero lacks strength and viability. Piachi is a metaphysical rebel; all he can do is combat evil with evil. But through the immensity of his revenge, the unflinching adherence to his dark purpose, he belongs in that gallery of strong-willed Kleistian heroes, such as Guiscard, Kohlhaas, and Arminius, whose revolt transcends personal interests.

"The Beggarwoman of Locarno" and "St. Cecilia, or the Power of Music"

Despite its conciliatory ending, Kleist's last drama [*Prinz Friedrich von Homburg*] contains many jarring notes of disquietude. The suggestion of the disturbing rupture between conscious actions and unconscious motives as well as Homburg's final expression of disbelief cast a pall of doubt on the ideal which the play depicts. In quick, furtive flashes Kleist bares the make-believe character of an idealistic philosophy. Its notion of a Rational State ensuing from the individual's enactment of moral freedom is at best a beautiful dream. But for a fleeting moment in his career as a writer Kleist acted as though the dream of Reason were valid. In one sense, his Idealistic legacy to the world shares the "as if" nature of Kant's moral philosophy. The notion of a Kingdom of Ends is viable only if it is assumed that nature itself is a kingdom governed by a teleological law and is so constituted as to guarantee and even promote man's moral activities. The Kantian moral faith makes some sense if one embraces the corollary belief in universal teleology. But Kant asserted emphatically that the idea of purpose can never be a constitutive principle of knowledge and therefore does not properly belong to the realm of "nature." He points the way to an existential view: against the uncooperativeness of nature to reveal its purposes, practical reason must stress the need for self-determination in accord with a normative and faintly teleological law. And although Kant attached to the exercise of the purposive faculty of the will the

promise of a future world and the existence of God, what remains prominent in his view of moral action is man's autonomy, his self-dependence, the human predicament of having to make choices in an ostensibly purposeless and impassive universe. The moral law is ultimately something quite apart from being. In Kant's ethical voluntarism, one can detect the germs of existential anguish.

In his last two stories, "The Beggarwoman of Locarno" ["Das Bettelweib von Locarno"] and "St. Cecilia, or the Power of Music," ["Die heilige Cäcilie"] Kleist reverts again to the anguished mood of his earlier works. They depict a world which, far from rational, is not only impassive to the purposive drive of man, but alien, absurd, even grotesque and strangely dualistic. "The Beggarwoman . . . ," little more than a brief anecdote, is literally a ghost story portraying the irruption of an incomprehensible, destructive force in human life. A marquis who had indirectly caused the death of an old beggarwoman finds a miserable end in his burning castle, which he had set afire himself, "weary of life," after he had vainly attempted to exorcize the spirit of the dead woman. Although there is a hint of moral justice in the story, the maniacal frenzy of the nobleman and other narrative elements create an atmosphere of unrelieved anguish. In this sense the anecdote is a transposition of Kleist's predominant inner mood into a succinct artistic metaphor.

"St. Cecilia, or the Power of Music" is a more complex and grotesque tale of an event taking place in the (imaginary) Cloister of St. Cecilia near Aachen during the time of the religious wars. Four brothers, iconoclasts, plan to destroy the cloister but are diverted from their intent by a strange miracle. Sister Antonia, believed to be seriously ill, suddenly appears, wan but healthy, and leads the congregation in an oratorio whose musical splendor forces the four marauders to their knees in reverent prayer. It turns out that Sister Antonia had laid unconscious in her cell the whole time, while St. Cecilia herself must have conducted the oratorio, a conjecture later sanctioned by the Pope. But it is the aftermath to the oratorio that is most puzzling. The miracle conjures up in the four brothers a state of mind that can only be described as religious hysteria. They spend the rest of their lives observing silence, fasting, worshiping the crucifix, and singing at regular intervals the *gloria in excelsis*. At a ripe old age, they die, a seemingly happy lot, but not before having sung once more the *gloria* with booming voices that reverberate grotesquely through the insane asylum to which they had been committed.

In his last two stories, Kleist depicts a world in which good and evil, the heavenly and diabolic, the fearful and exalted, live in confusing proximity, a stark contrast to Homburg's ideal world of moral purposiveness. Yet, when he finally made his choice to commit suicide, Kleist seemed to have regained a measure of confidence in the ultimate goodness of the world and the eternal purpose of the soul. His last letters, no doubt written in a state of euphoria, abound with metaphysical hopes and a joyous anticipation of happiness and the discovery of life's meaning in a blessed hereafter. If he did not possess it in this life, Kleist seems to have taken a certain faith in a Kingdom of Ends into his voluntary death. But one cannot help overhearing in his death litany some of the hysterical accents of the *gloria in excelsis* sung by the four brothers in **"St. Cecilia, or the Power of Music."**

"The Duel"

Thematically, **"The Duel"** ["Der Zweikampf"] with its complicated plot may well be the most ambiguous of Kleist's *Novellen.* As in *The Schroffenstein Family, Amphitryon,* and **"The Marquise of O——,"** factual evidence points in one direction and the inner feeling of the innocent victims in another. But here, the conflict between reason and feeling is compounded by the enigmatic outcome of a trial by combat said to reveal the will of God. In the ordeal, the evildoer is victorious but later dies from a festering disease caused by a paltry wound he received in the combat, while his mortally wounded opponent recovers miraculously. In this *Novelle,* God appears to be as ambiguous, though in a different way, as in **"The Earthquake in Chile,"** where He unleashes a natural catastrophe killing thousands of people in order to save two wayward lovers from certain death, only to have them slaughtered by a horde of religious zealots.

Set at the end of the fourteenth century in southern Germany, the plot of **"The Duel"** consists of two distinct threads brought together in an alibi offered by a suspected murderer in court. Accused of the assassination of his brother, Count Redbeard admits that the murder weapon, an arrow, is indeed his but insists that he had spent the night of the murder in the castle of Littegarde, a widowed noble lady living far away from the scene of the crime. As evidence he produces a ring which Littegarde had allegedly given him as a token of love. Littegarde, though recognizing the ring as hers, denies the allegations made against her by the unwanted suitor. Driven away and disowned by her family, she seeks refuge with Friedrich of Trota, a friend and protector, who takes up the cudgels for her and challenges Redbeard to a trial by arms. In the combat, Trota slips and is mortally wounded. Littegarde's dishonor seems to be proved beyond doubt, since God had spoken against her through the trial. But Friedrich recovers from his severe wounds, while his practically unharmed opponent slides ever closer toward death. Yet, the law demands that Littegarde and Friedrich be burned at the stake for their perjury before God, despite the strange sequel to the duel. As preparations for the supplice are made, the full truth is revealed. The ring had actually been given to Redbeard in the dark of night by Littegarde's scheming maid. She had succeeded in disguising herself as her mistress and letting herself be seduced by Redbeard, who thought all along that he had made Littegarde's conquest—a somewhat operatic and contrived occurrence reminiscent of the plot of *The Schroffenstein Family.* The ring episode, in casting a pall on Littegarde's honor, had almost eclipsed the original issue of Redbeard's culpability. But now that his alibi has been proved invalid and he is about to die, the contrite Redbeard confesses to the murder of his brother, whom he had had killed by a hired assassin. Littegarde and Friedrich are united in marriage

by the Emperor as Redbeard's body burns at the stake in their stead. Afterward, the Emperor affixes an amendment to the statutes governing trial by arms to the effect that an ordeal will immediately reveal truth "only if it be God's will."

It is readily apparent that the focus of the *Novelle* is not so much on the murder of Redbeard's brother as on Littegarde and the strange ways of God to man suggested in the unexpected aftermath of the duel. With obvious irony in mind, Kleist says explicitly at one point in the story that the law of holy combat will infallibly bring the truth to light, when he has actually constructed his plot in such a way as to make the outcome equivocal no matter who wins the duel. For Redbeard is as much convinced of the truth of his statement concerning the ring as are Littegarde and Friedrich of his dishonesty. In this respect, both accused and accuser are equally deceived. Under the circumstances, what is actually called into question is not the truth or untruth of their conflicting beliefs but the validity of the law of holy combat itself. In Kleist, things never are what they seem, the truth supposedly revealed in a trial by arms not exempt. Had Redbeard been worsted in the combat, he would have expiated the murder of his brother, but unbeknown to anyone but himself. Yet, legally, the ordeal was fought over his alibi and the doubt it cast on Littegarde's character, for which he had, in his opinion and the opinion of most observers, tangible and incontrovertible evidence, namely her ring. His defeat would have proved as little as did Friedrich's with respect to the actual events that produced the *corpus delicti.* Although it may be the clue to the mystery, the "eloquent object," in this case the ring, does not necessarily by itself speak the truth, not any more than the trial by arms. In addition to demonstrating once again that circumstantial or sensory evidence is often delusive, Kleist seems to satirize the human pretense under which man-made laws supposedly embody the divine will. This theme he emphasizes when he has the Emperor amend the law of holy combat with the highly ambiguous clause "only if it be God's will," which, in fact, makes a joke of the whole idea of ordeal by arms. Who is to tell when the outcome of a combat is sanctioned by the divine will or not?

The veiled satire is further reinforced by the inexplicable ebbing away of Redbeard's vital forces after the combat. Although hinting that the truth is not what it appears to be, the unexpected reversal of fate does not have the force of law and is therefore devoid of objective validity. It is only when Redbeard confesses, after the circumstances surrounding his attempt at seduction have been brought to light, that reality confutes legality.

On the other hand, one could justifiedly maintain that Kleist illustrates in this *Novelle* the implications of the religious adage "God moves in mysterious ways." The unexpected aftermath to the combat helps disclose the perpetrator of the real crime, while the immediate occasion for the duel, namely Littegarde's honor, only obfuscates the central issue of the murder of Count Redbeard's brother. As some interpreters have remarked, Kleist sees the way to God cluttered with the debris of man-made laws. Yet

God cannot be concerned with legalistic problems, Kleist seems to suggest, but rather with ultimate truth. God may be enigmatic, but not necessarily evil, as he chose to point out repeatedly. Sylvester in *The Schroffenstein Family* voiced such a belief openly; we encounter it directly in Kleist's letters, somewhat obliquely in the Gypsy motif in **Michael Kohlhaas,** and still less directly, though unmistakably, in other works. Nevertheless, in such *Novellen* as **"The Earthquake . . . ,"** **"The Beggarwoman of Locarno,"** or **"St. Cecilia . . . ,"** the ways of God to man lead to violent death and madness, which only intensifies the impression of bewilderment about God's designs we gain from Kleist's works. The inscrutability of the divine will is apt to evoke profound disquietude, which is illustrated in Littegarde's and even Friedrich's comportment. Nowhere else did Kleist depict so drastically the paralyzing grip of despair as in Littegarde, with the possible exception of Penthesilea at the moment of recovery from madness or the Prince of Homburg at the sight of his grave. Littegarde is not Alkmene. She cannot be. Though, like Alkmene, she knows herself guiltless, God has apparently found her guilty. Convinced of both truths, she passes through the most agonizing experience of inner schism. Faith in things unseen, when things seen and God's own judgment speak so eloquently against it, is more than she can bear. And she is a child of her time, because she does not doubt for a moment the validity of the ordeal by arms, as is evident in the invective she hurls at Friedrich when he visits her in her dank cell:

> "Madman! Maniac!" cried Littegarde. "Hasn't God's sacred judgment gone against me? Weren't you beaten by the Count in that fatal duel? Hasn't he vindicated with his arms the truth of what he accused me of before the court?"

She is on the brink of madness. Her inner schism is revealed when she violently rejects Friedrich's attempts at consoling her and in the same breath calls him her "darling":

> "Go away!" she cried, recoiling from him on her knees across the straw. "If you don't want me to go mad, don't touch me! You are an abomination to me; the hottest flames are less dreadful to me than you!"

> "Oh, Jesus!" Littegarde cried, flinging herself down in a frenzy of terror at his feet and pressing her face to the floor. "Leave the room, my darling, and forget me! . . ."

> "All the horrors of hell are pleasanter for me to look at than the love and kindness beaming at me out of the springtime of your face!"

Friedrich, on the other hand, is seemingly endowed with that strength of inner feeling we usually encounter in Kleist's women protagonists rather than the men. But even he must adopt a defensive attitude toward the factual evidence which belies his and Littegarde's inner conviction. He admonishes her in impassioned terms to " . . . rear up the feeling that you have within you like a tower of rock"— a well-known Kleistian phrase—and

> "cling to it and never waver, even if the earth below and the heavens above should founder. Let us believe the more intelligible and reasonable of the two ideas that baffle the understanding here, and, rather than thinking you guilty, let us think I won the duel. I fought for you."

Then he pleads with God to "keep [his] own soul from distraction," as if he were trying to suppress his own doubts as much as hers. Generally, Kleist's heroines withstand the adversity of the world in silence and a kind of inward directed stance, while Friedrich talks almost sanctimoniously, which is hardly a sign of inner assurance. This does not render him unsympathetic or weak, but it reveals a chink in his armor, symbolized in his sudden and inexplicable faltering during the combat. Yet, ultimately, his asseverations triumph over empirical deception, but only after the struggle had twice led him to the brink of despair—upon his defeat in combat and the near death at the stake.

In **"The Duel"** the problem of "trust" takes on decidedly religious dimensions. In contrast to Gustav and Toni or Agnes and Ottokar, Littegarde and Friedrich have no doubts about the immaculateness of each other's motives or the integrity of their actions. Among her suitors, Friedrich was "the dearest one of all in her eyes," and after her expulsion from her parental home she implicitly trusts his conviction of her innocence, which he in turn expresses movingly:

> Not another word to defend and justify your innocence! There is a voice in my heart that pleads for you more vigorously and convincingly than all your protestations, or even all the legal points and proofs that you will be able to marshal in your defense before the court in Basel.

What is obviously tested is their faith or trust in God. And the greater burden of generating faith against the assaults of despair is thrust upon Friedrich. If he nearly falters in his inward certainty, though not visibly in his outer bearing, we cannot blame him. Kleist has contrived a test of faith for his hero which in severity can stand comparison with Abraham's trial. This much at least can be inferred from the general course of events related by the narrator, especially from the scene in Littegarde's cell. Significantly, Kleist passes over in silence their inner journey from their prison to the stake, where, bound and garroted, they fully expect to die ironically, in an *auto-da-fé*. The artistic canons of the *Novelle* do not allow the writer to describe at length inner states of mind. He can only relate significant episodes which must speak for themselves.

Although the whole plot of **"The Duel"** amounts to an ironic comment on the religious claims made for human laws, Kleist does not take the reader into his confidence very early in the story, as in *Amphitryon* or *The Broken Pitcher,* to let him savor immediately some pungent ironies. Very much as in *The Schroffenstein Family,* we are for a long time kept in the dark about the real cause of the tragic deceptions. But by now we are sufficiently familiar with the underlying rhythm in Kleist's works to anticipate

perilous and ironic reversals at the very moment strong af-
firmations to the contrary are being made. We know the
accusation leveled against Littegarde is false, since it is
supported by so much visual evidence. When Friedrich starts
the combat with superior skill, we can assume he will go
down to defeat. Or when Littegarde haughtily affirms that
Friedrich could not be hurt even if he fought unarmed, we
begin to fear for his life. Finally, if all agree that the trial by
arms will dredge up the hidden truth, we must anticipate that
the truth will only become more obscured.

Thus, what is ultimately on trial is the *deus absconditus*
himself. Though the story leads to a relatively happy ending, and Friedrich, after the ill fated combat, refuses to
accuse God of injustice, seeking the reason for the tragic
turn of events in his own sins, we are nevertheless left
with a sense of disquietude about the reliability of the
divine will. This deep sense of the uncertainty of all things,
including God, is summarized in the final motto "if it be
God's will." The motif of the trial by arms allowed Kleist
to illustrate the ambiguity inherent in ultimate reality or
God. If, in this instance, God chose to save the innocent
and punish the guilty, it may have been a sheer caprice of
his will. In other instances, as in **"The Earthquake . . . ,"**
he chose to destroy the pure in heart. It would be intrepid
to say apodictically what the transcendental meaning of
Kleist's stories is, especially when they are placed side by
side. We come away from reading them with a sense of
anxiety and no certainties.

George M. Martin   (essay date 1978)

SOURCE: "The Apparent Ambiguity of Kleist's Stories,"
in *German Life & Letters*, Vol. XXXI, No. 2, January,
1978, pp. 144-57.

[*In the following essay, Martin explores the apparent contradictions in Kleist's short fiction, maintaining that there is
in fact an "underlying order" and that "Kleist's own views,
his fears and aspirations, emerge very clearly from a consideration of the overall arrangement, either of the individual story, or of the collection of stories."*]

In a paper delivered before the English Goethe Society in
1963 J. M. Ellis makes the claim that Kleist's **"Das Erdbeben in Chili"** *must* have different and contradictory
interpretations. He later qualifies this assertion:

> I may have been cheating a little in claiming that the
> story must have different and contradictory interpretations;
> the truth is that it invites them and knocks them down,
> one after the other. We are indeed led to interpret the
> story in a number of ways, each inconsistent with the
> other; but we should not . . . stick to any one of them,
> but instead see that all of them are provisional . . .

This, for Ellis, is the whole point of the story:

> . . . . the excitement of the story lies to a large extent
> in his [i.e. the reader] constantly having his explanations

overturned. . . . At the end we have almost given up
trying to see coherence . . . we are left sceptical. . . .

For Ellis then the very essence of the story lies in its
ambiguity, in the fact that no one interpretation does justice to the complexity of the subject-matter.

Now, it is not my intention to deny the presence of contradictory elements in **"Das Erdbeben"** or indeed in any
of Kleist's stories. But I should like to suggest that the
contradictions are merely apparent ones. Kleist may insist
on presenting his material from seemingly conflicting points
of view, but an underlying order can be detected behind
this apparent confusion: Kleist's own views, his fears and
aspirations, emerge very clearly from a consideration of
the overall arrangement, either of the individual story, or
of the collection of stories. Kleist's imagination inevitably
imparts to his material his poetic vision.

I should like to illustrate these points by looking firstly at
"Das Erdbeben in Chili." An element of ambiguity is
present, even in the opening paragraphs. There are moments when the narrator seems to support the lovers, there
are moments, however, when he appears to side with society. This element of ambiguity is emphasised by the
narrator's tendency to describe events purely from the point
of view of the character whose reactions he is portraying.
Thus, in the initial part of our story, we see the impact
made by the earthquake first on Jeronimo and then on
Josephe.

For Jeronimo, the opening through which he escapes is
merely a 'zufällige Wölbung", i.e. his escape, in his own
eyes, is mere chance. Once outside, he perceives merely
the wanton destruction all round him. . . . Jeronimo, initially at least, does not see the earthquake as evidence of
divine intervention. He is impressed solely by the destruction and human suffering caused.

Josephe, on the other hand, soon comes to the conclusion
that the earthquake has not struck indiscriminately. . . .
For Josephe—if not for Jeronimo—there is a very obvious
meaning to all the destruction. The earthquake in her eyes
has picked its victims, these victims being the representatives of the corrupt and inhuman society which had sought
to destroy her love. Josephe has no doubt that the earthquake is God's indictment on a wicked society, a vindication by God of her love.

Our story opens then on a note of ambiguity. But gradually we sense that Kleist is constructing his tale so as to
convey his own personal views. Thus Jeronimo is not
allowed to persist in his initial attitude towards the earthquake—this indicates that Kleist himself does not think all
that highly of Jeronimo's first reactions. Thus too the lovers
are allowed to escape and find happiness together—this
gives the impression that Kleist favours Josephe's interpretation that the earthquake had been sent to destroy an
inhuman society. This impression is confirmed when Kleist
breaks his narrative to share with the lovers the dream of
their new found happiness. In their dream Kleist evokes
some sort of Paradise from which evil has been complete-

ly removed and in which the natural goodness of man reigns supreme, a world of joy and happiness, of love and peace, a dream world in the possibility of which Kleist would so dearly like to believe. So much so that Kleist has to include it, as part of his poetic vision. But this idyllic passage is unique in Kleist's short stories. Within the framework of a Kleistian narrative it is obviously out of place, obviously artificial. This apparent "Stilbruch" nonetheless fulfils an important function in our story. For the artificiality of the style makes us sense the artificiality of the lovers' dream. It only *appears* that things have changed, it only *appears* that social barriers have been destroyed and a new brotherhood of man established. Kleist knows that the Paradise in which he would so like to believe is irretrievable.

This does not explain, however, why Kleist should depict Josephe and Jeronimo as being naive and presumptuous, even arrogant. Here we must remember that Kleist, since the time of the so-called Kant crisis, has been obsessed with the fact of human limitation, it being the curse of the human condition that man apparently cannot transcend his own subjective experiences. It is in Kleist's view arrogance that man nonetheless presumes to take action on the basis of these same subjective criteria and it is this human arrogance that Kleist sees as the root cause of so much of the suffering in the world, it is this arrogance of which Kleist believes we all are guilty, whether we have good intentions or not. And so it is that Kleist shows the lovers—whom he supports—and the congregation in the "Dominikanerkirche"—whom he detests—equally guilty of presumption. Both interpret the earthquake to suit themselves. And Kleist's attitude towards this fact of human arrogance becomes apparent in the terrible consequences he attributes to it in our story. The sequence of events in the cathedral is quite unpredictable, totally without rhyme or reason, dictated solely by chance. There are so many changes in fortune—all entirely fortuitous and yet so serious in their eventual consequences. This is a terrifying world, an absurd world, a world made meaningless, Kleist would have us understand, by man's arrogance and self-centredness. The horrible descriptions in this scene, particularly of the death of Fernando's child, are meant to make us sense Kleist's horror at the fact of human presumption.

But Kleist does not end his tale at this stage. He adds an epilogue, telling how the child of the lovers survives and is adopted by Don Fernando. This is Kleist's way of expressing his hope that God really does want a society in which more importance is attached to true love and natural emotions. Further, Kleist allows Fernando to overcome the bitterness he must feel towards Philipp as a result of the death of his own son. Kleist allows him to overcome the human, all too human reaction, he allows him to adopt the child. This is Kleist's way of expressing his hope that man may yet overcome his limitations.

The initial ambiguity of our story quickly gives way then to the deliberate and skilful presentation of Kleist's view of the world: the Paradise that has gone irretrievably and of which we can but dream: the horrors and chaos of the present, the horrors of a world made meaningless by man's

presumption and arrogance: the hope that the future will see the advent of a genuine and more natural society when man may yet overcome his limitations. The wisdom of **"Das Erdbeben"** reflects the triadic development in the history of mankind which was so typical of Kleist's age and which so often appears in his works. It is the expression of this vision, its plausible evocation (*not* of course its logical demonstration) that provides our story with its underlying unity and explains its content.

In **Michael Kohlhaas** too ambiguities abound, at least in the earlier part of the narrative. Kohlhaas is described in paradoxical terms and the narrator's attitude towards his attempts to win justice for himself is equally ambivalent. Everything in the opening half of the story is ambiguous. Indeed, when one compares **Michael Kohlhaas** with Kleist's main source—which is very much on the side of Kohlhaas, seeing him as the champion of the people against tyranny and oppression—one cannot help feeling that Kleist is deliberately confusing the issues, possibly in an attempt to evoke the ambivalent and fortuitous nature of the empirical world.

Thus in the opening stages great importance is attached to the element of chance. It is the chance factor (the unexpected arrival of the Schloßvogt) which in the final analysis goads Kohlhaas into action, not any matter of principle. It is the chance factor (the unfortunate death of Lisbeth) which finally determines Kohlhaas to set out on his war of revenge. But the world Kleist evokes in the first half of his story is ruled not only by chance but also by inconsistency. Lisbeth e.g. seems on the one hand to support Kohlhaas, indicating that he has a divine duty to challenge the Junker. Yet her behaviour when Kohlhaas is selling his property to raise money for his war of retribution suggests she does not really approve. Even her final gesture on her deathbed is ambiguous:

> und [sie] zeigte dem Kohlhaas, mit dem Zeigefinger, den Vers: 'Vergib deinen Feinden: tue wohl auch denen, die dich hassen.'

This can of course be taken as an indication that she would have her husband forgive the Junker. But the contempt she shows for the parson and for the Bible might equally well suggest the very opposite: for goodness' sake, do *not* forgive the Junker! This is certainly how Kohlhaas himself interprets her final gesture:

> So möge mir Gott nie vergeben, wie ich dem Junker vergebe.

This element of inconsistency is, however, perhaps best illustrated with reference to the figure of Martin Luther. There are very considerable differences between the letter sent to Kohlhaas by the historical Luther and the letter Kleist allows his Luther to send. The letter Kleist's Luther sends is confused and confusing, it is also unfair and unjust. Kleist's readiness to depart from his historical model, his willingness to show Luther in an ambiguous and ambivalent light is evidence of his desire in this first half of the narrative to suggest the ambiguity of life, its unpredictability, its confusion. Even a Luther, it transpires, is not the bastion of integrity one might expect. For we cannot help feeling that Kleist's Luther misuses his spiritual authority. He is concerned, we fear, neither with principle nor with the truth of Kohlhaas's situation, but with political expediency. In addressing his letter to Kohlhaas, Luther hopes that his authority alone will be sufficient to cow the rebel into passive submission.

But Kohlhaas, far from submitting, challenges Luther's allegations. He explains to Luther the purpose of his visit to Wittenberg:

> Eure Meinung von mir, daß ich ein ungerechter Mann sei, widerlegen! Ihr habt mir in Eurem Plakat gesagt, daß meine Obrigkeit von meiner Sache nichts weiß: wohlan, verschafft mir freies Geleit, so gehe ich nach Dresden und lege sie ihr vor.

Luther's reaction is that of someone whose bluff has been called and who now finds himself forced to take a course of action he would rather avoid. He has no answer to Kohlhaas's argument and finds as a result that he has no alternative but to help Kohlhaas obtain a safe conduct to Dresden. He drifts into a course of action the full implications of which he chooses to ignore. He is led, not by principle, but by short-term expediency. Hence the ambivalence of his attitude towards Kohlhaas during the scene in Wittenberg, hence too the confusion his actions cause.

If in the first half of our story Kleist deliberately makes things appear as confused and as ambiguous as possible, *Michael Kohlhaas* would seem nonetheless to meet Friedrich Schlegel's requirement that a work of art should represent a synthesis of apparent chaos and underlying order. For in the second half of our story confusion gives way to a clearly defined pattern the unity of which lies in the expression of Kleist's own personal views. Previously Kleist's own opinions, his assessment for example of Kohlhaas had been withheld. But now his own interpretation is revealed—through the way in which his story is structured.

The presentation and structure of the "Abdecker-Szene" for instance leave us in no doubt as to Kleist's feelings about Hinz and Kunz. The latter encourage Herr Wenzel to misuse his power as "Erb-, Lehns- und Gerichtsherr" to have the horses found and returned. Their aim in doing so is presumably to forestall the verdict of the courts, to avoid personal disgrace and humiliation and to make Kohlhaas and his cause appear ridiculous. Kleist's comment on ministers of state who abuse the authority invested in them for their own personal ends is contained firstly in the rather crude humour so characteristic of the "Abdecker-Szene". This note is introduced, we feel, to make us sense just how laughable and contemptible Hinz and Kunz are, just how pathetic are their efforts to use their office for their own personal benefit. Kleist's comment is reflected secondly in the development he gives the scene. We see the confusion resulting from Kunz's underhand methods. We see how quickly he loses control of the situation: he may flaunt his insignia of office but the crowd treats him with scorn and contempt. We see him reduced to a state where he cares little for propriety and legality—he wants for example to *force* Kohlhaas to inspect the horses, although Kohlhaas is still a free man and can do as he wishes. We see how little he cares for popular traditions—he tries for example to *force* one of his servants to take the horses away, although a curse still hangs over them, at least in the opinion of the people. And we see the result of such unprincipled conduct on Kunz's part: the chaos, the disrepute into which the state is brought, the threat to the state insofar as one of its representatives is assaulted. The development of the scene makes it clear that in Kleist's eyes it is the behaviour of Hinz and Kunz that constitutes the real threat to law and order, not the actions of a Michael Kohlhaas.

Kleist's condemnation of the Elector of Saxony is also shown in the development he gives his story. We see the Elector condoning Kunz and his actions, allowing Kohlhaas to suffer the consequences of the fracas on the city square. The Elector does not intervene: he allows the Tronkas to continue to obstruct Wrede's attempts to win Kohlhaas justice. He allows evil to prevail. He allows Kohlhaas so to despair of obtaining justice that he agrees, or at least appears to agree, to join up with Nagelschmidt. The serious repercussions given in this case to the Elector's lack of action reflect Kleist's condemnation. It becomes clear that in Kleist's opinion it is the Elector who is responsible for the confusion that arises—because of his reluctance to act as he knows he should, a reluctance that stems directly, it seems, from his unwillingness to give up his mistress, Heloise, wife of Herr Kunz. Once again, in Kleist's eyes at least, the confusion, chaos and injustices of this world are caused by man's selfishness and ruthless egotism.

So it is that in the conduct of the Elector of Saxony and of Hinz and Kunz Kleist evokes once more the pathetic spectacle of self-seeking human endeavour. This is part of his vision. But so too is his hope that the cosmic powers would have mankind enjoy happiness—if only man would overcome his own subjectivity and appreciate their plan. Hence the depiction of Kohlhaas in the closing sections—as someone who withstands the temptation of self-interest and self-preservation in order to restore justice in Saxony. Kohlhaas now emerges, in Kleist's eyes at least, as a hero. He had seemed to err in the methods he chose. But then Homburg had seemed to err—when he joined battle too soon. Alkmene had seemed to err—when she mistook Jupiter for Amphitryon. And yet in both cases Kleist made of the apparent error a positive achievement. Homburg, because of his error, is able to revitalise Brandenburg society by ensuring that the social contract is drawn up afresh between ruler and ruled; Alkmene's error becomes the basis for an apotheosis of Romantic love. The memory of their error fades: both plays end on a triumphant note tinged admittedly by the irony so typical of Kleist. So too in *Michael Kohlhaas*. Reservations as to the hero's methods are now muted. Kohlhaas dies a triumphant death, the death of a martyr who has helped restore earthly justice and transform society, the death of a man who has accomplished a divine mission. For the introduction of the gypsy suggests not only Kleist's unqualified support of Kohlhaas, it shows too that Kohlhaas's actions meet with divine approval. Kohlhaas may have to die, but he leaves behind a new Brandenburg and in addition Lisbeth holds out to Kohlhaas "the hope of a *Jenseits* in which love reigns unlimited and all life's perplexing questions are answered." Kleist once more ends with a reminder of the better world for which he can but hope.

While in *Michael Kohlhaas* and in **"Das Erdbeben in Chili"** initial ambiguity gives way to the expression of Kleist's personal hopes and fears, some of Kleist's tales are quite without confusion or ambiguity. One thinks for example of **"Der Findling,"** a story best appreciated when one bears in mind Kleist's most probable source—Molière's *Tartuffe*. Kleist was evidently intrigued by Tartuffe's behaviour, particularly by his attempt to order Orgon from his very own home. Kleist was perplexed: how could anyone who had been treated with as much kindness as had a Tartuffe behave so abjectly and so cruelly? **"Der Findling"** is Kleist's attempt to devise a set of circumstances in which such behaviour might become explicable. Thus our story is not realistic in the sense of naturalistic. It is constructed, artificial, symbolic. The events that occur are the events that Kleist causes to occur—in order to provide his explanation.

The opening paragraphs can thus be seen as an attempt to evoke a particular emotional situation. Piachi, it emerges, had been happily married but is now very unhappy in his marriage to his second wife, Elvire. A plague breaks out—a symbol of the unhealthy nature of Piachi's marriage and the danger it poses for Paolo, his son by his first wife. Piachi wishes to do all he can to save his son, but suddenly the foundling appears, asking for help:

> Piachi wollte in der ersten Regung des Entsetzens, den Jungen weit von sich schleudern; doch da dieser, in eben diesem Augenblick, seine Farbe veränderte und ohnmächtig auf den Boden niedersank, so regte sich des guten Alten Mitleid': er stieg mit seinem Sohn aus, legte den Jungen in den Wagen, und fuhr mit ihm fort, obschon er auf der Welt nicht wußte, was er mit demselben anfangen sollte.

Piachi was horrified initially and wanted to ignore the boy. But then his pity is aroused and he decides to take the boy with him. In doing so, Piachi is suppressing his own instinctive reaction, is acting against his better judgment. Piachi, it transpires, can be led astray by pity: the same false sentimentality which, as we may assume, had tempted him to marry Elvire now results in the death of his son.

The grief-stricken Piachi who had been repelled initially by Nicolo nonetheless now wants to take the boy home with him. We are suspicious of his motives, particularly when we read that he was distressed at this stage "beim Anblick des Platzes, der neben ihm leer blieb" and that he took the foundling back to Rome "an seines Sohnes Statt". Kleist is evidently suggesting that Piachi's reasons for taking the child stem neither from love nor charity. They

are essentially selfish. For while Piachi may genuinely grieve for the loss of his son, he is more afraid of facing the emptiness of a life without him. He needs someone on whom to heap love and affection. Piachi may be unaware of his subconscious motives, he may think he is being very kind and charitable. But Kleist would leave us in no doubt that for all his apparent magnanimity he is really using this boy as an object—as someone who will provide him with comfort and solace.

Elvire for her part welcomes the child with open arms. She treats Nicolo exactly like Paolo. By making her react in this way, Kleist is seeking to evoke a particular emotional situation. For fate had dealt Elvire a cruel blow. The Genoese knight who had saved her life had died and in her grief she had agreed to marry Piachi. Elvire, a young and beautiful woman, had substituted the compassion of an old man for the true love she would have shared with her knight. Although unhappy and emotionally unsatisfied, she refuses to admit consciously to the hypocrisy of her situation. She wishes to keep up appearances. She assumes outwardly the role of the faithful, virtuous wife. Thus she can treat the two children identically—because they serve for her an identical purpose. She is not interested in them as individuals. She welcomes Nicolo—because she needs him to help suppress her emotional frustration, because it is only by being a good mother that she can appear to fulfil the role of the good and devoted wife.

Nicolo then is accepted into the family, is adopted—because of the inadequacies of the marriage between Piachi and Elvire. Both hope, however subconsciously, that Nicolo will help them solve their emotional difficulties. In fact Nicolo's advent will have quite the opposite effect. Nicolo will expose the failings of both Piachi and Elvire and will reveal the hypocrisy of their marriage.

For this the treatment accorded Nicolo by his adoptive parents is in part responsible. They treat the child, on the surface at least, with great kindness and affection. Both, however, show themselves remarkably afraid that he might become not a reassurance against the inadequacy of their marriage, but a threat, a reminder of their own failings. Piachi fears that Nicolo's money might win him false friends—but then Piachi too is hoping to "buy" friendship and affection. Elvire fears that he might indulge in illicit "affairs"—but then Elvire too is having an illicit affair. Elvire and Piachi may treat Nicolo with great kindness—but only as long as he helps *them* cope with *their* emotional problems.

The child, understandably, becomes resentful. Deprived of the chance to express his own individuality, he becomes bitter and when his parents combine, as he believes, to humiliate him, he decides to avenge himself. The form his revenge takes is determined by the treatment his parents accorded him. For Nicolo has come to fulfil their worst fears: he has become the inverted reflection of their own failings. He tries to seduce his own adoptive mother: in this Nicolo is the negative reflection of Colino, his dastardly action showing just how wicked Elvire's spiritual adultery really is. He orders his own adoptive father out of the house: this terrible deed reflects the fact that Piachi, in marrying Elvire and later in adopting Nicolo, was acting possessively—for all his apparent magnanimity.

Both the manner of Nicolo's adoption and the treatment accorded him by his new parents combine in Kleist's interpretation to provide a possible explanation for behaviour similar to that of a Tartuffe. But Kleist does not end at this stage. He has Piachi kill Nicolo, he has Piachi die, determined to pursue his revenge, even in hell. Kleist's reason for ending his story on this discordant note is perhaps to make us sense the cruelty of life and to have us share in his protest at the injustice thereof. For Piachi is basically a good person, a man who at all times acted with the best of intentions. It is true of course that he was partly to blame for what happened. But poor Piachi did not know that he was using Nicolo selfishly; he thought he was doing good. This for Kleist is the injustice of life, the fact that it is impossible for us, especially in close human relationships, to know when we are doing the right thing. We know enough neither about ourselves nor about each other; all too often, in spite of the best intentions, we are pursuing merely selfish aims. Inevitably seemingly, we make mistakes but we only find out when it is too late. This for Kleist is the injustice of life: **"Der Findling"** represents his protest.

There is then nothing ambiguous about **"Der Findling"**. And yet this story has caused critics considerable difficulties. Because of its pessimistic and uncompromising ending it was long assumed that this must be one of Kleist's earliest tales. Kreutzer, however, has now shown that it was one of his latest. There is, however, no reason for surprise that Kleist should have written this story as late as 1811. For when we remember that **"Der Findling"** deals with the injustice of life and the inevitable fact of human limitation, i.e. with the theme central to the whole of Kleist's work, it seems wholly appropriate that this story should occupy the central position in the second volume of Kleist's stories. There is no ambiguity about **"Der Findling"** itself: ambiguity only arises when we see the volume as a whole. For we now find—in the tales encircling **"Der Findling"**—conflicting responses on Kleist's part to his central theme.

"Die Verlobung" for example is probably the most bitter of all Kleist's stories. Gone is the obvious sympathy with the human predicament that sustains even as grim a tale as **"Der Findling"**. In its place we have scorn, contempt, it seems, for the futility of all human endeavour. It has been pointed out—rightly—that the social and political background plays an important role in the development of this story. The reason is clear: the characters are pathetic, helpless individuals, totally unable to overcome the inhuman and destructive forces released by the social and political climate of the time, totally unable, or unwilling, to assert their own humanity.

The opening paragraph sets the theme. Congo Hoango is depicted as being by nature a good, honest and generous individual. But when political events make him aware of the iniquities of slavery, he becomes a monster, perpetuating acts of the greatest inhumanity, killing and plundering. He even encourages Toni to use her charms to entice white men to their death. Thus these opening lines reveal the corrupting influence exerted by the political situation. Even as kind a man as Congo becomes a monster: even as positive a value as that of love has become perverted.

It is against this background that the love affair between Toni and Gustav is set. Gustav is shown as a young man quite unable to cope with the difficulties of a tense political situation. He is naive, so quick to trust Babekan and to suppress his initial suspicions. But his naivety stems less from stupidity than from loneliness and fear. Gustav is terribly aware of his own inadequacies: his naivety, his effusive sentimentality, his excessive protestations of love all reveal someone looking pathetically for comfort and reassurance. He is prepared to believe anything that would give him a greater sense of security. He is so afraid and feels so inadequate that—in spite of himself—he will use love as a means of obtaining emotional reassurance.

Thus, because of the political situation, Gustav's love for Toni is a very shabby love indeed. And so Kleist, when describing the first signs of attraction between Gustav and Toni, reminds us in two flashbacks of the political background. We are told of the cruel, inhuman way in which Babekan was treated by white people. We sense her bitterness and resentment and see in the second flashback (the revenge of the young negress) the dastardly actions that can result. This mood of resentment and suspicion is the cloud hanging over the lovers, threatening their love even before it has begun.

Kleist's imagination inevitably imparts to his material his poetic vision.

—*George M. Martin*

Gustav's initial suspicions soon reassert themselves. He seduces Toni, not out of love but in an attempt to find reassurance. His lack of genuine feeling for Toni as a person is only too apparent. He keeps talking of the likeness he sees between her and his former fiancée, Mariane Congreve; he even presents Toni with a cross given him by Mariane. A third flashback tells how Gustav was responsible for the death of Mariane because of his rashness in condemning publicly the setting up of the Revolutionary Tribunal. He suffers as a result from a sense of guilt and in his love for Toni is seeking primarily to atone for his errors in the past.

The same political background which has made Gustav incapable of true love also causes Toni to betray her love. For Toni has grown up in an atmosphere of intrigue and finds herself unable to shake off its pernicious influence. She knows full well she should tell Gustav the truth of their situation. She even prays for the strength and courage to do so. But when it comes to the test, she is too weak to tell Gustav the unpleasant truth about herself. Like Gustav she is unable to rise above the evil influences of the time.

The lovers' weaknesses are revealed only too clearly when the unexpected happens and Congo returns home suddenly. Toni assumes all too readily the role of the intriguer. Gustav's fears and suspicions reassert themselves and his impetuosity prevails. The last scenes in our story are full of black humour: the cruel descriptions for example of the deaths of Toni and Gustav are meant to evoke the absurd futility of all human endeavour and to suggest just how ridiculous and pathetic people are. The idea of man's helplessness is further emphasised by the fact that Gustav's impetuosity once more causes the death of a girl: man, it seems, cannot learn from his mistakes, man is doomed. The characters in our story appeal as mere puppets, quite unable to stand up to the evil forces of their time. The love of Gustav and Toni is no love at all, their "Verlobung" being if anything a parody of love. And if our story ends with the news that a monument is to be erected to the memory of their love, this surely is the supreme irony, the bitter comment of a writer disgusted at the pathetic nature of human endeavour.

The cynicism of **"Die Verlobung"** is not, however, maintained throughout the second volume of Kleist's stories. The volume ends for example with **"Der Zweikampf"**, easily Kleist's most optimistic tale. Here we see man's greatness, his ability to triumph over the corrupting influence of society and fulfil his own humanity. Here we see that God is, after all, a good God. He really does care, even if his designs are not always clearly understood by man.

Kleist's source for **"Der Zweikampf"** was in all probability the story of Renato in Cervantes' *Persiles*. This tells how an innocent person lost a duel but yet won in the sense that he found through his apparent defeat the path to true happiness. In writing **"Der Zweikampf"** Kleist was attempting perhaps to offer a personal illustration of the truth of Cervantes' story.

The relevance of the opening section—often deemed superflous—now becomes apparent. Kleist in this introduction is creating the background to the duel. Jakob is shown to be a man of evil, the epitome of social man. And yet, to our surprise, he himself proposes going to court to answer the charges made against him. He feels confident, it transpires, because he thinks he has an alibi on one of the charges: he is convinced he spent the night in question with Littegarde. Thus when challanged to a duel on this issue, he feels confident. He may be guilty, but he is able to approach the duel with a feeling of innocence. The lovers, on the other hand, are not nearly so sure of themselves. Littegarde, for instance, is in love with Friedrich. But initially she attaches too much importance to the advice of her self-centred brothers and seems prepared to renounce her love. Littegarde in Kleist's eyes is too passive at this stage and is in danger of forfeiting her chance of happiness. Friedrich too is weak in the sense that he

challenges Jacob to a duel at all. To believe in the duel as a means of obtaining justice is a sign that he is blinkered by tradition, influenced too much by mere man-made institutions.

Kleist has thus devised a situation in which Jakob is superficially innocent but essentially guilty while the lovers are superficially guilty but essentially innocent. This anticipates and explains the apparently ambiguous outcome of the duel. On the superficial level the forces of an evil and corrupt society appear to triumph. Friedrich allows himself to be influenced by the reactions of the crowd. He listens to the "voice of society", changes his tactics and is struck down. The manner of Jakob's apparent victory may not be chivalrous but society nonetheless sees his success as perfectly "legitimate". Friedrich's "defeat" is seen as a clear indication of Littegarde's guilt: society fails to realise that trial by holy combat is merely a man-made institution and necessarily imperfect. When the lovers lose all confidence in themselves and in each other, we reach the nadir of the whole story. It seems that the power of love will not prevail and that society, with its corrupt and corrupting influence, will destroy two supremely innocent people.

It is now, however, that Friedrich shows his true greatness. His trust in Littegarde remains unimpaired—in spite of the outcome of the duel. He questions—not the innocence of Littegarde, but the justification behind man-made conventions. He alone senses the importance of believing in oneself and in one's own feelings and it is through his example that the love between Friedrich and Littegarde is renewed. The deeper level to the outcome of the duel now emerges. Society's verdict is replaced by God's judgement. Friedrich recovers from his wound and Jakob dies. The lovers find true happiness together and indeed are able to improve society. For their love has shown the inadequacy and fallibility of the laws regulating trial by holy combat. The words are now to be added: "Wenn es Gottes Wille ist." This addition effectively destroys the use of the duel as an instrument for the dispensation of justice, for no one can know when God will choose to make His wishes known. In this way Kleist has his lovers bring about the abolition of an inhuman custom. This is their great social achievement and it is for this that they receive the 'Gnadenkette.' **"Der Zweikampf"** is the expression of Kleist's hope that the evil and corrupting influence of society will be overcome and that man will succeed in restoring society to its original natural goodness.

It has now become clear that in Kleist's second volume of stories the element of ambiguity is not contained within the individual stories. Yet **"Die Verlobung"** and **"Der Zweikampf,"** while both dealing with Kleist's major theme, the subject of human limitation, do so from conflicting points of view. We have on the one hand the cynicism of **"Die Verlobung,"** on the other the hope and optimism of **"Der Zweikampf"**. What are we to make of this apparent ambiguity?

We must conclude, I feel, that Kleist's response to the fact of human limitation is essentially two-fold. Whilst on the one hand full of contempt for man in his helplessness, Kleist—in this respect not unlike Büchner, not unlike Hebbel—cannot help emotionally but seek a meaning to the apparently meaningless. The pessimistic view must always be tempered by a more optimistic outlook; we have the plus and the minus, Penthesilea and Käthchen, **"Die Verlobung"** and **"Der Zweikampf"**: Fernando's child dies a most horrible death, but the child of Jeronimo and Josephe survives.

We must realise therefore that in Kleist we are not dealing with an Either-Or situation. Far too much of the critical literature concentrates unduly on the one aspect—either on Kleist's fears or on his aspirations. We must realise we are dealing with a Both-And situation. Kleist is intent on evoking *his* poetic vision, i.e. on reminding us both of his fears *and* of his hopes. Hence many of the apparent ambiguities. It is not good enough to play the one aspect off against the other and conclude that nothing but inconsistencies and ambiguities emerge. Ellis for instance is opposed to an optimistic interpretation of **"Das Erdbeben"**:

> If it is admitted that it is God who has led one (child) to safety, then why could He not have done this with the other? ["Kleist's *Das Erdbeben in Chili,*" PEGS, 33, 1962-63]

To argue this, is to miss the point completely. We should remember that at all times Kleist is presenting his poetic vision, i.e. both his fears *and* his aspirations. When we remember this, the apparent ambiguities disappear.

John M. Ellis (essay date 1979)

SOURCE: "The Character of Kleist Criticism," in *Heinrich von Kleist: Studies in the Character and Meaning of His Writings,* The University of North Carolina Press, 1979, pp. 143-64.

[*Ellis is an English educator and critic. In the following excerpt, he presents a thorough survey of critical scholarship on Kleist's short fiction, and discusses the varying interpretations of several Kleist novellas and stories.*]

Abstracting motifs and ideas from their context in individual works is . . . a more than usually dangerous procedure in Kleist criticism since his works demand a close attention to their twists and turns. The very notion of a context is more complicated in works that continually change direction, and in which an idea can seem to have positive value on one page but be revalued later on. It is fruitless for the critic to try to trace a motif through all Kleist's works as if the motif had a constant value, because the complete context of a whole text rarely allows the abstraction of an idea that has any unambiguous value even in one of Kleist's works.

This has, however, been the standard procedure of Kleist critics, and it is the most serious flaw in Kleist criticism. It has been common to give a fixed value throughout his work to particular notions such as trust, error, or feeling.

This is not simply mistaken criticism but is in a way a recoil from Kleist's characteristic demand on his readers; for Kleist demands that the reader remain flexible and move with the texts' changes of direction, while his critics have generally responded to this disturbing openness only by taking refuge from it in fixed, rigid positions. Thus Kleist's meaning is reversed. He sets his readers a challenge—to deal with a constantly developing situation—and to grasp for firm orientation points from which each text can be judged is to fail that challenge.

Here we find the reason for the sometimes extraordinary degree of disagreement among Kleist scholars as to the meaning of a particular work—especially *Prinz Friedrich von Homburg* and **"Das Erdbeben in Chili."** The reduction of these complex works to the same simple messages, attitudes or ideologies, or to any other kinds of unambiguous assertions, can only be a very arbitrary procedure; one critic chooses one facet of the text as the key to interpretation while another chooses something else. Sometimes a particular reduction of the text is more tempting than others (the case, say, of the "education" theory in *Prinz Friedrich von Homburg*), and that may produce at least a majority viewpoint. In other cases, such as **"Das Erdbeben in Chili,"** the possibilities for reduction to a fixed viewpoint are so various that there is no majority tendency among critics. The texts clearly entertain (without finally allowing) various possible attitudes to and interpretations of them, and the great disagreement among critics on certain texts is simply due to the fact that individual critics seize on one or other possibility and on the particular limited context of the text that gives that possible interpretation its most tempting form; they then rigidify it to make of it *the* interpretation of the text. The subsequent arguments with others who have picked a different suggested interpretation always miss the point; while the critics argue over who has the better case, they do not see that the story is *about that argument,* not about the particular interpretation that they are trying to make the victor in the argument. Not all of Kleist's works have provoked this kind of controversy; **"Der Findling"** has not, for example. But this is because Kleist often makes one plausible explanation so explicit that it seems to offer the critic an unusually easy resting place. Here, to see only Piachi's altruism and Nicolo's depravity is an especially tempting way of avoiding the disturbing complications of the text.

So far, I have spoken in only very general terms of Kleist criticism; let me now turn to some examples to show what actually happens in typical instances. The first is a recent and relatively simple example of what I have been describing: Elmar Hoffmeister's *Täuschung und Wirklichkeit bei Heinrich von Kleist.* This title confirms a commitment to the prevailing manner of Kleist criticism, for it is clearly analogous to Friedrich Koch's *Bewußtsein und Wirklichkeit* and Walter Müller-Seidel's *Versehen und Erkennen,* to take only two examples. The double-barreled thematic title, incidentally, is a fad that seems to have originated with Gerhard Fricke's *Gefühl und Schicksal bei Heinrich von Kleist;* it appears to have carried over into journal articles (as in Hans-Peter Herrmann's

"Zufall und Ich") and to works in English (as in John Gearey's *Tragedy and Anxiety*), and it is still as strong as ever—a new title is Hermann Reske's *Traum und Wirklichkeit.*

What can be seen immediately in these titles (apart from a certain repetitiveness, for all tend to cover ground that is at least partly covered in the others) is a prevailing habit of abstracting a motif and tracing it throughout Kleist's work. Elmar Hoffmeister's case is typical: he goes through the texts one by one to show deception in each of them. Piachi is deceived by Nicolo in **"Der Findling"**; the Prince is deceived by his own dream in the *Prinz von Homburg;* the Marquise is deceived by events in **"Die Marquise von O . . ."** and so on. His conclusion, in general terms, can only be that there is much deception in Kleist. Two things can be said about such a book and about all the other examples of the genre. First, the general conclusion about Kleist is a very uninteresting one, and in that sense at least the idea of the book is unproductive. And second, this journey through the works with a fixed idea produces no interpretative insights into the individual texts. To take the former point first: one might look at Shakespeare's best-known plays and say that there is much deception in them. Iago deceives Othello, Lear is deceived by his daughters, Macbeth is deceived by the witches, and so on. None of this is very unique or interesting: there is no obvious value in taking very general and unremarkable ideas out of context simply to list their occurrence. There is deception in Kleist, in Shakespeare, in Goethe, and in everyday life: by itself, the notion is not startling. Some interest might be generated if the discussion could get at a specifically Kleistian use of the notion. But that would lead to a thorough interpretation of each text, with attention to the place of deception within the thematic structure of each text, and it is just such a procedure that books like Hoffmeister's seem designed to avoid: going through all the texts with a simple idea as an orientation point for each is not merely . . . a procedure that does not involve serious thought about each text. Hoffmeister's interpretative comments— and those of all such books—are in fact rarely new or original, and they generally follow well-known surface readings. A good example is his view of **"Der Findling."** Hoffmeister simply assimilates it to his framework by identifying Nicolo as a deceiver in a section entitled "Der Betrug des Verführers Nicolo in der Novelle 'Der Findling'"; that very formulation makes it clear that the interpretation offered is the superficial one that is well known from other general books of criticism. Evidently, this kind of work will have no impact on our understanding of the texts.

Hoffmeister's book is recent and not yet widely known. To show just how typical its failings are, I want now to turn to two cases that are superficially very different: Hans Matthias Wolff's book *Heinrich von Kleist als politischer Dichter,* and an article by Manfred Durzak, "Zur utopischen Funktion des Kindesbildes in Kleists Erzählungen." Wolff's book is a well-known, somewhat older general treatment of Kleist; Durzak's is a recent article which focuses narrowly on a particular motif.

Wolff's work is dominated by a political idea: the relation of individual to state in Kleist's work. His thesis is that Kleist first felt that the individual was more important but later came to feel that the reverse was the case. Wolff goes through all the works and discusses them in this light. Just as in Hoffmeister's case, it will readily be seen that the general idea that forms the framework of the study is a fairly simple one that lacks intrinsic interest as it stands. Indeed, it is only fair to say that the idea as presented and discussed does not achieve the level of interest and complexity that one would expect from an introductory course in political science, and a reader ignorant of Kleist could surely be forgiven for concluding that Kleist was a dull and unsubtle writer if that was what his work was about. Once more, the level of interpretative comment on the individual texts which is allowed by mechanical "coverage" with the aid of such an idea is very low. In *Der zerbrochne Krug,* for example, Wolff's main idea is that Adam is "nicht allein Mensch, sondern Richter, d.h. *Beamter,* und aus dieser seiner Stellung als Beamter ergibt sich die gesamte Problematik des Werkes . . . er ist der Beamte, der seine Gewalt mißbraucht." Here we can see only too clearly the way in which the pursuit of a general notion gets out of hand: that Adam is a state official—a trivial enough point—is suddenly the basis of "die gesamte Problematik des Werkes." It is easy enough to see (for example, in his very name) that Adam's being a human being is a rather larger issue than that of his being a bureaucrat. The discussion of Kohlhaas is in similar vein: according to Wolff, his troubles stem from his mistreatment by officials of the state. Together with *Der zerbrochne Krug,* then, **Michael Kohlhaas** shows how Kleist is for the individual and against the state at this stage. In *Prinz Friedrich von Homburg,* on the other hand, the Prince learns to accept the state, which means that Kleist himself now values the authority of the state over the individual. This all involves a sadly uninteresting view of all the works, and an avoidance of the really interesting issues of Kleist's texts; and in the process, no interpretative remark about the texts is made that is of any originality. Wolff's view of *Prinz Friedrich von Homburg* is simply the very familiar "education" theory; his view of **Michael Kohlhaas** is simply that there is injustice to Kohlhaas; and so on. Ironically, where **Michael Kohlhaas** questions whether it is possible to use abstractions like "the State" (a lofty abstraction that falls to pieces during the story), Wolff goes on using it regardless of what the story does to it. A determination to trace a general idea throughout all the works evidently makes this critic deaf to what any particular text is saying and to what it actually does with that idea. Wolff does not notice that one of the things that **Michael Kohlhaas** does is precisely to question the value of any analysis in the terms that he uses to examine Kleist's work; the notion of the individual versus the state evaporates in this story.

Durzak's analysis concerns the figure of the child in Kleist's work. He too traces this motif through several texts, assigning to it a fixed value—a positive one—each time it appears. This mean that he motivates critical events in any story simply in terms of Kleist's belief that children represent "reine Natur" regardless of what the context of the particular work demands. So, for example, he thinks the reconciliation of the Marquise and the Count is possible because of the child, who "repräsentiert reine Natur"; that Kohlhaas's sons are knighted so that "die Katastrophe in einem utopischen Kindesbild aufgehoben wird"; and that the ending of **"Das Erdbeben in Chili,"** too, is optimistic because of the survival of the child. None of this can be justified by the emphases of the context of the work. In each case, the critic substitutes what concerns him (the theme he is following through each text) for what concerns the work. In the **"Marquise von O . . ."** it is surely obvious that we must look to the whole history of what has gone on between Marquise and Count and see the ending as a result of all that; how could Kleist really motivate his story otherwise without seeming utterly arbitrary? In *Michael Kohlhaas*, the knighting of Kohlhaas's sons is surely part of the pattern contrasting the flourishing of his name and that of the house of Brandenburg with the future demise of Saxony's; there is again no trace of any emphasis on childish innocence in what happens. And in the **"Erdbeben in Chili,"** especially, the delicate balance of the ending is disturbed by the unambiguous assertion that the child represents a utopian solution. In this last case, to preserve his thesis, Durzak has to rewrite Kleist's crucial final sentence and see in Don Fernando's final statement "diese von Schmerz beschattete Freude." Kleist's own language is of course more guarded and much more interesting—its emphases are far removed from those of Durzak's theme. In commenting on the quality of this criticism it is not my purpose to find fault with any particular critic; my point is to stress that these are the inevitable results of a procedure in Kleist criticism that is very widespread. Criticism that seizes on a general idea and sets out to use it on all the texts, whether in the form of avowedly limited articles like Durzak's, or general works that take a specific view of Kleist and his work like Hoffmeister's and Wolff's, will of necessity only produce results that reduce and distort the meaning of that work.

So far, the flaw that I have diagnosed seems simple enough, and the question may arise: if it really is that simple, why is it not more obvious, and why have not more critics seen and overcome it? The answer to this question appears to me to lie in a feature of Kleist criticism that tends to conceal the true character of the situation. As if sensing that the basic content of their arguments is excessively simple, many Kleist critics elaborate it and restate it in ever more complex terminology. Hoffmeister, again, is a representative example: "Bei den Gestalten, die in guter oder böswilliger Absicht Irrtum stifteten, wurde schon deutlich, daß sie meist in einem unzulänglichen, verfehlten Verhältnis zur Realität als gegenständlicher und gesellschaftlicher Wirklichkeit standen." The impressive terminology tends to cast a spell on the reader, but it can be broken by determined reflection. Is to "stand in an insufficient relationship to reality as objective and social fact" really more than "to be in error"? Hoffmeister's verbal elaboration masks a thought so simple as to be hardly worth stating: "People spread mistakes because they themselves have made them." Hoffmeister's terminology is superficially impressive, and it may seem to lend his criticism some plausibility, but it really serves only to disguise that what he is saying is not remarkable. Another

means of infusing an appearance of complexity into what is in reality very simple lies in the elaboration of distinctions that have no real point to them; for example, "Irreführung in guter Absicht" is distinguished by Hoffmeister from "Irreführung in schlechter Absicht," without his explaining why anything is gained from doing so. Categories must surely be justified as useful and pertinent ones if they are to contribute anything to an understanding of Kleist.

The technique of creating a verbal complexity in the critic's own language to compensate for a lack of substance is by no means new, nor is Hoffmeister's case an extreme one. It was already very noticeable in the work of Friedrich Braig (1925), for example. When discussing Kleist's literary works, Braig would generally give a plot summary which was interspersed with a few comments such as: "Hier kämpfte der Dichter um Sein oder Nichtsein," or "Hier hat sich Kleist bis in die letzten Tiefen der Menschenseele hinabgebohrt." These remarks are virtually without content as far as interpreting or characterizing the text goes, and they represent an attempt to make the critic's statements seem interesting and impressive when he has in fact no real point to make. . . .

Herrmann's study elaborates the notion of chance events in Kleist mainly by adding linguistic complexity to an obvious thought, which is that many chance events in Kleist demand a response from those who experience them. But it is just as true of daily life anywhere, at any time, that chance events often compel a response to them; and since that is so, it cannot be very interesting to say that such is also the case in Kleist's world. Nothing is said here that is characteristic of Kleist. A good test in such cases is to see whether the study concerned involves or leads to interpretative comments that differ in any way from those that are standard in other general studies of Kleist. In Herrmann's study, none such is found—linguistic complexity super-imposed on the obvious is all that is there.

In some cases, the recourse to verbal complexity is recognizably a recoil from dealing with the problems of Kleist's texts. Max Kommerell's study is a case in point. Kommerell does indeed respond to the problematic nature of Kleist's texts, but he misplaces the source of this feature by locating it in the characters: "Kleists Personen sind Rätsel." Since we can say equally that Hamlet, Macbeth, Othello, and most other literary figures are "Rätsel," it is clear that Kommerell has not put his finger on the specifically Kleistian problematic character of these texts. This bad start prevents further progress, and Kommerell then shifts to endless playing on the compounds of "Rätsel": "rätselhaft," "Verrätselung," "Enträtselung," without thereby adding anything to the interpretation of the texts. In **"Der Findling,"** for example, he finds Nicolo "ruchlos," just as most others do, and his judgments are similarly unremarkable in other works. His discussion soon abandons any attempt to go beyond very well-known interpretative views to concentrate on developing its own linguistic texture per se; and a consequence of his concern with elaborating his own verbal system rather than looking at what Kleist wrote is that he begins to make serious factual errors in referring to Kleist's texts—an instructive example of where this kind of criticism is likely to lead. Let me give one example: Kommerell's discussion of **"Der Findling"** is essentially a plot summary using his special vocabulary ("rätselhaft," etc.), but during this he refers to Colino as the man who rescued Elvire from a fire and died of wounds received doing so "nach wenigen Tagen, während derer sie ihn nicht verließ." This is not only a bad factual error but a central one: a critic who wishes to come to terms with what is happening in this text, and what Elvire represents in it, could not possibly fail to be deeply impressed with her having spent three years (not a few days) constantly at the bedside of the dying Colino!

The examples I have discussed so far are typical of the field; quite how typical they are can be judged from the fact that all of the fundamental criticisms I have made of them can be made with equal justice of the work that is currently the best-known and most-quoted book on Kleist, Walter Müller-Seidel's *Versehen und Erkennen*. As his title suggests, Müller-Seidel's work is concerned with the abstraction of a motif from Kleist's texts: Kleist's characters first commit a "Versehen" and then experience "Erkennen." The notion that the characters first make mistakes and then see them is, here too, not by itself very promising; moreover, it derives . . . from earlier writers such as Kommerell and Koch. Elaboration is again the answer to this problem of lack of originality or inherent interest in his thesis, and Müller-Seidel pursues it by categorizing various kinds of "Versehen" and "Erkennen." One section of his treatise, for example, is on "Sinnengläubigkeit" as a subspecies of "Versehen," and he discusses as an important Kleistian problem "das Vertrauen in die Verläßlichkeit der fünf Sinne, das zur Ursache immer neuer Verkennungen wird. Es handelt sich um eine Art von Sinnengläubigkeit, der manche Figuren schlechterdings verfallen." This is either trite, or wrong. It is trite if it refers to people in general, wrong if it refers to Kleist's characters in particular. It is of course not a failing of Kleist's characters but a universal human habit to believe the evidence of the senses. No one put in the position of the Marquise or Alkmene would be other than baffled by what happens. The real issue is the misleading nature of what those characters see; they do not hallucinate, they merely draw normal conclusions from what they see, as anyone else would. Müller-Seidel has managed to make much ado about nothing. Another example of the same procedure can be seen when he begins to categorize and subsection the concept "Erkennen." Here there is first a linguistically complex title: "Die Enthüllung des rätselhaft-wider-spruchsvollen Sachverhalts und die Formen des Erkennens." He then proceeds to tell his reader that one of the forms of "das Erkennen" is "dadurch, daß die beteiligten Figuren den verrätselten Sachverhalt durchschauen." This could have been said more simply: one way out of a mistake is to see one's mistake. Once the polysyllabic terminology is cut through, only utter triviality remains. The function of the complex terminology is surely to disguise this fact.

Interestingly, Müller-Seidel makes the same kind of factual errors as does Kommerell when he refers to Kleist's text. For example, Müller-Seidel refers to Colino as "den geheimen Liebhaber dieser in einer Scheinehe lebenden Frau." To be sure, the memory of Colino is Elvire's secret obsession; but he is not and never was her secret lover. Colino never knew Elvire until he rescued her from the fire, in the process receiving wounds from which he died; and his death preceded her marriage. Again, this kind of example seems to confirm that criticism that strains to elaborate a simple idea, and therefore has all of its attention directed to the cultivation of its own texture, has very little time and energy left to give to what Kleist actually wrote. Müller-Seidel's interpretative judgments point to this conclusion just as surely as his inability to refer accurately to Kleist's text points to it, for those judgments are never innovative; they are in fact the reverse, always those most commonly found in previous critics. . . .

Because of the prestige enjoyed by Müller-Seidel's work, I have thought it worth-while to spend some time discussing his study as a representative example of Kleist criticism. I want now to turn to another very influential figure in Kleist criticism—Gerhard Fricke. Though his view of Kleist no longer enjoys the kind of universal acceptance once accorded it, Fricke did more than any other critic to create the conditions in which the criticism that I have described is able to flourish. For in Fricke's work, verbal elaboration is not simply a compensation for poverty of content, as in the case of Hoffmeister, Reusner, Müller-Seidel, and others; in his criticism the elaboration of a verbal system is an independent goal, and there is a delight in his own language that soon leaves behind any thesis about Kleist's texts. This might have made him irrelevant to Kleist criticism; instead, he was until recently the most influential of all Kleist critics, and he continues to exert influence through those who have absorbed a good deal of his manner, if not his doctrines. . . .

All too often then, verbal complexity compensates for a deficiency in real content in Kleist criticism; and that deficiency, in turn, has usually resulted from a desire to find a general idea with which to characterize all of his works, one by one, and from the misconceptions about the nature of his writing that must inevitably result from so reductive a procedure.

The basic ideas that have formed the framework of these studies have sometimes been derived from aspects of the texts themselves. This is the origin, for example, of "Gefühl," "Zufall," "Vertrauen," as well as the many different versions of error and illusion ("Versehen," "Täuschung," "Traum," etc.). I have argued above that Kleist's texts are badly misread if these ideas are taken as fixed and absolute ones, as authors of general studies have done in order to find a theme to trace through all the texts, rather than as material that Kleist exploits at one moment and drops at the next in the interests of his larger concerns. But the basic notions of many general studies do not have even this much legitimacy; they are not the result of a misreading of the way certain motifs function in the text but instead derive from sources outside the texts. Two main kinds of source can be seen: the first consists in biographical information, the second in the ideological and critical preoccupations of the particular critic.

Kleist's biography is obviously a main source of the view that his work is above all violent and tragic, the mirror of a tormented, sick mind; critics who take this view certainly have his suicide prominently in mind. But if they had looked only at the emphases of his writings, it would have been harder to reach this conclusion. *Penthesilea,* to be sure, might superficially invite such a description, but it is an exception among the major writings. If we look at *Prinz Friedrich von Homburg, Der zerbrochne Krug,* **Michael Kohlhaas,** **"Der Zweikampf," "Die Marquise von O . . . ,"** and even **"Das Erdbeben in Chili,"** we find ambiguous rather than solidly pessimistic works. One has only to compare the typically ambiguous endings of Kleist's works . . . with the black, claustrophobic helplessness of. . . . some works of Hebbel or Chekhov to see that he is indeed a serious and thoughtful writer but not an unreservedly gloomy one. Kleist's works present human life as something that must be thought and rethought, interpreted and reinterpreted; it is very much contrary to the drift of the great majority of his works to say that they present a consistently negative attitude to life.

A comparable biographically introduced notion is that Kleist's characters are extremists, "grenzenlose Menschen." In fact, there are very few of Kleist's characters who, looked at in themselves, might tempt the critic to use such a phrase. Aside from Penthesilea, Michael Kohlhaas is the only obvious other possibility, but to label him simply an extremist would be to misunderstand his position in the text, especially the way in which that position changes. Far from representing an ideal character for Kleist as an uncompromisingly self-reliant figure, Michael Kohlhaas is a character whose stance is questioned by the late developments of the story. Kleist's characters are far too diverse to be reduced to a single type: Adam, the Count F., Alkmene, Prince Friedrich, Friedrich von Trota, Michael Kohlhaas, Don Fernando, Jeronimo, and Nicolo are all very different people, and their all being found in Kleist's work involves only one generalizable fact, which does not remove those differences: they are all characters who are not easy to judge, and the reader must be prepared to change his attitudes to them as new situations develop within each text.

There is one area of Kleist's biography (or what is known of it) that has at least some points of contact with the most central aspects of his work. This is the so-called Kant crisis, which occurred when he was a student; he was severely shaken to discover in Kant's philosophy that absolute truth cannot be found. But the use of this by Kleist's critics shows only too well how even relevant biographical material can distort and limit critical understanding. For critics who proceed from the Kant-crisis and conclude from it that Kleist's works embody a despair of knowledge and truth have blinded themselves to that fact that Kleist in the next decade moved well beyond that simple beginning and added a great deal to it. His writings are not reducible simply to an expression of that early mood. Far from merely showing despair, they show a considerable fascination with how situations and people can never be judged in one authoritative way (the "truth" about them) but are instead the subject of a developing understanding that can involve several different viewpoints. This, then, is a case in which the biographical pointer does not actually lead the critic in the wrong direction; but the pointer is so rudimentary and undeveloped that for the critic simply to accept it and go no further, using it as a key to the texts and leaving them at that point, is finally just as bad as following a completely misleading biographical fact. Although that experience was obviously the earliest sign of the development of Kleist's characteristic concerns, a thorough look at the texts is necessary to see that his best work has developed so far beyond that stage that to use it as an interpretative key would restrict and limit the discussion to the point that nothing would be seen of the characteristic quality of Kleist's mature work. Despair of knowledge is a very simple and easily grasped notion with nothing distinctive or unusual in it; where Kleist went from that beginning, on the other hand, is something unique and valuable.

A practical demonstration of the value of adducing the Kant-crisis can be seen in the nature of the interpretative comments of critics who have approached the texts from this standpoint; they are rarely different from the standard judgments commonly made by critics of all persuasions. At best, the Kant-crisis points to a large, vague area within which we must think about Kleist's work; it does not substitute for thinking, and the results of such thinking will look very different indeed from the mere transformation of a fact of the young Kleist's experience into an interpretative comment on his mature work. Even this, then, the most promising of biographical pointers, is eventually as misleading as it is unnecessary. A thorough look at any of the texts would lead to the more appropriate and useful notion of how a *search* for understanding is built into their structure; the primitive biographical pointer by itself has only led to still more studies of "error" and "deceit" as motifs in Kleist's work.

The other biographical pointer that is followed with regularity in Kleist criticism is the essay "Über das Marionettentheater." Enough has been written on this essay and its relation to Kleist's work to allow a whole volume of studies to be collected and published together, and at least a nod in the direction of its importance for understanding Kleist seems to be obligatory in any general study. I have no wish . . . to discuss the essay in detail here; and it is unnecessary to do so. Only two points need be made. First, the whole undertaking has on its face the appearance of being fundamentally another reductive search for an easy solution to the understanding of Kleist's work, yet one more way of circumventing serious thought about the texts by seizing on a simple idea to trace through them all. Any easy external key to texts as different as **Michael Kohlhaas,** *Prinz Friedrich von Homburg,* and **"Das Erdbeben in Chili"** is impossible to imagine, whatever its source. Second, the impact of this approach on the interpretation of the works is in practice very little. Take the example of Johannes Klein: he proclaims the importance of the "Marionettentheater" essay for an understanding of Kleist, but when it comes to a discussion of the works, he gives his readers the same view of **"Der Findling,"** of **Michael Kohlhaas,** of **"Die Marquise von O . . . ,"** and so on, that can be found in the work of practically any other critic.

The only other category of general ideas that has been made the basis of general studies of Kleist is that deriving not from Kleist or his work but from the ideological or critical preoccupations of the critic himself. These inevitably are very general notions that occur equally as the basis of hundreds of other studies of other authors. The real source of these ideas, then, is critical practice in general. Michael Moering, for example, writes on irony in Kleist; Hans Heinz Holz, on Kleist's work as springing "aus einem sprachphilosophischen Problem"; Friedrich Braig introduces religious belief; and so on. But the studies that are numerically most important . . . are those whose framework is Marxist. That a critic determined to see definite religious viewpoints in Kleist's works will do so regardless of their meaning needs no further comment; and Moering's work and that of Holz are not sufficiently substantial to merit discussion. . . .

Marxist criticism . . . has achieved some prominence within German literary criticism and has even gained some regard from those who are not adherents: they tend often to view it as at least the work of genuine intellectuals. But the truth appears to be . . . that it shares the worst habits of the bourgeois, old-fashioned critics on whom Marxists generally pour scorn. Moreover, since it also tends to resist whatever has been progressive in criticism over the last few decades, it is a highly conservative and even reactionary form of criticism. Let us look at some examples; it is almost obligatory to start with George Lukács.

Lukács is concerned above all else with the political aspects of Kleist's work. He sees in *Der zerbrochne Krug* "die Mißhandlung der Bauern durch die Obrigkeit"; *Prinz Friedrich von Homburg* is about a "Konflikt zwischen Individuum und Gesellschaft"; *Michael Kohlhaas* is about the mistreatment of a normal individual by a corrupt ruling class. . . .

Before coming to the question of what is specifically Marxist here, we are first struck by the fact that these are the same kinds of judgments found in the writings of the stuffiest, most conservative bourgeois critics: they are almost identical with the views of Hans Matthias Wolff, for example, and exhibit all the drawbacks of this kind of criticism. Wolff too saw in *Der zerbrochne Krug* essentially no more than a corrupt state official oppressing the people, in *Prinz Friedrich von Homburg* no more than the individual versus the state, and in *Michael Kohlhaas* a struggle of an individual against corrupt state officials. Lukács even makes the same kind of comment on the allegedly unnecessary and unfortunate addition of the "romantic" ending of *Michael Kohlhaas*. The same very basic criticism apply to both Wolff and Lukács, therefore, and the fact that they are equally valid for both shows that they need not involve any kind of hostility to Marxism as a philosophy. Wolff and Lukács both read these texts in the same superficial manner, reducing the content to an idea that obsesses them, but which is only a small part of the material of the text. Both lift elements of the text out of context and consequently destroy its thematic structure; both are deaf to anything in the text that is not connected with their very simple idea. And in both, a symptom of their reductive attitudes is the need to reject the end of the text as an unfortunate addition for which they can find no reason. Lukács's Marxist reading is in fact just like any other reductive, superficial misreading caused by the critic's obsession with a simple idea instead of trying to understand more of the text; it is no different from typical bourgeois criticism.

There are, however, further reservations that are more specifically relevant to Marxism itself. For example, Lukàcs clearly cannot conceive of a historical subject being used for a *thematic* purpose; his comments on Luther show that he thinks Kleist's purpose was simply to give an accurate historical portrayal. Where even Wolff thought of the text in terms of a thematic idea, however simple, Lukács thinks of *Michael Kohlhaas* in terms of its accuracy as a portrayal of the ruling class of a historical period—a reduction that goes even beyond Wolff's. And Lukács's praising this as a literary masterpiece because it is historically accurate from a Marxist viewpoint is, of course, an indicator of how very seriously he means that reduction: there is, apparently, nothing more than literature could be, or be about, than just that.

There is a great irony involved in Lukács's view of Kohlhaas, one that shows only too well its weakness. Lukács praises Kleist's portrayal of the oppression of Kohlhaas by the ruling class, but it is precisely the insufficiency of this kind of thinking that is an important theme in the story. *Michael Kohlhaas* is a story that questions whether such abstractions as "the state" or "the government" are usable; its final scenes see all political abstractions and any notion of a political "system" crumble as the reader at last recognizes that there exists only an incoherent, disorganized scene filled with individuals having no very clear ideas of what they are doing. The early part of the story seems to allow an impression of a coherent class that opposes Kohlhaas in a consistent, disciplined way to preserve its interests as a class, and that is how Lukács speaks of the whole story; but the text as a whole is partly about the fact that this is an *illusion* that the individual has. The exposure of the lack of reality in a certain kind of political thinking—such as that of Lukács—is part of the very structure of the story; no wonder Lukács could not read this text adequately!

Lukács's watchword for literary texts is "Realism," but that is highly misleading. A term as broad as "reality" must concern the whole of human life, yet for him it concerns only a narrow segment of human experience—political circumstances. To be more correct, he looks for only one aspect of that, namely, the class situation. And as a consequence of his exclusive concern with whether an author has shown the "reality" (i.e., the class situation) of any given historical moment, he cannot read anything as a thematic study dealing with human life in a way that goes beyond experience at a particular moment in history (or beyond a certain aspect of politics). *Michael Kohlhaas* is a study of how an individual is almost bound to try to think of any system that confronts him as if it were another individual with its own outlook, attitude, and personality, even though this view is pointless and conceivably disastrous. To look instead in a literary work for a realistic picture of historical circumstances is to preclude any receptivity to a thematic study that uses historical material for its own purposes; and to look only for a validation of one's political ideology in a literary work is to preclude the possibility that it has anything of its own to say.

Some more recent Marxist critics have themselves criticized Lukács, but they fail to provide any superior version of Marxist criticism that avoids his fundamental misconceptions. Manfred Lefèvre, in a recent *Forschungsbericht,* written from a Marxist point of view, concedes that some of Lukács's judgments were indeed oversimple, and he takes the view that a more advanced Marxist criticism now exists in a series of recent writers. But these differences between Lukács and his successors are superficial only. What these newer Marxists quarrel with in Lukács is mainly his summary judgment that Kleist was a "borniert-er preußischer Junker" into whose works reality intruded only "gegen seine Absichten," which nonetheless made him an important Realist. But their concern is mainly that a somewhat more favorable judgment of Kleist be made from the same basic standpoint, not that the texts be read in a fundamentally different way. The newer writers of whom Lefèvre speaks in fact proceed much as Lukács did, and are guilty of much the same misreadings and simplifications that Lukács himself made. Ernst Fischer sees Kleist's works as being about ''die Wechselwirkung des Einzelnen und der Gesellschaft,'' with the early stories showing Kleist's negative attitude towards society but *Prinz Friedrich von Homburg* showing a final awareness of "gesellschaftliche Notwendigkeit"; Hans Mayer thinks Kleist's works embody Rousseauism and that *Prinz Friedrich von Homburg* is a final synthesis of "Staatsraison und Gefühlskraft"; Siegfried Streller too thinks the teachings of Rousseau, but also those of Adam Müller, are embodied in Kleist, and Lefèvre makes it clear when discussing Streller that he shares Streller's view. . . . Again, this is all utterly familiar: when Marxists look at the texts, they are most likely to repeat Wolff, and these are in fact all Wolff's judgments. The iconoclastic new viewpoint in practice rarely results in anything more than judgments borrowed from old-fashioned bourgeois critics. Even the elementary mistake of thinking that whatever Kohlhaas argues must be Kleist's view is Wolff's; neither Wolff nor the Marxists are able to resist taking a piece of political "Stoff" out of the work's context while ignoring its *use* in the work. But neither is this all really very far from Lukács. Lefèvre makes much of the fact that the judgments of the more recent Marxists are more sophisticated than those of Lukács. For example, where Lukács thought Kleist a "Junker" who portrayed social realism (read: the injustice of the class system) in spite of himself, Mayer sees in him a bourgeois artist who saw the limitations of bourgeois reality, and Fischer conceives of him as "vor allem ein Rebell." But these differences are mostly a matter of different summary attitudes by Fischer and Mayer based on readings of the texts that in most important ways are similar: they share fully with Lukács the tendency to read the texts without much regard for their own emphases and to pursue in them a simple political idea that distorts Kleist's characteristic way of writing.

The Marxist critics I have cited make a point of saying that they read Kleist's work in the historical context of his time, which in practice means the context of political history. There are well-known arguments for and against that procedure, but they are not relevant here, for that is not what these critics really do, and it is not the source of their readings or of their misreadings of Kleist's texts. The proof of this assertion can be seen in their results, which, as readings, are no different from those of non-Marxist critics. What is really happening is that they are placing the *results* of their reading the texts in the historical context (or rather, whatever their ideological view of that context is); and everything depends on the quality of those readings, which, if inadequate, render the whole procedure useless at the outset. In fact, then, they are setting readings that are superficial and distorted into a historical context, and that can never do anything to make the readings better. There is, in a way, no test here of the usefulness of a historical approach; this is in its essence standard superficial reductive academic criticism. Marxists brandish some new terminology—but then, their bourgeois counterparts make much use of that stratagem too—and they are full of righteous fervor. But they say very much the same things about the texts that other critics have said, and to just as little purpose. . . .

There are some hopeful signs in recent critical essays on individual works. While many such essays still tend to repeat the same interpretative views that have long predominated in Kleist criticism, a growing number of critics seem to be questioning the received opinion of the past and taking a more complex and subtle view of the texts. But as before, general studies of Kleist lag behind this interpretative progress and seem to seek only new ways of organizing familiar interpretations within a simplified and reductive thematic framework.

"Die Marquise von O . . ." presents a particularly striking case of improvement in recent criticism. In the first paragraphs of the interpretation of **"Die Marquise von O . . ."** included in this volume, I noted that the important and provocative scene of reconciliation between father and daughter was never mentioned in the critical literature on the story, and I argued that this was a measure of how much the traditional clichés of Kleist criticism had distracted attention from what he wrote. Since I wrote this, no fewer than four studies of the story have appeared that take this scene to be central to the interpretation of the text: Hermann F. Weiss, "Precarious Idylls: The Relationship Between Father and Daughter in Heinrich von Kleist's *Die Marquise von O. . . .,"* *Modern Language Notes,* 91 (1976); Thomas Fries, "The Impossible Object: The Feminine, the Narrative (Laclos' *Liasons Dangereuses* and Kleist's *Marquise von O . . .,"* *Modern Language Notes,* 91 (1976); Heinz Politzer, "Der Fall der Frau Marquise: Beobachtungen zu Kleists *Die Marquise von O . . . ,"* *Deutsche Vierteljahrsschrift für Literaturwissenschaft und Geistesgeschichte,* 51 (1977); Erika Swales, "The Beleaguered Citadel: A Study of Kleist's *Die Marquise von O . . . ," Deutsche Vierteljahrsschrift für Literaturwissenschaft und Geistesgeschichte,* 51 (1977). It is of course possible to have some reservations about these essays too. Mine would be, briefly, that Swales's treatment becomes rather rigidly concerned with the notion of order and Politzer's with the text's exemplifying Freudian concepts, while Weiss's short piece does little more than stress the importance of the role of the father, and Fries devotes far more time to Leclos than to Kleist in his comparative essay. None of the four quite sees how the reconciliation scene clashes with what has gone before it, stylistically and otherwise, and how it forces a rewriting of the assumptions on which the world of the Marquise and the story generally had seemed to be based. Even so, to see the importance of the reconciliation scene must and does lead to the question of the repressed emotions of the Kommandant, and to get this far is to be in an interpretative sphere well beyond that of all previous Kleist criticism. It is an odd fact that the importance of this scene is so obvious to all four of the latest critics of the story (five, including myself), for all previous critics had overlooked it in order to pursue the elaboration of concepts such as error or contradiction. This curious contrast is yet more proof of how such a style of criticism has led critics away from the problems and subtleties of Kleist's texts to ones of their own making.

Two examples of how general studies of Kleist still lag far behind critical essays on individual works are: Denys Dyer, *The Stories of Kleist: A Critical Study* (London, 1977), and Ilse Graham, *Heinrich von Kleist. Word Into Flesh: A Poet's Quest for the Symbol* (Berlin and New York, 1977). That Graham's book uses a formula all too familiar in Kleist criticism can be seen immediately from the publicity statement in the publisher's catalogue: "She isolates a primitive model of experience as being paradigmatic of him, and traces its two principal variants through Kleist's dramatic and narrative work." As so often before, it is Kleist's essay on the *Marionettentheater* which is made to yield this key to all that he wrote. Graham's book uses the standard model that I have described: a simple idea, traced throughout the works; interpretations of the texts that agree in most important outlines with those of previous Kleist critics; and compensatory verbal elaboration—indeed this work is written in an unusually self-indulgent style.

Dyer's book certainly avoids pretentiousness, and it represents a serious attempt to introduce the general reader to the world of Kleist and Kleist criticism without striving for originality of interpretation. Unhappily, the standard views of Kleist criticism, when set out baldly and directly, look somewhat uninteresting; Dyer's book suffers as a result. The absence of any real interpretative involvement in the texts leads to inaccurate quotation, frequently in ways that are crucial to the meaning of a text. Not once, but twice, Dyer says that in **"Der Findling,"** Xaviera had been discarded by the Bishop before she seduced Nicolo; but this only happens many years later, right at the end of the story. The parallelism of both Nicolo and Xaviera being in subservient roles is lost here.

The crucial phrase "zum Schauplatze seines vollen Glückes" in **"Das Erdbeben in Chili"** is misquoted as "ihres vollen Glückes" and, again, an enormously important interpretative point is missed.

The magnitude of the difference in subtlety between these two general books and the best recent critical essays on individual works emerges when the judgments made by Graham and Dyer on **"Die Marquise von O . . . "** are contrasted with those of Fries, Weiss, Politzer and Swales. Dyer speaks obsessively of the "purity" of the Marquise, and Graham in similar vein of her "serene acceptance." By contrast, the other four critics appear actually to be talking about human beings, not unreal black and white characters.

Two articles that have appeared recently on **"Der Findling"** also deserve special mention. They too point forward to better things in Kleist criticism: Erna Moore, "Heinrich von Kleist's 'Findling': Psychologie des Verhängnisses," *Colloquia Germanica,* 8 (1974); and Frank Ryder, "Kleist's *Findling*: Oedipus *Manqué?" Modern Language Notes,* 92 (1977). (Moore's study, though dated 1974, actually appeared in 1976 because the journal was well behind schedule.) Both Moore and Ryder deal with the real people of Kleist's story and not with the narrator's surface judgments or the one-dimensional cliché characters of previous Kleist critics. Ryder's essay is somewhat speculative, as he himself freely admits, but whether or not his speculations are absolutely sound in each case, his results are thought-provoking and illuminating to the reader who wishes to progress beyond the superficial traditional view of the story. Moore, in the best single interpretative essay on Kleist of recent years, also goes well beyond that view. She warns that we should not allow the narrator's superficial moral judgments to deflect our attention from the actual events that he relates, following the viewpoint on this question developed in my published essay on **"Der Zweikampf"** which she cites in her support. She also argues persuasively that Kleist's characters are not to be treated as pawns in a metaphysical chess-game but instead as people whose psychology and motivation are to be understood. Having begun in this way, she achieves what seems to me a far more satisfactory view of Elvire than any hitherto, and one that has many points of contact with the view I have developed in this [essay]. Differences between my interpretation and Moore's arise where Piachi and, to a lesser extent, Nicolo are concerned. In my view she does not go far enough in rejecting the narrator's surface judgments and looking at what the narrated events in themselves indicate. And on the more general question of the thematic basis of the story, our results are even more divergent. However, I find her essay most impressive.

If the six interpretative essays that I have discussed are an omen for the future, then Kleist criticism would seem recently to have become more promising. On the other hand, this selective discussion has dealt only with the best recent essays; there is still much evidence that unproductive criticism, of the kind discussed in the main body of this [essay], will continue to appear.

James M. McGlathery (essay date 1983)

SOURCE: *"Erzählungen I:* 'Michael Kohlhaas,' 'Die Marquise von O . . . ,' 'Das Erdbeben in Chili,'" in *Desire's Sway: The Plays and Stories of Heinrich von Kleist,* Wayne State University Press, 1983, pp. 76-88.

[*In the following excerpt, McGlathery examines the theme of sexual sublimation in* Michael Kohlhaas, *"Die Marquise von O . . . ,"* and *"Das Erdbeben in Chili."*]

Of the three stories which fill this volume of collected tales that Kleist published in 1810, only **"Die Marquise von O . . ."** obviously concerns sexual shame or guilt. This fact is especially surprising because all three tales were begun or finished in Kleist's middle period, between the writing of *Der zerbrochne Krug* and *Das Käthchen von Heilbronn,* when erotic psychology was most clearly his dominant interest. The departure from that focus is only superficial, however, for on closer inspection one finds that *Michael Kohlhaas* and **"Das Erdbeben in Chili,"** are love stories in which sexual sublimation plays no small part.

At first reading, *Michael Kohlhaas* seems little concerned with love. Kohlhaas' wife, Lisbeth, to whom he had been happily married, dies early in the story, and Kohlhaas does not take a new wife or become romantically involved. Thus, one certainly cannot speak here of any emotional conflict involving the suppression of awareness about desire that one finds in most of Kleist's other major works. Kohlhaas' grief over the loss of his wife seems quite outside the focus of attention, since the story concerns his grim quest for the punishment of Junker Wenzel von Tronka

for doing him an injustice. Kohlhaas began his search for retribution before his wife's death in connection with the matter gave him cause to pursue it with vengence. And yet the tale is perhaps best read as a love story in view of the fact that Kohlhaas is visited before his execution by an old woman who appears to be the ghost of his wife and that the whole of Kohlhaas' mad pursuit of justice is played out between Lisbeth's death and her uncanny return some seven months later, when her role as her husband's guardian angel during that period is finally revealed.

Lisbeth's role is one of Kleist's major deviations from the Kohlhaas story as he found it in his sources. Kleist's critics have occasionally considered the wife's part extraneous, and some have wondered why he bothered to introduce the supernatural element of her return from the dead into an otherwise realistic tale. It is precisely these critical objections that suggest that the key to an understanding of the story lies in Kohlhaas' devotion to his wife and his resulting determination to win justice and to humiliate Junker Wenzel.

Kohlhaas' likely motive for revenge following Lisbeth's death is his grief over her loss, although he does not allow himself to see the matter in those terms. Kohlhaas may unconsciously be intent on proving himself worthy of his dead wife's admiration, since it was Lisbeth who cast him in the role of avenging angel: "she said . . . that it would be God's work to put a stop to disorders like these; and that she herself wanted to get together the money to pay the costs that would result from his [Kohlhaas'] conduct of this case." (The historical Kohlhaas was named Hans, but Kleist changed his name to that of Michael, after the angel in Revelations, chapter 12, who wards off and then imprisons the satanic dragon while Mary is giving birth to Jesus.)

To be sure, Lisbeth subsequently has misgivings and begs her husband to renounce his quest for justice. But Kohlhaas recognizes that she does so not because she has begun to doubt the holiness of his endeavor; instead, she fears that it will cost them their livelihood and their home. Even when Lisbeth, on her deathbed, shows Kohlhaas the Bible verse (Luke 6:27), "Forgive your enemies, do good to them who hate you" (the Bible, including the Luther translation, has "Love your enemies"), she likely is thinking as much of the safety and well-being of him and their children as of their salvation and blessed reunion in heaven. In any case, it is clear that Kohlhaas' ensuing rage, which takes possession of him only after his wife's death and cools shortly thereafter, is largely an expression of grief over her loss in the form of a yearning to fulfill the role of angel of justice that Lisbeth had suggested for him. (The installment of *Michael Kohlhaas* that Kleist published in his journal *Phöbus* ended here, with the widowed horse dealer setting out to avenge not only the wrong done him but also the death of his wife, which had resulted from his initial efforts to secure justice.)

The turning point in Kohlhaas' career as a rebel comes with his public denunciation by Martin Luther. His resulting concern to meet with Luther suggests that he may be bothered by a guilty conscience about his murderous passion for revenge, although it has now subsided. Kohlhaas' role as avenging angel and the issue of whether or not retribution is sanctioned by the Bible were matters raised by his wife, so that Luther's condemnation may well remind him of Lisbeth's judgment of his quest. Indeed, Kohlhaas goes to Luther not to argue the justness or holiness of his cause, but to change Luther's opinion of him. To this end Kohlhaas proposes that he be granted safe conduct to plead his case against the junker in person in the Saxon capital, for Luther claimed in his public denunciation of Kohlhaas that the Elector had not concerned himself with Kohlhaas' complaint only because he had not been informed of the matter. Just as Kohlhaas was originally concerned less about God's opinion of him than his wife's, he is now seeking not so much a theological judgment from Luther as a token of the latter's respect and admiration. Luther therefore serves as a substitute for Lisbeth, whose opinion Kohlhaas can no longer ask.

The climax of this pivotal scene, and of the story as a whole, comes after Kohlhaas has justified his terrorist activities to Luther by exclaiming, as a tear rolls down his cheek, "Most worthy Sire! It has cost me my wife; Kohlhaas wants to show the world that she did not die in an unjust cause." The turning point follows when Kohlhaas replies to Luther's query that might not he have done better to have forgiven the junker "for the sake of your Saviour?" The horse dealer exclaims, "Maybe! and maybe not! If I had known that I would have had to use blood from my wife's heart to get them [i.e., his horses] back on their feet, maybe I would have done as you said." In other words, Kohlhaas explains that he might have refrained from turning outlaw for his wife's sake and thereby ignores Luther's point that he should have forgiven the junker out of devotion to Jesus.

This is not to say that Kohlhaas is unconcerned about his salvation, for as he is leaving he drops to his knees to ask Luther to hear his confession and give him communion. Kohlhaas' action here, too, seems motivated less from contrition engendered by Luther's admonitions than from a far more ordinary concern to stay right with God through the routine observance of required ritual. Kohlhaas' explanation of his request is that his "martial enterprises," as he offhandedly calls them, have kept him from taking the sacrament at Pentecost, which was his custom. Perhaps Kohlhaas feels guilty toward God and wishes to hide the fact from Luther, or even from himself. More likely, though, the widower-horse-dealer-turned-outlaw is concerned with doing what he can to see that if he should die—and under the circumstances he must feel that could happen very shortly indeed—he would be allowed to join his dear Lisbeth in heaven.

From the moment of his visit to Luther, which revived poignant memories of Lisbeth and thoughts of joining her after death, Kohlhaas undertakes no further violent actions in support of his complaint. He gradually loses interest in the matter, concerning himself instead with hopes of survival for himself and his and Lisbeth's children. Just after Lisbeth's death and before he took the law into his own hands, Kohlhaas had sent the children to relatives across the border for safekeeping. With his career as an outlaw behind him and having been assured of safe conduct in Dresden, Kohlhaas sends for his children immediately. Later, when he has lost hope of gaining satisfaction and has begun to fear for his life, the widower-father secretly makes ready to emigrate with his children to the Near East or the East Indies but is arrested before he can carry out his plan. Thus, following the interview with Luther, Kohlhaas' grief over Lisbeth's death appears to find relief in his bittersweet return to his role as father to their children.

The story's denouement begins with the Elector of Saxony's chance discovery, as Kohlhaas is being transported to Brandenburg for trial and execution, that the horse dealer possesses a capsule known to contain a prophecy regarding the fortunes of the Saxon ruling family. Here, too, the love between Kohlhaas and Lisbeth plays the key role, for immediately after her death and out of concern for her husband's safety, Lisbeth (to all appearances) assumed the role of his guardian angel, although without his knowledge. It evidently was Lisbeth, transformed as a fortune-telling hag, who held out to the Saxon Elector the prospect of learning the fate of his ruling house and who then gave Kohlhaas the capsule containing the prophecy as a means of making him safe from prosecution by the government of Saxony. When the hag later visits Kohlhaas in prison in Berlin shortly before he is to be executed there, she tells him about the contents of the capsule to persuade him to offer it to the Elector in exchange for his freedom (this tactic would not likely have succeeded since the Elector proves powerless to intervene when he attempts to do so). Kohlhaas, though, sees the capsule as a last means of revenge and is determined to take its secrets with him to the grave.

The hag first pleads with Kohlhaas to save himself for the sake of the children but then admits that Kohlhaas has a point in maintaining that it is more important the children should respect and admire him for having refused to bow to injustice. Thus, the hag's response in leaving the decision up to Kohlhaas is in keeping with Lisbeth's earlier, ambivalent attitude as revealed prior to her death. The focus here is once again on Kohlhaas' role as avenging angel, the role originally suggested to him by Lisbeth and one that doubtless appealed mightily to his desire to be a hero in her eyes. The hag's parting words to Kohlhaas, "You shall not lack for knowledge of all these things when we meet again," evidently refer to a reunion in the beyond, where her identity and the nature of her mission will be revealed to him. It was precisely this dream of their meeting in heaven which motivated Kohlhaas' climactic visit to Luther and his change of course in pursuit of justice.

Realistically speaking, of course, the hag can hardly be Lisbeth, but Kleist is careful to preface this part of his account with an indirect reminder that *Michael Kohlhaas* is a tale told on the testimony of older chronicles (one must remember the introduction of this supernatural element was Kleist's invention). Kleist's narrator pauses to comment that "at this point something had occurred which we report, to be sure, but must grant freedom to doubt to those who prefer to do so." Although the narrator himself thereby indicates that he believes what he is about to tell, there is no reason to think that Kleist was capable of such belief. The point seems rather to be that Lisbeth's miraculous appearance is a fitting end to this tale, especially when it is viewed as a love story, and not as an account of a man's determined quest for justice. Indeed, Kohlhaas' uncanny interview with his deceased wife may be considered a wish fulfillment which, had it not in fact happened, would have served as a projection of the unconscious dream of love that helps motivate Kohlhaas' behavior throughout.

The image of the beloved as angel of salvation or retribution plays a central role in **"Die Marquise von O . . . ,"** for here the heroine's rescue by a gallant officer is the event around which the action revolves. In this story Kleist's familiar theme of suppressed or unadmitted sexual guilt, which is uncharacteristically lacking in *Michael Kohlhaas,* proves as central as it was in *Der zerbrochne Krug* and *Amphitryon.* But while Judge Adam knew quite well that he had tried to seduce pretty young Eva and Alkmena was aware that she had enjoyed an incomparable night of love with a man she presumed was her husband, the Marchioness von O. is not conscious of having made love to anyone since the death of her first husband several years earlier and yet finds herself pregnant.

After the marchioness has finally discovered the identity of the man who violated her, and after she marries and forgives him, she lovingly declares to him one day that "he would not have appeared to her as a devil back then [i.e., at the time his identity as her violator was revealed], if he had not, on their first meeting, seemed to her to be an angel." The key to understanding the story is that if Count F., the gallant Russian officer in question, had not appeared to the marchioness on that first occasion in the sublimely erotic role of angel of rescue, she might not have fainted in his arms, thereby putting him in the way of temptation. Thus, it likely was not the fact that Count F. had saved her from being raped by his troops that prevented her from thinking of him as her potential violator, but instead her own suppressed sexual guilt, which caused her to faint rather than face the dread thought that she was experiencing stirrings of desire in his arms. When it is revealed that Count F. violated her, the marchioness's reaction to him as though he were the devil suggests that she projects onto her rescuer the sexual guilt she unconsciously feels over having swooned when she sensed desire's power taking possession of her.

The struggle within the marchioness is subconscious. The especially intriguing aspect of her emotional crisis is that, not only does she not know the identity of the man who sired the child she is carrying, she is not lying when she claims to her parents that she has no idea how she became pregnant. The parents' subsequent banishment of their daughter occurs not because she conceived a child out of wedlock but rather for what they perceive as her haughty withholding of the truth not merely from them, but from

herself. Such denial is a serious moral fault, and one that parents are especially at pains to correct in their children (in her parents' eyes the marchioness must seem like the proverbial child who, caught with her hand in the cookie jar, steadfastly denies the obvious). The unwed daughter's pregnancy does not much bother her parents; her claiming not to know how it happened is quite another matter.

Perhaps the best evidence that the marchioness does "know" that Count F. is the father of her unborn child is her reaction to his assurance, before he has revealed himself, that he has been told everything about her condition and is still completely convinced of her innocence. Until that moment in the scene between the two of them in her garden, she has been content to repose in the gallant count's embrace. Now, though, she rises and extricates herself as she exclaims, "What? And you have come anyway?" Doubtless her first thought is that the count cannot be serious or, if he is not mocking her, he must be acting out of pity and compassion, that is, as her angel of rescue once again. This thought, invoking the earlier situation in which he played a similar role and the suppressed memory of what she had felt then in his embrace, likely contributes to her urge to escape from his arms now. What ensues is equally to the point. As the count begins to hint at the truth by adding mysteriously, "As convinced, . . . Julietta, as though I were omniscient, as though my soul dwelt in your breast," the marquise demands that he leave and tries to escape him. And when he pleads, "One single, secret, whispered [word?]!" she replies, "I don't *want* to know *anything*" (Kleist's italics) and brushes him away violently. The marchioness must unconsciously sense that she knows the truth and that she has known it all along, though she cannot let such a recognition rise to the level of consciousness.

When Count F. appears in answer to the marchioness's newspaper advertisement (in which she promises to marry the man who violated her regardless of who he is, if only he will present himself), she reacts as though the Russian officer were the devil incarnate. Completely beside herself, she sprinkles the members of her family with holy water after he has departed. That she does not attempt to purify herself with the water as well suggests that the marchioness is projecting her own guilty susceptibility to the count's gallantry upon her mother, father, and brother. The marquise must know the devil is considered to have power only over those who have a chink in their moral armor.

As soon as the count has declared himself, the marchioness's mother recognizes immediately what must have happened and implies that each of the family members must unconsciously have known all along that the count was the guilty party. "Whom have we been expecting then?" she exclaims. Her daughter replies in embarrassed confusion, "Well? Why, not him?" suggesting perhaps that she is not sure that she, too, had not somehow known the truth. Granted, the other members of the family had been thrown off the track for the same reason as she, that is, by the count's gallantry in having rescued her from his troops. Still the marchioness must remember at some level what she had felt just prior to her swoon. Her failure, therefore, to think of the possibility that Count F. had violated her is different in kind and degree from her parents'.

That the parents have no objection to the count's suit, even after his revelation that it was he who took advantage of their daughter, suggests that they recognize he acted not out of base lust but out of romantic transport, as is shown by his many demonstrations of devotion to her. The marchioness's revulsion at the thought of marrying the count is perfectly understandable, since his disclosure destroyed her romantic image of him as her angel of rescue and perhaps because she feels he is now acting only out of chivalry. Considering that she eventually overcomes this revulsion and finds true happiness as the count's wife, the marchioness's deeper reason for her horror may have been unconscious shame over having felt so secure and so drawn to him at their first meeting that she had fainted in his arms. **"Die Marquise von O . . . "** would appear then to be a tale of love at first sight made interesting by the heroine's struggle with suppressed shame over having so suddenly, if unconsciously, surrendered to desire.

Count F.'s emotional situation is diametrically opposite that of his beloved. He alone, of all the characters, knows the secret of her pregnancy. He recognizes and accepts his guilt and wishes to atone for it. Since he is so thoroughly devoted to the young widow, he justifiably looks upon his violation of her as motivated by something like love at first sight. Proposing marriage to her and throwing himself at her feet in humble submission is therefore no embarrassment for him, especially because he feels he would be doing so even if he had been able to control himself earlier. There is no emotional conflict within the count and certainly no suppression of guilt or awareness. He passionately desires to wed the marchioness and pursues his aim singlemindedly, regardless of how embarrassing or humiliating the terms and conditions might be.

The shame and embarrassment the count feels concerning his dishonorable deed, though, is balanced by his amusement at the incongruity of the marchioness's pride considering the realities of her position, of which she of course is unaware. The count evidently feels that although she suffered his ravishment of her in a faint, on some level of consciousness she must have known what was happening to her, even though it seemed to be taking place in a dream. Long before he finally reveals himself, the count hints at the truth in an effort to raise her awareness to the conscious level. This obviously is his purpose in telling her how in a dream she had become associated in his mind with a female swan he had seen as a boy on his uncle's estates. He relates that he once threw mud at the swan which then dove underwater to come up with no trace of besmirchment. (Is the swan's dive a reference to the marchioness's faint, from which she arose cleansed of the memory of his passion and of her urge to surrender to it?) When he called the swan by name he was unable to lure her to him for "she took her pleasure simply in propelling herself through the water and preening."

The father's feelings toward his widowed daughter are also of considerable interest. Colonel von G. clearly was not amused by what he considered to be the daughter's haughty refusal to admit the truth, but his extreme reaction to her denials (especially his intent to drive her from the house with his pistols) seems to indicate some further motivation. The same is true of his behavior during the later scene of his reconciliation with her in which he seems to assume the role of his daughter's ravisher. She herself proves as passive and submissive toward his kisses and caresses as she had been rendered by her faint in Count F.'s arms earlier. During these poignant moments of reconciliation, Colonel von G. seems to be identifying with the daughter's still unknown violator, although in his own eyes—and, even stranger, in those of his wife—he is only behaving like the stereotypically doting father whose devotion causes him to go to foolish extremes. The colonel's excessive intimacies with his daughter, who is by then in an advanced stage of pregnancy, are perhaps not unrelated to thoughts of the passion she had inspired in her ravisher. His reaction is similar to Count F.'s earlier indiscretion, which resulted in part from his having witnessed the lust the marchioness had inspired in his soldiers: "summoned by the lady's cry for help, a Russian officer appeared and with furious blows scattered the dogs who were lusting after such booty."

"Das Erdbeben in Chili" is more clearly a love story than *Michael Kohlhaas* and even **"Die Marquise von O . . . "**—indeed so much so that the sexual subconscious seems at first glance to play little or no role. Thus, although Josepha has born a child out of wedlock, neither she nor her lover Jeronimo feel any guilt about having surrendered to desire, having consummated their love without a priest's blessing and, worse, having done so within the walls of a convent. On the contrary, the two young lovers come to believe that their survival in a terrible earthquake, which saved Josepha from execution and Jeronimo from hanging himself, was ordained by God as a sign of his approval of their union—a union which Josepha's father had evidently sought to prevent because Jeronimo, her tutor, was of lower social station.

If sexual fantasy is involved here, it concerns the young couple's vision of themselves and their union as being under God's special blessing and protection. There can be no question that Jeronimo's and Josepha's belief that their union was made in heaven is not only blasphemous but also irrational. God would hardly have wrought such destruction if his purpose had been to save them or to give his blessing to their love. In particular, the earthquake claimed among its victims those who had shown a measure of clemency toward Josepha, such as the abbess and the governor (*Vizekönig*).

When Kleist's story first appeared in Cotta's *Morgenblatt,* it carried the title "Jeronimo und Josephe," with the earthquake mentioned only in the subtitle. In his first volume of *Erzählungen,* however, he gave the tale its present title, as he may have intended originally. This later title directs attention away from the love story and focuses it on the earthquake and its effects on the mood of the populace. As in the case of Josepha and Jeronimo, sexual fantasy or sublimation plays a role in the reaction of the citizenry to the earthquake and indeed had already done so in their response to the news of Josepha's having given birth to an illegitimate child on the cathedral steps during the Corpus Christi procession. The projection and identification involved in the attitude of the female population toward the young couple as having yielded to temptation can be seen in the description of the eagerness with which "the pious daughters of the city" secured themselves a good view of Josepha's scheduled execution and of the matrons' and virgins' dissatisfaction that the sentence had been changed from death by fire to decapitation. Unadmitted male sexual envy and vicarious identification also took their part from the beginning, when Josepha's brother told their father, Asteron, of her romantic involvement with Jeronimo—the news that prompted the father to send her to the convent.

The most devastating result of such subterranean feelings is produced by the envy and sexual guilt felt unconsciously by Master Pedrillo, whose dashing of the infant's head against a wall forms the shocking culmination of the mob scene at the cathedral. Pedrillo knew Josepha in a far more humble capacity than did Jeronimo: he was the family's shoe repairman and must, if only unconsciously, have identified with Jeronimo as a fellow household servant who satisfied, with Josepha's consent, urges that the lowly cobbler must feel he himself could only have gratified by ravishing her. Such suppressed sexual envy would explain not only the cobbler's seizure of the bastard child as the special object of his rage but also the narrator's curious reference to Master Pedrillo's intimate knowledge of Josepha's feet: "a shoe repairman who had worked for Josepha, and who knew her at least as precisely as he did her little feet"; that part of a woman's body, especially in Kleist's day and before, was associated with cowardly, fetishistic desire). The cobbler's first words to Josepha at the cathedral suggest that her surrender to her desire for Jeronimo is on his mind, however unconsciously: "Who is the father of this child? he cried out, as he turned with insolent defiance to Asteron's daughter."

That sexuality at some level of consciousness preoccupies those members of the community eager to see the young lovers destroyed is indicated by the fact that the spark that ignites the mob violence at the cathedral comes with the elderly preacher's comparison of Santiago before the earthquake to Sodom and Gomorrah in which he cites as his chief example "the blasphemy that had been committed in the convent garden of the Carmelite nuns." After the preacher dwells "long-windedly" on this subject and condemns the forbearance with which the matter had been handled, Constanza, mistaken for Josepha, is struck down and killed by someone who yells, "Convent whore!" Jeronimo is then identified and clubbed to death by his own father. Such a violent action suggests that behind the father's rage lies an identification with the son as having tasted forbidden fruit from above his station and not simply the pious belief that God disapproves of the son's evident blasphemy. Finally, sexual obsession seems to lurk behind Master Pedrillo's fanatic rage as he slays Josepha and then yells, "Send the bastard after her to hell!"

Even when Don Fernando, at the story's end, attempts to come to terms emotionally with the mistaken murder of his own son, Juan, and the lucky survival of Josepha's and Jeronimo's illegitimate son, Philipp, in his stead, a trace of sexual guilt or revulsion may help explain the grieving father's rationalization that when he "compared Philipp with Juan, and how he had obtained the two of them, he almost felt as though he should rejoice." Since the story concludes with this ambiguous sentence, the nature of its ambiguity seems important. It is easy enough to see that since Don Fernando obtained Philipp through the grace of God (or through his own courageous actions), his piety would argue that the orphaned boy should be the more highly prized. The problem lies rather with the implied reference to how Don Fernando had obtained Juan. Thus, Don Fernando does not entirely lack the populace's demonstrated guilt regarding sexuality and its need to escape into piety—a psychic mechanism also evident in Josepha's and Jeronimo's unshakable belief in the holiness of their love. Most important, the orphan must remind Don Fernando of his appealingly gallant role as an angel of rescue, the role that provided a typical avenue of sexual sublimation in the novelistic literature of Kleist's day.

Clayton Koelb (essay date 1990)

SOURCE: "Incorporating the Text: Kleist's *Michael Kohlhaas,*" in *PMLA,* Vol. 105, No. 5, October, 1990, pp. 1098-107.

[*In the following essay, Koelb provides a stylistic and thematic analysis of* Michael Kohlhaas.]

It is a paradox of German literary history that Heinrich von Kleist's novella **Michael Kohlhaas** is perennially among both the most esteemed and the most frequently censured works in the modern canon. There is nearly universal admiration for the story of Kohlhaas's attempt to obtain redress for an injustice done to him by the Tronka family and of the final righting of his grievance only after he is condemned for taking the law into his own hands. But this simple, powerful tale is complicated by what many critics refer to as a "subplot," in which Kohlhaas receives from a gypsy woman a prophecy regarding the elector of Saxony and, by destroying the paper on which it is written, revenges himself for the wrongs committed by the elector's agents. Many critics have attacked this prophecy plot, and it continues to provoke critical displeasure in spite of attempts to defend it. [In *The Marquise of O— and other Stories,* 1978] David Luke and Nigel Reeves, for example, find the work "as Kleist might have completed it," without the prophecy material, to be wholly admirable: "the story of an individual grievance developing, with fascinating and dreadful realism, through ever-increasing complexities until it becomes a major affair of state and is then brought to a paradoxical but impressively logical resolution." But by 1810, when Kleist finally completed the project he had started perhaps as early as 1804, it had gone in another direction. "Unfortunately, . . . Kleist was not content to finish **Michael**

Kohlhaas on those lines, but introduced a bizarre and fantastic sub-plot which seriously damages the artistic structure of an already long and complex narrative." Luke and Reeves follow the precedent of, among others, Georg Lukács [in *Deutsche Realisten des 19. Jahrhunderts,* 1951], who finds that the potentially successful realism of the novella suffers a "derailment" (*Entgleisung*) in the last quarter of the text. Lukács therefore simply omits the prophecy material from his discussion, and other interpreters have clearly wished that they could do the same.

It is worth asking why so many readers are uncomfortable with the story as Kleist wrote it. It cannot merely be that Kleist makes use of fantasy, since he does so in other tales without provoking uneasiness. No one objects, for example, to the intrusion of the supernatural in **"Das Bettelweib von Locarno"** or in **"Die heilige Cäcile."** The judgment of Luke and Reeves is once again typical:

> The irruption of the inexplicable into an otherwise explicable world is here again [in **"Die heilige Cäcilie"** as in **"Das Bettelweib"**] very far from seeming to be a mere whimsical and stylistically alien digression: instead, it is once more the precise centre and appalling *pointe* of the whole tale.

But why is the confrontation between natural and supernatural, explicable and inexplicable, seen to be "whimsical" and "alien" in one story but central in the others? What is different about *Michael Kohlhaas* that sets the stage for such large-scale critical disappointment?

One answer certainly lies in the disposition of many readers, particularly in the twentieth century, to read the story as a realistic chronicle gone astray. After all, by subtitling *Kohlhaas* "aus einer alten Chronik" and **"Die heilige Cäcilie"** "eine Legende," Kleist seems to distinguish the works and perhaps to suggest that supernatural elements could be expected in the latter but not in the former. Modern readers hold a "chronicle" to a higher standard of verisimilitude than they do a "legend," and they may therefore suppose— wrongly as it turns out—that *Kohlhaas* will measure up to this standard. In any case, engagement with the story evidently produces expectations that are frustrated by the course the plot finally takes. Readers who assume that the narrative turns on the issue of Kohlhaas's horses find the rug pulled out from under them by the "whimsical" addition of the prophecy. Even those who defend the plot as Kleist wrote it see the story as divided conspicuously into two sections by the change in narrative attention from horses to prophecy. One of the most radical of recent defenses, Helga Gallas's Lacanian reading, provides a psychoanalytic motivation for the division whereby the scrap of paper bearing the prophecy functions as a figurative substitute for the horses. In Gallas's view [published in *Das Textbegehren des "Michael Kohlhaas": Die Sprache des Unbewassten und der Sinn der Literatur,* 1981] the division is only formal and superficial, since both the horses and the paper are already themselves metaphors of the phallus; but the division persists and indeed figures prominently in her analysis. Her interpretation may even depend on the presence of a division, since the process of metaphoric substitution and metonymic displace-

ment according to which the tale is said to function can be glimpsed only because Kleist stages so openly the move from one "object" to another.

All these readings, whether they attack or defend, assume that there is a prominent change in narrative attention. But this change may be not so much a structural element of the plot as a feature of the critical tradition attached to the text. If we listen at least as carefully to the *rhetoric* of the narrative as we do to the things narrated, we discern a unity that is perhaps otherwise obscured. A rhetorical reading of Kleist's story discloses a set of concerns that remain unchanged from beginning to end. The rhetorical analysis offered here suggests that structures embedded in and foregrounded by the text produce an unmistakable coherence, that there is no change at all in narrative attention, and that the story is explicitly "about" the same topic all the way through. We need not assume that Kleist went astray or even that he built on a pattern of figurative substitution and displacement.

The problem arises primarily because of the tendency to read the first half or three-quarters of the story as centering on Kohlhaas's horses. This reading is natural enough, since Kohlhaas himself makes so much out of them and since they function for him as the master trope, standing for both injustice and justice, power and impotence, obedience and rebellion. Kohlhaas turns the case of his horses into an affair of state and projects onto them all the fears and desires he feels toward the community. Quite understandably Gallas sees the horses as invested with a charge of emotion equivalent to the Freudian castration anxiety. The reader, however, need not accept that the issue of Kleist's story is the object at issue in Kohlhaas's struggle with the state. In fact, one of the principal effects of the prophecy material seems to be to deflect attention from the horses to what was intended all along to be the central concern—the possession of authoritative documents.

In the crucial opening scene, in which Kohlhaas comes into conflict with the Tronka family, the horses come into play mainly as stand-ins (that is, as collateral) for a missing document. It is Kohlhaas's lack of a *Paßschein* ("permit") that starts all the trouble:

> Der Burgvogt, indem er sich noch eine Weste über seinen weitläufigen Leib zuknüpfte, kam, und fragte, schief gegen die Witterung gestellt, nach dem Paßschein.—Kohlhaas fragte: der Paßschein? Er sagte, ein wenig betreten, daß er, soviel er wisse, keinen habe; daß man ihm aber nur beschreiben möchte, was dies für ein Ding des Herrn sei: so werde er vielleicht zufälligerweise damit versehen sein.

> The warden, still fastening a waistcoat across his capacious body, came up and, bracing himself against the wind and rain, demanded the horse-dealer's permit. "My permit?" asked Kohlhaas and added, a little disconcerted, that so far as he knew he did not possess one, but that if the warden would kindly explain what on earth such a thing was he just might possibly have one with him.

Kohlhaas's response to the warden's demand deserves careful attention. He does not simply state that he lacks the document in question; he claims not to know what sort of "Ding des Herrn" a *Paßschein* would be. From one perspective, Kohlhaas merely uses a commonplace idiom, an emphatic trope properly translated as "what in the world?" Kleist, however, frequently uses a complex rhetoric in which both tenor and vehicle in a figurative expression signify with equal force. For example, the heroine of his tragedy *Penthesilea* chews on the body of the slain Achilles and later remarks that she was simply putting into practice "Wort für Wort" the everyday locution "I love him so much I could eat him up." Kleist evidently thought that this feature is one of the most important of his play, for when he wrote to his cousin Marie von Kleist in the autumn of 1807 to announce that he had finished the work, he reminded her of its subject matter with a single sentence: "Sie hat ihn wirklich aufgegessen, den Achill, vor Liebe" 'She loved that Achilles so much that she really did eat him up.' Thus one suspects that the tropes used by Kleist's characters are important in a literal as well as a figurative sense. Here the suspicion that the permit the warden wants might literally be a "Ding des Herrn" is confirmed when he explains to Kohlhaas that "ohne einen landesherrlichen Erlaubnisschein, kein Roßkamm mit Pferden über die Grenze gelassen würde" 'without a state permit a dealer bringing horses could not be allowed across the border.' So the permit is really a "thing of the lord" in that it is issued by the appropriate *Landesherr*. This language implicitly invites the conclusion that a document might also be a "thing of the Lord," deriving its authority not merely from the will of a secular ruler but from the divine order itself. As the story develops, it becomes ever more clear that indeed the issue does center on Kohlhaas's relation to both the secular and the divine systems of order.

We must also read carefully Kohlhaas's apparently ironic request to be told what a *Paßschein* is so that he can see whether he was provided with one "by chance" (*zufälligerweise*). This is, to be sure, an example of using self-deprecation or affected ingenuousness to put an interlocutor at a disadvantage. Kohlhaas implies that the permit must be of such minute importance that he might have one lying about somewhere and not even know about it. At the same time, though, the wording suggests that this "Ding des Herrn" might come into one's possession quite by chance, and in this story (as it turns out) we must take that possibility very seriously. Kohlhaas does acquire, by chance, a document that enables him to bring the scales of justice into better balance. This document, the gypsy woman's scrap of paper, belongs to a realm clearly different from that of the requested *Paßschein,* since the scrap's origin is supernatural rather than secular. Each document, however, may be properly described as a "Ding des Herrn."

The permit issue remains central to the plot, but its meaning is steadily complicated by the rhetoric of its presentation. For example, Kohlhaas is required to leave his two fine black horses with Wenzel von Tronka as "ein Pfand, zur Sicherheit, daß er den Schein lösen würde" 'surety that he would get the permit.' Although the horse dealer

suspects that requiring such a permit is illegal, he is prepared to fulfill the clearly intended meaning of "den Schein lösen" by leaving the horses and purchasing a permit in Dresden. As it turns out, though, he enacts an entirely different significance of these words when he "dissolves the appearance" by learning that "die Geschichte von dem Paßschein ein Märchen sei" 'the story about the permit was a mere fabrication.' "Märchen" implies that the permit demanded by Tronka belongs to the world of the imagination, particularly the literary imagination, and not to the legal structure governing the everyday world. Kohlhaas's horses, then, have been held to guarantee the production of a document that neither exists nor can exist under the current legal system. The absence of the permit, so mightily deplored by the Junker's warden, is irremediable—except perhaps in the realm of *Märchen*.

For now, Kohlhaas can only temporarily fill this void with another sort of void, a complex rhetorical nullity, by obtaining a document attesting to the nonexistence of the permit: he persuades the disgruntled Dresden officials to issue "einen schriftlichen Schein über den Ungrund derselben" 'a written certificate of [the permit's] groundlessness,' which he duly carries back to Tronka castle and shows to the warden. Having thus procured a document that should properly serve as a replacement for the one initially demanded, Kohlhaas expects to get in return the *other* replacement, the horses. What he gets, however, is to his way of thinking another set of stand-ins that are, in fact, another void. Instead of the sleek, healthy, well-fed horses he left with the Junker, he is given "ein Paar dürre, abgehärmte Mähren . . . ; Knochen, denen man, wie Riegeln, hätte Sachen aufhängen können" 'a pair of scrawny, worn-out nags, their bones protruding like pegs you could have hung things on.' He declines to accept these horses as his and tells the Junker, "Das *sind* nicht meine Pferde, gestrengster Herr! Das sind die *Pferde* nicht, die dreißig Goldgülden wert waren! Ich will meine wohlgenährten und gesunden Pferde wieder haben!" 'Those are *not* my horses, my lord; those are not the *horses* that were worth thirty gold florins! I want my healthy, well-nourished horses back!' The horse dealer's language asserts that the horses offered are for all practical purposes nonhorses.

There is a symmetry in these events, even if it is not exactly justice. Kohlhaas has presented a nonpermit in place of the document demanded, and he has been given nonhorses in place of the horses he requires. The exchange comes close to balancing out, and Kohlhaas, in spite of his justifiable anger, is prepared to accept "den Verlust der Pferde, als eine gerechte Folge davon" 'the loss of the horses as a just consequence,' provided that his groom Herse indeed failed to tend them, as the Junker's warden and stableboy claim. But that charge, too, proves to be a rhetorical nullity: on learning that Herse was mistreated without cause while trying to perform his duty at the Tronka estate, Kohlhaas sees no alternative but to seek legal redress. The action he takes, perhaps not surprisingly, answers precisely the imperative that initiated the problem—the demand for a document. He sets about producing a variety of documents seeking remedy in the courts of law for the mischief done by the earlier nondocuments.

Hier verfaßte er, mit Hülfe eines Rechtsgelehrten, . . . eine Beschwerde, in welcher er, nach einer umständlichen Schilderung des Frevels, den der Junker Wenzel von Tronka, an ihm sowohl, als an seinem Knecht Herse, verübt hatte, auf gesetzmäßige Bestrafung desselben . . . antrug.

With the aid of a lawyer . . . he drew up a statement in which he gave a detailed description of the outrage committed against him and his groom Herse by Junker Wenzel von Tronka. He demanded punishment of the Junker in accordance with the law. . . .

After months go by without any news of his case, he produces more documents: he sends letters, receives letters, composes petitions, and receives more letters, all to no avail. At last he gets a letter transmitting a resolution from the chancellery that directs Kohlhaas to desist from his litigation about a pair of horses that the Junker von Tronka was quite prepared to return to him.

The rhetoric of the horse dealer's response to this resolution is instructive: "Kohlhaas, dem es nicht um die Pferde zu tun war—er hätte gleichen Schmerz empfunden, wenn es ein Paar Hunde gegolten hätte—Kohlhaas schäumte vot Wut, als der diesen Brief empfing" 'Since for Kohlhaas the horses were not the issue—he would have been equally aggrieved had they been a couple of dogs—this letter made him foam with rage.' Both dogs and horses may be said to "foam" (*schäumen*), though under very different circumstances. Persons do so only figuratively, in the everyday cliché *vor Wut schäumen* that Kleist uses here. The rhetoric of the sentence contradicts its explicit sense. Why is Kohlhaas metaphorically likened to a horse just when he is said to view the horses as beside the point? The sentence's self-deconstruction is by no means a self-cancellation, however; both terms in the ambivalent structure are valid. In what way is it correct to say that the horses both are and are not the issue? The sentence that in effect poses the question also offers the way toward an answer. The horses are not the issue in themselves, just as Kohlhaas asserts, but they are a metaphor for other matters of importance to the story—such as Kohlhaas's powerful emotions, or justice itself, or even (as Gallas would have it) phallic potency. To function in this way, however, the horses must first be transformed into a text. That is, of course, exactly what occurs in the opening scene when the warden proposes that Kohlhaas offer the horses in lieu of the missing permit.

The chronicle material gave Kleist the occasion for enlarging on a figurative equivalence of horses and texts that was already a part of his linguistic experience. In early January of 1808, at the time that *Phöbus,* a literary journal cofounded by Kleist, first appeared, containing portions of *Penthesilea,* Jean Paul declared himself ready to contribute to the periodical:

I will provide the best [horse] I can to hitch to the team of your *Phoebus*—no hobbyhorses of any sort— and if I cannot help either the team or myself, at least my [horse] can run alongside, the way people have single horses do in Naples, letting them trot along with the team just for the fun of it.

By publishing a fragment of **Kohlhaas** in *Phöbus* later that year, Kleist could well have bragged with Penthesilea that he had made Jean Paul's metaphor good "Wort für Wort." The figurative horses he puts in harness for his publishing enterprise are the "real" horses inscribed so prominently in the center of the tale of the justice-seeking horse dealer.

Kohlhaas is a story that connects horses and texts by both metaphor and metonymy, by representing horses (through publication in *Phöbus*) and containing them (as characters in the narrative). The horses were already textual artifacts before Kleist wrote the final version of his story. The tale, in fact, fills the space of a missing "horse" in that it occupies a place in the "team" proposed by Jean Paul's figure. It is little wonder, then, that the horses in the story act as stand-ins for a missing but necessary text, the permit that Kohlhaas discovers is only a "Märchen." At the story's beginning, this "Märchen" marks a space occupied at first by nothing, then by the horses, and then by a lengthy series of texts beginning with the "written certificate of . . . groundlessness" and ending only with the gypsy's prophecy and the reader's discovery that this tale is not the realistic narrative it first appeared to be but is instead itself the missing text, the "Märchen" indirectly demanded by the warden of the Tronka castle.

The considerable narrative space between the incident about the permit and the introduction of the theme of the gypsy's prophecy is filled to overflowing with documents that replace one another, answer one another, or cancel one another out. Nearly every turn of the plot is associated with some sort of *Schrift* initiated by Kohlhaas, by government officials, or by others involved in the dispute. There are contracts, writs, letters, receipts, petitions, edicts, declarations, resolutions, notices, proclamations, certificates, inquiries, passports, notes, reports, dispatches, sentences, verdicts, and more. When one begins to reckon up all the documents that figure in the story, one is prompted to exclaim with Judge Adam that they are "piled as high as the Tower of Babel." Certainly they seem to speak with a confusion of tongues equivalent to that which the Lord imposed on the builders of that tower and to lead Kohlhaas no closer to divine authority—not, that is, until the end.

The question of the relation of the texts to divine authority is opened up much earlier in the narrative, though the story does not offer an example of divine scripture until the tale of the gypsy woman is told. The question is, in fact, implicit in the novella's setting—Germany during the Reformation—and in the appearance among the dramatis personae of Martin Luther himself. Luther, author of the doctrine *sola scriptura,* is Kohlhaas's spiritual leader, since Kohlhaas and his wife had been among the early converts to Lutheranism. The great work of translating the Bible into German was, of course, motivated by the belief that scripture could serve as the means by which the individual establishes a personal relation with God, unmediated by doctrine, clergy, and other institutions of the church. No doubt that when Kohlhaas promulgates his first edict and declares that he does so "kraft der ihm angeborenen Macht" 'by virtue of the authority inborn in him' his reasoning derives in part from the Protestantism he has embraced. When he meets the great reformer face to face and hears him ask, "[W]ho gave you the right to attack . . . in pursuance of decrees issued on no authority but your own . . . ?" he is unable to offer more than an apologetic "No one, your Reverence." The reader, however, is at liberty to supply the answer Kohlhaas fails to give: "You, Martin Luther, gave me the right to find divine authority in myself."

Kohlhaas is perhaps wise in his reticence. Luther could not have accepted such an answer and would surely have replied that it is very difficult to be sure that the voice one hears within is God's and not the Devil's. The theologian is not certain whether the horse dealer is in touch with divine order or diabolical disorder, though Kohlhaas's actions incline Luther to suspect the latter. The former possibility cannot be dismissed, however, and Luther has to acknowledge that "was du forderst, wenn anders die Umstände so sind, wie die öffentliche Stimme hören läßt, ist gerecht" 'if the circumstances really are as public opinion has it, then what you demand is just.'

Holy Scripture makes its way into this mass of documents not only by implication—through the presence of Luther—and not only because Elizabeth, Kohlhaas's wife, as a good Lutheran, has the Bible read to her on her deathbed but perhaps most importantly because Kohlhaas's final act of vengeance against the elector of Saxony is an acting out "Wort für Wort" of a set of scriptural commandments. In the Old Testament, Ezekiel hears the voice of divinity offer him a text that he is supposed to eat:

> Then I saw a hand stretched out to me, holding a scroll. He unrolled it before me, and it was written all over on both sides with dirges and laments and words of woe. Then he said to me, "Man, eat what is in front of you, eat this scroll. . . ." So I ate it, and it tasted as sweet as honey. (Ezek. 2.9-3.3)

In the New Testament, the Revelation of John echoes this figure:

> The voice which I heard from heaven was speaking to me again, and it said, "Go and take the open scroll . . . and eat it. It will turn your stomach sour, although in your mouth it will taste as sweet as honey." So I took the little scroll from the angel's hand and ate it. . . . (Rev. 10.8-10)

When Kohlhaas, after reading the prophecy for the first time, eats the paper it is written on, he is doing more than simply keeping it from the elector; he is incorporating it into himself, making himself one with it. The deed is the physical fulfillment of and a figure for the act of reading he has just completed. The biblical texts quoted above are allegories of a kind of successful reading in which the word becomes part of the reader. Kohlhaas, by eating the prophecy, incorporates the mysterious text into himself,

especially into that part of himself which is supposed to survive the death of the flesh.

It is important to remember that the final scene of the story is not only or even primarily the narrative of Kohlhaas's execution. The execution itself does not even take up the whole of a single sentence. Most of what goes on in that scene is various acts of reading. After the sentence of death is read to Kohlhaas, a few days before it is to be carried out, he receives a letter from Luther, the contents of which are not revealed to the reader: the letter is "[ein] ohne Zweifel sehr merkwürdige[r] Brief, der aber verlorengegangen ist" 'without a doubt a very remarkable communication, all trace of which, however, has been lost.' He also reads a note delivered from an old woman, whom he initially supposes to be the gypsy, but it is signed "Your Elizabeth." The words of the note are quoted in the text, but an essential paratextual element gets lost. When Kohlhaas asks the man who brought the note for more information, a gap opens up:

> Doch da der Kastellan antwortete: "Kohlhaas, das Weib"—und in mitten der Rede auf sonderbare Weise stockte, so konnte er, von dem Zuge, der in diesem Augenblick wieder antrat, fortgerissen, nicht vernehmen, was der Mann, der an allen Gliedern zu zittern schien, vorbrachte.

> But just as the castellan was answering: "Kohlhaas, the woman . . . ," only to falter strangely in mid-speech, the horse-dealer was swept along in the procession [to the place of execution] which moved off again at that very moment, and could not catch what the man, who seemed to be trembling in every limb, was saying.

When he reaches the hill where he is to be executed, he is given the document containing the verdict of the court in Dresden, and he reads it through, "mit großen, funkelnden Augen" 'his eyes wide and sparkling with triumph,' taking special note of "auch einen Artikel darin . . . , in welchem der Junker Wenzel zu zweijähriger Gefängnisstrafe verurteilt ward" 'a clause condemning Junker Wenzel to two years' imprisonment.' Spying the elector of Saxony in the crowd, he

> löste sich, indem er . . . dicht vor ihm trat, die Kaspel von der Brust; er nahm den Zettel heraus, entisiegelte ihn, und überlas ihn: und das Auge unverwandt auf den Mann mit blauen und weißen Federbüschen gerichtet, der bereits süßen Hoffnungen Raum zu geben anfing, steckte er ihn in den Mund und verschlang ihn.

> strode up close to him, took the locket from round his neck, took out the piece of paper, unsealed it and read it; then, fixing his gaze steadily on the [elector] who was already beginning to harbour sweet hopes, he stuck it in his mouth and swallowed it.

All these engagements with texts, culminating in the reading/eating of the prophecy, establish reading as the means by which the story reaches its resolution. Kohlhaas does not simply decipher the marks in the various documents, he makes himself one with the writing's meaning and thereby puts himself in intimate contact with a power outside himself. It is in this union that he achieves a significant victory over the elector of Saxony. Paradoxically, the outcome of Kohlhaas's execution, in which the horse dealer's body is literally dismembered, is that the elector becomes "zerissen an Leib und Seele" 'physically and mentally a broken man.' Kohlhaas, in other words, becomes whole while the elector falls apart. The fall of the executioner's ax is thus of relatively little consequence in comparison with the unifying act of reading, and the proportioning of narrative space between the two processes reflects this valorization. . . .

The allegedly deraiding material about the gypsy woman and her prophecy is a semisecularized holy scripture essential to the project of the novella. This episode provides a genuinely authoritative document that can finally answer the demand made of Kohlhaas at Tronka Castle. We must recognize, however, that much of the prophecy plot's claim to authority rests for the reader on the enigma of the material and on the mystery surrounding the unheard words of the castellan about the gypsy woman's identity. Neither the reader nor Kohlhaas knows for sure whether the gypsy is in fact his wife somehow returned to life, and so the old woman and her prophecy hover on the boundary between the natural and the supernatural. Kohlhaas knows what the letter from Luther says and what the prophecy concerning the elector ordains, but the reader does not. The narrator's surmise that the letter is "without doubt a very remarkable communication" applies equally—or perhaps even more—to the prophecy. A message that is withheld must be very important indeed, rather in the way the "imperial message" of Kafka's little parable is. Kafka's story drives home the point that the ultimate guarantee of a text's transcendent authority is unavailability. "You" to whom the message is directed can only "sit at your window when evening falls and dream it to yourself." The poor elector of Saxony is in just this position, possessed of the certain knowledge that a text of the highest importance has been sent in his direction but that he can only imagine its contents.

Kohlhaas achieves a perfect symmetry—and therefore, in a sense, a perfect justice—by placing the elector in exactly the same position that the elector (through his servants and vassals) had placed him. Each is faced with the necessity of filling an essential void in the center of an authoritative document. A text that has been emptied of content must be filled, possibly by imagination, possibly by incorporation. As the story presents these alternatives, incorporation appears superior because of its remarkable fecundity. Not only does Kohlhaas produce an enormous quantity of documents, most of which survive and become incorporated into the body of **Michael Kohlhaas,** he begets as well a significant number of progeny who survive and also produce descendants, so that Kohlhaas's line apparently outlives the elector's. The final sentence of the novella notes that "von Kohlhaas aber haben noch im vergangenem Jahrhundert, im Mecklenburgischen, einige frohe und rüstige Nachkommen gelebt" 'in Mecklenburg some

hale and hearty descendants of Kohlhaas were still living in the century before this.' The story of the elector, for which the reader is referred "to history," remains a blank to be filled in.

Kohlhaas pays a high price for achieving unity with an authoritative text. Transcendence is uncompromising. In going beyond this world, it takes out of the world anything or anyone that incorporates transcendence. It is not simply to heighten the drama that Kleist delays Kohlhaas's reading of the prophecy until the execution; he means also to reemphasize the close relation between transcendence and emptiness. Having incorporated the scripture and thereby made himself one with it, Kohlhaas no longer belongs in this world. He belongs where Elizabeth is and where that *Paßschein* the Junker's warden demanded is: in the world of *Märchen.*

Kleist's story stages a drama of deep ambivalence about those objects that both promise unity, order, and fullness and threaten chaos, dismemberment, and emptiness—that is, about texts. A key paradox in the drama is that the solution to the horse dealer's problem (the gypsy's scrap of paper) belongs to the same category as the problem's origin (the required permit). More than a story of justice, this is a tale of reading and writing. There can be little doubt that the work puts into play an issue of urgent existential importance for Heinrich von Kleist, who was evidently hoping desperately to resolve through literature a crisis brought on by his commitment to literary activity. Kleist's choice of an intellectual rather than a military profession put him outside the aristocratic Prussian society into which he had been born. He was considered a renegade and a ne'er-do-well by his own family, not least for devoting himself to a career that tended to use up, rather than to produce, financial resources. Still, even though he was "a totally useless member of society in their eyes" because he spent his time writing, he nonetheless hoped "to give them joy and honor from [his] writing labors" (letter of 10 Nov. 1811). Literature was to be the homeopathic cure for an ill brought on by literature.

The chronicle of Kohlhaas, like the patriotic drama *Prinz Friedrich von Homburg,* attempts to inscribe Kleist's literary efforts within the circle of Prussian aristocratic society. The plot is set up so that Brandenburg, through its elector, comes out looking far superior to shabby Saxony, its neighbor and enemy. The surprising result of the horse dealer's career of apostasy from the norms of good citizenship is that his family actually rises socially. No sooner is Kohlhaas's body laid in the coffin than "rief der Kurfürst die Söhne des Abgeschiedenen herbei und schlug sie, mit der Erklärung an den Erzkanzler, daß sie in seiner Pagenschule erzogen werden sollten, zu Rittern" 'the Elector [of Brandenburg] sent for the dead man's sons and, declaring to the High Chancellor that they were to be educated in his school for pages, dubbed them knights forthwith.' These boys, now presumably called von Kohlhaas, take up precisely the place in the Brandenburg (that is, Prussian) social system that Kleist had abandoned first for science and then for literature. The rebel's descendants thrive as honored members of a thriving and honorable state. Many commentators have recognized the political intention behind the prophecy material, but frequently they imagine this motivation to be, like the "subplot" itself, "artistically extraneous" [David Luke and Nigel Reeves, eds. and trans. *The Marquise of O— and Other Stories,* by Heinrich von Kleist, Penguin, 1978]. Far from being extraneous, the political implications of the story go to the heart of the matter by offering an ameliorative and healing role for literature. As the gypsy's text helps Kohlhaas to achieve union with the order from which he has been alienated, so does the text of *Kohlhaas* seek to integrate Kleist's literary activity with a career of service to the state from which literature had apparently alienated him. The text of the story repeats the paradox of the texts in the story. It is a text that, in every way, incorporates the text.

By powerfully investing in the notion of textual incorporation, Kleist demonstrates how much he participates in one of the central concerns of European Romanticism.

Linda Dietrick (essay date 1990)

SOURCE: "Kleist's *Novellen:* Narration as Drama?" in *Momentum Dramaticum: Festschrift for Eckehard Catholy,* edited by Linda Dietrick and David G. John, University of Waterloo Press, 1990, pp. 289-303.

[*In the following excerpt, Dietrick assesses the dramatic elements in Kleist's short fiction.*]

It was once a virtual commonplace for critics to observe that Kleist's tales—or *Novellen,* as the tradition has come to designate what he simply called *Erzählungen*—have a "dramatic" quality about them. In a famous interpretation of **"Das Bettelweib von Locarno,"** the most prominent of those critics, Emil Staiger [in *Meisterwerke deutscher Sprache aus dem neunzehnten Jahrhandert,* 1942], wrote of this quality almost as if it were a matter of consensus among observant readers, something that one would expect from a dramatist of such stature or, indeed, from a writer devoted to the *Novelle,* if one assumes this to be the most dramatic of epic forms. Staiger's close stylistic analysis appears to support specifically this presumed consensus. He stresses Kleist's hypotactic syntax, in which the grammatical subjects stand isolated from their predicates, brief descriptions of objects resemble stage directions, and subordinated elements function in strict relation to the whole. Indeed, this principle of functionality appears to extend to the sequence of sentences as well. The effect is one of tension and anticipation, which culminates in the "dramatic" finale, the audible manifestation of the ghost:

> Im **"Bettelweib von Locarno"** [. . .] haben wir es offensichtlich mit einer dramatischen Novelle zu tun. Der Zweck des Dichters liegt am Schluß, an jener Stelle, wo das Präteritum in das Präsens übergeht. Die Teile sind unselbständig, in ihrer Auswahl, Ordnung und Abstufung überhaupt nur vom Ende aus zu begreifen.

To Staiger, the *Novelle* appears "fast als nacktes Schema dramatischen Stils".

In all of this, however, he has not just been elaborating upon what seems self-evident. Behind the stylistic analysis lies his theory of poetic "Grundbegriffe," ideal categories that designate basic attitudes—i.e. "dramatisch," "lyrisch," "episch"—of a writer toward his or her material, and hence a basic quality of the resulting literary work, regardless of the formal genre to which it is assigned. Of the "dramatischen Geist" he writes:

> Er steht dem Gegenstand nicht passiv gegenüber, wird aber auch nicht, wie der Lyriker, eins mit ihm, sondern er setzt sich mit ihm auseinander, er stellt ihn unter sein Gericht, indem er die Teile ordnet, bezieht, dies als Voraussetzung und als Absicht und jenes als Folge auffaßt, indem er aus dem Ganzen allen Sinn des Einzelnen bestimmt.

This is language from a different era of criticism: abstract, idealist, and above all, timeless. Because it assumes that a certain recognizable type of creative subjectivity will manifest itself in a text—a text of any epoch—it tends to beg the question of style. Since we already know that Kleist wrote works that we call dramas and *Novellen* (the latter also having been traditionally associated with the drama), are we not therefore predisposed to characterize them as dramatic? And however incisive Staiger's stylistic analysis may be, one must also ask: how useful is it, after all, to classify in this way all literary texts that, for instance, work with structures of confrontation and tension, or use syntactical and narrative techniques to prompt the anticipation of an ending?

Interestingly enough, what some other critics have meant by the dramatic in Kleist's prose has been quite various. [In *GRM,* 1961] Hans Peter Herrmann, for example, has argued that the "dramatic" effect of *Spannung,* of tension or anticipation, arises much more from the long reach of Kleist's individual sentences, with their characteristic "dergestalt, daß" or "es traf sich, daß," than from the series of narrated events. In a fictional world so governed by chance, by those abrupt, unmotivated turns of event to which Kleist's characters react, it is not so much the anticipation of a next step or an ending to the plot as it is the complex syntax that creates the tension and, at the same time, holds out the possibility of order and orientation. Wolfgang Victor Ruttkowski, following Staiger, also mentions *Spannung* as an element that seems to mark Kleist's *Novellen* as "Beispiele dramatisch überformter Prosa" [*Die literarischen Gattungen: Reflexionen über eine modifizierte Fundamental poetik,* 1968]. For him, it arises out of what he calls the principle of "dramatische[r] Koinzidenz," the temporal conjunction of apparently chance events: for instance, Kohlhaas' acquiring of precisely that object, the capsule with the fortune, that his nemesis the Elector of Saxony would most like to obtain. E. K. Bennett, on the other hand, sees in Kleist's *Novellen* a dramatic tension or conflict which is primarily thematic: in "the harshness of conflicting antitheses, which finds expression sometimes in the character of his persons, sometimes in the situation," we see presented "that inherent dualism of the universe of which the tragic dramatist is so acutely aware" [*A History of the German Novelle*, 1961]. Taken together, however, these various critical views invoke the notion of dramatic conflict or tension to describe phenomena so diverse as to make it seem too elastic to be useful. While one may be inclined to grant that Kleist's *Novellen* create by various means the effect of *Spannung*, I think that one can fairly question whether this is a specifically "dramatic" effect, or one common to many or all literary works to some degree.

Ruttkowski is indebted not only to Staiger but also to Wolfgang Kayser's observations [in *Die Vortragsreise: Studien zur Literatur,* 1958] about the narrator in Kleist. These observations remain one of the best formulations of this particular aspect of the *Novellen*:

> Der Erzähler steht ganz im Banne des Geschehenen, das er erzählt und das Wirklichkeit ist. Er steht im Banne: er besitzt keine Überlegenheit über die Figuren, wie wir es von Fielding und Wieland her kennen. Er überschaut nicht einmal das Ganze des Geschehens; seine Voraussagen sind nur partiell, und seine Wertungen [. . .] gelten fast immer der jeweiligen Situation [. . .]. Was am Erzählen zunächst auffällt, ist die Abwesenheit nicht nur von Wendungen ans Publikum oder von Erörterungen und Reflexionen, sondern auch von einer Sprechweise wie dem Beschreiben, ohne die doch kaum ein Erzähler auskommt [. . .]. Beherrschend ist der Bericht, das heißt die sachliche Angabe des in der Zeit verlaufenden Geschehens. Die Welt ist für diesen Erzähler im wesentlichen die Aufeinanderfolge von Begebenheiten, in der es keine Ruhe gibt.

Ruttkowski stresses the last two sentences: for him, the ceaseless temporal flow of the narrated events and the absence of leisurely description create *Spannung* and are typically "dramatic." He also notes how Kleist favours certain visual effects: scenes resembling historical tableaux and descriptions of facial expressions or other visible behaviour to suggest states of consciousness without narrating the characters' thoughts. Respective examples would be the arrival of Kohlhaas at the Erlabrunn cloister and the reaction of Lisbeth to Kohlhaas' plans to sell their house. These observations appear to be connected with a persistent critical assumption that Kleist is an "objective" story-teller who lets the visible facts and the raw, uninterpreted material of the narrated events speak for themselves, as if they were unrolling upon a stage. Similarly, Bennett, who rightly notes the conspicuous absence of a frame in Kleist's *Novellen,* is led by this fact to state that "there is no indication of the presence of a story-teller," for Kleist is "primarily a dramatist and not an epic writer."

There is, however, no getting around the fact that there *is* a narrator, the one formal feature that has distinguished narrative prose from drama, at least until Brecht and Wilder. It is the narrator's voice which calls Don Fernando "dieser göttliche Held," which claims that the Marquise, having left her father's house with her children, is "[d]urch diese schöne Anstrengung mit sich selbst bekannt

gemacht," and which is able to report how Nicolo thinks "mit den bittersten und quälendsten Gefühlen" of the secret lover whom he thinks Elvira has. Kleist's narrator does not avoid moral evaluation, the reporting of states of consciousness, or even, very occasionally, the direct address of the reader:

> Wohin er eigentlich ging, und ob er sich nach Dessau wandte, lassen wir dahingestellt sein, indem die Chroniken, aus deren Vergleichung wir Bericht erstatten, an dieser Stelle, auf befremdende Weise, einander widersprechen und aufheben [. . .].

Those critics who call Kleist, or more accurately the narrator, a strict "Chronist" who reports only the bare facts are clearly oversimplifying.

Nevertheless, as Kayser's carefully balanced formulation indicates, the narrative reporting of factual events and circumstances frequently predominates, and where this occurs, the reader is hardly aware of any distinct, personalized narrating voice. Where signals of a narrator's discourse do appear in value judgements, in reports of psychological states or in references to a "wir," the consciousness in which that discourse appears to originate is anything but omniscient. That is, the narrator's explicit evaluations, the attitudes he takes toward the events, and even his ability to say what "really" happened, are conditioned by a limited perspective. The reader realizes, for instance, that Don Fernando's divinely heroic status is somewhat compromised by his having led the fatal return to Santiago, that the Marquise has not become fully acquainted with herself, and that the description of Nicolo's thoughts as bitter and tormenting says nothing about why they are so. Kleist works with a narrator who appears no less human, and often no less subjectively involved in the events and lives of which he tells than the third-person characters. The narrator is not exempt from the problem of interpreting and understanding which is one of Kleist's persistent themes.

In view of this, it is not entirely implausible for Fritz Lockemann to suggest that Kleist's *Novellen* demonstrate the transformation of dramatic material into narrative terms. That is, there are certain aspects of human existence, especially the complex psychology of the subject and of intersubjective relationships, which Kleist can only *show* in a drama through the action and through the characters' struggles to bring into language what, for him, essentially cannot be said. One thinks, for example, of Penthesilea's physical tearing to pieces of Achilles' body, or of Alkmene's "Ach." If the incommunicability of subjectivity in discourse is one of Kleist's poetic concerns, then the discourse of his narrative works must itself reflect this limit. It does this, I think, not by strict adherence to the "objective" reporting of facts and events, as Lockemann asserts, but by using the figure of the narrator to raise the whole question of the communicability and interpretability of subjective experience. It is one thing, however, to say that Kleist found specifically narrative techniques for expressing concerns that also inform his dramas and quite another to conclude that his *Novellen* are "dramatic," or to speak with Staiger, that he himself is a "dramatischer Geist."

Although what the critics reviewed here consider to be "dramatic" is quite diverse, they all seem to assume that the term is a reasonably stable critical category. This may help to explain the relative disinterest in making such assumptions or assertions among more contemporary critics, for whom the description "dramatic" can no longer be a transparent and self-evident critical term. The semiotic, sociological and socio-historical approaches which have lately been making the most original and interesting contributions to the interpretation of Kleist's prose have no room in their idiom for a term which has not first been examined as an element in a cultural code and historicized. Admittedly, Staiger's idea of "das Dramatische" is a long way from the normative doctrine of genres of the seventeenth and eighteenth centuries, which sharply distinguished, for instance, drama from narrative prose, and could not conceive of ever-developing and historically specific variants and transformations of earlier forms. Staiger's *Grundbergriffe,* which allow for the so-called mixed forms, are a late reflection of post-Enlightenment conceptions of genre with their rejection of pure, "objective" forms and their affirmation of the shaping role of the writer's subjectivity. They provide no adequate point of reference, however, for a critical understanding of those very conceptions.

Thus, it may still be theoretically useful and meaningful to read Kleist's *Novellen* as "dramatic," but only in so far as one can account for their historically specific relationship to Kleist's dramas and, more importantly, to *the* drama as it was understood in that age. To do that, one would need a semiotics of the terms "drama" and "dramatic," that is to say, an analysis of them as culturally and historically determined signs. This would have to include a study not only of how Kleist's predecessors and contemporaries theorized about the drama and distinguished it from what was not drama (for instance, from narrative), but also of what underlying ways of thinking and signifying organized this theorizing, as well as poetic practice, in the first place. As the foregoing discussion has indicated, it is essential to examine not only what is said, but also what goes without saying. To develop a semiotics of the drama in the early nineteenth century, however, and to locate Kleist in this context, is clearly a large task. The following should therefore be viewed as a preliminary outline.

What did it mean to Kleist, to write dramas and to write prose narrative? As it happens, his literary production falls in a period when conceptions of these genres (and indeed of literature) were in profound transition. . . .

It can be observed . . . that alongside the programmatic efforts around 1800 to enhance the aesthetic status of narrative—or in Friedrich Schlegel's case, even to subsume the drama under the category of *Roman*—the old conception persisted of a hierarchy which sharply distinguished drama from narrative and valued drama more highly. This was evidently the case for Kleist. In a letter to Arnim, Clemens Brentano reported:

> Überhaupt werden seine Arbeiten oft über die Maßen geehrt, seine Erzählungen verschlungen. Aber das war

> ihm nicht genug, ja Pfuel sagt mir, daß sich vom Drama zur Erzählung herablassen zu müssen, ihn grenzenlos gedemütigt hat.

For Kleist, as for Otto Ludwig and Marie von Ebner-Eschenbach much later, the drama remained the privileged genre against which narrative prose and the aesthetic achievements of the prose writer were to be measured.

Why should this be so? From a sociological perspective, the explanation is clearly connected with the changing social function of literature, as drama or narrative, in Kleist's age. The drama had been (for the Enlightenment) and remained (for the Weimar Classicists) a public form of discourse, and for the dramatist it promised the prestige and the influence of a public role. Schiller had written about the dream of a national theatre:

> Unmöglich kann ich hier den großen Einfluß übergehen, den eine gute stehende Bühne auf den Geist der Nation haben würde. Nationalgeist eines Volks nenne ich die Aehnlichkeit und Uebereinstimmung seiner Meinungen und Neigungen bei Gegenständen, worüber eine andere Nation anders meint und empfindet. Nur der Schaubühne ist es möglich, diese Uebereinstimmung in einem hohen Grad zu bewirken, weil sie das ganze Gebiet des menschlichen Wissens durchwandert, alle Situationen des Lebens erschöpft, und in alle Winkel des Herzens hinunter leuchtet. ["Was kann eine gute stehende Schaubühne eigentlich wirken?" (1784), *Schillers Werke,* ed. by Benno von Wiese, 1962]

Kleist's intense desire for this kind of public influence and for the recognition it would imply is evident, for instance, in his verses dedicating *Prinz Friedrich von Homburg* to Princess Amalie of Prussia. Having to turn to the *Novelle,* when his dramas were coolly received, meant writing literature that was privately consumed and spoke to the isolated individual rather than to and for the community. He was thus forced to follow a path that the Romantics had freely accepted. As a rule, they did not look to the drama and the theatre for a binding public discourse, but to mythos, whereby the subjective esotericism of their project tended to weaken it. Kleist's dramatic ambition, on the other hand, was directed toward achieving a form of public, authoritative literary discourse that had been shaped by the Enlightenment.

Yet the authority of transparent signification which the Enlightenment had thought the drama could approximate was no longer possible. The old order of signification had ruptured: signs had become detached from the things they named, in a certain sense substitutes for something now inaccessible, carriers of subjective contents, and objects of knowledge in their own right. In 1801 Kleist seems to have undergone this paradigm shift as a personally traumatic encounter with the critical philosophy of Kant. Whereas a mind like Goethe's could harmonize with relative serenity the inner and outer worlds, and the Romantics could make a virtue out of philosophical necessity by embracing the perspectivism of irony and the infinite deferral of meaning, Kleist remained painfully aware of the intransparency of signs. Metaphorically, he understood this to mean that one apprehends the world like a mirror that is "schief und schmutzig" or like someone who, having green glasses for eyes, cannot tell if the green world he sees really *is* the world. Of his own aesthetic goals, he wrote:

> Nur weil der Gedanke, um zu erscheinen, wie jene flüchtigen, undarstellbaren, chemischen Stoffe, mit etwas Gröberem, Körperlichen, verbunden sein muß: nur darum bediene ich mich [. . .] der Rede.

> Sprache, Rhythmus, Wohlklang usw., und so reizend diese Dinge auch, insofern sie den Geist einhüllen, sein mögen, so sind sie doch an und für sich, aus diesem Gesichtspunkt betrachtet, nichts, als ein wahrer, obschon natürlicher und notwendiger Übelstand; und die Kunst kann, in bezug auf sie, auf nichts gehen, als sie möglichst *verschwinden* zu machen.

These are the words of a writer still committed to the Enlightenment telos of transparent signification, but now struggling with the notion that signs are and will always remain distorted by subjectivity and mired in materiality.

In both his *Novellen* and his dramas, this struggle is enacted in the tension between two virtually incompatible goals: to attain the authority of a perfectly true and transparent representation of the world, and to reflect critically the perspectivism of *every* discursive standpoint. Here, the pre-Romantic conception of the dramatic genre stands as model, but that transcendent, supra-individual truth which it holds out as its promise is continually relativized by the particular and often competing claims to truth of one point of view or another. To a modern mind, this might appear to be a good definition of the dramatic, but to Kleist and his age it must have looked like the dramatic principle under pressure from elements that were proper to narrative.

All of Kleist's characters are readers of signs. Kohlhaas must read the condition of his horses and the opaque bureaucracies of two electorates, the Marquise von O . . . her pregnant body, Santiago its earthquake, the Marchese the ghostly sounds, Friedrich and Littegarde the outcome of the duel, Alkmene the initialled diadem and two identical Amphitryons, Homburg and the Elector each other's actions and stratagems, Frau Marthe her broken jug, and so on. Here reading, that is to say interpreting, is no harmless, playful activity, but an urgent existential need, often with devastating consequences.

Yet where, in all the narratives created to gloss those signs, is the temporally and causally seamless narrative that can say what they "really" represent? Whereas the older Kleist criticism looked for principles of closure such as moral decision, pure feeling or divine purpose which, abstracted from isolated text passages, seem to organize Kleist's fictional world into a clear, meaningful whole, much recent criticism is prepared to argue for ambiguity, relativity, and fragmentation. At the same time, however, it is characteristic of such interpretations that they require considerable effort. Such readings are applied, so to speak, against

the grain of works that, both thematically and structurally, owe their existence to a compelling desire for transparent, authoritative discourse: the discourse of Enlightenment drama.

> **One could say, then, that in Kleist's *Novellen*, the process of narrating has been subsumed under the dramatic structural principle.**
>
> *—Linda Dietrick*

As *Novellen,* of course, these works differ from their Enlightenment and Classicist predecessors in that they are notoriously autonomous. They lack the traditional frame and feature narrators that seem at one moment barely present and at another no more blessed with insight than the figures. Kleist appears to dispense with all bridging, orienting contact with the reader, that is, with the social context within which his tales were received. Yet from the beginnings of its modern reappearance in eighteenth-century European writing, the *Novelle* was the one narrative form that made the social function of story-telling its conspicuous theme. In Goethe's *Unterhaltungen deutscher Ausgewanderten* (1795) and Wieland's *Hexameron von Rosenhain* (1805), for instance, this theme is reflected in the frame which encloses, but is outside of, the spatiotemporal world of the narrated *Novellen*. From the outset, the tales are clearly marked off as such, and the social activity of narrating them and responding critically to them is simultaneously reflected. While that critical response is not rigidly prescribed—there is a certain open-endedness acknowledged in these interrelated layers of discourse—it is still set within a relatively safe, self-restrained, civilized context. And while abjuring primitive didacticism, the entire fictional structure models a particular kind of discursive behaviour: through narration, the irrational events or the anti-social impulses of an individual presented in the fiction are absorbed and buffered by an embracing social order.

In Kleist's *Novellen,* none of this occurs, leading one critic to observe: "Seine Erzählungen weisen den Rezipienten als teilnehmenden und urteilenden Dialogpartner ab." Yet it is entirely in keeping with the dramatic aesthetic that the works should ignore their audience. For to acknowledge explicitly the narrative process as an aesthetic activity would undermine the reader's involvement in the illusion of seeing the world directly and transparently represented. At the same time, the process of narrating has by no means lost its social function. It has become a motivating factor in the dramatic action. What earlier *Novellen* tried to do at the level of the frame—to insert the activity of narrating into the context of critical reception—Kleist's *Novellen* try to do at the level of the narration itself. Here interpretation—reading and narrating human experience— is shown to be not a merely entertaining or edifying aesthetic activity, but an existential necessity with risky, even lethal consequences.

There are many examples. The Marquise von O . . .'s story is, from the very first paragraph, about the search for the "right" story behind her strange pregnancy. Kohlhaas' violent campaign is motivated by the story of his horses, but his story is constantly re-shaped by the conflict with an almost endless variety of other versions. **"Die heilige Cäcilie"** is structured around a mother's quest for the "real" story behind her sons' changed lives. In **"Die Verlobung in St. Domingo,"** Gustav turns his gun on Toni because he cannot construct the right version of what led her to bind him hand and foot. And in **"Das Bettelweib von Locarno,"** the Marchese is confronted with events that, for him, utterly resist rational narration in terms of cause and effect. In all these *Novellen,* moreover, there is no reliably omniscient narrator to act as ultimate guarantor of the story's coherence or correctness. The struggle to bring events and things into the language of narrative is not merely Kleist's subject matter, it is a central structuring principle and a motor that drives his plots.

One could say, then, that in Kleist's *Novellen,* the process of narrating has been subsumed under the dramatic structural principle. There is, however, another element which is less amenable to drama: *Zufall,* the chance event that is by definition blind, unmotivated, and not rationally explainable in terms of any prior temporal-causal sequence. For Kleist, it would appear to be the literary analogue of the intransparent sign, the sign that cannot show forth its meaning except by the conspicuous discursive effort of narration. Yet chance is indispensable to Kleist's *Novellen;* without it, there would be no way to generate a plot out of the struggle to narrate. (It could probably be argued that in the further history of the *Novelle,* the continued preoccupation with the strange, isolated, marginal event—with what tradition calls the "unerhörte Begebenheit"—serves a similar purpose.)

If Kleist's *Novellen* are to be called dramatic, then it can only be in the limited, historically specific sense that they strive to represent in a (relatively) continuous causal and spatiotemporal sequence the world directly as it "is." That kind of authoritative transparency became, however, an endlessly elusive goal as Kleist and others in his age crossed the threshold into modern modes of thought and words became detached from things. Yet he must still have thought it possible to plot discontinuity, to mirror by some algebra of language the temporal and causal arrangement of particular representations and acts of representing. The consequence is that "drama" threatens constantly to decay into narrative.

Anthony Stephens (essay date 1994)

SOURCE: "Das Erbeben in Chili—Die Verlobung in St. Domingo," in *Heinrich von Kleist: The Dramas and Stories,* Berg, 1994, pp. 194-211.

[*In the excerpt below, Stephens provides a thematic comparison of "Das Erdbeben in Chili" and "Die Verlobung in St. Domingo."*]

"Das Erdbeben in Chili" was the first of Kleist's stories to be published, being completed by autumn 1806, and may well have been the first to be thought out. There is no way of knowing whether any experiments in narrative form preceded it, and source studies have been characteristically unrewarding as far as the main plot is concerned. Kleist's control of complex narrative form in his first published story is even more astonishing than his precocity as a dramatist in *Die Familie Schroffenstein,* finished in 1802. By the time he wrote **"Das Erdbeben in Chili,"** he had been through the long battle to resolve the problems of tragic form in *Robert Guiskard* and had also completed *Der zerbrochne Krug.* His stories, as a whole, combine a penchant for tableaux, *coups de theâtre,* and 'set pieces' with a sophisticated control of perspective, and it is likely that his narratives benefited from his continual experiments in dramatic technique.

"Das Erdbeben in Chili" has attracted, and continues to attract, more critical exegesis than any other prose narrative of comparable length in German literature. Perhaps more tantalizing in its brevity and condensation than any other of Kleist's stories, it experiments with the masochistic gratification readers may derive from texts that do violence to genre-based expectations. It does this in three ways: first, it places the reader in the same situation as the fictional characters, forced to decipher a plethora of signs whose apparent meaning is misleading; second, it subjects the reader to an unreliable narrator who is by turns omniscient and partisan, inclusive and exclusive of the reader's position; third, it plays on the trope of a deferred ending in a way that has generated endless controversy and, properly, remains unresolved.

In 1979, John Ellis commented on the contradictory readings of this text [in *Heinrich von Kleist*] that 'previous interpretations achieve a special interest for a story whose very theme is interpretation. This is because the point of the story lies not in the meaning of the events themselves but in the attempts made by the narrator and the characters to give them meaning.' This is a good summation, and has the further interest of placing 'the narrator and the characters' in the same predicament, raising the question of whether this is possible in terms of narrative structure. There are no accidental narratives, and to posit a narrator struggling with thematics in the same way as the figures of the plot has the logical corollary of positing a further narrator who ironizes the limited perspective of the figure whose 'attempts' are analogous to those of other 'characters.' Writing on the story indeed drew this conclusion as soon as the critical apparatus became available, but, paradoxically, it has not meant an end to partisan or moralistic readings that imitate, at one or more removes, the attitudes taken by the foreground narrative persona to characters, actions, and events. Such interpretations still ignore the fact that this narrator, by imitating the attitudes of the characters, *at times* becomes one of them in a formal sense, and is thus subject to ironic treatment by the whole of the narrative structure. Most tantalizing to the reader is the fact that this effect is sporadic, rather than sustained, and I thus cannot agree with Bernd Fischer's ["Fatum und Idee Zu Kleists *Erdbeben in Chili,*" *DVjs,*

58, 1984] simplification of the foreground narrator into a figure in consistent opposition to the text's 'deeper intentions.' There would be less writing on the story if the narrative perspective were so predictable.

As with Kleist's first drama, the story begins with a family conflict that is heightened to yield violence on a cosmic scale. While *Die Familie Schroffenstein* begins as a variation on *Romeo and Juliet*, **"Das Erdbeben in Chili"** takes up the theme, familiar in German literature of the time and ultimately stemming from the story of Eloise and Abelard, of a tutor who falls in love with his pupil, thus calling forth the hostility of the family. In the case of Jeronimo and Josephe, Don Pedro Asteron responds by placing his daughter in a nunnery. Jeronimo scales the walls and gets her pregnant. The story opens at the moment Josephe is on the point of being executed and Jeronimo, in prison, on the point of suicide. The earthquake that supervenes, destroying the city of St. Jago and thousands of lives, unites the lovers and their child and defers the expected ending to this family tragedy.

In the aftermath, Jeronimo and Josephe are accepted by another aristocratic family, that of Don Ferando Ormez; they unwisely return to the city to join in a service of thanksgiving and are, together with Don Fernando's sister-in-law and infant son, massacred in a scene of mob violence. At the conclusion, Don Fernando has adopted their child in place of his dead son. Just as the plot falls into three clear divisions—events leading up to the earthquake and the destruction of the city; an idyllic interlude, with overtones of a utopian vision, among the survivors in the countryside; the return to the city, the massacre, and its aftermath—so the plot revolves around three families.

There is, first, Josephe's family of origin, the aristocratic household of Don Pedro Asteron into which Jeronimo, as an intruder from the lower classes, is denied acceptance and which asserts patriarchal authority to punish both the love affair across class barriers and, much more savagely, Josephe's motherhood. There is a strong parallel to *Die Familie Schroffenstein* in the theme of a paternal hostility to children that gets out of hand. When Josephe, walking as a novice in a religious procession, is overtaken by birth pains on the steps of the cathedral, the ensuing scandal results in her being subjected to torture on the command of the Archbishop and condemned to be burned alive. At this point, the text attributes the commuting of her sentence to beheading to 'die Fürbitte der Familie Asteron, noch auch sogar der Wunsch der Äbtissin selbst, welche das junge Mädchen . . . liebgewonnen hatte.' The Archbishop takes over the role of Josephe's father as punitive authority and carries it to an excess of cruelty, while the family now joins in the humane intercession of the abbess, whose affection for Josephe contrasts with the savagery of the patriarchal church.

There is, in Don Pedro's initial rage and subsequent attempt to mitigate its full consequences, something of the helplessness of the two fathers at the end of *Die Familie Schroffenstein*, when confronted too late with the murderous effects of their own aggression. If all social power in Kleist's works may ultimately be seen as deriving from paternal authority, it is equally the case that such power is always likely to exceed the control of individual fathers. The alignment of the family with the Abbess, however, does something toward restoring to it a measure of ambivalence, which becomes significant when Jeronimo and Josephe are accepted by the family of Don Fernando.

Philipp, Josephe's child, is conceived while she is still identified as the daughter of Don Pedro Asteron. His birth both makes her the victim of the violence inherent in the whole of Christian society, and places her in the center of a new family of her own with Jeronimo and the child, after all three survive the earthquake. While a Christian Archbishop has played a leading part in setting the destruction of this second family, Kleist's narrator appears to want to even the balance by giving the idyllic tableau of their reunion after the earthquake an equally religious aura by alluding to pictorial representations of Joseph, Mary, and Jesus—perhaps even to a 'Rest of the Flight to Egypt,' which Kleist may have seen in Dresden. Within the idyllic framework of the second part of the narrative, the second family is kindly received by the third, that of Don Fernando Ormez, and the narrator enhances this sign of the reconciliation of Josephe's new family, social pariahs before the earthquake, with an established aristocratic clan by an evocation of a harmonious society outside the ruined city in which the divisions of property and social class no longer have force: 'als ob das allgemeine Unglück alles, was ihm entronnen war, zu *einer* Familie gemacht hätte.' One of the chronic puzzles of motivation, so familiar from Kleist's dramas, is the question of whether Don Fernando's humane, and later heroic, conduct is simply to be read in terms of a code of aristocratic chivalry, or whether it represents one lasting effect of the utopian interlude.

The family of Don Fernando Ormez survives the catastrophe in the square in front of the cathedral, despite the murders of Donna Constanze and the infant Juan, for whom Josephe has been caring, and adopts Philipp in his place. In structural terms, the child Philipp connects the three families and thus the three segments of the story. His birth in scandalous circumstances effectively places Josephe beyond the reach of the family Asteron, for good or ill. As a bastard begotten on a novice in a convent, he at first shares the pariah status deriving from both his parents being branded as criminals, but is then included in the reconciliations of the second part of the story. He survives his natural parents to be adopted by a family very like the one from which his mother was rejected, with the difference that his adoption is an act of conscious choice and not, like his birth, a consequence of sexual desire. His transmission from family to family thus unifies the plot in terms of narrative syntax. Here Kleist stops short of his usual satirical portrayal of the idealization of parentage by adoption in the German Enlightenment, leaving Don Fernando's words and thoughts in the concluding sentences of the story a genuine enigma, which invites the reader to embark on a decoding of the rest of the story so as to resolve it.

Thematically, Don Fernando's adoptive fatherhood is opposed not so much to natural as to destructive paternity. The text's patent hostility to the hypocrisy and inhumanity of a professedly Christian and Catholic society led to the volume of Kleist's stories containing it being banned in Vienna on its first publication. Destructive paternity correlates with both the Christian church and mob violence, while natural paternity, in the person of Jeronimo, may take on the aura of a benign Christian icon in the scene beneath the pomegranate tree. Mob violence is unleashed by the sermon of the 'Chorherr' who, interpreting the earthquake as an anticipation of the Last Judgement, attributes it to God's vengeance on immorality, specifying Jeronimo and Josephe: 'und in einer von Verwünschungen erfüllten Seitenwendung, die Seelen der Täter, wörtlich genannt, allen Fürsten der Hölle übergab!' The consonance of religious authority and paternal vengefulness, which was first evident in the Archbishop's replacing Don Pedro Asteron as chief punitive agent, is quite deliberately restated in the massacre.

The mob violence turns the rhetoric of the sermon condemning Jeronimo and Josephe into actuality, and the sentence in which Jeronimo is killed reinforces this by having as its grammatical subject 'eine Stimme':

> Doch kaum waren sie auf den von Menschen gleichfalls erfüllten Vorplatz derselben getreten, als eine Stimme aus dem rasenden Haufen, der sie verfolgt hatte, rief: dies ist Jeronimo Rugera, ihr Bürger, denn ich bin sein eigner Vater! und ihn an Donna Constanzens Seite mit einem ungeheuren Keulenschlage zu Boden streckte. Jesus Maria! rief Donna Constanze, und floh zu ihrem Schwager; doch: Klostermetze! erscholl es schon, mit einem zweiten Keulenschlage, von einer andern Seite, der sie leblos neben Jeronimo niederwarf.

The syntax renders the murderers anonymous, but at the same time makes two connections clear: the 'voice' that strikes down Jeronimo is an extension of the voice that delivers the sermon; the same voice makes an unverifiable claim to being Jeronimo's father. The 'Chorherr' thus revives and intensifies, in his consigning the souls of the two lovers to 'all the Princes of Hell,' the previous actions of the Archbishop, which, in turn, had magnified the paternal indignation of Don Pedro Asteron. The mob violence is doubtless a quotation from accounts of similar scenes during the Terror in France, but we must be aware that the behavior of the populace at large is not tied to any one political model, but simply echoes the constellation of family relationships dominant in each phase of the story.

In the first segment, popular reaction is entirely consonant with the vengefulness of Josephe's father and the Archbishop:

> Man sprach in der Stadt mit einer so großen Erbitterung von diesem Skandal. . . . Man vermietete in den Straßen, durch welche der Hinrichtungszug gehen sollte, die Fenster, man trug die Dächer der Häuser ab, und die frommen Töchter der Stadt luden ihre Freundinnen ein, um dem Schauspiele, das der göttlichen Rache gegeben wurde, an ihrer schwesterlichen Seite beizuwohnen.

The emergence of a humane vision of the family in the second segment, with the idealization of the reunion of Josephe and her child with Jeronimo and their acceptance by Don Fernando and his relatives, is echoed by the evocation of a general reconciliation with strong Rousseauistic overtones. The third section is then introduced by a general movement of the surviving citizens back into the city for the thanksgiving service: 'Das Volk brach schon aus allen Gegenden auf, und eilte in Strömen zur Stadt.' The mob that, after the sermon, turns on the group led by Don Fernando and including Jeronimo, Josephe, and both children, thus cannot help but include some of the same 'Volk' who appear to form one, harmonious family in the idyllic sequence. Kleist's Rousseauistic allusions are, in his poetic works, consistently critical or ironical. This is one such irony, through subtle enough to be a trap for readers.

Political interpreters should always be aware that Kleist has given this 'Volk' a very different structural function from that of the identically named chorus in *Robert Guiskard*. There, the voice of the people is a consistent and distinctive expression of the needs of the whole community, as against the wrangling in the Ducal family and the evasions of Guiskard himself. In **"Das Erdbeben in Chili,"** this essential counterpoint is absent, and the populace, as chorus, simply enhances the prevailing emotional tone of whatever version of family relationships dominates the foreground of the story at any given time.

Criticism has long recognized that the story quotes the philosophical debate on Divine Providence and the Lisbon earthquake of 1755. There has been a strong tendency to see Kleist as continuing the debate as well. Certainly, the fictional characters restate the terms in which Voltaire, Rousseau, and Kant, to name only the most prominent contributors, had discussed the issue of how the terrible effects of the earthquake could be reconciled with the idea of a benevolent deity. What is missing from such interpretations is an awareness that Kleist, in *Die Familie Schroffenstein*, had already explored the work of art as a demiurgic creation, demonstrating that a fictional world could, on the one hand, exhibit all that symmetry characteristic of Newton's or Leibniz' vision of the cosmos, whilst, on the other, presenting nothing but meaningless destruction. I suggest, therefore, that Kleist quotes the debate in an ironic sense, fully aware that an aesthetic construct can offer a well-ordered appearance that in no sense satisfies a hunger for meaning in religious terms and in the real world.

In support of this, I draw attention to the fact that the two gestures toward calculating the effect of the earthquake on the sum of human happiness and suffering, which are most reminiscent of Rousseau's reply to Voltaire's poem on the Lisbon earthquake, are enmeshed with Jeronimo's and Josephe's complete misunderstanding of the realities they confront:

> und waren sehr gerührt, wenn sie dachten, wie viel Elend über die Welt kommen mußte, damit sie glücklich würden!

so war der Schmerz in jeder Menschenbrust mit so viel süßer Lust vermischt, daß sich, wie sie [Josephe] meinte, gar nicht angeben ließ, ob die Summe des allgemeinen Wohlseins nicht von der einen Seite um ebenso viel gewachsen war, als sie von der anderen abgenommen hatte.

They do not consistently misunderstand these realities in the central segment of the text, for they agree on the prudent plan 'lieber nach La Conception zu gehen, und von dort aus schriftlich das Versöhnungsgeschäft mit dem Vizekönig zu betreiben,' but their speculations on the sum of human happiness, in the manner of the 'philosophers' criticized by Rousseau, correlate with their misreading reality in terms of a special providence that safeguards them.

Reality as text and the unforeseen consequences of conflicting readings are always in the foreground of the story. The earthquake is read in the first and third segments in the context of the Last Judgement; in the second it suggests a regeneration of society in which the institutions of property and class pale into insignificance. Jeronimo and Josephe's relationship is read differently by Don Fernando and his family in the second segment from the way in which society at large reads it in the first and third segments. We are left to wonder as to how Don Fernando saw things prior to the earthquake. Kleist has infused the text of reality with a 'demonic' quality, which reminds one of Goethe's summary of the concept in the phrase: 'Nemo contra Deum nisi Deus ipse.' For the discourse of Divine Providence is only intelligible in such contradictory terms, thus leaving the question open as to whether this semantic axis, for all its insistent presence, yields any final sense at all.

Put another way, the fictional characters are steadily compelled to run the gauntlet of signs that encourage one or other reading. This is most blatant in the description of Josephe's progress through the ruined city:

> Sie hatte noch wenig Schritte getan, als ihr auch schon die Leiche des Erzbischofs begegnete, die man soeben zerschmettert aus dem Schutt der Kathedrale hervorgezogen hatte. Der Palast des Vizekönigs war versunken, der Gerichtshof, in welchem ihr das Urteil gesprochen worden war, stand in Flammen, und an die Stelle, wo sich ihr väterliches Haus befunden hatte, war ein See getreten, und kochte rötliche Dämpfe aus.

The consistent pattern of the text is to present the characters with events that may also be meaningful signs, in the manner in which Josephe is here confronted with the visible destruction of all the patriarchal authorities that have conjoined to condemn her to death. The model for the way in which the semiotics of the text treat the characters is given early in the story in the description of how Jeronimo is pursued through the collapsing city:

> Besinnungslos, wie er sich aus diesem allgemeinen Verderben retten würde, eilte er, über Schutt und Gebälk hinweg, indessen der Tod von allen Seiten Angriffe auf ihn machte . . . Hier stürzte noch ein Haus zusammen, und jagte ihn . . . in eine Nebenstraße; hier leckte die Flamme schon . . . und trieb ihn schreckensvoll in eine andere; hier wälzte sich . . . der Mapochofluß auf ihn heran, und riß ihn brüllend in eine dritte.

The verbs produce a state in which Jeronimo entirely forgets Josephe and their child, loses consciousness once he is in safety, and has to be reminded of them by catching sight of a ring on his hand: 'Drauf, als er eines Ringes an seiner Hand gewährte, erinnerte er sich plötzlich auch Josephens.' All this is signalled to the reader, in terms of the semantic patterns of the whole text, by the word 'besinnungslos,' with which the narrative sequence begins, for it is to recur at significant points. Josephe is similarly thrown into panic: 'Ihre ersten entsetzensvollen Schritte trugen sie hierauf dem nächsten Tore zu; doch die Besinnung kehrte ihr bald wieder, und sie wandte sich, um nach dem Kloster zu eilen, wo ihr kleiner, hülfloser Knabe zurückgeblieben war.'

After rescuing the child, she undergoes much the same ordeal as Jeronimo, and indeed is on the point of succumbing to helplessness when a narrow escape from death has the effect of clarifying her thoughts rather than throwing her into further panic:

> Sie schritt, den Jammer von ihrer Brust entfernend, mutig mit ihrer Beute [the child] von Straße zu Straße, und war schon dem Tore nah, als sie auch das Gefängnis, in welchem Jeronimo geseufzt hatte, in Trümmern sah. Bei diesem Anblicke wankte sie, und wollte besinnungslos an einer Ecke niedersinken; doch in demselben Augenblick jagte sie der Sturz eines Gebäudes hinter ihr . . . durch das Entsetzen gestärkt, wieder auf; sie küßte das Kind . . . und erreichte . . . das Tor.

Through 'Besinnung' she converts panic into heroism, thus offering one of the few and sporadic instances of a successful resistance to the structural factors within the text of reality that press toward misreading. Despite the clear contrast to Jeronimo's lack of 'Besinnung' and the tendency for 'helper' figures to be female, the motif is not gender specific. A variant of the word returns in the text at the moment when Don Fernando tries to capitalize on the mob's momentary confusion by implementing a strategy to confuse them still further: 'so antwortete dieser, nun völlig befreit, mit wahrer heldenmütiger Besonnenheit: "Ja, sehen Sie, Don Alonzo, die Mordknechte! Ich wäre verloren gewesen, wenn dieser würdige Mann sich nicht . . . für Jeronimo Rugera ausgegeben hätte."'

The strategy is less than fully successful, but this semantic axis suggests that 'Besinnung' is the only alternative to violence the characters may successfully employ to deal with the breathless course of events. The most cynical reading of the story would insist that Josephe and Don Fernando are permitted just enough 'Besinnung' as is necessary to effect the rescue of the child and his transmission to a new family—but no more. Whether a reader will recognize such signals or not is a moot point, and brings us to the problem of the narrator's behavior toward the reader.

The narrator in the foreground is liberal with value judgements and emotional epithets, and is quite willing, at times, to include the reader within the fiction of omniscience: 'Aber wie dem Dolche gleich fuhr es durch die von dieser Predigt schon ganz zerrissenen Herzen unserer beiden Unglücklichen, als der Chorherr. . . . ' In the coda to the catastrophe, by contrast, the narrator retreats from both this prior complicity with the reader and the tendency to leave nothing to the imagination into an enigmatic terseness that has produced a welter of conjecture and paraphrase in writing on the story: 'Don Fernando und Donna Elvire nahmen hierauf den kleinen Fremdling zum Pflegesohn an; und wenn Don Fernando Philippen mit Juan verglich, und wie er beide erworben hatte, so war es ihm fast, als müßt er sich freuen.'

The laconic conclusion invites the reader to re-examine the text for clues to a fuller understanding, but the problem is that there are too many of them. The reader tends to be inveigled into taking one semantic axis through the judgements of the characters and the narrator and aligning the conclusion with this, only to have a further reading choose another. Rather than pursue this course yet again, I prefer to consider the structural device of the deferral of ending in the text.

The earthquake itself forestalls the foreshadowed endings to a familiar tragedy: the execution of one lover and the suicide of the other. The pocket in narrative time that is thus created is captured in the following image: 'alle Wände des Gefängnisses rissen, der ganze Bau neigte sich . . . und nur der, seinem langsamen Fall begegnende, Fall des gegenüberstehenden Gebäudes verhinderte, durch eine zufällige Wölbung, die gänzliche Zubodenstreckung desselben.' Commentators usually point to other mentions of vaults or arches in Kleist's work, without realizing that these examples are purposely constructed to endure, whilst the whole point of the 'zufällige Wölbung' here is that it collapses in the next paragraph. Within the brief respite, which becomes the second segment of the story, the lovers have the opportunity to plan alternative endings for themselves, one of which is marked by a play on the word 'beschließen': 'Sie beschlossen . . . nach La Conception zu gehen, . . . von dort nach Spanien einzuschiffen . . . und daselbst ihr glückliches Leben zu beschließen.' However, the story opts against such a closure. The temptation of a reconciliation with the society of St. Jago is too strong; such 'Besinnung' as might be available in the warnings of Donna Elizabeth is ignored; and mob violence enacts the ending that the earthquake had deferred, with the sole difference that Philipp is preserved to be adopted by Don Fernando and his wife.

Some of the enigma of the deferred conclusion has been well described by John Ellis: 'The point of the ending is that even after so many attempts to construe the world in a positive way have failed, despair is impossible too. . . . Throughout, the story has moved us from one view of the world to the next; its ending serves not as a turn toward hope but as a reminder that the continual process of coming to terms with the world cannot ever stop. . . . ' Put in structural terms, the implication is that all endings are deferred or arbitrary.

The text here plays upon its own fictional quality, as it does elsewhere, most notably in the evocation of the idyll in the valley, for it has already provided a 'set-piece' ending, full of pathos and taking up motifs from earlier in the text, in the tableau in the wake of the massacre:

> Hierauf ward es still, und alles entfernte sich. Don Fernando, als er seinen kleinen Juan vor sich liegen sah, mit aus dem Hirne vorquellenden Mark, hob, voll namenlosen Schmerzes, seine Augen gen Himmel.

That the text proceeds beyond this to Philipp's adoption and Don Fernando's enigmatic comparison of the dead child with the living suggests an interplay between two narrative authorities. There is one narrator who is consistently close to the characters and who, in the scene of the massacre, becomes excessively engrossed in the action, bestowing extravagant epithets left and right: 'dieser göttliche Held . . . ; Sieben Bluthunde lagen tot . . . ; der Fürst der satanischen Rotte.' The tableau quoted above is this narrator's ending. But there is another narrator active in the text who appears to know better, or at least knows enough to regard omniscience as a sham and all endings as provisional, especially those that look like final tableaux. It is this narrator that restores ambiguity to the story.

It is tempting to see in this duality of narrative voices an analogy to that of Deity and Demiurge in Gnostic thought, for this offers the closest parallel I can see to Kleist's aversion to final authorities that are both unified and predictable. In his dramas, the fragmentation of paternal authority is, as I have shown, a recurrent theme. That his narrative authorities should succumb to the same malady produces structural effects in his stories that help account for their proverbial modernity. Readers who expect Kleist's narrators to keep to the rules are misled—or, to employ a term Ross Chambers has fruitfully applied to a series of 19th-and early 20th-century narratives, seduced.

They are seduced into thinking the text of reality always signals its own preferred reading. Since the negative connotations of a successful seduction become apparent only when the event is seen in retrospect, Kleist's stories demand at least one re-reading for this effect to become visible. To provoke a re-engagement with the text, Kleist uses what might best be termed irritants. Even a cursory reading of **"Das Erdbeben in Chili"** will produce an awareness that Divine Providence is invoked by the characters, but conspicuously does not deliver the outcome it appears to promise. A re-reading may then reveal that the prime structural authority in the text, namely the narrative perspective, is, by analogy, as equivocal and inscrutable as 'das Wesen, das über den Wolken waltet.' A similar irritant may be seen in the enigmatic terms of the story's final sentence, which has indeed sent readers back to the text in an effort to clarify its import. Readers may, of course, choose to ignore such factors and reduce the text's ambivalences to a linear understanding—but at the ironic cost of exchanging an impartial overview for the blinkered vision of a character within the fiction.

"Die Verlobung in St. Domingo" is linked thematically to **"Das Erdbeben in Chili"** in a variety of ways, though there is no indication of their being composed in proximity to one another. At the most basic level, both texts suggest the ambience of *Die Familie Schroffenstein* by engaging our sympathies for two young lovers brought down by a combination of an imperfect emancipation from their social provenance and of their misreading of the text of reality. More significantly perhaps, both texts quote versions of the aftermath of the French Revolution. While **"Das Erdbeben in Chili"** chooses a highly stylized analogy, **"Die Verlobung in St. Domingo"** is set in 1803, and is the only one of Kleist's fictions to present a world whose connection to Revolutionary France is not metaphorical. Finally, there are related motifs, such as a play on the semantic complex formed by variations on 'sich besinnen.' The narrator, at the outset, attributes the outbreak of warfare on the island of Haiti to 'die unbesonnenen Schritte des Nationalkonvents' in Paris, and Gustav, in his narration of the death of his first betrothed, Mariane Congreve, places his own guilt squarely on 'die Unbesonnenheit . . . , mir eines Abends Äußerungen über das eben errichtete furchtbare Revolutionstribunal zu erlauben.' The first printed version of the story had Herr Strömli and his two sons call Gustav 'Du unbesonnener Mensch!' after he shot Toni, whilst this was amended in the collected edition to 'Du ungeheurer Mensch!'

The recurrence of this motif leads us to expect that misreading the text of reality will be a dominant theme, since 'Unbesonnenheit' clearly implies in these contexts that an opportunity to pause and re-interpret the events of which the character is part has been missed. Indeed, the main shift of emphasis between **"Das Erdbeben in Chili"** and **"Die Verlobung in St. Domingo"** is in the degree of blindness that produces the tragic conclusion. Insight and misapprehension are more finely balanced in the former story, with Jeronimo and Josephe being lured away from prudent courses of action by an abundance of apparently encouraging signs.

"Die Verlobung in St. Domingo," by contrast, derives much of its power from exploiting the device much used in horror fiction since Bram Stoker's *Dracula,* namely, the stupidity of the good. Much of the story is narrated from the perspective of Gustav von der Ried, a Swiss officer in the French Army, and no effort is spared to deprive him of insight when he needs it most. Not only does his simple equation of moral qualities with skin color consistently lead him into pitfalls, but he himself narrates two stories that are obvious metatexts to the main action without making the obvious connections which might neutralize the fatal 'Unbesonnenheit' that has already cost the life of one woman he loves. As Sigrid Weigel observes [in 'Der Körper am Kreuzpunkt von Liebesgeschichte und Rassendiskurs in Heinrich von Kleists Erzählung *Die Verlobung in St. Domingo,*' in *KJb*, 1991],

the two stories may, together, have a profound effect on Toni, but Gustav can draw no conclusions from them for his own situation.

At times, Gustav's obtuseness suggests that the text, over the heads of the characters and the foreground narrator, is signalling a parodistic intention to the reader. It is incautious, but plausible, that Gustav's first question to Babekan is: 'seid Ihr eine Negerin?' It is surely somewhat sinister that Babekan, even before she asks who he is, should demand to know: 'seid Ihr herein gekommen, um diese Wohltat, nach der Sitte Eurer Landsleute, mit Verräterei zu vergelten?', since this initiates the whole process of mutual accusations of betrayal that culminates in the catastrophe. If Gustav, ignoring the fact that Babekan has just accused whites as a whole of consistently repaying good with evil, then proclaims: 'Euch kann ich mich anvertrauen; aus der Farbe Eures Gesichts schimmert mir ein Strahl von der meinigen entgegen'—then the crudity of his perceptions borders on parody. It says much for Kleist's skill that he can multiply examples such as these throughout the text without the parodistic dimension becoming more obtrusive.

That the character of Gustav retains credibility is due to the amount of genuine confusion the text presents. In complete contrast to the schematic succession of dystopian and utopian settings in **"Das Erdbeben in Chili,"** **"Die Verlobung in St. Domingo"** creates a world of obscurity that persists till the catastrophe has been reached. Gustav emerges, literally, from the 'Finsternis einer stürmischen und regnichten Nacht,' but remains metaphorically within the occlusion of his own racial prejudices and the chaotic situation on the island until he has killed Toni in a moment of extreme 'Unbesonnenheit.' Writing on the story has raised the question as to whether Kleist also had racial prejudices, to which the only sensible answer is that, if he had them, he did not have them here. The blunders and cruelties committed as a result of racist thinking in **"Die Verlobung in St. Domingo"** are as negatively marked as the excesses of the Catholic Church in **"Das Erdbeben in Chili,"** and no critic has yet suggested that that story be read as an apologia for Catholicism in Latin America in Kleist's own time.

Kleist, in representing the opposing sides in the racial conflict, returns to a device first used in *Die Familie Schroffenstein,* namely, of making the perceptions, language, and actions of the opposing parties symmetrical with one another. Both appeal to divine vengeance to annihilate the other; both pursue a futile kind of arithmetic of atrocity in trying to calculate who has most wrong on whose side; both sides prove able, after Toni and Gustav have died senselessly, to respect a pact involving hostages that ends this particular episode of bloodshed, whilst the war still continues.

This should have prevented critics from taking sides, yet part of Kleist's peculiar magic is to make literary scholars behave like characters in his stories, and so Ruth Angress [in 'Kleist's Treatment of Imperialism: *Die Hermannsschlacht* and *Die Verlobung in St. Domingo,*' in

Monatshefte, vol. 69 (1), 1977] has him siding with the blacks, while Gonthier-Louis Fink [in 'Das Motiv der Rebellion in Kleists Werk im Spannungsfeld der Französischen Revolution und der Napoleonischen Kriege,' in *KJb* 1988/89] has him justifying slavery as part of his aversion to the French Revolution. But what Kleist is presenting, impartially, is the confusion that allows Gustav to condemn, in one breath, 'das Gemetzel der Schwarzen gegen die Weißen,' while in the next he answers Toni's question as to why the whites have made themselves so hated by acknowledging it is 'das allgemeine Verhältnis, das sie, als Herren der Insel, zu den Schwarzen hatten.' Gustav's attempt to extricate himself from this confusion by telling an anecdote of vengeance in a racial context only enmeshes him further, so that at the end he is reduced to invoking a vision of angels deciding the issue. But every mention of divine vengeance or providence in the story functions as a signal that the character speaking cannot attain any clarity about purely human affairs.

The pivotal figure in the story is Toni, who begins as the natural daughter of Babekan and the adopted daughter of Congo Hoango and ends as the dead betrothed of Gustav von der Ried, who commits suicide after killing her in error. Until Gustav changes her view of things by his narrative of the death of his first betrothed, Mariane Congreve, she has acted as decoy for Congo Hoango, luring whites to stay in the house by her sexual attraction, so that Hoango can kill them. Her change of allegiances is abrupt and complete, and her fatal misreading is to expect Gustav to trust her despite all appearances.

Her position between the two fronts is an uneasy one, and nothing has prepared her for its ambiguities. The claims on her are symmetrical. The narrator concludes one of the last private exchanges between her and Gustav with the words: 'nannte er sie noch einmal seine liebe Braut, drückte einen Kuß auf ihre Wangen, und eilte in sein Zimmer zurück.' The words reinforce their sexual bond and are not lost on Toni, as the narrator assures us: 'Denn sie sah den Jüngling, vor Gott und ihrem Herzen, nicht mehr als einen bloßen Gast, dem sie Schutz und Obdach gegeben, sondern als ihren Verlobten und Gemahl an.' The irony that surrounds the word 'Gast' encompasses the whole tragedy of imperfect emancipation. For, as Babekan reminds her, she has been an accessory to the deaths of numerous white 'guests' in this household, and when Congo Hoango is deceived into thinking she has remained loyal to him, there is a disconcerting symmetry in the narration between his words and Gustav's farewell to her: 'und nannte sie sein liebes Mädchen; klopfte ihr die Wangen, und forderte sie auf, ihm den übereilten Verdacht, den er ihr geäußert, zu vergeben.'

Toni, while much more perceptive and certain of her feelings than Gustav, fails to perceive that her conversion may be less visible to him than it is to herself. Indeed, there is an element of exaggeration in the narrator's molding her into a heroine whose natural medium of expression is suddenly Schilleresque rhetoric. With a total lack of caution, she proclaims to her mother:

du hast sehr Unrecht, mich an diese Greueltaten zu erinnern! Die Unmenschlichkeiten, an denen ihr mich Teil zu nehmen zwingt, empörten längst mein innerstes Gefühl; und um mir Gottes Rache wegen alles . . . zu versöhnen, so schwöre ich dir, daß ich eher zehnfachen Todes sterben, als zugeben werde, daß diesem Jüngling . . . auch nur ein Haar gekrümmt werde.

Quite inadvertently, Babekan is doing Toni a favor by giving her an opportunity to re-read the text of her own experience in terms of her changed attitude to what now appears a criminal past. But conversions, in Kleist's work, involve dislocations of perspective, and the only unease Toni displays here is betrayed by swearing an oath before her mother, of all people, as if she needs to establish herself in her new role by asserting it in absolute terms— 'zehnfachen Todes sterben'—and in the face of an embodiment of her own immediate past. I have elsewhere discussed the role of oaths and other formal declarations in the story in the context of the shifting quality of language as a means of ordering reality in Kleist's fictions. Their ambivalence is here evident in the irony that, whatever inner strength Toni may draw from her own words, she has just endangered both Gustav and herself by making Babekan suspicious. The same words may stabilize Toni's inner turmoil, while having the opposite effect on her external situation.

The narrator in **"Die Verlobung in St. Domingo"** has attracted much less scrutiny than in **"Das Erdbeben in Chili,"** probably because the structure is less schematic and because the narrative perspective fulfills any expectations a reader might have of an appropriately dramatic ending, thus discouraging further enquiry in precisely the opposite manner to which the ambiguous ending of the other story provokes it. For the lovers are ceremonially united in death: 'nachdem man noch die Ringe, die sie an der Hand trugen, gewechselt hatte, senkte man sie unter stillen Gebeten in die Wohnungen des ewigen Friedens ein.' To ensure no cliché is omitted, they also receive a monument in Herr Strömli's garden in Switzerland: 'und noch im Jahr 1807 war . . . das Denkmal zu sehen, das er Gustav, seinem Vetter, und der Verlobten desselben, der treuen Toni, hatte setzen lassen.' The only discord is the fact that the narrator seems to have forgotten that the story is set in 1803.

There are many dissonances in the narrative perspective once one goes looking for them. The frequent value judgements and emotional epithets are not consistent. Omniscience tends to fade and reappear like the Cheshire Cat in *Alice in Wonderland,* obtruding, in one moment, by a gratuitously inappropriate image to capture Gustav's innermost feelings—'so legte sich ein Gefühl der Unruhe wie ein Geier um sein Herz'—while skilfully masking, in the next, the precise stages by which Toni frees herself from the role of decoy for a gang of murderers. Similarly, we are left in no doubt as to Gustav's confused attempts to reconcile his racial prejudices with an awareness that all wrong is not on the side of the blacks, whilst, from the moment he seduces Toni, we get only the most fragmentary glimpses of his motivations. His killing of Toni seems to involve one of those dislocations of consciousness that are common in Kleist's works, especially among his male protagonists, and the violence of his actions *after* he has shot her makes him as much of an enigma as Graf Wetter vom Strahl in *Das Käthchen von Heilbronn*: 'schleuderte er das Pistol über sie, stieß sie mit dem Fuß von sich, und warf sich, indem er sie eine Hure nannte, wieder auf das Bette nieder.'

There is thus no more reason to accept the narrative perspective at face value here than there is in any other of Kleist's stories. The foreground narrator is a piece on the board in a game the text plays with the reader. As in **"Das Erdbeben in Chili,"** there is no lack of axes along which the semantics of the text may be pursued, and it is arbitrary to opt for any single one. To indicate, by way of conclusion, a counterpoint to the narrator's professed indignation at the gruesome events he purveys, one may take the axis in the text that suggests that death is the entelechy of the main characters, rather than something they flee.

FURTHER READING

Biography

Baker, Joseph O. *The Ethics of Life and Death with Heinrich von Kleist*. New York: Peter Lang, 1992, 124 p.
    Examines Kleist's search for values, illuminating his literary motivation.

Cohen, Arthur A. "The Sufferings of Heinrich von Kleist." *The New Criterion* 2, No. 4 (December 1983): 26-34.
    Biographical piece that describes the impact of Kleist's unhappy life on his writings.

Maass, Joachim. *Kleist: A Biography*. Translated by Ralph Manheim. London: Secker & Warburg, 1983, 313 p.
    A straightforward biography.

March, Richard. *Heinrich von Kleist*. Cambridge: Bowes & Bowes, 1954, 60 p.
    A short biography that examines the phases of Kleist's life.

Zweig, Stefan. *Master Builders: A Typology of the Spirit*. New York: The Viking Press, 1930, 905 p.
    Includes a lengthy chapter on Kleist's life, focusing on his "struggle with the daimon."

Criticism

Bennett, E. K. *A History of the German Novelle*. Cambridge: Cambridge University Press, 1934, 296 p.
    Examines the history of the *Novelle* genre and categorizes Kleist's groundbreaking tales as "metaphysical" *Novellen*.

Clouser, Robin A. "Heroism in Kleist's *Das Erdbeben in Chili*." *The Germanic Review* LVIII, No. 4 (Fall 1983): 129-40.

Proposes that the heroic elements of "Das Erdbeben in Chili" have been neglected by critics and can be used to determine the main character and themes.

Dyer, Denys. *The Stories of Kleist: A Critical Study*. London: Duckworth, 1977, 205 p.
    Evaluates each Kleist *Novellen* and contains a detailed biographical chapter.

Ellis, John M. *Narration in the German Novelle: Theory and Interpretation*. Cambridge: Cambridge University Press, 1974, 219 p.
    Describes "Das Erdbeben in Chili" as an example of narration in the German *Novelle* genre.

Gausewitz, Walter. "Kleist's *Erdbeben*," in *Monatschefte* LV, No. 4 (April-May 1963): 188-94.
    Suggests that Kleist's "Das Erdbeben in Chili" is representative of the period of transition from the old to the modern *Novelle*.

Geary, John. *Heinrich von Kleist: A Study in Tragedy and Anxiety*. Philadelphia: University of Pennsylvania Press, 1968, 202 p.
    Surveys the elements of tragedy in Kleist's *Novellen*, plays, and minor writings.

Glenny, Robert E. *The Manipulation of Reality in Works by Heinrich von Kleist*. New York: Peter Lang, 1987, 245 p.
    A study of reality as it relates to Kleist's characters, their worlds, and their interaction.

Graham, Ilse. *Heinrich von Kleist—Word into Flesh: A Poet's Quest for the Symbol*. Berlin: Walter de Gruyter, 1977, 289 p.
    An attempt to clarify Kleist's spiritual quest as it informs the canon of his work.

Heine, Thomas. "Kleist's *St. Cecilia* and the Power of Politics," in *Seminar: A Journal of Germanic Studies* XVI, No. 2 (May 1980): 71-82.
    Examines inconsistencies in previous critical treatments of Kleist's "St. Cecilia, or The Power of Music."

Jacobs, Carol. *Uncontainable Romanticism: Shelley, Bronte, Kleist*. Baltimore: The Johns Hopkins University Press, 1989, 233 p.
    A critical look at the open parameters of the Romantic literature of Shelley, Bronte, and Kleist, examining Kleist's *Michael Kohlhaas*, "The Duel," and "The Foundling."

Landwehr, Margarete. "The Balancing Scales of Justice: Chance, Fate, and Symmetry in Kleist's Novellas." *Colloquia Germanica* 25, No. 3/4 (1992): 255-74.
    Discusses how justice is handled in Kleist's novellas through chance, fate, and symmetry.

Laurs, Axel. "Narrative Strategy in Heinrich von Kleist's *Die Heilige Cacilie Oder die Gewalt der Musik (Eine Legende)*." *AUMLA: Journal of the Australasian Universities Language and Literature*, No. 60 (November 1983): 220-33.
    Analyzes structure, composition, and narrative techniques in "Die Heilige Cacilie."

Lucas, Von R. S. "Studies in Kleist: *Michael Kohlhaas*." *Deutsche Vierteljahrsschrift Fur Literaturwissenschaft und Geistesgeschichte* 44, No. 1 (1970): 120-70.
> Studies the criticism on the complicated novella *Michael Kohlhaas*.

Mann, Thomas. "Kleist and His Stories." In *The Marquise of O— and Other Stories* by Heinrich von Kleist. New York: Criterion Books, 1960, 318 p.
> The preface to Kleist's collection of *Novellen*, which provides both biographical and critical overviews to the works.

Passage, C. E. "*Michael Kohlhaas*: Form Analysis." *The Germanic Review* 30, No. 3 (October 1955): 181-97.
> A close examination of *Michael Kohlhaas*.

Silz, Walter. *Heinrich von Kleist: Studies in His Works and Literary Character*. Philadelphia: University of Pennsylvania Press, 1961, 313 p.
> Critical studies of Kleist's prose and dramas.

Ugrinski, Alexej, ed. *Heinrich von Kleist—Studies*. Berlin: Erich Schmidt Verlag, 1980, 293 p.
> Explores studies on Kleist's dramas, prose, and biographical influences; includes critical as well as comparative studies.

Additional coverage of Kleist's life and career is contained in the following sources published by Gale Research: *Dictionary of Literary Biography,* **Vol. 90; and** *Nineteenth-Century Literature Criticism***, Vols. 2, 37**.

Paul Morand
1888–1976

French short story writer, novelist, nonfiction writer, travel writer, poet, screenwriter, biographer, and autobiographer.

INTRODUCTION

A globetrotter, diplomat, and bohemian, Morand specialized in short stories and travel essays and was one of the best-known French writers during the era between the two World Wars. His work evoked the cosmopolitan atmosphere and energetic social life of the postwar period while creating psychological portraits of hedonistic, often disillusioned characters. His witty, fast-paced descriptive prose is rich in imagery and has led some critics to categorize him as a French modernist and imagist. Like several modernist writers, Morand dispensed with transitions between poignant events and images in order to sustain narrative intensity. Despite his immense popularity in the 1920s, Morand had remained largely unknown to English-speaking readers until Ezra Pound's translations of two of Morand's most important works, *Tendres stocks* (*Fancy Goods*) and *Ouvert la nuit* (*Open All Night*), were belatedly published in 1984. These bold translations elicited excitement among critics, renewed interest in Morand, and introduced Morand's work to a new generation of English-speaking readers. In a review of these works, Richard Sieburth observed, "The Morand of these short stories is still news. . . . [He is] one of the great nomads of 20th-century French literature, racing through the apocalypse with the haste and glamour of an Orient Express."

Biographical Information

Morand was born in Russia, the only son of French parents who later established themselves in Paris. His father was a playwright, painter, Louvre curator, and director of the École des Arts Décoratifs. The young Morand was thus introduced to such French and international cultural luminaries as Marcel Schwob, Auguste Rodin, Sarah Bernhardt, Stéphane Mallarmé, Vance Thompson, Oscar Wilde, Frank Harris, Lord Alfred Douglas, and Jean Giraudoux, the latter of whom became Morand's tutor, lifelong friend, and a major influence on his work. From the time he was thirteen, Morand spent summers in England learning English. He undertook studies at the Écoles des Sciences Politiques in 1906 in prepararation for a career in foreign affairs, attended Oxford in 1908, and traveled to Italy, Spain, and Holland from 1909 to 1912. These travels had an important impact on Morand's personality and development as a writer, and he continued to be an avid traveler for most of his life. Capitalizing on his social privilege, Morand served as a cultural attaché to England at the outbreak of World War I, and later became a diplomat and ambassador for the French government; from 1914 to 1918, he lived variously in England, Rome, Madrid, and Paris, there frequenting Dada and avant-garde circles and beginning lasting friendships with Jean Cocteau and Marcel Proust; and he met a Romanian princess, who became his wife. After publishing two volumes of short, impressionistic poems, *Lampes à arc* (*Arc-Lamps*) and *Feuilles de température* (*Temperature Records*), Morand gained significant praise and attention for his first short story collection, *Tendres stocks*, and enjoyed tremendous success with *Ouvert la nuit*, which yielded 100 printings less than two years after its publication and has been reissued many times since. Although Morand was a popular and prolific writer during the 1920s and 1930s, he wrote sparingly after the onset of World War II. In 1958 Morand was nominated to the Académie Française, but was forced to withdraw his candidacy because he had acted as ambassador to Switzerland for the Vichy government of Occupied France during World War II, a role that had caused him to be banished from France. He was eventually elected to the Académie in 1968, at the age of eighty. Morand died in Paris in 1976.

Major Works of Short Fiction

Morand's short stories are products of Morand's wanderlust and reflections of the moral, physical, and spiritual devastation left by World War I. His stories are marked by eccentric characters, fast-paced narration, disorderly descriptions, and unexpected, humorous imagery. Each of the three stories in *Tendres stocks,* "Clarissa," "Aurore," and "Delphine," describes the experiences of three young women drifting in wartime London, while *Ouvert la nuit* contains six stories, each set in a different European city and featuring a different female victim of the moral and material disintegration of Europe. *Tendres stocks* keenly observes the evolution of morality and the relationship between the sexes and *Ouvert la nuit* unveils exotic and erotic themes. These were portraits of young women whom, as Proust pointed out, "we refused to consider as women before such artists as Renoir, Giraudoux, or Morand brought them to our attention." *Fermé la nuit* (*Closed All Night*), considered to be a male counterpart to *Ouvert la nuit,* similarly portrays the chaotic lives of four colorful men: a German, an Irishman, a Frenchman, and an Asian refugee in London. Morand's other short fiction collections include *L'Europe galante* (*Europe at Love*), in which the common themes are love and sexuality; *East India and Company*, twelve stories written in English and set in the Orient; and *Magie noire* (*Black Magic*), a series of stories in which African characters living in Western societies feel compelled to return to their African heritage.

Critical Reception

Although Morand's early short stories were praised by such literary figures as Pound and Proust, who wrote a preface for *Tendres stocks*, Morand's sporadic output after the 1930s contributed to the gradual decline of his reputation as a popular and critically respected writer. His importance in French literature is debated: critics acknowledge his command of style and technique and his descriptive powers, yet several contend that his themes are often superficial, his characters exaggeratedly eccentric, and his observations on cultural characteristics overly generalized. Other critics have pointed to what they consider misogynistic, racist, anti-Semitic, and pro-Nazi themes in Morand's work. Nevertheless, Morand's early stories continue to be regarded as representative of international literary and cultural tastes of the 1920s. George Lemaître, writing in 1938, commented: "Beyond any doubt Morand is the most typical representative and interpreter in French literature of the world of today. . . . His defects and his merits, are they not the defects and merits of the world today? . . . That is why his recording of our ordeals and woes will remain permanently one of the most invaluable and illuminating testimonies of the spirit of our age."

PRINCIPAL WORKS

Short Fiction

Tendres Stocks [*Green Shoots*; also published as *Fancy Goods*] 1921
Ouvert la nuit [*Open All Night*] 1922
Fermé la nuit [*Closed All Night*] 1923
*L'Europe galante [*Europe at Love*] 1925
East India and Company 1927
*Magie noire [*Black Magic*] 1928
Flèche d'Orient [*Orient Air Express*] 1932
Rococo 1933
Les extravagants [*The Eccentrics*] 1937
Nouvelles complètes. Vol. 1. (short stories, novels, poems, autobiography, and essays) 1992

Other Major Works

Lampes à arc [*Arc-Lamps*] (prose poems) 1919
Feuilles de température [*Temperature Records*] (prose poems) 1920
Lewis et Irène [*Lewis and Irene*] (novel) 1924
Poèmes (1914-1924) (poems) 1924
Rien que la terre [*Earth Girdled*; also published as *Nothing but the Earth*] (travel essays) 1926
*Bouddha vivant [*The Living Buddha*] (novel) 1927
New York (travel essay) 1929
*Champions du monde [*World Champions*] (novel) 1930
Londres [*London*] (travel essay) 1931
1900 [*1900 A.D.*] (history and memoirs) 1931
Papiers d'identité (autobiography) 1931

Air Indien [*Indian Air*] (travel essay) 1932
Mes débuts (autobiography) 1933
France-la-doulce [*The Epic-Makers*] (novel) 1934
Bucarest [*Bucharest*] (travel essay) 1935
Le flagellant de Séville [*The Flagellant of Seville*] (novel) 1951
Hécate et ses chiens [*Hecate and Her Dogs*] (novel) 1954
Venises [*Venices*] (autobiography) 1971
Les extravagants: Scènes de la vie de bohème cosmopolite [*The Extravagants: Scenes of a Cosmopolitan Life*] (novel) 1986

*These titles appeared under the collective title *La chronique du XXᵉ siècle* [*The Chronicle of the Twentieth Century*].

CRITICISM

Marcel Proust (essay date 1921)

SOURCE: A preface to *Fancy Goods,* in *Fancy Goods; Open All Night: Stories* by Paul Morand, edited by Breon Mitchell, translated by Ezra Pound, New Directions, 1984, pp. 3-12.

[*Proust's multivolume novel* À la recherche du temps perdu *(1913-27; Remembrance of Things Past) is among literature's works of highest genius. Renowned for its artistic construction, this masterpiece has been widely praised by readers and critics for conveying a profound view of human existence from the perspectives of social history, philosophy, and psychology. In the following excerpt taken from a preface that was originally published in* Tendres Stocks *(1921), Proust commends Morand's ability to "join things by new relationships" and lauds his portrayal of the women in* Fancy Goods, *but faults his imagery.*]

The Athenians are slow in execution. As yet only three young damsels, or dames, have been given up to Morand our Minotaur ["**Clarissa,**" "**Delphine,**" and "**Aurora**"— the title characters of the three stories collected in *Tendres Stocks*]; seven are specified in the treaty. But the year is not yet over. And many unavowed postulants still seek the glorious destiny of Clarissa and Aurora. I should like to have undertaken the useless labor of doing a real preface for these charming brief romances, which bear the names of these beauties. But a sudden intervention forbade me. A stranger has taken her abode in my mind. She goes, comes, and soon despite her mobility her habits are become familiar to me. And moreover, she has tried like a too long-sighted boarder to establish a personal relation with me. I was surprised at her lack of beauty. I had always thought Death beautiful. How otherwise should she get the better of us? However . . . she seems to be absent for the day, this day. Doubtless a brief absence, if one can judge by what she has left me. There are more prudent ways of profiting by the respite accorded me than to spend it writing a preface for an author already known and who has no need of my prefaces.

Another reason also should have deterred me. My dear master Anatole France, whom I have not, alas, seen for twenty years, has just written in *La Revue de Paris* that all "singularity of style should be rejected." Now it is certain that Morand's style is *singulier,* personal. If I were to have the pleasure of seeing M. France, whose past kindness is still present and living to my vision, I would ask him how he can believe in a unity (or uniformity) of style when men's sensibilities are *singulier* (personal, particular, individual, different one from another). The very beauty of style is the infallible sign that the thought has risen, that it has discovered and knotted the necessary relations of things which their contingence had left separate (inapparent). . . .

The truth (M. France knows it better than anyone, for he knows everything better than anyone else) is that from time to time a new and original writer arrives (call him if you like Jean Giraudoux or Paul Morand, since for some reason unknown to me, people are always bringing Morand and Giraudoux together like Natoire and Falconet in the marvelous *Nuit à Châteauroux,* without their having any resemblance). This new writer is usually fatiguing to read and difficult to understand because he joins things by new relationships. One follows the first half of the phrase very well, and then one falls. One feels it is only because the new writer is more agile than we are. New writers arrive like new painters. When Renoir began to paint people did not recognize the objects he presented. Today it is easy enough to say that he is an eighteenth-century painter. But in saying it one omits the time factor, and it needed a great deal of time, even in the nineteenth century, to have Renoir recognized as a great artist. To succeed, the original painter, the original writer, proceeds like an oculist. The treatment—by their painting, their literature—is not always agreeable. When they have finished they say: "Now look!" And there it is, the world which has not only been created once, is created as often as a new artist arrives, appears to us—so different from the old one—perfectly clearly. We adore the women of Renoir, Morand, or Giraudoux, whom before the artist's treatment we refused to consider as women. And we want to walk in the forest, which on the first day had looked to us like anything you like, except a forest—for example a tapestry with a thousand nuances, and lacking exactly the nuances of forest.

Such is the perishable, new universe which the artist creates and which will last till a new artist appears. To all which many things might be added. But the reader who has already suspected them will define them better than I could in reading **"Clarissa," "Aurora,"** and **"Delphine."**

The only reproach I might be tempted to offer Morand is that he uses images other than the inevitable images. No, all the "almost" images among images don't count. Water, in given conditions, boils at 100° centigrade. At 98° or 99° the phenomenon does not occur. In which cases he would do better to do without images. . . .

It seems as if our minotaur Morand had up to the present searched the detours of his "vast retreat," as Phèdre calls it . . . —in French and foreign palaces, built by architects inferior to Daedalus. From whence he watches the young ladies in dressing gowns, with sleeves fluttering like wings, young ladies who have had the imprudence to descend into the labyrinth. I know these palaces no better than he does, and would be of no use to him in solving their shrouded and fractious mystery. But if, before becoming an ambassador, or rivaling Consul Beyle, he will visit the Hôtel de Balbec, I might endeavor to lend him the fatal thread:

> "Tis, I, my prince, tis I whose useful aid
> Hath taught you the wrong turnings of the labyrinth."

Clément Pansaers   (essay date 1921)

SOURCE: "Paris Letter," in *The Dial,* Chicago, Vol. LXXI, August, 1921, pp. 209-12.

[*In the following excerpt, Pansaers places the work of Morand, particularly* Tendres Stocks, *alongside that of notable modernist artists and writers.*]

Marcel Proust is the neo-classicist, at the opposite pole from Francis Picabia, the extremist, the tumultuous innovator. Oscillating between the two and linking them are Paul Morand on one side and Jean Cocteau on the other, both trying to steer an intelligent course between these two extremes. . . .

In his *Feuilles de Temperature* M. Paul Morand seemed to place himself very close to the extreme advance guard; he now gives us in **Tendres Stocks** almost a return to the stable equilibrium, the manner of Marcel Proust. In three studies he depicts three successive states of his being, with assurance and by luminous images. He confesses that he prefers the fanciful Aurore to inconsistent and changeable Clarisse and to disquieting Delphine. His choice could not be otherwise. Imagination, in fact, is the motive force of the advanced literature with which Morand's work may be classed. Thus in his book he accumulates a really tender stock of substantial wealth, from which he complacently produces a fourth person whose name is Paul Morand. All we can do is to wait for the next volume which will undoubtedly assure us of the precise place to be occupied in the young literary movement by this author.

Frances Newman   (essay date 1923)

SOURCE: "Paul Morand," in *The Reviewer,* Vol. III, Nos. 11–12, July, 1923, pp. 932-39.

[*In the following essay, Newman declares Morand one of the great prose writers of the early twentieth century, citing many of his short stories as evidence.*]

The book-shops of Paris are not yet so numerous as the cafés and the coiffeurs, but from the celebrated angle of the Boulevard Montparnasse and the Boulevard Raxpail to the Rue des Petits Champs, following the most agreeable combination of the route of the autobus AE and the autobus AF, an eye more easily caught by books than by paint brushes and Brittany beds looks into twenty-nine windows—La Société Francaise des Ecoles du Dimanche and the stalls along the Quai Voltaire not counted—where the nineteenth century yellow octavos which routed the eighteenth century calf are not yet routed by the green, the white and red, the white and black, of the twentieth century. All of these windows may be supposed, naturally enough, to place in view the authors already most en vedette; and temperamental and topographical remoteness does not prevent the Librairie Le Souderie in the Boulevard St. Germain and Le Divan in the Rue de l'Abbaye from agreeing with the Librarie Stock in the Place du Théatre Francais that their clients will wish to read *Le Grand Ecart*, by M. Jean Cocteau, and *Le Diable au Corps*, by M. Raymond Radiguet, the French Scott Fitzgerald; that *La Belle que Voilá* is a worthy sister to *Maria Chapdelaine*, which has furnished six hundred and seventy-five thousand well-brought up young girls with romance and M. Jean Giraudoux with a Canadian name for his hero's fictitious passport; that there are people who can read and who have not yet read *La Garçonne*; that *Le Cycle de Lord Chelsea* is an excellent picture of English manners, for all that M. Abel Hermant ignores British law by marrying his lovers at midnight and British usage by addressing his duchess as Lady Saint Albans. They agree, furthermore, that the Prix Goncourt will reassure those Frenchmen who may be sufficiently like Americans to distrust so gay a tale as M. Béraud's *Le Martyre de l'Obése*; that even under the arches of the Odéon, even in sight of the House of Molière, no book which is not crossed, as chromatically as an ambassador's shirt front, by a rose colored band announcing the prize it has just gained can hope to be noticed unless it is crossed by a band inscribed VIENT DE PARAITRE.

But the arbiters of windows seldom present to view more than two or three examples of these notable fictions—the place of honour is reserved for the seventy-first edition of **Fermé la Nuit**, usually surrounding a photograph of M. Paul Morand and flanked by a few reminiscent copies of **Ouvert la Nuit** and of **Tendres Stocks**. There are sometimes proud little exhibitions, in privileged windows, of pages of M. Morand's manuscripts and of those rare items, *Lampes à Arcs* and *Feuilles de Température*—for M. Morand, like most writers and all nations except the American, commenced author as poet. M. Morand is also the fableur whom no bookish conversation ends without discussing; with whose wise words M. Cocteau timely opened the Séances d' Avant Garde at the Baraque de la Chimère; whose Prix de la Renaissance could scarcely increase the biographical and critical attention the literary journalists have been showing him even before the first reviews and the fortieth edition appeared on the day of publication. And since French reviewers still lean more heavily upon historical criticism than upon personal opinion, any one who pursues all the potential sources of the

---

Ezra Pound on *Tendres Stocks*:

Proust in his preface to Morand's **Tendres Stocks** has greeted Morand and Giraudoux as the standard bearers, or something of that sort, of the new prose. They are different enough, Giraudoux piling up objective detail in a welter of words, trying to construct, and succeeding, along lines which Laforgue had used in satirizing the overloading of Salammbo; Giraudoux writing almost obviously for his own pleasure and out of his own subjectivity; Morand with buddhic eye contemplating the somewhat hysterical war and post-war world and rendering it with somewhat hasty justness. His somewhat unusual title may perhaps be translated Fancy Goods; one has met his ladies *"de par le monde,"* and technically Aurora must be exceedingly good, for one can hear the English woman's voice and speech throughout the story, and it cannot be easy to convey these tones of voice and idiom in a foreign speech. Aurora is English, just as Delphine is not English, and in the later stories I think he has sustained his differentiation of nationalities exceedingly well. And he has surely the first clear eye that has been able to wander about both ends of Europe looking at wreckage, and his present news value need not fail ultimately of historic validity. His people are as definitely real, of the exterior world, as Giraudoux' are subjective mechanisms.

Ezra Pound, in The Dial, *October, 1921.*

---

form which his countrymen seem unable to believe that M. Morand can have created will learn a great deal about French literature—and nothing about any other literature. No critic has so far suggested that any one of M. Morand's nine women may be descended from the matron of Ephesus or that any one of his four men may be made in the image of the guests at Plato's banquet, but to M. Henri de Regnier, of the French Academy, M. Morand seems, without paradox and in his fashion, a distant successor of La Bruyère; to M. Francis Gérard, M. Morand seems to have passed from the subtle embroideries of La Bruyère to the reconstructive art of Balzac. To M. Charles Vildrac, still in their fashion, the nights of M. Morand seem less distant successors of the Comte de Gobineau's *Nouvelles Asiatiques*. To the more contemporary-minded, M. Morand continues to suggest M. Jean Giraudoux, despite M. Marcel Proust's express testimony that they have no resemblance. Undoubtedly, there is a surface resemblance between M. Morand and M. Giraudoux, but the essential quality which is M. Morand's distinction breaks through the thin veneer when **"La Nuit de Charlottenburg"** and **"Siegfried et le Limousin,"** a psychoanalytical portrait of the Gothic mind in defeat and a cartoon in the tone of a French newspaper, are read in the same week.

M. Morand has publicly stated that, "under a lyric form, the essence of his ideas and of his sensibility may be found in *Feuilles de Température*." This favored work is as slender as tradition could ask—seventy-eight pages with the list of its thirty-six brief poems whose dedications to Madame Marie Laurencin and M. Darius Milhaud sufficiently indicate M. Morand's pictorial and musical modernity—but tradition could ask that their author should have been less than thirty-two years old when they were published, only a year before *Tendres Stocks* and the preface of M. Proust carried his renown farther than Le Boeuf sur le Toit; that, at thirty-two, with the most liberal allowance for his years on the field of honour, a poet should have ceased to enjoy shocking the pious with such lines as "L'hostie est le plat du jour" and

> Pour 60 centimes, MODERN PHOTO vous tire
> en aviateur, ou en Jésus avec
> la couronne d'épines
> SANS AUGMENTATION De PRIX

—however much those years may justify shocking the patriotic with lines so typically Morand as

> l'espion de l'ambassade d'Allamagne
> est heureusement là pour porter les bagages.

The qualities of French poetry, particularly the lyrical qualities, are not always readily audible to an Anglo-Saxon ear, but it seems improbable that any very considerable idea or emotion should be lost under the lyricism of Don Juan or of Carte de Circulation.

M. Morand is also of the opinion that good prose must be as truly lyric as good verse—an opinion that he holds in common with Mr. Arthur Machen and Signor Croce, e pluribus. But the affection for the opiate wand of night which he has in common with Shelley and Keats does not make the prose **"Nuit de Portofino Kulm"** or the poetic **"Bénéfices de Guerre"** lyric in any English meaning of that word; and it is precisely the virtue of his prose and the fault of his verse that they are not. In the eighteenth century, when skepticism created the French prose that the world still venerates, Voltaire and Chamfort and Diderot owed a great deal of their acrimonious charm to the number and the exact variety of the beliefs which they failed to share with their contemporaries; but their disbeliefs were at least as important to them as his beliefs were to Savonarola or to the saintly Ignatius Loyola; they were, in spite of the celebrated warning against zeal, magnificent pamphleteers. And in nineteenth century England, the great prosateurs were the Huxleys, the Ruskins, the Arnolds—the men who could not suffer their fellow creatures to entertain erroneous ideas concerning either the present or the future life. The skepticism of M. Morand is the skepticism of the twentieth century, a century which in its literary manifestation has shown eagerness only in being born ten years before its time, a century to which convictions are not very important, a century which has tastes and distastes rather than beliefs and disbeliefs. M. Morand's thirteen brief fictions are, with one exception, records of something more than thirteen ideas which fail to awaken his enthusiasm.

There is another quality that good prose may share with good poetry, that the most sedentary tale, the most closeted drama, may share with the romances which, from Don Quixote to Jurgen and to M. t'Stersteven's *Vagabond Sentimental*, have found ecstasy and gusto more easily captured on the open road—the quality called magic; and **"La Nuit Turque"** shares that quality, however differently, however delicately, with "Saint Agnes' Eve."

Perhaps if M. Morand had not written for nearly twenty years without publishing the work that went to form his manner of writing—"very conscious, very premeditated"—he might have revealed a closer affinity with those impassioned geniuses who die gloriously at five and twenty. Perhaps, too, a diplomatist sees the world as it is earlier than other men: the first line in the portrait of Clarisse, first of the *Tendres Stocks*, already looks back to the happy days. The happy days, curiously enough, were the days when French cooks and French barbers were marching to Charing Cross with their flags, when the English, "unable to free themselves from the security natural to inhabitants of a place entirely surrounded by water," slowly awoke to the war. The subterranean supper club, where the matre d'hotel naturally addressed himself to Clarisse, where waiters stumbled over crutches while neutrals offered, under the cloth, two hundred thousand Mausers at once and cautiously took from their revolver pockets samples of the uniforms of the belligerents, is so much more than simply remembered that it becomes a predella (in the middle of the picture) rather than a background. The particular twentieth century taste which M. Morand amiably waves aside in the portrait, addressed to Clarisse in the second person, is the mania for collecting—reduced to a pleasant absurdity by Clarisse's preference for imitations. Aurore—M. Morand is not sufficiently denationalized to abandon his country's habit of refusing to acquire local color by leaving barbarians their vernacular names—reduces the simple life to an equal absurdity: Aurore remained in London to sing the praise of forests, she dined at the Carlton proclaiming that she delighted to cook her food between two stones. Delphine says again, under the fresher form of the consolable war widow, what Francis the First paused long enough on the threshold of his glass house to say of women; but it also records M. Morand's taste for that London "which does not give up what has given itself to her"—a taste that he acquired painfully, after months of enduring the Channel every Sunday for the satisfaction of passing some hours in Calais.

The best evidence that M. Morand is not merely another clever autobiographer is a second book incomparably better than his first. Re-read after the perfections of *Ouvert la Nuit*, *Tendres Stocks* becomes only the last of the labours which created the epoch-making form of those six Nights—not, according to any yet accepted definition, short stories. But the massacre by imitation of all the previous erectors of landmarks in the history of short fictions makes it extremely probable that **"La Nuit Turque"** (as most suitable to be put between all hands) will find itself, magisterially annotated, in one of those practical manuals which will still begin with the unfortunate "Necklace," but which may conceivably abandon "The Great Stone Face" and "The Gift of the Magi" for Chekov's "The Darling" and Mr. D. H. Lawrence's "Wintry Peacock" and Miss Mansfield's "Bliss." This portrait of Anna Valentinova owes its backdrop of the Bosphorus to the Russian Revolution, and it is, naturally, the record of a lack of enthusiasm for the present Russian Government, if only for its unusual tenderness and for one of those extraordinarily penetrating coups d'oeil, which fall alike on the Frenchman and the German and the Englishwoman, **"La Nuit Turque"** would be notable even between **"La Nuit Catalane"** and **"La Nuit des Six Hours"**—"Ardent," said Anna, "sensual and serious like all the French. Passion and security."

M. Morand is not, of course, the first Frenchman who has known that across the Pyrenees and the Rhine and the Channel there are undeniably human beings, but it is almost safe to say that he is the first Frenchman who has realized them. A mind fed by the life and the literature of Europe can not produce a prose like the prose of writers fed only by observation of themselves and their fellow-citizens and by the calm stream of a literature which, for a millennium and a half, has flowed contentedly under bridges more Roman than Greek. But the regulations of a language which reduces David the Psalmist to the stature of a Corneille and smoothes William Shakespeare into the likeness of a Racine would reduce even George Meredith, even Henry James, to a certain lingual order: and though Meredith has his admiration among English novelists, M. Morand is kept just within the bonds of French tradition, more by the necessities of his language than by the gaiety, the malice, the pelissonnerie which the Sorbonne officially proclaims the characteristics of the esprit gaulois. Like Chekov, to whom he has no resemblance, M. Morand gives an artfully deceptive impression of writing rather to his theme than to his form; and like Chekov, he may end **"La Nuit Nordique"** with a twist as unforeseen as Maupassant's, **"La Nuit Hongroise"** with the simplicity of tragedy, and **"La Nuit Turque"** with only "Elle me congédia avec douceur et ne fit qu'un instant une tache plus sombre que la nuit." His figures of speech, which did not seem to M. Proust quite inevitable, are sometimes so worn that they would seem to have been unconsciously picked up in English; more often they are extremely fresh—"magnolias, ces fleurs de peau, deviennent noire comme des pendus". . . . Lea, on the last night of the six day race, with "ses paupières de la couleur de 50 francs". . . . an English soldier in peace uniform passes, "éclatant comme un piment dans un bocal de pickles.". . . "ses deux chats persans qui dorment pres du foyer dont ils semblent les cendres." In these images, as definitely as in his themes and his vocabulary, M. Morand must inevitably be one writer to readers who know English and French literature, another to those who know only French and another and much less interesting one to those people who will first meet him in translation; the amusing Oxford slang that he writes in French—an achievement almost more remarkable than the faultless English Oxford slang of the Armenian Michael Arlen—could not be preserved by the most inspired translator—"anciens d'Eton" and "dinant en réfectoire" must lose their exotic flavor when they become again "old Etonians" and "dining in hall."

In *Ouvert la Nuit*, the images, the style, the form and the themes were one: **"La Nuit Catalane"** painted the portrait of Remedios, sometime companion of the legally assassinated Esteban Puig, with the same words that re-

nounced all adherence to the Internationalism which was her religion; **"La Nuit Nordique"** painted the golden-haired Aino with the same world that made quite plain its author's doubt that the French and the Scandinavian attitudes towards the human body lead to different results. In *Fermé la Nuit*, the images, the styles and the form have perhaps distanced all except one of the ideas: the portrait of O'Patah, protagonist of **"La Nuit de Portofino Kulm,"** is an admission of doubt concerning patriotism as a proper activity for poets; it is also a free fantasia on Irish airs and it begins with a description of vertical New York, which M. Morand will visit for the first time next year. **"La Nuit de Babylone"** admits a doubt of the advantages of diplomacy deplorable in a diplomatist, but it never quite settles between painting the disillusioned minister and Denyse, who always arrived a little late. **"La Nuit de Putney"** doubts nothing more serious than a Levantine doctor who proposes to stay time in its flight over women's faces, just as the peerless **"Nuit des Six Jours"** doubted nothing more serious (to a Frenchman) than sport; but the night in Putney fades from the memory and leaves only that literary ripe olive, the museum of the history of medicine.

"La Nuit de Charlottenburg" records the theme that is apparently M. Morand's unique belief—the belief of his century, psychoanalysis. The Freudian faith comes to the surface only of this one remarkably good parody of the Gothic spirit, of "la volonté de puissance" and of "l'arriére boutique de la conscience," but it is the invisible element which is the magic element and M. Morand is the first writer who has used psychoanalysis, not to produce fictions that might rather be documented cases, but as it will be used by the writers who will always have known the unconscious.

The Times Literary Supplement (essay date 1923)

SOURCE: "From the French," in *The Times Literary Supplement*, No. 1123, July 26, 1923, p. 500.

[*In the following excerpt from a review of* Open All Night, *the critic praises Morand's ability to describe his subjects vividly.*]

We should never suspect that we were reading a foreign work but for the imperturbable and un-English gesture with which M. Morand displays [in *Open All Night*] the aberrations and barbaric follies of civilization. In the **"Six-day Night"** which evokes the garish excitement of an international bicycle race—the resting teams in their dressing-rooms lit with a search-light so that the public may miss nothing, the thin circle of competitors ceaselessly sweeping round the illuminated track, the odours and manners of the despotic crowd—all is set down with such concreteness and colour that we can recall without fear the ranker pages of the *Satyricon*. M. Morand's prose is a development of the *écriture artiste* of the Goncourts as it was intensified by Huysmans. In spite of the difference (due to the fashion of the times) that he insists on seeming casual, there is the same search for the word which shall exactly transmit the sensation, the research for the bizarre in the familiar, and consequently a vocabulary crowded with terms from the workshops and the pavements.

A. B. Walkley (essay date 1923)

SOURCE: "Through French Eyes," in *More Prejudice,* William Heinemann Ltd., 1923, pp. 206-10.

[*In the following excerpt, Walkley commends Morand's knowledge and depiction of London, as illustrated in* Tendres Stocks.]

[Today] there are French writers who appear to be thoroughly at home among us and to know England "like their pocket." And yet, even with these knowing ones, England seems to assume an unreal, exotic air. I take up a book published by the Nouvelle Revue Française—*Tendres Stocks,* by Paul Morand—which is a triad of short stories or studies encircling three remarkable young ladies, and I find it crammed with the intimate topography, not to mention the manners and customs, of Oxford and London. Piecing the autobiographical fragments together, you learn that the author was at an English school (where he had to do battle for the national French nightgown against his pyjama'd school-fellows), was in England at the outbreak of war, went to the front, and returned to become an Oxford undergraduate (the indications point to Magdalen). He shows a peculiarly intimate knowledge of Oxford—the after-war Oxford, serious, laborious, that has displaced the pre-war Oxford with its Clarendon dances and its daily Clicquot (but in what college was *that?*), which in its turn displaced the Oxford of the early Georges, when the students ruined themselves in "turn-outs" and kept mistresses. He knows Mesopotamia, and Banbury Road, which he has learnt to call "Banbury"—as full, he says, of Wordsworth Houses and Keats Lodges as of nursemaids. He even knows that "town" come out on the river in the summer and assume the air of "gown," careful about feathering their oars and keeping the right side of the river, and calling one another "Sir." All this is simply prodigious in a Frenchman; you see how far you have got from the Venice-of-the-North generation!

But Oxford, after all, is (be it said with all reverence) a small place, and its anfractuosities, as Johnson would have called them, are soon penetrated. London is quite another thing. There are as many million Londons as there are Londoners. Many of us love it for the comparative ease with which you can live out of it and can avoid knowing more of it than your own particular little corner. And what is called London "life" (I mean the sort of life depicted in the illustrated papers and on the films and in agoramaniac plays and on the posters and in the "novel of the season") is for many of us a sheer nuisance and often only a rhetorical expression. Fortunately, there is enough of London to go round and to suit all tastes, and for my part I like even those parts of London that I have no intention of exploring, when Mr. E. V. Lucas writes about them.

M. Morand seems to know almost as much of London as Mr. Lucas and some Bohemian sides of it, I conjecture, even better. He says it is a town that never quite satisfies you, but that spoils all the others for you. He has wandered over it from Ebury Street to the confines of Epping Forest, from Upper Tooting to the route of Motor-bus No. 19, which (he asserts) takes you to Islington. He describes to me in detail a London which I only know vaguely by hearsay and revels familiarly in haunts which I have never had the temerity to approach. One of his young ladies inhabits an old court-house disused since the reign of George IV (it would seem to be Battersea way); another a house once the house of Lord Byron. He dines and dances at Murray's. Or he feeds at Old Shepherd's in Glasshouse Street, which he likes for its massive tables, low ceiling, toasting fork, and *buffet froid* decked with jonquils in ginger-beer bottles. In the next compartment he can see "la calvitie cossue de Sargent et la tignasse de Roger Fry." *Is* there such a place? He sups with Montjoye, or rather Aronsohn ("an old Norman family," says Daniel), who is private secretary to the Chancellor of the Exchequer, and has Adam-style rooms in the Albany, with black satin armchairs painted by Couder. *Is* there such a person? Perhaps M. Morand is intentionally mystifying us. And my "perhaps" only shows how easy it is for a Londoner not to know his London, not to be able to discriminate between fact and fiction about it. In any case, M. Morand obviously did not invent Ebury Street and Bus No. 19. He tempts me to go and inspect both—but perhaps they would be disappointing, without the glamour of youth. He is very young, M. Morand, and the rackety existence he appears to have enjoyed in London would be far too uncomfortable for an old fogey.

Frances Newman (essay date 1924)

SOURCE: A review of *Open All Night,* in *The Reviewer,* Vol. IV, No. 2, January, 1924, pp. 143-45.

[*In the following excerpt from a review of* Open All Night, *Newman discusses the difficulty of developing a true appreciation of Morand's writing when reading it only in translation.*]

For three good reasons, *Ouvert la Nuit* is a hard book to translate. . . . Unless it is possible to leave more Morand in a translation than [has been done to date] . . . , the descendants of the Pilgrim Fathers will never know why M. Marcel Proust found *Tendres Stocks* worthy of his languid introduction, or why *Fermé la Nuit* divided Parisian front pages with M. Poincaré and the Ruhr all of last spring. M. Morand's French is extremely post-graduate French, and even those Americans who once searched the dictionary for all the words in *L'Abbé Constantin* and *Le Voyage de M. Perrichon* will find his vocabulary no smaller than Signor d'Annunzio's and probably larger than William Shakespeare's—and constructed almost entirely of words unknown to the Academy's lexicon. The first reason, then, why *Ouvert la Nuit* is a hard book to translate is that it is a hard book to read. The second reason is that

M. Morand had the advantage of an Oxford education, of serving his government four years in London, and of an early admiration for the prose of George Meredith; that one of his style's chief charms, consequently, is the Anglican overtones of his French. . . . The third reason is that M. Morand has become entirely cosmopolitan without ceasing to be entirely Parisian. . . .

H. B. V. [the initials of an anonymous translator of *Open All Night*] has not helped unilingual Americans to understand why M. Morand failed of the Prix Flaubert only because he had just won the Prix de la Renaissance—instead, he has made comparatively bilingual Americans doubt that they were justified in thinking M. Morand ripe for the Prix Goncourt. No writer of plays can be quite proof against actors, and no writer of fictions can be proof against a translator who infallibly flattens "prit le parti" to some such platitude as "took up the cudgels" and "on le supprima" to "they made way with him". But if H. B. V. should decide to translate *Candide*, and heaven did not forbid him, there would certainly be more Voltaire left in a flayed *Candide* than there is Morand in these flayed Nights, although every one of them doubts some contemporary delusion as amusingly as M. Voltaire doubted that this is the best of all possible worlds. M. Morand's artfully inconspicuous formula, apparent only after the dissection of the thirteen specimens in his three books, is to choose as model a lady whose devotion to the doomed idea, or to a man who is possessed of that idea, allows him to paint the lady's portrait, and to tell her story in the same words that annihilate the idea: the Catalonian Remedios is devoted to the Third International because she is devoted to the memory of the legally assassinated Esteban Puig; Léa is devoted to *le sport* because she is devoted to that peerless sixdayman, Petitmathieu; only the Nordic Aïno is devoted to her own idea, and Mr. Seltzer [the publisher of H. B. V.'s translation] has omitted her "Night," doubtless as being entirely too clever a contrast between Scandinavian and Parisian interest in the divine human form.

But an incredulous mind is apparently not the only literary necessity: even after a peeling, such reasonable doubts should stand out like the muscles and tendons of the celebrated flayed Greek in the Milan Cathedral. No translator, surely, could dissever the idea of *Candide* from its surface so completely that anyone could suspect a well-glued veneering.

J. Middleton Murry (essay date 1924)

SOURCE: "Moralizings on Morand," in *The Dial*, Chicago, Vol. LXXVI, February, 1924, pp. 184-87.

[*Murry is recognized as one of the most significant English critics and editors of the twentieth century. Anticipating later scholarly opinion, he championed—through his positions as founding editor of the* Adelphi, *and as a regular contributor to the* Times Literary Supplement, *among other periodicals—the writings of Marcel Proust,*] *James Joyce, Paul Valéry, D. H. Lawrence, and Thomas Hardy. As with his magazine essays, Murry's book-length critical works are noted for their impassioned tone and startling discoveries; such biographically centered critical studies as* Keats and Shakespeare: A Study of Keats' Poetic Life from 1816-1820 *(1925) and* Son of Woman: The Story of D. H. Lawrence *(1931) contain esoteric, controversial conclusions that have angered scholars who favor more traditional approaches. Notwithstanding this criticism, Murry is often cited for his perspicuity, clarity, and supportive argumentation. In the following excerpt, he comments on Morand's moral attitude and use of images in* Open All Night.]

From what aspect are we to judge Paul Morand's work? As the thing in itself that is called a work of art? As a book whose astonishing success in France makes it a social phenomenon? As a symptomatic expression of the modern European mind? The material itself admits of all these approaches, or seems to admit of them; and the choice between them seems to depend upon the temperament of the critic.

I freely confess that I am incapable of a calm aesthetic estimate of *Open All Night*. When it first came out I was very much amused by it. It seemed to me then, and seems to me now, the kind of thing our own would-be cynical young writers (such as Aldous Huxley) would like to accomplish, but cannot. For it really is amusing—provided that you can keep yourself in the temper necessary to be amused by it. But that requires an effort which, eighteen months later, I find myself incapable of making. I am not very *raffiné*; I should never have been able to appreciate Nero's technique on the fiddle while Rome was burning. I should have been wandering about somewhere in the streets with a useless bucket in my hands.

In other words I am as good as disqualified for passing any sort of relevant judgment upon *Open All Night*. For M. Morand has improved on Nero. He stands on his head in the midst of the conflagration playing jazz music on a pocket banjo. It is rather prodigious. But the noise he makes is not loud enough to drown the crackle of the flames or the crepitations of collapse. Perhaps it is that I am too fond of Europe. I am never wholly attending. Even when I am laughing at one of M. Morand's outrageous epithets, my ears are otherwise intent. I hate Europe for collapsing, for going sick and passive and rotten; I pretend not to be sorry and make as if I knew it was all inevitable, but all the same—

And, because of this, in my heart of hearts I cherish a resentment against M. Morand. If there is any dancing to be done over the European bonfire, I don't want it to be the fox-trot or the Blues. Let it be something more demonic—whether in exultation and triumph or howling and lamentation does not matter, only let it be something of a bigness appropriate to the event.

I suppose very much the same resentment might have been cherished against Petronius Arbiter (if it was he who wrote the *Satyricon*) in the Roman days; and the obvious reply to it is that Petronius amused himself at a time when there was nothing else to do. Probably that elegant Roman felt pretty bitter about it all inside; the changes are that he was a disappointed Republican idealist whose secret delight was in reading about Cincinnatus at the plough. At all events I seem to remember in the *Satyricon* a smack of the savagery that most often comes of disillusion. Perhaps if M. Morand were a little more savage, I should feel more at home with him. As it is I don't. At moments I have quite a violent desire to feed him on a pound of bad bread and one rotten herring a week for a month or two and see what would happen to his attitude.

But that is not literary criticism; or if it is, it is literary criticism of the most primitive and elementary kind. The other sort, which is far more appropriate to these pages, begins by accepting M. Morand for what he is, and goes on to declare that what he does, he does very well. It then would speculate upon the precise extent of his debt to Jean Giraudoux, from whose manner and attitude M. Morand has certainly learnt a good deal. Not that he is an imitator. M. Giraudoux's trick of vision does not come naturally to many; to M. Morand it does. Or perhaps it is misleading to suggest that such a kind of vision could come *naturally* to anybody. It seems that it must be the outcome of a deliberate effort, which has already had time to become almost a tradition in the most advanced French literature. Its pedigree reaches back through Rimbaud to Baudelaire.

This trick of vision is not easy to define, except as a function of a peculiar use of its chief instrument—the image. Take a couple of examples from the hundreds in M. Morand's pages. The eyelids of Léa in **"The Six Day Night"** are "the colour of a fifty-francnote"; and again her "beautiful Jewish complexion" is "like a sulphur-dusted vine." In the baldest scientific terms, the process employed in these images is the assimilation of the organic to the inorganic; still more precisely, the reduction of the vital to the mechanical. Léa's eyelids can be turned out by the printing presses of the Banque de France, her complexion pumped on to her by a sulphur-spray. And this use of the image is strictly in keeping with an attitude to life. In Baudelaire, the originator of the method, the attitude to life determined the use of the image; it follows, with a kind of inevitability, from the passionate invocation of *"O mort, vieux capitaine!"* It is a mechanized world from which the poet seeks liberation in death; no wonder that he should describe it as such. But with the modern epigoni one is never quite sure. Have they built up an attitude on the foundation of an inherited trick of imagery? Or is the attitude really theirs by nature?

With M. Morand one cannot tell. Or rather, one is secretly pretty certain, but finds it almost impossible to give convincing reasons for the certainty. I should say unequivocally that M. Morand's was a pose rather than an attitude. And if I were asked to say why I believe this, I should have to fall back on that absence of savagery at which I have already hinted—the savagery that is in Baudelaire and Rimbaud, and indeed must be in the work of any one who really *feels* that the human universe is mechanical.

There is all the difference in the world between a man who really believes this and one who, like the arch-prestidigitator, Remy de Gourmont, uses it as an intellectual hypothesis on which to execute variations. M. Morand's variations are astonishing; he is, in his way, a great virtuoso. But it is only a game.

M. Morand is no doubt perfectly well aware of that. His answer would be, once more, that there is nothing else to do but play it. Nowadays you must treat the life of this old Europe as a spectacular kaleidoscope; if you take it more seriously, you are lost. You go mad, turn Second Adventist, or flee to the ends of the earth; or you do all three at once. *N'importe où hors du monde.* All which is highly indecorous and inartistic, not to be contemplated by a civilized Parisian. And yet—being no Frenchman—I cannot help believing that the only way out will be found by the people who are prepared to do indecorous and inartistic things. **Open All Night** makes me only the more convinced of it. When the pages are finished, and my half-smiles and my semi-admirations are over, I am embittered and weary. This play-boy business simply won't do. There is, after all, something horribly indecent about it. The real indecorum is here. Far better flee to the mountains and howl prophecies of doom: if that seems barbarous, it is only another proof added to thousands that our European tradition is *kaput*. Better still, perhaps, to sit tight and look inside ourselves. . . .

But that is moralizing once again. You are bound, if you belong to this side of the water, to be set moralizing by Morand. The very fact of him is a sign of the times. Once in the moralizing strain you forget—it is somehow irrelevant—that he is quite extraordinarily witty at moments (*Donna Nemedios,* "the mermaid in the sea of Marxism"!) and that his vision of the reality can come uncomfortably near to what the reality is.

Apollinaire, Claudel, Cocteau, Delteil, Duhamel, Durtain, Giraudoux, Romains, Soupault and others have done honor to the American scene, but few have rendered it as faithfully and enthusiastically as Paul Morand while on his cruises around the world.

—*Régis Michaud, in* Modern Thought and Literature in France, *1934*.

The Bookman (London) (essay date 1924)

SOURCE: A review of *Green Shoots,* in *The Bookman,* London, Vol. LXVI, No. 392, May, 1924, p. 130.

[*In the following review, the critic lauds Morand's powers of observation and feel for language in* Green Shoots.]

It is said that Monsieur Morand has been an official at the French Embassy in London. If he served under Cambon they were in one respect in very striking contrast with each other; for the Ambassador, admirable diplomat as he was, did not in his more than twenty years at Albert Gate master more than a few words of our language. Morand has the very soul of it. In these three studies of young ladies who, as Mr. Walkley in his entertaining preface [to **Green Shoots**] very truly says, are remarkable, he evidently wrote in his own tongue, for we are given the name of a translator. Possibly the rudiments of the language bore him a little, and you cannot be recondite all the time. His mode of writing is not for the groundlings, as everyone knows who has read **Open All Night**. And there is not a moment of the day or night when his intense powers of observation and deduction appear to slumber. Allusiveness is here and a most diverting method of description. The essence is admitted, but nothing else; and in this little volume there lies more treasure than in a great number of bulky tomes. "Crocodiles with little bellies round and soft like lettuces, brown bears more greedy for the soles of their feet than for honey, hyenas like bags stuffed with bones," are among the spoil which Aurore, one of these young ladies, brings from Africa. Now she has returned to the glimpses of the moon, so that she dines, with the imperturbable Morand, at a resort where it is possible to feast the eyes upon "Sargent's rich, substantial baldness and Roger Fry's shock head." Aurore, Delphine and Clarisse—they make the best of their worlds.

J. W. Krutch (essay date 1924)

SOURCE: "Two Sophisticates," in *The Nation*, New York, Vol. CXVIII, No. 3075, June 11, 1924, pp. 685-86.

[*Krutch is widely regarded as one of America's most respected literary and drama critics. Noteworthy among his works are* The American Drama since 1918 *(1939), in which he analyzed the most important dramas of the 1920s and 1930s, and the essay "Modernism" in* Modern Drama *(1953), in which he stressed the need for twentieth-century playwrights to infuse their works with traditional humanistic values. A conservative and idealistic thinker, he was a consistent proponent of human dignity and the preeminence of literary art. His literary criticism is characterized by such concerns: in* The Modern Temper *(1929) he argued that because scientific thought has denied human worth, tragedy has become obsolete, and in* The Measure of Man *(1954) he attacked modern culture for depriving humanity of the sense of individual responsibility necessary for making important decisions in an increasingly complex age. In the following excerpt from a review of* Green Shoots, *Krutch compares Morand to the author Ronald Firbank and finds their work humorous and stylish but lacking moral earnestness.*]

An elegant searcher after flamboyant decoration and highly piquant sauces, [Ronald Firbank] deliberately betook himself to the British West Indies in search of material, and this story [*Prancing Nigger*] of a Negro banana grow-er and his wife, who leave their hut in the country to seek social advantages for their daughter in the metropolis, is the result. Now the *fausse ingénue* is notoriously the most piquant of characters, and no ignorance was ever less innocent than that of the melting daughter of Mr. and Mrs. Mouth who, grown plump and languishing in voluptuous idleness, was ignorant of nothing which concerns the tender passion except clothes and the other civilized devices by which it is made more elaborate and perverse. Mr. Firbank leads her and her family across the savannahs, languid with heat and sleepy with the odor of voluptuous flowers, to the town of Cuna-Cuna, where the simplicity of the savage meets in the cafe, the dance hall, and the opera house with the corruption of civilization and manners are at once naive and decadent. With genuine humor and the utter sophisticate's thorough relish of the delicately scabrous, Mr. Firbank tells the story of their adventures there and he makes of it something utterly exotic, utterly fascinating, and, it must be admitted, utterly depraved—something as simple and as corrupt as "Daphnis and Chloe. . . ."

Paul Morand, who is taken very seriously indeed by Marcel Proust [in his preface to **Green Shoots**], is no less "civilized" than Mr. Firbank in his purely aesthetic attitude toward life but he is, I believe, younger and hence he can still find a land of unreal color closer home. A young Frenchman, who was a student at Oxford and who passed some of the early war years in London, he there discovered or imagined a Bohemia extraordinary enough and careless enough to intrigue his fancy, and he has described the adventures, comic and sentimental, of his sophisticated soul. A. B. Walkley [who wrote the introduction to **Green Shoots**] is somewhat amazed at the London described, contenting himself when the question of verisimilitude is concerned with a shrugging "perhaps." With like incredulity one may wonder if the originals of the three feminine portraits presented were really so remarkable. One suspects that, seen through eyes less determined to find the baffling, this collector of antiquities, this mysterious widow, and this sensational dancer might seem less unusual; but no doubt it does not matter. Mr. Morand has a personal and charming style and a very pretty talent at analyzing complexities, even if he does invent them first, so that when one comes to a passage like the following it would be merely churlish not to cry "Bravo."

> She paints her stuffs, dyes her carpets, bleaches her hair, tints her cats. Around her she has a thousand objects destined for other uses than one would suppose them, books which open into boxes, telescopic penholders, chairs which become tables, tables which transform themselves into screens, and also those innumerable surprise-box trinkets which we owe to the bad taste of the Italians and Japanese. . . . "I am planning an artificial garden," she says. . . . "One would lie down on moss of that beautiful green that only dyed moss has, warm and powdery to the touch. All round there will be flower beds of colored beads, tissue-paper flowers, and beneath oil-cloth foliage, in a cast-glass pool, the congealed frolicking of guttapercha carp."

In addition to humor, both Mr. Firbank and Mr. Morand have a very complicated sensibility, but their aesthetic attitude is without either moral or immoral enthusiasm. I should rest content with praise of their entertaining quality did not the portentousness with which their sponsors discuss their "art" give me pause. Both of the writers under discussion are intensely occupied with "style"; both produce "pure literature" without any implications for life; and hence their books will be hailed as among the important events of the season by that group of critics to whom whatever literature touches life as it is lived seems always a little vulgar. But to me, I confess, it seems that a literature so "pure" is somewhat anemic, and that really great books do come home to men's bosoms and concern themselves with their affairs. Men can write well and still have something to say, can produce art which is not above but a part of life. For such I reserve my highest admiration because they alone can be passionate, and passion alone is great. "Moral earnestness" is a terrible phrase but writers as diverse as Anatole France, D. H. Lawrence, H. L. Mencken, and Aldous Huxley have it; and what important writer has not? The literature of escape is still but a minor affair, whether it escape into a nurse-maid's paradise or transport the most impeccable aesthete into a far region of art whither the prayers and curses of his fellow-men never penetrate.

Joseph Collins (essay date 1924)

SOURCE: "Some French Writers of the Present Day: Paul Morand," in *Taking the Literary Pulse: Psychological Studies of Life and Letters,* George H. Doran Company, 1924, pp. 231-38.

[*In the following excerpt, Collins praises the verisimilitude of Morand's works* Tendres Stocks, Ouvert la Nuit, *and* Fermé la Nuit.]

Monsieur Paul Morand is not only a literary sign of the times in his country, he is a mirror of French mentality. He was more than thirty years old before he published anything and he had been a wanderer in the world. Both his maturity and *wanderlust* are reflected in his writing. He has no morbidity, no desire to shock, little inclination to instruct, but he has an uncontrollable urge to tell what he has thought, seen or done that he may please the reader and promote his own satisfaction.

"Novels are mirrors walking on a road; sometimes they reflect sunlight, sometimes mud puddles," said Stendhal. M. Morand's stories reflect both, but chiefly sunlight. He is a realist of the school of La Bruyère. . . .

Morand's characters, like those of La Bruyère, are human; they talk, eat, drink, come, go and struggle to make money like real folks; they rarely overstep the limits of propriety and their conduct never transcends that of real life. His first two books of poems, *Lampes à Arc* and *Feuilles de Température,* caused a mild sensation in the reading circles of France and gave rise to hopes which have been

realised by *Ouvert la Nuit* and *Fermé la Nuit*. In addition to being an unusually keen observer, he is possessed of a singularly light and vigorous style and has the ability to paint a picture with fewer strokes of the brush than most of his fellow authors. He reminds one of those crayon artists who do their stunts upon the stage by sketching world characters on a blackboard with photographic accuracy and fidelity. There are few details of life and few activities of the world, few moral or mental tendencies of humanity that his alert mind does not register and his facile pen does not describe. . . .

With **"Clarisse," "Delphine," "Aurore,"** [in *Tendres Stocks*], Paul Morand played trump cards and won. Marcel Proust wrote a laudatory preface to *Tendres Stocks*. In it, he reviewed the writers of the last century, and those of the present generation. He did it to refute Anatole France that there have been no good writers since the eighteenth century. Proust says there are several but his preface may be interpreted as a panegyric of Baudelaire whom he discusses in detail, throwing here and there a look on the past of literature. "The only criticism that I feel tempted to make of Morand is that he sometimes employs images other than inevitable images." This criticism is light. What seems a little whimsical in his style is not always displeasing, and what seems dangerous to Proust is natural to Morand: he loves speed, a stroke of his pen is substituted for a long discourse, he likes abridged comparisons and makes antipodes touch each other in his vision.

Although Marcel Proust does not see any likeness between Paul Morand and Jean Giraudoux, *Tendres Stocks* has a slight resemblance to *L'Ecole des Indifférents,* Morand's English girls offer their hands, smiling, to the selfish and lazy fatalists of Giraudoux. In *Tendres Stocks,* the author is still sensitive to his remembrances of college and does not display the cruelty with which he will look back on them, later. The softness of the banks of the Thames surrounds the silhouettes of the young girl, of the widow, of the dancer; the whistle of the engines does not make the reader deaf, it only adds a melancholy to the country.

The reader feels that somewhere in his mind he has pictured a woman like Aurore—he has felt pity for a Delphine—he has realised the superiority of Clarisse, but he has not encountered any of them. Those who do not know *Tendres Stocks* have still to discover the charm of dawn in Morand, and the pity, always ironical, which he has not chosen to impart to his nocturnal expeditions; in these two books, he discovered the world, and discovered himself.

In *Ouvert la Nuit* he writes of his adventures with women in his wanderings. They are not love affairs in the true sense of the term. They are occurrences incident to mood and passion. There is no deep sentiment and a cynical and bitter mood stifles and colours all feeling. Love and its ways are viewed with eyes that transmit to the spirit distorted images, and these characters do not stir our hearts. We can look at the Cupid as a clown and smile with the author as he intends we should.

Ouvert la Nuit opens with **"The Catalan Night"** and its most interesting features are the account of political unrest in Catalonia and the flavour of the Spanish Inquisition that pervades the last pages. **"The Roman Night"** is Roman only in its setting. Rome is as real and as vivid in it as a photographer's painted background, but the heroine, a French moron, is totally devoid of charm and interest.

The vibrations of life's sorrows seem to reach the author's spirit without loss. Love is a farce but sorrow is a reality. It is particularly in **"The Turkish Night"** and in **"Hungarian Night"** that the note of sorrow rings clear. The reader is convinced that the latter as well as the **"Night of Six Days"** are real experiences. It bristles with slang, that extraordinary and breezy argot which requires long association with Parisians to acquire or to understand. The dialogue is picturesque and vigorous. The best episode in the book is the last, **"The Nordic Night."** Its portrayal demands all the lightness of touch, the subtilty of hues and the adroit fingering of the author: it is a success; alone, it would have made the reputation of the writer, but as a climax to the series that it follows, it places him on the top rung of the ladder. He describes the ethics of the Diana-Bund Society, a return-to-Nature organisation, his shyness when he first appeared among the members of the Society, his eventual enjoyment of their revels, and his own experience with Aïno, one of the most ardent champions of the Diana-Bund. She called him a "cochon international," perhaps not inappropriately, although in his preface he says that, in his wanderings "he thought only of French women," which is an avowal of his purely French mentality. He deals with a custom that has been more or less conventionalised in certain communities and especially in some Northern ones of Europe, but the thoughts and sensations of a young man of Gallic inflammability who is suddenly thrust into a Society clad as Adam and Eve were before their fall and his descriptions of the different members of this association are most amusing and entertaining; Aïno reacts to normal life and accepted conditions of living, as the author has reacted to the environment of the feminine members of the Society, which causes an unexpected contrast. . . .

M. Morand's style in *Ouvert la Nuit* is vivid, full of humour. At one moment, he reminds one of Heine because of the dissonances full of effect, and at another moment of M. Jacob. He is very apt to play a few lyric notes and then interpolate a strain of jazz. He lifts the reader momentarily into the empyrean and then seems to enjoy dropping him into the mud. He is youth testing his strength and suppleness. His humour has a decided acridity and he sees the weaknesses of his characters more than their strengths.

In *Fermé la Nuit* he is a mature development who knows what he can do. If he essays to scale a height, to ford a stream, to breast a gale, he will accomplish it. In four brief stories which constitute the volume, he has expressed, without venom and without pity, the dominant infirmity (which the possessor deluded himself was virtue) of four types of successful modern men.

O'Patah, the Irish Bard and Liberator in **"La Nuit de Portofine Kulm,"** suggests a creation of ancient youth—part monster, part god; part dinosaur, part poet; part savage, part genius; part child, part philosopher. A giant in physical and mental stature and dynamic power, apparently a seer in native wisdom who could not be tutored by example or taught by experience; with the vanity of a tenor stage idol and the bombast of a Tammany chief, he turns out, with the ease of a well-oiled machine, verse full of the human appeal that makes him a poet for the millions; and at the same time he follows the lead of his basic instincts with the naïveté and unconcern of a primitive.

These are stories of men, but the writer takes the pitch, as it were, from the women. Ursula, of the Portofino Kulm episode, is like one of those sketches that a facile artist makes with a dozen strokes of the pencil; not only is it a somatic likeness, it is a soul revelation. M. Morand has a literary technique that recalls Whistler. In the same way that the latter made use of a spot or patch of colour or a tone to lead the observer's eye propitiously on and off his canvases, M. Morand uses a woman. **"The Charlottenburg Night"** gives M. Morand opportunity to say "things" about the Huns. He says them so adroitly, so politely, so tactfully that a "neutral" scarcely appreciates their sting, their venom, but the German reader would no doubt sense them on first reading.

Only one who knows the mystery of the human heart could have described Denyse of **"The Babylon Night,"** Denyse for whom the young politician would sacrifice an ambition, but who, poor unfortunate, was forsworn from birth— from countless births—to burn incense to perverted gods.

It is a gem and youths who feel the sap of literature rising in their sinews would do well to make it their *vade mecum*.

The closing episode reveals the apogee of M. Morand's art. No writer could parallel **"The Putney Night"** save Mr. Shaw or Signor Pirandello. In it the author shows an amazing familiarity with beauty parlours and a most extraordinary understanding of the adaptability and versatility of the Levantine: "One of the successes of all of us Orientals," said Habib, "is that the idea of doubting ourselves never enters our heads, and the idea of doubting others is always there."

M. Morand is fond of travelling, sleeping-cars and leather hand-bags; he uses modern machinery like a virtuoso poet who is not quite "fooled" by his own game; he is keen, clever, he has talent and he has written "the right book at the right time.". . .

The Saturday Review of Literature (essay date 1927)

SOURCE: A review of *East India and Company,* in *The Saturday Review of Literature,* Vol. III, No. 46, June 11, 1927, p. 901.

[*In the following excerpt from a review of* East India and Company, *the critic lauds Morand's narrative technique and judges him a contemporary master of the exotic tale.*]

The jacket of this book [***East India and Company***] promises the reader "bizarre oriental adventures with the utmost ultra-modern European spices." There is nothing in it that can be called "spicy," as that adjective is usually applied to French novels. Indeed, it is in the class of innocuous novels of which the French publishers say, *peut être mis entre toutes les mains.*

"Bizarre oriental adventures," however, we find, and in good measure. Three ghost stories and four other corking good yarns for which China furnishes a brilliantly sketched background, a gruesome chapter on Malay poisons, stories in which a Spaniard lives as a god on a mysterious island in the Indian Ocean, a Parisian finds the haunted skull of the horse of Ghengis Khan, an Englishman is tricked by a cunning Oriental in the Kingdom of Indrapura, an American girl in Manila is unable to love anyone but herself, two Scotsmen of the same family, but a hundred and fifty years apart, feel the fascinating lure of Tahiti,—these clever and cosmopolitan tales should appeal to readers of all nationalities and all tastes.

Paul Morand, already widely known as the talented author of ***Open All Night*** and ***Closed All Night,*** ranks with Claude Farrère as the contemporary master in France of the exotic tale. Neither Morand nor Farrère can vie with Pierre Loti in ability to reproduce the soul of foreign lands; but both make an equal, if not superior, appeal to the general reader, for they have what Loti lacked: an art of composition, a sense of the dramatic, in a word, excellent narrative technique.

William A. Drake (essay date 1927)

SOURCE: "Paul Morand," in *Contemporary European Writers,* The John Day Company, 1928, pp. 66-71.

[*In the following excerpt from a study written in 1927, Drake compares Morand to the Roman writer Petronius and perceives Morand's work as moral rather than depraved, but lacking in conviction and depth.*]

Anatole France, in a preface much quoted by reviewers, once called Marcel Proust "a depraved Petronius." As much might be said, with much more truth, of Paul Morand, but with this difference: that Morand's talent is by instinct moral, and not depraved. In the collections of character sketches which are his most natural and as yet his most satisfactory expression, ***Tendres Stocks, Ouvert la Nuit, Fermé la Nuit*** and ***L'Europe Galante,*** we have a long sequence of brilliant clinical notes on post-war European society. His single novel, *Lewis et Irène,* is little more than an elaboration upon the same theme, in the same manner. Perhaps no living writer has savored more completely than Paul Morand every flavor of contemporary European urban life. Few have absorbed so much, with such accurate perception, and with such superb discrimination. This life he describes, not with the detail of orthodox Realism or the subtle revelation of psychology, but directly, as it is focused in its exceptional characters, and as these appear to him. He gives us the outposts that more sober art has not yet reached.

The analogy between Paul Morand and Petronius Arbiter is as close as the historical similarity (which Spengler has noted) of modern Europe and Rome in the Decadence. Sidonius Apollinaris states that Petronius lived in the Greek colony of Massalia, the present city of Marseilles, which came under Roman influence at the time of the Punic Wars and under Caesar's yoke in A.D. 49. He was, therefore, in youth, either an expatriate Roman upholding the traditions of his fathers in a foreign city, or he was a provincial Tory. In either case, he was a cosmopolite. Very like Morand is the sketch given by Tacitus of this keen-eyed, humane young ironist, who

> passed his days in sleep, his nights at his official duties or at amusements, and by his careless life, became as famous as other men by the sweat of their brows. He was regarded as no commonplace profligate, but as a finished master of voluptuousness. His reckless freedom of speech, being regarded as frankness, procured him popularity. Yet, during his proconsulship of Bithynia, and later as consul elect, he displayed vigor and a capacity for affairs. Afterwards returning to his life of indulgence, he became one of the chosen circle of Nero's intimates, and was looked upon as an absolute authority on questions of elegance, whose sanction alone divested pleasure of vulgarity and luxury of grossness.

Morand knows the upper stratum of post-war Europe as Petronius knew his Rome—from the point of view at once of outsider and participant. Like Petronius, he is an artist in sensation. He has recorded, as did the author of the

Satyricon, a large variety of isolated cases, wherein the malady of the society which he describes may be isolated and diagnosed.

A perfect cosmopolitan by temperament, education, occupation, and the accident of birth; an exquisite in every function of life; and withal, an eminently sensible young man, with ethical sympathies and a certain moral squeamishness which his irony and his pretended indifference cannot quite conceal, and with a soundly normal attitude to life in general, Paul Morand is in the way of making an exceedingly interesting contribution to our still meager knowledge of our own times. If the types which he chooses as the vehicles of his disclosures are eccentric and exceptional, they are so because his talent, superficial alike in its excellences and in its shortcomings, tends to the exaggeration of caricature. He has answered this objection:

> I am reproached for treating only of the exceptional, for failing to look for the human and the permanent when I write. But it is the duty of the reader to look for that, to discover the conclusions which I deliberately conceal because I will not impose them upon the reader to his boredom. For me, the exceptional is a manner of attaining to the permanent. Literature should be, above all, a means of international locomotion, the most highly perfected and the most aërial.

It is clearly evident that the author of the *Satyricon* felt some remorse for Rome as he read the unmistakeable signs of her decay in the features, in the words, in the deeds of his companions. It is patent to one who takes pause to tell the signs, that the dismay and confusion of post-war Europe fill Paul Morand with a similar repugnance. Remotely underlying and morbidly shimmering upon the brilliance which he describes, there is the horrible phosphorescence of death; there is a certain depraved insanity goading his people upon their aimless courses, a deliberate frenzy in their refusal to think and see, and a dark blight impending. Morand, as a completely aware child of his age, feels with bitterness the Dionysian inevitability of this procession toward the night. No word of protest escapes him; he will not even confess the verdict of his mind; but the inner knowledge of this decline, sharpens and directs his vision and lays a mystery upon his spirit. He gives himself away only once: in the little fable of the Bolshevik child teaching the old Frenchman how to work, and being taught in turn how to play, with which *L'Europe Galante* closes. The rest is only light, spicy, ironic observation. The garish lights of the cabarets twit the menacing clouds above their roofs. But in his spirit, Morand watches these clouds gather; and it is his instinctive acceptance of the inevitable tragedy which they presage that links him, as an artist, with Charles Baudelaire.

Morand does not presume to judge the age nor to appoint judges for it. He confesses the finite, and is contented simply to record. Because his conceptions are not clear, perhaps because, to an extent, he lacks, with his own creatures, the courage to rationalize his subjective decisions, his irony is deficient in edge, in the savage impact of

conviction. He does not love man well enough to care greatly what his destiny may be. These are the infirmities of Paul Morand's spirit and the deficiencies of his literary art, which, in consequence, remains rather symptomatic than intrinsically important. But he does not strive for more. He is satisfied to observe the night clubs of a city, the external aspect of a chance companion, the whimsical combats of hypocritical love, without attempting to penetrate those false but significant surfaces, to uncover indelicate depths. He is far too civilized to become passionate, far too social to be introspective, far too casual even to desire the heights. He has gone where his talent and his taste have taken him. They have at least led him to originality in thought and expression.

Morand's early poems, in *Lampes à Arcs* and *Feuilles de Température,* disclose the first tendencies of his talent. Influenced by Blaise Cendrars (*Le Panama*) and André Salmon (*Prikaz*), though by neither to a considerable extent, these early productions—contributed to the Dada movement, yet so far from it in technique and destination—may be said to be in the direct current of Morand's Petronian endeavor. The story of **"Clarisse,"** in ***Tendres Stocks,*** bears some recollections of Jean Giraudoux, who is associated with Morand in his work at the Quai d'Orsay; but, despite everything that may be said to the contrary, the similarity between the two writers ceases precisely there. Beyond the accidental references of **"Clarisse,"** the field, for praise and blame, is Morand's own. An agreeable, ironical, urbane annotator of extreme contemporary types, he is instinctively aware of the quicksands which threaten post-war Europe, and conveys his apprehension of calamity, without the pompousness of prophecy, in the normal process of sophisticated realistic exposition.

Uffington Valentine (essay date 1929)

SOURCE: A review of *Black Magic,* in *The Saturday Review of Literature,* Vol. V, No. 48, June 22, 1929, p. 1130.

[*In the following review of* Black Magic, *Valentine assesses Morand's portrayal of Blacks as detached but knowledgeable.*]

Paul Morand's attitude towards the negro is typically Gallic in its absence of those prejudices which are apt to enter into our own view of him. [*Black Magic*] consists of a group of negro studies which gain value from the detachment of their author, and which had their inception in the fascination exerted upon him by jazz. Drawn by the ineluctable urge of the music he traveled over half the globe and visited nearly two score negro countries. The knowledge of negro nature and the occult powers that possess it gained from his wanderings he has set down in this book.

Unstinted pains are not, however, always attended by adequate reward. The voodooism that M. Morand divined lay at the background of jazz largely remained, despite his assiduous efforts to uncover its sources, the mystery it was to him before he set forth on his journeying. What one finds in **Black Magic** is not an interpretation of voodooism, but merely a vivid dramatization of its effects. However, the volume is not meant to be a scientific exposition of negro thaumaturgics, and perhaps one should not complain if the revaluation of the negro's soul is not what might be expected from the writer's contacts with it under such varied circumstances. At best, research into the spiritual make-up of primitive natures leads to *impasses*; their depths are instinctively guarded. What such research has for the most part brought to light is the fear-motive that dominates the primitive mind, the belief in the inimicalities of life, in an evil power that must be propitiated and thwarted.

This Paul Morand realizes and he has made it the thesis of the first story of his volume. In it he demonstrates the persistence of fear as a spiritual dominant even in evolved negro types subjected to highly civilized influence. The story revolves about a Lousiana-born negress whose dancing has made her the idol of Paris. The triumph of her position, all that she has imbibed from white surroundings, falls away under the atavistic terror aroused by discovering a "voodoo hand" in her bed. She seeks the evil-warding prophylactics of a witch-doctor, goes to a negro sabbat, and there, thrown into hypnosis, she receives an ominous message from her dying grandmother that carries her back to her birthplace, where the shadows of voodooism close in on her. In a spasmodic endeavor to defy them she takes a Mississippi ferry-boat, with the intention of returning to Paris. But voodooistic forewarning confirms itself. She is drowned in the river. The story has more of the accessories of negro necromacy and its preventatives than appear elsewhere in the book.

The second tale is one to which Americans are likely to take exception, though it is inferable that Paul Morand classes the woman who figures in it among the psycho-neurotics rather than holds her typical of American femininity. The story plays on the French Riviera, where a negro, a band leader at a casino, is found on the roadside riddled with bullets, with a paper having the words "Respect for White Women! K. K. K.," pinned to his shirt-front, and in his arms a white woman from Charleston, South Carolina. The story is in large part a monologue of self-justification on the woman's part, with interjections by her auditor that bring out frankly the clashing American and French points of view about miscenegation and all that pertains to it. There is much food for thought in the story. Though written in a polemical vein, it is as dramatically effective as any in the volume.

American feeling in regard to the negro is the subject of two other stories. In both is unsparingly presented the persecution that is the fate of the educated, well-mannered, white-skinned members of the negro race who have sought social acceptance in white circles. The negro's facile reversion to race primitiveness is the theme of a third story, **"Syracuse, or the Panther-Man."** That M. Morand entertains doubt of the negro's value as a factor of civilization may be deduced from the outstanding story of the group, **"The Black Tsar,"** in which, in the vein of Swift's

Voyages of Gulliver, he creates a future negro-ruled West Indian republic. In Occide, its hero, he apparently forecasts what, in his opinion, would be the result of dominance by the negro. "Absolute power intoxicates him," he says. "It gives reign to his instincts, and his will to power explodes."

Régis Michaud (essay date 1934)

SOURCE: "Adventures, Globe-trotters, and Imagists: Valery-Larbaud, Pierre Mac-Orlan, Paul Morand, Jean Giraudoux," in *Modern Thought and Literature in France,* Funk & Wagnalls Company, 1934, pp. 122-48.

[*A French-born American critic and eductor, Michaud specializes in French literature but also has published studies of contemporary American literature and the modern American novel. In the following excerpt, he finds Morand's employment of description and imagery original though tending toward excess.*]

[In] 1921 **Tendres Stocks** [**Green Shoots**] appeared with a preface by Marcel Proust, a quaint title for three portraits of modern young women in an English setting. Proust, in his preface, pointed adroitly to what already appeared as Morand's qualities and defects. His sketches revealed a clever imagist and a magician, but perhaps he exaggerated the trick to the point of eccentricity. To fight routine he did not hesitate to twist reality and subject it to *maquillage,* and his methods were those of the cubist painters. Like Clarissa in the book, he preferred artificial flowers and rubber goldfish to real ones, and enjoyed wearing imitation pearls. Travesty and *trompe-l'oeil* became an artistic process. The world had become too callous, obsolete and ready-made, and it could be renewed only through being deformed and falsified. So it was in his **Nuits,** the great literary sensation of the 1920s: **Ouvert la Nuit** [**Open All Night**] (1922), **Fermé la Nuit** [**Closed All Night**] (1923), to which must be added the stories in **L'Europe galante** [**Europe in Love**] and **Rococo**.

The corrosive acids and other chemicals which Morand used to paint those sensational scenes seem to have deteriorated somewhat. The rare monsters, men and women, in his aquarium may well not be so common nowadays, yet the world is still sufficiently chaotic and strange to make them actual. "Harsh and metallic" were Morand's nights, as he himself confessed, and they were fantastic enough. The world had gone mad, and the war had mixed many oddities in its big tumbler. Here were "blood, voluptuousness and death" (. . . to, borrow Maurice Barrès's title), in catastrophic French prose, and one shudders to think that Loti, Anatole France and Barrès himself were still alive to read such books. Morand's world was that of hallucination, but his hallucinations were true to life. "Men had become soldiers and women crazy, while destiny had thrown a pretty lot of catastrophes of its own into the bargain." Barcelona, Constantinople, Rome, Paris, Budapest, New York, Berlin and Scandinavia, each city or country was summed up in a representative man or woman, and the characters were as eccentrically drawn as the settings. They seemed to have just awakened from an earthquake or a volcanic eruption. Morand's flash-light pictures had snapped all the most revealing and suggestive features. He disregarded traditional methods of investigation and description and went straight to deformities and vices depicted in what seemed sometimes like fantastic cartoons. He was too sensational and violent not to be limited, and he had the greatest difficulty afterwards to free himself from his own imitators.

Marie Scheikévitch   (essay date 1935)

SOURCE: "Paul Valéry—A Post-War Publisher: Bernard Grasset—Paul Morand—Julien Green," in *Time Past: Memories of Proust and Others,* translated by Françoise Delisle, Houghton Mifflin Company, 1935, pp. 286-303.

[*In the following excerpt, Scheikévitch assesses Morand's literary talent and influences.*]

It was in the first year of the War, during one of his short stays in Paris, that I met the young diplomat, Paul Morand. It was difficult not to notice a young man so strikingly frank and intelligent, shrewd of judgment, and with a turn of mind so synthetic. His neat and swift way of looking at people, events, and their relations to each other at once gave the impression that he moved only by flying. His gift for gathering together, through comparisons, ideas, facts, elements, and for linking them up by a striking detail, rendered his talk both spirited in delivery and adorned by a vast store of knowledge acquired through insatiable inquisitiveness. He seemed to have opened all doors and scanned all possible horizons. He expressed himself simply, choosing by preference concrete terms. While listening to the working of such an original mind, one wondered what had been his education and in what surroundings he had grown.

His father, Eugène Morand, painter and poet, had, after the fashion of certain symbolists, felt the influence of the Pre-Raphaelites. His vast erudition and his interest for experimenting in the realms of art had made him in turn take up decorative art, oil painting, and pastel. . . .

The little Paul was a solitary child, and, if we are to believe him, very lazy. At fourteen he loved reading, but mostly realist writers: Zola, Maupassant, Huysmans. Then for a short period he was full of sports and his mind remained undeveloped. However, somewhere about twenty, he attempted a few poetical productions, much influenced by English literature (translations of Francis Thompson, Shelley, and English mediaeval mystery plays). Then he chose a diplomatic career, from no special liking, but so as not to live in France, for he wanted to know various civilizations. His whole outlook was very 'Oxford'; that is to say, very Oscar Wilde and Walter Pater—'Art for Art's sake,' 'The artist apart from life.' All he had written so far bore the imprint of his reading: Baudelaire, Henri de Régnier, Albert Samain, and the Médan school. After getting acquainted with Jean Giraudoux in Munich, he read

essays in *La Nouvelle Revue Française,* then just beginning publication, and, comparing their novelty with his early work, realized that he had to unlearn everything, and he stopped writing for six to seven years. It was during that period that, having chosen a diplomatic career, he no longer gave thought to literature. But entering upon an active life and practical studies, being suddenly thrust into a new world, contributed more than anything else to alter his style and his outlook on life.

'I suddenly became thirty or forty years younger,' he told me one day when I was questioning him. 'I lived in London during 1913 and 1914 as a young attaché, in the company of pleasant women who were my early models for *Tendres Stocks.*'

During the summer of 1916, he came to Paris on Briand's departmental staff. In the preceding year he had met Marcel Proust and was admitted into society on the confines of both the world of letters and that of politics.

Paul Morand was, after the War, among those young writers who felt the originality of a period picturesque and fertile as none before, and where a new poetry was finding expression. He brought to it his telescopic vision of life at full speed, with such haste as to seize on the passing moment, and produced a profusion of photographic impressions revealing the spectacle of a world completely renewed. When he speaks of the outset of his career he admits:

> To date from 1920, after the world revolution, cropped up numerous youthful generals from the army of men of letters. Grasset and Gallimard daily produced new Klébers or Marceaux. The "modest beginning" advocated by Boileau offers advantages; but, after the War, it was the public who, above all, with a passion for something new, instigated the flamboyant attempts of several writers. I quite understand that today, when we are no longer in a hurry, when the ground has been cleared, when God can once more recognize the faithful, an author prefers to take his time before launching out. But there was no choice for us; a special hour, one of the most bewildering in history, was speeding away in front of us: we had to snap it, take photographs of it: two worlds clashing in thunder. A writer lives by contacts; there was a need for prompt action, in fear of the spectacle disappearing, this spectacle without precedent: new frontiers, countries the day before unknown, a Babel of confused races, emancipated women, doomed men, inflation producing upon manners unsuspected and crushing effects, enemies making friends after four years of silence, revolution at our door, the downfall of the West, and many such apocalyptic marvels.

This outlook on the world has been shared by other minds, but none have given it expression with as much aptness as Paul Morand. His descriptions are as pleasing as cocktails skilfully mixed and spiced. What is more, his relish for the precise and picturesque information keeps curiosity constantly quickened. . . .

Every one of Morand's attitudes is an indication that he can never remain still, but must seize hold of whatever is essential at the place he happens to find himself and proceed always further. One day, when one of Anna de Noailles's admirers was praising her on her prodigious gifts, she stopped him short: 'What you forget, Monsieur, is to praise me for my very good sight; physically I observe much quicker and far better than most people.' This power of observing better, Paul Morand possesses more than anyone else. His intuition made him foresee, as far back as 1925, that the post-War period was virtually closed.

He has set the idea of the narrow dimensions of the earth against the exaltation of the romantic globe-trotter. He has aimed at freeing his narratives from the rubbish of exoticism and local colour, so as to react against the arbitrary fashion through which certain writers have come to conceive people, landscapes, and manners.

> What we came to ask of the earth was not a justification for some mental or sentimental disorder; we had, on the contrary an evident need of order, a longing to take stock anew of this earth on which we were to live, and which we hoped to enjoy more fully than ever had been done so far. To watch a world go to pieces does not perforce compel the observant artist to go to pieces himself. His duty is to take note that this chaos does not prevent the earth spinning round according to the eternal laws which rule submissive Nature, even though Man is unruly.

His varied travel books—*Toute la Terre, Paris-Timbouctou, L'Hiver Caraïbe, L'Air Indien,* and *New-York,* and so on—move with inimitable impetuosity. Anyone reading his *Londres* makes a deep study, all the more interesting since Paul Morand mingles with his images a documentation almost encyclopaedic. One feels how much he loves the English capital, and that all the occasions he has had of living there he has used with eagerness in his ardent desire to learn. Success has not caused him to limit himself to a fixed type of work; his constant researches prove, on the contrary, that he remains many-sided and attentive in his understanding of the writer's trade. As 'observer,' he should be granted a first prize, while also being looked upon as in the front ranks of the narrators and journalists of our days.

Georges Lemaitre   (essay date 1938)

SOURCE: "Paul Morand," in *Four French Novelists: Marcel Proust, André Gide, Jean Giraudoux, Paul Morand,* 1938. Reprint by Kennikat Press, Inc., 1969, pp. 303-92.

[*An Algerian-born American educator and critic, Lemaitre published numerous works on French literature, including* From Cubism to Surrealism in French Literature *(1941) and studies of the authors Pierre Beaumarchais, André Maurois, and Jean Giraudoux. In the following excerpt, Lemaitre provides an overview of Morand's short fiction and lauds his ability to capture "the spirit of our modern time."*]

[Morand's] first publications—*Lampes à Arc* (1919) and *Feuilles de Température* (1920)—were collections of short poems, most of them referring to circumstances or impressions of the war and the armistice period, many being obviously inspired by Morand's own experiences in England, Italy, and Spain. They all bore the stamp of a fundamental pessimism and of a restless imagination; with their jerky, syncopated style they sounded an unmistakable note of challenge to *bourgeois* common sense and the rational conception of things. Morand was then in the vanguard of the young artists who thought that the old civilization was dying and that a hard, cold, shoddy, industrial, banal new system was about to take its place. Between the two worlds, one already moribund and the other yet to be born, these young artists were striving to create a strange new language of their own to express their agony and their forebodings.

Tendres Stocks (1921) was conceived somewhat in the same spirit. The three short stories about three young women, drifting in war-time London, were but a pretext for an indictment of the precarious state of contemporary morals; yet the style was less frantic and dislocated than in Morand's previous writings, and his evolution in the direction of the ideals of *La Nouvelle Revue Française* was clearly marked.

Ouvert la Nuit (1922) and *Fermé la Nuit* (1923) brought Paul Morand instantaneous and lasting fame. In these two collections of short stories, he conjures up with haunting intensity the very atmosphere of some typical social groups in turbid, post-war Europe. *Lewis et Irène* (1924), a full-length novel in similar vein, was not an unqualified success. *L'Europe Galante,* though not published until 1925, belongs to the same group of works; in it the themes previously presented in the *Nuits* were repeated in a more daring key, fully justifying the translation of the title used in the English version, *Europe at Love*.

At this stage of his moral and literary evolution, Morand appeared as the most typical representative of the fascinating though unbalanced post-war period and also as its most genuine and adequate interpreter. . . .

[A trip around the world in 1925] was for Morand the starting point of a new life and the beginning of an almost entirely different outlook on people and things. Up to 1925, he had travelled to and fro all over Europe, but in most cases these journeys had been made as rapidly as possible from one capital to another, and the main experience gathered from these various trips was a thorough knowledge of the ways and uses of international trains and of the comparatively small steamers which threaded the narrow European seas. . . .

His travels no longer consisted of rapid dashes from one point of Europe to another, but took the form of extensive and costly journeyings to distant countries, such as the United States, the West Indies, and even Central Africa. His writings during this period were of two kinds. Some were direct accounts of his travels up and down the earth; *Rien que la Terre* (1926), *Le Voyage* (1927), *Paris—Tom-*

bouctou (1928), *Hiver Caraïbe* (1929). Others were more elaborate studies of the moral characteristics of the large human groups, with which Morand had come into contact in the course of his travels outside Europe, and which seem to hold within themselves the future of mankind: the yellow races in *Bouddha vivant* (1927), the black in *Magie Noire* (1928), the American people in *Champions du Monde* (1930). In these ethnical studies which are presented in the form of novels, Morand did not try so much to expound theories or to make predictions as to offer an objective picture of the most typical aspects of the modern world. Appropriately he gave to this series of studies, recording the outstanding features of contemporary civilization, the collective title of *Chronique du XXe Siècle*. The book *L'Europe Galante* is included in the series, though in truth this selection of short stories concerning the ways and byways of love in post-war Europe, belongs to an anterior and different stage of Morand's outlook on life, and seems to have been linked rather artificially to the three other volumes of the *Chronique du XXe Siècle*, perhaps merely for the sake of symmetry, in order to include Europe along with Asia, Africa, and America. . . .

The modern writer is no longer sedentary, keeping to his study or the salons. The younger men—for instance Paul Morand—travel over the world, add sport to travel, and are active in as many new fields as their elders were curious about the past.

—*Marie Scheikévitch, in* **Time Past: Memories of Proust and Others, *1935*.**

[The] many different and sometimes quite divergent directions which Paul Morand's writings have taken . . . have been a puzzle to the reading public and have made it difficult to determine the real import of his work. Yet his work does carry a meaning and possesses an original value of its own. Its unity does not lie in the formal similarity of the various subjects treated but in the identity of spirit which inspires all his books—the spirit of our modern time. Beyond any doubt Morand is the most typical representative and interpreter in French literature of the world of today, with its manifold and rapidly changing phenomena, with its over-intellectual culture, its crude and callous display of efficiency and power, its sharp and violent racial and national antagonisms, its fundamental restlessness, its moral frailty, and its fervent longing for a recovery of order and balance. All these complex and sometimes contradictory feelings and aspirations Morand has experienced within himself, because the circumstances of his life have moulded his personality in such a way as to make him particularly apt to understand and to express the idiosyncrasies of his time. . . .

Two entirely different views of modern life are presented by Morand. They are not by any means contradictory nor even divergent; they simply correspond to two successive stages in the author's life experience, and at the same time to two different periods in contemporary civilization. The first is a picture of post-war Europe, permeated by an atmosphere of confusion, immorality, and despair. The second embraces the whole world, in a somewhat steadier ambit, notwithstanding the trepidations caused by the rapid march of technical progress and the ominous tremors heralding the approach of major transformations.

The picture of post-war Europe is forcibly presented in the volumes published between 1919 and 1926, and is especially effective in *Ouvert la Nuit, Fermé la Nuit, Lewis et Irène,* and *L'Europe Galante*. To these may be added *Flèche d'Orient* in which a state of mind typical of the post-war period is curiously combined with air-travel impressions obviously of a much later date.

Ouvert la Nuit narrates episodes, some insignificant, others highly dramatic, in the lives of six women, victims of the moral and material disintegration of Europe. Each episode is named after a definite 'Night.' The first, the 'Catalonian Night,' centres round Doña Remedios, formerly the mistress of a Catalonian agitator who had been executed for his part in a revolutionary uprising. Returning from an international socialist congress in Lausanne held in his honour, she reaches Barcelona intent upon retaliation. A professor of history, who has been in love with her for many years, agrees for her sake to conceal a bomb inside a bouquet of her favourite flowers, and to hurl it into the King's carriage.

The aristocratic and refined Anna Valentinovna is living in the most sordid poverty among other White Russian refugees in Constantinople. After many gruesome and heart-rending adventures she has become a waitress in a cabaret. She had in her possession a few securities, which she had sewn into the lining of her fur coat, with the intention of holding them until she could escape from Constantinople. To her dismay the fur coat had been pawned in a most disreputable part of the city by a poverty stricken relative in order to obtain money for drink. By chance she meets an old friend and admirer—now married—and with the money she has saved goes under his escort to recover the coat. She finds the securities still intact. What is she going to do with them? Keep them in the hope that better times will come? No!

"I shall go to Paris alone for my own purposes," says Anna. "This will be my one last happiness. For look," and pointing over the Golden Horn, and beyond the Bosphorus and the sea, she indicated the route she had followed in coming, "I shall never go back there. I shall never see my own country again. . . . I am young, but no longer very young, and I know what I am saying. . . . In Paris I shall stay at the hotel on the Quai Voltaire, because the Louvre is truly regal in the evening towards five o'clock at the end of the autumn; I shall settle some family affairs; I shall go and see the church in the rue Pierre-le-Grand, where I was baptized. In the second week following my arrival I shall be almost penniless. Then I intend to hang myself and to have done with this misery I know only too well. . . . Farewell."

And she goes off into the darkness of the night—the Turkish night.

The attractive, eccentric Isabelle, who is a consumptive and a neurotic, is determined to remain in Rome, obstinately refusing to return home to France—nobody knows why. She consorts with strange and questionable people. She spends a great deal of time with an excessively handsome cinema star, and then in the doubtful company of a powerful mulatto. An aura of mystery surrounds her. One day she disappears completely. Some of her friends going to look for her at the villa she has rented in a deserted suburb of Rome, find her there—this Roman night—lying murdered on the floor, 'naked, motionless, with black marks about her neck.'

Then there is Léa, the thoroughly unprincipled yet curiously sentimental lady-love of a bicycle racer, and her sordid yet laughable adventures in the **'Six Day Night'**—also Zaël, the homesick, little Jewish dancing girl, who, on returning to her native Budapest, is kidnapped by anti-Semites and thrown into the Danube, in the **'Hungarian Night'**—and lastly the blonde Aïno who has the questionable distinction of being the secretary of a nudist club, in the **'Nordic Night.'** One and all drift helplessly towards catastrophe or shame.

Fermé la Nuit is the counterpart of the above, presenting pictures of four men—all of them new 'vaniqueurs,' in the mad turmoil of the post-war period. O'Patah, an Irish patriot and revolutionary agitator, after a life filled with sordid adventures, violent struggle, and epic triumph, descends into hopeless debauchery and is struck down at last by general paralysis and insanity in his exile at Portofino Kulm on the Italian Riviera. Baron Egon von Strachwitz is a product of the era of defeat and demoralization in Germany. He is an aristocrat, who has been ruined by the revolution. He is tied to an hysterical wife. He indulges in many strange hobbies, one of the less abnormal of which is to keep scores of live snakes in glass cages attached to the walls of his apartment in Charlottenburg. In **'Nuit de Babylone'** a French politician is depicted who enjoys life in his own particular French way, while the Ministry of which he is a member is being turned out of office. Lastly we have the Levantine, Habib Halabi, beauty specialist and quack, who has skyrocketed to a position of wealth and secret power among the élite of high London society. In a case of dangerous and suspicious hæmorrhage, when death threatens the sufferer, he is called in, rather than a doctor or surgeon, and amazingly succeeds in his most unorthodox cure. . . .

The characters and circumstances described in Paul Morand's books of this period should not be taken as representing the average general state of European society after the war. They are merely abnormal and extreme cases, valuable only as signs and symptoms of the underlying deterioration. The mass of European people, then seething and bubbling, as it were, with all sorts of internal ferments, was throwing up to the surface a scum of miserable and depraved individuals, in the same way as the froth rises to the surface of a liquid in fermentation, covering and concealing everything that lies beneath. Though the froth does not constitute the whole liquid, it is because the liquid is fermenting that the scum can form and spread; moreover, the scum alone is visible to the observer and from its nature and composition the kind and the degree of the fermentation going on beneath can be indirectly, but none the less surely determined.

In the same way, the world pictured by Morand was not the whole European scene but only a small fraction of it—a thin but obstreperous layer of disorderly people, adventures and crooks, loose women, or just frail victims of circumstance, all of them falling an easy prey to abnormal vices, alcohol, cocaine, secret diseases, living recklessly in an atmosphere of perpetual excitment and feverish pleasure, lest they should sink at once into blind despair. Morand shows that many of them had been driven into exile by revolutionary outbreaks, by rank poverty, or by personal restlessness. Abroad their original national features had often become accentuated—aggravated, as it were, by the restraints put upon them through contact with uncongenial surroundings. They flocked instinctively to the great capitals, but occasionally some migrated to the cosmopolitan seaside resorts, dwelling, according to the vagaries of circumstance, either in wretched slums or in luxurious hotels, haunting night clubs, gambling dens, low dives, or nickel-plated modern bars. They lived on caviar and champagne—when they were not starving. As shown in *Ouvert la Nuit* and *Fermé la Nuit* many turned night into day and spent the greatest part of their conscious existence under the garish lights of the big, fast living cities. They made up a world of their own, a world of artificiality and brutality, of corruption and decay, exhaling under the reek of cheap perfumery a perceptible smell of 'high venison.' '"Tu a vieilli, mûri . . ."—". . . Mûrir? On durcit à de certaines places, on pourrit à d'autres: on ne mûrit pas."' '"You have grown older, more mature . . ."—". . . Mature? One becomes hard in places, one rots in others: one does not mature."' Among them, working for a living was a cross between an exciting gamble and sheer robbery. . . . Yet in most instances it was much less a case of deliberate wickedness than of desperate surrender in face of the crushing brutality of a hostile destiny. 'C'est une génération sacrifiée, Madame: les hommes sont devenus soldats, les femmes sont devenues folles. Le destin y a encore ajouté un joli lot de catastrophes' [**'La Nuit Romaine'**, *Ouvert la Nuit*]. Not infrequently the immoral abandon of their lives is relieved by some deep, and, to the onlooker, absurd yet touching sentimentality, while at the same time it may be absolved by their heart-rending distress and suffering. Since the war men had been at a premium and women had to fight for them. 'Je lui dis que depuis la guerre la situation est renversée et que ce sont les hommes qui deviennent une denrée précieuse pur laquelle les femmes doivent se battre' [**'La Nuit de Portofino Kulm,'** *Fermé la Nuit*]. In this concert of misery and extravagance, the shrill notes of sensuality and sex, perpetually recurring like a maddening motif, compellingly suggest an acute, almost painful obsession of impurity and shame. Aïno, in **'La Nuit Nordique,'** aptly though rather crudely sums up this impression when she says to her admirer—who is also the narrator of the story—'Vous êtes un cochon international.'

Such unbalanced and picturesque characters have not been peculiar to post-war Europe. Similar characters did exist before, and even at the present day are not altogether lacking—though they display somewhat different features to be sure. Yet, immediately after the great upheaval, the universal uneasiness bred these people suddenly in such numbers, dramatic circumstances gave their lives such unexpected twists and turns, that they may be considered among the most typical manifestations of that period of moral confusion and unrest. Then extraordinary specimens of weird humanity stood out clearly against the hard, cold brightness that lit the sky after the storm. There was little that was beautiful and attractive in them, but they embodied the reckless and desperate spirit of an era, and they presented a rich display of vivid colours, sharp outlines, intense and striking contrasts, that might well tempt the brush of an artist like Paul Morand.

The morbidity characteristic of post-war Europe faded away after a few years. The picture Morand has drawn of that now vanished world remains as a most invaluable testimony to the final moral tragedy of a sacrificed generation. . . .

Magie Noire represents an effort to grasp and to record some of the typical features common to all the representatives of the negro race at the present stage of world evolution. Morand's first important contact with negroes was made in 1927, in the course of a long itinerary through the southern part of the United States and also during a trip taken to the islands of the West Indies. In 1928 he went to Central Africa and found there what seemed to be the answer to certain psychological problems about the negroes which puzzle and disturb the minds of enquiring white men.

Two main aspects struck him as fundamental. Their relations with the white race are obviously a dominant factor in the life of all negroes but especially in the case of those belonging to the American group. Morand, as many others have done, endeavoured to show the elements of hatred and admiration, the internal conflict of the halfcaste, and the sense of inferiority and inordinate pride, which enter as components of the complex emotions roused in the coloured people by the whites. He showed more originality and insight, however, when he set himself to study the manifestations of another, more mysterious, side of their soul—revealing itself in the mystic strain that runs through negro music, which all but conquered America and the whole modern world in recent years; in the compelling rhythm of negro dances; in the superstitious practices of witchcraft or 'Vaudou' in the Antilles; in the incomprehensible transports which sway the African soul; and above all, in the mystic link which, despite history and distance, still secretly unites all those who partake of negro blood. Morand shows the real unity of all these apparently different factors, and traces them to their source in the deep, atavistic spirituality of the race. He shows that among the blacks there exists a universal sympathy which resolves the individual existence of man, animals, plants, and even minerals, into a magic whole, and that it is from the intimate, all-embracing communion with Nature that the negro draws his power of appeal, and derives some of his amazing beliefs and the incentives for his extravagant actions. 'Fais la paix avec les animaux, les végétaux, les minéraux. Tous même famille. Reconnais tes parents. Sans eux on ne peut rien,' says a master of 'Vaudou' to his disciple. In the words 'Magie noire' Morand finds a key to the soul of the race. 'La race noire, la plus matérielle du monde, est en même temps une race magique.'

Eight short stories illustrate these mysterious impulses of the black race. The tales are not all of equal merit but some of them have intense dramatic power and almost symbolical value. In **'Le Tzar Noir'** we find the character of Occide, a mulatto from Haiti, who, underneath a veneer of French culture, instinctively adheres to the darkest superstitions of the Antilles. Though cunning and crafty as a politician he is nevertheless childishly sincere; and he loathes the whites, while assiduously aping them. He becomes the dictator of his island and then introduces all sorts of absurd measures which seem to be a challenge to reason and common sense, and which actually spring from an inherited memory of primitive African life, that still haunts him subconsciously even though for generations the Atlantic has separated his own forefathers from the land of their origin.

In **'Adieu, New-York!'** the refined and fascinating Mrs. Pamela Freedman is taking an African cruise on the luxurious and ultra-exclusive American liner 'Mammoth.' She shows no desire to cultivate the acquaintance of any of her fellow passengers, with the exception of one young man, the son of a senator and the best-looking man on board. General curiosity and jealousy are aroused. Then a passenger who knew her mother reveals that Mrs. Freedman has some coloured blood in her veins. A conspiracy is immediately hatched. Her cavalier is intimidated into shunning her. When the ship touches at a lonely spot on the coast of Africa, it happens that, on her copy of the printed notice informing passengers when the ship is due to sail, some unknown hand has altered the time of sailing from 10 a.m. to 10 p.m. Pamela Freedman takes a long trip into the jungle, and when she returns she finds that the boat has left. There is nothing for her to do but to seek the hospitality of the local French administrator. At first she is furious at the trick of which she is the victim, but gradually the spell of Africa works upon her, and she feels strangely at home, at peace. . . . Soon she feels the call of the blood. She finds herself irresistibly drawn towards one of the household servants, a supremely handsome and powerful specimen of manhood, who is in reality the son of a tribal chieftain and is being held prisoner because he is suspected of practising witchcraft. As if hypnotized, she runs away with him, follows him into the jungle, to be one of his wives, and there finds complete contentment. 'Elle se sentait rentrer dans le monde noir, elle se noyait en lui. . . . Elle en avait assez d'être une fausse Blanche! Pourquoi s'enorgueillir d'un progrès emprunté? Son progrès à elle, c'était de revenir, par une étonnate et harmonieuse union, à la terre ancestrale. . . .'

The tale of **'Le Peuple des Etoiles Filantes'**—the People of the Shooting Stars—offers an impressive picture of a village in Central Africa. All the inhabitants of the village are seized by a superstitious frenzy of destruction; they burn the stores, the plantations, their own huts, in the belief that inexhaustible plenty will magically follow the annihilation of all that has been so painfully created and carefully organized under the direction of civilized whites. How such a conception could come into the minds of simple people, normally peaceful and harmless, seems to baffle ordinary understanding. Nevertheless, the colonial administrator, who has for many years been in contact with the mystic spirit of the country and the race, and perceives a deep cause behind this temporary craze, explains 'Les esprits détestent les coupes de bois, les routes, les semailles tout ce qui amoindrit la vie magique.'

The process of simplification and generalization used by Morand in *Magie Noire* to account for so many apparently heterogeneous and irreducible actions and impulses may seem at first somewhat arbitrary and superficial. Yet it has the merit of rendering intelligible facts which have a mysterious common root in the deep consciousness of the whole race, beyond the reach of the ordinary casual observer. The very speed with which Morand—as he proudly informs us—visited '28 pays nègres,' covering '50,000 kilomètres,' enabled him to grasp, behind changing exteriors, some elements which are probably truly fundamental. Moreover, as he retained throughout this varying pageant all the vivid colours tingeing each particular scene, the book is on the whole one of unusual interest and no little fascination. . . .

[The] whole picture which Morand has given us of the modern world is remarkably clear and precise. The irregular and discursive pace of the presentation leaves the reader with an impression of the complexity and disjointedness of the universe, yet there is never any confusion or vagueness in Morand's descriptions. With cool and alert intelligence he arranges all his details, setting each in its proper place and in the light that will most vividly reveal its character. There is no sign of any artificial organization or distortion of facts for the sake of a thesis. Sometimes a warm flash of imagination illuminates one aspect or another of his subject; but more often the facts are left exposed under the cold hard glare of Morand's relentless scrutiny. Frequently the scrutiny does not penetrate much beneath the surface; indeed it would be difficult for anyone to cover as much ground as Paul Morand did and to penetrate far beneath the surface at the same time. True, in places, Morand has shown that he is capable of delving deeply, but such 'excavations' are not much to his taste. He prefers to travel fast, to take a general, broad, synthetical view of the most striking aspects of our contemporary world and to bring home to his readers the results of his life-long enquiry into the mentality of the various nations and races he has had the opportunity of observing;—and while exposing the hardness and ferocity of our modern civilization to display its often unsuspected, yet peculiar and compelling beauty.

Paul Morand's remarks on the psychology of different races and nations are among his most original contribu-tions to contemporary literature. He knows of course that certain fundamental traits are common to practically all normal men in all parts of the world; but he is not greatly interested in the abstract types of universal humanity, which the French writers of the classical school have studied with so much predilection in past centuries. . . . [The] essentials of a man's attitude towards his fellow men originate, according to Morand, in external, almost superficial characteristics—characteristics which are stamped on each individual by national and racial influences. Such characteristics are to a large extent inborn, though environment also plays an important part in their formation and in the determination of their various modalities. Yet whatever their origin, they undoubtedly represent the most active and sensitive part of the modern man's reaction to the universe; and to them Morand has devoted much care and attention, as being perhaps the outstanding typical features of our contemporary world.

In his studies of racial and national psychology, Morand's most original method is to take the case of a human being who has been uprooted and transplanted into foreign surroundings; the most typical traits of national or racial character become, for a while at least accentuated, almost exaggerated, in opposition to unfamiliar circumstances. So they are shown up more clearly to the observer against the contrasting background of different manners and alien mentalities. Sometimes also, Morand looks at people deliberately from the standpoint of a foreigner and thus easily perceives the most striking and individual points of their national character. These features are illustrated in Morand's tales and novels mainly by the action and speech of his individual characters themselves, but often he presents also in a few short, sharp statements a gem of keen and shrewd observation. . . .

[The] contrasts in outlook and mentality found among the denizens of the modern world interest him, not so much on account of their bearing on social or political problems, as because they constitute in themselves the most colourful and striking element in the rich and checkered pageant presented by our planet today. And this pageant Morand, the artist, finds at every point fascinating. The denunciation of the modern world as harsh and unpoetical has become a commonplace in literature; in particular those aspects of contemporary civilization which are linked with labour and machinery are usually accepted as unavoidable and perhaps even convenient, but they are not as a rule held to be beautiful. Morand feels their beauty keenly and sincerely and one of the great merits of his works is that he makes us aware of the inherent poetry in the most decried spectacles—the feverish atmosphere of a six-day bicycle race, the garish display of a bullfight, the doubtful appeal of a night club. . . .

Even the bleakest aspects of a huge modern city during a shower are transfigured by Morand's poetical vision. 'Paris was swamped by the rains of a muggy November, the houses being reflected to their very roofs on the wet asphalt. The foggy mist around the street lamps was turned into a rose-hued dust. Along the flooded side-walks battered trees were bending themselves in the wind' [**'La**

Nuit Catalane,' in *Ouvert la Nuit*].... In this frame of mind Morand appears not as the chronicler of a decaying universe but as the pure artist, the great poet of the modern world he loves so well....

'Il reste la littérature. Elle vit de contrastes.' Contrasts are the very life of literature, so thinks Paul Morand. All his own literary achievements illustrate this theory of his. The mere juxtaposition of elements which are not usually found in association arouses his interest and his artistic curiosity. He is prompt to discover beauty in all the colourful and variegated aspects of modern reality, as when nations and races mingle or clash violently together, or when past, present, and future come into collision and overlap one another in picturesque confusion. The æsthetic value of these contrasts is brought out and enhanced in Morand's works by the forceful presentation of the characters, the rich quality of the background against which they move, and the intensity and vividness of his own literary expression and style.

The characters which he depicts are, in most cases, drawn from direct observation of life. But he never merely transfers bodily into his books the actual portrait or biography of any person he has known in his own experience. A measure of artistic and imaginative elaboration goes into the transposition, whereby the original data are combined and transformed into an entirely new character. Actual human beings have provided him with a mass of working material, but not with definite individual models. This material is, of course, entirely distinct from Morand's own personality and remains so even when the artistic creation is completed. It would be idle to attempt to find in Morand's characters any reflection of his own obsessions, aspirations, or desires. Those who have tried that experiment have only succeeded in fabricating a composite figure, either grotesque or odious, according to the aspect considered—but in no wise related to the man's own idiosyncrasies. The characters presented by Morand are objectively constructed; they stand each for some aspect of the modern world and not for the moods and opinions of their author. Yet the author does not disappear altogether behind the characters of his creation; rather he remains at their side, in the modest and subordinate capacity of a witness, pursuing them with his sharp irony, and his subdued emotion, in all their antics and adventures. We learn very little about the personality of this unassuming companion—in fact, we are not interested in him; the characters portrayed readily concentrate upon themselves all our direct curiosity.

As a rule, Morand's heroes are not too easily understood. He does not draw a full length, self-contained portrait of any of his characters after the manner of La Bruyère. Their personality is revealed to some extent by their behaviour; but their behaviour is often so strange and disconcerting that it calls for an explanation instead of providing the reader with one. Morand does not employ the hackneyed subterfuge of unveiling the innermost thoughts and intentions of his characters, as if he had the magic power of reading their minds and hearts. His method is more natural and at the same time more complicated. Almost every

character feels impelled to talk, to explain his actions, to present himself as he sincerely believes himself to be, or as he wants other people to think he is—but not as he really is....

The physical aspect of each of Morand's characters often stands out almost with the expressiveness of a caricature. For instance, young Isabelle in **'La Nuit Romaine'** is described thus: 'Immediately below her shoulders she appeared divided into two thin, tapering legs, like a pair of compasses, and she moved forward by sticking the points into the pavement.' The face of the Levantine, Habib, in **'La Nuit de Putney'** is depicted in the following manner: 'From a point just below the hair-line there appeared one single streak of eyebrow and a hook-like nose, holding up thick lips resembling a piece of red butcher-meat. Below this, was a full, heavy chin, and bluish cheeks which, under their coating of *rachel* face-powder, took on a shade of verdigris.' ...

Notwithstanding the diversity of their external appearances [Morand's characters] possess a number of characteristics in common. Most of them have been uprooted from their natural environment. As a rule they are sharp and clever, showing more cunning and shrewdness perhaps than broad human intelligence. Generally they display excessive sensuality, but they lack the frank, natural—even if over-rich—vitality which is to be found for instance in the powerful creations of a Rabelais. They seem to live in a perpetual state of excitement, and they are inclined, all too often, to follow devious and abnormal paths in seeking to satisfy their cravings. Moral scruples do not stand in their way; religions hardly seem to exist for them; superstitions beset them on all hands. They are seldom moved by any deep sentiments; their affectation is to be rather 'matter of fact,' though, being highly emotional and rather unbalanced, they often act on sudden and violent impulse. They rarely indulge in analytical or contemplative moods; they belong to an era in which action seems to have first claim; and they throw themselves into activity, if not with any definite and clear purpose, at least with all the impetus of a dramatic destiny.

Upon this common background are superimposed in each particular case the more specific traits which go to complete the picture of the revolutionary agitator, the political *émigré*, the professional sportsman, the beauty specialist, the decayed aristocrat, the successful business woman, and so on—all representative types of our age. The writings of Paul Morand could furnish a gallery of the most striking and typical characters of the modern world.

Yet these characters by no means represent average or normal types of modern humanity. They are all exceptional, and in cases abnormal, specimens of their kind. But precisely because they are exceptional, they perhaps disclose more truly the most fundamental aspects of our society, which cannot be readily detected in the 'average' man. Modern psychologists have shown that our most basic tendencies are normally concealed and only appear in exceptional circumstances when some mistake, some unforeseen slip unexpectedly betrays us, thereby revealing their existence; it is therefore necessary to concentrate attention on these apparently insignificant symptoms of an important hidden reality. Morand employed a very similar method: the unusual people he has chosen to depict are not presented as normal types; but through them he is able to disclose the hidden substrata of modern civilization. 'I am often accused of keeping to the exceptional and not seeking in my writings to establish the human and permanent elements. . . . Is it possible today, when all the new psychology teaches us that the deepest abysses of our moral life are never revealed on the surface but are revealed by actions that have apparently miscarried—actions that are illogical, unexplainable—is it possible to take young writers to task for commencing on the same lines? For me the study of the exceptional is a way of reaching the permanent.'

The artistic setting in which Morand places these exceptional yet typical human examples is no less exceptional and at the same time no less typical than they themselves are. He overlooks the familiar and commonplace aspects of the surroundings he describes. He retains and evokes only those which are highly coloured, rich in contrasts—those which surprise the reader and strike the imagination because of their novelty or their strangeness. The word 'exotic' has sometimes been employed by critics with reference to the literary effects achieved by Morand when describing the bizarre habits of some little known group of people, either near or remote—or when painting peculiar features of scenery in strange and distant lands. He has vehemently protested against the use of such a term in criticism of this phase of his art. Indeed the term 'exotic' has become associated with the idea of a rather gaudy ornament, added more or less artificially to a description for the sake of picturesqueness, and having neither meaning nor value in itself. For that kind of local colour, plastered only too often on the surface of modern novels, Morand has nothing but contempt. He avers that in his own case every detail presented expresses a significant aspect of reality and helps us to grasp the fundamental relationship between ourselves and the outside world. . . .

In Morand's short stories and novels the action usually presents the same surprising singularity in characters and in environment. The progress of events is neither definite nor logical. Adventure, with its complex and alluring possibilities, seems to lead on at random the shiftless and ill-conditioned individuals. The plot in each case follows a sinuous course, sometimes turning aside abruptly, sometimes stopping for no obvious reason, sometimes branching off by way of a detour, as it were, and then picking up again the original direction. Important, dramatic sequences do occur; but in Morand's presentation of them, chance seems to be the only arbiter of their occurrence. Is this, we may ask, the fitting and adequate interpretation of an age in which facts tumble over one another, unforeseen, unconnected, and yet compelling? Or is it that Morand is displaying merely the modern gambler's love and expectation of sheer luck? . . . Or once more, does it arise from an artistic predilection for the colourful web of events that only chance can pro-

duce? . . . Or again is not it rather that Morand's instinctive feelings coincide with the very spirit of our time, expressing both the fundamental impotence of man to control his own destiny and the fantastic beauty of the capricious patterns into which our life is woven by some mysterious, all-powerful influence?

Morand's style to a large extent reflects this conception of existence. His sentences are not at all regular, organized, or well composed. They sparkle with intelligence; but the grammatical construction is constantly dislocated for no obvious reason. He pays little attention to the rhythmic cadence of his phrases; he never cares to round off a nice period with well chosen and sonorous words. From time to time, however, there surges up unexpectedly some intense, rich, pungent expression in which all the evocative and suggestive power of the passage is concentrated, giving the reader the shock or the thrill of a direct and entirely unconventional vision of reality.

To achieve these effects, Morand uses the following method: he first writes in a connected manner a full and fluent account of what he has to relate. Then, in the very middle of his text, he deliberately cuts out all the transitions and connexions,—all the spontaneous but superfluous literary padding that has grown round his original, simple, clear thought. He goes even further and strikes out a number of those words that find their way into a clause in order to satisfy the exigencies of the syntax but which do not in themselves carry any particularly interesting signification. For instance, the verb *est* and the expression *il y a* are very often omitted, and many a formal sentence is cut down to a noun followed by several grammatically unconnected attributes. Approximately one third of a first version is eliminated by this method; the rest is given to the public untouched and unpolished, in a sketchy but extremely arresting form.

This manner of composition conveys to the reader an impression of great rapidity. The mind has to leap quickly from one idea to another; all the intermediary stages of thinking have been suppressed; in many a clause only the indispensable element has been retained; throughout the whole the reader is rushed along at full speed as though by a telegraphic impulsion. Yet speed must not be taken here as a synonym for conciseness. Morand does not possess the art of expressing a great deal in a few well chosen and highly significant words. His technique is one of suppression rather than of compression—though the result for the casual reader amounts to practically the same thing.

The reader is not led step by step along an easy and well defined road. He receives naturally indications and hints, all perfectly clear and fairly numerous; but nevertheless his mind has to be constantly on the alert in order to keep on the right path, to supply the missing links in the development of the tale, or to turn sharply and without much warning, should Morand suddenly take a fancy to explore some secluded nook or corner by the wayside. So the reader is made to collaborate, as it were, with the author, and the mental activity required of him, which is tactfully measured to keep his mind nimble and yet is not so arduous as to make him feel unpleasantly taxed, goes far towards imparting to Morand's writings a remarkably stimulating, enlivening quality.

But the most striking feature of Morand's style is his abundant, queer, and aggressive imagery. The most surprising, far-fetched yet often illuminating comparisons give his prose an entirely personal accent. Many critics have protested against his extraordinary metaphors—among others Marcel Proust, who wrote: 'Le seul reproche que je serais tenté d'adresser à Morand, c'est qu'il a quelquefois des images autres que des images inévitables' [Preface to *Tendres Stocks*]. The literary images presented by Morand are certainly not inevitable ones; they cannot even be called natural; they rest upon artificiality. For instance, he will quite systematically assimilate some physical feature of a human being, or some normal aspect of natural scenery, to a manufactured object,—and invariably to one, not only of the most trivial use, but also of the most emphatically modern application. Yet after the first shock of surprise one is bound to recognize that these seemingly irrelevant suggestions often indeed disclose subtle, realistic affinities between persons and things apparently very far remote from each other. Thus Morand compares the discoloured eyelids of a *femme galante* to the yellowish-grey French fifty-franc notes. 'J'aimais ses mains plébeiennes, ses paupières de la couleur des billets de cinquante francs.' ['**La nuit des six jours,**' in *Ouvert la nuit*]. . . . During a storm the sky is split by a flash of lightning as if it were a piece of silk suddenly rent in twain. 'Le ciel se fendit comme une pièce de soie.' The watery eyes of a bilious and observant professor are likened to a photographic plate in the yellow fluid of a developer. 'Il descendait le boulevard Saint-Michel . . . posant sur le monde des yeux gris et noirs pareils à une plaque de photographie et qui baignaient dans l'eau jaune d'un révélateur' ['**La nuit Catalane,**' in *Ouvert la nuit*]. . . .

Fatigue and strain too often result from prolonged contact with Paul Morand's works. A multiplicity of vivid splashes of colour, brilliant touches, and startling contrasts, more or less disconnected, without any toning down whatever of their lurid intensity, flash past our eyes at almost cinematographic speed. The spectacle is exciting, fascinating, intoxicating; but even if new aspects of beauty are revealed now and then, the hard, pitiless light falls more often than not on dismal and distressing objects. The quickness of the pace seems to multiply their occurrence. Contrasts are too sharp, clashes too frequent, changes too rapid—the procession dissolves itself into a dizzy, fluttering show. But who among us would not recognize in these features the very characteristics of our modern times? Morand offers a typical case of perfect adaptation of an author to his chosen topic. His defects and his merits, are they not the defects and merits of the world today? That is why he has been able to express so well its anxieties and its forebodings. That is why his recording of our ordeals and woes will remain permanently one of the most invaluable and illuminating testimonies of the spirit of our age.

Edgar C. Knowlton, Jr. (essay date 1964)

SOURCE: "Chinese Elements in Paul Morand's 'Mr. U'," in *Chinese Culture,* Vol. V, No. 3, March, 1964, pp. 34–41.

[*Knowlton is an American educator, translator, and critic. In the following excerpt, he praises Morand's short story "Mr. U" as an excellent example of Chinese-French literary contact and cites passages that illustrate Morand's detailed knowledge of Chinese culture.*]

There are important French men of letters in the twentieth century who illustrate China's influence on European literature, in the tradition of earlier French writers like Voltaire. . . . Among these an honorable place must be accorded Paul Morand, whose early literary contributions to European fiction of this century have been surveyed by Milton H. Stansbury in *French Novelists of Today*. Stansbury stresses the cosmopolitanism of Morand, but pays little attention to China as reflected in the novelist's work. The short story by Paul Morand discussed in this paper, "**Mr. U,**" is a brilliant example of the result of Chinese-French literary contact. . . .

"**Mr. U**" is mentioned as a literary product of Paul Morand's trip in 1925 to the Far East on page 356 of Kurt Jackel's study, "Paul Morand und die Erneuerung des Exotismus in der französischen Literatur der Gegenwart," *Zeitschrift für französische Sprache und Literatur*, LX, 1937. The story exemplifies the hope expressed by William Leonard Schwartz at the close of his work entitled *The Imaginative Interpretation of the Far East in Modern French Literature, 1800-1925*: "From this evidence of progress in France one may therefore predict that the time is approaching when imaginative writing in all languages on Far Eastern subjects will be accurate interpretations of Oriental civilization and thought."

In retelling the story briefly, specific instances will be given which show the detailed knowledge of China displayed by Morand. Reference to an additional relevant source will also be provided.

The story concerns the nocturnal adventure of Mr. Doolittle, a tipsy Irishman in New York, who, one morning at three o'clock, is addressed by Mr. U, a ghost from ninth-century China, who has come to New York City leading a white cock on a leash. The cock is the ghost's guide, as we learn from Harry T. Morgan's *Chinese Symbols and Superstitions*: ". . . a pure white cock is an emblem of purity and is the only capable guide of transient spirits."

Mr. U informs Doolittle of his dilemma; his tomb had included terra cotta statuettes in his service. T'ang dynasty terra cotta funeral statuettes are treated by Madeleine Paul-David in her *Arts et styles de la Chine*. . . .

The artistic beauty of the statuettes was unfortunate because this beauty attracted a New York antique dealer's eye. Morand here quotes a pertinent Chinese proverb: "Une femme laide est un trésor dans la famille." ("An ugly wife is a treasure in the family.")

More complete Chinese and English versions of this proverb are found in Arthur H. Smith's *Proverbs and Common Sayings from the Chinese*. His English rendering of the proverb is as follows:

> For peace in one's domestic life
> No treasure like an ugly wife,
> While one most beautiful and fair
> Will fill your days with grief and care.

The New York dealer opened up Mr. U's tomb and robbed it of the terra cotta statuettes. This left Mr. U without protection from other spirits, and he himself became an unfortunate "esprit mendiant" (mendicant ghost). N. B. Dennys describes these "pauper spirits" or "disreputable Ghosts" on page 77 of his *The Folk-lore of China*.

Mr. U goes on to explain to Mr. Doolittle that he has tracked down the grave-desecrater to 489 Fifth Avenue. If New York were China, he would have committed suicide at the thief's home. The attitude of the Chinese towards suicide as an effective way of taking vengeance is explained on pages 623-624 of James Dyer Ball's *Things Chinese*.

[Morand's] cosmopolitanism is well known, and literary cosmopolitanism was quite in vogue in the twenties. Equally characteristic of the period was public awareness of the increased tempo and complexity of life, a feeling which Morand was exceptional in translating into prose fiction.

—Charles B. Osburn, in Revue des langues vivantes, *Vol. XLII, No. 2, 1976.*

Mr. U now needs the help of Mr. Doolittle, who is to call out an imperial order, in Chinese, to the statuettes to return to Mr. U's tomb: *"Yu-tche ki-k'o chang kan-sou k'iu. K'inn tse."*. . .

Students who wish to see French romanizations as well as the Chinese characters may consult Father Séraphin Couvreur's *Dictionnaire classique de la langue chinoise*. Morand's first two syllables correspond to Couvreur's *iú tchèu*, given as a compound meaning "édit impérial" (imperial edict). . . . Next, we find *li k'o*, glossed as "bientôt" (soon). . . . The fifth syllable or character is *chàng*, meaning "aller à" (go to). This is followed by the name of the province written with characters transcribed by Couvreur as *kān* and *siŭ*. Completing the verbal idea of the fifth syllable is the next character, *k'iú*, also glossed "aller" (go). The final characters make up another compound: *k'in ts'èu*, rendered in Couvreur's dictionary as "On doit respecter cet ordre ou cet édit" (One must respect this order or this edict). The second character of the compound, *ts'èu*, is assigned meanings "celui-ci, ceci" (this

one, this). . . . It is clear that Morand's choice of syllables was not haphazard. He was helped with the invention of the plausible sentence in Chinese. . . .

Mr. Doolittle does as exhorted by the ghost, with the result that there ensues a "fracas épouvantable" (frightful din).

Mr. U thanks him; he must take leave because the white cock is about to crow. This concurs with V. P. Burkhardt's statement in *Chinese Creeds and Customs,* VIII: "Ghosts are essentially nocturnal, and fade at cockcrow which heralds the dawn."

As he departs, he gives Mr. Doolittle some money, as he says. Mr. Doolittle returns home, and the next morning reads in his copy of the *New York Times* that the funerary statuettes have disappeared from their Fifth Avenue temporary abode. He checks the bag of money given him by the ghost and discovers that it contains Chinese funeral paper money. This special paper money is described on page 714 of the second volume of J. J. M. de Groot's *The Religious Systems of China*.

We have mentioned that **"Mr. U"** was written following the author's trip to the Far East in 1925; Paul Morand has sketched more specifically the impetus for this story in a letter to me dated April 20, 1961: "J'admire, depuis mon voyage à Péking 1925, le père Léon Wieger, que St. John Perse et Philippe Berthelot appréciaient, surtous pour ses contes folkloriques." (I have admired since my trip to Peking in 1925 Father Léon Wieger, whom St. John Perse and Philippe Berthelot appreciated, especially for his folklore tales.)

Indeed, Paul Morand dedicated **"Mr. U"** to this same Father Léon Wieger (1856-1933), eminent French Sinologist.

It is possible to find on page 294-296 of Father Wieger's *Folk-Lore Chinois Moderne* in French and in the original Chinese a folk-tale which has many of the elements of Morand's story. The same folk-tale from the tenth century *Kwang I Ki* is given in Chinese as well as in English on pages 809-810 of the second volume of de Groot's *The Religious System of China*.

Father Wieger's explanatory note following his French translation of the old Chinese folk-tale provided Paul Morand with the idea of earthly authority over the dead: "Par ordre impérial, les figurines se laissèrent décapiter. Sans cela, elles auraient résisté. Extension de l'autorité terrestre sur les êtres infernaux." (By imperial command, the figurines let themselves be beheaded. Otherwise, they would have resisted. Extension of earthly authority over the beings in hell.)

Note the use of the same words in the ghost's explanation to Mr. Doolittle: ". . . vous ne savez peut-être pas qu'il y a extension de l'autorité terrestre sur les êtres infernaux . . ." (. . . you do not perhaps know that there is extension of earthly authority over the beings in hell . . .)

Lest this similarity be thought to suggest that Morand was guilty of plagiarism, we hasten to assure the reader that Morand's use of the folk-tale is original and creative; it is imaginative re-working of the Chinese original and deftly coördinated with the contrasting depiction of Mr. Doolittle, the twentieth-century Irishman in New York City.

Elements which we have noted as evincing detailed knowledge of China on Morand's part such as the white cock, the proverb about the advantage of having an ugly wife, the reference to the pauper spirits, suicide as a form of vengeance, the crowing of the cock are not found in the Chinese folk-tale which may be summarized briefly.

A traveling merchant becomes acquainted with a stranger who reveals himself to the merchant as a ghost; he asks him to do him a favor so as to discipline the unruly figurines that were buried with him in his tomb. The merchant is to cry out: "Ordre impérial de décapiter toute cette racaille d'or et d'argent!" (Imperial order to decapitate all this gold and silver rabble!)

The merchant, like Mr. Doolittle in Morand's story, complies with the request of the ghost. As reward he receives some decapitated gold and silver men and horses. When the merchant reaches Ch'ang-ngan city, he tries to sell the objects but is suspected of having stolen them from a tomb. When he explains what had happened, the tomb is opened and inspected; hundreds of gold and silver decapitated men and horses are found there.

The voicing of the imperial order to funerary statuettes by a living person in order to help a ghost in distress is the pivot about which each story turns. In both cases the order is obeyed, and in both the ghost rewards his helper.

Another parallel is afforded by the immediate result of voicing the imperial order. Corresponding to the "fracas épouvantable" (frightful din) of Morand is the "bruit sourd que rend le glaive du bourreau aux grandes exécutions" (muffled noise made by the executioner's sword at big executions).

But the total effect of the Morand story is very different from that of the Wieger folk-tale. Part of the virtue of the former is the result of the contrast between the representative of ancient China's past and the twentieth-century Westerner. Wit and mockery add to the Morand treatment.

An example of the play on words for which Morand is famous is the following:

> "Je me sens perdu dans votre contrée lointaine où les maisons ont plus d'un étage et les femmes de grands pieds plats, où l'on ne rencontre aucun lama jaune ni aucun chameau . . ." (I feel lost in your distant country where the houses have more than one story and the women large flat feet, where one does not meet any yellow lama or any camel . . .)

It may not be necessary to dwell upon the effectiveness of the understatement in the description of the houses in New York City as having more than one story, but it may be useful to point out the humor of the ambiguousness of the word *lama* in this context.

The English translation of **"Mr. U"** which was published in *Living Age* (CCCXXX, No. 4280, July 17, 1926) on pages 154-157 chooses to render Morand's *lama* as "llama." It is, however, unlikely that a Chinese ghost would have "llama" in mind; it is much more likely that the Tibetan "lama" is meant. The modern French reader associates both Peruvian "llama" and Tibetan "lama" with the word *lama,* and the appearance of the word *chameau* humorously accentuates the possibility that this *lama* is the South American one. The humor of Morand's sentence is of more than one level here: the implied comparisons between the *maisons* and the *femmes,* the *étages* and the *pieds,* as well as the ambiguous application of *jaune* (because of the "yellow hats" of the *lamas,* their complexion, or the color of the fur) are mirth-rousers.

"Mr. U" appeared in a different English version in M. E. Speare's edition of *Great French Short Stories* and probably elsewhere. Morand's story has been published in French several times, and, as far as I can determine, no one version is exactly like any other. . . .

This study of **"Mr. U"** has demonstrated that Chinese influence, direct or indirect, on a twentieth-century European writer may result in an inspiring glimpse at Chinese civilization. At the same time it has afforded an insight into Morand's technique, which not only makes effective use of an exotic theme, but handles the smallest details with craftsmanship. It represents the appreciation of the work of a French Sinologist, Father Wieger, by a distinguished literary artist. The balanced mixture of folk-lore and satire set against the background of ancient China and modern New York make **"Mr. U"** as readable today as it was almost forty years ago.

Kirkus Reviews **(essay date 1984)**

SOURCE: A review of *Fancy Goods; Open All Night: Stories,* in *Kirkus Reviews,* Vol. LII, No. I, January 1, 1984, p. 12.

[*In the following excerpt, the critic delivers a harsh assessment of* Fancy Goods; Open All Night: Stories.]

Written in 1921 and 1922 by French writer Morand (1888-1976), these sketches of Parisian flappers [in *Fancy Goods; Open All Night: Stories*] would hardly be a candidate for 1980s rediscovery—if it were not for the fact that they were translated by Ezra Pound; those translations never saw print back in the 1920s but were found in a trunk in Virginia in 1976. And it's not difficult to see why (financial reasons aside) these two groups of stories might have appealed to Pound—considering his interest in the condensation of linguistic imagery. (An example of Morand's prose: "No hollow whitewashed apple tree could avoid bending over water reflecting the clouds, weighted with a boat and the odors of an alcohol lamp.") But Morand's work itself—portraits of seductive, neurotic women—is thin, mannered, recherché; only one story ("**Borealis,**" the last piece in **Open All Night**) has a flavor of comedy and oddness about it—with musings on German nudism adding to the sketch of yet another burstingly *interesting* young woman. So this is a literary curiosity-item for the most part, complete with Marcel Proust's preface to *Fancy Goods*—which hardly mentions Morand's work . . . but later was to become an intelligent section of *Contre Sainte Beuve*.

Patrick McCarthy (essay date 1992)

SOURCE: "The Evils of Modernity," in *The Times Literary Supplement,* No. 4678, November 27, 1992, p. 17.

[*In the following review, McCarthy perceives misogynistic, racist, and anti-Semitic themes in the works collected in Morand's* Nouvelles complètes.]

This new volume [*Nouvelles complètes,* edited by Michel Collomb] in the Bibliothèque de la Pléiade contains Paul Morand's early short stories, from *Tendres Stocks* (1921) to *Flèche d'Orient* (1932). Since his stories are better than his novels and his early writing better than his later, the *Nouvelles complètes* contains Morand's best work. His novels are tedious, because he was convinced that the modern world was dazzling but appalling; his characters do not evolve, their dreams die and we no longer believe in them. Morand's talent resembles a brief, penetrating glance, which isolates a fragment but is simultaneously aware of all that it is omitting.

Tendres Stocks consists not even of stories, but sketches: three portraits of women living in First World War and post-war London. The setting is wilfully exotic: American heiresses first with Bolshevik spies in the Café Royal or during the Oxford and Cambridge boat race. The depiction of the fashionable world, in which Morand chose to spend a good deal of his life, was so convincing that several elegant women, among them Nancy Cunard, wondered whether the author had used them as models. Morand also parodies himself when he describes how the man-hating huntress, Aurore, who has dispatched countless Canadian deer, is reduced to ambling through the New Forest wearing nothing but a scanty tunic. The language of these sketches is mannered, yet behind their intelligent kitsch lies the serious theme of the war between the sexes, which has somehow been provoked by the Great War itself. When the narrator asks Clarisse whether she loves him, she replies that she is merely displeased when he is absent from London. Although she is a caricature, Aurore too is a model of the self-sufficient woman who does not need men either in or out of bed. In all three sketches the narrator fails to understand, much less to conquer, the heroines, and, despite the title, there is little tenderness in this precociously mature first book (whose introduction, significantly, was by Proust).

Ouvert la Nuit (1922) and *Fermé la Nuit* (1923) continue to use the male language of seduction and domination in order to demonstrate how remote women really are. Isabelle makes love with the narrator in a taxi on the evening they first meet, but just as quickly betrays him with other partners, one of whom is a woman. Lesbianism indeed haunts Morand's narrators, because it is a realm which they are not allowed to enter. Another of these narrators is a government minister who cannot concentrate on the collapse of the government because he is wondering whether his Denyse is making love with another woman. Morand mocks himself in a story in which the narrator pursues the mistress of a cycling champion. At the moment when she takes it into her head to surrender to him he decides he prefers the cyclist, who has sweaty thighs and smells of iodine. One doubts whether Morand has many feminist readers.

One reason why women readers may spurn Morand is that his discomfort at the revelation of sexual difference takes the form of hatred. His heroines turn out badly: Isabelle is murdered by a male lover, while Anna, a Russian aristocrat who has been ruined by the Bolsheviks, plans to come to Paris in order to commit suicide. Several others of his heroines have nervous breakdowns, presumably as a punishment for their rejection of men; just as often the punishment is inflicted directly by a man. Again, Morand parodies this theme in a story in which Habib, a plastic surgeon, tortures the bodies of his female patients. As he heaps mud on their faces or sends electric shocks through a dancer's long legs, he is expressing Morand's resentment of a beauty which men cannot possess.

When *Tendres Stocks* appeared, reviewers compared Morand with Valery Larbaud, and the parallels between the two writers are obvious: the themes of travel, cosmopolitanism and luxury and the flippant tone. However, the differences are more significant, and they appear in the way that women are depicted. In Larbaud's post-war stories, *Amants heureux amants,* the heroes' pursuit of fresh conquests is also a flight from women, but this fear is avowed and never turns into hatred.

Larbaud was able also to relish the modernity of the 1920s and to see in avant-garde culture a fresh upsurge of liberation. By contrast, Morand, although he was born in 1888, only seven years after Larbaud, perceives the pre-war period as a vanished Utopia of stability, and is obsessed by the war as the harbinger of a new and dangerous era. It has spawned the breed of emancipated women: "A generation has been sacrificed; the men have become soldiers and the women have gone mad." More generally, it marks the destruction of the old order: Habib, the plastic surgeon, has arrived in London precisely when "the good things of this world are passing from the hands of English lords into the hands of Russian Jews". Where Larbaud sees unity, Morand sees disintegration. Coming from a family which had lived in St Petersburg, he was struck by the plight of the Russian *émigrés*. Married to Hélène Soutzo, who came of a rich Greek banking family and had been married to a Romanian nobleman, he was attentive to the disorders in Central Europe which followed the collapse of the Habsburg Empire. As a diplomat, he studied such catastrophes but was sheltered against them.

By the time he published *L'Europe galante* in 1925, Morand's best work was already done and he was starting to repeat himself. His descriptions of women become predictable: "Paula is all white. She accentuates it. Her face is a disk of white velvet criss-crossed with red lines." When one reads a story of three women describing the men they love, one has a shrewd suspicion that although the men seem very different, they will turn out to be one and the same person.

A more serious defect is Morand's growing racism. Michel Collomb suggests that because he saw modernity as disintegration, Morand sought points of stability in the concepts of gender and race. He read Gobineau and decided that each race had its own order, which it must follow if it is not to be destroyed. From here it was a short step to asserting that humans with black skins should live in jungles and practise voodoo, that the mixture of races was a bad thing and that the disease of modernity was transmitted by black American jazz musicians. The second of these propositions had already been suggested in *Ouvert la Nuit,* where Isabelle's murderer is of mixed parentage. Fuller treatment comes in *Magie noire* (1928), where an American woman, whose mother was black and father white, abandons white America, depicted by Morand as riddled with prejudice, and finds happiness in an African tribe as the concubine of a handsome medicineman.

The idea that blacks—like women—are responsible for modernity is made with the usual complacent irony that renders it palatable rather than ridiculous: "Ours is an age of blacks. Consider the general laziness, the contempt young people feel for work, the nudity whether at the Lido or at Palm Beach." The standard-bearer of egalitarianism is the black American dancer Congo, modelled on Josephine Baker, who launches Paris into a frenzy of joy, where notions of social hierarchy and of individualism itself are abolished. However, here again punishment is at hand. By exchanging the Mississippi Delta for Paris and by not returning to embrace her dying grandmother, Congo has offended the voodoo gods. At the end of the story the waters of the great river close over her and over her luxurious automobile. White civilization, one supposes, has been saved.

Despite such dangerous absurdities, Morand does offer insights into Europe's dealings with other cultures. Later in *Magie noire* he depicts an African tribe that burns down its village. Although it is acting in blind obedience to instructions from its medicine-men, it is also rebelling against the introduction of a colonial economy, in which it will grow cash crops in return for an individual wage.

However, the blame for this aggression is placed not on the French colonial officials but on two greedy, rootless Syrian traders.

But Morand's resentment of modernity is more often directed against the Jews. In *Ouvert la Nuit* he depicts the murder of a Jewish woman in Admiral Horthy's Hungary and shows an understanding of the appalling arbitrariness of anti-Semitic violence. But this did not prevent him from publishing *France la Doulce* (1934), an anti-Semitic novel about Jewish refugees from Germany who take over the French film industry. Here again, Morand's ability to analyse the evils of the inter-war period did not grant him immunity to them.

It was no coincidence then that he should have become an ambassador under the Vichy regime. In June 1940, he was in London at the head of a French delegation dealing with economic warfare. He received overtures from the Gaullists, to which he responded by attacking de Gaulle, while the new Vichy government asked him to stay in London as its contact with the British authorities. Instead, Morand went scuttling back to France. The irritated Quai d'Orsay would not give him another post, but he went over the civil servants' heads to none other than Pierre Laval. On his return to power in 1942, Laval first appointed Morand as his adviser and then got him the job of special envoy to Romania. Morand arrived in Bucharest in August 1943, and seems to have spent most of his time dodging the Allied bombing and wondering how he could leave the capital before the Red Army marched in. In May 1944, he fled again, having pulled enough strings to get himself appointed ambassador to the rather safer country of Switzerland. He remained ambassador there until the Vichy government itself fled in August of that year. The moral of this tale is not Morand's comic blend of opportunism and political ineptitude but rather that Vichy accorded him special treatment because it recognized in him a natural supporter.

Michel Collomb also offers us a literary curiosity in this volume: *East India and Company,* a series of stories which Morand wrote for *Vanity Fair* in 1926-7 and which he never published in French. These are slight pieces that repeat his usual themes, such as the perils of interracial marriages. A Chinese man who marries an Irish woman locks her up in a cage, where she is presumably delighted to play out her own racial role as victim. The curious feature of these stories is that, in order to make his work more accessible to the American public, Morand has adopted many of the mannerisms of Somerset Maugham. They are, however, mere mannerisms, and, if one were to seek out an English author with whom to compare Morand, the most likely candidate would be Evelyn Waugh. Morand could not have written the Guy Crouchback trilogy but his best books remind one of *Black Mischief* and *Vile Bodies.* This is no small achievement.

Additional coverage of Morand's life and career is contained in the following sources published by Gale Research: *Contemporary Authors,* Vols. 69-72; *Contemporary Literary Criticism,* Vol. 41; *Dictionary of Literary Biography,* Vol. 65; and *Major 20th-Century Writers.*

Mary N. Murfree
1850–1922

(Full name Mary Noailles Murfree; wrote under the pseudonyms Charles Egbert Craddock and R. Emmet Dembry) American short story writer and novelist.

INTRODUCTION

Murfree was one of America's foremost "local color" writers of the nineteenth century. Although she wrote about many themes, including the Civil War, Southern society, and colonial history, her reputation rests primarily on her unique stories of life in the mountains of Tennessee. In such works as the acclaimed collection of stories *In the Tennessee Mountains* and the novel *The Prophet of the Great Smoky Mountains,* Murfree used elaborately detailed descriptions and distinctive dialect in the speech of her characters to vividly evoke the singularity of her remote settings and their inhabitants. In her day Murfree was hailed as a highly original writer who brought to life a little known but characteristically American milieu.

Biographical Information

Murfree was born in Murfreesboro, Tennessee, into the prominent family after which the town was named. Both her father, lawyer William Law Murfree, and her mother, Fanny Priscilla Dickinson Murfree, were devoted patrons of the arts, and Murfree grew up in a cultured atmosphere that nurtured her literary interests. Throughout her childhood Murfree and her family spent the summer months at a resort in the Cumberland Mountains; there she encountered the rural life that would figure prominently in her later writings. In 1857 Murfree's family moved to Nashville, where Murfree attended the Nashville Female Academy. At seventeen she was admitted to the Chegary Institute in Philadelphia, a finishing school for girls. During her two-year attendance there she developed a passion for music and began to write poetry. She returned to Nashville in 1869, and three years later moved back into the family home in Murfreesboro which had been rebuilt after being destroyed during the Civil War. Murfree began writing in earnest in 1872 and published her first story two years later in *Lippincott's* magazine. Her first volume of stories, *In the Tennessee Mountains,* was published in 1884. Between that year and 1914, Murfree produced twenty-five books: eighteen novels and seven story collections. In 1922, the year in which she received an honorary degree from the University of the South, Murfree fell ill and was confined to a wheelchair. She died in July of that year.

Major Works of Short Fiction

In the Tennessee Mountains is widely regarded as Murfree's finest volume of short stories. Featuring eight stories,

including "The Dancin' Party at Harrison's Cove" and "The 'Harnt' That Walks Chilhowee," this collection was her greatest popular and critical success. Her first book, *In the Tennessee Mountains* established the themes, character types, moods, settings, and style that Murfree would employ in many of her novels and later stories. The pieces in the collection typically present a portrait of mountain life, providing closely observed descriptions of the circumscribed lives of the rustic men and women who inhabit the remote hill country of Tennessee. Confined to a narrow sphere of experience, Murfree's characters are governed principally by their relations to the natural world and the traditional modes of behavior they have inherited. As a result of their circumscribed situations, Murfree's figures are often simple stereotypes rather than fully realized individuals; nevertheless the author does infuse some of them with a certain dignity. This quality is evident, for instance, in Murfree's crediting the "sympathetic heart of the multitude, so quick to respond to a noble impulse" for Rufus Chadd's electoral victory in "Electioneerin' on Big Injun Mounting." Also characteristic of the short stories in *In the Tennessee Mountains* is Murfree's intense focus on describing the mountain scenery. Her elaborate, often poetic descriptions of the mountains; the sun, moon, and stars; and other natural phenomena in effect render nature one of the major characters in the stories. Moreover, Murfree often used nature imagery and juxtapositions with natural elements as devices to characterize her human figures. As William Malone Baskervill has pointed out, "the scenery of the mountains is essential to the comprehension of the gloom of the religion, the sternness of life, the uncouthness of the dialect, and the harshness of the characters presented in her stories."

Critical Reception

In the Tennessee Mountains was the basis for Murfree's reputation as an important local colorist. Baskervill has stated that when the book was released, "it was at once recognized that another Southern writer of uncommon art, originality, and power had entered into a field altogether new and perfectly fresh." Many reviewers admired the apparent authenticity of Murfree's sympathetic depictions of the ordinary lives of mountaineers with their exotic yet uniquely American dialect and traditions. However, as Murfree repeatedly returned in her novels and short stories to the limited world she had created, reviewers became disaffected and her popularity declined. Today her works are regarded as of historical interest only, important merely as a part of the local color movement at its height.

PRINCIPAL WORKS

Short Fiction

In the Tennessee Mountains 1884
The Phantoms of the Foot-Bridge and Other Stories 1895
The Mystery of Witch-Face Mountain and Other Stories 1895
The Young Mountaineers 1897
The Bushwhackers and Other Stories 1899
The Frontiersmen 1904
The Raid of the Guerilla and Other Stories 1912

Other Major Works

Where the Battle Was Fought (novel) 1884
Down the Ravine (novel) 1885
The Prophet of the Great Smoky Mountains (novel) 1885
In the Clouds (novel) 1886
The Story of Keedon Bluffs (novel) 1887
The Despot of Broomsedge Cove (novel) 1888
In the "Stranger People's" Country (novel) 1891
His Vanished Star (novel) 1894
The Juggler (novel) 1897
The Story of Old Fort Loudon (novel) 1899
The Champion (novel) 1902
A Spectre of Power (novel) 1904
The Storm Centre (novel) 1905
The Amulet (novel) 1906
The Windfall (novel) 1907
The Fair Mississippian (novel) 1908
The Ordeal: A Mountain Romance of Tennessee (novel) 1912

The Story of Duciehurst: A Tale of the Mississippi (novel) 1914

CRITICISM

William Malone Baskervill (essay date 1897)

SOURCE: "Charles Egbert Craddock," in *Southern Writers: Biographical and Critical Studies, Vol. 1,* M. E. Church, 1897, pp. 357-404.

[*In the following excerpt, Baskervill surveys Murfree's work, noting influences on her writng, and commenting on her characterizations, descriptions, use of humor, and literary style in general.*]

[Murfree perceived the] elemental qualities of our common humanity, but also the sturdy independence, integrity, strength of character, and finer feelings always found in the English race, however disguised by rugged exterior or hindered by harsh environment. Their honesty, their patriotism, their respect for law, their gloomy Calvinistic religion, their hospitality were in spite of the most curious modifications the salient points of a striking individuality and unique character. The mountains seemed to impart to them something of their own dignity, solemnity and silence. . . .

No phase of [their] unique life escaped the keen eye and powerful imagination of the most robust of Southern writers in this most impressible period of her life.

The growth of Craddock's art can not now be traced with certainty, though it is known that she served an apprenticeship of nearly ten years before her stories began to make any stir in the world. The general belief, therefore, that her literary career began with the **"Dancin' Party at Harrison's Cove,"** which appeared in the *Atlantic* for May, 1878, is incorrect. She used to contribute to the weekly edition of *Appleton's Journal,* which ceased publication in that form in 1876, and it is a little remarkable that her contributions were even then signed Charles E. Craddock. Two of her stories were left over, and one of them, published in *Appleton's Summer Book,* in 1880, **"Taking the Blue Ribbon at the Fair,"** rather indicates that she had not yet discovered wherein her true power lay. Although it is a pleasing little story, it is not specially remarkable for any of the finer qualities of her later writings; and it appears out of place in a collection of stories published in 1895, as if it were a new production. The assumed name which her writings bore was finally determined upon by accident, though the matter had been much discussed in her family. It was adopted for the double purpose of cloaking failure and of securing the advantage which a man is supposed to have over a woman in literature. It veiled one of the best-concealed identities in literary history. More than one person divined George Eliot's secret, and the penetrating Dickens observed that she knew what was in the heart of woman. But neither internal nor external evidence offered any clue to Craddock's personality. The startlingly vigorous and robust style and the intimate knowledge of the mountain folk in their almost inaccessible homes, suggestive of the sturdy climber and bold adventurer, gave no hint of femininity, while certain portions of her writings, both in thought and treatment, were peculiarly masculine. . . .

Miss Murfree's literary success really began with the publication of her collection of short stories, *In the Tennessee Mountains,* in May, 1884. It was at once recognized that another Southern writer of uncommon art, originality, and power had entered into a field altogether new and perfectly fresh. Only here and there was discernible the slightest trace of imitation in conception or manner, while the atmosphere was entirely her own; and to the rare qualities of sincerity, simplicity, and closeness of observation were added the more striking ones of vivid realization and picturing of scene and incident and character. Her magic wand revealed the poetry as well as the pathos in the hard, narrow, and monotonous life of the mountaineers, and touched crag and stream and wood and mountain range with an enduring splendor. All the admirable qualities of her art are present in this volume. The spontaneous, instinctive power of telling a story for its own sake proclaimed close kinship with Scott, while the exquisite word-painting and beautiful descriptions of mountain scenery, with all the shifting phases of spring and autumn, of sunset, mist, storm, and forest fire, could have been learned only in the school of Ruskin and of nature. In the profound and tragically serious view and contemplation of life she is the child of George Eliot and of the battle-scarred South. But her real power, as is true of every writer that has been either an enriching or an uplifting force in human lives, rests upon a sympathetic understanding of human life. Her insight into the ordinary, commonplace, seemingly unpoetic lives of the mountaineers, her tenderness for them, her perception of the beauty and the wonder of their narrow existence is one of the finest traits in her character and her art. Through this wonderful power of human sympathy the delicately nurtured and highly cultured lady entered into the life of the common folk and heard their heart-throbs underneath jeans and homespun. She realized anew for her fellow men that untutored souls are perplexed with the same questions and shaken by the same doubts that baffle the learned, and that it is inherent in humanity to rise to the heroic heights of self-forgetfulness and devotion to duty in any environment. Indeed, the key-note of her studies is found in the last sentence of this volume: "The grace of culture is, in its way, a fine thing, but the best that art can do—the polish of a gentleman—is hardly equal to the best that nature can do in her higher moods."

Each of these stories embodies a "higher mood" of some uncultivated, simple soul influenced by a noble motive, and the good lesson taught with equal art and modesty stirs the heart with refining pity and admiration. Cynthia Ware's long journeys on foot and heroic exertions are rewarded with the pardon of the unjustly imprisoned man whom she loves, only to find that he has never taken the trouble to ask who secured his release, that his love was

but a little thing which he had left in the mountains, and that while she was waiting for him he was married to some one else. Through Craddock's skill we become witnesses of this heart tragedy and enter into the inner experience of a human soul which through suffering learns to adjust itself anew, "ceases to question and regret, and bravely does the work nearest her hand. . . ." Again it is the weak and slender Celia Shaw who painfully toils at night through the bleak, snow-covered woods to save the lives of the men whom her father and his friends had determined to "wipe out." Again and again in Craddock's writings the strange miracle of this sweet, trustful, loving, yet heroic girlhood appears amid the lonely, half-mournful life of the mountain folk, intensified by the attitude of the faded, gaunt, melancholy older women, "holding out wasted hands to the years as they pass—holding them out always and always empty"—with the grace, the beauty, and the pervasive fragrance of a wild rose in the wilderness. Our author seems to agree with George Eliot in thinking that "in these delicate vessels is borne on through the ages the treasure of human affections."

Craddock's heroes—blacksmiths, constables, herders, illiterate preachers, and other rude mountaineers—are equally attractive in their way, and are drawn with an even tenderer and more skilful hand. She is a master in depicting those situations which touch the springs of pathos or thrill the heart with a generous elation. . . .

The central idea or the strong situation, however, is not unduly stressed. The touches of incident and of humor and the exquisite landscapes leave unfading impressions. . . .

The large and solemn presence of Nature is never lost sight of, her various moods and manifestations being used, as a kind of chorus to interpret the melancholy or the emotion of the human actors. The narrative is inlaid with exquisite bits of landscape, serving not so much to disclose the range and minuteness of the author's observation—at least in her earlier works—as to give expression to the fitting sentiment or development to the appropriate passion. When the great beauty of the style with which these fresh and robust stories were clothed is taken into consideration, something of the present pleasure and the richer anticipation of the readers of 1884 may be imagined. . . .

[Almost] every year since that time has witnessed the appearance of some new volume. . . .

Though the result is on the whole disappointing—the rare promise of the author's earlier work not being fulfilled in her later more labored efforts. Miss Murfree has taken a place among the very best writers of purely American fiction. The too great regularity of production in which she has indulged has led her into dreary wastes of repetitious shallows, and still more frequently has weighted her stories with mannerisms which mar the beauty and perfection of their art. . . .

A still more serious complaint may be urged against the author's tendency to overdo landscape pictures, and to make needless digressions. Miss Murfree is, above all things, a painter, and particularly in her earlier works has given abundant evidence that she is a real artist in adapting story and landscape to each other. Her description, too, serves a literary purpose, now expressing the fitting sentiment, anon developing the appropriate passion. She seizes and interprets physical features and natural phenomena in their relation to various aspects of human life with at times unerring precision, vigor, and dramatic force. Indeed, the scenery of the mountains is essential to the comprehension of the gloom of the religion, the sternness of the life, the uncouthness of the dialect, and the harshness of the characters presented in her stories.

> **Murfree's insight into the ordinary, commonplace, seemingly unpoetic lives of the mountaineers, her tenderness for them, her perception of the beauty and the wonder of their narrow existence is one of the finest traits in her character and her art.**
>
> **—*William Malone Baskervill***

All her digressions are not irrelevant. Oftentimes what seems to be a mere digression is according to nature, and used with significant effect in the presentation of mountain scene, life, and character. The result is a complete and perfect picture. The mountaineers are proverbially slow of speech and of thought, and during their long reflective pauses in conversation the skilful narrator must interest the mind of the reader just as in real life the listener would seek something for his mind to dwell upon. This gives lifelikeness to the picture, and, like a sweet interlude in music, a charming bit of description serves to fill in delightfully the intervening moments which would otherwise seem unreasonably long and tedious. The opening pages of *The Despot of Broomsedge Cove* reveal the author at work in her happiest vein and making the best use of this extraordinary gift. With a few skilful touches the corn-field, the winding road, the three mountaineers, each with his salient features of look, gait, and character, made known in the fewest possible words, and the glorious mountain view, are made to stand out before us as in real life, so that the reader becomes identified with the story and naturally shares in the conversation. . . .

But far too often in her later stories the author's descriptions of natural scenery and observations of natural phenomena are excessive. . . . In this particular novel they reach the point of downright padding. The pictures are exceedingly well done, and the observations are sometimes very acute and perfectly true; but they are altogether out of place, and serve only to interrupt the action and to make the reader chafe, till he learns to skip. . . . It may readily be acknowledged that Miss Murfree's people are the people of the district she describes. Folk and mountains belong together. But she deals with life rather as a whole, as a community, a class, at best as a type. She has not succeeded in creating any individual or distinct character. Even Cynthia Ware, Dorinda Cayce, Alethea Sayles, Letitia Pettingill, and Marcelly Strobe, the heroines in as many different stories, are but variants of one and the same type. Slight changes are introduced in adapting them to different situations, but the characters all seem to be drawn from the same model. A graver defect is noticeable in the author's treatment of her heroes, wherein she shows a fatal inability to sustain character. When the Prophet is introduced, revealing in the quick glance of his eye "fire, inspiration, frenzy—who can say?" the reader is thrilled at the prospect of a masterly delineation. He expects to travel along the narrow border-land between spiritual exaltation and insanity. But in only one of Miss Murfree's stories, **"The Dancin' Party at Harrison's Cove,"** does she reveal a sympathetic understanding and appreciation of the character of the minister. With the circuit-riders and pa'sons she seems to have had no personal acquaintance. They are drawn just as we would expect them to be depicted by one whose sole information was based on tradition, hearsay, and imagination. Nor does Craddock at any time exhibit that profound knowledge of the human heart and sympathetic insight into spiritual matters revealed by George Eliot in the character of Dinah Morris. Pa'son Kelsey remains hazy and indistinct throughout the story, the reader is left in doubt as to his sanity, and the catastrophe throws little light upon his character.

The Despot [in *The Despot of Broomsedge Cove*] offered even a greater opportunity for masterly portraiture. In conception this is one of the most original and striking figures to be found in contemporary literature. . . .

After a few chapters, however, the author seems to lose interest in the working out of her original conception. The hero is discarded for other matters, while at the same time the author's grip of the narrative suffers loss, and the way is paved for irrelevant landscapes and digressions. Even the hero's connection with the tragedy of the story is accidental, and the heroine gradually absorbs the interest and the attention of the reader. The author almost invariably leaves her chief characters looking sadly, if not hopelessly, into the future.

Perhaps Miss Murfree has attempted an impossible task in seeking to invest the meager life and primitive character of the mountaineers with an annual interest. . . .

But the sweep and power of Miss Murfree's narrative in all her finer stories is sufficient to carry the reader over greater difficulties than these. Story-telling is her true vocation. She is no essayist or historian drawn by the fashion of the time into the facile fields of fiction. Fresh material and picturesque character lend, it is true, their unique charms; but, after all, we are interested in this writer chiefly on account of the stories she has to tell of the lives of men and women whose traits are in common with those of all times and all places. While, however, the reader's desire is to reach the end of any of her stories and "see how it comes out," still there are many places where he delights to linger. There are whole chapters in which scene, situation, and incident are handled without a flaw. The situations are admirably planned, the incidents inimitably related. The author can be descriptive or dramatic at will, and shows the command of a humor which has the tang but not the deep thought and mellow wisdom of George Eliot's. . . .

Nor would it be true to life if the humor were left out. . . . It is a characteristic of the race. The Tennessee mountaineer is noted for his dry, caustic speech, and under his slow drawl and rustic manners are concealed no little practical wisdom and shrewd observation. Of course geniality and playful fancy do not flourish in so harsh a region, but there is no lack of pungent, pithy sayings. This humor pervades the mountains. . . .

Without this pungent humor the distinct flavor of the inner life of the strange, unique inhabitants of the mountains would be lost.

Here, then, we have originality, robust vigor, womanly insight, and the charm of a born story-teller brought to bear with genuine art upon a fresh field and a unique civilization. Much of her later work may have suffered from an attachment to the narrow sphere of the mountain folk; but such are her strength of purpose and great capability that it is not unreasonable yet to expect the complete fulfilment of the promise of her earlier work, if the larger world may demand a share of her attention and energies.

The New York Times Book Review (essay date 1899)

SOURCE: "Miss Murfree's New Book," in *The New York Times Book Review*, July 29, 1899, p. 499.

[*The anonymous critic, evaluating* The Bushwhackers and Other Stories, *finds the volume stylistically weaker and less interesting oveall than Murfree's previous work.*]

Charles Egbert Craddock is the pen name of a lady who writes many interesting stories, and it is only fair to say that most of them are more interesting than those which go to make up [*The Bushwhackers and Other Stories*]. Nevertheless these are a fairly good lot, as the auctioneers would put it. The title of the volume is taken from a story in which it must be said that the "Bushwhackers" do not play a very conspicuous part. Perhaps the author has been going to the theatre and has learned that the name of a play is not always indissolubly associated with the subject matter. This acceptance of a side issue as a

suggestion for a title is, however, more frequently met with in the profession which always has the billboard in mind than in that which has only the newspaper advertisement to consider.

"The Bushwhackers" is a dialect story. The author having made a reputation as a writer of tales of the Tennessee mountains, must perforce remain forever among those who say "we-uns" and "you-uns." The hero of this little tale talks in a manner which will delight all those who find no comfort in plain English. He would probably prove to be a highly uninteresting youth in real life, but in this tale he is a character study, and therefore he is to be accepted as something out of the ordinary. He is full of ambition to go to the war and serve as a cavalryman. He accomplishes his purpose, and loses his arm through the treachery of one of his comrades. He afterward saves this same fellow when he is caught in a tight place. That is what makes him a hero. The heroine is a pale and indefinite figure, who serves no good purpose in the tale except to refuse to admire a man with one arm, and afterward to take pity on him and accept him. This is a truly feminine performance, but it is not at all new in fiction.

The story is written in a very plain and unvarnished style. Indeed, it would probably be regarded as a thin and weak style if it had been put forth by one of the unknown. But a famous author may do many things which a young and yet uncelebrated one would not dare to think of attempting. Here is a specimen of the author's descriptive writing as shown in the present volume.

> There was a fine panorama once in the twilight when a battery on the heights shelled the woods in the valley, and tiny white clouds, with hearts of darting fire described swift aerial curves, the fuses burning brightly against the bland blue sky, ere that supreme moment of explosion when the bursting fragments hurtled wildly through the air.

It is not kind of an author to startle a reader by such an abrupt transition from the figurative to the literal. How is the reader to know from anything which the author says that the author is aware of the great natural truth that clouds do not have fuses? And then that wild hurtling of fragments through the air has been done to death by the newspaper correspondents. The Spanish war brought out all those old familiar formulas which had rested since the civil war. Perhaps, as the author now under discussion was writing about the civil war, she had the right to use the expression of the time.

The other stories in this volume are entitled **"The Panther of Jolton's Ridge"** and **"The Exploit of Choolah, the Chickasaw."** Of these two the second is the stronger tale. The first lacks directness of purpose and celerity of action. The second is stronger in the matter of character delineation. In style the three stories are much the same, and they are interesting without being striking. If the author was not already a person of repute, these tales would not make her so.

E. F. Harkins and C. H. L. Johnston (essay date 1902)

SOURCE: "Charles Egbert Craddock," in *Little Pilgrimages among the Women Who Have Written Famous Books,* L. C. Page & Company, 1902, pp. 75-90.

[*In the following excerpt, the critics recount Murfree's association with the* Atlantic Monthly *magazine.*]

It was in May, 1878, during the administration of Mr. Howells, that the readers of the *Atlantic* were treated to a most delightful, a most refreshing surprise, a story of the Tennessee Mountains, called **"The Dancin' Party at Harrison's Cove,"** by a new author, Charles Egbert Craddock.

The quaint and unprecedented strain was noticeable in the first colloquial sentence:

"'Fur ye see, Mis' Darley, them Harrison folks over yander ter the cove hev' determined on a dancin' party.'"

Mr. Howells was pleased with his discovery; the *Atlantic* readers—then the most critical literary company in America—hailed the coming of a promising author; the professional critics hesitated at first and then echoed the popular applause.

Time passed, and Mr. Aldrich took Mr. Howells's chair in the *Atlantic* office, and one of the first official acts of the new editor was to write to Charles Egbert Craddock inviting more contributions. Then, pending an answer, he ordered in two Craddock stories that had been left over by reason of a superabundance of somewhat more important material.

The response to his invitation came in the shape of a series of as excellent American stories as ever was published—**"The Star in the Valley," "The Romance of Sunrise Rock," "Over on the T'other Mounting," "The 'Harnt' that Walks Chilhowee," "Electioneerin' on Big Injun Mounting," "A-Playin' of Old Sledge at the Settlemint,"** and the exceptionally long and powerful **"Drifting Down Lost Creek,"** which ran through three numbers of the *Atlantic.* Later there appeared a novel, *Where the Battle was Fought,* a work hardly worthy of its predecessors. In time the name of Charles Egbert Craddock was signed to three books: the novel just mentioned, a collection of short stories (***In the Tennessee Mountains***), and to *Down the Ravine,* a tale for the young folks, in whom the author then took a lively interest. All in all, they were profoundly interesting stories, revealing a deep insight into the manners of the pent-up, ignorant, law-flaunting, hard-headed, and pure-hearted mountaineers. Palacio Valdes calls attention to that "beautiful spectacle"—a virginal man of eighty. John Fox, Jr., who has been walking in the footsteps of the author of ***In the Tennessee Mountains,*** once said to us that he had met Southern mountaineers who, at thirty, were as chaste as angels.

But aside from the virility of the Craddock sketches, there were more substantial marks of the author's masculine sex. There was legal acumen, for instance, which led to the assumption that Craddock was a lawyer who turned to literature for recreation. And there was the bold, manly handwriting—inky handwriting—a bottle of ink to a page. So inky, indeed, that when Mr. Aldrich thought of asking the Southerner for a serial (*The Prophet of the Great Smoky Mountains*) he remarked, "I wonder if Craddock has laid in his winter's ink yet; perhaps I can get a serial out of him. . . ."

She could not fairly be characterized as a dialect writer; her narration is generally excellent; and her power of description is especially praiseworthy. Note, for example, the life and the grace in the first lines of **"The 'Harnt' that Walks Chilhowee"**:

> The breeze freshened, after the sun went down, and the hop and gourd vines were all astir as they clung about the little porch where Clarsie was sitting now, idle at last. The rain-clouds had disappeared, and there bent over the dark, heavily wooded ridges a pale blue sky, with here and there the crystalline sparkle of a star. A halo was shimmering in the east, where the mists had gathered about the great white moon, hanging high above the mountains. Noiseless wings flitted through the dusk; now and then the bats swept by so close as to move Clarsie's hair with the wind of their flight. What an airy, glittering, magical thing was that gigantic spiderweb suspended between the silver moon and her shining eyes! Ever and anon there came from the woods a strange, weird, long-drawn sigh, unlike the stir of the wind in the trees, unlike the fret of the water on the rocks. Was it the voiceless sorrow of the sad earth? There were stars in the night besides those known to astronomers: the stellular fireflies gemmed the black shadows with a fluctuating brilliancy; they circled in and out of the porch, and touched the leaves above Clarsie's head with quivering points of light. A steadier and an intenser gleam was advancing along the road, and the sound of languid footsteps came with it; the aroma of tobacco graced the atmosphere, and a tall figure walked up to the gate.

Note—above the engaging swing of the words—the masculine touch, "the aroma of tobacco graced the atmosphere." Surely Mr. Aldrich and his associates, not to mention the readers of the *Atlantic,* were justified in thinking of "Mr. Craddock." And in the same story you will find another remarkably vivid picture, not large and overwhelming—that is not the author's style; but small and delicate, with all the scenery of a photograph but even a more impressive appearance of reality—the picture of Clarsie sitting at the window in the moonlight.

Miss Murfree's brother is our authority for the statement that "Her pictures of people are of types, not individuals; and where it is thought an individual has been drawn, it is because that person possesses, in a large degree; the peculiarities of his class." The vital fact, however, is the author's success in portraiture; her skill in infusing vitality into her picturesque characters; her artistic employment of a cultivated imaginative temperament. Her natural gifts quite suit her choice of subjects, it might be said, superficially; but beneath the surface of her success is to be seen the artistry that adorns all subjects. She is an artist, as we would say of Miss Jewett or Miss Wilkins. Like them, she would successfully hold the mirror up to nature,—anywhere. . . .

Her work is a valuable as well as entertaining contribution to American literature. Indeed, she has covered her field so well that any hope of improving upon her standard, or even of emulating it as laudably, is almost futile.

The New York Times Book Review (essay date 1904)

SOURCE: "With the Pioneers," in *The New York Times Book Review,* May 28, 1904, p. 359.

[In the following essay, the reviewer provides a favorable evaluation of The Frontiersmen.*]*

With a large class of novel readers there is always a keen sympathy with the men and women who blazed the trail on the frontier; those who defended their homesteads and stockades against fierce American Indians. . . . These readers prefer reminiscences of homely and adventurous life to the conventional society novel. Among such, Charles Egbert Craddock has made the pioneers in the frontier region that is now Tennessee a field peculiarly her own. Her newest book [*The Frontiersmen*] deals with persons and scenes with which all her readers are familiar in the Great Smoky Mountains and the Blue Lick Springs. There are eight stories about them in their log cabins, buckskin clothes and primitive forts. Each story holds the genuinely American flavor of the soil and the native wilds.

"The Linguister" is the first and the main story in the volume. The heroine of it is Peninnah Penelope Anne Mivane. No one, except her sweetheart, Ralph Emsden, ever thought of shortening it; for the wits of Blue Lick Station declared it had been given to her in the hope of adding something to her fairylike stature. Her father had been a victim to the crafty Cherokees, consequently the daughter had spent most of her girlhood in molding bullets. Her lover did his courting while he helped her. She, in turn, stood at his elbow in the bullet-riddled stockade and rammed each successive charge home with a ramrod as tall as she was. In fact, the momentous question was popped amid a bloodcurdling shout from the invading Indians as they received a charge of the bullets made by the lovers. There is a novelty in the way of a proposal, if you please.

The course of true love is sadly interfered with, in this instance by an obstreperous old Irish grandfather, who could be as deaf as an adder when he chose to be. Emsden goes off for a week's hunting and has an exciting hand-to-hand fight with a wolf. His shot maddened the cattle, which stampeded off beyond the control of the ranchmen. This was a calamity in those parts and caused no end of trouble. Grandpa Mivane was valiant enough to offer himself as ambassador to the infuriated herders and intercede for his grandchild's lover. Through him, as deftly manipulat-

ed by the wily Peninnah Penelope Anne, news was spread of a French invasion. The ranchmen promptly forgot their grievance against Emsden and rode off to protect Blue Lick Station from the French.

A messenger was hurried off to the British Commandant at Fort Prince George. The Commandant summoned, among others, Peninnah Penelope and all the rest of it, to tell the news. So bravely and deftly did she plead that she was called the little linguister. Soldiers sent out from the fort found no French, but a common cause united the cattlemen and Emsden's friends at Blue Lick Station. The girl's bravery won the day and the lovers were happy. The other stories are annals of the same adventurous Southwestern people, and are of varying interest.

G. H. Baskette (essay date 1907)

SOURCE: "Mary Noailles Murfree," in *Library of Southern Literature, Vol. VIII, Madison-Murfree,* edited by Edwin Anderson Alderman and Joel Chandler Harris, The Martin and Hoyt Company, 1907, pp. 3721-745.

[In the following excerpt, Baskette judges Murfree's mountain stories fresh and unique, and believes they constitute her strongest claim to a lasting place in Southern literature.]

In general, it may be said that Miss Murfree's writings are marked by an originality of style and method that places her among the *creative* authors of America as distinguished from many other writers of fiction who have attained reputation and popularity. This is especially true in reference to her stories of mountain life, which comprise her most noteworthy work and constitute the strongest claim to recognition of her genius and to the permanency of her place in literature. These stories are unique in their freshness of literary atmosphere, in their charm of description, and in their compass of a hitherto undeveloped and unrevealed theater of human interest. In this field the gifted author has in many respects wrought with a strikingly realistic accuracy and yet with an investment of idealism and poetic fancy that appeal very strongly to the imagination of the reader. Skilfully and wonderfully she has depicted the mountain scenery in its varying shades and aspects. With fine narrative art, with intense dramatic power, and with the touch of keen human sympathy, she has given an insight into the lives, customs, traditions, superstitions, struggles, loves and longings of a curiously quaint, yet sturdy people, who, at least before the inroads of modern enterprise had brought them into a closer contact with a progressive civilization, were singularly separate from the unfamiliar world outside their restricted environment. It must be said, however, that Miss Murfree has taken an author's license, and, by confining her delineations of character and conduct to the more uncouth representatives of the mountain people, has given the impression that there is a more general and unvarying class life than actually exists. Her characters, while in many instances subtly portrayed and differentiated, are in the main of such a uniform type that they all appear, as another writer has said, to be drawn from the same model. Nevertheless, the fact that she deals with a community class which, because of the peculiarities of its environment and mode of life, is distinct from like grades of people in districts more accessible to educational and refining influences, only emphasizes the author's art and resources. Out of the monotony of general awkwardness and uncouthness, the overshadowing pervasiveness and sameness of the mountain impression, and the drawl of persistent and unchanging dialect, she has cleverly fashioned personalities, incidents, plots, and *dénouements,* with scenic settings that are marvelous in their picturesqueness and variations. Her heroes, whether they be tillers of the scantily productive hillsides, or whether they be "moonshiners," herders, blacksmiths, traders, fanatical preachers, or refugees from justice, are given individualities that are clearly asserted in their rude manners and conduct under the influences of motives and passions that appeal to a common human nature.

Miss Murfree's mountain women are drawn with a realistic skill that makes a pathetic picture of their narrow lives and limitations. Faded old women who have worn themselves out in the routine of drudgery are especially well depicted. Her heroines, the younger women, whose characters are portrayed usually under the stress of depressing experiences, are in instances made quite attractive in native feminine grace, despite the handicap of ignorance and poverty, but in the main they are remindful of a common mold, and are made the victims of unfulfilled desires and disappointed hopes. Cynthia Ware, the heroine of **"Drifting Down Lost Creek,"** may be taken as a type. In her trustful heroism and patient suffering she makes as pathetic a figure as can be found in literature. As has been indicated, a pervading, if not dominant feature of this class of Miss Murfree's stories, and one made prominent in all her works is her descriptive writing. Her descriptions of mountain scenery are exceptionally fine—indeed, unsurpassed—and they are multiplied throughout her stories with wonderful frequency. As Dr. Baskervill says in his sketch of the author: "The large and solemn presence of nature is never lost sight of, her various moods and manifestations being used as a kind of chorus to interpret the melancholy or the emotion of the human actors. The narrative is inlaid with exquisite bits of landscape, serving not so much to disclose the range and minute detail of the author's observations—at least in her earlier works—as to give expression to the fitting sentiment or development to the appropriate passion." These exquisite descriptions of the mountain views and cloud effects occur so often one is made to marvel how the author can avoid making them but thinly disguised repetitions, or how she can make available a vocabulary sufficiently full for her purpose. And yet, similar as some of the scenes may appear, the descriptions are remarkably dissimilar. It is true, however, that in so much of this kind of writing Miss Murfree has apparently exhausted the language, and has made the too frequent use of such words as "vague," "vibrant," "lucent," "opaque," "opalescent," etc., a serious defect. In fact, she overdoes her landscape-painting, and at times it becomes tiresome. She, too, often interrupts her story and stops its movement to indulge her *penchant* for scene-painting. The impression made on the reader is that, conscious of her power in this respect, she wishes to make the most of it on every possible occasion. Nevertheless, the power is there, and it is not confined to landscape-painting, for many of her finest and most vivid pictures are those of a different character, such as the interior of the homes of mountain dwellers, moonshiners' caves, and other scenes of human interest and struggle.

Of Miss Murfree's books that are distinct in scope and scene from her stories of mountain life, her latest novel, *The Fair Mississippian* (1908), may be taken as a test of her matured powers. This is a well-sustained story with the scene laid in Mississippi near the bank of the great river with its bayous and adjacent marshes and cypress sloughs, giving the author ample range for her descriptive habit. The descriptive passages, however, that are not strictly parts of the story, are less frequent, and are briefer and less suggestive of interrupting nature choruses than in many of her other books. The plot of the story, like most of Craddock's plots, is simple rather than intricate, and it is not strikingly original. The feature of adventure is made prominent, and there are some tense and stirring scenes. The characters are well portrayed and the motives well elucidated, but the book cannot be called a study of Southern life—and perhaps it was not so intended—as the action is restricted to an isolated spot, and the personages of the social set are, with a few exceptions, not representative, but distinguished mainly by their oddities. The story evinces the author's care for detail and her study of her subjects, notably in regard to the legal complications concerning a will, and throughout it holds the interest of the reader. As a literary production it may be classed with the best of current American fiction.

Miss Murfree's stories are wholesome and pure, without a hint of the erotic, or of prurient suggestion, or any appeal to maudlin sentimentality. In this respect they are models of healthy, entertaining, and often instructive fiction. Her style is robust, vigorous, and original, clear and accurate in expression, but elaborate, and given to adjectivity, with a diction that often suggests a drain upon the vocabulary and smacks of affectation. But to those who know the author personally as a vivacious and engaging conversationalist, her writing is recognized as in accord with her natural manner of speech.

Miss Murfree is entitled to a high place among American novelists. Her work promises to maintain a hold upon the more intelligent and discriminating readers of fiction; and, as she is still in the vigor of life and activity, a large class of readers will look forward with interest to further productions from her prolific pen.

Harry Aubrey Toulmin, Jr. (essay date 1911)

SOURCE: "Charles Egbert Craddock," in *Social Historians,* The Gorham Press, 1911, pp. 59-97.

[*In the following excerpt, Toulmin assesses Murfree's role as social historian.*]

Nowhere have more notable expositions been presented of the character and scenes in any particular locality, than those in the volumes of Charles Egbert Craddock dealing with the Tennessee Mountain folk. The inhabitants of the Great Smoky Mountains entered their forest homes with ideas and equipment modern a century ago. To-day, they maintain virtually the same aspect and the identical implements of their forefathers barely modified by the marvels of outside invention. It is scant wonder that the delineation of such characters in the accurate and precise manner of Craddock proved of intense literary interest.

Miss Murfree attacked her intricate problem with a scientific spirit. The mountaineer's nature was an unexplored tract in the studies of social psychology. She applied a keen intelligence and an active imagination to the analysis of this reticent, uncouth and backward division of society until she faithfully unravelled the subtle mass of customs, unwritten laws, childish prejudices, and superstitions. In her record of this effort she has embodied a faithful reproduction of the actual conditions with little perversion for artistic purposes. At first glance such a course would presuppose a treatise of interest to the student of social conditions utterly antagonistic to any pretence to literary success. This is not the case. To portray the individuality of this primitive community is to unfold a novel type of Anglo-Saxon, at once fundamentally the exponent of personal liberty and ready justice, together with undeveloped capacities for extraordinary progress, making the work a veritable revelation.

The study of these mountaineers of pure English ideals is an uncanny thing. We see ourselves more than a century ago, arrested in the development by some supernatural neglect, put under the microscope, and every point of our national traits and organism illumined fully in the light of modern information. Miss Murfree spent a part of her life amongst these people, and, in so doing, she served an apprenticeship in a stupendous human laboratory. Her books are laboratory records of a distinctive investigation in generic psychology which gives her the credit of a genuine contribution to the science of the social organization as well as to the creation of an artistic and literary success.

The question of the characters in Craddock must inevitably recall the frequent statements that her works are marred by their sameness of view and similarity of character development. Unconsciously this was in the main a genuine compliment to the success of the author's effort to execute a sane and rational sketch of mountain men and women. A people left to themselves for decades in the boundless wilderness outside the pale of any progress, exchanging no views except those that originate within the community, living no life but the simple routine of a barren rural existence, could hardly be expected to evolve any considerable amount of original thought or produce a race of versatile conversationalists. The superficial events of the district—its laws, its customs, and social happenings—could only agree with that same monotony of that life. A more complicated scheme of society might naturally originate in a varied cosmopolitan life, yet the equity of the situation would preclude the opposite in any society distinguished for nothing, except its primitive simplicity. So, while in one light the criticism is technically defensible as to the montony of the external phases of the mountain life—the dialect, the customs and superstitions, the duties and the manners of the community members—yet the analytic mind of the writer has brought to light the more delicate and personal shadings of the actual internal thought of those people.

A modern American critic has presented as a qualification of a literary production that it shall be of "enduring interest." No more striking illustration of this literary truism could be found than in Craddock's [writing], for beneath the routine, superficial shell of the mountain life the characters of her [stories] are vitally real and human individuals. Every figure carries an eager and insistent claim of "enduring interest" by the simple virtue of its humble humanity, and appeals to the American mind in particular because every movement and every motive of the personages is actuated by staunch ideals of personal liberty and innate justice. Here the social institutions of the nation are moulded in the rough.

Diversity of character is everywhere evident in fullest measure. Without the bounds of the conventional customs, each man and woman is developed as a distinctive, personal unit fashioned in his own particular mould and responding to the complication of his life in his own particular manner. While Miss Murfree has been hampered in the matter of routine happenings, she has widely diversified her characters in the relation of their personal traits and individual inclinations. It would be as just to criticise the handling of [George Meredith's] "Richard Feverel," dealing with life in an intricate civilization, with the usages and mannerisms of conventional English society, as it is to deprecate the continual use of the inherent features in a simple mountain existence—both must of necessity maintain the atmosphere, the reality of the setting, by retaining the staple fixtures of their respective societies.

In the same manner that Dickens and Scott in the British Isles and Cooper in America treated the types in the lower and more ignorant strata of the community with such realistic skill, Craddock has presented with deserved success the same cast of intellect. These mountaineers may lack the polish and education of their more fortunate brethren, but by the genius and justice of the author's pen the ennobling features of their lives stand out in brilliant contrast in their humble love for their children in their wretched cabins on the barren declivities, their efforts to rear them in order that they may become efficient members of the household, their patient, ignorant but none the less pathetic efforts, to save them from the ravages of disease and hardship, savoring strongly of that potent, touching humanity which strikes the sympathetic emotions in every section, lending to their life a keen and vital interest. It is the same world-wide spirit in the humble prose and in the humble dialect of the uncouth countryman, as that pervading the polished verses of Hugo's "Lorsque L'Enfant Paraît."

Each volume has its quota of rural types. The officers of the law, the moonshiners, and the murderers; farmers, millers, and blacksmiths; storekeepers, hunters, and the itinerant preacher; all are commingled into the elemental mosaic; Miss Murfree has succeeded admirably in etching accurately with the methodical attention to detail of a De Maupassant. She presents, however, her subjects with something of a sweeter, nobler enthusiasm than that superb artist.

And there is still another point in favor of her delineation in the sphere of country character. . . . In handling characters plainly identified with the surroundings and treating them from such a perspective, Craddock has wrought a result of potential effect.

Beneath the rude exterior of the Tennessee mountaineer there is a wealth of superior qualities. Shy and sensitive as he is, the cursory view of the chance traveler affords little ground for an adequate appreciation of the tangible virtues possessed by the inhabitants of the Great Smoky and the Chilhowee. Craddock has depicted these people with infinite finesse and subtle delicacy of workmanship. They become under the magic of her revealing studies men of genuine nobility, of lofty and inspiring character, full of loyalty and of deep devotion to every tie. Men not inspired perpetually by a bloodthirsty desire to kill and slay their fellows upon the whim of some fancied provocation, men not animated by spirits antagonistic to every canon of law and order, but inspired with sentiments and ideals creditable to a more polished society. The distance they are removed in the scale of real worth from their more fortunate compatriots is one existing in the imagination solely, for the true mountaineer as portrayed in Craddock's novels is a man little withdrawn in political and religious sentiment from the "valley man." "The ennobling difference between one man and another,—between one animal and another,—is precisely in this, that one feels more than another," and, despite the crudity of his education, the Tennesseean of the hills in the pages of Craddock as well as in his native slopes is a man capable of deep and pure emotions.

Miss Murfree maintains a firm grip upon the "spine of the story," finally turning the trivial incidents, the petty occasions, the community events, into a harmonious composition wherein truth to life and perfect versimilitude are commingled into one graceful unity.

—Harry Aubrey Toulmin, Jr.

No more attractive study of rural personalities can be found in the treatment of American characters than those figures

of the *Prophet of Great Smoky* and the *Despot of Broomsedge Cove*. Moral power of a high order is at home in these men. Miss Murfree has skillfully sketched the religious ecstasy, the faithful devotion, and the moral sublimity of men by nature large and generous, yet whose every action is hindered by accident of birth, by lack of competent education.

On the rougher side of the community's life the daring and fortitude of the fugitive from justice, the moonshiner and the falsely accused are fitting partners of Dandie Dinmont, Rob Roy, and Claverhouse. Border farmer, freebooter, soldier in a bad cause they may have been, nevertheless the lofty, kindly natures that were the mainsprings of each have their counterparts in the identical qualities of the Tennessee Mountaineer, for "these men touch the ideal of heroism only in their courage and faith, together with a strong, but uncultivated, or rather mistakenly applied intellectual power." Self-confident, bold, hardy men they appear in Craddock's pages and justly so, for a man's personality can be but the intimate reflection of his environment.

As in the countless scenes of literature, the character of woman is treated with something of a finer appreciation, of a rare gift of gentleness that makes the creation glow with perpetual interest. The heroines of Miss Murfree's romances are no exception to this literary tradition. . . .

It is equally true to speak of Miss Murfree as Brownell speaks of [James Fenimore] Cooper, "some, at all events, of those gentle and placid beings that he was so fond of creating are very real." Nevertheless, the placidity and the amiable bending to the moods of fate so evident in the women of Cooper is markedly lacking in the heroines of Craddock's tales, who are more nearly the primitive, bold, and virile offspring of a civilization in its first youth, accustomed to contend with the rigours of an unsettled existence. The sacrifices of their placidity and amiability does not imply, however, any corresponding sacrifice of reality which is, to the contrary, enlivened and revitalized to a still greater extent. . . .

The plots of [her] tales are all simple. There is nothing especially intricate or involved, for it is merely a section of real life removed from its physical surroundings to the printed page, done in a manner, however, to command intense interest in the trivialities of a rather uneventful existence. Following the method of George Eliot, she draws the scenes as a series of every day incidents happening in their natural sequence without any apparent regard as to the literary effect. Craddock moves from incident to incident in the routine of the mountain dweller's life as George Eliot let her fancy make much or little of the inconsequent flurries in the 19th century middle English country life. The culminations of the plots, the dramatic scenes, and unexpected denouements are all vivid witnesses to the writer's art. Many situations rise to the plane of dramatic intensity terminating in a strong, emotional denouement, realizing in maximum measure the several possibilities of the actor's parts. It would be very easy to degenerate into melodramatic rant and bombast in these sketches of elemental passions. Miss Murfree maintains to the contrary a firm grip upon the "spine of the story," finally turning the trivial incidents, the petty occasions, the community events, into a harmonious composition wherein truth to life and perfect versimilitude are commingled into one graceful unity.

The plots, and the situations in which they are laid, demand moderate length. In this aspect of the work Craddock has erred somewhat. Her inclinations to be accurate and to faithfully represent the actual state of mountain life have led her to trespass upon the reader's good will in a too large a degree; for it would be well if she realized, "not that the story need be long, but that it will take a long time to make it short." The capacity for sustained attention is exhausted by the lengthy exposition of "pathetic circumstance and dramatic relations" wherein the successive incidents are fraught with their own particular high, emotional tension. It is undoubtedly this tedium of emotional crises or series of continually exciting situations that is largely responsible for the impression that the volumes suffer from sameness or monotony.

Individually these movements are of considerable intrinsic worth. Commanding scenes replete with pure dramatic fire stand out in silhouette against this varied background. . . .

Miss Murfree's plots are constructed with an idea of presenting a whole group of characters, their friends and kindred of the clan, and the miscellaneous what not that may perchance drift across the rural horizon. She is apparently determined to give the characterization of the existence accurately, fully, and with a dispassionate scientific method tempered by whatever art such a course would permit. She is not tempted primarily by any allurements of artistic perversion for art's sake. It is this very quality that lends the most valuable property and enduring attraction to her romances. [Nathaniel] Hawthorne had no such particular mission of psychological investigation, yet the spirit of Craddock is of the same artistic type. As a consequence of the former's freedom from giving such an absolute portrayal, his plots have "a unity, an unwavering creative purpose" which is not the fortunate possession of Craddock.

This is not intended to deny the creative ability to Craddock. It is observed merely to illustrate the material difference in the limiting circumstances, for Miss Murfree is undoubtedly one of the most original, most creative of the Southern writers. Hawthorne constructed primarily with an artist's eye; Craddock with the finely adjusted ideal of a scientific delineation. The former possessed an infinite capacity for subordination and synthesis—in large measure indicative of his talent; the latter writer, from the nature of her material, could not produce such artistic contrasts and dramatic unities.

Within the realm of the humble mountain tragedies lies the corresponding germ, the identical primitive spark that burst into such immortal flame in the closing scenes of [Victor Hugo's] *Hernani*. The same pride of race and racial instinct, the same elemental passions pulsate in the minds

of actors, the same devoted, self-sacrificing love of woman throbs in the untutored mountaineers as in the more polished players of Hugo. Consequently, it is a matter for little amazement that the romances and tales of Craddock instantly attracted serious literary attention.

Able and extraordinary powers of description have proved a fruitful source of dispraise. In the majority of Miss Murfree's works the unwarrantable use of numerous descriptions is a very serious detriment, one that has furnished much ground for those who are inclined to depreciate her powers. That she is endowed with a nicety of imagination, a sharpness of perception, alert at once to detect the most subtle shades and tints in the natural kaleidoscope, and, at the same moment, to translate her impressions into passages of inspiring beauty, is not to be denied. Perhaps it is her purpose so to imbue the whole fabric of the sketches with the dominating beauty of the mountain scenery that the entire composition is laden with the natural atmosphere. To produce such a result her facility in this direction would demand far less of nature descriptions than she has used; doubtless the temptation to employ such a faculty, over which she has the most complete mastery, was one she found difficult to resist. . . .

Her skillful depicting of interior arrangements, of mountain dens and moonshiner's retreats, of the simple household duties and domestic difficulties, reflects a dexterous use of the scenic properties. No one watches the setting of the stage with more care than Miss Murfree. She has the faculty of differentiating between the several values of light and shade, of delicate colorings and transient reflections in the natural setting, so that the entire background may be in harmony with the figures in the rural stage. Everywhere there are the most tangible signs that Craddock is making a determined effort to follow the commandment of Poe—constant creation of an atmosphere.

Miss Murfree possesses that remarkable power to transmute the illusive witchery of mountain grandeur into the dispassionate garb of prose. Her love of nature is a dominant, vitalizing bond which she submits to with grace and genuine love for it.

Through her inclination to the beauties of the sky, Miss Murfree has made herself a veritable literary astronomer. The stars and comets, the manifestations of celestial phenomena, are made to do duty as agents of the plot machinery. *His Vanished Star* and many other tales utilize the superstitious awe in which the ignorant and unlettered hold the terrifying oddities in the natural scheme of things. She is a well informed and competent observer of the celestial happenings. The use and reference to the sky and cloud effects, to the sunsets and the commingling of color in the heavens, are frequent and ably done—a masterly and experienced hand executing charming descriptive effects. . . .

Craddock's powers of description are not confined, however, to the portrayal of natural phenomena. The physical characteristics of the people, the oddities of speech and dress, the interiors of their homes and the illicit stills, are masterfully presented to the eye. There is the pervading evidence of an artist's sense for harmonious color schemes and vivid contrasts reveling in this unexplored field of creative work.

A robust style, distinguished by its unusual clarity and masculine method, is the salient feature of this author's exposition. A generous use of epithet, varying from the prosaic to the most poetic turns of speech, as she becomes inspired with the grandeur of the gorgeous panorama spread before the eye on every hand. At times her remarkable power in describing the superb solitudes of the Bald and Chilhowee leads her into digressions and lengthy ramblings in the very execution of which the style loses its chief virtue, seeming to share in the vacillating forgetfulness. It matches in tone and color the ecstasy of the author, who seems at intervals utterly enraptured with the scenery, oblivious of every other claim; instead of the terse, clear Anglo-Saxon words mated to a distinctly American landscape and a particularly English people, she borrows from all sources terrifying, high-sounding phrases inappropriate for such an occasion. Phrases too lengthy, too sonorous, making of each scene that should have been distinguished for its simplicity, instead, a top-heavy, irrelevant word display.

This feature has worked a most pernicious result. In those very passages of superb descriptive analysis, she demolishes the true ring of each sentence by either some characteristic repetition which has occurred numberless times elsewhere or some ill-chosen vagrant from another type of vocabulary. While the author has in general handled well the descriptive phrases, the delicately modulated structures, the perfectly adapted sentences, nevertheless, the perfection of the entity has been visibly marred by such lapses from a purely graceful style. . . .

Yet rarely has dialogue been more finely rendered in native dialect than in Craddock's lines. Everywhere resplendent with the gift of interpreting the myriad lineaments of the shy mountaineers, bounteously supplied with an experience calculated to penetrate the mysteries of their reticent, retired dispositions, nurtured in the solitude of these coves and forests, Craddock has accomplished a marvelously accurate exposition of the countless phases of human nature in the hill country. The ability to keep in true perspective the slow, ruminating conversation of this hasteless people, with their countless seeming digressions and irrelevant statements, while concurrently to maintain the interest of the spectator, finally using each digression, every single reference, as a separate pigment for the closing dramatic composition, requires the mastery of an essentially delicate art. Within a single speech the reproduction of a dialect and the psychologic interpretation of the speaker's character are reflected in the drawling intonations, the somnolent manner of enunciation, or the flitting from topic to topic in the speech of some of the characters. . . .

Miss Murfree has been charged with an undue amount of such conversational digressions as well as the unnecessary wealth of description. This particular criticism is not well founded. The numerous digressions have been made be-

cause of the need to insert suitable agents which should be at once attractive in themselves and at the same time maintain the semblance of real conditions in the mountaineer's method of speech. A cursory view of the speeches and tales as a production conforming to some particular rule of dramatic unity is highly unjust; there are real lives portrayed in these volumes and fidelity to actual conditions must in justice be well considered also.

Again, these digressions furnish in large measure a means of indicating those lapses into slow thought between his fitful efforts at conversation when the mountaineer is aroused, perchance, from his constitutional apathy. Thus it is that, in numerous cases, the apparently purposeless digressions and unwarranted employment of nature descriptions, faultless and beautiful in themselves, have in reality a justified use, demanded by actual conditions. . . .

To Miss Murfree's everlasting credit she has been the most faithful expositor of her characters in reproducing the genius of their primitive American life in the tangible form of a perfect dialect. Whatever service in the perpetuation of the Hoosier dialect and the spirit of the Middle West James Whitcomb Riley has performed, it has been duplicated in point of historical trustworthiness by Charles Egbert Craddock.

With the combination of a faultless dialect and a thoroughly intimate knowledge of the laws, customs, and superstitions, Miss Murfree has succeeded in presenting a singularly accurate delineation. Historians may come and social philosophers may go, but it may be safely ventured that no more intrinsically worthy contribution to the annals of the nation has been made than the perpetual embodiment of a little known section of people in the Southern Mountains through the accurate agency of their simple dialect. What an intimate reflection of their nature for those who may pursue the records in the future!

One definitive feature of every piece of writing in this author's work is her profound knowledge of things legal. . . .

This knowledge of the law was gained as a part of her education, which included a large reading course on legal subjects. Her association with her brothers must have given her the markedly masculine view which is a prominent characteristic of all her writings. From this source, also, must have come her grasp of boy character which she has so fittingly used in mountain personages. . . .

[Throughout her writing] there is the infinite pathos of life, full red-blooded life, pulsating with very human foibles and emotions, throbbing with very personal ambitions and desires. Features of this stamp make the books intensely interesting. It is the genuine humanity in every tale that makes the constant, vital appeal to every one with a spark of interest in his fellows. To the most indifferent of readers, whether he prefers the romance or no, there must be borne in upon him the realization that these speeches are not the smoke of an artist's fancy, but are the intensely human utterances of a vigorous people.

Conforming to the main purposes in a series of tales like these, Miss Murfree has realized them both. The first is an artistic one; the other is a consciously ethical, intellectual ideal. Craddock has shown power versatile enough to execute an excellent story, full of dramatic possibilities, to pursue the plan with scientific methods, and to induce a lively interest throughout the narrative. She possessed the ability to transmit to paper the seductive charm of mountain color, the murmur of a hidden rill, a sketch of homely domestic life, or a fiery speech of a religious fanatic, mingling these factors into an entity of surprising beauty. Of the two purposes, the purely educational or didactic is the most superior feature, the most lasting recommendation. Both purposes have many faults in execution. The latter purpose, however, is a possession of more than transient interest. The works are distinctly social studies. Craddock has written many stories about several localities in the South, but such volumes as these will be the basis of her reputation as a Southern writer. There is ample justification for this type of works, if justification is needed at all, in that such stories are a trustworthy impersonation, a memorable record, of a little known division of the English race whose ancestors a few generations removed dared to conquer the wilderness, to aid in rearing a stupendous fabric of human liberty; of men many of whom furnished hosts of the bravest in the ranks of the Federal and Confederate armies distinguishing themselves by signal service and uncompromising rectitude of character. A romantic history of such a society takes its place with the lives of great men and the narrations of great events; it makes a distinct contribution to national annals. That is the essential reason for its creation and is the argument for the perpetuation of these books as a vital part of the literature.

In fact, this is the point whereon this whole group of writers on Southern subjects rest much of their claim to continued recognition. Allen, Cable, Harris and Page each has devoted himself to a particular phase of Southern existence, whether of a whole state or of a large section of his home land; and Miss "Craddock" has likewise conspicuously devoted her talents with keenness and success. As Mill philosophizes upon the economics of national policy, "no nation in which eccentricity is a matter of reproach can be in a healthy state," so we see in the variety and mixture of our own eccentrically assembled peoples and communities a healthy and prosperous phase of the Southland. The study of the oddly mixed factions and races is one of considerable worth to the nation, besides its historic value or because it is an artistic addition to the literature.

This school could be aptly termed, therefore, the *Social Historians*. They have deviated from the beaten course in historical novels where a war, a revolution, or the gaining of an empire is the basic fabric for the construction of the drama. Their mission is the recording of the social history of many phases and angles of Southern life through the vehicle of a story or romance whose most permanent interest lies in its relation to actual conditions, not primarily to the rules of an art or to the progress of some national aggrandizement.

Miss Murfree belongs distinctly to this school of *Social Historians*. In this particular field, her power is wide and far-reaching. Here is an unique addition to national, to Southern literature. She may have made some errors, may have committed many mistakes in technique; but when the entire evidence is brought in, the tales of Charles Egbert Craddock will stand specimens of high creative ability and of high dramatic development replete with a wealth of humor, a wealth of human appeal, a wealth of genuine eloquence.

Fred Lewis Pattee   (essay date 1915)

SOURCE: "The Era of Southern Themes and Writers," in *A History of American Literature since 1870,* 1915. Reprint by Cooper Square Publishers, 1968, pp. 294-321.

[*Pattee was a widely respected educator, editor, and critic. He is considered one of the most influential figures in the decline of English literary colonialism and the subsequent declaration of American literary independence in the early years of the twentieth century. In the following excerpt, originally published in 1915, he offers a stylistic analysis of Murfree's work.*]

Criticism of the Craddock novels must begin always with the statement that their author was not a native of the region with which she dealt. She had been born into an old Southern family with wealth and traditions, and she had been reared in a city amid culture and a Southern social régime. The Tennessee mountains she knew only as a summer visitor may know them. For fifteen summers she went to the little mountain town of Beersheba, prototype undoubtedly of the "New Helvetia Springs" of her novels, and from there made excursions into the wilder regions. She saw the mountains with the eyes of the city vacationist: she was impressed with their wildness, their summer moods with light and shadow, their loneliness and their remote spurs and coves and ragged gaps. She saw them with the picture sense of the artist and she described them with a wealth of coloring that reminds one of Ruskin. In every chapter, often many times repeated, gorgeous paintings like these:

> A subtle amethystine mist had gradually overlaid the slopes of the T'other Mounting, mellowing the brilliant tints of the variegated foliage to a delicious hazy sheen of mosaics; but about the base the air seemed dun-colored, though transparent; seen through it, even the red of the crowded trees was but a somber sort of magnificence, and the great masses of gray rocks, jutting out among them here and there, wore a darkly frowning aspect. Along the summit there was a blaze of scarlet and gold in the full glory of the sunshine; the topmost cliffs caught its rays, and gave them back in unexpected gleams of green or grayish-yellow, as of mosses, or vines, or huckleberry bushes, nourished in the heart of the deep fissures.

> Mink, trotting along the red clay road, came suddenly upon the banks of the Scolacutta River, riotous with

the late floods, fringed with the papaw and the ivy bush. Beyond its steely glint he could see the sun-flooded summit of Chilhowee, a bronze green, above the intermediate ranges: behind him was the Great Smoky, all unfamiliar viewed from an unaccustomed standpoint, massive, solemn, of dusky hue; white and amber clouds were slowly settling on the bald. There had been a shower among the mountains, and a great rainbow, showing now only green and rose and yellow, threw a splendid slant of translucent color on the purple slope. In such an environment the little rickety wooden mill—with its dilapidated leaking race, with its motionless wheel mossgrown, with its tottering supports throbbing in the rush of the water which rose around them, with a loitering dozen or more mountaineers about the door—might seem a feeble expression of humanity. To Mink the scene was the acme of excitement and interest.

A picture of summer it is for the most part painted lavishly with adjectives, and presented with impressionistic rather than realistic effect. Every detail is intensified. The mountains of eastern Tennessee are only moderate ridges, yet in the Craddock tales they take on the proportions of the Canadian Rockies or the Alps. . . .

Always the scenery dominates the book. It is significant that all of her early titles have in them the name of a locality,—the setting is the chief thing: Lost Creek, Big Injun Mounting, Harrison's Cove, Chilhowee, the Great Smoky Mountains, Broomsedge Cove, Keedon Bluffs. In stories like **"The Mystery of Witch-Face Mountain"** the background becomes supreme: the human element seems to have been added afterwards by a sort of necessity; the central character is the great witch-face on the mountain.

It reminds one of Hardy, and then one remembers that when **"The Dancin' Party at Harrison's Cove"** appeared in the *Atlantic*, *The Return of the Native* had for three months been running as a serial in *Harper's Monthly*, and that, somewhat later, In the "Stranger People's" Country and *Wessex Folk* ran for months parallel in the same magazine. It is impossible not to think of Hardy as one reads *Where the Battle Was Fought*, 1884. The battle-field dominates the book as completely as does Egdon Heath *The Return of the Native*, and it dominates it in the same symbolic way. . . .

The title of the book—*Where the Battle Was Fought*—makes the battle-field central in the tragedy, and so it is with the short stories **"'Way Down on Lonesome Cove"** and **"Drifting Down Lost Creek."** Nature is always cognizant of the human tragedy enacted before it and always makes itself felt. . . .

But such effects in her work are fitful: one feels them strongly at times, then forgets them in the long stretches of dialect conversation and description seemingly introduced for its own sake. Of the art that could make of Egdon Heath a constantly felt, implacable, malignant presence that harried and compelled its dwellers until the reader at last must shake himself awake as from a nightmare, of this she knew little. She worked by means of brilliant sketches; she relied upon her picturing power to carry the story, and as a result the effect is scattered.

In her characterization she had all the defects of Scott: she worked largely with externals. She had an eye for groups posed artistically against a picturesque background as in that marvelous opening picture in **"'Way Down on Lonesome Cove."** She expended the greatest of care on costume, features, habits of carriage and posture, tricks of expression, individual oddities, but she seldom went deeper. We see her characters distinctly; not often do we feel them. In her major personages, like the Prophet, the Despot, the Juggler, we have little sympathetic interest, and it is impossible to believe that they were much more than picturesque specimens even to the author herself. To get upon the heart of the reader a character must first have been upon the heart of his creator. Here and there undoubtedly she did feel the thrill of comprehension as she created, a few times so keenly indeed that she could forget her art, her note book, and her audience. The one thing that seems to have touched her heart as she journeyed through the summer valleys and into the remote coves seems to have been the pitiful loneliness and heart-hunger of the women. Could she have done for all of her characters what she did for Celia Shaw and Madeline and Dorinda and a few other feminine souls, the final verdict upon her work might have been far different from what it must be now.

Her stories necessarily are woven from scanty materials. In the tale of a scattered and primitive mountain community there can be little complication of plot. The movement of the story must be slow, as slow indeed as the round of life in the coves and the lonesome valleys. But in her long-drawn narratives often there is no movement at all. She elaborates details with tediousness and records interminable conversations, and breaks the thread to insert whole chapters of description, as in Chapter VI of *The Juggler*, which records the doings at a mountain revival meeting seemingly for the mere sake of the local color. Nearly all of her longer novels lack in constructive power. Like Harte, whom in so many ways she resembled, she could deal strongly with picturesque moments and people, but she lacked the ability to trace the growth of character or the slow transforming power of a passion or an ideal or a sin.

Her style was peculiarly her own; in this she was strong. It is worthy of note that in an age rendered styleless by the newspaper and the public school she was able to be individual to the extent that one may identify any page of her writings by the style alone. It is not always admirable: there is a Southern floridness about it, a fondness for stately epithet that one does not find in Harris or in others of the Georgia group. She can write that the search light made "a rayonnant halo in the dim glooms of the riparian midnight," and she can follow the jocose observation of a woman washing dishes with this tremendous sentence: "'What fur?' demanded the lord of the house, whose sense of humor was too blunted by his speculations, and a haunting anxiety, and a troublous eagerness to discuss the question of his discovery, to perceive aught of the ludicrous in the lightsome metaphor with which his weighty spouse had characterized her dissatisfaction with the ordering of events." It may be interesting to know that the woman vouchsafed no reply. Rather, "she wheezed one more line of her matutinal hymn in a dolorous cadence and with breathy interstices between the spondees."

She is at her best when describing some lonely valley among the ridges, or the moonlight as it plays fitfully over some scene of mountain lawlessness, or some remote cabin "deep among the wooded spurs." In such work she creates an atmosphere all her own. Few other writers have so made landscape felt. One may choose illustrations almost at random:

> On a certain steep and savage slope of the Great Smoky Mountains, the primeval wilderness for many miles is unbroken save for one meager clearing.

> Deep among the wooded spurs Lonesome Cove nestles, sequestered from the world. Naught emigrates from thence except an importunate stream that forces its way through a rocky gap, and so to freedom beyond. No stranger intrudes; only the moon looks in once in a while. The roaring wind may explore its solitudes; and it is but the vertical sun that strikes to the heart of the little basin, because of the massive mountains that wall it round and serve to isolate it.

> The night wind rose. The stars all seemed to have burst from their moorings and were wildly adrift in the sky. There was a broken tumult of billowy clouds, and the moon tossed hopelessly among them, a lunar wreck, sometimes on her beam ends, sometimes half submerged, once more gallantly struggling to the surface, and again sunk. The bare boughs of the trees beat together in a dirgelike monotone.

Nowhere is she commonplace; nowhere does she come down from the stately plane that she reaches always with her opening paragraph. Even her dialect is individual. Doubtless other writers have handled the mountain speech more correctly, doubtless there is as much of Charles Egbert Craddock in the curious forms and perversions as there is of the Tennessee mountaineers, yet no one has ever used dialect more convincingly than she or more effectively. She has made it a part of her style.

The story of Charles Egbert Craddock is a story of gradual decline. *In the Tennessee Mountains* was received with a universality of approval comparable only with that accorded to *The Luck of Roaring Camp.* In her second venture, *Where the Battle Was Fought,* she attempted to break from the narrow limits of her first success and to write a Hardy-like novel of the section of Southern life in which she herself belonged, but it failed. From all sides came the demand that she return again to her own peculiar domain. And she returned with *The Prophet of the Great Smoky Mountains.* It was praised, but with the praise came a note of dissatisfaction, a note that became more and more dominant with every novel that followed. Her first short stories had appealed because of their freshness and

the strangeness of their setting. Moreover, since they were the first work of a young writer they were a promise of better things to come. But the promise was not fulfilled. After *The Juggler,* her last attempt on a large scale to create a great Tennessee-mountains novel, she took the advice of many of her critics and left the narrow field that she had cultivated so carefully. She wrote historical romances and novels of contemporary life, but the freshness of her early work was gone. After 1897 she produced nothing that had not been done better by other writers.

Her failure came not, as many have believed, from the poverty of her materials and the narrowness of her field. Thomas Hardy deliberately had chosen for his novels a region and a people just as primitive. A great novel should concern itself with the common fundamentals of humanity, and these fundamentals, he believed, may be studied with more of accuracy in the isolated places where the conventions of polite society have not prevented natural expression. . . .

The failure of Charles Egbert Craddock came rather from her inability to work with large masses of material and coordinate it and shape it into a culminating force. She was picturesque rather than penetrating, melodramatic rather than simple, a showman rather than a discerning interpreter of the inner meanings of life. She could make vivid sketches of a moment or of a group or a landscape, but she could not build up touch by touch a consistent and compelling human character. Her genius was fitted to express itself in the short story and the sketch, and she devoted the golden years of her productive life to the making of elaborate novels. A little story like "**Way Down on Lonesome Cove**" is worth the whole of the *The Juggler* or *In the Clouds.* The short stories with which she won her first fame must stand as her highest achievement.

The Outlook (essay date 1922)

SOURCE: "The Romance of the Tennessee Mountains," in *The Outlook,* Vol. 131, No. 16, August 16, 1922, p. 626.

[*In the following essay, the critic outlines Murfree's career.*]

A generation ago, when Mary N. Murfree wrote her romance of Tennessee, *The Prophet of the Great Smoky Mountains,* the emphasis in American short-story writing was being placed on local color. Mary Wilkins and Sarah Orne Jewett gave us the local color of New England; George Cable, that of Louisiana; and so over almost every section of the country. But the Southern mountains and the life and character of their people were then practically an unknown subject in fiction. It was before the time when John Fox had utilized the Kentucky mountains and before the same region had been treated, less dramatically but far more realistically and feelingly, by Lucy Furman in her *Mothering on Perilous,* lately followed by her equally delightful tale, *The Quare Women,* which again is most interestingly supplemented by Laura Spencer Portor in the current *Harper's Monthly* in her bit of reminiscence called "In Search of Local Color."

Miss Murfree really discovered a new field. She utilized it to the full from the romantic and the descriptive point of view in her first book. Yet the vigor of the book was such that her pen-name, Charles Egbert Craddock, was generally accepted at its face value and the author was believed to be a man.

Other novels followed *In the Tennessee Mountains* and *The Prophet of the Great Smoky Mountains,* varying of course in ability and interest, but none attained anything like the popularity of the first two romances. The reason was that Miss Murfree, like many other writers of fiction, abandoned her natural line of writing and attempted to be over-subtle and to deal too philosophically with life problems. Even in her best books she also inclined to rest too strongly on descriptions of marvelous scenery. She was often accused of hauling the moon over the Tennessee mountains too often and too lingeringly, and in one instance, if we remember rightly, of causing it to rise in a part of the sky never intended by nature for moonrise. One or two of her books attempted historical themes, but with no very great success. On the other hand, many of us remember with pleasure Miss Murfree's short stories, afterwards collected in book form; they reproduced the primitive and sturdy character of the Tennessee mountaineers as well as anything she did. Her stories for children were also of excellent quality.

Fred Lewis Pattee (essay date 1923)

SOURCE: "The Reign of Dialect," in *The Development of the American Short Story: An Historical Survey,* Harper & Brothers Publishers, 1923, pp. 268-90.

[*In the following excerpt, Pattee discusses Murfree's place in what he calls "the reign of dialect" during the 1880s and her influence on the subsequent generation of writers.*]

The final avalanche of [writing in] dialect which came with the 'eighties was precipitated by a curious bit of uncontracted-for advertising. In 1878 a story had come in to *The Atlantic* from the Southwest over the unheard-of name of "Charles Egbert Craddock." There was dialect in the very title, **"The Dancin' Party at Harrison's Cove,"** and large parts of it were told in an argot, a leisurely tedium of barbarous wordiness, strange to Northern readers.

> Ef he don't want a bullet in that pumpkin head o' his'n he hed better keep away from that dancin' party what the Harrisons hev laid off ter give, 'kase Rick say he's a-goin' ter it hisself, an' is a-goin' ter dance too; he ain't been invited, Mis' Darley, but Rick don't keer fur that. He is a-goin' ennyhow, an' he say ez how he ain't a-goin' ter let Kossute come, 'count o' Kossute's sass an' the fuss they've all made 'bout that

bay filly that war stole five year ago,—'t war five year an' better. But Rick say ez how he is agoin', fur all he ain't got no invite, an' is a-goin' ter dance too, 'kase you know, Mis' Darley, it's a-goin' ter be a dancin' party; the Harrisons hev determined on that. Them gals of theirn air mos' crazed 'bout a dancin' party. They ain't been a bit of account sence they went ter Cheatham's Cross-Roads ter see thar gran'mother, an' picked up all them queer new notions. So the Harrisons hev determined on a dancin' party; an' Rick say ez how he is goin' ter dance too; but Jule *she* say ez how she know thar ain't a gal on the mounting ez would dance with him; but I ain't so sure 'bout that, Mis' Darley; gals air cur'ous critters, ye know yerself; thar's no sort o' countin' on 'em; they'll do one thing one time, an' another thing nex' time; ye can't put no dependence in 'em.

The sketch manifestly had been accepted on account of its unusual materials and the wild new atmosphere which enveloped it. Of plot there was practically none: the inevitable fight between Rick and Kossute, prevented forcibly by a man-handling old circuit preacher who had been Rick's regimental chaplain during the war—that was all: the rest was local color of a rather startling variety. Other sketches followed at long intervals; the public responded as slowly as a few years earlier they had responded to Cable's southern sketches. After six years, eight of them had accumulated, enough for a small volume. *In the Tennessee Mountains* was the title decided upon, and in the spring of 1884 the author went to Boston to make final arrangements. Then had come the climax: to the amazement of T. B. Aldrich, the *Atlantic* editor, and of Oliver Wendell Holmes, who happened to be in the office, Charles Egbert Craddock proved to be a woman—Miss Mary Noailles Murfree, of the historic family that had given its name to Murfreesboro', Tennessee. The story of this dramatic moment, spread broadcast over America, advertised the new book tremendously. Perhaps no collection of American short stories, save only the *Sketch Book* and *The Luck of Roaring Camp,* was ever launched with more of impetus or was awaited by the reading public with more of curiosity. Its success precipitated a veritable downpour of local-color fiction.

Miss Murfree's rank as a writer of short stories must be determined almost solely by this single volume. She followed her success with a series of Tennessee Mountain novels, and it is as a novelist rather than a short-story writer that she must finally be judged. Short lengths of fiction were imperative for her during the uncertain days when she was acquiring a market: most of the young writers of the period were forced to try the currents with skiffs before launching the five-decked galleons of their dreams; later, when her popularity had declined and she was no longer sure of a market, she again was forced to use the smaller unit. Strictly speaking, her short stories are not short stories at all save in the one element of shortness. She records simple, everyday incidents in their natural sequence and stops when the space allotted to her has been filled. She moves leisurely from incident to incident in the monotonous vacuity of mountain life, as a minutely written journal might move.

In all of her fiction, materials come first. Her titles are usually expressed in terms of landscape: "T'other Mounting," "Lonesome Cove," "Sunrise Rock," "Chilhowee," "Harrison's Cove," "Witch-Face Mountain"—the setting first and then the action. On the cover of her first edition was the impressionistic design of a ragged landscape with an eagle hovering above it in mid-foreground. Everywhere the strikingly novel: barbarous locutions, strange fashions of dress, manners, traditions: wild mountain passes and coves and ravines, savage and forbidding—everywhere the unique. The reader is in charge of a competent guide who calls attention constantly to local peculiarities and is voluble with his explanations. Manner—art, plot—is secondary. She begins with landscape, a landscape always in some vague extreme of beauty, or vastness, or wildness: she introduces characters to match, sometimes whole neighborhood clans, each individual minutely described—impressionistically—in terms of his uniqueness; and then rambles on and on until the reader loses himself in an atmosphere that at last is like nothing he has ever known before. She has created a new world and it all seems curiously real at first, and yet a second reading in cold blood is very apt to reveal an artificiality that is repellent. It is a trick of style we feel, not an actuality, that has captured us.

> **Murfree's minute pictures of mountain life, for all their minuteness, cannot be classed as realistic. She was not a mountaineer herself; she studied the region not sympathetically, but curiously, as a summer visitor who went about with a notebook.**
>
> —*Fred Lewis Pattee*

It was this impressionistic manner of presenting materials, this wild mountain haze over all things, this new conception of landscape, that made Charles Egbert Craddock so important a figure in the fiction of the 'eighties in America. Part of it undoubtedly was her own personality, but part of it was Thomas Hardy, whose *Return of the Native* was contemporary with her first tales in the *Atlantic*. In both writers the landscape is used symbolically, impressionistically; it becomes in reality the leading character in the tale, the ruling motif in the plot. Cynthia Ware is but the human counterpart of Lost Creek. The grim mountain range held her in its grip just as Egdon Heath held Eustacia Vye and Wildeve till they died. "Whether the skies are blue or gray, the dark, austere line of its summit limits the horizon. It stands against the west like a barrier. It seemed to Cynthia Ware that nothing which went beyond this barrier ever came back again." And at the close of the tale, her hopes of escape forever blasted, "it seems to her that the years of her life are like the floating leaves drifting down Lost Creek, valueless and purposeless and vaguely vanishing in the mountain."

Her minute pictures of mountain life, for all their minuteness, cannot be classed as realistic. She was not a mountaineer herself; she studied the region not sympathetically, but curiously, as a summer visitor who went about with a notebook. She heightened all her pictures. Her mountains are hills, but she makes them tower into the very skies. In the words of an early reviewer, "they are purpler, bluer, and yellower than any other mountains; they are at times more remote and forbidding, at times more close and tender, than the peaks and summits of other ranges; their moon is distinctly superior, and, unlike other moons, constant. Their inhabitants bear little resemblance to the natives of other altitudes and gorges." She is a colorist splashing with broad strokes: she dashes all her pages with a profusion of lurid adjectives—her imagination runs riot amid her materials. Her genius is epic rather than dramatic or lyric: she works at her best with the sweep of great mountain vistas and elemental men and elemental passions. "Behind the crowd was the immensity of the unpeopled forests; below, the mad fret of the cataract; above, the vast hemisphere of the lonely skies; and far, far away was the infinite, stretching o'er those blue ranges that the Indians called the Endless"—this is her setting. She is wholly masculine in her treatment of the sentimental and the feminine. She is almost without humor—as austere, indeed, and as cold as her mountain ranges and her lonesome coves. She is at her best when describing desolation, *genre* pictures with impressionistic detail.

One is never moved by the tales of Charles Egbert Craddock except perhaps intellectually. One may exclaim, *This is vivid,* or, *This is well-nigh poetry,* or, *This is Johnsonian English, rare at this late day,* but there is no other emotion. We feel that she is self-conscious, that she is adding ornament to ornament with deliberation, that she is exhibiting rather than sharing. A style that alludes to cows as "bovine vagrants," that describes a scene in terms of "interfulgent sunbeams," that, instead of "dancers," has "sinful votaries of Terpsichore," that can begin a paragraph with, "There was a prolonged silence in the matutinal freshness," or, again, with "The hairy animal, whose jeans suit proclaimed him man, propounded this inquiry with a triumphant air. There was a sarcastic curve on the lips of his interlocutor"—a style that is everywhere like this can hardly carry conviction. At a dramatic moment in the action she pauses for a page, two pages, to paint a picture.

> The sudden flight of a bird cleft the rainbow; there was a flash of moisture on his swift wings, and he left his wild sweet cry echoing far behind him. Beetling high above the stream, the crags seemed to touch the sky. One glance up and up these towering, majestic steeps—how it lifted the soul! The Settlement, perched upon the apparently inaccessible heights, was not visible from the road below. It cowered back affrighted from the verge of the great cliff and the grimly yawning abysses.

And so on and on. A touch of this now and then may be used with Shakespearean effect to relieve the emotional tension or to show how nature harmonized with the mood of the moment or was in contrast with it, but after page after page of such material, inserted at every possible point, we feel that with her the picture was first and the drama incidental. It is artificial: it does not move us.

Unquestionably her work is not of short-story texture. It may be even used, brilliant as it is at times in its impressionism, as a warning and as an example of fundamental rules ignored and broken. Even had she been more perfect in her technique, from the very nature of her material, she was headed toward ultimate failure. Her material was even more attenuated than Harte's. The California mines *did* afford a variety of characters drawn from the whole of the civilized and the uncivilized world, but the Tennessee Mountains had only one variety, and their social system was austerely uncomplex. A half dozen sketches she might make, a half dozen motifs for fiction there might have been: the primitive murder for revenge or jealousy, the outlaw adventurer and his deeds, the drama of the moonshine still raided by revenue officers, the shooting of strangers who had wandered for various reasons into the mountains—there could be little variety. It was not long after her first book that reviewers were charging her with "plowing ground which already she had plowed to barrenness." She lived to see herself forgotten save by a few of her early readers, and her books unable to command for any length of time a uniform publisher. Yet in the history of American fiction she is still notable. At a single moment in the drama she was the central figure, and she created a profound impression. Her influence upon the rising young school that was to rule the 'nineties cannot be overlooked by one who would write the history of the closing years of the century.

Van Wyck Brooks   (essay date 1947)

SOURCE: "The South: Miss Murfree and Cable," in *The Times of Melville and Whitman*, E. P. Dutton & Co., Inc., 1947, pp. 378-94.

[*Brooks was an American poet. In the following excerpt, he praises Murfree's writing for its realistic rendering of a previously "unknown human sphere," but finds the use of dialect nearly "unreadable."*]

In [Mary Murfree's] many stories, long and short, the same characters reappeared that one met in her first book, *In the Tennessee Mountains,* but this and *The Prophet of the Great Smoky Mountains* revealed an unknown human sphere in a way that was singularly real, impressive and poetic. One of the recurring themes was that of the cultivated stranger who meets the unsophisticated mountain girl, and many of the stories dealt with the conflicts of the mountain folk and the world outside which the revenue-officer and the sheriff represented. Among the other local types were the blacksmith and the horse-thief, who mysteriously disappears, like the revenue-spy; for one of the unwritten laws of the moonshiners was that the informer should perish, and outsiders in general were the enemy in the moonshiners' minds. For the rest, they knew nothing

of social classes and their speech was full of poetry, and especially the biblical metaphors of Old Testament people for whom dancing was more sinful than killing a man in a quarrel and who bore such names as Abednego and Jubal. The preacher was omnipresent and one of the best of Miss Murfree's characters was the infidel prophet Kelsey with his second sight who thought he was the only unbeliever in a Christian world and whom Satan hunted through the mountains like a partridge. A few of the other mountaineers were admirably drawn, the fugitive Rick Tyler who was falsely accused and who looked like a hound in the middle of the hunting season, and Groundhog Cayce and his giant sons, the moonshiners with their forest arts, who recalled the Tennessee brood of Cooper's Ishmael Bush. Some of the scenes were idyllic and many abounded in fine descriptions of the forest, the flowers and the mountains that towered over all. The stories were vibrant as often as not with the violent feelings of the mountain folk, whether anger, love, loyalty, resentment or the thirst for revenge.

Now and then Miss Murfree's stories were marked by great dramatic power, **"The 'Harnt' that Walks Chilhowee,"** for example, the tale of the fugitive cripple who was taken for a ghost, and some of her historical writing was interesting also. . . .

But, interesting as much of it was, the best of this writing was scarcely readable, two generations later, for the very same reason that many other gifted writers were unreadable also, because of their abuse of dialect. . . .

There were many reasons for this study of dialect,—the spread of the philological mind and especially the wish to commemorate the local life and preserve the local speech that seemed destined to be lost with the growth of the industrial system and the national feeling. . . .

It was the pains that writers took to reproduce dialect exactly that blighted many books which might otherwise have survived if the writers had used a little more tact, less science and more art, and suggested the dialect merely by occasional touches. The attempt to convey it literally defeated its own end because what was intended for the ear was presented to the eye. Unable to see the sound, one resented the obstruction.

William B. Dillingham   (essay date 1962)

SOURCE: An introduction to *When Old Baldy Spoke*, by Charles Egbert Craddock, in *The Emory University Quarterly*, Vol. 18, No. 2, Summer, 1962, pp. 93-106.

[*In the following excerpt, Dillingham links Murfree's short fiction with both the genteel tradition and the school of realism.*]

In 1885, the year when William Dean Howells published *The Rise of Silas Lapham* and the Statue of Liberty was being assembled on Bedloe's Island, a young woman walked calmly into the offices of the *Atlantic Monthly* and informed the editor, Thomas Baily Aldrich, that SHE was the Mr. Charles Egbert Craddock who had been writing stories for his magazine. Neither *Silas Lapham* nor the Statue of Liberty caused much more of a stir that year than this literary disclosure. In Boston the news that Charles Egbert Craddock was actually a woman, Mary Noailles Murfree, made the front page, and the young lady from Murfreesboro, Tennessee, found herself whispered about and stared at when she walked down the street. She had won recognition mainly with several short stories in the *Atlantic Monthly* beginning in May 1878, and she steadily gained reputation as one of the most competent of the new regional writers. These stories were collected and published in 1884 as *In the Tennessee Mountains*. The book was widely admired, not only by the writers and readers of the genteel tradition but also by the new adherents of "realism" in literature. Miss Murfree had satisfied the genteel with her tendency to moralize, and she had appealed to the Howells school of realism with her depiction of the commonplace, the Tennessee mountain people, their language and ways. The next year she published her best-known novel, *The Prophet of the Great Smoky Mountains*, and her fame was assured. . . .

Before she died in 1922, Mary Noilles Murfree published some twenty-four books, including historical romances and collections of juvenile stories. All her books were widely read, but the earlier works are the most vital, and many of her later plots and characters are weak repetitions of those in *The Prophet of the Great Smoky Mountains* and *In the Tennessee Mountains*. Like so many other local colorists of her time, she could not extend her art beyond a rather limited range. Her later works, consequently, are today all but forgotten.

"When Old Baldy Spoke" is not an eminent addition to the published stories of Mary Noailles Murfree, but it is representative of the mountain tales for which she is remembered. Jim Hoxie, a youth of eighteen, is fascinated by the life and talk of the local moonshiners. In fact, he is so strongly attracted to their tall tales and big brags around the copper still that he neglects his own work to join in their drinking and loafing. When the still is discovered by revenue officers, Jim is carried off to jail. His sentence served, he finds no welcome at home, and he strikes out alone, trying to begin a new life. Day after day he cultivates his small crop in the shadow of Old Baldy. His family and community finally accept him after he discovers the moonshiners trapped in a cave and informs the authorities. Although the moonshiners try again to implicate him, his efforts at honest toil are evident in the earth he has cultivated. The law and the community accept the argument of Lawyer Green: "And it stands to reason . . . that a boy who works in the field CAN'T STAY AWAKE at night to moonshine."

In the story of Jim's growth to responsibility, the author teaches an obvious lesson of diligence and hard work. She seldom wrote without a strong didactic purpose, which the modern reader is likely to find objectionable. But the moral which seems to pervade **"When Old Baldy Spoke"** may

partially spring from the character of the mountain people, in whom religious superstition is as basic as their appetites. The frightening movement of the earth, which closes the chasm in the mountain side, causes the people to reexamine their lives. Jim learns how to act and how to find a place in his community. For Jim's grandfather the voice of Old Baldy is the Mighty Host warning him not to judge his grandson too severely. Melindy believes that God's judgment has been pronounced against her for coddling her pet bear "when humans air needy an' folks hold thar hands from givin'." The miller runs out, his face as white as the flour on his clothes, to confess his sins. The strange but forceful voice of the supernatural rumbles through the stories of Mary Noailles Murfree, and as in this tale it affects profoundly the primitive folk of the mountains.

The author who could thus portray so well the mountaineer's deep superstitions had an unfortunate conception of her own rôle as narrator. She apparently wished her readers to think of her as distinguished by erudition and sophistication, and she filled her stories with purple eloquence, supplied in juxtaposition to the homely language of the mountain people. The extreme distance between her lofty descriptions and the dialect creates an effect of artificiality or even comic incongruity. In describing the mountains, she writes: "On every hand loomed in massive sublimity the Titanic peaks." She speaks of the earthquake as a "tumultuous crash" which "rent the air—deep sepulchral with strange cavernous vibrations." Her language in depicting the humble Melindy is almost comically exalted: "To a tutored imagination her beauty, as she stood there in the rugged field with her hand on the brute's head, might have suggested the goddess Ceres." In spite of her flaws as an artist, however, Mary Noailles Murfree left many stories, including **"When Old Baldy Spoke,"** in which she managed to create an atmosphere, a definite impression of time and place.

Richard Cary (essay date 1967)

SOURCE: "Mystique of the Mountains," in *Mary N. Murfree*, Twayne Publishers, Inc., 1967, pp. 45-78.

[*In the excerpt below, Cary discusses the significance of the mountain milieu in Murfree's short fiction.*]

The overwhelming central fact of life in Miss Murfree's tales of Tennessee are the mountains. Their presence is felt within the first page of all but one of these eight stories [in *In the Tennessee Mountains*]. . . .

The effect of the mountains is unquestionably pervasive, for Miss Murfree has marvelous evocative powers. Yet, even in this collection, the press of too many recurrences and too many adjectives becomes onerous. She fails not in fidelity to detail so much as in artistic balance. Often she breaks off in the middle of a crucial dialogue or dramatic action to take still another glimpse at a rugged vista. She said in extenuation of this defect that "one observes most keenly and remembers most vividly in a crisis." Be that as it may, it is not always the beauties of landscape that catch the sense.

Miss Murfree sets one of these stories in the Cumberlands, another in a wild spur of the Alleghenies, a third in the Great Smoky Mountains. These are purely nominal designations. The prospect is all of a piece, with infinitesimal variations. The sky by day is lustrously blue and changes to crimson, purple, gold, and saffron as evening verges into night, then makes way for moons of every phase and hue. In the vast phalanxes of towering ranges, majestic summits intercept the horizon. A wilderness of dark evergreens and deciduous trees casts dense shadows over sheer precipices, great projecting ledges, treacherous chasms, and unexplored caverns. Cataracts spurt out of immense fissures and smash tumultuously against giant boulders. Stony roads curve downward to basin-like valleys. Birds, foxes, wolves, deer, and an occasional bear slip lightly through thick foliage, which is deeply colored in keeping with the season. "Her Tennessee mountains are purpler, bluer, and yellower than any other," wrote one critic in exasperated disparagement [anonymous review of *The Mystery of Witch-Face Mountain, The Nation,* February 27, 1896].

Undeniably, Miss Murfree accentuates to the point of affectation the exquisite aspects of landscape. However, all does not fall within Addison's dictum that "we find the works of nature still more pleasant, the more they resemble those of art." She is most successful when allying external nature with man in his obscurer moods and meditations, when man merges with environment in harmonious acceptance of the mystery of existence. This inexpressible coordination, here best demonstrated in **"Over on the T'other Mounting"** and in **"The 'Harnt' That Walks Chilhowee,"** is given full tribute by William Malone Baskervill: "Her description, too, serves a literary purpose, now expressing the fitting sentiment, anon developing the appropriate passion. She seizes and interprets physical features and natural phenomena in their relation to various aspects of human life with at times unerring precision, vigor, and dramatic force. Indeed, the scenery of the mountains is essential to the comprehension of the gloom of the religion, the sternness of the life, the uncouthness of the dialect, and the harshness of the characters presented in her stories" [*Southern Writers: Biographical and Critical Studies,* 1897].

This effect of interrelationship she accomplishes in part by adducing Gothic horror as an ever-present concomitant of loveliness in nature, illustrating the duple sides of man's nature and influencing his thoughts and actions. Among the over-all sublimities a peak "beetles" bare and grim. Gigantic walls of rock loom "gloomy and sinister" over denuded forests of desolate black-branched trees. "Grisly yawning abysses" lay in wait for unwary riders, and the primeval magnificence is shrouded in somber neutral hues. When offered in apposition to dour expectations or emotions, these atmospheric details become more than mere geographic adjuncts, more than mere local color. They serve as true portents and indices of human sensitivity.

Less abstruse in its application is the use of metaphor to substantiate the invisible affinity of man and nature. Lifting his gaze to a star or to a mountaintop, man feels his soul and imagination lifted. Watching empty nights succeeding empty days ratifies his own loneliness; hearing foxes bark in a moonlit autumn wood relieves it. The grace of a woodland flower is reflected in that of a young girl. Man's imperceptible aging mimics erosion in nature, and his misery is not unlike that of a freezing bird or a wounded deer. A creek disappearing into a mountain recess is seen as a human life lost in the eternal enigma. The calm of the forest restores the calm of a harassed heart and spirit.

The moon, which later contends with the mountains in frequency of appearances, calls attention to itself in five of the stories. Everyone has had his little joke about "Mary's moon," as her mother dubbed it; but most reviewers condemn it offhand as a meretricious stage prop. "She was often accused of hauling the moon over the Tennessee Mountains too often and too lingeringly and in one instance, if we remember rightly, of causing it to rise in a part of the sky never intended by nature for moonrise," noted the *Outlook* [August 16, 1922]. "As somebody has said, she works her moon too hard," echoed the *Atlantic Monthly* [July, 1889]. This is irrefutable but, as in other facets of Miss Murfree's writing, there is more here than meets the uncritical eye. In her preoccupation with the moon she is a true "lunatic" with, however, method in her madness.

When not hung out purely as decoration, the moon's major function is to act as a spotlight. In a district devoid of central artificial lighting, what more natural way exists to illuminate outdoor drama at night? Miss Murfree utilizes moonglow strategically to focus the area of action and to pick out imperative details of topography. She turns the rays on people's faces to expose emotions or significant changes of expression. A "drowning" moon accompanies the bitter reflections of a misfit over his persistent failures, a "sinking" moon corresponds with sudden fright, and a "red" moon shines on a ruffian, hands dripping with blood, who is running from the forest. Like Hawthorne, she causes the moon to obscure as well as to elucidate, casting ambiguous beams on elements to be disclosed later. Like him, she also certifies the moon as a moral agent. It smiles "right royally" on the jocund dancing party and withholds approval of the outlaw band which rides into "the gloom of the shadows."

In this breathless domain of "clifty heights" the typical abode is a log hovel clinging uncertainly to the mountainside. A vagrant path leads to the rickety fence upon which perches a motionless man. Hounds, calves, "soprano pigs," chickens, and horses roam the yard—but the hounds and chickens are as often in the house. The porch is occupied by broken chairs, cooking utensils, discarded garments. In the fireplace, which takes up almost one side of the house, a hickory fire is usually burning. The rough, uncovered floor, with one or two loose puncheons, supports inverted washtubs and splint baskets used for seats, a bedstead with sagging mattress and patchwork calico quilt, some rushbottomed chairs, perhaps a spinning wheel. From the rafters dangle strings of bright red peppers, ears of corn, hanks of woolen and cotton yarn, bunches of medicinal herbs, brown gourds, and little bags of seeds. Ranged on shelves along the walls are pots, pans, and drinking vessels. Miss Murfree stresses the marked cleanliness of these interiors.

A store and a blacksmith's shop may be found at road junctions together with a smattering of cabins within walking distance of one another. Often just called "Cross-Roads" or "the Settlemint," these hamlets epitomize the extent of mountain community. By reverting to such generic names—and others such as Big Injun Mountain and Colbury, the county center—throughout these stories, Miss Murfree creates a sense of unbroken tissue. Each story becomes a separate incident in a protracted, haphazard epic of life in this beautiful, violent, backward country.

. . . . .

The mountain men and women seen briefly in **"Taking the Blue Ribbon"** and in **"The Panther of Jolton's Ridge"** take on added dimensions in *In the Tennessee Mountains,* and we are introduced to several other basic types. Notwithstanding, Miss Murfree restricts her range to a small segment of the variegated mountain populace. She knew best those she met around Beersheba Springs and concentrates on those along the lowest social-economic margin, ignoring the better educated, the more affluent and adaptable citizens with minor appeal to far-off magazine readers. Mountain aristocrats were too much like their upcoming town counterparts, so she exploits the Boeotian qualities of the unaltered rustics. She achieves a tiring repetition before she leaves them for other fields, but there exists sufficient testimony that she faithfully retained most of the realities within her narrow bailiwick.

Men dominate the forefront. They hunt, fish, fight, loaf, or disport themselves with primal disregard for domestic obligations. All are congenitally shiftless although some work sporadically around their depressed homesteads. The smith, the miller, and the moonshiner seem the only ones who apply themselves steadily. Fierce independence and a fine contempt for the law are promiscuous. Only a minority, however, are actually lawless. Of these the representative in **"The Dancin' Party"** is horse-thief and brawler Rick Pearson, who is an outgrowth of the panther, John Brice. His person, with some scant deviations, foretokens a long line of intrepid, immoral, blunt, bluff, not unattractive demiheroes to follow.

> He was dressed, like the other mountaineers, in a coarse suit of brown jeans somewhat the worse for wear, the trowsers stuffed in the legs of his heavy boots; he wore an old soft felt hat, which he did not remove immediately on entering, and a pair of formidable pistols at his belt conspicuously challenged attention. He had auburn hair, and a long full beard of a lighter tint reaching almost to his waist; his complexion was much tanned by the sun, and roughened by exposure to the inclement mountain weather; his eyes were brown, deep-set, and from under his heavy brows they

looked out with quick, sharp glances, and occasionally with a roguish twinkle; the expression of his countenance was rather good-humored,—a sort of imperious good-humor, however,—the expression of a man accustomed to have his own way and not to be trifled with, but able to afford some amiability since his power is undisputed.

The more tractable male adults are listless, recurrently drunk, wear a grave mien, talk in a monotonous drawl, see ghosts, abuse their wives, indulge their beasts. Younger men have tremendous build and strength, are quicker to anger, livelier in banter, and tenacious in courting.

There are three ranks of females in this masculine realm: the young maiden, the young wife, the older woman. The young mountain maiden expands into a highly controversial figure later in Miss Murfree's work. In five stories in **In the Tennessee Mountains** the lineaments of the larger portrait begin to emerge. The young mountain girl before marriage is extraordinarily beautiful, has the grit and determination of her forebears, a propensity for misfortune in love, and a strong strain of resignation.

Mandy Tyler [in **"The Dancin Party at Harrison's Cove"**] is least characteristic, with black hair and too much vivacity. As yet an unbridled coquette, she plays practical jokes with impunity on her clumsy swains. Clarsie Giles [in **"The 'Harnt' That Walks Chilhowe"**] is a step closer to the composite. Although also a brunette and untameable, she is tall, lithe, with "delicately transparent complexion" and large, liquid eyes. She turns out to be the norm of mountain girls who marries the norm of mountain boys. Celia Shaw [in **"The Star in the Valley"**] is the first full step toward the ultimate mountain-flower type. One of the mountaineers pictures her succinctly: "She's a mighty good, saft-spoken, quiet sort o' gal, but she's a pore, white-faced, slim little critter." Obviously alien to her own world, she is incapable of entering the one above her. Puzzled neighbors dismiss her as "teched in the head." She has a fair, ethereal face, bronze hair, opaline eyes, and a voice with the cadence of autumn winds. Miss Murfree calls her a "woodland flower." Selena Teake [in **"The Romance of Sunrise Rock"**] is her immediate complement: delicate crimson lips, limpid eyes, and—a salient feature hereafter—masses of yellow hair. Cynthia Ware [in **"Drifting Down Lost Creek"**] combines the spunk of the first pair with the pulchritude of the second. Her brilliant auburn hair is accounted a defect by the mountaineers; it sets her aside as "different." She sacrifices valiantly for love, loses, and takes her medicine without rancor.

The general run of mountain girl, who does not share the pluck, the radical beauty, or love-tragedy of the mountain-flower type, marries early, settles into an unsightly shanty, produces a troop of children, and sinks into the muck of immutable routines. It does not take long to enter the next stage. The mother of Clarsie Giles is "a slovenly, indolent woman, anxious, at the age of forty-five, to assume the prerogatives of advanced years. She had placed all her domestic cares upon the shapely shoul-

Murfree during the visit to Boston when her identity was revealed: (left to right) Edwin Booth, Murfree, Thomas Bailey Aldrich, Lilian Woodman Aldrich, Fanny Murfree, Miss Houghton, and James M. Bugbee, 1885.

ders of her willing daughter, and had betaken herself to the chimney-corner and a pipe." The married mountain woman quickly becomes thin and sallow, with deeply sunken eyes, jutting cheekbones, and a set expression of hopeless melancholy. . . .

As often as not the women work in the fields, more industriously than their husbands. Pitiably, they are caught between the forces of contending men and frequently suffer the brunt of the consequences. In time, however, they establish for themselves a kind of hearthside immunity. From this vantage the older crones release incessant streams of shrewd, shrewish comments on affairs of the home or around the Settlemint. They interrupt and derogate everyone. Aggressive, crisp in judgment, they enjoy astonishing toleration from their menfolk. Once in a while a garrulous grandfather arrogates this role, but he inclines to be minutely anecdotal and less caustic. Children do not usurp the center of attention as they do in many subsequent Murfree stories. When noted at all here, they are peripheral groups of "boisterous tow-headed children."

Another cementing element in Miss Murfree's encircled world is its peculiarities of speech. As with the landscape, she amalgamates impressions from several sections. She also pretends that mountaineers of every class consistently speak one dialect. At first Charles Forster Smith, most vigilant critic of her usages, exhorted her indiscriminate mixing of localisms and arbitrary coinages. Later he admitted being too pedantic and placed her with Joel Chandler Harris and George Washington Cable as the best dialect writers of the South [*Southern Bivouac,* November, 1885].

The base of mountaineer language in the time of her stories was a combination of Anglo-Saxon and Celtic, with Chaucerian overtones; but Miss Murfree incorporated no

great number of esoteric expressions. The reader is seldom jogged by utterly unfamiliar locutions, for she favors recognizable words, idioms, and similes from conventional contemporary English and American sources. Whatever her distortions, she succeeds in producing verisimilitude through reproductions of the slow, dry, digressive drawl of the region, deceptively somnolent yet barbed with pungent country wisdom. She employs it patently and excessively, but her most grievous error lies in cacography—the inelegant misspellings accepted by her generation as genuine transcription of colloquial speech and as a legitimate form of humor. Piquant to begin with, it grows tiresome as all unabated idiosyncrasy does. Before long it nullifies much of its value as a characterizing device.

In three of these stories she uses vernacular to dynamic advantage in the opening sentence—a native statement which immediately sets tone, gives an inkling of custom, and points the direction of plot. The best example is her first: "Fur ye see, Mis' Darley, them Harrison folks over yander ter the Cove hev determined on a dancin' party." For the rest, she falls back on only two words that may give pause ("chouse," "cymlin'") and two that are determinable in context (a mountain range runs "spang up into Virginny," and "plumb catawampus"). Mild malapropism occurs when a mountaineer "hev hed the insurance" to associate with townspeople. "Drag me through hell an' beat me with a soot-bag" has the tune and stride of backland lingo, but "tuk ter the work like a pig ter carrots" and "perlite an' smilin' ez a basket of chips" smell of professional polish.

Despite the exceptional freedom to talk granted the people in these stories, not many escape Miss Murfree's possessive grip and take shape as personalities on their own power. In the manner of earlier nineteenth-century novelists, she furnishes full formal credentials with each character at initial entry into the action. Some few are anticipated by remarks of their familiars, but this introduction does not obviate summary treatment afterward. She overdoes the method of *oratio oblique,* arriving at antecedent and internal determinants of character from an external third-person stance. A man's attributes and psychological development are described in so many words. Looks are equated with qualities. Her nobler people *look* different, *i.e.,* the mountain-flower type. Also, a mountain lad turned lawyer has chiseled Grecian features. There are now and then people with subsurface rumblings, persons with problems not amenable to solution by intoxication or physical violence. While Miss Murfree indicates her belief in a double self and permits some introspection, she continually reverts to exposition rather than self-revelation.

The characters in *In the Tennessee Mountains* are largely stereotypes. Less than half a dozen can be recalled as individuals. Rick Pearson in **"The Dancin' Party"** is merely picturesque; Kenyon, a showcase of blunt moral and physical manliness. Mandy Tyler raises expectations of conflict and comedy, but she fades out both as a personality and an activator. Rufus Chadd emerges from the massed background of types as a man torn by inner tumult. "A harrassing sense of doubleness" invests him with vitality absent in the host of mountain mothers and mountain-flower girls who acquiesce mutely to their condition of social and emotional bondage. **"The 'Harnt' That Walks Chilhowee"** contains three figures who reveal levels of consciousness which go deeper than their narrative and environmental functions: Simon Burney with his awkward, fruitless courtship of a much younger girl, his tender concern for Clarsie's lawbreaking, and his thankless philanthropy; Mrs. Giles with her acidulous tongue, invented folklore, and crafty usurpation of decision-making in the household; Reuben Crabb with his deprived, lonely soul and presumptuous acceptance of gratuities as though they are his due—all give suggestions of subterranean currents, of complexities and contradictions conducive to speculation. Budd Wray undergoes a psychological dilemma, but the hand of Miss Murfree too heavily guides the outcome. Every city man and woman is to some degree a mouthpiece of Miss Murfree's attitudes and opinions—the women keen but shallow, the young men particularly leaden.

. . . . .

The powers of routine, inertia, and ignorance shape most of the activities and attitudes of Miss Murfree's mountaineers. So positive are these influences that not even those who leave the mountains are exempt from their dictation, but one notable exception is the opportunist Evander Price who shakes himself clear to his own irreparable injury. The two most noticeable traits of these mountaineers are their sloth and their pride. Completely content with things as they are, the men pass from one day to another as English squires might: hunting, racing horses, drinking, shooting for prizes, telling and retelling tales of their exploits. Only dire emergency can move them to more practical exertion. Intensely individualistic, they carry pride to inordinate lengths; and they are undisposed to combine in enterprise except for avoidance of liquor taxes, which they regard as an intervention in their personal affairs. They acknowledge no superiors, social, moral, or physical, and will resist with their lives any attempts at domination.

Pride infiltrates family feeling, potent and unspoken. Respect for the aged is second nature, and solidity of clan is demonstrated in a supper where four generations—ranging from two to eighty years of age—sit together in unceremonial communism. The effect is one of continuity and homogeneity, visible in their absorption with events of the past (possibly as compensation for the scanty happenings of the present) and in xenophobia. The latter takes on two contrary semblances. Stemming from their insulated existence, they view every unaccounted stranger with suspicion, if not hostility; anyone may be a revenue agent or an informer in the pay of the government. No questions are asked and none answered. Even the nearby valley people are held to be "cur'ous critters," and the mountaineers become "sifflicated" in lowland air. Yet, stemming from family pride, they respond with instant and total hospitality to all, including doubtful "furriners" who come to their door. Food, lodging, or aid is extended ungrudgingly.

Guests get the best the house can offer and are accompanied by expressions of regret as they leave. Privacy of background is inviolate; a stranger need only tell as much as he chooses about himself.

Violence is the primary principle of reaction and a customary occurrence. Under the slow talk and the sluggish gestures throb currents of ungovernable emotions. Stabbings and shootings are conventional. Blood is no deterrent; passions run red. Revenge is a personal prerogative, and murder is planned as casually as one might review yesterday's weather. A mother foresees impassively the extermination of her son by a bandit gang: "They'll slaughter the boy." Women develop stoic acceptance of their place as chattel. Beaten and slashed by their drunken husbands, they loyally defend them from retaliation by male relatives. Any demonstration of courtesy or filial affection is out of order, and women traditionally refrain from displays of feminine delicacy in public. Spinsters are openly condemned and pitied, as are slight or redhaired women.

Originally Presbyterians, the mountaineers have gravitated to evangelical creeds propagated by the flamboyant circuit riders who seasonally breach their remote borders. Eagerly they await the next visitation and the "bloody-minded sermons." The mountaineers interpret Scripture literally and subscribe to Calvinistic predestination. The resultant of these periodic revivals is a moral code strict in statement, lax in observance, and relative in values. As against murder, a venial infraction, dancing and gambling are grave transgressions directly punishable by God. Murder contemplated over the stealing of a mere bay filly is censured, but "ef it war the roan three-year-old now, 'twould be different." In a conflict between earthly and heavenly criteria the response is overt piety and sly expediency. The mountaineers are careful not to jeopardize future reward for present profit—however, why not try for the best of both worlds? For the most part, all laws except those against bootlegging are obeyed. And with uncomplicated trustfulness they expect immunity from prosecution by the county attorney as their due for having elected him.

Fearless in physical pursuits, they are incorrigibly superstitious. Life in a state close to nature fraught with inexplicable movements, noises, and consequences has bequeathed a repository of lore about human "harnts," screeching owls, and prophecy by ritual. The devil is ubiquitous by night and to him is ascribed all prodigies and most mishaps. On the mountaineers' calendar the day of judgment has an indeterminate but rubrical place. Mrs. Harrison, for instance, fears that the house will fall on them as a reproof of their wickedness in dancing.

. . . . .

Out of this locale, these people, and their practices, Miss Murfree embodies a plausible world in which comedy, pathos, politics, grief, love, religion, and brutality intermix in proportions determined by the special temperament of this special generation. The stories in *In the Tennessee Mountains* contain only rudiments of her fuller construct, but they provide infallible guidelines to her subsequent manner. The materials, techniques, and themes of the stories that comprise this volume leave no doubt that she perceives the impelling forces of mountaineer life and that she sympathizes with her subjects. They also indicate that she could never be much more than a responsive stranger in a country too crude for her ingrained sensitivity.

The ruling method of management in five of these eight stories is a contrast of urban and rustic cultures. The first story, in point of publication, most nearly approximates her own experience. The central altercation in **"The Dancin' Party at Harrison's Cove"** occurs between two mountaineers, but it also involves directly and indirectly summer visitors from the resort hotel at New Helvetia Springs. Mrs. Johns, a mountain wife whose chief occupation is to sell Indian peaches to the city vacationers, returns to the hotel one day to secure medicines for her ailing husband. She goes into a long account of her son's imminent danger—he insists on attending the dancing party in defiance of Rick Pearson's threat to kill him if he does. Her sallow face, expressionless voice, and shabby, faded calico are juxtaposed to Mrs. Darley's plump round arms, flowing black dress ("all furbelows and flounces"), and animated manner. They make "a wonderful contrast," says Miss Murfree, illustrating further the enormous cleft that separates their speech and social discretions. An intermediate standard is inserted later when the Harrison girls enjoy a brush with sophistication at Cheatham's Cross-Roads and develop a desire to emulate "fashion." Pitiful by Mrs. Darley's estimation, the Cross-Roads is a filter through which the most backward may acquire a modicum of metropolitan style. Male qualities come under profounder scrutiny. Ambrose Kenyon, the city man who by raw physical courage prevents gunplay between young Johns and Pearson, elicits respect from the mountaineers because they mistake him for a preacher—he is a lay reader—and tally his dour visage and platitudinous moralisms with those of a circuit rider. An outsider, he would probably have been slain except that he stills the dissonance between town and mountain by evincing an indigenous virtue: "He had grit enough to belong to the gang." Pearson espies in him "a parallel of his own belligerent and lawless spirit." Country courage in whatever dress is country courage.

In **"The Star in the Valley"** Miss Murfree again favors the ruder culture. Reginald Chevis, a sensitive city sportsman camping in the mountains, looks down on Celia Shaw "with a mingled pity for her dense ignorance, her coarse surroundings, her low station." He is appalled when she encourages her father and his friends to drink to excess. When he learns later that she did so in order to gain time enough to warn a man they intended to murder, "he began to have a glimmering perception that despite all his culture, his sensibility, his yearnings toward humanity, he was not so high a thing in the scale of being." Miss Murfree rates bedrock virtues above finishing-school manners, and she is reasonably proud that "differences of caste are absolutely unknown to the independent mountaineers." Chevis prides himself on this humanity, Celia actually has it; he talks about it, she acts. When she dies not long after

her mission in the snowstorm, she assumes, for Chevis, the symbolic status of a star.

Miss Murfree now embraces a wider scope of comparisons. In **"The Star"** Chevis' companion Ned Varney does not figure strongly enough to constitute an attitude, but in **"The Romance of Sunrise Rock"** John Cleaver and Fred Trelawney project two distinct reactions of the city to the country: Trelawney is sympathetic; Cleaver, inimical. In the byplay of development, the good and bad of both ways of life are weighed—and the simpler existence comes off better once more. The contrast begins on a deceptive note when the native is referred to as a "hairy animal" and Cleaver as "this fine young fellow." Within minutes, however, he drops his unexpressed disdain of country dullness, admitting that "Greek and Latin do not altogether avail." As for his elaborate edifice of education, why, the happy sheep-farmer does not need it. Through Selina Teake, a sad and lovely mountain-flower, the onus of frivolity is placed squarely on girls who pursue "society." Trelawney shrinks at what Selina might think of them, and Miss Murfree launches a long self-incriminating satire on the uselessness of fashionable education which enables city women "to interject commonplace French phrases into their daily conversation, and render their prattle an affront to good taste." (Like most dilettante ruralists, she derogates polite attainments while never really abandoning them; she feels secretly superior in her possession of them. In short order, ironically, she interjects a French and a Latin expression.) Regardless of paradox, she makes her overt point in the resolution of Trelawney and Cleaver. Trelawney decides to remain in the mountains, sheds the skepticism of his college days, and acquires calm and strength from his environment "very like the comfort of religion." On the other hand, Cleaver returns to the city, is surrounded by an envious crowd that disparages his success, and lives bleakly in the knowledge of their pettiness.

Using a *Tom Jones* technique of cross-sectioning society, Miss Murfree presents a new set of variants in **"Drifting Down Lost Creek."** Cynthia Ware's pilgrimage to Sparta to effect the release of Evander Price from jail permits views of life on the mountain, along the sparsely settled valley area, and in the county seat. The differences are less striking than those between mountain and metropolis; but Cynthia, in perfect harmony on the mountain, is the object of suspicion on the road and of pity in the town. Like all good mountaineers, she is out of place away from the mountain. By the time she arrives in Sparta, "all her grace and pliant swaying languor [are] lost in convulsive, awkward haste and a feeble, jerky gait." Only after she glimpses the mountain again does she feel "the supreme exaltation" and recover her poise. The lover she rescues rejects her, adopts town life, and marries a town woman. Once an ambitious inventor, he settles down to a routine job and is harassed by lurking doubts of his powers. He is proud of his wife's "school l'arnin'," but she considers him uncouth and depressing. On a brief visit back to the mountain he is no longer capable of seeing its beauties, only weather signs. He has lost the better girl and the more wholesome place. In the beginning the mountain "stands against the west like a barrier. It seemed to Cynthia Ware that nothing which went beyond this barrier ever came back again." Prophetically, this is the story of her loss. Evander crosses the barrier, grows hard and calculating. His native quality is totally vitiated.

In the return-of-the-native theme of **"Electioneerin' on Big Injun Mounting,"** Miss Murfree sets up yet another scheme of contrast, buttressed by a psychological conflict. Rufus Chadd, a mountain dweller until he is twenty, moves to town, becomes a lawyer, and is elected district attorney. His native instincts and primal experiences help him outstrip city antagonists. Gradually, constant contact with the worst phases of human nature harden him; he becomes a pitiless prosecutor. When he returns to his old bailiwick to campaign for re-election, he discovers that his book talk and store clothes repel his former neighbors. He is attacked and almost killed by a vicious bully, Isaac Boker. When Chadd declines to identify Boker as his assailant and demands that he be freed, sentiment flows back in Chadd's favor. Like Kenyon in **"The Dancin' Party,"** Chadd demonstrates an indigenous virtue and wins deference. Although a civil officer, he pays allegiance to the mountain code of silence. (His motivation goes deeper, but the mountaineers accept at face value his refusal to inform.) Such reversion to regional mores is proof sufficient to the mountaineers that Chadd is still one of them. He is the obverse of Evander Price for, in this struggle between old and new, the old prevails. Chadd is eventually re-elected by the heaviest majority ever polled on Big Injun Mounting.

Of the three remaining stories in *In the Tennessee Mountains* only **"A-Playin' of Old Sledge at the Settlemint"** offers no specific regional oppositions; in **"Over on the T'other Mounting"** Miss Murfree arbitrarily injects the opinion that the "magnificent pageant of the four seasons . . . was a gracious recompense for the spectacular privileges of civilization," thus aligning herself again with the mountains. And she appends this clearly inconsequent aphorism as last paragraph to **"The 'Harnt' That Walks Chilhowee"**: "The grace of culture is, in its way, a fine thing, but the best that art can do—the polish of a gentleman—is hardly equal to the best that Nature can do in her higher moods."

One of the severely divisive factors in these stories is Miss Murfree's inability to establish a point of view and thereafter maintain it consistently or shift it strategically to best advantage. Her principal perspective is that of a spectator on the perimeter of the action who is obviously not autochthonous but acquainted with the ways of the natives and inclined to appreciate their finer, often invisible endowments. Her tendency in this role of overseer is to manage people and affairs too firmly and to deny them development in their own essential directions. When, as in **"The Dancin' Party,"** she permits a mountaineer to divulge the basic situation, she invariably relegates this narrator to a far corner and resumes control. The fracture that results is disturbing to the mood of unity, for Miss Murfree cannot refrain from extraneous commentary about the characters or course of events.

As a literary artist she makes every conscious effort to enter the nerve center of this strange world, but her training as a Southern lady simply will not let her. The closest she comes is arm's length. In a burst of spontaneous approbation, she exclaims: "Here are the true republicans!" or indeed, "Here are the only aristocrats!" Yet this forthright glorification cannot cancel out the insidious reappearance of the phrase "these mountaineers"—and worse, "these people"—in her less guarded, less rhapsodic moments. Frequently, she emits inadvertent condescension through surrogates such as Mrs. Darley in **"The Dancin' Party,"** Reginald Chevis in **"The Star in the Valley,"** Rufus Chadd in **"Electioneerin' on Big Injun Mounting,"** and John Cleaver in **"The Romance of Sunrise Rock,"** Chevis, for instance, reflects the attitude of patrician to pleb that creeps willy-nilly into all Miss Murfree's mountain stories when he lifts his hat "with that punctilious courtesy which he made a point of according to persons of low degree." Did Miss Murfree realize the import of her offhand remark that "even a 'mounting' woman is susceptible of the sting of wounded pride," including the obloquy of the single quotation marks? She approaches the brink of self-analysis when she wonders whether Cleaver is a snob because he sees the mountaineers as bull-headed, ludicrous, and unkempt. Soon, however, she is back regarding the scene as a stage and herself as an applauding spectator.

A second disjunctive practice is Miss Murfree's truly extraordinary use of formal language. O. Henry dabbles in grotesque polysyllables for the pure fun or irony they provide, but she sets them down in utter seriousness. Fairly sparing to begin with, she progressively increases the number of arcane words and phrases in later stories and novels. In these stories the reader stumbles over such horrendous Latinisms as "febrifuge," "interfulgent," "exercitations," "stellular,"and a "fulvous-tinted" deer. French falls trippingly into the text and sits cheek by jowl with Italian: "stupendous alto-relievo in silver repoussé." Jogging country dancers are "votaries of Terpsichore." The academic resonance and the halting rhythms are incompatible with the coarse fluidity of native speech. The ornate adjectives only make natural splendor a gaudy spectacle.

The contrast of elevated and corrupt language undoubtedly helps to accentuate the great gap between the worlds of city and mountain, but its effect upon tone and continuity is destructive. In **"Over on the T'other Mounting"** a long vulgate passage runs without transition into a stylized depiction of "a subtile amethystine mist," and is succeeded by "Waal" and another expanse of dialect. Even more harsh is the collision of the first and second paragraphs of **"The Romance of Sunrise Rock."** "Moons waxed and waned; nations rose and fell; centuries came and went. And still it faced the east, and still, undimmed by storm and time, it reiterated the miracle and prophecy of the rising sun." This grandiose description of Sunrise Rock collapses abruptly against the jagged sharpness of Selina's, "'Twar painted by the Injuns,—that's what I hev always hearn tell." The shock of disparity is out of proportion to any intended impression. Like melodrama, it tempts the reader to laugh in the wrong places. . . .

The awesome immensity of the mountains fills these stories with a sense of infinite space and slow, timeless movement. Under eternal skies the natives live out drab lives, take without complaint the buffets of fate, and thank whatever God there be for their immortal souls. Not all, however, is wonder and gloom. Through the unwinding days and nights they find in their work and in their sport occasions to jest, to laugh. They make amusing analogies between themselves and their animals, domestic or wild. Coquettes twit their suitors unmercifully. Men and women jibe coarsely at each other. And their dialect, though natural to them, provides another dimension of comedy for the reader.

Rustic jocularity is not to Miss Murfree's own taste. She prefers the slimmer blade of drawing-room wit. Standing above and to one side of the defenseless mountaineers, she insistently jabs them with glittering ironies. She creates discordance by interposing remarks about the alleged superiorities of city over country, by coupling the potency of mountains with women's suffrage, by grinning over some yokel blunder. It is all kindly meant, and the irony heightens because she does not realize its end effect.

She develops irony of situation in the tensions of choice between mundane and spiritual values, in native rationalizations of crimes, in verifying the uselessness of bookish education in a rural plight, and in exposing a fearsome 'harnt' as a frightened, one-armed sniveler. She exploits irony of theme in **"The Romance of Sunrise Rock"** (Selina loves the wrong man and Cleaver never knows how happy Trelawney is); in **"Electioneerin' on Big Injun Mounting"** (the mountaineers vote for Chadd for the wrong reasons); in **"A-Playin' of Old Sledge"** (the community makes undeserved presumptions about Wray's renunciation of revenge); in **"Over on the T'other Mounting"** (Britt's attempt to murder Hoxie leads to reconcilement of their long-standing feud); in **"The Star in the Valley"** and **"Drifting Down Lost Creek"** (one girl dies and one girl recedes into herself while neither male protagonist ever comprehends their pathetic intensity). In this last category of ironic usage Miss Murfree succeeds in implementing her theme of common humanity least pretentiously.

Miss Murfree did not subscribe to Poe's conception of the short story as a vignette of single accumulating effect or a single incident with decisive impact upon character. Says Fred Lewis Pattee: "Strictly speaking, her short stories are not short stories at all save in the one element of shortness. She records simple, everyday incidents in their natural sequence and stops when the space allotted to her has been filled. She moves leisurely from incident to incident in a monotonous vacuity of mountain life, as a minutely written journal might move" [*The Development of the American Short Story,* 1923]. Sarah Orne Jewett, who used to "nibble all round her stories like a mouse," refers to Miss Murfree's "big" stories. They are in many cases, now and later, two stories indeterminately fused; they are aborted or condensed novels. The bastard term *novelette* would suit a good number. They offer excessive antecedent data, digress too far afield, and go on long after the unifying action is concluded.

"Drifting Down Lost Creek" is an outstanding example of Miss Murfree's disregard of prescriptive principles. It is less a short story, even in length (seventy-nine pages), than an attenuated novel. She does not focus on a single turbulent or understated incident for a flash of insight; instead, she presents a developmental chronicle of the changes wrought in the lives of two young lovers over the course of a decade. She imparts an appearance of unity to this domestic tragedy of Puritan stoicism by repeated correspondence of humanity and nature—Cynthia's life and the purposeless drift of leaves on the surface of Lost Creek—and through the cyclic effect of this basic symbol in the opening and closing paragraphs. But the prolongation of Cynthia's ordeal and Miss Murfree's obtrusive explanations diminish its power as a short story.

"The Star in the Valley" proceeds with deliberate, convincing intensification from a static scene of idealistic meditation to a static scene of realistic threats to a kinetic scene of escape and pursuit. Miss Murfree then allows the story to strangulate in turgid recapitulation and explication, rendered unnecessary by her fugal interplay of the "star" in the valley (Cynthia Ware), the "star" on the mountain (Reginald Chevis), and the first ascendant star of evening. **"The Romance of Sunrise Rock"** takes long in starting, progresses to an exciting height of hallucination, then similarly flags into a redundant epilogue.

Mrs. Johns's introduction to the evolving climax of **"The Dancin' Party"** constitutes a narrative frame which Miss Murfree might better have extended to infold the entire story or not have used at all. The vital, central duel is thus seen through the screen of an omniscient tenderfoot rather than through the eyes of an implicated, native witness. Suspense is capably broached and upheld in the manner of Hardy's "The Three Strangers" by a dynamic series of three contrastive entrances. Pearson and his armed comrades do not disturb the dancers, for they are all insiders. Kenyon gives momentary pause to the fiddler and the dancers, for he is an outsider who stirs conscience and raises discomfortable possibilities. His reassuring bromides restore equanimity and prepare the scene for a drastic dislocation. Johns's appearance at the door stops the music and brings the dancing to a standstill, for he carries the spark of abeyant catastrophe.

"A-Playin' of Old Sledge" is also based on a vivid central duel, but Miss Murfree somewhat bedims its vigor by distending it into a moral application. Wray's psychological reflexes, plausible in the card game, become improbable in his cancellation of revenge. Miss Murfree's proclivity to follow more than one thread in a short story is again visible in **"The 'Harnt' That Walks Chilhowee,"** but she strikes a highly satisfying balance between the pathos of Reuben Crabb's life-in-death quandary and the comedy of a December-May rivalry in courtship. With its overlay of forest shadows, local superstitions, pithy characters, domestic genre details—and Miss

Murfree's forbearance as narrator—it is in so many respects the best story in this volume.

Within its formal frame, **"Over on the T'other Mounting"** has the loose weave, circuitous pattern, and primary colors of a folk tale. Miss Murfree adopts the anecdotal method of arriving at the core incident and leaves promise at the conclusion of further tangents to be explored. After accepting the first premise that witches fired T'other Mounting, the subsequent adventures and ironies follow as logically as any deadpan tomfoolery. Violence and hilarity blend with the supernatural and the vernacular in a tale without dominant didactic motive except for reasserting the inequality of power in the partnership of man and nature.

The resolution of **"Electioneerin' on Big Injun Mounting"** comes nearest to matching the type most frequently encountered in the contemporary short story. Miss Murfree relinquishes none of her ceremonious procedures, but cuts through cleanly to a throbbing nerve of motivation. Chadd's decision not to testify against his assailant Boker is determined by one fleeting glimpse of piteous Mrs. Boker standing in the doorway; his experience tears away the accretions of town life from his heart and opens a flow of restorative group memory. Neither the preliminary or posterior apparatus obscures the validity of this instinctive reversion, which marks a point of rare discernment in Miss Murfree's early interpretation of mountaineer behavior.

. . . . .

After *In the Tennessee Mountains* Miss Murfree published some fifteen stories in this category (three others with Civil War components are discussed under that head). Seven of the stories appeared in the period 1885-1895; the others, between 1908-1920. Although she introduces few new elements, she perceptibly strengthens her rhetorical and structural techniques. There is less emphasis on the contrast of cultures; she presents the mountaineers more often in situations undefiled by outside influences; and she more often dispenses with her *alter ego* commentator from the city. Although she continues to trespass as author-critic, she moves in point of view closer to her subjects; she is more the prober than the thrilled spectator. If anything, she is more persistently pietistic, and she inclines more readily to the hoax. After a decade of toiling in other literary vineyards, she returns to the mountains. In this last era she re-creates the scenic prodigies, the unorthodox natives, the romance and outlawry of the region; and she conjures up again the tinted names of the mountains, and Colbury, Cross-Roads, Kildeer County, Tomahawk Creek. Nevertheless, the feeling of strain in the stories is due to a manifest attempt to recapture the magic of the old, successful formula. Sadly, the once heady compound has lost its potency.

Five stories are informed with the spirit of Christmas and ring slight variations on the gospel of man's regeneration through love. They all turn on the same device of feud or ill-will melted by the sight of a Tennessee mountain recrudescence of the Child in the Manger. The repetitive quality of this determining scene and the excess of sentimentality is accounted for by the fact that each appeared in the December issue of a national periodical and was undoubtedly contrived with that specific occasion in mind.

The hatred of one man for another in **"Way Down' Lonesome Cove"** (1885) feeds on rivalry in love and a stolen horse. The second circumstance rekindles the feud which had arisen over the first. Gunfighting ensues. When Luke Todd comes to kill Tobe Gryce, he discovers him hiding in an abandoned saltpeter cave with his little daughter and the horse. Todd's trigger finger is stayed by "A soft aureola with gleaming radiations, a low, shadowy chamber, a beast feeding from a manger, and within it a child's golden head." His heart gives a great throb: "Somehow he was smitten to his knees. Christmas Eve!" The objective correlative of child, animal, and holiday wreaks this somewhat disputable effect upon a hardened mountaineer bent on murder. The conversion is too abrupt to be convincing—Bret Harte's "The Luck of Roaring Camp" with a Christmas confection. Far more credible is the poignant confrontation between Mrs. Gryce, once an "azalea-like girl," now faded by unceasing work and worry, and the younger Mrs. Todd. Here Miss Murfree presents with unusual cogency two stages in the metamorphosis of a mountain-flower to a crone. Mrs. Gryce sees in Mrs. Todd a vision of herself when beautifully young; Mrs. Todd espies in Mrs. Gryce's face the forecast of wrinkles to come in her own. Another standby in many stories and novels—the monarch baby who tyrannizes everyone within the ken of his clenched fist and defiant stare—also makes a first full-fledged entrance in Gryce's daughter, the "Colonel," who is a cut more obstinate, imperious, and greedy than most of her breed. Knowing Miss Murfree's inveterate fondness for irony, one wonders at the utilization of this little Tartar as a Christ likeness, as well as the names Gryce (Christ) and Todd (God).

Sentimentality and stereotypes overwhelm this story. Miss Murfree lapses ineptly into the historical present tense. She reveals prior events through flashback conversation, a creditable technique except that Mrs. Gryce recalls the details to her mother, who must surely have been familiar with them. And yet this story has saving graces in the scene between the two wives and in such symbolic touches as the sinister light from the flares of the mob falling now and then on the holly bushes, a provocative inverse prefiguration of the happy denouement.

Discounting some minor changes, **"His 'Day in Court'"** (1887) is a facsimile of the foregoing story but is, perhaps, less believable. This feud has extended over several generations of killings and maimings, includes all members of the Quimbey and Kittredge families, and is currently bitter, whereas Todd and Gryce had never fought and Todd had not seen Mrs. Gryce in ten years. Renewing the Montague-Capulet heresy, Absalom Kittredge marries Evelina Quimbey. When they have a falling out, Absalom kidnaps their baby. Forced by court order to restore the boy to his mother, Absalom creeps up to the Quimbey home one night intent on stealing him back. Evelina had placed the golden-haired child temporarily in its piggin on the straw-covered ground in the stable, surrounded by cattle and sheep. The over-all grouping reminds Absalom that this night is Christmas Eve. He steals away quietly, the Nativity scene having had its due effect upon his vindictive heart.

Miss Murfree revives every cliché of Christmas magazine fiction, even alluding to the Babe in the Manger and the Star of Bethlehem; but again there are aspects of excellence. As in the preceding story, she brings her knowledge of legal technicalities skillfully into play; and she lifts the curtain on a fascinating, populous "underfoot world" of children, dogs, poultry, and other oddities on the kitchen floor only dimly significant to adults. Several short scenes, done with faultless restraint, have a power greater than the totality: the gurgling child captivating the huge, brute Quimbeys (like "The Luck" grabbing Kentuck's finger); old Quimbey's vilification of Absalom in the courtroom; the reunion of Evelina and her father, and his gentle, diplomatic threat of murder to mediator Joe Boyd. Old Mrs. Kittredge creates an unforgettable impression of classic tragedy and remorse after she permits Evelina to carry off the baby: "She was terrified by her own deed, and cowered under Absalom's wrath. . . . She flung her apron over her head, and sat still and silent—a monumental figure—among them."

"Who Crosses Storm Mountain?" (1908) is shallow anecdote exemplifying the Christian lesson of peace on earth, goodwill toward men but this time in O. Henry farce-irony vein. The lost baby of one feudist, Gilhooley, is picked up by a drunkard, placed in a mail pouch (the presumptive manger), and then unknowingly adopted by the second feudist, Petrie. When identity is established, Gilhooley comes to claim the child. The two sworn enemies—mollified by his immaculate innocence—patch up their differences and are last seen on all fours, barking for the infant's delectation. Miss Murfree's disposition to pontificate, to give ex officio explanations of motive, and to underscore theme explicitly destroy movement and humor.

"The Riddle of the Rocks" (1886) is, by contrast, solemn in tone and embraces a fundamental concern of the mountaineers—prophecy based on signs. The feud, children, and Christmas Eve play habitual parts in the eventuation of this story; but all are subordinated to the arduous struggle of a man to regain his faith. Roger Purdee, a totally ignorant herder gifted with "the fires of imagination," is sincerely confident in his ability to read the Scriptural messages imprinted on two blocks of sandstone which he and others believe are the tables of the Law flung down from the mountain top by Moses. He achieves impressive local reputation by passing on the revelations of these hieroglyphs. Grinnell, an envious neighbor whose family has feuded with the Purdees for many years, convinces the community that the alleged runes are no more than the erosions of weather and the depredations of worms. Purdee undergoes sickening disillusionment, withdraws into deep depression, and broods uncommunicatively for days. His internal agonies are interrupted by Grinnell's claim to his lands. It turns out, ironically, that Grinnell's house and farm are on Purdee's ground. With revenge at hand he is reminded of the season by a glimpse of the beguiling Grinnell child and sheep huddling in the door of a rude stable. Christ-like, he forgives his persistent persecutor. Through this magnanimity Purdee's shaken faith is restored. Once again he begins to descry a familiar letter, a developing word, and finally the phrase "Peace on earth, good will to men" carved in the rocks.

The trend and upshot of this story are not forced as in the others. Purdee's regenerative act is solidly motivated in his strong religious nature. The Nativity tableau merely prompts him to behave according to his principles; it does not precipitously reverse a lifetime of malice (as in previous cases). Miss Murfree's desire to tell two stories at a time occludes a profounder view of Purdee's ordeal. As she approaches intimate commitment with his ruminations, the exigencies of the feud break in and she veers off on another tack, the emphasis reverting to action rather than characterization. Although the two threads have a common denominator that in the end connects them, the psychology of Purdee's revivification gets short shrift and the story suffers a sense of integral disunity.

Miss Murfree endows the Tennessee mountains with height and mystery of universal stature through these implications of Biblical miracle and revelation. Purdee's belief—shared by many others—that the Old Testament prophets roamed these mountains and that the Lord spoke to Moses in the Great Smokies invests them with awe more primal than that inspired by ephemeral "harnts." Shelley's "Ozymandias" comes to mind when Miss Murfree sets man's brief contumacious moment against nature's impervious, limitless dominion.

She occasionally discharges ponderous sarcasms to belittle native affectations (referring to one man as "the advanced thinker" and never dignifying him with a name), but in general her witticisms are less pointedly directed from one class to the weaknesses of another class. Through the spontaneous affection of the Grinnell and Purdee children she testifies that they have "not the sense enough to know anything about hereditary enemies," that society perpetuates the very prejudices it so piously deprecates. Adroitly too she links the themes of feud and faith: "With the ramrod of his gun he sought to follow the fine tracings of the letters writ by the finger of the Lord on the stone tables."

She tries to resuscitate this fine combination of animus and conversion in **"His Christmas Miracle"** (1911), a retelling of the grasshopper-ant fable. She succeeds in establishing a firm basis for thrifty Jubal Kennedy's change of heart toward the improvident, lovable Bedell family, so well in fact that the replica of the nativity scene is wholly inutile. Kennedy, a thoroughgoing philistine, cannot realize he has witnessed two miracles—the Bedells and their house spared utter destruction when it slides over the precipice; his own selfless heroism in their behalf—and is still hankering for an abrogation of natural law as the story ends. To be sure that the implied doctrine is not lost, Miss Murfree declares sententiously that "The kingdom o'

Christ is a spiritual kingdom"; and faith, not works, is the key to the miracle of existence.

Politics vies with religion as a claimant of the mountaineers' attention. Elections give them an unassailably egoistic moment of glory during which their favor is sought and their opinions solicited. **"The Casting Vote"** (1893) derives its drama from a deadlocked election and a perfidious brother. Confined to these elements, this account could have been an effective one of local attitudes and passions. Unfortunately, Miss Murfree disregards every restriction of the short story and instead creates what amounts to a skimpy novel. Action preceding and following the crisis is everlasting, and numerous other thematic considerations crowd the main issue. The story starts out to be a Christian parable on the texts of honor thy brother and turn the other cheek. Soon it deviates into a tangle of familiar bypaths.

Justus Hoxon is an all-sacrificing, all-suffering Christ, as the anagram of *just* and *Jesus* in his first name would indicate. He has surrendered his own ambitions in order to bring up his brother Walter and is now electioneering for him. In remuneration, Walter steals and marries his sweetheart Theodosia, a vain, vacillating mountain-flower without the usual martyr complex. Walter loses the election when the deciding voter hears of his unprincipled behavior. The couple returns to the mountains; he becomes a slothful drunkard, she a dowdy crone. Justus dismisses thoughts of revenge, takes a job as night watchman in a city factory, and spends his time conning the sky for another sight of the comet that blazed at him on election night. Miss Murfree appears to place immense symbolic weight on this fleeting body but, as in the novel *His Vanished Star,* the reader finds it difficult to decode its relation with the major theme beyond the vague implication that God's eye is twinkling down on good Justus. The sky is an open scroll from which, she says, "all men of receptive soul . . . have read there of the mystery of the infinite, of the order and symmetry of the plan of creation, of the proof of the existence of a God." We are now far afield from the original thesis that Walter, somewhat like Hollis in **"Taking the Blue Ribbon,"** wins the cheapest prize while losing his marvelous brother and the election. There is certain satisfaction in the poetic quality of retributive justice: goodness is rewarded, and evil is permitted to punish itself. Justus prospers serenely in his new environment while Walter and Theodosia come to pieces quickly in material squalor that matches their moral flabbiness.

Miss Murfree's proneness to see landscape with the eyes of a painter is beautifully exhibited. "The scene was like some great painting . . . so elaborate and perfect in the coloring of the curves of purple, and amethyst, and blue mountains afar off." But there is a point where her romantic propensity gives way to the realistic: "where the rail fence drew the line of demarcation, Art seemed to fail." Nature is paradisic; man, his hovels and chattel, a blot on perfection. Discreetly she adds a human figure or two against this delicately vistaed Hudson River-school backdrop, blending when it is the mountain-flower girl, discordant when it is the utilitarian backwoodsman. Thus, despite the patent estheticism of her concept, the final effect is one of mystic intercommunication between nature and natives and author and reader. In this instance, at least, the peevish ejaculation of the New York *Times* (February 24, 1895)—"picture, picture, always picture"—is misdirected.

Miss Murfree is supposed to have written this eighty-page story in one evening, which may explain some of its weaknesses and baldly repetitive designs.

Two stories revolve around the accepted vocation of bootlegging in the mountains. The earlier one, **"The Moonshiners of Hoho-Hebee Falls"** (1893) is long on plot and short on motive, local color with a generous sprinkling of sermon. It is indeed two stories: Leander Yerby's relations with Mrs. Sudley, his foster mother; his Uncle Nehemiah's altercation with the moonshiners. The only bond between the two is the boy's presence in both. The story is peopled by a cluster of types, except Mrs. Sudley, who rules her household with continuous melancholy, no arguments or objurgations, and sometimes a hymn tune; and Nehemiah, a sanctimonious fraud, the most guileful and falsefaced mountaineer yet encountered in Miss Murfree's gallery, who descants endlessly against sin while ruthlessly maneuvering for his own profit. Although mostly drawn from without, the inhibited woman and the doltish hypocrite are achieved portraits. More than in other stories, individuals are characterized by what other individuals say about them.

In several places the shadow of Hawthorne's method falls across this story. When Nehemiah writes his informing letter to the revenue agents, a moth comes whisking in, moves up and down the sheet befouling itself with ink, circles again and again about the candle, passes through the flame, then falls quivering on the page. The moth is Nehemiah portending the failure of his own adventure. He circles around the dangerous flame (the furnace) of the moonshiners and collapses when they capture him. The furnace in the still below the falls is utilized in the same manner as the one in "Ethan Brand." The flare from its open door points up details of place, actions, and expressions vital to the evolution of the story. A prefiguration of the raid may be seen when the firelight is obscured by the moonlight, signalizing the ascendancy of heaven over hell, good over evil. And Hilary Tarbetts stands off from the other mountaineers by virtue of his white, ascetic face and cleaner accent, "like some rustic pietist, with strange theories and unhappy speculations and unsettled mind." Like Brand, he has been absent from his native heath a long season.

"The Moonshiners" seems to have been written as yet another substantiation of the Christian tenets that the rogues of the world eventually get their comeuppance and the meek inherit the earth. **"His Unquiet Ghost,"** published eighteen years later, treats the same constituents of moonshine and revenue agents with far less solemnity. To foil the agents, Walter Wyatt agrees to pretend he is dead until they leave the area. Eavesdropping at a forge, he hears himself reviled by several men he had counted as friends. Disillusioned, he goes to the cemetery where his body is supposed to be buried. There he sees his purportedly faithless sweetheart grieving distraughtly. Thinking him dead, she confesses her love for him. These antithetical scenes—comic at the forge, pathetic at the grave—comprise an amusing strophic movement in this leisurely, poker-face folk tale. Wyatt is downgraded and exalted, he gets bad and good views of himself, he undergoes dejection and jubilation in alternate doses. But Miss Murfree's heavy-handed dispensation of moral precepts countermands much of the humor in Wyatt's Faustian interludes. In a coda dreary with explicit preaching, she pounds the theme of Wyatt's reformation, wrought by the power of true love, while admitting that it caused no permanent change in his prankish temperament.

Hoax gives primary momentum to two other stories published about this time. **"Wolf's Head"** (1910) is a provincial corruption of the classic dryad myth. It manifests the ingenuity of a young woman in helping her lover escape the law and entrapping him for herself. This straight-line narrative has ingredients garnered from earlier works, a hoary denouement, a jovial spirit throughout, and a laconic O. Henry ending. The cast of characters is standard. The loquacious grandfather—now a stock figure—carries the burden of introducing the situation. Point of view shifts thereafter to an urban sportsman who plays surrogate for the author. Bloated polysyllabics offend when they come directly from Miss Murfree; for instance, the moon's "peculiar untranslated intendment which differentiates its luminosity." In other cases, it entertains. The city man hears the story about the fugitive "what war growed up in a tree" and muses about "the dryadic suggestions of a dendroidal captivity."

"A Chilhowee Lily" (1912), another anecdote, involves stronger factors of city-county contrast than had appeared for some years. However, it is only a feeble refrain on the hopeless yearning of the country girl for the city man, with just two notable effects: (1) Evanescent Loralinda Byars, the mountain-flower, is correlated feature for feature with the Chilhowee lily in opening, middle, and closing paragraphs to create a sturdy, if obvious, envelope structure; (2) The conflicting romantic-realistic impulses of local color are strikingly and succinctly demonstrated. After displaying a mountain cabin under "the annihilating magnificence of the moon," Miss Murfree trends to the other extreme:

> By daylight the dreary little hut had no longer poetic or picturesque suggestion. Bereft of the sheen and shimmer of the moonlight its aspect had collapsed like a dream into the dullest realities. The door-yard was muddy and littered; here the razorback hogs rooted unrebuked; the rail fence had fallen on one side, and it would seem that only their attachment to home prevented them from wandering forth to be lost in the wilderness; the clapboards of the shiny roof were oozing and steaming with dampness, and showed all awry and uneven; the clay and stick chimney, hopelessly out of plumb, leaned far from the wall.

In dealing with native superstitions Miss Murfree catches the feeling of awesome mystery engendered by the overpowering mountains, the darkness of forests, and the prim-

itive remoteness of the mountaineers. Without straying from rational interpretation, but not always providing one, she succeeds in permeating her stories with a legitimate sense of the weird. **"The Phantoms of the Foot-Bridge"** (1893) is in the best tradition of murky ghost stories. It proceeds on a plane of hint and repetition, of expectation working toward fulfillment. Every scene of importance has its presage in symbol or miniature. Millicent's apparition is preceded by three haunts that heighten probability and whet anticipation; her mystical appearance with a lighted candle prefaces the tragic shooting of Emory Keenan in the deserted hotel; her cap prefigures death by association for Keenan or John Dundas; the screech owl, a harbinger of death, recurs ominously. Miss Murfree's technical skills, almost completely ignored in criticisms of her work, show here to fine advantage.

John Dundas is an imposing physical specimen out of dandified romantic fiction, with Byronic appeal of silence and sadness for the lovely, simple mountain maid. His carefully shaven face, his immaculate cuffs, his black cloak with bright-blue lining, and his ring and gloves are derisively labeled feminine by roughcut Keenan, who would no more wear gloves than a petticoat. His clumsy red finger and Dundas' delicate hand illustrate by synecdoche the vast separation of town and mountain. Nevertheless, the theme is negligible and none of the characters displays distinguishing marks except the superficial Dickensian feature of a jaunty soldier's cap on Millicent's pretty golden head. Miss Murfree's penchant for explanation fills the final page with unneeded details of aftermath.

In **"The Mystery of Witch-Face Mountain"** (1895), a fully plotted novelette with no deviation in its narrative momentum, the activities of two juries—the coroner's, reviewing the murder of the city stranger, and the jury of view investigating possibilities of building a road—induce essential unity; for the murder and the discovery of oil form a central strand upon which every element hangs. The mystery is revealed as anti-climactic afterthought and the story straggles on to a redundant conclusion, an infirmity Miss Murfree cannot seem to overcome. Barring that and the gratuitous pedagogy, this is one of her least congested, smoothest flowing stories.

The parallel with Hawthorne's "The Great Stone Face" is unavoidable even though the face in **"The Mystery"** is formed by accidental juxtaposition of several natural phenomena and appears only when the oil content in a nearby stream is ignited. There is no inspirational intent as in Hawthorne; instead the face has an aspect of snarling mockery, and the mountaineers expect bad luck any day it is visible. Allegorical nomenclature is present in Constant Hite, perfect pun for a mountain dweller, and in Nick Peters, the bandit with whose devilry the murder may be associated. And right out of "Young Goodman Brown" are the conjectures about witches in the woods and the series of ambiguous rhetorical questions regarding the nature of the miraculous fire.

Miss Murfree leans speciously on classical names, frequently straining to elevate her mountain heroes and heroines by inconceivable analogies with Greek deities. Minerva Slade is twice blessed in that she is specifically compared with Hebe (as Millicent had been with Diana). Although Narcissa Hanway does gaze once into "the lustrous dark surface of a tiny pool" and blenches from her own image, her qualities owe less to mythological than to horticultural allusion. Her "flower-like face" is invoked at least three times.

The machinery of law and the natives' attitude toward law form a strong motif here, but the contrast of cultures surpasses it. The initial note is struck when the nameless city stranger realizes "that sense of distance in mind and spirit which is the true isolation of the foreigner, and which even an identity of tongue and kindred cannot annul." The other alien, Alan Selwyn, is an ineffectual valley man flawed by tuberculosis, the stigma of city existence. His secrecy is resented by the mountaineers, and his clothes are considered "fantastic toggery." Neither man survives the mountain experience; Hite, Narcissa, and her brother endure. After Selwyn's death, jealous Hite perceives that Narcissa's grief is not for a departed lover but "a sympathy akin to his own and to her brother's." Mountain vitality and solidarity are upheld. Hite will probably marry Narcissa in time.

Superstition, hoax, and the wily Indian share equal interest in Miss Murfree's last published mountain story, **"The Herder of Storm Mountain"** (1920). In language largely crisp and simple (leaving out "holophrastic" and "intervenient") she unfolds a story not unlike **"Over on the T'other Mounting,"** bedecked with Cherokee lore she had acquired in the intervening years. It is an effortless pleasantry, with one jarring facet: the constable's outspoken disgust over Lem Forsey's insistence on making a legal and burdensome matter out of a mere Indian casualty. For his departure from local mores, Lem is dismissed as "teched in the head."

"Una of the Hill Country" (1912), a lightweight satire on male vanity and female discretion in playing up to it, is a feminist dig at a man's bleeding ego with little observable value except as a local-color daguerreotype set in a frame of culture contrast. Town-country tension is subordinated to ridicule of the mountebank mountaineer. Valeria Clee, an explicit mountain-flower (to paraphrase Gertrude Stein, a wild rose is a wild rose is a wild rose), renews the action and theme which Miss Murfree had rehearsed at full novel length five years previously in *The Windfall*. Valeria is plucked out of her mountain surroundings and established as consort to a lion in a traveling circus. Her "ethereal figure, poetic type of beauty" captivate audiences everywhere, but she is not taken in by "the glitter and gauds of her tinsel world." Not one of these allures "could withstand the simple goodness of the unsophisticated girl." They retreat before "the power of her fireside traditions of right thinking and true living which she had learned in her humble mountain home." In such naïve terms Miss Murfree projects the assumption that simplicity is purity and ignorance innocence—an anti-intellectual, pseudo-pastoral pose of part-time peasants. Unique manifestations such as the barbecue-barn dance,

snatches of folk ditties, and the infirm grandparents lend solidity to the story; but anomalous references to Endymion and Hercules restore the air of artificiality.

Last of the mountain short stories engaged in comparison of values is **"Them Old Moth-Eaten Lovyers,"** published in *Century* (May, 1913) but never collected. A controlled effort far superior to many in her volumes, this tale sings the heartwarming Darby-and-Joan ballad of a lovable old couple who savor moments of glory during a visit in town, have their first quarrel in forty-five years of marriage, then reconcile in the intimate atmosphere of their lifelong mountain home. Somewhat like the two sisters in Jewett's "The Dulham Ladies," Editha and Ben Casey have lived inbred lives together (only one separation since childhood) and now seem like fatuous valetudinarians to all but themselves. Editha, in fact, is one of the most fetching old ladies in Miss Murfree's fiction, having none of the customary crone attributes.

Miss Murfree maintains a tone of light jollity while presenting the comedy of retrospective youth sympathetically but evading the inherent sentimentality in the homely theme of indestructible love between two elderly people. She goes back to the hickory logs in the deep fireplace and the scarlet peppers swinging from the ceiling, and to dialect popping with vivid idioms ("plumb jokified," a "hirpling old codger"). She balances scenes of sacred and profane love, of past and new generations, of speakeasy and log cabin with a restraint uncommon in her earlier local-color writing. And she unites all elements with a trite but apposite enveloping symbol of Cupid in the first and last passages.

Harry R. Warfel (essay date 1970)

SOURCE: "Local Color and Literary Artistry: Mary Noailles Murfree's *In the Tennessee Mountains*," in *The Southern Literary Journal*, Vol. 3, No. 1, Fall, 1970, pp. 154-63.

[*Warfel was an American educator, editor, and critic with a special interest in tracing the development of American intellectual and literary life. In the following essay, he explores Murfree's role as a local colorist and praises the organization of her stories.*]

It is good to have a new reprinting of *In the Tennessee Mountains*, originally published in 1884. Not only do the eight stories demonstrate the geographical and human substance of local-color fiction, which Professor Nathalia Wright analyzes in detail in her Introduction, but they also make clear the fact that Mary Noailles Murfree was more concerned to manipulate artistic literary techniques than to photograph the places and people. Less than most local colorists did she compel attention through attempts at verisimilitude; mountains, rivers, roads, clearings, villages, and houses have no precise location. The mountain people are types endowed with a single usable fictional trait; none except the crippled Reuben Crabb could be identified if a town meeting should bring them all together. Yet Miss

Murfree was one of the best local colorists because she was not misled into striving for "realism." . . .

What Miss Murfree did was to fuse in proper quantity the elements of local color. First is a setting so geographically unique as to provide for actions (like Bret Harte's outcasts' behavior in a snowstorm) which seemingly could occur nowhere else. It is of less importance, of course, that the setting be identifiable as a particular place than that it shall energize the imagination of the author and serve as symbol as well as fact. The scene exists not for itself but for what the author can do with it in making it subserve the unified totality of the composition. Characters form the second element; they must be appropriate to, if not indigenous to, the geographical area. Since local color is a branch of the fictional representation of manners, focus is upon odd, whimsical, semi-literate, wilful, non-urban people whose often strange behavior gives rise to conflict with each other and with the law. Beyond the particular settlement is an organized society, of some sort, whether the Vigilantes in Harte's mining camp stories or the "revenuers" in Joel Chandler Harris's Georgia mountain narratives or the county government in Miss Murfree's tales; this power operates, generally speaking, in a high-handed fashion in meting out punishment for actions which the unorganized people consider proper, even if these actions include murder. Miss Murfree occasionally is eloquent in describing the democratic and humanitarian quality of her mountaineers in contrast with the callous and pitiless "justice" of the legal system. The conduct of the characters is always seen in contrast with the established rules of society; stress is laid upon laziness, upon ignorance of the simplest facts of the physical and social sciences and a resultant superstition, upon a settled strangeness of disposition generally characterized as "tetched in the head," and upon a proneness of the men to quarrel with knives and fire arms. The old women, usually gnarled in body, are gossips, and the beautiful young girls are bashfully or pertly seeking husbands. Contrast is at times provided by bringing to the fictional area an outsider or two. Implicitly and explicitly local color emphasizes the differentness of the native characters from the norms of society at large. "As to artificial distinctions of money and education,—what do the ignorant mountaineers care about money and education?" exclaims Miss Murfree.

The third and most necessary element in local color is a dialect appropriate to the locale. Few authors were capable of phonetically respelling the speech sounds or of accurately rendering the total syntax and vocabulary of a region. Indeed, this kind of precision, best seen in Harris's Uncle Remus fables, might have been self-defeating; the local colorist was not an anthropologist or linguistics scholar but an imaginative creator of types of behavior. Hence the humor tricks—misspelling, malapropisms ("insurance" for "assurance," for example), and outrageous word coinages—go along with local words, unusual metaphors, local idioms, and respelling for pronunciation and vocal effects. As Miss Wright correctly states in an aside: "In figurative expression, however, the mountain people themselves are far more vivid than the characters in [Miss Murfree's] stories", and it might have been added that,

despite the complete analysis given in the Introduction, the total speech quality is suggested rather than presented. Dialect is the most colorful aspect of local color, but it rarely has—and need not have—the linguistic validity ascribed to it by some scholars.

Upon the aforenamed three elements the author impresses his philosophy, his outsider's point of view, and his pastel shades of humor and pathos. An idealism or romanticism marks all local-color fiction, for the writer sets up his contrasts to emphasize the virtues of love, fidelity, duty, honor, obedience, and so on through the long list of affirmative moral abstractions. Normally, therefore, he finds among his chosen characters some traits superior to those found in urban people. Miss Murfree intervenes in her stories again and again to pass judgment upon the people and their social customs, as in "Human nature is the same everywhere, and the Wilkins settlement is a microcosm" and "The secret history [archaeology] of the hills among which they lived was indeed a sealed book to these mountaineers."

It is at this point, therefore, that there becomes apparent an important distinction between Miss Murfree's (or any Romanticist's) ethical views and those of Howells and James (and other so-called Realists). Where Miss Murfree passes judgment upon her people's conduct, Howells and James remain neutral as if to say, "This is the way the ball bounces. In the Naturalism of Crane and Dreiser the characters' deviations from virtuous action are condoned or at least explained on the ground that the abstract forces of biology and environment are responsible. Authors' attitudes toward moral behavior, therefore, explain much more about a story than does any amount of discussion about verisimilitude, and the terms Romanticism, Realism, and Naturalism take on a greater definitiveness when employed as types of ethical attitude. Each implies something more than factual accuracy in reporting, for each attitude draws to itself wholly different fictional materials and methods. "Realism" as generally employed ought to be dropped as a synonym for verisimilitude; since there is really no degree in truth or in truthfulness in recording experience, attempts to discriminate types of literature by depths and heights of moral heroism and turpitude always fail of their purpose. The metaphor of the potato—clean if Romantic, a little begrimed if Realistic, and covered with dirt if Naturalistic—is fanciful but incorrect. Most of Dreiser's stories have less "dirt" than Miss Murfree's.

The local colorist normally is an outsider who views his characters with a superiority and sometimes even with a derogatory aloofness. Certainly Miss Murfree, while discovering fictional value in the Tennessee mountaineers, made no effort to associate with them or to accept their mode of living as a socially satisfactory pattern. The New Regionalists of the 1930's like Marjorie Kinnan Rawlings became a part of their fictional society, living in it, reporting it with sympathetic understanding, and viewing it—certainly in the life of the Baxters in the Florida Big Scrub in the 1870's in *The Yearling*—as defensible and worthy. Possibly the greatest shift in authorial attitude, apart from the development of Realism and Naturalism, was the insistence upon a harmony between the author and his material. Sinclair Lewis and others, despite their satiric thrusts, knew and understood their people and found reason to accept, to a degree, the normalcy of their characters' mental confusions and moral deviations. Miss Murfree's aloofness was appropriate to her chosen art form, and it is not just to find fault with it.

Associated with and possibly dependent upon her outsider's point of view is the intermingling of humor and pathos; they function together as essentially as do characters and setting. Most of the humor in Miss Murfree's stories emerges in the dialect statements rather than in the action. . . .

The substance and the author's attitude in themselves would not make Miss Murfree's stories memorable. . . . Miss Murfree was an artist who shaped her materials with something of the dexterity of Henry James, the great teacher and exemplifier of the rules of fictional structure. Just as he usually chose high-society characters whose deviations from normality made them interesting, so Miss Murfree selected most of her main characters from among the mountaineers or used these people as foils to outsiders. In the eight stories in *In the Tennessee Mountains* the main characters possess or go through abnormal mental states, a subject matter which permitted her, like Henry James, to attain narrative effects not available to writers of action stories. Her main people in the eight stories are as follows. Cynthia Ware, doomed never to wed, adjusts to her fate. Josiah Tait is an embittered revenge-seeking jilted lover. Celia Shaw suffers and dies from unrequited love. The stern and unrelenting lawyer Rufus Chadd, an expatriate mountaineer, seeks re-election as State's Attorney despite his childhood companions' hostility. An unsuccessful physician John Cleaver during a depressive reaction retreats from organized society to the mountains and there lays the foundation for a successful career as a psychiatrist among his own people. An elderly ex-soldier, Ambrose Kenyon, who is also a lay preacher, puts an end to a mountain feud. Tony Britt, harboring revenge, becomes insane from remorse after trying to murder a neighbor. Simon Burney, a harshly just man, becomes an angel of mercy in rescuing and protecting a cripple accused of murder.

Having these characters and these suggested lines of action, Miss Murfree organized her stories into the classical pattern, the sequence perfected in ancient Greek tragedy and notably exemplified in *Antigone*. The fundamental situation, the first of the four main segments, is at the beginning and consists of ten elements that may be presented in any order: the setting, the metaphor of the story line, the main character, the theme, the mood or over-all emotional quality of the story, the tone (whether serious, humorous, or ironic), the method of narration (symbolic, allegorical, impressionistic, stream-of-consciousness, etc.), the author's ethical attitude or philosophical stance, the style (including use of dialect), and the framing of the problem or conflict. These elements can occupy a few paragraphs or many. The second segment, usually the longest in a story, is the development of the problem through the successive steps in the conflict. The third segment, a few sentences normally, presents the climax or show-down and the decision. Finally is the denouement or conclusion

or resolution. In American fiction Washington Irving first used this formula in "Rip van Winkle"; Hawthorne and Poe perfected the formula in their stories, and Poe gave some of the rules, especially those relating to singleness of effect and the over-riding significance of the initial and final sentences. Any other arrangement, whether historical or biographical, is likely to be a series of incidents or episodes and sometimes is called episodic fiction. Local colorists employed both formulas.

Miss Murfree shaped her materials to adapt the setting to present the metaphor and the mood of the story. All scenes are emotionally toned, so that they serve both as setting and as images interpreting the characters' thoughts and actions. The varied subjects and themes provide for a variety of beginnings and scenic sequences, so that much of her art is concealed from the eyes of the casual reader. No turn in the events is unsupported by imagery of this kind. The opening paragraph of **"Drifting Down Lost Creek"** illustrates the multilevel quality of her writing:

> High above Lost Creek Valley towers a wilderness of pine. So dense is this growth that it masks the mountain whence it springs. Even when the Cumberland spurs, to the east, are gaunt and bare in the wintry wind, their deciduous forests denuded, their crags unveiled and grimly beetling, Pine Mountain remains a sombre, changeless mystery; its clifty heights are hidden, its chasms and abysses lurk unseen. Whether the skies are blue, or gray, the dark, austere line of its summit limits the horizon. It stands against the west like a barrier. It seemed to Cynthia Ware that nothing which went beyond this barrier ever came back again. One by one the days passed over it, and in splendid apotheosis, in purple and crimson and gold, they were received into the heavens, and returned no more. She beheld love go hence, and many a hope. Even Lost Creek itself, meandering for miles between the ranges, suddenly sinks into the earth, tunnels an unknown channel beneath the mountain, and is never seen again. She often watched the floating leaves, a nettle here and there, the broken wing of a moth, and wondered whither these trifles were borne, on the elegiac current. She came to fancy that her life was like them, worthless in itself and without a mission; drifting down Lost Creek, to vanish vaguely in the mountains.

Lost Creek Valley, hemmed in by the somber barrier of Pine Mountain, symbolizes the situation of Cynthia Ware, who knows—and thus metaphorically states the story line— that "nothing which went beyond this barrier ever came back again." The initial image is reinforced by the disappearance of Lost Creek into a tunnel. The mood, already implied, is defined as "elegiac," so that the ending of the forthcoming action is foreshadowed. Lest the reader fail to grasp the meaning of the picture, the final sentence provides an analogy of Cynthia's life to floating leaves and a moth's broken wing. Not verisimilitude, not local scene painting but artistic preparation for the quality of the entire story and especially for the effect to be gained at the end was Miss Murfree's purpose in the opening paragraph. In later paragraphs come the mill-wheel, preparatory for the blacksmith shop, and the weekly task of laundering, an image of Cynthia's lifelong homely repetitive toil in contrast with her dreams. When Mrs. Wray begins to speak, it becomes apparent that the narrative will emerge more through conversation than through description, and that the emotionally toned picture will interpret the action. The remainder of the story merely illustrates, through Cynthia's loss of Evander Price as a potential husband, the story line and theme. The final paragraph returns to the images set forth in the beginning:

> At length he [Evander] was gone, and forever, and Cynthia's heart adjusted itself anew. Sometimes, to be sure, it seems to her that the years of her life are like the floating leaves drifting down Lost Creek, valueless and purposeless, and vaguely vanishing in the mountains. Then she remembers that the sequestered subterranean current is charged with its own inscrutable, imperative mission, and she ceases to question and regret, and bravely does the work nearest her hand, and has glimpses of its influence in the widening lives of others, and finds in these a placid content.

Miss Murfree ends the story with something of a sentimental affirmation that lonely spinsterhood need not be embittered, indeed can be filled with humanitarian service to others. This conclusion is in accord with her idealistic philosophy and also, of course, with the Victorian mores and fictional moralizing of her time. To have ended otherwise would have destroyed the quality of the story. Nor need a reader assume that a presentation of the materials in another tone or to subserve another mood, such as in John Steinbeck's "The Chrysanthemums," a story remarkably similar in artistic procedures and substance, would have been better. Working within the framework of her own capabilities and interests, Miss Murfree composed a remarkably fine story. Burne-Jones and Rossetti have their place among the great artists as well as Breughel. It is not the substance or the philosophy which is of most significance; it is the management of all the artistic procedures available to the artist in terms of his own vision.

Among the minor matters of artistry which have evoked some negative commentary is Miss Murfree's elevated style and allusiveness in contrast to the mountaineers' homely dialect. Styles and tastes vary through the generations. If the editors who printed her work had felt strongly that so romantic a presentation needed some softening of the brilliant coloring effects, no doubt she would have yielded to blue pencil marks. The fact is, however, that her contemporaries—Bret Harte, Mark Twain, William Dean Howells, and Henry James, as well as fellow local colorists—secured many of their best effects by the same means. One may smile at a phrase like "a stupendous alto-relievo in silver repousse," but to substitute a common term would be like striking out an ornate detail from a romantic painting.

Each of the other seven stories in *In the Tennessee Mountains* is as carefully and as artistically composed as is the first one. Local color in and for itself was not Miss Murfree's aim or achievement, although no other writer has equaled her thus far in capturing something of the quality and magic of the scenery and in giving an indication of the character of the mountain people. It is as a romantic artist who, while seeming to be local in subject matter and dialect, transcended the immediate into the universal that Miss Murfree is memorable.

Richard Cary   (essay date 1971-72)

SOURCE: A review of *In the Tennessee Mountains,* in *The Mississippi Quarterly,* Vol. 25, No. 1, Winter, 1971-72, pp. 94-7.

[*In the essay below, Cary offers a favorable assessment of* In the Tennessee Mountains.]

As a purveyor of attractive fictions, Mary Murfree's heart was indubitably in the highlands. Of the eighteen novels and seven volumes of collected short stories she published in almost half a century of unrelenting "literary" effort, ten and six, respectively, dealt specifically with the folk and folkways of the Tennessee mountains. On the wave of local-color writing engendered by the expansion of national self-consciousness following the Civil War, she rode with the leading exponents of the genre: Harte and Twain of the Western mining camp, Hay and Eggleston of the Midwest hamlet, Jewett and Freeman of the New England coast and farm, Page, Harris, and Cable of the Southern quarter. Expressly motivated—she "wanted the world to know the East Tennessee mountaineer before the railroad reached the mountains"—she strove, as they did, to preserve intact a small parish of unique America at a pristine moment, before it was irreversibly homogenized by the proliferating incursions of mass transportation, mass communication, mass culture.

Handicapped physically, Miss Murfree wrote out of a quenchless passion to excel mentally. As a child she reveled in her singular ability to spell 'Popocatepetl' correctly, a tendency she later translated into gratuitous blobs of erudition and polysyllables, almost always alien to the context and jarring to the sensibility. Indeed, her account of how she settled on her métier acutely demonstrates the egocentricity that guided and dominated her identity as author: "I struck upon the mountaineers as a topic at hap-hazard, perhaps because I was myself greatly interested by them; but I did not then appreciate how very little was known of them elsewhere. I was early familiar with their customs, dialect, and peculiar views of life, for I used to spend much time in the mountains long before I knew of the existence of such a thing as 'literary material.'" The angle of perception is unfortunate. Had her interest focused on the subjects for *their* sake rather than on the titillations they afforded *her,* the unwitting snobbery in her treatment of a class "lower" than her own would not so often provoke readers less convinced of their membership in a superior order. Despite her protestations, Miss Murfree, scion of the landed gentry, never did rid herself of ingrained attitudes toward "these people." When she realized their potential in the current markets, she used them for profit as long as the traffic would bear.

In the Tennessee Mountains contains not the first mountain stories Miss Murfree wrote, but the first eight published in the *Atlantic Monthly.* Issued by Houghton Mifflin in 1884 on the suggestion of Thomas Bailey Aldrich, the volume received acclaim comparable to Bret Harte's prototypical *The Luck of Roaring Camp,* and in the opinion of one respected historian of the short story "marked another important mile-stone in regionalist writing." The operative word is 'regionalist,' for after only two apprentice efforts Mary Murfree had polished her localized effects of people, place, language, lore, mores, tone, and point of view to a high glow fascinating to inhabitants of areas outside the Tennessee mountain ranges. Distressed experts in the topography, sociology, and patois of the immediate scene might quibble over details of her descriptions and dialects, but Miss Murfree put together a construct which, if not meticulously true to the letter of life, is often larger than life and notably persuasive as art. At least during these seven primal years (1878-1884) she managed to sustain a freshness and variety of presentation which in the course of time degenerated to stereotype and eventually into a parody of itself.

Yet, even in this initial cluster of stories her virtuosity veers now and again into unfertile repetition. The overpowering mountains, the ubiquitous decorative or symbolic moon, the untidy log hovel, the crossroads store and blacksmith shop, the rugged, lawless demihero, the mountain-flower maiden, the prematurely bedraggled mother, the testy old crone, the brainless violence and puerile superstitions—all these recur, as they must in so circumscribed a situation. Out of these limited staples Miss Murfree contrived a stock community primitive in code and behavior, over which she imposed a sheen of her own interpretations and sophistication. Except sporadically in her stories, and in two novels (*The Prophet of the Great Smoky Mountains, In the "Stranger People's" Country*), she never wholly succeeded in seeing the world from the mountaineers' stance.

These eight stories, in matter and manner unalterably of the 1870's, nevertheless propound enough universals to warrant rereading in the 1970's. There are the themes of nature as spiritual restorative, of the mystical correspondence between external and human nature, and the democratic proposition of a common humanity regardless of birth or status. There is the contemporaneous conflict of urban-rural cultures, predominantly resolved in favor of the latter. There is Rufus Chadd, mountain boy who "makes it" as district attorney but in the pinch reverts to indigenous sympathies; Fred Trelawney, unsuccessful young lawyer who drops out of the rat race and finds regeneration as a successful sheep farmer; the T'Other Mounting, emblematic of our duple, uninhabitable self, alive with horrors we prefer not to scrutinize, though inescapably there; Reuben Crabb, mutilated refugee from society, hounded unjustly for a crime he did not commit; and Lost Creek, eternal flux of life and death upon which we float ineluctably, unfit to understand or control the mystery of existence. Stylistically and perspectively Miss Murfree is frequently out of joint with the ambience she creates. However, these and other reminders of constancy in the

human circumstance, whether by mountain stream or city sewer, retrieve her lesser aberrations and may well inspire further revivals of her work by generations yet to come.

Mary Nilles   (essay date 1972)

SOURCE: "Craddock's Girls: A Look at Some Unliberated Women," in *The Markham Review,* Vol. 3, No. 4, October, 1972, pp. 74-7.

[*In the essay below, Nilles examines Murfree's stereotypical heroines.*]

> ". . . gals air cur'ous critters, ye know yerself; thar's no sort o' countin' on 'em . . ."
> **—"Dancin' Party at Harrison's Cove"**

Even a cursory look at the heroines in the fiction of Charles Egbert Craddock (Mary Noailles Murfree, 1850-1922) reveals that they were the antithesis of "modern" or "liberated" women. These female characters were often shallow and shadowy repetitions of each other, usually simple and uneducated, dependent upon and completely submissive to males. They had little chance to determine their own lives and were considered weak beings, inferior to the stronger males in their fictional realm. In a rural Tennessee milieu of nearly a century ago, they were "charmin" and proper foils for the rounder, more believable men. Only a few possessed a hardy pioneering spirit and spoke out forthrightly in that indomitable dialect Miss Murfree could imitate with precision.

Yet eighty-five years ago the writings of Miss Murfree were internationally popular. The *New York Times* [July 29] declared her in 1899 "a famous author . . . already a person of repute." William Dean Howells thought "[s]he was the first to express a true Southern quality in fiction." Today the rambling plots and rustic characters of her twenty-five novels and her many short stories often are found too conventional, romantic, boring, silly or irrelevant to invite and sustain reading pleasure. Even for the student of local color literature, entry into her work, with its beetling crags, sprawling vistas and unusual speech, is no easy feat. Yet viewed beside the more "serious" fiction about women which Southern writers produced after romanticism like Miss Murfree's died, a glance at some of these characters provides not only a look at some interesting period fiction; it also lends to readers now involved in literature and protest movements far more "relevant" a moment of comic relief and an idea of how far literature and society have come.

An examination of some female characters created within *In the Tennessee Mountains* (1884) can quite easily lead one into Miss Murfree's unusual literary world. Defining and evaluating the personalities of the women in this closely-knit collection of short stories can develop a better understanding and appreciation of Craddock's general themes and stylistic peculiarities, her literary ethos, as well as the color, freshness, excitement and humor of her unique local color artistry.

Miss Murfree's females were never too believably developed. Yet a few verged beyond cardboard stereotypes. Two such "rounder" characterizations appear in **"Drifting Down Lost Creek"**: Cynthia Ware, an auburn-haired, brown-eyed, frail but hard-working young girl, and her shrewish, sharp-tongued mother. Miss Murfree's work often depicts this mother-daughter combination. The graceful Cynthia, though "densely ignorant," possesses, typically for Miss Murfree, an "ethereal fairness." Poverty clothes her in homespun, but her beauty thereby is only increased. Her bright hair, lithe figure, bare round arms and deft hands stirring batter make her appear "the very genius of home." The mountaineers even admire her unusual determination: "She ain't got a red head on her for nothin." But she is indeed no independent urbane career girl.

Cynthia hopelessly loves Evander Price, a blacksmith's apprentice. When he is unjustly accused of murder, she investigates the "crime," and tries to gain his pardon. The panoramic landscape symbolizes her unhappiness; Pine Mountain mourns with the "threnody" of her sufferings as Evander's unjust sentence goes unchanged. Cynthy resumes seasonal farm work in her confining "primitive community," reasserting fidelity to him.

Almost three years later, word of his pardon arrives. But now he seems "mighty glad ter git shet o' the mountings." He has also married. After ten years Evander returns and reveals his loss of an innate sensitivity; as he speaks with the heroine he mentions only briefly and unthinkingly their old romance. The pathos of Cynthy's situation is indeed great; she can only listen to him with familiar, patient understanding; she dares not reveal her undying love. . . .

The pathetic, and, from a more contemporary angle of vision, the almost unbelievable dedication of a female like Cynthia to a man who hardly notices her is one of Miss Murfree's most popular themes. The strong, silently suffering, simplistic mountain girl is often her best wrought female characterization. None of these females ever experiences the depth and complexity of suffering endured by the heroines of Ellen Glasgow, Elizabeth Madox Roberts or Willa Cather. Yet a few, like Cynthia, are endowed with a degree of kindness, compassion, intelligence, and longsuffering. Her self-sacrifice is in keeping with her role; yet, the genuine pathos she engenders is surprisingly intense. Her speech is crisp and witty, her personality quite warm and endearing. Unfortunately, like all other Murfree females, she lacks psychological depth, and, especially for modern readers, a good deal of verisimilitude. She ranks as one of Miss Murfree's most charming, delightful girls, but one hopelessly shackled to the stereotype of the long-suffering maiden who is unhappy in love. . . .

Selina Teake, another vision of typical Craddockian loveliness, appears in **"The Romance of Sunrise Rock."** In blue homespun, with flushed cheeks and lips of delicate crimson, her masses of yellow hair part to reveal eyes like limpid pools. Fred Trelawney, a city lawyer, soon falls in love with her, but it is John Cleaver, a doctor fleeing the pressures of an urban practice, who unknowingly wins her heart. Cleaver berates hill life and folk but Selina grows more deeply infatuated. The blind young man cannot recognize her love; he wants only "the world of men and action."

Trelawney, however, openly expresses his admiration for the area and Selina. He lambasts the education of the "accomplished" society women he has known and confesses that she is the "ideal of a modest, delicate young girl . . . the only sincere woman I ever saw," the woman he loves and wishes to marry. Meanwhile, as Selina contracts diphtheria, her tender deathbed glances and words of kindness to the doctor betray her love. As this rambling story ends, Cleaver realizes that, like Trelawney, he will never forget the mountain girl who suffered so long for his unrequited love.

Selina is again a foil to the hero. Her long suffering nature stands antithetical to his educated, complex, introspective and harried personality; her innocence and ignorance contrasts with the charm of sophisticated urban women. Yet again, Miss Murfree favors the males and Selina is never probed deeply enough to hold the reader's attention. She is only a finely drawn type. The pathos she engenders is noteworthy; she is comparable to Celia of **"The Star in the Valley."** But her attractiveness would have been greatly enhanced had the reader been shown her musings and motivation. Since she lacks dimension her deeds are easily forgotten.

"Electioneerin' on Big Injun Mounting" depicts another class of female character: the tired, overworked wife. Mrs. Isaac Baker is a woman who has had to endure slashes at the hands of her husband; with him there is obviously little real "communion." This antithesis of the young wife who shares life with her husband must support her family almost singlehanded. She is dominated by her husband's every whim; "She hev had ter do all the work fur four years,—plowin', an' choppin' wood, an' cookin', an' washin', an' sech." She is likely modeled upon one of those Tennessee mountain wives whom Miss Murfree saw die early because of overwork. But though this woman is worn and exercises no rights as an individual, she chooses to remain with her husband. Although she may be bowing to social convention, she is still "powerful tuk up with him." . . .

In short, most females in this collection, and in the body of Miss Murfree's writing, lack psychological complexity, variety and the potential to sustain lasting interest. They represent a type of womanhood popular in Southern fiction during Miss Murfree's era, but remain highly unbelievable as "real" persons. With the hindsight of almost a century it seems somewhat remarkable that these characters were so widely acclaimed. These beautiful, sometimes stubbornly determined, but always resigned females enjoyed no deep emotionally or psychologically realistic relationships with males. Their masculine counterparts hunted, fished, made moonshine, or happily loafed away hours, forgetful of any familial responsibilities. Meanwhile

Murfree's young girls pined for them, defended their name and vowed them fidelity; the older, tired but stoic wives cared for an often shabby house and their brood of children: old crones, almost free of the ravages of overwork and loneliness, made witty but caustic comments about life, love and marriage in the mountains. Spinsters and red-headed females enjoyed an even harder lot. They were scarcely noticed by anyone and their lives were especially repressed and resigned, sober and never articulated. Most of these women did not develop close relationships with other females either, and lived their sheltered lives secure within only the vogue of romanticism.

Miss Murfree was surely no feminist writer; she created her characters safely inside the confines of a set tradition. Yet a few of her women are entertaining in terms of this tradition and noble in their subdued reflection of a period in American literature in which women, at least in Miss Murfree's special world, were accredited an unenviable status. Shadowy, awesome mountains and strict social conventions held even the most inventive and outgoing of these women prisoner while romantic Southern local color fiction reached its zenith.

Reese M. Carleton (essay date 1974)

SOURCE: "Mary Noailles Murfree (1850-1922): An Annotated Bibliography," in *American Literary Realism 1870-1910,* Vol. 7, No. 4, Autumn, 1974, pp. 293-378.

[*In the following excerpt, Carleton evaluates Murfree's place in American literature and discusses her ultimate inability to fulfill the promise of her early short fiction.*]

Mary Noailles Murfree submitted her first short story for publication in 1878, and during the next twenty years, under the pseudonym "Charles Egbert Craddock," she produced many stories and novels dealing with the mountaineers of Tennessee. In the 1880s and early 1890s, when a regional focus was popular in American literature, Murfree achieved prominence. By using the Tennessee mountain dialect, the details of the mountain people's daily lives, and by emphasizing the poverty and harsh existence in the isolated clearings and settlements of her chosen locale, Murfree, along with writers such as Cable, Harte, Chopin, and Jewett, contributed to the development of realism in American fiction. At the same time, however, she adhered to the standards of the genteel tradition, thus assuring a place for her work in the leading magazines of the day. Then, when regional fiction became less popular in the late 1890s, Murfree began writing historical novels and romances; and for the first fifteen years of the twentieth century the name "Charles Egbert Craddock" remained prominent among writers of popular fiction.

Although in general Murfree was highly respected at home and even gained an international following, critics early recognized the conflicting romantic and realistic features of her fiction, and contemporary opinion fluctuated between enthusiastic interest, approval with reservations, and absolute dissatisfaction. At the beginning of her career, her high potential as a writer was consistently acknowledged, but the degree to which she achieved this potential as time passed was debatable. During the last two decades of the century, critics argued about such problems as her excessive use of nature and her apparent inability to expand beyond the Tennessee locale and character even after she seemed to have exhausted their usefulness. Eventually she did expand her range somewhat by shifting focus to Tennessee history and by introducing a new interest in the Cherokee Indians, but her later historical novels and romances never received as much attention as her stories about the Tennessee mountaineers. By 1900 the mountaineer stories had become so firmly established as a part of American literature that Murfree was included in most general discussions of contemporary writing, and in some quarters her novels were considered as significant as those of Twain, Howells, and James. Gradually, however, she came to be viewed more as a part of a specific literary movement, especially in Southern literature, than as the great American novelist that some critics found her to be in the 1890s, and twentieth-century literary histories have placed her in the position of a minor writer whose contribution to American literature appears slight when compared to the work of her more prominent contemporaries.

One factor which may have kept Murfree from realizing her early promise was her failure to listen to the right voices. She seems to have lacked good judgment concerning her abilities and her limitations, and she evidently paid little attention to unfavorable reviews and to critics who liked her work but who also recognized its weaknesses and offered suggestions for improvement. On the other hand, she was sensitive to the dictates of the traditional genteel society and to popular taste. Because she was dependent on her writing for her livelihood, she was alert to what would sell best. Instead of attempting to avoid excesses and to develop new characters and situations called for by the critics, she followed popular demand. Yet even as she did so, her work consistently reflects her ability to go much further into serious writing than did the usual popular writer. Emphasizing the control of the environment over her characters' lives, Murfree depicted the social, religious, and political events of an isolated region characterized by an underlying violence which often erupted to create tragedy. Although a romantic film glosses most of the stories, Murfree also portrayed the poverty which dominated the mountain life, and at times she offered implicit criticism of sophisticated society by contrasting valley life unfavorably with that of the simple mountain inhabitants. All of this is evidence that she might have worked, had she chosen to do so, in the main stream of realism and so secured for herself a larger role in the development of American fiction.

Benjamin Franklin Fisher IV (essay date 1981)

SOURCE: "'The Visitants from Yesterday': An Atypical, Previously Unpublished Story from the Pen of 'Charles Egbert Craddock'," in *Tennessee Studies in Literature,* Vol. 26, 1981, pp. 89-100.

[Fisher is an American educator and critic. In the following excerpt, he provides a thematic and stylistic overview of Murfree's "The Visitants from Yesterday."]

The name "Charles Egbert Craddock," Mary Noailles Murfree's familiar pseudonym, inevitably suggests the Tennessee mountains and mountaineers. Indeed she may be called the laureate of the Great Smokies. Less commonly known are her writings that delineate Mississippi and, in fewer cases, other environs; and, perhaps more significant, her fiction in the supernatural vein. . . . [A] story entitled **"The Visitants from Yesterday,"** throws a larger perspective upon Murfree's authorial talents. It is neither mountain nor outdoors fiction, has none of those famous digressions into rhapsodizing upon natural phenomena that have so exercised contemporaneous reviewers and more recent students, and, finally, resembles the "ghostly tales" of Henry James. . . .

"The Visitants from Yesterday" exists in a typescript consisting of nineteen leaves, with minimal autograph alterations. . . . **"The Visitants"** was a title listed in a table of contents for *Mountain and River: Stories and Sketches,* a volume projected for publication during Murfree's last years. Perhaps her liking for the material and a desire to publish this particular story account for the typescript state. A point of interest is that the first leaf was reworked, as the different typeface shows, with significant change resulting. . . . Other fiction written late in Murfree's life survives only in handwriting. One such, a variant version of **"The Herder of Storm Mountain,"** her last published story, indicated thoughtful revision. So far as I am aware, the only other mention of **"The Visitants from Yesterday"** occurs in Edd Winfield Parks's biography of Mary Murfree [*Charles Egbert Craddock,* 1941].

"The Visitants from Yesterday" shows Murfree as the "old-fashioned modernist" Parks describes. What she attempts is a "ghostly" tale like Henry James's "The Romance of Certain Old Clothes," "De Grey: A Romance," or "The Jolly Corner," though she lacks the subtle sophistication unfolded in those psychological dramas. Another unmistakable feature is borrowed from popular magazine and newspaper sensational stories, which in their turn derive from earlier Gothic fiction. **"The Visitants"** provides not merely another thriller, but also sheds light upon the handling of materials different from "Charles Egbert Craddock's" well-known mountain lore.

One measure of Murfree's deftness crops up in what initially seems to be her inconsistency in naming the protagonist: he is first Jack Trent, then Jack Rosney. As I stated above, the first page of the manuscript bears a different typeface from what appears on the others; the name Jack Trent appears only on this first sheet, and I doubt that it is an oversight by an aged person—as Murfree then was. I rather suspect that she considered extensive revisions, began but never completed them, among which this name shift was important, because in **"The Visitants"** she once more addresses the themes and character types of an earlier novel, *The Story of Duciehurst.* . . .

Components in the novel central to the later story are the use of a crucial concealed document (a mortgage settlement rather than a will); a shadowy old house (decayed to ruin as Mrs. Derwent's opulent city residence is not, but with a great front staircase reaching to the third floor, as in the story); the blond, yet not wholly sympathetic lady (whose thinking and conversation run to divorce); the name Rosney (actually the villain in *Duciehurst* is Edward Floyd-Rosney; otherwise he and Jack, both Mississippians, share many characteristics in matters of age and temperament, though Jack is the hero); and touches of supernaturalism (more readily explained away in the novel than in **"The Visitants"**).

Murfree's technique is sound, betraying no earmarks of clumsiness or disproportion that often mar her published short stories. There is an economic balance of the descriptive and the dramatic, the atmosphere of foreboding and the supernatural occurrences to which it leads, with relief of a mundane and intermittently comic species. The "tragedy" of the opening, the "melancholy" arising in the middle-aged protagonist returning to scenes of a happy past (akin to James's Spencer Brydon's return to confront the "ghost" of his past), are offset by the gaily colored awnings and balcony flowers of the imposing old house. Moreover, Jack's anxieties upon beholding the house are "altogether unwarranted by the facts." This language recalls the opening of "The Fall of the House of Usher." True, the Derwent mansion lies in no remote locale, but "haunted" it is, we quickly learn.

Rosney's "vague expectations of encountering faces and forms that he had known here long ago" are more than fulfilled by the appearance of the "visitants." He is so eager to confront the past, notably in the forms of the "old residents," that they must ultimately come forth, much like familiars or spirits summoned through more lurid practices. Mrs. Huntley's chatter at luncheon pleases Jack, and her remark about "read[ing] the characters of these people to a more discerning effect, looking at their environment and their completed lives" foreshadows the actual "visitations" from Mrs. Derwent and Grilson. It is therefore reasonable to speak of the disputed estate, because there is no will, and Jack's declaration that he continues to think of his benefactress "always as living . . . a most vital presence" is at once plausible and ironic. Not surprisingly, she shortly appears before him. Although he is shaken, Jack tries to shrug it off as "nerves," and we do not yet comprehend the significance of this visitation. Suspense builds, although its full impact is delayed, during the automobile ride, and a bit of ironic word-play may exist in Mrs. Huntley's teasing of Rosney: "I can't undertake to keep you in spirits as well as Tom." To be sure, Jack is kept "in spirits," if the visions of old Grilson and then of the old man and his evil intents—which cause the death of Mrs. Derwent—may be termed such.

Jack's subsequent encounters with the "visitants" are skillfully presented. The abundant darkness and shadows that hover around as he returns to the house, the thought of respite—in the proposed evening's entertainment—that quickly disperses as the shades of Mrs. Derwent and old

Grilson appear once more (this time in a situation of tense sensationalism), and the ambiguities offered in the close of the story, all are marshalled by a steady authorial hand. The overall result is our enjoyment of a chronicle of "supernatural" events, which are finally presented as explainable on the basis of scientific reasoning—although there is the nagging note of those who persist in divining supernatural underpinnings for Jack's fright and illness, not to mention the discovery of the will.

Had **"The Visitants from Yesterday"** seen print during Murfree's lifetime, it might have altered certain critical views of her literary abilities. An attempt to recast other material, the story reveals its author's ability to improve in this tale of effect, so like one of Poe's in achieving unity—and like Poe's in that the effect is one of anxiety and terror. Murfree produced in **"The Visitants"** a piece that, although not of her usual mountain-fiction variety, is, nevertheless, a creditable piece of Tennessee fiction.

Benjamin Franklin Fisher IV (essay date 1985)

SOURCE: "Mary Noailles Murfree's 'Special' Sense of Humor," in *Studies in American Humor*, n.s., Vol. 4, Nos. 1-2, Spring-Summer, 1985, pp. 30-8.

[*In the excerpt below, Fisher surveys the comic elements in Murfree's short fiction.*]

Placing Mary Murfree as a humorist is analogous to the similar positioning of one of her American literary predecessors, Edgar Allan Poe. His comedy was readily noted by contemporaries; then, for better than a century, it was largely ignored or lamented as an excrescence. Mid-twentieth-century critics, like Clark Griffith and Richard P. Benton, however, initiated revaluations that have spurred wide recognition and admiration for Poe's subtleties in irony and other comic techniques. Murfree, on the other hand, still awaits a similar reassessment, and that in despite of repeated, but too terse, reviewers' and anthologists' notice that humor is neither infrequent nor execrable in her works. I propose that Murfree's comic elements are substantial, and that she keenly comprehended and modified literary backgrounds like the "Big-Bar" School as well as analogous works from Irving, Poe, and Dickens. Murfree, moreover, can display a savagery that stems from these earlier, male authors, but her savagery highlights features less revolting in details of violence and physical pain. Any bawdiness in her fiction is also much less overt, although it does appear from time to time. Thus Murfree manifests indeed a "special" sense of humor. . . .

Her work in fact could as easily place her without as within the genteel tradition in later nineteenth-century American literature—where with casual dismissal she is usually located. Exemplary of divergences from genteelness are her presentations of social pleasures like gander-pulls, horse-swaps or sales, gambling, or drinking (and moonshining among Tennessee mountaineers), the common fare in W. T. Porter's *The Spirit of the Times* and other kindred sporting/racing journals circulating male authorship to male audiences. With a twist here and a turn there, though, Murfree effects what is altogether her own in creating humor. . . . Divergences also occur over what is "masculine" and what "feminine" in Murfree's fiction, but . . . such rage for taxonomy—and the ensuing confusion—is of small consequence. Suffice it to say here that Murfree's attracting the literary world under a male pseudonym grew unimportant after her revelation in Boston that "Charles Egbert Craddock," notwithstanding a bold, "masculine" hand, was a woman.

Negligible as great literary art, Murfree's first published sketches are social satires throughout, with settings and characters different from what one expects to find in writings by this Laureate of the Smokies. They are of interest because they reveal their creator's penchant for wordplay, here by means of transparent names among the personae as targets for satire. . . . **"Flirts and Their Ways,"** includes a "Miss Demureness," whose characteristics place her as one type of flirt. Better humor resides in names among the more sophisticated creations peopling . . . **"My Daughter's Admirers."** There the Reverend "Mr. Yawn-Your-Head-Off" serves as foil to the witty "Mr. Sparkle." "Jack Olwell" exemplifies Murfree's satire employing skillful sound effects; as either "all-well" or "oil-well," his bland fawning upon "Mr. Regulus," whom he "oils well" or attempts to convince that, because of their friendship, all is well, furnishes amusement. More deft, the name "Regulus" derives from the Latin "little king"; more precisely, it is diminutive for "rex" or ruler. Such denotations succinctly encompass the petty tyranny Regulus exercises. The English senses of "regulation" and "regular" add further dimension to this portrait. Regulus, we quickly divine, is a confidence man, whose boasts about his masculinity are empty. Indeed, in terms of manliness he may be no "regular guy," so to speak; simultaneously his calculated regulation of an outward demeanor may as regularly guy or deceive the ingenuous.

Murfree did not continue in the path of an Austen or a Thackeray, as these early sketches suggest that she might have, in delineating urban sophisticates in witty prose. She did continue strong, however, in featuring con men, and women, and in other comic propensities, when she turned to local color in the Tennessee mountains and, less often, the Mississippi delta. Her great predecessor in fictionalizing Tennessee-mountain folk was that Pennsylvanian-turned-Southerner, George Washington Harris, whose Lovingood yarns and like tales by other Southwest humorists she evidently knew. Thence and from other writers named above, derive much of the duplicitousness, imagery, and macabre integral to Murfree's own humor. She also recalls those writers' repeated sly mockery of superstition and supernaturalism through conscious exaggerations or through ridiculing and surprise deflations. Her skepticism is no less clear-cut, and she indicates a keen divination of the ludicrous potential amidst the mundane circumstances and homey occupations of her characters.

Routine life in a Murfree tale, though, may not dovetail with our own conceptions of such existence; nor, in all likelihood, would "homey" within related contexts seem familiar. The worlds of her fiction are generally remote, often inimical:

> Always enwrapped in the illusory mists, always touching the evasive clouds, the peaks of the Great Smoky Mountains are like some barren ideal, that has bartered for the vague isolation of a higher atmosphere the material values of the warm world below. Upon those mighty and majestic domes no tree strikes root, no hearth is alight; humanity is an alien thing, and utility set at naught. Below, dense forests cover the massive, precipitous slopes . . . and in the midst of the wilderness a clearing shows here and there, and the roof of a humble log cabin; in the valley, far lower still, a red spark at dusk may suggest a home, nestling in the cove.

Weird influences are paramount in such regions, and here the prose itself, in its halting movement, conveys a sense of slow, uncertain surveying of the elements as they appear in descending importance. In so fantastic a locale, it is no great wonder that Rick Tyler, a fugitive from justice, ruefully (and to us amusingly) compares his flight with diabolic pursuit: "'Satan's mighty active, considerin' his age, but I'd be willin' ter pit the State o' Tennessee agin' him when it kem ter huntin' of folks like a pa'tridge.'" Rude life combines with unsophisticated acceptance of folksy religion to make such mountaineers think that the devil, or for that matter more positive biblical personages, could be their near neighbors, perhaps to be met along roadways and paths among the strange reaches of the great mountains. Murfree undercuts so easy a credence for the spirit-world, however, when she puts into her characters' minds, no matter how well-versed about otherwordly salvation or damnation they may be, thoughts of more immediate, but just as weighty, sufferings devised by non-supernatural antagonists like the law. Although Tyler's notion of personal hardship, emanating from the state and not hell, is wryly phrased, the wording leaves us in no doubt of his being as sore tried and used by his own kind as by Satan and his minions. In like manner, Clarsie Giles, heroine of Murfree's best-known story, **"The 'Harnt' That Walks Chilhowee,"** when informed that she could be jailed for aiding a living criminal, and not, as she supposed, the Chilhowee ghost, ponders the former condition as "infinitely more terrifying than the awful doom which follows the horror of a ghost's speech." She had previously suffered anguish because in mountain lore speaking to a ghost brings instant death. In these vignettes Murfree domesticates the spectral into the comic to strengthen her realism. Replacing the horrifying supernatural agents of earlier Gothic fiction, she shows us how the thoroughly ordinary and plausible may be distorted by superstitious minds. The concision in these passages promotes a mirth that would be muted in more extended treatment, just as it does in a later story, **"The Visitants from Yesterday."**

Readers, of course, readily perceive Murfree's finely wrought irony. Clarsie's ignorance permits her no alternative to her belief that she has encountered the ghost of the misshapen dwarf, the tellingly named Reuben Crabb. We discerningly align with the narrator's perspective, whose

language (describing Reuben's realization of his power over the girl and its advantage) alerts us to his living state. Here is none of the tricky hilarity or loopholes in apparent supernaturalism that is suddenly discovered to result from dreams, drunkenness, or drugs. Instead of induced visionariness, as it might be found in, say, Harris, Murfree, rather, makes tensile such superstitious lore as the mountaineers seldom gainsay. This example of explained supernaturalism pulses with a risibility never to be found among the explanations of Mrs. Radcliffe and her emulators. Just so, in **"Over on the T'other Mounting,"** the fighting between Tony Britt and Caleb Hoxie recalls the bullying of Reuben by Sam Grim, in that comic relief alleviates what could actually become grisly with gore. Offhanded remarks by spectators distance the beatings and give a dead-pan tone with effects like those in Huck Finn's recounting his adventures. Tony's pugilistic tendencies are mitigated by the necessity to gather money for a fine: "'An' it kept him so busy a-scufflin' ter raise the twenty dollars that he never hed a chance ter give Caleb Hoxie more'n one or two beatin's the whole time he was a-scrapin' up the money.'" Had these fisticuffs engaged Sut Lovingood or one of the "ring-tailed roarers," rough-housing to the last degree might predominate, with fond care to list each detail of pain inflicted. Murfree's lighter touch conveys the dramatics with none of the disgusting elaboration favored by others.

Another tie binding Murfree to earlier humorists, rather the converse of those just discussed, because savgery is depicted straightforwardly (suggesting no authorial affinities strictly for the smiling side of life), occurs in the Mississippi surroundings and characters of two late novels, *The Fair Mississippian* and *The Storie of Duciehurst*. If marked by some noticeable flaws in style, these books call up from Southwestern humor characters whose animal features and traits function significantly. Gone, however, are the endearing roguishness of a Ramsey Sniffle, Sut Lovingood, Jim Doggett, or a host of others who are "half-horse, half-alligator," replete with the blurring of distinctions separating human from animal worlds. Murfree here offers none of the winning qualities of these earlier types. . . .

Finally, our attention should be turned to another variety of Murfree's humor, a combination of down-to-earth domesticity with mirth, unified by the author's peculiar turn of phrase and offering of particulars. An excellent example, from the novel *His Vanished Star,* centers on the noteworthy care lavished upon a sickly turkey poult by Widow Larrabee, whose motivation incorporates motherly feelings and an eye to her table. Mock-heroics contribute signally to the comedy. This "infant turkey"—as if it were human—is accorded such solemnity in the setting forth of its circumstances that what is a common incident in farm life (care of ailing animals) verges on burlesque. . . .

To conclude, I trust that the foregoing illustrations have demonstrated Mary Murfree's "special" sense of humor. Working on ground common to many earlier humorists, and without failing to recognize its vitality, she adapted from it and toned down its excesses. Rather than hammer down with replete details the frequently overt bawdy from earlier frontier humor, Murfree leaves much to our own imaginations. . . . Murfree tends to repeat comic situations, just as she tended to overwork descriptive materials or to note appearances of the moon. What provides relish in reading an individual work may diminish when the aggregate of her fiction is surveyed. Nevertheless, since her characters are "ancestors of Li'l Abner and Snuffy Smith," they are worthwhile in considerations of American humor.

FURTHER READING

Biographies

Cary, Richard. *Mary N. Murfree.* New York: Twayne Publishers, Inc., 1967, 192 p.
    Comprehensive biography.

Parks, Edd Winfield. *Charles Egbert Craddock.* Chapel Hill: University of North Carolina Press, 1941, 258 p.
    Biographical and critical work on Murfree.

Bibliography

Carleton, Reese M. "Mary Noailles Murfree: An Annotated Bibliography." *American Literary Realism 1870-1910,* 7, No. 4 (Autumn 1974): 293-378.
    Annotated bibliography with short critical introduction.

Criticism

Becker, May Lamberton. Introduction to "Electioneerin' on Big Injun Mounting." In *Golden Tales of the Old South.* pp. 175-76. New York: Dodd, Mead and Co., 1930.
    Biographical introduction with positive assessment of Murfree's style.

Ensor, Allison. "The Geography of Mary Noailles Murfree's *In the Tennessee Mountains.*" *Mississippi Quarterly* XXXI (Spring 1978): 191-99.
    Focuses on places and place names in Murfree's short stories.

Orgain, Kate Alma. "Mary Noailles Murfree (Charles Egbert Craddock)." In *Southern Authors in Poetry and Prose*, pp. 214-23. New York: Neale Publishing Co., 1908.
    Overview of Murfree's life with a few critical remarks.

Payne, William Morton. A review of *The Mystery of Witch-Face Mountain and Other Stories. The Dial* (16 March 1896): 173-74.
    Maintains that while the stories in this volume retain much of the quality of her earlier work, Murfree tends to stretch "too far" for synonyms.

Simpson, Claude M., ed. Introduction to "The 'Harnt' That Walks Chilhowee." In *The Local Colorists: American Short Stories, 1857-1900*, pp. 204-05. New York: Harper and Brothers, 1960.
    Comments on the principal themes, style, and characters of this short story.

Additional coverage of Murfree's life and career is contained in the following sources published by Gale Research: *Contemporary Authors,* Vol. 122; and *Dictionary of Literary Biography,* Vols. 12, 74.

Luigi Pirandello
1867–1936

Italian playwright, short story writer, novelist, essayist, and poet.

INTRODUCTION

One of the most important dramatists of the twentieth century, Pirandello was also a prolific writer of short stories. He planned to write a story for each day of the year and to collect them in a series entitled *Novelle per un anno*, intended to contain twenty-four volumes, each of which would comprise fifteen tales. In all, Pirandello succeeded in completing two hundred and thirty-three stories before his death. Through this vast body of work, he worked out in many variations the quotidian struggles of characters trying to grasp the significance of life. Early in his career Pirandello was associated with a school of regional realist writers, and many stories are set in the author's native Sicily, with vividly rendered landscapes of sun-baked fields and oppressive sulphur mines. Yet Pirandello's short stories often have a tinge of irony and absurdity as well as an intellectual complexity that sets them apart from the work of typical realist writers. The preoccupations of Pirandello's characters are generally cerebral, and the action of the stories often hinges less on action or a climactic event than on the significance of a word or gesture. Pirandello was awarded international acclaim for the philosophic probing of his plays, and the same themes are found in his short stories, many of which he subsequently adapted for the stage.

Biographical Information

Pirandello was born in Sicily to a prosperous sulphur merchant. Although his father initially sent him to study commerce at the local technical institute, Pirandello lacked interest in the subject and transferred to an academic secondary school, where he excelled in oratory and literature. He began writing at a young age, and by the time he was twelve had produced his first play, *Barbaro*, with siblings and friends. He also wrote poetry and fiction, publishing his first poem in 1883 and his first story a year later. After graduation, Pirandello attended universities in Palermo, Rome, and finally Bonn, where he earned a doctorate in Romance philology. He then returned to Rome, living on a remittance from his father while trying to establish himself as a writer. Here he became a member of the literary circle of Luigi Capuana. Capuana, along with another well-known Sicilian writer Giovanni Verga, followed the precepts of Émile Zola's Naturalism (*verismo* in Italian) and attempted through fiction to recreate the people, customs, and landscapes of their native Sicily. Though Pirandello's later theoretical writings show that his thought evolved

beyond *verismo*, landscape remained a striking feature of his narrative works. In 1894 Pirandello's father arranged his marriage to Antonietta Portulano, the daughter of a business partner, and the couple settled together in Rome and had three children. Pirandello published his first book of short stories, *Amori senza amore* (*Loves without Love*), in 1894. Two novels followed, *L'Esclusa* (*The Outcast*), published serially in 1901, and *Il Turno* in 1902. Then in 1903 Pirandello suffered a dramatic financial reversal when his father's sulphur mine was destroyed in a landslide and flood. His family wealth was wiped out, and the catastophe pushed his wife into mental collapse. Antonietta never recovered, but became paranoid and delusional. Pirandello initially refused to have her hospitalized, and he took refuge from her irrational abuse by escaping to his study to write.

In 1904 Pirandello published his novel *Il fu Mattia Pascal* (*The Late Mattia Pascal*) to great acclaim, as well as a volume of short stories. More short story collections followed in 1906, 1910, 1912, 1914, and two in 1915. He also published an important critical work *L'umorismo* (*On Humor*) in 1908, and three more novels by 1916. Pirandello began to have success with his dramas also. His first full-length play was performed in 1915, and two Sicilian dialect plays, *Pensaci, Giacomino!* (*Think It Over, Giacomino!*) and *Liolà*, were successfully produced the next year. More plays were staged in the following years, including two which were adapted from his short fiction, *Cosí è (se vi pare)* (*Right You Are (If You Think So)*) and *La patente* (*The License*). Pirandello's reputation swelled enormously in 1921 with the Rome performance of his play *Sei personaggi in cerca d'autore* (*Six Characters in Search of an Author*). With this play and *Enrico IV* (*Henry IV*) Pirandello came to international fame. Pirandello joined the Fascist Party in 1925 and received government sponsorship to form the Art Theatre of Rome. This company toured throughout Europe and America with productions of his plays. The Art Theatre dissolved in 1928, and Pirandello's plays suffered decreasing popularity. In 1934 Pirandello was awarded the Nobel Prize for literature, while that same year a Fascist claque booed his *La favola del figlio cambiato* (*The Fable of the Changeling*) off the stage in Rome. He continued to write short stories up until his death in 1936.

Major Works of Short Fiction

In all his work Pirandello probes the conflicts between reality and appearance, the individual and society, art and life. Influenced by *verismo*, Pirandello's early fiction unceremoniously exposes the lives of villagers—miners, clerics, olive farmers, an old man captured by bandits, distressed brides and widows—and highlights salient features of Sicilian society: strict Catholicism, an uncompromising code of honor, well-defined social roles, and an underlying violent temperament. He skillfully described the landscape and inhabitants of Sicily in a naturalistic style while simultaneously commenting on the paradoxical and contradictory aspects of life and the restrictions of social identity. Later stories are more overtly philosophical. "Canta l'epistola" ("He Who Chants the Epistle") describes a youth who, after losing his faith in God, develops pantheistic love for a blade of grass. The enormity of the universe and the folly of ordinary people are described through the eyes of the boy, whose behavior—incomprehensible to others—leads to his death. Other stories, such as "War" from *The Medals, and Other Stories*, are masterpieces of dialogue, with little physical description or narration. The verbal interplay of the characters is so highly developed that Pirandello was able to fashion plays out of some short stories with only minor alterations. The fiction from Pirandello's last years differ from his earlier work. Pirandello toured the world with his theater company, and some later stories are set outside his native Italy, most notably in New York. His very last stories are also surreal and metaphysical. In the story "All'uscita" ("At the Gate"), the dead souls of a philosopher and an obese man converse. The philosopher, as in life, philosophizes, and the stout man too is still interested in the preoccupations of his former life. In Pirandello's last story, "Una giornata" ("A Day"), the narrator lives an entire life in a single, bewildering day, from a strange birth in a train station to old age and death in a dusty armchair. In these final stories Pirandel-

lo abandoned his preoccupation with factual reality to explore psychological and metaphysical issues.

Critical Reception

Pirandello achieved fame because of his plays, and his reputation still rests principally on his dramatic works. The majority of critical studies since his death have concentrated on his plays, yet he was a popular short story writer in Italy in his day. Many of his stories were first published in daily newspapers, where his novels were also serialized. His short fiction began to appear in English in the 1930s, when his international reputation as a playwright increased interest in his career. However, no new English translation has appeared since 1965. Pirandello wrote enough for two careers, one as a playwright, one as an author of fiction, and the immense success of his dramas is at least partially responsible for the relative neglect shown his short stories by general readers.

PRINCIPAL WORKS

Short Fiction

Amori senza amore [*Loves without Love*] 1894
Beffe della morte e della vita [*Jests of Death and Life*] 1902
Quand'ero matto [*When I Was Mad*] 1902
Bianche e nere [*White and Black*] 1904
Erma bifronte [*The Two-faced Herma*] 1906
La vita nuda [*Naked Life*] 1910
Terzetti [*Tercets*] 1912
Le due maschere [*The Two Masks*] 1914
Erba del Nostro Orto [*Grass from Our Garden*] 1915
La trappola [*The Trap*] 1915
E domani, Lunedi [*And Tomorrow, Monday*] 1917
Un cavallo nella Luna [*Horse in the Moon*] 1918
Berecche e la guerra [*Berecche and the War*] 1919
Il carnevale dei morti [*The Carnival of the Dead*] 1919
Novelle per un anno. 15 vols. [*A Story for Every Day of the Year*] 1922-37
Horse in the Moon 1932
Better Think Twice about It, and Twelve Other Stories 1933
The Naked Truth, and Eleven Other Stories 1934
The Medals, and Other Stories 1939
Short Stories 1959
Short Stories 1965

*The stories in these collections were selected from the series *Novelle per un anno.*

Other Major Works

Mal giocondo [*Joyful Ills*] (poetry) 1889
Il fu Mattia Pascal [*The Late Mattia Pascal*] (novel) 1904

L'esclusa [*The Outcast*] (novel) 1908

L'umorismo [*On Humor*] (essay) 1908

I vecchi e i giovani [*The Old and the Young*] (novel) 1913

Liolà (drama) 1916

Si gira [*Shoot*] (novel) 1916

Cosí è (se vi pare) [*Right You Are (If You Think So)*] (drama) 1917

Il piacere dell'onestà [*The Pleasure of Honesty*] (drama) 1917

L'uomo, la bestia e la virtù [*Man, Beast and Virtue*] (drama) 1919

Sei personaggi in cerca d'autore [*Six Characters in Search of an Author*] (drama) 1921

Enrico IV [*Henry IV*] (drama) 1922

Vestire gli ignudi [*Dress the Naked*] (drama) 1922

Ciascuno a suo modo [*Each in His Own Way*] (drama) 1924

Uno, nessuno e centomila [*One, None, and a Hundred Thousand*] (novel) 1926

Come tu mi vuoi [*As You Desire Me*] (drama) 1930

Maschere nude. 10 vols. [*Naked Masks*] (drama) 1930-38

Questa sera si recita a soggetto [*Tonight We Improvise*] (drama) 1930

I giganti della montagna [*The Mountain Giants*] (drama) 1937

CRITICISM

The Times Literary Supplement (essay date 1933)

SOURCE: "Stories from Pirandello," in *The Times Literary Supplement*, No. 1623, March 9, 1933, p. 164.

[*In the following review, the critic extols the collection* Better Think Twice about It.]

Thirteen stories from Signor Pirandello's vast output of tales are included in [**Better Think Twice about It**]. Almost all of them are scenes of Sicilian life, humorous or tragic; and one would have been glad to see some of the other stories, which are equally characteristic and contain many germs of Signor Pirandello's later plays. Nevertheless, this small selection illustrates his mastery of the short story, the queer twist of his humour and the grimness of his tragedy.

Except for the immortal **"La Giara,"** it is not likely that any of these stories are well known in England: in its English dress, however, that comic tale of the avaricious farmer and the old jar-mender who riveted himself up in the oil-jar does not preserve its raciness quite so well as the two tales of husbands and wives, **"The Call to Duty"** and **"The Quick and the Dead."** Both are *contes drolatiques* discreetly told, but the latter is more than a mere anecdote. It tells how a skipper came into port to find a crowd awaiting him with the news that his first wife, who had been reported drowned three years before at Tunis,

had come home alive. In the interval the skipper had married her sister, who was about to bear him a child. The skipper is a pious and God-fearing man and he faces the problem with all the dignified seriousness of a Southern race, while the two women behave like sisters, not like rivals. The solution that he finds and the effect of it on the townspeople is deliciously told. Pirandello gives a far more varied picture of the Sicilian temperament than does Verga in his great tragic stories, although Verga could not have found a more tragic theme than that of **"The Other Son."** Here, as in **"The Captive,"** the foundation of the tragedy is the cruelty of brigands: but, whereas in the first the horror is unmitigated, in the second there is a humorous sadness that only a Sicilian and a philosopher could have attained. The brilliant little story that gives the volume its title tells how an old professor who has married a young wife, provided her with a young lover and recognized the child, comes to reprove the young lover who is thinking of deserting his old love and marrying another. The professor's impassioned appeal to the young man's good sense has in it that paradoxical justice that may well be called Pirandellian.

It is to be hoped that the reception of this volume will encourage the translators to produce another; for it is impossible properly to appreciate the Pirandello of the plays without understanding the masterly narrator of the stories and the background of simple, passionate, comic and often paradoxical island life that they illustrate. Moreover, whereas the characters of his later plays are little better than abstractions, those of his stories are very much flesh and blood.

Percy Hutchison (essay date 1934)

SOURCE: "The Short Stories of Pirandello," in *The New York Times Book Review*, September 9, 1934, p. 2, 12.

[*In the following review, Hutchison judges the collection* The Naked Truth *"truly great," asserting that Pirandello conveys the messages of his stories very subtly.*]

The twelve stories which comprise [**The Naked Truth, and Eleven Other Stories**] have been selected from the series by Luigi Pirandello called *Novelle per un Anno*. In adopting what is the title of the second piece as a caption for the collection the translators chose wisely. Signor Pirandello has long been occupied with that illusive matter, truth; discussing the concept from various angles, probing for reality, studying effects. *As You Desire Me*, as those who saw the play, or the cinema based on the play, will recall, was an ingenious and intensely human dramatization of a highly metaphysical question—namely, what is one's real self? There is less of metaphysical in this dozen of stories than lies behind the play; the tales seem rather to concern themselves with the effect of truth and, still more often, the absence of truth.

It might be argued, therefore, that the collection has a moral purpose, as, indeed, seems to be the case. But Pirandello is an artist, in fact, a consummate artist; if each piece seems to have its separate moral, and to participate in the moral common to them all, there is no didactic intrusion. The reader has not been taken by the ears and dragged into a Sunday school. He will find, however, that this astute, capable and gorgeously witty Italian has, with Machiavellian cunning, compelled him to do some individual thinking while resting under the delusion that he was merely being entertained or horrified, as the case might be.

As we have already spoken of the title-piece as a key to the whole, we shall turn first to **"The Naked Truth."** It is less masterly than several other stories in the book. It is, in fact, Pirandello in his gayest mood; witty in the extreme, nevertheless of a transparent type of wit which leaves it an inferior piece. Two sculptors, Ciro Coll and his friend Pogliani, find themselves favored with a visit by a lady and her bereaved daughter, for the latter's fiancé had accidentally shot himself while hunting, and since he has bequeathed his vast fortune to the girl, they desire a fitting monument to his memory. The girl has made a sketch of her idea for the monument. All her thoughts are of her dead lover: she feels that she is married to him, though he is dead, and her figures are to show Life marrying Death.

> The skeleton [she explains] stands rigid, but between the folds of the winding-sheet comes out one of his hands, only just visible. It holds the wedding ring. And Life, looking modest and timid, presses up against the skeleton and holds out her hand to receive the ring.

Getting away from the light banter of the piece, for this is, as Pirandello intended it should be, the very ultimate of sentimentalism, what is the author going to do with such sentimentalism? He is going to cast such ridicule upon it—by rousing up truth naked—that no one reading his farcical narrative shall mistake his purpose.

We must make a not-long story shorter still. The figure of the girl (Life) is to be clothed, and the face is to be molded in her own likeness. The artists insist that Life should be nude. But no, again and again, no; that cannot be, she insists. And then the girl, really a bit of an artist, starts taking lessons from Pogliani. The tale ends with Ciro Coli talking to the skeleton he has borrowed from the medical school for his model for Death. Pogliani and the girl are to be married, and his brother-artist, pretending the skeleton is that of her former lover, concludes with these words:

> They want Life naked now—it's to be nude Life, as nude and as crude as Life can be. Now it's to be you clutching at her, my fine fellow, and she refusing to have anything to do with you. Ah! Just you tell me now—why on earth did you have to go out shooting?

In no sense a remarkable piece, **"The Naked Truth"** achieves its purpose and a little more—the destruction of false ideas (here, sentimentality, which is always false), through the simple process of placing them in juxtaposition to the truth.

In the story which leads the collection, **"The Annuity,"** we find the wit of Pirandello at its height, a truly salty wit, Continental rather than English or American. **"The Naked Truth"** might have been done by an Anglo-Saxon; it is doubtful if **"The Annuity"** could have been. One feels in the narrative, with its amused and tolerant understanding of racial qualities and tradition, much the same rare sagacity which so distinguished the work of Alphonse Daudet.

The story is about an aged peasant farmer who sells his farm to a rich Maltese for an annuity of 2 lire a day for life. The Maltese had previously taken on the adjoining farm at 1 lira a day. And not only that, but the annuitant had promptly and most obligingly died. Don Michelangelo Scinè trusts that Maràbito will be just as obliging. But no. Moreover, the neighbors, detesting the Maltese interloper, take an interest in keeping the old man alive!

> You live on to a hundred, just to spite him [they cry]. May our Blessed Lord and His most Holy Mother keep you alive to make the man die of fury. A blood-sucker, that's what he is. *You* suck *his* blood, as he's sucked the blood of so many of the poor.

And Maràbito not only does live to be a hundred, but still beyond that. And Scinè himself dies, and also Zagara, the lawyer, who takes over the property and the obligation of the annuity, and the farm comes back into the possession of the old man!

Apart from the deeply human significance of the story, and the mordant wit in the conception, we like even more the delicate etching in of the Italian countryside, of the peasants, their wives and families, the very animals on the place, the old man's love for them—

> The mules and donkeys * * * they were used to hard work, poor animals, but they were also accustomed to their daily ration of barley and bran, in addition to their straw.

And poor Maràbito speculates as to what treatment they will receive from their new master.

In two or three of the stories, notably one called **"The Fly,"** Pirandello is not content even with being sardonic. One sees the relation to truth in **"The Annuity"**—Scinè had not been honest even with himself. If he had not expected Maràbito to die, as had Ciuzzo Pace, speedily, he would not have taken over the farm at 2 lire a day. In **"The Fly,"** Zaru, dying of glanders transferred to him by a fly, watches the insect feeding on a cut on the face of his cousin Neli, well knowing that Neli also will die, speedily and horribly, and wishing his death, so that he shall not have the pleasure of marriage, for Zaru and Neli were to have been married on the same day.

> Ah! Now they would really get married together! A grim jealousy, a dull envy had come upon him at the sight of his young cousin so healthy, so full of the promise of life—life from which he himself was suddenly to be cut off.

Like **"The Annuity"** this story is Continental, Gallic. But it is not Daudet we find in the story, it is de Maupassant. **"The Fly,"** as a pure achievement in horror fiction, leaving aside for the moment the Pirandello philosophic slant, must be ranked as one of the world's masterpieces within that disagreeable genre.

The mordant note is dominant throughout all the stories in the book, whether Signor Pirandello occupies himself with men or women, or both; with merchants, peasants, or priests. In **"The Wax Madonna,"** for example, whimsically, delicately humorous, not in any wise irreverent, the good Father Fiorica is tempted—very mildly tempted—by the Devil. For instance, just one little pinch, while he is in the pulpit, from the beautiful snuff-box a parishioner has given him, and then "forty sneezes, sending the whole congregation into fits of laughter."

But the wax Maddona! It was raffled for once a month, and then borne in procession to the house of the winner. And the good Padre did so wish that little Duccio, whose father was so violently opposed to the church, should win the holy figure! Who could tell? Might it not bring the parents back into the fold? So, tempted of the same cunning devil, Father Fiorica reads out little Duccio's name as that of the winner, when, as it turns out, the boy had not taken a ticket that week, having given his penny to a poor child of the village. So the parents send back the Madonna, and Father Fiorica does not see his little friend, of whom he had become so fond, again. Truth—truth is better at all times, says Pirandello's charming allegory. Was any bitter pill ever more dedicately sugared?

"Va Bene," one of the longer stories in the collection, does not entirely fit into the pattern of the book as we have drawn it. The gentle Professor Corvara Amidei seems to have been drawn by Pirandello in a moment of fierce rebellion. It is not that the kind schoolmaster transgresses against truth at any point. If possible, he is too truthful in his simplicity. He is taken advantage of at every turn, the butt of a malign fate.

It is not easy, therefore, to make out precisely what is Pirandello's purpose behind **"Va Bene."** Certainly the good man does not triumph, the meek does not inherit the earth. Instead, the schoolmaster is dragged off to prison for throwing his wife out of the window where he overheard her making an assignation with her lover below. In his sudden insanity, the professor had no thought but to hasten her into her lover's arms. The story is a rich jest—the sort of jest the devil likes to play on mortals. Hence, there is savage anger concealed beneath the limpid flow of the narrative. Yet the author, his lips curling in scorn, nevertheless is looking upon life with pity in his eyes. Why had God made so sweet and trusting a soul as that of the professor only to cast it to Satan for a plaything. **"Va Bene"** is a cry of revolt; a searing, bitter cry. Yet the humor of the tale is infinite; without this healing salve of humor the story would be intolerable.

We have been able to touch, and barely to touch, on but a few of the many facets of these tales. Not in a long time

has one so able as Luigi Pirandello poured his genius into the short story. The truly great writers of the short story can be counted on the fingers of one's hands. How puny by comparison appears the average tale in our magazines! Seldom does it go below the surface; still more seldom is there anything behind it in the least resembling ideational power. In *The Naked Truth* we find something of the artistic genius of Boccaccio plus the mind of Pirandello.

Publishers are in the habit of saying that collections of short stories do not readily sell. There may be a pleasant surprise here. Beneath the author's studied lightness of manner there is grim insistence on the verities that are eternal; behind the sallies of wit, a hand armed with righteousness and indignation. It may be said without fear of exaggeration, here is a collection of stories truly great.

Elizabeth Hart   (essay date 1935)

SOURCE: "Luigi Pirandello, 1934 Nobel Prize Winner," in *New York Herald Tribune Books,* January 6, 1935, p. 3.

[*In the following review, Hart hails* Better Think Twice about It *as a testament to Pirandello's skill as a short story writer.*]

It is probably to the Nobel Prize judges that we owe most of our thanks for getting another batch of Pirandello stories so soon after the appearance of that superb collection *The Naked Truth,* but a very special bow should be reserved for the publishers, the translators, or whoever selected the contents of [*Better Think Twice about It*]. The prestige of a literary prize winner can be counted on—for a short time—to bring a certain section of the public running to buy whatever is issued over his name, no matter how inferior and unrepresentative it may be, and more than one publisher has gathered his rosebuds by delving hastily into the past work of the author of the hour and coming forth with whatever his hand touches first. But the publishers have played fair with Pirandello and with old Pirandello enthusiasts and their reward certainly ought to be a whole new host of converts. When I say that the level of these stories is as high as that of *The Naked Truth* I am making a statement that should work two ways, for any one who has read the former collection will want to get this one and any one who hasn't will want to rectify the error after reading *Better Think Twice About It*.

Indeed the two books extend and supplement one another in a way absolutely essential to the reader who hopes to get any idea of the range and versatility of Pirandello's genius for the short story. There is not between them any such striking and obvious contrast as either offers to the noetic pyrotechnics of the plays, nothing to arouse exclamations of incredulity at their having been written by the same man. The pre-Mussolini peasants and villagers, the obscure professors and petty tradesmen and little men of all sorts that make up the caste of this volume, as they did of that of its predecessors, bear the stamp of the same creator. It is a familiar face that *Better Think Twice About It* turns toward us, but a set of new expressions.

There are four stories out of the thirteen, for instance, whose *raison d'etre* is pure laughter. We have had humor in Pirandello stories before, certainly, and very effective humor, but it has always served as an incidental or an equalizing quality to something else—to irony, or tenderness, or horror or tragedy—and hence has not prepared us for the genuine comic gift displayed in **"The Jar"** and **"The Call to Duty."** Both these tales are wholly and irresistibly funny, and it is worth noting as another example of Pirandello's subtle variety, his infinite capacity for never being quite the same, that they are created in entirely different moods. **"The Jar"** might have been told by one of Chaucer's most joyous and simple-hearted peasants. It is a true Gothic tale, earthy, shrewd, full of a frank, bouncing delight in the troubles of the ridiculous Don Lallo, starter of law suits, and the uncomfortable physical predicament of old Zi Dema, mender of broken pottery. **"The Call to Duty"** is urbane and sly, handling its robust theme of cuckoldry and aphrodisiacs with a mocking politeness, gaining its most mirthful and ribald effects by elaborate indirections. Then there is **"The Quick and the Dead"** which is concerned with the knotty problem of Skipper Nino Mo, when his first wife whom he had believed drowned in a shipwreck turned up hale and hearty after he had married and got with child her younger sister Rosa. How the Skipper, who was fond of both sisters, and the sisters who were devoted to one another, found a solution satisfactory to them, but highly upsetting to the Registrar of births and deaths is related with a humor quieter and more difficult of analysis than the aforementioned brands—perhaps because Pirandello achieves it without once wavering from his attitude of sincere respect for the scrambled trio he describes. Fourthly, there is **"It's Nothing Serious"**; but the less said about that the better. It is amusing in spots, but too thinly so to make up for the triteness of its point.

And, now that the captious note has been sounded, I might just as well admit that nothing has been added to the collection by the inclusion of the two animal stories **"Black Horses"** and **"The King Set Free."** In fact, I will go further and say that the former is a distinct drawback. Very few authors seem to be able to make animals talk without setting one's teeth on edge.

"The Captive" seems to me both inspired and touching. An old man, well-to-do according to the modest standards of his village, is kidnaped by three poor and hitherto respectable peasants, taken to a cave on a lonely mountainside and threatened with death unless he writes a note requesting ransom. But as old Guarnotta sadly tells these clumsy criminals, no one will pay out money for his life when they have everything to gain by his death. His wife, her nephews, will merely pretend that they never received the threatening letter, and wash their hands of him. If he is set free, however, he swears to meet his captors within two days at any spot they may appoint and hand over the sum they desire. Furthermore, by all that is holy, he will not betray them to the police. The bandits, however, although they already realize that they have bungled the whole affair hopelessly, are not willing to trust him. Since they have repented their crime (chiefly because it was unsuccessful) they cannot bring themselves to commit another and kill him. Hence they compromise by deciding to keep the old man in the cave until God sees fit to terminate their period of expiation by summoning their captive to heaven.

At considerable sacrifice to themselves and their families they bring him daily bread. They make him as comfortable a bed as possible, they do everything for him except listen to his pleas for release. And little by little Guarnotta no longer desires to return to his former life. His captivity is less lonely, less boring, less empty of warmth and affection. He has grown fond of his captors, he has found pleasure in ministering to their eager thirst for information on all kinds of subjects with the superior knowledge he possesses. Meanwhile the men too have formed a deep affection for their captive "quite apart from the duty imposed on them by their consciences . . . regarding him as their own private possession in which no one else had any claim." When at last he dies, playing with the children of one of them, they mourn him bitterly and long. And for the rest of their lives when his name is mentioned they say "He was a saint that man. I'm sure he was admitted straight to Paradise."

Those are the bare bones of **"The Captive,"** but for the breathing, lovely flesh you must go to Pirandello. And so it is with **"Chants the Epistle,"** whose beauty is as frail, as self-contained, and as perfect as the blade of grass that Tomasino Unzio "overwhelmed by the most tender pity for all those little things which come to life and last but a brief space" grew to love with "an almost motherly tenderness" as he followed "its slow upward growth . . . timidly at first in its quivering slenderness above the encrusted stones . . . then up, up ever taller, bold and jaunty with a little reddish plume on its head like a cock's comb." Pirandello can make you understand what happened within Tomasino when a careless girl "put out her hand and picked just that very blade of grass and put it between her teeth with its head hanging plume downward," but I cannot. I can only repeat helplessly "Read it!"

And read the others, particularly **"The Wet Nurse"** and **"The Other Son."** They do not rank with the tales I have just mentioned, but they would be the highlights of many another short-story writer's collected works.

Walter Starkie (essay date 1937)

SOURCE: "Pirandello, Novelist and Short-Story Writer," in *Luigi Pirandello*, revised edition, John Murray, 1937, pp. 94–126.

[*An educator and critic who specialized in the Romance languages, Starkie is best known for his tales of gypsy life, drawn from his own experiences living among them in Europe. In the following excerpt, he provides an overview of Pirandello's short fiction.*]

[In the early stage of his literary career, Pirandello could have been classified] as a regional writer interpreting and expressing the customs and mode of life of the inhabitants of his native Sicily. But Pirandello was not fated to continue treading the path of Verga or even Capuana. He soon turned away from describing the folk and its primitive passions, and began to examine morbid psychological problems such as present themselves in the crowded lives of our soul-tormented twentieth century. The rural communities of Sicily with their simple village life did not give Pirandello the opportunity which he ceaselessly demands, of expressing his own torturing doubts and fears; he was not satisfied, as Verga was, with the objective description of character. Pirandello regards each of his characters as a symbol ready to express the distracting ideas that agitate his mentality. He seems perpetually to ask the question, "What is character? Does it exist?" When he looks at an individual he sees him in duple, triple or quadruple, and so he tells us that character, as writers have considered it up to this, is a pure illusion. In reality every man bears within himself two, three, four men, each of which, at a given time, dominates the others and determines an act. Pirandello in many of his stories shows the multiplicity of the individual and how unjust it is to judge a man only from the point of view of one out of his many personalities. And this idea of the multiplicity of the individual does not appeal to Pirandello as an abstract philosophical problem: it is an agonizing obsession which tortures him so unceasingly that each little story, each play, becomes a piece of self-expression undertaken in order to give relief to himself. No writer has ever been so obsessed by this problem as Pirandello, and it is the sense of inner conflict which causes these works to produce such a vivid impression on readers. It is absurd to see in Pirandello the philosopher whose works must be considered manuals for the student. Nothing could be farther from the truth: he might well say to the public who have listened to his plays what a famous actress once said of her enthusiastic audience: "They do well to applaud me, for I have given them my life." In his descriptions of morbid soul-torture Pirandello has given us his life and exposed every corner of his complex personality. If we look on his work in this light, we shall not disturb ourselves at the manifold contradictions that arise in every manifestation of his genius. So far from ascending to the higher ether of philosophical speculation, the Pirandellian threads his weary way through inextricable maze and chaos. He is driven this way and that by his notions of reality and illusion, and yet in the depths of his mind he believes positively in Life. . . .

How different Pirandello is to the great masters of creative art! We imagine Beethoven in the act of writing the *Fifth Symphony* or Wagner writing the drama of *Tristan and Isolde*—both of them entirely absorbed by their subject. It never comes into their mind to doubt the reality of their idea, for it is at the moment the one reality of their life, and their problem is how they may attain complete self-expression. Look, on the other hand, at Pirandello: as soon as his imaginative brain seizes an idea and he begins to revel in its fantasy, then there appears that malicious little imp who follows him like his shadow, breathing the chill breath of doubt, and thus most of the fantasy withers as beneath a shrivelling frost. Francesco Flora in his study [*Dal Romanticismo al Futurismo,* 1925] states the case: "Pirandello constructs men from one set idea. After having constructed them, he does his best to make them live. He distributes abroad false syllogisms dressed up as men. All the characters of Pirandello theorize on their own life: they are pseudo-philosophers, every man and woman of them.". . .

[Let] us examine some examples from his great output of short stories of *novelle,* as they are traditionally called in Italy. Italy is the country *par excellence* for the short story, and from Boccaccio to Pirandello, Italian authors have always known how to adapt their inspiration to this most difficult form of literature. English writers have never been able to make a complete success of the short-story form. The neatness of finish, the lightness of touch, the vivid style, seem far truer to the genius of Latin peoples, whose qualities are of the spontaneous kind. Northern nations produce novel writers in abundance, because in the North men brood over their sorrows and there is calculation even in their joy. Just as their lives in sunless climes are governed by will-power, so their literature is above all things an expression of their inner thoughts, an analysis of their passions. In the South, where the sun shines and where men's passions rise high, happiness, as Nietzsche once said, is short, sudden and without reprieve. There is less calculation and analysis, and more spontaneity. There is less sustained effort, but more frequent flashes of inspiration. This is especially true of Pirandello. In his longer novels there are many prolix passages which fatigue even the most hardened Pirandellian. In his short stories, on the other hand, Pirandello is rarely prolix, and he has a variety of methods of treatment worthy of Guy de Maupassant. But it is only the outer technique that resembles the Parisian writer: whereas Maupassant the malicious and sarcastic novelist deserves, according to Croce, the name of ingenuous poet, Pirandello must not be considered thus. The adjective "ingenuous" is the antithesis to his self-conscious art. Maupassant suffers and rejoices with his characters—he is all sensibility. Pirandello rarely shows any pity openly. The pity we feel for his characters is derived from our sense of pain at the heartlessness of the author. Both authors are profoundly pessimistic and a-religious. God is absent from both, and we have a sense of desolation and sadness. Guy de Maupassant watches the sad destiny of humanity with pity and with composed serenity; Pirandello is never serene, because he suffers ceaselessly in himself. He is more egotistical than Maupassant and thinks for ever of his own woes, not of those of his characters. Every short story of Pirandello is, as it were, a myth in the Platonic sense, to explain his subjective philosophy. And this philosophy is the philosophy of the individual, because Pirandello, like most of the moderns, would deny that there is a real world of things and persons, existing by itself outside the spirit which knows it. Like Maupassant, Pirandello would refuse to be called a realist, saying that "the great artists are those who display to other men their illusion," but he would go farther in his statement. For him the world is only a dream, a mirage, a phenomenon, an image created by our spirit. There are no such things as fixed characters, for life is ever changing, ever ebbing and flowing. Thus we find it very difficult to seize hold of these characters: they often resemble those modernist pictures wherein the painter has tried to paint the subjects in motion. It is for this reason that Pirandello is a symbol of all our present age: his fantastic stories are symbols of the struggle that goes on ceaselessly in all the minds of modern men. There is no dolorous serenity in his work, because the mind of to-day cannot rest: there are few men of flesh and bone in his novels, because flesh and bone are of no account. The world of Pirandello resembles that of Lucretius: shimmering myriads of atoms that combine by chance with one another and produce now a tree, now a man, now a beast— all according to the rules of chance.

Pirandello has been unceasing in his production of short stories ever since the first years of the present century. In these stories we can see his evolution as an artist. In the earlier collections, such as *Quand'ero matto* (1902), *Bianche e Nere* (1904), *Erma Bifronte* (1906), *La Vita Nuda* and *Terzetti,* many of these stories are . . . Sicilian. They are in many cases simple and unaffected in style and purged of rhetoric, as if he had attempted to cultivate the short rhythmic style of Maupassant. Gradually then we notice a tendency to prolixity and rhetoric—towards dialogue which announced the future dramatist. In many of the later volumes of stories, such as *Berecche e la guerra* (1919) and *Il carnevale dei Morti* (1919), the story is the merest excuse for long pieces of tortuous sophistry. The early editions of the Pirandellian *novelle* are difficult to obtain, and it is very fortunate that Bemporad the Florentine publisher undertook the task of issuing a complete collection under the title of *Novelle per un anno,* or *Stories for Every Day in the Year*.

First of all let us consider some stories in the earlier editions which might seem to reappear again and again with slight variations through the author's entire production. One of his favourite plots for his short stories is to show how "the best-laid plans of mice and men gang aft agley." In **"La Vita Nuda"** (**"Life in its Nakedness"**), a story which has given its name to a volume, a young girl whose fiancé on the eve of the wedding has died suddenly, visits a sculptor to order a memorial in honour of the dead man. Stricken with grief, her one thought is to symbolize eternally her sorrows by representing Life in the form of a young girl resigning herself to the embraces of Death, represented as a skeleton holding out the bridal ring. At first, under the influence of sorrow, the lady insists, contrary to the wishes of the sculptor, that the figure of Life should be clothed, but later on, when she falls in love with the sculptor's friend and her recollection of the dead finacé has begun to fade, she insists that Life should be shown in its symbolic nakedness resisting the contact of Death.

On other occasions Pirandello takes the opposite course, and makes his characters lament over the past that will never return. In **"Prima Notte"** (from the first volume of *Novelle per un Anno*), he describes the marriage between Lisi Chirico and Marastella, village folk of Sicily. Lisi was a widower, and Marastella had been in love with a

youth who perished in a shipwreck. The bridal couple spend their first night in the graveyard; she weeps over the tomb of her lost love, he calls on his dead wife by name: "The moon gazed from heaven down on the little graveyard in the uplands. She alone on that fragrant April night saw these two black shadows on the yellow little path near two tombs. Don Lisi, bending over the grave of his first wife, sobbed: 'Nunzia, Nunzia, do you hear me?'"

Such a story, in spite of the morbid and rather unnatural thesis it develops, is a good illustration of Pirandello's power. More than most modern authors he is able to convey to his readers a haunting sensation of sadness that does not leave us even when we have laid aside the book. Lisi Chirico and Marastella are not normal human beings: they are too neurotic, too highly strung for country folk; but so subtly does the author paint the background that they stand out in bold relief. And this skill of the author in drawing his background does not appear by direct touches, after the manner of a Thomas Hardy. Except for the last few lines which we have quoted there is no pictorial description. We infer the setting of the story from the dialogue bandied about by the characters. Pirandello's skill in producing the atmosphere he requires for his story or drama recalls the methods adopted by Jacinto Benavente, another master of the indirect description. As in the case of Benavente, too, if we probe deeply the mind of our Pirandello, we reach sentimentality—a modern sentimentality which hides away from the light of day and erects a structure of irony and cynicism as a barrier to protect its sensitiveness. The last story we treated showed traces of the sentimental, but perhaps the most characteristic example occurs in the story, **"Il lume dell' altra casa,"** from the collection *Terzetti*. Tullio Butti, the hero, like eighty per cent of the Pirandello heroes, is a queer, grotesque fellow. It is a good thing that the world of Pirandello is the stuff of dreams: what a miserable place real life would be if all men were like Mattia Pascal or Tullio Butti! Tullio Butti seemed to have a feeling of rancour against life. Nobody was ever able to make him take any interest in anything or relax his sullen, introspective gaze. Even his talkative landlady and her daughter were unable to humanize him. From the window of his room Tullio could see into the house at the opposite side of the street. In the evening, looking out at the windows of the house, he saw a family sitting round the dinner-table, and at the head sat the father and mother. The children were waiting in eager impatience for their food to be served. All were laughing gaily, and the mother and father laughed too. Every evening Tullio sat in darkness and gazed at the lighted window opposite, and it became his one joy in life. But the inquisitive daughter of his landlady, noticing that he used to remain hours in his room without a light, did a very excusable thing under the circumstances: she looked through the keyhole and saw Tullio standing gazing at the lit-up window. And forthwith she rushed off in hot haste to her mother to relate that he was in love with Margherita Masci, the lady opposite. Soon afterwards Tullio saw with surprise his own landlady enter the room opposite when the husband was not there and talk to the lady. The same evening, as a result of that conversation, the lady came to the window and whispered across to him good night. From that day onwards Tullio did not wait eagerly in his room for the illumination of the window opposite: nay, he waited impatiently until that light should be extinguished. With terrible suddenness the passion of love raged in the heart of that man who had been for so long a stranger to life. He left his lodgings, and on the same day as he left, the tidings came that the lady opposite had abandoned her husband and three children. Tullio's room remained empty for some months, but one evening he returned bringing the lady with him. She begged for leave to stand at the window and look across at the other house, where sat the sad father surrounded by the three downcast children. In this tale there is a warmth of sentiment that is lacking in many of the stories, but even here there is the sting characteristic of Pirandello. The tragedy arises, as usual, from the meddling curiosity and gossip of people who are not concerned. It is the talkative landlady who lights the fatal fuse. The moral is the same as in countless modern plays where evil gossip breaks up the peace of families.

It is absurd to see in Pirandello the philosopher whose works must be considered manuals for the student. Nothing could be farther from the truth. . . . In his descriptions of morbid soul-torture Pirandello has given us his life and exposed every corner of his complex personality.

—*Walter Starkie*

The same tender sadness appears in **"La Camera in Attesa"** (contained in the collection *E Domani Lunedi*). Three sisters and their widowed mother have been awaiting for some years the return of the brother and son, Cesarino, who went off to Tripoli on a military campaign. For fourteen months they have had no news of him, and as a result of repeated inquiry it has been ascertained that Cesarino has not been found among the dead or the wounded or the prisoners. Ever awaiting his return, the four women have kept his room ready for him. Every morning the water in the bottle is changed, the bed is remade, the nightshirt is unfolded, and once a week the old clock is wound up again. Everything is in order for his coming. Nothing shows the time that has elapsed except perhaps the candle, which in weary waiting has grown yellow, for the sisters do not change it as they do the water in the bottle. At first all the neighbours were greatly moved by this case, but little by little their pity cooled and changed to irritation, even in some a certain sense of indignation for what they called play-acting. But the neighbours forget that life only consists in the reality that we give to it. Thus the life that Cesarino continues to have for his mother and sisters may be sufficient for them, owing to the reality of the acts they perform for him here in the room which awaits him, just as it was when he left. The reality of Cesarino's existence remains unalterable in this room of his and in the heart and mind of his mother and sisters,

who outside this reality have no other. Time is fixed immutable were it not for Claretta, the betrothed of Cesarino. The thought of her makes the four women note the passing time. In the first days she used to visit them daily, but gradually, as time dragged on, her visits became rarer. The old mother, who counts the days that elapse between each visit, is surprised that whereas the departure of Cesarino seems only yesterday, so much time passes for Claretta. The culminating point of the tragedy arrives when the news is brought that Claretta is getting married. The mother lies dying; the three daughters look at her with sad envy. She will soon be able to go and see if he is over there; she will be relieved of the anxiety of that long wait: she will reach certainty, but she will not be able to return and tell them. The mother, though she knows for certain that she will find her Cesarino over there, feels a great pity for her daughters, who will remain alone and have such need to believe that he is still alive and will return soon. And thus with her last breath she whispers to them: "You will tell him that I have waited so long." And on that night in the silent house the room is left untouched, the water is not changed, the date on the calendar marks the previous day. "The illusion of life in that room has ceased for one day and it seems for ever." Only the clock continues to speak of time in that endless waiting.

Again and again the same theme recurs in the *novelle* in different forms. "What makes life is the reality which you give to it." Thus the life that Cesarino Mochi's mother and his three sisters live in that room of his is sufficient for them. If you have not seen your son for some years, he will seem different to you when he returns. Not so Cesarino; his reality remains unchangeable there in his room that is set in expectation of his coming. In the concluding story of the ninth volume of *Novelle per un Anno*, entitled **"I Pensionati della Memoria"** (**"The Pensioners of Memory"**), Pirandello treats the same idea, but takes it up where the former story left off. Supposing even that the mother and sisters had been present at the death of Cesarino and had watched his coffin being lowered into the grave, would they not feel that he had departed for ever, never to return? But no, gentlemen, Pirandello tells us that Cesarino's mother and sisters and many of us would find that the dead man comes back behind us to our homes after the funeral. He pretends to be dead within his coffin, but, as far as all of us are concerned, he is not dead. He is here with me just as much as you are, except that he is disillusioned. "His reality has vanished, but which one? Was it the reality that he gave to himself? What could I know of his reality—what do you know about it? I know what I gave to him from my own point of view. His illusion is mine." And yet those people, though I know that they are dead, come back with me to my house. They have not got a reality of their own, mark you; they cannot go where they please, for reality never exists by itself. Their reality now depends on me, and so they must perforce come with me: they are the poor pensioners of my memory. Most people, when friends or relations die, weep for them and remember this or that trait in their character which makes the feeling of bereavement seem greater. But all this feeling of bereavement, this sorrow, is for a reality which they believe to have vanished with the deceased.

They have never reflected on the meaning of this reality. Everything for them consists in the existence or in the non-existence of a body. It would be quite enough consolation for these people if we made them believe that the deceased is here no more in bodily form, not because his body is buried in the earth, but because he has gone off on a journey and one day he will return from that journey. This will be their consolation. The real reason why we all weep over our dead friend is because he cannot make his presence a reality to us. His eyes are closed, his hands are stiff and cold: he does not hear or perceive us, and it is this insensibility that plunges us in sorrow. Owing to his death our one comfort has departed—the reciprocity of illusion. If he had only gone off on a journey, we could live on in hope like Cesarino's sisters, saying to ourselves: "He thinks of me over there and thus I live for him."

In the stories we have considered there are traces of a kindlier Pirandello. Sometimes he produces a deep emotional effect on his reader when he ceases to try to solve a problem or work out a knotted intrigue. In **"Il Ventaglino"** (**"The Little Fan"** in *Novelle per un Anno,* Vol. I) we see a little scene in a public park in Rome on a hot and dusty afternoon in August. So subtle is the author's method of description in this story that we visualize the scene. The park is dusty and the yellow houses nearby are forlorn and desolate; men are slumbering in the sultry atmosphere. On one seat a thin little old man with a yellow handkerchief on his head is reading a paper; nearby a workman out of work sleeps with his head leaning on his arms. On the other side an old woman listens to the sad tale of a woman nearby, and then departs after giving her a piece of bread. Then there is a red-haired girl who walks up and down impatiently: she is evidently waiting for somebody. All these people Pirandello describes for us impressionistically. Amongst them appears poor Tuta with her baby in her arms. Tuta is alone in the world with her baby. She has but a penny in her pocket and the child is famished. "Not a single person would believe that she was in such hopeless want. She could hardly believe it herself. But it had come to that. She had entered that park to find a shady spot and had loitered there for the past two hours: she could remain on until evening, but then . . . where was she to spend the night with that child in arms? And next day? And the day after that? . . . Ah, Nino, there is nothing for it but the river for both of us." Then Tuta watches mechanically the people crowding into the park in the cool of the evening: children skipping, nurses carrying babies, governesses, soldiers in uniform. Something seemed to change her line of thought. She looked up at the people and smiled. She unbuttoned the neck of her coat and uncovered a little of her white neck. Just then an old man passed by selling paper fans. With her last penny she bought one. Then "opening still more of her blouse and starting to fan slowly her uncovered breast she laughed and began to look invitingly and provokingly at the soldiers who were passing by."

Such a story shows us Pirandello at his best, because in it he avoids any criticism of his characters. He limits himself to exposing objectively the results of his observations. In the majority of the stories the author tries to justify himself, and he insists on criticizing and interpreting his characters to us. In such exquisite stories as **"Il Lume dell' Altra Casa," "La Camera in Attesa"** or **"Il Ventaglino,"** the characters and the atmosphere they create round themselves tell us all the inferences to be drawn. Pirandello tells us more about his characters than any preceding novelist: he allows them to blurt out all the thoughts that are passing through their minds. One of the reasons why nearly all his characters are abnormal is because he will not content himself with exposing their exterior, obvious personality, but tries to reach even their subconscious thoughts and actions. Pirandello never stops short at the objective observation of character: irresistibly he is driven on to interpret and comment critically upon the children of his imagination. And this critical and interpretative attitude of mind often chills the inspiration and kills the character. When Pirandello the critic and dilettante metaphysician appears on the scene, Poetry in fright takes to her heels and flees away. . . . [The] whole basis of Futurism consists in pitiless criticism of the past. The Futurists believe that "Passéisme" (one of Marinetti's coined words) is synonymous with all that is evil, because its devotees in their thought and art are incapable of understanding the essence of modern life. It is therefore not surprising that Pirandello's works should be full of the close reasoning and criticism of the modern mind, especially as he himself is a vacillating Futurist—one who belongs to the older generation and yet has found a place at the table of the present-day youths.

Sometimes Pirandello's stories are feasts of dialectic and there is no attempt at weaving a story. They are, as it were, dialogues between the author and himself about metaphysical problems, and no abnormality is too exaggerated to illustrate his point. We find a woman of forty years of age who allowed herself to be seduced by a peasant youth of nineteen and became *enceinte*. Then after marrying him to calm the scandal, she commits suicide rather than allow him to possess her again [**"Scialle Nero"** in *Novelle per un Anno,* Vol. I]. In another story [**"Canta L'Epistola"** in *Novelle per un Anno,* Vol. III] a youth who is in Holy Orders loses his faith and goes back to his country village, to become the butt for the ridicule of all. But he sees the folly of everything and minds not their jeering insults. His sensitive mind becomes pantheistic and turns to all the manifestations of Nature, especially those plants and flowers that bloom for but one short day. The more fragile and humble those plants or insects, the more they excited his compassion and moved him to tears. Sometimes it was an ant or a fly or even a blade of grass. All these tiny things set off the enormous vacuity of the universe, the unknown. For a month he had been watching intently a blade of new grass growing between two stones in a ruined chapel. Every day he went to see it and protect it from marauding goats and sheep. One day he saw a young lady in the chapel, and distractedly she picked the blade of grass and put it in her mouth. Then the youth felt irresistibly impelled to hurl the epithet "stupid" at her. After hearing about this insult, her fiancé challenged the youth to a duel and wounded him fatally. When the priest was hearing the poor boy's confession at the point of death, he asked him why he had acted thus. He replied gently,

"Father, for a blade of grass." And all thought that he was continuing still to rave. In other stories Pirandello draws on all his fund of grotesqueness in order to produce his "creepy" effect: peasants filled with insane hatred against rich neighbours who have lately arrived, or else a man who feels such loathing for his wife because of her infidelity that he locks her in the upper part of the house while below he brings in drunken prostitutes to sleep with him. In those stories life seems to be a hideous nightmare and everything is out of focus. Every character suffers from some fixation to the point of madness. The irony of Pirandello disappears, and all that we see is one of those grinning masks which frighten children. Such stories often produce a terrifying effect on readers, because these abnormal beings have a complete logic of their own—the logic of the madman. More than any writer of to-day Pirandello is able to convey to us the emotion of horror. Let us quote one story called **"E Due"** from the first volume of *Novelle per un Anno*. A young man one evening, while walking on the outskirts of the city near the bridge over the river, sees a man climb on to the parapet, lay down his hat there, and then cast himself into the river. Diego hears the terrible splash in the water beneath—then not a sound—absolute silence on all sides. And yet the man was drowning there beneath him. Why did he not move or shout for help? It was too late. Pirandello in masterly manner suggests the surroundings as they appeared to the horror-struck youth. The houses opposite in darkness, in contrast to the lights of the city: in the silence not a sound except far off the chirrup of crickets, and beneath him he heard the gurgling of the dark waters of the river. And that hat—the hat which the unfortunate man had left on the parapet—it fascinates us as it fascinated Diego: he cannot drive it from his thoughts. Later on we find him on the parapet again. He took off his hat and placed it in the same place as the other had been:

> He went to the far side of the lamp to see what his hat looked like on the parapet, under the light of the lamp like the other. He stood for a few moments, leaning over the parapet and looking at it, as if he himself was not there any more. Then suddenly he gave a grim laugh; he saw himself stuck up there like a cat behind the lamp, and his hat was the mouse. . . . Away, away with all this tomfoolery! He climbed over the parapet: he felt his hair stand on end—his hands quivered as they clung tightly on to the ledge. Then he loosened his grip and threw himself into the void.

In such a story Pirandello shows qualities of subtle analysis and description which rival Maupassant; it is only at the end, when the character watches itself act, that we see the cloven hoof of the Pirandellian. At other times our author touches the chord of Anatole France and leads us into a garden of Epicurus. The last *novella*, **"All Uscita"** (**"At the Gate"**), of the collection *E Domani, Lunedi* will be a fitting conclusion to our examination of Pirandello's short stories. We are at the gate leading from a cemetery, and we meet the phantoms of the Fat Man and the Philosopher who have recently died. The Philosopher, true to his vocation, starts immediately to weave his sophistries for the benefit of his grosser friend. He will continue for ever in the next world to reason and reason, just as the Fat

Man will continue to wear his vesture of adipose tissue. The latter, however, will not be satisfied to be fat: he sees still the little garden of his house in the sunlight, the little pond in the shade with the goldfish swimming about; he smells the fresh perfume of the new leaves and then the red and yellow roses, the geraniums and the carnations. All the philosophy in the world will not prevent the nightingale from singing or these roses from blooming. All these joys made this Fat Man accept the sorrows and the worries in his past life. They enabled him to accept with resignation the caprices of his wife, her infidelities that were legion. Life for him was possible because he had no illusions. He had even been relieved to hear that his wife had a lover, because he knew that all her hatred of him would be transferred to her lover. But that lover is not a fat man: he is jealous, and in one of his fits he will kill his mistress. And lo, she appears, a bloodstained phantom, running along as though pursued by her mad lover. All these phantoms relate their experiences, their desires which have never been satisfied. And death does not solve the riddle, because it is nothing but total disillusion. Thus the end is the same as in Anatole France's story "In the Elysian Fields" when the shades, gathered together in a field of asphodel, converse about death as if they knew nothing of it and were as ignorant of human destinies as when they were still on earth. "It is no doubt," as the smiling cynic Menippus said, "because they still remain human and mortal in some degree. When they shall have entered into immortality, they will not speak or think any more. They will be like the gods." But the philosopher Pirandello will not become a god: he will be left behind at the gate to continue his reasoning for all eternity.

Percy Hutchison (essay date 1939)

SOURCE: A review of *The Medals, and Other Stories*, in *The New York Times Book Review*, May 14, 1939, p. 7.

[*In this review, Hutchison praises* The Medals, and Other Stories, *noting that Pirandello's work is distinct from that of other short fiction writers.*]

Strange and eerie, as is everything written by Luigi Pirandello, fabricator of that compelling drama *Six Characters in Search of an Author,* and of *As You Desire Me,* which also was put upon the screen, this new culling [*The Medals, and Other Stories*] from his two hundred short stories is as provocative as all that has gone before. For this winner of the Nobel Prize in Literature is not kin to any other writer of fiction, either in the past or in the present. He belongs to no school; his works, whether short or long, whether plays or stories, cannot be pigeon-holed. Pirandello is neither realist nor romanticist. He defies all labels. He does, however, belong very definitely in a certain category of philosophy, although he writes so disarmingly that the reader is conscious at first only of having been immensely entertained.

Put briefly, Pirandello is an idealist in the strictest academic sense. He outdoes Kant himself. He does not pretend to know, and does not care, whether there is a *Ding-an-sich,* a "Thing-in-itself," as Kant averred. But he does insist, as did the Sage of Koenigsberg, that appearance may be called reality, the test being, is this or that true for the beholder? All that Pirandello would like to discover; all that he wishes to put forth is essential truth. But not in the entire range of literature has any one else, save, perhaps, Cervantes, conveyed essential truth so engagingly, with such unfailing humor.

Including the title-piece, there are nineteen stories, or novella, in this volume. This brings the total in English translation up to something over threescore out of the 200 left behind by the author. One is forced to use the term "short story" for this type of piece; yet the connotation is inaccurate, for the English words suggest much more a "set piece," more of plot, fuller characterization, than is require here.

Take, for example, the title-piece. **"The Medals"** shows us a fine old gentleman in reduced circumstances who has been masquerading as a Garibaldi veteran when all that he actually did was to follow after a brother who was but 15 years old at the time in order to care for the lad should he be wounded. The boy was killed; and the brother took his medals. After all, we hear the author say, why not? He was offering his life to the cause as truly as was the other. And the upshot of the story is that at the end the Garibaldian Veterans Association, which had discovered that it had been tricked, realizes this—Pirandello's essential truth—and gives the old chap a magnificent burial.

The humor of Pirandello has few counterparts today. In a story called **"Sicilian Honor"** a peasant is on trial on the charge of having murdered his wife, whom he had found consorting with a lover. He makes a lengthy speech at the termination of which the judge asks him if it is his defense. "No, Your Honor," comes the reply. "It is not my defense. It is the truth. Merely the truth." A Daniel come to judgment, one might say; and not be far wrong. Pirandello is an ironist; yet if his irony is keen, it is seldom, if ever, barbed.

It could not be expected that in so great a list as two hundred titles all pieces could be of equal merit or of equal interest, and the reviewer has an uneasy feeling that the two preceding collections of translations from the novella stack up a trifle better than this one. But the difference is not great, and he, for one, would welcome each and every piece down to the very least.

There is one bit in **"The Medals,"** written only shortly before the author's death. It is a sort of allegory about death; brave, whimsical, not shouting defiance to the universe, yet defiant. This is one of the most beautiful prose-poems on death it has been my lot to encounter.

Alfred Kazin   (essay date 1939)

SOURCE: "Italy and England Appear in New Fiction," in *The New York Herald Tribune Books,* May 21, 1939, p. 6.

[*A highly respected American literary critic, Kazin is best known for his essay collections* The Inmost Leaf *(1955) and* Contemporaries *(1962), and particularly for* On Native Grounds *(1942), a study of American prose writing since the era of William Dean Howells. In the following review of* The Medals, and Other Stories, *he finds the stories for the most part tiresome.*]

Luigi Pirandello spent the first half of his life looking at Italians from a classroom, and the last half giggling at them from Olympian heights. Olympus is not in the Fascist atlas; and that was his good fortune. By identifying all men as freaks, he was saved from feeling for them as citizens of Italy. But this appearance of remoteness, of finding all systems equally vain and damnable in the sight of eternity, was not a form of escape. Pirandello might often have resembled Noel Coward, but he could never have been a Bernard Shaw.

What Pirandello had was a gift of capturing not the great things that men cannot reach, but the little things they will not see. The short end of the telescope became his access to reality. It was as if he had walked so long under the legs of men that the things they betrayed became more important than the principles they declared. This gave him at once his freedom and his charm. It enabled him to grasp life at the toes, to watch the wigglings, the half-beginnings, to titter at the gap between man's aspiration and his vanity. Pirandello did not seek what was absurd; he found in absurdity the pattern of destiny. He had as a first belief what Emily Dickinson raised to a poetic principle—the feeling that man is a funny and gentle little animal, less important than he knows and less cruel than he will believe, who perpetually leaps at the walls of the prison-house that he calls his consciousness.

Gentleness rules Pirandello's stories. It was impossible for him not to feel sympathy for his characters: but it was also impossible for him to be moved by them. He did not offer them with the confidence that they were important; he merely hoped that they would prove reminiscent. He saw the dwarf in human beings so clearly that he could as ill afford to jeer at them as to respect them. Laughter was man's acknowledgment of his own inferiority; and to laugh at oneself was to admit that a writer could be as silly as his own characters.

Pirandello, as everybody knows, was obsessed by this proximity to his characters. He not only made one of his most famous plays out of the idea, but rang its changes in several stories. At his best this provided him with an original and dashing idea; at his worst, it resulted in coyness. Pirandello's worst fault was a tendency to be absorbed in his own charm. It made him cute, and when he wanted to ask "Now what shall I write about today?" he admitted that he had nothing to say, and then wrote about the difficulties of saying nothing. He brought his characters in, he smiled at them, coaxed them; he turned to the reader with a frank and smiling face, his hands outstretched, a Latin shrug distending his shoulders. It was his way of scratching the soul in public; and the result was not always pretty.

Most of the stories in [*The Medals, and Other Stories*] are familiar. One of the best, **"An Oversight,"** I do not remember seeing before. It illustrates perfectly Pirandello's use of incongruities. On a sultry afternoon in Rome, a third-class hearse is bearing to the grave the last remains of some obscure professor. Only his cook remembers to follow him. The driver, a good-natured fellow who was formerly a cabman, dozes in his seat. The hearse jostles its way through the hot and deserted streets, a few neighboring women clucking, urchins jeering, the cook stolidly following her master to his grave. As the hearse crosses a large thoroughfare, the pedestrians see a tall, emaciated gentleman with dark spectacles throw his package angrily at the driver. There is an altercation, but the hearse is allowed to go its way. The cabman was dozing, and had forgotten that he was driving a hearse. When he saw the tall, emaciated gentleman he mechanically nodded, and asked "Fare?"

Some of the stories are bedroom farces and bedroom mock-tragedies in the style that provided titters thirty years ago and are only embarrassing to read today. In **"A Wronged Husband"** the little lamplighter rushes home to expose his wife and finds the Minister of the Interior hiding on a window precipice. He turns to his wife and berates her bitterly for not secreting His Excellency in a safer place. In **"Sicilian Honour"** the poor dumb peasant who has been wronged by the local count murders his wife and tells his story so naively that he goes to jail for thirty years. In **"A Widow's Dilemma,"** one of the best in the collection, an old man and woman who have been lovers secretly for years go to the cemetery to visit the graves, he to his wife's and she to her husband's. The man has already arranged to be buried at his wife's side, the tombstone arranged, and the proper inscription outlined. But the woman forces him to marry her, and his plans are spoiled. Whereupon she arranges for the two men to be buried together, and after her own death, the two women.

Most of the famous stories have been included here. **"A Mother-in-Law"**; **"Sicilian Tangerines"**; and Pirandello's last poignant essay in autobiography, **"My Last Journey."** It is a useful collection, if not always a judicious one, but the translations are bad.

Renato Poggioli   (essay date 1958)

SOURCE: "Pirandello in Retrospect," in *Italian Quarterly,* Vol. 1, No. 4, Winter, 1958, pp. 19–47.

[*Poggioli was an Italian-born American critic and translator. Much of his critical writing is concerned with Russian literature, including* The Poets of Russia: 1890-1930 *(1960), which is one of the most important examinations of that literary era. In the following excerpt, Poggioli discusses the Italian author Giovanni Verga as the literary progenitor of Pirandello.*]

During the period between the end of the last century and the first World War, two great Italian novelists, and one of them undoubtedly the greatest, were islanders: the Sicilian, Giovanni Verga, and Grazia Deledda from Sardinia. While the best known authors of their generation were striving, often in vain, to approximate universality either by withdrawing from life entirely or by offering their readers refined and frequently false quintessences of life, Verga and Deledda achieved universality almost without conscious effort, by turning toward what to others seemed too humble and restricted a form of existence.

Those who wished to ape Europe or Paris succeeded in being merely provincial. But these two writers, each of whom had no thought but for his own island, amply asserted his full right to enter into the temple of *Weltliteratur.* They had encompassed universal values by stressing their own regionalism. In evangelical terms, we may say that they entered heaven along the straight and narrow path.

Of the two binomials Deledda-Sardinia and Verga-Sicily, the second is of greater interest to us now, not on account of Verga's superiority, but because Pirandello, with whom we are concerned, stems from Verga and Sicily.

D. H. Lawrence helps us to clarify the origins of Pirandello who is Verga's spiritual son and a Sicilian too, for Lawrence knew both Sicily, where he lived for a while, and Verga's writings. He decided to translate Verga and published two volumes of the Italian's short stories in English, as well as the great novel *Mastro Don Gesualdo.* For this last work Lawrence wrote an introduction which remained unpublished until after his death. In it we see that Lawrence was still under the influence of the great Russians, and he used the impression created by that contact to make us understand, by contrast, the Sicilian soul and the art of Verga.

> . . . In *Mastro Don Gesualdo* you have the very antithesis of what you get in *The Brothers Karamazov.* Anything more un-Russian than Verga it would be hard to imagine, save Homer. Yet Verga has the same sort of pity as the Russians. And, with the Russians, he is a realist. He won't have heroes, nor appeals to gods above or below. The Sicilians of today are supposed to be the nearest thing to the classic Greek that is left to us; that is, they are the nearest descendants on the earth.

In order further to emphasize the relationship between Verga and Pirandello delineated above, I shall quote the testimonial of the French critic, Benjamin Crémieux, who once stated that "Pirandello's humoristic subject begins where the naturalistic subject of Verga ends." Actually, it is in Pirandello's social and moral experience rather than in his art that Crémieux's statement is true, for Pirandello's Sicilians are no longer ancient Greeks, but modern men. They no longer belong to the generations which could recall the rule of the Bourbons, as did the characters of *I Malavoglia*; they are citizens of the Kingdom of Italy. They are no longer peasants or shepherds or men from distant farms, but the inhabitants of villages or small provincial towns. In short, from Verga's pastoral world we are taken to the world of the petit bourgeois, from the shepherd's crook and the nomadic life to the pen and the table of sedentary people, whether they dwell in Palermo, the island's metropolis, or in Rome, the capital.

Verga's shepherds and Pirandello's petit bourgeois represent the artistic synthesis of two contrasting generations, or more accurately, the historical and social evolution of Sicily during the last sixty years. In part, Pirandello's task consisted in pointing up the psychological changes brought about by the transition from country to province, from the simple, almost feudal relationship between citizen and State. Pirandello traces the course from a life of innocent ignorance to that of a sad awareness. In other words, the playwright aimed at showing that the Sicilians felt rising within them those terrible diseases designated by Lawrence as "intellect" and "soul."

Though Verga's Sicilians were, indeed, deprived of a consciously developed intellect, we must admit that they too possessed a soul of sorts. Thus we cannot push the critical game of paradox to its logical conclusion. Verga's heroes, immersed in the flow of events, are idyllic spirits, epic and tragic at times, but without drama, without history. Unlike Pirandello's description of his own heroes, their souls do not watch themselves live, but are simply *souls that live.* Pirandello's heroes, too, will let themselves be swept along by the current, but they are directed not by the laws of nature but by those of society, conscious that their time is no longer reckoned by the agricultural calendar of the seasons, but by the bureaucratic timetable of a daily servitude.

Something similar to the phenomenon that had taken place among the Sicilians of Verga's generation, transforming them into the Sicilians of Pirandello's, took place also among the inhabitants of another island, Corsica. As soon as it became a part of the French nation, this island gave its most adventurous sons to the administration of France and her Empire. From a pastoral idyll, praised even by Rousseau who at one time cherished a dream of becoming the Moses of the Corsican people, its inhabitants had turned to a life of action. Since Buonaparte, every Corsican leaves the island, not with a dream, but with a Napoleonic program.

Sicily fulfilled a more useful, though less brilliant, role. After sending her strongest sons to America, she detailed the remaining share of her human crop to the administration of the Italian nation, but, unlike Corsica in its relation to France, Sicily has given Italy great writers and remarkable philosophers, as well as statesmen.

Sicilian emigration to America and the continent had, for a long time, the same effect on the social life of the island that the steady pursuit of a new frontier toward the Far West had had in the history of the United States. But finally, the Sicilians too found their California, and not at the extreme border, but at the very heart of their island. Unmerciful Nature suddenly proved that even volcanoes and geological catastrophes may be in some way useful. It revealed to the islanders their own volcanic and phospho-

rescent gold, sulphur. The Sicilians knew they owned sulphur, but had never realized that it could be turned into gold. The beginnings of a primitive industry had already been noted by Verga who, after the *Malavoglia,* gave us *Mastro Don Gesualdo.* At that time the self-made men of the new industry began to appear in Sicily. In fact, the two men who were to become Pirandello's father and father-in-law were among the owners of sulphur mines.

This social evolution is artistically evidenced in a synthetic way, and not by analysis, in Pirandello's early works. We shall point to those evidences, not as to simple historical documentation, but as to indications of the real nature of Pirandello's art, too often regarded as abstraction or cerebral fancy. Aside from the literary experience terminating with Verga, Pirandello's starting point was also, I repeat, a new social and moral experience that Verga had barely discerned. Crémieux wisely warns the readers and critics to remember this "realistic, experimental and un-ideological basis of the art and thought of Pirandello."

In one of Verga's short stories, "La Roba" ("Property") the author describes the vast tracts of land owned by Don Mazzarò, an illiterate peasant, who has become rich through toil and sacrifice. Wherever one went, one learned that the surrounding land belonged to Don Mazzarò. Verga remarks, with epic humour: "It seemed that Don Mazzaro was spread out as wide as the surface of the earth, and that we were walking on his belly." Don Mazzarò, in grabbing as much land as possible, was not motivated by covetousness or avarice, but by the impulse which moves others to the conquest of love or power. His pride of acquisition was of such purity that he submerged his own identity in the object conquered: "After all, he did not care for money; he said it was not real property and as soon as he had accumulated a certain sum, he bought land. He wanted to own as much land as the king and be even better off than the king, who can neither sell it nor call it his own." Mazzarò's feeling for property is that of a primitive man, part patriarch, part pioneer. The fact that he does not consider money as wealth shows that he still belonged to that social pre-history when the conception of *homo oeconomicus* had still to be evolved.

Let us consider now one of Pirandello's short stories which he later developed into a one-act play of the same name, **"La Giara"** (**"The Jar"**). The hero, Don Lollo, could be Don Mazzarò's brother. He too loves the land and, like Don Mazzarò, oversees the peasants who are lazy and negligent in their work. He treats them badly, punishes them whether or not it is warranted. One day, Don Lollo buys a large jar which is to hold the surplus oil expected from a bumper crop of olives. The jar is enormous, and Don Lollo is so proud and jealous of it that he forbids anyone to touch it for fear that it might be broken. Suddenly some peasants discover that the jar is cracked. At first, Don Lollo is infuriated, but then he becomes resigned to having it repaired by Don Zima, who is expert at this kind of work. Don Zima has invented a magic putty which, according to him, will make the jar as good as new, with no trace of a crack. But Don Lollo insists that he repair it the old way by stapling the parts together with wire. Protesting, Don Zima obeys. He climbs into the jar to mend it from within and when he wants to get out, he realizes that the neck of the jar is too narrow for his shoulders. At the sight of Don Zima, imprisoned in the jar much as Jonah was in the whale, Don Lollo is once more infuriated. He feels that this is an entirely new situation, an "interesting case," to use legal jargon. Rather than set Don Zima free, he sends for a lawyer.

The lawyer advises Don Lollo to free Don Zima, in other words, to break the jar again; otherwise, Lollo will be guilty, by definition of law, of sequestration of person. Don Lollo concurs, but points out that it is Don Zima's own fault that he has been caught inside the jar. The lawyer's judgment is worthy of Solomon; he decrees that Don Lollo is to break the jar and Don Zima is to pay for it. Don Zima objects that the jar is worthless, first, because he found it broken, and secondly, because Don Lollo insisted that it be repaired in his own way. The lawyer then decides that Don Lollo must break the jar and Don Zima pay a third of its value. Don Lollo gives in, but Don Zima refuses to pay and prefers to remain in the jar until Don Lollo changes his mind. Don Lollo goes off in a fury, but Don Zima gaily sends for some wine and settles down to joking with the peasants dancing about his prison. Don Lollo, finally seeing that they are making fun of him, rushes down in a rage and kicks the jar to pieces amid the laughter of the peasants and a bellow of triumph from Don Zima.

What is the difference between the worlds of Don Mazzarò and Don Lollo? Don Mazzarò conceives of property as a relationship between men and things, a struggle between man and nature. Don Lollo, instead, regards it as a relationship between men and society, a contest between man and man, a right that can be conferred or removed by law. He conceives of the law, not as an expression of justice, but as the sanction or denial of a privilege. He plays the law against the law to maintain or to defend a privilege, to enforce the subordination or even the humiliation of a rival, of a competitor, in other words, of a peer. Don Zima, in order to oppose Don Lollo's legalism, falls back on obstructionism and crawls into the jar, like a snail into its shell. From this haven, he proves to his adversary that the law may be a blunted weapon, a useless instrument. In literary terms, we may say that we have passed from the epic, austere world of Verga into an ironic, dramatic world; or, in sociological terms, from a primitive, patriarchal society, into the world of bourgeois civilization. We have passed from an old feudalism which maintained itself by the law of violence to a new feudalism which defends itself by the violence of the law. And at least sometimes the law is defeated and broken into as many pieces as the fragments of the jar.

Pirandello describes this world with a malicious smile which lurks, like Don Zima, at the very bottom of the jar. From there the author smiles unnoticed at Don Zima, but mostly at Don Lollo and the lawyer. On closer observation, however, Pirandello's position is revealed as not too different from that of the lawyer, who listens to the argument rather indifferently. That indifference is a sceptical reflection on the law of which he is the representative and interpreter. Pirandello, in his turn, smiles because he realizes that men always act like puppets, whether they be moved by the strings of instinctive passion or by those of the indirect and repressed emotions which burgeon beyond the pale of the law.

The true discovery in the short story **"The Jar"** is that law is not a rule which tends to discipline and check the strife between men but is, of itself, a new instrument for strife. Pirandello took the legal and social battle symbolized by the Sicilian Don Lollo as a point of departure and from that battle he later evolved the eternal dissent, not between man and man, but in the very soul of man with man himself. Thus a new dissension was revealed, of which the author was to give us further proofs in deeper and richer personalities.

From Verga's final position, which was a return toward the simple, Pirandello moved in the opposite direction toward the heterogeneous and complex. Although his goal was different, Pirandello's itinerary coincided, in direction at least, with that of so many men from his island who abandoned the white houses of the Sicilian countryside for the uniform gray beehives of the capital. In this hostile world, Pirandello's Sicilians defend themselves with dialectics, as did those of Verga with a knife.

The really important word is *dialectic*. Contrary to what his father probably wished him to do, Pirandello did not choose a law career, a career considered by simple minds both useful and dignified, like the army or the priesthood. He chose, instead, to follow the road of literature and culture, not as a journalist or amateur, but seriously, as a philologist and a scholar. He went from the University of Rome to that of Bonn in Germany, where he graduated as a Doctor of Philosophy with highest honors. In his final dissertation, Pirandello had reconciled the love of his island with the love of science in a work of scholarly research on the systematic and historical phonetics of the dialect of Girgenti, his province. In Germany, he continued to write poetry and began to read the classics of philosophy. Perhaps it was at that time that the shadows of abstract ideas and the romantic seeds of modern thought began to take shape in his southern soul.

Although written much later, a true synthesis *a posteriori,* **"The Jar"** appears to us today a symbol of his awakening consciousness. Between his experiences of the period and his new studies, there was the same transition, we might say, that there is between legal and pragmatic dialectics and pure oratory. Yet Pirandello, the student of philosophy, as well as Pirandello the artist, was always to retain a little of the wrangling dialectic of Don Lollo. That scepticism which was later to form the basis of his logic was to lead that same logic to the most abstract and general conclusions. But the force which had first started that scepticism in motion will always be the force that the heroes of the master, Verga, left as inheritance in the souls of the Sicilians portrayed by his disciple, Pirandello. That force is the instinctive suspicion felt by every simple soul when faced with official justice and its instruments, that is to say, the police, courts, judges, and official documents, and the suspicion felt toward that very justice which is, in the final analysis, governmental authority.

The shadow of law and government power is present in Verga's stories too, but it remains in the background. In most of Verga's tales, the predominant passion is not desire for possession, but for love. If the instinct for possession finds in man's law or in nature's catastrophe its own sentence (earthquakes, landslides, floods like the one which was to inundate the sulphur mine of Pirandello's father and to destroy his wealth), then too the violent and volcanic instinct of love carries in itself its own implicit punishment, jealousy. However, in almost every instance, the instinct for possession as well as that of love, is dominated and checked, despite its strong compulsion, by a supreme law, a noble and unyielding moral code, the code of honor. The Malavoglia family does not suffer and work in order to get rich, but in order to pay back its debts, to win back public esteem. In "Cavalleria Rusticana" the rustic duel is fought to erase with blood the wound inflicted on honor. Everybody knows the subject of "Cavalleria Rusticana." It is one of Verga's many short stories, which, according to Lawrence are, "one after the other, stories of cruel killings . . . it seems almost too much, too crude, too violent, too much a question of mere brutes." As a matter of fact, the judgment is unjust. Turiddu is not a brute; nor is Alfio. Both are men of sensitive and even honorable nature. Turiddu knows he is wrong and would even let himself be killed, he says, "but for the thought of his old mother . . ." When Alfio discovers that Turiddu is his wife's lover, he challenges him to a duel without harsh words and with an extreme moderation of gesture. Turiddu accepts the challenge, thoughtfully, almost silently, with only a nod and a half-phrase. Their instinctive and primitive self-mastery acquires a character of epic spontaneity and dignity when compared to the sophisticated elegance of a "gentleman" in an affair of honor. And they tread, not with the heavy step of a peasant or a carter, but softly, like shadows, to their death or to inflict death for love and honor.

The same eternal theme of adultery and jealousy is the theme of Pirandello's comedy *Il berretto a sonagli* (*Cap and Bells*), and of the short story from which it grew. But here we see enormous changes at the very outset and in every detail. In Verga's tale the villagers witness, in a respectful and stern silence, the scandal and drama unfolding before their eyes. Blood and sin are matters too grave to be the subject of much conversation, but the crux of Pirandello's plot is gossip. It is through slander that Beatrice, the wife of Mr. Fiorica, learns that her husband is carrying on an intrigue with the wife of one of his clerks, a humble book-keeper, Ciampa. During the latter's absence, arranged by Beatrice herself, she has his house raided by the police and the lovers are caught, but not precisely in a compromising situation. Ciampa returns just in time to witness the outburst of scandal. Poor Ciampa had known that his wife had been unfaithful to him for years but he had always pretended to be unaware of it and by this feigned ignorance, which made him the object of universal pity, he had provided himself with a mask of respectability. Once the scandal becomes public knowledge and everyone is aware that his wife's unfaithfulness can no longer be unknown to him, Ciampa finds himself cornered and faced with two alternatives: the primitive law of honor and vengeance, or the supine acceptance of the accomplished fact and the consequent dishonor. Unlike Compar Alfio, Ciampa hesitates before bloodshed, but his extreme awareness of society prevents him from choosing the second alternative.

Then, in a moment of brilliant lucidity, he decides to exploit Beatrice's jealousy which, though justified, is so morbid and exaggerated that it carries her to the verge of insanity. With this to work on, he convinces the wretched heroes of the petty scandal that the only solution lies in establishing Beatrice's insanity and in asserting that, in her insanity, she has taken for fact something that was but a figment of her imagination. With devilish ability, carried by suggestion and logic to the very verge of absurdity, Ciampa succeeds in convincing everybody that Beatrice is mad and that she must be sent to an asylum. Thus, instead of Ciampa being forced to wear the mask of dishonor, it is Beatrice who is forced to wear on her head the cap and bells of folly.

Frances Keene (essay date 1958)

SOURCE: Introduction to *Short Stories* by Luigi Pirandello, translated by Lily Duplaix, Simon and Schuster, 1959, pp. vii–xiv.

[*In the following excerpt from an essay written in 1958 as an introduction to the collection* Short Stories, *Keene perceives Pirandello's stories to be about the human condition.*]

Before Pirandello ever wrote a play, he wrote poetry and short stories. The form his thoughts took at their grandest and most expressive—as in *Six Characters in Search of an Author* and *Henry IV*—was clearly foreshadowed in the dramatic juxtapositions which characterize his stories, and the tone of the plays at their best has the thin, pure echo of poetry. Thus to know and not merely to skim the works of this uniquely thoughtful dramatist a reader should have access to a fair cross-section of the short stories.

Easier said than done, for Pirandello wrote over three hundred and sixty-five short stories (he once told French critic Benjamin Crémieux that there was "a fair choice of extras for Leap Year"). Collections have been made and will continue to be made since the *opera omnia* remains untranslated. This book gives an organically sound, perceptive choice and, while not pretending to offer any final distillation, includes stories representative of Pirandello's major themes.

"Obsession" is not too strong a word to describe Pirandello's concern with the nature of reality. But if this, the dominant theme in all his work, is obsessive, it is the kind of obsession a suspended prism exerts on the curious eye of the beholder: the sides turn without the viewer's intervention and the surfaces reflect sun or shade, refract this or that sudden gleam of light in inexhaustible kaleidoscopy. Pirandello was the viewer; the prism was man's nature, his identity, turning apparently at will its many facets toward the beholder. But was the prism truly moving "at will"? Remember that it was suspended. Just so does the individual move before the author in apparent freedom, yet conditioned by who knows what cord that suspends him in his particular situation, his appointed place. Pirandello never sought to alter the movements of his prisms: there is no finger smudge on the clear planes, for the characters are never pushed or prodded by the author's nudge. Their motivation lies in the nature of *das Ding an sich*. Thus they turn and sway of their own momentum, yet within limits prescribed by their particular unalterable situation.

And by what casual interaction do the beams of light intertwine as two or more suspended prisms move in relation to each other! How transitory this tangled, indistinguishable light! From which prism comes the dominant glow? Who is to say which is the "perfect," the "right" reflection? What is the "truth" of this strange interplay?

Understanding and accepting this view of the relationship between author and subject, the reader at once sees clearly why Pirandello never overtly expresses compassion in either stories or plays. Can the viewer in all conscience feel compassion for the prism? By extension, this explains too why the writer never tells reader or audience which side he wishes taken. How can you choose one side when man is, by his very nature, multiform, no less different to different individuals than to his different selves?

Yet human nature craves certainty, and certainty implies choice. Thus we see exposed the root conflict of the human drama in these two antithetical and indeed mutually exclusive "truths": the prismatic nature of man and his devouring need for certainty. Am I what my wife sees, what my child "knows" is me, what my associate rubs elbows with daily, what my priest hears at Confession, what I understand me to be as I keep my journal by night? What manner of creature am I and of how many faces? Does my beloved know if even I cannot know which of these faces is the "right," the "true"—and to which of these is he or she, in fact, *the beloved?* (This question of identity is treated par excellence in *Right You Are . . .* and is most theatrically plausible in *As You Desire Me.*)

Certain conclusions inevitably result from Pirandello's preoccupation with the nature of man, chief among them that the human being is nearly always uncomfortable in time and place but that, given his "suspension cord," there is little if anything he can do about it. These two unwelcome conditions of place and time are interwoven to form the background against which the character is pinioned. In the short masterpiece **"The Soft Touch of Grass,"** Pirandello takes a bereaved and lonely man presumably in his early sixties and observes him in circumstances that twist a casual action into a gesture of apparent lewdness. The supposed intent is less stunning for the reader than is the appalled man's realization of what, by an accident of time and place, the young girl thinks he is up to. Wickedness in the eye of the beholder has seldom been more nakedly portrayed nor has an aging individual's plight seemed more poignantly unbearable.

"Cinci" goes to the other end of the chronological scale. Here Pirandello portrays a boy in early adolescence whose loneliness, natural at that age, is compounded by the wretched circumstances in which he and his mother live. Just as a young caged lion may pause before his bars and, for kicks, send up a frightening roar into the faces of his gaping, apprehensive oglers, so Cinci goes into the little church opposite the hospital and unleashes the frightening thunderclap of his dropped books. Having petrified the old people, he sees "no further need [sic] to gall the patience of those poor scandalized worshipers" and wanders on his way just as the young lion resumes his pacing. But the bars are still there.

Some measure of peace, a peace so restless that it can be broken at the slightest intrusion, settles on Cinci at the top of the hill where he lounges against a wall. He is not a violent boy, a lover of violence for its own sake, and this is made clear by his stifled cry of protest when the farm lad kills the lizard. He is not so much animated by pity as affronted by the wantonness of the gesture which does not even permit the boys to indulge human curiosity about the creature's darting looks and antics. The fight which this act unleashes and the controlled fear it awakens in Cinci give the silent struggle there in the white moonlight on the newly harrowed field a classic simplicity and terror. Cinci kills almost inadvertently; he fights for his life instinctively, kills, and frees himself as if it were happening to someone else. He "awakens" from the act as from a dream and leisurely resumes his return to loneliness, having tasted in that instant's action the bitterness of death—a recognition he will carry with him all his days. In that moment of truth he has passed from adolescence to manhood and there is no going back, although he has wilfully obliterated from his consciousness the events which precipitated the change.

"The Rose" takes the theme of human frustration to still another level. Signora Lucietta, the young widow, is caught like a fly in amber in the alien town where she has gone to earn her living. The elements in this story which bring it to the verge of tragedy are not of the spectacular, easily recognizable kind but are of an infinitely subtle, almost evanescent nature. Lucietta senses all that she is foregoing in turning down the one man who might have rescued her from perpetual exile in the narrow provincial world and who might have brought her, through his intelligence, to some sort of spiritual and emotional maturity. That her "suspension cord" forces her to complete the gesture which closes the escape hatch forever is as inevitable as the news of the fall of kings in Greek tragedy. Lucietta's true widowhood begins then.

Pirandello shared Thoreau's view that nearly all of us "lead lives of quiet desperation" and, again like Thoreau, he found that the epitome of man's self-torture was most often achieved in cities. There everything seems to conspire to thwart man's reaching for the sun and light, for warmth, and the simple relief of unsuspicious communion both with others and with nature. The cliché that man is nowhere more alone than in a crowd has, when examined in single instances of desperate isolation, elements in it which range from the grotesque to the terrifying.

Pirandello shared Thoreau's view that nearly all of us "lead lives of quiet desperation" and, again like Thoreau, he found that the epitome of man's self-torture was most often achieved in cities.

—*Frances Keene*

Although from different social strata, Signor Bareggi in **"Escape"** and the grandfather in **"The Footwarmer"** know equally well the bleak, cheerless streets of the Roman periphery at night. Though the news vendor would never seek physical escape as does Bareggi, the old man's withdrawal into the womb of warmth and silence that is his kiosk is as complete an immolation as is Bareggi's inevitable destruction in the mad chase that spells his deliverance. Not only is the situation in **"Escape"** magnificently ludicrous, but the key character is never allowed to become so. The power of the story lies in the fact that Bareggi's life is indeed so unbearable that we tacitly agree to his own estimate of it, and find his choice of a Pegasus perfectly in keeping with the hideous monotony, the bleak vulgarity of his round of days. His escape is no less grand for being accomplished in a milk wagon. And the very coherence of the solution precludes in both writer and reader any trace of pity or sentimentality.

In all his work, including the ironic and humorous, Pirandello underscores the inevitability of this human frustration—human discomfort and discontent with place or time or both. The human drama implies frustration, thanks to the irreconcilable dichotomy we talked of earlier, and, since Pirandello recognizes it as endemic to life itself, he pulls it from the shadows and places it where it belongs. This is no backwater, the author asserts repeatedly, but an essential part of the main stream: no man can pursue his life and be ignorant of it.

The Sicilian tales have a place of their own in Pirandello's work, for in them physical atmosphere is more an integral part of the story than props and background are otherwise allowed to be. In **"Fumes"** and **"A Mere Formality"** we feel at all times the threatening presence of the sulphur mines, the acrid stench of the burning stuff and the peculiar devastation its extraction from the earth wreaks not only on the land but on the lives of those who seek to exploit that land. We may see the mines only from a distance, hear of the rigors of plant management in an office adjacent to a bank, but the crude, uneven struggle of man against nature is as present as if it were played out an arm's length away. Gabriele's ruin in **"A Mere For-mality"** has been brought about by the unwise assumption that he could step into his father's shoes and acquire, by will power and dedication alone, sufficient expertise to wrest a living from the pits for himself, his family, his employees. He is in pitched battle with the natural forces of his native island, and Nature, with blind unconcern for the affairs of men, has slapped him down. We see him on the verge of disaster, brought to this pass by the apparent vengefulness of a world which has refused to yield up its secrets to one who has never truly become a part of it. Gabriele is one of a series of protagonists in the author's many Sicilian tales and plays who hate the métier they must perform yet who, for reasons of middle-class solidarity and family duty, tempt fate by allowing themselves to be maneuvered into a family profession. Pirandello felt that this was a particularly frequent exploitation in Sicilian middle and upper bourgeois life. Sons who were sent to the mainland, to the Universities of Naples, Rome, Bologna, Milan—even as far afield as Paris or Bonn, where he himself went—risked returning strangers to their homeland, deracinated, unfit to consider confidently living out their lives there and yet unable, because of the matrix of Sicilian society, to cut the cord entirely.

Yet another aspect of the difficulty of being Sicilian is exposed in **"Bombolo."** This story of knight-errantry on behalf of the downtrodden peasant proves its perennial validity if one remembers the late highwayman, Giuliano, who, like Bombolo, took from the rich to give to the poor. A Sicilian by birth, Bombolo returns to his native island after successful years presumably as an illicit trader in the Levant. Disquieted and eventually goaded to action by the terrible inequities he sees all about him, Bombolo decides to bring "justice" at least to his own area. The tale reveals conclusions Pirandello must have found hard to swallow: the man who seeks to bring relief to the peasants is fighting a losing game, and the reasons why he can't win lie within the distorted nature of the peasants themselves. The *Why* of this distortion is self-evident, nor has the recent creation of a World Bank altered its immediate relevance.

The sharp contrast between the intelligence of some of Pirandello's female characters and the roles society allows them to occupy is reminiscent of Ibsen. Nowhere is this closeness more apparent than in **"The Rose."** Signora Lucietta trying vainly to rally her strength sufficiently to compete for a living in the world of men finds that, though she may win employment and even respect, she is inevitably defeated on the social plane. This is Nora in more contemporary situations—but underlying such situations is the great, timeless question: has she, Lucietta, any more right than Nora or Williams' Blanche, for that matter, to her own complex identity?

Pirandello presents us with a somewhat similar case in the slighter story, **"The Umbrella."** Ostensibly, this tender little story tells of a young widow and her two small daughters, of her inability to buy a full complement of winter clothes for both children, and of the elder girl's yearning to possess the single new umbrella the mother can afford. But behind this thin veil of tear-jerking plot—complicated by the child's believable death—lies the writer's perpetual probing into the emotional motivation of human behavior: the mother is brusque with the elder child because she senses that it is this child, with her brooding, speculative glance, who will prevent her remarriage. The young widow is desperately lonely, insecure. In every sense, she admits the frustration the presence of Dinuccia causes her; she even admits that she yearns for her "not to die, God forbid," but simply not to have been born. Her consequent guilt at the child's coincidental death can only be imagined, for Pirandello will not trim his sails to a particular readership: the mother never reappears after she sends the maid for the doctor. . . . [This story] is important, for it shows the range of Pirandello's appeal. Even the superficially trite situational story has its flashes of depth and perception, the same glow which so totally illumines the greater work. As many writers eke out an insufficient income by popularizing certain themes they treat more profoundly in their major productions, so Pirandello popularizes—and pinpoints—in this little story the theme of woman's fate. That this theme preoccupied him all his life is given monumental proof in one of his key works, **"Such Is Life."**

Frustration, encroaching age, perpetual loneliness, misunderstanding, death—*la condition humaine*—are, then, the recurrent subjects. The forms range, as we know, from the wildly, hilariously burlesque through the ironic, the gently satiric, the quasidocumentary, to the dramatic and, in the classic sense, tragic. Details, too, run like cues for action through the gamut of the stories. There are cricket sounds at night, the play of moonlight on steel, the great sound of silence (which Leopardi caught so well), the pointlessness, the hopelessness, of hope. Over all, there is man's boundless inhumanity to man.

Is there, then, no end to man-inflicted, self-inflicted pain? There is, the author believes, but it lies in no faith, in no "right," in no assurance from within; it lies in patience, tolerance, maturity and compromise. **"The Wreath"** is . . . [a rare example] of Pirandello's personal formula for a fit survival. In it the husband wins grandeur and purity in his wife's eyes by acting above, beyond the formulas of the day, by dropping all the recommendations society would have given him and by acting, indeed, like a clement and loving god.

But a god's love—even if our gods are made in our own best image—is impersonal, benign—above all, unpossessive. And there it is, Pirandello's answer, arrived at with infinite greatness of spirit, infinite patient scrutiny of the poor whirling prisms with their irrevocably separate identities, their apparently autonomous gyrations. To the earlier question "Can one feel compassion for a prism?" the author would answer, "Yes, and even love, for strife-torn, strife-inflicting life is bearable only if love—not possessiveness—rule."

Irving Howe (essay date 1959)

SOURCE: "Some Words for a Master," in *The New Republic,* Vol. 141, No. 2341, September 28, 1959, pp. 21–4.

[*A longtime editor of the leftist magazine* Dissent *and a regular contributor to* The New Republic, *Howe is one of America's most highly respected literary critics and social historians. He has been a socialist since the 1930s, and his criticism is frequently informed by a liberal social viewpoint. In this review of the 1959 collection* Short Stories, *Howe relates Pirandello's work to nineteenth-century realism.*]

About half a year ago, when a collection of Pirandello's stories appeared in English, I began to read them casually and with small expectations. Like other people, I had once looked into a few of his plays and been left cold; had accepted the stock judgment that he was clever theatrically but lacking in literary range and depth; and had disliked him because of his friendliness to Italian Fascism.

Two or three stories were enough to convince me that here, beyond doubt, was the work of a master. Not all the stories in [**Short Stories by Pirandello**] are first-rate; some show the marks of haste or fatigue, others are finger-exercises in which Pirandello plays with his main themes yet does not fully release them. But even in the slightest of these twenty-two stories—only one had previously been translated into English—there is that uniqueness and assurance of voice which is the first sign of a major writer. And in the best of them there is writing which can bear comparison with the masters of the short story, Chekhov and Joyce.

Now this is not an estimate for which modern criticism has prepared us. Outside of Italy, there is little Pirandello criticism; the books about him in English range from Italianate rhapsody to American academic, but none provides enough material or adequate criticism. A good but too brief essay by Eric Bentley helps one find direction in the labyrinth of Pirandello's vast production, and equally helpful are some incisive reviews by Stark Young, written in the twenties for *The New Republic* and reprinted in his *Immortal Shadows.* But for the most part, in America Pirandello is a name, not a force. He has seldom been welcomed to the pantheon of modernism, and those of us raised on modernist taste have suffered a loss.

Nor is this true in regard to Pirandello alone. Taste can be a tyrant, even the best or most advanced taste. Literary people who reached maturity two or three decades ago often felt zealous in behalf of writers like Eliot, Stevens and Joyce, for they, in Harold Rosenberg's phrase, had established the "tradition of the new" and it was this tradition which roused one's excitement and loyalties. Soon, however, the tradition of the new was being shadowed by a provincialism of the new.

The *avant garde* impulse was the most vital in the literary life of our century, but by now we might as well admit that it also exacted a price in narrowness of interest, sometimes in smugness of feeling. Because its spokesmen told us so forcibly which poets and novelists were relevant to an age of terror and war, we assumed a little too quickly that other writers could be left to molder in darkness. Now, by way of penance, middle-aged writers regularly—

and if they have any humor about themselves, ruefully—announce literary "discoveries" based on reading with pleasure the writers whom they had felt free to dismiss in their youth.

So here are some notes—inexpert, rueful—on Luigi Pirandello.

Pirandello's stories are in the main tradition of 19th Century European realism. Except for those set in Sicily, which have a distinctive regional flavor, they often seem close in manner and spirit to the writings of the French realists and naturalists. Ordinary social life forms their main setting. The frustrations of the city, the sourings of domesticity, the weariness of petty-bourgeois routines, provide their characteristic subjects. Like Flaubert, though with less fanatic insistence, Pirandello cuts himself out of his picture. His prose is neither elevated nor familiar; it is a middle style, denotative, austere and transparent, the style of an observer who achieves sympathy through distance rather than demonstration.

Far more than we have come to expect in the modern short story, the impact of Pirandello's stories depends upon their action, which sometimes contains enough incident to warrant a good deal of expansion. There are rarely Joycean epiphanies of insight or Chekhovian revelations through a massing of atmosphere. The function of Pirandello's style is to serve as a glass with a minimum of refraction or distortion; and whatever we may conclude as to his purpose or bias must come not from a fussing with details of metaphor but from a weighing of the totality of the action. In this respect, Pirandello the story writer is not quite a "modern" writer.

He is not quite "modern" in still another way. Though Pirandello in his plays would break with the psychology and epistemology of 19th Century realism, abandoning the premises of both a fixed individual character and the knowability of human relationships, his stories were still accessible to educated people of his generation who had been brought up on rationalist assumptions. Such readers may have found them excessively bleak—one does not leave Pirandello in a mood to embrace the universe—but they had no difficulty in grasping them, as later they might with his plays.

The stories deal with human problems, but do not threaten the reader with a vision of human lot as beyond comprehension or as open to so many meanings that there follows a paralysis of relativism. Pirandello has a sharp eye for absurdities, but this is still far from the view that life is inherently absurd. One can find anticipations of existentialism in these stories, as one can find them in many writers of Pirandello's day who were oppressed by the collapse of 19th Century certainties; but precisely those writers, like Pirandello, who seem to have anticipated the existentialist posture of an affirmed insecurity are the ones, in the end, who resist its full display. They stopped short, often at a depressed stoicism, a sense of life as weariness. And this, in turn, has some relation to their having been raised in a more or less Christian culture: for if they no longer had a radiant or sustaining faith they preserved from it a feeling for duties, burdens, limits.

Fantasy, playfulness, sexual pleasure, religious emotion, any sort of imaginative abandon or transcendence—these seldom break through in Pirandello's stories, though some of them can at times be heard pulsing quietly beneath the surface. A full tragic release is rare. Much more characteristic are stories in which the final sadness arises from the realization of characters that they will have to live on, without joy or hope. In a five-page masterpiece, **"The Soft Touch of Grass,"** a bereaved, aging man is mistakenly suspected by a girl of having lewd intentions; overcome by a sense of the hopeless entanglements of life, he returns to his lonely room and "turned his face to the wall."

The function of Pirandello's style is to serve as a glass with a minimum of refraction or distortion; and whatever we may conclude as to his purpose or bias must come not from a fussing with details of metaphor but from a weighing of the totality of the action.

—*Irving Howe*

In **"Such Is Life,"** a masterpiece that would do honor to Chekhov, a hopeless marriage, long broken, is hopelessly resumed. This story, written with a repressed austerity and unrelieved by a rebellious gesture or tragic resolution, stays terribly close to life; in a sense, its power depends upon Pirandello's scrupulous decision not to allow either his emotions or imagination to interfere with what he sees. At the end, the central figure is left with "an ever-present torment . . . for all things, all earthly creatures as she saw them in the infinite anguish of her love and pity, in that constant painful awareness—assuaged only by fleeting peaceful moments which brought relief and consolation—of the futility of living like this. . . ."

There are humorous stories too, such as **"The Examination,"** in which a good-tempered glutton studying for a state examination is regularly deflected from his work by friends tempting him to share their pleasures. One smiles at the end, for Pirandello manages it with suavity and tact. But it is a humor of sadness, a twist upon the idea of incongruity as the very heart of life, and it brings little gaiety or relief. Of the pleasure that can come from simply being alive Pirandello's stories have little to say, certainly nothing to compare with his one marvellously lighthearted play *Liola,* in which youthful energies bubble without restraint or theory.

Stark Young, in a review of the play *Henry IV,* has described the Pirandello theme as

> . . . the dualism between Life on one hand and Form on the other; on the one hand Life pouring in a stream,

unknowable, obscure and unceasing; on the other hand forms, ideas, crystallizations, in which we try to embody and express this ceaseless stream of life. Upon everything lies the burden of its form, which alone separates it from dust, but which also interferes with the unceasing flood of Life in it.

This description, partly drawn from Pirandello himself, is an excellent one, though some amendment is required in regard to the stories, for there the stream of Life is much weaker than the barrier of Form. In Young's version, the Pirandello theme is concerned with constants that apply to any moment in history, and there is plenty of evidence in both the stories and plays that Pirandello sees it this way. But I think that a sharper focus can be had upon the stories if one also regards the Life-Form theme as closely related to the stresses and tensions of late 19th- and early 20th-century life in Europe.

To all of this, one group of Pirandello stories is something of an exception. Those set in Sicily are comparatively buoyant and combative, not because Pirandello, himself a Sicilian, glosses over the misery of his homeland or indulges in peasant romanticism, but simply because here the human drama plays itself out with quick violence. Men rise, men fall; but they do not know the dribbling monotonies of an overly-rationalized mode of existence, as do so many characters in Pirandello's urban stories. In **"Fumes,"** the best of the Sicilian group, a decent hard-working farmer, to frustrate the local money-lender, agrees to sell his land to a sulphur-mining company, appalled though he is at the thought of the fumes that will now blight the whole region. The spectacle of a man being pressed beyond endurance is a familiar one in Pirandello's stories; but the farmer, while hardly a Promethean figure, does cry out at the end, "Neither he nor I!"

Behind Pirandello stands his master in fiction, the Sicilian Giovanni Verga, from whom he learned to disdain rhetoric and grandeur. Reading Verga's stories one feels they are not so much "made-up" fictions as communal fables, the record of a people born to catastrophe. Reading Pirandello's stories, one feels they have been wrought by a man increasingly estranged from a world he knows intimately. Pirandello does not achieve the virile spareness of Verga; no one does. In Verga everything is subordinated to the decisiveness of the event; in Pirandello one must always be aware of his psychological motives, even if these seldom appear on the surface of the story, and then mainly as a film of melancholy. Verga's happenings are much more terrible than Pirandello's, yet are easier to take, since in Verga men scream and howl as they suffer. Only a few decades separate the two writers, but the distance between them reflects a deep change in the spiritual temper of European life, a certain loss of zest and will.

Writers, like the rest of us, do not choose their moment of birth, and it would be absurd to relate Pirandello too closely with the depressing qualities of his stories. So quick an intelligence must have been aware of the difference in the literary possibilities open to Verga and himself, and realized that most of the advantage did not lie with him. But

no serious writer chooses his subject; he can only choose whether to face it. And that Pirandello did with exemplary courage and honesty.

Marian Seldin   (essay date 1959)

SOURCE: "The Near Tragic," in *The Commonweal,* Vol. LXXI, No. 1, October 2, 1959, pp. 28–9.

[*In the following review of* Short Stories, *Seldin identifies qualities that distinguish Pirandello's successful short fiction from his weaker stories.*]

Most volumes of short stories involve for the reviewer a built-in hazard in that space forbids the particular comment and justice the general. However, these twenty-two stories [in ***Short Stories by Pirandello***] mitigate the difficulty because Pirandello's preoccupation in them, as in his plays and novels, is remarkably constant. Human experience, as he saw it, is at best ironic, at worst not quite tragic, but rather frustrating. For men, who need to communicate, are unheard, misunderstood or, when grasped a little too well, made vulnerable to those who wish them ill.

The stories gain their force from the fact that the anguish their characters endure comes through human acts, willed acts proceeding from motives not fully understood and leading to consequences not entirely foreseen. Pirandello's people, then, are fully men and women, not mechanisms subject to drives nor pawns in the clutches of the doomsters. This is true even of the Sicilian stories in which environment, the impoverished land pockmarked and contaminated by sulphur mines, plays a significant role. In **"Fumes,"** for instance, Don Mattia destroys the green hill he loves to benefit the mines he hates, but he is driven to the act not by an inexorable nature but through the malice of an enemy who, having injured him once, can justify himself only by injuring again.

The short story, though, is a limiting form, particularly for an author whose concern is just this sort of probing into what men make of the human condition. Thus, none of these stories has to me the impact of *The Outcast,* one of the best of his novels, or of the famous *Six Characters in Search of an Author.* The best of them are the longer ones, those which approach *novella,* for in them Pirandello has time not only to establish character—which he does with finesse even in the shorter pieces—but also to prepare adequately for his ironic insight.

A few of the shorter pieces, such as **"Cinci"** or **"Escape,"** which focus on only one character are virtuoso achievements, so brilliantly do they marshal mood and event to achieve their bitter moments of truth. And those lighter in mood, like **"Watch and Ward,"** an ironic anecdote, or **"Who Pays the Piper . . . ,"** a "folk" tale, are wryly successful. However, some of the more serious ones too short to permit the pathetic or the ironic to make itself felt gradually end by being only sentimental. Or worse, they end falsely, invoking an irony not validly present. In **"A**

Mere Formality" a sick man's stratagem to deny his innocent wife her equally innocent lover after his own death seems to me to be inadequate to its end. And Lucietta, the appealing young widow in **"The Rose,"** in spite of her naive frivolity and her neighbors' malicious willingness to take advantage of it, *could* possibly come through happily, marry the man who loves her instead of being consigned to perpetual matelessness through an incident essentially trivial. We suffer an inundation of authentic agony and ought not also have to endure insistence upon anguish where it need not be.

But on the whole the stories are rich in justified emotion, in moments of acute sympathy for the plight especially of women and, most tenderly, of the old. And Pirandello's pervasive awareness of the absurd shows itself most effectively in his serious pieces where incidents which out of context would be Mack Sennet comedy serve to intensify rather than to mitigate the tragic.

Ulrich Leo (essay date 1963)

SOURCE: "Pirandello between Fiction and Drama," translated by Glauco Cambon, in *Pirandello: A Collection of Critical Essays,* edited by Glauco Cambon, Prentice-Hall, Inc., 1967, pp. 83-90.

[*Leo was a leading German scholar of Romance literature. In the following excerpt from an essay that was originally published in* Romanistiches Jarbuch *in 1963, he compares the short story "Mrs. Frola and Her Son-In-Law, Mr. Ponza" to its stage adaptation,* Right You Are (If You Think So), *while asserting that Pirandello's short fiction is more artistically powerful than his dramas.*]

. . . In . . . *L'uomo, la bestia e la virtù (Man, Beast and Virtue)* we [can see] how the poetical sense of a work of narrative fiction vanished once that work was adapted for the stage, to make room for theatrical animation: the play had not grasped in its essence the short story from which it was derived. In . . . **"O di uno o di nessuno" ("Either of One or of No One"),** we [can see] that the relevant play, confined as it was to the dramatic genre's only form of speech, i.e., direct discourse, could not do justice to the rich expressive resources of narrative fiction, which include silence, though on the other hand, thanks to the unity of time which is more germane to theater than to a tale the play in question managed to fulfill the structural unity of a given theme much better than the source story had.

Now we shall see . . . how the short story—by going beyond its genre limits with no loss of poetical force—has become something like a nonnarrative prefiguration of the play; indeed, that it *is* already the play, at the potential stage. . . . The story in question is **"La signora Frola e il signor Ponza, suo genero" ("Mrs. Frola and her Son-in-Law, Mr. Ponza"),** while the play it generated is *Così è (se vi pare) (It Is So, If You Think So).* We are reminded of the question "Who had it been?" which abruptly opens the short story **"O di uno o di nessuno" ("Either of One or of No One").** That question seemed to issue in all likelihood from both male protagonists of the story, though the possibility remained that it was the narrator himself who uttered it. At any rate he was the one that began to tell the story after the short initial paragraph. Instead, in the case of **"La signora Frola"** . . . we find ourselves from beginning to end in a speech atmosphere which—with the exception of few passages to which we shall return—is no longer that of a fictional narrative in the proper sense of the word: because the narrator, far from occupying the obvious center, is simply "not there." And while in a play the playwright not only does not have to, but actually cannot be "present," . . . a fictional narrative without narrator remains to this day, despite all the transformations this genre has gone through, a contradiction in terms. Let us then consider the literary form as it shows itself here.

What we see here is no narrative—and no I-narrative either—it is a *dramatic monologue.* And if we ask who is the monologue's persona, everything seems to refute the possibility of its being the author himself. Obviously the subjective participation expressed by the monologue—and in direct discourse, not just in free indirect discourse—is too naïve and immediate for that. Besides, this participation involves a group of what could be defined as "masked people," i.e., a compact mass of average men and women who confront two (or rather, three) "unmasked" ones with a curiosity stubborn and merciless to the point of fanaticism. The "unmasked" ones, on their part, want nothing but to live their own life outside the so-called "normal" sphere, yet they cannot do it in the eyes of the "masked" people (the impersonal, anonymous subject that Heidegger would label "das Man," as in *Man sagt,* "people say . . ." while Pirandello here says "Tutti [All]). The "speaker" of the monologue is obviously a member of this group and seems to endorse unconditionally their well-known (to him) viewpoints, prejudices, and ways of conduct. Thus how could this speaker be Pirandello, who, rather, always and everywhere takes the side of the "unmasked," of the defenseless and lonely? Pirandello indeed, who in *It Is So, If You Think So* will introduce Laudisi (the short story has no character by that name) as a kind of counsel against the busybodies, and patently on the author's behalf?

But even if we did not know that the short story **"Mrs. Frola and her Son-in-Law"** is by Pirandello and that *It Is So, If You Think So* constitutes its stage version, we could distinguish the speaker of the monologue, on stylistic grounds, from the author—for the manner of utterance bears the unmistakable mark of the dramatic farce. "But really, can you imagine? all of us will go crazy if we don't manage to find out which of the two is crazy, this Mrs. Frola or this Mr. Ponza, her son-in-law. Things like that happen only at Valdana, unlucky town, the magnet of all eccentric strangers!" Thus it begins, and thus it goes on; and thus quite evidently no author speaks (regardless of which author it may be); this is the voice of an anonymous citizen of a backwoods small town, which to him is the hub of world events (". . . Things like that happen *only at Valdana*. . . ."); and he is speaking in the tone of carping criticism familiar to his cronies. Yes, the anonymous persona speaks not only in the context of that nameless collective which Heidegger calls "das Man": he represents it, he himself is the voice of that collective. He even emphasizes himself to the point of literal equivalence with it: ". . . we all here looking into one another's eyes, like lunatics? . . ." Irrefutably, the speaker is himself part of the impersonal group. And to whom does he speak? Not to his own group (as Laudisi will do in the play when he tries to convey to the naïve and fanatical mass his skepticism concerning truth, Pirandello's own skepticism). This speaker evidently has nothing to tell or to teach that his fellow gossips do not already know. Those he addresses, instead, . . . are the readers (one might almost say the listeners). To them—almost as a delegate of the nameless collective—he tells with great excitement whatever eccentricities happen to be afoot in Valdana at the moment.

This, then, is our "first reading impression"—after we have noticed that what we read here is, with regard to genre, no story but a dramatic structure. Yet the "second reading impression" modifies the first, without of course canceling it. By listening more carefully we still find something in the "monologue" that cannot be so unquestionably attributed to a naïve member of the "People say . . ." impersonal group. The speaker at some points seems to be half conscious of what will be the basic thesis of Laudisi in the play: that truth is defined just by its being unknowable. This naturally would never occur to any really harmless member of the "Tutti" busybodies: for they actually live on the certainty that the secret of Signora Frola and Signor Ponza can be clarified if one but delves enough; that one can know whether Signora Ponza is the first or the second wife of her husband; and whether, according to the answer, Signora Frola or Signor Ponza is the crazy one. This is how the "Tutti" think. But the speaker of the monologue has a phrase which in the course of his talking becomes an actual *leitmotiv,* and it expresses something like a first secret doubt on such a naïve certainty: "not to be able to discover . . . where the phantom is, where reality"; "where is reality? where the phantom?" ". . . where the phantom, where reality may be" (the dubitative question is thereby raised to the status of an overall motto). Still another particularly revelatory passage is to be found right at the beginning: "Naturally, in everybody the fateful suspicion rises that, things being so, reality is *worth just as much* as the phantom, and that every reality may very well *be* a phantom, and vice versa." This "suspicion" is already almost Laudisi's doctrine; and if it really came to life in "everybody's" mind, then the anonymous "people say" attitude would lose its impact. In this connection it pays to observe that, while the keyword for the anonymous speaker in the short story is "realtà" (reality) (with its negative counterpart "fantasma" [phantom]), Laudisi's keyword in the play is "verità" (truth) (without an antithetical concept; at each act's end, and often elsewhere too). "Truth" stands cognitively above "reality" and "illusion."

These doubts on the possibility of seizing truth (reality), within our "monologue," do modify for us as readers the first impression of the speaker's persona: he appears now less naïve, more thoughtful and independent, spiritually a bit closer to the author Pirandello. Another stylistic trait modifies the genre form we have called "monologue," in that it brings that form closer to an authentic narrative: the speaker, that is, does *narrate* the antecedents in fragments inserted between his outbursts, instead of just dissolving all the preliminary facts into exclamations, questions, self-objections, addresses to the fictive audience. That he, and not Pirandello, is the narrator may be seen in his initially twice repeated self-admonition to "order": "But no, it is better to relate everything first in an orderly way"; "But let us proceed with order." (In a formally opposite way Pirandello himself, without any such transition, had begun to narrate from the second paragraph of the short story **"Either of One or of No One."**) When the speaker narrates coherently, then, he himself interrupts his own impressionist speech, whose center is the reaction of "Valdana" to the events described—but not so much the events themselves; he remembers ever anew that his fictive "listeners" (the readers) must be initiated to what he and his familiars already know. Such narrative pieces are to be found all over, shading always into the reflections of the curious people (especially of the ladies), so that it is never easy to distinguish the objectively narrated facts from the subjective reactions to such narration, whether retold or directly uttered by the speaker himself: another proof that we are dealing with one speaker and one and the same monologue. But the very fact of narration does bring the persona closer to the figure of the author (Pirandello), who in a "normal" short story would have been himself the narrator; on the other hand it distances the persona from the undifferentiated crowd, which is generally present in the monologue only insofar as the persona speaks of it ("le *signore*" [the ladies]; "tutti" [all]; "Valdana"). In the context of these narrative fragments there actually occur the speeches of Mrs. Frola and of Mr. Ponza in the guise of free indirect discourse (on the cue of their visits as reported by the speaker, visits which then are directly enacted in the play). Even a bit of dialogue (between Mrs. Frola and her supposed daughter) is rendered in the form of direct discourse; and there is also a direct discourse by Mrs. Frola. But always from the lips of the monologue's persona, not of the author.

Who, then, utters the monologue? My answer will surprise those who know (as I myself said before) that a character called Laudisi appears only in the play and not in the story. However, I answer the question: the speaker of the "monologue" is neither one of the "masked" people, nor Pirandello: it is rather Laudisi and no one else. Of course not the same Laudisi who in the play will act as mouthpiece of the author against the nameless collective, but his embryonic and still unnamed predecessor in the "short story." I figure for myself the process (which perhaps even Pirandello the author did not consciously realize—we explicators must serve some purpose after all!) somewhat as follows. The cue to the project came—as is known—from a tragic *fait divers*: the destruction of a small town in the Marsica region of Abruzzi by an earthquake in 1915. In the face of this reality the whole idea developed. Pirandello shows, without introducing them directly as he will later do in the play, the ladies and gentlemen of the small, imaginary town of Valdana in their excitement about the consequences of that event for their town. He does this in perspective, through the words of one of them. This person, while speaking as one of them, starts having his spiritual doubts: since an individual by himself is apter to think things over than a crowd. While he intermittently and fragmentarily recounts antecedents and story proper in his monologue, he gets (as if behind his own back) a broader view of the facts narrated by him than is possible to the thoughtless crowd of busybodies for whom he speaks, and who on their part can only see the fleeting moment. Thus the phase of reflection has penetrated the naïveté that can only experience what is momentary; and it has done this—since it's a matter of investigating reality—in the guise of methodic skepticism, even though in its first dawning. The speaker has, unawares, already distanced himself a bit from his impersonal crowd; and this means that the short story already contains, in a nutshell, the "Laudisi" of the play to come. Comparable in this way to the later Laudisi, the speaker already stands a little disengaged from the nameless collective for which he nevertheless speaks; and this with regard to the writer as well as to the reader. (This of course by no means implies that Pirandello had developed his philosophy right then for the first time. I am describing a literary process, not an ideological one.) The speaker of the "short story" is "a Laudisi *avant la lettre*." Let us not forget that the wholly developed Laudisi, the skeptic of the play, is also a member of the "crowd": for he is familiar, related, bound to the group of the "masked people" (the busybodies). He is no "unmasked" one, because he knows how to defend himself. He is, besides, no recent arrival, no "Ingénu," "Micromégas," or "Candide": he is from "Valdana" like the others; to that extent he constitutes a legitimate literary descendant of the "short story's" anonymous speaker, who on his part spiritually somewhat prefigures him.

A close examination of the text confirms this from language and style. The expression through which the speaker of the "monologue" finally reveals himself as part of the "Tutti" (". . . *a guardarci tutti negli occhi*. . . .") recurs almost unchanged on the lips of the play's Laudisi: "*Vi guardate tutti negli occhi?* . . ." (You all look into one another's eyes?). Yet a basic difference is there. The anonymous speaker said "*guardarci,*" to look into one another's eyes (meaning *ours*), because he considered himself part of the "Tutti"; Laudisi says "*vi* guardate," *you* look into one another's eyes, because he consciously excludes himself from the "Tutti." That speaker of the short story, then, has been organically reshaped into the Laudisi of the play. The latter will be hopelessly split from his erstwhile "peers" by his basically antithetic way of feeling and thinking, while his forerunner in the "short story," despite his spiritual "temptations," does remain a member of the crowd to the very end of the monologue.

If my explication is viable, then "Laudisi"—the singular polemical character of the dramatic piece *It Is So, If You Think So,* and certainly in his own right one of Pirandello's liveliest creations—is already latently, potentially there

in the pseudo-short-story **"Mrs. Frola and her Son-in-Law."** The same is now true of almost everything that will otherwise go into the three acts of the play. Since the "short story"—as is by now clear—really is dramatic in nature, we can safely call it a one-acter which prepared the matter of the later three-acter by allusion rather than actual execution. This holds even though Pirandello included the work in question among his "short stories"; and it would not be the only case of its kind.

The play is already potentially present in the "short story." It is not a case of the play's having misunderstood the short story and robbed it of its existential sense; nor is it a case of the short story (which here already has dramatic quality and works mainly with direct discourse) being utterly different from the play in the matter of expression. Some tender nuances do of course get lost in the dramatic elaboration: ". . . she concludes with a sigh which on her lips takes the shape of a sweet, utterly sad smile." This is given in the short story by the speaker's narrative report, but in the play could only have been salvaged (or buried) in a stage direction, for the actress to *show*. Yet such cases are, as we saw, exceptions, because both elaborations of the subject belong to the same expressive sphere, the dramatic one. They effectively relate to each other as a sketch does to a fuller rendering of the same subject.

With such assumptions let us note again the motifs, scenes and acts that are at best hinted at in the "monologue," but constitute structural elements of the play. First of all (to say it once again), the collective "Tutti," who populate the play, are present in the "monologue" only through the mouth of the speaker. The earthquake, natural cause of the whole story, is mentioned only once in the "monologue," and only as "a grave mishap," while in the play it becomes the object of the "people say" group's discussions, and what's more, documents are sought in the devastated small town with a view to unveiling the "secret"—this being one of the two main motifs of Act III (especially scene 1 and 2 with foreshadowings in Act II, scene 1). The attribution of evidential power to documents, which is holy dogma to the "masked" ones, will be one of Laudisi's arguments against the knowability of "truth." In the "monologue," the documents hardly come up, even by way of allusion. The play on its part needed a "third act," and thus there was a reason to extend the action by introducing motifs which the psychologically oriented model had not used. But, unlike the earlier cases, this time the new motifs grow organically from the central idea by which the model was determined in its turn; they do not obscure, they develop it.

As for the other leading theme of Act III and great climax of the whole piece—the personal appearance of the controversial Mrs. Ponza—the very end of the "monologue" suggests just the possibility of questioning her as a last resort to solve the riddle; but the lady herself does not show up, even in the speaker's narrative. Such is the difference between the genre requirements of a dramatic monologue taking the place of the short story on the one hand, and of a full-fledged theatrical piece on the other, however little aimed at extrinsic effects. Act III, the climax of the play, is mainly missing from the "monologue," save for a few hints. Even the *prefetto,* a prominent figure of the "people say" group in Act III of the play, is only mentioned in the "monologue." And the three great scenes in which both "unmasked" persons pay visits to their tormentors, the "Tutti", in an attempt to save something of their secret from the fury of the busybodies, appear as "scenes" only in the play, effectively offsetting each other (I, 4-6). In the "monologue," as we earlier saw, these visits have already taken place and appear only retrospectively in the recollective talk of the speaker, partly in narrative form, partly in free indirect discourse, at times even in reported direct speech; and therefore they are much less sharply divided into contrasting scenes, for they rather make up phases of the development, in a general recapitulation of Valdana's "eccentricities."

I have endeavored to define something like a new genre by means of this "dramatic narrative monologue" disguised as "short story," from which later a three-act play was to emerge. That in the end, however, the author stands behind the speaker (though at quite a distance); that it is after all Pirandello who makes himself heard through the mouth of this anonymous and still naïve group spokesman, need not be doubted. It is not only the identity of "reality" and "phantom" (i.e. the unknowability of "truth"), as sensed by the "speaker," that betrays the author hiding behind him. The excitement, the perplexity of the speaker as such, who means to report just the group opinion, indirectly mirror the first shock of the author at the "tragic *fait divers*" to which he owed his inspiration. Into the scurrilous petty-bourgeois group language of his "Laudisi before the fact" the author translates his own first reaction as man and poet: "What shall I do with this process that reality is throwing at me?" In this sense (but then quite indirectly) one might call our pseudo-short-story, in the end, an "author monologue": different in genre from an I-narrative, different from a journal of the kind published by André Gide and Thomas Mann in connection with the writing, respectively, of the *Counterfeiters* and of *Dr. Faustus,* different as well from a personal letter. It is in fact a little genre unto itself. . . . At any rate I must count myself among those who say Pirandello went astray when he left narrative fiction for the drama . . . Pirandello's short stories and also his novels comprise a wealth of poetical gems, while in his plays the search for effect only too often has overruled the spiritual thoughtfulness and the voice of poetry. . . .

Jørn Moestrup   (essay date 1972)

SOURCE: "1910-16. Renewal," in *The Structural Patterns of Pirandello's Work,* Odense University Press, 1972, pp. 90–121.

[*In the following excerpt, Moestrup highlights some of the most significant stories written by Pirandello between 1910 and 1916, a period that the critic perceives as the middle phase of Pirandello's career as a short fiction writer.*]

SHORT STORIES 1910-1916

The short stories of this period will be divided into [separate] groups: first the seven which, by reason of their quality, are superior to the rest; then four that are of almost as high a quality; then the short stories which, though of less aesthetic value, contain important clues as to attitudes and ideas. . . .

Because he has lost his faith, Tommaso Unzio [in **"He Sings the Epistle"** (1911)] has left the seminary where he was studying. He thus deprives himself of an annuity, which had been given him by an uncle, conditional on his making a career in the church. Tommaso is now without resources and is disapproved of by his family. His father even uses violence in an attempt at giving Tommaso his faith back, and he spends as little time at home as possible. He wanders about in the countryside around his hometown, which is situated on the slopes of Monte Cimino in the north of Latium. On the rare occasions on which he meets people, they make fun of the naïve young man and get him to repeat what a sub-deacon's (Tommaso's ecclesiastical rank) duties are during Mass. He sings the epistle, Tommaso explains, and the sentence sticks to him as a nick-name.

As time passes Tommaso becomes more and more isolated and he spends his days in solitary meditation in the woods. He is attracted by the phenomena of nature—they live and die unconcerned by any moral or philosophical speculations. He feels that their existence is the only thing he can accept because it is eternal and immutable. Whatever dies in nature returns to the source which it came.— For an entire month he observes a blade of grass growing between two stones near his village. Every day he watches its growth with a mixture of excitement and wonder. One day he sees someone sitting on one of the stones, a Miss Olga Fanelli, who is presumably waiting for her fiancé, Lieutenant De Venera. As Tommaso does not seem inclined to disappear, she leaves in irritation after having carelessly torn up his blade of grass and put it in her mouth. Tommaso is shocked and shouts "idiot" (stupida) at her as she passes. Then he is set upon by her fiancé and challenged to a duel. In accepting the challenge he sets conditions which will almost certainly lead to the death of one of the participants. Tommaso is tired; he knows that the lieutenant is an excellent shot and that he has been offered a way out of his insoluble problems. His expectations are fulfilled: he is shot in the breast and dies soon after. For his religious mother's sake he agrees to allow a confessor to come to his deathbed. When, however, the priest asks him the question, the answer to which everyone is longing to hear, as to why he shouted "idiot", he answers with a smile, "Because of a blade of grass" (per un filo d'erba), and everyone thinks that his last words are the product of delirium.

"He Sings the Epistle" is the first short story in which the metaphysical landscape is the central theme. It is permeated by an intense feeling of longing; for the first time in his life Pirandello gives free expression to his incessant striving towards the absolute, while at the same time creating perfection. There is a contrast between the works of his youth and **"He Sings the Epistle"** and the following short stories of the same kind. In the latter he has found the way for and the goal of his search, in the attempt at identification with nature. The traditional elements of romanticism are absent. The mountains the wind and the grass maintain their actual existence and are not anthropomorphized. They have nothing to tell mankind; they have merely a way of existing, a self-sufficiency that is without question. There is a strength and fascination in the unshakeable calm of their being, in their unconditional acceptance of the conditions of life and in their complete self-identification. The writer feels this to originate from some link, not defined or explained, but felt, with the absolutes towards which his entire life is irresistibly drawn. Pirandello never surpassed this small group of short stories written in the period immediately after 1910, in which the metaphysical landscape appears; they stand comparison with the best of his plays. In its movement towards death, which does not come as a misfortune and is not felt as a tragedy, but as a final liberation, Tommaso's fate is presented with a passionate sensitivity. This, then, is a writer's expression of the spiritual state of Europe in the years before the First World War was to bring an epoch to a definitive close.

In its structure and style the short story is a good example of Pirandello's way of writing. It begins with a comic dialogue about Tommaso's nick-name, which immediately places the reader in medias res, and ends with the sharp irony of Tommaso's explanation as to why he had insulted Miss Fanelli. Two classical narrative passages follow the opening dialogue. The first deals with Tommaso's time at the seminary and his arrival home, while the second describes his life at home after he has given up the idea of becoming a priest. Then come two long inner monologues containing Tommaso's thoughts while he wanders around in the mountains; they are separated by a short passage of narrative concluded by a rejoinder. A pause marks the end of this gentle development of the story. Then the story is resumed at a completely different level. A passage of narrative is followed by a lively dialogue in which some townsfolk discuss the incredible scandal, Tommaso's behaviour towards Miss Fanelli, the duel and so on. This is a characteristic Pirandellian device: instead of continuing with narrative and inner monologue in his description of the blade of grass and the unfortunate meeting with Miss Fanelli the author switches over to dialogue. After this the story continues with straightforward narrative interrupted now and again by passages which refer Tommaso's thoughts until the story ends with Tommaso's final answer to the question as to why he had insulted the lieutenant's fiancée. Thus the two sharply separated parts of the story have roughly the same structure: dialogue—narrative—inner monologue—rejoinder, a structure that is highly conducive to lively, direct and varied narration.

Despite its somewhat banal introduction the second half of [**"The Fish Trap"** (1912)], concluding as it does with an astonishing twist, is so impressive that the story as a whole must be considered one of Pirandello's best. Bernardo Morasco has wasted his life. As a painter he has betrayed the artistic ideals of his youth in order to be able to provide for his family. At last, after twenty years have passed, he receives an inheritance which frees him from his slavery, but it is too late. The action takes place in the course of a day. Bernardo has left his house in order to commit suicide; he is too old to make an attempt at being a real artist again, and the money he has inherited has made him superfluous as a bread-winner.

For many hours he wanders around in Rome and finally goes down to the Tiber, past Ponte Flaminio, and continues along the bank. There is now no parapet and a narrow path makes it possible to get right down to the river. There he sees an odd piece of fishing-tackle, a kind of rotating trap consisting of two large baskets. It is driven by the current in such a way that the baskets alternate above and below the water. Bernardo decides to carry out his plan and jumps into the water, but the trap stops. A moment later the current starts the trap rotating again—slowly at first. This moment has been enough for Bernardo to be seized by terror at the imminence of death. With a desperate movement he avoids the trap by grabbing hold of a stake that is sticking halfway out of the water. As soon as Bernardo has freed himself from it and the trap is no longer slowed down by his weight, it begins to rotate at full speed and spurts a dollop of water over Bernardo, a gesture of warning and contempt. Reality suddenly begins to look quite different to the suicide candidate. Once he is safely on the bank, he becomes aware of the mildness of the spring evening, the stars in the sky and the silence. The proximity of death has made it impossible for him to kill himself.

It has often been said that Pirandello was obsessed by the thought of death. In **"The Fish Trap"**, as in a story written shortly before—**"Distraction"**—death is represented as sudden and irrevocable annihilation, a power that man is unable to face. Death is the most serious obstacle in his search for the absolute, a search which is also an urge to resist annihilation. This urge is victorious in a story like **"He Sings the Epistle"**. Through his long contact with nature Tommaso develops an attitude to life which permits him to await annihilation as if it were a deliverance. The calmness with which he meets death is that of natural objects. Death, for him, means a return to his point of origin.

The fact that **"He Sings the Epistle"** and **"The Fish Trap"** were written in successive years shows Pirandello's constant need to verify his position; a new standpoint will always be in danger and will be confronted with its antithesis—death as a deliverance in **"He Sings the Epistle"**, as annihilation in **"The Fish Trap"**. Tommaso's attitude to death is the direct opposite of Bernardo Morasco's.

Silvestro Noli [of **"Night"** (1912)] was born in Piemonte, in Torino, but like so many teachers before him, he began his career in Southern Italy. After some years he gets a post in a town in Abruzzi, and here, under the pressure of loneliness, he makes the enormous mistake of marrying a local girl, and thus, from an intellectual and spiritual point of view, signs his own death warrant. He will never be able to escape his treadmill in this remote province, because his wife refuses to move. She has never left her native town, not even to visit her in-laws. Seven years after having left Torino, Silvestro returns home for a short visit. Sitting in the train on his way back to wife and child in Città Sant'Angelo in Abruzzi, he feels completely crushed. At a station on the Adriatic coast he has to wait an entire night for the train that will take him up into the mountains and he meets, by chance, the widow of a colleague of his, who had died leaving her with three children and very little money. She has been on a fruitless errand to the Ministry of Education in Rome. At first she clings to him, but when she learns that he is married and that his wife is a local girl, she immediately understands the situation. No explanation is necessary—she herself comes from Bagnara Calabra on the southernmost point of the peninsula.—To pass the time they go down to the beach and spend the night there. As the mountains, trees and wind make Tommaso Unzio resign himself to his fate because he identifies himself with natural objects, so sea and stars give the couple a kind of strength. But while Tommaso had wished for death, they acquire a feeling of cosmic solidarity, which gives them renewed strength with which to support their lot. Their pain expands and fills the universe; they become fused with their environment and feel that their own unanswered questions are those of nature itself; and as a grey dawn slowly breaks their sense of affinity with the water at their feet and with distant planets enables them, at least momentarily, to feel less hopeless and despairing.

A clear indication of how Pirandello changed in the decade 1900–1910 can be obtained by comparing the atmosphere in this story with, for example, night as it is described in an another story in which the subject matter invited a similar treatment. The story . . . is **"First Night"** (1900). As a short story it is not inferior to **"Night"**, merely different. The poetic spring night has no power to help Marastella and Don Lisi [in **"First Night"**]. It is simply a framework, and its soft harmony serves to emphasize the loneliness and deep sadness with which the author imbues his characters. They live in a universe which has not as yet opened itself and there is no sense of cosmic affinity—there is only loneliness. In 1900 nature is not, as it is in 1912, an intermediate link with the absolute.

[In **"Ciàula Discovers the Moon"** (1912)] the nature theme of **"He Sings the Epistle"** and **"Night"** reaches unsurpassed heights, and **"Ciàula"** is one of Pirandello's most masterly stories, perhaps his best. Contact between man and nature is achieved in abrupt and shocking fashion despite the fact that the gulf between them was originally greater than ever before. This time Pirandello is not dealing with people possessing intellectual qualities that are far above average as was the case with Tommaso Unzio and Silvestro Noli. The main character Ciàula is a feeble-minded Sicilian, who slaves all day in the sulphur mines. He is a *caruso,* a workboy, for Zi' Scarda, whose sulphur he carries up to the surface. He is obedient and strong and does a good job. He got his nickname of Ciàula because

he has a marvellous way of imitating the cry of crows. Once after an accident in the mine which cost Zi' Scarda's son his life and Ciàula an eye, he ran away and hid himself in a remote passage. He did not emerge until after sunset and was seized by terror of the great empty darkness that surrounded him and was quite different from the familiar and innocuous darkness of the mine.

One day Zi' Scarda and Ciàula are obliged to work late and spend the night in the mine. Ciàula is deeply worried by the thought of the darkness that will meet him when he has climbed up the steep stairs with the sack on his back. His alternating states of mind are described with great sureness of touch. When he finally reaches the top everything is brightly illuminated, and he finds not the empty night but the full moon; its light makes night day. Ciàula calms down completely; so great is his wonder that his sack slips off his shoulder, while he himself, sitting on the ground and looking at the moon, begins to weep. "And Ciàula began to weep, without any volition, at the great consolation, the great relief (dolcezza), he felt at having discovered it, there, while it rose in the sky, the moon, with its veil of white light, unknowing of the mountains, the plain, the valleys that it lit up, unknowing of him, who, at least, because of it, was no longer afraid, was no longer tired, in the night that was full of his wonder".

It is posited of Ciàula that he is a poor idiot, who has never experienced any feelings that were not connected with the elementary necessities of life, but in the face of absolute reality the distinctions between different kinds of people are eradicated, and the moon has an even greater effect on Ciàula than the night on Silvestro Noli.

There is always a solid basis of reality in all that Pirandello wrote, except for his last period after 1925. In all stages of his work his naturalistic starting point constitutes a solid foundation on which to base his ethico-philosophical commitment. Thus in **"Ciàula"** the final catharsis is reinforced by the milieu in which the events take place. The miners' bleak existence is described with the ferocious precision that Pirandello knew how to use when it was his intention to describe the life of social outcasts.

Behind the aspiration towards the absolute that underlies Pirandello's metaphysical landscape is an abhorrence of life in its usual forms. In the previous decade this reality had been the major theme in Pirandello's work. It was described as a repulsive spectacle which, nevertheless, still had so much of the interest of novelty that the major part of Pirandello's creative energy had been taken up in depicting it, in plotting the role played by chance and instinct. Gradually his relationship to reality altered. There is no abrupt change, for even after 1910 Pirandello wrote stories in which the attitude to reality corresponds closely to that in the stories of the previous decade and which limit themselves to giving examples of cruelty and chance. But in stories like **"Ciàula"**, **"Night"** and **"He Sings the Epistle"** various ways of escape from reality are explored; this escape can also take place in a more direct manner. Thus, in **"The Long Dress"** [1913], the main character's suicide springs from a feeling of disgust that life has inspired in her. She refuses to subject herself to its desolate monotony and moral degradation. Resignation is no longer an acceptable attitude and the revolt is carried out. This new type of short story is characteristic of Pirandello's writing in the years after 1910 with its total and uncompromising rejection of an existence that evokes only repulsion and despair and no longer arouses even a documentary interest.

The story takes place in a first-class compartment on a train journey to the central part of Sicily. Didi, 16 years of age, accompanied by her father and brother, is travelling to Zúnica to make the acquaintance of the rich Marquis of Nigrenti. He is 45 and her father hopes that they will get married. Her father is also a nobleman, but has no capital. The lucrative post as an administrator that he has held for the past twenty years is to come to an end in the near future. That is why he is now attempting to establish his children—his son is to marry the Marquis' sister if possible, a prospect that he accepts with equanimity. No one is forcing Didi to do anything she does not want to do. Her father is far from being a tyrant, but her brother has explained to her with resigned humour how the land lies. It is merely a matter of a wise and far-sighted plan that her common sense must surely make her willing to co-operate in.—It is hot in the compartment. The sun burns mercilessly from a cloudless sky. Her father and brother fall asleep and Didi sits alone, wide awake, and thinks of her life in recent years, how she has become a grown-up and has at last been given a full-length dress (the title). All this culminates in thoughts about the future awaiting her, and she feels her spirits sink in despair and repulsion. She carefully takes a bottle out of her father's bag. It contains a poison of which he takes a couple of drops at a time for his weak heart. Slowly she takes the top off, raises the bottle to her mouth and drains it to the dregs.

> Suddenly the hand that was holding the bottle fell heavily down into her lap. As if her ears had just been opened she noticed the noise of the train, thunderous, enormous, deafening, so loud that she feared it would stifle the scream that tore her throat . . . No . . . now her father and brother started from their sleep . . . they were by her side . . . How could she hold on without them?

> Didi stretched out her arms, but grasped nothing, saw nothing, heard nothing.

> Three hours later the dead little girl in her long dress arrived at Zúnica, the dream-village of her happy childhood.

The moving and dramatic finale makes an unforgettable conclusion to this account of a young girl's revolt against the way things are.

"Revenge for the Dog", 1913, resembles, as regards content, the short stories of the previous period. It is yet another example of how mercilessly chance deals with human beings, but its uncompromising hardness, its total lack of humour, its terrifying control only became possi-

ble at a point in Pirandello's life when resignation had ceased to play a major role and had given way to negation and revolt.

Jaco Naca is a poor farmworker and seriously ill with malaria. Suddenly he happens to become the owner of a barren piece of land just outside Agrigento. It consists of a steep slope, which is full of boulders, so he sells most of it for a song to a man who builds two houses on the plot. The houses contain attractive flats with a magnificent view. When Jaco sees this, he feels that he has been cheated and he tries to get what he believes to have been his due, and when the attempt fails, he takes revenge in another way. He begins to plant various crops on the piece of land he has retained and he places a watchdog there, which he seldom feeds. It barks and howls with hunger every night and keeps the occupants of the two houses awake, but they can do nothing. Jaco has not broken any regulation. One night one of the tenants, a Signor Barsi, shoots at the dog with the result that next morning Jaco appears before the two houses and threatens to shoot anyone who harms his dog. It is a mortal insult to kill a Sicilian peasant's dog. In one of the flats there live a widow and her ten-year-old daughter Rorò. They disapprove strongly of the attempt at killing the poor innocent, hungry dog, despite the fact that it ruins everybody's sleep. Barsi is deeply indignant at this attitude, not least because he is interested in the widow, who does not want to have anything to do with him, and now his chances have been ruined completely. One day Rorò summons up her courage and goes down to feed the terrible dog. Her mother and some of the other tenants, including Signor Barsi, watch her at a distance. That night, for the first time for many weeks, the dog does not bark, and Rorò and her mother think, of course, that this is because it is no longer hungry. But there is another reason. Rorò's feeding of the dog is a challenge for Barsi, and the same evening he has crept down to it with some poisoned food. Next morning the little girl goes down to her new friend and sees it lying with its legs sticking out as though it were asleep. She goes closer and suddenly sees Jaco: he is lying in wait and the next moment there is a shot. From above, the mother and the other tenants see Rorò's dead body roll down the slope until it comes to rest beside the dog.

On probably no other occasion did Pirandello succeed in giving his pessimistic conception of the relationship between cause and effect more consistent expression. The impetus to the tragedy stems from what originally seemed to be a piece of good fortune—Jaco's unexpectedly becoming a landowner. And another factor that is usually a last refuge in the general wretchedness of the world, love, in the form of Barsi's interest in the widow, helps to provoke the catastrophe. The victims, the child and the animal, are completely innocent, while the person who will suffer most is, after Rorò and the dog, the least guilty, the malaria-plagued, half-mad, miserable illiterate, Jaco, who acted from instinct. He will either spend the rest of his life in prison or wander around as an outlaw in the mountains, where he cannot survive long. Next after him in the table of suffering comes the mother, who, widowed when young, has now lost her child as well. Last comes Barsi, the man who bears the actual guilt and who is at the most accountable only to his own conscience, which will, presumably, soon acquit him.

That the tragic drama of Jaco Naca was followed a few months later by one of his wittiest and most elegant stories bears witness to Pirandello's range and versatility as a writer of short stories.—As in by far the great majority of cases ["**The Little Black Goat**" (1913)] has a precise conceptual basis, which, in a way that is characteristic of Pirandello's style, is supported by a convincingly real background. His philosophy springs directly from reality and it seldom seems to have been set into a framework. The ideas do not become abstractions, as they are tied to concrete situations from the very beginning. It must be this fact that Gramsci is referring to in an often quoted sentence [A. Gramsci, *Letteratura e vela nationale*, 1950: "questi punti di vista sono necessariamente di origine libresca, dotta, presi dai sistemi filosofici individuali, o non sono invece esistenti nella vita stessa, nella cultura del tempo e persino nella cultura popolare di grado infimo, nel folclore?" (are these points of view—i.e., Pirandello's idealistic philosophy—necessarily of literary or scholarly origin, taken from the individual philosophical systems, or do they exist instead in life itself, in the culture of the time and even at the lowest level of folk culture, in folklore?)—Here is the source of Sciascia's view (expressed in *Pirandello e la Sicilia*, 1961) that Pirandello is primarily a *Sicilian* writer; the basic features of his work are seen to be specifically Sicilian and not broadly European, characteristic of the period, etc.]. This time the theme is the movement in things, ceaseless change, and by contrast rational man's static picture of the world, which fails to take change into account. Some people are able to adapt themselves, others are not. Among the latter is Charles Trockley. He has been the English Vice-Consul in Agrigento for many years and is a paragon of punctiliousness and objectivity. One day he receives a visitor who causes him much annoyance. She is a Miss Ethel Holloway, the daughter of an English aristocrat, and is on the obligatory tour of Europe as a part of her education. The tour includes Sicily, where the Doric temples in Girgenti are not to be missed. But during her visit to the majestic temple ruins Miss Ethel shows more interest in the sheep and goats which continue to profane the holy place despite Trockley's repeated complaints to the local council. When she sees a little black kid, she is beside herself with delight, buys it and has it sent to her hotel, where they promise to look after it until she has returned to England and can send for it. Eight months later the Vice-Consul, who has in the meantime happily forgotten the unfortunate episode, receives a letter from London: a request from Miss Ethel for her little black kid. After lengthy investigations the animal is identified and Trockley is presented with a horrible, horned brute, a scratched and evil-smelling beast, which he dutifully sends off to England with the result that shortly after he receives a letter from Sir John Holloway filled with the most furious abuse, because the Vice-Consul has dared to send his daughter such a monster.

In a comic dialogue at the end of the story the narrator, who is a close acquaintance of Mr Trockley's, carefully tries to get him to understand that logic and facts are not of his world. He should have bought another black kid for the foolish, spoilt girl or written to her that her graceful playmate had unfortunately died of longing for her kisses and caresses.

Except for a slightly sluggish introductory scene the story is thoroughly enjoyable reading. A sensitive description of the landscape and the temples is combined with humorous portraits of the two main characters with their widely different ideas of reality, and Pirandello seems to have an inexhaustible fund of drastic and ludicrous epithets with which to describe the change in the charming little black kid.

The above are not the only stories of splendid quality from this period, 1911-1913. There is no doubt that there is a decline in quality in the last years before Pirandello's breakthrough as a dramatist. The stories written in 1910-1913 are on the whole decidedly better than those written in 1914-1916. Pirandello wrote some very good short stories after 1913, but only one of them is up to his highest standard.

"**The Little Red Book**", 1911, gives an incredible account of the treatment of foundlings in a provincial town in Sicily at the beginning of our century. A foundling is put out to nurse with a woman, who receives a monthly sum for breastfeeding it, her "red book". She immediately pawns it—this traffic has for some reason become the speciality of enterprising businessmen from Malta—for a couple of hundred lire, which go to her daughter's dowry. The foundling very often dies if, for example, the nurse, does not have enough milk. This is quite common, but the local authorities look the other way; the money has at least been used to start a new marriage. Thus a reasonable balance between departure and arrival is maintained.— Especially striking is the tone in which this hair-raising story is told. The tone of voice is slightly regretful, but at the same time neutral and objective. There is no note of accusation in the ironic resignation of the narrator, who at no point allows his indignation to appear directly. This merciless coolness is intensely effective. The usual narrator is placed at the same level as the inhabitants of Nisi (Porto Empedocle); he appears to reason as they do and he reacts to what happens as they react, that is to say that any emotional reaction is speedily adjusted to the inhuman conditions of life. What energy they have is not used on moralizing or protesting but on ensuring, as far as possible, their own and their family's survival.

"**The Truth**" [1912] is one of the short stories that might seem to confirm Sciascia's view that Pirandello is primarily a Sicilian writer [Sciascia, *Pirandello e la Sicilia*, 1961], that is to say that the conceptual problems with which he deals derive from the environment in which he grew up and its behavioural characteristics. The subject is a difficult one because it raises questions that are of principle importance and that have far-reaching implications, in this case the relationship between the local and the universal. A given conviction is often formulated in such a way that the depth of penetration into local (and private) conditions is directly related to the degree of universality achieved. It is clear that the environment in which he grew up had enormous importance for Pirandello. This can be seen from the simple fact that much of the material for his writing is taken from Sicily. But one can further agree with Sciascia that there are clear parallels between his philosophy and characteristic features of the Sicilian behavioural pattern. **"The Truth"** is an example of this. The main character Tarallà has been accused of the murder of his wife and makes no attempt to deny his guilt. The important question however, is his motive. If it was a crime passionel, caused by his discovery of her infidelity, the penalty will only be a couple of years in prison, but a lengthy prison sentence awaits him if it was a case of premeditated murder. Tarallà, who has no understanding of such legal subtleties, naïvely admits that he committed the murder not because he had discovered his wife's infidelity, which he had known about for a long time, but because her lover's wife had blazoned the news abroad to others in the town. In this way Tarallà's spotless reputation was defiled, and he was forced to act in accordance with the rules of his environment. By killing his wife he has removed the blemish from his "honour". When the judge has heard this explanation, Tarallà is sentenced to 12 years in jail.—The most important part of this impressive story is Tarallà's long confession, which he is convinced will gain him an acquittal. With penetrating psychological insight Pirandello has given us a brilliant portrait of the individual who defends his behavioural reflexes with warmth, simple eloquence and complete confidence in the moral solidarity of the society in which he lives. He is a complete victim of his assumptions, his basic beliefs, for his actions are conditioned reflexes rather than willed actions. There is a clear connection between the Sicilian behavioural norms, which are solely concerned with externals—the only thing that matters is form, the surface, while substance is unimportant, a matter for the individual to arrange as he thinks fit—and Pirandello's conviction that personality in the usual meaning of the word does not exist: people put on masks to conceal the chaos beneath and everyone constructs his own mask (this is a theme that Pirandello did not exploit until he began to write drama and it plays no role in his *best* narrative prose). This connection does not constitute sufficient grounds for establishing a causal relationship and maintaining that Pirandello's conception of the problem of identity derives from his childhood surroundings.—Much time was to pass before the idea of the personality as an assumed mask became a determining element in his work. In fact this did not occur until Pirandello was more than 50 years of age. By that time he had been using Sicilian material in his short stories for many years without, however, using Sicilian concepts of honour to further a particular philosophical thesis. There is, moreover, one important difference between the sociological pattern and Pirandello's ideas. For him the problem of identity, as it manifests itself after 1910, is part of a total view of life, the main component of which is the idea of the inacessibility of reality. Reality cannot be apprehended and each of us creates his own reality and his own personality. This point of primary importance has no connection with Sicily; the local

formalism certainly does not exclude the idea of a tangible reality, since the real world is deeply rooted for Tarallà, and facts are under no circumstances to be questioned.

For these reasons it is difficult to see any basic influence operative in the behavioural structure with which he grew up. Not until about 1910 when his ideas on reality had matured did Pirandello draw his inspiration from an area of experience with which he was thoroughly acquainted. Sicilian ideas about honour could be used when the time came, but they are not his point of departure. That is why **"Truth"** and, for example, **"Certain Considerations"** (**"Certi obblighi"**) 1912, which treats a similar problem, were written at this time.

"Big Swallow and Little Swallow", 1913, is a charming story about two foreigners, who are apparently not married, but who spend their holidays every year in a small town in Tuscany. The inhabitants of the town are very sympathetic towards them and have christened them Big Swallow and Little Swallow, because he is very large, she very small, and they fly away at the end of the summer.

The two foreigners come every summer for six years. There is something poetic and secret about the irregularity of their situation and their faithful love. They bring a fairy-tale atmosphere to the little Tuscan town, and its inhabitants, who derive a kind of strength from their ideal relationship, feel sad when they do not come in the seventh year. It is not until late in the summer that Little Swallow comes—together with her boring legal husband. She is very ill and has come to die in the house, where she had been happy for six successive summers.

The story is written in an extraordinarily attractive style—with a light but sure hand. It deals with the subject of double existence, but it is difficult to classify together with other of Pirandello's stories. The important point about it is not that it is an example of a social masque, but its poetically ideal atmosphere, which is continually controlled and kept in check by the sympathetic but matter-of-fact narrator. The result is a bitter-sweet humoresque, in which romantic love is permitted only a brief span of life. The narrator finds it sad that love is doomed to defeat, but this was a foregone conclusion, and the case in question is in itself so unusual that it can almost be considered as a fairy-tale.

"Since It's Not Raining", 1913, is a highly amusing story about Pirandello's native town. Every December a statue of the Madonna is taken in procession from its usual church to the cathedral, whence, after a stay of a certain length, it returns home with pomp and circumstance. But the Madonna can only be brought home on a Sunday and at that time of the year there is a good deal of rain on Sicily, which means that it often has to spend rather a long time at the cathedral waiting for a fine Sunday. Its prolonged stay at the cathedral is a source of much bother and expense to the Chapter, and the story describes one of the most disastrous cases, when the Virgin plagued the poor cannons for eleven whole weeks.

There is much satire at the expense of the clergy in Pirandello's work and it is frequently to be found in stories of
high comedy, among others the two stories that together
with **"Since It Is Not Raining"** were given the subtitle
"Clerical Vestments in Montelusa" ("Tonache di Montelusa = Agrigento"). The two stories are **"Meola's Defence"**, 1909, and **"The Fortunate Ones"**, 1911. Anti-
clericalism is a constant feature of his work, and nearly all
the priests who appear in it are unsympathetic or comic.
His relationship to the official religion is clearly defined.
He does not believe in Catholicism or any other organized
religion, and he seems to have given up his childhood
faith at an early point in his life. There is no trace of a
crisis in his first collection of poems (1889) or later. [In
his study *L'uomo segreto: Vita e croci di Luigi Pirandello,* second edition, 1944] Nardelli relates an anecdote which
purports to describe how as a boy Pirandello came into
conflict with the church and religion. It is taken from the
short story **"The Little Madonna"**, 1914, which suggests
that it is autobiographical. Pirandello shows great respect
for other people's religious feelings, even when they appear within the framework of the official religion. Strong
conviction deserves respect in itself, as is shown in the
story **"Faith"**, 1914.

In the years immediately after 1910 Pirandello wrote a
group of short stories which, without having any particular artistic value, are important for the understanding of
his basic ideas. These ideas were already fully developed,
but were not to receive their authentic artistic expression
until the dramas. The most important of these stories is
"Stefano Giogli, One and Two", 1909, **"The Answer"**,
1912, and **"The Trap"**, 1912.

"Stefano Giogli, One and Two" is of historical importance in being the first of Pirandello's works in which
relativism is the major theme. Stefano is aware that we do
not see things as they are, but merely form some kind of
picture of them. At the same time he knows that the chaos
that prevails inside him, in his own supposed personality,
is no less a fiction than the way in which he perceives his
surroundings. [In a footnote, the critic adds: "The connection between these two levels cannot be emphasized too
strongly. Each of the others views me in his own way, and
the many different views arouse doubt as to the existence
of the personality as an entity in the usual meaning of the
word; is this existence not a postulate, a fiction? Thus the
step is taken from an external problem, the way in which
relativism complicates existence, to an inner problem, the
dissolution of the personality."] The story documents that
the two themes are, for Pirandello, very closely connected. Stefano falls head over heels in love with Lucietta. He
is obsessed by her and can think of nothing else during the
three months that precede their wedding. Then his brain
slowly begins to function again, and he discovers that he
has married a girl who has not the slightest understanding
of the relativity of her own ideas. Lucia is completely
unable to imagine that what she thinks might not be totally
correct and real, indeed, far righter than what anybody
else might happen to think. She is incredibly opinionated
and has formed an impression of Stefano which it is impossible for him to change. He can, of course, see that the

ridiculous individual his wife has constructed has no connection with "reality", but what is he to do? Logical argument makes no impression on Lucia, and he himself is not
sure that he knows what he is like; besides, since he loves
his wife, dare he run the risk of destroying the picture of
him she has created? It is the picture she loves, and if it
collapsed, what would happen to her feelings for him?
The result is that Stefano becomes jealous of the imaginary fool his wife is in love with—that is jealous of his
doppelgänger. Pirandello did not include this story in the
edition of his collected short stories, and its first appearance was in a posthumously published volume in 1937.
This may have been because of its modest artistic value,
or the reason may have been that it too obviously foreshadows the novel *One, None, A Hundred Thousand.*—
The story is completely divorced from reality; the ideas
remain mere ideas and the two main characters are abstractions, not living people. The situation in which they
are placed is artificial and unspontaneous, because it has
so evidently been based on an idea.

"The Evil Spirit", 1910, is related to **"Stefano Giogli"**
but lacks its philosophical expositions. It deals with a man
who is honest and generous, but who is fortunate in such
a peculiar way that his fellow-citizens come to regard him
as an unscrupulous trickster. Later he becomes the victim
of a malevolent stroke of fortune which places him in a
number of situations which can only strengthen the others'
unfavourable opinion of him. He is ascribed a personality
that he does not have but can do nothing to escape this
personality, and the story ends with an account of yet
another chance incident in which his evil spirit plays yet
another malicious trick on him. At the point of transition
between two periods in his writing this story combines
two of Pirandello's main theses—chance and relativity—
which characterize respectively the period before and the
period after 1910. This combination is also to be found in
other of his works.

In a story of a quality considerably superior to that of the
two that have just been discussed—**"The Diploma"**,
1911—the theme is once again what other people think
about us, but here Pirandello is not directly concerned
with the concept of relativity. The main character's problem is not, in fact, that other people have an incorrect
view of his personality, but that they consider him to be
in possession of "il malocchio", the evil eye. This is a
form of superstition that is far from extinct in Italy.—He
saves himself, like Spatolino in **"The Tabernacle"**, but
consciously and after mature consideration, by exploiting
his tragic situation and winning people's respect through
the fear they feel of him.

In **"Stefano Giogli"** and similar stories the theme is the
reality which other people force on us, their idea of a
given person who is unable to recognize himself in the
versions of himself with which he is confronted. But, as
has been mentioned, a weakness of the person who feels
himself misinterpreted is that he is unable to give a better
description of his own character; his self-portrait is no
less arbitrary, a fact that Stefano is quite aware of; the
personality is susceptible of many interpretations and con-

sists of heterogeneous elements which can never be made the object of an exhaustive description. A two-way movement can, therefore, be observed: 1) other people misunderstand one from outside—each in his own individual fashion; 2) from inside only chaos and mutually contradictory elements are to be observed, and this strengthens the misconceptions of others while it makes self-defence impossible.—The theme of **"The Answer"** is the connection between the various external interpretations and the inner contradictory elements. Marino believes that he has never completely understood Anita because on a certain occasion she suddenly turns out to be completely different from what he had imagined. But he has merely been guilty of an inadequate interpretation of her character; he has isolated a part of her personality and believed that this part constituted the whole. He has no reason to feel disappointment or indignation when she suddenly seems to be different, for she fulfils her new role with the same sincerity as that with which she fulfilled her previous role. It is just as much *her*.

Other short stories are variations on similar themes, for example **"The Journey"**, 1910, **"Bobbio's Ave Maria"**, 1912, **"In the Maelstrom"**, 1913, and **"The Train has Whistled"**, 1914. Chance and the problem of identity are combined in **"The Journey"**. Adriana Braggi has spent her entire life confined to a provincial Sicilian town. Here she has grown up and married. Illness, that is chance, is the cause of a journey she makes—first to Palermo and later to Naples and other towns. On this journey she discovers herself and becomes aware of a potential that would never have appeared if she had stayed at home. Before she dies, she has time to experience a passionate love affair.—The remarkable thing about her experiences is that this time the depths of the soul do not appear as something threatening, as a disturbing and heart-breaking chaos. The discovery of a new dimension of the soul is described as a sudden insight, an immediate and stimulating contact with infinity, which can, therefore, be attained not only via nature but also via instinct: "and at this breath of air a great wonder-filled stillness made her mind expand enormously; and as if a light from other worlds (cieli) had suddenly been lit in the inconceivable emptiness, she felt, at that moment, close to eternity, and with an infinite clarity she felt conscious of everything, the infinity that conceals itself in the depth of the mystery of the soul, and she felt that she had lived—for a moment, for that moment, she had been eternal".

In **"Bobbio's Ave Maria"** the main character discovers that without knowing it he bears within himself elements of the past, fragments of childhood experiences, which have buried themselves deep in his personality and reveal themselves on certain occasions. **"In the Maelstrom"** was later to yield material for one of Pirandello's last plays, *You Don't Know How*, 1934. The theme here is the sexual instinct which can suddenly take control of a human being. One's normal behaviour, the personality that everybody (including oneself) has assumed to be permanently established can be broken down, irresistibly and without warning, by an uncontrollable impulse.—In **"The Train has Whistled"** Belluca suddenly becomes a new person

because his imaginaion has been awoken. Until this moment his life has been that of a slave's, and his constant preoccupation with finding food for the people he is responsible for has not left him a free moment. One day a chance sound, a train-whistle, suddenly penetrates his consciousness and he revolts against his inhuman existence.

Chance and change of personality appear again in **"By Oneself"** as cause and effect, while the presence of natural elements give the story a metaphysical perspective. Matteo Sinagra has always been well-off and popular, but a sudden and inexplicable catastrophe lays his life in ruins, and afterwards he feels his helplessness. Not only has he suddenly changed in the eyes of his closest relatives, but he himself has the feeling that he has changed totally, both physically and intellectually. He chooses to commit suicide and to save the survivors trouble he goes to the churchyard (the title) to do so. On the way he picks up a stone and puts it in his pocket. It is a fragment of the universe, and he inhales the air as no other person could, as "living, present, vibrating (fremente) eternity".

The idea of existence as a contrast between movement and form is formulated in **"The Trap"**. The existence lived by the natural elements is incessant movement; mankind's life is form, a form that stiffens more and more and ends in death.

> Life is the wind, life is the sea, life is the fire; not the earth, which becomes a shell and takes on form.

> All form is death.

> All that is removed from the condition of suffering and stiffens amidst this ever-glowing, uniform stream is death.

> We are all beings that have been caught in a trap, taken out of the stream that never stops, formed to die.

Here the connection between various elements of Pirandello's philosophy is clear. Things and, therefore, the personality are not susceptible of cognition, and the reason is to be found in the constant movement that is the main principle of existence. Man consists of two component parts, mind and body, and the latter slowly decays. What happens to the mind is less clear; it is always unknowable, but does not degenerate in the same way as the body. From other sources it appears that it is preserved and returns to its point of origin, merges once again with the lifestream. It has already been mentioned that in this loosely connected complex of ideas attention should be directed not to the synthesis, but to certain fundamental elements. The attempt at building up a logical scheme of things is less important. What is fundamental is the idea of chaos, the impossibility of forming an unequivocal view of oneself and things, that is the world that surrounds one. And beyond this world the existence of another world is assumed. One can, of course, not *know* anything about this world, but it is possible to achieve a connection with it through instinct and, especially, nature. And as a philosophical common denominator for these things, for extra-terrestrial existence, for nature, for oneself the concept "flusso", the lifestream that embraces everything, is used.—The relationship between the individual ideas is of varying intensity; close between relativism and identity, loose between these ideas and the form-movement concept, which is formulated far less clearly, appears far less frequently and does not have the central placing ascribed to it by [the noted Italian drama critic Adriano] Tilgher.

Olga Ragusa (essay date 1973)

SOURCE: "Pirandello's Haunted House," in *Studies in Short Fiction,* Vol. X, No. 3, Summer, 1973, pp. 235–42.

[*An Italian-born American educator and critic specializing in Italian literature, Ragusa is the author of* Narrative and Drama: Essays in Modern Italian Literature from Verga to Pasolini *(1976) as well as book-length studies on Pirandello, Giovanni Verga, and Alessandro Manzoni. In this essay, she explicates Pirandello's ghost story "Granella's House" as a commentary on the limits of reason and science.*]

Richard Kelly's recent "The Haunted House of Bulwer-Lytton" (*Studies in Short Fiction,* Vol. 8) calls to mind Pirandello's **"La casa del Granella,"** a story first published in 1905 and which later became part of Pirandello's short story *summa, Novelle per un anno.* It appears to have been translated into English twice, once with the title of **"Granella's House"** and the second time as **"The Haunted House."** Aside from inclusion in collections of Pirandello stories published in the United States and England, it also found its way into *Strange to Tell,* an anthology subtitled "Stories of the Marvelous and Mysterious," edited by Marjorie Fischer and Rolfe Humphries.

As the second English title reveals, **"La casa del Granella"** is a ghost or mystery story with at least some of the conventional ingredients of the genre. But early as it came in his career, it already bears the peculiar Pirandellian stamp, and it is therefore a ghost story with a difference. Like Bulwer-Lytton's "The Haunted and the Haunters" it shows its author to have been conversant with the spiritualist movement of the mid- and late nineteenth century, but in contrast to Bulwer-Lytton's rationalist examination of the supernatural with the consequent dissolution of the mystery and the actual and figurative laying of the ghost, it proclaims the defeat of science and recognizes the irreducible presence in life and in the experience of life, of the unexplainable and the mysterious.

The story begins with a metaphorical direction sign that alerts the reader to the presence of a meaning beneath the surface of plot and characterization. To the actions of a mouse who has fallen into a trap and unaware of the finality of its plight is desperately trying to get out, is contrasted the behavior of men who have recourse to the law, know that they are stepping into a trap and are yet able to present an impassive face to the world, while all the time inside them their feelings go scurrying about madly, worse than the mouse.

The setting of the scene that follows is a lawyer's reception room in a small town in Sicily, specifically Agrigento, Pirandello's birthplace, as we come to learn later. It is hot, the room is crowded; and every time the door opens, lawyer Zummo's prospective clients surge forward, then disappointedly sink back, as the chosen one is admitted while the rest must return to their extenuating wait in the shadow of dusty bookcases overloaded with "old litigations and proceedings, the wrack and ruin of so many once happy families." To make things worse, Zummo's ten-year old son has on this particular morning invaded the room and is busy harassing those who are waiting with needling questions and impertinent remarks.

Three individuals stand out from the rest: they show no sign of impatience, and to their neighbors' surprise and discomfiture three times already they have permitted newcomers to take their turn. The husband, gloomy, almost funereal in appearance, is wearing an old frock-coat just out of moth balls. The wife, "stout, thriving, with a full bust and a whiskered red face," flashes looks of "defiant, self-satisfied stupidity" about her. While the daughter, pale, emaciated, squinting like her father, sits hunched forward and distraught like him, both of them looking ready to keel over were it not for the mother's amplitude between them holding them up. Three early Pirandello grotesques, reminiscent, for instance, of his portrayal of Batta Malagna or of the *vedova* Pescatore in *Il fu Mattia Pascal (The Late Mattia Pascal).* "What disaster could have befallen them?" asks the impersonal narrator. "What persecution were they subjected to? What violent death was crying to be avenged? Or was financial ruin staring them in the face?" The answer to the last question at least is negative, for the mother is generously bejewelled.

Around these three figures Pirandello has created the space that sets them off as within a magic circle. Later in his work that same space will isolate Signor Ponza and Signora Frola from the chorus of small-town gossips around them, and will encircle the Six Characters, keeping their life-in-art inviolate. In Zummo's waiting room the other clients try to push the pestering boy in the direction of the three, but he is unwilling to get close to them, repulsed by their mournful gloom and perhaps even by something else—but if there is a something else, it lies at this point tightly encapsulated within the normal suspense of story telling that Pirandello has so far created.

The tempo of the story changes abruptly as the three are admitted to the office, and dialogue replaces the narrative voice. The second part of the story is almost exclusively dramatic encounter, and Zummo shows himself at once to belong to that group of hyper-active, emotionally volatile, intellectually alert, restless and irascible men that are part and parcel of Pirandello's portrayal of the Sicilian world. Mention of only one other such instance will have to suffice here: the unforgettable *don* Lollò Zirafa in **"La giara"** (**"The Jar"**).

The case the three are bringing to the lawyer concerns the summons for breach of contract and defamation with which the landlord Granella has served them because they moved out of a house they had rented and paid for when they discovered that it was inhabited by ghosts. "By what?" Zummo interrupts incredulously. "By ghosts, yes sir!" the wife repeats defiantly, waving her hands in the air. Zummo's indignation knows no bounds: people who believe in ghosts belong in insane asylums and not in a lawyer's office. Suddenly he remembers that it is after his lunch hour, that he is tired and hungry. But the three won't let him go. They surround him and force him to listen to the details of the persecution to which they have been subjected: chairs moving about the room of their own accord, objects hurled through the house as though by invisible hands, cupboards moaning and straining, mocking laughter issuing from dark corners. "Playful ghosts," Zummo muses, showing that for all his scepticism he knows something of the subdivisions of the species. "Playful!" the wife retorts indignantly. "Not playful at all! Infernal!" The upshot is that at the end of an hour's arguing, Zummo capitulates. Contrary to what the Author does when he sends the Six Characters packing, Zummo agrees to become the Piccirilli's spokesman. Attracted by the novelty and the speciousness of the case, as he himself describes it, he will take up the Piccirilli's defense: "You understand, of course, that I cannot accept your story of the ghosts. Hallucinations, old wives tales. But I'm considering the legal side of the question. . . ."

The legal side of the question takes Zummo further than it takes Judge D'Andrea, for instance, who in **"La patente" ("The License")** is faced by quite as disconcerting a case, this one involving a form of primitive magic: the evil eye. In spite of the pressures that are brought to bear on him, Judge D'Andrea remains on the side of reason, interpreting the phenomena he witnesses as the results of superstition and psychological coercion and aberration, not of the supernatural. Zummo's mind, instead, wanders immediately to childhood memories, to the irrational: ghost stories he had been told as a child and that had frightened him. But to believe in ghosts, he now reasons with himself, one must first believe in the immortality of the soul. And does he or doesn't he believe in it? When, as a matter of fact, has he ever given these problems serious thought? No more than anyone else does he have time to think about death: "Even science stops at the threshold of death, as though death did not exist and one should not worry about it. Science says: 'You're still here; concern yourselves with being alive. The lawyer should worry about being a lawyer, the engineer about being an engineer . . .'." And rebelling at what we recognize as a general emphasis on role to the exclusion of self, it is with relief that Zummo welcomes the possibility of the existence of ghosts: how narrow his life in that provincial town had become! How wasted are his energies among the petty concerns of his fellow-citizens! And so the ghosts that are now knocking at his office door fill him not with apprehension but with glee. Through them he is beginning to understand things that his colleagues don't even know exist! The ghosts whisper to him insinuatingly:

"We're here, too, you know. You, men of reason, materialists who believe only in what you can touch, you don't want to bother with us, do you? You don't want to worry about death? But here we come, gaily, from the kingdom of the dead, knocking at the doors of those who are still alive, making fun of you, making chairs and tables dance around the room, frightening your clients, laughing at them from the depths of some old wardrobe, puzzling you today, my learned lawyer, and puzzling tomorrow a body of equally learned judges who will have to try a most novel case. . . ."

In preparing his case, Zummo spends more time on the literature of the occult than on his law books. The latter have quickly convinced him that he will have to prove the actual existence of the ghosts, that only if the landlord can be considered responsible for having rented a house unfit for human habitation can the Piccirillis win their case. He applies himself with boundless zeal. He first reads "a history of spiritualism from the origins of mythology to the present," and then a work on the wonders wrought by fakirs. After that there follows, pell mell, the whole international roster of writers on the supernatural, all of whom Pirandello mentions by name: Crookes, the British physicist who in the '70's and '80's estranged the scientific community by his research into mediumship; Aksakov, the Russian statesman who translated Swedenborg and conducted experimental seances with his friends; the professors of chemistry and zoology at the University of St. Petersburg (Pirandello names the latter of the two: Wagner); Zoellner, professor of astrophysics at Leipzig and enthusiastic exponent of spiritualism; Janet, professor of philosophy at the Sorbonne, follower of Victor Cousin, anti-positivist and anti-materialist; Rochas, ex-army officer and administrator at the Ecole Polytechnique, who conducted experiments on psychical phenomena and wrote extensively of parapsychological subjects; Richet, professor of physiology at the Medical School of the Sorbonne, founder of the *Annales des Sciences Psychiques,* coiner of the term "metapsychique" (the French equivalent of parapsychology), and later winner of a Nobel Prize in physiology; Morselli, anthropologist, neurologist and psychiatrist, author among other works of the 1906 *Psicologia e spiritismo*; and Lombroso, the famous criminologist and psychiatrist, author of the controversial *Genio e follia* (1864), whom Pirandello had already had occasion to cite in his 1893 essay, "Arte e coscienza d'oggi."

What amazes Zummo and fires him with uncontrollable enthusiasm is that what he had been in the habit of dismissing as old wives tales he now finds supported, defended, and rationally explained by reputable scientists, educated as he has been in accordance with the tenets of Positivism. But what is characteristic for him—as well as for Pirandello—in the attraction he feels for the new field of knowledge he has just discovered, is the total absence of frivolity. He is in deadly earnest, convinced that he has found a clue to the ultimate mystery, death, that he has found an answer to what he calls Hamlet's "terrible question," *to be or not to be.* Thus of what might be considered the three components of the science of the occult—spiritualism, theosophy, and the study of psychic or psychological phenomena—it is the first, spiritualism or, to be more precise, spiritism, that has the strongest appeal for him. This is borne out by two details in the story: Zummo's initial rejection of the "biological explanation" for psychic phenomena in favor of the "metaphysical hypothesis"; and his invoking of Allen Kardech as the new messiah [in a footnote, the critic adds: "Allen Kardech was the name taken by Denizard Rivail (1804-1869) after his conversion to spiritualism. In his *Livre des esprits* (1857) he laid the foundations of his doctrine, further exemplified in the pages of the long-lived *La Revue spirite*."] in the course of his impassioned peroration in court, which loses him the case but wins him the great moral victory to which he aspires:

> He spoke of Allan Kardech as of a new messiah. He defined spiritism as the new religion of humanity. He said that science with its solid but cold instruments, with its too rigorous formalism had overwhelmed nature; that the tree of life nourished artificially by science had lost its leaves and grown sterile, or else was bearing small and wrinkled fruits that shrivelled up, tasting of ashes and poison because no warmth of faith matured them. But now, behold, the mystery was beginning to unclose its dark gates: tomorrow they would stand wide open! Meanwhile through this first narrow slit uncertain and fearful shadows were appearing to reveal to mankind in its dismay and anguished longing the world beyond: strange lights, strange signs. . . .

But before this *dénouement* is reached—reminiscent in its spectacular *coup de scéne* of the court scene in *Il turno* (*The Merry-Go-Round of Love*)—Pirandello has had occasion to weave yet another cultural and ideological clarification into the texture of his fiction. Zummo's proud rejection of the "biological explanation" had been followed by his unsettling discovery that *signorina* Piccirilli was a "portentous" medium. Therefore the appearance of the ghosts in the house was not Granella's fault but the Piccirillis'. Undismayed, however, Zummo turns this defeat into an advantage for his passion: he is now in a position to witness the phenomena he had so far only read about. With merciless single-mindedness he forces the Piccirillis to engage in experiment after experiment, subjecting them to the very persecution from which they had tried to escape. Pirandello underlines the irony of the situation: while Zummo exults at having discovered proof of the immortality of the soul, the Piccirillis, *terre à terre* in their faith, having never doubted the immortality of "their tormented, paltry little souls," are overcome with guilt at what to them is "commerce with demons." The established religions, in other words, looked upon this growth of interlocking para-scientific endeavors and beliefs with even greater suspicion and revulsion than science itself.

With the trial scene the story that had begun in the lawyer's waiting room comes to an end. The Piccirillis have served their function and can now move back into their anonymity. But Granella, technically the winner, is left standing center-stage. He has been rewarded by the law but humiliated by that public opinion that Zummo, lawyer turned magician, bearer of charisma, has succeeded in convincing of the existence of "something beyond." The

coda to the story generalizes the experience and asks the Pirandellian epistemological question, "Fiction? Reality?"

As in all good ghost stories the reader is now taken into the haunted house itself. To hearsay and report will be added direct, personal experience. The agent of the experience is Granella. He has won his case, but the reputation of his house has been effectively ruined. Not even the old servant who has been with him all her life has the courage to return to it. It is up to him to show that the house is *not* haunted, and he challenges the ghosts derisively: just let them show their faces! Contrary to what is often the case with haunted houses, this house is in an urban and not a country setting, and though it gives the impression of being solitary, situated as it is in an open space with an abandoned shed opposite, it is actually but a few steps from one of the town's most populous districts. The location is determined on one level of Pirandello's creative strategy by the exigencies of the plot whose thrust is towards a direct encounter between Granella and Zummo in which the roles of winner and loser will be inverted. And on a different level, by his recurrent concern with the problem of "conscience"—a particularly difficult concept to translate but which we could perhaps for the sake of clarity subdivide into its dual aspects of soul and consciousness.

For what happens now happens within the walls of Granella's house, but it happens there exclusively within his consciousness. He has a few pieces of furniture brought to the empty house and that evening, after a leisurely stroll through the neighborhood to make sure that everyone knows where he is going, he retires for the night. As Zummo at an earlier juncture in the story had remembered the ghost stories he heard as a child, so Granella at this point cannot completely dispel the impressions made on him at the trial just a short time before: the sudden general turn-about-face, the solid phalanx of new believers who had excluded him from their ranks. Neither the deserted square in front of the house, nor the single street lamp flickering in the darkness, nor yet the flame of his candle wavering as though someone were blowing on it, reassures him. The empty rooms echo to his step. The monstrous shadow of his body plays upon the walls. As he sets about making his bed, his heart beats faster and he jumps at every sound heard or imagined: a knock at the door or the bedpost bumping against the wall? the flight of a bat or a hissing in his ear? an enormous white tongue appearing from behind a door or a roll of wall paper unwinding on the floor? Suddenly he can endure the alternation of fear and self-reassurance no longer and, having made sure that out in the square no one is spying on him, he flees from the house.

But it so happens—a chance circumstance which has all the flavor of the haphazard chain of events in a Boccaccio novella—that he was not unobserved. In an urban setting there is always a good chance that someone is wakeful at night. Word of what has happened reaches Zummo, and at once he sees an opportunity for having the verdict reversed: in fact, he will use Granella himself as a witness for the Piccirillis! The trap is laid for the following night. With a group of supporters Zummo takes up his post in the abandoned shed. It is not even midnight before the door opens and Granella, in shirt sleeves, his shoes in his hands, holding up the trousers he had been in too great a hurry to button, sneaks out. Zummo's moment of triumph is at hand. But triumph as what? As lawyer or as exponent of a new faith? It is as lawyer that he gathered around him the handful of companions who are now sneering and scoffing at Granella. But it is as proselytizer that he invests him: "And now, you idiot, do you believe in the immortality of the soul? Justice in its blindness gave you the verdict. But now *you* have opened your eyes. Tell me. What did you see?" With the same economy with which he was to end *Sei personaggi*—"Fiction? Reality?"—Pirandello ends **"La casa del Granella"**: "But poor Granella, crying and trembling, was unable to answer."

The ghost question remains unsolved. Are there or aren't there ghosts? Was Granella frightened by an actual apparition, as Zummo's question would seem to imply? Or was it auto-suggestion that affected him, as a rehearsal of the phenomena Pirandello describes for his first night in the haunted house would indicate? And is there really any difference between the two? In the post-Kantian universe is what we imagine any less real than what we "know"?

No doubt one of the reasons, if not *the* reason, why Pirandello was attracted to the area of the occult was the tension set up in its theoretical foundations and in the experience of its practitioners between fact and fiction. If Bulwer-Lytton sought, as Richard Kelly concludes, "to rationalize that indefinable something," to bring "the supernatural within the boundaries of the believable," then Pirandello sought instead to undermine the solidity of the rational and to enlarge the boundaries of the believable so that it could include the supernatural without it having to be reduced to anything else. In the course of the story, the image of the mouse falling into the trap has been extended to the Piccirillis falling into the trap of legal disputation, to Zummo falling into a trap of his own making, and to Granella falling into the trap that awaits every man, the awareness to the existence of "that indefinable something" that scientific probing has not yet been able to dispel.

Douglas Radcliff-Umstead   (essay date 1978)

SOURCE: "The Jests of Love and Death," in *The Mirror of Our Anguish: A Study of Luigi Pirandello's Narrative Writings,* Fairleigh Dickinson University Press, 1978, pp. 108–22.

[*An American educator and critic, Radcliff-Umstead is the author and editor of numerous studies of Romance literature. In the following excerpt, he analyzes some of Pirandello's later short stories, to which the critic attributes a distinctly mythic quality.*]

Several of Pirandello's final novelle—written during the years of his most intense theatrical activity—reveal a desire to evade everyday reality in a higher plane of experience. What was examined in earlier tales like

"Quand'ero matto" of 1901 as an escape into insanity became a mythic realm that the novelistic characters longed to enter. The dream world of these later tales recalls the higher reality that the contemporary school of French surrealists wished to explore. Like the poet Paul Eluard, the Italian author endeavored to recreate the death of the ego in a mirror (Eluard's *"mirroir sans tain"*), which absorbs the conventional personality image. Along with the surrealist school Pirandello accepted the coexistence of contradictory entities within the human psyche. Just as the surrealists turned to the clinical research of Charcot on hysteria, Pirandello had earlier found confirmation in the theories of Marchesini and Binet on the contradictions and multiplicity of the individual personality. Pirandello's preoccupation with fortuitous events resembles the "objective hazard" of surrealists like André Breton, who probed the apparently inexplicable forces that determine a certain course of events. The Italian writer shared with the surrealists a total distrust for logical order, which tried to arrest the vital flux. Pirandello wished to investigate how the secret life of the instincts could invade consciousness and produce a dreamlike state while destroying the ordinary perceptions of time and space. The writer hoped to re-create that marvelous movement when the psyche would be displaced in opposite directions at once. Through the instantaneous spasm of the marvelous, Pirandello aimed at reaching those moments of lapse when persons were restored to possession of an authentic inner life. Although the titles of his late tales deceptively relate to his earlier stories of conventional reality by referring to concrete objects like a commonplace flower or to everyday occurrences like a visit, the Sicilian writer was pursuing a journey across strange vistas that could not be predicated on the structures of chronological time and where the psyche had to undergo a constant experience of disintegration. The frightening realm of the late novelle is one in which the public self becomes submerged in the struggle between the waking ego and the no longer suppressed instincts. But in his effort to create a mythic representation of the conflict between the marionette of Culture and the anarchical beast of Nature that is fought in the mind of every person, Pirandello differed fundamentally from the surrealists in that he never practiced automatic writing. Conscious rational control is evident in almost every line he ever wrote. The oneiric visions of his later novelle are captured in a style over which the author exercised full mastery.

Pirandello's desire to fashion myths for modern times reflected the mood of Italian writers during the Fascist era, when political reality was so oppressive and demoralizing that a literature of fantasy alone could effectively elude government censorship. Surrealism in Italy possessed a political dimension that was unnecessary in France, where writers rebelled against bourgeois values but did not have to seek refuge from the agents of a dictatorship. Political necessity compelled many Italian writers to veil sense with non-sense, to cross that literary frontier which, as Freud observed, would arrive at "wit": a frontier where, as Lacan was later to mention, "man tempts his very destiny when he derides the signifier." Among the authors of this special wit between the two world wars was Pirandello's friend

Massimo Bontempelli (1878-1960), editor of the cosmopolitan review '900. In tales like "La Scacchiera davanti allo Specchio" ("The Chessboard before the Mirror," 1922) Bontempelli experimented with a style that he called "realismo magico"; in that work persons become objects and objects take on human personality during a journey through the mystery world behind a looking glass. Magic realism begins with a situation of conventional reality that is steadily demolished as the fictitious characters carry their absolutely logical designs to absurd outcomes. Bontempelli aimed at creating fables of persons imprisoned by time and death. The atmosphere of miracle that suffused the semi-realistic, semi-fantastic universe of Bontempelli's writings also came to characterize the borderland between daily reality and hallucination in the later Pirandellian tales.

The discovery of a terrifying power removes the protagonist of **"Soffio"** (**"A Breath,"** 1931) from the everyday world and transforms him into a fatal instrument, perhaps Fate itself. The tale has all the disturbing force of Kafka's *Metamorphosis* as it recounts the protagonist's shocked awareness of his ability to cause death merely by joining his thumb and index finger and blowing lightly on them. This novella is in the first person, and the astonished narrator relates his initial lack of comprehension on discovering his death-dealing might after he first made the fatal gesture and blew the lethal breath upon an acquaintance who had just told him about the sudden death of a mutual friend. Again and again the protagonist repeated the identical gesture, with the same deadly results, until the newspapers declared that a mysterious epidemic was ranging through the city and decimating the population. Afraid for his sanity, the protagonist stopped his experiments, and the city returned to normal. After two weeks the narrator decided to conduct a crucial test. With the detachment of a scientist practicing eugenics, he chose as the subject of his experiment a deformed child, who died with a smile on his face after the fatal breath touched him. By then the narrator understood that he had become Death, impartiality killing persons without any feeling of hatred. The situation of this tale seems a logical conclusion to Pirandello's preoccupation with the relationship between life and death. Death figures as the force of negation because it is the persistent negative power residing in being itself. To demonstrate his fairness, the protagonist performed the gesture on himself by standing before a store mirror. Here the motif of the mirror portends self-annihilation, for the narrator's image vanished forever after the mortal breath blew across the glass surface. The individual consciousness, on mirroring itself, has passed through reflection to complete dissolution. This novella, which began in the matter-of-fact tone realistic narration, moves from relating the protagonist's uneasy recognition of his deadly gift to a nightmare atmosphere when he became pure disembodied spirit. His frantic distress, rendered all the more effective by the first-person technique with at times anguished repetitions of forms of verbs of urgency like *scappare* (to run away), diminished only after his spirit floated away to the countryside where he could introduce Death as a gentle force. While the physical self has crossed the line to disintegration, outer nature remains. Arrival at cosmic unity must result in total dispersion. A

yearning for annihilation dwells at the center of Pirandellian art. Its paradox is that absorption into the cosmos acts as a form of re-creation, and absolute indetermination appears not a menace but a temptation. In this tale as in most of the mythic novelle, a language of shock predominates, especially as expressed by adjectival past participles like *sbalordito* (astonished), *alterato* (changed), *annichilito* (annihilated), *respinto* (pushed back), which delineate the changes that suddenly overcome the protagonist. Despite his ever-increasing anxiety, the narrator kept seeking rational explanations for the epidemic he seemed to cause; like most Pirandellian characters, he resisted becoming an excluded one. Here the signifying function of language undergoes a deliberate crisis that parallels the physical disintegration as language moves toward non-sense in the narrator's bewildered voice. Like Poe and Maupassant in their epidemic tales, Pirandello searches here the mystery between life and death.

Death as a floating away into nothingness is the message of the novella **"Di Sera, un geranio"** (**"At Evening, a Geranium"**) of 1934, which so transcends the conventional sense of narrative as to acquire an evanescence of style as the disembodied spirit wanders across a familiar realm that is rapidly becoming remote. A man who feared a dangerous operation has died. To die is exactly to lose contact with the material objects that go into the construction of life. The bewilderment of the spirit floating around the death chamber is shown in the adverbs of place like *qua* (here), *giù* (down), *là* (there), which establish a staccato rhythm for the forcible flight of the consciousness. As a sentient form it used to find identification in thought and in the outer world but never with the body, toward which it feels rancor in death. Living consists in the immaterial flash of the thinking process and in the images that others project upon an individual. Dying is a dissolution into formlessness, the fading away of all constructs. The structures of life that the mind and the senses try to grasp—like a clock, a picture hanging on the wall, the rose color of a lamp—were all illusions that must vanish into death's nothingness. Pirandellian characters do not experience that alienation from physical objects which forms the illness of Antoine Roquentin in Sartre's *La Nausée* (1938) and the painter Dino in Alberto Moravia's novel *La Noia* (1960). The Pirandellian aspiration is to escape the condition of the conscious *être-pour-soi* to acquire the inertness of *être-en-soi* in the object's resistance to the *néant* that death threatens. Whereas Sartre's protagonist recoils before pebbles and tree roots, and Moravia's anti-hero confesses to an object-malady that has plagued him since childhood, the dying spirit in the novella wishes—before it completely disappears—to reside in something like a stone or a flower. Instead of being superfluous, objects in their thingness possess a formal structure that is denied to the thinking spirit. Just as in the story of the man with a flower in his mouth, in this novella a flower serves as the symbol of death but also as a blazing moment of eternity. For a second the spirit enters into the life of a geranium, which suddenly catches fire and flames brilliantly until the spirit has faded altogether away. The momentary flickering of mortality ends. Language and poetic image capture death's phenomenology and psychology. Although this novella points out how death is the horrifying chasm of nothingness, it shows the act of dying as holding no terror, but only a melancholy sense of separation from the objects that impart a transient meaning to life.

Time and death are both conquered through the dream vision of the tale **"Visita"** of 1935, where the waking world merges with the irreality of an hallucination. The novella opens with an extremely brief interchange between the narrator and his butler, who has announced the visit of a Signora Anna Wheil. But the narrator knows from an obituary notice that Anna Wheil died the day before in Florence. In a parenthetical paragraph the narrator admits that he may never have held that interchange with the butler, that the scene may well have been a dream caused by reading the obituary notice. All that he recalls for certain is that he saw Anna Wheil in a dream, in which she appeared clothed in the chaste whiteness of a cloud that started to dissolve, exposing the rose-toned nudity of her body. Anna Wheil was indeed the object of the narrator's erotic desires, which could be satisfied only in dreaming; the very Germanic form of her name makes of her an exotic figure who remains forever elusive. When the narrator discovers her waiting for him in his study, he at once understands the appearance of the white cloud, because she is wearing the same white summer dress from three years before at the time of their sole meeting during a garden reception. Pirandello here reproduces the way dreams transform objects of conventional reality, almost magically remaking the world and investing it with the seductive attractiveness of desire. This dreamlike mood of voluptuous confusion is self-generating as a complex of sensations of color that annihilate the ordinary sense of temporal incompleteness by merging past and present. The fusion of past and present appears in what the narrator calls an "eternal present" when he makes a grammatical play between the present tense "La conosco appena" ("I scarcely know her") and the imperfect "La conoscevo appena" ("I scarcely knew her"), as he succeeds in recapturing with all the vividness of present time the enchantment of that garden party on an afternoon in late springtime. That garden served as his terrestrial paradise, the *locus amoenus* where the narrator represented Man and Anna became the supreme Lady, the object of adoration who can never be attained. As he was introduced to Anna, she was bent over, playing with some children, and he glimpsed the white beauty of her breasts. With their eyes alone he and Anna exchanged a silent communication that bound them together for eternity. The language of the narrator's worshipful appreciation of Anna's feminine loveliness adds an erotic refinement to the religious devotion for a sacred lady that medieval poets of the Italian Sweet New Style like Dante and Petrarch used to address to the *donna angelicata* of their sonnets and canzoni. Anna is the *"ewig weibliche"* that no man will ever truly possess to the depths of her being. Her breasts were like the promise of a gift that Heaven granted man to console him for his sufferings on earth. Yet, in the atmosphere of the tale, where the levels between dream and reality are blurred, Anna remained a woman of everyday society who had a husband, and the narrator understood that he would have

to have been twenty years younger to take her away from her husband. Thus the respectful distance that separated him from Anna resembles the detachment of the medieval love poets, who always chose another man's wife as the object of their affections.

As he emerges from the splendid dream of the past, the narrator hears Anna speaking to him with the familiar pronoun. At that present moment, following the notice of her death, he seems to discover her there in the green-tinged light that filters into the study through the trees outside his home and gives the objects in the room the harmonious color of hope. But Anna now reveals to him how cancer has deprived her of those breasts which he admired at the reception. When he looks, however, the narrator sees only the whiteness of the newspaper which included the obituary, for his Anna has disappeared. That whiteness becomes the color of annihilation. To some critics Anna's breasts have appeared as those of a mother figure, and the cancer which ravaged them is interpreted as an incest prohibition. Pirandello's mythic novella may be seen apart from a Freudian interpretation. The cancer which mutilated and eventually killed Anna is another of death's preliminary visits. Her beauty will, nevertheless, be everlasting because it has entered the narrator's unconscious from which it can be summoned for a dream visit. The haunting image of the lovely female at the garden party represents in the novella the erotic transformation of creative visual energy from a supremely transitory experience. Anna's breasts are the gifts of ripe abundance, with a complex of effete impulse, desire and aspiration that they arouse in the narrator, only to vanish in the disintegration of the dream vision. As often in Pirandello the tale is constructed around an absence revealed through the narrator's consciousness that remains "opened" to discourse. The chaos of elements such as the swirling colors works upon the narrator, who stays a passive figure through whom the dream transformation takes place. In the art of this mythic narration death and the ravages of disease are defeated as a mortal creature like Anna Wheil is elevated to an atemporal sphere, which corresponds to the crystaline life aspired to by Breton and that concrete universe closed to casual passersby which Aragon sees as the surrealistic state of grace.

The gloomily obsessive atmosphere of a nightmare haunts the tale **"C'è qualcuno che ride"** (**"There's Someone Who Is Laughing"**) of 1934. This novella may very well represent a political satire of the spirit of conformity that characterized life in Italy under the Fascist regime. It bears a striking similarity to the allegorical satires of Mussolinian Italy in Moravia's *Racconti surrealistici e satirici,* where the self-satisfied adherents of the dictatorship appear as greedy monsters intent only on gratifying their many lusts. In a deliberately unnamed city an official proclamation has invited (commanded) the people to attend a reception (rally) at a ballroom. Not even the brilliance of chandeliers nor the liveliness of dance tunes could succeed in dispelling the feeling of uneasy apprehension at that evening's ball. The restlessness that pervaded the gathering derived from the fact that no one knew the reason for the invitation. Like the defendant in Kafka's *The*

Trial, the guests were left perplexed by the machinations of a superior power who made all the decisions for them. At the orders of official photographers some of them were dancing to create the impression of a festive occasion; they were merely performing the dutiful obligation of pleasing the authorities who had invited them to the ball. From time to time a guest had to disappear into a secret chamber where everyone supposed a serious decision was being reached. The door to that chamber recalls the heavenly gate in *The Trial:* symbol of frustration for those forbidden to enter it an emblem of the aspiration toward a nonexistent meaning. All that most of the guests could do was perform a funereal masquerade where the dancers resembled old toys that had been stored away for years and were then unpacked for the event. While they awaited a public announcement that might bring clarification, the passive guests appeared to share a tacit agreement to maintain the grave decorum that alone would be appropriate under the weighty circumstances. In the ballroom's claustrophobic atmosphere, oppressed by seventeenth-century frescoes of menacing nocturnal scenes, the guests were reduced to dancing automata.

All the counterfeit solidarity of the crowd—founded as it was on fear and ignorance—was threatened by three persons who broke from the norm of automatic gestures and openly laughed aloud. The laughter of a father, his university-age son, and his adolescent daughter seemed an affront to the event's solemnity, and all the other guests soon became convinced that the act of nonconformity was the result of a conspiracy to create embarrassment. While everywhere else the ballroom's mirrored walls reflected the "emperor's-clothes" ignorance and paranoia of the crowd, the laughing expression of those three insouciant guests alone disturbed the mindless harmony of the reflections. To punish the three for their defiance, the entire crowd arose in perfect robot unanimity and started to hem them into a corner. Three official figures who were robed in domino hood and mask appeared from the secret chamber and took the lead of the crowd. With their hands burlesquely shackled together by napkins, the dominoes stood before the terrified family in the sarcastic attitude of criminals begging for mercy—the dominoes thus became the mirror reflection of the posture that the laughing trio had to be intimidated into assuming. After a loud sardonic laugh burst from the crowd intent on teaching the family a lesson for their bad manners, the father barely managed to take hold of his children and escape. The whole tale is structured on a series of repetitions and imagery to convey a nightmare experience. Here the narrative must turn upon itself to distort and exhaust discourse until it is reduced to the insignificant communication code of totalitarianism.

Public derision and banishment from the communal assembly of the ballroom were the only penalties that the nonconformists suffered, but the crowd's aggressiveness betrayed a ruthless desire to suppress all dissent. The laughing trio made the supreme mistake of enjoying the reception without fearing the consequences of their conduct, which must have seemed normal to them but to the majority that laughter could be viewed only as overt disrespect.

Bergson observes that laughter indicates a slight revolt on the surface of social life, which in Pirandello's tale is choreographed as a robots' ball. Laughter works to convert rigidity into plasticity, but it can also repress any separatist tendency, as in the laugh that the crowd returns to the family. Under a dictatorship the normal becomes abnormal and suspect. In the climate of a totalitarian state, the most natural act could be interpreted as a challenge to official policy. Pirandello's novella anticipates studies of conformism like Ionesco's play *Rhinoceros.* In every dictatorial regime "spontaneous" emotions must be the result of careful planning and orchestrating; otherwise the chaos of genuine feelings might disturb the public's submission. If this novella is to be regarded outside the traumatic context of the Fascist era, it should be classified along with the nightmare novelle of the Italian writer Dino Buzzati (b. 1906) for its representation of the vague fear that has obsessed individuals in the mass societies of the twentieth century.

A few months before Pirandello's death, the *Corriere della Sera* published the novella **"Una Giornata" ("A Day"),** which proved to be the author's farewell to the world. The "day" of the title is the symbolic day of an entire life-span, from birth to death. Through first-person technique the narrator surveys the confusing panorama of his life. At night-time he is tossed from a train coach into a strange station; he must have been asleep for some time because he cannot recall boarding the train. Nocturnal darkness here is that of birth and childhood. The choice of a train station as the bewildering point of arrival for life is of course typical of the author, who saw in such a setting all the agony of life's puzzling activities. In the darkness the narrator becomes aware of a light, which moves, seemingly of its own volition, to the train that leaves without him: from infancy every individual recognizes certain forces that operate beyond human control. Before he ventures into the unknown city, the narrator examines himself just as an infant will explore the unknown territory of his own being. After dawn, on the busy downtown streets, he observes how other persons rush frenetically about as if they were absolutely certain about the seriousness of what they are doing. The narrator resolves to act like others and appear to be fully convinced about the significance of his acts. Here conformity is not acquiescence to a dictatorial society but the simulation of life. The narrator will let others be the mediators of his actions and goals, imitating the patterns of behavior that he observes to be acceptable to others.

To his astonishment persons seem to recognize the narrator. He wonders if they are greeting him or his suit. Is it only the social mask that others acknowledge? In the breast pocket of his jacket he finds an old wallet that must have fallen once in a puddle since he cannot make out the blurred name on the water-stained identification cards. The narrator also discovers the photograph of a lovely girl in a bathing suit; somehow he thinks that the girl in the photo is throwing a greeting meant especially for him. The position of the photo next to a religious Sunday-School card would seem to indicate his fiancée. The wallet also contains a large bank note—perhaps an inheritance or his first earnings; since the time is already past noon, more than half of life has passed. In a restaurant, in a bank, the narrator continues to be recognized, and he plays his part in the comedy of life by taking directions from others in the hope that they are in the know and possess the vital secret. A car drives up, and the chauffeur takes him to an elegant older house where the same family must have dwelt for several generations. Yet he still feels an intruder in that traditional setting. In the bedroom the beautiful girl of the photograph is waiting for him to join her. At dawn of the following day she is gone, and the bed feels as cold as a tomb, since the death that has already overtaken her draws close at hand for the narrator. The mirror on the wall—always the Pirandellian mirror, which shatters any illusions—tells him that he is an old man. The vital cycle completes itself when his children and grandchildren invade the silence of the dusty old room where he once enjoyed the warmth of love. And while the elderly narrator still has the strength, he watches his grandchildren standing near his armchair. Before he even realizes it, they too have grown old.

In that final novella Pirandello traced the allegorical journey of life, using the modern machines of alienation like the locomotive and the automobile. The protagonist passes through life like an amnesiac who never emerges from his hypnotic trance. Time is never arrested in the tale, for it moves away like the light from the train. Brief clauses re-create the staccato, panting thoughts of the bewildered narrator. Short periods of restoration along the journey produce illusions of order that quickly vanish. Life attains its fullest moment in the consummation of the love-death in the bed that becomes a grave: here the acts of love and dying are free of the physical repulsiveness that torments many of the author's protagonists, and the lovers almost seem to be taking part in the ritual of a medieval romance. But much of life is a sequence of ritualistic gestures whose significance eludes the pilgrim. Rather than stressing the nihilistic conviction of life's futility, however, this novella of leave-taking emphasizes the bewilderment of the human pilgrimage in a post-Christian universe. The vital quest for understanding closes with a recognition of the confusing nature of earthly existence. Humankind must forever pursue a journey for which there is no close except in death.

With the final mythic novelle, Pirandello left behind the Veristic preoccupation with factual reality to create an art form that demolishes the physical barriers of the exterior world to undertake a voyage of exploration through the inner landscape of the mind. Escape from life's entrapment characterizes both the Veristic and mythic tales, which respectively display the contradictory conclusions of Romanticism in Naturalism and Surrealism. With those last tales Pirandello actually succeeded in fashioning the new mythology that Tommaseo hoped to be the goal of his writings. Pirandello's novelle create a discourse about nothingness as they define the edges of the void menacing modern life. The novellistic language seeks to go beyond the confines of realistic reference to open new dimensions of psychic and social signification. Through his novelle the author had been able to examine individual cases of

the failure or success of his fictional characters to reach an accord with life. Each tale traced the absurd, circular pattern of social existence or the brutalizing conformism with stifling codes and customs. But by the very limitations of its condensed form, the novella could merely suggest the relationship of the individual character to the social environment in which he or she thought himself or herself to be a prisoner or outcast. It was to the expansive technique of the novel that Luigi Pirandello turned when he sought to study in depth the conflict between personal aspirations and societal constraints.

Mark S. Finch (essay date 1979-1980)

SOURCE: "Life and Form in Pirandello's Short Prose: An Existential Atmosphere," in *Revista/Review Interamericana,* Vol. 9, No. 4, 1979–80, pp. 615–21.

[*In the following essay, Finch perceives in Pirandello's short fiction a tension between the spontaneity of life and the boundaries—both social and psychological—that humans impose upon themselves.*]

It would be difficult to determine what influence if any Pirandello had on the modern existentialists. However, there can be no doubt that he must be considered a precursor of the modern literary men who propound this philosophy. Thomas Bishop and Erminio G. Neglia both note that Pirandello exemplifies much of the chaos, anxiety, grief and absurdity so central to existential thought [Bishop, *Pirandello and the French Theater,* 1960; Neglia, *Pirandello y la dramática rioplatense,* 1970]. Pirandello himself has said [in his essay "On Humor"] that "life is a changing equilibrium, a continuous awakening and slumbering of feelings, tendencies and ideas. It is an incessant fluctuation between contradictory terms, an oscillation between opposite poles: hope and fear, truth and falsehood, beauty and ugliness, right and wrong, and so on." Even Sartre praised Pirandello as one of the world's most important dramatists, saying that he was well ahead of his times in much of his writings [Sartre, "A Paris et Ailleurs," *Les Nouvelles littéraires,* April 24, 1952].

Existentialism distinguishes between essence (*what* a thing is) and existence (*that* it is). Existence precedes essence. A man *is* before he *is something.* He exists before he defines himself. Within this atmosphere of existing there is freedom, common in Sartre's plays, for example, to control and decide how one will act in this world. One must decide continually the course of action in daily existence. In the process of existing, one is constantly developing one's essence. This creation of essence only stops at death. Likewise, death is the final act of freedom, as seen in Sartre, for the ultimate of existence is to be able to accept death with mental strength and fortitude.

That existence precedes essence seems to be an underlying premise of Pirandello's short fiction. Certainly his short stories are not *exactly* like Beckett's or Sartre's whose settings always evoke more a *condition humaine* than a specific locale, but in Pirandello's stories one is always keenly aware of the relativity of all systems, whether religious, philosophical, social or personal.

But if relativity and a denial of *a priori* essence are constants in his stories, Pirandello always locates them in a particular place with many different character types, thereby avoiding an abstract, philosophical kind of story such as Beckett's "Watt." Pirandello delights in portraying life concretely, the way it appears to the senses. For Pirandello, man is an animal who rationalizes about the circumstances in which he finds himself and this is precisely the point at which his art takes its cue, portraying characters in a complex social context (invariably Sicily) and showing their thoughts, ideals, rationalizations and hopes.

In the process of determining the essential aspects of Pirandello's art, Adriano Tilgher, in his seminal article "Life Versus Form" [in *Pirandello: A Collection of Critical Essays*, 1967], has attempted to expound perhaps the central theme in Pirandello's work, namely, how thought arises from the Pirandellian, and existential, flow of life. Tilgher begins his essay by asking what distinguishes man from nature in Pirandello's view, and he concludes: "This, and only this: that man lives and feels himself live, while the other beings of nature just live, live purely and simply." For Pirandello, life rises to thought or consciousness in man, pours itself into stiff modes of thought, and then becomes our concepts and ideals. Pirandello himself has said the following:

> Life is a continuous flow which we continually try to stop, to fix in established and determinate forms outside and inside of ourselves because we are already fixed forms, forms that move among other immovable ones, which follow the flow of life until the point when they become rigid and their movement, slowed, stops. The forms in which we try to stop and fix this continuous flow are the concepts, the ideals, within which we want to keep coherent all the fictions we create, the condition and the status in which we try to establish ourselves. ["On Humor"]

These rigid forms, as a result of our concepts and ideals, become the conventions, mores, traditions and laws of society. These forms are relative to the incomprehensible, and possibly absurd, flow of life. Tilgher concludes that Pirandello's art exemplifies the idea that life in its infinite "nakedness and freedom," is quite impossible to enjoy outside of the preconstructed (or perhaps existentially predetermined) forms into which society, history and individual existence have been channeled.

Now, within the philosophical atmosphere of existentialism regarding existence preceding essence, and the Tilgherian theory regarding the rigidity of form and flow of Pirandellian life, it will be shown, upon the discussion of several short stories, that these two elements are delicately and artistically interwoven in Pirandello's works of even lesser importance.

In the short story **"The Jar"** we find Lollo Zirafa, a wealthy farmer who has a notorious reputation for filing law suits against people, and commonly losing them. Within the absurdity of this jurisprudential fiasco, he has great anxiety regarding the forthcoming olive harvest, which has every indication of being one of the best ever. He decides he will purchase a new giant jar, one large enough to hold the bumper crop. Almost immediately after its arrival, however, Zirafa finds it broken and consequently enlists the aid of a handy-man named Licasi to mend it. Licasi claims to have a secret cement that would repair the jar so well that people could barely discern the hairline fracture. Zirafa insists that Licasi also rivet the jar to ensure that the jar hold oil. Over Licasi's protests, Zirafa has his way, but poor Licasi, in the process of wiring, riveting and cementing the broken piece, has sealed himself into the vessel. After consulting his legal advisor, Zirafa is left in a perplexing and absurd dilemma. Licasi refuses to pay for the destruction of the jar in getting him out. He says he would rather stay there than pay. Both individuals seem to be possessed and belligerent within their own structured mental and societal forms.

> **Pirandello is not a naive nihilist. He has the ability to see *all* of reality. Indeed happiness is as much an objective fact of life as sorrow. For Pirandello, life is not simple, but an incomprehensible flow, a tapestry of infinite complexity**.
>
> —*Mark Finch*

That night Zirafa sees his farm workers dancing and singing around the jar, drinking wine and *looking* like demons. This is most symbolical of the incomprehensible flux of life. In his rage Zirafa runs out to the jar and kicks it down a hill. When it strikes a tree it breaks, thereby freeing Licasi. The story thus represents two conceptions, or forms, which collide quite irrationally, or absurdly, causing the senseless and symbolic destruction of an artifact, itself a symbol of the objectification of life (existence) into rigid, crystalized form. Within this form, there is destruction of character and a chaos of warring forces. This, thematically, is quite existential.

In **"The Jar"** neither Zirafa nor Licasi understand each other's thought structures; they are both rather unperceptive. But for Pirandello even the "perceptive" human being's insights and determinations are seen to be subjectively absurd. In the delightful story **"It's Nothing Serious"** he takes for his protagonist a young sophisticate who displays considerable ability to see through the surface reality of things to the more elementary primitive levels of everyday existence. Pirandello's portrait of Perazzetti may even be something of a self-parody.

In **"It's Nothing Serious,"** Perazzetti is an intellectual and he plays an amusing mental game that often causes him to laugh in public for no apparent reason. His game is to realize that there is the "Cave of the beast" in us all and so he tries to guess which beast belongs in which cave—whether, absurdly, it be a turkey or another kind of animal. His game, or form, extends one level higher, however. When he meets someone whose higher civilized functions he finds intolerably stuffy and illmannered, he imagines that person, absurdly enough, squatting, performing that function that marks us all as unavoidably animals.

There are certain times when Perazzetti is not himself though; times when this laughter mechanism is suppressed. This invariably happens when he is in love, and since he has been engaged six times already, that is quite often. After his last engagement, which ended when he noticed disturbing resemblance between his fiancee and her brother, Perazzetti decides to marry Filomena, an idiot girl. He then sends her to the country to be well cared for, agreeing with his friends that it will cause him some distress. But he argues that that pain will be a blessing for it "will mean that I have fallen in love once more, so deeply in love as to be prepared to commit the greatest of stupidities, that of taking a wife." When his friends reply that he already has a wife, he responds that that was nothing serious.

Perazzetti thus married to protect himself from the danger of taking a wife. This story is an example of thought rising from the irrational flow of life, into the mind of a young man. The humor of the story arises from his ultimate solution deviating from social norm—one usually marries the woman one loves. What is even more ironical, however, is that Perazzetti, the one who espoused the bestial theory of life, actually divorces himself from that elemental source through the use of intellect. Perazzetti, the rational mind *par excellence* (at least between love affairs), dooms himself to live apart from the source of vitality—and love. Perazzetti's solution is a deadening intellectual form and although he may be able to maintain a certain comic distance from reality, his laughter is doomed to become sadness. There is opposition between Perazzetti, the individual, and his image as construed by others. The rigidity of societal structure has forced him to take a wife, but he has done this only to in reality avoid the norm, or societal demand. The intellectual level of Perazzetti as opposed to Zirafa, for example, is most distinct. However, the existential atmosphere and rigidity of form seem to be rather similar.

Such stultifying thought-structures occur in other than intellectuals in Pirandello's stories. For example, in **"Sicilian Honour,"** Pirandello examines the effect that the objectification of honor can have. The story concerns itself with the trial of Saru Argentu, a Sicilian farmer accused of murdering his wife. Although he believes himself to be completely innocent, because he killed his wife for having an affair, under questioning by the judge it is learned that Saru had known of his wife's affair for a long time. He had absurdly known that his wife was prostituting herself; he even encouraged it. Often he would send word home that he would be coming home early, so that his wife had time to get rid of her client. The reason he had killed her, then, is because the incident had become public—because his honor had been impeached.

To Saru, this was justification enough to bury a hatchet in his wife's skull.

In all three stories so far discussed, we have seen that destructive things can happen when a *form* becomes an obsession. Pirandello, however, does not judge his characters. For even in Saru Argentu his purpose is to examine the complexity, often the incongruities, of consciousness as it rises mysteriously from that existential undercurrent of flux. Certainly to Argentu, he was perfectly justified in killing his wife, and he feels no guilt at all. Saru is not an intellectual *per se,* as Perazzetti, yet he too is trapped by a form so rigid as to cause his obsession and ultimate death of his wife.

In the story **"The Husband's Revenge,"** Pirandello presents another way still within the framework of existentialism, the forms can arise to affect behavior of people. In this unique case it is a wife's memory of her husband which becomes crystallized into an obsession. A young man named Bartolino is betrothed to a young widow, Carolina. She asks him if he would refer to her as "Lina," as did her first husband; also that they honeymoon in Rome, as she had done with her first husband, and also that they sleep in the same hotel—and even the same room! After the honeymoon, poor Bartolino comes to realize the extent of his new wife's obsession with her former husband. She talks constantly about him, how he did this or that, how he in fact *formed* her. Bartolino by this time has become obsessed himself with a photograph of her deceased husband in which he is smiling pleasantly and tipping his hat.

Almost in an absurd kind of self-defense, Bartolino decides to have an affair with a recently widowed woman named Ortensia, who, coincidentally, lives nearby. His scheme is easily carried out, since it was Ortensia's wish as well. But as he lies in her bed, he notices a shining object on the floor. He picks up the gold locket with the intuition of giving it back to her, but as he sits waiting for her, he opens it. Inside, he sees a miniature copy of the troubling photograph of Cosimo, still smiling and tipping his hat. And so Cosimo, although he is absurdly dead, continues his influence beyond the grave, first embodied in his wife's obsession with his memory, and secondly, in the effect that that memory has on Bartolino.

Pirandello, in this short fiction, delights in *presenting* such wry occurrences objectively, with form, underlined with existential absurdity, without editorial comment or authorial intrusion. He does not always present reality as mildly grotesque, or ironic in this way, however.

In the short story **"The Captive,"** Pirandello creates a tale of exceeding beauty and tenderness. Vice Guarnotta, a well-liked and wealthy old man, is abducted from his holdings at the edge of the sea. On the way, he had been thinking that the "Whole world was now as lonely as that highway and his own life grey as that twilight." He had lost his only son and he had sworn to wear black for the rest of his life. Within this existential harshness, he is always thinking about how intolerably boring life is. At this very moment he is abducted.

He awakens to find himself bound with ropes in a cave. When the kidnappers, one of whom Vice recognizes as Manuzza, demand a ransom of three thousand florins, he tells them that he would have to sell everything he owns, something that he would have to do for himself. He also adds that his nephews and nieces would not help because if he were dead, they would inherit the money. Vice then suggests quite honestly, that if they would let him free, he would sell everything he had and give it to them, and he promises he would not reveal their identity. The amateurish bandits vote against this and thereby find themselves in a predicament since they do not want to kill the old man; and neither can they set him free for fear that he might tell somebody. Within the absurdity of the kidnapping, even the bandits are caught in an existential dilemma, namely, a confrontation with the societal form of "law" and honor. They finally decide to keep Vice incarcerated in the cave for the rest of his life.

As the months go by, Vice realizes that keeping him supplied with food and water *is* a burden on these men. This is compounded by the fact that one of three must always guard him, while the other two work. Gradually he develops a fatherly love for the men, meets their wives, and frolics with his "grandchildren." He totally forgets his past life with its intolerable boredom. One day, however, as he is playing with the children, he collapses on the ground dead. As for the kidnappers: "during the rest of their lives, if anyone happened to mention Vice in their presence and speak of his mysterious disappearance, they would say: He was a saint that man . . . I'm sure he was admitted to paradise."

In a sense, the bandits, absurdly enough, had done Vice a favor. Vice had been obsessed with the loss of his own son and nothing brought him happiness—neither his wife nor his possessions. His oath to wear black for the rest of his life indicates the extent of his servitude to the memory of his son. In this story, through a series of blunders by amateur kidnappers, a man is actually delivered into happiness. As those men came to replace his lost son, Vice is given back to the life of feeling, and deciding, and consequently he enjoys his last days immensely.

It can be seen here that Pirandello is not a naive nihilist. He has the ability to see *all* of reality. Indeed happiness is as much an objective fact of life as sorrow. For Pirandello, life is not simple, but an incomprehensible flow, a tapestry of infinite complexity. It rises mysteriously into forms or structures—either intellectual, as in Perazzetti's case, or from memory, as in "Lina's" case, or finally out of pragmatic need, as the jar in Zirafa's case. The form can also be social as in **"Sicilian Honour."** If men can seem existentially ludicrous because of life being poured into still molds, they can also occasionally be redeemed from them. Surely in Vice's case, although there is required an almost absurd series of coincidences, he is actually better in the cave-life than the one he was leading.

Curiously enough the two hundred fifty short stories of Pirandello have not been studied in depth. Of course, his drama has received most of the attention. Yet within the discussion of these five particular stories it has become evident that within an atmosphere of existentialism, coupled with the ever-present dichotomy between life and form, there is in Pirandello a delicate balance between these two elements. To this extent it is hoped that further light has been given to the ultimate aesthetics of Pirandello.

Paolo Valesio (essay date 1987)

SOURCE: "A Remark on Silence and Listening," in *Oral Tradition,* Vol. 2, No. 1, January, 1987, pp. 288–95.

[*In the following excerpt, Valesio closely examines the short story "Canta l'epistola."*]

One of the least known among the many short stories that Luigi Pirandello published in literary magazines around the turn of the century and started issuing in book-length collections from 1901 on is the one titled **"Canta l'Epistola"** (**"He-who-intones-the-Epistle"**), a phrase which is the nickname of the defrocked seminarian who is the hero of the little story.

Tommasino, who because of his change of heart has become an object of scorn and ridicule for his father and for the other inhabitants of his village, leads a chaste and solitary life, a life for which the term "contemplation" could be used—with the specification, however, that Tommasino's experience is not a systematically religious one (he has left organized faith), but an asystematic way of looking at, listening to, things.

In the course of his musings, Tommasino concentrates his attention on one single blade of grass, growing wild near a little abandoned church, in a hilly spot he regularly visits in his walks. It is not that he takes care of it in an active way (watering it, for instance): he simply follows its life, rejoicing in its growth and duration. But one day a young lady passes by, sits in that spot and, getting up to continue her walk, absent-mindedly rips off that blade of grass, putting it between her teeth.

"You idiot!" cries out Tommasino in exasperation. The young lady, astonished at this insult on the part of a person with whom she never exchanged a word, reports the episode to her fiancé, an army lieutenant who happens to be a very good shot. He asks for an explanation that naturally the young man cannot offer: slapped by the officer, Tommasino accepts the challenge to a duel, and is mortally wounded by a pistol shot. To the priest who kneeling by his death-bed asks him meaning of all this ("But why, my son? Why?"):

> Tommasino, with half-shut eyes, with a weakened voice, in the midst of a sigh which turned into a very tender smile, simply answered: "Father, it happened because of a blade of grass. . . ." And everybody believed that he had remained delirious until his dying hour.

Such are the closing lines of what I do not claim to be one of Pirandello's greatest achievements, although it is a remarkable story. The initial part of this short story is a little too didactic and expository in tone; given the brevity of the text, this weakens the concentration. But I am not putting together an essay on Pirandello (and at any rate, the minor texts of an important writer are crucial for his or her critical assessment); my purpose is to implement a certain way of thinking about literature, and this intelligently sensitive story is a significant emblem. Let me then briefly sketch certain basic critical responses which are possible here.

A first possibility is what can be called a naive reading. Such a reading would not look behind or beyond the text: what it would see is a bizarre anecdote, wry and faintly moving—in short (according to the circular move characteristic of a certain handbook style) a "typically Pirandellian" text. As most naive readings, this one is essentially right. But, again, as most naive readings, it does not have enough force to restrain the questing or questioning reader as he or she is drawn to go deeper: with all the attendant risks (and challenges) of tortuosity, of endless erring through the maze of interpretation.

Indeed, the possibility of what might be called an astute reading quickly emerges here. Consider.

Contrary to the coarsely voiced suspicions about the reasons behind his leaving the seminary, Tommasino is (as noted) completely chaste: ". . . no woman could have claimed to have received as much as a passing glance from him." A post-Freudian reader will immediately suspect repression at work here; and such suspicions would be rewarded, given the way the growth of that blade of grass is described—the blade of grass which Tommasino

> had followed almost with a motherly tenderness in its slow growing among the other and shorter ones which were around it; and he had seen it rise—shy at first, in its quivering slenderness—above the two encrusted rocks, as if it were fearful and at the same time curious, in its admiration of the sight that opened up beneath it—the green, boundless plain; and then he had seen it stand up taller and taller, bold and self-confident, with a small reddish tassel on its top, like the comb of a young rooster.

Indeed, the phallic symbol seems so blatant here that the reader could incline to regard this too explicit delineation as further proof of the relative immaturity of the author's narrative skills at this stage. Such an impression could be confirmed by the following images:

> Tommasino's joy at finding it every time intact, with its defiant small tassel (*pennacchietto*) on top, was indescribable. He stroked it with the utmost delicacy, he smoothed it using only two fingers; it was as if he guarded it with his soul and breath. And in the evening, on leaving the stalk, he entrusted it to the early stars which began rising in the dusky sky, so that they and all their sisters would watch over it during the night.

And really, with his mind's eye, from afar, he saw that blade of grass of his, between the two rocks, under the thickly crowded stars sparkling in the black sky, which kept watch over it.

Once again, it would seem that the symbolic infrastructure of the tale is ("and thereby hangs a tale") almost embarrassingly clear. With this kind of preparation the culminating image in the story, which triggers Tommasino's insult, appears almost to quiver on the edge of pornography. The young lady

> absent-mindedly stretching her hand, had pulled up precisely that blade of grass and had stuck it between her teeth, with the small tassel hanging out. Tommasino Unzio had felt his soul tear, and he had not been able to resist the impulse to cry out to her: "You idiot!" when she had passed in front of him, with that stalk in her mouth.

No further elaboration is necessary here: the whole development of a certain kind of critical reading is already unfolding before your eyes. Such a reading I would define as hypercritical. Now, the kind of listening criticism that I am proposing avoids both the *hypocriticism* (if I may use this new coinage) of the naive reading—which at any rate is certainly not hypocritical, in the current sense of the word—and the hypercriticism of the astute reading.

But such a characterization does not imply any condescending or polemical attitude toward the readings which have been sketched. Anxiously setting one interpretation against the other is typical of that *phônomakhein* ("waging battles of words") which has been already defused and refused by the ancient Greek Skeptics; and at any rate such an attitude would be clearly contrary to the listening approach advocated in this essay. Indeed, in order to be serious, such a listening must be understanding and comprehensive: it must listen not only to the texts but, with equal attention and respect, to all interpretations that have grown, or can grow, around them. The rhetorical ontology recovers the whole textual complex (including, I repeat, critical interpretations) as part of a common effort—to bring things to expression, to transform Being into forms of being. This enterprise is objectively shared by all the components of textual work, beyond all appearances of division, of competitive struggle.

Within such a restorative enterprise there is no neglect of differentiations (indeed they are developed and discussed, as we just saw); but there is no space for the sharp, absolutist polemics that removes and discards. So much is this true, that the reading of **"Canta l'Epistola"** that I am going to briefly delineate in the next few lines grows out of a careful listening to the possible readings sketched above, and is meant as an integration of them, not as a way of scoring points with respect to them.

What does it mean, in this specific case, to listen? To say that one listens to the text is not specific enough; if we leave it at that, what we have is a slightly more intense way of repeating what (in a different parlance) literary criticism has been saying for a long time. What we actually have to do is *to listen to what Tommasino is listening to*: the voice of mute things.

It could be objected that this is a counter-intuitive way of describing the situation, for what Tommasino is doing is not listening to, but looking at; the whole text in fact is (as my quotes from it have shown) textured on images that have to do with sight. But precisely this is the epistemological turning point.

If we confine ourselves to looking at what Tommasino is looking at, then we are in the same position as all the other people around him: we do not see *anything* (because nobody, under normal conditions, really *sees* a blade of grass); therefore we conclude, quite reasonably, that Tommasino is crazy; and his reaction to Miss Olga (the lieutenant's fiancée)—who, as all of us normally do, handles the blade of grass without really seeing it—appears as totally arbitrary. But what really explains Tommasino's behavior is that he is listening to a message. Only if we accept this are we ready to grant a human value to his actions. So long as he is seen as merely looking at the stalk, his attitude appears as a perverse one, as a way of avoiding mature relationships between human beings, stooping down to a form of life which lies below such relationships; it would be, then, a one-way connection which, although definitely not brutal, looks brutish—a stunting and impoverishing attitude. And yet—"The religious sentiment arises from . . . a brute conation of human nature," as is noted in a series of philosophical reflections of those years (The Gifford Lectures at Glasgow, 1916-1918; see Samuel Alexander, *Space, Time, and Deity,* 1920).

More specifically, if we accept the fact that in doing what he does Tommasino is listening to a voice, then this very act of listening confers human dignity on this relationship. "Human dignity," I said—but how can one speak of this, when the relationship at issue does not take place between two humans, two full persons? The answer is found in a religious notion which can also be considered as a paradox: the predominantly Judaeo-Christian concept of rooting human dignity in a relation with the transcendental. It turns out, then, that Tommasino's loss of faith is not a mere sociological fact in the background of the story; much less is it a kind of stage to be passed through on one's way to a more sophisticated view of the world. Tommasino is, to be sure, thinking/feeling in the wake of the abandonment of an institutionalized, confessional faith, but his thinking/feeling is still a response to that faith.

This situates our text in its appropriate context, which is a very broad spiritual landscape. In this sense, Pirandello's short story comes to look like that stalk of grass, and the context necessary in order to really listen to what it is saying appears now as that great plain which spreads below; recall the passage about the blade of grass that grows "as if it were fearful and at the same time curious, in its admiration of the sight that opened up beneath it—the green, boundless plain." Like every intense interrogation in the territory of Christianity, Tommasino's experience is on the verge of heresy; that is, it holds commerce with one of the great rivals, and nourishing alternatives, of the Christian confession. In this case, the nourishing alternative is that of pantheism. Thus Tommasino's listening to the voice of the stalk of grass is one more episode in a very long and complex story which crosses the history of philosophy, and of theology, *and* of poetry: the story of the several efforts to recover a sense of the sacred in the adherence to all the things in the world, from the largest to the tiniest. . . .

Let us get back, for some moments, from this broad context to the specific rhetorical strategy at hand: this story is also an effective reminder of how, in the actual implementation of sacred images and themes (what I have called elsewhere "theorhetoric"), irony and even the grotesque can play a decisive role, without diminishing (on the contrary . . .) the spiritual tension of discourse. The image of the "blade of grass" as a symbol of the tiny but important things in the world is, by the time Pirandello writes, a philosophical topos. The interesting theorhetorical twist of this novelette consists in *literalizing* the metaphor: the "blade of grass" thus becomes a blade of grass—no longer a passing nod to the variety of the world, a hurried way of speaking, but the motor of the whole sequence of events. This makes for a mixture of serious and grotesque elements. There is also another stab here, aimed at the rhetoric of "rest and recuperation," with its description of the weary man-immersed-in-the-world (intellectual, political, or simply mundane man or woman) who goes to the country in order to bathe in the spontaneous and innocent simplicity of nature.

This is a vital and persisting discourse, to be sure. (One still reads letters from friends and colleagues, many of them professional writers, who talk in these terms of their experience of retired living in the country.) Yet this discourse is questioned by a modern rhetoric which points up the element of illusion implicit in such a move, and the many petty or sordid realities which are to be found in the places apparently most close to nature. In this sense, Pirandello's text has close antecedents in texts like a well-known narrative essay by Giovanni Verga, "Fantasticheria," in the short story collection *Vita dei campi* or an acidly intelligent novel like the one by Joris-Karl Huysmans, *En Rade* (1887). The ironization of this kind of return of the native is not an isolated case in Pirandello's short stories. But this one is remarkable in its heightening of the colors—and I refer not only to the element of grotesque, but also to that of deadly violence. . . .

A final point on the story—which turned out not to be such a minor text, after all. . . . If we do not simply listen to Tommasino listening, but (as I proposed) listen to what he is listening to, then we have a right (indeed, an obligation) to maintain a critical attitude. I refer to Tommasino's abrupt reaction against Miss Olga.

Let us dare ask a question that is often disdained, as if it were too naive, by literary criticism: what passed through Tommasino's mind between the moment in which he saw the blade of grass being ripped off and the moment of his exclamation? It is not absurd to surmise that Tommasino, who had studied in the seminary, may have thought along the lines of reflections like the following:

> . . . nothing the world has to offer
> —the sensual body,
> the lustful eye,
> pride in possessions—
> could ever come from the Father
> but only from the world
>
> (1 John 2:16).

Indeed, Miss Olga with the stalk hanging from her mouth must have been an emblem of what the Vulgate (with a phrase that rings deeper than the "pride of possessions" of the Jerusalem Bible version) calls *superbia vitae*: "life-pride," or "pride of life."

But isn't Tommasino's reaction to that life-pride a bit too strident, too uneasy? (We thus recover what is fruitful, and cannot be ignored, in the astute reading.) Isn't this reaction somewhat inconsistent with the terms of Tommasino's own experience, which is teaching him a fully sympathetic acceptance of all things and creatures in the world? This is certainly not said in order to score a point on Tommasino—but rather, in order to underscore the necessity for constant self-criticism (isn't this, actually, a weaker synonym for soul-searching?) in the pursuit of the experience of listening.

Luisetta Chomel (essay date 1989)

SOURCE: "Pirandello's Notion of Time," in *Canadian Journal of Italian Studies,* Vol. 12, Nos. 38-9, 1989, pp. 26–31.

[*In the following excerpt, Chomel discusses Pirandello's treatment of the theme of time in several of his short stories.*]

The Pirandellian man, trapped in the flux of time, condemned to endure an incessant chain of transformations, vainly tries to resist time and fix himself in a lasting form. Institutions, traditions, social masks, even prejudices and hypocrisy are but devices he uses in his attempt to stop the flow of time. The time motif punctuates Pirandello's writings from the poetic beginning to the last plays, in different forms and various degrees of intensity. . . .

The novelle, being the result of direct observation of life, communicate to the reader a peculiar sensation of immediacy and authenticity. They are instantaneous pictures of a chaotic reality, inhabited by a variety of individuals caught in a particular moment of their struggle with life. Although in the majority of the novelle the word "time" is not even mentioned, the narrative structure always points to one of the many facets that mirror the same vision of time. Usually, the characters in the novelle appear on the scene with a very light baggage of past memories and disappear without having the chance to manifest their conscious intentions. From the rapid sketch the author draws, we know just enough to situate them in an approximate frame of existential necessities. Then, something happens, and the characters are confronted by a haphazard, gratuitous event, totally unrelated to the logical chain of cause and effect. In this narrative frame past and future appear irrelevant and only the instant remains. The characters, deprived of the continuity and duration of a psychological inner time, are completely absorbed into the fleeting moment, and the next moment they disappear, carried by the flux of linear time. In Pirandello's words, this is the dimension of human time: "The just and the unjust, the ingenuous and the deceitful, the prudent and the rash, all meet with same end, and no one triumphs except accident." The accidental event narrated can be comic, humorous or tragic; it can be relevant to the life of the characters or simply an anecdote. It always stands out vividly from the succession of the other moments.

Time is, at first, envisaged as the irresistible force that brings mutations to things and individuals. In **"Lumìe di Sicilia"** the young girl who has been swept into the merry life of a courtesan, has changed so much as to efface from memory her previous feelings and commitments. For Micuccio, on the contrary, the past is still a living part of himself, and he feels betrayed by Teresina's easy oblivion. The two protagonists stand as symbols of time in the country and time in the city, since the disparity of their characters in relation to the past is clearly associated to their different way of living. Micuccio has lived in the country; time, paced with the seasonal cycle, has passed slowly for him, allowing the fusion of successive moments into a form of psychological duration. Teresina, instead, has been exposed to the accelerated rhythm of urban life, and the flux of time has rapidly changed her feelings and her personality.

The past has no weight in the present life of people. Many of the characters arrive out of nowhere, such as the three carefree people who dare to laugh for no reason stirring the indignant reaction of the most dignified crowd, in **"C'è qualcuno che ride"**. Or the young boy who, driven by an unreasonable impulse, kills a girl with the nail he has found in **"Il chiodo"**. Or the man and the woman in **"Rondone e rondinella"**, caught in their seasonal meetings of love and tenderness, whose lives and even names are unknown.

In other novelle, the instant in which the "accident" happens is endowed with a particular significance and assumes the value of an epiphany. This is the case in **"La visita"** where the moment of complicity and understanding between the narrator and the beautiful Signora Wheil has the impact of a revelation. He has perceived of her something essential that death has not destroyed. The epiphanic mode also prevails in **"La tartaruga"**. Mr. Mishkow is a well-intentioned man who leads a miserable family life, alienated from his wife and children by their contemptuous indifference. One day he comes home with a turtle, supposedly an animal that brings good luck, only to provoke the fury of Mrs. Mishkow who threatens to leave the house if he does not get rid of the disgusting reptile. He first accepts her conditions but, while he wanders in the city trying to find an appropriate place to leave the animal, he suddenly decides to confront his wife. For nine years, since he has married Mrs. Mishkow, he has been living on tiptoe, somehow ashamed of his naive spontaneity and love for life, constantly apprehensive to displease his impenetrable wife, or to provoke the gelid disapproval of his frightfully aged children. In a flash, he realizes what he has tried to ignore for many years: his wife wants to leave him. The ridiculous, little animal is only a pretext; after the turtle his wife will find another excuse. But the revelation does not shock him; instead, he vaguely senses an opening for his dreary existence. Following his impulse he comes back home, and defiantly deposes the turtle in front of his outraged wife. She immediately departs, leaving Mr. Mishkow with the vague sensation that the turtle has indeed brought him good luck.

Also **"Il treno ha fischiato . . ."** exemplifies the significance of the epiphanic instant. The train whistle in the night awakens the dormant consciousness of an ordinary man with an ordinary life. Suddenly he realizes the oppressive parameter of his miserable existence, and is shaken by a confused desire of freedom and openness. It is a sparkle of awareness that makes him see the truth; he will never be the same, even if he is obliged to carry on the burden of his inane life. In **"La carriola"**, the sudden awakening of awareness also represents a turning point in the life of a man. One day the man, stepping in front of the door of his house, is struck by a revelation: he is a stranger in this house, a stranger to himself. He is someone else who has never lived that life or any life. Exteriorly, he maintains his habitual behaviour, but interiorly the feeling of extraneity becomes a certitude. As a spectator, he sees himself acting according to the usual role. He lives only when, in full awareness, he secretly transgresses the bounds of the role, playing "wheel barrow" with the old dog. For all these characters the confrontation with the present moment is the only reality. A few follow their momentary intuition and transform their life. Others sink in their torpid existence not because they feel their past as an integrating part of themselves, but because necessity or the force of habit, with its reassuring predictability, reabsorb them.

The past remains a shadowy zone of life, a construction of the mind rather than a reality. In **"La signora Frola e il signor Ponza"**, the past of the newly arrived trio, anxiously sought by the little community of the town, has practically disappeared with the documents destroyed by the earthquake. What remains of it are the opposite versions given by Signora Frola and Signor Ponza. Where is the truth? Or what is the past? The past is not what really happened but how the individual, now, perceives it. Only the present has an indisputable value while previous events vanish in the imponderable night of subjective consciousness. Reciprocal compassion for the common folly appears to be the single attainable goal of human experience. The same conclusion is reached in **"Sedile sotto il vecchio cipresso"**. Here the past, far from being a mystery, is accurately represented in a cumulus of meaningless and ferocious actions. After a life torn by the obses-

sion of revenge, the old man semi-paralyzed, meets his ancient rival again, a wreck, half blind, and reduced to begging. He calls him, and they sit together on the old bench. They do not talk, but a slight touch tells their mutual understanding. The two men, united in their misery, feel a sort of disparate compassion for each other. Their past actions are cancelled by this moment of "disperata pietà".

In other stories the past assumes a menacing aspect. In **"Vittoria delle formiche"**, the protagonist, a man rejected by his family and reduced to poverty by his irresponsible conduct, leads a carefree existence in the countryside. Oblivious to the past, without a program, he abandons himself to the flux of time, enjoying each moment, totally absorbed in the rhythm of nature:

> Aveva scoperto questa nuova ricchezza, nell'esperienza che può bastare così poco per vivere; e sani e senza pensieri; con tutto il mondo per sè, da che non si ha più casa nè famiglia nè cure ne affari; sporchi, stracciati, sia pure, ma in pace; seduti la notte al lume delle stelle, sulle soglie di una catepecchia; e se s'accosta un cane, anch'esso sperduto, farselo accucciare accanto e carezzarlo sulla testa; un uomo e un cane, soli sulla terra, sotto le stelle. (*Novelle per un anno*).

But when, during the night, the past emerges from oblivion, the man falls prey to remorse, regrets, and guilty feelings. Memory acts negatively, bringing the man back into the intricate web of human relations, individual responsibilities, and antagonistic forces. After a night worse than the others, the ants, which he has first contemplated with amused curiosity, suddenly appear as enemies that should be fought and destroyed. He tries to burn the anthill, but the wind unexpectedly starts blowing and sets his miserable shack on fire. Like a madman, he throws himself into the flames vainly hoping to extinguish the fire, and dies after a few hours, denouncing in his delirium the alliance of the wind and the ants.

A contrast between time-awareness and time-ignorance implicity lies in the development of the story. Until the protagonist fully participates in each present moment, without apprehension for the future or regret for the past, he joyfully savours his freedom but, when the ghosts of the past reappear, he again becomes a slave of the time chain, which brings back the notions of guilt, fear and struggle.

The same concept of time-ignorance as the only possibility of relative happiness is projected in **"Fortuna di essere un cavallo"**. The old horse, abandoned by his master and chased by the village, peacefully browses on the grass growing on the edge of the road, seemingly happy to satisfy his most immediate need, thoughtless and unaware of past and future. Again **"Una giornata"**, the last of Pirandello's novelle, addresses the theme of chronological time. A man, just before dying, sees his past life in a flashback, and a long span of time is reduced to one day. Like a man thrown from a train in an unknown station, he wanders in the city, a stranger to his surrounding and to himself. He does not recall anything of his life, not even his name.

The busy life of the city appears meaningless, almost laughable to him. He looks at the other people, incapable of understanding the reasons for their activity. Some people greet him but he has no memory of them. His past has totally disappeared; only the old picture of a beautiful young woman he finds in a pocket of his jacket stirs a sweet emotion. When, driven by the others, he reaches his home, he does not recognize anything: the objects are extraneous and the house foreign. He sees the beautiful young woman of the picture and, for a moment, he feels again the warmth of love, but she too fades away. He finally understands that he is dying; his children and grandchildren surround him. He has completely forgotten them and now his only feeling is compassion: ". . . rimango a guardare finchè posso, con tanta tanta compassione, ormai dietro questi nuovi, i miei vecchi figliuoli." The past has no weight and human time resolves in a succession of estranged moments, until the sum of the presents dissolves into a timeless, infinite darkness.

The novelle, although they do not convey a specific notion of time, leave the overall impression of a fragmented reality lacking a connective tissue of memories and perspectives. . . .

Franz Rauhut (essay date 1989)

SOURCE: "Pirandello's Short Story 'La Rosa' as a Work of Art," translated by Giovanni R. Bussino, in *Canadian Journal of Italian Studies,* Vol. 12, Nos. 38–9, 1989, pp. 67–73.

[*In the following essay, Rauhut analyses the structure, theme, and literary devices of Pirandello's story "The Rose."*]

Because of its significant human value, Pirandello's short story **"La rosa"** (**"The Rose"**), first published in *La Lettura* in November 1914, merits an aesthetic analysis.

For the sake of orientation I will summarize the plot. Lucietta, the twenty-year-old widow of Loffredi (a journalist who was murdered), lives alone with her two children and has to face the problem of supporting herself and them. By winning a competition, she succeeds in obtaining the position of telegraph operator in the small town of Pèola. In the drowsy village the attractive young woman becomes a stimulating element. From the very beginning Fausto Silvagni, the thirty-five-year-old town secretary, courts her. She accepts his invitation to the local club's annual ball. The ball provides the unfortunate woman with a happy and thrilling evening, which she enjoys in all innocence, while the young men of the town press around her with passionate interest. When the rose she is wearing in her hair falls to the floor, it is picked up and returned to her, and she is told to present the flower to a man of her choice. The erotically aroused men turn the situation into a cruel joke: the woman's gesture is supposed to signify a declaration of love. In order to get out of her predicament, she presents the flower to the town secretary,

but the possibility of the two forming a lifetime bond is forever thwarted because of the man's pessimism.

The work portrays a crescendo of events that culminates in a dramatic decision concerning the lifetime destinies of the two protagonists. Both of these characters, having modest social occupations, hold such great human significance for the reader that he is compelled to use the word "tragic" in describing them. As is often the case in short stories, the artistic style unifies narration, description and dialogue. An analysis of the story's four parts should therefore show that the total structure contains exceptionally interesting qualities as well.

Part I introduces the situation, the setting and the two main characters, Signora Lucietta Nespi (the widowed wife of Loffredi), and Fausto Silvagni (the town secretary). Signora Nespi is sitting with her children on a slow-moving train bringing her to the place of her future employment. Description, narration and dialogue are used to create the ambience, the characters and the human situation.

Let it be said in advance that a heavy mood permeates the entire work. Already the very first sentence serves to vaguely prepare the mood for the negative outcome of the short story. Just as the slow little train arrives very late, so too will the protagonist utterly fail to attain her happiness in life. "*Nel bujo fitto della sera invernale il trenino andava col passo di chi sa che tanto ormai non arriva piú a tempo.*" ("In the dense darkness of the wintry night the little train traveled with the pace of one who knows that by now he will no longer arrive on time.")

As she travels to her place of employment, the woman is musing over her past in Genoa. She wants to be worthy of her former marriage with the respectable journalist who was murdered, but, since his death, she has experienced disillusionment. Now the pitiful locomotive in the night becomes a symbol both of her loneliness as well as of the miserable place of residence that awaits her. In the howling of the locomotive, she hears "the voice of her destiny," but this woman with her "small, bold nose" is a courageous soul.

Through the author's use of coincidence, the woman on the train meets the man who will affect her destiny, namely, the town secretary. In this, Pirandello employs the device of contrast. The woman's first impression of the man is negative. He has sad eyes and this automatically gives her the feeling that the world which she needs will always remain alien to her ("*lontanissimo e ignoto*"). This is another, even clearer hint of the negative end. And in conversation he reveals that he has a skeptical, pessimistic outlook on life; obviously he is a Pirandellian philosopher. The contrast between the two characters is indeed vast, and precisely for this reason the author's psychological acumen is all the greater in that, as the travelers converse, he allows an essential change of mood to take place in the man's opinion of the woman. Thus it happens that in discussing the murder of the widow's husband (a deed probably politically motivated) the town secretary feels he understands the woman well. He derives satisfaction from this and experiences a feeling of tender sympathy for the courageous widow.

The relationship between the two quickly takes a positive turn and the man opens up. He discusses the fact that the provincial town is plagued with boredom, which finds visible expression in the numerous dogs sleeping in the streets and in the squares. He also gives her some good news: the local club will soon be holding ball. At the end of the conversation, the man, who introduced himself as the town secretary, lets his "intense melancholy" show, and the locomotive greets the small train station of Pèola with a "mournful whistle."

In this fashion the story writer has introduced all the motifs of his work, except, of course, the one designated by the title as the most important. Viewed technically, the introduction is constructed with the use of contrasts, symbols and psychological insights. The contrast is extreme between the woman who shows courage despite her misfortune, and the dreary town represented by the middle-aged, pessimistic man. This contrast arouses in the reader a great liking for the woman and the secret wish that, despite all the difficulties, the two unfortunates will become a happy couple.

As I have pointed out, components of the environment are used as expressive symbols, but despite the many descriptions of the gloomy ambience, it is the psychological depiction of the characters that dominates, making these characters perfectly transparent. This is especially true in the case of young Lucietta. Here Pirandello repeatedly uses a striking stylistic device found in several of his other works. The first example of this device in **"La rosa"** is seen soon after the beginning of the story. Reflecting on her previous home in Genoa, the woman experiences a sense of disappointment expressed with the words *"Che tradimento!"* ("What a betrayal!"). First the narrator reveals what the woman is thinking about. This is immediately followed by the character's words, which are no longer part of the narration but simply what the woman is literally thinking. This constitutes a sudden leap on the author's part. He no longer keeps an objective distance but instead has jumped into the mind of the character he is describing. By becoming one with her, so to speak, he tells us with absolute certainty that what is being expressed is factual. In this way, Pirandello goes against his own psychological tenet, namely, that no individual can know any other, that we attribute only fictional personalities to people. But this anomaly can easily be discarded. No author is required to write creatively in accordance with his own theories. It is interesting to note that Pirandello's psychological belief is also at variance with the plot of **"La rosa"** in that the town secretary really understands the young woman and therefore gains a liking for her. I would like to define this stylistic device, which was especially valuable in the creation of this short narrative, as an identifying leap into the thoughts of the character being described by the narrator.

There are at least two more examples of this technique occurring in the work. 1) "I suoi due bimbi orfani, *loro sí,*

On Pirandello's portrait of Sicily:

[If the stories of **Better Think Twice about It**] have a definite locale, reflect the lives of a sharply defined group, they are, nevertheless, not mere surface reflections. The characters, and there is an almost endless parade of them, are fully etched. Even the animals—the poor, scraggy donkeys, the meagre horses, the dogs and the hens—walk in and out of these tales. In fact, more than one story in the book is satire of the sort so common in the Middle Ages in which animals were portrayed as leading very human existences or, given the gift of speech, as commenting on their human companions. There is never lengthy description in these tales, which are told with a fine economy of words; but Pirandello, now with a single line, now with a brief paragraph, so contrives to fill in the landscape that before one has finished one has a better picture of Sicily than many a travel book has to offer. That wit for which Luigi Pirandello is famous is here in abundance. Indeed, except for the first story, **"The Other Son,"** the collection could be described as merry throughout; the merriment, however, often conceals deep scorn, and is everywhere tempered with pity.

Percy Hutchison, in "Pirandello's Tales of Sicilian Life," in The New York Times Book Review, *January 6, 1935.*

poveri amorini, s'erano addormentati . . ." ("Her two orphan children, *yes, they, poor little darlings,* had fallen asleep.") Here the woman's sorrow regarding the fate of her children is expressed.

2) "Il sedile di fronte serbava l'impronta de' suoi piedini, che vi avevano trovato un comodo sostegno, prima che fosse rientrato a prender posto *ce n'erano tante di vetture, nossignori!proprio lí,* un omaccione su i trentacinque anni, barbuto, bruno in viso, ma con occhi chiari, verdastri: due occhi grandi, intenti e tristi." ("The seat in front retained the impression of her little feet, which had found a comfortable place of support there, before a man entered to find a place—*there were so many coaches, but, no sir!— right there,* a big fellow about thirty-five years old, bearded, dark-complexioned, with bright, greenish eyes: two large eyes, intense and sad.")

The interpolations in question (the italics are mine) are often followed by an exclamation point revealing that they are thoughts which aroused excitement. The latter example has yet another important and special quality. The woman thinks: "ce ne sono tante di vetture, nossignori!— proprio lí." (This means in effect: There *are* coaches with plenty of seats. The fellow does not have to sit right there and disturb me!) But the author employs the descriptive past tense *"erano"* ("were") and mixes the identification of his own "self" with his objective narration. Whoever allows this psychological device to work on himself feels the author's intense participation and is affected by it because he is drawn into the identification. Through its repeated use, Pirandello gives the characters in his work a heightened emotional vivacity.

In the next section, what happens to the special qualities we have already found? Here the theme of the narration is the stimulating effect the young woman has on the provincial town, as well as the reciprocal effect the changed town has on her. She enjoys a great deal of respect not only because she is the widow of the murdered man widely discussed by the Italian press, but also and above all, because she is youthful and charming. There are several contrasts here. There are both young and old men who are excited by Lucietta's presence. There are also a number of ugly women who react against the mood of the town, which has changed because of the young beauty. The motif of the sleepy dogs lazing about, already introduced as the symbol of the boredom affecting the town, changes its meaning in that it becomes the symbolic symptom of the "*aria nuova*" ("new mood"). The dogs are kicked and stones are thrown at them to scare them away from their places of rest, and they are pitied by the ugly women who feel a sense of solidarity with them. On the street, the men straighten their collars, vests and ties to improve their appearance. The married men say to their wives, "Dear, why don't you fix your hair a little better?" The subtle humor of this motif scarcely needs to be mentioned.

The town secretary courts the telegraph operator by conversing discreetly with her. Psychologically, this woman is the most interesting character. The repercussions on her of the new mood she has generated are amply represented. Naturally, she notices the interest she has aroused in the townsmen and is quite taken by it; the various new circumstances *"inebriarono in breve anche lei"* ("soon intoxicated her too.") At the same time, the woman, who, as we know, is a widow with two children, is in a state of emotional helplessness. Everything she experiences, both internally and externally, is portrayed by the author by means of his psychological identification with her. This is a clever stylistic device; it makes us witness a change occurring in her character which is incomprehensible even to herself. One moment she is crying without knowing why; the next she is laughing, again without knowing why. This swing in moods underscores the fact that deep mental processes are incomprehensible to the rational mind. This Pirandello's "self", which emerges periodically in the work, acts as a psychologist who represents fact to the reader and serves simultaneously as both author and scientist.

I should mention here that the end of the second part of the short story presents the positive element of an insistently offered invitation to the local club's ball, which at first the woman offers no certainty of accepting.

Part III, with its psychological portrayal of the woman, is devoted to a new motif, the one already intimated by the title of the short story. While debating whether she should go to the ball, she spots a magnificent red rose in front of a window of her house. Since it has bloomed despite the season's cold, the psychological effect of this strange contrast turns it into a decisive symbol for her: "*Vide vivo lí in quella rosa il suo desiderio ardente di godere una notte almeno.*" ("She saw vividly there in that rose her

ardent desire to enjoy at least one night.") This is a case of what psychologists call "escape". To be sure, she hopes to escape her mental distress by seeking a moment of happiness. All at once she overcomes the negativism of her inhibitions. "*Sí, là! Con quella sola rosa tra i capelli sarebbe andata alla festa, e i suoi vent'anni, e la sua gioja vestita di nero . . .*" ("Yes, there! She would go to the ball with that single rose in her hair, and with her twenty years and her joy—dressed in black . . .") She still dresses in black because, even though the traditional year of mourning has just ended, she feels very much like a widow. Here, too, artistic contrast is not absent. Moreover, in the sentence just quoted, the "identifying leap", that important stylistic technique, is used superbly.

The concluding fourth part, the night of the ball, also does not suffer from a lack of effective contrasts. There are both old and young men, dancers and spectators, as well as dignified ladies who are hurt by the effect the young lady is having on the men and who therefore leave the ball. There is the innocent enjoyment of the widow who keeps the bestial hunger of the men in check by her unassailable virtue. But above all there is the contrast between Lucietta and Fausto Silvagni, which is fundamental to the stories outcome. In the unfolding of the plot, especially in the fateful outcome, a very interesting psychological representation dominates. Such artistic richness calls for a step by step commentary.

The men, losing their heads in a mass psychosis, press around the woman, who arrives somewhat late. The reader may liken the "bestiality" of the erotically aroused men to the sleeping dogs. Although the narrator himself does not point this out, whoever reflects on this realizes that man is more dangerous than animals, and that civilized behavior hides this fact. In contrast, the twenty-year-old beauty, who is innocently swept away by the dancing at the ball, is all the more appealing. After such a grave tragedy, she deserves to enjoy life again. The town secretary does not dance but looks on pensively. He focuses his thoughts on the extremely negative experiences of his youth which have made him an isolated, inactive, pessimistic observer, and, at the same time, he thinks about Lucietta who, as he knows, is in need of help, just like himself. "*Non era forse volata da suoi sogni lontani, questa cara folle fatina vestita di nero, con una rosa di fiamma tra i capelli?*" ("Had not this crazy little sprite dressed in black, with a flaming red rose in her hair, flown out of his dreams of long ago?") In this way the narrator suggests an emotional connection between the "little sprite" and the secretary, which opens up for the reader the prospect of a lifetime bond. Thereby the rose, which up until this point was simply a symbol of the woman's zest for life, becomes such a symbol for the man as well.

The last part of the short story is the richest in psychology. Through the use of his innovative technique, the author allows us to look into the hearts and minds of the two protagonists. However, we are also made privy to the different experiences of the other men and women at the ball. This is a pluralism of inner vision that contributes importantly to the powerful effect of the final episode.

Lucietta dances without a pause, tiring the men, and afterwards there comes the surprise ending in a concentrated dramatic form. The rose falls from the woman's hair, whereupon the elderly mayor picks it up, gives it back to her and orders her to present the flower to the man of her choice. Everybody believes that this should be a declaration of love; the sexually excited young men want the woman, who is aloof, to promise herself to one of them. This is suggested by the words "The choice of Paris!" (naturally, a female Paris), uttered by one of the men. But thus the rose, which from the beginning has been the symbol of the woman's zest for life (and which now could also symbolize the same for the man), acquires the additional function of serving as a symbol of the young men's extremely tactless joke. Lucietta, however, finds a solution. She will simply present the flower to one of the men who have only sat there and looked on the entire time. However, at that moment, she spots the town secretary and spontaneously hands him the flower, which she merely intends as an expression of her affection for him. The young men maliciously insist that her gesture is a declaration of love given the notorious courtship paid by the town secretary to the telegraph operator. In this way the rose becomes the symbol of a fateful decision for the two. The situation forces the man to quickly choose between his pessimism and his feelings of love. Although his dilemma is shown only in his turning pale, she immediately grasps the entire situation. Now, not only he but she too is in a state of emotional conflict. Pressured externally, she hastens to ask him whether he believes that the presentation of the rose can be a declaration of love. In this way she herself induces the man's negative answer, which springs from his pessimism. His act is an act of renunciation, the voluntary surrender of a desired love that would mean life's happiness for both of them. He gives her back the rose and asks her to throw it away. She immediately does this with complete awareness of the significance of her gesture. In effect, the poor woman transforms the symbol of her innocent zest for life (of a night's duration) into the symbol of the destruction of her life's happiness forever.

No doubt the mood of the short story's ending puts the Pirandellian philosopher in the wrong. A reader who thinks about it might wonder whether the final symbolic gesture must be totally decisive in its meaning. Might not the two, who are suited to one another, still find each other later on? Or might not the provincial town have another suitable man to offer the woman? But such considerations should not be made since they transcend the author's intentions.

I would like to conclude my analysis with the following observation: The aesthetic elements that have attracted my attention in this short story are wonderfully combined in the dramatic ending as a pluralism of contrasts, symbols and psychological depiction.

Douglas Radcliff-Umstead (essay date 1991)

SOURCE: "Luigi Pirandello as Writer of Short Fiction and Novels," in *A Companion to Pirandello Studies*, ed-ited by John Louis DiGaetani, Greenwood Press, 1991, pp. 344–67.

[*In this excerpt, Radcliff-Umstead employs two examples, "The Journey" and "Happiness," to illustrate his assertion that Pirandello's focus in his stories is "the failure or success of his fictional characters to reach an accord with life."*]

Before his death Pirandello hoped to write a novella for each day of the year and to gather them in the series *Novelle per un anno* (*Stories for a year*). By 1937, the year after the writer's death, fifteen volumes had appeared in print. In all the author succeeded in completing 233 tales. The earliest story dates from his seventeenth year, and the final surrealistic dream stories belong to the last five years of the writer's life. Before being included in volumes, many of the tales originally appeared on the story page of major daily Italian newspapers like Milan's *Corriere della sera* as well as the provincial *Giornale di Sicilia*. The writer directed his stories to a reading public of the professional and semi-professional middle class, for whom the novellas were intended as little mirrors of their aspirations and frustrations.

In composing his tales, Pirandello had behind him the long Italian narrative tradition of novelistic art that arose in the late thirteenth century and early attained near perfection with Boccaccio's *Decameron* of 1350. The stories tend to concentrate on a single central event that determines the course of the protagonist's life by exposing the main character's inner strengths or weaknesses. Pirandello had before him the recent literary experience of his fellow Sicilian writer Giovanni Verga (1840-1922), whose collections *Vita dei campi* (*Life of the Fields*, 1880) and *Novelle rusticane* (*Rustic Tales*, 1883) marked the shift of emphasis in the novella from exterior action and verbal witticism, as in Boccaccio's tales, to an examination of inner motivation and the influence of environment. Both Verga and his Sicilian compatriot Luigi Capuana (1839-1915) were associated with *verismo*, the literary school of regional realism that stressed fidelity to truth. Many of Pirandello's tales study the same insular Sicilian world as is depicted in the narrative works of Verga and Capuana. Despite the veristic aim to achieve objectivity, all three Sicilian authors display a fatalistic attitude that seems to be inherent to the novella and that distinguishes it from the regional short stories of other nations like Russia or the American South. The art of the novella lends itself to an irrational presentation of life, where chance or fate strikes the protagonist. With his humoristic vision Pirandello represented life as a cruel practical joke, and his tales are histories of the jests that mock his characters.

Neither in the early volumes nor in the definitive editions of the *Novelle per un anno* is any attempt made to place the tales in a frame story as occurs in the *Decameron*. Pirandello realized that in the twentieth century encircling the chaotic material of life in a harmonious frame would have been artistically false. Instead, his novellas should be experienced as isolated moments of intense agony or brutal irony as filtered through humorism. The wretched characters in the world of his tales appear as calculating peasants, hypocritical clergymen, disillusioned artists, game-playing entrepreneurs, lonely students, shrewd lawyers, disappointed war veterans, unfulfilled teachers, exploited sulfur miners, reactionary aristocrats, neglected wives, unloved children, and the elderly longing only to die. For the settings of his tales, Pirandello moved from the fetid peasant huts of his earliest veristic tales of Sicily to the swarming tenements of modern Rome in the stories of his midcareer to the apartments of black Harlem and Jewish Brooklyn in his final novellas. Quite often the scene takes place in a train compartment, usually second class, or a railroad station restaurant where the restless reach out in vain to each other. A large number of characters suffer from myopia, both physical and (by symbolic extension) spiritual, and are thereby hampered in their quest for self-realization. Whatever the social roles may be, wherever the tale is set, the characters frequently remain separate from each other. The stories can be classified according to certain predominating themes or situations; fables where animals stare with amazement at the inane rituals of human life; graveyard tales with obligatory scenes in cemeteries or at funerals; stories of nihilism that explode in violence; pictures of life's barrenness often ending in suicide; exposés of the falseness of bourgeois customs (especially in marriages); and visions of a super-reality transcending everyday experience.

Even in his earliest stories, Pirandello tended toward dramatic enactment of scene. Indirect discourse is almost totally missing as lively dialogue or interior monologue (in the first or third person) take its place. As some critics have pointed out, there exists in Pirandello's narrative writing an entire language of silence made up of nonverbal communication through gestures and expressions of the eyes as well as represented voice inflections. Syntax, the use of tenses, and the choice of verbal modes (particularly the subjunctive to express emotional expectations) all contribute to creating a language of deception, to oneself and others, that Pirandello's humoristic art unmasks.

Between 1894 and 1920, before the writer conceived the plan for the comprehensive *Novelle per un anno,* Pirandello published his stories in volumes with antithetical titles like *Amori senza amore* (*Loves Without Love*); *Beffe della morte e della vita* (*Jests of Death and Life*); *Quand'ero matto* (*When I Was Mad*); *Bianche e nere* (*White and Black*); *Erma bifronte* (*The Two-faced Herm*); *La Vita nuda* (*Naked Life*); *Terzetti* (*Tercets*); *Le due maschere* (*The Two Masks*); *La Trappola* (*The Trap*); *Erba del nostro orto* (*Grass from Our Garden*); *E domani, lunedì* (*And Tomorrow, Monday*); *Un cavallo nella luna* (*A Horse in the Moon*); *Berecche e la guerra* (*Berecche and the War*); and *Il carnevale dei morti* (*The Carnival of the Dead*). On opening any of these volumes, the reader soon discovers that death plays a role in about two-thirds of the stories. Pirandello's obsession with death differs from the nightmare tales of Poe, Heine, and Maupassant as the Sicilian author focused on the empty rituals and the often pompous settings associated with death. While for a few of the characters in the novellas a tomb may provide a consoling sense of permanence, in many

cases the grave fails to testify to enduring sentiments of attachment and comforting eternal rest. Death often occurs on an August afternoon as the result of a heat stroke when the African scirocco wind blows across the blazing fields of Sicily or the burning concrete streets of Rome. A recurring situation in the tales is that of the death watch where relatives and acquaintances gather at the home of a moribund person to wait out the final hours. Although the certainty of dying may offer release from the pain of living, the realization of immediate fatality can intensify the awareness of life.

Two tales that strikingly illustrate Pirandello's novelistic art are **"Il Viaggio"** (**"The Journey,"** 1910) and **"Felicità"** (**"Happiness,"** 1911). A critical analysis of each story will reveal the writer's investigation of a subterranean world of human anguish and expectation. Adriana Braggi, the protagonist of **"Il Viaggio,"** begins to reawaken to her instinctual longing for life and love at the very time she receives a sentence of death from cancer of the lung. This tale reflects the influence of *verismo* on Pirandello as the author takes pains during the first two pages to detail the monotonous mode of life within the environment of a small town (called, pejoratively with the diminutive suffix, a *"cittaduzza"*) in the interior of Sicily. The heroine appears to be an unconscious prisoner of time-honored custom in the narrow community where women lead a claustrophobic existence, usually leaving their homes only once a week to attend Sunday mass. In that rigid society women do not function as persons in their own right but merely as extensions of their husbands' being. The fashionable gowns and jewels, ordered from Palermo or Catania, that the women wear on their weekly expedition to church are intended to impress the townspeople with the prosperity of the husbands. Throughout the opening passages, the tense that predominates is the imperfect ("she used to go out," "she used to dress," "they used to see each other") to indicate the eternal monotony and unchanging character of village life. Upon describing the region's drought-ridden conditions the author establishes a leitmotif for the story:

> In all the houses, even in the few lordly ones, water was lacking; in the vast courtyards, as at the end of streets there were old cisterns at the mercy of the heavens; but even in winter it rarely rained . . .

This story's inner structure is based on the principle of water as the source of life and death, such as the French phenomenologist Gaston Bachelard has traced in his text *Water and Dreams*. As the tale's title suggests, this is the story of a journey that the heroine will make to escape that land of drought and life-denying inflexible customs. Throughout Pirandello's novellas, the journey motif marks the attempt to discover a hitherto repressed reality.

Before her departure from the village Adriana Braggi lived in a state of unawareness, unquestionably obeying social demands for proper behavior. Her brief marriage of four years had been a silent and voluntary martyrdom of fidelity without love for a tyrannically jealous husband. What Pirandello emphasizes is that almost all the women in that empty provincial world suffer the identical fate as Adriana, except that they are never called to a journey of self-knowledge. Along with the aridity of their existence there is an atmosphere of oppressive silence that seems to annihilate the passing of time itself within the imprisoning walls of their homes "where time seemed to stagnate in a silence of death." After her husband's death, Adriana continues the routine of a provincial homemaker, staying on in the same house with her two sons, her mother, and her brother-in-law Cesare who according to village custom is the actual master of the home. It never occurs to her to deviate from time-honored custom or to rebel against a stultifying existence of being buried alive. Pirandello does not intervene directly into the tale; instead of commenting, he allows thoughts and events to take place as in a natural process. Indirect free style conveys how the death of Adriana's mother causes her to acknowledge the loss of her youth at age thirty-five. Premature old age, a drying up of vital energies, appears to be the inevitable destiny of those who accept provincial life.

Pirandello's obsession with death differs from the nightmare tales of Poe, Heine, and Maupassant as the Sicilian author focused on the empty rituals and the often pompous settings associated with death.

—Douglas Radcliff-Umstead

Adriana's routine of living according to the village code is interrupted when she has to seek medical consulation and travels with her brother-in-law to Palermo. Away from the little town's suffocating environment, Adriana changes her apparel and her coiffure, as if she were starting a new life. The scene where she stands before a mirror and shows her new traveling outfit to her teenaged sons and astonished brother-in-law is an example of Pirandello's art of dramatic enactment: all four individuals take part in an experience of discovery, wherein Adriana realizes that she has not withered away in her silent widowhood. Although her new outfit is black for mourning, its elegance makes everyone aware of the youthful vitality previously submerged under the melancholy mask of provincial existence. Through brief snatches of dialogue Pirandello allows the scene to unfold for the reader as if it were a stage performance.

This tale of Adriana's journey is one of overcoming barriers. The first barrier is passed as Adriana leaves on her first train trip and watches the narrow houses of her arid village disappear from the window of her coach. She is leaving behind a life of unconscious captivity to village tradition. With the train trip all the solidity of life vanishes, a solidity which a writer like Verga saw symbolized by the domestic hearth but which Pirandello viewed as an illusion. After a medical specialist in the island's capital city pronounces a fatal diagnosis, Adriana refuses to suc-

cumb to the lethargy that had earlier oppressed her. As she stands by the Fountain of Hercules in Palermo's public garden, the widow undergoes a mystical experience on beholding the jets of water spraying over the statue of the demigod. The joy of a seemingly endless moment permits the woman to dominate the dread of death and for the first time in her life she opens her being to all the elusive magic of rich sensations: the brilliant colors of the capital city's streets at sunset, the exciting commotion of crowds of shoppers, and at the fountain a voluptuous feeling of eternity. At last, as life and death confront each other in her consciousness, Adriana ends her stagnation.

Rather than allow Adriana to return to the slow death of living in the village, Cesare takes her with him to Naples. Crossing the sea to reach the continent marks the passing of the second barrier, for the widow, with the primitive insular mentality of Sicilians, feels that the trip across the water must signify a turning point in her life. In Naples a mere touch of each other's arm as they promenade on the street one night suffices to reveal to Adriana and Cesare the affection which earlier they would never have acknowledged. Previously, the two were "masked" to each other and to the world of their home village, but now the certainty of death permits them to violate a traditional way of life which both had accepted without question. Adriana can cross the barriers of social taboos to discover the freedom of surrender to rapture. Transgression follows naturally upon reawakening.

With the collapse of moral strictures Adriana starts out on what will be both a journey of Eros and Thanatos for her—"a journey of love toward death." Pirandello deliberately brings his tale to a swift close to represent the heroine's frenetic journey through Rome, Florence, and Milan in a delirium of passion, where every moment becomes more precious than the one before since it might be the last the lovers will share. At Venice, the city most symbolic of decay and death, Adriana spends a day of velvet voluptuousness: the velvet of gondolas which, however, reminds her of the velvet lining of coffins. No longer able to elude the mirror image of death on her face, Adriana passes the ultimate barrier by poisoning herself. Her love for Cesare could never know the disenchantment that usually follows the rapture of passion in Pirandellian tales. From the imprisonment of life in a Sicilian village, Adriana has moved to the final confinement of death to end her journey of self-discovery. Water dominates throughout the tale: the arid village where rainfall seems like a holiday, mystical rebirth at the Palermo fountain, the liberation of the steamer trip, the dreamlike vision of Venice emerging proud and melancholy from its ever silent lagoons. The passionate journey to the source of life in water frees Pirandello's heroine from entrapment but ironically leads her to the surrender of death.

According to Pirandello, a sensual and sentimental relationship between a man and a woman can never end in enduring happiness. Instead, one of the few sources of lasting contentment, Pirandello suggests, is maternal love when it is permitted to blossom. The story **"Felicità"** illustrates how the satisfaction of the maternal instinct en-

ables a woman to withstand social humiliation and poverty. This tale also demonstrates Pirandello's art of contrasting sadness with warmth and intimacy. It, too, is a
story of barriers, in this instance, the barriers that the
characters raise to isolate themselves from each other. The
story opens in a zone of nearly explosive tension: at Palermo in the town palace of Duke Gaspare Grisanti, whose
last hope for financial salvation has vanished after his
only son deserted a wealthy wife to run off with an actress. An air of decay hangs over the gloomy rooms of the
palace, made all the more oppressive by the stuffy odor of
old furniture. Pirandello makes the tense atmosphere an
almost tactile experience where a violent electric charge
seems about to burst forth from every familiar object. All
her childhood the duke's daughter Elisabetta lived in the
palace's shadows, knowing her father did not love her
because her lack of beauty would not attract a rich match
to restore the family fortune. When Elisabetta asks for her
father's consent to wed a tutor (a man from a far inferior
social class), the duke agrees to the shameful marriage but
banishes her forever from the palace. This tale then is
concerned with the distances that people build between
themselves. Pirandello portrays in spatial terms the spirit
of exclusion that leads the duke to separate others (including his own child) from his aristocratic presence. Consequently, the son-in-law can enter the palace only by the
servants' staircase to collect the meager checks granted to
him in place of a dowry. Since the duke never intends to
look at Elisabetta again, he arranges for his wife to meet
her in a rented carriage. Here the author emphasizes how
some individuals stubbornly attempt to manipulate reality,
to the point of determining the space others can occupy
and share with each other.

After Elisabetta's husband deserts her and flees Sicily to
avoid prosecution for theft, the young woman rises above
misery to radiant joy when she gives birth to a boy. She
does not seek reconciliation with the duke, who continues
to make his pompous daily appearance in public riding
through the streets in a coach attended by footmen in
perukes and livery. She has already established a humble
"*casetta*" ("the little house"—the diminutive stresses both
the impoverishment and the warm intimacy of the home),
feeling no need to return to the palace's melancholy darkness. Mother and child can live at the outskirts of town,
near a countryside of cheerful sunlight and fragrant flowers. The tale closes with Elisabetta's resolute dismissal of
her mother's hope that the duke might relent and readmit
his daughter and grandson to the palace. For in the little
house a sense of sunny openness predominates, in contrast
to the palace's dark constriction. As the story's title indicates, Elisabetta has created her own corner of happiness,
such as Bachelard studies in his treatise *The Poetics of
Space*. With a strength of will Pirandello thought unique
to mothers, Elisabetta can bear exclusion from her aristocratic heritage because the truly vital identity she has discovered in maternity allows her to construct a zone of
private contentment. Motherhood can then offer a release
from the anguish of living.

Throughout his novellas Luigi Pirandello examined individual cases of the failure or success of his fictional char-

acters to reach an accord with life. Adriana Braggi of **"Il
Viaggio"** discovers renewal and annihilation simultaneously, while Elisabetta Grisanti finds liberation in banishment. In his short fiction the writer explored situations of
distress and alienation in a naturally condensed literary
form.

Maria Rosaria Vitti-Alexander   (essay date 1991)

SOURCE: "Nature as Structural-Stylistic Motive in *Novelle per un anno*," in *A Companion to Pirandello Studies,* edited by John Louis DiGaetani, Greenwood Press,
1991, pp. 385–95.

[*In the following essay, Vitti-Alexander maintains that a
symbolic connection exists between Pirandello's characters and nature as it is depicted in his stories.*]

In the preface to *Six Characters in Search of an Author,*
Pirandello calls himself a philosophical writer because he
aims to give his "figure, vicende, paesaggi" (characters,
vicissitudes, landscapes) a universal value, a "patricolare
senso della vita" (a particular sense of life). Driven by a
"profondo bisogno spirituale" (a profound spiritual need),
he continually probes, dissects, and analyzes everything,
be it man, vicissitude, or nature.

This [essay] shows how nature in the Pirandellian short
stories does not stand alone, for a "paesaggio" (landscape)
is not presented "per il solo gusto di descriverlo" (for the
simple reason of a mere description). Rather, it acts within the limits of narration, as a structural motive, almost
always a catalyst for the action of the characters. In several short stories, the character finds the only possibility
of development—that is, escaping his present predicament—through a specific reference to nature. In other
stories, nature becomes an important tool for emphasizing
the characters, and in so doing, clarifies and completes
their personalities. This completion is sometimes achieved
by focusing on various aspects of the character's personality and at other times through a humoristic opposition to
nature itself.

This use of landscape is particularly effective because of
the characteristics of the short story genre. By definition
the short story must keep within a limited narrative space
and make maximum use of its content by concentrating on
a close sequence of events. Because Pirandello's focus is
on his preoccupation with man and his ensnarement in the
incongruous ways of life, everything else, including nature, becomes subjected to this central focus. By nature I
mean the natural elements around us, such as the sky, the
sea, and the earth, which can be either experienced first
hand or filtered through the imagination of the artist.

In the preface to **Novelle per un anno,** Corrado Alvaro,
close to Pirandello through many years of friendship, talks
of the man Pirandello—of his ways of living, seeing, and
understanding things. For Alvaro, Pirandello was a lover
of humankind, an indefatigable observer of the infinite

meanderings of the human mind, one who "lasciava parlare e ascoltava" (would let others talk while he listened). Alvaro also recounts that Pirandello, after having visited much of the world, remembered only people from these trips, rarely the things he saw:

> Non lo sentii mai parlare di mobili, di oggetti, di decorazioni, ma molto di uomini, dal fondo di tutte le città che aveva vedute, e come seguitando ad aver da fare con essi, contrastarvi, accordarsi, inveire.

> I never heard him speak of furnishings, of objects, of decorations, but a lot of men, from the background of all the cities he had seen, and as if continuing to have to deal with them, oppose them, agree with them, inveigh at them.

Even the memories of his son Stefano emphasize this aspect of the writer's interest—that desire to know, penetrate, and understand the human mind, paying little attention, so it seems, to the outside world. Stefano recounts that his father would remain taciturn during parties and reunions, only to return to his study and recall precise and revealing details about all those present.

This curiosity about man, whom Pirandello thought both simple and complex, comprehensible and incomprehensible, has always been at the center of his interest and the focal point of his writings. In all his works, the main focus is always on the character of man, humoristically Pirandellian, because

> il giudizio che dava sugli uomini glielo dettava il momento, la circostanza, l'umore; e non era mai definitivo. A un giorno di distanza diceva l'opposto.

> the judgment he would give on men was dictated to him by the moment, the circumstance, the mood; and it was never final. A day later he would say the opposite.

A glance at Pirandello's writings reveals this insatiable preoccupation with man and the workings of his mind. In the later preface to *Il fu Mattia Pascal*, Pirandello himself acknowledges this penchant when he says that the humorist goes out and looks for specimens with a wooden leg, or a glass eye, because for him man is not an abstraction or a type, but an individual with faults, shortcomings, and imperfections. His last novel, *Uno, nessuno e centomila* (*One, None and a Hundred Thousand*), is about a dissolution of personality which the reader follows through the mentality of the main character. The play *Trovarsi* is built entirely on the mental anguish of the protagonist who finally realizes the double aspect of human experience.

Pirandello's own personal life played an important part in his disposition toward the workings of the mind. From 1903 until 1913, Pirandello lived with a mentally ill wife, always feeling himself divided into two—the man he thought he was and the man his wife saw. Later, these tormented years gave birth to many works that focus on man and his psyche—*Diana e la Tuda*; *Cap and Bells*;

Her Husband, Shoot, to mention a few. Pirandello felt his southern origin might also account for his preoccupation with the dialectics of the mind; in the short story **"Il Professor Terremoto"** one of his characters reminds us that:

> Sono così tormentosamente dialettici questi nostri bravi confratelli meridionali. Affondano nel loro spasimo, a scavarlo fino in fondo, la saettella di trapano del loro raziocinio, e frù e frù e frù, non la smettono più.

> They are so tormentingly dialectical these good Southern brethren of ours. They drive the point of the drill of reason deep into their sorrow to dig to the very bottom, and they go and go and go at it without ever stopping.

Given the extensive collection *Novelle per un anno,* I will limit myself here to only a few short stories as examples. The short story **"Fuga"** is a beautiful example of nature determining the action of the character. In this story the natural elements of the outside world push the main character, Bareggi, to accomplish his escape from his personal world. Nature offers him the only possibility of development. Bareggi is locked in by an oppressive world of stressful work and by an impossible family life caused by the presence of three women dependent on him economically and psychologically. Nature provides him with the stimulus and resolve to act against his circumstances. Note how the dim light of a rural world incites him to flee his unsustainable situation:

> appena nelle nari avverti il fresco odore fermentoso d'un bel fascio di fieno nella rete e il puzzo caprigno del cappotto del lattajo . . . : gli odori della campagna lontana, che immaginò subito, laggiù, laggiù, oltre la barriera nomentana, oltre Casal dei Pazzi, immensa, smemorata e liberatrice.

> as soon as his nostrils caught the fresh, fermenting odor of a nice bundle of hay in the feedbag and the stench of goats on the milkman's coat . . . : the smells of the distant countryside, which he imagined immediately, over there, over there, behind the barrier of the Nomentana, behind Casal dei pazzi, immense, forgetful, and liberating.

A rural odor and the presence of a country object excite the character's imagination and compel him to escape the asphyxiating, immediate reality. Arriving home from work tired, suffering from nephritis, and harassed by the thought of his daughters and wife, Bareggi seizes a horse-drawn milkman's cart parked outside a home and scurries into the country:

> Volò Ponte Nomentano, volò Casal dei Pazzi, e via, via, via, nella campagna aperta, che già s'indovinana nella nebbia.

> Ponte Nomentano flew by, Casal dei Pazzi flew by, and on and on into the open countryside, which was dimly visible through the fog.

Bareggi's escape is accomplished through a tumultuous crescendo of sounds and through continuous references to the outside world. The horse's neighs are echoed by the tremendous noise of the cans and the jugs in the cart which "doveva sembrare una tempestà quel carretto in fuga con tutti quegli arnesi che, traballando, s'urtavano" (it must have seemed a racket, that cart in flight with all those tools which, bumping, hit one another). Above it all rises Bareggi's voice, accompanying "la pazza corsa" (the mad flight) with long, repeated laughs; "rideva il signor Bareggi, pur nel terrore . . . rideva di quel terrore; . . . E rideva, rideva, . . ." (He was laughing, Signor Bareggi, even in his fear . . . he was laughing at his own fear; . . . and he kept on laughing and laughing . . .) At the same time there is the constant reference to the fog which "si faceva sempre più fitta col calar della sera" (was becoming always ever more heavy with the approaching nightfall), and "che gli impediva di veder perfino le lampade elettriche" (which prevented him from seeing even the electric lamps). The fog both heightens the sensation of the flight toward an "immensa," "smemorata," and therefore "liberatrice" countryside, and displays the symbiosis between the confused psychological state of the character, who runs away unconscious of where he is going and of what is happening to him, and the landscape which, wrapped in a cotton-wool cloud, hides the reality of things. His unconsciousness is reaffirmed by the fact that the horse, not he himself, is the agent of the mad escape. It is only the horse and the empty milk wagon that the reader sees at the end of the story. What has become of Bareggi the reader is never told:

> Quando il cavallo si fermò davanti al rustico casalino, col carretto sconquassato e senza più né bidone né un orcio, era già sera chiusa.

> When the horse stopped in front of the rustic farmhouse, with the ruined cart, but with neither the milk can nor the pitcher, it was already late night.

As Bareggi's unconscious mental state is evidenced by a sharp, dense, and assailing fog that wraps and hides the world, the meticulous and repetitive presentation of aspects of nature emphasize the conscious decision Matteo Sinagra reaches in "**Da sé.**" In this short story, the fusion between character and landscape is continued and amplified, so that nature becomes an absolute and the character's state of mind is explained and understood through the repeated lists of natural elements.

Matteo Sinagra, having lost all confidence in himself after experiencing a bankruptcy, and feeling "dead" for all practical purposes, decides to resolve his miserable existence by taking his own life. Not having money for his funeral, Sinagra decides to walk himself to the graveyard, as a "corpse" walking to his own funeral. It is during this walk that Sinagra, a dead-man-alive, as he calls himself, experiences quite a different world around him, now that he is detached from his own subjective conceptions. In his condition as a "living corpse" he observes the world for the first and last time. The nature he sees is the everyday elements: trees, rocks, clouds, flowers, the sea, and the

mountains. But the presentation of these elements illustrates the character's new perspective. The character himself has changed. Mundane aspects of the surrounding world reveal themselves to him from a different perspective because they were seen with different eyes. As a dead person, Sinagra is amazed by a world he had never seen before. With newfound innocence, he rediscovers known aspects of nature that his mundane familiarity with nature had taught him to neglect:

> Gli alberi . . . o guarda! erano così gli alberi? E quei monti laggiù . . . perché? quei monti azzurri, con quelle nuvole bianche sopra . . . Le nuvole . . . che cose strane! . . . E là, in fondo, il mare . . . Era così? Quello, il mare?

> The trees . . . oh look! Were the trees like this? And those mountains down there . . . why? Those blue mountains, with those white clouds on top . . . Clouds . . . what strange things! . . . And there, at the bottom of the sea . . . It was like this? That, the sea?

In the position of a corpse walking himself to his grave, Sinagra's condition becomes as absolute as the nature he focuses on; because nature is seen through a fresh and unbiased perspective, it becomes an object that exists in itself.

The symbiosis between nature and character finds an ulterior and more complex application in "**Un cavallo sulla luna,**" where the characters' personalities are presented and developed through a humoristic opposition to nature. In this short story the narrator utilizes nature for a double purpose; he uses it to show the symbiosis of the characters' souls with the rural world, and he exploits it to focus on the characters' humoristic differences. Nino Berardi, an older man of noble Sicilian descent, has married a young, naive northern girl. They have chosen to spend their honeymoon in an old family house located in the Sicilian countryside. The short story opens with the rural landscape of an arid and dry farmland:

> Di settembre, su quell'altipiano d'aride argille azzurre, . . . la campagna già riarsa dalle rabbie dei lunghi soli estivi, era triste: ancor tutta irta di stoppie annerite, con radi mandorli e qualche ceppo centenario d'olivo saraceno qua e là.

> In September, on that plain of arid, blue clay, . . . the countryside, already parched by the rage of the long summer sun was gloomy: yet all was bristling with blackened stubbles, with a few almond trees and some centennial Saracen olive trees here and there.

The landscape so particularly introduced does not exist per se but is instead employed mystically as an explicative mirror of the protagonist's mental state. It is through the exterior representation of nature that the character's internal parching thirst finds its expression. The "campagna riarsa dalla rabbia dei lunghi soli estivi" (the countryside, parched by the rage of the long summer suns) mirrors Nino's volto infocato, che guardava qua e là coi piccoli occhi neri, lustri, da pazzo, e non intendeva più nulla, e non mangiava e non beveva e diventava di punto in punto più pavonazzo, quasi nero.

excited face, that looked here and there with small glowing black eyes, those of a madman, and he was no longer hearing anything, and was not eating and not drinking and was becoming from moment to moment more purple, almost black.

Nino is not a groom capable of understanding "la giovanissima sposa . . . una vera bambina ancora, fresca, aliena" (the very young bride . . . truly a little girl still, fresh, aloof), but rather a mature man who burns with desire for "una bambina."

The humoristic employment of the natural aspects of the countryside becomes evident when applied to the other character, Ida:

Ida dietro le spesse siepi . . . sentiva, invece, correndo, come strillavano gaje al sole le calandre, e come, nell'afa dei piani, nel silenzio attonito, sonava da lontane aje, auguroso, il canto di qualche gallo; si sentiva investire, ogni tanto, dal fresco respiro refrigerante che veniva dal mare prossimo.

Ida, as she ran, heard how gaily the wood-larks sang in the sun, from behind the thick hedges . . . she heard also, in the sultriness of the plain, and in the astonished silence, the crow of cocks, full of prophecy from distant barnyards; she felt assailed now and then by the fresh, cool breath coming from the nearby sea.

While for Nino the narrator uses nature to describe his uncontrollable passion, for the innocent Ida that same nature reflects her gentleness and docility. Ida sees neither aridity nor rage, only peace. While the dense, pungent, heavy breath of nature is truly a detailed visual and olfactory representation of the man's burning sexual desire, nature also signifies Ida's innocence. It is only at the closing of the short story, when she panics at seeing her husband dying, that the surroundings become the operating motive of Ida's escape. The countryside is hostile now, with a large, menacing moon, which

sorgeva lenta da quel mare giallo di stoppie. E, nera, in quell'enorme disco di rame vaporoso, la testa inteschiata di quel cavallo . . . mentre i corvi, facendo la ruota, gracchiavano alti nel cielo. . . .

was rising slowly from that yellow sea of stubbles. And, black, against that enormous vapory copper disk, the skull-like head of that horse . . . while the crows, circling above, croaked, high in the sky . . .

Ida wants to flee and calls for the father "a gran voce il padre, il padre che se la portasse via . . . via, via, via" (in a loud voice to her father, her father to take her away . . . away, away, away).

The presence of landscape in Pirandello's narrative has been studied at length. Yet the operating function of nature in relation to the protagonist has been ignored. In many cases nature acts as a determining aspect of Pirandello's narrative because the final action of the protagonist—even though precarious—finds expression and explanation in the only landscape description present. Such short stories are usually narrations of human misery (such as a tormented life or a boring or insufficient job), which are almost totally deprived of landscapes but always end with an image of nature or a simple reference to it. In many cases the image and reference are short and incisive because they are symbolically tied to the main character of the story. It is, in fact, this mention of the outside world that offers the character the only possibility of development, of freeing himself from his world.

An example is the short story **"La distruzione dell'uomo,"** where Pirandello presents the complex and totally absorbing existential suffering of a man. Petix, the main character, can neither accept nor explain humanity's insistence on procreation, even when it means raising children in poverty. Petix's atrocious suffering is dissected and analyzed thoroughly. The world that obsesses him, and in which he is condemned to live, is populated by the poor, who in Petix's eyes are completely lacking in dignity and decorum. While the object of study in this short story is the misery of this world, and the nausea that Petix feels toward it, Pirandello provides the only possibility of action through the landscape descriptions, and thereby allows Petix to escape the hated world of procreation.

Signora Porrella, a forty-seven-year-old woman, is pregnant for the sixteenth time in her life and completely unconscious of her repulsively deformed body. She comes to symbolize, for Petix, the world of his suffering. At the end of her ninth month, Signora Porrella, accompanied by her husband, takes daily walks through the city toward a river nearby where she stops to rest on a rock by the river bank. The river, the only reference to nature in this otherwise totally closed and inescapable world of mental suffering, provides Petix with the only way to carry out his revenge. One day Petix, provoked to the limits by the strolling couple,

non disse nulla; e tutto si svolse in un attimo, quasi quietamente. Come la donna s'accostò al pietrone per mettervisi a sedere egli l'afferrò per un braccio e la trasse con uno strappo fino all'orlo delle acque straripate; là le diede uno spintone e la mandò ad annegare nel fiume.

said nothing; and everything happened in an instant, almost quietly. As the woman came close to the big stone to begin to sit down, he seized her by the arm and with one tug dragged her to the edge of the flooding river; there he gave her a strong shove and sent her to drown in the river.

That landscape, seemingly introduced by chance, is an integral part of the motive for Petix's homicidal act, the only action that the narrator provides for him to free him-self of this woman who symbolizes, with her pregnancy, the world of bestial procreation that he so despises. The river, so opportunely introduced in the narration, offers him the way to freedom. The presence of the water, the big rock on the river bank, Petix's shove, and the death of the woman are all fused in the short but necessary de-scription of the natural landscape. Petix's violence to the woman, impetuous and without escape, mirrors the vio-lence of the turbulent current that inexorably drags away the body of the victim.

Nature can also be used to continue a character's life, as in the case of the short story **"La morte addosso."** The protagonist, condemned by a mortal illness, knows he cannot escape his cruel fate. Death tells him, after having put "un fiore in bocca," a cancerous growth on his lip, that "ripasserò tra otto o dieci mesi!" (I will be back within eight or ten months). The only action the narrator assigns him is to wait until death returns. But as in the previous story, the escape comes from nature. One night the dying character meets a man who is waiting in a train station for the next train. The two spend the night speaking together and in the morning, before the casual companion of a night leaves to return to the country, the dying man turns to him and asks him to help him find a way to escape his death and so continue to live:

> E mi faccia un piacere, domattina, quando arriverà. . . All'alba, lei può far la strada a piedi. Il primo cespuglietto d'erba su la sponda. Ne conti i fili per me. Quanti fili saranno, tanti giorni ancora io vivrò. Ma lo scelga bello grosso, mi raccomando. Buona notte, caro signore.

> Do me a favor. Tomorrow morning, when you get back. . . At dawn, you can make the rest of your journey on foot. The first small tuft of grass by the roadside. Count the number of blades for me. The number of those blades will be the number of days that I have yet to live. But, I implore you, choose a nice, big tuft. Good-night, dear signore!

Again in this short story it is a glimpse of landscape, of nature, that widens the perspective of the protagonist and offers him a means to escape death. A "cespuglio campes-tre," a tuft of grass, in a faraway place will be the char-acter's lifeline.

The landscape description also stimulates the character's imagination to the point where his fantasy actually be-comes reality. This is the case in **"Rimedio: la geogra-fia,"** whose character, desperate because of his family condition, a dying mother, a wife with whom he cannot communicate, and a meager family budget, finds an es-cape by wandering through the pages of his daughter's atlas. The character's wanderings around the globe are not only mental flights, but they become for him real escapes from which he returns with an impression so concrete and tangible that his nostrils still sense "il tanfo caldo e grasso del letame nelle grandi stalle" (the warm and heavy stench of the manure in the big stables). The mental flights are

real enough to cause the character to contrast them to the sad reality of his household.

Even though the landscape presented here is not real but imagined, it equally carries out its function for the char-acter. When his wife becomes intolerable and begins to request things he cannot provide, he immediately replaces her with the image of a place, Lapland, where conjugal conduct is different because

> I Lapponi, . . . sudici cani, cara mia! . . . Ti basti sapere che, mentr'io ti tengo così cara, essi tengono così poco alla fedeltà coniugale, che offrono la moglie e le figliuole al primo forestiero che capita. Per conto mio, cara puoi star sicura: non son tentato per nulla, cara, a profittarne.

> The Laplanders, dirty dogs, my dear! . . . It is enough for you to know that, while I am so fond of you, they are so little interested in conjugal fidelity, to offer the wife and their daughters to the first foreigner who comes by. As for me, dear, you can be sure I am not at all tempted, dear, to take advantage of that.

The wife can neither follow him in his mental escape from the immediate reality, nor can she understand his humor-istic answer:

> Ma che diavolo dici? Sei pazzo? Io ti sto doman–dando. . . . Sì, cara. Tu mi stai domandando, non dico di no. Ma che triste paese, la Lapponia!

> But what in the world are you saying? Are you crazy? I am asking you. . . .

> Yes, dear. You are asking me, I am not denying it. But what a sad country Lapland is!

As Corrado Alvaro reminds us in his preface: "gli uomini lo interessavano . . . nessun ricordo di paese, molti sugli uomini" (men interested him . . . not one remembrance of a country, many of the men). Yet it would be unjust to say that Pirandello was insensitive to nature and that he felt detached from it. For Pirandello nature provides the vehi-cle through which he develops his characters. Even in those short stories where it is man, as character, who dominates, nature is never absent but is represented sym-biotically by the character himself. Pirandello's memories of people he met during his frequent trips around the world and of his countrymen, that "contrastarvi, accordarsi, in-veire con essi" (to oppose them, agree with them, inveigh at them), is all transformed in a remembrance dense as a landscape. Unfailingly, the reader leaves the Pirandellian short stories with a vision of nature, a smell of earth, and an indelible feeling of landscape because it is part of the subconscious of the characters themselves.

In many Pirandellian short stories nature is a function of human thought—not as a direct representation but mir-rored. Although the short story **"La giara"** takes place in the countryside, among olive groves and planted fields, there is not one direct description of the landscape itself.

We do not see the bountiful olive trees, but we know of their presence through the voice of the narrator who instead describes an "annata buona," a good harvest year, and lined-up jars ready to be filled with oil. Such an indirect presentation of nature continues throughout the story. It is men working, the coming and going of the olive pickers and the mule-drivers who "con le mule cariche di concime da depositare a mucchi su la costa per la favata della nuova stagione" (with the mules loaded with manure to deposit on the slope by the field where he was going to sow beans next year), which suggest an image of a rural Sicilian countryside. A description of the olive groves, of the fields to be cultivated, does not interest the narrator. More important are the thoughts of the characters toward the groves and the countryside. The result is a fusion, a symbiosis between men and nature, that does not allow us to see one without the other. An old peasant is therefore seen as a tree, "vecchio sbilenco, dalle giunture storpie e nodose, come un ceppo antico d'olivo saraceno" (a misshapen old man, crippled and gnarled, just like an ancient Saracen olive tree).

In **"Notte"** we see the casual encounter of two wretched individuals, an unhappily married man and a young widow. While waiting for their train, the two spend the night on a deserted beach, sharing their miseries and sorrows. But in a moment of silence the two become aware of the nature in front of them, and through nature their individual sufferings take on a universal meaning, an existential suffering shared by all humankind:

> di tutti gli esseri e di tutte le cose, . . . di tutta la vita che non può sapere perché si debba nascere, perché si debba amare, perché si debba morire.

> of all the human beings and of the things, . . . of all life which cannot know why one should be born, should love, or should die.

At dawn the two are ready to resume their journey and to continue with their own miserable existence; but now they have learned to find in the surrounding nature a consoling force for their unhappy lives.

Because of Pirandello's predilection for short stories, and his lifelong writing of them, he has been called Boccaccio's successor in the tradition of Italian short prose writing. Indeed, like Boccaccio, Pirandello has found in this literary genre a most suitable mode of narration. But while Boccaccio often describes nature, landscape, and the environment, Pirandello makes character prevalent over landscape. In his essay *L'umorismo* Pirandello says:

> Dopo aver considerato il cielo, il clima, il sole, la società, i costumi, i pregiudizzi, ecc., non dobbiamo forse appuntar lo sguardo sui singoli individui e domandarci che cosa siano divenuti in ciascuno di essi questi elementi, secondo lo speciale organamento psichico, la combinazione originaria, unica, che costituisce questo o quell'individuo? Dove uno s'abbandona, l'altro si rivolta; dove uno piange, l'altro ride; ride; e ci può esser sempre qualcuno che ride e piange a un tempo. Del mondo che lo circonda, l'uomo,

in questo o in quel tempo, non vede se non ciò che lo interessa; fin dall'infanzia, senza neppur sospettarlo, egli fa una scelta d'elementi e li accetta e accoglie in sè; e questi elementi, più tardi, sotto l'azione del sentimento, s'agiteranno per combinarsi nei modi più svariati.

After having considered the sky, the climate, the sun, society, customs, prejudices, etc., don't we really have to turn our gaze to the single individuals and ask ourselves what these elements have become in each one of them, according to the special psychic organism, the original, unique combination, which constitutes this or that individual? Where one lets himself go, the other rebels; where one cries, the other smiles; and there can always be someone who laughs and cries at the same time. Of the world which surrounds him, man, in this or in that time, sees only what interests him: since childhood, without even suspecting it, he chooses elements, accepts them, and makes them his own; these elements, later, under the action of feeling, will be stirred to combine themselves in the most varied ways.

With regard to the relationship between Pirandello and nature, Corrado Alvaro says that "Pirandello transferì ogni sentimento della natura in una legge fatale del cuore e dei sensi, . . ." (Pirandello transferred every feeling for nature into a fatal law of the heart and the senses, . . .). But such a transference must not be seen as the author's insensitivity to the natural world; it must be seen, rather, as a will to see and understand nature through its relationship with humankind, because

> l'arte è la natura stessa, ma proseguente l'opera sua nello spirito umano. E da questo appunto deriva l'amore dell'artista per la natura: egli si riconosce in essa, e al contatto di lei assume coscienze del proprio genio.

> art is nature itself, but continuing its work in the human spirit. In fact, from this derives the artist's love for nature: he recognizes himself in her, and through this contact with her he assumes consciousness of his own genius.

Maria Grazia Di Paolo (essay date 1993)

SOURCE: "Women's Marginality and Self-Obliteration in Some of Pirandello's *Novelle*," in *Forum Italicum*, Vol. 27, Nos. 1–2, Spring–Fall, 1993, pp. 204–13.

[*In the following excerpt, Di Paolo assesses Pirandello's characterizations of women in his short stories, finding them stereotypical and limited in variety.*]

When reading Pirandello's *novelle* (and his other works as well), we become more and more convinced that his female characters convey traditional myths, which can broadly be so identified: woman as Flesh, as Nature, as Muse. Under these categories we encounter images of women in a variety of roles common to a male-dominated tradition. The most common among them are those of mother, caretaker, and fallen woman. Consequently, I intend to discuss here some *novelle* not only because they are important in themselves, but because, more than others, they illustrate modes of discourse in which both narrator and narratee are, in one way or another, engaged in some kind of gender-inflected dialogue. These *novelle* have a common theme—the marginality of women. As we shall see, women are outsiders, "escluse," totally dependent upon men for support and approval.

Let us first examine **"La veste lunga."** The narrative perspective of this story—as well as that of the others to be discussed here—is third-person limited (also called selective omniscience), and the events are being relayed through the eyes and mind of a female protagonist. The story centers around Didì, who wears her first long dress when the men in her life (her brother and her father) take her to Zùnica, where they hope to marry her off to the Marchese Andrea Nigrenti di Zùnica, "in una cittaduzza morta, in un fosco palazzo antico, accanto a un vecchio marito dai capelli lunghi . . . ." During the trip to Zùnica, Didì has time to reflect as she feels left out, alone:

> Da un pezzo, cioè dalla morte della madre, avvenuta tre anni addietro, Didì aveva l'impressione che il padre si fosse come allontanato da lei, anzi staccato così, che lei, ecco, poteva osservarlo come un estraneo. E non il padre soltanto: anche Cocò.

While the train slowly moves on through desolate, arid fields, without a drop of water nor a blade of grass, under an ominous blue sky, Didì, observing the two men comfortably asleep, ponders silently: "Dove la conducevano quei due, che anche lì la lasciavano così sola? A un'impresa vergognosa; E dormivano!" On that long eight-hour train ride, oppressed by the heat and burdened by her long dress, Didì finds it all too unbearable. In despair, therefore, she frantically gulps down her father's medicine. Three hours later the train reaches its destination with a "piccola morta con quella sua veste lunga a Zùnica, al paese di sogno della sua infanzia felice."

Conflict is a central element in this story, which pits Didì (the female protagonist) against her father and brother (the male protagonists), by opposing male and female realms against each other. Didì's entire life unfolds inside a house: "Le pareva che fosse rimasta lei sola a vivere ancora della vita della casa, o piuttosto a sentire il vuoto di essa . . ."; her father's and brother's, outside: "Il padre, il fratello s'erano messi a vivere per conto loro, fuori di casa, certo." Didì's role is obviously a passive one, severely curtailed by her womanhood, as the symbolic signification of her long dress (referred to so often in the course of the narration), so clearly indicates. The role of the male protagonists is, instead, an active one, since it is they—not she—who decide on, and choose, Didì's behavioral tenets. In Derridian terms, the story is built, then, on a set of hierarchical oppositions in which males hold a position of privilege. Finally, trapped in a convention that allows her no authoritative self, Didì must either succumb or take her own life, the only possession still completely hers. However de-

plorable, her suicide is an act of rebellion that may suggest the acquisition, on her part, of a female identity.

There are a few examples in Pirandello's *novelle* where occasionally women do step out into the world, from which they were barred, in order to quench what Pirandello calls the natural thirst for life: "ce lo sentiamo tutti qua, come un'angoscia nella gola, il gusto della vita," he writes in **"La morte addosso."** Yet, that only happens in extreme circumstances, the outcome of which is usually fatal. Adriana Braggi of the story **"Il viaggio,"** we are told from the very beginning, is a widow: "Da tredici anni Adriana Braggi non usciva più dalla casa antica, silenziosa come una badìa, dove giovinetta era entrata sposa."

Later Pirandello explains the reason for her total seclusion by illustrating the social restrictions in which Adriana (exemplifying womanhood) is bound to live, apart from the social amenities of the male experience:

> A—Di questa clausura nessuno si meravigliava in quell'alta cittaduzza dell'interno della Sicilia, ove i rigidi costumi per poco non impedivano alla moglie di seguire nella tomba il marito. Dovevano le vedove starsene chiuse così in perpetuo lutto, fino alla morte.

> B—Gli uomini, tanto o quanto, trovavano nella varia vicenda degli affari, nella lotta dei partiti comunali, nel Caffé o nel Casino di compagnia, la sera, da distrarsi in qualche modo; ma le donne, in cui fin dall'infanzia s'era costretto a isterilire ogni istinto di vanità, sposate senz'amore, dopo avere atteso come serve alle faccende domestiche sempre le stesse, languivano miseramente con un bambino in grembo o col rosario in mano, in attesa che l'uomo, il padrone, rincasasse.

But Adriana is more fortunate than most women of her time: taken ill, she enters the outside world when her brother-in-law escorts her to Palermo for a more accurate diagnosis of her illness. The trip opens up Adriana's eyes to the wonders of an unknown world. The voyage, in Pirandello's words, becomes "viaggio d'amore, senza ritorno; viaggio d'amore verso la morte." Life reveals its wonders to Adriana, for she discovers not only a world she does not know—she discovers love. Adriana surrenders to these discoveries with all the passion of a dying woman who thirsts for life, vanishing as soon as envisioned. Unable to face the reality that awaits her, she too, like Didì, chooses to end her own life by drinking the entire potion she was to have taken drop by drop in the few remaining days of her existence.

The same point of view links this story to the previous one—third-person limited. Through Adriana, the protagonist, we see most of its action—a narrative mode ideal for the kind of fiction wherein narrator and narratee express one single view point. The conflict basically occurs between woman and society that dictates her code of conduct. Again we have two different and conflicting realms governed by male-dictated canons: "E allora ella non poté più replicare: vide in sé la donna del suo paese che non deve mai replicare a ciò che l'uomo stima giusto e conveniente." In both *novelle* the author employs archaic variations of the "two suitors' convention," a nineteenth-century novelistic mode wholly patriarchal in nature, for its structure implies the inferiority and necessary subordination of women. This convention implies "the binary opposition of two suitors," provided that the term "suitor" is taken loosely to mean a potential mate for the female character, whose maturity is evaluated in terms of her response to her suitors. In **"La veste lunga,"** of course, we have only one suitor, and the conflict arises precisely from that premise, since the heroine, having been left without a choice, must prevent the impending unwanted marriage through her untimely death. In **"Il viaggio,"** instead, the "two suitors' convention" proves quite efficacious, insofar as the heroine has learned the value of gentility, silence, and self-denial. She has picked the "wrong" suitor for herself, but the "right" one for society, as she does exactly all that is expected of her. Once widowed, she is free to love the man of her choice. However, this is not the result of the emancipation of her "self" or the acquisition of a new consciousness, but rather of a process of "internalization." According to Lacanian theories, a sense of identity ensues from the "internalization" of perspectives others may have of one. Adriana has fully succeeded in internalizing male desire, that is to the extent that she imagines herself as men imagine her. She follows the male-authored canon to the letter: before going to Palermo, a new wardrobe is bought for her, presumably by her brother-in-law, who also gives her instructions as how each article of clothing is to be worn. Her suicide, therefore, cannot be deemed an act of rebellion like Didì's of **"La veste lunga,"** but, in view of her illness and what awaits her at home, should be seen as an act of renunciation dictated by her total concern for social demeanor: "riconobbe i caratteri del maggiore dei suoi figlioli: si portò quella busta alle labbra e la baciò disperatamente; poi entrò nella sua camera; trasse dalla borsa di cuoio la boccetta con la mistura dei veleni intatta; si buttò sul letto disfatto e la bevve d'un sorso."

"The literary landscape is strewn with dead female bodies" [Elizabeth Showalter, "Toward a Feminist Poetics," in *The New Feminist Criticism,* edited by Showalter, 1985] is a phrase that aptly describes the frequency with which these characters commit suicide. Yet not all of Pirandello's heroines are doomed by the same fate of untimely death. Besides physical death, some of them suffer spiritual death. Such is, for example, the case of Lucilla, the character that gives the title to a *novella,* beginning, in *medias res,* with a climax (the segment in which the tension builds up and leads to a turning point). Lucilla is an orphan who has lived with nuns the first twenty years of her life, as we learn from a series of flashbacks on her life as a little girl in the convent that had taken her in after her mother's death. The child-like quality, which so often Pirandello ascribes to women, is here carried out to extremes:

> ma a vederla, è rimasta come una bambina: tanta così . . . con la sua testina ricciuta sul collo svelto, che può girarla di qua e di là, come vuole, e tutti i riccioli intorno, come tanti serpentelli . . .

Having come of age, she feels a burning desire to leave the convent and go out into the real world. Like Adriana and Didì, she, also, thirsts for life. Lucilla feels she could keep house for Nino, the young man who teases her when passing by the convent on his way home. But as Lucilla reaches the place where he lives, she finds a room-full of drunk, excited men who, together with Nino, have fun tossing her about like a rag doll. The story, third-person limited like the others, ends with a thought report in which the narrating self as well as the experiencing self both seem to merge into the same voice—that of the inevitable vulnerability of the female as "otherness":

> Lucilla non sa più quanto tempo sia passato; che cosa le sia veramente accaduto là; s'è dibattuta, s'è svincolata, liberata, mordendo, graffiando, e ora va nella notte, non sa dove, piccola piccola, per strade grandi, deserte, ignote; è come impazzita, inebetita; e guarda, così piccola, i tronchi giganteschi degli alberi, di cui a stento riesce a scorgere le cime, e più su, più su, finestre vane illuminate come nel cielo, dove vorrebbe sparire, sparire, se Dio, come spera, vorrà alla fine darle le ali.

Lucilla's life had been confined within the walls of a convent, a world of only women, presented in the story vis-à-vis and in antithesis to Nino's lodging, which, instead, consisted entirely of men. Her very entering into that world—unknown and in absolute contrast with the only one she knows—signifies a breach of the social code. Thus, the independence that Lucilla is seeking ends with the annihilation, rather than the development, of the self.

A similar, though less painful, destiny awaits Tuta of **"Il ventaglino."** In the story, we witness a scene in a public park in Rome. On a scorching summer afternoon, Tuta ventures into the park, with her baby in her arms. She is jobless and all alone in the world with her child. As she happens to explain to an old lady, her husband had sent her to the city to fend for herself: "Da un pezzo, difatti, quell'uomo voleva liberarsi di lei, e per forza l'aveva mandata a Roma, perché cercasse di allogarsi per balia." Here Pirandello is at his best. In this story he minimizes the role of the narrator; consequently, we see a more extensive use of dialogue and stream of consciousness in the form of thought report. Particularly effective, in this context, is the following passage:

> Proprio nessuno voleva credere che ella non sapeva più come fare, dove andare? Stentava a crederlo lei stessa. Ma era proprio così. Era entrata là, in quel giardinetto, per cercarvi un po' d'ombra; vi si tratteneva da circa un'ora; poteva rimanervi fino a sera; e poi? dove passar la notte, con quella creatura in braccio? e il giorno dopo? l'altro appresso?

In seeking a solution to her predicament, she takes the "due soldi" she has been given and buys a paper fan. Then, she begins to look invitingly at the soldiers passing by:

> prese il ventaglino e, tirandosi più giù la rimboccatura sul petto, cominciò a farsi vento vento vento lì sul

seno quasi scoperto, e a ridere e a guardare spavalda, con gli occhi lucenti, invitanti, aizzosi, i soldati che passavano.

In these stories, Pirandello shows, indeed, much sympathy for his heroines. Let it be recalled here that he voiced his support of Sibilla Aleramo's book *Una donna* with a review in *La Gazzetta del Popolo* of April 26, 1907. Nonetheless, in our Christian tradition women were perceived as corrupt and corrupting. Pirandello seems to adhere to this belief when he writes: "La donna, per sua natura (salve, s'intende, le eccezioni) è tutta nei sensi. Basta saperla prendere, accendere e dominare" (See **"La realtà del sogno"**). This is why I feel that, inasmuch as Pirandello shared the sorrow of these women's wretched lives, there is still in his fiction a sense of the inescapability of women's nature. In **"Il ventaglino,"** Tuta is aware of the injustice but is made submissive and resigned by the process of internalization of the different sexual standards governing men's and women's lives: "Be', l'ho fatto e Dio m'ha castigato. Ma patisce pure lui, pôro innocente! E c'ha fatto, lui? Va', Dio nun fa le cose giuste. E si nun le fa lui, figurete noi. Tiriamo a campà!"

In view of all this, it is no wonder that even people of her own sex mistrust her: "Raccontava alla vecchia la sua sventura. Il marito . . . Fin da principio la vecchia le rivolse un'occhiata, che poneva i patti della conversazione, cioè: uno sfogo, sì, era disposta a offrirglielo; ma ingannata, no, non voleva essere, ecco."

Actually, women must relinquish ambition in favor of motherhood, which, in these stories, is the only fulfilling aspect of being a woman. Most touchingly indeed, Pirandello portrays countless mother figures. This is, for example, how Didì of **"La veste lunga"** remembers her mother:

> Tuttora Didì ne sentiva un desiderio angoscioso, che la faceva piangere insaziabilmente, inginocchiata innanzi a una antica cassapanca, ov'erano conservate le vesti della madre. L'alito della famiglia era racchiuso là, in quella cassapanca antica, di noce, lunga e stretta come una bara; e di là, dalle vesti della mamma, esalava, a inebriarla amaramente coi ricordi dell'infanzia felice.

Another example is in the story **"Felicità,"** where Elisabetta, as the very title suggests, can finally find an answer to her unhappy life through motherhood:

> Quando però ella si vide salva col bimbo, quando vide quella sua carne che palpitava viva . . . quando poté porgere al suo bimbo la mammella, godendo che entro a quel corpicino uscito or ora dal suo corpo entrasse subito quella sua tepida vena materna . . . parve veramente che volesse impazzire dalla gioia.

On the importance of such a role in Pirandello's works, several studies have been made. Kelly's conclusion regarding motherhood in Pirandello seems to be the most cautious, especially if applied to the last story discussed: "La donna madre diventa allora la perfetta incarnazione di questa soluzione pirandelliana: il suo essere si trasforma

e si perpetua in un altro, e il multiforme ritmo vitale non è interrotto." Subsequently life becomes valid "perché continua, mutevole e varia, nel suo flusso eterno" [Kelly, "Una rivalutazione della maternità nelle protagoniste pirandelliane," *Le ragioni critiche,* 7 (1976)]. Elisabetta of **"Felicità"** understands this idea in its entirety when she says, "voleva vivere, vivere: cioè, esser madre, voleva: un figlio voleva, suo, tutto suo," because the only claim to a life of her own is through her offspring. Only then does she become one with nature: "Non voleva risentirsi di nulla, a nulla badare per non turbare affatto l'opera santa della natura, che si compiva in lei." Motherhood and suffering are in fact the two main positive signifiers of the wretched lives of many a heroine in Pirandello's short stories.

In spite of these recurrent motifs, he does not spare his contempt for men who victimize women. In this very story, for example, the male characters (the father, as dictator, and the son-in-law, as parasite) are depicted as morally inferior to the female characters. The father, the absolute ruler of the household, clings firmly to a traditional view of women: "Forse perché donna e secondogenita, forse perché non bella, così timida in apparenza, umile di cuore e di maniere, schiva e taciturna, non era stata mai calcolata da lui come una figliuola, ma piuttosto come un ingombro lì per casa, un ingombro di cui provava fastidio solo quando si sentiva guardato." As the proper sphere of Pirandello's women was the home, what gave them dignity was self-sacrifice and resignation, the very qualities that George Eliot herself, after all, had listed as the traditional and desirable womanly virtues.

Such are, then, Pirandello's women, allowed to live only vicariously, through their own men and their children. Having had no life of their own, the void overwhelms them if left alone. That is why in **"La camera in attesa"** three sisters and their mother, for fourteen months have prepared, and continue to prepare, the room for the return of the male offspring:

> Il fatto è che da quattordici mesi quelle tre sorelle e la loro madre inferma credono di potere e di dovere aspettare così il probabile ritorno del fratello e figliuolo Cesarino, sottotenente di complemento nel 25° fanteria.

Thus, his room is kept "così puntualmente in ordine, finanche con la camicia da notte stesa sul letto rimboccato." Through a dialogue which Pirandello establishes between writer and reader, we are reminded of a recurrent theme in his works: what makes life is the reality which you give to it. Yet, for these women, the only reality they are able to assure for themselves is in that room, "La camera in attesa" (where the reality of Cesarino's existence never suffers change): outside that room, there is no other.

But nowhere is this role of women living through their loved ones more vivid than in the *novella* **"Ho tante cose da dirvi . . . ,"** in which Pirandello paints the humorous yet poignant story of Signora Mommina. She has lived a comfortable life, happy in seeing her husband slowly achieve success and recognition as a musician, and pleased to watch her daughter grow into a beautiful woman. But with her husband dead and her daughter emigrated to Buenos Aires, she is left all alone. Once she had many friends who crowded around her famous husband and her beautiful daughter; yet, Signora Moma keeps inviting them over. Every day she rushes down the street to remind them: "Ma avevate promesso di farvi vedere! Venite! Venite! Dalle quattro alle sei. Ho tante cose da dirvi . . . ." No one ever shows up. The reason is, as the narrator explains:

> Altra vita, lì, una *sua* vita, non era possibile; perchè in realtà lei, la signora Moma . . . lì, nella sua casa, non aveva mai avuto una vita *sua* e quasi non c'era mai stata.

It is interesting to note the author's italics of *sua,* with which he wants to underline the fact that, in that house, Signora Moma had been so completely selfless as not to be able to construct a life of *her* own. And although she now instinctively feels the need to function independently, she does not realize that, given the premises on which her existence was built, she will not be allowed to do so. Translated into Lacanian terms, the object of human desire is the desire of "Other" in at least two senses: the desire for the Other and the Other's desire. In other words, Signora Moma's unconscious desires had been subordinated to the Other's desires, so that her presence was in reality a non-presence.

As shown in the course of our brief discussion, all these stories reveal the compassion and love the author surely felt for his heroines, in spite of his anti-feminist statements. We must observe that women's marginality was a reality Pirandello was concerned with, just as he was with that of all the outcast who populated his kaleidoscopic imagination. Nevertheless, as we have seen in these *novelle,* the female characters are all depicted almost exclusively vis-à-vis their relationships with men. Their roles as caretakers, mothers, or fallen women are, in fact, construed in terms of some kind of service to be performed for the male provider of the household. They are, moreover, described, in most cases, in terms of their physical appearances (see **"Il viaggio," "Lucilla," "Il ventaglino," "Felicità"**), which ultimately determine the type of life they are to lead. But as regards their psychological make-up, they tend to be depersonalized when functioning as objects of desire and/or commodity (see, in particular, **"Il viaggio," "Il ventaglino," "La ventaglino," "La camera in attesa"**). Divested of a positive sense of self, these women's stories lead to self-effacement, either physical or spiritual. Deprived of an authoritative self, they are as if cloistered in a patriarchal system that determines the boundaries of their lives, their non-presence and ensuing self-obliteration. Thus, encoded in the text, as Pirandello inscribes the character in the narrative as female, the latter's marginality is clearly deciphered and inevitably sanctioned.

FURTHER READING

Biography

Guidice, Gaspare. *Pirandello: A Biography,* translated by Alastair Hamilton. Oxford: Oxford University Press, 1975, 221 p.

Abridged translation of the standard critical biography.

Criticism

Aste, Mario. "Two Short Stories of Pirandello: Their Sources and Their Relationship to the Essay *Umorismo*." *Perspectives on Contemporary Literature* 7 (1981): 64-72.

Traces two fables by Pirandello to several literary and folklore sources, and considers the fables in light of Pirandello's philosophy of humor as it is detailed in *L'umorismo.*

Brooks, Cleanth, and Warren, Robert Penn. "Luigi Pirandello: 'War.'" In their *Understanding Fiction,* Meredith Corporation, 1959, pp. 155-58.

Brooks and Warren analyze Pirandello's short story "War," which is also translated and reprinted here.

Jepson, Lisa. "Filling Space: The Trauma of Birth in Pirandello's Existential Novelle." *Italica* 68, No. 4 (Winter 1991): 419-33.

Perceives psychological and existential imagery in Pirandello's short stories. Jepson states: "Pirandello's novelle offer a unique portrayal of the phenomenological struggle to construe meaning and secure freedom despite the physical and psychological limitations the human condition imposes upon the individual."

May, Frederick. An introduction to *Short Stories* by Luigi Pirandello, translated by Frederick May, pp. ix-xxix. London: Oxford University Press, 1965.

Surveys Pirandello's short fiction, emphasizing the dreamlike quality of his stories.

Moestrup, Jørn. *The Structural Patterns of Pirandello's Work.* Odense: Odense University Press, 1972, 294 p.

Overview of Pirandello's short fiction. Moestrup organizes and discusses the stories according to the periods during which they were written in Pirandello's career.

Moore, M. J. "Sicily in the 'Novelle' of Luigi Pirandello." *The Modern Language Review* XL, No. 3 (July 1945): 174-79.

Examines the local color of Pirandello's stories set in Sicily.

Patten, Mercury. A review of *Better Think Twice about It. The New Statesman and Nation* V, No. 105 (25 February 1933): 224.

Favorable assessment of Pirandello's collection. Patten concludes: "[This] volume shows that Pirandello is not only a great master of the theater and a most original and successful experimenter, but he is also a really great storyteller as well."

Ragusa, Olga. "Pirandello's *La Patente*: Play and Story." In *Petrarch to Pirandello*, edited by Julius A. Molinaro, pp. 202-28. Toronto: University of Toronto Press, 1973.

Compares the play *The License* to the short story upon which it is based. Ragusa views her study as "a contribution to the so far all too brief tradition of the close study of the transformation of narrative into drama within the Pirandello corpus."

Stone, Jennifer. "Pirandello's Scandalous Docile Bodies." *Review of National Literatures* 14 (1987): 79-92.

Employs the theories of the psychoanalysts Sigmund Freud and Jacques Lacan to explicate Pirandello's short fiction, focusing primarily on the stories "The Tortoise" and "The Challenge."

Additional coverage of Pirandello's life and career is contained in the following sources published by Gale Research: *Contemporary Authors,* **Vol. 104;** *DISCovering Authors;* *Drama Criticism,* **Vol. 5;** *Twentieth-Century Literary Criticism,* **Vols. 4, 29; and** *World Literature Criticism.*

"The Fall of the House of Usher"
Edgar Allan Poe

American short story writer, novelist, poet, critic, and essayist.

The following entry presents criticism of Poe's short story "The Fall of the House of Usher," first published in *Burton's Gentleman's Magazine*, September, 1839. For an overview of Poe's short fiction, see *SSC*, Volume 1.

INTRODUCTION

Poe's stature as a major figure in world literature is based in large part on his ingenious short stories and critical theories, which established highly influential models for the short form in both fiction and poetry. Regarded by literary historians as the architect of the modern short story, Poe is credited with the invention of several popular genres: the modern horror tale, the science fiction tale, and the detective story. Twentieth-century scholars have discerned in such well-known short stories as "The Fall of the House of Usher" a seminal contribution to the development of various modern literary themes, including the alienation of the self and the nature of the subconscious. The critic Allen Tate has even identified the tormented Roderick Usher as a prototype for the self-conscious hero in modern fiction. Although nineteenth-century critics generally failed to recognize the full extent of Poe's contribution to the form, he is now acclaimed as one of literature's most original and influential practitioners of the short story.

Plot and Major Characters

Summoned by a mysterious note, the unnamed narrator of "The Fall of the House of Usher" arrives to find his childhood friend Roderick Usher fearful and depressed in his decaying family mansion. Roderick attributes his morbid condition to the influence of the gloomy house and the imminent death of his beloved twin sister Madeline, his only surviving relative. The narrator's futile attempts to distract his host with art, literature, and music are interrupted when Roderick abruptly announces that Madeline has died. Anxious to preserve her corpse before burial, Roderick persuades the narrator to help him convey the coffin to a former dungeon beneath the house. In the next few days, Roderick's state declines into madness. Increasingly unnerved himself, the narrator is woken one night by certain curious noises. He finds Usher in a state of escalating hysteria and attempts to calm him by reading "Mad Trist," the story of a dragon-slaying knight. At the climax of the story, both hear an ominous clanging sound within the house. The door opens to reveal the emaciated, blood-spattered figure of Madeline, who had been buried alive. Tottering on the threshold, she falls forward heavily, kill-ing her brother in her violent death agony. As the narrator escapes from the house, a zigzag fissure opens in the structure and the house of Usher collapses in on itself.

Major Themes

"The Fall of the House of Usher" is known for its remarkable structure, in which major themes emerge through an elaborate network of repeated images. The prominent theme of duality is expressed primarily in several parallel structures, including the symbiotic bond between Roderick and his sister Madeline. The theme also appears in the opening image of the mansion reflected in a dark tarn, as well as in the metaphor of a mind infected with madness, suggested by Roderick's poem "The Haunted Palace." Also, while Roderick's declining mental condition is echoed in the crumbling house, overgrown with parasitic plants and wrapped in a sort of unpleasant swamp gas, the fissure which finally destroys the Usher mansion literally brings the theme of dualism to a crashing climax. Roderick's extreme sensitivity to Romantic literature and his inordinate desire to preserve Madeline's corpse hint at other important themes, those of decadence and decay. Thus,

Poe presents Roderick as a tragic aesthete, who, though completely alienated from mundane reality, succeeds in arousing pathos in the reader. As more than one critic has observed, the fall of the house of Usher describes the decline of an incestuous, decaying family, with all of its psychological implications, as well as an actual, if improbable, physical event.

Critical Reception

Readers of "The Fall of the House of Usher" have long associated the melancholy Roderick Usher with Poe himself. Indeed, the story's themes of destructive division, family decline and morbid imagination offer intriguing parallels to the author's fragmented life. However, Poe's own book reviews from this period indicate his preference for suggestive, "mystic" literature over didactic allegory—an attitude that explains the multiple interpretations which "The Fall of the House of Usher" continues to elicit. While critics such as Richard Wilbur and Louise Kaplan have seen the story as an exploration of the frightening depths of the human psyche, other scholars have detected a more parodic note. Much of the controversy over the meaning of "Usher" has centered on the reliability of the story's anonymous narrator. Where Patrick F. Quinn sees the narrator as a model of common sense, G. R. Thompson and Frederick S. Frank propose a naive—even malign—aspect to this character. Recent criticism has focused on the sadistic, possibly perverse, overtones of Usher's relationship with his sister and some feminist critics have interpreted the story as a parable of patriarchal destructiveness.

CRITICISM

D. H. Lawrence   (essay date 1919)

SOURCE: "Edgar Allan Poe," in *The Symbolic Meaning: The Uncollected Versions of 'Studies in Classic American Literature,'* Centaur Press Limited, 1962, pp. 115-30.

[*Lawrence was a modern English novelist, poet, and essayist noted for his introduction of the themes of modern psychology to English fiction. In his lifetime, he was a controversial figure, both for the explicit sexuality he portrayed in his works and for his unconventional personal life. Much of the criticism of Lawrence's works concerns his highly individualistic moral system, which was based on absolute freedom of expression, particularly sexual expression. Human sexuality was for Lawrence a symbol of the Life Force, and is frequently pitted against modern industrial society, which he believed was dehumanizing. In the following excerpt, originally published in 1919, Lawrence describes Poe's portrayal of love as a "destructive force" in his short stories.*]

It seems a long way from Fenimore Cooper to Poe. But in fact it is only a step. Leatherstocking is the last instance of the integral, progressive, soul of the white man in America. In the last conjunction between Leatherstocking and Chingachgook we see the passing out into the darkness of the interim, as a seed falls into the dark interval of winter. What remains is the old tree withering and seething down to the crisis of winter-death, the great white race in America keenly disintegrating, seething back in electric decomposition, back to that crisis where the old soul, the old era, perishes in the denuded frame of man, and the first throb of a new year sets in.

The process of the decomposition of the body after death is slow and mysterious, a life process of post-mortem activity. In the same way, the great psyche, which we have evolved through two thousand years of effort, must die, and not only die, must be reduced back to its elements by a long, slow process of disintegration, living disintegration.

This is the clue to Edgar Allan Poe, and to the art that succeeds him, in America. When a tree withers, at the end of a year, then the whole life of the year is gradually driven out until the tissue remains elemental and almost null. Yet it is only reduced to that crisis of perfect quiescence which *must* intervene between life-cycle and life-cycle. Poe shows us the first vivid, seething reduction of the psyche, the first convulsive spasm that sets-in in the human soul, when the last impulse of creative love, creative conjunction, is finished. It is like a tree whose fruits are perfected, writhing now in the grip of the first frost.

For men who are born at the end of a great era or epoch nothing remains but the seething reduction back to the elements; just as for a tree in autumn nothing remains but the strangling-off of the leaves and the strange decomposition and arrest of the sap. It is useless to ask for perpetual spring and summer. Poe had to lead on to that winter-crisis when the soul is, as it were, denuded of itself, reduced back to the elemental state of a naked, arrested tree in midwinter. Man must be stripped of himself. And the process is slow and bitter and beautiful, too. But the beauty has its spark in anguish; it is the strange, expiring cry, the phosphorescence of decay.

Poe is a man writhing in the mystery of his own undoing. He is a great dead soul, progressing terribly down the long process of post-mortem activity in disintegration. This is how the dead bury their dead. This is how man must bury his own dead self: in pang after pang of vital, explosive self-reduction, back to the elements. This is how the seed must fall into the ground and perish before it can bring forth new life. For Poe the process was one of perishing in the old body, the old psyche, the old self. He leads us back, through pang after pang of disintegrative sensation, back towards the end of all things, where the beginning is: just as the year begins where the year is utterly dead. It is only perfect courage which can carry us through the extremity of death, through the crisis of our own nullification, the midwinter which is the end of the end and the beginning of the beginning.

Yet Poe is hardly an artist. He is rather a supreme scientist. Art displays the movements of the pristine self, the living conjunction or communion between the self and its context. Even in tragedy self meets self in supreme conjunction, a communion of passionate or creative death. But in Poe the self is finished, already stark. It would be true to say that Poe had no soul. He lives in the post-mortem reality, a living dead. He reveals the after-effects of life, the processes of organic disintegration. Arrested in himself, he cannot realise self or soul in any other human being. For him, the vital world is the sensational world. He is not sensual, he is sensational. The difference between these two is a difference between growth and decay. In Poe, sensationalism is a process of explosive disintegration, phosphorescent, electric, refracted. In him, sensation is that momentary state of consciousness which concurs with the sudden combustion and reduction of vital tissue. The combustion of his own most vital plasm liberates the white gleam of his sensational consciousness. Hence his addiction to alcohol and drugs, which are the common agents of reductive combustion.

It is for this reason that we would class the "tales" as science rather than art: because they reveal the workings of the great inorganic forces, disruptive within the organic psyche. The central soul or self is in arrest. And for this reason we cannot speak of the tales as stories or novels. A tale is a concatenation of scientific cause and effect. But in a story the movement depends on the sudden appearance of spontaneous emotion or gesture, causeless, arising out of the living self.

—Yet the chief of Poe's tales depend upon the passion of love. The central stories, **"Ligeia"** and **"The Fall of the House of Usher"** *are* almost stories; there is in these almost a relation of soul to soul. These are the two stories where love is still recognisable as the driving force.

Love is the mysterious force which brings beings together in creative conjunction or communion. But it is also the force which brings them together in frictional disruption. Love is the great force which causes disintegration as well as new life, and corruption as well as procreation. It brings life together with life, either for production or for destruction, down to the last extremes of existence.

And in Poe, love is purely a frictional, destructive force. In him, the mystic, spontaneous self is replaced by the self-determined ego. He is a unit of will rather than a unit of being. And the force of love acts in him almost as an electric attraction rather than as a communion between self and self. He is a lodestone, the woman is the soft metal. Each draws the other mechanically. Such attraction, increasing and intensifying in conjunction, does not set up a cycle of rest and creation. The one life draws the other life with a terrible pressure. Each presses on the other intolerably till one is bound to disappear: one or both.

The story of this process of magnetic, self-less pressure of love is told in the story of **"Ligeia"**, and this story we may take to be the clue to Poe's own love-tragedy. The motto to the tale is a quotation from Joseph Glanville: "And the will therein lieth which dieth not. Who knoweth the mysteries of the will, with its vigour? For God is but a great will pervading all things by nature of its intentness. Man doth not yield himself to the angels, nor unto death utterly, save only through the weakness of his feeble will."

> **It would be true to say that Poe had no soul. He lives in the post-mortem reality, a living dead. He reveals the after-effects of life, the processes of organic disintegration. Arrested in himself, he cannot realise self or soul in any other human being.**
>
> **—*D. H. Lawrence***

If God is a great will, then the universe is a great machine, for the will is a fixed principle. But God is not a will. God is a mystery, from which creation mysteriously proceeds. So is the self a unit of creative mystery. But the will is the greatest of all control-principles, the greatest machine-principle.

So Poe establishes himself in the will, self-less and determined. Then he enters the great process of destructive love, which in the end works out to be a battle of wills as to which can hold out longest.

The story is told in a slow method of musing abstraction, most subtle yet most accurate. Ligeia is never a free person. She is just a phenomenon with which Poe strives in ill-omened love. She is not a woman. She is just a re-agent, a re-acting force, chimerical almost. "In stature she was tall, somewhat slender, and, in her later days, even emaciated. I would in vain attempt to portray the majesty, the quiet ease, of her demeanour, or the incomprehensible lightness and elasticity of her footfall. I was never made aware of her entrance into my closed study save by the dear music of her low, sweet voice as she placed her marble hand upon my shoulder.". . .

Having recognised the clue to Ligeia in her gigantic volition, there must inevitably ensue the struggle of wills. But Ligeia, true to the great traditions, remains passive or submissive, womanly, to the man; he is the active agent, she the recipient. To this her gigantic volition fixes her also. Hence, moreover, her conquest of the stern vultures of passion.

The stress of inordinate love goes on, the consuming into a oneness. And it is Ligeia who is consumed. The process of such love is inevitable consumption. In creative love there is a recognition of each soul by the other, a mutual kiss, and then the balance in equilibrium which is the peace and beauty of love. But in Poe and Ligeia such balance is impossible. Each is possessed with the craving to search out and *know* the other, entirely; to know, to have, to possess, to be identified with the other. They are two units madly urging together towards a fusion which must break down the very being of one or both of them. Ligeia craves to be identified with her husband, he with her. And not until too late does she realise that such identification is death.

"That she loved me I should not have doubted; and I might have been easily aware that, in a bosom such as hers, love would have reigned no ordinary passion. But in death only was I fully impressed with the strength of her affection. For long hours, detaining my hand, would she pour out before me the overflowing of a heart whose more than passionate devotion amounted to idolatry. How had I deserved to be blessed by such confessions? How had I deserved to be cursed with the removal of my beloved in the hour of her making them? But upon this subject I cannot bear to dilate. Let me say only that in Ligeia's more than womanly abandonment to a love, alas! all unmerited, all unworthily bestowed, I at length recognised the principle of her longing with so wildly earnest a desire for the life which was now fleeing so rapidly away. It is this wild longing—it is this vehement desire for life—*but for life*—that I have no power to portray—no utterance capable of expressing."

Thus Ligeia is defeated in her terrible desire to be identified with her husband, and live, just as he is defeated in his desire, living, to grasp the clue of her in his own hand.

On the last day of her existence Ligeia dictates to her husband the memorable poem, which concludes:—

"Out—out are all the lights—out all!
  And over each quivering form
The curtain, a funeral pall,
  Comes down with the rush of a storm,
And the angels, all pallid and wan,
  Uprising, unveiling, affirm
That the play is the tragedy 'Man,'
  And its hero the Conqueror Worm."

"'O God!' half shrieked Ligeia, leaping to her feet and extending her arms aloft with a spasmodic movement, as I made an end of these lines, 'O God! O Divine Father!—shall these things be undeviatingly so? Shall this conqueror be not once conquered? Are we not part and parcel in Thee? Who—who knoweth the mysteries of the will with its vigour? Man doth not yield him to the angels, *nor unto death utterly,* save only through the weakness of his feeble will.'"

So Ligeia dies. Herself a creature of will and finished consciousness, she sees everything collapse before the devouring worm. But shall her will collapse?

The husband comes to ancient England, takes a gloomy, grand old abbey, puts it into some sort of repair, and, converting it into a dwelling, furnishes it with exotic, mysterious splendour. As an artist Poe is unfailingly in bad taste—always in bad taste. He seeks a sensation from every phrase or object, and the effect is vulgar.

In the story the man marries the fair-haired, blue-eyed Lady Rowena Trevanion, of Tremaine.

"In halls such as these—in a bridal chamber such as this—I passed, with the Lady of Tremaine, the unhallowed hours of the first month of our marriage—passed them with but little disquietude. That my wife dreaded the fierce moodiness of my temper—that she shunned me and loved me but little—I could not help perceiving; but it gave me rather pleasure than otherwise. I loathed her with a hatred belonging rather to a demon than to a man. My memory flew back (Oh, with what intensity of regret!) to Ligeia, the beloved, the august, the entombed. I revelled in recollections of her purity," etc.

The love which had been a wild craving for identification with Ligeia, a love inevitably deadly and consuming, now in the man has become definitely destructive, devouring, subtly murderous. He will slowly and subtly consume the life of the fated Rowena. It is his vampire lust.

In the second month of the marriage the Lady Rowena fell ill. It is Ligeia whose presence hangs destructive over her; it is the ghostly Ligeia who pours poison into Rowena's cup. It is Ligeia, active and unsatisfied within the soul of her husband, who destroys the other woman. The will of Ligeia is not yet broken. She wants to live. And she wants to live to finish her process, to satisfy her unbearable craving to be identified with the man. All the time, in his marriage with Rowena, the husband is only using the new bride as a substitute for Ligeia. As a substitute for Ligeia he possesses her. And at last from the corpse of Rowena Ligeia rises fulfilled. When the corpse opens its eyes, at last the two are identified, Ligeia with the man she so loved. Henceforth the two are one, and neither exists. They are consumed into an inscrutable oneness.

"Eleanora", the next story, is a fantasy revealing the sensational delights of the man in his early marriage with the young and tender bride. They dwelt, he, his cousin and her mother, in the sequestered Valley of Many-coloured Grass, the valley of prismatic sensation, where everything seems spectrum-coloured. They looked down at their own images in the River of Silence, and drew the God Eros from that wave. This is a description of the life of introspection and of the love which is begotten by the self in the self, the self-made love. The trees are like serpents worshipping the sun. That is, they represent the phallic passion in its poisonous or destructive activity. The symbolism of Poe's parables is easy, too easy, almost mechanical.

In **"Berenice"** the man must go down to the sepulchre of his beloved and take her thirty-two small white teeth, which he carries in a box with him. It is repulsive and gloating. The teeth are the instruments of biting, of resistance, of antagonism. They often become symbols of opposition, little instruments or entities of crushing and destroying. Hence the dragon's teeth in the myth. Hence the man in **"Berenice"** must take possession of the irreducible part of his mistress. "Toutes ses dents étaient des idées," he says. Then they are little fixed ideas of mordant hate, of which he possesses himself.

The other great story somewhat connected with this group is **"The Fall of the House of Usher"**. Here the love is between brother and sister. When the self is broken, and the mystery of the recognition of *otherness* fails, then the longing for identification with the beloved becomes a lust. And it is this longing for identification, utter merging, which is at the base of the incest problem. In psychoanalysis almost every trouble in the psyche is traced to an incest-desire. But this will not do. The incest-desire is only one of the manifestations of the self-less desire for merging. It is obvious that this desire for merging, or unification, or identification of the man with the woman, or the woman with the man, finds its gratification most readily in the merging of those things which are already near—mother with son, brother with sister, father with daughter. But it is not enough to say, as Jung does, that all life is a matter of lapsing towards, or struggling away from, mother-incest. It is necessary to see what lies at the back of this helpless craving for utter merging or identification with a beloved.

The motto to **"The Fall of the House of Usher"** is a couple of lines from De Béranger.

> "Son coeur est un luth suspendu;
> Sitôt qu'on le touche il résonne."

We have all the trappings of Poe's rather overdone vulgar fantasy. "I reined my horse to the precipitous brink of a black and lurid tarn that lay in unruffled lustre by the dwelling, and gazed down—but with a shudder even more thrilling than before—upon the remodelled and inverted images of the grey sedge, and the ghastly tree-stems, and the vacant and eye-like windows." The House of Usher, both dwelling and family, was very old. Minute fungi overspread the exterior of the house, hanging in festoons from the eaves. Gothic archways, a valet of stealthy step, sombre tapestries, ebon black floors, a profusion of tattered and antique furniture, feeble gleams of encrimsoned light through latticed panes, and over all "an air of stern, deep, irredeemable gloom"—this makes up the interior.

The inmates of the house, Roderick and Madeline Usher, are the last remnants of their incomparably ancient and decayed race. Roderick has the same large, luminous eye, the same slightly arched nose of delicate Hebrew model, as characterised Ligeia. He is ill with the nervous malady of his family. It is he whose nerves are so strung that they vibrate to the unknown quiverings of the ether. He, too, has lost his self, his living soul, and become a sensitised instrument of the external influences; his nerves are verily like an aeolian harp which must vibrate. He lives in "some struggle with the grim phantasm, Fear," for he is only the physical, post-mortem reality of a living being.

It is a question how much, once the rich centrality of the self is broken, the instrumental consciousness of man can register. When man becomes self-less, wafting instrumental like a harp in an open window, how much can his elemental consciousness express? It is probable that even the blood as it runs has its own sympathies and responses to the material world, quite apart from seeing. And the nerves we know vibrate all the while to unseen presences, unseen forces. So Roderick Usher quivers on the edge of dissolution.

It is this mechanical consciousness which gives "the fervid facility of his impromptus." It is the same thing that gives Poe his extraordinary facility in versification. The absence of real central or impulsive being in himself leaves him inordinately mechanically sensitive to sounds and effects, associations of sounds, association of rhyme, for example—mechanical, facile, having no root in any passion. It is all a secondary, meretricious process. So we get Roderick Usher's poem, "The Haunted Palace," with its swift yet mechanical subtleties of rhyme and rhythm, its vulgarity of epithet. It is all a sort of dream-process, where the association between parts is mechanical, accidental as far as passional meaning goes.

Usher thought that all vegetable things had sentience. Surely all material things have a form of sentience, even the inorganic: surely they all exist in some subtle and complicated tension of vibration which makes them sensitive to external influence and causes them to have an influence on other external objects, irrespective of contact. It is of this vibrational or inorganic consciousness that Poe is master: the sleep-consciousness. Thus Roderick Usher was convinced that his whole surroundings, the stones of the house, the fungi, the water in the tarn, the very reflected image of the whole, was woven into a physical oneness with the family, condensed, as it were, into one atmosphere—the special atmosphere in which alone the Ushers could live. And it was this atmosphere which had moulded the destinies of his family.

In the human realm, Roderick had one connection: his sister Madeline. She, too, was dying of a mysterious disorder, nervous, cataleptic. The brother and sister loved each other passionately and exclusively. They were twins, almost identical in looks. It was the same absorbing love between them, where human creatures are absorbed away from themselves, into a unification in death. So Madeline was gradually absorbed into her brother; the one life absorbed the other in a long anguish of love.

Madeline died and was carried down by her brother into the deep vaults of the house. But she was not dead. Her brother roamed about in incipient madness—a madness of unspeakable terror and guilt. After eight days they were suddenly startled by a clash of metal, then a distinct, hollow, metallic, and clangorous, yet apparently muffled, reverberation. Then Roderick Usher, gibbering, began to express himself: "*We have put her living into the tomb!* Said I not that my senses were acute? I *now* tell you that I heard her first feeble movements in the hollow coffin. I heard them—many, many days ago—yet I dared not—*I dared not speak.*"

It is again the old theme of "each man kills the thing he loves." He knew his love had killed her. He knew she died at last, like Ligeia, unwilling and unappeased. So, she rose again upon him. "But then without those doors there *did* stand the lofty and enshrouded figure of the Lady

Madeline of Usher. There was blood upon her white robes, and the evidence of some bitter struggle upon every portion of her emaciated frame. For a moment she remained trembling and reeling to and fro upon the threshold, then, with a low moaning cry, fell heavily inward upon the person of her brother, and in her violent and now final death-agonies bore him to the floor a corpse, and a victim to the terrors he had anticipated."

It is lurid and melodramatic, but it really is a symbolic truth of what happens in the last stages of this inordinate love, which can recognise none of the sacred mystery of *otherness,* but must unite into unspeakable identification, oneness in death. Brother and sister go down together, made one in the unspeakable mystery of death. It is the world-long incest problem, arising inevitably when man, through insistence of his will in one passion or aspiration, breaks the polarity of himself.

The best tales all have the same burden. Hate is as inordinate as love, and as slowly consuming, as secret, as underground, as subtle. All this underground vault business in Poe only symbolises that which takes place *beneath* the consciousness. On top, all is fair-spoken. Beneath, there is the awful murderous extremity of burying alive. Fortunato, in **"The Cask of Amontillado,"** is buried alive out of perfect hatred, as the Lady Madeline of Usher is buried alive out of love. The lust of hate is the inordinate desire to consume and unspeakably possess the soul of the hated one, just as the lust of love is the desire to possess, or to be possessed by, the beloved, utterly. But in either case the result is the dissolution of both souls, each losing itself in transgressing its own bounds.

The lust of Montresor is to devour utterly the soul of Fortunato. It would be no use killing him outright. If a man is killed outright his soul remains integral, free to return into the bosom of some beloved, where it can enact itself. In walling-up his enemy in the vault, Montresor seeks to bring about the indescribable capitulation of the man's soul, so that he, the victor, can possess himself of the very being of the vanquished. Perhaps this can actually be done. Perhaps, in the attempt, the victor breaks the bounds of his own identity, and collapses into nothingness, or into the infinite.

What holds good for inordinate hate holds good for inordinate love. The motto, *Nemo me impune lacessit,* might just as well be *Nemo me impune amat.*

In **"William Wilson"** we are given a rather unsubtle account of the attempt of a man to kill his own soul. William Wilson, the mechanical, lustful ego succeeds in killing William Wilson, the living self. The lustful ego lives on, gradually reducing itself towards the dust of the infinite.

In the **"Murders in the Rue Morgue"** and **"The Gold Bug"** we have those mechanical tales where the interest lies in following out a subtle chain of cause and effect. The interest is scientific rather than artistic, a study in psychologic reactions.

The fascination of murder itself is curious. Murder is not just killing. Murder is a lust utterly to possess the soul of the murdered—hence the stealth and the frequent morbid dismemberment of the corpse, the attempt to get at the very quick of the murdered being, to find the quick and to possess it. It is curious that the two men fascinated by the art of murder, though in different ways, should have been De Quincey and Poe, men so different in ways of life, yet perhaps not so widely different in nature. In each of them is traceable that strange lust for extreme love and extreme hate, possession by mystic violence of the other soul, or violent deathly surrender of the soul in the self.

Inquisition and torture are akin to murder: the same lust. It is a combat between conqueror and victim for the possession of the soul after death. A soul can be conquered only when it is forced to abdicate from its own being. A heretic may be burned at the stake, his ashes scattered on the winds as a symbol that his soul is now broken by torture and dissolved. And yet, as often as not, the brave heretic dies integral in being; his soul re-enters into the bosom of the living, indestructible.

So the mystery goes on. La Bruyère says that all our human unhappiness *vient de ne pouvoir être seuls.* As long as man lives he will be subject to the incalculable influence of love or of hate, which is only inverted love. The necessity to love is probably the source of all our unhappiness; but since it is the source of everything it is foolish to particularise. Probably even gravitation is only one of the lowest manifestations of the mystic force of love. But the triumph of love, which is the triumph of life and creation, does not lie in merging, mingling, in absolute identification of the lover with the beloved. It lies in the communion of beings, who, in the very perfection of communion, recognise and allow the mutual otherness. There is no desire to transgress the bounds of being. Each self remains utterly itself—becomes, indeed, most burningly and transcendently itself in the uttermost embrace or communion with the other. One self may yield honourable precedence to the other, may pledge itself to undying service, and in so doing become fulfilled in its own nature. For the highest achievement of some souls lies in perfect service. But the giving and the taking of service does not obliterate the mystery of otherness, the being-in-singleness, either in master or servant. On the other hand, slavery is an avowed obliteration of the singleness of being.

Darrel Abel (essay date 1949)

SOURCE: "A Key to The House of Usher," in *Interpretations of American Literature,* edited by Charles Feidelson, Jr., and Paul Brodtkorb, Jr., Oxford University Press, 1959, pp. 51-62.

[*In the following essay, originally published in 1949, Abel offers a symbolic interpretation of "The Fall of the House of Usher."*]

By common consent, the most characteristic of Poe's "arabesque" tales is **"The Fall of the House of Usher."** It is usually admired for its "atmosphere" and for its exquisitely artificial manipulation of Gothic claptrap and décor, but careful reading reveals admirable method in the author's use of things generally regarded by his readers as mere decorative properties. . . .

I

Too much of the horror of the tale has usually been attributed to its setting superficially considered. But the setting does have a double importance, descriptive and symbolic. It first operates descriptively, as suggestively appropriate and picturesque background for the unfolding of events. It later operates symbolically: certain features of the setting assume an ominous animism and function; they become important active elements instead of mere static backdrop.

Descriptively the setting has two uses: to suggest a mood to the observer which makes him properly receptive to the horrible ideas which grow in his mind during the action; and to supply details which reinforce, but do not produce, those ideas.

The qualities of the setting are remoteness, decadence, horrible gloom. Remoteness (and loss of feature) is suggested by details of outline, dimension, and vista. Decadence is suggested by details of the death or decrepitude of normal human and vegetable existences and constructions, and by the growth of morbid and parasitic human and vegetable existences, as well as by the surging sentience of inorganism. Gloom and despair are suggested by sombre and listless details of colour and motion (at climactic points, lurid colour and violent action erupt with startling effect from this sombre listlessness). The narrator points out in the opening passage of the tale that the gloom which invested the domain of Usher was not sublime and pleasurable (which would have made it an expression of "supernal beauty" in Poe's opinion), but was sinister and vaguely terrible.

Five persons figure in the tale, but the interest centres exclusively in one—Roderick Usher. The narrator is uncharacterized, undescribed, even unnamed. (I shall call him Anthropos, for convenient reference.) In fact, he is a mere point of view for the reader to occupy, but he does lend the reader some acute, though not individualizing, faculties: five keen senses which shrewdly perceive actual physical circumstances; a sixth sense of vague and indescribable realities behind the physical and apparent; a clever faculty of rational interpretation of sensible phenomena; and finally, a sceptical and matter-of-fact propensity to mistrust intuitional apprehensions and to seek natural and rational explanations. In short, he is an habitual naturalist resisting urgent convictions of the preternatural.

The doctor and valet are not realized as characters; they are less impressive than the furniture; and Anthropos sees each only once and briefly. No duties requiring the attendance of other persons are mentioned, so our attention is never for a moment diverted from Roderick Usher. His sister Madeline's place in the story can best be explained in connection with comment on Usher himself.

The action of the story is comparatively slight; the energetic symbolism, to be discussed later, accomplishes more. Anthropos arrives at the House of Usher, and is conducted into the presence of his host. Usher has invited Anthropos, a friend of his schooldays, in the hope that a renewal of their association will assist him to throw off a morbid depression of spirits which has affected his health. Anthropos is shocked at the ghastly infirmity of his friend. He learns that Madeline, Roderick's twin and the only other living Usher, is near death from a mysterious malady which baffles her physicians. Presently she dies and Roderick Usher, fearing that the doctors who had been so fascinated by the pathology of the case might steal her body from the grave, places it in a sealed coffin in a subterranean vault under the House of Usher. Anthropos assists in this labour.

Immediately there is an observable increase in the nervous apprehensiveness of Roderick Usher. He finds partial relief from his agitation in the painting of horribly vague abstract pictures and in the improvisation of wild tunes to the accompaniment of his "speaking guitar." For seven or eight days his apprehensiveness increases and steadily communicates itself to Anthropos as well, so that, at the end of that time, a night arrives when Anthropos' state of vague alarm prevents his going to sleep. Usher enters and shows him through the window that, although the night is heavily clouded, the House of Usher's environs are strangely illuminated. Anthropos endeavours, not very judiciously, to calm him by reading aloud from a romance that might have come from the library of Don Quixote. At points of suspense in this romance, marked by description of loud noises, Anthropos fancies that he hears similar sounds below him in the House of Usher. Roderick Usher's manner, during this reading, is inattentive and wildly preoccupied; at the noisy climax of the romance Usher melodramatically shrieks that the noises outside had actually been those of his sister breaking out of the coffin in which she had been sealed alive. The door bursts open; Madeline appears and, falling forward dead in her gory shroud, carries Roderick Usher likewise dead to the floor beneath her. Anthropos rushes from the House of Usher, turning in his flight to view its shattering collapse into the gloomy tarn beneath it. How these events become invested with horror can only be understood by discerning the meanings which the symbolism of the tale conveys into them.

II

Roderick Usher is himself a symbol—of isolation, and of a concentration of vitality so introverted that it utterly destroys itself. He is physically isolated. Anthropos reaches the House of Usher after a whole's day's journey "through a singularly dreary tract of country" that is recognizably the same sort of domain-beyond-reality as that traversed by Childe Roland and his medieval prototypes. Arrived at the mansion, he is conducted to Usher's "studio" "through many dark and intricate passages." And there "the eye struggled in vain to reach the remoter angles of the chamber" in which his host received him.

Usher is psychologically isolated. Although he has invited his former "boon companion" to visit and support him in this moral crisis, clearly there has never been any conviviality in his nature. "His reserve had always been habitual and excessive," and he has now evidently become more singular, preoccupied, and aloof than before. "For many years, he had never ventured forth" from the gloomy House of Usher, wherein "he was enchained by certain superstitious impressions." ("Superstitious" is the sceptical judgment of Anthropos.) Thus, although his seclusion had probably once been voluntary, it is now inescapable. His sister Madeline does not relieve his isolation; paradoxically, she intensifies it, for they are twins whose "striking similitude" and "sympathies of a scarcely intelligible nature" eliminate that margin of difference which is necessary to social relationship between persons. They are not two persons, but one consciousness in two bodies, each mirroring the other, intensifying the introversion of the family character. Further, no collateral branches of the family survive; all the life of the Ushers is flickering to extinction in these feeble representatives. Therefore no wonder that Anthropos cannot connect his host's appearance "with any idea of a simple humanity."

Roderick Usher is himself a symbol—of isolation, and of a concentration of vitality so introverted that it utterly destroys itself.

—Darrel Abel

The isolation and concentration of the vitalities of the Ushers had brought about the decay of the line. Formerly the family energies had found magnificently varied expression: "His very ancient family had been noted, time out of mind, for a peculiar sensibility of temperament; displaying itself, through long ages, in many works of exalted art, and manifested, of late, in repeated deeds of munificent yet unobtrusive charity, as well as in a passionate devotion to the intricacies, perhaps even more than to the orthodox and easily recognizable beauties, of musical science." For all the splendid flowering of this "peculiar sensibility," its devotion to intricacies was a fatal weakness; in tending inward to more hidden channels of expression, the family sensibility had become in its current representative morbidity introverted from lack of proper object and exercise, and its only flowers were flowers of evil. It was fretting Roderick Usher to death: "He suffered much from a morbid acuteness of the senses; the most insipid food was alone endurable; he could wear only garments of a certain texture; the odors of all flowers were oppressive; his eyes were tortured by even a faint light; and there were but peculiar sounds, and these from

stringed instruments, which did not inspire him with horror." These specifications detail the hyper-acuity but progressive desuetude of his five senses. The sum of things which these five senses convey to a man is the sum of physical life; the relinquishment of their use is the relinquishment of life itself. The hyper-acuity of Roderick Usher's senses was caused by the introverted concentration of the family energies; the inhibition of his senses was caused by the physical and psychological isolation of Usher. It is noteworthy that the only willing use he makes of his senses is a morbid one—not to sustain and positively experience life, but to project his "distempered ideality" on canvas and in music. This morbid use of faculties which ought to sustain and express life shows that, as Life progressively loses its hold on Roderick Usher, Death as steadily asserts its empery over him. The central action and symbolism of the tale dramatize this contest between Life and Death for the possession of Roderick Usher.

III

Some of the non-human symbols of the tale are, as has been mentioned, features of the physical setting which detach themselves from the merely picturesque ensemble of background particulars and assume symbolical meaning as the tale unfolds. They have what might be called an historical function; they symbolize what has been and is. The remaining symbols are created by the "distempered ideality" of Roderick Usher as the narrative progresses. These have prophetic significance; they symbolize what is becoming and what will be. The symbols which Usher creates, however, flow from the same dark source as the evil in symbols which exist independently of Usher: that evil is merely channelled through his artistic sensibility to find bold new expression.

All the symbols express the opposition of Life-Reason to Death—Madness. Most of them are mixed manifestations of those two existences; more precisely, they show ascendant evil encroaching upon decadent good. On the Life-Reason side are ranged the heavenly, natural, organic, harmonious, featured, active qualities of things. Against them are ranged the subterranean, subnatural, inorganic, inharmonious, vague or featureless, passive qualities of things. Although most of the symbols show the encroachment of Death-Madness on Life-Reason, two symbols show absolute evil triumphant, with no commixture of good even in decay. One of these is the tarn, a physically permanent feature of the setting; the other is Roderick Usher's ghastly abstract painting, an impromptu expression of the evil which has mastered his sensibility. There are no symbols of absolute good.

The House of Usher is the most conspicuous symbol in the tale. It displays all the qualities (listed above) of Life-Reason, corrupted and threatened by Death-Madness. It stands under the clouded heavens, but it is significantly related to the subterranean by the zigzag crack which extends from its roof (the most heaven ward part of the house) to the tarn. The trees about it connect it with nature, but they are all dead, blasted by the preternatural evil of the place; the only living vegetation consists of "rank sedges" (no doubt nourished by the tarn), and fungi growing from the roof, the most heavenward part. The house is also a symbol of the organic and harmonious because it expresses human thought and design, but the structure is crazy, threatened not only by the ominous, zigzag, scarcely discernible fissure, but also by the perilous decrepitude of its constituent materials, which maintained their coherency in a way that looked almost miraculous to Anthropos: "No portion of the masonry had fallen; and there appeared to be a wild inconsistency between its still perfect adaptation of parts, and the crumbling condition of the individual stones." In the interior of the house, the furnishings seemed no longer to express the ordered living of human creatures: "The general furniture was profuse, comfortless, antique, and tattered. Many books and musical instruments lay scattered about, but failed to give any vitality to the scene." That is, the human life it expressed was not ordered and full, but scattered and tattered. The "eyelike windows," the most conspicuous feature of the house, looked vacant from without, and from within were seen to be "altogether inaccessible"; they admitted only "feeble gleams of encrimsoned light." Life and motion within the house were nearly extinct. "An air of stern, deep, and irredeemable gloom hung over and pervaded all."

Roderick Usher resembles his house. It is unnecessary to point out the ways in which a human being is normally an expression of Life-Reason—of heavenly, natural, organic, harmonious, featured, and active qualities. The Death-Madness opposites to these qualities are manifested in interesting correspondences between the physical appearance of Usher and that of his house. The zigzag crack in the house, and the "inconsistency" between its decayed materials and intact structure, are like the difficultly maintained composure of Usher. Anthropos declares: "In the manner of my friend I was at once struck with an incoherence—an *inconsistency* [my italics]; and I soon found this to arise from a series of feeble and futile struggles to overcome an habitual trepidancy—an excessive nervous agitation." The "minute fungi . . . hanging in a fine tangled web-work from the eaves" of the house have their curious counterpart, as a symbol of morbid vitality, in the hair of Usher, "of a more than web-like softness and tenuity . . . [which, as it] had been suffered to grow all unheeded, . . . floated rather than fell about the face, [so that] I could not, even with an effort, connect its Arabesque expression with any idea of simple humanity." (We are reminded of the hair reputed to grow so luxuriantly out of the heads of inhumed corpses.) Usher's organic existence and sanity seem threatened: his "cadaverousness of complexion" is conspicuous; and he not only attributes sentience to vegetable things, but also to "the kingdom of inorganization" which he evidently feels to be assuming domination over him. His most conspicuous feature was "an eye large, liquid, and luminous beyond comparison"; after Madeline Usher's death, Anthropos observes that "the luminousness of his eye had utterly gone out." It was thus assimilated to the "vacant eyelike windows" of his house. And the active qualities of Usher were also fading. We have noticed that his malady was a combined hyper-acuity and inhibition of function of the five senses which main-

tain life and mind. Altogether, the fabric of Usher, like that of his house, exhibited a "specious totality."

The only other important mixed symbol is Usher's song of the "Haunted Palace." It is largely a contrast of before and after. Before the palace was assailed by "evil things, in robes of sorrow," it had "reared its head" grandly under the heavens:

> Never seraph spread a pinion
> Over fabric half so fair!

It displayed several of the characteristics of Life-Reason. But after the assault of "evil things," the Death-Madness qualities are triumphant. Order is destroyed; instead of

> Spirits moving musically
> To a lute's well-tuned law,

within the palace are to be seen

> Vast forms that move fantastically
> To a discordant melody.

Instead of a "troop of Echoes" flowing and sparkling through the "fair palace door," "a hideous throng rush out for ever" through the "pale door" "like a rapid ghastly river." Reason has toppled from its throne, and this song intimated to Anthropos "a full consciousness on the part of Usher of the tottering of his lofty reason upon her throne." The perceptible fading of bright features in the palace is like the fading of the features and vitality of both Usher and his house.

The principal symbols of decrepit Life-Reason having been explicated, it remains to comment on the two symbols of ascendant Death-Madness—the tarn, and Roderick Usher's madly abstract painting. These show the same qualities that we have seen evilly encroaching upon the Life-Reason symbols, but these qualities are here unmitigated by any hint or reminiscence of Life-Reason. The juxtaposition of the tarn-house symbols is crucial; the zig-zag fissure in the house is an index to the source of the evil which eventually overwhelms the Ushers. The tarn is an outlet of a subterranean realm; on the surface of the earth this realm disputes dominion with the powers of heaven and wins. This subnatural realm manifests itself in the miasma that rises from the tarn. "About the mansion and the whole domain there hung an atmosphere peculiar to themselves and their immediate vicinity—an atmosphere which had no affinity with the air of heaven, but which had reeked up from the decayed trees, and the gray wall, and the silent tarn—a pestilent and mystic vapor, dull, sluggish, faintly discernible, and leaden-hued." This upward-reeking effluvium has its counterpart in the "distempered ideality" of Usher while he is producing his mad compositions after the death of Madeline: they are products of "a mind from which darkness, as if an inherent positive quality, poured forth upon all objects of the moral and physical universe in one unceasing radiation of gloom."

"Radiation of gloom" is as interesting an idea as "darkness visible." It reminds us that another mark of this emanation of evil was lurid illumination. The feeble gleams of light that entered Usher's studio were encrimsoned. The "luminous windows" of the "radiant palace" became the "red-litten windows" of the "haunted palace." Oddly, even Usher's mad music is described in a visual figure as having a "sulphureous lustre." On the catastrophic last night of the House of Usher, the environs are at first illuminated, not by any celestial luminaries, but by the "unnatural light of a faintly luminous and distinctly visible gaseous [so our matter-of-fact Anthropos] exhalation which hung about and enshrouded the mansion." And finally, the collapse of the house is melodramatically spot-lighted by "the full, setting, and blood-red moon, which now shone vividly through that once barely perceptible fissure."

Roderick Usher's dread of the "kingdom of inorganization" as a really sentient order of existence reminds us of the animate inanimation of the tarn. Activity and harmony are really related qualities; harmony is an agreeable coincidence of motions. The tarn's absolute stillness is the negation of these qualities. Water is a universal and immemorial symbol of life; this dead water is thus a symbol of Death-in-Life. It lies "unruffled" from the first, and when at last the House of Usher topples thunderously into it, to the noisy accompaniment of Nature in tumult, its waters close "sullenly and silently over the fragments." This horrid inactivity is the condition toward which Usher is tending when he finds the exercise of his senses intolerable.

The tarn is as featureless as any visible thing can be; its blackness, "unruffled lustre," and silence are like the painted "vaguenesses" at which Anthropos shuddered "the more thrillingly" because he shuddered "not knowing why." Here are blank horrors, with only enough suggestion of feature to set the imagination fearfully to work.

This leads us to the only remaining symbol of importance, Usher's terrible painting. It is more horrible than the "Haunted Palace" because, whereas the song described the lost but regretted state of lovely Life and Reason, the painting depicts Death-Madness horribly regnant, with no reminiscence of Life and Reason. The scene pictured is subterranean (Madeline's coffin was deposited in a suggestively similar vault): "Certain accessory points of the design served well to convey the idea that this excavation lay at an exceeding depth below the surface of the earth." It is preternaturally lurid: "No torch or other artificial source of light was discernible; yet a flood of intense rays rolled throughout, and bathed the whole in a ghastly and inappropriate splendor." The picture shows a lifeless scene without features—"smooth, white, and without interruption or device."

Before these remarks on the symbolism of the tale are concluded, some notice should be taken of the part which musical symbols play in it. Poe uses his favorite heart-lute image, from Béranger, as a motto:

> Son coeur est un luth suspendu;
> Sîtot qu'on le touche il résonne.

The "lute's well-tuned law" symbolizes ideal order in the "radiant palace," and the whole of that song is an explicit musical metaphor for derangement of intellect. For Poe, music was the highest as well as the most rational expression of the intelligence, and string music was quintessential music (wherefore Usher's jangled intellect can endure only string music). Time out of mind, music has symbolized celestial order. His conception was not far from that expressed in Dryden's "Song for St. Cecilia's Day," with "The diapason closing full in Man." The derangement of human reason, then, "sweet bells jangled out of tune and harsh," cannot be better expressed than in a musical figure.

IV

I have thus tediously but by no means exhaustively exposed the filaments of symbol in **"The Fall of the House of Usher"** to show how much of its effect depends on the artfully inconspicuous iteration and reiteration of identical suggestions which could not operate so unobtrusively in any other way. Human actions in the story are of much less importance, but one or two events deserve notice. The depositing of Madeline's coffin in the underground vault provides Anthropos with an opportunity to compare the appearance of Roderick and Madeline Usher. She had on her face and bosom "the mockery of a faint blush" and on her lips "that suspiciously lingering smile . . . which is so terrible in death." In contrast, the "cadaverousness of complexion" of Roderick Usher had been repeatedly remarked. Thus is indicated how nearly triumphant Death is in the Ushers from the moment when Anthropos first enters the house, how scarcely perceptible is the difference between a live Usher and a dead one. Consequently, Madeline's rising up from her coffin to claim her brother for death really suggests that he had mistakenly and perversely lingered among the living, that the similitude of life in an Usher was merely morbid animation. He needed only to cross a shadowy line to yield himself up to Madness and Death.

The night of catastrophe, then, witnessed this transition. The reading of "The Mad Trist" shows a mechanical, not a symbolical, correspondence between Usher's ruin and external things; it is the only piece of superimposed and unfunctional trumpery in the tale, though it does serve, perhaps, to explain and justify the suspenseful doubt and surprise of Anthropos when he hears the weird sounds of Madeline's ghastly up-rising. The storm which rages outside is not a supernatural storm, but a tumult of natural elements impotently opposing the silent and sullen powers which in that hour assert dominion over the House of Usher and draw it into their Plutonian depths.

The tragedy of Roderick Usher was not merely his fatal introversion, but his too-late realization of his own doom, the ineffectuality of his effort to re-establish connection with life by summoning to him the person most his friend. When at last he shrieks "Madman!" at this presumably sane friend, he crosses the borderline between sanity and madness. In a moment he dies in melodramatic circumstances, and immediately thereafter is carried into the tarn by the culminatingly symbolical collapse of his house.

V

It is expedient to review the impressions of Anthropos the determined doubter, who leaves the domain of Usher with a sense of supernatural fatality accomplished. Throughout the tale he scrupulously tries to find rational explanations for the horror which agitate him. He explains his depression of spirits when he first views the House of Usher by reference to the gloomy combination of "very simple natural objects." That the tarn deepened this depression he accounted for psychologically: "The consciousness of the rapid increase of my superstition—for why should I not so term it?—served mainly to accelerate the increase itself." In the house he is puzzled to account for the fact that, although the furniture is all of a sort to which he has been accustomed throughout his life, it has an "unfamiliar" effect of gloom; and it is difficult for him to connect any "idea of simple humanity" with Usher's ghastly appearance, although he dutifully tries. He tells us that Usher "admitted" that his "superstitious impressions in regard to the dwelling which he tenanted" might be traced to "a more natural and far more palpable origin" than the malign sentience which he attributed to the place, that is to his grief at his sister's hopeless illness. The music which Usher composes during his bereavement is characterized by his common-sensible friend as distempered and perverted, and Usher himself is called a hypochondriac. The limited tolerance of Usher for sound is described in Anthropos' medical jargon as "a morbid condition of the auditory nerve." Usher's conviction of the sentience of the "kingdom of inorganization" is regarded by his friend as a pertinacious but not altogether novel delusion. Usher's agitation is partly ascribed to the influence of the fantastic literature which he reads. The sounds which interrupt the reading of "The Mad Trist" are, Anthropos thinks (before the apparition of Madeline changes his opinion), hallucinations prompted by the wild story and his own state of excited suggestibility. The lurid, upward-streaming illumination of the environs of the House of Usher on the night of catastrophe is explained as a natural phenomenon—a "gaseous exhalation." And, if we wish, we can attribute the stupendously shattering collapse of the ancient House of Usher itself to merely physical and natural causes—the violent thrust of the storm against its frail fabric and almost dilapidated structure. But, significantly, our matter-of-fact Anthropos does not suggest any natural explanation; he merely flees "aghast.". . .

Allen Tate (essay date 1950)

SOURCE: "Three Commentaries: Poe, James, and Joyce," in *Memoirs and Opinions, 1926-74,* The Swallow Press, 1975, pp. 155-69.

[*Tate's criticism is closely associated with two critical movements, the Agrarians and the New Critics. The Agrarians were concerned with political and social issues as well as literature, and were dedicated to preserving the Southern way of life and traditional Southern values. The New Critics, a group which included Cleanth Brooks and Robert Penn Warren, among others, comprised one of the most influential critical movements of the mid-twentieth century. A conservative thinker and convert to Catholicism, Tate attacked the tradition of Western philosophy, which he felt has alienated persons from themselves, one another, and from nature by divorcing intellectual from natural functions in human life. For Tate, literature is the principal form of knowledge and revelation that restores human beings to a proper relationship with nature and the spiritual realm. In the following excerpt, originally published in 1950, he identifies Roderick Usher as a prototype of the modern fictional hero.*]

["**The Fall of the House of Usher**"] is perhaps not Poe's best [story], but it has significant features which ought to illuminate some of the later, more mature work in the naturalistic-symbolic technique of Flaubert, Joyce, and James. Poe's insistence upon unity of effect, from first word to last, in the famous review of Hawthrone's *Twice-Told Tales,* anticipates from one point of view the high claims of James in his essay "The Art of Fiction." James asserts that the imaginative writer must take his art at least as seriously as the historian takes his; that is to say, he must no longer apologize, he must not say "it *may* have happened this way"; he must, since he cannot rely upon the reader's acceptance of known historical incident, create the illusion of reality, so that the reader may have a "direct impression" of it. It was toward this complete achievement of "direct impression" that Poe was moving, in his tales and in his criticism; he, like Hawthrone, was a great forerunner. The reasons why he did not himself fully achieve it (perhaps less even than Hawthorne) are perceptible in "**The Fall of the House of Usher.**"

Like Hawthorne again, Poe seems to have been very little influenced by the common-sense realism of the eighteenth-century English novel. What has been known in our time as the romantic sensibility reached him from two directions: the Gothic tale of Walpole and Monk Lewis, and the poetry of Coleridge. Roderick Usher is a "Gothic" character taken seriously; that is to say, Poe takes the Gothic setting, with all its machinery and *décor,* and the preposterous Gothic hero, and transforms them into the material of serious literary art. Usher becomes the prototype of the Joycean and Jamesian hero who cannot function in the ordinary world. He has two characteristic traits of this later fictional hero of our own time. First, he is afflicted with the split personality of the manic depressive:

> His action was alternately vivacious and sullen. His voice varied rapidly from a tremulous indecision (when the animal spirits seemed utterly in abeyance) to that species of energetic concision . . . and perfectly modulated guttural utterance, which may be observed in the lost drunkard, or the irreclaimable eater of opium, during the periods of his most intense excitement.

Secondly, certain musical sounds (for some unmusical reason Poe selects the notes of the guitar) are alone tolerable to him: "He suffered from a morbid acuteness of the sense." He cannot live in the real world; he is constantly exacerbated. At the same time he "has a passionate devotion to the intricacies . . . of musical science"; and his paintings are "pure abstractions" which have "an intensity of intolerable awe."

Usher is, of course, both our old and our new friend; his new name is Monsieur Teste, and much of the history of modern French literature is in that name. Usher's "want of moral energy," along with a hypertrophy of sensibility and intellect in a split personality, places him in the ancestry of Gabriel Conroy, Stephen Daedalus, John Marcher, J. Alfred Prufrock, Mrs. Dalloway—a forbear of whose somewhat showy accessories they might well be a little ashamed; or they might enjoy a degree of moral complacency in contemplating their own luck in having had greater literary artists than Poe present them to us in a more credible imaginative reality.

I have referred to the Gothic trappings and the poetry of Coleridge as the sources of Poe's romanticism. In trying to understand the kind of unity of effect that Poe demanded of the writer of fiction we must bear in mind two things. First, unity of *plot,* the emphasis upon which led him to the invention of the "tale of ratiocination." But plot is not so necessary to the serious story of moral perversion of which **"The Fall of the House of Usher," "Ligeia,"** and **"Morella"** are Poe's supreme examples. Secondly, the unity of tone, a quality that had not been consciously aimed at in fiction before Poe. It is this particular kind of unity, a poetical rather than a fictional characteristic, which Poe must have got from the Romantic poets, Coleridge especially, and from Coleridge's criticism as well as "Kubla Khan" and "Christabel." Unity of plot and tone can exist without the *created, active detail* which came into this tradition of fiction with Flaubert, to be perfected later by James, Chekhov, and Joyce.

In **"The Fall of the House of Usher,"** *there is not one instance of dramatized detail.* Although Poe's first-person narrator is in direct contact with the scene, he merely reports it; he does not show us scene and character in action; it is all description. The closet approach in the entire story to active detail is the glimpse, at the beginning, that the narrator gives us of the furtive doctor as he passes him on "one of the staircases." If we contrast the remoteness of Poe's reporting in the entire range of this story with the brilliant re-creation of the character of Michael Furey by Gretta Conroy in "The Dead," we shall be able to form some conception of the advance in the techniques of reality that was achieved in the sixty-odd years between Poe and Joyce. The powerful description of the facade of the House of Usher, as the narrator approaches it, sets up unity of tone, but the description is never woven into the action of the story: the "metaphysical" identity of scene and character reaches our consciousness through *lyrical assertion.* The fissure in the wall of the house remains an inert symbol of Usher's split personality. At the climax of the story Poe uses an incredibly clumsy device in the effort to make the collapse of Usher active dramatically; that is, he employs the mechanical

device of coincidence. The narrator is reading to Usher the absurd tale of the "Mad Trist" of Sir Lancelot Canning. The knight has slain the dragon and now approaches the "brazen shield," which falls with tremendous clatter. Usher has been "hearing" it, but what he has been actually hearing is the rending of the lid of his sister Madeline's coffin and the grating of the iron door of the tomb; until at the end the sister (who has been in a cataleptic trance) stands outside Usher's door. The door opens; she stands before them. The narrator flees and the House of Usher, collapsing, sinks forever with its master into the waters of the "tarn."

We could dwell upon the symbolism of the identity of house and master, of the burial alive of Madeline, of the fissure in the wall of the house and the fissure in the psyche of Usher. What we should emphasize here is the dominance of symbolism over its visible base: symbolism external and "lyrical," not intrinsic and dramatic. The active structure of the story is mechanical and thus negligible; but its lyrical structure is impressive. Poe's plots seem most successful when the reality of scene and character is of secondary importance in the total effect; that is, in the tale of "ratiocination." He seemed unable to combine incident with his gift for "insight symbolism"; as a result his symbolic tales are insecurely based upon scenic reality. But the insight was great. In Roderick Usher, as we have said, we get for the first time the hero of modern fiction. In the history of literature the discoverer of the subject is almost never the perfector of the techniques for making the subject real.

Richard Wilbur (essay date 1959)

SOURCE: "The House of Poe," in *The Recognition of Edgar Allan Poe: Selected Criticism Since 1829,* edited by Eric W. Carlson, University of Michigan Press, 1966, pp. 255-77.

[*In the following essay, originally delivered as a lecture to the Library of Congress in 1959, Wilbur discusses Poe's allegorical representation of the poetic soul in conflict with the external world, especially as it is demonstrated in "The Fall of the House of Usher."*]

A few weeks ago, in the *New York Times Book Review,* Mr. Saul Bellow expressed impatience with the current critical habit of finding symbols in everything. No self-respecting modern professor, Mr. Bellow observed, would dare to explain Achilles' dragging of Hector around the walls of Troy by the mere assertion that Achilles was in a bad temper. That would be too drearily obvious. No, the professor must say that the circular path of Achilles and Hector relates to the theme of circularity which pervades *The Iliad.*

In the following week's *Book Review,* a pedantic correspondent corrected Mr. Bellow, pointing out that Achilles did not, in Homer's *Iliad,* drag Hector's body around the walls of Troy; this perhaps invalidates the Homeric example, but Mr. Bellow's complaint remains, nevertheless, a very sensible one. We are all getting a bit tired, I think, of that laboriously clever criticism which discovers mandalas in Mark Twain, rebirth archetypes in Edwin Arlington Robinson, and fertility myths in everybody.

Still, we must not be carried away by our impatience, to the point of demanding that no more symbols be reported. The business of the critic, after all, is to divine the intention of the work, and to interpret the work in the light of that intention; and since some writers are intentionally symbolic, there is nothing for it but to talk about their symbols. If we speak of Melville, we must speak of symbols. If we speak of Hawthorne, we must speak of symbols. And as for Edgar Allan Poe, whose sesquicentennial year we are met to observe, I think we can make no sense about him until we consider his work—and in particular his prose fiction—as deliberate and often brillilant allegory.

Not everyone will agree with me that Poe's work has an accessible allegorical meaning. Some critics, in fact, have refused to see any substance, allegorical or otherwise, in Poe's fiction, and have regarded his tales as nothing more than complicated machines for saying "boo." Others have intuited undiscoverable meanings in Poe, generally of an unpleasant kind: I recall one Freudian critic declaring that if we find Poe unintelligible we should congratulate ourselves, since if we *could* understand him it would be proof of our abnormality.

It is not really surprising that some critics should think Poe meaningless, or that others should suppose his meaning intelligible only to monsters. Poe was not a wide-open and perspicuous writer; indeed, he was a secretive writer both by temperament and by conviction. He sprinkled his stories with sly references to himself and to his personal history. He gave his own birthday of January 19 to his character William Wilson; he bestowed his own height and color of eye on the captain of the phantom ship in **"Ms. Found in a Bottle"**; and the name of one of his heroes, Arthur Gordon Pym, is patently a version of his own. He was a maker and solver of puzzles, fascinated by codes, ciphers, anagrams, acrostics, hieroglyphics, and the Kabbala. He invented the detective story. He was fond of aliases; he delighted in accounts of swindles; he perpetrated the famous Balloon Hoax of 1844; and one of his most characteristic stories is entitled **"Mystification"**. A man so devoted to concealment and deception and unraveling and detection might be expected to have in his work what Poe himself called "undercurrents of meaning."

And that is where Poe, as a critic, said that meaning belongs: not on the surface of the poem or tale, but below the surface as a dark undercurrent. If the meaning of a work is made overly clear—as Poe said in his "Philosophy of Composition"—if the meaning is brought to the surface and made the upper current of the poem or tale, then the work becomes bald and prosaic and ceases to be art. Poe conceived of art, you see, not as a means of giving imaginative order to earthly experience, but as a stimulus to unearthly visions. The work of literary art does not, in Poe's view, present the reader with a provisional arrangement of reality; instead, it seeks to disengage the reader's mind from reality and propel it toward the ideal. Now, since Poe thought the function of art was to set the mind soaring upward in what he called "a wild effort to reach the Beauty above," it was important to him that the poem or tale should not have such definiteness and completeness of meaning as might contain the reader's mind within the work. Therefore Poe's criticism places a positive value on the obscuration of meaning, on a dark suggestiveness, on a deliberate vagueness by means of which the reader's mind may be set adrift toward the beyond.

Poe's criticism, then, assures us that his work does have meaning. And Poe also assures us that this meaning is not on the surface but in the depths. If we accept Poe's invitation to play detective, and commence to read him with an eye for submerged meaning, it is not long before we sense that there *are* meanings to be found, and that in fact many of Poe's stories, though superficially dissimilar, tell the same tale. We begin to have this sense as we notice Poe's repeated use of certain narrative patterns; his repetition of certain words and phrases; his use, in story after story, of certain scenes and properties. We notice, for instance, the recurrence of the *spiral* or *vortex*. In **"Ms. Found in a Bottle"**, the story ends with a plunge into a whirlpool; the **"Descent into the Maelström"** also concludes in a watery vortex; the house of Usher, just before it plunges into the tarn, is swaddled in a whirlwind; the hero of **"Metzengerstein,"** Poe's first published story, perishes in "a whirlwind of chaotic fire"; and at the close of **"King Pest,"** Hugh Tarpaulin is cast into a puncheon of ale and disappears "amid a whirlpool of foam." That Poe offers us so many spirals or vortices in his fiction, and that they should always appear at the same terminal point in their respective narratives, is a strong indication that the spiral had some symbolic value for Poe. And it did: What the spiral invariably represents in any tale of Poe's is the loss of consciousness, and the descent of the mind into sleep.

I hope you will grant, before I am through, that to find spirals in Poe is not so silly as finding circles in Homer. The professor who finds circles in Homer does so to the neglect of more important and more provable meanings. But the spiral or vortex is a part of that symbolic language in which Poe said his say, and unless we understand it we cannot understand Poe.

But now I have gotten ahead of myself, and before I proceed with my project of exploring one area of Poe's symbolism, I think I had better say something about Poe's conception of poetry and the poet.

Poe conceived of God as a poet. The universe, therefore, was an artistic creation, a poem composed by God. Now, if the universe is a poem, it follows that the one proper response to it is aesthetic, and that God's creatures are attuned to Him in proportion as their imaginations are ravished by the beauty and harmony of his creation. Not to worship beauty, not to regard poetic knowledge as divine, would be to turn one's back on God and fall from grace.

The planet Earth, according to Poe's myth of the cosmos, has done just this. It has fallen away from God by exalting the scientific reason above poetic intuition, and by putting its trust in material fact rather than in visionary knowledge. The Earth's inhabitants are thus corrupted by rationalism and materialism; their souls are diseased; and Poe sees this disease of the human spirit as having contaminated physical nature. The woods and fields and waters of Earth have thereby lost their first beauty, and no longer clearly express God's imagination; the landscape has lost its original perfection of composition, in proportion as men have lost their power to perceive the beautiful.

Since Earth is a fallen planet, life upon Earth is necessarily a torment for the poet: neither in the human sphere nor in the realm of nature can he find fit objects for contemplation, and indeed his soul is oppressed by everything around him. The rationalist mocks at him; the dull, prosaic spirit of the age damps his imaginative spark; the gross materiality of the world crowds in upon him. His only recourse is to abandon all concern for Earthly things, and to devote himself as purely as possible to unearthly visions, in hopes of glimpsing that heavenly beauty which is the thought of God.

Poe, then, sees the poetic soul as at war with the mundane physical world; and that warfare is Poe's fundamental subject. But the war between soul and world is not the only war. There is also warfare within the poet's very nature. To be sure, the poet's nature was not always in conflict with itself. Prior to his earthly incarnation, and during his dreamy childhood, Poe's poet enjoyed a serene unity of being; his consciousness was purely imaginative, and he knew the universe for the divine poem that it is. But with his entrance into adult life, the poet became involved with a fallen world in which the physical, the factual, the rational, the prosaic are not escapable. Thus, compromised, he lost his perfect spirituality, and is now cursed with a divided nature. Though his imagination still yearns toward ideal beauty, his mortal body chains him to the physical and temporal and local; the hungers and passions of his body draw him toward external objects, and the conflict of conscience and desire degrades and distracts his soul; his mortal senses try to convince him of the reality of a material world which his soul struggles to escape; his reason urges him to acknowledge everyday fact, and to confine his thought within the prison of logic. For all these reasons it is not easy for the poet to detach his soul from earthly things, and regain his lost imaginative power—his power to commune with that supernal beauty which is symbolized, in Poe, by the shadowy and angelic figures of Ligeia, and Helen, and Lenore.

These, then, are Poe's great subjects: first, the war between the poetic soul and the external world; second, the war between the poetic soul and the earthly self to which it is bound. All of Poe's major stories are allegorical presentations of these conflicts, and everything he wrote bore somehow upon them.

How does one wage war against the external world? And how does one release one's visionary soul from the body, and from the constraint of the reason? These may sound like difficult tasks; and yet we all accomplish them every night. In a subjective sense—and Poe's thought is wholly subjective—we destroy the world every time we close our eyes. If *esse est percipi*, as Bishop Berkeley said—if to be is to be perceived—then when we withdraw our attention from the world in somnolence or sleep, the world ceases to be. As our minds move toward sleep, by way of drowsiness and reverie and the hypnagogic state, we escape from consciousness of the world, we escape from awareness of our bodies, and we enter a realm in which reason no longer hampers the play of the imagination: we enter the realm of dream.

Like many romantic poets, Poe identified imagination with dream. Where Poe differed from other romantic poets was in the literalness and absoluteness of the identification, and in the clinical precision with which he observed the phenomena of dream, carefully distinguishing the various states through which the mind passes on its way to sleep. A large number of Poe's stories derive their very structure from this sequence of mental states: **"Ms. Found in a Bottle,"** to give but one example, is an allegory of the mind's voyage from the waking world into the world of dreams, with each main step of the narrative symbolizing the passage of the mind from one state to another—from wakefulness to reverie, from reverie to the hypnagogic state, from the hypnagogic state to the deep dream. The departure of the narrator's ship from Batavia represents the mind's withdrawal from the waking world; the drowning of the captain and all but one of the crew represents the growing solitude of reverie; when the narrator is transferred by collision from a real ship to a phantom ship, we are to understand that he has passed from reverie, a state in which reality and dream exist in a kind of equilibrium, into the free fantasy of the hypnagogic state. And when the phantom ship makes its final plunge into the whirlpool, we are to understand that the narrator's mind has gone over the brink of sleep and descended into dreams.

> Poe sees the poetic soul as at war with the mundane physical world; and that warfare is Poe's fundamental subject
>
> —*Richard Wilbur*

What I am saying by means of this example is that the scenes and situations of Poe's tales are always concrete representations of states of mind. If we bear in mind Poe's fundamental plot—the effort of the poetic soul to escape all consciousness of the world in dream—we soon recognize the significance of certain scenic or situational motifs which turn up in story after story. The most important of these recurrent motifs is that of *enclosure* or *circumscription*; perhaps the latter term is preferable, because it is Poe's own word, and because Poe's enclosures are so often more or less circular in form. The heroes of Poe's tales and poems are violently circumscribed by whirlpools, or peacefully circumscribed by cloud-capped Paradisal valleys; they float upon circular pools ringed in by steep flowering hillsides; they dwell on islands, or voyage to them; we find Poe heroes also in coffins, in the cabs of balloons, or hidden away in the holds of ships; and above all we find them sitting alone in the claustral and richly-furnished rooms of remote and mouldering mansions.

Almost never, if you think about it, is one of Poe's heroes to be seen standing in the light of common day; almost never does the Poe hero breathe the air that others breathe; he requires some kind of envelope in order to be what he is; he is always either enclosed or on his way to an enclosure. The narrative of William Wilson conducts the hero from Stoke Newington to Eton, from Eton to Oxford, and then to Rome by way of Paris, Vienna, Berlin, Moscow, Naples, and Egypt: and yet, for all his travels, Wilson seems never to set foot out-of-doors. The story takes place in a series of rooms, the last one locked from the inside.

Sometimes Poe emphasizes the circumscription of his heroes by multiple enclosures. Roderick Usher dwells in a great and crumbling mansion from which, as Poe tells us, he has not ventured forth in many years. This mansion stands islanded in a stagnant lake, which serves it as a defensive moat. And beyond the moat lies the Usher estate, a vast barren tract having its own peculiar and forbidding weather and atmosphere. You might say that Roderick Usher is defended in depth; and yet at the close of the story Poe compounds Roderick's inaccessibility by having the mansion and its occupant swallowed up by the waters of the tarn.

What does it mean that Poe's heroes are invariably enclosed or circumscribed? The answer is simple: circumscription, in Poe's tales, means the exclusion from consciousness of the so-called real world, the world of time and reason and physical fact; it means the isolation of the poetic soul in visionary reverie or trance. When we find one of Poe's characters in a remote valley, or a claustral room, we know that he is in the process of dreaming his way out of the world.

Now, I want to devote the time remaining to the consideration of one kind of enclosure in Poe's tales: the mouldering mansion and its richly-furnished rooms. I want to concentrate on Poe's architecture and decor for two reasons: first, because Poe's use of architecture is so frankly and provably allegorical that I *should* be able to be convincing about it; second, because by concentrating on one area of Poe's symbolism we shall be able to see that his stories are allegorical not only in their broad patterns, but also in their smallest details.

Let us begin with a familiar poem, "The Haunted Palace." The opening stanzas of this poem, as a number of critics have noted, make a point-by-point comparison between a building and the head of a man. The exterior of the palace represents the man's physical features; the interior repre-

sents the man's mind engaged in harmonious imaginative thought.

> In the greenest of our valleys,
> 　By good angels tenanted,
> Once a fair and stately palace—
> 　Radiant palace—reared its head.
>
> In the monarch Thought's dominion,
> 　It stood there!
> Never seraph spread a pinion
> 　Over fabric half so fair!
>
> Banners yellow, glorious, golden,
> 　On its roof did float and flow
> (This—all this—was in the olden
> 　Time long ago),
> And every gentle air that dallied,
> 　In that sweet day,
> Along the ramparts plumed and pallid,
> 　A wingéd odor went away.
>
> Wanderers in that happy valley,
> 　Through two luminous windows, saw
> Spirits moving musically
> 　To a lute's well-tunéd law,
> Round about a throne where, sitting,
> 　Porphyrogene,
> In state his glory well befitting,
> 　The ruler of the realm was seen.
>
> And all in pearl and ruby glowing
> 　Was the fair palace door,
> Through which came flowing, flowing, flowing,
> 　And sparkling evermore,
> A troop of Echoes, whose sweet duty
> 　Was but to sing,
> In voices of surpassing beauty,
> 　The wit and wisdom of their king.

I expect you observed that the two luminous windows of the palace are the eyes of a man, and that the yellow banners on the roof are his luxuriant blond hair. The "pearl and ruby" door is the man's mouth—ruby representing red lips, and pearl representing pearl white teeth. The beautiful Echoes which issue from the pearl and ruby door are the poetic utterances of the man's harmonious imagination, here symbolized as an orderly dance. The angel-guarded valley in which the palace stands, and which Poe describes as "the monarch Thought's dominion," is a symbol of the man's exclusive awareness of exalted and spiritual things. The valley is what Poe elsewhere called "that evergreen and radiant paradise which the true poet knows . . . as the limited realm of his authority, as the circumscribed Eden of his dreams."

As you all remember, the last two stanzas of the poem describe the physical and spiritual corruption of the palace and its domain, and it was to this part of the poem that Poe was referring when he told a correspondent, "By the 'Haunted Palace' I mean to imply a mind haunted by phantoms—a disordered brain." Let me read you the closing lines:

> But evil things, in robes of sorrow,
>   Assailed the monarch's high estate.
> (Ah, let us mourn!—for never morrow
>   Shall dawn upon him, desolate!)
> And round about his home the glory
>   That blushed and bloomed,
> Is but a dim-remembered story
>   Of the old time entombed.
>
> And travellers, now, within that valley,
>   Through the red-litten windows see
> Vast forms that move fantastically
>   To a discordant melody,
> While, like a ghastly rapid river,
>   Through the pale door
> A hideous throng rush out forever,
>   And laugh—but smile no more.

The domain of the monarch Thought, in these final stanzas, is disrupted by civil war, and in consequence everything alters for the worse. The valley becomes barren, like the domain of Roderick Usher; the eye-like windows of the palace are no longer "luminous," but have become "red-litten"—they are like the bloodshot eyes of a madman or a drunkard. As for the mouth of our allegorized man, it is now "pale" rather than "pearl and ruby," and through it come no sweet Echoes, as before, but the wild laughter of a jangling and discordant mind.

The two states of the palace—before and after—are, as we can see, two states of mind. Poe does not make it altogether clear *why* one state of mind has given way to the other, but by recourse to similar tales and poems we can readily find the answer. The palace in its original condition expresses the imaginative harmony which the poet's soul enjoys in early childhood, when all things are viewed with a tyrannical and unchallenged subjectivity. But as the soul passes from childhood into adult life, its consciousness is more and more invaded by the corrupt and corrupting external world: it succumbs to passion, it develops a conscience, it makes concessions to reason and to objective fact. Consequently, there is civil war in the palace of the mind. The imagination must now struggle against the intellect and the moral sense; finding itself no longer able to possess the world through a serene solipsism, it strives to annihilate the outer world by turning in upon itself; it flees into irrationality and dream; and all its dreams are efforts both to recall and to simulate its primal, unfallen state.

"The Haunted Palace" presents us with a possible key to the general meaning of Poe's architecture; and this key proves, if one tries it, to open every building in Poe's fiction. Roderick Usher, as you will remember, declaims "The Haunted Palace" to the visitor who tells his story, accompanying the poem with wild improvisations on the guitar. We are encouraged, therefore, to compare the palace of the poem with the house of the story; and it is no surprise to find that the Usher mansion has "vacant eye-like windows," and that there are mysterious physical sympathies between Roderick Usher and the house in which he dwells. The House of Usher *is,* in allegorical fact, the physical body of Roderick Usher, and its dim interior is, in fact, Roderick Usher's visionary mind.

The House of Usher, like many edifices in Poe, is in a state of extreme decay. The stonework of its facade has so crumbled and decomposed that it reminds the narrator, as he puts it, "of the specious totality of old woodwork which has rotted for long years in some neglected vault." The Usher mansion is so eaten away, so fragile, that it seems a breeze would push it over; it remains standing only because the atmosphere of Usher's domains is perfectly motionless and dead. Such is the case also with the "time-eaten towers that tremble not" in Poe's poem "The City in the Sea"; and likewise the magnificent architecture of **"The Domain of Arnheim"** is said to "sustain itself by a miracle in mid-air." Even the detective Dupin lives in a perilously decayed structure: the narrator of **"The Murders in the Rue Morgue"** tells how he and Dupin dwelt in a "time-eaten and grotesque mansion, long deserted through superstitions into which we did not enquire, and tottering to its fall in a retired and desolate portion of the Faubourg St. Germain." (Notice how, even when Poe's buildings are situated in cities, he manages to circumscibe them with a protective desolation.)

We must now ask what Poe means by the extreme and tottering decay of so many of his structure. The answer is best given by reference to **"The Fall of the House of Usher,"** and in giving the answer we shall arrive, I think, at an understanding of the pattern of that story.

"The Fall of the House of Usher" is a journey into the depths of the self. I have said that all journeys in Poe are allegories of the process of dreaming, and we must understand **"The Fall of the House of Usher"** as a dream of the narrator's, in which he leaves behind him the waking, physical world and journeys inward toward his *moi intérieur,* toward his inner and spiritual self. That inner and spiritual self is Roderick Usher.

Roderick Usher, then, is a part of the narrator's self, which the narrator reaches by way of reverie. We may think of Usher, if we like, as the narrator's imagination, or as his visionary soul. Or we may think of him as a *state of mind* which the narrator enters at a certain stage of his progress into dreams. Considered as a state of mind, Roderick Usher is an allegorical figure representing the hypnagogic state.

The hypnagogic state, about which there is strangely little said in the literature of psychology, is a condition of semi-consciousness in which the closed eye beholds a continuous procession of vivid and constantly changing forms. These forms sometimes have color, and are often abstract in character. Poe regarded the hypnagogic state as the visionary condition *par excellence,* and he considered its rapidly shifting abstract images to be—as he put it— "glimpses of the spirit's outer world." These visionary glimpses, Poe says in one of his **Marginalia,** "arise in the soul . . . only . . . at those mere points of time where the confines of the waking world blend with those of the world of dreams." And Poe goes on to say: "I am aware of these 'fancies' only when I am upon the very brink of sleep, with the consciousness that I am so."

Roderick Usher enacts the hypnagogic state in a number of ways. For one thing, the narrator describes Roderick's behavior as inconsistent, and characterized by constant alternation: he is alternately vivacious and sullen; he is alternately communicative and rapt; he speaks at one moment with "tremulous indecison," and at the next with the "energetic concision" of an excited opium-eater. His conduct resembles, in other words, that wavering between consciousness and sub-consciousness which characterizes the hypnagogic state. The trembling of Roderick's body, and the floating of his silken hair, also bring to mind the instability and underwater quality of hypnagogic images. His improvisations on the guitar suggest hypnagogic experience in their rapidity, changeableness, and wild novelty. And as for Usher's paintings, which the narrator describes as "pure abstractions," they quite simply *are* hypnagogic images. The narrator says of Roderick, "From the paintings over which his elaborate fancy brooded, and which grew, touch by touch, into vaguenesses at which I shuddered the more thrillingly because I shuddered without knowing why—from these paintings (vivid as their images now are before me) I would in vain endeavor to educe more than a small portion which should lie within the compass of merely written words." That the narrator finds Roderick's paintings indescribable is interesting, because in that one of the *Marginalia* from which I have quoted, Poe asserts that the only things in human experience which lie "beyond the compass of words" are the visions of the hypnagogic state.

Roderick Usher stands for the hypnagogic state, which as Poe said is a teetering condition of mind occurring "upon the very brink of sleep." Since Roderick is the embodiment of a state of mind in which *falling*—falling asleep—is imminent, it is appropriate that the building which symbolizes his mind should promise at every moment to fall. The House of Usher stares down broodingly at its reflection in the tarn below, as in the hypnagogic state the conscious mind may stare into the subconscious; the house threatens continually to collapse because it is extremely easy for the mind to slip from the hypnagogic state into the depths of sleep; and when the House of Usher *does* fall, the story ends, as it must, because the mind, at the end of its inward journey, has plunged into the darkness of sleep.

We have found one allegorical meaning in the tottering decay of Poe's buildings; there is another meaning, equally important, which may be stated very briefly. I have said that Poe saw the poet as at war with the material world, and with the material or physical aspects of himself; and I have said that Poe identified poetic imagination with the power to escape from the material and the materialistic, to exclude them from consciousness and so subjectively destroy them. Now, if we recall these things, and recall also that the exteriors of Poe's houses or palaces, with their eye-like windows and mouth-like doors, represent the

physical features of Poe's dreaming heroes, then the characteristic dilapidation of Poe's architecture takes on sudden significance. The extreme decay of the House of Usher—a decay so extreme as to approach the atmospheric—is quite simply a sign that the narrator, in reaching that state of mind which he calls Roderick Usher, has very nearly dreamt himself free of his physical body, and of the material world with which that body connects him.

This is what decay or decomposition mean everywhere in Poe; and we find them almost everywhere. Poe's preoccupation with decay is not, as some critics have thought, an indication of necrophilia; decay in Poe is a symbol of visionary remoteness from the physical, a sign that the state of mind represented is one of almost pure spirituality. When the House of Usher disintegrates or dematerializes at the close of the story, it does so because Roderick Usher has become all soul. **"The Fall of the House of Usher,"** then, is not really a horror story; it is a triumphant report by the narrator that it *is* possible for the poetic soul to shake off this temporal, rational, physical world and escape, if only for a moment, to a realm of unfettered vision.

We have now arrived at three notions about Poe's typical building. It is set apart in a valley or a sea or a waste place, and this remoteness is intended to express the retreat of the poet's mind from worldly consciousness into dream. It is a tottery structure, and this indicates that the dreamer within is in that unstable threshold condition called the hypnagogic state. Finally, Poe's typical building is crumbling or decomposing, and this means that the dreamer's mind is moving toward a perfect freedom from his material self and the material world. Let us now open the door—or mouth—of Poe's building and visit the mind inside.

As we enter the palace of the visionary hero of the **"Assignation"**, or the house of Roderick Usher, we find ourselves approaching the master's private chamber by way of dim and winding passages, or a winding staircase. There is no end to dim windings in Poe's fiction: there are dim and winding woods paths, dim and winding streets, dim and winding watercourses—and, whenever the symbolism is architectural, there are likely to be dim and winding passages or staircases. It is not at all hard to guess what Poe means by this symbol. If we think of waking life as dominated by reason, and if we think of the reason as a daylight faculty which operates in straight lines, then it is proper that reverie should be represented as an obscure and wandering movement of the mind. There are other, and equally obvious meanings in Poe's symbol of dim and winding passages: to grope through such passages is to become confused as to place and direction, just as in reverie we begin to lose any sense of locality, and to have an infinite freedom in regard to space. In his description of the huge old mansion in which William Wilson went to school, Poe makes this meaning of winding passages very plain:

> But the house—how quaint an old building was this!— to me how veritable a palace of enchantment! There

was no end to its windings—to its incomprehensible subdivisions. It was difficult, at any given time, to say with certainty upon which of its two stories one happened to be. From each room to every other there were sure to be found three or four steps either in ascent or descent. Then the lateral branches were innumerable—inconceivable—and so returning in upon themselves, that our most exact ideas in regard to the whole mansion were not very far different from those with which we pondered on infinity.

Dim windings indicate the state of reverie; they point toward that infinite freedom in and from space which the mind achieves in dreams; also, in their curvature and in their occasional doubling-back, they anticipate the mind's final spiralling plunge into unconsciousness. But the immediate goal of reverie's winding passages is that magnificent chamber in which we find the visionary hero slumped in a chair or lolling on an ottoman, occupied in purging his consciousness of everything that is earthly.

Since I have been speaking of geometry—of straight lines and curves and spirals—perhaps the first thing to notice about Poe's dream-rooms is their shape. It has already been said that the enclosures of Poe's tales incline to a curving or circular form. And Poe himself, in certain of his essays and dialogues, explains this inclination by denouncing what he calls "the harsh mathematical reason of the schools," and complaining that practical science has covered the face of the earth with "rectangular obscenities." Poe quite explicitly identifies regular angular forms with everyday reason, and the circle, oval, or fluid arabesque with the otherwordly imagination. Therefore, if we discover that the dream-chambers of Poe's fiction are free of angular regularity, we may be sure that we are noticing a pointed and purposeful consistency in his architecture and décor.

The ball-room of the story **"Hop-Frog"** is circular. The Devil's apartment in **"The Duc de l'Omelette"** has its corners "rounded into niches," and we find rounded corners also in Poe's essay "The Philosophy of Furniture". In **"Ligeia,"** the bridal chamber is a pentagonal turret-room; however, the angles are concealed by sarcophagi, so that the effect is circular. The corners of Roderick Usher's chamber are likewise concealed, being lost in deep shadow. Other dream-rooms are either irregular or indeterminate in form. For example, there are the seven rooms of Prince Prospero's imperial suite in **"The Masque of the Red Death."** As Poe observes, "in many palaces . . . such suites form a long and straight vista"; but in Prince Prospero's palace, as he describes it, "the apartments were so irregularly disposed that the vision embraced but little more than one at a time. There was a sharp turn at every twenty or thirty yards, and at each turn a novel effect." The turret-room of **"The Oval Portrait"** is not defined as to shape; we are told, however, that it is architecturally "bizarre," and complicated by a quantity of unexpected nooks and niches. Similarly, the visionary's apartment in **"The Assignation"** is described only as dazzling, astounding and original in its architecture; we are not told in what way its dimensions are peculiar, but it seems safe to assume that it would be a difficult room to measure for wall-to-wall carpeting. The room of **"The Assignation,"** by the way—like that of **"Ligeia"**—has its walls enshrouded in rich figured draperies which are continually agitated by some mysterious agency. The fluid shifting of the figures suggests, of course, the behavior of hypnagogic images; but the agitation of the draperies would also produce a perpetual ambiguity of architectural form, and the effect would resemble that which Pevsner ascribes to the interior of San Vitale in Ravenna: "a sensation of uncertainty [and] of a dreamlike floating."

Poe, as you see, is at great pains to avoid depicting the usual squarish sort of room in which we spend much of our waking lives. His chambers of dream either approximate the circle—an infinite form which is, as Poe somewhere observes, "the emblem of Eternity"—or they so lack any apprehensible regularity of shape as to suggest the changeableness and spatial freedom of the dreaming mind. The exceptions to this rule are few and entirely explainable. I will grant, for instance, that the iron-walled torture-chamber of **"The Pit and the Pendulum"** portrays the very reverse of spatial freedom, and that it is painfully angular in character, the angles growing more acute as the torture intensifies. But there is very good allegorical reason for these things. The rooms of **"Ligeia"** or **"The Assignation"** symbolize a triumphantly imaginative state of mind in which the dreamer is all but free of the so-called "real" world. In **"The Pit and the Pendulum,"** the dream is of quite another kind; it is a nightmare state, in which the dreamer is imaginatively impotent, and can find no refuge from reality, even in dream. Though he lies on the brink of the pit, on the very verge of the plunge into unconsciousness, he is still unable to disengage himself from the physical and temporal world. The physical oppresses him in the shape of lurid graveyard visions; the temporal oppresses him in the form of an enormous and deadly pendulum. It is altogether appropriate, then, that this particular chamber should be constricting and cruelly angular.

But let us return to Poe's typical room, and look now at its furnishings. They are generally weird, magnificent, and suggestive of great wealth. The narrator of **"The Assignation,"** entering the hero's apartment, feels "blind and dizzy with luxuriousness," and looking about him he confesses, "I could not bring myself to believe that the wealth of any subject in Europe could have supplied the princely magnificence which burned and blazed around." Poe's visionaries are, as a general thing, extremely rich; the hero of **"Ligeia"** confides that, as for wealth, he possesses "far more, very far more, than ordinarily falls to the lot of mortals"; and Ellison, in **"The Domain of Arnheim,"** is the fortunate inheritor of 450 million dollars. Legrand, in **"The Gold Bug,"** with his treasure of 450 thousand, is only a poor relation of Mr. Ellison; still, by ordinary standards, he seems sublimely solvent.

Now, we must be careful to take all these riches in an allegorical sense. As we contemplate the splendor of any of Poe's rooms, we must remember that the room is a state of mind, and that everything in it is therefore a thought, a mental image. The allegorical meaning of the costliness of Poe's decor is simply this: that his heroes are richly imaginative. And since imagination is a gift rather than an acquisition, it is appropriate that riches in Poe should be inherited or found, but never earned.

Another thing we notice about Poe's furnishings is that they are eclectic in the extreme. Their richness is not the richness of Tiffany's and Sloan's, but of all periods and all cultures. Here is a partial inventory of the fantastic bridal-chamber in **"Ligeia"**: Egyptian carvings and sacrophagi; Venetian glass; fretwork of a semi-Gothic, semi-Druidical character; a Saracenic chandelier; Oriental ottomans and candelabra; an Indian couch; and figured draperies with Norman motifs. The same defiance of what interior decorators once called "keeping" is found in the apartment of the visionary hero of **"The Assignation"**, and one of that hero's speeches hints at the allegorical meaning of his jumbled decor:

To dream [says the hero of **"The Assignation"**]—to dream has been the business of my life. I have therefore framed for myself, as you see, a bower of dreams. In the heart of Venice could I have erected a better? You behold around you, it is true, a medley of architectural embellishments. The chastity of Ionia is offended by antediluvian devices, and the sphynxes of Egypt are outstretched upon carpets of gold. Yet the effect is incongruous to the timid alone. Proprieties of place, and especially of time, are the bugbears which terrify mankind from the contemplation of the magnificent.

That last sentence, with its scornful reference to "proprieties of place, and . . . time," should put us in mind of the first stanza of Poe's poem "Dream-Land":

> By a route obscure and lonely,
> Haunted by ill angels only,
> Where an Eidolon, named NIGHT,
> On a black throne reigns upright,
> I have reached these lands but newly
> From an ultimate dim Thule—
> From a wild weird clime that lieth, sublime,
> Out of SPACE—out of TIME.

In dream-land, we are "out of SPACE—out of TIME," and the same is true of such apartments or "bowers of dreams" as the hero of **"The Assignation"** inhabits. His eclectic furnishings, with their wild juxtapositions of Venetian and Indian, Egyptian and Norman, are symbolic of the visionary soul's transcendence of spatial and temporal limitations. When one of Poe's dream-rooms is not furnished in the fashion I have been describing, the idea of spatial and temporal freedom is often conveyed in some other manner: Roderick Usher's library, for instance, with its rare and precious volumes belonging to all times and tongues, is another concrete symbol of the timelessness and placelessness of the dreaming mind.

We have spoken of the winding approaches to Poe's dream-chambers, of their curvilinear or indeterminate shape, and of the rich eclecticism of their furnishings. Let us now glance over such matters as lighting, sound-proofing, and ventilation. As regards lighting, the rooms of Poe's tales are never exposed to the naked rays of the sun, because the sun belongs to the waking world and waking consciousness. The narrator of **"The Murders in the Rue Morgue"** tells how he and his friend Dupin conducted their lives in such a way as to avoid all exposure to sunlight. "At the first dawn of the morning," he writes, "we closed all the massy shutters of our old building; lighting a couple of tapers which, strongly perfumed, threw out only the ghastliest and feeblest of rays. By the aid of these we then busied our souls in dreams. . . ."

In some of Poe's rooms, there simply are no windows. In other cases, the windows are blocked up or shuttered. When the windows are not blocked or shuttered, their panes are tinted with a crimson or leaden hue, so as to transform the light of day into a lurid or ghastly glow. This kind of lighting, in which the sun's rays are admitted but transformed, belongs to the portrayal of those half-states of mind in which dream and reality are blended. Filtered through tinted panes, the sunlight enters certain of Poe's rooms as it might enter the half-closed eyes of a day-dreamer, or the dream-dimmed eyes of someone awakening from sleep. But when Poe wishes to represent that deeper phase of dreaming in which visionary consciousness has all but annihilated any sense of the external world, the lighting is always artificial and the time is always night.

Flickering candles, wavering torches, and censers full of writhing varicolored flames furnish much of the illumination of Poe's rooms, and one can see the appropriateness of such lighting to the vague and shifting perceptions of the hypnagogic state. But undoubtedly the most important lighting-fixture in Poe's rooms—and one which appears in a good half of them—is the chandelier. It hangs from the lofty ceiling by a long chain, generally of gold, and it consists sometimes of a censer, sometimes of a lamp, sometimes of candles, sometimes of a glowing jewel (a ruby or a diamond), and once, in the macabre tale **"King Pest,"** of a skull containing ignited charcoal. What we must understand about this chandelier, as Poe explains in his poem "Al Aaraaf," is that its chain does not stop at the ceiling: it goes right on through the ceiling, through the roof, and up to heaven. What comes down the chain from heaven is the divine power of imagination, and it is imagination's purifying fire which flashes or flickers from the chandelier. That is why the immaterial and angelic Ligeia makes her reappearance directly beneath the chandelier; and that is why Hop-Frog makes his departure for dreamland by climbing the chandelier-chain and vanishing through the sky-light.

The dreaming soul, then, has its own light—a light more spiritual, more divine, than that of the sun. And Poe's chamber of dream is autonomous in every other respect. No breath of air enters it from the outside world: either its atmosphere is dead, or its draperies are stirred by magical and intramural air-currents. No earthly sound invades the chamber: either it is deadly still, or it echoes with a sourceless and unearthly music. Nor does any odor of flower or field intrude: instead, as Poe tells in **"The Assignation,"** the sense of smell is "oppressed by mingled and conflicting perfumes, reeking up from strange convolute censers."

The point of all this is that the dreaming psyche separates itself wholly from the bodily senses—the "rudimental senses," as Poe called them. The bodily senses are dependent on objective stimuli—on the lights and sounds and odors of the physical world. But the sensuous life of dream is self-sufficient and immaterial, and consists in the imagination's Godlike enjoyment of its own creations.

I am reminded, at this point, of a paragraph of Santayana's, in which he describes the human soul as it was conceived by the philosopher Leibniz. Leibniz, says Santayana, assigned

> a mental seat to all sensible objects. The soul, he said, had no windows and, he might have added, no doors; no light could come to it from without; and it could not exert any transitive force or make any difference beyond its own insulated chamber. It was a camera obscura, with a universe painted on its impenetrable walls. The changes which went on in it were like those in a dream, due to the discharge of pent-up energies and fecundities within it. . . .

Leibniz's chamber of the soul is identical with Poe's chamber of dream: but the solipsism which Leibniz saw as the normal human condition was for Poe an ideal state, a blessed state, which we may enjoy as children or as pre-existent souls, but can reclaim in adult life only by a flight from everyday conciousness into hypnagogic trance.

The one thing which remains to be said about Poe's buildings is that cellars or catacombs, whenever they appear, stand for the irrational part of the mind; and that is so conventional an equation in symbolic literature that I think I need not be persuasive or illustrative about it. I had hoped, at this point, to discuss in a leisurely way some of the stories in which Poe makes use of his architectural properties, treating those stories as narrative wholes. But I have spoken too long about other things; and so, if you will allow me a few minutes more, I shall close by commenting briskly on two or three stories only.

The typical Poe story occurs within the mind of a poet; and its characters are not independent personalities, but allegorical figures representing the warring principles of the poet's divided nature. The lady Ligeia, for example, stands for that heavenly beauty which the poet's soul desires; while Rowena stands for that earthly, physical beauty which tempts the poet's passions. The action of the story is the dreaming soul's gradual emancipation from earthly attachments—which is allegorically expressed in the slow dissolution of Rowena. The result of this process is the soul's final, momentary vision of the heavenly Ligeia. Poe's typical story presents some such struggle between the visionary and the mundane; and the duration of Poe's typical story is the duration of a dream.

There are two tales in which Poe makes an especially clear and simple use of his architectural symbolism. The first is an unfamiliar tale called **"The System of Dr. Tarr and Prof. Fether,"** and the edifice of that tale is a remote and dilapidated madhouse in southern France. What happens, in brief, is that the inmates of the madhouse escape from their cells in the basement of the building, overpower their keepers, and lock them up in their own cells. Having done this, the lunatics take possession of the upper reaches of the house. They shutter all the windows, put on odd costumes, and proceed to hold an uproarious and discordant feast, during which there is much eating and drinking of a disgusting kind, and a degraded version of Ligeia or Helen does a strip-tease. At the height of these festivities, the keepers escape from their cells, break in through the barred and shuttered windows of the dining-room, and restore order.

Well: the madhouse, like all of Poe's houses, is a mind. The keepers are the rational part of that mind, and the inmates are its irrational part. As you noticed, the irrational is suitably assigned to the cellar. The uprising of the inmates, and the suppression of the keepers, symbolizes the beginning of a dream, and the mad banquet which follows is perhaps Poe's least spiritual portrayal of the dream-state: this dream, far from being an escape from the physical, consists exclusively of the release of animal appetites—as dreams sometimes do. When the keepers break in the windows, and subdue the revellers, they bring with them reason and the light of day, and the wild dream is over.

"The Masque of the Red Death" is a better-known and even more obvious example of architectural allegory. You will recall how Prince Prospero, when his dominions are being ravaged by the plague, withdraws with a thousand of his knights and ladies into a secluded, impregnable and windowless abbey, where after a time he entertains his friends with a costume ball. The weird decor of the seven ballrooms expresses the Prince's own taste, and in strange costumes of the Prince's own design the company dances far into the night, looking, as Poe says, like "a multitude of dreams." The festivities are interrupted only by the hourly striking of a gigantic ebony clock which stands in the westernmost room; and the striking of this clock has invariably a sobering effect on the revellers. Upon the last stroke of twelve, as you will remember, there appears amid the throng a figure attired in the blood-dabbled grave-clothes of a plague-victim. The dancers shrink from him in terror. But the Prince, infuriated at what he takes to be an insolent practical joke, draws his dagger and pursues the figure through all of the seven rooms. In the last and westernmost room, the figure suddenly turns and confronts Prince Prospero, who gives a cry of despair and falls upon his own dagger. The Prince's friends rush forward to seize the intruder, who stands now within the shadow of the ebony clock; but they find nothing there. And then, one after the other, the thousand revellers fall dead of the Red Death, and the lights flicker out, and Prince Prospero's ball is at an end.

In spite of its cast of one thousand and two, **"The Masque of the Red Death"** has only one character. Prince Prospero is one-half of that character, the visionary half;

the nameless figure in grave-clothes is the other, as we shall see in a moment.

More than once, in his dialogues or critical writings, Poe describes the earth-bound, time-bound rationalism of his age as a disease. And that is what the Red Death signifies. Prince Prospero's flight from the Red Death is the poetic imagination's flight from temporal and worldly consciousness into dream. The thousand dancers of Prince Prospero's costume ball are just what Poe says they are— "dreams" or "phantasms," veiled and vivid creatures of Prince Prospero's rapt imagination. Whenever there is a feast, or carnival, or costume ball in Poe, we may be sure that a dream is in progress.

But what is the gigantic ebony clock? For the answer to that, one need only consult a dictionary of slang: we call the human heart a ticker, meaning that it is the clock of the body; and that is what Poe means here. In sleep, our minds may roam beyond the temporal world, but our hearts tick on, binding us to time and morality. Whenever the ebony clock strikes, the dancers of Prince Prospero's dream grow momentarily pale and still, in half-awareness that they and their revel must have an end; it is as if a sleeper should half-awaken, and know that he has been dreaming, and then sink back into dreams again.

The figure in blood-dabbled grave-clothes, who stalks through the terrified company and vanishes in the shadow of the clock, is waking, temporal consciousness, and his coming means the death of dreams. He breaks up Prince Prospero's ball as the keepers in **"Dr. Tarr and Prof. Fether"** break up the revels of the lunatics. The final confrontation between Prince Prospero and the shrouded figure is like the terrible final meeting between William Wilson and his double. Recognizing his adversary as his own worldly and mortal self, Prince Prospero gives a cry of despair which is also Poe's cry of despair: despair at the realization that only by self-destruction could the poet fully free his soul from the trammels of this world.

Poe's aesthetic, Poe's theory of the nature of art, seems to me insane. To say that art should repudiate everything human and earthly, and find its subject-matter at the flickering end of dreams, is hopelessly to narrow the scope and function of art. Poe's aesthetic points toward such impoverishments as *poésie pure* and the abstract expressionist movement in painting. And yet, despite his aesthetic, Poe is a great artist, and I would rest my case for him on his prose allegories of psychic conflict. In them, Poe broke wholly new ground, and they remain the best things of their kind in our literature. Poe's mind may have been a strange one; yet all minds are alike in their general structure; therefore we can understand him, and I think that he will have something to say to us as long as there is civil war in the palaces of men's minds.

Lyle H. Kendall, Jr. (essay date 1963)

SOURCE: "The Vampire Motif in 'The Fall of the House

of Usher'," in *College English,* Vol. 24, No. 4, March, 1963, pp. 450-53.

[*Kendall is an American educator and critic. In the following essay, he views Madeline Usher as a vampire.*]

The often expressed conventional interpretation of [**"The Fall of the House of Usher"**] is summarized and expatiated upon in Arthur Robinson's "Order and Sentience in 'The Fall of the House of Usher.'" My own view of the story, although admittedly whimsical, is that in concentrating upon symbolism, upon psychological aberration, upon its connection with *Eureka* (first published some years after the story) and with certain aspects of nineteenth-century culture, critics of **"The Fall of the House of Usher"** have almost universally failed to recognize that it is a Gothic tale, like **"Ligeia,"** and that a completely satisfactory and internally directed interpretation depends on vampirism, the hereditary Usher curse. Madeline is a vampire—a succubus—as the family physician well knows and as her physical appearance and effect upon the narrator sufficiently demonstrate. The terrified and ineffectual Roderick, ostensibly suffering from pernicious anemia, is her final victim.

It is not my purpose here to trace sources and analogues, for example, the body of a murdered person hidden in a makeshift coffin in the haunted wing of a castle (Clara Reeve, *The Old English Baron,* 1777), or the climactic and cataclysmic description of eerie, horrible sounds (the final chapter of Charles Maturin's *Melmoth the Wanderer,* 1820). Poe was sufficiently familiar with Gothic materials and techniques (effectively summarized in chapter seven of James R. Foster's *History of the Pre-Romantic Novel in England,* 1949), and both male and female vampires abounded in literature by the time he published his contribution to the genre in 1839. The bibliography of poetry, fiction, and drama appended to Montague Summers' *The Vampire* (1929) lists at least twenty-five separate works that Poe could have read, or known about, by the time he came to invent Roderick and Madeline. Among these are Southey's *Thalaba the Destroyer* (1801), Byron's *The Giaour* (1813), Polidori's *The Vampyre: A Tale by Lord Byron* (1819), Scribe's *Le Vampire* (1820), Keats's *Lamia* (1820), Hugo's *Han d'Islande* (1823), Merimee's *La Guzla* (1827), Liddell's *The Vampire Bride* (1833), Gautier's *La Morte Amoreuse* (1836), and a host of German works— mostly bearing the title *Der Vampyr,* or something close to it—published in the 1820's. And although it was not published until 1847, I cannot forbear mentioning Thomas Prest's enormously popular *Varney the Vampire.*

Roderick is the central figure of the narrative, Poe seeming at first glance to devote less than passing attention to Madeline as a character. Her personality seems unrealized, for she appears only three times: toward the middle of the story she passes "through a remote portion of the apartment"; some days after her supposed death she is seen in her coffin, with "the mockery of a faint blush upon the bosom and the face, and that suspiciously lingering smile upon the lip which is so terrible in death"; in the final paragraph but one she reappears to die again, falling "heavily inward upon the person of her brother." These brief appearances are nevertheless fraught with darkly suggestive significance, enough to inspire D. H. Lawrence's impressionistic diagnosis, although he takes a wrong turn: "The exquisitely sensitive Roger, vibrating without resistance with his sister Madeline, more and more exquisitely, and gradually devouring her, sucking her life like a vampire in his anguish of extreme love. And she was asking to be sucked."

Roderick, neither consumed by love nor acquiescent, faces a classic dilemma. He must put an end to Madeline—the lore dictates that he must drive a stake through her body in the grave—or suffer the eventuality of wasting away, dying, and becoming a vampire himself. As an intellectual he regards either course with growing horror and at length summons an old school friend, the narrator, whom Usher tentatively plans to confide in. From the outset the evidences of vampirism are calculated to overwhelm the narrator. Even before entering the house he feels the presence of supernatural evil. Reining in his horse to contemplate the "black and lurid tarn," he recalls Roderick's "wildly importunate" letter, speaking of *bodily* as well as mental disorder. He remembers that the Usher family has "been noted, time out of mind, for a peculiar sensibility of temperament, displaying itself, through long ages, in many works of exalted art, and manifested, of late, in repeated deeds of munificent yet unobtrusive charity" (a typically ironical Poe commentary upon charity as expiation). Before he rides over the causeway to the house, the visitor reflects further upon "the very remarkable fact, that the stem of the Usher race . . . had put forth, at no period, any enduring branch; in other words, that the entire family lay in the direct line of descent, and had always, with very trifling and very temporary variations [accounting for the twins], so lain."

Once within, the narrator wonders "to find how unfamiliar were the fancies which ordinary images were stirring up." On the staircase he meets the family physician, whose countenance wears a "mingled expression of low cunning [denoting knowledge of the Usher curse] and perplexity." He finds Roderick "terribly altered, in so brief a period," (an inconsistency: earlier the narrator says, "many years had elapsed since our last meeting") with lips "thin and very pallid," a skin of "ghastly pallor," oddly contrasting with the "miraculous lustre of the eye"; his manner is characterized by "incoherence—an inconsistency" and nervous agitation. He has, in fact, all the symptoms of pernicious anemia—extreme pallor, weakness, nervous and muscular affliction, alternating periods of activity and torpor—but it is an anemia, as Usher now makes perfectly clear, beyond the reach of mere medical treatment. He explains "what he conceived to be the nature of his malady . . . a constitutional and a family evil and one for which he despaired to find a remedy." He confesses that he is a "bounden slave" to an "anomalous species" of terror. Roderick discloses, further, that he is enchained by superstition in regard to the Usher house, and that "much of the peculiar gloom which thus afflicted him could be traced to a more natural and far more palpable origin—to the severe and long-continued illness—indeed to the evidently approaching dissolution—of a tenderly beloved sister." And the invalid reveals immediately

that *tenderly beloved* is ironically intended by speaking with a "bitterness which I can never forget" of Madeline's impending death.

When Madeline herself now appears, at some little distance, the guest regards her with "an utter astonishment not unmingled with dread; . . . A sensation of stupor oppressed me [a characteristic reaction to the succubus] as my eyes followed her retreating steps." Roderick himself is quite evidently terror-sticken. Reluctant to grasp the import of the plain evidence with which he has so far been presented—not to mention the supernatural assault upon his own psyche—the narrator learns that Madeline's illness has been diagnosed as "of a partially cataleptical character," which is to say, to even the most casual student of necromancy, that she has the common ability of witches to enter at will upon a trance-like, death-like state of suspended animation. Her "settled apathy" and "gradual wasting away of the person" are to be accounted for by the corresponding condition in her victim.

Following Madeline's presumed death the friends occupy themselves with poring over old books that have a curiously significant connection with Usher's dilemma. Among them are the "Chiromancy" of Robert Flud, Jean D'Indagine, and De la Chambre (dealing with palmistry). Even more significantly, "One favorite volume was a small octavo edition of the 'Directorium Inquisitorium,' by the Dominican Eymeric de Gironne" (on exorcising witches and ferreting out other sorts of heretics). But Usher's "chief delight, however, was found in the perusal of an exceedingly rare and curious book in quarto Gothic—the manual of a forgotten church—the *Vigiliae Mortuorum secundum Chorum Ecclesiae Maguntinae.*" The "wild ritual of this work"—the *Watches of the Dead according to the Choir of the Church of Mainz*—is, of course, the "Black Mass."

These books fail to provide a text for Roderick, who decides to imprison Madeline, as he says, by "preserving her corpse for a fortnight (previously to its final interment,) in one of the numerous vaults within the walls of the building." Here the plodding narrator at last scents the truth: "The brother had been led to his resolution . . . by consideration of the *unusual character of the malady of the deceased, of certain obtrusive and eager inquiries on the part of her medical men, and of the remote and exposed situation of the burial-ground of the family.* I will not deny that when I called to mind the sinister countenance of the person whom I met upon the staircase on the day of my arrival at the house, I had no desire to oppose what I regarded as at best but a harmless, and by no means an unnatural precaution" (italics mine).

Alone the two friends encoffin the body and bear it to the vault. One last look at the *mocking* features of Madeline, and then the lid to the coffin is screwed down, the massive iron door secured. "Some days of bitter grief" ensue, but soon, sensing danger from a wonted quarter, Roderick Usher spends his restless hours consumed by the old horror, which he verges on confiding to the narrator: "There were times, indeed, when I thought his unceasingly agitated mind was laboring with some oppressive secret, to divulge

Aubrey Beardsley's drawing of Roderick Usher, from a limited edition published in 1894-95.

which he struggled for the necessary courage." As he confesses later—"I *now* tell you that I heard her first feeble movement in the hollow coffin" (*hollow* in the sense that its vampiric occupant is scarcely physical in nature)—Usher is perfectly aware of Madeline's impending escape. And on the final night the guest himself suffers an experience which suggests that her evil spirit is already abroad. Endeavoring to sleep, he cannot "reason off the nervousness which had dominion over me." The room, he feels, is exerting a bewildering influence: "An irrepressible tremor gradually pervaded my frame; and, at length, there sat upon my very heart an *incubus* of utterly causeless alarm. *Shaking this off with a gasp and a struggle,* I uplifted myself upon the pillows" (italics mine), and now he hears "low and indefinite sounds." Shortly he is joined by Usher, radiating "mad hilarity" and restrained hysteria, who rushes to a casement window and throws it "freely open to the storm." It is not difficult to imagine that all the old fiendish Ushers in the distant cemetery are, disembodied, somehow present. A whirlwind (traditionally signalizing a spiritual presence) "had apparently collected its force in our vicinity; for there were frequent and violent alterations in the direction of the wind; and the exceeding density of the clouds . . . did not prevent our perceiving the life-like velocity with which they flew careering from all points against each other."

The last of the Ushers is persuaded to leave the window, which is closed against electrical phenomena of "ghastly origin," and the guest begins to read aloud from the "Mad Trist," whose descriptions of sound are horribly reproduced by Madeline as she leaves her prison and approaches the listeners. Roderick's final words are "a low, hurried, and gibbering murmur" punctuated by extraordinarily meaningful phrases: "'I *dared* not speak! . . . Oh! whither shall I fly? . . . Do I not distinguish that heavy and horrible beating of her heart?'" (Again, the slow and heavy pulse is traditionally characteristic of preternatural creatures.) Poe's accentuation of the miraculous aspects of the tale continues to the end. The sister reels upon the threshold, "then, with a low moaning cry, fell heavily inward upon the person of her brother, and in her violent and now final death-agonies, bore him to the floor a corpse, and a victim to the terrors he had anticipated." She is a vampire to the finish, and there is no escaping the shock of absolute recognition in "From that chamber, and from that mansion, I fled aghast."

In this view **"The Fall of the House of Usher"**—typical of Poe in its exploration of abysmal degradation—creates an experience that possesses, within itself, credibility and unity of technique once the basic situation is granted. And from the artist's treatment of the theme, the active existence of malignant evil in our world, emerges his partly optimistic and partly ironic commentary: Evil in the long run feeds incestuously upon itself, and it is self-defeating, self-consuming, self-annihilating; the short run is another matter.

Joel Porte (essay date 1969)

SOURCE: "The Haunted Palace of Art," in *The Romance*

in America: Studies in Cooper, Poe, Hawthorne, Melville, and James, Wesleyan University Press, 1969, pp. 60-9.

[*Porte is an American educator and critic. In the following essay, he observes a conflict between Romantic and Realist attitudes in "The Fall of the House of Usher."*]

Beginning with Poe and continuing as a strong current in the works of Hawthorne, Melville, and James, the desire to test and evaluate the opposing claims of novelistic "good sense" and romance "wildness" finds expression in the very fabric of American fiction. "Art" as an implied or explicit theme and the frequent use of "artist" figures become characteristic of the American romance—indeed, are among the criteria that define it—as our authors argue out for themselves the question of daylight versus night.

It might seem odd to mention **"The Fall of the House of Usher"** in connection with such a formulation, but this familiar tale is an especially interesting illustration of the foregoing thesis. The reader first must be asked to shift his attention slightly from the gothic horrors depicted in the story to the subtle opposition set up between the character of Roderick Usher and that of the narrator. Usher is a portrait, somewhat caricatured, of the artistic temperament in its most decadent—that is, romantic—state. He has a "remarkable" face, with large and liquid eyes, lips "of a surpassingly beautiful curve," and a fine nose "of a delicate Hebrew model." Phrenologically considered, his "finely moulded" chin shows "a want of moral energy" (clearly suggestive of his capacity to indulge in forbidden practices), and the "inordinate expansion above the regions of the temple" bespeaks great intellectual powers. He is morbidly sensitive:

> The most insipid food was alone endurable; he could wear only garments of certain texture; the odors of all flowers were oppressive; his eyes were tortured by even a faint light; and there were but peculiar sounds, and these from stringed instruments, which did not inspire him with horror.

His emotional life is characterized by a preponderance of the darkest of all human states, absolute *Angst*. "I dread the events of the future," he explains lucidly, "not in themselves, but in their results." This "intolerable agitation of soul" makes every incident and experience pregnant with unnameable terror for him. "I feel that the period will sooner or later arrive," he confesses, "when I must abandon life and reason together, in some struggle with the grim phantasm, FEAR."

Usher is thus admirably suited by nature to exploring and giving expression to the direst aspects of human life, and his beliefs and training are what we should expect. He holds an opinion, we are told, concerning the "sentience of all vegetable things": nature for him is not only a force, animated and alive, but a source and reflection of hidden powers at work in the world. And the titles of his favorite books—of which Poe supplies a carefully constructed (and partially invented) list—read like a card catalog of subjects and materials for the most lurid of romancers, apt illustrations of the notion that there are more things in heaven and earth than are dreamt of by the most sagacious of novelists. Usher reads "the Heaven and Hell of Swedenborg; the Subterranean Voyage of Nicholas Klimm of Holberg"; several volumes of "Chiromancy"; the "Journey into the Blue Distance of Tieck; and the City of the Sun of Campanella," as well as a volume on the Inquisition by a Dominican friar. Most suggestive of all, perhaps, "there were passages in Pomponius Mela, about the old African Satyrs and Œgipans, over which Usher would sit dreaming for hours," while "his chief delight" was in perusing the "rare and curious . . . *Vigiliae Mortuorum secundum Chorum Ecclesiae Maguntinae.*" Usher's favorite fantasy material—undoubtedly connected, any psychoanalytically inclined reader would say, with his excruciatingly intense anxieties—is a combination of sexuality and death.

As an artist—he is at once poet, painter, and musician—Usher adheres strictly to the school of the fantastic and the extreme. His guitar impromptus are either perverse variations on familiar tunes or "wild improvisations." And his paintings and poems, at least judged by the two detailed examples that Poe supplies, are the very type of the romancer's art: lurid symbolism verging on hideous allegory, or ominous allegory heightened by weird symbolism. Roderick's creations hint at the terrible secret about the House of Usher, presenting an intolerably dark view of human nature.

Into this house of horror enters Poe's narrator, the sort of man who in happier days and more cheerful circumstances might have written the novels of Anthony Trollope. Although by no means unemotional or unfeeling, he is an eminently, even doggedly, reasonable person with a great need to make sense of his experiences, or at least to believe that everything ultimately is capable of some rational explanation. Strange occurrences fascinate him—he is the kind of man who is frequently tempted to peer over the brink of an oddity—but he is finally disturbed enough by the inexplicable to want only to avoid it. His speech is formal, complicated, and intricately logical, as if to express a hope that the coherences of grammar might make up for the incoherencies of life. He is intelligent, but his intelligence is more often used to protect himself from knowledge than to explore the unknown.

Numerous concrete instances of all these characteristics are provided by Poe throughout the tale. When the narrator first sees the House of Usher, its melancholy aspect depresses and unnerves him, and that he should be so affected strikes him as "a mystery all insoluble." He is assailed by "shadowy fancies," and to escape them resorts to what we learn is his usual expedient, an attempt at rational explanation: "I was forced to fall back upon the unsatisfactory conclusion, that while, beyond doubt, there *are* combinations of very simple natural objects which have the power of thus affecting us, still the analysis of this power lies among considerations beyond our depth." The explanation, admittedly "unsatisfactory," offers the appearance rather than the substance of intellectual acuteness, but it at least temporarily allays the narrator's fears and protects him from a darker conclusion—that the ca-

pacity for *Angst,* seemingly groundless and unreasoning fear, is part of everyone's human makeup. Later, when the narrator finds Usher in just such a state, he can only term it "anomalous"—that is, abnormal and unwarranted. And toward the end of the tale, when he himself is finally infected with the "incubus of utterly causeless alarm," his only resource is to attempt to shake it off "with a gasp and a struggle," since the sentiment is "unaccountable yet unendurable." Our narrator has no power against the "unaccountable," and his "yet" is beautifully characteristic; that a horror without an apparent cause should be unendurable (indeed, worse than an explainable horror) makes no sense to him. He has not learned to accept the awful truth—Usher's truth—that the world's worst horrors are unendurable *because* they are unaccountable.

The narrator perpetually shies away from the suggestion of inexplicability and ultimate mystery in human affairs. Disturbed by his first vision of the house, he attempts to calm himself by resorting to the "somewhat childish experiment" of observing, instead of the house itself, its reduplicated image in the tarn. The experiment fails, his nervousness is only increased, and he feels compelled to explain: "There can be no doubt that the consciousness of the rapid increase of my superstition—for why should I not so term it?—served mainly to accelerate the increase itself. Such, as I have long known, is the paradoxical law of all sentiments having terror as a basis." He is content to rest in a general "law," no matter how paradoxical, and to account himself a victim of "superstition," rather than confront a profound personal puzzle. But his solicitude extends beyond himself to the reader. His explanations are clearly meant to reassure us, and he avoids exploring the ambiguous, we may understand, mainly for the sake of our peace of mind. The "equivocal hints" he receives from Usher concerning the latter's mental state which relate to "certain superstitious impressions" about the house are, we are told, "conveyed in terms too shadowy here to be re-stated." Usher's strange theory of vegetable "sentience," especially in regard to the malign influence exercised over him by the very stones of the house, is brushed aside: "Such opinions need no comment, and I will make none." And whatever the narrator may have learned from Usher's "few words" about the "sympathies" existing between himself and his sister, he is not eager to go beyond reporting that they were "of a scarcely intelligible nature." Poe's main purpose in all of these instances is, of course, to heighten the sense of implied horror by being suggestive rather than explicit. And the narrator serves this purpose splendidly, in spite of himself, since his attempt to allay our fears by overlooking the "anomalous" only increases the air of the sinister. As with his first vaguely disquieting impression of the house, the narrator prefers consistently to shake off the inexplicable intimations that he believes "*must* have been a dream" and turn his attention to the "real aspect" of things, hopefully to dispel the atmosphere of unreality.

"The naked Senses," Poe wrote in **Marginalia,** as if he were thinking of his narrator, "sometimes see too little—but then *always* they see too much." The narrator of **"The Fall of the House of Usher"** has a "noticing" eye which, clearly in defiance of his conscious intention to enlighten and demystify, weaves a pattern of surrealistic detail that contradicts any common-sense view of reality. What he sees, without apparently being fully aware of it, is a barely definable similarity between the house and its master. The "minute fungi" which cover the exterior of the house (and which play a part in Usher's theory of sentience) overspread the building, "hanging in a fine tangled web-work from the eaves," while Roderick's hair, "of a more than web-like softness and tenuity," had been "suffered to grow all unheeded" and floated wildly about his face. The house gives the impression of a "wild inconsistency between its still perfect adaptation of parts and the crumbling condition of the individual stones"; likewise, in Roderick's behavior, the narrator is "at once struck with an incoherence—an inconsistency." The atmosphere reeking from the mansion is that of a "pestilent and mystic vapor, dull, sluggish, faintly discernible, and leaden-hued"; Roderick's voice is "leaden," and from his mind "darkness, as if an inherent positive quality, poured forth upon all objects of the moral and physical universe in one unceasing radiation of gloom." ("A sense of insufferable gloom pervaded my spirit," reports the narrator as he first approaches the house.) And, worst of all, "perhaps the eye of a scrutinizing observer might have discovered a barely perceptible fissure, which, extending from the roof of the building in front, made its way down the wall in a zigzag direction, until it became lost in the sullen waters of the tarn." That "scrutinizing observer" is of course our narrator, sharp enough to perceive, and willing to report, this obscure sign of inherent instability in the house, but not eager to divine for himself, or convey to us, that "oppressive secret" which is the parallel cause and sign of instability in the decaying Roderick. "The eye," says the narrator entering Usher's room, "struggled in vain to reach the remoter angles of the chamber." Some things are too dark even for his scrutinizing eye.

The nightmarish view of reality suggested by the resemblance of house and master defies the narrator's explanations and discourages him from attempting to draw any conclusions, but we are not ultimately left to rest contentedly in his limited point of view. Instead, we are offered Roderick Usher's own artistic productions as oblique elucidations of the mysteries everywhere adumbrated in the tale. Usher's poem, "The Haunted Palace," seems to be a flat allegory, with an "under or mystic current" of meaning, as the narrator suggests, insinuating "the tottering of his [Usher's] lofty reason upon her throne." The verses do equate a reasonable head that has gone bad with a "Radiant palace . . . In the monarch Thought's dominion" which has been assailed and captured by "evil things, in robes of sorrow." (The palace once had "banners yellow" for fair hair, "two luminous windows" for eyes, a "pearl and ruby" door for teeth and lips, and a king full of "wit and wisdom" for sanity.) But it is worth noting that the loss of reason is signalled by a shift from "Spirits moving musically / To a lute's well-tuned law" to "Vast forms that move fantastically / To a discordant melody"—the shift from "lawful" music to the "wild fantasias" of Usher's improvisation. The poem thus represents Usher's fate as a romantic artist: he may begin in joy and gladness, but he inevitably moves to despondency and madness as his vision darkens and he becomes aware of the "evil things" in himself and others—truths that cannot be overlooked by the artist who descends into the human depths. The narrator's visit to the House of Usher is not only a visit to the soul of Roderick Usher but a glimpse into the "Haunted Palace" of the romancer's art itself.

As an example of the kind of experience necessarily encountered in the realm of romance, we are offered one of the "phantasmagoric conceptions" painted by Roderick Usher:

> A small picture presented the interior of an immensely long and rectangular vault or tunnel, with low walls, smooth, white, and without interruption or device. Certain accessory points of the design served well to convey the idea that this excavation lay at an exceeding depth below the surface of the earth. No outlet was observed in any portion of its vast extent, and no torch or other artificial source of light was discernible; yet a flood of intense rays rolled throughout, and bathed the whole in a ghastly and inappropriate splendor.

Looking ahead to Hawthorne's *Marble Faun,* we might wish to name this painting "Subterranean Reminiscences." But by itself it sufficiently suggests that realm of the submerged—the underside of human consciousness—which is the peculiar province of romance. Ordinarily dark and inaccessible, it is now exposed and illuminated by the "ghastly" light of the romancer's imagination.

The narrator of "The Fall of the House of Usher" has a "noticing" eye which, clearly in defiance of his conscious intention to enlighten and demystify, weaves a pattern of surrealistic detail that contradicts any common-sense view of reality.

—Joel Porte

In the tale the picture adumbrates the dungeon-tomb reserved for Roderick's sister, Madeline, and thus suggests that the particular kind of underground experience which lies at the heart of this (and, as it turns out, most other) romance art involves the darkest aspects of sexuality. Roderick Usher's secret subject, with an obvious but unacknowledged borrowing from Byron, concerns what can be called the Manfred Syndrome: the artist-brother's illicit and finally murderous passion for his twin-sister, usually identified—as in Byron's poem—with Astarte, the eastern Venus. (Ultimately, as in Melville's *Pierre,* the underlying suggestion is drawn out that the artist's narcissistic love for his female mirror image symbolizes his infatuation with his own psyche—a destructive involvement with his own unconscious which is at once the romancer's inspiration and his undoing.)

Since Poe's tale is, at its deepest level, a kind of fictional debate which argues for the seriousness of romance as a way of exploring the secret soul of man (Roderick's point of view), it is altogether fitting that the awful truth about the House of Usher should be most fully revealed by a romance within the larger romance: "the 'Mad Trist' of Sir Launcelot Canning." Poe underlines the narrator's common-sensical obtuseness and his imperviousness to the serious implications of the romance form by having him choose to read to Usher, in order to calm him, a tale which exacerbates him to the point of madness and, ultimately, death. The narrator himself at first calls the tale one of Usher's "favorite romances," and then adds, characteristically, that he was joking, "for, in truth, there is little in its uncouth and unimaginative prolixity which could have had interest for the lofty and spiritual ideality of my friend." In fact, the "Mad Trist" is a highly imaginative symbolic representation of the sordid reality of Usher's psychosexual nature. And it is Usher himself who spells out its meaning for the bewildered narrator, as the incidents read out of Canning's tale coincide with the final events of Poe's tale in one final ghastly demonstration of the power and living truth of romance.

The "Mad Trist" relates an episode in which the hero Ethelred comes upon and slays a "scaly and prodigious" dragon, with "fiery tongue" and "pesty breath," which has been polluting the precincts of a golden and silver "palace." While the narrator reads, the details of this last horrible night in the house mingle with those of the "Trist" as the ravished and dying sister Madeline makes her way, with many a clinking and clanging, up to the chamber containing Usher and his friend. The tortured, terrified Roderick himself makes the connections: "Ethelred—ha! ha! . . . the death-cry of the dragon, and the clangor of the shield!—say, rather, the rending of her coffin, and the grating of the iron hinges of her prison, and her struggles within the coppered archway of the vault!" In Roderick's version of the "Mad Trist" (the wonderfully ambiguous title suggesting both insane sorrow and a mad love meeting)—and here we must gather up the repetitive elements of the fantasy woven throughout Poe's tale—the sexually tempting sister is the "dragon" that has infested and corrupted the "palace" of his soul. Roderick's own haunted palace can be restored to its pure use only by the slaying of this evil thing "in robes of sorrow" ("the lofty and enshrouded figure of the lady Madeline" appears at the end with "blood upon her white robes"). For Madeline, of course, the sexual dragon is her lustful and attacking brother.

But the assigning of blame is ultimately of no importance. Since Roderick and Madeline are twins—that is, one person—Ethelred / Roderick's confrontation with the dragon/ sister represents a symbolic confrontation with his own sexuality. It is an awareness of his own secret and forbidden desires that has darkened the imagination of the artist, and the romancer can never return to the "pure" state when he was free of such knowledge. Roderick's determination

to slay the dragon/sister coincides with his own death. Illicit sexuality, for Roderick Usher, is inseparable from life.

For Poe's narrator, however—the rational man of daylight sensibility, whose experience of the self is blissfully free of such dark knowledge—the revelation in the House of Usher is not a truth about human existence but a bad dream that can be shaken. He arrives there on a "dark" and "soundless" day, having traveled into the "shades of evening." His first ghastly impression of the House seems to him the "after-dream" of an opium eater. It "*must* have been a dream," he insists. He sees the lady Madeline for the first time with a "sensation of stupor" and listens to Roderick's wild guitar "as if in a dream." He can scarcely believe the strange world he has entered, and yet he finds it difficult not to be affected by and caught up in it: "I felt creeping upon me, by slow yet certain degrees, the wild influences of his [Usher's] own fantastic yet impressive superstitions."

The danger of being permanently infected by so dark a vision increases with time; long dreams are hardest to forget. And so he must rouse himself with a violent effort to escape the horrors he has viewed, fleeing "aghast" "from that chamber, and from that mansion," and thereby releasing himself cataclysmically from the grip of nightmare: "—my brain reeled as I saw the mighty walls rushing asunder—there was a long tumultuous shouting sound like the voice of a thousand waters—and the deep and dank tarn at my feet closed sullenly and silently over the fragments of the 'HOUSE OF USHER.'" For the narrator, the ghastly world of romance is dissolved as the dark waters of night close over the fragments of his shattered dream. But for the reader, and for Poe, this world continues to live.

G. R. Thompson (essay date 1972)

SOURCE: "The Face in the Pool: Reflections on the Doppelgänger Motif in 'The Fall of the House of Usher'," in *Poe Studies*, Vol. 5, No. 1, June, 1972, pp. 16-21

[*In the following essay, Thompson offers a reading of "The Fall of the House of Usher" that highlights its parallel structures and ironic tone.*]

In *Heart of Darkness* (1898-99), Joseph Conrad's first narrator comments on the conception of the meaning of a narrative held by Marlow, who is himself the narrator of the basic tale of his pursuit of his psychological double, Kurtz, and to whom Conrad's first narrator listens as one sitting in darkness waiting for light. The first narrator comments that Marlow, unlike other tale-spinning sailors, saw the significance of a narrative not as a core meaning of some kind but as a system of structures: "The yarns of seamen have a direct simplicity, the whole meaning of which lies within the shell of a cracked nut. [But to Marlow] the meaning of an episode was not inside like a kernel but outside, enveloping the tale which brought it out only as a glow brings out a haze, in the likeness of one of these misty halos that sometimes are made visible by the spectral illumination of moonshine." So it is with Poe's **"The Fall of the House of Usher"** (1839), a tale that bears a number of similarities in theme, imagery, and structure to *Heart of Darkness*. Poe's tale is a structure of interpenetrating structures that shifts its aspect with a slight shift of perspective by the reader. Given the initial focus of a reader, the primary answer to any question presented by the story varies, though the relationships among the various structures of the story do not.

This can be partially illustrated by reference to the recurrent concerns of critics of the tale; most of the critical commentary returns obsessively to a few central points, compulsively repeating with slightly altered angles of vision the same set of haunting questions. What is the significance of the close resemblance of Roderick Usher and his sister, and are the two the products of and, simultaneously, guilty of incest? Did Roderick intentionally try to murder Madeline, and did Madeline actually return from her tomb, vampirelike, to claim her brother's life? Is the physical House actually "alive" and by some preternatural force of will controlling the destinies of the Ushers? Or is the story not a tale of the supernatural at all, but rather a work of psychological realism? What then is the precise role of the narrator? And can the work be read in Freudian or Jungian terms? If the tale is a psychological or symbolic work, what is the meaning of the interpolated story of "The Mad Trist" of Sir Launcelot Canning? What significance have the titles of the books in Usher's library, and what significance are we to attach to Usher's strange, neurasthenic art works? The very fact that these questions persist year after year suggests that at the dark heart of the story lies an essential ambiguity, carefully insinuated and carefully wrought.

The present essay . . . is no exception to this eternal return to the same questions. But it is misleading to conceive of the meaning of the tale as developing solely upon, say, the supernatural character of the House, or of Madeline Usher, *as opposed* to a Gothic homily on the neurasthenia of the ultimate in narcissistic artist-heroes, or *as opposed* to the incestuous guilt and hereditary curse of the family. The tale is a concatenation of all these, and not an either/or question. Nevertheless, there is, I submit, a basic structure that integrates all the others, a set or system of relationships that remains constant and primary, enveloping the rest with a further meaning without disturbing each as a coherent system within itself. This primary structure is the product of the objective synthesis generated by our perceiving as readers the double aspects of the tale as simultaneously supernaturalistic (symbolic of deep structures in the human mind or not) and yet also "realistic" in a conventional sense. This multiple perception of the simultaneous or parallel levels of the tale derives primarily from our perception of the subjectivity of the narrator. That is, we experience a series of "supernatural" events (which have Freudian and Jungian resonances) through the mind of the narrator whom we recognize as disturbed— so that we simultaneously are subjectively involved in and detached from these experiences.

Poe's method in his Gothic tales, I have argued elsewhere, is in the American tradition of the "ambiguously explained supernatural," in which clues to the basic psychological action of the tale are carefully insinuated into the Gothic atmosphere of supernaturalism. Thus, underlying or enveloping a typical "supernatural" tale by Poe, there is, on one level, a rational explanation of the seemingly supernatural events, on a second level, a psychological explanation, and on a third level, an insinuated burlesque (under or around the whole structure of explanations) of both the content and the mode of the tale. That is, the whole system of interpenetrating levels or structures of the tale leads ultimately to Poe's mockery of the ability of the human mind ever to know anything with certainty, whether about the external reality of the world or about the internal reality of the mind.

Much of the present discussion of **"Usher"** derives from the brilliant analysis of the tale as a psychodrama of the mutual hysteria of the narrator and Roderick Usher by Darrel Abel [in "A Key to the House of Usher," *University of Toronto Quarterly* 18 (1949)]. What I offer as progressive to our understanding of the tale is principally addenda to such evidence in terms of a reconsideration of the principal symbols of the tale within the primary structural context proposed—that is, the structure wherein the subjectivity of the narrator provides the basic system of structures holding in tension all the others. I shall attempt to demonstrate the pervasiveness of this primary structure principally by reference to the pattern of the double and its redoubled manifestations (Roderick and Madeline, Roderick and the House, Roderick and the narrator, Madeline and the narrator, the narrator and the House). This pattern is further redoubled by the imagery of the face or skull, which ultimately inverts back on the self as a symbol of the "reality" seen from the inward perspective of characters caught in a labyrinth of mental surmise.

On its most obvious level, the tale is concerned with the traditional Gothic subjects of death and madness and fear. The matters of madness (especially Roderick's) and fear have been frequently (though not definitively) commented on, but the other pervading subject of death (physical, familial, spiritual, and mental) has not been closely enough linked to the themes of fear and madness. It is curious, for example, that no one has ever seen fit to remark that when the narrator rides up to the House of Usher, he is immediately confronted with a death's-head looming up out of the dead landscape. The image of the skull-like face of the House Poe obviously intended to dominate as the central image of the tale, for he returns to it again and again, placing the most extended descriptions of it at symmetrically located places in the narrative. Eventually, the pervasive image of the psychically split face reflects the internal landscape of the narrator himself (rather than just Usher), so that the primary structure of the tale merges with its central image. Even when the House sinks into the pool at the end, the motifs of the skull and face (Usher's, the House's, that of the mind gone mad in "The Haunted Palace," and the narrator's) represent the internal spiraling of the complete subjectivity of consciousness. That is, the sinking of the House into the reflective pool dramatizes the sinking of that rational part of the mind, which has unsuccessfully attempted to maintain some contact with a stable structure of reality outside the self, into the Nothingness that is without and within.

Usher's weird painting of what might be a tomb for the burial of the body of Madeline, imaging nothing but rays of light rolling throughout a passage without outlet, is also reflective of the death and burial of consciousness and rationality themselves; thus it is a painting of Usher's internal void, which is objectified by the final collapse of the House into the image of itself in the pool. The spiraling further and further inward leads us to the mocking irony of the ultimate theme of Nothingness, which is all the mind can ever truly know, if it can know anything. The Nothingness without (in the landscape) and the Nothingness within (in the minds of Usher and the narrator) are nothing less than mirror images or doubles reflecting the theme of Nothingness in the tale. And the collapse of the universe of Roderick Usher includes the double collapse of his mind along with the narrator's—productive of an overall structure of collapse mirroring the pattern of the universe itself, as expressed in *Eureka*.

That Usher's mind disintegrates as the tale progresses is obvious. Both Usher and the narrator comment variously on the matter. The inciting event, in fact, is Usher's written appeal to the narrator to preserve him from the final collapse of his mind. Moreover, as mentioned, a major concern in the tale is the mechanism of fear itself, which has perversely operated on Roderick Usher before the narrator arrives, and which operates on the narrator through Usher afterwards, so that we apprehend the basic dramatic action of the tale as psychological—the presentation of the progressive hallucination of the two protagonists. In the supernaturally charged atmosphere of the first level of the story, the narrator seems to serve as a corroborating witness to the actual return of Madeline, and to the strange, simultaneous "deaths" of the Ushers and of their House. But Poe meticulously, from the opening paragraph through to the last, details the development of the narrator's initial uneasiness into a frenzy of terror, engendered by and parallel to Usher's terrors. The tale opens with the narrator's account of his lonely autumn journey through a "singularly dreary tract of country" in response to a "wildly importunate" summons from Usher. At nightfall, as the "melancholy" House of Usher comes into view, the narrator feels a sense of "insufferable gloom" pervading his spirit. He pauses to look at the "mere house," trying to account rationally for its total weird effect. But the scene still produces in him "an utter depression of soul, which I can compare to no earthly sensation more properly than to the after-dream of the reveller upon opium . . . an iciness, a sinking, a sickening of the heart—an unredeemed dreariness of thought . . . it was a mystery all insoluble; nor could I grapple with the shadowy fancies that crowded upon me as I pondered." The primary effect of the opening paragraphs, of course, is to suggest something horrible and supernatural about the House of Usher. But, as in Poe's other tales, there is no overstepping of the real; the strange impression of the scene is relegated to the "fancies" of the narrator. Because the narrator tries to

account for the effect rationally, however, we are led, for the time being, to attribute the weirdness of the scene not to his subjective impressions but to the scene itself.

Yet Poe uses this apparent rationality to heighten the irrational. The narrator reflects on the possibility that "there *are* combinations of very simple natural objects" that have the power to affect the mind, but "the analysis of this power lies among considerations" beyond our "depth"; and at this moment, he looks down into "a black and lurid tarn," to see the reflected, remodelled, and inverted images of "the gray sedge, and the ghostly tree stems, and the vacant and eyelike windows." The effect of this vision in the pool is to produce in him a "shudder even more thrilling than before" and to "deepen the first singular impression." He comments to himself that "There can be no doubt that the consciousness of *the rapid increase of my superstition*—for why should I not so term it?—served mainly *to accelerate the increase itself*. Such, I have long known, is the paradoxical law of *all sentiments having terror as a basis*" (my italics). After this objective recognition of an inward self-division that results in yet further subjectivity, he again lifts his eyes "to the house itself, from its image in the pool" and he becomes aware of a "strange fancy" growing in his mind: "I had *so worked upon my imagination as really to believe* that about the whole mansion and domain there hung . . . a pestilent and mystic vapor, dull, sluggish, faintly discernible, and leaden-hued" (my italics). But Poe then reasserts the narrator's rationality: "Shaking off from my spirit what *must* have been a dream, I scanned more narrowly the real aspect of the building." The paragraph that follows is organized, however, so as to bring the "real" description back again to the "impression" the scene makes upon the narrator's "fancy." Although the narrator begins his "analysis" of the House at the (rational) roof, with its fine tangled web-work of fungi, his eye travels down along a zigzag fissure to become again "lost in the sullen waters of the tarn," by now clearly emblematic of the subconscious mind.

The apprehensive, fanciful, superstitious, but "rational" narrator then goes into the House to meet Usher, where, during the course of the next several days, he comes increasingly under the influence of Usher's own wild superstitions. "In the manner of my friend," the narrator says, "I was at once struck with an incoherence—an inconsistency. . . ." He continues: "To an anomalous species of terror I found him a bounden slave. 'I shall perish,' said he, '. . . in this deplorable folly. . . . I have, indeed no abhorrence of danger, except in its absolute effect—in terror. In this unnerved—in this pitiable condition—I feel that the period will sooner or later arrive when I must abandon life and reason together, in some struggle with the grim phantasm, FEAR.'" Usher's statement of his own condition applies also to the narrator, who struggles with the same phantasm, heightened by Usher's own phantasms. It is Usher, for example, who remarks to the suggestible narrator that the House is *alive* and has exerted a malignant influence on his mind. Later the narrator, looking for something to read, finds that the only books in Usher's library are accounts of strange journeys, eerie meetings, and death-watches. Then Usher reads his weird poem about the decay of reason, the single extended metaphor of which suggests the "face" of the House of Usher itself, and extends the pattern of descent from roof to basement, of rationality to irrationality, and the inverse ascent of irrationality welling up to overwhelm the rational. Soon after the reading, Madeline dies, and Usher and the narrator bury her in a crypt in the cellar. She has the "mockery of a faint blush of life" upon her skin and a terrible "lingering smile" upon her lips, phenomena that the "rational" narrator attributes to the peculiar ravages of her cataleptic disorder but which Usher intimates is something less natural. Then, as Usher's behavior becomes even more distracted (a continual "tremulous quaver, as if of extreme terror, habitually characterized his utterance"), the narrator confesses to himself his own increasing apprehensiveness. Slowly, although he tries to see in Usher's behavior "the mere vagaries of madness," the narrator feels growing in himself a vague fear that Usher has some horrible "oppressive secret" to divulge. "Rationally," however, the narrator acknowledges that Usher's "condition terrified . . . it *infected* me. I felt creeping upon me, by slow yet uncertain degrees, the wild influences of his own fantastic yet impressive superstitions."

Symmetrically, the psychological themes of the first part of the tale are exactly repeated in the second, but with the fears of both Usher and the narrator at a higher pitch. Shortly after Madeline's burial, the narrator is unable to sleep, especially since, as with the reflected image of the House in the tarn, he is aware of his increased terror: "an irrepressible tremor gradually pervaded my frame; and, at length, there sat upon my very heart an incubus" of "utterly causeless alarm." "Overpowered by an intense sentiment of horror," the narrator begins pacing nervously; suddenly he is startled by a light footstep outside his door. But it is only Usher. Usher's intensely agitated condition, however, is the more unnerving, especially when he suggests that a supernatural and luminous vapor has surrounded the House in spite of the rising wind without.

What is perhaps the clearest of clues to the theme of doubled and redoubled fear comes next. The narrator, in an attempt to calm Usher, reads from a volume called "The Mad Trist." The title calls attention to the basic situation in which the narrator finds himself. Usher is about to keep a mad trist with Madeline, even as the narrator has kept his mad trist with Usher. The tale, this "Mad Trist," is an absurd parody of a Medieval romance about the delusive meeting of the knight Ethelred with a hermit who disappears and changes his form into that of a fearful dragon. The narrator's reading of "The Mad Trist" to Usher is interrupted by strange sounds of creaking wood, of shrieking, and of grating metal. These sounds, beginning at the bottom of the House and moving upward toward them, eerily (and ludicrously) correspond with the sounds evoked in the chivalric romance. The sounds, of course, are supposed to be the results of the cataleptic Madeline's efforts to free herself from her tomb. Usher, at least, tells the narrator that this is so and that she is, in fact, now standing outside the door. And, in the end, the narrator sees her too: bloody, frail, emaciated, trembling, and reeling to and fro, falling upon Usher in her "now final death

agonies" and bearing Usher "to the floor a corpse, and a victim to *the terrors he had anticipated.*" As a last emphatic psychological detail, Poe has the narrator tell us that "from that chamber and from that mansion, I fled aghast." Thus we do not know for sure that the House splits apart and sinks into the tarn in a lurid blaze, for the narrator has by now been revealed to be totally untrustworthy.

Yet, even here, Poe provides one more turn of the screw: for, buried in the details about the House, is the information that the oxygenless dungeon has been a storage place for gunpowder or "some other highly combustible substance." Thus *if* the House cracks open and crumbles, rather than a necessarily supernatural occurrence, as it seems to the hysterical narrator, it is explainable as the combustion generated when the lightning of the storm crackles near the previously airless crypt—the inrushing electricity being conducted along the copper floor and igniting the remnants of powder. Yet these mocking clues are not all. The miasma enshrouding the House provides yet another, for marsh gas was then thought to have *hallucinatory* effects, and Poe elsewhere mentions this very effect.

**The ghosts in the tale of Usher
are those of the mind**.

—*G. R. Thompson*

If the stated terrors of the narrator are not convincing enough for a complete psychological interpretation of the supernaturally charged events, the recurrent dream imagery and the very order of the opening paragraphs regarding the images of the House in the pool should confirm such a reading. The dream images culminate in the return of Madeline and in the "Mad Trist." Madeline, supposedly the victim of a cataleptic fit, is presumably not a ghost or other supernatural manifestation, even though her appearance at Usher's door produces a ghost-like effect in the best tradition of supernatural Gothic. We *do* get our Gothic thrill, even though she is not a supernatural being. Yet, if she is not, then how, in her frail and emaciated condition, would she be capable of breaking open the coffin, the lid of which the narrator specifically tells us they screwed down tightly? Or of pushing open the door, "of massive iron" and of such "immense weight" that its movement "caused an unusually sharp, grating sound, as it moved upon its hinges"? These details of Madeline's entombment, given us at the midpoint of the tale, underscore the dream motif and link her dreamlike manifestation directly to the psyche of the narrator; for Poe also makes a point of having the narrator tell us that Madeline's tomb is at great depth, immediately beneath that portion of the building in which was "my own sleeping compartment." The images of sleep, mist, water, and descent, recurring throughout the tale, forcibly suggest Poe's focus on the subconscious mind. The night of Madeline's return, just before the reading of the "Mad Trist," the narrator cannot sleep, and a detailed description of his troubled drowsiness is given. Neither can Usher sleep, for he is troubled by the dreamy mist enshrouding the House. Finally, the events, the disappearances, the transformations, and the correspondences of sounds in the tale of the "Mad Trist" which follows, all have the order of a dream, and, moreover, move from the depths of the House upward toward Usher and the narrator.

Yet the "Mad Trist" is made purposefully ludicrous; it reads like a parody, and even the narrator comments on its absurdity. The correspondence of sounds, especially, heightens the ludicrous effect. But the intruded tale of the "Mad Trist" also has a clear ironic effect; it destroys the Gothic illusion. As in **"Ligeia,"** Poe intrudes an ironic distance clearly and rather suddenly between the narrator and the reader, here calling attention to the real psychological situation of the two protagonists engaged in their own mad trist.

Connected with the dream images and reinforcing the suggestion of subconscious action is the dreamlike reflection of the House of Usher in the pool and its parallel in Usher's "Arabesque" face. In fact, Usher's famous face (supposedly a pen portrait of Poe's own according to biographically oriented critics), with its parallels in the appearance of "The Haunted Palace" of Usher's wild poem and in the appearance of the House itself, provides a major clue to the irony insinuated into, under, and around the apparent Gothic surface of the story. Usher's face in a sense is the image of the narrator's own, whose mind, if not disintegrating also, is capable of slipping in an instant into the same kind of madness or hysterical fear to which Usher is subject. The narrator, as he becomes absorbed in his "superstitious" reflections, says that he had to shake off from his fancy "what *must* have been a dream." The narrator's first impression of the House is that it is like a human face, especially with its two vacant eye-like windows. Then he looks down into the pool, but sees only the reflection of the "face" of the House. What is equally likely, of course, is that he should see imaged there his own reflected features, since Poe is careful to point out that the narrator wheels his horse up to "the precipitous brink" of the tarn and thus gazes straight down. Then he remembers Usher's hysterical letter and mentions, along with Usher's "mental disorder," that he had been Usher's close and only friend. Next he remembers that the peasants refer to both the House and the family as the House of Usher and immediately returns to the image of the "face" in the pool. When he looks up at the House again, he tries to "analyze" its weird effect, and describes once more its prominent details, especially the overspreading fungi "hanging in a fine tangled webwork from the eaves." The nervous narrator, conscious of his own vague terror and therefore the more apprehensive, goes into the House to meet Usher, and his attention is focused on the weird appearance of Usher's face. Usher's face has a generally decayed aspect, like the House itself, but especially noticeable are his large and luminous eyes and his hair "of more than web-like softness and tenuity." This tangled, "web-like," "silken hair," of a "wild gossamer texture," thus

imagistically merges the facelike structure of the House with Usher's face, the "Arabesque expression" of which the narrator cannot "connect with any idea of simple humanit." As we have seen, the narrator grows "terrified" and "infected" with Usher's hysteria. He becomes like Usher. In meeting Usher, he is symbolically staring into the face of his psychological double, and when he steps through the "Gothic" archway of Usher's house into the dark, black-floored hall with its carved, niched, fretted architectural features, lit by "feeble gleams" of "encrimsoned" light that barely makes its way through elaborately "trellised panes," it is clear that the narrator has stepped into the confused, subjective world of Gothic terror and horror. Once inside, in another absurdist touch, he is taken by a servant who "ushers" him into Usher's presence. Thus, Usher's "Arabesque" face and the face of the House are the same, and when the narrator gazes into the pool, the reflected "Arabesque" face is merged with his own— symbolically *is* his own. The image of the face is then reemphasized in Usher's poem about the attack of "madness" on the "haunted" castle.

The ghosts in the tale of Usher, then, are those of the mind. Such an analysis does not deny the supernaturalistic surface level of the tale, nor other significant patterns such as the incest motif, the eerie hint of vampirism, the use of abstract art to suggest sexuality, entombment, or Nothingness, or the carefully balanced themes of order and sentience that other critics have noted. Rather, such a reading incorporates them into its overall pattern, while wrapping a layer of dramatic irony about the whole. As in other of Poe's Gothic tales, the delusiveness of the experience is rendered in and through the consciousness of the narrator so that we participate in his Gothic horror while we are at the same time detached observers of it. In the image of the House as skull or death's-head, and the merging of the narrator's face with the face of the House which is also Usher's face in the pool, we see as so often in Poe the subtly ironic paralleling of the narrative structure of the tale to its visual focal point. And by having the facelike House of Usher sink into its own image, the final collapse into that void which is both the self and the universe simultaneously is complete. This, then, is the larger pattern of meaning generated by the overall narrative system enveloping the other levels of narrative. And yet there is, by implication, a further enlargement. Since it is clear that we do not know that anything the narrator has told us is "real," the whole tale and its structures may be the fabrication of the completely deranged mind of the narrator. Nothing at all may have happened in a conventional sense in the outside world—only in the inner world of the narrator's mind. Of this redoubled Nothingness, then, also comes Nothing. And this further perception of the structures of Nothingness becomes our ultimate perception of the tale as simultaneously involved and detached observers.

Frederick S. Frank (essay date 1979)

SOURCE: "Poe's House of the Seven Gothics: The Fall of the Narrator in 'The Fall of the House of Usher'," in *Orbis Litterarum*, Vol. 34, No. 4, 1979, pp. 331-51.

[*Frank is an American educator and critic with a special interest in Gothic literature. In the following essay, he argues that the true villain of "The Fall of the House of Usher" is the narrator himself, who has failed to recognize the limitations of his narrowly rationalistic mind.*]

Between the meditative arrival of the friend of Roderick Usher and his panic-stricken exodus from the vanishing mansion there lies the story of the humiliation of reason within the palace of art. Like his counterpart, the curiosity-driven hero who descends into the maelström, the naive voyager who narrates **"The Fall of the House of Usher"** makes the special journey inward which demands a reversal of vision and a relinquishment of ego in order to attain what Emerson called "an invisible, unsounded centre in himself." Both explorers enter the deadly mouth of an apparently chaotic world and both explorers are confronted with the necessity for absurd choices in order to pass the aesthetic test and solve the problem in form posed by the dissolving house and the perilous whirlpool. While the maelström narrator deliberately *descends* into an aquatic version of the Gothic castle, the Usher narrator merely *falls*. The aesthete who surrenders to the fatal grip of the whirlpool is rescued by his veneration of form and actually ascends to a higher awareness of beauty, but the trespassing materialist who invades the House of Usher sets in motion a sequence of falls culminating in the destruction of the domicile of art itself, Usher's ideal world which the narrator disparages as "the kingdom of inorganization." Within such a precarious kingdom of aesthetics the rationalist is clearly out of his element and he poses a threat to invisible order and higher beautiful form unless he can develop an aesthetic response to Gothic experience. Such a restructuring of attitudes is the primary transcendental accomplishment of the maelström descender while the refusal to see beyond the immediate Gothic hazards of his own concern for sanity and safety mark the Usher narrator as the tale's unconscious villain and the secret agent of disorder within inorganization's kingdom. In short, the House of Usher falls because the alien intruder fails to rise to a new consciousness of aesthetic responsibility. It is he and not the Ushers or their house who is both victim and victimizer although this inversion of roles is beyond the limits of the narrator's imagination.

The narrator's mansion sojourn is a Gothic ordeal for him precisely because he chooses to view it Gothically and to treat his analytic helplessness as conclusive evidence of a nightmare world full of insoluble Gothic dilemmas and governed by decay, absurdity, and death. What is beyond analysis must be intolerably fearsome to such a skeptical intellect. Like previous orphans of the castle in Gothic fiction, the Usher narrator regards his adventure as a typical Gothic entrapment and comes to see the Ushers as a pair of castle spectres. Once within the kingdom of inorganization, he consistently refuses to become a part of it and is an insider only in the superficial sense of being present as an observer. A master of external detail, he nevertheless fails to see the duty he owes toward the crumbling house and its febrile occupants. By his obtuse reliance upon reason he annihilates the prospective dreamworld and by his Gothic reactions to the double threat of madness and disintegration the narrator precipitates all of the falls in the story. No mere spectator or witness to the collapse of the house, he may really be the causal agent whose aesthetic insensitivity and rejection of visionary habits of seeing bring about the catastrophe of amorphousness at the climax of the tale. The more the narrator seeks to apply rational postulates to the mysteries surrounding the palace of art, the weaker the structure enclosing him becomes until the dreamworld melts into the tarn having been dematerialized by the alien visitor's obtuse perceptions of his mission at Usher. Most of Poe's best serious tales are concerned with how to see or how to expand visionary consciousness while making a fatal journey or while confined to the circumscribed turbulence of a Gothic building or chamber. In **"The Fall of the House of Usher,"** Poe has written his grandest parable of defective vision and imaginative timidity, for in the voice of the storyteller we recognize the defeated rationalist who has violated the kingdom of aesthetics, who has sinned against the reality of the supernatural, and who has caused a resurgence of primordial chaos by his failure to use his imagination once he enters the portals of the palace of art. It has been observed [by James W. Gargano] that "Poe often so designs his tales as to show his narrators' limited comprehension of their own problems and states of mind." But nowhere in the Poe canon are the consequences of a narrator's imaginative deficiencies and his refusal to participate in the transcendental dreamworld that "lieth sublime, Out of SPACE—out of TIME" so complexly treated as in the vain quest of the Usher narrator.

Although many critics have called attention to the flawed mind of the Usher narrator, no student of the tale has yet argued that his presence within the House disturbs the fragile triangle of aesthetic order that still exists when he arrives. But in regarding the storyteller merely as a spectator or witness to the holocaust the crime of the narrator is overlooked and the inner meaning of the Usher narrator's flight from the kingdom of inorganization is missed. Thoroughly horrified and Gothified by the weird events that he thinks he has witnessed, the Usher narrator deserts the palace of art at the crucial moment and refuses to succeed Roderick as the future artist-monarch over this kingdom of dreams. Aesthetic heroism involves a willingness to remain within the House not as a guest or as a skeptical investigator but as a new resident who is prepared to put the quest for beauty ahead of all mortal considerations. But unlike the maelström descender who saves himself by seemingly dooming himself, the friend of the Ushers is incapable of the act against reason and self-preservation that can disclose a world of higher form amidst Gothic turmoil. For him, the case of the Ushers remains unsolved while his own imaginative cowardice is never examined. He handles internal or psychic events as if they were external happenings and in his effort to reconstruct the experience he omits the most significant fall among the seven falls that occur in the story: the collapse of his own arrogant confidence in the infallibility of reason as a shaping power. As it disappears into the tarn, the House is both a symbolic reminder of the faulty psycho-architecture of the rationalist and an emblem of a permanently lost world within the narrator himself. For all of its factual minutiae and medical data, the narrative itself remains a perplexed fragment of what really took place at Usher,—the distressed monologue of a frustrated analyst who can see parts but never the whole. In the poem, "Dream-Land," Poe had reflected upon the fact that divine unity can only be reached through the dreamer's irrational crossover into the regions of sleep. "Never its mysteries are exposed / To the weak human eye unclosed." It is the "weak human eye unclosed" of the Usher narrator which distorts the value of the fatal experience and transforms a potential dream of beauty into a fragmentized Gothic nightmare for himself.

By concentrating upon the narrator's abuse of the dream experience we may be able to answer in aesthetic terms several provoking questions which **"The Fall of the House of Usher"** poses concerning the superiority of the synthetic over the analytic outlook in Poe's hierarchy of mental functions. If the House of Usher finally falls because of the reluctance of the narrator to submit to the dream experience and to unite himself organically and spiritually with Roderick Usher's kingdom of aesthetics, we can extend this hypothesis to a pair of Dupin-like questions about the anti-imaginative voyager's true position in the aesthetic scheme of the story. First, what kind of criminal is the Usher narrator and where does he belong in Poe's catalogue of maniacs? And second, what is the exact nature of the crime and punishment of this [man who, in Barton Levi St. Armand's words, is an] "unwilling initiate who has failed to comprehend the significance of the Mysteries he has witnessed and the passion-drama in which he has participated?" Such an approach means that the story really belongs to the narrator and is far more about his unknowing desecration of the palace of art than he himself realizes. Ironically, the fearful disintegration which he believes has overtaken and swallowed up the Ushers and their House has actually befallen the blasphemous pilgrim whose attempt to impose a rational control over his sojourn is a failure.

The architectural cataclysm of the sinking of the House into the tarn is preceded by several anticipatory falls. Beginning with the fall of the narrator's eyes into the dark unyielding mirror of the tarn, each subsequent fall is the result of his attempt to order the transcendental world by applying rational criteria and each fall further undermines the palace of art. In arranging for the narrator to move through a sequence of seven falls Poe may have had in mind a septenary design for the story to suggest the perversion of aesthetic vision by a non-believer who rejects seven chances to ascend to the throne of art. The numerology underlying the seven falls has a deep religious significance just as the one life shared by the three bodies of Roderick, Madeline, and the House is a bizarre play on the doctrine of the trinity. In their order of occurrence, the seven falls may be enumerated as follows: the peer downward into the "remodelled and inverted images" of the tarn, an initial invitation to see all that lies over the tarn in reverse; the narrator's Gothic interpretation of the "Haunted Palace" rhapsody in which he thinks he

detects "the tottering of his [Usher's] lofty reason upon her throne," when it is actually the narrator's own rationality which is beginning to fall; the dropping of the narrator's spirit into Gothic premonitions of sleepless horror and his overpowering by terrifying noises as he struggles within the solitude of his apartment "to arouse [himself] from the pitiable condition into which [he] had fallen, by pacing rapidly to and fro" in his unconscious mimicry of Roderick Usher's "hurried, unequal, and objectless step;" the twin falls featured in the Gothic inset legend of Sir Launcelot Canning, "'the head of the dragon, which fell before him'" and the brazen shield adorning the castle wall which "'fell down at his feet upon the silver floor, with a mighty great and terrible ringing sound'," the repeated double fall of Madeline atop Roderick in a ghastly parody of the classical sexual posture as she "fell heavily inward upon the person of her brother;" the outer fall of the dream edifice into the tarn, the visible result of the narrator's chaotic impact on the palace of art; and the inner fall of the narrator's self-assured belief in the power of reason as he flees "aghast" from the Gothic crisis his mind has created. The multiple connotations of falling throughout the story again suggest the narrator's aesthetic delinquency and his capitulations to Gothic terror. From each successive trial of the imagination the purely analytic temperament recoils in horror until it literally fragmentizes the visionary opportunity of beholding primal unity. What we see through the eyes of the narrator at the end of the tale is precisely what we see through his eyes as he studies the facade of the House at his arrival: a confusing spectacle of disparate parts that lies beyond his depths.

Clearly, it is the prolonged gaze downward into the tarn, the probing of the depths of self, that furnishes the clue to all of the other inversions of reality contained in the story. Within the so-called kingdom of inorganization all of the laws of empirical reality are reversed. Much madness is divinest sense, stone truly is alive, the dream power supersedes the waking state as a route to knowledge, illusion takes precedence over reality, and dying by diving into the image of the House shimmering in the tarn becomes the preferred mode of behavior. A total immersion of his mind in the beckoning pool of imagination followed by further attemps to fuse himself with the dreamworld of the Ushers ought to prevent all of the various falls. By conjoining himself with the kingdom of inorganization he could then endow his words with the poetic energy required to sustain the structure through [what Poe defines in "The Poetic Principle" as] the "rhythmical creation of beauty." Indeed, it is the unnamed narrator's duty, just as it is the esoteric obligation of all potential visionaries and dreamers in Poe, to merge himself with the higher world through the power of words. In the cosmic fantasy, **"The Power of Words,"** Poe has the celestial voyager, Agathos, show his companion, Oinos, how wisdom and beauty must be sought in "the abyss of nonentity." Agathos proclaims the law of opposites by which the suicidal hero can transform various kingdoms of inorganization into trancendental paradises. His powerful words to Oinos correspond almost exactly to the sort of mystic appeal exerted by the tarn upon the inquisitive yet hesitant Usher narrator. Agathos says, "Look down into the abysmal distances!—attempt to force the gaze down the multitudinous vistas of the stars, as we sweep slowly through them thus—and thus—and thus! Even the spiritual vision, is it not at all points arrested by the continuous golden walls of the universe?—the walls of the myriads of the shining bodies that mere number has appeared to blend into unity?" Descending and not falling then, first with the physical eye and then with the entire mind and soul is the proper path for the Usher narrator to follow as he contemplates the individual particles that compose the Usher universe. But in his thoroughgoing hostility to reverie, he does not tell or order events properly. In his very way of remembering his nearly fatal occupancy of the mansion he uses the power of words negatively to demolish the palace of art.

The House of Usher falls because the alien intruder fails to rise to a new consciousness of aesthetic responsibility. It is he and not the Ushers or their house who is both victim and victimizer although this inversion of roles is beyond the limits of the narrator's imagination.

—*Frederick S. Frank*

The Usher narrator's crime, therefore, lies in the manner of the telling. From the first words of the overture passage in which he fights off the temptation to fall asleep and to enter the magic castle as a reverent dreamer, the tone of his account never goes beyond the traditional Gothic hero's emotions of horrified perplexity and a losing struggle with the tenebrous and demonic forces which hold him prisoner. His vocabulary is an unpoetic mixture of the medical and the hysterical as he speaks a language highly inimical to the poet's idiom. Habituated to classification, he clings desperately to the old diction falling back upon such terms as "hypochondriac," "maladies of a strictly cataleptical character," "restrained *hysteria*," and "settled apathy" to protect his reasoning self from the absurd possibilities which intimidate his "lofty reason." Or in describing his dire situation he retreats into the maudlin rhetoric of the typical Gothic victim who finds himself cut off from air, light, and hope in the bowels of some murky Gothic dungeon. Such phrases as "the hideous dropping off of the veil," an echo of the major device of suspense in Mrs. Radcliffe's *The Mysteries of Udolpho* (1794), and "there sat upon my very heart an incubus of utterly causeless alarm" not only revert to the frantic style of the English Gothic novel from which they are derived but underscore Poe's stress upon the verbal constrictedness of the narrator. Plainly, his power of words is limited to two inadequate voices: the voice of the scientist-analyst-physician which wants to busy itself "in earnest endeavors to alleviate the melancholy of [his] friend;" and the voice of the Gothic victim who dreads live burial just as much as one of Monk Lewis's incarcerated maidens and who longs to escape from the haunted castle before it

can consume him. Recital of the tale within the confines of these two voices is an act of destructive retrospection. Rather than serving as a verbal defense against encroaching madness, his words deprive him of the artist's insight. Standing in bewilderment on the threshold of chaos and nothingness at the close of the tale we are left to ask the romantic poet's question which the narrator declines to utter: "Whither is fled the visionary gleam? / Where is it now, the glory and the dream?"

By failing to reflect deeply enough upon the mystic signal given to him by the tarn to "invert and remodel" his consciousness the narrator dooms his quest to failure from the outset. All that will now befall him as he proceeds across the tarn and penetrates the head of Roderick Usher will by its very nature be irreducibly symbolic like the stylized movements of a religious ritual or self-exploratory dream. By venturing boldly through the sleeping mind's Gothic corridors the acolyte of beauty might eventually pass into a higher degree of wisdom and share the mysteries of the castle. A passage in Freud's work *On Dreams* explains the process of inversion which accompanies the transition through which the narrator passes when he enters the dream temple of art and is "ushered" into "the presence of his master." For Freud, the reversal of vision induced during the dream state leads to a *"new unity,"* the proper goal for the Usher narrator within the kingdom of inorganization.

> Ideas which are contraries are by preference expressed in dreams by one and the same element. "No" seems not to exist so far as dreams are concerned. Opposition between two thoughts, the relation of *reversal,* may be represented in dreams in a most remarkable way. It may be represented by some *other* piece of the dream content being turned into its opposite—as it were by an afterthought. We shall hear presently of a further method of expressing contradiction. The sensation of *inhibition of movement* which is so common in dreams also serves to express a contradiction between two impulses, a *conflict of will.*

By ignoring the law of opposites as projected in the tarn reflection he brings himself into direct conflict with the artist-ruler of the inner world and by clinging to empirical categories he menaces and finally destroys the poetic entity symbolized by the House. The narrator's failure to invert the Gothicism of his experience also justifies Roderick Usher's desperate epithet, "'MAD-MAN,'" because from Usher's point of view the visitor has not grasped the salvational law of opposites upon which the palace of art rests and has lost all contact with the aesthetic realities of Usher's dreamworld. Both the painting and the poem within the poem, "The Haunted Palace," are efforts on the part of Roderick Usher to reveal to the narrator his own shortcomings but he overlooks the self-reflective quality in these symbols just as he cannot or will not allow himself to be converted to the law of reverse vision on the brink of the tarn.

If the universe of Roderick Usher is a pure poetic abstraction that can be imagined into existence, it then follows that it can be reasoned out of existence by an uncooperative observer who repeatedly reduces the whole to parts or fragments by his way of visualizing the challenge of the Gothic fortress. Although on the edge of annihilation, the architectural and psychological parts of the House of Usher nevertheless do possess a totality when the House first comes into the narrator's view. Just how heavily strained the delicate triangle of order is when he beholds its face is indicated by the zig-zag fissure which scars the House's countenance. The slightest disturbance of the taut harmony underlying the aesthetic composition of the House and owner will insure the destruction of the whole. Mysteriously, and contrary to any known physical law, the structure of the House as well as its interior synthesis are literally kept in place by an exertion of Roderick Usher's poetic imagination. Conversely, the imagination of the artist is held in place by the palace of art. By an imaginative analogy which defies all of the analytic speculations of the narrator Roderick Usher is like a poet and his House is like the divinest structure of the mind at its highest condition of creation, or like a poem. Such a relationship can be discerned only by discarding sensory prejudices and Gothic fears in order to see the House and master synthetically. Between Usher and his House there is a tension that is both creative and fatal, a private universe of form resting upon the supra-rational principle of the perfect psychic congruity of the two worlds of mind and matter. For the Usher narrator to understand his aesthetic obligation toward this precarious oneness he should immediately embrace the dreamer's timeless selfless perspective. For only a reversal of rational safeguards and a release of the imagination can preserve the coalition of art and artist symbolized visually in the fragile condition of the House and its lord. Roderick Usher's imaginative vitality, long burdened by such immense creative strain now stands threatened with a breakdown. The atrophy of Usher's aesthetic energies is accurately diagnosed by the narrator as a downward pressure of the senses upon his mind, "a morbid acuteness of the senses" accompanied by "a host of unnatural sensations." Sensing that his imagination cannot maintain the balance much longer, Usher has summoned his friend in the hope that he will be able to envision the artistic problem in form and will then ascend to Usher's stewardship of the mansion as new keeper of order in the kingdom of inorganization. If Usher can somehow transfer the responsibility of imagination to the skeptical and frightened visitor, as indeed he tries futilely to do, then coherence and unity might be retained and the kingdom of aesthetics continue to stand though Usher himself perishes.

It is precisely such an absurd collaboration between the external structure of the House and the internal structure of a sensitive and gifted mind that the puzzled narrator cannot or will not acknowledge. Seeing such a connection would require not only a suspension of his Gothic preconceptions toward the frowning and ominous castle which rises up before him, but also an absurd decision, the cardinal act against reason which enables certain Poe questers to elevate their identities by choosing death over life. What the House demands of its tenants is not siege or conquest but the *outré* reverence of the artist who is willing to dwell inside the timeless and tenuous world of the poem.

None of these duties are perceived by the Usher narrator.

During his analytic appraisal of the grim visage of the House he is much taken with its "vacant eye-like windows," an overt organic feature dating back to the incredible aliveness of architecture in Gothic fiction as well as a masonic sign made to him by the House to go "beyond [his] depth." Chagrined by the eruption of certain irrational dreads within himself the narrator's feelings are much like those of any typical Gothic victim contemplating the horrors that await him within the haunted castle as he approaches its sinister bastions. But if the law of reverse vision is applied, the stare of the House is not vacant but replete with sentience and not merely eye-like but genuinely ocular in its urgent appeal and invitation to the narrator. As the contest of eyes continues the visitor's eye travels to the base of the House where there lie "a few white trunks of decayed trees," a brilliantly surrealistic image of bones scattered before a mighty stone face. Since Poe ends **"The Fall of the House of Usher"** by echoing a passage from *Ezekiel* 43:2 ("And his voice was like the noise of many waters") it seems plausible given his sense of singularity of impression that he has chosen to begin the story with the image of the wanderer in the valley of the dry bones. And given the ironies of the narrator's own rational madness the House ceases to be an objective reality in his mind's eye and becomes a traumatic projection of his own secret insecurities and desires. Somewhere behind the apparent Gothic hideousness of the House's "Arabesque expression" there lurks an occult totality which the narrator can sense but cannot articulate in scientific language. Unable to tabulate the Gothic data before him into a logical whole or to reduce his wild feelings to a formula he is obstinately committed to putting things in their right order as he probes for an explanation: "What was it—I paused to think—what was it that so unnerved me in the contemplation of the House of Usher?" Shortly thereafter, his scrutinizing eye will single out the "barely perceptible fissure," the ultimate fractional detail in a mental picture consisting of disquieting fragments. The more intently he gazes the more diminished his vision grows as his unsympathetic outlook and the power of his words accelerate the sublimal processes of disintegration already at work within Usher's kingdom of inorganization.

Once inside the House itself the Usher narrator pursues a campaign to determine and relieve the malady of the Ushers. Having shaken off the temptation to dream and to see in reverse he assumes that he is still in the "real" world although his unexpressed Gothic fears that the House can see, feel, think, and change shape at will continue to trouble him. Unwittingly, he is the author of a series of miniature falls which lead to major deterioration of aesthetic sensibility at the climax. The narrator's close analysis of Roderick Usher's head, for example, is a repetition of the facial perusal undertaken by him prior to the glance into the tarn. And just as he misreads the symbolism of the House by failing to enter into the attitudes of the dreamer, so he misjudges the symbolism of Usher's forehead and eye. The cranial details which the narrator reports form a composite of pallid Byronic outcasts and Gothic men of feeling. The strange virility of Monk Lewis's Ambrosio, the crepuscular grandeur of Mrs. Radcliffe's

Montoni and Schedoni, the cryptic eye of Beckford's Vathek, the equivocal handsomeness of Byronic heroes such as Cain and Manfred, the preternaturally powerful voice of Brockden Brown's Carwin in *Wieland* (1798), and the wild hair and volcanic eyes of Maturin's Melmoth the Wanderer seem to have coalesced in the super-human features of Roderick Usher, Poe's penultimate reproduction of the English Gothic villain. While the desperate malice of the Gothic tradition's satanic hero appears to be perfectly duplicated in Usher's Gothic face, Poe has inverted the meaning behind this mask of evil. Transplanted from the pages of the Gothic novel to the contorted phrenology of Roderick Usher the standard Gothic face loses all previous moral significance as an index to the struggle of good and evil within the tempest tossed soul of the Gothic novel's tormented tormentor. What the Gothic face symbolizes in the inverted context of Usher's world is not guilty anguish coupled with an all-consuming passion for evil but a terminal fatigue of imagination. Although he resembles the Gothic villains outwardly Usher's inner tension is much closer in kind to a wasted figure such as Kafka's hunger artist. For the attentive observer, the face of Usher spells out the intimate nexus between creativity and death. The miraculous organ of sight in particular, Usher's "eye, large, liquid, and luminous" contains the answer to the riddle of survival within the house of art. Preoccupied with his medical inspection of Usher's extraordinary cranial properties, the narrator does not make the vital symbolic connections between Usher's eyes and the tarn. The tarn is also "liquid and luminous" and a deeper look into its depths will lead to illumination for the quester. Introspection of Usher's remarkable face will also illuminate and carry the observer beyond the horror to a new depth of soul. Certainly, there is no more compelling facial image of the exhausted artist to be found in Poe's work as he has converted the conventional grimace, glare, and pallor of the Gothic novel's evil men into a figure of aesthetic depletion. When the narrator notes that the "finely moulded chin" shows "a want of moral energy," he once more reveals his inability to see symbolically and his reluctance to go deeper than the literal levels of experience. He is guilty of moralizing over Usher's features when the eye like the tarn is exerting the key command to "invert and remodel" in order to transcend horror.

Further analysis by the narrator is bound to push art and artist into a disastrous disharmony. Yet, with each phrase that he utters about his host's head, or Madeline's cataleptic peregrinations, or the Gothic acoustics which seem to be approaching a hellish crescendo, he weakens the artistic structure and falls further into aesthetic insanity. With each degree of descent into the whirlpool the maelström descender was able to beautify the horrible through the power of words; his philosophical opposite, the Usher narrator, insists upon Gothicizing all that is potentially beautiful within the palace of art. Having twice been confronted with his aesthetic alter-ego, first in the face of the House and then in the face of the host, he denies himself the higher identity that the maelström decender achieves. Looking at the various falls he causes, it is possible to see the friend of Usher as a satiric embodiment of the "heresy of *The Didactic*" to which Poe [in "The Poetic Principle"]

attributes a debasement of the sense of the beautiful. Although not wholly lacking in imagination, the narrator distrusts it as an impractical and dangerous faculty. To use the imagination is to indulge in a "somewhat childish experiment" that can only deter the moralist from his mission to save the Ushers from their peculiar disease. Vexed by a twinge of the irrational within himself as he gazes into the tarn he quickly makes a rational recovery to scan "more narrowly the real aspect of the building." This counterpointing of vision and revision is the basic psychological pattern into which the narrator's mind falls throughout the story. And nowhere is his vacillation between imaginative action and rationalistic reaction so destructive to the kingdom of aesthetics as in the central conversation he has with Usher concerning the preposterous theory of inorganic sentience.

Usher's heady discourse on "the sentience of all vegetable things" is perhaps the most complicated moment in the story for the narrator. For him, Usher's impassioned disclosure of this wild theory is the omega point of unreason in "the mental existence of the invalid." In reviewing the incident with his customary factual precision the narrator admits that he "lack[s] words to express the full extent" of Usher's bizarre ideas. In all other respects, the narrator's recollection is complete:

> I well remember that suggestions arising from this ballad led us into a train of thought wherein there became manifest an opinion of Usher's which I mention not so much on account of its novelty (for other men have thought thus), as on account of the pertinacity with which he maintained it. This opinion, in its general form, was that of the sentience of all vegetable things. But, in his disordered fancy, the idea had assumed a more daring character, and trespassed, under certain conditions, upon the kingdom of inorganization. I lack words to express the full extent, or the earnest *abandon* of his persuasion. The belief, however, was connected (as I have previously hinted) with the gray stones of the home of his forefathers. The conditions of the sentience had been here, he imagined, fulfilled in the method of collocation of these stones—in the order of their arrangement, as well as in that of the many *fungi* which overspread them, and of the decayed trees which stood around—above all, in the long undisturbed endurance of this arrangement, and in its reduplication in the still waters of the tarn.

To the narrator, the psychological damage of such bold imaginings is obvious in the impending insanity which threatens Usher. He conceives of his duty to be the relief of such psychotic enthusiasm in order to prevent a total disunity of self from overpowering his friend. Because Roderick Usher knows that his own reign over the kingdom of inorganization is about to end, the supreme task in his view is the successful transfer of aesthetic trusteeship to the narrator, his potential artist-successor. But the mere possibility that the House is far more than a physical structure, that it is the living symbol of all artistic endeavor and higher imaginative activity, is so repugnant to logic that the narrator must dismiss the idea as mad or risk madness himself. Never understanding that Usher's belief in the aliveness of the House is absolutely valid inside the inverted world he cannot take this crucial conversation seriously. Instead, he extends his earlier "feeling half of pity, half of awe into a moral contempt for such eccentric ravings. All chance for aesthetic rapport with Usher is lost as the narrator rationalizes away the wild lecture by abruptly declaring that "such opinions need no comment, and I will make none."

Sometime previous to the discussion of organic sentience Usher must have attempted to convince his guest of the truth of this supernatural proposition, for the narrator remembers that he was "enchained by certain superstitious impressions in regard to the dwelling which he tenanted." Earlier examination of his patient has also led the narrator to conclude that Usher's environmental delusions are cannibalizing his sanity. His morbid anxiety, for example, is diagnosed by the narrator as "an effect which the *physique* of the gray walls and turrets, and of the dim tarn into which they all looked down, had, a length, brought about the *morale* of his existence." Communication or an alliance between the rational and the aesthetic sensibilities is imperative at this pivotal point in the tale if the balance between artist and work of art is to be restored. Furthermore, it is vital that the outside narrator now go beyond his former depths and engage freely in unreason in order to assume the House's legacy. He must quickly consent to take Usher's place for if he procrastinates or moralizes, then the energy-starved mansion will drain off Usher's dwindling power of words. That is, the architectural organism will overfeed itself, the creation will turn upon its creator, and the aesthetic universe of the Ushers will revert to an inchoate mass. To see his appointed part in such a non-rational crisis means of course that the narrator would have to transmogrify both his vision and his vocabulary. But the narrator lacks the poet's daring; he will not pursue his own anti-rational impulses to a fulfillment of form; he cannot give himself over to that absurd gesture of faith in irrational descent which brings revelation. According to the law of opposites as fixed by the tarn mirror, Usher's eyes, and the colloquy on inorganic sentience, it is the narrator who is indeed the Gothic madman of the tale. If the palace is haunted, it is haunted by the phantom of reason. The term, "inorganization," which ambiguously refers both to inorganic substance such as stone and metal and to disorder or disorganization is also subject to the law of reverse vision which governs the House of Usher. Beheld with the imaginative eye, the kingdom of inorganization becomes the exact reciprocal of itself,—a kingdom of transcendent order or a poetic unity. Beheld as the narrator beholds it via the "weak human eye unclosed," it is indeed a chaotic spectacle.

After the crucial and abortive conversation with Usher, the negative forces represented in the narrator cause the remainder of the tale to deteriorate into Gothic melodrama. Premature burial, cadaverous resurrection, diabolic sound effects, a mounting spiral of terrified helplessness, lurid radiance, visceral disturbances in the Gothic substructure of the building, and the mandatory tempest all precede the narrator's expulsion from the castle. Rather than simply escaping from his Gothic predicament, the vain quester is literally disgorged or vomited forth by the submerging House as if he were some profane, foreign object. Also before his flight from the mansion all further demonstrations of inverting and remodelling assume a Gothic form. For example, the imbalance between art and artist, between the microcosm of poetic structure and its dying god, is now evidenced by the horrific fact that House and Master are beginning to exchange their metabolisms. Upon examining his patient on their last fatal night together in the House the narrator is astonished to discover that "throughout his whole countenance there reigned a *stony rigidity*" [italics mine]. Such a symptom of petrifaction is not just an indication of the onset of some weird variety of *rigor mortis* although such a paroxysmal stiffening would by no means be an unexpected medical development. What is unexpected, however, is the Gothic fact that Usher and his House are trading bodies in a perverse defiance of all the laws of nature. As Usher becomes progressively stony and inorganic, his counterpart and other self, the House, becomes increasingly corpuscular, plastic, and organic until the point of oversaturation is reached and the House liquefies into primal nothingness. With this final unbalancing of the equation between thought and feeling or between science and art, a universe comes to an end and a god is dead. And the party responsible for the aesthetic tragedy is the disconcerted narrator who entered the House of Usher with such noble intentions.

As for the lethal embrace of brother and sister, their posthumous reunion might compel the narrator to abandon his spectator's role and look beyond the ghastliness of this supernatural event. But once more his inability to use his imagination when faced by a Gothic crisis keeps him from seeing the reunion as something more than Madeline's retribution upon her incestuous sibling, the necro-rapist raped and murdered by his undead sister. The narrator has already experienced a visual analogue of the sister atop the brother in the image of the House astride its reflection in the tarn. In a higher sense, this death clasp is yet another "combination of very simple natural objects" whose mystic principle of arrangement eludes the rationalist. It never occurs to the narrator as he watches this horrible liaision that the House and its patrons are making a final plea to him to look beyond the horror he is now witnessing and rise above his spectator's role. Can be afford to take the absurd risk of remaining within the House at this climactic moment and become the new sovereign of the aesthetic realm? Looking to his own mortal survival, his tone is typically horror-struck as he recalls this gruesome *Liebestod* which completes his nightmare and drives him from the citadel of his innermost self. Gouted with blood and energized with a superforce from beyond the grave that is reminiscent of Ligeia, Madeline "bore him to the floor a corpse, and a victim to the terrors he had anticipated." So reads the rational deposition of this erstwhile doctor in residence now become makeshift coroner. He remains unenlightened to the fact that what he has concluded about Usher's extinction really applies to the higher aspects of himself, for the capacity to dream Poe's dream of supernal beauty is forever shattered.

The sudden appearance of the "blood-red moon" wedged into the fissure and boring like some mad eye through the corroding masonry of the House is a final Gothic beacon in which all previous signs and hints of aesthetic lunacy come to a destructive focus. In signalling the fall of the rational consciousness, the eye-like, crimson orb is a fine objective correlative for the narrator's own eye and gaze throughout the story. His fascination with the ruby moon as it seems to trickle down the gaping wound on the face of Usher's House like some impossible bubble of blood oozing from fractured stone is a last instance of mishandled symbolism. What he sees as an objective event is in truth a subjective event for he is now looking back upon his own fragmented consciousness or his own internal collapse. As denoted by the lunar eye, he is both the "red slayer" of Emerson's famous poem ["Brahma"] and the slain. But none of the internal meaning of his symbolic experience within the kingdom of inorganization is clear to him. In *Marginalia,* Poe would write: "It is the business of the critic so to soar that he shall *see the sun.*" Since solar revelation is Poe's figure for critical lucidity, the lunar opposite at the finale of "**Usher**" must symbolize aesthetic consternation and loss of self. Pausing again on the edge of the tarn to survey the world which he has helped to destroy (actually he is scientifically curious about the nature and origins of the "wild light") the House dematerializes within his mind's eye. The Biblical overtones inherent in the signature of the "long tumultuous shouting sound like the voice of a thousand waters" imply that the Day of Judgement is at hand—certainly a day of damnation for the once-proud reasoning self. Like the earth itself on the eve of creation, the House of Usher is "without form, and void; and darkness was upon the face of the deep."

As shown in the seventh fall in the final paragraph of the story, the Usher narrator's quest terminates in a grotesque cul-de-sac for the inquiring mind as the dreamworld disintegrates. Rationally depressed, verbally exhausted, and scientifically frustrated, he will never again be able to enjoy the *Todestraum* or dream of creation through death. While his fellow voyager, the intrepid mariner who descends into the maelström, designs his higher experience within the Gothic vortex to his own visionary satisfaction, the Usher narrator cannot stabilize or unify the imaginative elements of his adventure into the dark center. The limited central intelligence who repeats the tale within the tale that is "**The Fall of the House of Usher**" is hopelessly alienated from the aesthetic wonders of the universal mind and overwhelmed by feelings of rational impotence. According to Maurice Lévy, "The vocation of Gothic heroes is essentially that of *losing their way.*" Standing in awe on the "safe" and solid periphery of the liquid and lethal domain of art, the vain quester is not just another anonymous Gothic hero who has lost his way but the ultimate outcast of Poe's private universe.

Patrick F. Quinn (essay date 1981)

SOURCE: "A Misreading of Poe's 'The Fall of the House of Usher'," in *Ruined Eden of the Present, Hawthorne, Melville, and Poe: Critical Essays in Honor of Darrel*

Abel, edited by G. R. Thompson and Virgil L. Lokke, Purdue University Press, 1981, pp. 303-12.

[*In the following essay, Quinn opposes G. R. Thompson's contention that the narrator of "The Fall of the House of Usher" is unreliable.*]

D. H. Lawrence advised trust the book and not the author, but he neglected to say what or who should be trusted when the book consists of a story told by a narrator who is unreliable. Presumably one then looks for guidance from that convenient abstraction, the critic, who, along with his other duties, attempts to clarify the author's intention and to unmask narrators with bogus claims to credibility. In *Poe's Fiction: Romantic Irony in the Gothic Tales* (1973), G. R. Thompson argues that it was part of Poe's intention as an ironical author to make the most of the unreliable narrator device, and that he did so in a good many of his most famous tales, including "**MS. Found in a Bottle,**" "**Ligeia,**" and "**The Fall of the House of Usher.**"

Having long believed that Poe wanted his readers to give credence to, indeed to the identify with, the visitor to Usher's house, and finding myself unpersuaded by the opposite proposals in Thompson's book, I should like to review the matter in some detail. Taking up four points that are worth more or less discussion: the appearance of the house, the narrator's experience, the ending of the story, and its theme, I shall try to show that in this case it may be the critic of the story rather than its narrator whose reliability is more open to question.

THE APPEARANCE OF THE HOUSE

"It is curious," Thompson writes, "that no one has ever seen fit to remark that when the narrator rides up to the house of Usher he is immediately confronted with a death's head looming up out of the dead landscape. Poe obviously intended the image of the skull-like face of the house to dominate as the central image of the tale, for he returns to it again and again, placing the most extended descriptions of it at symmetrically located places in the narrative."

There can be no objection to describing as "dead" the landscape in which the house is sited, but two other assertions are made here which are not so self-evident. To take the house first: what does it look like? Very few architectural specifications are given, but it is obvious that the house is very old and very large. It dates back to feudal times and, though no doubt remodeled since then, remains what it originally was, a castle. Poe's misuse of the recherché words *donjon* and *donjon-keep* does not inspire one with confidence in his expertise about castles, but he conveys, nonetheless, a sufficiently graphic picture: the house of Usher is a castellated mansion of medieval origin. And of considerable size. "Vast" is the narrator's word for it, when, in the final paragraph, he records his last look at the front of the house. Approximately *how* vast may be inferred from the dimensions of Usher's "studio," the windows of which are at "so vast a distance from the black oaken floor as to be altogether inaccessible from within." If this is only the studio, imagine the scale of the great hall! But the question is whether a vast, castellated mansion, seen from in front, where the entrance is, can have a plausible resemblance to a death's head. I would say no. The proportions of the building, its generally rectilinear structure, its turrets, and above all its dimensions make this resemblance extremely difficult to visualize. And so I, for one, do not find it curious that the alleged house-skull resemblance has, prior to Thompson, gone unremarked.

Nor can I go along with Thompson's other contention, that the image of the skull-like facade of the house dominates the tale, with Poe returning to it again and again to give it more extensive treatment. The disagreement here may be reduced to a matter of statistics. **"The Fall of the House of Usher"** has 41 paragraphs. Counting "The Haunted Palace" as part of paragraph 18, and scrutinizing the text for evidence Thompson would use to support his view, I come up with only paragraphs 1, 4, 5, 18, possibly 19, and 41. In these paragraphs I do not find "extended descriptions," nor do I find them, as Thompson does, "at symmetrically located places in the narrative."

THE EXPERIENCE OF THE NARRATOR

It is of importance to Thompson's case that a close link be discerned between the narrator and his host, since the essence of the case is that the two are psychological doubles and hence the initial uneasiness felt by the narrator develops into a "frenzy of terror, engendered by and parallel to Usher's terrors." As evidence of such a link, Thompson adduces the three-way relationship he sees between the face of the narrator, the facade of the house, and the face of Usher. He pairs the first two this way: "The narrator's first impression of the house is that it is like a human face, especially with its two vacant eyelike windows. Then he looks down into the pool, but sees only the reflection of the 'face' of the house. What is equally likely, of course, is that he should see imaged there his own reflected features, since Poe is careful to point out that the narrator wheels his horse up to 'the precipitous brink' of the tarn and thus gazes straight down."

So far there is no mention of a *three*-way connection, but two passages on a later page deal with this emphatically: "Usher's 'arabesque' face and the face of the house are the same, and when the narrator gazes into the pool the reflected 'arabesque' face is merged with his own—symbolically is his own . . . [plus] the image of the house as skull or death's head and the merging of the narrator's face with the face of the house which is also Usher's face in the pool."

In my opinion, the evidence offered for a three-way tie-up is unconvincing, for these reasons:

1. The narrator's first impression of the house is that it is "melancholy," and to such a degree that he feels overcome by a "sense of insufferable gloom." Neither in the first scene nor elsewhere does he allude, even distantly, to

a resemblance between the house and a human face, much less a skull. To be sure, there would be some basis for imputing to the narrator the impression of such a resemblance if the text read, per Thompson's paraphrase, "two vacant eyelike windows." In fact, the numeral *two* is not used by the narrator. (It is probable that Thompson borrowed it from the third stanza of "The Haunted Palace," but Usher's poem is hardly relevant evidence about the narrator's first impression of the house.)

2. When the narrator gazed at the tarn, could he have seen his face reflected, overlaid, as it were, on the reflected image of the house? It seems to me that, given his initial position, across the water from the house, he could have seen one or the other, but not both. Only after crossing over the causeway, standing with his back to the house, and *then* looking down could he have seen his reflection, within the frame of the reflected facade of the house. But since he does not cross the causeway until after his visual experiment is made, the laws of geometric optics would seem to rule out the possibility of the double-reflection phenomenon.

3. Another reason for questioning the face-facade theory may be worth mentioning. When the narrator enters the house and meets his host, his attention, Thompson says, "is focused on the odd appearance of Usher's face," which recalls to the reader "the facelike structure of the house." In a very general way this deduction is correct, for a basic *donnée* of the story is that some kind of occult connection, necessarily imprecise, exists between the house and its owner. But by giving such minute attention to Usher's face— its luminous eyes, its curved lips, its delicately shaped nose (distinguished, moreover, by an unusual "breadth of nostril")—the description negates Thompson's earlier suggestion that, *de rigueur,* an association is to be made between the house and a skull or death's head.

A more important contention in Thompson's argument is that the story is essentially about the mental collapse of the narrator, and that the stages of the collapse are given careful documentation: "Poe meticulously . . . details the development of the narrator's initial uneasiness into a frenzy of terror," etc. The word *uneasiness* is perhaps not sufficiently strong to do justice to the state of mind of the narrator when he has a *mauvais quart d'heure* in the opening scene. But once he is inside the house does this uneasiness augment by differentiated stages and eventually partake of the terrors that afflicted Usher? This is not shown.

Between paragraphs 6 and 24 the narrator's account does not reflect any progressive deterioration of mind or feeling. How could it? For his account is concerned almost entirely with Usher, his appearance, behavior, and obsessions with several varieties of fear. And rather than respond to and interiorize these obsessions, the narrator attempts to distract Usher from them. For several days after his arrival, he says, "I was busied in earnest endeavors to alleviate the melancholy of my friend." Following the interment of Madeline, "some days of bitter grief having elapsed," Usher's condition takes a serious turn for the worse. As he reads the symptoms, the narrator is unsure whether to diagnose their cause as "extreme terror" or "the more inexplicable vagaries of madness." Either way, Usher's condition has become terrifying, and it is *now,* after perhaps a week of residence in the house, that the narrator begins to feel real distress. Up to this point there has been no meticulous recording of a developing uneasiness. The development starts now, but it does not approach the intensity ("frenzy of madness") of Thompson's estimate.

Thompson's version of what takes place at this crucial juncture (paragraphs 24, 25, 26) adds some details to the text and, inexplicably, ignores others. The text reads: "There were times, indeed, when I thought his [Usher's] unceasingly agitated mind was laboring with some oppressive secret, to divulge which he struggled for the necessary courage." In Thompson's version of this statement the emotional ante is raised considerably: ". . . the narrator feels growing in himself a vague fear that Usher has some horrible 'oppressive secret' to divulge." Recognizing that Usher's terror is becoming contagious, the narrator says: "I felt creeping upon me, by slow yet certain degrees, the wild influence of his own fantastic yet impressive superstitions." Thompson renders this as "slow yet uncertain degrees"; but whether certain or uncertain, the degrees by which the infection spreads are not itemized. Instead, Poe at once sets his final scene, which is enacted a week or so after Madeline's burial.

The scene begins with the narrator's account of experiencing "the full power of such feelings"—that is, those induced by Usher's condition. He is, to quote Thompson again, "unable to sleep, especially since, as with the reflected image of the house in the tarn, he is aware of his increased terror: 'an irrepressible tremor gradually pervaded my frame; and, at length, there sat upon my very heart an incubus [of] utterly causeless alarm.'" What the resumé as quoted does not reflect are two sentences in the text which describe the narrator's efforts to deal with, to dispel, his feelings of terror. The resumé continues: "'Overpowered by an intense sentiment of horror,' the narrator begins pacing nervously; suddenly he is startled by a light footstep outside his door. But it is only Usher. Usher's intensely agitated condition is the more unnerving, especially when he suggests that a supernatural and luminous vapor has surrounded the house in spite of the rising wind without."

Here also is an omission of some consequence. The narrator does not pace to and fro *because,* as Thompson seems to imply, he feels "overpowered by an intense sentiment of horror." Rather, he resorts to this action as a means of fighting back, "to arouse myself," as he puts it, "from the pitiable condition into which I had fallen." He is not "startled" (nor could he be) by Usher's light footstep; the sound merely "arrested [his] attention." He does not find Usher's distraught appearance "the more unnerving." What he says is quite simply and credibly this: "His air appalled me—but anything was preferable to the solitude which I had so long endured, and I even welcomed his presence as a relief."

Usher does not "suggest that a supernatural and luminous vapor" has surrounded the house; all he does, without comment, is open a casement window. The narrator sees for himself an "unnatural" light glowing about the house. It seems, then, that one of Usher's specific fears—that the house would become increasingly sentient, with increasingly ominous implications for himself—is in fact borne out. But instead of succumbing to this fear the narrator tries to explain away both it and the apparent basis for it. The phenomenon, he tells Usher, is only hallucinatory. "You must not—you shall not behold this!" he exclaims, and further to deflect Usher's attention he begins reading aloud from the "Mad Trist." As things turn out, the reading proves less than therapeutic, but the intention behind it was certainly sane.

At this point the action of the story is within a few moments of its close. Surely by now, if Thompson is right, the narrator, despite himself, would reveal how he is being victimized by a "frenzy of terror" on a par with Usher's. He is not so victimized. Usher is the one who succumbs, "a victim to the terrors he had anticipated." The narrator, on the other hand, "unnerved" and "aghast" as he understandably is, retains sufficient *sang-froid* to get out of the house in time and witness what happened to it.

WHAT HAPPENED TO THE HOUSE?

The question is not as frivolous as it looks, for it involves one of the major theses of Thompson's book. The thesis is that Poe, as an ironical writer in the romantic mode of irony, characteristically provides in his tales one kind of meaning for the average, untutored reader, and plants, or "insinuates," another meaning, which, in Poe's words, "only minds congenial with that of the author will perceive." In the present instance, the thesis applies in this way: The reader of average gullibility will not think of questioning the veracity of Usher's visitor, and his account of what took place will be appreciated for the uncanny kind of excitement the tale gives rise to; whereas an inner circle of readers, aware that Poe's technique is one of "deceptive, ironic, psychological realism," will read the story for its clues (Thompson's word), just as a detective does in a mystery story. Therefore we either accept the narrator's word about what happened to the house, or, following Thompson's lead, we "clue in" to a different hypothesis.

According to the narrator, the house of Usher, almost immediately after his exit from it, split into two great sections and sank into the tarn. Since Thompson's opinion is that the man is revealed as "completely untrustworthy," he sees no reason why this professedly eyewitness report should be accepted as definitive. He offers an alternative explanation. The copper-floored vault in which Madeline was interred, he points out, was once a storage place for powder or some other highly combustible substance. This is textually exact. And so, Thompson continues, "if the house cracks open and crumbles, rather than a necessarily supernatural occurrence, as it seems to the hysterical narrator, it is explainable as the combustion generated when the lightning of the storm crackles near the previously airless crypt—the inrushing electricity being conducted along the copper floor and igniting the remnants of powder." This is an ingenious explanation, but it depends on too many improbabilities.

It seems improbable, for instance, that there was enough residual gunpowder in what is described as a small and damp vault to cause (when ignited) an explosion adequate to blow up the house; for the house, it can be assumed, is "vast." I have no idea what critical mass of gunpowder would be required to blow up a castle of even average size, but what Thompson refers to as "remnants of powder" would not seem to be nearly enough, for the phrase suggests only a few scattered, unswept grains. (The text, incidentally, makes no mention of such "remnants." It was apparently the copper sheathing that led the narrator to infer that the place had once been a powder magazine.)

If we assume that there was gunpowder in sufficient quantity to cause, when ignited, the blowing up of the house, a question arises as to the agency that might have caused the ignition. Thompson's theory is that a lightning bolt, finding access to and then conducted along the copper flooring, provided the spark. What is not explained is how such a bolt could have found access to the burial vault. Located "at great depth" underground, and therefore windowless, and of course damp, it would seem as lightning proof as any interior chamber could imaginably be.

There is the further (or rather preliminary) question as to whether the storm produced lightning. Rain is not mentioned, or thunder, and as for lightning, all that is said on this score is: "nor was there any flashing forth of the lightning." Thompson would certainly have a better case if the statement were less negative. I think it is possible that one reason why the tempestuous final night of the story is described as "wildly singular" is that all the makings of a thunderstorm were present—but, singularly, there was neither rain, nor thunder, nor lightning. Since, however, the text is not absolutely negative on this point, the possibility may be entertained that there was lightning that night. It was not seen as "flashing forth" because, presumably, it was concealed by the cloud cover, which was very dense and hung low enough to "press upon the turrets of the house." Such lightning as there may have been, therefore, was of the cloud-to-cloud variety, for flashes from cloud to ground, given the unnatural visibility of the occasion, would have been seen. So perhaps a bolt or two may have struck one of the turrets. But an explanation is still in order as to the route and the conducting material by which an electric charge traversed the anfractuous distance between turret level and the vault, sequestered well below ground level. The text offers no basis for such an explanation.

THE THEME OF THE STORY

In **"The Fall of the House of Usher,"** as Thompson interprets it, Poe, through the narrator's account of his experience, ironically mocks "the ability of the human mind ever to know anything with certainty, whether about the external reality of the world or the internal reality of the mind." I find it impossible to reconcile this definition of the story's theme with the contention, variously phrased, that the narrator of the story is mentally unstable, disturbed, prone to hysteria and hallucination—that he is, in fine, "completely untrustworthy." Surely it was as obvious to Poe as it is to us that a deranged mind, mired in its own subjectivity, is unable successfully to perceive objective reality, much less cope with it. There would be no point, ironical or otherwise, in mocking such inability. Therefore, only if the narrator's mental credentials are in good order, and the story he tells is accepted as reliable, can there be any possibility that the thematic drift of the story is as Thompson describes it.

Benjamin Franklin Fisher IV (essay date 1981)

SOURCE: "Playful 'Germanism' in 'The Fall of the House of Usher': *The Storyteller's Art,*" in *Ruined Eden of the Present, Hawthorne, Melville, and Poe: Critical Essays in Honor of Darrel Abel*, edited by G. R. Thompson and Virgil L. Lokke, Purdue University Press, 1981, pp. 355-74.

[*Fisher is an American educator and critic with a special interest in the work of Edgar Allan Poe. In the following essay, he analyzes "The Fall of the House of Usher" as a parody of Gothic literature.*]

During the past thirty years, few approaches to Poe's great tale have failed to pay respects to Darrel Abel's "A Key to the House of Usher," first published in 1949 and several times reprinted, wherein he analyzes the centrality of symbolism embodying the conflict between life-reason and death-madness. In no way will I challenge this or other readings that argue for serious import inherent in **"Usher,"** although I wish to examine a facet of Poe's technique not charted by Abel, nor by many others who use his justly famous essay as a foundation for their theories. My aim is to illuminate Poe's comic impulses, as I discern them, in this tale. Comedy and burlesque, to be sure, have been noticed, but not extensively treated, by James M. Cox, G. R. Thompson, and, implicitly, Daniel Hoffman. External and internal evidence support a comic perspective within **"Usher,"** as I will show. Although my "key" may unlock only the back door of the house of Usher, I trust that it will nevertheless afford entrance to yet another area of Poe's artistic imagination.

I

What is the "text" of **"Usher"**? Recent critical theory suggests that "textuality" is also a matter of "contextuality." External evidence places **"Usher"** inescapably within the realms of Gothic tradition. Indeed, Abel's critique begins with the "exquisitely artificial manipulation of Gothic claptrap and décor," but careful reading reveals admirable and clever method in Poe's handling of materials generally regarded as mere decoration. Recent critics have paid attention to the "otherness,"—if I may so term the artistry that surpasses the mere horrific, as the Gothicism in **"Usher"** does—while noting the abundant cli-

Poe's burial site in Baltimore, Maryland.

chés from the tradition. Clark Griffith mentions Poe's drawing upon older Gothicists, like Radcliffe and Walpole, as well as upon the *Blackwood's* variety of his day, although he emphasizes the former. An equally certain influence was the vastly popular novelist of contemporaneous fame, G. P. R. James, whose numerous "solitary horsemen" stand as literary brethren to the narrator, who reins in before the house of Usher to survey the scene and begins to register fears for his readers, eager for the anticipated thrills in terror literature. If we admit that Poe embraced the entirety of Gothicism, we might, in the light of recent studies, perceive **"Usher"** as parodic of not just the Gothic in general but, like some of his other tales, a hit at some of his own characteristic tendencies as a fictionist. If we also admit that **"Usher"** betrays its creator's ambivalent attitudes toward his art, as Roppolo suggests, we might see the tale as one of many examples of American romantic writing that simultaneously uses and attacks the Gothic legacy from European literature.

An important aspect of the European impact on American literature, by way of its British parent, is "Germanism," or Gothicism, that oft mentioned term of disapprobation in critical circles. In the autumn of 1839, the time in which **"Usher"** appeared in the September issue of *Burton's,* Poe had good reason to think of "Germanism," and think of it he did, as is attested in the repeatedly cited (and perhaps as often misunderstood) preface to his collected fiction, *Tales of the Grotesque and Arabesque*. Poe's

assertion that "terror is not of Germany, but of the soul" may imply (whatever else it indicates) that the "soul," given his current frame of mind, is that of a humorist, so far as one level of **"Usher"** (and perhaps other tales) is concerned—a connotation that does not exclude possibilities of equal sobriety in any given piece. Furthermore, if "Metzengerstein" or "Von Jung" comes more readily to mind as the "single exception" to Poe's disclaimers of "that species of pseudo-horror which we are taught to call Germanic," we must remember that he called no attention to them in the critical extracts he included in volume II. **"Usher,"** however, was highlighted, more than any other tale, with five notices that called attention to it and, moreover, emphasized its stern, somber, and terrible elements. One commentator states that it "would have been considered a *chèf d'oeuvre* if it had appeared in the pages of *Blackwood*." Reasonably, we may wonder whether Poe presented all these encomiums for clues to alert readers as to what lay under the *Blackwood* article surface of **"Usher."**

The charge of "Germanism" was hurled at Poe from the time he began to publish fiction in the *Southern Literary Messenger*. He quickly had to apologize to editor White for the horrors in **"Berenice,"** his first tale for the journal, though he justified his creation by pointing out how common (and remunerative) such Gothicism was in the literary marketplace. With the appearance of **"Morella"** in the next number came adverse criticism of Poe's ventures into "the German school," which recurred over the next several years.

Such hostility toward German Gothicism had a long history by the time Poe got around to countering it, and for examples (surprising ones, no less), let us look to the beginning of the nineteenth century. In the preface to *The Bravo of Venice,* Monk Lewis stated that the original German might be "too harsh for the taste of English readers"; consequently, he altered passages to soften them. But his bowdlerization failed to deter critical stricture [such as J. F. Hughes' complaint]: "The writers of the German school have introduced a new class [of novel], which may be called the electric. Each chapter contains a shock; the reader not only stares, but starts, at the close of every paragraph." Apologetics like Lewis's continued; apparently, no respectable British writer wished to be bracketed with German excesses. Maturin, for instance, remarked in his first novel, *The Fatal Revenge; or, The Family of Montorio* (1807): "Whatever literary articles have been imported in the *plague ship* of German letters, I heartily wish were pronounced contraband by competent inspectors. Turning the pages of this lurid novel, we must conclude that Maturin's practice and preaching diverged. He continues, though, in phraseology anticipating Poe's notions of "Germany": "I question whether there be a source of emotion in the whole mental frame, so powerful or universal as *the fear arising from objects of invisible terror.*" Thirty-three years later, Poe said much the same thing: "I maintain that terror is not of Germany, but of the soul,—that I have deduced this terror only from its legitimate sources, and urged it only to its legitimate results." The rub may be in determining the precise nature of those sources and results.

Another circumstance that is relevant to Poe's sensitivity about "Germanism" is his practice of alternating serious with comic Gothic tales. We know that such tales as **"Ligeia," "How to Write a Blackwood Article,"** and **"A Predicament,"** published prior to **"Usher,"** provide clues to his divided aims in writing terror fiction. So do later tales, such as **"The Premature Burial," "Tarr and Fether,"** and **"The Sphinx."** Why not, then contemplate possibilities for perceiving a mixed mode in **"Usher"**?

I believe that in **"Usher"** we find an allegorical (dare I say it?) presentation of the baneful effects of taking the sensational aspects of "Germanism" too seriously. As in **"Silence—A Fable,"** we are spectators as a man (the narrator) looks at another man (Roderick) whose story is his own. In **"Usher,"** too, what happens to the second man symbolizes what happens within the first. In meeting again his childhood friend who is named, interestingly enough, for the last of the Goths (in Poe's sly manner of wordplay) and whose all too "Gothic" adventures amidst all too "Gothic" surroundings quite literally enchant him, our narrator resembles earlier Gothic personages who were duped because of their credulity, such as Catherine Moreland or Cherry Wilkinson. That Poe's two characters were previously acquainted might be apprehended as a revelation by the narrator (carefully manipulated by Poe) of his immature reading tastes. Although he has become a man,

he has not put away childish things, and in remaining too near his Gothic background, as exemplified in **"Usher,"** he has paved the way for yielding to the effects of irrationality. Like the heroes in **"The Man Who Was Used Up"** and **"Tarr and Fether,"** this narrator is used up in the course of events—not so much as to preclude his telling his tale again but enough to indicate to readers the hazards in subscribing wholeheartedly to "Germanism." Sensing that it is going askew, he can do nothing to break the spell, so to speak, and, like Coleridge's wedding guest, he cannot choose but to participate in the drama (the tragedy) of collapse.

II

With these matters in mind, let us scrutinize the text of **"Usher."** Some of the exaggerations and repetitions, the veritable gallery of Gothic horrors, may make better sense if we consider their comic potential. I mentioned above the solitary horseman; other elements are equally recognizable as primary features of Gothicism: the supersensitized narrator-protagonist; the persecuted, frail maiden; the diabolic villain, modified in Roderick (à la Byron and Bulwer) into a latter-day hero-villain; the minor characters; the hyberbolic language; the eerie setting; the weird art and music; and the "supernatural." All are constituents of a fine "German" tale, and I suggest that Poe worked his materials for as much comic, ironic value as for any Gothic impact.

First, the teller of the tale could not be more appropriate. By means of this figure, Poe burlesques the quenchless sensibility of those virtuous, high-minded, sexless, arty types in Gothicism, whose curiosity always outruns their rationality in prompting them to actions and emotions altogether rash, daring, or ridiculous in the face of what readers readily size up as horrors for out-Heroding Herod (to use one of Poe's favorite phrases). The narrator approaches the house of Usher through a foreboding countryside (to understate its negative implications), surely passing beyond the natural scenery of a Radcliffe or Maturin and into the spooky *qua* spooky. Those "few rank sedges . . . and . . . few white trunks of decayed trees" partake of the "desolate and terrible," not because they convey "half-pleasurable" sensations of the well-known "Sublime" but because they do not. Their sole inspiration is "insufferable gloom" for our narrator, who, as the tale runs its course, proves unable to suffer (in the biblical sense) any terrors, present or future. Later, he is moved to tell his story, after the manner of Poe's other confessional narrators, because he is actuated by the worst features in his chronicle. And if the overt aim of Gothic fiction is to arouse a sense of gloom, this tale fulfills, and overshoots, that aim.

We also sense that, gloomy or not, the narrator relishes the substance of his tale. Like other Gothic protagonists, he unceasingly conveys sensations of uneasiness, but his repetition of such stock "Germanisms" as "singular," "gloom," "melancholy," and "ghastly" causes us to wonder whether his reiteration is not more than "half-pleasurable." Also, it may be no accident that several times he tells us he "found" himself confronting menacing phenomena, as Gothic protagonists always do. He is ripe, we quickly discover, for his first "view of the melancholy House of Usher" (a haunted castle that out-Gothicizes many of its species), which to him appears to be human (or inhumanely human)—a fine touch in a tale wherein the characters look like their haunted house and vice versa. The narrator's function, first and foremost, is to tell a story, which he does with gusto, festooning his tale with rhetoric that passes beyond the edge of credibility, in comparison with most terror tales. For example, the visual persuaders commence "within view" of the Usher mansion and intensify with such phraseology as "first glimpse," "I looked upon the scene before me," "I reflected," "gazed down." These and other like passages urge that we realize Poe is manipulating the narrator, in such fashion that this character seems almost an avid reader of a terror tale, who, like the central figure within, is only too willing to register trauma. Maybe Poe intends another turn of the comic Gothic screw, in that he creates a figure who resembles an ordinary reader, eager for thrills, as well as (simultaneously) epitomizing all that is worst in Gothic protagonists.

Significantly, the narrator states that "in this mansion of gloom I now proposed to myself a sojourn of some weeks" and that the "proprietor, Roderick Usher, had been one of my boon companions in boyhood." Twice, he emphasizes the "personal" nature of their friendship, adding: "As boys, we had been even intimate associates." Can such rhetoric be Poe's subtle dropping of clues, implying immaturity among fans of "Germanism," who he knows cannot subdue their propensities for the horrific? That is, we behold in the narrator a being who is long familiar with thrillers and who nonetheless enters the house of Gothic fiction, as symbolized in the Usher mansion, only to become enmeshed in its toils. The bond between the narrator and comic Gothicism is strengthened when we remember that Roderick is modeled upon a doomed hero, well known to Poe and his audience through contemporary literary sources.

Elsewhere, the narrator unwittingly reveals his intent preoccupation with sensationalism. For example, in language that echoes a more overtly burlesque Poe character, the Signora Psyche Zenobia, he remarks, after yet another glance at the mansion: "There grew in my mind a strange fancy—a fancy so ridiculous, indeed, that I but mention it to show the vivid force of the sensations which oppressed me. I had so worked upon my imagination. . . ." Those devilish terms, "fancy," "sensations," "imagination," all obviously hallmarks of overstrained sensibility, add bold relief to the personality through whom **"Usher"** is sketched for us. He suggests, on one hand, his uneasiness with the environment that we (and doubtless he himself) understand as Gothic, or "German," and, on the other, he undercuts his reasons for such agitation in betraying the subjectivity with which he creates this atmosphere. Perhaps his penchant is enjoyment of grim Gothic mansions.

By now, we should be ready to conclude that we are dealing with a "sick" narrator, whose malady stems from over-indulgence in the "pseudo-horrors of Germanism." In this light, the journey into the self, perceived by numerous readers of **"Usher,"** may be viewed as a journey by someone akin to the stock types travestied by Jane Austen, E. S. Barrett, or T. L. Peacock. Poe's Mr. Lackobreath also comes to mind as one of their literary descendants. Such questers encounter comic Gothic situations (to us, if not them), and may embody salient traditional traits, combinations that heighten the fun for readers who can laugh at the ludicrous, ever lurking near the fringes of terror tales. The **"Usher"** narrator falls into these ranks. He is irresistibly drawn to the house of Usher, earmarked for extremes with Gothic appurtenances or by what he ingenuously accepts as such.

His relish for the Gothic or "Germanic" is more evident after he enters the house. His familiarity with the environs of foreboding and decay becomes apparent when he informs us: "The carvings of the ceilings, the sombre tapestries of the walls, the ebon blackness of the floors, and the phantasmagoric armorial trophies which rattled as I strode, were but matters to which, or to such as which, I had been accustomed from my infancy." In tandem with his boyhood ties to Roderick, this exposition hints of another facet of our narrator, steeped in matters "Germanic" and smacking of the apartments in **"Metzengerstein."** Furthermore, he is so "practiced" upon (in the Elizabethan sense) that, by the end of the tale, he can no longer function, except as a participant in the spirit of Gothicism, which Poe presents at its most exaggerated. Our narrator articulates a welter of hyperboles as he reads the "Mad Trist," certainly a farrago of Gothic nonsense and a parody of the same in **"Usher."** The "Mad Trist" resembles "The Haunted Palace," but contains none of the serious undercurrent in the poem. The narrator continues to purvey sensationalism in "seeing" Madeline's return from the tomb, in witnessing the "fall" of the mansion into the tarn, and in going through it all again in telling "the fall of the house of Usher."

These experiences result from his enchantment by the Gothic tradition, so to speak, and, implicitly, a similar fate awaits others (characters within tales as well as the unwitting, who are eager to read about them) who succumb to the witchery of overdone Gothicism. As the narrator flees the scene of Madeline's overpowering of Roderick, amid a barrage of Gothic props, he "finds" himself again, this time in crossing the causeway; in other words, he realizes that he was attempting to escape the mansion of gloom. But he has taken flight too late; the Gothic spell has undone him. His brain reels, and his last, emphatic impression is of "fragments of the '*House of Usher*'"—or what he designates as such (as Poe indicates in the punctuation). Like the too curious, sensation-oriented visitor to the madhouse in **"Tarr and Fether,"** whose perceptions are battered by the close of the tale, the narrator of **"Usher"** is spiritually drubbed because of his febrile submission to "Germanism."

Two more anomalies attest the narrator's unreliability, implying that his sensations are prone to irrationality. First, one may ask where he learns that "House of Usher" is "a quaint and equivocal appellation . . . in the minds of the peasantry who used it." Had he perchance lingered to gossip with such persons as he journeyed toward the mansion, or does this inconsistency align him with Melville's Ishmael (who cannot be present in certain situations he details as if he were on the scene) as a first-person narrator whose authority many readers would not dispute? This discrepancy in **"Usher"** is functional, if Poe intends the character's recountings of this circumstance to appear valid to readers who revel uncritically in the supernatural.

Poe satisfied two audiences in "Usher." For one, he provided the horrors they expected and enjoyed. For the other, he created a work that embodies (among much else) a moral about succumbing to the extravagances of the Gothic.

—Benjamin Franklin Fisher IV

Second, what are we to make of the narrator's statement that "many years had elapsed" since his last meeting with Roderick and, shortly afterward, continuing: "Surely, man had never before so terribly altered in so brief a period as had Roderick Usher!" A lapse may not be apparent, were we to discern in Usher's malady a submerged commentary upon the decadence of Gothicism. If he represents the last stages of the tradition, then, so far as the span of the tradition goes, his rapid decline is plausible because of the mode's sudden decline from favor. Poe's censors believed that "Germanism" was passé and wished he would heed their criticism.

We may ask, then, what initially drew the narrator into this "Germanic" atmosphere. A letter, of course (which often substitutes for the "mouldering ms."), and a strange one. It is "wildly importunate," revealing "nervous agitation . . . acute bodily illness" and, as Poe originally phrased it, "pitiable mental idiosyncrasy." A good Gothic come-on—and unable to resist, the narrator responds with a "personal reply" by journeying to visit Roderick. The consequence of this personal involvement is the narrator's growing awareness of his increasing superstition, which multiplies because of his "infection" from the "wild influences of [Roderick's] fantastic yet impressive superstitions." These terrors wax noticeably after his assistance with the premature burial of Madeline, as if participation in another bit of shopworn Gothic horror topples his rational faculties and prepares for his direct attendance in the uproar of her "return." Maybe the repeated use of "wild" and compounds incorporating it is another device by which Poe calculated to insinuate comedy relevant to the crazy developments in the chronicle of the Ushers and their guest.

Having drawn the narrator through a landscape "horrid" enough to titillate Catherine Moreland and into the frights within the Usher mansion, Poe involves him with characters who are hackneyed personages of Gothicism. At the same time, Poe contrives to lead his narrator farther and farther from the mundane world outside of romance. The narrator meets the other *dramatis personae* in a series of encounters that are staged with Poe's subtlest artistry.

At the entrance to the house, his horse is taken by "a servant in waiting," who does not enter the mansion. His presence may symbolize normal humanity. Then, as if Poe wished to sketch lightly with the brush of suspense, our narrator is led by a "valet of stealthy step" (why "stealthy," if not to indicate that this opinion is the narrator's subjectivity?) to the master of the strange house. Along the way, they meet the family physician, whose "countenance, *I thought* [italics mine], wore a mingled expression of low cunning and perplexity," who "accosted me with trepidation and passed on." This storyteller's imagination grows irrational and untrustworthy because of his eagerness "to think Gothically," as it were.

Next, the narrator is greeted by Roderick, whose physique and emotions epitomize the decadence of Gothic hero-villains as a type, engendering in his friend that "species of pseudo-horror, which we are taught to call Germanic." Indeed, the description of Roderick is a visual aid to such instruction. With Poe arranging these meetings in ascending order of importance for their terrifying effects upon the narrator and those who enjoy his tale, our quester attains a high "Germanic" peak when, finally, he watches Madeline glide through a distant section of her brother's apartment and sees her as Roderick's feminine counterpart. Of course, the narrator stands upon the "German" summit, in terms of his emotional responses to the terrors that surround him, when (later) he "sees" Madeline come back from the tomb.

III

We must now attend to Roderick Usher and his sister. Years ago, Mabbott emphasized the significance of his name, which derives from the last great ruler of the Visigoths. As the last master of his weird, tottering house, where the commonplace traits of hero and villain of Gothic romance are confusedly intermingled, Poe's Roderick may be intended to exemplify the last "Goth" of another decadent tribe, the timeworn literary populace of terror tales. Lest my reading be considered "ingenious," we must not overlook the implications in Usher's premature burial of his twin sister. Siblings and premature burials were linked phenomena, with parricides or near parricides (only slightly less sensational) occurring frequently among the cast of Gothic figures from the days of Walpole. Twins seemed especially fated to come to early and awful ends, and Madeline's "illness" triggers Roderick's downfall. Just so, the grim atmosphere in the opening scenes may symbolize more "sickness"—not only of the twins, whose contagion affects the narrator, but of the tale and, through it, Gothicism in general.

To detect a travesty of Gothic hero-villains in Roderick is no absurdity. Like the narrator, whose makeup as a Gothic hero he shares, he is sensitive to art, music, poetry, romance (if we may so designate the "Mad Trist"), and architecture—in this case the overdone Gothic variety, his house. Because he epitomizes his type at the end of its tether, Roderick allows his "home" to dominate him (haunted castles often assume dimensions of characters), until he can no longer resist its evil charms. The approaching dissolution of the mansion is evident in the fissure in its facade and its crumbling stones. Like the one-hoss shay, this house, undeniably a Gothic castle, has endured, but its time draws nigh. Like the narrator, Roderick also is "practiced" upon and, more readily, acknowledges the baneful influence of his house and the sensations it engenders: "I *must* perish in this deplorable folly . . . I must inevitably abandon life and reason together, in my struggles with some fatal demon of fear."

Like many another Gothic character, Roderick encounters a "fatal demon," and his characteristics from this point become more and more those of the villain, with his deliberate burial of Madeline deepening his fears, until he becomes a madman, though sufficiently forceful to persuade his companion, the narrator, that the vision of vengeful Madeline is genuine. Roderick portrays the necromancer or magician, common in terror tales. If we have difficulty accepting that Madeline can not only survive the airlessness of her tomb but manage her incredible escape, we might perceive her as a genuine supernatural being (as she is in the narrator's mind), drawn from her grave by the fears of her brother, which effect the "spell" that can summon spirits. These fears, in turn, are symbolized in the great storm. That they ought to be viewed by readers as rationally explainable is clear in the narrator's words to Roderick: "'These appearances, which bewilder you, are merely electrical phenomena not uncommon,'" and miasma from the tarn may account for the terrifying atmosphere. Once more the narrator unwittingly reveals the truth. A debilitated hero-villain, from a decayed tradition, however, will have none of such explanations. Roderick persists in "Germanically" interpreting the "Mad Trist" of multiple meanings and, consequently, falls prey to its suggestions of his own situation, with disastrous results.

It is proper now to turn our attention to the lady Madeline, because all interpreters of **"Usher"** see Roderick's fate inextricably linked to hers. Her name, so redolent of Maddalenas and Rosalinas in earlier Gothic works, bears special import here, because it derives from "Mary Magdalen" and means "a tower" and "a lady of house." Madeline, as lady of the house of Usher, unfolds additional ironies. Initially, she brings qualities of passivity together, typifying Gothic heroines with features of the dying consumptive, another stock figure. Of course, her baffling malady recalls the catalepsy that afflicts Berenice and Ligeia, as well as their innumerable sisters in literature of the age. Perhaps this fated maiden is Poe's ironic bow to still another hackneyed aspect of "Germanism," particularly in the terms that describe her appearance in the tomb, with "the mockery of a faint blush upon the bosom and the face, and that suspiciously lingering smile upon the lip which is so terrible in death." To alert readers, the mockery and the smile might intimate a "hoaxical" aspect in this seemingly ordinary Gothic heroine.

Remembering that Mary Magdalen was among those at the Crucifixion, should we conclude that Poe, ever alert to scriptural themes, added another irony in naming Roderick's sister for one who was present at a colossal sacrifice? Madeline's reappearance as a terrible "ghost," which frightens Roderick to death and the narrator *nearly* to death, is couched in terms that suggest hallucination (in Roderick or the narrator, as the case might be). In the ornate, hysterical language, detailing a perfect medley of "sensations," we may discern Poe's wily hand pulling all stops for a crescendo conclusion. Literally and figuratively, this crescendo brings down the house.

Well it might, considering the probable exacerbation of Poe's imagination after several years' charges of "Germanism" had rung in his ears. His imagination could set forth literary Gothicism in well-appointed forms yet, simultaneously, jeer at its excesses. Such is the tenor of the preface to *Tales of the Grotesque and Arabesque*. Nor need we wonder, as we perceive his conscious manipulation of the **"Usher"** narrator's sensibilities, undone by overexposure to Gothic castles, abbeys, and mansions and peopled by such haunting types as Roderick, Madeline, the valet, and the doctor. Poe's artistry leads the narrator, himself a cliché figure of Gothicism, a kinsman of the Cherry Wilkinsons and Catherine Morelands, to pull the house down around his ears. With it falls (figuratively) the accumulated nonsense of overdone Gothicism, a lineage, to be sure, as time-honored as the Usher family itself. Perhaps Poe insinuated another sly bit of wordplay in **"Usher,"** with its connotation of "bringing in" a new era of fiction after the demise of a debilitated stock. As the protagonist-narrator of **"Tarr and Fether"** concludes his chronicle on an ironically rueful note, the narrator in **"Usher"** closes his: with the implied moral that outrageous "Germanism" is indeed treacherous.

IV

That the narrator senses the weaknesses inherent in typical Gothicism, in terror for terror's sake, is by no means assured at the end of his tale. Like many of his Gothic relatives, he seems compelled by the onslaught of terrors he endured to retell them to others. Unlike Catherine Moreland, he has no Jane Austen to chasten his discernible *Blackwood*'s *raison d'être*. He remains a creature of feeling, or, in Poe's descriptive phrase, "all soul"—a proper consort for the ridiculous Signora Psyche Zenobia. She, in turn, serves to lampoon Poe's more serious portraits of Psyche and, with the **"Usher"** narrator, repeatedly reminds us how thin is the line differentiating the serious from the ludicrous.

If our **"Usher"** narrator possessed a broader outlook, he would not view his situation so Gothically. Doubtless from his "childhood" (read "immaturity"), acquaintance with the fantastic—that is, steeping himself in Gothic romance—has unbalanced his vision. Thus he enters and is overwhelmed by the "world" controlled by Roderick's wizardry. Although this storyteller senses that something is amiss within the world of his tale (it's too Gothic), he cannot comprehend the nature of its defects. This subservience to the witchery of the *roman noir* is highlighted in the reading of the "Mad Trist," an evident (to perceptive readers of Poe's tale) distillation of all the hokey "medieval" ingredients of the Gothic. Mad it is, and mad its readers grow, if they are not already halfway there—so that they "see" the specter of the lady Madeline.

Again, we must examine some of Poe's phraseology. Dubbing the "Mad Trist" a favorite romance of Roderick, the narrator seems to derive greater pleasure in its perusal than does his companion. What Usher detects, and much more quickly than his impercipient friend, is his own death knell, sounding in this overdone tale. How ironic that a Gothic romance signals the end of Gothic romance! And as with many others of its ilk, this Gothic tale evinces "uncouth and unimaginative prolixity," which had been under fire from the days of Mrs. Radcliffe. Scott's review of Maturin's *The Fatal Revenge; or, The Family of Montorio* censured its length, and Poe was later to lament "the devil in 'Melmoth,' who plots and counterplots through three octavo volumes for the entrapment of one or two souls, while any common devil would have demolished one or two thousand."

In such light we return to our too-Gothic narrator, exhorting his too-Gothic friend: "I will read, and you shall listen;—and so *we will pass away* this terrible night together" (italics mine). Recalling that the physician, whose brief appearance is colored by the narrator's subjectivity, had also "passed on," we may read this passage as covert, sly mockery of dying Gothicism. Such wordplay keeps good company if we also remember that, earlier, the valet "threw open a door and *ushered* me into the presence of his master," or that, previously, the narrator had "entered the *Gothic* archway of the hall." With final italicizing for my emphasis, I note that Roderick's favorite reading was "an exceedingly rare and curious book in quarto *Gothic*," perhaps not uncoincidentally the *Vigils for the Dead* of an old German church. Other books that are listed among Roderick's delights may also hint at comic undertones, one a burlesque that features a comic parrot.

It may not be amiss to comment that Roderick's painting of nothingness is deemed worthy of emphasis by the narrator and that the "last Waltz of Von Weber" is recalled as a sample of his performances. The painting ought to alert us to absurdity, because it depicts glaring light where no light can shine. The music was composed just prior to its supposed creator's death; as such it is a swan song for Usher and all that he represents of faded Gothicism. Poe had elsewhere engaged in such innuendoes, and I think we should not discount their importance in **"Usher."** Indeed, all these things, every one redolent of "Germanism," will pass away.

From the foregoing, it should be evident that Poe's comic impulse was active in **"Usher."** Although in his famous preface to *Tales of the Grotesque and Arabesque* he apparently eschewed the "Germanic," we cannot pretend that he never served it up liberally in some of his tales (witness **"Metzengerstein,"** **"Berenice,"** and the Mesmeric tales). Given the brief time between conception and pub-

lication of **"Usher,"** and then between the *Burton's* and *Tales of the Grotesque and Arabesque,* we cannot ignore implications in this tale of covert lampooning of the Gothic tradition, tied to Poe's commentary on "Germanism," like a pudding richly studded with Gothic clichés. Not the first, or last, attempt by Poe to mock the very sort of fiction that earned him a (meager) living, **"Usher"** accomplishes far more subtle humor at the expense of Gothicism than, say, **"Loss of Breath"** or **"The Premature Burial."**

Disenchanted with the terror tale that was so much in demand but unwilling to lay down the reins with which he could so ably steer its course, Poe satisfied two audiences in **"Usher."** For one, he provided the horrors they expected and enjoyed. For the other, he created a work that embodies (among much else) a moral about succumbing to the extravagances of the Gothic. Thus, to paraphrase Abel, **"Usher"** is a matchless example of "Poe's . . . art which conceals art." Although he composed other tales that mingle tragic with comic substance, nowhere else was he so artistic.

George R. Uba   (essay date 1986)

SOURCE: "Malady and Motive: Medical History and 'The Fall of the House of Usher'," in *South Atlantic Quarterly,* Vol. 85, No. 1, Winter, 1986, pp. 10-22.

[*In the following essay, Uba diagnoses the cause of the Ushers' strange maladies by relating them to medical and psychological knowledge current at the time Poe wrote "The Fall of the House of Usher."*]

When the narrator of Poe's **"The Fall of the House of Usher"** first glimpses the Ushers' manor and demesne, he suffers a marked depression, which he likens to a "bitter lapse into everyday life—the hideous dropping off of the veil" of the opium eater. This description is surprising in light of the tale's subsequent developments, with their stark removal from the "everyday" and the hallucinatory quality of their description, but it points to Poe's own clear perception of how his tale's dramatic tension is to be maintained. For if **"The Fall of the House of Usher"** is distinguished by its forays into the fantastic and the grotesque, it also remains tethered to the real. What I am calling reality is most usefully apprehended in this case from the perspective of medical history. An understanding of such history not only affords insight into the maladies of both Roderick and Madeline Usher but suggests both how and why the latter suffers premature burial at the hands of the one person who loves and needs her most.

Thrice in the course of the narrative, Roderick Usher is referred to as a "hypochondriac." David W. Butler has demonstrated that Usher suffers not so much from a morbid belief in imaginary ills (the popular conception of hypochondria) as from hypochondriasis, a serious medical disorder widely known and discussed for centuries as well as during Poe's own time. It is evident that Poe was familiar with the various symptoms of the malady, for they recur in nearly textbook fashion in the story. Among these symptoms were the predilection to look on the dark side of things and to fall under the influence of environment and habit; fluctuations between high spirits and depression; a sudden acuteness of the senses; and the fear of impending doom. Benjamin Rush, the prominent American physician (and signer of the Declaration of Independence), commented on the alternation of high spirits and depression as an early stage of hypochondriasis and singled out "despair" as the "most awful symptom." Roderick Usher possesses "a mind from which darkness, as if an inherent positive quality, poured forth upon all objects of the moral and physical universe, in one unceasing radiation of gloom." His behavior, at least prior to his sister's demise, is "alternately vivacious and sullen"; he suffers from a "morbid acuteness of the senses" which at one juncture even allows him to "distinguish that heavy and horrible beating of [Madeline's] heart"; and he is convinced that he must soon perish. Hypochondriasis was also commonly linked to cultivation and personal refinement, qualities which Usher, with his "lofty and spiritual ideality," possesses in abundance. Even the commonly understood "remedies" for the malady, which included the pursuit of fine arts and an agreeable course of reading, along with the cultivation of cheerful society, are attempted by Usher, an erstwhile musician and painter who solicits the "cheerfulness" of the narrator's "society" in an effort to gain "some alleviation of his malady."

But neither Butler's valuable essay, which posits a connection between the mind-body disorder of hypochondriasis and the Romantic's faith in the ability of the imagination to affect the corporeal world, nor an earlier discussion by I. M. Walker about the medical implications of the "miasma" that surrounds the house and tarn fully accommodates Poe's complex handling of pathology. Neither Butler nor Walker, for example, explores the implications of Poe's use of medically cognate terms such as "melancholy" and "madness" in further describing Roderick Usher. And neither examines the malady that torments Madeline Usher while baffling her physicians. Yet Poe enumerates several specific symptoms of Madeline's distress and otherwise encourages us to believe that it has a definite basis in reality. By understanding this malady and by further examining the implications inherent in the descriptions of Roderick Usher, we may arrive at a clear understanding of the medical basis for Madeline's unhappy fate and Roderick's mysterious behavior.

Poe is at pains to show the similarities between the two Ushers. When the narrator notices the "striking similitude between the brother and sister" as he gazes down upon what he imagines to be Madeline's corpse, he learns at once that the two not only are more alike than most siblings but are in fact twins—twins in whom "sympathies of a scarcely intelligible nature had always existed." Just as the Ushers are closely allied in sympathies, it follows that their ailments may be related in some way as well. This notion is consistent with what we have earlier learned about Roderick: that he suffers not merely from a "constitutional" but a "family" evil. Throughout the course of its medical histo-

ry hypochondriasis was consistently linked with one other common malady: hysteria. The eminent seventeenth-century English clinician Thomas Sydenham declared that hypochondriasis was as like hysteria "as one egg is to another." Bernard Mandeville's *A Treatise of the Hypochondriack and Hysterick Diseases* (1730) took for granted the twin nature of the two maladies, as did such later eighteenth-century productions as George Cheyne's popular *The English Malady or a Treatise of Nervous Diseases of All Kinds as Spleen, Vapours, Lowness of Spirits, Hypochondriacal, and Hysterical Distempers* and Robert Whytt's more clinical *Observations on the Nature, Causes, and Cure of those Disorders which have been commonly called Nervous, Hypochondriac, or Hysteric*. And during Poe's lifetime the association between hypochondriasis and hysteria remained sufficiently widespread that when the Royal Society of Medicine of Bordeaux attempted to ascertain whether there were any difference at all between the maladies, a writer in the *Foreign Quarterly Review,* reporting on the Society's efforts and positively affirming the differences between the two disorders, immediately assumed that he was correcting the misimpression of the multitudes. For most people, he readily acknowledged, the "identity" of hypochondriasis and hysteria remained intact up to the present.

Probably the most conspicuous difference between the two maladies was that hypochondriasis was believed to afflict men and hysteria to afflict women. This difference is of course consistent with the hypothesis of twin ailments, for if Roderick Usher suffers from hypochondriasis, it is Madeline Usher who suffers from hysteria. But it was also believed that "sympathy" between the nervous systems of different individuals could lead to the transference of symptoms from one person to another through the organ of the mind; in particular hysteria was "found to be catching." Upon Madeline's supposed demise, Roderick exhibits a marked change of behavior. When the narrator encounters him near the start of the tale's climactic scene, he notices "a species of mad hilarity in his eyes—an evidently restrained *hysteria* in his whole demeanour" (Poe's italics). Poe's use of the nominative rather the adjectival form of the word "hysteria" and particularly the emphasis he places on it through the expedient of italics suggest an actual malady rather than a temporary type of aberrant behavior. So deep are the "sympathies" between the twins that upon Madeline's "death" she bequeaths her brother the ravages of her own distress. He in turn confers upon the narrator, who rapidly reaches the limits of his own reason, a portion of that same abundance.

While it might be supposed that any medical authority versed in the history of pathology and observant of the close ties between Roderick and Madeline Usher should have been able to diagnose the latter's disorder, such is not the case here, where "the disease of the lady Madeline had long baffled the skill of her physicians." There are two reasons why this is so. The first is the difficulty of arriving at the initial diagnosis even under the best of conditions because of the malady's protean nature. Sydenham remarked succinctly on this point: "The frequency of hysteria is no less remarkable than the multiformity of the shapes which it puts on. Few of the maladies of miserable mortality are not imitated by it." Even in Poe's day the difficulty of diagnosis was conceded. As the writer in the *Foreign Quarterly Review* noted, "the attacks of hysterical pain are sometimes so sudden and so violent as . . . to excite, even in the mind of the practitioner, much doubt as to their possible origin and tendency." While Madeline's symptoms are consistent with those most commonly associated with hysteria—she is stricken in "the maturity of youth" and suffers from "a gradual wasting away" and a variety of catalepsy—the very paucity of these symptoms, as well as her "settled apathy," which would tend to occur between rather than during episodes of hysteria, could militate against proper diagnosis. Her current physician's "perplexity," however, is coupled with an appearance of "low cunning," which strongly suggests a second reason why the correct diagnosis is not made. Simply, this physician is one of a small legion of medical practitioners who, during Poe's day, were known to "prey upon the weakness and credulity" of both hypochondriacal and hysterical patients. By constantly altering his treatment of his patient, he ensures himself of the largest possible retainer. It is no wonder, then, that upon the entrance of the narrator, an outsider, the physician evinces "trepidation." For all he knows, his unethical practices are about to be exposed.

Poe's handling of Madeline's disorder, no less than his handling of her brother's, is both sophisticated and medically correct. Moreover, his decision to make Madeline a victim of catalepsy (twice in the story, as if to emphasize the point, he notes the cataleptical nature of her malady) affords us a medically credible way of explaining how she is buried alive. For centuries, catalepsy had been regarded as one of the most prominent, certainly in its more extreme manifestations the most dramatic, of hysterical symptoms. In a cataleptic or hysterical fit, the patient experienced a muscular paroxysm which froze the body and limbs in whatever position they happened to be placed last. Sometimes the patient lost consciousness. Breathing often slowed and the pulse rate diminished to the point where they were scarcely perceptible or at times even brought to a temporary halt. In the more extreme cases, no doubt aided and abetted by the motionlessness of the victim, the cataleptic fit was widely assumed to be capable of imitating death itself. The description offered by the sixteenth-century French surgeon Ambroise Paré of this extreme manifestation of hysteria was one that may fairly be said to have persisted in the popular imagination for centuries:

> it bringeth a drousiness, beeing lifted up unto the brain, whereby the woman sinketh down as if shee were astonished, and lieth without motion, and sense or feeling, and the beating of the arteries, and the breathing are so small, that sometimes it is thought they are not at all, but that the woman is altogether dead.

Paré went on to suggest that in the severer manifestation the body could also turn cold. The famous nineteenth-century German phrenologist Johann Christoph Spurzheim, in his early classic on mental derangement, *Observations*

on the Deranged Manifestations of the Mind or Insanity, agreed that in the convulsive, hysteric, and hypochondriac fits the patient might seem "almost dead" and added that the fit itself could last for several hours. In regard to this latter point, the English physician Alexander Crichton went even further, noting instances of sleep "of the comatose kind, or mixed with catalepsy" in which the "state of torpor" continued for several days, during which the person afflicted took no food whatever. Such a feature would be consistent with Madeline Usher's "emaciated frame" upon her reappearance at the end of the tale. In brief, whatever substance there may have been to the fairly common reports during Poe's time of "*trances* in which patients have been supposed to be dead," there is no doubt that the belief in such trances was widespread and that those trances were "of the family of hysteria." Indeed, as the century advanced, papers on "Hysteria Simulating Death" appeared in reputable medical journals. When Roderick Usher, awaiting in dread the return of his buried sister, cries out in horror, "*We have put her living in the tomb!*" (Poe's italics), there is, then, medical reason to suppose that he may be taken at his word.

Of course the question remains as to whether Roderick knew that his sister was still alive at the time of burial. Given both medical and popular opinion on the matter, as well as the contributing effects of environment, of mental derangement, and of forebodings of death, it is not unreasonable to suppose that Roderick at first imagines his sister to be dead when he entombs her in the donjon-keep in a remote region of the family manor. Assuming that Madeline has suffered a particularly severe seizure of the type described above, it would have been difficult even for an expert to determine at once whether the victim were alive or dead. When the narrator views Madeline, it is in the darkness of the vault with only "half smothered" torches affording light and with "little opportunity for investigation." At that, the glances of the narrator and Roderick Usher "rested not long upon the dead." There seems little doubt that Poe means to suggest, even at this early juncture, the possibility that Madeline may still be alive. He reminds us at this point that hers was a malady "of a strictly cataleptical character" and proceeds to describe both "the mockery of a faint blush" and a "suspiciously lingering smile" upon her face. Even Madeline's physical appearance at the end of the tale, with the blood staining her white robe, may appertain here, for Spurzheim reported cases of catalepsy that had been cured by spontaneous hemorrhages. The bloodied robe may be taken as the sign of Madeline's momentary recovery from the seizure itself.

But though Poe implies that Madeline may still live, the degree to which Roderick suspects that his sister is alive at the time of the burial remains unknown. The likelihood persists that he is deceived by the apparent signs of death, but there is no way of proving conclusively that this is so. A more material point is the fact that *eventually* he believes that his sister still lives—yet fails to do anything about it. Within a few days of the burial, we are told, Roderick undergoes "an observable change," his utterance marked by "a tremulous quaver, as if of extreme terror." Even the rather slow-witted narrator perceives that Usher's "unceasingly agitated mind was labouring with some oppressive secret, to divulge which he struggled for the necessary courage." During periods of relative calm, Roderick gazes about him "for long hours, in an attitude of the profoundest attention, as if listening to some imaginary sound," the sound, presumably, of his sister struggling to free herself. Poe continues to drop broad hints until Roderick openly confesses to having detected his sister's movements in the coffin for many days past, although not, it should be added, to having known that she was alive at the initial moment of burial. The obvious question is, why does Roderick, upon learning the truth, make no attempt to rescue the one person in the world whose life he most despairs of losing? To understand his motive—for it is a motive and not merely an exaggerated case of fright—we must turn again to Roderick's malady, this time placing it in the wider medical perspective Poe provides.

There is evidence that Roderick suffers not only from hypochondriasis but from the related disorder of melancholia. The afflictions had long been tied to one another, probably because of their similar symptoms and mutually uncertain etiology. In the early nineteenth century, the terms "melancholy" and "spleen" were often assumed to be synonymous with "hypochondriasis." Even when the disorders were not seen as strictly alike, they were viewed as associative or causative. Benjamin Rush classified hypochondriasis and melancholia as differing grades "of the same morbid actions in the brain"; Spurzheim bracketed "hystery" and "hypochondry" (as well as dyspepsia) under the broader division of melancholia; and Crichton saw melancholy as frequently giving rise to and commingling with hypochondriasis. Poe uses the term "melancholy" twice in the course of his narrative. Once he applies it to Roderick in reference to the narrator's attempts to "alleviate the melancholy" of his friend, and again he uses it in reference to the house itself, along with its inhabitants, in the phrase, "the melancholy House of Usher," For his part, Roderick evinces symptoms and behavior clearly in accord with those of melancholia as it was then understood: he suffers from profound uneasiness; tends to avoid society and bodily exercise; and, conversely, seeks out solitude, quiet, and darkness, where he can spend long hours in brooding. In addition, he suffers from extreme distress, extravagant ideas of persecution, and innumerable imagined objects of terror—all of which were among the common symptoms of melancholia.

Poe's fusing of the hypochondriacal and melancholic disorders is, once again, medically correct. But the term "melancholy" gains added currency from its close association with suicide. In fact, Spurzheim declared that "the morbid inclination to suicide" was no less than "the same disease which is commonly called melancholy." Certainly Roderick Usher is inordinately embittered and demoralized by the prospect of his twin's impending demise. Madeline's death, he says with a "bitterness" the narrator "can never forget," will "leave him (him the hopeless and the frail) the last of the ancient race of the Usher." Roderick also speaks of Madeline's prostration with "inexpressible agitation." It is apparent that he believes himself about to be deserted by his beloved sister. Coupled with

his melancholic symptoms, there is a clear motive here for desiring his own death. Yet Roderick does not die at his own hands. Once again the medical literature helps to explain why. While some melancholics committed suicide, Spurzheim noted that most suicidal patients of this type were timorous and pusillanimous, and the German physician Johann Christian Heinroth observed that sufferers of melancholia, despite their tendency to self-destructiveness, usually do not commit suicide because of an attendant loss of will power. Roderick Usher appears to be exactly this sort of pusillanimous soul. Faced with the prospect of living alone, the melancholic Roderick wants desperately to join Madeline in death but lacks the will power to kill himself. The most that he can do, by burying his twin, is to act out the "promise" of his own death. By burying Madeline, Roderick symbolically terminates his own life.

Symbolically but not actually. In actuality Roderick continues to face the terrifying prospect of a life utterly alone. Yet Madeline's first stirrings in the coffin afford him a means of bringing his death wish to fruition. These means, as it turns out, are those of the madman, but then madness is nothing less than the cumulative effect of Roderick's maladies. Of course the suspicion of Roderick's madness is present throughout the tale and made explicit when the narrator says of Roderick, "At times, again, I was obliged to resolve all into the mere inexplicable vagaries of madness." But this suspicion, divorced from a medical context, constitutes little more than a crude device intended to enhance the narrative's emotional appeal. It is instead the virtual certainty of Roderick's insanity from a medical standpoint, the way that Poe's allusions to his hypochondriacal and melancholic character comprise mutually converging efforts to certify this insanity, that allows us to appreciate the full extent of Roderick's psychological disorganization and the bizarre logic behind his willingness to keep Madeline entombed.

> If the external effects of "The Fall of the House of Usher" remain largely a function of the tale's gothic extravagance, to a considerable extent its moral and imaginative substance is a function of its close ties to medical history."
>
> —*George R. Uba*

Just as hypochondriasis enjoyed a close association with melancholia in medical history, both maladies were consistently linked to insanity. Hypochondriasis and hysteria, for example, had long been seen either as possible preliminaries to insanity or as modifications of it. Benjamin Rush observed how hypochondriacs sometimes sought *relief* through madness; Thomas Upham, the American philosopher and psychologist (and a contemporary of Poe), removed hypochondriacal delusions from the realm of general misapprehensions and placed them in a category that we would recognize today as psychosis. Likewise, melancholia had a long history of association with insanity, dating at least from Hippocrates, who designated melancholia and mania as divisions of insanity, and continuing on through Spurzheim, who designated idiotism, mania, and melancholia as insanity's three common forms. Poe conveys the connection between melancholia and insanity through the device of Roderick Usher's poem, "The Haunted Palace," wherein the "Radiant palace," a metaphor for the sovereign reason, is "assailed" by "evil things in robes of sorrow." That is to say, reason is assaulted by the evil of madness ("a hideous throng") exteriorized in the form of melancholia ("robes of sorrow"). Other observations also pertain. Crichton might have been describing Roderick Usher himself in observing that the melancholic commonly grew more absent and silent and at the same time "wild and alarming in his looks" before succumbing finally to a "violently disordered state of the brain." In the same way, with the high attainment of his art, poetry, and music alternating with his episodes of despondency, Roderick is the classic example of the person of sensibility and genius who was thought to be particularly susceptible to the melancholic's fluctuations between "mental brilliancy and a state bordering on moody madness."

The fact that hypochondriasis and melancholia were aspects of or precursors to a more general derangement (what Rush called "general madness") and that Roderick Usher clearly falls victim to this latter disorder offers a clue to some of the tale's perplexities. Assuming, for example, that Madeline has also fallen victim to madness (her name alone implies that this is the case), the medical literature may "explain" how she manages to free herself despite the fact that her coffin lid was screwed down and the tomb secured. Poe may have been playing on the fact that one of the symptoms of insanity or madness was long believed to be an inconceivable strength. Spurzheim, for example, confirmed instances in which the "muscular energy" seemed "almost supernatural" and in which "the strongest bands yielded to the efforts of the maniac." Moreover, medical history points to the particular route to death that Roderick takes. His willingness to bury his sister alive or at least to keep her buried alive is not a function of malice or overtly murderous design but of a profound desire to die himself. Spurzheim noted that the propensity to commit suicide appeared under three basic modifications: actual suicide; murder of another (especially a relative), followed by suicide; and murder of another "in order to be put to death." Roderick's pusillanimous character rules out the first two alternatives. Recognizing his inability directly to terminate his own life, he in effect chooses the third, and in electing to keep his sister buried despite his belief that she still lives, commits, in the eyes of the law, a murder. Such linking of murder and suicide as a manifestation of insanity was well known in Poe's day. Crichton observed the connection between an insane person murdering "the one he is most fond of" and the primary "wish of putting a period to his own existence," a circumstance, he added, "too notorious to be denied."

This circuitous route to death offers certain advantages to the psychopath. For one thing, it allows for the fragment-ing of the self: Roderick purposely blurs the boundaries between his own identity and his sister's. By fragmenting the self in this way, the individual simultaneously abdicates all responsibility for being. Roderick joins himself to the tide of dissolution on which his sister is relentlessly conveyed. Paradoxically, by keeping her buried he denies the need to come to terms with the prospect of his own survival. Along with the fragmentation of the self, Roderick's means of achieving death allow him to abdicate all decision-making and assertive action. It was not uncommon, according to the medical literature, for "those who begin with destroying their relations or others" subsequently to "surrender themselves to justice, and request to be punished with death." While Roderick does not surrender to legal justice, he nevertheless courts retribution. That is, he takes advantage of his twin's condition to improve the possibility of his own death—by fright. Whether he knowingly or unknowingly buries his sister alive at the start, eventually he does all that he can do to increase the terror of his environment: he throws open the casement to the storm, swings his chair round to face the door of the chamber through which Madeline must pass, and generally does whatever he can to stoke his own deepest fears. Thus prepared, he becomes a perfectly passive vessel at the moment of Madeline's reappearance. The sister metes out justice, the brother receives it willingly. With a minimum of assertive action on his part, Roderick is borne to death, "a victim to the terrors he had anticipated."

In setting up his own death, the mad Roderick not only ends the threat of solitary existence but also the nightmare of inherited history. As D. H. Lawrence once suggested in regard to the tale, this nightmare or family curse is incest. Certainly the tale makes it easy to suspect an unnatural relationship between the two Ushers. As Roderick grieves, for example, over his "tenderly beloved sister—his sole companion for long years," the narrator perceives how "a far more than ordinary wanness had overspread the emaciated fingers through which trickled many passionate tears." And as the tale climaxes, we are told that Madeline, "with a low moaning cry, fell heavily inward upon the person of her brother." In this latter case, the sexual component seems unmistakable.

And yet seen in this light, the incest motif tells us remarkably little. We do not know, for example, whether the incest has been previously consummated—or not. We do not know whether the impulse is cause or effect of the Ushers' maladies, or what, if any, relationship it bears to primordial sin. However, an understanding of the medical history of hysteria lends insight into each of these matters while confirming that incestuous desire is at the source of the Ushers' relationship. Throughout most of medical history, hysteria was linked to sexuality, and starting with Galen was expressly tied to enforced sexual abstinence. The ancients regarded the uterus as a virtually independent organism or "animal" that might become displaced, at times literally ascending in the body and causing emotional instability and other symptoms of hysteria. Galen refuted the notion of uterine displacement, maintaining that the female's retention of a secretion analogous to the male's semen was the primary cause of hysteria and that males who retained their semen could suffer from a companion disorder. Despite their differences, both the ancients and Galen were in implicit agreement that a resumption of sexual relations was therapeutic. Around the early seventeenth century, the term "vapours" originated in reference to the emanations from a disordered uterus that were now presumed to ascend through the body. Subsequently the term "vapours" became synonymous with hysteria itself (significantly, it is a "vapour" that surrounds the Ushers' house and has "reeked up"). By the end of the eighteenth century the eminent French psychiatrist Philippe Pinel, working on the basis of empirical observations, reaffirmed the connection between hysteria and sexual abstinence. And during the nineteenth century the repression of sexuality and of erotic desire as an etiological agent in hysteria continued to receive medical support. The notable interregnum occurred during the Middle Ages, when all organic disease was seen as a manifestation of innate evil, consequent upon original sin. Since during this period a new distinction also arose between physical union for the purpose of procreation and union for the unholy purpose of carnal gratification, the therapeutic value of sexual activity was of course sharply challenged. Particularly in the case of hysteria—for many people the visible token of bewitchment—both the means and ends of medical treatment were called into question.

Poe conjoins these two views—one tracing its lineage back to antiquity, the other to the Middle Ages—through the motif of incest. Early on in the tale we learn that "the entire family lay in the direct line of descent, and had always, with very trifling and very temporary variation, so lain." This "deficiency . . . of collateral issue" violates probability and hints at a pattern of repressed sexuality. In particular, Madeline's hysteria, coupled with her singular attraction for her brother, implies an unrealized sexual desire. A pattern of such unauthorized desire would be consistent with the family's curious genealogical development and would, in its presumed realization at some earlier period, account for Roderick's hereditary madness. The point here, though, is that Roderick and Madeline have attempted to breach this pattern of family incest. The medical evidence strongly suggests that the Ushers have not consummated their incestuous desires; on the contrary, they have abstained from sexual activity. In the process, Madeline has succumbed to hysteria, the ailment of sexual abstention, and Roderick to hypochondriasis, the male's counterpart to hysteria. The Ushers' maladies, in short, are the product of a refusal. Nevertheless, the illicit desire remains so strong that the Ushers finally do achieve the equivalent of sexual consummation when at last it is safe to do so, as Madeline's "violent and now final death-agonies, bore him to the floor a corpse." Such a dark impulse, so malign and ineradicable, serves the same function as disease itself did in the Middle Ages: it is the signature of innate depravity in a world otherwise suffused with inexplicable suffering and doom. It is the dark fate that Roderick Usher hints at when he refers the narrator to the "terrible influence which for centuries had moulded the destinies of his family, and which made *him* . . . what he was" (Poe's italics). It is the fate signified too by the house, with its "atmosphere which had no affinity with the air of heaven" and with its apocalyptic "fall." Where sexual abstinence constitutes the organic cause of the Ushers' maladies, human sinfulness constitutes the moral counterpart.

An understanding of medical history sheds valuable light on Poe's famous tale of the doomed Ushers. It helps in identifying the Ushers' maladies and in providing a medical basis for supposing that Madeline is indeed buried alive. A full understanding of Roderick's disorders helps account for his curious willingness to leave his still-living sister entombed, while a knowledge of the history of hysteria helps locate the Ushers' mutual doom in a pattern of incest, itself a token of a darker fatality to which all mankind is heir. If the external effects of **"The Fall of the House of Usher"** remain largely a function of the tale's gothic extravagance, to a considerable extent its moral and imaginative substance is a function of its close ties to medical history.

Mark Kinkead-Weekes (essay date 1987)

SOURCE: "Reflections On, and In, 'The Fall of the House of Usher'," in *Edgar Allan Poe: The Design of Order*, edited by A. Robert Lee, Vision Press Ltd., 1987, pp. 17-34.

[*Kinkead-Weekes is a South-African born English educator and critic. In the following essay, he focuses on the reliability of the narrator in "The Fall of the House of Usher."*]

What is immediately impressive about **'The Fall of the House of Usher'** is the care with which it sets out to establish the kind of reader it requires. As opposed, it turns out, to Coleridge's notion of an aeolian lute, which resounds to every capricious gust of feeling or idea, there is to be scruple and discrimination, a challenge to put imagination, and feeling, and critical intelligence to work, in controlled harmony. The mode then is not merely Gothick, but rather a 'Gothick' which at every turn signals a consciousness of its own operation, its own language and vision. From the outset we have before us, too, a narrator we must both respond to, and carefully watch responding:

> During the whole of a dull, dark, and soundless day in the autumn of the year, when the clouds hung oppressively low in the heavens, I had been passing alone, on horseback, through a singularly dreary tract of country, and at length found myself, as the shades of the evening drew on, within view of the melancholy House of Usher. I know not how it was—but with the first glimpse of the building, a sense of insufferable gloom pervaded my spirit.

This could be the opening script for a thousand 'horror' stories and films: the adjectival atmospherics, the *compositio loci* as the titles come up, the dreary landscape, the gathering darkness, the melancholy house, the lonely horseman, the preternatural feeling of gloom.

But just as the sense of something worked-up becomes conscious, becomes overdone with the word 'insufferable'—we are made aware of it as a word through a scruple, made to stand back and *look,* at both the Gothick and the motives of its audience. In other words, Poe keeps a controlling distance on what the opening paragraph terms 'that half-pleasurable, because poetic, sentiment with which the mind usually receives even the sternest natural images of the desolate or terrible'; this story will be no mere sensationalist exercise in 'horror'. Still less are we offered that darker romanticism which seeks in hallucination or drug some goading or torturing of the imagination into the sublime—but rather something more like the aftermath of that: the hideous awakening from illusion into sick depression and hangover, so that everyday reality seems poisoned and bitter. The narrator is both suspect and comes through. If there is a touch of 'romantick' or even decadent expertise, of one who has known the pull of the Gothick theatre and the opium den, nevertheless the outcome is a clearing away, from what we are to attend to, of those self-pleasing but necessarily falsifying and even sickening kinds of veil. We can hope for good Poe when the temptations to what can be bad in him are so clearly renounced.

From beginning to end in **'The Fall of the House of Usher'** Poe requires of us a peculiarly double kind of reading response, at once attuned to the depressive qualities of the story, yet aware that we are being asked to think and to feel more than simply 'sensation'. That double note can be felt simply in looking

> upon the mere house, and the simple landscape features of the domain—upon the bleak walls—upon the vacant eye-like windows—upon a few rank sedges—and upon a few white trunks of decayed trees—.

Something is there, both in and behind the detail of the passage, a horror certainly but a horror conscious of its own effect, its own elusive power. Something. . . .

'What was it—I paused to think—what was it that so unnerved me . . . ?' Again the narrator anticipates by a split second the thoughtful (not Gothick) reader; but only to discover that rational 'analysis' cannot explain the strange 'power' of that 'combination of very simple natural objects'. Indeed it is that inability that can cause 'shadowy fancies' to accompany the realization of being out of one's depth. But just as there was a challenge to a different quality of imagination from the falsely 'romantick', so now the narrator tries a different kind of 'thought': contemplation, or more exactly, *reflection.* This shares with 'analysis' (i.e. taking to pieces) a kind of objectivity, an ability to stand outside an experience to see whether by deliberately rearranging its elements and shifting perspective, the experience can be made clearer. But this 'reflection' is unlike analysis in that it seeks not to dissect or explain but to re-cognize, seeing again but more whole, because mirrored against greater and darker depth. The lake suggests the bowl of the mind, in which reality can be not only reflected but reflected on, in a medium whose depth is not merely rational but holds darker and even

ominous fathoms of consciousness below the surface, giving deeper focus to the image on the retina. In such reflection (it seems) imagination can join mind and what we now call the subconscious, in a wholeness of cognition.

The immediate effect however is to increase disturbance. In the dark medium the reflection of sedge and trees has become greyer and more 'ghastly', though still without explanation. It is nevertheless clearer. About now, if not before, the nature of what was caught in the original seeing and the inverted image ought to be graspable. Was it not an intimation of something deathly?—because what is in itself merely bleak and vacant, inorganic, becomes deathly if you see it as what has happened to a face and eyes?—and what is organic, still growing, is even more deathly if you see it as rank grey or ghastly white like mortifying flesh and bone? What we glimpsed was no mere seasonal decay, but death-in-life or living deathliness, further confirmed and increased by the sense of life inverted, perceived in reflection, though not yet articulated by more than a shudder.

Then, through a process of association, the narrator's mind produces the further fathoming for his reflection to work more fully: the intuition of the connection between his response to the scene before him, and what he has learned of the state of Roderick Usher, disordered in body, nerves and mind, inheritor of a whole process of dynastic life and growth now withering into a last death-in-life—the connection between the 'family', its last representative, and the 'house', that is implicit in the name the locals have given it. So that, returning to his 'reflection', the narrator not only feels his apprehension heightened to a kind of terror, but is able to pin down more precisely three of its causes. He is frightened that he is about to encounter, indeed is already encountering in the House of Usher, an atmosphere not only deathly but infectious; a disintegration already almost complete beneath what still feels whole; and worst of all, that he himself may be already implicated in that infection and disintegration, entering the House. The atmosphere peculiar to the family mansion, and almost palpable like a miasma reeking up, is not merely death-in-life but 'pestilent', and evil, with 'no affinity with the air of heaven'. The extraordinary combination of total decay ('Minute fungi overspread the whole exterior') with still 'perfect adaptation of parts', becomes threatening with the discovery of the 'barely perceptible fissure', which can nevertheless be seen to run from top to bottom and into the tarn below the surface. The concealed threat of the comparison with 'the specious totality of old woodwork which has rotted for long years in some neglected vault, with no disturbance from the breath of the external air' is that the first breath of air from outside will bring instant disintegration—and there is the narrator entering. But most sinister of all is the possibility that it may not, after all, be a matter of the outsider risking infection or introducing an alien element.

For the House of Usher seems terribly *familiar,* a world he is used to, as well as producing unfamiliar and frightening fancies. If what seems living can be deathly, and what seems whole be about to disintegrate, might this not be true of the narrator?—it is his mind, after all, that is mirrored in the tarn. There is another but also possible irony in the evil physician he meets on the stair; for the narrator, too, purports to be coming to heal. Yet his scruple and capacity for self-examination do seem reassuring; this man who keeps accusing himself of childishness, superstition, fancy, dream, surely shows a sane mind and a good heart as well as imagination and intuition? But it is also true that, having renounced false forms of imagination and feeling, his language keeps trembling near the brink of indulgence in them; the tarn in which his reflection is mediated is 'lurid' as well as deep, and may be poisoned. And most disturbing of all is his own sense of disturbance, and of recognition, much exceeding ours—suggesting that he does feel peculiarly implicated and threatened, as though he somehow belonged to the 'House' and the 'Family', as more than just a childhood friend. We cannot tell yet how to feel, but one thing is more and more certain: the questioning or response is not only continuous, but increasing.

However, our introduction to Roderick Usher (though of course we see him only through the narrator) begins to clarify the difference between them. He is the protagonist of the Gothick/Romantick which the story began by distancing: at the centre of its 'intricate' passageways; its dark spaces and recesses beyond inspection; its in-turned enclosure; its 'encrimsoned light' from windows not meant to see out of, but rather to transform the daylight artificially into a richer atmosphere of inner sensation. Indeed Roderick is the *artist* in these modes, the culmination of a long line—but both the narrator and Usher himself proceed to clarify what that development of imagination and sensibility may cost, in the loss of vitality and the reduction of fully human being:

> Many books and musical instruments lay scattered about, but failed to give any vitality to the scene. I felt that I breathed an atmosphere of sorrow. An air of stern, deep, and irredeemable gloom hung over and pervaded all.

We soon discover why. The one-sided development of that kind of artist clearly involves a loss of physical vitality, indeed an atrophy of the body, so that the narrator can hardly recognize the 'wan being' Usher has become. Intuitions about the House are reinforced and diagnosed in the impressions made by its owner. His extraordinary luminous eyes may seem very different from the vacancy of the house-face (though we have just had a hint of how they might look from outside in the daylight) but the 'cadaverous complexion' and hair 'of a more than web-like softness and tenuity', floating about the high temples—everybody remarks on the resemblance to Poe himself—also irresistibly and horribly remind one of the previous sense of grey substance and floating fungoid growth, living but corpse-like, a death-in-life now located in the poet and musician as well as in his House. Moreover the delicate mouldings of lip and nostril, bespeaking beauty and sensibility, are at odds with the lack of moral energy betrayed by the chin. The cost of lustrous eye and Arabesque expression is a radical splitting of 'simple human-

ity': a deep division of personality betrayed by inconsistency and incoherence of behaviour, attitude, voice. Roderick's 'cordiality' is both 'overdone' and sincere; he both deeply needs and deeply rejects human contact and relation:

> His action was alternately vivacious and sullen. His voice varied rapidly from a tremulous indecision (when the animal spirits seemed utterly in abeyance) to that species of energetic concision . . . which may be observed in the lost drunkard, or the irreclaimable eater of opium, during the periods of his most intense excitement.

Apathetic hangover and drugged excitement appear again—and it becomes clear that it is the willed and unnatural over-development of the senses in the artist that has caused his 'malady'. As his capacity for sensation has become more acute, it has also become not only 'unnatural' but 'morbid'. Alexander Pope imagined how a more-than-human sense of smell might become fatal, so that one might 'die of a rose in aromatic pain'. In Usher the artist's over-developed senses have indeed made him helplessly vulnerable—like the lute which cannot help resounding—to all their objects in the sensible world, so that, in self-preservation:

> the most insipid food was alone endurable; he could wear only garments of certain texture; the odours of all flowers were oppressive; his eyes were tortured by even a faint light; and there were but peculiar sounds, and these from stringed instruments, which did not inspire him with horror.

Moreover, the over-development not only defeats itself, but strikes Usher as certain to be fatal. The trembling nervous agitation, which had seemed partly excitement at communicating himself to his friend, reveals itself more deeply as terror: terror of *anything* 'other', not in itself, but in its deadly impact on his own excitability, so that responsiveness has become the risk of self-annihilation.

> I shudder at the thought of any, even the most trivial, incident, which may operate upon this intolerable agitation of soul. . . . I feel that the period will sooner or later arrive when I must abandon life and reason together, in some struggle with the grim phantasm, FEAR.

Still worse, it is dawning on Usher, in the guise of 'superstitious impressions' about the influence of the 'mere form and substance' of the grey house and dim tarn upon him, that things which seem merely in the dimension of '*physique*' (of the body) can actually affect the '*morale*' of existence (of the soul). He has begun to suspect that the Gothick/Romantick habitation, 'by dint of long sufferance' of its influence, may not only have produced physical deterioration, morbid over-sensitivity, and nervous agitation, but an effect upon his spiritual being.

And finally in this catalogue of gloom—confessed with the greatest hesitation—is the dying of his 'tenderly beloved sister' which will leave him the last of the Ushers—the most 'natural' and 'palpable' sorrow of all, as it seems.

At this point the narrator seems wholly vindicated. His first intuitions have been confirmed, not only by what he finds in Roderick Usher, but also by what Usher himself has made explicit. And however he may have been familiar with and even tempted by Usher's world in the past, his perception of its disastrous consequences is now clear, and keeps him clear of it. But just here we find a paradox. At the moment of the reader's greatest confidence in the narrator's power of 'reflection', he suddenly produces a wholly inexplicable response, as never before. As the Lady Madeline

> passed slowly through a remote portion of the apart-ment, and without having noticed my presence, dis-appeared. . . . I regarded her with an utter aston-ishment not unmingled with dread; and yet I found it impossible to account for such feelings. A sensation of stupor oppressed me, as my eyes followed her retreating steps.

There is some kind of intuition at work; but why 'dread'? and 'stupor'? Moreover the strangeness of response is immediately followed by a mystery of event; and one which recalls the previous suspicion about the possible effect of the narrator's intrusion into the House of Usher. 'Post hoc' may not be 'propter hoc', but on the very evening of his arrival the Lady Madeline takes finally to her bed. 'For several days ensuing, her name was unmentioned by either Usher or myself'—which seems highly peculiar, from both sides. Again, why? Before we know where we are, the news comes 'abruptly' that she is dead . . . but even before that, the mystery has deepened by our sense, along with the narrator, that the blackness which 'pours' like a fountain from Roderick Usher must spring from some source darker than we have yet fathomed. For:

> as a closer and still closer intimacy admitted me more unreservedly into the recesses of his spirit, the more bitterly did I perceive the futility of all attempt at cheering a mind from which darkness, as if an inherent positive quality, poured forth upon all objects of the moral and physical universe in one unceasing radiation of gloom.

There is no explanation. Just as we determine that we can trust the narrator, we are left to ourselves.

Or rather, we are given Roderick Usher's *art* as our clue to the deeper source of such darkness. The narrator imparts only vague suggestiveness: 'An excited and highly distempered ideality threw a sulphureous lustre over all'—'a certain singular perversion and amplification of the wild air'—'vaguenesses at which I shuddered the more thrillingly, because I shuddered knowing not why'—'there arose out of the pure abstractions . . . an intensity of intolerable awe, no shadow of which felt I ever yet in the contemplation of the certainly glowing yet too concrete reveries of Fuseli'. He is obviously out of his depth; both his language and in the last instance his syntax have gone soggy. He clearly intuits something 'distempered', 'sulphureous',

'perverted' and shudderingly awful behind what he insists is ideal and abstract—the adjectives are very telling when one looks. But he is clearly unable to pin down what that *is*. Or perhaps he is subconsciously unwilling to do so, feeling that vagueness is safety and preserves the glow; the remark about Fuseli being too concrete may be significant.

It is all the more striking after this that Roderick's poem and his picture should be so specfic; even, in what the narrator admits is 'the nakedness of their designs', an exposure, demanding interpretation. The poem is only superficially disguised in allegory and very quickly unlocks itself into explicitness, as soon as one recognizes that once again the 'building' is a way of bodying forth the inner nature of the human being within. It is a confession of the inner corruption and perversion of a human being. We first see the 'Haunted Palace' in its Eden-state, a green and fertile valley, a fair palace-of-man where, because 'the monarch Thought' is on the throne, there is also always spiritual power and protection, radiant light, golden movement and liveliness, sweet fragrance. How different from the dreary country, the ruined and fissured house, the most ungolden fungoid-hair, the reeking pestilential tarn where the Artist of Sensation has ruled! The contrast is further underlined in terms both of consciousness and the art that springs from it. Here the 'luminous windows' of the eyes are clear and open to the day, and one can see into an interior behind them where spiritual energies move musically to 'a lute's well-tuned law'—as opposed to the automatism of the aeolian lute resounding to every impetus of sensation. Where Mind/Spirit, born to the purple, rules, the song that comes through the pearl and ruby of the mouth is both an everflowing of 'surpassing beauty' and also specifically a celebration of wit and wisdom. (We are to imagine Usher's song, conversely, as performed with 'fervid facility' and, in the notes of accompaniment, as a 'wild fantasia'.) But in the Haunted Palace the monarch has been overthrown and is dead, the old times are 'entombed', and the palace has been transformed to the House of Usher. There, in the final stanza, are the 'red-litten' windows of Roderick's Gothick habitation, eyes still luminous, but behind which portentous fantasies spring in discordant melody; there, the 'ghastly' spate of speech and hysteria of the man close to mental and nervous breakdown. The narrator cannot but recognize 'in the under or mystic current of its meaning . . . a full consciousness on the part of Usher of the tottering of his lofty reason upon her throne'. The diagnosis of Usher's malady has come a step further; the hypertrophy of the senses comes about *through* atrophy of the High Reason (which includes both the rational and the spiritual), so that there has not only been a splitting apart of faculties which belong in harmony when the hierarchy is right, but an overthrow of the highest part of the self followed by its death and burial. But what the narrator fails to recognize is that Usher is exposing his awareness, not only of mental breakdown and the growth of sorrow, but of having given domination to *evil* things in sorrow's garb, a 'hideous throng'. That apprehension has been touched on once or twice, but it is becoming more and more explicit; we have to attend to more than physical and nervous breakdown, more than mental breakdown, to the growth of something redder-litten in the Red-man of Usher, something infernal. Moreover, as the Romantic is always aware that the human being creates, or at least partly creates the world, so that 'sentience' flows between him and a living rather than inorganic universe, so Usher has come to believe that his line of development has indeed created in their House—which we can now define as Gothick/Romantick art—an almost palpable 'atmosphere' of artifice and reflection which has an 'importunate and terrible influence' on any inhabitant. The 'darkness' we have to see into is blacker than mere sorrow.

We are yet however to seek for the nature of what (to use the words the narrator is unwilling to follow up) might be 'sulphureous', or 'perverted'. What could have filled him with such stupefying dread that he will not even make enquiries? Suddenly we are reminded of his strange response to the Lady Madeline . . . and then discover that we too know more than we thought we knew, when we confront her brother's picture. For if we once imagine that the picture might be 'about' the relation of the brother with the sister, it becomes far from 'phantasmagoric' let alone 'abstract'. We already know that Roderick and Madeline are the last representatives of a family which had for generations no 'collateral' branches; that is, had only the most minimal relations and connections with other people. This chimes with Roderick's terror of anything 'other': a terror both physical and psychological which would be bound to affect the possibility of any relationship, unless with someone who felt least 'other'. If it is something 'perverted' we are looking for, the possibility exists in the ambiguity of 'his only *relative*'.

We turn to the picture to guess at the resonances of the 'vault or tunnel', the smooth whiteness, the intense light, which have no access to the outside world but are buried far underground. The suggestions are (are they not?) of intense possessiveness or even imprisonment, and of intense secrecy or repression; and it seems to be the enclosure that makes the light, so intense and splendid in itself, seem 'ghastly and inappropriate'. (The vault or tunnel may also be a sex-symbol—though that might be Freudian stock-response, and 'rectangular' is discouraging!)

But as the word 'incest' forms as a possibility in one's mind, it would be as well to be careful, since the most interesting part of the chain of deduction is the psychological explanation rather than any Gothick sexual frisson. And we have established nothing about the Lady Madeline herself, or *her* malady. The only clue to the nature of the Lady is her name—but fortunately that says a great deal. For if Usher represents an overdevelopment of the senses at the expense of High Reason and Spirit, the Magdalen who lies behind all forms of the name is the archetype of the refining of the fleshly into saintliness—she is, although of the same flesh as her brother, the opposite kind of development. (It should be no surprise to learn, a page or two later, that they 'had been twins, and that sympathies of a scarcely intelligible nature had always existed between them'.) If we think of the story as monodrama like the poem in it—as it seems increasingly

useful to do—we could see them as the twin dimensions of human being which require to be harmonized in the Fair Palace of an integrated personality. But then, incest really is a perverter of the psyche and the soul, since, far from the higher faculty being enthroned, far even from its otherness being respected, it is usurped, possessed, pent in and submerged, kept from relating to the world or even existing in its own light, and made complicit in Usher's own sensationalism. The Magdalen, too, might be made mad-line.

We begin to sense what the effect on the Lady might be, and catch the resonances of first 'apathy', and then 'catalepsy'. But this is to bring out a second 'horror' metaphor: the vampire, who bleeds his victim's life-blood away until she becomes passive, devitalized, paralysed, and dies. If the narrator, who is sensitive to the Gothick, intuited anything remotely of this nature from the apparition of the lady and its effect on Usher, it is hardly surprising that he—who betrays a distant resemblance to the House of Usher and a familiarity with their kind of habitation—should dread and repress what he will not dare to think. Only (one repeats) the point is not to create Gothick frisson, but to diagnose the evil that its one-sided development has brought about by deranging the psyche of its habitués, and the art which it produces. Since the story clearly is about a kind of art, its protagonists can be seen as three dimensions of an artist's self-inquisition, in order to grasp its consequences. The narrator will be the daylight self, but still attached to the others below the surface, and likely to repress knowledge of what they have been up to, that is 'insufferable'.

> **From beginning to end in 'The Fall of the House of Usher' Poe requires of us a peculiarly double kind of reading response, at once attuned to the depressive qualities of the story, yet aware that we are being asked to think and to feel more than simply 'sensation'.**
>
> —*Mark Kinkead-Weekes*

All this of course is sheer speculation as one reads—the evidence is only what fits with the details that have gone before. As the story now goes on, with the abrupt news of the Lady's death and the plan to entomb her in the dungeon (which the narrator readily accepts, to guard against the sinister doctor who might try to dig her up and conduct an investigation), the only thing that will perhaps strike every reader is the uneasy reminiscence of the vault in the cellarage to the vault in the picture, though this one is far more confined and there is no light in it whatever. The body of the Lady also creates disquiet because of 'the mockery of a faint blush upon the bosom and the face' but especially because of the 'suspiciously lingering smile upon the lip which is so terrible in death'. It is appropriate enough to her character, since the final mark of the Fair

Palace is that its 'pale door' should 'smile'; but it is not at all appropriate in what is supposed to be dead, and being buried.

Moreover the effect of the death and burial on Usher is disastrous. The luminousness in his eyes, which seemed the one compensation for the bodily decay and the incipient nervous and mental breakdown, goes out altogether. The division in the self seems to have disappeared, but only because he is possessed altogether by an even more extreme terror than before. He seems 'labouring with some oppressive secret', or like a madman 'gazing upon vacancy for long hours, in an attitude of the profoundest attention, as if listening to some imaginary sound'. The narrator begins to feel 'infected'. 'I felt creeping upon me, by slow yet certain degrees, the wild influences of his own fantastic yet impressive superstitions.' Then suddenly we are plunged into the full Gothick experience: the sleepless night, the gloomy furniture, the tattered draperies swaying fitfully in the draught, a tempest brewing outside, the awakening—with uncontrollable and inexplicable shuddering—to mysterious sounds in the intervals of the storm. After being held at a distance for so long, the full Gothick flesh-creeping seems to have taken over, with the narrator leading the required response, as the door opens to reveal the Gothick protagonist in a state of 'restrained *hysteria*'. (Usher himself of course had predicted a 'species of mad hilarity' as the end of the process described in his poem.) As he now throws open the window to the storm, it is clearly a reflection of the inner tumult now reaching its climacteric, and an admission of both its beauty and its terror. If it images a psychological state, the significant feature would seem to be that the densely oppressive cloud-cover is now being visibly disintegrated by 'frequent and violent alterations in the direction of the wind' to produce a contention in which, with 'life-like velocity' the warring energies 'flew careering from all points against each other, without passing away into the distance'. Not only can the clouds no longer 'prevent our perceiving', but the 'under surfaces' of the issueless war are 'glowing in the unnatural light of a faintly luminous and distinctly visible gaseous exhalation which hung about and enshrouded the mansion'—an electric manifestation of what one might call spiritual energy turned lurid. The whole universe seems to be at war, and Roderick Usher, throwing the window open, seems to insist on the correspondence of 'outside' with 'inside'.

But the narrator will have none of this. He tries to insist that the storm is a merely physical phenomenon with natural causes, or at worst the result of miasmas from the tarn; and that 'You must not—you shall not behold this.' The daylight self, shuddering, insists that the cover-up continue. He even thinks that a milder form of romantic experience could be useful therapy; and reads from the 'Mad Trist' of Sir Launcelot Canning in the 'vague hope' that, however little its 'uncouth and unimaginative prolixity' may interest 'the lofty and spiritual ideality' of his friend, it may act as a kind of inoculation, a mild dose of the disease of folly, to calm his fevered excitement.

Now there is an entirely new note; and critics who find the 'Mad Trist' a lapse in what they take to be a truly Gothic

offering, tend to miss both its meaning and its comedy. For this is the point at which the attentive reader passes decisively beyond the narrator's limitations, indeed begins to convict him of short-sighted complacency. He failed before, by not daring to enquire about the Lady Madeline and Usher's art; but now a blind optimism makes his self-assurance comic, though we only see this fully on a second reading. For the 'Mad Trist' is just what its title suggests, a crazy trust or confidence misplaced. Its kind of Gothick depends on the belief that the knight-errant can safely engage with the powers of evil and come off, magic-shielded and victorious, rescuing the Maiden of Innocence in the end. Sir Launcelot is a secular author, not Sir Galahad or even Sir Perceval. Waxing doughty on wine—the note of self-intoxication again—his errant knight does not bother to come to any understanding with the 'obstinate and maliceful' reclusiveness that imprisons the Lady, but with sturdy confidence merely breaks the door down. He is just as confident in dealing with the evil dragon that takes the hermit's place, guarding the treasures and the Maiden—again he bluffly knocks it on the head.

Is there not a parallel with the assurance of the narrator that he can open up, control, and cure, the House of Usher and its owner, and his refusal, now, to heed the sinister warning echoes which accompany each stage of Sir Launcelot's story? He feels superior to its 'uncouth and unimaginative prolixity'—but he exactly shares and mirrors it. He fails altogether to identify the hermit, and the dragon, because he persists in a fiction of Usher's 'lofty spirituality' against all the evidence: the poem, the picture, the self-diagnosis, and the hysterical affinity with the dark tempest. But insofar as he does recognize something of his friend's 'mental disorder' (though he persists in trying to think it 'hypochondriac') he has Sir Launcelot's utterly misplaced belief in his ability (with 'gentle violence') to control, shield, and cure it. He is, and has been, blundering into a situation he does not in the least understand; unaware especially how each move makes things worse, as the dragon is worse than the hermit, and the next manifestation will be more dangerous still. When one re-reads, there will be a grotesque comedy of complacency in the language—as against the sinister echoes which comment on each phase of the 'Mad Trist' and its reading of the situation. Of the first sinister sound of breaking open in the House of Usher he remarks:

> It was, beyond doubt, the coincidence alone which had arrested my attention . . . the sound, in itself, had nothing, surely, which should have interested or disturbed me. [There is no question mark.] I continued the story. . . .

After the 'most unusual screaming or grating sound' he congratulates himself that he

> retained sufficient presence of mind to avoid exciting, by any observation, the sensitive nervousness of my companion. I was by no means certain that he had noticed the sounds in question; although, assuredly, a strange alteration had, during the last few minutes, taken place in his demeanour. . . .

In fact the utter fear of Usher, the turning of his whole body to face the door, the hysterical rocking, betoken somebody in the last extremity of terror; but simply do not register with the voice that can say 'I knew he was not asleep', or describe the agonized rocking as 'a gentle yet constant and uniform sway'.

Moreover the narrator, and Sir Launcelot, have also quite mistaken the nature of the 'shield'. Far from enabling anybody to rescue the Lady Soul from enchantment, the dropping of the shield is the falling of the last scale of protection from *their* eyes, to reveal a condition unrescuable and incurable, a psychological disaster reaching its inevitable end in total destruction. Far from rescuing the Maiden, it is necessary to recognize that she has been dangerously, fatally transmuted, and for ever.

Now the secret comes out, in the 'distinct, hollow, metallic and clangorous, yet apparently muffled, reverberation' which cannot be ignored, and the gibbering confession which accompanies the Lady's approach up the stairs and into the open.

> Ethelred—ha! ha!—the breaking of the hermit's door, and the death-cry of the dragon, and the clangour of the shield!—say, rather, the rending of her coffin, and the grating of the iron hinges of her prison, and her struggles within the coppered archway of the vault! Oh whither shall I fly?

What followed incest and vampirism was attempted murder. The coming of the narrator (we may deduce) so greatly increased Roderick Usher's anxiety—partly desiring cure, but mostly terrified of exposure—that he hastened, on the Lady's latest catalepsy, to bury her, alive. Both his poem (about not only the overthrow but the evil death of the monarch) and his picture (imagining the means) show some premediation and awareness of how repression could become final burial. His confession, now, proves that even if he only subconsciously knew what he was doing at the time, he knew beyond question soon afterwards and did nothing. And now:

> Have I not heard her footstep on the stair? Do I not distinguish that heavy and horrible beating of her heart? . . . 'MADMAN! I TELL YOU THAT SHE NOW STANDS WITHOUT THE DOOR!'

It is not quite clear whether 'Madman' is addressed to himself or to the narrator, but it does not matter, it will do very well for both (especially if both are sides of the same person). Usher's madness is beyond question. The narrator's consisted in imagining that he could control or cure such disintegration: of relationship on one level; or on the other, monodramatically, such preying on one side of the psyche by another, with the inevitable reaction. In case one had forgotten . . . the last result of vampirism is the creation of another vampire. The red one has tried to devitalize, paralyse, bury the white one—and there she stands now, with 'blood upon her white robes', in a doorway that opens like jaws. As she falls 'heavily inward upon the person of her brother, and in her violent and now

final death-agonies, bore him to the floor a corpse . . .', we watch the inevitably destructive reaction of that which has been buried alive against its repressor; an appalling parody of the sexual act by what had been the saintly Lady; and the ineluctable movement back into unity of that which had been split. (As Poe was to write in *Eureka* a decade later, 'in the original unity of the first thing lies the secondary cause of all things, with the germ of their inevitable annihilation'—though here the splitting of the soul has been so unnaturally violent that the return to unity is correspondingly appalling.)

There can be no cure or compromise as death-in-life completes itself—only the narrator's headlong flight in self-preservation. As he crosses the causeway his final glimpse of the Fall of the House of Usher exactly images how, after such splitting, unity can only be regained in annihilation. As the zig-zag fissuring opens wider and wider, the radiance that comes through and sheds its 'wild light' along the narrator's path is that of a blood-red and setting moon: red-and-white in a moment of fusion but at the price of annihilation. The House disintegrates and the deep tarn closes over its fragments—the last 'reflection', the last conscious act of the narrator precipitately fleeing back to his daylight world, is to cover a ruinous process in unconsciousness.

But because Poe is so much more than the narrator and the actors (those sides of himself who play out his deliberate nightmare of disintegration), it is possible for the reader to become more fully *conscious*—so as neither to evade, nor to succumb to, the Fall of the House of Usher. The story itself tells us how to read it: not as an indulgence in the Gothick, but as an imaginatively critical exploration into the implications, the fascinations, and the price of the Gothick artist's over-development of imaginative sensationalism at the expense of body, thought and spirit. Poe was fascinated by the genre, and its exaggeration of certain aspects of 'the romantic poet' offered a persona that clearly had its appeal. But what is the real distinction of this story above all his stories, is the capacity for self-scrutiny with which he set out both to explore, and to understand and criticize, that appeal, to grasp what was deathly and dehumanizing in it through admitting, but also examining, its fascination. I can think of no story which offers its author, its narrator, or its reader more opportunity for Gothick indulgence and frisson. But it is not only meticulously made, so that every detail counts, but also, and on a much deeper level, it has real psychological penetration. I take it that it is the House of *Usher* because it is also a prophecy, of what uncritical indulgence in that kind of imaginative over-development would usher in, and cost. Here (as not always in Poe or his critics) it is clear that art must be more than a sounding-board for gusts of 'feeling' or 'idea' masquerading as inspiration; must make more intelligent, aware, and more deeply humane and spiritual music than [that in Coleridge's, 'Dejection: Anode']:

> The dull sobbing draft, that moans and rakes
> Upon the strings of this Aeolian lute,
> Which better far were mute.

And the artist needs to be intelligent and self-critical too; able to peer into the abyss of his own psyche, but also to build a Coleridgean Fair Palace, not merely a haunted one.

Leila S. May   (essay date 1993)

SOURCE: "'Sympathies of a Scarcely Intelligible Nature': The Brother-Sister Bond in Poe's 'Fall of the House of Usher'," in *Studies in Short Fiction,* Vol. 30, No. 3, Summer, 1993, pp. 387-96.

[*In the following essay, May undertakes a feminist analysis of the relationship between Madeline and Roderick Usher, and its implications in Victorian society.*]

Matthew Arnold was in a distinct minority when, in 1853, he criticized the action of Sophocles's *Antigone,* saying that it "is no longer one in which it is possible that we should feel a deep interest." Arnold finds that we moderns cannot use as a model "that which is narrow in the ancients, nor that with which we can no longer sympathize." Unfortunately, he thinks, such is the case with *Antigone,* "which turns on the conflict between a heroine's duty to her brother's corpse and that to the laws of her country." Arnold's condemnation is uncharacteristic—both of Arnold himself, who revered everything classical, and of his age. For, as George Steiner, in his work *Antigones,* says:

> Between c. 1790 and c. 1905, it was widely held by European poets, philosophers, scholars, that Sophocles' *Antigone* was not only that finest of Greek tragedies, but a work of art nearer to perfection than any other produced by the human spirit.

Steiner goes on to point out that, after 1789, the Antigone legend became "talismanic to the European spirit," even if the fascination for it seemed to erupt *ex nihilo* (In the 35 years prior to that date no painting exhibited in the salons of Paris had that motif). Why did this theme so suddenly transfix the gaze of nineteenth-century artists and critics? What was it about this "'most sisterly of souls' (Goethe's invocation of her in his 'Europhrosyne Hymn' of 1799)" that held such an allure?

This generation of readers found in *Antigone* an idea that thrilled them because they desired its truth and yet, at the same time, they knew it could not be true. It is the "truth" that Hegel had unveiled—that the sister in her virginal, untainted purity can, through self-sacrifice for her brother, sustain that most "natural" of all structures, the family, even against the legitimate demands of structures of authority that surround and threaten to engulf it. In their exaltation of this text there also might well have been a guilty acknowledgment of its falsehood, and at some level a recognition that the lie pointed to an indictment of the very centerpiece of their culture—an indictment, in other words, of the family, and particularly of its synchronic cross-section, sibling relationships as they had been structured in that culture and called "natural."

A study of sibling relationships in nineteenth-century literature, particularly those in which a sister is the primary pole of the relationship, can provide a key to understanding much about that period's complicated and contradictory conception of the family. As a response to the social upheaval created by the industrial revolution, the nuclear family was restructured as a hyperreal and hypersensitive organization that could serve both as a unit for energizing the activities required on the new economic battlefield and, paradoxically, as a moral refuge from the public sphere. As such, it was imperative that the roles within the family be clearly demarcated and strictly disciplined— that the family be organized in such a way as to convince itself and its sub-units, the individual members of the family, both of the legitimacy of the familial organization of authority and of their duty to fortify and perpetuate it. That authority was, of course, patriarchal, as were the social structures to which the family responded and corresponded; yet the energy to maintain the unit was matriarchal. Feminine desire—the desire of the mother—had to be contained and channeled in such a way as to create the home as a sphere of moral perfection so elevated above the predatory struggle of the new economic strife as to seem to justify that very struggle (whose main goal was conceived as the protection of the family and its purity), while offering respite, relaxation, love and servitude to at least one of the bloodied warriors, and offering a training-ground to new warriors for the coming battles. That is to say, feminine desire had to will its own constraint and negation, had to will itself as a kind of impossible purity and virtuousness. Such purity and virtuousness were unattainable for the mother, who had already been "sullied," contaminated by the unwholesome desire of another who had himself been contaminated by his contact with the ferociousness of the world beyond the walls of the home. Only in heaven could there exist a truly Virgin Mother; but such a vestal vessel was nevertheless required to be elevated, touted, and sacrificed, and could exist on earth only in the being of the sister, a sanctum sanctorum of moral virtue, whose desire would be molded to fit the necessary ends. This disciplining (and often self-disciplining) of sororal desire was relatively successful in the nineteenth century, but the tremendous pressures brought to bear on the family unit, and particularly on its female members, created deep anxieties and fears—anxieties from without concerning the true nature of the feminine desire that was being purified and distilled, anxieties from within based on the dread of the yet unimagined potential of that same desire—the unimagined potential of the liberation of female selfhood and sexuality.

In nineteenth-century literature, sisterhood itself is conceived in the same contradictory fashion as is the family—viz., as both an ideological justification of the patriarchal system and a potential subversion of those same structures; and, in its most hysterical lauding of the sister's virtue, nineteenth-century patriarchy registers its deepest fears and allows in them to be painted a very different portrait of sisterhood and of feminine desire from the one it means to depict. These fears and anxieties take the form of a dread—that is, of a horrible attraction to the thing feared—and this dread is revealed in the fiction of the period. The failure of disciplined feminine desire results in the instability, slippage, uncertainty and unreliability of desire within the family, as assigned roles lose their boundaries, overlap, and confound themselves. In the literature of the fantastic, this phenomenon is raised to a feverish pitch as the principle of individuation itself collapses, taking along with it the very possibility of the family and the social system that it sustains, and prefiguring a release and discharge of feminine desire in new and revolutionary forms—hinting at the subversive forms of sisterhood that may have been precisely the ones that lay hidden and smoldering in the deepest fears of Victorian patriarchy itself.

"The Fall of the House of Usher," written mid-century, is prophetic in its anticipation of a vision of the collapse of a society built on the seemingly secure foundations of the family. One might say, in a certain sense, that Poe heralds—or, if you will, "ushers" in—a new era. Although innumerable studies have analyzed the symbolism of Poe's **"House of Usher,"** and particularly that of the Usher twins, no one has yet discussed the twins as "simply" representing themselves: the apogee of the nineteenth century's figuration of the brother-sister dyad. Poe, unlike many of his contemporaries, makes not even a nominal attempt to include a parental presence; we have entered a world in which the nineteenth-century family has been reduced to its most basic unit: the sibling dyad. In this work we witness, with Poe's narrator, "the hideous dropping off of the veil," wherein the fundamental building block of the Victorian family—the "ideal" brother-sister relation—once revealed for what it is and taken to its logical extreme, must necessarily (and horribly) self-destruct. As in texts as diverse as *Antigone, Frankenstein,* and *Wuthering Heights,* it is significantly the *sister* who must be sacrificed—here literally entombed, buried alive deep within the foundations of the familial edifice—and it is her breaking free from that entombment that provokes the collapse of the entire structure.

Poe's tale begins in twilight, "in the autumn of the year"—at a moment, in other words, of twofold transition. When Poe's narrator first comes upon the house, he gazes at the "vacant eye-like windows" and wonders, "what was it that so unnerved me in the contemplation of the House of Usher?" The narrator muses over his friend's "very ancient family" which,

> all time-honored as it was, had put forth, at no period, any enduring branch; in other words, . . . the entire family lay in the direct line of descent, and had always, with very trifling and very temporary variation, so lain. . . . [I]t was this deficiency, perhaps, of collateral issue, and the consequent undeviating transmission, from sire to son, of the patrimony with the name, which had, at length, so identified the two as to merge the original title of the estate in the quaint and equivocal appellation of the "House of Usher"—an appellation which seemed to include, in the minds of the peasantry who used it, both the family and the family mansion.

The "House of Usher," then, is explicitly meant to "stand for" family as well as estate; and both of these entities are equally deathly, equally verging on collapse. G. R. Thompson points out that the house is described as a "death's-head looming out of a dead landscape," and asserts that Poe "obviously intended the image of the skull-face of the house to dominate as the central image of the tale, for he returns to it again and again, placing the most extended descriptions of it at symmetrically located places in the narrative." The narrator takes note of the "pestilent and mystic vapor, dull, sluggish, faintly discernible, and leaden-hued," which hangs about the manor house. He then goes on to describe the mansion itself:

> Its principle feature seemed to be that of an excessive antiquity. The discoloration of ages had been great. . . . Yet all this was apart from any extraordinary dilapidation. No portion of the masonry had fallen; and *there appeared to be a wild inconsistency between its still perfect adaptation of parts, and the crumbling condition of the individual stones. . . .* Beyond this indication of extensive decay, however, the fabric gave little token of instability. Perhaps the eye of a scrutinizing observer might have discovered *a barely discernible fissure,* which, extending from the roof of the building in front, made its way down the wall in a zigzag direction, until it became lost in the sullen waters of the tarn. (emphases added)

One can scarcely imagine a more apt description of the nineteenth-century familial institution—a reeking, crumbling, and decaying structure that nevertheless remains seemingly intact on the surface. As Marilyn Chandler observes, "[c]omparing the house to woodwork in a neglected vault that no 'breath of external air' can reach suggests by association that this environment, too, is somehow mysteriously hermetically sealed." This, I would add, further enhances the image of the "hermetically sealed" familial enclosure.

The interior of the house is equally airless, dismal, and repellent. Its entire contents are in a state of deterioration, the furniture "profuse, comfortless, antique, and tattered." Even the "[m]any books and musical instruments . . . failed to give any vitality" to the place wherein an "air of stern, deep, and irredeemable gloom hung over and pervaded all." The house's proprietor, Roderick Usher, is himself rendered in precisely the same terms of de-generation. His beautifully delicate, refined features are marred by a "cadaverousness of complexion," "lips somewhat thin and very pallid," and "a want of moral energy." Roderick ambiguously describes to his friend "the nature of his malady" as "a constitutional and a *family evil*" my emphasis—an "evil" that "enchain[s]" him to his house, from which he has not ventured for many years. He then admits, "although with hesitation" (why?), that his "family" ailment can be "traced to a more natural and far more palpable origin"—namely, to his "tenderly beloved sister—his sole companion for long years—his last relative on earth." Although at this very juncture the object of discussion slowly drifts past, we are not privy to any physical description of her—a striking contrast to the earlier detailing of her brother's appearance. Yet we know already what Madeleine looks like, for we sense that her portrait is contained within the one we have been given of Roderick. The narrator has described Roderick as possessing lips of a "surpassingly beautiful curve; a nose of a delicate Hebrew model . . . ; a finely moulded chin . . . ; hair of a more than web-like softness and tenuity; . . . [a] ghastly pallor of the skin. . . . silken hair . . . [which] in its wild gossamer texture . . . floated rather than fell about the face." There is at least as much to suggest a woman's appearance in this depiction as there is a man's; indeed, one might construe that the narrator is himself hinting at precisely this when he remarks upon Roderick's "peculiar physical conformation." Of course, Madeleine and Roderick are twins, and hence there is bound to be a close physical similarity. Yet it is telling that it is the *sister*'s appearance that defines the brother's—much as Catherine Earnshaw's "look" is etched onto other characters in Brontë's text.

As in other nineteenth-century texts about sibling bonds, like *Frankenstein* and *Wuthering Heights,* **"The Fall of the House of Usher"** presents us with a persistent doubling, thematically and structurally, as characters, events, and the narrative structure itself, repeat one another. Poe's story, like Shelley's and Brontë's, is inundated with the blurring—indeed, complete breakdown—of boundaries between identities. And, once again, it is the sibling axis across which this collapse of distinctions so critical to the bourgeois ideology of the period takes place. . . .

With this unraveling of (hierarchical) distinctions between male/female, culture/nature, inside/outside, sameness/difference, we are presented with a simultaneously terrifying and potentially liberating vision. Yet because it is Poe and not Brontë who is writing, the emphasis is certainly placed much more firmly on the terrifying. The question as to whether Poe himself was aware of the radical implications of his tale is beyond the bounds of the discussion at hand. Nevertheless, his portrayal of this brother and sister with their "sympathies of a scarcely intelligible nature" is so central to the issues and debates of his day that it might appear as though he were directly engaging them.

Such a distillation of the family into its most concentrated and undiluted element would indeed be, Poe seems to be telling us, more than sufficient cause for the "horror" and "dread" so repeatedly evoked in his narrative. When the narrator lays eyes on Madeleine, he inexplicably regards her "with an utter astonishment not unmingled with dread—and yet [he] found it impossible to account for such feelings." In a peculiar sense, it is as though in this text the sister is simultaneously all-pervasive and hollowed out—already a ghost. Her desire is never expressed, yet is everywhere felt. The pressure put on the sister in the nineteenth-century is brought to its logical conclusion in Poe's dreadful tale, in which "the disease of the lady Madeleine had long baffled the skill of her physicians. A settled apathy, a gradual wasting away of the person, and frequent although transient affections of a partially cataleptical character" are the symptoms of this sister's malady. Although we are told that "[h]itherto she had steadily borne up against" it, Madeleine does at last succumb "to the prostrating power of the destroyer." The precise nature of this "destroyer," I want to argue, is none other than that

"family evil"—nineteenth-century bourgeois domestic ideology itself—"that silent, yet importunate and terrible influence which for centuries had moulded the destinies of [Usher's] family, and which made *him* . . . what he was."

The sister's body is the very site upon which this ideology so crucial to the perpetuation of patriarchy is enacted, and its effects are expressed nowhere more clearly than in the "apathy" and "gradual wasting away" of the ghostly, ghastly Madeleine. The bedrock of the nineteenth-century middle-class family is the sister, and her desire must be buried deep within the very foundation of the familial edifice itself. When Roderick informs the narrator "abruptly that the lady Madeleine was no more" the latter aids the bereaved brother in entombing his sister's body within a vault "half smothered in its oppressive atmosphere"—an uncannily fitting description of the metaphorical entombment of the sister in Victorian society. This sister, too, like many of her fictional and nonfictional contemporaries, is buried alive, but, unlike Antigone, she breaks free, and, when she does, brings the entire structure down with her. The "once barely-discernible fissure" is rent asunder, and there is "a long tumultuous shouting sound like the voice of a thousand waters"—a voice representing perhaps a thousand sisters emerging from their airless vaults.

Louise J. Kaplan   (essay date 1993)

SOURCE: "The Perverse Strategy in 'The Fall of the House of Usher'," in *New Essays on Poe's Major Tales,* edited by Kenneth Sliverman, Cambridge University Press, 1993, pp. 45-64.

[*Kaplan is an American psychoanalyst. In the following essay, she presents a psychoanalytic interpretation of "The Fall of the House of Usher."*]

Edgar Allan Poe was a dissembler, a hoaxter, a liar, an impostor, and plagiarizer. He was secretive about his true identity and frequently masqueraded under one of several aliases. Deception and mystification were Poe's stock-in-trade. Nevertheless, about some things we take him at his word. He truly was, as he boasted, a master of perversion, that most deceptive of mental strategies. We have only to recall his persistent and active pursuit of mental and physical self-destruction—the drinking, his habits of provocative and violent argumentation, the alienation of his guardian and other authority figures who might otherwise have given him support, the pedophilic-incestuous undercurrents of his marriage. Then there is the miasma surrounding his death—was it the outcome of one of his provocations, or disease, alcoholism, suicide, dementia? In living his life and even in his manner of negotiating death, Poe was a captive of the imp of perversity. But with Art as his shield, the realms of perversity became a haven for his troubled soul. He left to posterity a documentation of the spirit of the imp who held him enthralled.

In **"The Imp of the Perverse,"** Poe explained the logic beneath the apparent unreasonableness of this "innate and primitive principle of human action" which prompts us to act solely "for the reason that we should *not*." Whereas all other faculties and impulses of the human soul could be seen as expressions of the human need for self-preservation, in the instance of perversity "the desire to be well is not only not aroused, but a strongly antagonistical sentiment exists."

With that cagey "not only not," Poe renders precisely the double negative duplicity of the perverse strategy. From a psychoanalytic perspective, perversion is not only not simply (or necessarily) an aberration of the sexual life, or merely some irresistible impulse to perform an act insidious to the moral order. Perversion is a complex strategy of mind, with its unique principles for regulating the negotiations between Desire and Authority. To achieve its aims, the perverse strategy employs mechanisms of mystification, concealment, and illusion, devices characteristic of the tales of Edgar Allan Poe. The perverse strategy is, as Poe might have put it, a faculty of the human soul.

Among the elements of the perverse strategy that we will encounter in **"The Fall of the House of Usher"** are certain literary devices aimed at revealing truth by way of concealment. Poe believed that truly imaginative literature locates its deepest meaning in an *under*current. The surfaces of his tales are always deceptions. Initiated readers of Poe relish the deceptions and anticipate having to pore diligently over his texts to detect the embedded secrets. The tale of Usher is shrouded in mystifying atmospheres, references to obscure texts, and hints of enigmatic events. Poe's impish invitation to detect hidden meanings in one place distracts the reader from other crucial events going on behind the scenes. Whatever enigmas Poe brings into focus in **"The Fall of the House of Usher"** there are always the shadows of the unseen, the uncanny, the unknowable, implications of some darker secret that is being kept from us.

Indeed, to apprehend the ambiguities in **"The Fall of the House of Usher"** a reader must possess the analytical skills of a good detective. A few years after his account of the fall of Usher, Poe invented the detective story and created the prototypical detective, Monsieur C. Auguste Dupin. Dupin is "found of enigmas, of conundrums, of hieroglyphics; exhibiting in his solutions of each a degree of *acumen* which appears to the ordinary apprehension praeternatural." Poe cautions, a person of *mere* ingenuity may be incapable of analysis. Despite his lavish (and duplicitous) displays of scientific reasoning, Dupin arrives at his solutions by way of imaginative leaps and an uncanny attunement with the mind of the criminal. Roderick Usher is at once an imaginative artist and a criminal. Although a certain fondness for enigmas is necessary to appreciate **"The Fall of the House of Usher,"** it is our grasp of the perverse strategy that provides an attunement with Usher's troubled soul.

Poe was not above employing puzzles and enigmas as seductions into the mere ingenuity he disdained. In the history of Poe criticism, these seductions have been all too successful. For example, those not wise to the di-

versionary tactics of the imp have attributed Poe's facility with the logic of perversity to the primal traumas of his infancy and early childhood. When Poe was about eighteen months old, his alcoholic father abandoned the family. Shortly thereafter, Edgar witnessed the sickness, decay, and death of his mother. He became an orphan and his sister and brother disappeared. Poe's tales are convincing depictions of the castrations, separations, abandonments, and annihilations that constitute the typical anxieties of childhood, anxieties that in Poe's case must have reached overwhelming and therefore traumatic proportions. Poe's portrayals of body mutilations, smotherings, drownings, entombments of the living, the wasting away and rotting away of bodies, situations emptied of human dialogue, are calculated to re-evoke in the reader the archaic fears of childhood. It would not be farfetched to conjecture that Peo embraced these themes as a way of mastering the passively suffered traumas of his childhood.

We miss the point of all this, however, if we reduce **"The Fall of the House of Usher"** to Poe's personal traumas or his inclinations to sexual aberration and violence. Instead, as I said, I will take Poe at his word. I will use the tale of Usher as a demonstration of Poe's mastery of the perverse strategy, with its mystifications and concealments, its ambiguous relationship to the moral order, its pretense of a fundamental antagonism to representational reality. As I assess the currents and undercurrents of **"The Fall of the House of Usher,"** my interpretations of the moral and aesthetic plights of the artist protagonist, Roderick Usher, will be guided by the principles of the perverse strategy. Nevertheless, in this tale, where specters of incest and necrophilia hover in the background, perversion in its narrower and customary sense—as sexual aberration—will inform my concluding interpretations.

First printed in 1839 in *Burton's Magazine,* **"The Fall of the House of Usher"** was six years later included in Poe's *Tales of the Grotesque and Arabesque*. The very terms Poe chose to describe his tales are expressive of the confusions between the real and the imaginary, the animate and the inanimate that characterize the perverse strategy. Arabesque is derived from Arabian and Moorish art and refers to an elaborate design in which highly stylized human and animal figures are embedded among intertwined branches, foliage, and fanciful scrollwork. Crucial to the complexity of the artistic design of **"The Fall of the House of Usher,"** is the way in which Usher's person and fate are intertwined with the decaying foliage and crumbling ornate architectural scrollwork of his House. We are repeatedly reminded of the sentience of nonliving matter and the decay of living matter back into nonbeing. Grotesque is an ornamental style of antiquity, which one of Poe's lesser known critics [Wolfgong Kayser] has described as "something playfully gay and carelessly fantastic but also something ominous and sinister, in the face of a world in which the realm of inanimate things are no longer separated from those of plants, animals and human beings and where the laws of statics, symmetry, and proportion are no longer valid." **"The Fall of the House of Usher"** depends for its emotional effects on the dissolving of the boundaries between the inanimate and animate realms and the breaking down of the laws of everyday reality. Though this tale could hardly be recommended for its playful gaiety, the reader is playfully engaged in solving mysteries, protected until the very end from the full knowledge of the ominous and sinister events going on behind the scenes.

The tale's epigraph from De Béranger warns of a potential dissolution of the borders between illusion and reality. We learn at once that the heart of the artist, Roderick Usher, is like a lute that resonates to all that touches it:

> Son coeur est un luth suspendu:
> Sitôt qu'on le touche il résonne.

Poe, the creator of Roderick Usher, does not lose his boundaries. Through the trickery, call it technique, of mystification and enigma, Poe achieves the deceptions, call them illusions, that comprise his artistic strategy. In **"The Fall of the House of Usher"** various illusory devices are employed to preserve the borders of the moral order, even as they mischievously render a picture of moral disintegration.

The House of Usher decays, crumbles, and falls into oblivion but it does so in a manner eminently lawful and orderly. The tale is partitioned, one could say precisely measured, into three equal and distinct acts. The events take place within a month, beginning with the desolation and gloom surrounding the narrator's approach to the House and ending with the abrupt, noisy, and violent circumstances of his departure.

Act One introduces the characters, depicts the eerie effect the House of Usher has on its viewers and inhabitants, and apprises us of Roderick's family background and the general nature of his illness. The first character we meet is the narrator, who, in response to an agitated letter from his childhood companion Roderick Usher, has set off on a journey to his House. He has certain misgivings and the closer he comes to the House the more these misgivings increase. Nevertheless he hopes that his presence will help alleviate his old friend's maladies—a mysterious bodily illness accompanied by an oppressive mental disorder. We learn that Roderick and his sister, Lady Madeline, are the last of the Ushers, a family known for its inbreeding and deficiency "of collateral issue" as well as for its unassuming deeds of charity and devotion to the intricacies of musical science. As the narrator moves through numerous, winding passageways to the studio of his friend, he encounters a valet with a stealthy step and the Usher family physician, whose expression of "low cunning and perplexity" further enhances the mood of suspicion, gloom, and FEAR that envelops the Usher mansion. Save for the peculiar dialogues between the narrator and Rodrick, the universe of ordinary human dialogue is notable for its absence. Aside from the brief appearances of the valet and physician the staff of the mansion is invisible and uncannily silent. Madeline utters not one word. But the canny dialogue of detection between Poe and his reader is vibrant.

Harry Clarke's drawing of Lady Madeline for
"The Fall of the House of Usher."

Roderick tells the narrator that his sufferings stem from a disorder of the senses: He is oppressed by every odor, even of flowers. His tastebuds can endure only the most insipid food; his skin can tolerate only garments of the slightest texture; his eyes are tortured by the faintest of lights, and save for the tones from his own stringed instruments, every sound inspires Roderick with horror. Existence itself is a torment for Rodrick. He lives with the dread that this pitiable condition of his senses will eventually lead him to "abandon life and reason together, in some struggle with the grim phantasm, FEAR." He is possessed by a superstition that the form and substance of the House itself, the very sentience of the stones and foliage, have obtained a power over his spirit. Finally Rodrick hints that his gloom could be attributable to the severe and lengthy illness of his beloved sister, "his sole companion for long years—his last and only relative on earth". As Rodrick utters these words, Lady Madeline passes through a remote corner of his large studio and vanishes.

In Act Two the narrator quickly discovers the futility of "cheering a mind from which darkness, as if an inherent positive quality, poured forth upon all objects of the moral and physical universe, in one unceasing radiation of gloom." Nevertheless he does not give up on his mission of salvation. He spends several days alone with Roderick, reading from the esoteric texts in his library, watching him paint, listening to the wild improvised dirges his friend plucks from his speaking guitar. Most of this act is given over to detailed descriptions of Roderick's paintings, music, and poetry. It concludes with the "death" of Madeline and her entombment in a vault at the bottommost reaches of the House of Usher. As the narrator and Roderick go about the preparations for Madeline's burial, the reader learns that she is Roderick's *twin* sister, and also the disquieting fact that her features still glow from the blush of life. Immediately following Madeline's entombment, Roderick's mental condition deteriorates and the narrator becomes infected with his friend's fantastic imaginings and superstitions.

Act Three takes place on a stormy night about a week after the entombment of Lady Madeline. Usher comes to the narrator's room in a state of "mad hilarity" and hysteria. In an attempt to calm him, the narrator reads aloud from the tale of the "Mad Trist." The sounds described in this tale are soon echoed by the sounds of Madeline escaping from her tomb. Roderick exclaims, *"We have put her living in the tomb!"* Madeline appears in the doorway, and in her final death agonies, falls inward on her brother, bearing him "to the floor a corpse, and a victim to the terrors he had anticipated." The narrator flees in terror from the chamber and from the mansion. He looks back to see the mighty walls of the House of Usher burst asunder and fall into a dank tarn that closes over its fragments.

The tale of Usher is shrouded in mystifying atmospheres, references to obscure texts, and hints of enigmatic events. Poe's impish invitation to detect hidden meanings in one place distracts the reader from other crucial events going on behind the scenes.

—Louise J. Kaplan

With sin and violence so much in the foreground of Poe's tales, we are apt to forget that they are as much about the structures of reason and moral order as they are about the forces that undermine those structures, causing them to totter and collapse in on themselves as they do in **"The Fall of the House of Usher."** The protagonist, Roderick Usher, is an artist and the central conflicts concern the artist's ambiguous relation to the moral order. In a tale of an artist, matters of Art cannot be incidental. The decay and eventual fall of the House of Usher are inextricably linked to the crumbling away of the borders between reality and illusion in Roderick's art. The lengthy descriptions of his paintings, musical performances, and poetry are crucial to the *under*currents of **"The Fall of the House of Usher,"** and to the affinities between creativity and perversion. Poe's tale of the life and death of the artist, Roderick Usher, depicts the creative processes that enabled Usher's art along with the moral nihilism his art was striving to regulate and contain.

In his essay "The Poetic Principle" Poe stated that the highest art is to be "found in *an elevating excitement of the Soul*—quite independent of that passion which is the intoxication of the Heart—or that Truth which is the satisfaction of the Reason." Richard Wilbur, in "The House of Poe," distinguished between Poe's proclaimed aesthetic of repudiating the human and earthly in favor of *poésie pure*—the visionary uncontaminated by passion, the imaginative unconstrained by logic or reason—and his more down-to-earth literary method of posing moral riddles in the form of prose allegories. Wilbur deplored the aesthetic expressed by the visionary Poe in his essays on music and poetry, but honored the method employed by the logical Poe in allegories such as **"William Wilson," "Ligeia," "MS. Found in a Bottle,"** and **"The Fall of the House of Usher."**. . .

Whereas Poe's aesthetic entails a conscious undermining of reality and authority in order to attain the rhythms of a pure visionary art, his prose allegories derive their effects from the vibrancy of the negotiations between Desire and Authority. In other words, "the civil war" in the palace of the mind acts as a resistance to the wish for pure gratification. In the absence of such resistance, without moral conflict, the aesthetic of *poésie pure* is the equivalent of a moral nihilism.

Analogously, we might say that sexual aberration with its conscious claim for unrestrained gratification is the aesthetic of perversion, whereas the perverse strategy is an unconscious method that regulates the life of Desire. In contrast to the sexual aberrations which have, as a conscious aim, an undermining of Authority, the strategy of perversion is an attempt to preserve the moral order. Paradoxically then, the interests of the moral order—what some psychoanalysts call "ego and superego" and others "the symbolic order" and still others "the structures of language"—are served by the perverse strategy. In a canny duplicity, the perverse strategy achieves its moral aims by permitting a token expression to Sin and even to the torments, anxieties, melancholia, and violence that accompany moral disorder. As in all Poe's allegories, in the tale of Usher these frightful states of mind are given a due measure of expression—but all regulated and contained within the boundaries of art.

Like Usher, who evinces a fundamental antagonism to earthly reality in favor of imaginative purity, Poe spurned realistic descriptions and representational devices in favor of setting tones and creating moods that would engender abnormal states of mind. He wanted to shake readers loose from the moorings of everyday earthly life so their imaginations might be freed; so they might suspend disbelief and accept as true something patently untrue. In **"The Fall of the House of Usher"** Poe engenders illusion and yet preserves a sense of reality; he replaces what otherwise might be a feeling of overwhelming dread with playful shudders, thrills, excitements. Literary devices that confound what is true by masking it with the untrue, or substitute pleasurable emotions for painful ones, are analogous to fetishism, the paradigmatic instance of the perverse strategy.

Imposturing, petty lies, plagiarism, in fact, any act, object, thought, or artistic device that wards off the perception of an unwelcome or unbearable reality and substitutes instead perceptions that facilitate ambiguity and illusion can be thought of as the equivalent of a fetish.

In sexual fetishism, for example, a fetish—a garter belt, boot, slipper, whip, corset, negligee—is employed to counteract the unwelcome and frightening reality of a woman's actual body and to engender the illusion of a phallic woman, a person who is female but whose genitals nevertheless are identical to those of a male. This act of fetishizing a woman's body protects the fetishist from the anxious reality of the differences between the sexes. However, this shield against the "real" reality, though it enhances an illusion that rescues the capacity for sexual intercourse, can only be accomplished through a dehumanization and deanimation of the sexual partner. Thus in fetishism an experiencing, breathing body is deadened, entombed as it were, like the still blushing, earthly body of Madeline Usher, in the realm of the living dead. My concluding interpretations will stress how Roderick Usher's break with the moral order is connected with his need to repudiate the reality of Madeline's sexuality. For now I am using the model of fetishism to show how Roderick Usher's artistic devices contrasted with those of his creator, Edgar Allan Poe. In his quest for a pure aesthetic, Usher eventually loses his connection with the moral order. Poe never does.

The fetishist's apparent antagonism to reality is not so absolute and fundamental as it first appears. Nor is Poe so wholeheartedly committed to the aesthetic of pure Supernal Beauty he promulgates in "The Poetic Principle." Poe demonstrates his divided loyalties by always acknowledging the principles of reason and logic even as he creates an atmosphere of illusion and mystification. With his fetishistic devices, the fetishist is *disavowing* the reality of differences between the sexes, while simultaneously *avowing* that reality. His fears engender an illusion of identity between the sexes. The passions of his heart, his earthly sexual desires, are an acknowledgment of the sexual difference. With one part of his mind working to conceal differences, another part is still aware of reality. There is what is called in psychoanalysis "a split in the ego," a fissure or rupture in the mind, but not a full departure from the world of reality. The fetishist is not a madman who simply denies or *repudiates* reality, as Roderick Usher eventually does. Nor is he one of your standard neurotics, like perhaps the narrator of Poe's tale, who *represses* any knowledge that frightens or humiliates him.

In the life of Edgar Allan Poe, artistic creation served as a version of disavowal, a kind of fetishistic device that enabled him to conceal and yet still reveal the unbearable secrets and phantoms that haunted his mind. Moreover, the lies, tricks, conundrums, enigmas, and mystifications characteristic of Poe's tales function like a fetish. In **"The Fall of the House of Usher,"** various artistic media and art objects are employed in a fashion analogous to a fetish. Like translucent veils placed between the reader and what would otherwise be a full knowledge of some dark,

unwelcome reality, the ambiguity and illusory quality of Roderick's works of art serve to distract and conceal. Yet, and this is the heart of Poe's artistic strategy, these same art objects simultaneously reveal in a symbolic form what would be too unbearable to acknowledge directly. While readers are kept busy detecting the enigmas suggested by Roderick's art (and the esoteric books in his library), Lady Madeline is being de-animated, buried alive, entombed in the land of the living dead. Yet, just as an analysis of the symbolic structure of a sexual fetish would tell us about the unconscious mental life of the fetishist, so the symbolic structure of Roderick's art reveals his unconscious forbidden wishes.

Poe tells us that Usher's heart is like a lute that can only quiver helplessly and passively to the throbs of nature. Usher himself laments that his body, his very soul is being pervaded by the atmosphere of his house, but this complaint to the narrator may very well be a vast deception, a clever subterfuge. In Usher's ascetic avoidance of sensuous earthly pleasures is he not, in fact, inviting a merger with spirits, phantoms, foliage, stones, atmospheres? Would our earthbound narrator ever dare such risky excitements of the soul?

When the House of Usher first comes into sight, the narrator finds it impossible to erect any cover of illusion between the decaying images before his eyes and his soul. In fact the very opposite occurs. There is "a hideous dropping off of the veil." The narrator experiences "an iciness, a sinking, a sickening of the heart—an unredeemed dreariness of thought which no goading of the imagination could torture into aught of the sublime."

Though the narrator strives to impress us with his altruism and therapeutic zeal, one suspects that he has responded to Roderick's summons in order to gratify his personal quest for the sublime. With a mental contrivance that merely impersonates Art, the narrator turns his eyes away from the awe inspiring spectacle of the House and interposes an illusory arrangement of its features. He stops before a tarn that reflects the inverted image of the house with its grey and ghastly foliage and "vacant and eyelike windows." His gaze into the tarn does not, however, entirely dispel his anxiety; it transforms anxiety into a more tolerable fear. Indeed, the new visual arrangement brings "a shudder even more thrilling than before," but thrilling is a distance from the overwhelming melancholy and sinister import of the actual images. Poe's "thrilling" is all the seduction his readers require. We will not be disappointed. We are in for a bit of excitement. Our playful quivering apprehension will capture the essence of some terrible anxiety and shield us from the displeasure and terror we might otherwise experience. A roller coaster ride may scare us to death, but we gladly defy death for the elation of the thrills it promises. We enter the illusion willingly, even daringly, assured that we are not actually going to be smashed to pieces and die. In the tale of Usher, elated feelings of risk and excitement replace the mental sufferings—anxiety, depression, madness—we might otherwise experience if we were to actually feel as Roderick feels.

Poe invites us to resonate with Roderick's "FEAR." The thrilling tale the narrator relates will be the artifice that shields the reader from Roderick's unbearable moral plights. Poe, the artist, renders a tale that both reveals and conceals the torments of a soul that loses the boundaries of the symbolic order.

The logical Poe sides with truth and reason, but from the point of view of the visionary Poe, Roderick's release from reason and descent into madness is an act of artistic courage. The narrator who tells Usher's tale in his earnest, measured, reasonable way, is a coward who flirts with the dangerous process of Art and then furtively shrinks into the shadows of normality.

At each step of the way, from the moment the narrator has the inspiration to rearrange the particulars of the scene by inverting them, Art is evoked to conceal yet reveal the gradual but inexorable dissolution of Roderick's tie to the world of ordinary mortals. The art forms, poetry, painting, music, and even the obscure scholarly texts on the sentience of the inanimate world, books which "had formed no small portion of the mental existence of the invalid," express and reflect Roderick's plight, while by their continued connection to the symbolic order, they veil the horrors they express. As the last of his futile efforts to protect Roderick from the terrors encroaching on his mind and consuming his soul, the narrator reads aloud from the "Mad Trist," a vulgar grotesque by Sir Launcelot Canning. In this choice, the narrator confesses to an ingenuous duplicity: "I had called it a favorite of Usher's more in sad jest than in earnest; for, in truth, there is little in its uncouth and unimaginative prolixity which could have had interest for the lofty and spiritual ideality of my friend." The subtly "thrilling" shudders of Poe's **"The Fall of the House of Usher"** rouse the imagination and we accept as real and actual the ghastly sounds of Madeline Usher clawing her way out of her tomb. However, the blatant clangings and rattlings of the merely fanciful "Mad Trist" are so cheaply obtained as to be laughable.

Roderick's art, his music, his paintings, his poetry strive for aesthetic purity. Roderick is willing to risk his soul for Art. His bodily asceticism serves as a protection against earthly human desires. With his art, Roderick seems to be deliberately negating the palpable representational world. This negation of tangible reality is Roderick's effort to achieve a more intimate attunement with nature and even go so far as to dissolve his being in the sentience of non-living matter. Only with this painful and frightening dissolution of the boundaries of the self can Roderick free his imagination and create new art forms. As D. H. Lawrence said in his essay on Poe, "old things need to die and disintegrate . . . before anything else can come to pass . . . Man must be stripped even of himself. And it is a painful, sometimes a ghastly, process."

A contemporary reader might well wonder if Roderick did not invent abstract expressionism. The sounds and images created by Roderick overpower the ordinary, definitive, and concrete realities, replacing them with perceptions that facilitate ambiguity and illusion. "An excited and highly

distempered ideality threw a sulphureous lustre over all." Even when his images lean on reality, Roderick distorts that reality beyond any ordinary recognition. An example is his "singular perversion and amplification of the wild air of the last waltz of Von Weber."

The narrator is enthralled as he watches Roderick's paintings grow "touch by touch into vaguenesses." The more abstract and ambiguous they become "the more thrillingly" the narrator shudders. Of these "phantasmagoric conceptions" the narrator recalls one painting that was "not so rigidly of the spirit of abstraction." The imagery was just sufficiently representational to allow the narrator to "shadow forth, although feebly, in words," a description. The image the narrator recalls is the interior of an immensely long and rectangular vault that lay at an exceeding depth below the surface of the earth. Though no source of light is discernible, "a flood of intense rays rolled throughout, and bathed the whole in a ghastly and inappropriate splendor." We later learn that this chiaroscuro image is a harbinger of Madeline's tomb.

Another of Roderick's productions is far less abstract and more obviously premonitory. With the advantage of hindsight, the narrator, now comfortably distant from the frightening events he relates, recollects the words of one of the ballads Roderick sang as he strummed his singing guitar. In its conventional phrasing and structure "The Haunted Palace" evidences a mind capable of the "collectedness and concentration" the narrator admires. When he wrote the ballad Roderick was still in command of the formal properties of poetry. His madness was still only incipient. Yet the words imply, at least to the conventional and cautious narrator, that Roderick is aware of the fate that awaits him. "In the under or mystic current of its meaning, I fancied that I perceived, and for the first time, a full consciousness on the part of Usher, of the tottering of his lofty reason upon her throne."

Whereupon the narrator recites the verses of Usher's ballad, an abbreviated version of a poem written by Poe for another occasion and self-plagiarized to express the plight of Roderick Usher. Inevitably, the avid detectives who delight in fathoming Poe's deeper meanings note that all his mansions and buildings are structured like the human body, parts of the human body, or as layers or aspects of the mind. Often as not, the Usher mansion or the haunted palace of the mind in Roderick's ballad are cited as epitome and proof of this interpretation. The first four stanzas are said to represent a head, moreover a head with a lawful and orderly mind still capable of uttering words of authority; the flowing, glorious, golden banners are likened to hair, the windows through which wanderers might see "Spirits moving musically / To a lute's well-tunéd law" are linked to luminous eyes, the pearly and ruby doorway giving forth the wit and wisdom of the king is, of course, a mouth. The two concluding stanzas, which depict "red-litten windows" and "forms that move fantastically / To a discordant melody," are said to represent a sick and disordered mind. Like the narrator who is himself a missionary from the land of law and order, many of Poe's critics interpret "The Haunted Palace" as

Poe's lament to the tottering of Roderick's mind, his loss of connection to the life of reason. Surely, however, there must be an undercurrent beneath the current so easily and ingeniously detected by our reasonable narrator.

Let us consider "The Haunted Palace" from the point of view of the artist, Roderick Usher, rather than from the perspective of the frightened traveler who turned aghast from the revelations of Usher's Art, running as fast as he could back to civilization with its clear boundaries between real and not real, animate and non-animate, to tell an orderly tale. For Usher, as for any imaginative artist, the lyrics of his ballad might be less a lament to lost reason and more a tribute to innocence and free imagination. In this light, the "glory that blushed and bloomed" and now will "smile no more" could be interpreted as the innocent soul of the child. The child is the king who utters wisely, whereas the adult, the moral authority who enforces the life of reason, depriving the child of his contact with the world of sensate flux, is the corrupt one. The "evil things, in robes of sorrow" that "assailed the monarch's high estate" are the forces of civilization.

Poe, like the poets he idealized to the point of plagiarism, envisioned childhood as a time of glorious innocence, an innocence betrayed by the laws of reason and morality. Childhood was discovered (some say invented) in the eighteenth century in response to the dehumanizing trends of the industrial revolution. By the nineteenth century, when artists began to see themselves as alienated beings trapped in a dehumanizing social world, the child became the symbol of free imagination and goodness. Blacke and Wordsworth, and soon Dickens and Twain, were preoccupied with themes of childhood innocence. The image of the child was set in opposition to the prison of civilization. By peering into the soul of the child, the artist hoped to rediscover some divine state of selfhood. The artist looked to the child as the representation of that original True Self that was lost when man became a social being. Whatever is noble and pure and good about the human being could be found in the child, who, living freely in the world of sensate flux, a world uncorrupted by language and reason, is closest to the natural world, the realm of existence where soul and imagination flourish.

Clearly the narrator and Usher are at odds, not only in their attitudes to art but also in their moral values. The narrator is a conventional moralist, who even as he follows Usher into vaults and cellars and underground passages and thrills to the shudders they evoke, still clings desperately to the world of reality. Usher, on the other hand, has deliberately isolated himself from the world of earthly delights and from the moral order itself, in order to create visionary abstractions. The narrator, who has entered this heart of darkness on a mission of rescue, is frustrated by Usher's passive surrender to his illness. He suspects that Usher is nourishing the dark melancholy that he projected "upon all objects of the moral and physical universe" as if it were a positive force. With a mind still fettered by the temporal, physical world that Usher has shaken off, the narrator cannot apprehend "The Haunted Palace" as anything other than a sign of Usher's descent

into madness. Finally it is Usher who turns to the narrator, crying out "Madman." But who is the madman?

Recall that the perverse strategy encourages an illusory excitement that approximates madness in order to shield the mind against a more profound madness. To appreciate the nature of this other madness, let us return to the narrower meaning of perversion, perversion as sexual aberration.

Fetishism, in its literal, narrow sense enables sexual intercourse through a displacement of sexual desire away from the whole identity of a woman to some accessory or garment, some object ancillary to her being—a shoe or a garter belt. Why should a man be unable to experience sexual desire for a woman without the protection of a fetishistic device?

Until quite recently when psychoanalysts began to scrutinize the symbolic structure of the sexual fetish, the need to create a fetish was taken as presumable evidence of the castration anxiety evoked by the frightening vision of the absent and therefore castrated female genitals. It was assumed that there is something innately horrifying about the female body, something about her life-giving passages of sexuality and procreation that would inevitably bring to men's minds the stigmata of humiliation, degradation, multilation, and death. However, this perennial theme of the female stigmata is now appreciated as a disguise, a cover-up we might say, for a man's secret and forbidden unconscious wishes—to merge with woman, to be her, to never leave the Garden of Eden of Childhood where sacred mother and innocent child are united for eternity. In Eden the mother is pure and asexual. To acknowledge the mother's sexuality and her earthly desire is equivalent to a banishment from Eden. The fetish object conceals and disguises the sexual difference, thereby granting simultaneously an earthly passion of the Heart and the exalted spiritual wish to be reunited with the mother.

Whatever enigmas Poe brings into focus in "The Fall of the House of Usher," there are always the shadows of the unseen, the uncanny, the unknowable, implications of some darker secret that is being kept from us.

—*Louise J. Kaplan*

These currents of Poe's tale surface in the relation between Madeline and Roderick. Although much intervenes to intrigue and distract the reader of **"The Fall of the House of Usher,"** the specter of incest is omnipresent from the beginning. We are told at once that the barely perceptible fissure down the center of the mansion and the decay of its stones are expressions of the deficiency "of collateral issue, and the consequent undeviating transmission from sire to son, of the patrimony with the name." In a tale heavy with ambiguities, Poe's words to describe the incestuous family background of Madeline and Roderick are ominously ambiguous:

> [T]he stem of the Usher race, all time-honored as it was, had put forth, at no period, any enduring branch; in other words, . . . the entire family lay in the direct line of descent, and had always, with very trifling and very temporary variation, so lain.

Unless the twins, Madeline and Roderick, surrender to their earthly passions and commit incest, they are doomed to be the last of the Usher line. Was Roderick's asceticism, his avoidance of all bodily temptations, aimed at avoiding incest? Or did he endure the ghastly process of self-disintegration in order to create new forms of art? D. H. Lawrence introduces his essay on Poe by saluting the forces of dissolution, disintegration, and death, declaring them vital to the life of free imagination. However, Lawrence recognized that as much as **"The Fall of the House of Usher"** is about the risky ecstasies of a genuine artistic sensibility, it is also a tale of love. This is where the moral ambiguities lie. The spiritual ecstasy that is essential to Roderick's creativity becomes a force of evil in his love for Madeline. To put these issues another way: The tale of love in **"The Fall of the House of Usher"** reveals the terrible consequences of an aesthetic of pure gratification, when that aesthetic no longer engages the resistance of the moral order.

Lawrence warned, "There is a limit to love." He grasped precisely the force of evil in the spiritual bond between the two last survivors of the House of Usher. In sensual love, there is never a complete fusion or merger. The boundaries between self and other never completely dissolve. In spiritual love, however, the lovers vibrate in unison and their beings merge. [As Lawrence writes], in the vibrating, spiritual love between Madeline and Roderick:

> the mystery of the recognition of *otherness* fails, [and] the longing for identification with the beloved becomes a lust. And it is this longing for identification, utter merging, which is at the base of the incest problem. . . . In the family, the natural vibration is most nearly in unison. With a stranger, there is greater resistance. Incest is the getting of gratification and the avoiding of resistance.

Both Madeline and Roderick are dying of asceticism, of their mutual need to banish every sign of sensuality or earthly desire. Madeline's physical presence is a reminder to Roderick of his earthly passions. She is slowly wasting away, but her skin still blushes with the blood of life. In light of Roderick's conflicted feelings toward his sister, I would interpret "The Haunted Palace" as an expression of his wish to restore the spiritually of his love for Madeline. The contrasting images in this ballad represent two images of Madeline: the Madeline of childhood in her days of glorious innocence, and the bloody, lewd Madeline, the Madeline of sexual desire and the wild intoxications of the Heart.

Childhood innocence is about the life of Desire before the knowledge of female sexuality and the male-female sexual difference. It is the oedipal child, the child who must leave the world of sensate flux and free imagination and enter the symbolic order with its rules of language, reason, and morality, who resurrects the earlier uncomplicated infantile wish to merge with the mother, now as a defense against the knowledge of the irrevocable and irreversible differences between the sexes. With a full acknowledgment of these differences would come the painful acknowledgment that the life of Desire can never be pure. Once the child enters the moral order, the elevating excitements of the Soul cannot exist independently of earthly passions and the intoxications of the Heart— or the Truth of Reason.

Asceticism, the total avoidance of sensual pleasure, is an avoidance of the complex negotiations between Desire and Authority. When the effort to banish passion through asceticism fails, as eventually it must, there is either a fulfillment of a forbidden sexual desire or something worse— the madness of total emotional surrender to the other and a loss of identity.

Emotional surrender entails a total dissolution of the boundaries between the real and the not real. Thus, in ridding himself of the intoxications of the Heart, the passions of incestuous desire, Roderick is attempting a more insidious violation of the moral order. For, as Lawrence detected, latent in the undercurrent of an apparent sexual incestuous wish is the wish for a spiritual merger with the other. Roderick's deepest and most frightening wish is to merge with Madeline, to be eternally united with her in some smooth womblike utopia where the rough realities of earthly existence would no longer disturb his peace. Our most profound fears are always a reflection of our unconscious forbidden wishes. Roderick's "FEAR" of total annihilation resides in his wish to be one with Madeline, to dissolve his being in the sentience of non-living matter.

Alongside my own interpretive version of Madeline, I am ready to acknowledge a grain of truth in previous interpretations of her as double or doppelgänger, or as representation of Roderick's darker consciousness, or unconscious desires, or as witch or vampire. They all miss the essential point of the perverse strategy employed in **"The Fall of the House of Usher."** This prose allegory is about the regulation of Desire through the fetishistic devices of Art. Roderick's aspiration for a Supernal Beauty, the pure excitement of the soul expressed in his music and painting, is the counterpoint of his bodily asceticism. By ridding himself of all earthly passion he is attempting to repudiate his incestuous longing for Madeline. However, Roderick's sublime art only disguises and conceals his forbidden wishes and in the end the Truth is out—revealed. Roderick's effort to bury the life of Desire by deanimating his still living, breathing sister is doomed to fail. Madeline's return from her walled-off place beneath the House of Usher represents the return of Usher's repudiated desires and the granting of his forbidden wishes.

The nature of Madeline's dying gesture is ambiguous. When Madeline falls inward on Roderick is it a fulfillment of their sensual passions? Or is her apparently violent gesture an act of blanketing generosity, an affirmation of their spiritual bond, a granting of her beloved brother's wish to merge with her? Either way, Madeline's final enactment represents a destruction of the symbolic order and a violation of social morality. The civil war in the palace of the mind is over. The perverse strategy has failed.

The perverse strategy employs a symbolic structure. The perverse strategy enables illusion but also still retains a connection with the moral order and reality. The price is a split-in-the-ego, much like the barely perceptible fissure that extends down the walls of the House of Usher. On the other hand, a repudiation or total denial or earthly reality entails a breakdown of symbolic structures and always invites a return of the repudiated in its most archaic and awesome guises. Whether as witch or vampire or as the specter of incestuous desire, the terrifying, emaciated, white-shrouded, bloody Madeline returns from her tomb to grant her brother's forbidden wishes. The twins are reunited in death, merged as one for all eternity. With Madeline's substantiation of the aesthetic of pure Desire, her overthrow of moral Authority, Heaven cries out, venting its full wrath on the House of Usher, which cracks apart along its fissure, collapses like a house of cards— and is no more.

FURTHER READING

Criticism

Blackmur, R. P. "Afterword to 'The Fall of the House of Usher and Other Tales.'" In *Outsider at the Heart of Things: Essays by R. P. Blackmur*, edited by James T. Jones, pp. 223–30. Urbana and Chicago: University of Illinois Press, 1989.

> Comments on the extraordinary appeal of Poe's stories, with reference to "The Fall of the House of Usher."

Booth, Wayne C. "Manipulating Mood." In *The Rhetoric of Fiction*, pp. 200–05. Chicago: The University of Chicago Press, 1961.

> Analyzes the rhetorical development of mood using "The Fall of the House of Usher" as an example.

Caws, Mary Ann. "Tarn and Tunnel: Falling into Text." In *Reading Frames in Modern Fiction*, pp. 109–14. Princeton, N.J.: Princeton University Press, 1985.

> Offers a deconstructionist reading of frame devices in "The Fall of the House of Usher."

Dayan, Joan. "The Dream of the Body." In *Fables of Mind: An Inquiry into Poe's Fiction*, pp. 199–200. New York: Oxford University Press, 1987.

> Briefly comments on Madeline as representing the idea of the body.

Haggerty, George E. "Poe's Gothic Gloom." In *Gothic Fiction/ Gothic Form*, pp. 81–106. University Park: The Pennsylvania State University Press, 1989.

> Discusses Poe's fascination with the mechanics of Gothic literature, with reference to "The Fall of the House of Usher."

Herrmann, Claudine and Nicholas Kostis. "'The Fall of the House of Usher' or the Art of Duplication." *Sub-Stance* 26, No. 1 (1980): 36–42.

> Analyzes the significance of mirroring effects in "The Fall of the House of Usher."

Hoffman, Michael J. "The House of Usher and Negative Romanticism." *Studies in Romanticism* 4, No. 1 (Autumn 1964): 158–68.

> Examines "The Fall of the House of Usher" as an example of the post-Enlightenment loss of faith in human reason.

Lynen, John F. "The Death of the Present: Edgar Allan Poe." In *The Design of the Present: Essays on Time and Form in American Literature*, pp. 205–72. New Haven, Conn.: Yale University Press, 1969.

> Argues against allegorical interpretations of "The Fall of the House of Usher," and of other Poe stories.

Matheson, Terence J. "Fatalism in 'The Fall of the House of Usher.'" *English Studies in Canada* VI, No. 4 (Winter 1980): 421–29.

> Defends the common-sense attitudes of the narrator of "The Fall of the House of Usher."

Pahl, Dennis. "Disfiguration in 'The Fall of the House of Usher'; or Poe's Mad Lines." In *Architects of the Abyss: The Indeterminate Fictions of Poe, Hawthorne, and Melville*, pp. 3–24. Columbia: University of Missouri Press, 1989.

> Employs deconstructionist techniques to argue that "The Fall of the House of Usher" resists ultimate interpretation.

Smith, Herbert F. "Usher's Madness and Poe's Organicism: A Source." *American Literature* XXXIX, No. 3 (November 1967): 379–89.

> Identifies a source for Roderick Usher's belief in "the sentience of all vegetable things."

Thompson, G. R. "Poe and the Paradox of Terror: Structures of Heightened Consciousness in 'The Fall of the House of Usher.'" In *Ruined Eden of the Present: Hawthorne, Melville, and Poe*, edited by G. R. Thompson and Virgil L. Lokke, pp. 313–40. West Lafayette, Ind.: Purdue University Press, 1981.

> Rebuts Patrick F. Quinn's critique of his earlier essay "The Face in the Pool."

Voller, Jack G. "The Power of Terror: Burke and Kant in the House of Usher." *Poe Studies* 21, No. 2 (December 1988): 27–35.

> Interprets the "The Fall of the House of Usher" as a critique of the aesthetic of the sublime.

Voloshin, Beverly. "Transcendence Downward: An Essay on 'Usher' and 'Ligeia.'" *Modern Language Studies* XVIII, No. 3 (Summer 1988): 18–29.

> Discusses "The Fall of the House of Usher" and "Ligeia" as reactions against American Transcendentalism.

Woodson, Thomas, ed. *Twentieth Century Interpretations of "The Fall of the House of Usher."* Englewood Cliffs, N. J.: Prentice-Hall, 1969, 124 p.

> Collects important essays on "The Fall of the House of Usher" from the first half of the twentieth century.

Additional coverage of Poe's life and career is contained in the following sources published by Gale Research: *Authors and Artists for Young Adults,* Vol. 14; *Concise Dictionary of American Literary Biography,* 1640-1865; *DISCovering Authors;* *Dictionary of Literary Biography,* Vols. 3, 59, 73, 74; *Poetry Criticism,* Vol. 1; *Something about the Author,* Vol. 23; *Short Story Criticism,* Vol. 1; and *World Literature Criticism.*

Reynolds Price
1933–

(Full name Edward Reynolds Price) American short story writer, novelist, poet, playwright, essayist, memoirist, translator, and critic.

INTRODUCTION

Price is considered among the most accomplished contemporary authors of the American South. His short stories and novels, which are frequently set in the rural regions of his native North Carolina, are complex character studies that address such universal themes as the consequences of familial and sexual love, the need for independence, the effect of the past upon the present, and the mystique of place. Although some consider Price's use of symbolism and irony to be overwrought, many critics laud his unsentimental characterizations and acute depictions of regional traditions. While Price disclaims comparisons made between his work and that of most other Southern writers, particularly William Faulkner's, Price acknowledges Eudora Welty's influence on his career. Critics frequently cite similarities to the work of Welty and Flannery O'Connor in the spiritual and mythic subtext underlying Price's deceptively simple regional stories.

Biographical Information

The son of a traveling salesman, Price was born in Macon, North Carolina. During his undergraduate years at Duke University, he composed his first short story, "Michael Egerton," which received high praise from Eudora Welty, whom Price respected highly. After graduating from Duke University, Price attended Merton College, Oxford, as a Rhodes scholar. While residing in England, Price composed his first novel, *A Long and Happy Life* and several of the short stories that would comprise his first collection, *The Names and Faces of Heroes*. After three years at Oxford, Price returned to North Carolina. He took a position as teacher and writer-in-residence at Duke University. In 1984, Price's life quickly changed when he was diagnosed with spinal cancer. For two years he battled the disease and for several months he did not write. Fearing that he would not live to see the publication of his work-in-progress *Kate Vaiden*, Price returned to the novel while undergoing chemotherapy and radiation treatments. Price's illness left him confined to a wheelchair. Instead of crippling his artistry, this crisis has resulted in a prolific burst of poetry, drama, fiction, and autobiography. Price currently resides in Durham, North Carolina, and continues to teach at Duke University.

Major Works of Short Fiction

Price acknowledges Tolstoy, Flaubert, and Welty as major influences during the formative years of his writing and traces the roots of his metaphoric style to Milton and the Bible. Throughout his literary career, Price has explored manifestations of familial and sexual love as they affect a character's simultaneous desires for independence and fulfillment, as well as the imperfect communication among loved ones that leads to isolation and occasionally miraculous moments of understanding. These themes are played out in stories where the character's relationships span differences in age, class, race, and personality. The stories in his first collection, *The Names and Faces of Heroes*, reflect these signature issues, incorporating Price's native Southern setting and his autobiographical impulse. Critics praise Price's deft portrayal of male relationships and male adolescence in stories such as "The Names and Faces of Heroes," "Michael Egerton," and "Troubled Sleep." *Permanent Errors*, Price's second short fiction collection, differs in subject matter from the earlier fiction, as it focuses on academic and intellectual protagonists who forsake emotional involvement to pursue professional ambitions. The stories, in Price's words, attempt "to isolate in a number of lives the center error of act, will, understanding which, once made, has been permanent, incurable, but whose diagnosis and palliation are the hopes of continuance." This volume includes such frequently anthologized pieces as "Waiting at Dachau" and "The Happiness of Others."

Critical Reception

Early in his career Price was lauded for the optimism of his fiction in *The Names and Faces of Heroes* and the novel *A Long and Happy Life* which won the William Faulkner Award. With the appearance of *Permanent Errors*, critics noted a more somber tone. This collection depicts characters whose lives are shaped by a destiny that they can only partially control. Both Price's writing style and his role as Southern writer have been recurring issues among critics. Because of the poetic and metaphoric quality of his fiction, some critics have questioned his realism and characterization of southern culture. Others have defended his prose style as a method for presenting a multi-dimensional world that encompasses the physical, emotional, spiritual, and psychic realities of being human. Another recurring issue among critics is the extent to which Price's work is like that of William Faulkner's. Some make the comparison favorably, while others consider Price's work a less-successful imitation of the renowned Southern writer's work. Price comments on this frequent comparison thusly: "All Southern writers who have written in the last twenty years have had to bear the burden of being called Faulknerian. But the truth, if anyone is interested, is this, certainly and simply: they write about the South, which is their home as well as Faulkner's."

PRINCIPAL WORKS

Short Fiction

The Names and Faces of Heroes 1963
Permanent Errors 1970
Home Made 1990
The Forseeable Future 1991
The Collected Stories 1993

Other Major Works

A Long and Happy Life (novel) 1962
A Generous Man (novel) 1966
Late Warning: Four Poems (poetry) 1968
Love and Work (novel) 1968
Things Themselves: Essays and Scenes (essays) 1972
Presence and Absence: Versions From the Bible (nonfiction) 1973
The Surface of the Earth (novel) 1975
Early Dark: A Play (drama) 1977
Lessons Learned: Seven Poems (poetry) 1977

A Palpable God: Thirty Stories Translated from the Bible with an Essay of the Origins and Life of Narrative (essay and translations) 1978
The Source of Light (novel) 1981
A Start (miscellany) 1981
Private Contentment (drama) 1982
Vital Provisions (poetry) 1983
August Snow (drama) 1984
Kate Vaiden (novel) 1986
A Common Room (essays) 1987
Good Hearts (novel) 1988
The Laws of Ice (poetry and autobiography) 1988
Clear Pictures: First Loves, First Guides (memoir) 1989
New Music: A Trilogy (drama) 1990
The Tongues of Angels (novel) 1990
The Use of Fire (poetry) 1990
Blue Calhoun (novel) 1992
The Honest Account of a Memorable Life: An Apocryphal Gospel 1994
The Promise of Rest (novel) 1995
A Whole New Life (autobiography) 1995

*These novels, along with the short story "A Chain of Love," were collected in *Mustian*, 1983.

CRITICISM

R. G. G. Price (essay date 1963)

SOURCE: A review of *The Names and Faces of Heroes*, in *Punch,* Vol. CCXLV, No. 6423, October 16, 1963, pp. 577–78.

[*In the following positive review of* The Names and Faces of Heroes, *the critic contends that while Price's stories examine many of the same themes as those of other Southern writers, he does it "with an individual eye which sees everything freshly."*]

The Names and Faces of Heroes looks [to be] dividing opinion as sharply as Mr. Reynolds Price's first novel, *A Long and Happy Life.* Is his writing just dilute Faulkner, adrip with Southern charm, hinting at religious profundities, flabby and commercial, or is it, as I believe, the work of a mind sufficiently independent not to avoid material because other writers may have used it for banalities? In I. A. Richards's *Practical Criticism* he reports an experiment in which he gave a class a poem of Lawrence's without any indication of the author. Because it was set in a cosy, lamplit family atmosphere with a piano, many of the comments were derisive, *"Pears Annual,"* "Sentimental." etc. I feel something of the same stock response is blocking appreciation of the originality and force with which Mr. Price examines his particular patch of earth. It is true that in other books one finds North Carolina, ageing negroes, poor whites and, come to that, religion. What matters is that they are explored with an individual eye which sees everything freshly so that the ageing negroes are people, as distinguishable from other ageing negroes as Chardin's apples are from other apples. It is possible that in time Mr. Price may become just another Southern dollar-spinner; the point is that he isn't now, and that guilt-by-association isn't criticism. When I read the opening story, **"A Chain of Love,"** in *Encounter* I felt I was going to remember it for the rest of my life. Of course, vivid memories are not always a test of merit. Good tosh can be vivid, must be. But what I remembered about the story of the girl taking her grandfather to die in hospital— it is the girl who is the heroine of *A Long and Happy Life*—was not just the freshness and the compassion; it was the obstinacy with which it did not take the easy way, even at the risk of having reviewers assume that it did.

John W. Stevenson   (essay date 1966)

SOURCE: "The Faces of Reynolds Price's Short Fiction," in *Studies in Short Fiction,* Vol. III, No. 3, Spring, 1966, pp. 300–06.

[*In the following essay, Stevenson traces the theme of love as it is manifested through kinship, hospitality, and generosity in* The Names and Faces of Heroes.]

The controlling theme of Reynolds Price's fiction is the revelation that comes through the quest for self-knowledge, not in any intellectual sense but in the discovery that meaning and identity are found in giving, and in giving is learned the fulfilment of love. Price constructs everything in his stories around the dramatic contrast between all those human and natural forces that defeat and wear down and those moments of devotion and commitment found only in love. And this love is not a towering, raging, self-destroying passion, but the kind of love nurtured and made real in the relationships found in kinship, whether they be family or community. I know of no way to describe this deepest of all emotions than to see it as not so much a force but a current. Its reality is in an attachment, simple and uncomplicated, whose beginnings touch the heart of a character; and his devotion is such that he can no more expel it than he can contrive it.

Price reveals this theme of love through an emphasis on setting and on character in which the fictional technique is all reminiscence. He reveals theme through character, and the subjects of his stories are studies in the obligations of love. The discovery of this obligation, achieved through a type of ritual act, becomes at the same time an insight into the nature of hospitality. It is never an intellectual discovery; the characters come to their knowledge through a simple act of selflessness, as if out of each one's private suffering and alienation from being gradually emerges the shared humanness of a common guilt, a guilt redeemed through an act of grace.

All of Price's published short stories are collected in a volume entitled **The Names and Faces of Heroes** (1963). The first in the collection, **"A Chain of Love,"** is an episode in the lives of the Mustian family of Price's first novel, *A Long and Happy Life,* and more particularly it is a story of Rosacoke Mustian and her instinctive sensitivity toward the needs and wants of others. It is a study in contrasts, between the easy familiarity of family custom in the unfamiliar setting of a hospital room (Rosacoke and her half-witted brother, Rato, volunteer to sit with the sick grandfather for a week in a Raleigh hospital) and the lonely vigil, the solemn mystery of death faced by another family; between Rosacoke's friendliness and spontaneous sympathy and the formal stiffness and isolation of a young boy who waits silently outside the room of his dying father. Because Rosacoke can sense this family's plight— not so much the fact of death, but their facing it without friends and in a strange city—she feels obliged to make some gesture of hospitality. The need to show a sign focuses on the final scene of the story when with flowers brought from home she slips unseen into the dying man's room to offer her token of sympathy only to witness the strange rites of extreme unction—strange for one reared in Delight Baptist Church. She watches the ritual from the shadows, and then because she instinctively understands the intrusion of "looking on this dying which was the most private thing in the world," she laid the flowers on a chair and left "without saying a word." But the revelation is there in the simple act, clumsy perhaps and ill-timed, and the recognition of a stranger's need is linked to the elemental bond of human love seen in the fragile beauty of the althea blooms. The formal sacrament of the church through its external form achieves reality in its contrast with Rosacoke's instinctive recognition of the need to be named. Her simple gesture (althea blooms raised during the winter in a washtub placed in the kitchen) renders the profound nature of the sacrament of love—the knowledge that all relationships are personal. Later in the quiet but certain security of her grandfather's sick room, where death held no lonely fear, Rosacoke could console her own sorrow at the death of Mr. Ledwell, "who had died in that dark room" with the knowledge that "She had done what she could, being away from home, hadn't she, and didn't she know his name at least and hadn't he died not cut up or shot or run over but almost in his sleep with his wife and his boy there, and with all that beautiful dying song, hadn't he surely died sanctified?"

One discovers much of the underlying meaning in Price's short fiction in the more subtle drama of a character's developing moral awareness. Price reveals the significant action in what is going on in the character's consciousness: the discovery of his private obligation, his need to act out of a human responsibility to those who are if not in fact then in truth his kin. The commitment to action is the discovery that all action involves relationships. In many of the stories Price realizes this private discovery through the contrast between the young, for whom the knowledge of mortality is the awakening demands of love, and the middle-aged and elderly, for whom the knowledge is no longer an end but a beginning. The tension that dramatizes this contrast in all the stories is the nostalgia, the memory of an enfolding relationship that death cuts off. Because this loss involves a break up of the security and sense of community, the character perceives, if only briefly, the fragileness and the strength of the "chain of love." This is his passion, his discovery of the turning of time.

Another meaningful and important characteristic of Price's fiction lies in his setting. All of the stories are placed in the rural county of Warren, North Carolina—a setting which dramatizes through its simplicity and inherited moral values the source of kinship, the true place of hospitality. He contrasts the personal and inherited moral values of the rural setting with the nameless and impersonal urban morality, with those who live apart because of their fear of personal relationships. Rosacoke senses instinctively this impersonality; in a passage from Price's novel *A Long and Happy Life,* she sadly contemplates what life in the city with Wesley Beavers will be like:

> He said he would ride me to Dillon tonight and take me to Norfolk after Christmas to spend my life shut up in a rented room while he sells motorcycles to fools—me waiting out my baby sick as a dog, eating Post Toasties and strong pork liver which would be all he could afford and pressing his shirts and staring out a window in my spare time at concrete roads and folks that look like they hate each other.

All of Price's fiction grows out of a rural, Protestant fundamentalism, a setting which Miss Flannery O'Connor used for another purpose. While Price underlines the simple virtues that give the character dignity and a name, Miss O'Connor, through distortion and violence, dramatizes the folly of smug ignorance. She underlines a fanatic, superstitious pride exorcising evil in rites of holy zeal. The horror of Miss O'Connor's setting is in its revelation of the demonic set loose to assert a greedy salvation: so much destructive passion to consume the body of Christ, as if salvation were a cheap pillowcase bought in a ten-cent store and the words "Jesus Saves" emblazoned on its red silk cover in yellow cotton thread to comfort the homesick soul. There is no sacramental ritual in this setting, only suspicious aloofness and a fear of death. The terror is suffocating.

Price gives particular focus to this awareness of place as the source of knowing in his fiction in two stories about Negroes. Both of the stories are told by a first person narrator who as a young man has a strong family tie with two Negro servants. In the one, **"The Warrior Princess Ozimba,"** the action is in the present (rather than following Price's usual device of reminiscence), and the narrator takes on the family obligation started when his father was a boy of making an annual pilgrimage to the cabin of an aging and serene Negro woman. The occasion is her birthday, the Fourth of July, a day the old woman had selected for her birthday fifty years earlier, "not knowing what day she had been born and figuring that the Fourth was right noisy anyhow and one more little celebration wouldn't hurt if it pacified my father who was a boy then and who wanted to give her presents." And the gift, as it always had been from the very first, is a pair of blue tennis shoes. The crux of the story hangs on the immense dignity and respect, on the unspoken wisdom of devotion that binds a relationship no one needed to define or explain. Each year,

then, in the almost ludicrous yet childlike gift of blue tennis shoes there is renewed an unwritten covenant, a silent token of the obligation of love. For one brief moment the helpless, aged servant (blind, almost deaf, toothless) reveals to the heir of those whom she served all those years the nobility of service, that ultimate humility which gives her the exalted title, The Warrior Princess.

Like **"The Warrior Princess," "Uncle Grant,"** the other story of a Negro servant, is a deeply moving study of the fidelity and childlike devotion of a man who becomes the means through which a family discovers the meaning of kinship, the tie that binds. Here again is the recognition, revealed suddenly in later years and far away from the original setting, of the strangely paradoxical knowledge of dependence found in the dependent, of strength in simplicity, of wisdom in innocence. In such characters as Uncle Grant and Aunt Zimby, (The Warrior Princess), Price is not rendering an ideal of American primitivism; rather, like the old Negro woman in Eudora Welty's "A Worn Path" or Faulkner's Dilsey, these rural servants more nearly define the true pastoral character; their actions more specifically uphold the agrarian virtues and are in contrast to the stylized urban manners. It may well be that in modern American literature the only truly pastoral character is the Southern rural servant—presented not as a sentimentalized stereotype or as a subject for pity (hence, qualified for organized charity)—but as a way of measuring the order of myth (the past) against the fact of mortality (the present), of seeing pride in humility, hospitality in service.

The rural setting dramatizes the sense of nostalgia for a place once known and left behind, and these innocents recall this simpler world where a man knew who he was (knew without really knowing at the time) and accepted without calculation the obligations of love. It is, in fact, this technique of reminiscence that most effectively points up the contrast between the false and the real, the past and the present, the revelation of love and the knowledge of death that give dimension and force to Price's theme. None of Price's short stories presents this theme more sensitively than the one entitled **"The Names and Faces of Heroes."** He renders all of the action through the consciousness of a young boy as he searches his father's face for some one answer to the question he has set himself to discover. Riding through a dark, February night along a deserted North Carolina highway, the boy and his father are returning from a distant city where the father had gone to hear a famous Baptist preacher. The boy rides with his head in his father's lap staring up into his face; and although he cannot know the complexity of his search, he is aware of the need to know somehow the nature of his father's identity. "I search it for a hero. For the first time. I have searched nearly every other face since last July, the final Sunday at camp when a minister told us, 'The short cut to being a man is finding your hero, somebody who is what you are not but need to be. What I mean is this. Examine yourself. When you find what your main lack is, seek that in some great man.'"

The story is a vision story, and it works because Price believes in the reality of the boy's final revelation and because the authority of the story comes from his never violating the limits of the boy's consciousness. The boy's painful dilemma is not resolved until he first strips away all the masks that disguise not only himself from his father but also his father from him. A significant incident of the story is the boy's recalling and describing the father's ability to mock. Aware that men adopt disguises to hide their fears and believing that "you do not seek heroes at home," he has studied the faces of the past, men of legend and history. "I have not read books that do not show faces because I study a man's face first. Then if that calls me on, I read his deeds." But the deeds always reveal some moral flaw, some selfish misuse of power, and he concludes "All the dead have failed me. That is why I study my father tonight." What he discovers in the long reflection of his father's deeds and in his own need to earn his right as his father's son is the face of love, the source of his own being, and the name of his own identity.

Price's style—the natural and native syntax, the imagery—is like the prose of Eudora Welty, as is his sensitivity to character and his technique of dramatizing theme through character.

—John W. Stevenson

The boy discovers one other thing. In a tortured dream (he falls asleep during the long ride) he foresees as in a vision the death of his father; and filled with the sense of pain and despair at the rending of this bond, he perceives at the same time the overpowering obligation toward the physical and symbolic tie that joins them in love but which he must drain and take if he is to be redeemed through the very act of creation that by its commitment takes on its own destruction. It is the supreme act of hospitality. In the beginning of the story, the young boy thinks: "We are people in love. We flee through hard winter night. What our enemies want is to separate us. Will we end together? Will we end alive?" And at the end, knowing the blight man was born for and the promise of his vision, the boy accepts the need of the present. As they arrive at the end of their long night's journey (for him both real and symbolic) facing the warm light of their home and the mother's quiet welcome, the father stands in the snow holding out his arms to the boy who turns to climb from the car. Too old to be carried like a small child (he is nine), he asks, "What do you mean?" The father replies only "I mean to save your life, to carry you over this snow." And the boy says to himself—"silent, in the voice I will have as a man"—"They did not separate us tonight. We finished alive, together, whole. This one more time."

Price's style—the natural and native syntax, the imagery (". . . mainly because the Christmas pageant had fallen through when John Arthur Bobbitt passed around German measles like a dish of cool figs at the first rehearsal. . . .")— is like the prose of Eudora Welty, as is his sensitivity to

character and his technique of dramatizing theme through character. He has also Miss Welty's ability to render character by a fine selection of a few details that give the characters dimension and naturalness. Aunt Zimby, as seen by the narrator, is like an old snapshot in a family album: " . . . suddenly she was still as before, and then a smile broke out on her mouth as if it had taken that long for the story to work from her lips into her mind, and when the smile was dying off, she jerked her hand that was almost a great brown bird's wing paddling the air once across her eyes." Or Uncle Grant, as the narrator recalls the old Negro's image while looking at a postcard picture of the Egyptian pharaoh Amenhotep IV:

> . . . on a black background an Egyptian head, the tall narrow skull rocked back on the stalky neck, the chin offered out like a flickering tongue, the waving lips set in above (separate as if they were carved by a better man), the ears with their heavy lobes pinned close to the skull, and the black-rimmed sockets holding no eyes at all. . . . I bought the card and left the shop and walked ten yards and said to myself in the street what I suddenly knew, "It's the one picture left of Uncle Grant."

If Price finds his theme in the rural setting of northeastern North Carolina, he found also, I suspect, the place from which to explore in a less sweeping way the grandly epic theme of that other North Carolina writer Thomas Wolfe. Wolfe's restless energy and his cosmic agony for the lost home is refined and controlled in the nostalgia of Price's fiction. Perhaps it is the younger writer's knowledge of and belief in Wolfe's tremendous vision that gives him the stage to work out his own private need to define the quest for innocence and the obligations of love. Price selected, in fact, a sentence from Blake to introduce his collection of stories: "I met a plow on my first going out at my gate the first morning after my arrival, & the Plowboy said to the Plowman, 'Father, The Gate is Open.'" I cannot help thinking that the epigraph is Price's recognition of the seed of his literary source, the seed from which his fiction earns its right to sustain the vision Wolfe expressed in his large theme of "wandering forever and the earth again"—by which, Wolfe explained in a letter to Maxwell Perkins, "I mean simply the everlasting earth, a home, a place for the heart to come to, and earthly mortal love, the love of a woman, who, it seems to me, belongs to the earth and is a force opposed to that other great force that makes men wander, that makes them search, that makes them lonely."

Reynolds Price with Wallace Kaufman (interview date 1966)

SOURCE: An interview in *Shenandoah*, Vol. XVII, No. 4, Summer, 1966, pp. 3–25.

[*In the following excerpt, Price discusses his early career, Eudora Welty's influence on his career and work, and gives his reaction to being labeled a Southern writer.*]

[Kaufman]: . . . . *Most reviewers now consider you as a Southern writer. What do you think your relationship is to the first generation of modern Southern novelists? People like Faulkner, Carson McCullers, Robert Penn Warren, Katherine Anne Porter and Eudora Welty?*

[Price]: I should say that my relation to all those names, except Eudora Welty, is a relationship of varied admiration and respect. But a distant relation. Those were not the people I was reading when I was young and formable. Those were not, and have not become, the people I have returned to and read continually at moments of curiosity and leisure in my life. Faulkner, of course, is a special and enormous case. All Southern writers who have written in the last twenty years have had to bear the burden of being called Faulknerian. But the truth, if anyone is interested, is this, certainly and simply: they write about the South, which is their home as well as Faulkner's. Reviewers who lament the "influence" of Faulkner are really only asking that all other Southern writers arrange to be born outside the South. It is a curse, of a sort, to be born a writer in the same region and at the same time as a great regional novelist. Imagine being born in southwest England in the lifetime of Thomas Hardy and trying to write your own novels about Wessex, the world that you also knew. You would have been cursed with being "influenced by Hardy" for the rest of your life, called that at least. I am serious in speaking of "a curse" only to the extent that the cry of Faulknerian influence has become a conditioned reflex among literary journalists, even serious critics; the application of influence labels being—as any college English major knows—the easiest way to (a) write your 3,000 words and (b) to avoid at all costs *facing* a work of art, its new vision, its new and necessarily terrible way of stating the injunction of Rilke's Apollo: "You must change your life!" I can say, quite accurately, that Faulkner has been no influence, technical or otherwise, on my work. I admire the work of Faulkner that I know—by no means all—but with a cold, distant admiration for a genius whom I know to be grand but who has proved irrelevant to my own obsessions, my own ambitions. The writer in your list who did affect me greatly, and continues to do so, is Eudora Welty. I had read a few of her stories in high school. I remember especially that "A Worn Path" was in one of our high school anthologies, but it was in my senior year in college that I read her stories in quantity. They were an instantaneous revelation and a revelation about my life, not about literature nor the methods and techniques of fiction. They revealed to me what is most essential for any beginning novelist—which is that his world, the world he has known from birth, the world that has not seemed to him in any way extraordinary is in fact a perfectly possible world, base, subject for serious fiction. I recognized in those stores of Eudora Welty's which I read as a senior in college a great many of the features of the world I had known as a child in rural eastern North Carolina, and so I felt confirmed by her example in the validity of my own experience as a source of art. That was her great service to me, and I shall always be grateful to her for that service she rendered me unknowingly but most deeply grateful for the fact that she came to Duke to give a lecture—"Place in Fiction"—in the second semester of my senior year and

kindly asked to see some student writing. One of my stories (the only serious story that I had written, **"Michael Egerton"**) was given to her by William Blackburn. She read it, encouraged me, offered to send the story to her agent Diarmuid Russell, who has since been my agent, and championed my work in the early years when no one in America was interested in publishing it. What she offered me was what any young writer demands in varying ways at various times in his career—adequate judgment. I knew that she was a sound judge; and I knew it because she was judging my work as *art,* not as the product of a favorite student or a friend. Her mind was filled with the example of her own work and all the work she had seen and read in her life, and she was still able to say to me what was utterly valuable, utterly meaningful at that time— that my story was a good story. Not "This is the best story by a college senior which I have read in the past five years," but "This is an excellent *story*. Let me see the rest of your stories." I said truthfully that there were no other stories because to that time I had only written eight pages of fiction; but at her request I very rapidly went to work and began writing another story—**"A Chain of Love."** And in the next three years, the years of my study at Oxford, I produced about a hundred pages of short stories, all of which were later published in a volume called ***The Names and Faces of Heroes***.

What about the new Southern writers, your contemporaries like William Styron and Walker Percy, Fred Chappell and Shirley Ann Grau? Do you read these people conscientiously? Are you conscious of them as Southern writers?

I read them because I think they are serious writers but very different writers. I feel no duty to read them because they are in any sense "fellow Southern novelists." I have never felt myself a "Southern novelist." I am a novelist— who was reared and has lived most of his life in the South. Insofar as the South is a unique world, my work reflects that uniqueness; but my work is not, has never been *about* the South. Some of the Agrarians in the 20's, early 30's may have thought of themselves briefly as "Southern"; but I don't think it's been the feeling of anyone in the last twenty years, not any serious writer certainly. No, I read the writers you mentioned, and two or three of them are friends of mine, but I don't feel that their work has any special relationship with my work. I don't feel any dialogue between my work and theirs, except that dialogue which exists between all honest artistry—a relationship not of imitation but of emulation. One reads good work and that good work invites not imitation but a parallel effort of quality.

Why do you still live in the South? You often make trips away from it. What does the South offer you as a writer? Does it offer you something culturally or something more intangible?

Because the South is my home. It is where I was born. It is where I spent the first twenty-two years of my life and where I've spent the rest of my life with the exception of four years in Europe. The South is a place; and that place has been the scene of most of the crucial events of my life, both external and internal. Therefore I remain in that part of the world which has been—and seems likely to be—the site of my life.

Both your novels and the stories take place in the South, mainly in the area where you grew up. How close does the material in your fiction come to real people and real events? I guess what I'm asking is—to what degree are you a chronicler?

Every character in the novels is invented; and even the stories which appear to be autobiographical are really a kind of historical fiction, a drastic arrangement, re-invention of memory. No, I have no sense of being a conscious chronicler—either of Southern life or of human life as I've known it in my lifetime, which has after all been an enormous time in human history (I was born in 1933). What I've chronicled is my own world, that world which has seemed to me (since I began to see at all) to exist *beneath* the world perceived by other people, that world which seems to me to impinge upon, to color, to shape, the daily world we inhabit. . . .

[You] introduce the supernatural into **The Names and Faces of Heroes**. *Do you believe in the supernatural? And how can you create it if you don't really understand what it is?*

There are a great many things in the universe which we don't understand but make constant use of—electricity, the energy of the atom. We make use of our bodies every moment of our lives; and we certainly don't understand a tenth that there is to know about our eyes, our hearts, our kidneys. I suppose what you're referring to in **The Names and Faces of Heroes** would be that in the end of the title story, the child has a vision of the twelve years which wait between now and his father's death. And in *A Generous Man* there is the appearance to Milo of someone who has been dead for years, whom Milo had never seen in that person's earthly life. It's obviously difficult to discuss one's own relation to what you call the supernatural without sounding fishy in the extreme. I'd rather say this much and then pass on: that I do strongly suspect, even avow the existence and presence of forms of reality quite beyond those forms which we encounter in our daily routines. And whether or not those forms do manifest themselves—ever, in observable, sensually perceptible ways—certainly there can be no question that the dead linger, most powerfully, in our lives; the meaningful dead, those people who by the time most men have reached the age of twenty-one stand as one's ancestors on the black side of death in relation to our present continuing lives. That's all.

Where do you think all this strange stuff belongs in the larger context of literature? . . . What about your contemporaries and other twentieth-century writers? Where do you think the supernatural or at least the extranatural fits in?

There's a long and continuing tradition of the supernatural, not only in the epic, the lyric, and poetic drama but in the novel itself. Very obviously, the novel before the late 19th century was not committed to realism. The novels of 18th century England, the great Victorian novels—the Brontës, Dickens—are highly "unrealistic" visions of human existence. Dickens makes as profound and revealing and convincing use of the supernatural as Kafka. His coincidences alone are acts of God. And to mention Kafka is to mention the great modern student of the supernatural. I wouldn't claim that there are many serious novelists who are presently employing ghosts in their novels—there is a credible and necessary ghost in Agee's *A Death in the Family,* and there are the ghosts and demons in Isaac Singer—but I do claim that the supernatural in the form of ghosts is still a possible, occasionally a necessary component of a serious novelist's vision.

Most of your work is quite serious fiction, yet in all of it there's a great deal of comedy. In fact, I believe A Generous Man *started as an attempt at a comic novel. What role do you see comedy playing in your work?*

All my work is comic—not by conscious choice but because in attempting to embody the world that I've known, I have portrayed a comic world. Comedy is almost always a function of experience, a function of life. Even in the intensest moments of despair, pain, grief, wild bursts of laughter will insist upon rising and asserting themselves. And any literary form which abolishes or ignores the laughter at the heart of human life—even the laughter on the edges of human life—does so at the expense of its own truthfulness. Certain very large and important kinds of literary art have eliminated comedy, at least so far as we can see. For instance, with the possible exception of two or three scenes, there seem to be no elements of the comic in Greek tragedy. The laughter of life was simply postponed for plays which were comedies or for the satyr plays which were performed in cycle with the tragedies. But the fullest, therefore truest, most useful picture of human life is a picture which will necessarily and gladly contain much that is hilarious, mocking and satyric—satyric in the oldest sense: a picture of satyrs, grinning, hairy, ithyphallic dancers, cruel (no, indifferent) witnesses of man's only-partially-relevant existence.

Theodore Solotaroff (essay date 1970)

SOURCE: "The Reynolds Price Who Outgrew the Southern Pastoral," in *Saturday Review*, New York, Vol. LIII, No. 39, September 26, 1970, pp. 27–9, 46.

[Solotaroff is an American critic and educator. In the following excerpt, he reviews the development of Price's themes in Permanent Errors.*]*

In its deeper reaches, *Love and Work* is a novel about the unconscious and its circuits of love, fear, and punishment—what used to be called God. There is more than a hint of the spiritual in Price, rather like that in E. M. Forster or Rilke, which takes a psychological rather than a theological form: a powerful sense of dark unseen forces and influences that are only partly explained by the description of emotions and that require not just attention but supplication. This preoccupation comes increasingly into the foreground of *Permanent Errors,* a collection of stories and other pieces that, written over a period of seven years, lead up to and away from the issues of *Love and Work.*

In a brief, rather cryptic introduction Price tells us that the pieces are joined by a common intention: "the attempt to isolate in a number of lives the central error of act, will, understanding which, once made, has been permanent, incurable, but whose diagnosis and palliation are the hopes of continuance." Most of the errors in the book are committed by writers, who share Eborn's view that a writer needs solitude and detachment as a fish needs water (which happens to be true), but who use this need as a cover for vanity, timidity, selfishness, blindness, and other modes of withdrawal and assault.

There are two, possibly three, main examples. The first is Charles Tamplin, a young American writer living in England, who is involved in four pieces collectively titled **"Fool's Education."** Tamplin is something of an esthete and a prig who tends to view his experience from a self-protective literary attitude and to take his knowledge of life from the happiness and the scars of others. But he is not merely foolish: he has a quick, relevant understanding of what he sees, and though it comes too late to profit him in his life, it can, once recognized, accepted, and grieved over, perhaps help to strengthen him in his vocation. His situation is beautifully rendered in the first story [**"The Happiness of Others"**], which deals with the last day of his long-standing affair with a girl from home, a Rosacoke who has been to Vassar. To Tamplin, it is a day to get through, to kill gracefully and lightly, like the affair itself, and round it to a close. From their failure "to meet, to serve one another, to delight in the work" he will now gain his freedom to make art from it. They visit a favorite church near Oxford and end up trading, rather bitterly, the epitaphs on the tombs. His is an elegy by Ben Jonson for a friend who died young, in which the poet finds consolation in the very brevity of the life:

> In small proportions, we just beauty see;
> And in short measures, life may perfect be.

Sara's inscription is from a family tomb and speaks of the ties of love under the aspect of death:

> And they that lived and loved either
> Should die and lie and sleep together.
> Go reader. Whether go or stay,
>   Thou must not hence be long away.

"It's a truer poem," she says. "It could change whole lives." Tamplin is unimpressed. A short while later their car almost collides with a flock of sheep. A young shepherd follows them, apparently just awakened, refreshes himself with a last patch of snow, and calmly says, "Sorry." It is enough to light up Sara, who smiles and waves him pardon. A few small images of life's transience, but enough

to make Tamplin realize that Sara will recover in ways he won't—or only enough to write truly about the burden of this day.

Tamplin's pitfalls and recognitions deepen as his chronicle moves along. He is a young man in flight, one foot out the door of any entangling relationship, ready to pull the door of his privacy shut at any sign of invasion. He closes it on a desperate woman who wants to use his bed to steal a few moments of love, but he ends up worshiping the bitter mysteries of her love-scarred life. For there is a stern beneficence operating in his fate that drives him out of his shell, turns his timidity to a certain kind of strength, leads him, some years later, to abandon his stiff-necked pride and ask forgiveness for not forgiving Sara's rightful distrust of him.

This difficult movement from grievance to grief surges powerfully through the last two stories in the book, which deal with an older writer, not unlike Tamplin, whose wife first attempts and then commits suicide. **"Good and Bad Dreams"** is an extraordinary tracing of the borderland of the conscious and the unconscious that lies between a husband and a wife who have reached a terrible ultimate stage, in which her life hangs in the balance of their love/hate, but who can only communicate in their sleep.

"Walking Lessons," a long story, picks up the husband's legacy of rage after her death and takes him to an Indian reservation and to certain ordeals that his wife's act has reserved for him. The theme of an intolerable but seemingly unbreakable connection is doubled by the situation of the friend he visits there, a lapsed medical student who has a hopeless job as a VISTA worker and a more hopeless relationship with an Indian girl with multiple sclerosis. To Dora and the other Indians, the writer is a new affliction, the husband of a suicide, whose ghost, according to their lore, will follow him by night. To his friend, Blix, he is an unfeeling monster, "the killing kind." I won't try to trace the complex movement of this story or its mystical undertow, by which the writer is dragged to the admission of his responsibility, then to his atonement for it. I suspect that **"Walking Lessons"** brings to an end a long, grueling phase in Price's career, deeply though not congruently related to his own moral accounting, and bearing in its searching, potent artistry the healed scars of his own suffering.

Guy Davenport (essay date 1970)

SOURCE: A review of *Permanent Errors*, in *The New York Times Book Review*, October 11, 1970, p. 4.

[*Davenport is an American scholar, poet, essayist, illustrator, and fiction writer. In the following review, Davenport identifies the problems of intimacy and communication faced by characters in* Permanent Errors.]

The permanent errors of these bitter stories are suicide, the refusal to forgive and that violation of the heart's privacy whereby we know so much about a person's misery that we cannot know the person. All knowledge of others, Reynolds Price seems to say, is tragic. Then tension between human beings is a matter of distance, both real and psychological. All of these stories are about crossing the perimeters that may not be crossed without terrible responsibilities; love, compassion, confession are wounds, and their scars are permanent.

These stories are not easy to read or to comprehend. Except for **"Waiting at Dachau"** and **"Walking Lessons,"** they are elliptical and sketchy. Mr. Price prefers the oblique slant and the quick glimpse. The tone throughout is that of heartsick anxiety, hot nerves and of strained tempers about to snap: "She reached for his wrist. He gave her his hand. But she did not take it—'I was looking for the time,' she said. He extended his watch. She studied it carefully, returned it to his side, gave him the sum, 'Eighteen hours till I rest on the bosom of the deep.' They both gave the brief statutory grin—they spoke of her sailing, their permanent parting, in jokes . . ."

Modern literature has for years been closing the distance between stage and audience; obviously the artist feels the need for this emboldened intimacy. The Victorian novel was set in long perspectives; resonant voices boomed across rooms. Mr. Price, a North Carolinian, has a claustrophobic obsession with nearness, which to any Southerner represents chaos and moral disorder. All good manners and sane conduct begin with distance. It is precisely in the negation of traditional distances that Mr. Price finds the confusion in the souls of his characters.

The first four stories deal with lives that touch intimately but without understanding—the peril of love being that passion arrives helter-skelter where intelligence can't even begin to follow. In **"Waiting at Dachau"** two lovers thrash at each other's minds, furious that they are different, unique and inviolable. Imbedded in the story, which is set at

Dachau 12 years after the closing of that *stalag,* are certain betrayals of kin known to have happened there, which can only be explained by the absolute distinctness of each soul. The most futile cry of man is the impossible wish to be understood. Mr. Price poises his characters just at the tragic demarcation where they imagine they can be understood by others, and he lets them smash their innocence against the ineluctable fact that they are forever opaque and incomprehensible to the world.

"Walking Lessons," the long story which ends the collection, is about a young man whose wife has committed suicide. To escape his grief he visits a friend who is a VISTA worker among the Navajo, and who is keeping a Navajo girl as a mistress. Despair, altruism and an alien psychology—Mr. Price allows this triangle of disparities to diagram the human condition as he has studied it throughout this tough-minded book. The understanding among the three is marginal. Yet to communicate at all, we must surrender some of our own mind to participate in the ideas and attitudes of the mind we think we are addressing. This strange game drove the philosopher Wittgenstein to assume that human beings cannot communicate at all, and Mr. Price shows that human beings succeed in communication, if at all, as Homer's heroes fought, by main force and superhuman strenuousness. And even then we do not communicate, but in the effort we at least define to ourselves what we cannot impart.

The permanent errors of the title are therefore, once we have taken in the implications of Mr. Price's bleak book, any action whatsoever. To do is to err; to speak is to address the deaf. The way out of this dilemma, of course, is to be content to do and speak without being understood; one is then on the way to the paradox that understanding comes in channels of its own choosing, in its own good time. Perhaps at least one of Mr. Price's characters learns this, for a brief moment; by the last sentence of the story he has forgotten it.

Permanent Errors must take its place as a pivotal book in our literary history, as one of the brave steps beyond the fiercely Calvinist pessimism of Southern writing in general, which has consistently presented the only alternative in American thought to charismatic liberalism. Mr. Price's step is into an even more iron Calvinism. It may be that the South presents a more constant spectacle of man's fall from grace than the rest of the Republic; and it may be that tradition, which, as long as it is alive, deepens and refines its insights, insists in the work of Mr. Price on an ultimate vision of human blindness. No Southern writer of genius from Poe to Flannery O'Connor has ever depicted man as other than damned and complacently unaware of it.

Allen Shepherd (essay date 1973)

SOURCE: "Notes on Nature in the Fiction of Reynolds Price," in *Critique: Studies in Modern Fiction,* Vol. XV, No. 2, 1973, pp. 83–94.

[*In the following excerpt, Shepherd traces the various connections between the natural world and human consciousness in Price's short fiction.*]

Reynolds Price is not a writer in whose work nature and the relation of man and nature seem of the first importance, as they do, in different senses, in the fiction of Faulkner, Warren, Wolfe, O'Connor, or Dickey. Whatever the difficulties, though not because of them, Price is not given to celebrating nature. Beyond the dark pastoral of *A Long and Happy Life* (1962) and the jokes-in-character turned rather grim romance of *A Generous Man* (1966), an engagement with nature is consistently evident in Price's fiction through which characters receive or miss messengers, signs, emblems from the world of nature, whole lives changed in the process. "It was messenger, sign" [Reynolds Price, *Permanent Errors* (New York: Atheneum, 1970). Subsequent references are to this edition.] registers the protagonist's perception that a dying bat he has discovered on the lawn, lice-covered, weak, frightening, subsequently killed and buried, intimates his wife's approaching suicide. She does kill herself: the sign is true. So indeed are they all, though some are inconsequential and many are misapprehended. Where do these signs originate? "The world of nature" is an answer, true as far as it goes but incomplete. More comprehensively, one says the Great World, the supernatural, whose existence, presence, and force are intimated, even affirmed, most clearly in Price's recent work. One might indeed consider the stories collected in *Permanent Errors* (1970) or *Love and Work* (1968), the author's best novel, as religious statements, though not of a conventional variety.

When to the dying bat of Price's story one adds certain prominent deer, dogs, snakes, hawks, herons, and blood suckers, one may begin to visualize a company out of Thornton W. Burgess. Such is not to be found, of course; nor are any gigantic, ageless bears or enormous heroic marlin in residence. Price is not ecological nor allegorical nor consistently symbolical. . . .

Price's two volumes of short stories, *The Names and Faces of Heroes* (1963) and *Permanent Errors*, illustrate several strategies in the delineation of man's relation to nature, man's heightened perception of his own identity in that relation. With the exception of **"A Chain of Love"** and the title story, *The Names and Faces of Heroes* seems an effort, largely successful, at the revivification of cliches, Price undertaking to make the worn and familiar new and his own. In **"The Anniversary"** Miss Lillian Belle decorates the grave of one William (Pretty Billy) Williams, who died, under not so mysterious circumstances, on the day before their wedding, years before. To receive her narrative and to offer increasingly broad hints of Billy's regular destination in his unaccompanied, all-day horseback rides in the week preceding the wedding, a young Negro boy, Wash, is introduced. Although Miss Lillian Belle, by her own assertion, is "a mighty good forgetter," Nettie Pitchford, in whose house he expired, was clearly on Pretty Billy's mind. As the story closes, Miss Lillian Belle returns home

towards what she could see—the light, that was all, the sun on the spilled paint, the sudden flashing reaching out to her even down here, shining like Christmas all those years ago or like her own old eyes as bright now in remembering as some proud mountain yielding the sun its flanks of snow or some white bird settling its slender wings with the softest cry into dying light.

The two similes at the end (eyes/ proud mountain/ white bird) serve largely to decorate, seem an ill-considered grace note. We do not require to be told who or what Miss Lillian Belle is or resembles; the passage is cited, then, not so much because it fails to do what was done elsewhere—Rosacoke and the hawk, Milo and the weasel skull—but because it represents another strategy, considerably less successful.

Permanent Errors, as Price notes in a foreword, represents "the attempt to isolate in a number of lives the central error of act, will, understanding which, once made, has been permanent, incurable, but whose diagnosis and palliation are the hopes of continuance." By and large the stories are fine, intense, complex, sterner stuff than those in *The Names and Faces of Heroes*. Two of them will display different yet complementary perspectives on man and nature. In **"Good and Bad Dreams,"** a six-part sequence, the first, **"A Sign of Blood,"** introduces a husband and wife, well into the worst of times, the wife ultimately to commit suicide, the husband to survive. The wife departs the house in the first sentence yet neither escapes the other in what follows. He, feigning sleep until she is safely away, anticipates with narcissistic pleasure a free, solitary day, nine hours alone, reading, drawing, listening to music. Standing before the mirror, "an archaic Apollo," he communes with his image: *"You must change your life."* Not in the mirror but out in the yard his eye catches something, unidentifiable at a distance, to be—potentially—an agent of change, and "he felt the day begin to leak from his grip."

It is a bat, broken, nearly—or as he thinks at first, wholly—dead, lice-infested, the first he has ever seen up close. "He felt instantly stripped again and vulnerable, precisely in his eyes and throat." Once prodded, it stretches its wings, bares pink gums and needle teeth, "and—surely—screamed."

> He knew it would rush at his face—his eyes—and he dropped the shovel to run; ran three steps. Then he stopped to see, remembering her—as though she were there in the window above him, his panic slamming at her.

Here the complex and central structure of association which directs the story is identified. Without exercising excessive ingenuity, one may say that the bat, near death, intimates the wife, approaching suicide; that the husband's instinctive fear for his eyes and throat, the image in the mirror, relates to his need to protect himself from his wife, from her pain; and that in dispatching the bat, as he shortly does, he is, in his panic, "slamming at her."

Not yet a "permanent error," the husband's extant errors are, possibly, still correctable. Restoring himself through reflection on why the bat so frightens him—"Childhood icons? Halloween, vampires? Or older even, archetypal?"— the husband concludes that the bat must be removed before his wife returns, because, as he is pleased to think with perhaps some self-serving justice, the sight would be too much for her. But why, he asks, ought he have to protect her? "Let her grow her own rind or shrink from sight. God knew he'd grown *his*."

He kills the bat, easily, buries it, and shortly discovers why, as he thinks, it would change his life: "It was messenger, sign." "She will kill herself." Messenger perhaps, and reflecting, again perhaps, "the celestial joker's usual taste." To read the bat's advent thus is both legitimate in the story and validated by the author's practice elsewhere. The reader is also at liberty, even compelled, to consider this climactic revelation in light of the husband's known fears and desires, in terms of the association previously developed, and with respect for his insulated self-regard. That things *will* happen, that his wife is to die, may obviate certain problems for a man likely to be in attendance, even as the awareness creates others.

"A Sign of Blood" is not only amenable to comprehensible summary and fairly close analysis but represents a kind of *locus classicus*. The setting is not notably rural, as might be observed by way of objection to my remarks on Price's first two novels (deer, hawks, weasels, and herons *live* near Rosacoke and Milo). The story illuminates, complexly but clearly, one point of connection between man and nature. We see both how and why the husband interprets the sign and are left not with ultimate truth but with complementary possibilities.

The last story, of some ninety-five pages, to be considered is **"Walking Lessons,"** which treats a young man, much resembling the protagonist of **"A Sign of Blood,"** whose wife has recently committed suicide. To outdistance his grief he goes to visit a friend, a lapsed medical student, Blix Cunningham, now a VISTA worker among the Navajo, who has taken up with Dora Badonie, a young Navajo girl suffering through the early stages of multiple sclerosis. Understanding among the three is marginal, discontinuous; their futures bleak; the Arizona setting beautiful, awesome, ultimately desolate, terrible. The Indians are, by the VISTA man's testimony, "weirder than snakes" and survive, barely and miserably, on Coke, Roma Tokay, Skoal Wintergreen Flavored Chewing Tobacco and other unknown resources. To the Indians the writer-protagonist is simply another affliction, husband of a suicide whose ghost, according to their belief, will follow him by night. He is a witch, dangerous. To Cunningham, he is an unfeeling monster, fatal.

The crisis and climax of the story evolve from the attempt of Blix, the narrator, Dora, and a few drunken hangers-on to recover Dora's grandmother's pickup truck, stuck in the mud somewhere far up the Zuni road. After failing and losing their own truck, the original three walk out, while the narrator has cause to wonder whether he will be able

to make it, be deserted, or simply be killed. The long march across country, through an alien and hostile environment, is important not as it represents a struggle of man with nature but as it affects mental processes, psychological displacement. Through the first hour of walking the cloud cover holds, the cold is bearable, even exhilarating, and keeps the snow frozen. "I had won, would win. Won what?—freedom, competence." Another hour brings more penetrating cold, a new rhythm, "the coded message any fool could read: *It is possible to die. Here. Soon.*" Such awareness brings closer to acceptance ties that have not previously bound the narrator to his wife, dead; to Dora, knowing of her death, though she ascribes her illness to touching a snake; to Blix and Dora and their doomed union, recalling and chastising his own marriage. But the end is not yet: during a break Cunningham asks what he must do, not about getting out, but about Dora and the rest of his life; the narrator can only say that he had made *his* way out because he wanted to.

The sky opens "like a gullet, black and bottomless," the "fierce stars" by the tens of thousands stream their "titanic ray-therapy," the power line, inviolate, hums overhead, the airport beacon at Gallup lifts away. The saving truth offers itself, but not as a means of escape: the narrator wanted his wife dead, but he cannot, as he is invited to do by his would-be victim, kill Dora. Finally, he asks forgiveness of his dead wife's surrogate, and—as someone begins to shoot at them from a house nearby—he steps in front of Blix. He is happy, "if being past fear and with all debts paid is a brand of happiness." There remains only the last confession: "She is dead and dumb. Hammer-dead. Her name was Beth."

The end, when it comes, is as radical a conversion and nearly as mystical: a new man emerges and departs for the motel. Such communication as has occurred is a triumph, framed, drawn out, properly diminished and almost cut off by miles and miles of the Zuni road up to 7,000 feet, mud, snow, freezing cold, moonlight, cliffs. All of nature is more than backdrop, other than animate force, more concrete than influence: it is *there,* to be known, contended with, powerful, alien, instinct with life, with that of the narrator's wife among them, and clearly it is not—for a man like the narrator—to be lived with too long.

Constance Rooke (essay date 1983)

SOURCE: "*Permanent Errors,*" in *Reynolds Price,* Twayne Publishers, 1983, pp. 87–110.

[*Rooke is an American critic and short story writer. In the following excerpt, she examines the series of errors that lead to isolation and imperfect love in* Permanent Errors.]

Permanent Errors is, according to Price, an "attempt to isolate in a number of lives the central error of act, will, understanding which, once made, has been permanent, incurable, but whose diagnosis and palliation are the hopes of continuance." Loosely defined, it is a collection of stories divided into four parts. The first part, however, is really four stories which combine to form a discontinuous novella; the second is described by Price as "narrative poems of personal loss, therefore elegies"; the third contains one conventional story and six interrelated, surrealistic fragments; and the fourth is a novella. The "central error" throughout is a failure in love, whose "diagnosis and palliation" occur largely through art. Two of the protagonists are writers, "quasi-interchangeable lenses" with obvious optical similarities to Eborn and Price. In *Love and Work* Eborn recognizes both that "'mistakes can be permanent'" and that his work will continue. *Permanent Errors,* with its multiple perspectives and techniques all converging upon a single pattern of error, is concerned with the continuing, obsessive pattern of that error and with the compensations of art.

The epigraph for *Permanent Errors* is Price's own free translation of Rilke's "The Alchemist." An artist's parable, it draws upon a variety of alchemical traditions to describe the costs and conditions of artistic creation. Most centrally, it equates the *"crumb of gold"* that an alchemist employs as seed for his desired transmutation with the artist's own experience: he trades his life, that is, for the hope of something larger. The experiment recorded here leaves the Faustian artist *"babbling"* in disappointment, craving the life that he has sold away. But that conclusion is modified by an alchemical tradition which allows for intermediate success, and the suggestion that something of this current effort (though it falls short of the desired end) has nevertheless risen *"past him to God."* The reference to a *"crystal crib"* evokes yet another tradition, according to which the philosopher's stone is seen as a kind of homunculus, an infant born solely of the hermaphroditic alchemist; thus some defense is offered of the artist's solitude, although on this occasion his child (the work of art) is seen as a *"monster,"* born unnaturally. The artist's purpose is to become attuned perfectly with reality, to balance male and female principles, and to accept the paradox that his *"free and sovereign"* mind is *"fiercely ruled."* Finally, the epigraph serves to defend the author's choice of art as well as to admit its awful cost.

"Fool's Education" is the collective title of the four stories that comprise Part One. In the first story, "The Happiness of Others," we are introduced to Charles Tamplin on the eve of his separation from Sara. An irony attaches to the definition of Tamplin as a fool, since he is an Oxford scholar securely aimed at a brilliant writing career. Put simply, Tamplin is a fool because he is willing to let Sara go, and his education involves the recognition of that error. But Tamplin's error is not an accidental one, a simple mistake of judgment; it proceeds from the kind of person he is, one who manipulates and welcomes Sara's departure so that he can get on with his work. A genuine education, therefore, would necessarily involve more than a reversal of his decision to let Sara go. He would have to relinquish enough of his self-protective pride to make space for a recalcitrant, living woman—or Sara would herself be foolish to return.

An important clue to this abiding difficulty is the motif of competition which begins in "The Happiness of Others" and becomes still more conspicuous in "Waiting for Dachau." The first story describes the efforts made by Tamplin to "kill a day as painlessly as possible," his last day with Sara, which is "like a baby dumped on their doorstep, gorgeous but unwanted, condemning as an angel." He rejects the sun's alchemical gilding of Sara as deceitful; he will not allow the transmutation of Sara into the object of his desire, nor will he nurture the infant day. Tamplin wants to kill time, and at first the narrative voice implies that Sara is his accomplice. Gradually, however, we discover that it is only Tamplin who rejects their union; Sara has agreed to end it precisely because that is Tamplin's deepest wish and because she desires growth and reciprocity. This difference becomes clear when Tamplin and Sara read their chosen mottoes in a church near Oxford. Tamplin recites to himself Ben Jonson's lines on the bust of Cary, which Sara has not shown the wisdom to appreciate. Jonson's poem offers the aesthetic view of life; it prefers the shapely *"small proportions"* of beauty to long continuance. Sara's choice is of an aesthetically inferior poem, an epitaph for a communal grave which she discovers for the first time that day. It serves as her triumphant reply, proof that Sara has a vision of her own which spans the whole life cycle, which is available to all, and which shows love as so enduring that it can remove death's sting.

Tamplin runs from the church, reminded by Sara's lines that death *"reconciles all difference,"* that he will die alone and his brilliance fade to ashes. Previously, Jonson's lines had seemed "a kindness to himself," evidence that he might survive the truncation of his affair with Sara and turn it into art. He had supposed, however, that the failure of their relationship was mutual: their story, which he would tell for the rest of his life, was "only the oldest story of all—the simple entire failure to meet, to serve one another and delight in the work." Now Sara has proposed another story as older and more universal: the story of love, which she charges him with having willfully destroyed. Sara dislikes Cary's bust, its features "vapid as a baby's," and charges that "'Any man of thirty with a face bare as this, deserves to die.'" Implicitly, Tamplin is Cary—"'half a man'" because he has chosen to avoid the buffetings of life. Tamplin, retreating into art, is condemned to a living death (the denial of growth) and then to a solitary death for his refusal to endure the give-and-take of life with another person. Tamplin has refused to grant Sara's otherness, which would deflect him from a solitary course; he has been willing to accept Sara as his life's companion only on condition that she accommodate his vision entirely. And that is impossible for two reasons: Sara is an autonomous human being, with an impressive intelligence of her own, and the vision that Tamplin asks her to share is essentially a vision of love's failure.

The next scene confirms Sara's alliance with "a world older, simpler, deeper than he'd known." They are out driving together, and Tamplin has retreated from "their airless symbiosis" into satisfaction with the story he will make of their day when Sara again jolts him into reality.

At first Tamplin does not recognize the world as hers: the sheep and "green and gold" landscape she points out are aesthetically pleasing, like "'effects' in a nineteenth-century play." Green nature and golden art seem reconciled, a blessing designed for Tamplin. But he is vaguely perplexed by the "profitless choice" of sheep crossing the road; since the other side is not greener, it makes no sense to Tamplin that they should move together into an uncertain future. Tamplin is himself more cautious. Next, a shepherd appears, "a credible David" in a space and time which "might as easily be Galilee as Oxfordshire"; he also crosses the road, rubs snow in his eyes to wake himself up, and then mouths an apology for the delay to Sara. The description of the shepherd suggests something magical: an awakening not from ordinary sleep, but from myth. And this explains why Tamplin is so devastated by the shepherd's choice of Sara. Art and nature, continuous in this boy who "staged his grace as natural as breath," flow more readily to Sara than to Tamplin. Like the shepherd, she is capable of growth and motion. Tamplin sees a door opening for Sara, access to happiness through others since he has failed them both, and he "shift[s] gear quietly." He accepts the "crushing, stifling but just and most beautiful" tale that it will be his fate to recount: he will "describe, celebrate, adore at a distance" the happiness of others. . . .

In **"Elegies"** Price turns his attention to the deaths of his parents ("Late Warnings"), of a writing friend ("Invitation for Jessie Rehder"), and of his own innocence in childhood ("Summer Games"). We are aware of deep connections throughout the book and are accustomed to a discontinuous mode of narration, so that the autobiographical note struck by **"Elegies"** seems to reverberate throughout the whole. The photograph of the author's parents and his "sifting the debris of [his] mother's death" in "Late Warnings" are familiar from *Love and Work;* thus we associate Price to some degree with Eborn and with the various male protagonists who resemble Eborn. The difficulty that Eborn has with his marriage, his fear of contingency, and his identity as artist seem to be played out in the rest of *Permanent Errors,* while "Late Warnings" asserts the essential role of the parents in the psychodrama of the whole.

"Elegies" as a whole enforces our recognition that throughout *Permanent Errors* love is examined within the context of death. The threat of death is felt as a motive for human love, which in turn is threatened by death in several ways. Our vulnerability to death is increased if we love others, for they become "hostages" to fate; but if that fear causes us to retreat from love, our best defense against death's sting may be lost. If our task as human beings is to love one another, then death becomes an enemy in another sense: it may descend at any moment, before love's failures have been repaired. We can be left with permanent errors on our hands. Still more frightening is the possibility that we are attracted by death's power to sever human ties and to reveal our ultimate solitude.

In "Late Warnings" Price meditates upon the photograph of his parents, which on the cover of *Permanent Errors* is superimposed upon a drawing of a Chinese symbol for unity, the cohesion of Yin and Yang (the male and female principles). His mother's hip is thrust out in a curve against his father's body to echo that design. But Price is troubled by the photograph, despite evidence that his parents were successfully joined: he asks "Why does their shadow not resemble them?" and notes that his father's leg is obscured, as if these peculiarities were evidence of mutability. He wants them to "*take shelter in time,*" and then asks "shelter from what?" What we sense here is Price's own uncertainty: is love eternally triumphant, or is death? Premonitions of death (familiar from **"Scars"** and *Love and Work*) are seen as futile, since he "could still not save [his] love from death."

In the tender Jessie Rehder elegy Price again suggests that we live in the shadow of death. Jessie knew that: she kept a "medieval Dance of Death" in which she saw the likeness of herself dancing with two skeletons and a mysterious young man. The acknowledged pain of Jessie's life is seen as her solitary state, imaged by the fact that the young man is anonymous, unrealized; still she dances, "free *and* sentenced" to death, and keeps her eyes clean—as does Price, her friend. The final elegy is only loosely that, but is the darkest of all: it describes how Price as a child playing at war games discovered that death is not purely an external threat. There is something murderous in human beings, he says, something "which sets us wild against ourselves . . . [and] worst of all our love."

Set in eastern North Carolina, **"Truth and Lies"** (the first part of **"Home Life"**) offers another variation on the book's theme: this time a female protagonist, as unreliable as Tamplin in her presentation of self and history, is assigned Eborn's "hole in the heart" and finds that her life is "'*stopped*'" by error. Sarah Wilson is married to Nathan, one of the author's unhappy, alcoholic buccaneers, and is herself miserable. In her husband's pocket Sarah finds proof of his most recent infidelity and decides to take Nathan's place in a rendezvous with Ella. When Sarah first sees the girl she appears "giant," but we are told "she shrank as she came" until she "reached her natural size." So it seems that this obstacle to the continuation of Sarah's pitiful marriage can be dealt with after all—that Ella is "'nothing but an ignorant child'" her husband has "'tinkered with.'" By the end of the story, however, we recognize that Ella's strength is superior to Sarah's: "whatever her debts, she owned herself." Ella is "free" as Sarah is not—in part because she has escaped from childhood without that painfully unresolved relationship to her father that spelled Sarah's doom. Ella is fertile; she can go on, that is, to the work of the next generation. But Sarah is locked in the sterility of the past.

Like Tamplin, Sarah relies on facility with speech. She anticipates, in questioning Ella, responses that match her own dramatic conception of the affair; but the truth she receives from Ella deflates her, revealing Ella's dignity (like Sara's in **"Fool's Education"**) and her more natural approach to life. At first the drive that the two women take is intended merely as an occasion for talk. Sarah realizes, however, that mere confrontation may not suffice to end the affair, so she takes advantage of the direction in which her car has ominously traveled—to Kinley, the site of her childhood. She decides to tell her story, a pitiable tale which will prove to Ella that she has the right at least to keep her own husband.

Although the lie that Sarah later tells Ella may cause us to distrust her tale, probably Sarah's only distortions are interpretive. Most noticeable is her sense of betrayal, centering on the house that her father sold to fund her education. Though Sarah indicates that her relationship to both parents was happy and that she wishes only to "'make as good a life as [her] parents had had,'" we begin to doubt that Sarah felt herself sufficiently included in the family's happiness. We are told, for instance, that she would ask her mother for "'brothers, company'" and that her mother would reply "'Sarah, I thought we were happy. Why aren't you satisfied?'" Her mother eventually dies from trying to fulfill Sarah's wish for siblings, and Sarah's unacknowledged sense of guilt, revealed by her feeling that she "'must have looked bad—dirty and torn,'" contributes to our growing sense that Sarah misconceives her past. Significantly, she believes that the three years after her mother's death "'were the happiest'" simply because she does not remember them: "'I have never forgotten one painful thing.'" But she also questions whether her father felt as she did, that father and daughter "'were sufficient to one another and would go on being.'" She is like Tamplin, who "dreams of extracting love from . . . the boneyard of [his] childhood." And the house of love becomes for Sarah, as it does for Eborn, an emblem of dispossession. Like Eborn, she is incapable of moving on (as her father had hoped she would) to a mature life of her own.

At the beginning of the story we are told that Sarah has a "hole at the core of her chest." This hole is understood as a sensation indicative of fear, but Price develops a chain of hole images suggesting that the hole is related to Sarah's immaturity: an unassuaged pain makes it impossible for her to go forward with her life. Ella's sister's failure to produce a living child affected her heart, and Sarah's mother's heart was "'poisoned'" in the same way. But Sarah's sterility, associated with the hole in her heart, is emblematic of something larger: the arrested development that had destroyed Sarah's marriage, despite her attempt at "'healing wounds.'" Nathan also needs someone to "'plug up his chest'" to release him from the guilt that he feels for his past; but Sarah has failed in that because of her own exaggerated grievances and because her failure to give Nathan a child (or a real marriage) has led him to continue with his self-destructive drinking. Probably she does not know who is responsible for their childlessness, but she lies to Ella—describing the sterility she imputes to Nathan as "'one more hole through the middle of him.'" That lie rebounds, however, when Ella reveals that she has just aborted Nathan's child.

Sarah's guilt stems from her own rapacious need for love and the willingness to blame others for her own lack. The permanent error that she commits with the lie stands for that larger error, which began long ago. Her journey into the past with Ella, through desolate country and into the heart of her tale, serves ironically to reveal Sarah as one who demanded more than she was able to give. She begins the story with a sense of herself as a victimized avenger, set to spring upon Ella as the rabbit with its "eye congealed in terror." And she thinks for a while that she has triumphed over Ella with her lie. But Sarah ends as her own prey, when her car (the engine of a self-destructive journey into the past) strikes another rabbit, and she feels in the "fine bones" of her hands on the wheel "its brittle death." Sarah has finally become aware that it was she who "'*stopped*'" her life with Nathan.

The second part of **"Home Life"** provides an even more harrowing look at the domestic scene, in which suicide comes into focus as both a permanent error and a response to the male protagonist's permanent failure in love. The question of Lucas's culpability in his wife's suicide attempt is the central issue in the six fragmentary scenes of **"Good and Bad Dreams."** Our first sight is of Lucas alone, at home on "his first free solitary day in months," and the elation he feels suggests that the forced intimacy of marriage is abhorrent to him. Lucas occupies as much as he can a separate world, but even to breathe the same air as his wife seems a painful compromise and a restriction of his freedom: alone, Lucas can adjust the temperature of the room to suit his own taste exactly. He can indulge in fears he would hide from his wife and take jubilant pleasure in his own body.

His day is interrupted when he sees a dying bat in the backyard. At first he attempts to ignore it, to retreat into his own space. Later, he decides to dispatch and bury the animal which he fears; and suddenly he understands that the bat is "messenger, sign," of his wife's approaching suicide. As he kills the bat, so effectively does Lucas speed his wife's death. The bat is a parasite or vampire; and Lucas sees his marriage, "his promise to her," as having "sapped" every day of his life for years, just as the bat had "hogged his day." Alone and naked in his room, Lucas peers through his legs to see that his "dangling sex" has "transfixed the unmade bed—stake in the heart of the vampire." The bed as symbol of their sexual union is for Lucas a symbol of his wife's debilitating and parasitical attachment to him; but the image permits us to see also that it is the peculiar nature of Lucas's sexuality that thrusts the stake in her heart. In a later scene she appears as "a mouth on his helpless chest, dull-toothed, draining." Standing before the bat, Lucas feels "vulnerable, precisely in his eyes and throat," as Tamplin had when beckoned by Sara to witness the Andromeda galaxy. Eborn too feels threatened by women attached to him as mouths "to his throat, toothless, warm." (The line between mother and sexual partner, revealing each woman as victim and judge of the male protagonist, continues from *Love and Work* and **"Fool's Education"** in the glimpse that Lucas has of his mother's death in his wife's dreaming face.) All three men feel a need to "grow [their] own rind," to flee the demands of contingency; and all three are uncomfortable with sexual union, better able to deal with their erotic impulses by solitude. Lucas attempts narcissistically to kiss his own penis and then his mirrored lips, believing that they "could use the greeting"; the neglect he feels stems not from a dearth of opportunity to employ his wife's "facilities," but from a wish to make love to himself in blessed solitude. Sexually, Lucas feels that he belongs "to another species with analogous parts but incomprehensible needs"; in making love to his wife, he is like "the priest of a heresy who entered to perform his rite on her altar," obtaining finally a "reward" that is "sealed from her." The heresy, it would seem, is not Lucas's masculinity on a feminine altar, but his onanism.

The description of the suicide attempt is chilling, offered by an anonymous narrative voice; behind that, however, we sense both Lucas and his wife taking some final, gruesome satisfaction in the details of the scene. Lucas attempts to contain and defuse the threat of his own complicity by clinical analysis. He cannot, however, rid himself of guilt. Having earlier seen himself as Rilke's "archaic Apollo," issuing the familiar edict "*You must change your life*," and wishing to change in the direction of greater solitude, Lucas is now faced with the need to achieve greater intimacy with his wife. He must forestall a second attempt at suicide, but cannot even ask her motive for the first. Only when his wife is asleep can he extract the fact of his guilt; and in these still appallingly distant circumstances, his "pitiful humping amends" cannot suffice to save her. In one dream his wife appears as vampire-angel come to judge and kill him; Lucas makes himself vulnerable to her, while she draws forth "speech not blood, one word 'Pardon.'" In a subsequent dream vision, when Lucas would "rush to save her," his "heart refuses." Pardon cannot be granted, Christ in another dream cannot find the water he needs to wash Lucas's feet in forgiveness, and so must use His scalding spit, because Lucas cannot genuinely wish to save his wife.

"Walking Lessons" is the single entry in the book's final section, which is called "The Alchemist" because of the dark aesthetic powers displayed by the writer-protagonist. The unnamed narrator has arrived in Arizona to visit his friend Blix, a VISTA volunteer with the Navaho, and to avoid Christmas at home: his wife has committed suicide two weeks before. The pace of his tale is leisurely because the narrator's goal is to delay confrontation with the question of his wife's death. He labors, for example, to order the chaos of Blix's quarters so that the "contagion" he senses there cannot force his head "to acknowledge its own mess." Yet he is aware of the sensational figure he must seem to others as the mate of a suicide, and exploits this shamelessly in his dealings with Neely, the VISTA agent, and Dora, his friend's Navaho mistress. Inexorably, the story moves its narrator into precisely the psychological landscape he requires and had wished to escape.

It is tempting to view "Walking Lessons" as a sequel to "Good and Bad Dreams." It seems, for example, that Price is mirroring the two stories by withholding in each the name of one of the partners and by assigning mystical importance to the single occasion in each story where he does reveal a name—Lucas or Beth. The narrator's peculiar assertion that Beth might have intended only to warn him with an attempted suicide, although her method was a fail-safe pistol in the mouth, can be explained if we decide that indeed he is Lucas and that he cannot admit to his wife's previous attempt. It would be a mistake, however, to insist upon this equation. Price encourages us to detect resemblances throughout *Permanent Errors* and also establishes the autonomy of each story in order to make an important point about the artistic process. The alchemist's glory and his ordeal are to perform the feat of transformation again and again, but each time differently; each fresh try involves infinite, subtle variations upon his single basic experiment.

One obvious change as we move from "Good and Bad Dreams" to "Walking Lessons," from an attempted to a successful suicide, is the narrator's anger at his wife for leaving him "dumb with guilt and mystery, unable to answer the final indictment flung at the living by a suicide." The enormity of his wife's crime, her refusal to grant him fair trial, threatens to distract the narrator from his necessary task of self-indictment and eventual self-forgiveness. We do not see and he does not analyze the marriage. In place of Lucas's response to his wife's proximity, however, we have the narrator's response to the ideal of contingency as exemplified by Blix; and so we are prepared for the narrator's discovery that he has in part willed Beth's suicide for the sake of his solitude.

Blix is a foil for the narrator's emphasis on self-preservation, personal survival. His motive in coming to Arizona is antithetical to the narrator's; an ex-medical student, Blix has come to help the Navajo, not to appreciate the possibility that he is more fortunate than they. He has learned that the sense of guilt with which he began is essentially onanistic and has progressed from "'self-service,'" a euphemism for masturbation, to a sexual relationship with Dora, which signals his active involvement with the fate of the Navajo. But Dora has just discovered that she is dying slowly of multiple sclerosis, and her condition becomes a metaphor (particularly in the narrator's mind) of the hopelessness of Blix's efforts to help other people. While Blix is aware of his own inefficacy, he persists in his charitable course—despite mockery and despite being tempted by the doctrine of solitary self-preservation which the narrator espouses. Doctors and lovers alike play a losing game: sooner or later, they are defeated by death. Ultimately, however, Blix recognizes that he cannot retire from love or service to others on that account.

The narrator's solitude is half chosen and half a belief that people have no choice but to be alone. The foreign world of the Navajo, where "interlingual misfires" are a common occurrence, confirms for him the essential isolation of human beings. As Tamplin is "a fish in air," however, so the narrator cannot "'speak the language, can barely breathe the air'" for reasons that may be peculiar to himself. Blix diagnoses the narrator's reaction to his wife's death as curable because "'to be scraped . . . bare—owing nobody life, help'" is what he has always sought. Even sex, Blix suggests, was ultimately a separate and selfish experience for the narrator: "'Did you ever *come* for her, ever donate that much?'"

Shaken by this accusation, and by the macabre suggestion that he take Dora as the "'petrifying'" vessel of his next sexual donation, the narrator fears that Blix will "be converted, by his own life and the nearness of mine, to monstrosity." The vision of the narrator as monster is sustained by references to him as "'Mr. Scorch,'" in whose wake everything "'*stiffens*'" or "'bleeds,'" as the "'Prince of Darkness,'" as a "Halloween" ghoul, and as "'some kind of witch or something.'" When asked by the narrator what kind of monster he is, Blix replies "'There's only one—the killing kind.'" The narrator's monstrosity is in his willingness to stand back and watch as others suffer. His vision is of a bleak world where a five-year-old "Polyneices with a plastic bow and arrow" strives eternally to kill his brother—and, we know from Sophocles' *Antigone,* is in turn murdered by his brother; no reprieve seems possible to the narrator, for these Navajo children are surrounded by "immortal American litter." Blix and Dora, the narrator believes, will become "two more litter factories" in this permanently blighted landscape. They will succumb to entropy or the "second law of thermodynamics," an inevitable loss of heat: Dora's "'warm hole'" is already "'cooling.'" The question, of course, is whether the monstrous vision is the true one—or whether the narrator, "'Frozen—Birdseye Brains,'" simply imposes his own chill on others.

The narrator's stance is that of the observer. Watching Dora, he wishes "to be transparent . . . a witness clear as a pane of glass"—recalling Tamplin's glass barrier. His narration is punctuated by attempts to frame his experience, to title it. He wonders "who would be the ideal painter to paint us," settling on Brueghel; and for the spectacle of Indians toiling in the mud while he is safely enclosed behind the truck's window, he offers as title *The Drones and the Mate.* Seeing himself as "the consort chosen . . . and groomed for union," the narrator regards himself as infinitely precious, deserving of all possible protection; the union toward which he is aimed, however, is with his work rather than with other creatures. His object in **"Walking Lessons"** is to come to terms with these two conflicting images of himself, as monster and superior person. To do this he must make himself vulnerable: he must face his role in Beth's death and permit his superior suede shoes to be ruined in the common mud. He must walk for a time with people who seem to him of another species altogether.

The journey to rescue Dora's truck, which he undertakes with Blix and Dora and a motley crew of Navajos, supplies this opportunity. His powers as an artist, linked to the dark forces which are assigned to him by the Navajo as one pursued by his wife's ghost, metaphorically suffice to accomplish one miracle: safe behind glass at the wheel of Blix's truck, he manages to extract the truck from the mud in which it has been swamped. Blix then permits him to drive the truck, and "piloting at last—not ideally, not alone . . . but at least at nobody's mercy but [his] own," the narrator feels reasonably safe. At this stage of the journey the narrator has acknowledged his rage—his wish to consign all suicides to the "*Ninth* Circle" of Dante's hell as "'Traitors to Their Kin'"—and has been prompted by Blix to the recognition that he is "'left alone because [he] wanted to be,'" that he wants to be "free not to yield

again to Love the Great Occupation, Time-Passer, Killer." But he has not yet put those facts together. He can exorcise that rage and what he sees as his wife's vindictive try at spoiling the rest of his life if he sees that he has "foiled her death, her punishment by the simple expedient of desiring it, *requiring* it." To achieve that perspective, however, he must first be seriously threatened with extinction. He must sink into the mud which threatens all in order to see how badly he wants to get on with his own life.

Blix describes himself as "'fighting . . . not explaining human life'"; in his long, cold walk back to civilization, the narrator must do some fighting of his own. Still, the explanations persist. Justifying himself as writer, he asserts a preference for describing the psychological rather than the physical dimensions of his struggle for survival. But it is clear that the one comes into focus for him through the other. Previously, the narrator had thought he could escape the entropy which he sees as operative in the lives of Blix and Dora: through art, he "could radiate, steady and generous, for years without visible exhaustion—the radiance of simple knowledge . . . the wasteless conversion of mass into power." With chill death a distinct possibility, he now sees himself as one of "three running-down lives in a running-down world." Shared vulnerability leads him to a greater sympathy for others and an acceptance of their divergent paths when the threat of death recedes.

The physical dangers of cold and gunfire which the narrator must endure are parallel to the psychological exposure to his wife's chilly, hostile ghost; thus he acknowledges that the shot fired at his party by a defensive landowner is not "'the first shot ever fired'" at him, but "'the second.'" His reference, of course, is to his wife's suicidal shot, which he believes was aimed at him. But he discovers that this second shot is aimed at Dora (his wife's double), and this leads to his recognition that Beth committed suicide for reasons of her own which he can never entirely know. He is not the center of the universe, not the only cause of her death. Dora becomes Beth in the peculiar lunar landscape, the "Death Valley," through which these travelers journey. Like Beth, she considers suicide: she asks the narrator to kill her, and we gather that she has also made this request of Blix. Both Dora and Blix, in the narrator's imagination, seem agents of Beth's desire for vengeance; he senses that this whole excursion has been staged to punish him. Beth is everywhere—in the watchful satellite above (an ironic version of the Star of Bethlehem) and in the humming of the electrical wires whose power is "scary and disembodied," whose force is ended when the narrator grants the justice of his wife's complaint against him and begs her pardon through Dora.

As the story ends, we realize that the journey has had another meaning for Blix and Dora. Blix had asked the narrator's help, seeing him as one who had found the "'way out'" of contingency. The advice offered is that Blix may "'never walk alone,'" but he "'sure as Hell can *run*'" from a love as doomed as that which Dora offers. Both Dora and Blix, however, opt for continuance: Dora chooses to live, and Blix chooses to accompany her for as long as her journey lasts. Their experience in "Death Valley" has led all three characters to value their lives and has confirmed them in solitude or the paired life, the two divergent paths which are possible to human beings. Death comes sooner or later, whichever route is taken. Dangers such as are imaged by Dora's disease or by Beth's ghost must be faced down; people must accept who and what they are; the goal is continuance, for however long it lasts. In the end the characters agree to differ. The narrator is happy, he tells Blix, because he has realized "'There are people like me'"; and Blix replies, "'So what . . . there are more like me.'" The phrase "so what" is Beth's; it signals for the narrator an unanswerable difference between human beings, which he will not allow to stop him in his tracks. The last title that he assigns to their common venture is "'*Happy Though Breathing.*'" Breathing for different purposes, in adversity of different kinds, both sorts of people are finally happy to be alive.

Carl Ficken (essay date 1985)

SOURCE: "Reynolds Price: 'A Chain of Love'," in *God's Story and Modern Literature*, Fortress Press, 1985, pp. 151–61.

[*In the following excerpt, Ficken discusses how Price uses humor and descriptive narrative to the examine the painful reality of death in "A Chain of Love."*]

Reynolds Price is a contemporary Southern writer who

A former student on Price's attitude toward academia and teaching:

There was about Price when I was his student, and still is, a boyish ingenuousness, a kind of natural yet calculated indifference to classroom propriety. Not that he wasn't proper on his own terms. It was rather that the conventions he observed in his own classroom were entirely his own. The first thing he told us was that he was not a "doctor," that he had no Ph.D. We came very quickly to realize that there are few things Price holds in greater contempt than the trade-union traditions of American academic "scholarship"—a prejudice that I eagerly imbibed and have cultivated ever since. He was ready to take the ideas of a nineteen-year-old undergraduate just as seriously as those of any hoary academic with accreditation from Harvard or Yale. The point was (I think) that scholarly accreditation in and for itself had as little to do with literature as with life. One realized very quickly that, in this man's classroom, literature was powerful, even potentially dangerous stuff, but that to *do* it, to read it, you couldn't get away with holding it at arm's length. No "academic" distance would do. You had to get it on your clothes, your face, your hands, take it home with you, eat it, drink it, and sleep it.

Jefferson Humphries in "Taking Things Seriously," in Southwest Review, *Vol. 74, No. 1, Winter, 1989.*

---

has translated some biblical stories and has written about the value of narrative for human survival—whether a person is listening to or telling the tales. He cites the earliest narratives we have, those from the Hebrew Scriptures—the stories of Genesis and Judges, for example—and links the hearing and telling of those narratives with the growth and nurture of a people. His point is that the stories we hear as we mature can be the instruments by which we sense our own worth and learn what is necessary for our lives. Precisely through the story, a reader can be caught up in mystery, rescued from danger, given the word that matters. Further, by attempting to recover the order of past events and by asking for explanations, human beings not only come to understand their world and lives but are carried beyond themselves to deeper realities. For Price, then, as a writer of fiction, a strong story line is crucial. In making such a case, he does not stand in the avant-garde of modern fiction, where traditional narrative forms are sometimes devalued and where the nonsense and chaos of human experience are prominent. But he does work within a long tradition of storytelling that, indeed, goes back to biblical times and that has been renewed in many countries through many centuries, not least in the American South in this century. . . .

"A Chain of Love" was one of Reynolds Price's earliest stories. It is the first story in *The Names and Faces of Heroes* and is about the same Mustian family, from rural North Carolina, who were central characters in *A Long and Happy Life*. Both Price's comic spirit and his seriousness of purpose are evident in this story. Told from the point of view of Rosacoke Mustian, a girl of high-school age, the story records Rosacoke's grandfather's admission to a hospital in Raleigh, her stay with him through several nights and days, and her experience with the illness and death of a man across the hall. In one sense, nothing much *happens* in the story; the plot is certainly not involved, though a great deal is going on inside Rosacoke, and what goes on there is available to the reader and forms the major strength of the narrative. The characters of the story really come alive: Rosacoke, her grandfather (Papa), her Mama, and her two brothers, Rato and Milo, are believable partly because of what we know of their life circumstances and partly because of the language Price uses, both the descriptive language and the words he puts in their mouths. Along with the humor of the story, the reader also is confronted, as Rosacoke is, with the painful reality of death. The humor keeps the story from becoming melodramatic or sentimental and, in a way, forms the framework from which both author and characters examine life.

That the story might be about death is evident from the opening paragraphs. The first paragraph alone contains four allusions to death: the time of year identified as "the dead of winter," Rato almost freezing "to death" making hand-turned ice cream for Papa's birthday, Papa saying "he would die at home if it was his time," and mention of the death of Papa's wife. The references continue, sometimes serious, sometimes casual. The doctor tells the family they won't need "a full-time nurse with two strong grandchildren dying to sit" with Papa at the hospital.

Rosacoke recalls the Saturday night date she will miss with her boyfriend Wesley, and she remembers that as they sit in his Pontiac in front of her house the "rain frogs would be singing-out . . . and then . . calming as if they had all died together." There is a sentence about the death of Rosacoke's own father and the note that Rato "had seen a lot of things die."

Despite all these references to death, the tone at the beginning of the story seems lighthearted, even comical. That comes about partly because of the language Price uses and partly because of the interesting details and implications: we are given information that is suggestive of another story somewhere beneath the surface, and we are told some things that may seem irrelevant to the present story but in their vividness and reality make the present story more believable. For example, look at the reason Mama cannot stay at the hospital with her father-in-law:

> It worried her not being able to stay when staying was her duty, but they were having a Children's Day at the church that coming Sunday—mainly because the Christmas pageant had fallen through when John Arthur Bobbitt passed around the German measles like a dish of cool figs at the first rehearsal—and since she had organized the Sunbeams single-handed, she couldn't leave them then right on the verge of public performance.

The details of that sentence contribute to both the humor and the realism of the story.

The narrative perspective is not really clear until the third paragraph, when we learn that Rosacoke "almost liked the idea" of staying with her grandfather. Her one problem, we learn, will be missing her Saturday night with Wesley and "telling him goodbye without a word." In a very short space and through an indirect method, the narrator reveals that Mama does not entirely approve of her dating Wesley; that "telling him goodbye" was the "best part of any week" and had a special, almost mystical quality about it; that she would be happy to miss school for a week; that she liked being with Papa; and that she could not really remember much about her own father, who had been "run over by a green pick-up truck one Saturday evening late a long time ago." Thus, in the first paragraph, where we recognize the central consciousness of the narrative, we learn a great deal about her, and we get it almost incidentally. We are not directly told Rosacoke's feelings; rather, we seem to be listening in on her thoughts and catching implications. That Rosacoke is always spoken of in the third person contributes to this sense of indirection.

The heart of the story, however, has to do with Rosacoke's experience with death in a room near Papa's. Early in the week the room had been empty, and while Papa slept she had gone there to look out the window at a statute of Jesus on the hospital lawn. Though she couldn't see the face on the statue from this window, she had remembered from their arrival at the hospital that it was the "kindest face she had ever seen," and she had stood in the room to "recollect his face the way she knew it was"; (this

scene prefigures events in the final story of the collection, the title story, **"The Names and Faces of Heroes"**). Later, when a man with lung cancer is given the room, all the Mustians become interested in what is happening over there, as though somehow that man's health were related to Papa's health. Rosacoke especially follows the action across the hall, attracted in part by the dying man's son, who reminds her of Wesley, and drawn by both curiosity and sympathy to the death itself. When, on the next Sunday, Rosacoke takes the flowers she has asked Mama to bring and attempts to give them to the man's family, she walks in on a priest administering last rites. Rosacoke is at once embarrassed and struck with awe at the mystery of the candles, the annointing, the chanted Latin phrases, the black-robed priest, and the death before her. When Rosacoke returns to Papa's room and Rato comes in to tell them that the man has died, the focus turns to their own family and the face of death: Rosacoke watches Papa play solitaire a little more slowly, and she knows he is thinking:

> It wasn't as if he didn't know where he was going or what it would be like when he got there. He just trusted and he hoped for one thing, he tried to see to one last thing—for a minute he stopped his card playing and asked Mama could he die at home, and Mama told him he could.

The tone of the story becomes more serious by the final paragraphs, but Price still handles the scene on a low key, revealing a great deal about the characters, showing depth of emotion without manipulating the reader's feeling, and ending the story by a slight turning away from the somberness. The next-to-last paragraph ends with the passage quoted just above. The final paragraph draws us even further into Rosacoke's own reflections, as she tries to understand her feelings about the man's death. She knows there is something good about his death: "With all that beautiful dying song, hadn't he surely died sanctified?" But she has kept everything about it, including her visit to the man's son or to his family, and she has not even spoken her own sorrow at the death of this stranger. She finally says, there in Papa's room, that the death just didn't "seem right," that she felt as though she had gotten to know the man "real well." The final sentence of the story describes, again indirectly, the depth of her feeling and the impact of the whole experience on her family:

> And her words hung in the room for a long time— longer than it took Papa to pick the cards up off the bed and lay them without a sound in the drawer, longer even than it would have taken Rosacoke to say goodbye to Wesley if it had been Saturday night and she had been at home.

This is a story about death. It is also a story about some real human beings as they face death, and without saying it all explicitly, Price manages to describe the "chain of love" that binds not only this family but all humanity.

Is this, in any sense, a Southern story? Perhaps it is mainly the language and the setting that make it Southern.

Rosacoke's gesture of giving fresh flowers to the dying man is characteristic of people for whom hospitality and outward expressions of kindness seem natural and unaffected, but those are not traits only of Southerners, or for that matter of all Southerners. Several incidents raise a regional emphasis, but they do so only in a minor way and serve to reinforce the realism of the story. Mama brings candy to the hospital for Papa because, as she says, "nurses hung around a patient who had his own candy like Grant around Richmond." The dying man had only recently moved to Raleigh from Baltimore—which is clearly "north" to these Carolina folks—and his being a stranger contributes to Rosacoke's desire to visit and take flowers and makes her a little conscious of her own region: "She might be from Afton, N.C., but she knew better than to go butting into some man's sickroom, to a man on his deathbed, without an expression of her sympathy. And it had to be flowers." The relationship of the Mustians to Papa's black orderly may also mark a regional flavor of the story: there is some condescension as Papa speaks to "Snowball Mason" (as the man introduces himself), but there is also easy comradery between him and the Mustians; and when, on one occasion, Papa speaks harshly to the orderly, Rosacoke feels badly and is sensitive to Snowball's feelings: "He walked out of Papa's room with his ice-cream coat hanging off him as if somebody had unstarched it." The story is decidedly Southern in its language, characterization, and setting, all of which make it a realistic narrative. Nevertheless, it moves beyond regionalism to deal with universal circumstances and basic human emotions. Furthermore, the humor of the narrative keeps those universal elements from becoming ponderous and saves the story from sentimentality.

Reynolds Price with the students and faculty of Hendrix College (interview date 1988)

SOURCE: An interview, edited by Ashby Bland Crowder, in *The Southern Quarterly,* Vol. XXVI, No. 2, Winter, 1988, pp. 12–26.

[*Following is an excerpt from a lecture Price gave at Hendrix College in Arkansas where he answered questions from the faculty and staff. Price discusses his relationship to the setting and characters in "Waiting at Dachau" and offers insights into the characters and events of the story.*]

"Waiting at Dachau" is the fourth story in a volume of Reynolds Price's short stories entitled *Permanent Errors* (1970) and is grouped with three other stories—**"The Happiness of Others," "A Dog's Death"** and **"Scars"**—which together constitute the first division of the book, **"Fool's Education."** This "fool" is an American living in England working on a university degree and on becoming a writer. The fool, Charles Tamplin, is involved in a relationship with a girl named Sara, and some years after the Third Reich they visit together the Nazi concentration camp at Dachau.

In a recent visit to Hendrix College in Arkansas, Reynolds Price entertained questions from students and faculty on **"Waiting at Dachau."** In his opening remarks, Price said, "I had visited myself the remains of the concentration camp at Dachau in the summer of 1956. So there was a gap of thirteen years between my seeing the place and having a strong emotional response to it and having those emotions mingle with a number of other emotions and observations in my life and produce this story." This comment led to the following question, even though in his essay "To the Reader" at the beginning of *Permanent Errors,* the author had denied that the stories were autobiographical:

Q: Is **"Waiting at Dachau"** about yourself?

A: Well, let's say something I think is really basic to understanding all literature, certainly all literature written in the first person. That is, be very careful that you don't assume that the "I" in any story, novel or poem is the author. Charles Tamplin is by no means me. I just told you that I went to Dachau. I did in fact myself spend four years in England doing graduate work at Oxford—three years doing graduate work and one year just on my own. So Charles Tamplin will embody a number of things that I've thought and no doubt a number of things that I've felt, but you'll have to trust me when I say that he really is a very different person from me. I don't necessarily subscribe to everything he says, especially not in this story. He's obviously operating in this story under a strong head of quite intense personal emotional steam; and I may, myself, in 1969, have associated myself with some of that steam. But it's been thirteen years ago, and I would find it very hard to remember how much of that material I actually would have subscribed to at the time. I think, when Tamplin deals with that passage about the de Wieks, that he feels that theirs is somehow an enviable and emblematic human relationship; and I, myself, in that particular case, I think, would sympathize with that. I don't think one ought to try to provide any recipes for any two human beings as to how they conduct their own particular emotional relationship, aside from hoping that they won't cause each other unavoidable pain. I think very few human beings are placed, thank God, in the appalling situation in which those people found themselves being transported toward certain destruction. One wouldn't look at them and say everyone should behave like this because, luckily, very few people are ever going to be faced with anything quite that appalling, certainly not that dramatic. It's a very moving episode, and I remember myself when I first encountered that particular passage in some excerpts from a book about Anne Frank in Life magazine years ago, I remember being very moved by it. It obviously stuck in my mind so that when I was writing this story I went back and tracked that passage down and quoted it in my own story.

It's been a long time since I've written or read the story, but I think that obviously its major theme is a tormented set of questions about what love is between human beings, what it can be, what sorts of strains it can take and really how the great holocaust experience reflects upon our own cliches about love. I think Charles in the story asks a number of questions about what happens to what we call human love, romantic love, love between men and women or parents and children, when love appears to conflict with individual survival. . . .

Q: Can you tell us what Sara was thinking, why she didn't want to go into the camp?

A: Anybody got any ideas? I don't want to be coy about this, but I'm not sure that I have the complete answer to that. You might read the other stories in this series called **"A Fool's Education"**; the title is purposely ambiguous: does it mean you take a fool and educate him into something else, or does it mean you educate somebody to be a fool?—which obviously a great deal of education is dedicated towards doing. I myself would vote for the fact that Charles gets a lot of the foolishness educated out of him, not by academic institutions but by his own experience. My guess is that, if you've read what comes before about Tamplin and Sara and then read this, you're faced with several things, one of which is that Sara realizes that Charles is setting this up as some kind of elaborate emotional test, that they really are going to do this pretty awful thing. At the time they go into Dachau—does the story give the date? I said I was there in '56. I think they're there in '55 or '57, a year before or a year after I was there for some reason. At that particular time it was only twelve years after the liberation of the camp, twelve years after the whole world found out really what was going on there. I myself was twelve years old at the time the camp was liberated, so I have vivid memories of suddenly seeing in *Life* magazine or in the newsreels the piles of corpses being pushed together by bulldozers. That was really the absolute first time that any civilians in the western world knew that the concentration camps existed, or at least existed as dead ends for that many Jews and gypsies or other "impure" elements.

I should have brought along my little leaflet that I found in a Holiday Inn day before yesterday. There was an American Nazi group spending the night in the local Holiday Inn in their Nazi uniforms with their swastikas on; and they left little leaflets around the tables, about racial purity and the necessity of exterminating the Jews from around the world, and so on. It's hardly an idea that ended in 1945, as you probably know. This was a group of people in Idaho; I'm happy to say they weren't from Arkansas, but they might get some sympathy in certain parts of Arkansas, as they might get some sympathy anywhere in America for that matter.

Anyway, Charles and Sara were there at a time when the camp was still a kind of physically raw place. The story talks about the fact that literally nothing had been done to prettify it or make it into a kind of national park. Have any of you been to Dachau? A number of American tourists who go to Germany now—especially to Munich, which is only a few miles from Dachau—take a little side trip over there. I myself haven't been since 1956 and don't want to go, but I gather from what students of mine have told me and from photographs I've seen that it has indeed been decorated quite a lot. All sorts of museums have

been built, and statues have been put up, flowers have been planted. That's only natural; but at the time I was there it looked essentially the way it looked on the day of liberation, except the bodies were all gone. So you just saw this absolutely stark—and as I say in the story—this surprisingly small thing. You always think that if you hear of some great event, you're going to go there, and the place is going to be physically as grand and frightening as the whole thing has become in your imagination. In 1956 Dachau looked like a little Arkansas brick factory. You couldn't imagine that millions of people had passed through.

So I think Charles in his own rather dramatic, poetic way, has built this thing up in his mind as some sort of symbolic testing of their own love. Sara knows him well enough to resent that, to resent that romanticism in him; and really when the crunch comes, when they get there to the parking lot, she's just independent enough to resist it. It's not some elaborate plan that she's made to stage a refusal at that point; it's just a spontaneous choice. Charles reads it quite correctly. He reads it as some sort of symbolic rejection of their whole relationship, and it does become a sort of watershed that is the end of their relationship. They go on—though actually there is one story that comes after this in the series, called **"Happiness of Others"**—they go on to England and part there but have essentially parted for good at Dachau, which is what the story says; it invites Sara back, it begs her back, but there's no indication that she's coming. . . .

Q: What is the scene in which Charles and Sara discuss the "old chalk fingerprint" in the sky ("the great spiral galaxy in Andromeda") supposed to suggest about them—that they (and all of us) are a part of nature?

A: That and the opposite of that, which is the standard thing you say upon looking up at the stars—"Gee, what am I so upset about my own little problems for, when the whole thing is this big and this grand and this mysterious and this inscrutable? Why am I so depressed about, you know, what Bobby Jo said to me today in the cafeteria?" That, added to the fact that we are all to some extent literally the same *thing* as the galaxy in Andromeda; we're made out of the same hydrogen and oxygen and carbon atoms; and, I think, any kind of satisfactory human relationship probably needs to have some sort of, not necessarily conscious, awareness of those facts. Yet, in the end, Charles appears to go beyond all that rationalization and all that intellectualization and just say, "Sara, come back." What the hell, what's the point of depriving ourselves of the consolation that personal commitment and personal loyalty can bring, the sort of consolation that presumably the de Wieks got out of being who they were to one another.

And there's nothing at all implicitly or explicitly anti-Semitic in saying that one of the amazing things about the holocaust is how easy it was for Hitler to bring it off. Certainly the Western European powers and the United States made it a lot easier, for various complicated political reasons that you may or may not know anything about (very fascinating and horrible reasons). But the Jews of central and eastern and western Europe also made it much easier for Hitler to bring it off by their own refusal to believe that Hitler really meant what he said, that he was really going to do this, and by their refusal to get out. If these guys at the Holiday Inn suddenly became a political majority, would those of us who were running contrary to their program, would we pack up our toothbrushes and our favorite two pieces of clothing and leave the United States and emigrate to Canada or Mexico? It's unthinkable that somebody's going to pull a truck up to your house and haul you away and convert you to ashes just because you're a Jehovah's Witness or a homosexual or a Jew or a black or a gypsy, or whatever the particular program happens to condemn as being racially impure. That's what was happening.

Q: Would you explain about Sara's writing on the mirror?

A: That's something that happened to me. I once was with a friend at a bar, and the friend was telling me about the serious problem he was having. The problem didn't involve me; it was a problem with another relationship in his life. He got up and went to the men's room and came back; and half an hour later I got up and went to the men's room, and I saw in his handwriting (he had very distinctive, unmistakable handwriting)—I saw that written on the bathroom wall, and I couldn't resist putting it in the story. So I don't quite know what it's doing there except obviously Sara is at a very serious emotional crisis in her own life. She's deciding whether or not to give up on this relationship that has been the center of her young adult life to this point; and at this particular time in America, the '50s, it was much more fashionable for people that age, in their early '20s, to go steady and get engaged and have . . . I mean the fashion's beginning to come back but certainly through the '60s and '70s relationships of that sort weren't nearly as common as they are now—these very intense engagement experiences when people were in great detail planning the next sixty years together in their neat little house and their little children and their little car and little jobs and what not. So she's making a very crucial decision that she thinks is of the greatest importance to her future life, and she just phrases that prayer. I don't really mean to imply that she has some sort of mystical experience in the ladies' room. She's just feeling very intense, and she's probably had a little wine, and she just writes it. Do women's bathrooms have a lot of graffiti in them?

Q: Could you comment further on Sara and her relationship with Charles?

A: If you'd read the other stories about them, you'd see that the relationship has altered. She's begun to feel pretty rejected. She's tried to catch up with what seems to be his rejection of her. . . . I think she would have been much more willing to try to hold on for the whole trip than he.

If you really want to read a full expansion on a relationship of this sort, you might look at my novel published a few years ago called *The Source of Light*. It really is very much about a young man and a young woman a lot like Charles and Sara. They have different names, but I really think in many ways **"Waiting at Dachau"** is a kind of sketch for the later novel, *The Source of Light*. It's set in virtually the same time period, and is about very intense, thoughtful young people.

Q: Why do Charles and Sara travel to Dachau in the first place?

A: I don't think they necessarily planned it to produce any great discoveries. Charles is a graduate student in England. Sara has come over there to visit him. They take a trip, just what you do when you're in Europe: you sort of get in a car or bus; you ride around and look at the great scenes. Charles has this rather bizarre idea that they should go and look at this one rather awful scene; most people would not include Dachau on their travel itineraries any more than you would include the State electric chair on your itinerary around Arkansas. Few people would. But Charles did that. As the trip moves along—I don't know whether you've noticed or not, but nothing in the world is harder on a relationship than traveling together; it's the ultimate test of any relationship from friendship to roommates to romance. Sara and Charles experience a lot of that travel abrasion. And then poor old Charles—he's a fool—decides to stage this one big showdown—the showdown at the Dachau corral. Sara realizes that he is trying to stage a showdown, and she just says, "I'm not going to play. This is some kind of elaborate romantic game. The woman is supposed to be the romantic, and you're the man, and you're not supposed to be; but you've gone a little bananas, and I'm not going to play your game." Then she regrets it and realizes that she's rained on his parade, and that's why that very peculiar scene follows when they're in the restaurant and the lion bites her, which again is something I really saw. Could I ever have invented anything like that? I was once in a restaurant on the French Riviera; and some men came in with a lion, exactly as described in the story. "Does anybody want to have their picture taken with a lion?" This one woman, not with our party, said "Sure" and picked it up and held it in her arms; the flashbulb went off, and the lion chomped into her shoulder, and she was absolutely magnificent. The men who owned the lion went absolutely haywire. They were screaming. The woman stood there and kept stroking the lion until he finally turned her loose. She had this row of teeth prints and blood streaming down her arm.

You know, if you're a writer, you go through life like a magnet, or an electrically charged comb: all sorts of little bits of paper or metal filings start clinging to you; and when you come to write something as complicated as this, you suddenly think, "Oh, there's that whole lion business—that was interesting, that was weird. Suppose that happened now in this story."

I like Sara a lot. She's a very strong, admirable character. And obviously so does Charles. She's much stronger and more realistic than he—which is frequently the case in male-female relations. It is our stereotype that men are supposed to be strong, rational people, and women are the weak romantics. But it's almost invariably the other way around, I find. And Charles comes to realize it years later when he writes the story and presumably sends it to her, wherever she is. Maybe I should write a sequel to it. I always wonder what happened, what she does. Does she acquire a condominium in Florida and live happily ever after? Presumably Sara has gone on about her own life in the interval. Charles certainly doesn't tell us at the end of the story where Sara's been. That's one of the unspoken messages that the story contains—that is, again, that Charles is continuing to think of the world entirely as it relates to him and not as it relates to Sara or anybody else. . . .

Q: What was the experience of visiting Dachau like for you?

A: Pretty powerful. It's one of the top five most powerful places I ever visited. One of the strange things, I think, about scenes of great suffering—have any of you ever been to a place where there has been an enormous amount of concentrated suffering over a substantial period of time? There're not a lot of such places in America. God knows there's plenty of suffering; but America tends to be a violent country and, if there's going to be suffering, it tends to happen fast. Somebody gets lynched in an hour, or we mow down X number of Sioux Indians in a five minute encounter. We don't tend to put people in a single place and keep them there. You can say slavery went on for 300 years, but you probably can't quote me one single place where X number of slaves were made to suffer for X number of years.

There's only one place I can think of—it's in the South, Andersonville Prison in Georgia. If you ever go to Americus, Georgia, ride out about ten miles in the country and see the National Cemetery at Andersonville. It was a concentration camp kept by the Confederates. I've forgotten how many people died at Andersonville but far too many, maybe eight or nine thousand prisoners (northern prisoners were kept there). It was not maintained as a conscious extermination place the way the Nazi camps were. It was just largely the result of incredible mistakes. The Confederates got all these people in one place, and the sanitation conditions got so appalling. They were losing the war, and they couldn't feed or take care of these prisoners, so enormous numbers of them died. My point is, if you go to something like Dachau years later or Andersonville or any one of the battlefields of the First World War, almost invariably the scene now has the most incredible peacefulness to it. The birds are singing and the flowers are blooming, and you think: this is unimaginable. What I felt at Dachau is what Charles feels: something's all wrong. He's read about this place as being the scene of all this concentrated suffering, and yet it seems like the world's nicest picnic ground. Andersonville is one of the loveliest places you'd ever want to go to now. Yet all the photographs hanging in the museum at Andersonville show this appalling hogwallow that it was in 1865 when men were dying like flies.

Q: What is the significance of "waiting" in the title?

A: Well, there's got to be some significance if I put it there, but I'm not sure at the moment I can exactly remember. I think what Charles really means is that in a sense what he's saying in the story is "I'm still waiting. I'm still waiting *for you* to enter this commitment with me." And you see from the end of the story that Charles *has* changed and matured some, but the old Charles is still very much there. The fact that he calls the story **"Waiting at Dachau"** means that he still is clinging to this very romantic notion that love is this very titanic commitment—total loyalty, total suffering, total togetherness—whereas Sara has a much brisker, more realistic notion of what they're up to.

Patricia Hampl (essay date 1991)

SOURCE: "The Walking Wounded," in *The New York Times Book Review,* July 7, 1991, p. 5.

[*Hampl is an American poet. In the following excerpt, she praises the introspective quality of the stories in* The Foreseeable Future.]

Less than a generation ago, the short story, having lost its home in America's popular magazines, seemed also to have lost its place in contemporary writing. *The New Yorker* was the only weekly still publishing and paying well for short fiction, along with monthlies like *The Atlantic* and a handful of women's magazines. The baleful warning of the Visiting Writer comes back, telling a short-story-writing class: "The market has dried up." The year was 1969. His advice to the room filled with graduate students with thin piles of short fiction before them on the seminar table: "Write novels."

But dried-up market or no, the short story refused to bite the dust. Maybe the popular magazines that seemed to sustain the short story earlier in the century were not real friends, after all. True, they paid well and they had readers. But they imposed restrictions of style and length that stifled voice and even material. The essentially poetic, even spiritual, tendencies of the genre were suppressed in favor of narrative action. But left to its own devices, short fiction has resurfaced now as a narrative genre with keen meditative and retrospective powers.

Reynolds Price, in this graceful collection, *The Foreseeable Future,* presents three long stories that display this contemplative aspect of the form with dignity and beautiful gravity.

Only the final story (also the shortest), **"Back Before Day,"** has much built-in suspense, and even that is quickly abandoned. Instead, each story exhibits an intense respect for the characters' inner lives. These modest but passionate people spend their days largely in a silence punctuated by intense exchanges with men and women as isolated as themselves. The introspection and the interior lives of these figures provide them with a method of survival in the ordinary world, and even a kind of salvation.

Interestingly, although there are interior monologues, none of the stories are written in the first person, that much-favored voice of current short fiction. This is a wise, if unfashionable, choice. In the first two (and best) stories, in particular, the third-person narration creates an intimate atmosphere that a first-person voice might easily have made merely introspective or oppressively confessional.

"The Fare to the Moon" and the book's title story are set late in World War II near Raleigh and in the Carolina low country. They have the faint aura of period pieces about them without, however, being at all nostalgic. Both stories seem drenched in a time as well as a place. The fatefulness of wartime becomes an active presence in the characters' lives (something missing in **"Back Before Day,"** which is set in a less specified post-Vietnam War present).

Leah, in **"The Fare to the Moon,"** is the black true love of white (and married) Kayes Paschal. As the story begins, she has risen early to see her lover off to the Army. He has been drafted—at one level a deliverance from a desperate social situation, but more deeply a separation tragic beyond their ability to discuss.

This story is not the longest in the collection, but it is the most novelistic. Mr. Price manages to shift point of view from Leah to Kayes, to Kayes's brother, to his embittered wife and finally to his estranged son, Curtis. He even deftly works in vignettes from the shared childhoods of Leah and Kayes that serve to underscore the inevitability of their attachment.

Mr. Price accomplishes all of this without rushing, keeping that meditative voice that attests to the necessity of telling the story in the first place. Tone is everything for these carefully nuanced characters. "Easy, child," Leah says to Kayes's brother toward the end, when he mistakes her bravery for lightheartedness. "We're all too sad. Let's show some respect."

Kayes Paschal goes off to war, and in **"The Foreseeable Future,"** the collection's centerpiece, Whit Wade has just returned. His problem is an inability to feel quite alive since he was wounded in France. The doctors told him, he says, "for practical purposes, I was dead when they found me."

Whit has come home to his devoted wife, June, and adored child, Liss, in Raleigh, and to his job as an insurance adjuster. Using the frame of Whit's work-week on the road settling claims, Mr. Price lays out the story's chapters as days of the week, sending his hero away from home and safety where he battles wrecked, suicidal sensations. "Nothing," he says early in the story, "tastes good to me but the sight of my child."

The story moves from day to day in a vivid series of encounters with people adrift in their own loneliness, some of them touching Whit's early life, while others are strangers almost occult in their capacity to comprehend his life-and-death passage. Most of these characters—women especially—offer, as Whit says, "kind thoughts—sweet cheer, maybe lies." They also offer him their own versions of feeling alive and yet dead, their wounds as serious as his, if more subtle than those inflicted in war.

Late in the week, deep "out here in the beautiful lonesome sticks," Whit meets a frail man old enough to have opened the door to a Union officer. This "scared old boy with a mind like a blade, pushing ninety and ready for more," provides him, almost casually, with "the secret visible truth."

But in fact, each of the real and yet fabulous figures Whit meets along his way offers a paradoxical truth about how to keep on keeping on. None of these people are chummy, none wish to buttonhole an audience or even a listener.

That is part of the power of the book's overall effect and the source of its gravity: these people have stories because they have lives. They must recount them in order to live on, past the wounds and dislocations of their histories.

They are speaking, then, to themselves, yet everything they say has to do with the love they bear—or are unable to bear—others. It seems entirely right that these are people who have the habit of praying, for what is this kind of urgent interior voice but prayer?

Greg Johnson (essay date 1991)

SOURCE: "Homecomings," in *The Georgia Review,* Vol. XLV, No. 4, Winter, 1991, pp. 778–86.

[*Johnson is an American novelist and short story writer. In the excerpted review below, he notes Price's preoccupation with the theme of homecoming and praises his writing style.*]

One of the salient traits of Southern fiction has been its ongoing, obsessive fascination with home. Although such major non-Southern writers as Melville, James, Hemingway, and Fitzgerald tended to focus upon rootless wanderers whose sense of home is either attenuated or irrelevant, the imaginations of Southern writers have seldom strayed far from their origins. Thomas Wolfe's *You Can't Go Home Again* is surely the emblematic Southern title, since the works of Caldwell, Faulkner, McCullers, O'Connor, Warren, Welty, and dozens of lesser writers have focused with loving but troubled nostalgia on the traditional Southern homestead. In such various guises as the faded Compson mansion in Faulkner's *The Sound and the Fury,* the tumbledown Georgia farmhouses in O'Connor's stories, and the Vaughn homeplace evoked with such unforgettable lyricism in the opening pages of Welty's *Losing Battles*— "The house was revealed as if standing there from pure memory against a now moonless sky"—Southern writers have depicted home as the symbolic repository of the human heart and as the object of both their most embittered criticism and their fiercest emotional longings.

One of the most distinguished contemporary explorers of the homecoming theme is Reynolds Price. Beginning with *Kate Vaiden* (1986), winner of the National Book Critics Circle Award, Price has published an astonishing nine books in the past five years, adding to an already distinguished body of work that includes such acclaimed novels as *A Long and Happy Life* (1962) and *The Surface of Earth* (1975). Although most of his work has been set in his native North Carolina, none has been more obsessively concerned with homecoming than his fine new book, *The Foreseeable Future*. This gathering of three long stories dramatizes the lives of ordinary but conflicted men who endure personal crises in the domestic and spiritual realms.

The title piece, set in 1945, features a man shaken by his experiences in World War II. An insurance adjuster, Whit Wade is attempting to relearn his life—how to relate to his family, his work, and his past. "The Foreseeable Future" follows Whit through one crucial week, as he doggedly adheres to his routine of investigating insurance claims and tending to his family's needs. Slowly, his week's experiences—especially his encounters with a variety of sharply characterized clients—return the traumatized Whit emotionally and spiritually to the life he'd known before the war. Price's incisive but gentle prose evokes this healing process: "All the news he'd learned this week . . . aimed at prying his shut heart open to life. Life as risky as any French field and at least as strange, though he knew the common language here."

Throughout this collection, such haunting passages suggest the spiritual dimension of his characters' humanity. At a time when contemporary fiction is drenched in random sexuality, it is heartening to see a serious author dealing with sex in the context of genuine intimacy and healing. Whit's sexual reunion with his wife is conveyed in language that captures far more than the physical pleasure of his relief from loneliness:

> Here for the first time in—what? three years?—was an actual woman so fine he could not believe her. Yet his body was telling him, this hot instant, she was way too real for any dream. It craved all of her. So he tried to cool down, though he still watched her eyes. Rebecca Barksdale, you are too fine. Let me watch you from here, with both of us safe. Clear as it sounded in his mind, Whit said it over three slow times like a gift she'd never know he gave. For the first time in longer than he could remember, he was in one place—and happy there—not strewn through a field or longing for somewhere calm and dark.

The other two stories are equally impressive. In "Fare to the Moon," also set in the 1940's, Kayes Paschal is heading for the war instead of returning, and he leaves behind a complicated domestic situation: he has become involved in a love affair with a local black woman. Now that Kayes is leaving, his resentful wife and teenage son are forced to deal with the situation, and the story becomes a tautly

dramatic investigation of Southern attitudes toward race, family, and fidelity. As a family man in the 1940's, Kayes must negotiate between his own sense of guilt and his awareness that his relationship with the black woman, Leah, is perhaps the most significant of his life. His leaving for the war heightens this recognition almost unbearably: "This much was true—he had spent from eight to twenty-four hours a day, these six months, beside a kind intelligent person who fit against his mind and body, and chose to fit, in every way a sane human being would pray to find this side of death."

Throughout *The Foreseeable Future* Price displays his thorough understanding of his characters, their social context, their region. Though acknowledging pain and discord, his work repeatedly evokes the possibility of redemption.

—Greg Johnson

Even more compelling is the story that closes the volume, "Back Before Day." Unlike Whit Wade and Kayes Paschal, the protagonist here, Dean Walker, is prone to jealousy and violence. A football coach who deeply loves his wife and young son, he is tormented by the wife's continuing friendship with her high-school sweetheart, Clyde Bowles. Price includes a sexual scene in this story, too, but here the lovemaking becomes an expression of the couple's mutual rage and frustration: "They were as close as two people manage to get, short of skinning each other, eating the choice meat and wearing the hide. Yet though they could not have told you in words, their separate furious aims were alike. They each one wanted to forestall loathing or the need to seize one near human being and strike him or her in the brittle teeth or grind some former loved one to pulp and scrub his face, her hair and eyes, out of memory or notice." Delving masterfully into Dean's troubled mind, Price suggests that the man's self-doubt lies at the heart of his jealousy. "I've turned out less than average," he tells his wife, "a D-plus well-intentioned slack boy." Only in the powerful climactic scenes, in which a moment of random violence shakes Dean to the core, does the story suggest a possible resolution for this troubled family.

Throughout this book, Price displays his thorough understanding of his characters, their social context, their region. Though acknowledging pain and discord, his work repeatedly evokes the possibility of redemption, even in such small moments as a father's loving glance at his daughter, taking in her "long deep hair, fine as the day that had just shut behind them, and green eyes welcome as the world's first leaves." Such prose is the hallmark of this remarkable book, suggesting why Price has become one of the South's most important and revered writers.

James A. Schiff (essay date 1993)

SOURCE: "Fathers and Sons in the Fiction of Reynolds Price: A Sense of Crucial Ambiguity," in *The Southern Review,* Louisiana State University, Vol. 29, No. 1, January, 1993, pp. 16–29.

[*Schiff is an American educator and critic. In the following excerpt, he examines the bond between fathers and sons in Price's fiction and reveals the characterisitic role of eroticism established in "The Names and Faces of Heroes."*]

Since the 1962 publication of his first novel, *A Long and Happy Life,* which not only won the Faulkner Award but was also printed in its entirety in *Harper's,* Reynolds Price has been a visible presence in contemporary American letters, yet for some critics the promise of his career has never been fully realized. Though this attitude has changed somewhat in recent years, particularly with the publication of *Kate Vaiden* in 1986, Price still has not received a great deal of critical attention—certainly less than other members of his literary generation such as John Updike, Philip Roth, Thomas Pynchon, Toni Morrison, and Don DeLillo. Why?

Price's prose style explains the neglect in part. Not only is his style, in the words of Constance Rooke, "highly pronounced, unusual, and quite often difficult," but in an age and environment which favors more idiomatic, casual, and realistic prose, Price's writing strives for an impressive sound which reminds one, more than any other example from contemporary American literature, of *Paradise Lost* or the Bible. Related to this is the fact that one does not find a detailed sense of the *contemporary* world in Price's writing, as one does in say Updike's Rabbit novels or DeLillo's *White Noise.* Those writers are expert at incorporating sociology into their narratives, utilizing, often in a metaphorical sense, a wealth of information from newspaper headlines, television programs, and social trends. Relatively speaking, Price's fiction relies little upon sociological details; there is a chiseled bareness to his vision; his characters are depicted at the emotional core, with little regard for the trappings of contemporary life. Thus, for readers eager to find detailed sociology in fiction, Price may be something of a disappointment.

Another explanation for the neglect of Price's work stems from his early and mistaken casting into the role of a "minor Faulkner" (I say mistaken because John Milton, Leo Tolstoy, Eudora Welty, and the Bible are far greater influences). Without any careful scrutiny of his work, critics placed Price under the enormous shadow of the Mississippian simply because both are southerners. Geographically, Price's home and the area he writes about are closer to New York City than to Oxford, Mississippi, yet from the perspective of a northeastern literary establishment, North Carolina and Mississippi are joined, just as Colombia and Peru are joined and then called "Latin America" (note that the suburbs of Boston and New York are considered separate entities, as we see in the fiction of Updike and Roth; the same should hold true in the fiction of

North Carolinians and Mississippians). My point, however, is not to denounce the literary establishment, but rather to point out that hasty decisions and generalizations are sometimes made about writers whose geographical status is unfamiliar.

I wish to demonstrate, by focusing upon a central mystery that recurs in his fiction, that Price's vision is indeed unique and bold, and that more attention needs to be paid. My inquiry in these pages concerns the relationship between fathers and sons, the bond of kin which appears to interest Price most. Though all novels are to some degree about family life, Price's work focuses upon the family with an intensity that reminds one of Greek drama and biblical narrative, and at the center of familial relations is what I find to be one of the central mysteries in Price's fiction: the charged eroticism that exists between fathers and sons. I say "mystery" because Price is intentionally ambiguous about the nature of such an Eros, particularly in regard to the nature of physical contact.

"The Names and Faces of Heroes" (1963), a story from the collection of the same title, was Price's initial attempt at understanding an intimate relationship between father and son. Years after it was written, Price said of the largely autobiographical story, which is arguably his finest:

> I'm certainly aware that it's a very complicated and in many ways a difficult story, perhaps a little more difficult than it ought to be. It's certainly a love story. It's certainly a story containing an enormous amount of Eros. And I may say that I think it's one of those very rare stories in English which deals with the reality that English and American writers have found almost impossible to face or talk about, which is the degree of Eros, the overwhelming amount of Eros, that exists between many fathers and sons.

The story, delivered in the first person present by a nine-year-old boy named Preacher, documents a nighttime car ride in which Preacher and his father are headed home from Raleigh after having heard a sermon by a man who claims to have seen Christ. The opening line, in which Preacher says, "We are people in love," leads the reader, who is not yet aware that the "lovers" are a father and son, to imagine presumably some sort of more common adult heterosexual relationship. The reader is then tripped up when he learns who the lovers actually are, but simultaneously he is forced to consider whether it is not indeed natural for fathers and sons to be "lovers" of some sort. One's first inclination is to imagine a kind of brotherly love or Agape between father and son, but there is indeed Eros here as we learn that Preacher is lying with his head in his father's lap: "I the thin fork of flesh thrust out of his groin on the seat beside him, my dark head the burden in his lap." The physical and erotic nature of their love is continually stressed as Preacher's father, while driving, explores the body of his son: "He drops a hand . . . slipping between two buttons of the coat to brush one breast then out again and down to rest on my hip. His thumb and fingers ride the high saddle bone, the fat of his hand in the hollow *I* have, heavy but still on the dry knots of boyish

equipment waiting for life to start." There is, however, no
sense of sexual molestation or abuse in the tone or in the
language, and no action is taken which is not desired;
instead, Preacher and his father are as comfortable and
familiar to one another, both physically and emotionally,
as old lovers.

Though atypical for a nine-year-old in regard to his intelligence and perception, Preacher is nevertheless a typical
child both in his anxiety over his father's mortality and in
his fear of abandonment and separation; both, of course,
are also common fears of lovers. Preacher worries that his
father will leave him and "take up his life in secret," a
worry that is not completely without reason since his father has a history of being "drunk and wild." Driving beside
his father through the winter night and remembering the
words of a camp minister who urged him to find a hero
and "chin [himself] on his example," Preacher considers
his father as a possibility (the historical and the famous
have proven too distant). Though it is never resolved
whether his father fits the role (one could perhaps argue
this point either way), Preacher nevertheless sees him as
a larger-than-life figure whom he loves more than anyone
else. Jesus, another fatherly figure who plays a large role
in Preacher's life, springs forth as an alternative hero, and
here Price proves himself adept at pulling off a rather
difficult correspondence: Preacher's father, by virtue of
his ability to change faces, and by the wound in his hand
(from a childhood accident), is linked mystically to Christ.
In Preacher's eyes, his father is a kind of flesh-and-blood
representation of Christ, and by studying his father's face
Preacher moves closer to an understanding of divinity.

Near the end of the story, his head buried in his father's
lap, Preacher falls asleep, only to wake and realize his
greatest nightmare: "my father is gone." Fearing that some
enemy has succeeded in separating them ("They have
caught us, come between us"), or that his father has abandoned him, Preacher searches through the car windows
and then prays for his father's return. Soon a man appears
out of the snow, his "head wrapped in black, a black robe
bound close about him," and Preacher, still not fully awake,
mistakes him for the hero about whom they just finished
speaking, Jesus (recall that they are returning from hearing a minister who claims he has *seen* Christ). The man,
of course, is only Preacher's father, who has just returned
from urinating. Though his father senses Preacher's disappointment, there is once again a connection, in Preacher's
mind, between Jesus and his father.

At this point the strangest moment of the story occurs,
which links father and son together physically and mystically. With his hand cupping his groin, Preacher once again
falls asleep and this time dreams of his hand, which has
been transformed into its adult form while still wrapped
about his groin. The hand, which at one moment appears
to be his own and at the next seems to be his father's, is
molding the "kernels" of life, or more literally the genita-
lia. It is the hand which appears to generate creation, and
in this part of the dream Preacher is able not only to
anticipate his own adult self and his future powers of
creation, but also to experience vicariously his own cre-

ation as generated by his father. The dream then transports him into a room in which his adult self examines the
body and holds "the core" of what appears to be his dead
father (he also recognizes himself and his own mortality
in his father). In attempting to bring his father back to life
and "set him free," Preacher and his father are joined in
a sexual sense: "A shudder begins beneath my hand in his
core our core that floods through his belly."

Just as Preacher emerges from his father's groin, he attempts to bring life back to his father by stimulating that
groin. Though he appears temporarily successful, his father once again goes "cold" like "hard ice, final as any
trapped in the pole." Faced with the terror of his father's
mortality, Preacher makes a promise that he "will change
[his] life," an utterance that mirrors and answers to an
identical promise made by his father during Preacher's
difficult birth: "I . . . told Jesus, 'If you take Rhew [my
wife] or take that baby, then take me too. But if You can,
save her and save that baby, and I make You this promise—I will change my life.'" Through this mystical dream
sequence Price demonstrates the unique and intense bonds
between fathers and sons, particularly in regard to how
they are connected physically through the groin, which
functions as a kind of "core." Though it is common for
mothers to experience a physical link to their offspring
through the womb, connections of this sort are seldom
made between fathers and their children.

"The Names and Faces of Heroes" concludes with father and son arriving home. Freshly awake from the dream
of his father's death, Preacher is "flooded" with "sudden
need": "to rise, board him, cherish with my hands, my
arms while there still is time this huge gentle body I know
like my own, which made my own." Because the ground
is covered in snow, Preacher is then carried from the car
to the house by his father: "I go . . . into arms that circle,
enfold me, lift me, bear me these last steps home over
ice." With his face pressed against his father's heart,
Preacher, despite the knowledge of his father's future death,
experiences a sense of triumph: on this night they have
arrived home "alive, together, whole."

George Garrett (essay date 1993)

SOURCE: "Here is Heartbreak, and Here is Laughter," in
The New York Times Book Review, July 4, 1993, p. 8.

[*In the following review, Garrett praises the complexity
and scope of Price's short stories.*]

Reynolds Price has been a significant figure on the American literary scene for more than 30 years. He has been
recognized as one of our most gifted writers since his first
published book, the novel *A Long and Happy Life* (1962),
appeared and won the William Faulkner Foundation Award.
(It has been in print ever since.) Well before that, in 1954,
while he was still an undergraduate at Duke, he earned the
attention, interest and practical support of the visiting
writers Elizabeth Bowen and Eudora Welty for the story

"**Michael Egerton.**" A few years later, while Mr. Price was at Oxford on a Rhodes scholarship, Stephen Spender published his story "**A Chain of Love**" in *Encounter.*

Both of these tales are among a gathering of 50 stories making up *The Collected Stories,* his 25th book in a dedicated and productive career in letters that has included poetry, nine novels, plays, essays, translations, memoirs and three earlier collections of stories—*The Names and Faces of Heroes* (1963), *Permanent Errors* (1970) and *The Foreseeable Future* (1991). All of the stories from the earlier two collections are part of the "Collected Stories." *The Foreseeable Future,* consisting of three long stories, is perhaps too recent to be included, and would probably have made the new collection unmanageably abundant.

In a brief, evocative and very useful note to the reader, Mr. Price tells us that except for slight editorial corrections, "the older stories stand as they first appeared," adding that "all of them stand in a new order—one which attempts an alternation of voices, echoes, lengths and concerns that would prove unlikely if I held to the order of the prior volumes or set the stories by date of completion."

Thus the earlier stories are well scattered among the new and uncollected ones, and remarkably, except for some old favorites and widely anthologized pieces among them ("**The Warrior Princess Ozimba,**" "**Waiting at Dachau,**" "**The Names and Faces of Heroes**"), it is not easy for the reader to guess which stories came early and which are most recent. There is an unusual kind of uniformity demonstrated here, the uniformity of sustained, unflagging artistic excellence, all the more impressive since the author's arranged sequence and context stress variety of form and content.

There is no real model for Mr. Price's work. In interviews he has acknowledged the powerful influence of Eudora Welty, but in a special and complex manner—"I felt confirmed by her example in the validity of my own experience as a source of art." Mr. Price has described her in interviews as "the living writer I admire most," and he dedicated *Permanent Errors* to her.

Mr. Price belongs to no school or movement. From first to last, his stories are technically straightforward in the telling and accessible. At the same time, they manage to be subtle and adventurous in the complex experiences dealt with, the subjects explored. They are linked to one another (and to his other work) by somewhat similar ways and means of telling and, more deeply, by clusters of common concerns.

Most of Mr. Price's stories are told by first-person narrators, each with a different, distinctive and appropriate voice, yet sharing some characteristics, chief among which is a delicate balance, an almost perfect blending of spoken and written discourse. The sentences are solid and shapely, but always credible, convincing. There are brilliant, virtuoso stylistic moments, but they are fully earned, and

do not divert attention from the tale. Similes (a strict test of artistic self-indulgence) evolve naturally and infrequently, at once apt and surprising, as, for example, in "**Endless Mountains**": "It felt like I was the last live soul on a planet swept of the human race except for me, a lone man normal as milk in a bucket but the lord of all" or "a gentle shine like the memory of your best deed or dusk on the summer river, floating slow."

Setting is a vital force in Mr. Price's work. Most often that setting is North Carolina, the farms and towns and cities he has lived in and around; but there are first-rate stories firmly set in England and Europe. Contemporary Israel is beautifully evoked in "**Long Night**" and "**An Early Christmas.**" Most of the stories are set during the decades of Mr. Price's lifetime, but the range is, in fact, from the 1860's to the present, allowing for sudden allusions to an even deeper, more shadowy history, as in this tourists' vision (in "**Night and Silence**") of Rome, where "the Field of Mars still rocked in the dark to three millennia anyhow of soldier's feet—wide-eyed delicate bird-voiced Etruscans, sun-kilned Roman legionnaires, the shaggy Goths (drunk on clear light) and us this past slow afternoon; polo-shirted, maps in hand."

Mr. Price tends to be particular in time, not only in the setting of the stories, but also in the exact time of telling. When the tale is told matters almost as much as who the witness doing the telling is. "**The Company of the Dead**" begins: "Eighty-some years ago when I was a boy, Simp Dockett and I were in modest demand as reliable and inexpensive all-night 'setters.'"

All of these things add to the authenticity of the stories, an authority reinforced by clearly autobiographical elements. Several stories have a character named "Reynolds" in them, and others play close to the edges of the public facts of Mr. Price's life. This, in turn, allows him to enjoy the freedom of unabashed nostalgia without sentimentality. He has established his reliability, and the reader will gladly follow wherever he goes. Sometimes, with undiminished credibility, he goes deeply into the precincts of dreams and dream visions (not surprising for a man who teaches Milton), and there are ghosts in any number of these stories. In "**This Wait,**" a ghost is the believable narrator.

But as in all worthy texts, it is, finally, the *spirit* and not the letter of Mr. Price's stories that lifts them to achieve a grace beyond the art and craft of all but the finest few of his contemporaries. Nobody I know writes so well about the joys and sorrows of the family. Nobody else can so deftly capture the lyric intensity of simple happiness. To do so, of course, he must come face to face with grief, loss and pain. There are plenty of stories here that will break your heart, but there are precious few without the gift of laughter.

Above all, Mr. Price writes his best work about all kinds of love—obsessional love and lasting love, love in the family, love between men and women, men and men, old and young, interracial love—all treated with respect and without vulgarity or cynicism. In "To the Reader," Mr. Price writes: "From the start my stories were driven by heat—passion and mystery . . . and my general aim is the transfer of a spell of keen witness, perceived by the reader as warranted in character and act." The result of the aim is the accomplishment of this spellbinding collection, a book to be treasured.

Ron Carlson (essay date 1994)

SOURCE: "The Collected Stories of Reynolds Price," in *The Southern Review,* Louisiana State University, Vol. 30, No. 2, Spring, 1994, pp. 371–78.

[*In the following review, Carlson emphasizes the effective realism and emotional intensity of Price's stories.*]

I have become certain of one thing in the last half-year: the rich collection of stories in **The Collected Stories** of Reynolds Price—the galley copy of which I have absolutely torn apart, used up, wrecked—will exist somewhere as a thread in the fabric of twentieth-century American literature. The fifty stories here were written over the span of almost forty years (though Price notes in his introduction that he wrote exclusively in other forms between 1970 and 1990), and half of them come from his earlier collections, **The Names and Faces of Heroes** (1963) and **Permanent Errors** (1970). Price has been known as a "Southern Writer," and these stories for the most part would confirm that in their locale, in the situation of the characters (picking ticks, chewing snuff, eating hominy), and in that thing most often evoked by the name of Faulkner, that is a sense of familial mystery and loss—told in a form which many times overtly addresses its own identity as story. That last is exactly the kind of sentence which tries to bale fifty stories with one piece of wire, and it will not work. That ancient sins and secrets are hot for the characters in these stories, that the characters have a keen sense of regret which roils and simmers within them, an urgent need to testify, a fear of being damned and a stoic wonder for the ways they are redeemed—these may start to make this the book of a southern writer, but there is as much Sherwood Anderson here as Faulkner, and there's another thing throughout the stories, the thing most appreciated perhaps, and that is Reynolds Price's ability to infuse his stories with candor, a simple but powerful sense transcendent fiction has that confronts, invades the reader with the knowledge that if one sits at the table long enough with this writer he's going to show all his cards, unexpected as they may be, and in a beautiful way make something true.

The old word "duty" appears frequently in the stories, family duty—to take in an aging aunt, to be a good father, to pay a visit to a relative, to find the missing inner strength. In fact, there are several stories in which a young man calls on an old woman who used to work for his family. In **"The Warrior Princess Ozimba"** and **"Two Useful Visits,"** secrets are hinted at, revealed. The latter opens, "Back then your kin could lean down on you with the weight of the world and still not quite say, 'Get yourself up here to see Mary Greet; she's dying fast, and it's your plain duty.'" Both "visit" stories offer the men glimpses of the lost world of the South, and both men are suffused with a kind of gratitude for the care and trust the women have bestowed. These are short stories, the visits almost vignettes, yet news is exchanged and the young men are affected. Throughout the stories, which range in length from two to almost one hundred pages, Price is able to work very well in a small space. Part of this is because of his profound understanding of the scenes he creates and the depth of human potential in each, and part is his ability to marry language and the moment. There are a few stories with the pure lyric reach of prose poems and, of course, there are sections of others which brim with a diction so fluent and apt as to be arresting in themselves. In the last paragraph of **"Bess Waters,"** a story in eight short sections which spans one hundred years, 1863-1963, in the life of the former slave, the title character tries to answer the request of a young visitor (he is named Reynolds Price) to tell her story:

> And honest to God, Bess tries to tell it. Her dry lips work and her mind sends words—she only recalls these scattered hours—but what comes out is dark shine and power from her banked old heart and the quick of her bones, dark but hot as a furnace blast with a high blue roar. It burns the boy first. Bess sees him blown back and starting to scorch; then it whips round and folds her into the light till both of them sit in a grate of embers, purified by the tale itself, the visible trace of one long life too hard to tell.

The longest story in the book, **"Walking Lessons,"** is set, surprisingly, in the desert Southwest and begins with one of Price's stunning openers: "My wife killed herself two weeks ago, her twenty-sixth birthday. . . ." In Price's stories, most often people *start* in trouble, and things get worse. The twenty-eight-year-old writer and college teacher who, deep in fresh grief, flies to see his college friend Blix Cunningham where he works on the Navajo reservation in Arizona, meets a world so dark, troubled, and squalid as to be the physical manifestation of his sorrow. Blix lives in a hovel with an Indian woman, Dora Badonie, whose own maladies rival anybody's. **"Walking Lessons"** follows the three through a rough mission of mercy, a trek really, that becomes—in its magnitude, calamity, and poor weather—life-threatening. There are, the narrator discovers, no easy answers to the quandaries in which any of them are lost. And with convincing realism of scene and of voice, Price is just that tough-minded as he moves toward the resolution of the story. Redemption isn't something found suddenly on the ground like a coin, but something that breaks imperceptibly into a life like the gradient degrees of dawn. Here, as in many of the stories, the protagonist is a writer, and Price is unafraid of talking like one, breaking frame to be a storyteller and to address the reader. Here, after the travelers are first stranded, their walking lessons begin:

> I'm capable of spelling it out for you, in every increasingly pressurized moment—finding stripped

howling language to compel your company every step of my way toward agony, physical and mental desperation; but you've read Jack London, you've seen Yukon movies (Preston Foster, Bruce Cabot—eyelashes frosted). May I leave it to you? You have all the elements; build it around me—the night, the struggle.

Elsewhere in the book (frequently, it seems), Price speaks as a storyteller long past the pivotal events, using the accrued gravity of time to add weight and substance to happenings, as in one of my favorites, **"The Company of the Dead,"** a story about two teenage boys who become "setters," those hired to sit up with corpses to keep watch and offer company all the long night before the funeral. Near the start, the narrator says, "By the time Simp and I had our truly wild night—the one I must tell before too late—we were good sized boys, fifteen years old." There is a "must-tell" quality about many of the stories in this collection, as if they were insistent testimonies burning their ways out of a storyteller's heart. **"The Company of the Dead"** ends with this: "I'm ninety-two years old, writing this line, a man at peace with what he's done and what comes next. I leave this story, in both its parts, as my best gift to a world I've liked and thank, here now, but have never pressed for the black heart's blood of actual love." Parallel passages resound in the stories, "all these many years since" and "Thirteen years on, I tell whoever reads these lines," and this swift, poignant coda which closes **"A Full Day"**:

> In four months Buck will die from a growth that reached decisive weight in his body this full afternoon and threw him down. His elder son has made this unreal gift for his father on the eighty-ninth passing of Buck's birthday, though he died these thirty-five years ago.

The effect of this narrative strategy is clear: in a world of such scope, the dead affect the living (one character says about his life that it's like the Bible: there're more ghosts than good women), and the powerful sweep of time in these stories is as real as the weather. Price, in his form and narrative traits, demonstrates the long reach.

Three short pieces lodged a hundred pages apart in the collection are couched as letters from fathers to sons. Each is an emotional tour de force, as the men try to say in writing those essential things that can't be said aloud. **"The Last News"** is a graphic confession by an alcoholic father of personal crimes he committed long ago. He's not exactly looking for forgiveness, but for something deeper—the paying of a debt. "If you want to kill me once I'm out of here, be my guest," he says, and means it. And listen to the last line, the last word a knife-thrust: "I'm waiting to know your answer, sir." **"Breath"** is similar, being a brief, brutal history, a request for pardon by a father caught in an ongoing cycle of abuse, and it contains the slight hope that father and son might reconcile, "breathe in the same room." What is remarkable in these stories is how urgent the messages feel, how heartwrenching, how guileless. These are broken men speaking from the depths, and they are what gives so much of Price's fiction an edge that cuts. **"A Final Account"** shows us a third father, this one

writing a letter of gratitude and explanation moments after meeting with his grown son twenty-four years after walking away from his wife and baby. The father is dying of AIDS, alone among strangers, and he says, "Son, you count the most to me of anybody left alive. I knew if I said that straight to your face, blind as I am, I'd just seize up." Writing is the deeper way, these stories show us. The other note that sounds so clearly in this work, in these letters, is that as irremediable as the crimes and as permanent as the regret and as late as the hour may seem, there is still a shred of something to be salvaged.

Sometimes it is a bit of mercy. In **"An Evening Meal"** Sam Traynor, after five years fighting stomach cancer, has won the battle, and he celebrates his cure by going to dinner at a café. Years before he met and had a brief, intense affair with one of the waiters, who, startlingly, is still there. But the surprise of the story comes after the meal when, as he leaves, Sam sees the desiccated shell of one of his first loves, Richard Boileau. The young man hunched in the booth is obviously late in his struggle with AIDS. And the tableau Price leaves us with could have been painted by Hopper: it's dark, and the world is empty, but isn't that a light in the window? This broad summary is a disservice to a delicate story, one of the finest in the collection.

I have become certain of one thing in the last half-year: the rich collection of stories in *The Collected Stories of Reynolds Price*—the galley copy of which I have absolutely torn apart, used up, wrecked—will exist somewhere as a thread in the fabric of twentieth-century American literature.

—*Ron Carlson*

The motif of betrayal figures prominently in the stories of Reynolds Price. **"Truth and Lies"** is an intense confrontation between Sarah Wilson and her former student Ella Scott, who is sleeping with Sarah's husband, Nathan. The women spend all but two pages of the 5,000-word story closed in Sarah's car. The interview came about because of a note Sarah found in her drunken husband's pocket: "I have got something to tell you and will be on the tracks tonight at eight o'clock." Sarah meets Ella instead and comments, "Well, your writing's improved." From there the interview works through the layers of the Wilsons' marital history and through the pride and hopes of young Ella Scott. Both women come away changed in ways they could not have imagined—and with more resolve. In **"Nine Hours Alone,"** it's the teacher who bears the guilt and the consequences of betrayal. Here Price uses her goodbye letters to tell her secrets. Secrets—regardless of how deep they are buried—will out in Price's world, and once out, they demand reckoning. Once alerted to betrayal, we find the truly human character in the heady and powerful **"Serious Need,"** a fitting title for thirty-six-year-old Jock Pittman's unabashed tale of the way he conducted himself with an old classmate's sixteen-year-old daughter. In that story there is an epiphany (or what I'll call one) in a cemetery that I'm going to teach from here on in, but don't let that diminish your energies toward this story.

There is one Civil War story in this collection. **"Endless Mountains"** starts with the wound that is the source of every sentence for the thirty pages—and some months—of the story: "The shot went through the white inside of my right thigh on Wednesday near noon." The scavenger who stands over the wounded man a while later rifling his wallet says, "Well, Trump, it's your goddamned birthday." Trump experiences a tormented, half-waking dream brought on by fear of amputation and then by fever. He then flees—such as he can—not sure he isn't dead. The writing here is close and convincing in its delirium and pain as Trump stumbles across a ridge into the mountains. It's really a quest he's on, though he's not sure for what besides survival. The story grows into the metaphoric parallel to **"Walking Lessons"**; Trump is the damaged soul here, and his descent into pain is intended to cauterize him from the harm war and regret can bring. His "cure" includes one long night wrestling with a naked angel who takes the fever away, a beautiful, frightening scene which is magnified by Trump's stunned and desperate state of mind. His recovery is laden with memory of his own family, and Price describes Trump's courtship in a scene that gets as much out of snow and memory as Joyce. Finally, like the writer-narrator of **"Walking Lessons,"** Trump sees he will go on, must go on, "done with war." These two long stories form a kind of spine for this book; they are poetic and stark examinations of how one might proceed when all is lost.

My favorite stories in the book, however, are those where Price engages early manhood and adolescence. His talent for seeing into the secret heart of men and women is magnificent, but the way he portrays the hot cusp of manhood is unnerving. **"The Enormous Door"** would be a good story to read first, as it offers a sense of the expectations many of Price's male characters bring to their world. The month the narrator turns twelve, his family moves into a small hotel. "From the word go," he says, "I loved the air of mystery in the building." And there are mysteries, many in his own head. "What are grown men like, truly, in secret?" he wonders. The narrator's desire for a model of manhood (and some quirks in the hotel itself) lead him into a delirious career as a voyeur, spying on his neighbor, a teacher named Simon Fentriss whose magnetism overpowers the boy. Oh, it's a charged time all around, and add to it a purloined copy of *Sacred Joy: The Marital Beacon,* a four-inch-thick reference book, orange in color, with chapters covering the "beauty" of sexual congress and "The Oral Tradition" and you've got a twelve-year-old in a stew. Then Price, again, turns his story toward a greater place when the things the boy sees in his peeping become genuinely magical, astounding (if that were still an effective word), and lead to the kind of realization

Price approaches again and again in his fiction, that is, one not easily captured in a phrase or a moment, but applied instead to the span of life ("As I write this tale, I'm sixty years old . . ."), a larger understanding of love and flesh that wants to elude language forever.

Two other boy/men stories require mention. One is the homage to father-son love, **"The Names and Faces of Heroes,"** which is tender and vast—and encompassed in one long automobile ride home at night. The narrator is nine years old and lies with his head on his driving father's lap. "The short cut to being a man," a minister said to the boy the summer before, "is finding your hero, somebody who is what you are not but need to be." Swimming in the boy's mind are appropriate models: Helen Keller, Abraham Lincoln, Enos Slaughter. But the lessons of the night will go beyond conventional notions into that region of conscience nine-year-olds own: the terrible responsibility of knowing who will die (this is illustrated again, beautifully, in **"A New Stretch of Woods"**). **"The Names and Faces of Heroes"** is one of the best stories of its kind, truly required reading. It does not claim more than it earns.

"Troubled Sleep" is also narrated by a nine-year-old, Edward Rodwell, who spends a hard evening in the secret glen he shares with his unreliable and flashy cousin Falcon Rodwell. Their talk about travel and death is more comic than any we've seen in Price's stories, colored as it is by Falcon's imagination, reminiscent of scenes from Twain. This poignant story explores the thin line between innocence and romance; for Falcon, things are play, but the narrator drinks it all deep:

> When we played cowboys, everybody else who had to die died of bullets or arrows, but Falc never died of anything but blood poison or brain fever or milk leg and even then only after he had called me over to where he lay and whispered his Last Will and Testament, leaving me his radio . . . and making me give my oath to bury him in a copper casket and go to Sunday School and church weekly and turn into a great scientist and destroy germs. I would cry and offer to go with him . . . thinking to myself, "No radio on earth will ever be what Falcon Rodwell was to me."

Thumbing through this big red book again to type some of the above has further harmed the volume, and soon pages will be loose. There are dozens of stories I have not mentioned which another reviewer might, stories which carry a reader through different doorways of the fine big house I have tried to describe. I have become certain of one thing about these collected stories over the past five months, and that is that I'd rather meet them on my own terms. I wish I'd encountered Price's stories one by one like the many little seasons of a life, but I didn't, and getting them now at once, in such a way that ruined the physical book, well, there's something real about that, believe me. Reynolds Price has assembled a moving book of stories, not an unambitious paragraph in over seven hundred pages. His accomplishment lives. I'm glad to have this book, which will have a rubber band around it for a while, and I plan to do more than this review to share my luck at having had such a noble companion.

The last story in the collection, **"An Early Christmas,"** is a journey by a painter on Christmas Eve into the dark and dangerous labyrinth of modern-day Bethlehem. He finds—by all the evidence—the very place of Christ's birth and emerges to have his life and art changed. The last paragraph of this story, indeed the book, came to me as what Price has been up to in his story writing, a kind of artist's credo. The painter claims "the driving will to show this world its visible likeness, front and back, crown to toe from where I've stood, in the clean new mirrors of honest pictures that mean to be guide lights usably placed in the frequent, sometimes permanent, dark."

Jeffrey J. Folks (essay date 1994)

SOURCE: A review of *The Collected Stories,* in *World Literature Today,* Vol. 68, No. 2, Spring, 1994, pp. 370–71.

[*Folks is an American scholar with a special interest in Southern literature. In this positive review, he remarks on Price's continuing interest in the human struggle against a threatening reality of loss, illness, and death.*]

Now recognized as one of the South's finest living writers, Reynolds Price is author of the Mustian trilogy—which includes *A Long and Happy Life* (1962), *A Generous Man* (1966), and *Good Hearts* (1988)—and of the highly acclaimed novel *Kate Vaiden,* which received the National Book Critics Circle Award in 1986. The stories collected here [in *The Collected Stories*] range from **"Michael Egerton,"** first published in 1954, to **"An Evening Meal"** from 1992. These four decades of writing, however, were broken by almost twenty years from 1970 to 1990 in which Price wrote no short stories while he produced novels, poems, plays, essays, and translations. Price's return late in life to the more concentrated short-story form is connected with his condition of spinal cancer, diagnosed in 1984, which has confined him to a wheelchair but, as he insists, has led to an augmented emotional life in which memory has been sharpened and vision broadened.

The breadth of Price's interests is demonstrated by **"Waiting at Dachau,"** one of several important stories with locales and characters outside the South (although narrated by a Southern male from Price's own cultural background). As in many of the stories, the narrative structure of **"Waiting at Dachau"** reveals a fabulistic quality (in the girlfriend's refusal to visit Dachau, which leads to the breaking off of a marital engagement and to the narrator-as-artist's truer engagement with existence). Other stories are more personal in orientation but address equally crucial moments of existence. **"Deeds of Light"** relates the brief encounter of the fourteen-year-old Marcus Black with a twenty-year-old soldier on leave, Deke Patrick. Their ambiguous relationship, both filial

and potentially erotic, records a sensitive adolescent's coming of age to the ultimate value of friendship in opposition to the external world of loss and terror which two events, World War II and the death of Marcus's father, embody. Marcus's evolving "credo"—"Take what you need and hold on hard"—surely reflects the threatening quality of reality that Price attempts to counterbalance in his "hopeful" tales.

Two of Price's recent stories attest to the continuity of the author's interests and how his struggle with cancer has perhaps imbued his fiction with a greater sense of humanity's pain. **"Two Useful Visits"** records conversations with Mary Greet, a dying black woman, possibly born in slavery times. Still in his thirties, Hilman has recently lost his wife and child, yet his pain is countered by hers, the memory of slavery, which was "more hopeless than any of mine." The story **"Uncle Grant,"** a tribute to Grant Terry, to whom *The Collected Stories* is in part dedicated, describes the friendship of Price's father with an older black man, born around 1865. The narrator's father presents his friend with a short-wave radio, which Grant and the young narrator enjoy together—tuning in the larger world (albeit in undecipherable French and Spanish) which the child is later to explore in Europe just as Grant dies in North Carolina. The story's subtext of repressive economic and racial circumstances is figured in the Price family's move into a "smaller" apartment in Asheboro during the thirties, thus forcing Uncle Terry to return to Macon, where he finds work tending gardens and where he lives without electricity. The beloved radio, the objective symbol of communication among three men, is left with Mr. Price under the fiction that Grant will reclaim it as his living conditions improve.

Two further stories reflect Price's emphasis on friendship and the struggle against death as central themes. **"Troubled Sleep"** details the narrator's youthful friendship with Falcon Rodwell ("Falc"), the cousin who visits every summer and with whom the adolescent narrator shares troubling new discoveries of death, parental discord, sexuality, and identity. It is Falc's friendship, his greater vitality and connection with ordinary existence, that leads the narrator out of his "troubled sleep." The lyricism and nature symbolism of this story, as well as its thematic conclusion of affirmation and love, particularly resemble those qualities of Eudora Welty's fiction which Price has mentioned as an influence on his writing. **"The Last of a Long Correspondence"** interweaves public and private events, finding analogy between diplomatic restraint of the superpowers tempted by global destruction and the modest destruction averted by the narrator Timson in his relation to the child Kit. The story's optimistic conclusion, in which two human beings tempted by despair and need "left each other thoroughly clean and open-eyed," is not uncommon in Price's fiction. The distinctive stance and voice of Reynolds Price's fiction replicate such struggles of hope against despair. In his most recent stories Price remains, as he described the fictionalized protagonist Timson during the Cuban missile crisis, "following myself the usual way, dreaming of hope."

FURTHER READING

Bibliography

Flora, Joseph M. and Bain, Robert. *Contemporary Fiction Writers of the South: A Bio-bibliographical Sourcebook.* Westport, Conn.: Greenwood Press, 1993, 571 p.
   Provides biographical and a primary bibliography.

Wright, Stuart and West, James L. W. *Reynolds Price: A Bibliography, 1949-1984.* Charlottesville: University Press of Virginia, 1986, 122 p.
   Primary bibliography containing descriptions of Price's work and intial critical reactions to them.

Criticism

Humphries, Jefferson. "Taking Things Seriously: Reynolds Price as Teacher and Writer." *Southwest Review* 74, No. 1 (Winter 1989): 10–24.
   Traces the development of Price's writing style.

Kimball, Sue Leslie, and Sadler, Lynn Veach, eds. *Reynolds Price: From 'A Long and Happy Life' to 'Good Hearts.'* Fayetteville: Methodist College Press, 1989, 154 p.
   Collection of essays by various critics examining Price's career.

Rooke, Constance. *Reynolds Price.* Boston: Twayne Publishers, 1983, 158 p.
   Overview of Price's life and literary career through 1981.

Sadler, Lynn Veach. "The 'Mystical Grotesque' in the Life and Works of Reynolds Price." *The Southern Literary Journal* XXI, No. 2 (Spring 1989): 27–40.
   Examines supernatural and religious elements in Price's work and his connection to the Southern Gothic tradition.

Interview

Humphries, Jefferson, ed. *Conversations with Reynolds Price.* Jackson: University Press of Mississippi, 1991, 294 p.
   Collection of interviews from 1966 to 1989.

Additional coverage of Price's life and career is contained in the following sources published by Gale Research: *Contemporary Authors*, Vols. 1-4 (rev. ed.); *Contemporary Authors New Revision Series*, Vols. 1, 37; *Contemporary Literary Criticism*, Vols. 3, 6, 13, 43, 50, 63; and *Dictionary of Literary Biography*, Vol. 2.

Appendix:

Select Bibliography of General Sources on Short Fiction

BOOKS OF CRITICISM

Allen, Walter. *The Short Story in English.* New York: Oxford University Press, 1981, 413 p.

Aycock, Wendell M., ed. *The Teller and the Tale: Aspects of the Short Story* (Proceedings of the Comparative Literature Symposium, Texas Tech University, Volume XIII). Lubbock: Texas Tech Press, 1982, 156 p.

Bates, H. E. *The Modern Short Story: A Critical Survey.* Boston: Writer, 1941, 231 p.

Bayley, John. *The Short Story: Henry James to Elizabeth Bowen.* Great Britain: The Harvester Press Limited, 1988, 197 p.

Bruck, Peter. *The Black American Short Story in the Twentieth Century: A Collection of Critical Essays.* Amsterdam: B. R. Grüner Publishing Co., 1977, 209 p.

Burnett, Whit, and Burnett, Hallie. *The Modern Short Story in the Making.* New York: Hawthorn Books, 1964, 405 p.

Canby, Henry Seidel. *The Short Story in English.* New York: Henry Holt and Co., 1909, 386 p.

Current-García, Eugene. *The American Short Story before 1850: A Critical History.* Twayne's Critical History of the Short Story, edited by William Peden. Boston: Twayne Publishers, 1985, 168 p.

Foster, David William. *Studies in the Contemporary Spanish-American Short Story.* Columbia, Mo.: University of Missouri Press, 1979, 126 p.

Gerlach, John. *Toward an End: Closure and Structure in the American Short Story.* University, Ala.: The University of Alabama Press, 1985, 193 p.

Harris, Wendell V. *British Short Fiction in the Nineteenth Century.* Detroit: Wayne State University Press, 1979, 209 p.

Kilroy, James F., ed. *The Irish Short Story: A Critical History.* Twayne's Critical History of the Short Story, edited by William Peden. Boston: Twayne Publishers, 1984, 251 p.

Lee, A. Robert. *The Nineteenth-Century American Short Story.* Totowa, N. J.: Vision / Barnes & Noble, 1986, 196 p.

Mann, Susan Garland. *The Short Story Cycle: A Genre Companion and Reference Guide.* New York: Greenwood Press, 1989, 228 p.

Matthews, Brander. *The Philosophy of the Short Story.* New York, N.Y.: Longmans, Green and Co., 1901, 83 p.

McClave, Heather, ed. *Women Writers of the Short Story: A Collection of Critical Essays.* Englewood Cliffs, N. J.: Prentice-Hall, 1980, 171 p.

Moser, Charles, ed. *The Russian Short Story: A Critical History*. Twayne's Critical History of the Short Story, edited by William Peden. Boston: Twayne Publishers, 1986, 232 p.

New, W. H. *Dreams of Speech and Violence: The Art of the Short Story in Canada and New Zealand*. Toronto: The University of Toronto Press, 1987, 302 p.

Newman, Frances. *The Short Story's Mutations: From Petronius to Paul Morand*. New York: B. W. Huebsch, 1925, 332 p.

O'Connor, Frank. *The Lonely Voice: A Study of the Short Story*. Cleveland: World Publishing Co., 1963, 220 p.

O'Faolain, Sean. *The Short Story*. New York: Devin-Adair Co., 1951, 370 p.

Orel, Harold. *The Victorian Short Story: Development and Triumph of a Literary Genre*. Cambridge: Cambridge University Press, 1986, 213 p.

O'Toole, L. Michael. *Structure, Style and Interpretation in the Russian Short Story*. New Haven: Yale University Press, 1982, 272 p.

Pattee, Fred Lewis. *The Development of the American Short Story: An Historical Survey*. New York: Harper and Brothers Publishers, 1923, 388 p.

Peden, Margaret Sayers, ed. *The Latin American Short Story: A Critical History*. Twayne's Critical History of the Short Story, edited by William Peden. Boston: Twayne Publishers, 1983, 160 p.

Peden, William. *The American Short Story: Continuity and Change, 1940-1975*. Rev. ed. Boston: Houghton Mifflin Co., 1975, 215 p.

Reid, Ian. *The Short Story*. The Critical Idiom, edited by John D. Jump. London: Methuen and Co., 1977, 76 p.

Rhode, Robert D. *Setting in the American Short Story of Local Color, 1865-1900*. The Hague: Mouton, 1975, 189 p.

Rohrberger, Mary. *Hawthorne and the Modern Short Story: A Study in Genre*. The Hague: Mouton and Co., 1966, 148 p.

Shaw, Valerie. *The Short Story: A Critical Introduction*. London: Longman, 1983, 294 p.

Stephens, Michael. *The Dramaturgy of Style: Voice in Short Fiction*. Carbondale, Ill.: Southern Illinois University Press, 1986, 281 p.

Stevick, Philip, ed. *The American Short Story, 1900-1945: A Critical History*. Twayne's Critical History of the Short Story, edited by William Peden. Boston: Twayne Publishers, 1984, 209 p.

Summers, Hollis, ed. *Discussion of the Short Story*. Boston: D. C. Heath and Co., 1963, 118 p.

Vannatta, Dennis, ed. *The English Short Story, 1945-1980: A Critical History*. Twayne's Critical History of the Short Story, edited by William Peden. Boston: Twayne Publishers, 1985, 206 p.

Voss, Arthur. *The American Short Story: A Critical Survey*. Norman, Okla.: University of Oklahoma Press, 1973, 399 p.

Walker, Warren S. *Twentieth-Century Short Story Explication: New Series, Vol. 1: 1989-1990*. Hamden, Conn.: Shoe String, 1993, 366 p.

Ward, Alfred C. *Aspects of the Modern Short Story: English and American*. London: University of London Press, 1924, 307 p.

Williams, Blanche Colton. *Our Short Story Writers*. New York: Moffat, Yard and Co., 1920, 357 p.

Wright, Austin McGiffert. *The American Short Story in the Twenties*. Chicago: University of Chicago Press, 1961, 425 p.

CRITICAL ANTHOLOGIES

Atkinson, W. Patterson, ed. *The Short-Story*. Boston: Allyn and Bacon, 1923, 317 p.

Baldwin, Charles Sears, ed. *American Short Stories*. New York, N.Y.: Longmans, Green and Co., 1904, 333 p.

Charters, Ann, ed. *The Story and Its Writer: An Introduction to Short Fiction*. New York: St. Martin's Press, 1983, 1239 p.

Current-García, Eugene, and Patrick, Walton R., eds. *American Short Stories: 1820 to the Present*. Key Editions, edited by John C. Gerber. Chicago: Scott, Foresman and Co., 1952, 633 p.

Fagin, N. Bryllion, ed. *America through the Short Story*. Boston: Little, Brown, and Co., 1936, 508 p.

Frakes, James R., and Traschen, Isadore, eds. *Short Fiction: A Critical Collection*. Prentice-Hall English Literature Series, edited by Maynard Mack. Englewood Cliffs, N.J.: Prentice-Hall, 1959, 459 p.

Gordon, Caroline, and Tate, Allen, eds. *The House of Fiction: An Anthology of the Short Story with Commentary*. Rev. ed. New York: Charles Scribner's Sons, 1960, 469 p.

Greet, T. Y., et. al. *The Worlds of Fiction: Stories in Context*. Boston, Mass.: Houghton Mifflin Co., 1964, 429 p.

Gullason, Thomas A., and Caspar, Leonard, eds. *The World of Short Fiction: An International Collection*. New York: Harper and Row, 1962, 548 p.

Havighurst, Walter, ed. *Masters of the Modern Short Story*. New York: Harcourt, Brace and Co., 1945, 538 p.

Litz, A. Walton, ed. *Major American Short Stories*. New York: Oxford University Press, 1975, 823 p.

Matthews, Brander, ed. *The Short-Story: Specimens Illustrating Its Development*. New York: American Book Co., 1907, 399 p.

Schorer, Mark, ed. *The Short Story: A Critical Anthology*. Rev. ed. Prentice-Hall English Literature Series, edited by Maynard Mack. Englewood Cliffs, N. J.: Prentice-Hall, 1967, 459 p.

Simpson, Claude M., ed. *The Local Colorists: American Short Stories, 1857-1900*. New York: Harper and Brothers Publishers, 1960, 340 p.

Stanton, Robert, ed. *The Short Story and the Reader*. New York: Henry Holt and Co., 1960, 557 p.

West, Ray B., Jr., ed. *American Short Stories*. New York: Thomas Y. Crowell Co., 1959, 267 p.

Short Story Criticism Indexes

Literary Criticism Series
Cumulative Author Index

SSC Cumulative Nationality Index
SSC Cumulative Title Index

How to Use This Index

The main references

Calvino, Italo
1923-1985.....CLC 5, 8, 11, 22, 33, 39,
73; SSC 3

---

list all author entries in the following Gale Literary Criticism series:

BLC = *Black Literature Criticism*
CLC = *Contemporary Literary Criticism*
CLR = *Children's Literature Review*
CMLC = *Classical and Medieval Literature Criticism*
DA = *DISCovering Authors*
DAB = *DISCovering Authors: British*
DAC = *DISCovering Authors: Canadian*
DC = *Drama Criticism*
HLC = *Hispanic Literature Criticism*
LC = *Literature Criticism from 1400 to 1800*
NCLC = *Nineteenth-Century Literature Criticism*
PC = *Poetry Criticism*
SSC = *Short Story Criticism*
TCLC = *Twentieth-Century Literary Criticism*
WLC = *World Literature Criticism, 1500 to the Present*

The cross-references

See also CANR 23; CA 85-88;
obituary CA 116

---

list all author entries in the following Gale biographical and literary sources:

AAYA = *Authors & Artists for Young Adults*
AITN = *Authors in the News*
BEST = *Bestsellers*
BW = *Black Writers*
CA = *Contemporary Authors*
CAAS = *Contemporary Authors Autobiography Series*
CABS = *Contemporary Authors Bibliographical Series*
CANR = *Contemporary Authors New Revision Series*
CAP = *Contemporary Authors Permanent Series*
CDALB = *Concise Dictionary of American Literary Biography*
CDBLB = *Concise Dictionary of British Literary Biography*
DAM = *DISCovering Authors: Modules*
    DRAM: Dramatists Module; MST: Most-Studied Authors Module;
    MULT: Multicultural Authors Module; NOV: Novelists Module;
    POET: Poets Module; POP: Popular Fiction and Genre Authors Module
DLB = *Dictionary of Literary Biography*
DLBD = *Dictionary of Literary Biography Documentary Series*
DLBY = *Dictionary of Literary Biography Yearbook*
HW = *Hispanic Writers*
JRDA = *Junior DISCovering Authors*
MAICYA = *Major Authors and Illustrators for Children and Young Adults*
MTCW = *Major 20th-Century Writers*
NNAL = *Native North American Literature*
SAAS = *Something about the Author Autobiography Series*
SATA = *Something about the Author*
YABC = *Yesterday's Authors of Books for Children*

Alcott, Amos Bronson   1799-1888 .. NCLC 1
See also DLB 1

Alcott, Louisa May
1832-1888 .... NCLC 6; DA; DAB;
DAC; WLC
See also CDALB 1865-1917; CLR 1, 38;
DAM MST, NOV; DLB 1, 42, 79; JRDA;
MAICYA; YABC 1

Aldanov, M. A.
See Aldanov, Mark (Alexandrovich)

Aldanov, Mark (Alexandrovich)
1886(?)-1957 .... TCLC 23
See also CA 118

Aldington, Richard   1892-1962...... CLC 49
See also CA 85-88; CANR 45; DLB 20, 36,
100, 149

Aldiss, Brian W(ilson)
1925- .... CLC 5, 14, 40
See also CA 5-8R; CAAS 2; CANR 5, 28;
DAM NOV; DLB 14; MTCW; SATA 34

Alegria, Claribel   1924-........... CLC 75
See also CA 131; CAAS 15; DAM MULT;
DLB 145; HW

Alegria, Fernando   1918-........... CLC 57
See also CA 9-12R; CANR 5, 32; HW

Aleichem, Sholom .... TCLC 1, 35
See also Rabinovitch, Sholem

Aleixandre, Vicente
1898-1984 .... CLC 9, 36; PC 15
See also CA 85-88; 114; CANR 26;
DAM POET; DLB 108; HW; MTCW

Alepoudelis, Odysseus
See Elytis, Odysseus

Aleshkovsky, Joseph   1929-
See Aleshkovsky, Yuz
See also CA 121; 128

Aleshkovsky, Yuz .... CLC 44
See also Aleshkovsky, Joseph

Alexander, Lloyd (Chudley)   1924- .. CLC 35
See also AAYA 1; CA 1-4R; CANR 1, 24,
38; CLR 1, 5; DLB 52; JRDA; MAICYA;
MTCW; SAAS 19; SATA 3, 49, 81

Alfau, Felipe   1902-............... CLC 66
See also CA 137

Alger, Horatio, Jr.   1832-1899..... NCLC 8
See also DLB 42; SATA 16

Algren, Nelson   1909-1981 .... CLC 4, 10, 33
See also CA 13-16R; 103; CANR 20;
CDALB 1941-1968; DLB 9; DLBY 81,
82; MTCW

Ali, Ahmed   1910-................ CLC 69
See also CA 25-28R; CANR 15, 34

Alighieri, Dante   1265-1321 .... CMLC 3, 18

Allan, John B.
See Westlake, Donald E(dwin)

Allen, Edward   1948-............... CLC 59

Allen, Paula Gunn   1939-.......... CLC 84
See also CA 112; 143; DAM MULT;
NNAL

Allen, Roland
See Ayckbourn, Alan

Allen, Sarah A.
See Hopkins, Pauline Elizabeth

Allen, Woody   1935-.......... CLC 16, 52
See also AAYA 10; CA 33-36R; CANR 27,
38; DAM POP; DLB 44; MTCW

Allende, Isabel   1942- .... CLC 39, 57; HLC
See also CA 125; 130; CANR 51;
DAM MULT, NOV; DLB 145; HW;
INT 130; MTCW

Alleyn, Ellen
See Rossetti, Christina (Georgina)

Allingham, Margery (Louise)
1904-1966 .... CLC 19
See also CA 5-8R; 25-28R; CANR 4;
DLB 77; MTCW

Allingham, William   1824-1889 ... NCLC 25
See also DLB 35

Allison, Dorothy E.   1949-......... CLC 78
See also CA 140

Allston, Washington   1779-1843.... NCLC 2
See also DLB 1

Almedingen, E. M. .... CLC 12
See also Almedingen, Martha Edith von
See also SATA 3

Almedingen, Martha Edith von   1898-1971
See Almedingen, E. M.
See also CA 1-4R; CANR 1

Almqvist, Carl Jonas Love
1793-1866 .... NCLC 42

Alonso, Damaso   1898-1990 .... CLC 14
See also CA 110; 131; 130; DLB 108; HW

Alov
See Gogol, Nikolai (Vasilyevich)

Alta   1942-..................... CLC 19
See also CA 57-60

Alter, Robert B(ernard)   1935-...... CLC 34
See also CA 49-52; CANR 1, 47

Alther, Lisa   1944-.............. CLC 7, 41
See also CA 65-68; CANR 12, 30, 51;
MTCW

Altman, Robert   1925-............. CLC 16
See also CA 73-76; CANR 43

Alvarez, A(lfred)   1929-.......... CLC 5, 13
See also CA 1-4R; CANR 3, 33; DLB 14,
40

Alvarez, Alejandro Rodriguez   1903-1965
See Casona, Alejandro
See also CA 131; 93-96; HW

Alvaro, Corrado   1896-1956 .... TCLC 60

Amado, Jorge   1912-..... CLC 13, 40; HLC
See also CA 77-80; CANR 35;
DAM MULT, NOV; DLB 113; MTCW

Ambler, Eric   1909-............ CLC 4, 6, 9
See also CA 9-12R; CANR 7, 38; DLB 77;
MTCW

Amichai, Yehuda   1924- ...... CLC 9, 22, 57
See also CA 85-88; CANR 46; MTCW

Amiel, Henri Frederic   1821-1881 .. NCLC 4

Amis, Kingsley (William)
1922-1995 ..... CLC 1, 2, 3, 5, 8, 13, 40,
44; DA; DAB; DAC
See also AITN 2; CA 9-12R; 150; CANR 8,
28; CDBLB 1945-1960; DAM MST,
NOV; DLB 15, 27, 100, 139;
INT CANR-8; MTCW

Amis, Martin (Louis)
1949- .... CLC 4, 9, 38, 62
See also BEST 90:3; CA 65-68; CANR 8,
27; DLB 14; INT CANR-27

Ammons, A(rchie) R(andolph)
1926- .... CLC 2, 3, 5, 8, 9, 25, 57
See also AITN 1; CA 9-12R; CANR 6, 36,
51; DAM POET; DLB 5; MTCW

Amo, Tauraatua i
See Adams, Henry (Brooks)

Anand, Mulk Raj   1905-.......... CLC 23
See also CA 65-68; CANR 32; DAM NOV;
MTCW

Anatol
See Schnitzler, Arthur

Anaya, Rudolfo A(lfonso)
1937- .... CLC 23; HLC
See also CA 45-48; CAAS 4; CANR 1, 32,
51; DAM MULT, NOV; DLB 82; HW 1;
MTCW

Andersen, Hans Christian
1805-1875 .... NCLC 7; DA; DAB;
DAC; SSC 6; WLC
See also CLR 6; DAM MST, POP;
MAICYA; YABC 1

Anderson, C. Farley
See Mencken, H(enry) L(ouis); Nathan,
George Jean

Anderson, Jessica (Margaret) Queale
.... CLC 37
See also CA 9-12R; CANR 4

Anderson, Jon (Victor)   1940- .... CLC 9
See also CA 25-28R; CANR 20;
DAM POET

Anderson, Lindsay (Gordon)
1923-1994 .... CLC 20
See also CA 125; 128; 146

Anderson, Maxwell   1888-1959 ..... TCLC 2
See also CA 105; DAM DRAM; DLB 7

Anderson, Poul (William)   1926- .... CLC 15
See also AAYA 5; CA 1-4R; CAAS 2;
CANR 2, 15, 34; DLB 8; INT CANR-15;
MTCW; SATA-Brief 39

Anderson, Robert (Woodruff)
1917- .... CLC 23
See also AITN 1; CA 21-24R; CANR 32;
DAM DRAM; DLB 7

Anderson, Sherwood
1876-1941 .... TCLC 1, 10, 24; DA;
DAB; DAC; SSC 1; WLC
See also CA 104; 121; CDALB 1917-1929;
DAM MST, NOV; DLB 4, 9, 86;
DLBD 1; MTCW

Andouard
See Giraudoux, (Hippolyte) Jean

Andrade, Carlos Drummond de ...... CLC 18
See also Drummond de Andrade, Carlos

Andrade, Mario de   1893-1945..... TCLC 43

Andreae, Johann V.   1586-1654 ...... LC 32

Andreas-Salome, Lou   1861-1937... TCLC 56
See also DLB 66

Andrewes, Lancelot   1555-1626 .... LC 5
See also DLB 151

Andrews, Cicily Fairfield
See West, Rebecca

Andrews, Elton V.
See Pohl, Frederik

Andreyev, Leonid (Nikolaevich)
1871-1919 .... TCLC 3
See also CA 104

Andric, Ivo 1892-1975 .... CLC 8
See also CA 81-84; 57-60; CANR 43;
DLB 147; MTCW

Angelique, Pierre
See Bataille, Georges

Angell, Roger 1920- .... CLC 26
See also CA 57-60; CANR 13, 44

Angelou, Maya
1928- .... CLC 12, 35, 64, 77; BLC; DA;
DAB; DAC
See also AAYA 7; BW 2; CA 65-68;
CANR 19, 42; DAM MST, MULT,
POET, POP; DLB 38; MTCW; SATA 49

Annensky, Innokenty Fyodorovich
1856-1909 .... TCLC 14
See also CA 110

Anon, Charles Robert
See Pessoa, Fernando (Antonio Nogueira)

Anouilh, Jean (Marie Lucien Pierre)
1910-1987 ...... CLC 1, 3, 8, 13, 40, 50
See also CA 17-20R; 123; CANR 32;
DAM DRAM; MTCW

Anthony, Florence
See Ai

Anthony, John
See Ciardi, John (Anthony)

Anthony, Peter
See Shaffer, Anthony (Joshua); Shaffer,
Peter (Levin)

Anthony, Piers 1934- .... CLC 35
See also AAYA 11; CA 21-24R; CANR 28;
DAM POP; DLB 8; MTCW; SAAS 22;
SATA 84

Antoine, Marc
See Proust, (Valentin-Louis-George-Eugene-)
Marcel

Antoninus, Brother
See Everson, William (Oliver)

Antonioni, Michelangelo 1912- ..... CLC 20
See also CA 73-76; CANR 45

Antschel, Paul 1920-1970
See Celan, Paul
See also CA 85-88; CANR 33; MTCW

Anwar, Chairil 1922-1949 .... TCLC 22
See also CA 121

Apollinaire, Guillaume .. TCLC 3, 8, 51; PC 7
See also Kostrowitzki, Wilhelm Apollinaris
de
See also DAM POET

Appelfeld, Aharon 1932- .... CLC 23, 47
See also CA 112; 133

Apple, Max (Isaac) 1941- .... CLC 9, 33
See also CA 81-84; CANR 19; DLB 130

Appleman, Philip (Dean) 1926- ..... CLC 51
See also CA 13-16R; CAAS 18; CANR 6,
29

Appleton, Lawrence
See Lovecraft, H(oward) P(hillips)

Apteryx
See Eliot, T(homas) S(tearns)

Apuleius, (Lucius Madaurensis)
125(?)-175(?) .... CMLC 1

Aquin, Hubert 1929-1977......... CLC 15
See also CA 105; DLB 53

Aragon, Louis 1897-1982....... CLC 3, 22
See also CA 69-72; 108; CANR 28;
DAM NOV, POET; DLB 72; MTCW

Arany, Janos 1817-1882........ NCLC 34

Arbuthnot, John 1667-1735 .... LC 1
See also DLB 101

Archer, Herbert Winslow
See Mencken, H(enry) L(ouis)

Archer, Jeffrey (Howard) 1940- .... CLC 28
See also AAYA 16; BEST 89:3; CA 77-80;
CANR 22; DAM POP; INT CANR-22

Archer, Jules 1915- .... CLC 12
See also CA 9-12R; CANR 6; SAAS 5;
SATA 4, 85

Archer, Lee
See Ellison, Harlan (Jay)

Arden, John 1930- .... CLC 6, 13, 15
See also CA 13-16R; CAAS 4; CANR 31;
DAM DRAM; DLB 13; MTCW

Arenas, Reinaldo
1943-1990 .... CLC 41; HLC
See also CA 124; 128; 133; DAM MULT;
DLB 145; HW

Arendt, Hannah 1906-1975 .... CLC 66
See also CA 17-20R; 61-64; CANR 26;
MTCW

Aretino, Pietro 1492-1556 .... LC 12

Arghezi, Tudor.................... CLC 80
See also Theodorescu, Ion N.

Arguedas, Jose Maria
1911-1969 .... CLC 10, 18
See also CA 89-92; DLB 113; HW

Argueta, Manlio 1936-............ CLC 31
See also CA 131; DLB 145; HW

Ariosto, Ludovico 1474-1533........ LC 6

Aristides
See Epstein, Joseph

Aristophanes
450B.C.-385B.C......... CMLC 4; DA;
DAB; DAC; DC 2
See also DAM DRAM, MST

Arlt, Roberto (Godofredo Christophersen)
1900-1942 .... TCLC 29; HLC
See also CA 123; 131; DAM MULT; HW

Armah, Ayi Kwei 1939-.... CLC 5, 33; BLC
See also BW 1; CA 61-64; CANR 21;
DAM MULT, POET; DLB 117; MTCW

Armatrading, Joan 1950-.......... CLC 17
See also CA 114

Arnette, Robert
See Silverberg, Robert

**Arnim, Achim von (Ludwig Joachim von
Arnim)** 1781-1831 .... NCLC 5
See also DLB 90

Arnim, Bettina von 1785-1859.... NCLC 38
See also DLB 90

Arnold, Matthew
1822-1888 ..... NCLC 6, 29; DA; DAB;
DAC; PC 5; WLC
See also CDBLB 1832-1890; DAM MST,
POET; DLB 32, 57

Arnold, Thomas 1795-1842 ...... NCLC 18
See also DLB 55

Arnow, Harriette (Louisa) Simpson
1908-1986 .... CLC 2, 7, 18
See also CA 9-12R; 118; CANR 14; DLB 6;
MTCW; SATA 42; SATA-Obit 47

Arp, Hans
See Arp, Jean

Arp, Jean 1887-1966............... CLC 5
See also CA 81-84; 25-28R; CANR 42

Arrabal
See Arrabal, Fernando

Arrabal, Fernando 1932- ... CLC 2, 9, 18, 58
See also CA 9-12R; CANR 15

Arrick, Fran...................... CLC 30
See also Gaberman, Judie Angell

Artaud, Antonin (Marie Joseph)
1896-1948 .... TCLC 3, 36
See also CA 104; 149; DAM DRAM

Arthur, Ruth M(abel) 1905-1979.... CLC 12
See also CA 9-12R; 85-88; CANR 4;
SATA 7, 26

Artsybashev, Mikhail (Petrovich)
1878-1927 .... TCLC 31

Arundel, Honor (Morfydd)
1919-1973 .... CLC 17
See also CA 21-22; 41-44R; CAP 2;
CLR 35; SATA 4; SATA-Obit 24

Asch, Sholem 1880-1957 .... TCLC 3
See also CA 105

Ash, Shalom
See Asch, Sholem

Ashbery, John (Lawrence)
1927- ...... CLC 2, 3, 4, 6, 9, 13, 15, 25,
41, 77
See also CA 5-8R; CANR 9, 37;
DAM POET; DLB 5; DLBY 81;
INT CANR-9; MTCW

Ashdown, Clifford
See Freeman, R(ichard) Austin

Ashe, Gordon
See Creasey, John

Ashton-Warner, Sylvia (Constance)
1908-1984 .... CLC 19
See also CA 69-72; 112; CANR 29; MTCW

Asimov, Isaac
1920-1992 ... CLC 1, 3, 9, 19, 26, 76, 92
See also AAYA 13; BEST 90:2; CA 1-4R;
137; CANR 2, 19, 36; CLR 12;
DAM POP; DLB 8; DLBY 92;
INT CANR-19; JRDA; MAICYA;
MTCW; SATA 1, 26, 74

Astley, Thea (Beatrice May)
1925- .... CLC 41
See also CA 65-68; CANR 11, 43

Aston, James
See White, T(erence) H(anbury)

Balzac, Honore de
1799-1850 .... **NCLC 5, 35, 53; DA;
DAB; DAC; SSC 5; WLC**
See also DAM MST, NOV; DLB 119

Bambara, Toni Cade
1939-1995 ...... **CLC 19, 88; BLC; DA;
DAC**
See also AAYA 5; BW 2; CA 29-32R; 150;
CANR 24, 49; DAM MST, MULT;
DLB 38; MTCW

Bamdad, A.
See Shamlu, Ahmad

Banat, D. R.
See Bradbury, Ray (Douglas)

Bancroft, Laura
See Baum, L(yman) Frank

Banim, John 1798-1842 .... **NCLC 13**
See also DLB 116, 158, 159

Banim, Michael 1796-1874 ...... **NCLC 13**
See also DLB 158, 159

Banks, Iain
See Banks, Iain M(enzies)

Banks, Iain M(enzies) 1954- .... **CLC 34**
See also CA 123; 128; INT 128

Banks, Lynne Reid .... **CLC 23**
See also Reid Banks, Lynne
See also AAYA 6

Banks, Russell 1940- .... **CLC 37, 72**
See also CA 65-68; CAAS 15; CANR 19;
DLB 130

Banville, John 1945- .... **CLC 46**
See also CA 117; 128; DLB 14; INT 128

Banville, Theodore (Faullain) de
1832-1891 .... **NCLC 9**

Baraka, Amiri
1934- .... **CLC 1, 2, 3, 5, 10, 14, 33;
BLC; DA; DAC; DC 6; PC 4**
See also Jones, LeRoi
See also BW 2; CA 21-24R; CABS 3;
CANR 27, 38; CDALB 1941-1968;
DAM MST, MULT, POET, POP;
DLB 5, 7, 16, 38; DLBD 8; MTCW

Barbauld, Anna Laetitia
1743-1825 .... **NCLC 50**
See also DLB 107, 109, 142, 158

Barbellion, W. N. P. .... **TCLC 24**
See also Cummings, Bruce F(rederick)

Barbera, Jack (Vincent) 1945- ...... **CLC 44**
See also CA 110; CANR 45

Barbey d'Aurevilly, Jules Amedee
1808-1889 .... **NCLC 1; SSC 17**
See also DLB 119

Barbusse, Henri 1873-1935 .... **TCLC 5**
See also CA 105; DLB 65

Barclay, Bill
See Moorcock, Michael (John)

Barclay, William Ewert
See Moorcock, Michael (John)

Barea, Arturo 1897-1957 .... **TCLC 14**
See also CA 111

Barfoot, Joan 1946- .... **CLC 18**
See also CA 105

Baring, Maurice 1874-1945 .... **TCLC 8**
See also CA 105; DLB 34

Barker, Clive 1952- .... **CLC 52**
See also AAYA 10; BEST 90:3; CA 121;
129; DAM POP; INT 129; MTCW

Barker, George Granville
1913-1991 .... **CLC 8, 48**
See also CA 9-12R; 135; CANR 7, 38;
DAM POET; DLB 20; MTCW

Barker, Harley Granville
See Granville-Barker, Harley
See also DLB 10

Barker, Howard 1946- .... **CLC 37**
See also CA 102; DLB 13

Barker, Pat(ricia) 1943- .... **CLC 32, 91**
See also CA 117; 122; CANR 50; INT 122

Barlow, Joel 1754-1812 .... **NCLC 23**
See also DLB 37

Barnard, Mary (Ethel) 1909- .... **CLC 48**
See also CA 21-22; CAP 2

Barnes, Djuna
1892-1982 ... **CLC 3, 4, 8, 11, 29; SSC 3**
See also CA 9-12R; 107; CANR 16; DLB 4,
9, 45; MTCW

Barnes, Julian 1946- .... **CLC 42; DAB**
See also CA 102; CANR 19; DLBY 93

Barnes, Peter 1931- .... **CLC 5, 56**
See also CA 65-68; CAAS 12; CANR 33,
34; DLB 13; MTCW

Baroja (y Nessi), Pio
1872-1956 .... **TCLC 8; HLC**
See also CA 104

Baron, David
See Pinter, Harold

Baron Corvo
See Rolfe, Frederick (William Serafino
Austin Lewis Mary)

Barondess, Sue K(aufman)
1926-1977 .... **CLC 8**
See also Kaufman, Sue
See also CA 1-4R; 69-72; CANR 1

Baron de Teive
See Pessoa, Fernando (Antonio Nogueira)

Barres, Maurice 1862-1923 .... **TCLC 47**
See also DLB 123

Barreto, Afonso Henrique de Lima
See Lima Barreto, Afonso Henrique de

Barrett, (Roger) Syd 1946- .... **CLC 35**

Barrett, William (Christopher)
1913-1992 .... **CLC 27**
See also CA 13-16R; 139; CANR 11;
INT CANR-11

Barrie, J(ames) M(atthew)
1860-1937 .... **TCLC 2; DAB**
See also CA 104; 136; CDBLB 1890-1914;
CLR 16; DAM DRAM; DLB 10, 141,
156; MAICYA; YABC 1

Barrington, Michael
See Moorcock, Michael (John)

Barrol, Grady
See Bograd, Larry

Barry, Mike
See Malzberg, Barry N(athaniel)

Barry, Philip 1896-1949 .... **TCLC 11**
See also CA 109; DLB 7

Bart, Andre Schwarz
See Schwarz-Bart, Andre

Barth, John (Simmons)
1930- ...... **CLC 1, 2, 3, 5, 7, 9, 10, 14,
27, 51, 89; SSC 10**
See also AITN 1, 2; CA 1-4R; CABS 1;
CANR 5, 23, 49; DAM NOV; DLB 2;
MTCW

Barthelme, Donald
1931-1989 ...... **CLC 1, 2, 3, 5, 6, 8, 13,
23, 46, 59; SSC 2**
See also CA 21-24R; 129; CANR 20;
DAM NOV; DLB 2; DLBY 80, 89;
MTCW; SATA 7; SATA-Obit 62

Barthelme, Frederick 1943- .... **CLC 36**
See also CA 114; 122; DLBY 85; INT 122

Barthes, Roland (Gerard)
1915-1980 .... **CLC 24, 83**
See also CA 130; 97-100; MTCW

Barzun, Jacques (Martin) 1907- .... **CLC 51**
See also CA 61-64; CANR 22

Bashevis, Isaac
See Singer, Isaac Bashevis

Bashkirtseff, Marie 1859-1884 ... **NCLC 27**

Basho
See Matsuo Basho

Bass, Kingsley B., Jr.
See Bullins, Ed

Bass, Rick 1958- .... **CLC 79**
See also CA 126

Bassani, Giorgio 1916- .... **CLC 9**
See also CA 65-68; CANR 33; DLB 128;
MTCW

Bastos, Augusto (Antonio) Roa
See Roa Bastos, Augusto (Antonio)

Bataille, Georges 1897-1962 .... **CLC 29**
See also CA 101; 89-92

Bates, H(erbert) E(rnest)
1905-1974 ...... **CLC 46; DAB; SSC 10**
See also CA 93-96; 45-48; CANR 34;
DAM POP; DLB 162; MTCW

Bauchart
See Camus, Albert

Baudelaire, Charles
1821-1867 .... **NCLC 6, 29, 55; DA;
DAB; DAC; PC 1; SSC 18; WLC**
See also DAM MST, POET

Baudrillard, Jean 1929- .... **CLC 60**

Baum, L(yman) Frank 1856-1919 ... **TCLC 7**
See also CA 108; 133; CLR 15; DLB 22;
JRDA; MAICYA; MTCW; SATA 18

Baum, Louis F.
See Baum, L(yman) Frank

Baumbach, Jonathan 1933- ...... **CLC 6, 23**
See also CA 13-16R; CAAS 5; CANR 12;
DLBY 80; INT CANR-12; MTCW

Bausch, Richard (Carl) 1945- ...... **CLC 51**
See also CA 101; CAAS 14; CANR 43;
DLB 130

Baxter, Charles 1947- .... **CLC 45, 78**
See also CA 57-60; CANR 40; DAM POP;
DLB 130

Baxter, George Owen
See Faust, Frederick (Schiller)

Baxter, James K(eir) 1926-1972 .... **CLC 14**
See also CA 77-80

Baxter, John
See Hunt, E(verette) Howard, (Jr.)

Bayer, Sylvia
See Glassco, John

Baynton, Barbara 1857-1929 ..... **TCLC 57**

Beagle, Peter S(oyer) 1939- .... **CLC 7**
See also CA 9-12R; CANR 4, 51;
DLBY 80; INT CANR-4; SATA 60

Bean, Normal
See Burroughs, Edgar Rice

Beard, Charles A(ustin)
1874-1948 .... **TCLC 15**
See also CA 115; DLB 17; SATA 18

Beardsley, Aubrey 1872-1898 ..... **NCLC 6**

Beattie, Ann
1947- .... **CLC 8, 13, 18, 40, 63; SSC 11**
See also BEST 90:2; CA 81-84; DAM NOV,
POP; DLBY 82; MTCW

Beattie, James 1735-1803 .... **NCLC 25**
See also DLB 109

Beauchamp, Kathleen Mansfield 1888-1923
See Mansfield, Katherine
See also CA 104; 134; DA; DAC;
DAM MST

Beaumarchais, Pierre-Augustin Caron de
1732-1799 .... **DC 4**
See also DAM DRAM

Beaumont, Francis 1584(?)-1616 ...... **DC 6**
See also CDBLB Before 1660; DLB 58, 121

**Beauvoir, Simone (Lucie Ernestine Marie
Bertrand) de**
1908-1986 .... **CLC 1, 2, 4, 8, 14, 31, 44,
50, 71; DA; DAB; DAC; WLC**
See also CA 9-12R; 118; CANR 28;
DAM MST, NOV; DLB 72; DLBY 86;
MTCW

Becker, Carl 1873-1945 .... **TCLC 63:**
See also DLB 17

Becker, Jurek 1937- .... **CLC 7, 19**
See also CA 85-88; DLB 75

Becker, Walter 1950- .... **CLC 26**

Beckett, Samuel (Barclay)
1906-1989 ...... **CLC 1, 2, 3, 4, 6, 9, 10,
11, 14, 18, 29, 57, 59, 83; DA; DAB;
DAC; SSC 16; WLC**
See also CA 5-8R; 130; CANR 33;
CDBLB 1945-1960; DAM DRAM, MST,
NOV; DLB 13, 15; DLBY 90; MTCW

Beckford, William 1760-1844 .... **NCLC 16**
See also DLB 39

Beckman, Gunnel 1910- .... **CLC 26**
See also CA 33-36R; CANR 15; CLR 25;
MAICYA; SAAS 9; SATA 6

Becque, Henri 1837-1899 .... **NCLC 3**

Beddoes, Thomas Lovell
1803-1849 .... **NCLC 3**
See also DLB 96

Bedford, Donald F.
See Fearing, Kenneth (Flexner)

Beecher, Catharine Esther
1800-1878 .... **NCLC 30**
See also DLB 1

Beecher, John 1904-1980 .... **CLC 6**
See also AITN 1; CA 5-8R; 105; CANR 8

Beer, Johann 1655-1700 .... **LC 5**

Beer, Patricia 1924- .... **CLC 58**
See also CA 61-64; CANR 13, 46; DLB 40

Beerbohm, Henry Maximilian
1872-1956 .... **TCLC 1, 24**
See also CA 104; DLB 34, 100

Beerbohm, Max
See Beerbohm, Henry Maximilian

Beer-Hofmann, Richard
1866-1945 .... **TCLC 60**
See also DLB 81

Begiebing, Robert J(ohn) 1946- ..... **CLC 70**
See also CA 122; CANR 40

Behan, Brendan
1923-1964 .... **CLC 1, 8, 11, 15, 79**
See also CA 73-76; CANR 33;
CDBLB 1945-1960; DAM DRAM;
DLB 13; MTCW

Behn, Aphra
1640(?)-1689 ...... **LC 1, 30; DA; DAB;
DAC; DC 4; PC 13; WLC**
See also DAM DRAM, MST, NOV, POET;
DLB 39, 80, 131

Behrman, S(amuel) N(athaniel)
1893-1973 .... **CLC 40**
See also CA 13-16; 45-48; CAP 1; DLB 7,
44

Belasco, David 1853-1931 .... **TCLC 3**
See also CA 104; DLB 7

Belcheva, Elisaveta 1893- .... **CLC 10**
See also Bagryana, Elisaveta

Beldone, Phil "Cheech"
See Ellison, Harlan (Jay)

Beleno
See Azuela, Mariano

Belinski, Vissarion Grigoryevich
1811-1848 .... **NCLC 5**

Belitt, Ben 1911- .... **CLC 22**
See also CA 13-16R; CAAS 4; CANR 7;
DLB 5

Bell, James Madison
1826-1902 .... **TCLC 43; BLC**
See also BW 1; CA 122; 124; DAM MULT;
DLB 50

Bell, Madison (Smartt) 1957- ...... **CLC 41**
See also CA 111; CANR 28

Bell, Marvin (Hartley) 1937- ..... **CLC 8, 31**
See also CA 21-24R; CAAS 14;
DAM POET; DLB 5; MTCW

Bell, W. L. D.
See Mencken, H(enry) L(ouis)

Bellamy, Atwood C.
See Mencken, H(enry) L(ouis)

Bellamy, Edward 1850-1898 ...... **NCLC 4**
See also DLB 12

Bellin, Edward J.
See Kuttner, Henry

Belloc, (Joseph) Hilaire (Pierre)
1870-1953 .... **TCLC 7, 18**
See also CA 106; DAM POET; DLB 19,
100, 141; YABC 1

Belloc, Joseph Peter Rene Hilaire
See Belloc, (Joseph) Hilaire (Pierre)

Belloc, Joseph Pierre Hilaire
See Belloc, (Joseph) Hilaire (Pierre)

Belloc, M. A.
See Lowndes, Marie Adelaide (Belloc)

Bellow, Saul
1915- ...... **CLC 1, 2, 3, 6, 8, 10, 13, 15,
25, 33, 34, 63, 79; DA; DAB; DAC;
SSC 14; WLC**
See also AITN 2; BEST 89:3; CA 5-8R;
CABS 1; CANR 29; CDALB 1941-1968;
DAM MST, NOV, POP; DLB 2, 28;
DLBD 3; DLBY 82; MTCW

Belser, Reimond Karel Maria de
See Ruyslinck, Ward

Bely, Andrey .... **TCLC 7; PC 11**
See also Bugayev, Boris Nikolayevich

Benary, Margot
See Benary-Isbert, Margot

Benary-Isbert, Margot 1889-1979 ... **CLC 12**
See also CA 5-8R; 89-92; CANR 4;
CLR 12; MAICYA; SATA 2;
SATA-Obit 21

Benavente (y Martinez), Jacinto
1866-1954 .... **TCLC 3**
See also CA 106; 131; DAM DRAM,
MULT; HW; MTCW

Benchley, Peter (Bradford)
1940- .... **CLC 4, 8**
See also AAYA 14; AITN 2; CA 17-20R;
CANR 12, 35; DAM NOV, POP;
MTCW; SATA 3

Benchley, Robert (Charles)
1889-1945 .... **TCLC 1, 55**
See also CA 105; DLB 11

Benda, Julien 1867-1956 .... **TCLC 60**
See also CA 120

Benedict, Ruth 1887-1948 .... **TCLC 60**

Benedikt, Michael 1935- .... **CLC 4, 14**
See also CA 13-16R; CANR 7; DLB 5

Benet, Juan 1927- .... **CLC 28**
See also CA 143

Benet, Stephen Vincent
1898-1943 .... **TCLC 7; SSC 10**
See also CA 104; DAM POET; DLB 4, 48,
102; YABC 1

Benet, William Rose 1886-1950 ... **TCLC 28**
See also CA 118; DAM POET; DLB 45

Benford, Gregory (Albert) 1941- .... **CLC 52**
See also CA 69-72; CANR 12, 24, 49;
DLBY 82

Bengtsson, Frans (Gunnar)
1894-1954 .... **TCLC 48**

Benjamin, David
See Slavitt, David R(ytman)

Benjamin, Lois
See Gould, Lois

Benjamin, Walter 1892-1940 ...... **TCLC 39**

Benn, Gottfried 1886-1956 .... **TCLC 3**
See also CA 106; DLB 56

Bennett, Alan 1934- ..... **CLC 45, 77; DAB**
See also CA 103; CANR 35; DAM MST;
MTCW

Bennett, (Enoch) Arnold
1867-1931 . . . . TCLC 5, 20
See also CA 106; CDBLB 1890-1914;
DLB 10, 34, 98, 135

Bennett, Elizabeth
See Mitchell, Margaret (Munnerlyn)

Bennett, George Harold 1930-
See Bennett, Hal
See also BW 1; CA 97-100

Bennett, Hal . . . . CLC 5
See also Bennett, George Harold
See also DLB 33

Bennett, Jay 1912- . . . . CLC 35
See also AAYA 10; CA 69-72; CANR 11,
42; JRDA; SAAS 4; SATA 41, 87;
SATA-Brief 27

Bennett, Louise (Simone)
1919- . . . . CLC 28; BLC
See also BW 2; DAM MULT; DLB 117

Benson, E(dward) F(rederic)
1867-1940 . . . . TCLC 27
See also CA 114; DLB 135, 153

Benson, Jackson J. 1930- . . . . CLC 34
See also CA 25-28R; DLB 111

Benson, Sally 1900-1972 . . . . CLC 17
See also CA 19-20; 37-40R; CAP 1;
SATA 1, 35; SATA-Obit 27

Benson, Stella 1892-1933 . . . . TCLC 17
See also CA 117; DLB 36, 162

Bentham, Jeremy 1748-1832 . . . . . NCLC 38
See also DLB 107, 158

Bentley, E(dmund) C(lerihew)
1875-1956 . . . . TCLC 12
See also CA 108; DLB 70

Bentley, Eric (Russell) 1916- . . . . . . CLC 24
See also CA 5-8R; CANR 6; INT CANR-6

Beranger, Pierre Jean de
1780-1857 . . . . NCLC 34

Berendt, John (Lawrence) 1939- . . . . CLC 86
See also CA 146

Berger, Colonel
See Malraux, (Georges-)Andre

Berger, John (Peter) 1926- . . . . . . CLC 2, 19
See also CA 81-84; CANR 51; DLB 14

Berger, Melvin H. 1927- . . . . CLC 12
See also CA 5-8R; CANR 4; CLR 32;
SAAS 2; SATA 5

Berger, Thomas (Louis)
1924- . . . . CLC 3, 5, 8, 11, 18, 38
See also CA 1-4R; CANR 5, 28, 51;
DAM NOV; DLB 2; DLBY 80;
INT CANR-28; MTCW

Bergman, (Ernst) Ingmar
1918- . . . . CLC 16, 72
See also CA 81-84; CANR 33

Bergson, Henri 1859-1941 . . . . TCLC 32

Bergstein, Eleanor 1938- . . . . CLC 4
See also CA 53-56; CANR 5

Berkoff, Steven 1937- . . . . CLC 56
See also CA 104

Bermant, Chaim (Icyk) 1929- . . . . . . CLC 40
See also CA 57-60; CANR 6, 31

Bern, Victoria
See Fisher, M(ary) F(rances) K(ennedy)

Bernanos, (Paul Louis) Georges
1888-1948 . . . . TCLC 3
See also CA 104; 130; DLB 72

Bernard, April 1956- . . . . CLC 59
See also CA 131

Berne, Victoria
See Fisher, M(ary) F(rances) K(ennedy)

Bernhard, Thomas
1931-1989 . . . . CLC 3, 32, 61
See also CA 85-88; 127; CANR 32;
DLB 85, 124; MTCW

Berriault, Gina 1926- . . . . CLC 54
See also CA 116; 129; DLB 130

Berrigan, Daniel 1921- . . . . CLC 4
See also CA 33-36R; CAAS 1; CANR 11,
43; DLB 5

Berrigan, Edmund Joseph Michael, Jr.
1934-1983
See Berrigan, Ted
See also CA 61-64; 110; CANR 14

Berrigan, Ted . . . . CLC 37
See also Berrigan, Edmund Joseph Michael,
Jr.
See also DLB 5

Berry, Charles Edward Anderson 1931-
See Berry, Chuck
See also CA 115

Berry, Chuck . . . . CLC 17
See also Berry, Charles Edward Anderson

Berry, Jonas
See Ashbery, John (Lawrence)

Berry, Wendell (Erdman)
1934- . . . . CLC 4, 6, 8, 27, 46
See also AITN 1; CA 73-76; CANR 50;
DAM POET; DLB 5, 6

Berryman, John
1914-1972 . . . . . . CLC 1, 2, 3, 4, 6, 8, 10,
13, 25, 62
See also CA 13-16; 33-36R; CABS 2;
CANR 35; CAP 1; CDALB 1941-1968;
DAM POET; DLB 48; MTCW

Bertolucci, Bernardo 1940- . . . . CLC 16
See also CA 106

Bertrand, Aloysius 1807-1841 . . . . NCLC 31

Bertran de Born c. 1140-1215 . . . . . CMLC 5

Besant, Annie (Wood) 1847-1933 . . . TCLC 9
See also CA 105

Bessie, Alvah 1904-1985 . . . . CLC 23
See also CA 5-8R; 116; CANR 2; DLB 26

Bethlen, T. D.
See Silverberg, Robert

Beti, Mongo . . . . CLC 27; BLC
See also Biyidi, Alexandre
See also DAM MULT

Betjeman, John
1906-1984 . . . CLC 2, 6, 10, 34, 43; DAB
See also CA 9-12R; 112; CANR 33;
CDBLB 1945-1960; DAM MST, POET;
DLB 20; DLBY 84; MTCW

Bettelheim, Bruno 1903-1990 . . . . . . CLC 79
See also CA 81-84; 131; CANR 23; MTCW

Betti, Ugo 1892-1953 . . . . TCLC 5
See also CA 104

Betts, Doris (Waugh) 1932- . . . . CLC 3, 6, 28
See also CA 13-16R; CANR 9; DLBY 82;
INT CANR-9

Bevan, Alistair
See Roberts, Keith (John Kingston)

Bialik, Chaim Nachman
1873-1934 . . . . TCLC 25

Bickerstaff, Isaac
See Swift, Jonathan

Bidart, Frank 1939- . . . . CLC 33
See also CA 140

Bienek, Horst 1930- . . . . CLC 7, 11
See also CA 73-76; DLB 75

Bierce, Ambrose (Gwinett)
1842-1914(?) . . . . TCLC 1, 7, 44; DA;
DAC; SSC 9; WLC
See also CA 104; 139; CDALB 1865-1917;
DAM MST; DLB 11, 12, 23, 71, 74

Billings, Josh
See Shaw, Henry Wheeler

Billington, (Lady) Rachel (Mary)
1942- . . . . CLC 43
See also AITN 2; CA 33-36R; CANR 44

Binyon, T(imothy) J(ohn) 1936- . . . . CLC 34
See also CA 111; CANR 28

Bioy Casares, Adolfo
1914- . . . CLC 4, 8, 13, 88; HLC; SSC 17
See also CA 29-32R; CANR 19, 43;
DAM MULT; DLB 113; HW; MTCW

Bird, Cordwainer
See Ellison, Harlan (Jay)

Bird, Robert Montgomery
1806-1854 . . . . NCLC 1

Birney, (Alfred) Earle
1904- . . . . CLC 1, 4, 6, 11; DAC
See also CA 1-4R; CANR 5, 20;
DAM MST, POET; DLB 88; MTCW

Bishop, Elizabeth
1911-1979 . . . . . . CLC 1, 4, 9, 13, 15, 32;
DA; DAC; PC 3
See also CA 5-8R; 89-92; CABS 2;
CANR 26; CDALB 1968-1988;
DAM MST, POET; DLB 5; MTCW;
SATA-Obit 24

Bishop, John 1935- . . . . CLC 10
See also CA 105

Bissett, Bill 1939- . . . . CLC 18; PC 14
See also CA 69-72; CAAS 19; CANR 15;
DLB 53; MTCW

Bitov, Andrei (Georgievich) 1937- . . . CLC 57
See also CA 142

Biyidi, Alexandre 1932-
See Beti, Mongo
See also BW 1; CA 114; 124; MTCW

Bjarme, Brynjolf
See Ibsen, Henrik (Johan)

Bjornson, Bjornstjerne (Martinius)
1832-1910 . . . . TCLC 7, 37
See also CA 104

Black, Robert
See Holdstock, Robert P.

Blackburn, Paul 1926-1971 . . . . . . CLC 9, 43
See also CA 81-84; 33-36R; CANR 34;
DLB 16; DLBY 81

Black Elk 1863-1950 . . . . TCLC 33
See also CA 144; DAM MULT; NNAL

Black Hobart
See Sanders, (James) Ed(ward)

Blacklin, Malcolm
See Chambers, Aidan

Blackmore, R(ichard) D(oddridge)
1825-1900 . . . . TCLC 27
See also CA 120; DLB 18

Blackmur, R(ichard) P(almer)
1904-1965 . . . . CLC 2, 24
See also CA 11-12; 25-28R; CAP 1; DLB 63

Black Tarantula, The
See Acker, Kathy

Blackwood, Algernon (Henry)
1869-1951 . . . . TCLC 5
See also CA 105; 150; DLB 153, 156

Blackwood, Caroline 1931- . . . . CLC 6, 9
See also CA 85-88; CANR 32; DLB 14;
MTCW

Blade, Alexander
See Hamilton, Edmond; Silverberg, Robert

Blaga, Lucian 1895-1961 . . . . CLC 75

Blair, Eric (Arthur) 1903-1950
See Orwell, George
See also CA 104; 132; DA; DAB; DAC;
DAM MST, NOV; MTCW; SATA 29

Blais, Marie-Claire
1939- . . . . CLC 2, 4, 6, 13, 22; DAC
See also CA 21-24R; CAAS 4; CANR 38;
DAM MST; DLB 53; MTCW

Blaise, Clark 1940- . . . . CLC 29
See also AITN 2; CA 53-56; CAAS 3;
CANR 5; DLB 53

Blake, Nicholas
See Day Lewis, C(ecil)
See also DLB 77

Blake, William
1757-1827 . . . . NCLC 13, 37; DA; DAB;
DAC; PC 12; WLC
See also CDBLB 1789-1832; DAM MST,
POET; DLB 93, 163; MAICYA;
SATA 30

Blake, William J(ames) 1894-1969 . . . PC 12
See also CA 5-8R; 25-28R

Blasco Ibanez, Vicente
1867-1928 . . . . TCLC 12
See also CA 110; 131; DAM NOV; HW;
MTCW

Blatty, William Peter 1928- . . . . CLC 2
See also CA 5-8R; CANR 9; DAM POP

Bleeck, Oliver
See Thomas, Ross (Elmore)

Blessing, Lee 1949- . . . . CLC 54

Blish, James (Benjamin)
1921-1975 . . . . CLC 14
See also CA 1-4R; 57-60; CANR 3; DLB 8;
MTCW; SATA 66

Bliss, Reginald
See Wells, H(erbert) G(eorge)

Blixen, Karen (Christentze Dinesen)
1885-1962
See Dinesen, Isak
See also CA 25-28; CANR 22, 50; CAP 2;
MTCW; SATA 44

Bloch, Robert (Albert) 1917-1994 . . . CLC 33
See also CA 5-8R; 146; CAAS 20; CANR 5;
DLB 44; INT CANR-5; SATA 12;
SATA-Obit 82

Blok, Alexander (Alexandrovich)
1880-1921 . . . . TCLC 5
See also CA 104

Blom, Jan
See Breytenbach, Breyten

Bloom, Harold 1930- . . . . CLC 24
See also CA 13-16R; CANR 39; DLB 67

Bloomfield, Aurelius
See Bourne, Randolph S(illiman)

Blount, Roy (Alton), Jr. 1941- . . . . . CLC 38
See also CA 53-56; CANR 10, 28;
INT CANR-28; MTCW

Bloy, Leon 1846-1917 . . . . TCLC 22
See also CA 121; DLB 123

Blume, Judy (Sussman) 1938- . . . CLC 12, 30
See also AAYA 3; CA 29-32R; CANR 13,
37; CLR 2, 15; DAM NOV, POP;
DLB 52; JRDA; MAICYA; MTCW;
SATA 2, 31, 79

Blunden, Edmund (Charles)
1896-1974 . . . . CLC 2, 56
See also CA 17-18; 45-48; CAP 2; DLB 20,
100, 155; MTCW

Bly, Robert (Elwood)
1926- . . . . CLC 1, 2, 5, 10, 15, 38
See also CA 5-8R; CANR 41; DAM POET;
DLB 5; MTCW

Boas, Franz 1858-1942 . . . . TCLC 56
See also CA 115

Bobette
See Simenon, Georges (Jacques Christian)

Boccaccio, Giovanni
1313-1375 . . . . CMLC 13; SSC 10

Bochco, Steven 1943- . . . . CLC 35
See also AAYA 11; CA 124; 138

Bodenheim, Maxwell 1892-1954 . . . TCLC 44
See also CA 110; DLB 9, 45

Bodker, Cecil 1927- . . . . CLC 21
See also CA 73-76; CANR 13, 44; CLR 23;
MAICYA; SATA 14

Boell, Heinrich (Theodor)
1917-1985 . . . . CLC 2, 3, 6, 9, 11, 15, 27,
32, 72; DA; DAB; DAC; WLC
See also CA 21-24R; 116; CANR 24;
DAM MST, NOV; DLB 69; DLBY 85;
MTCW

Boerne, Alfred
See Doeblin, Alfred

Boethius 480(?)-524(?) . . . . CMLC 15
See also DLB 115

Bogan, Louise
1897-1970 . . . . CLC 4, 39, 46; PC 12
See also CA 73-76; 25-28R; CANR 33;
DAM POET; DLB 45; MTCW

Bogarde, Dirk . . . . CLC 19
See also Van Den Bogarde, Derek Jules
Gaspard Ulric Niven
See also DLB 14

Bogosian, Eric 1953- . . . . CLC 45
See also CA 138

Bograd, Larry 1953- . . . . CLC 35
See also CA 93-96; SAAS 21; SATA 33

Boiardo, Matteo Maria 1441-1494 . . . . LC 6

Boileau-Despreaux, Nicolas
1636-1711 . . . . LC 3

Boland, Eavan (Aisling) 1944- . . . CLC 40, 67
See also CA 143; DAM POET; DLB 40

Bolt, Lee
See Faust, Frederick (Schiller)

Bolt, Robert (Oxton) 1924-1995 . . . . CLC 14
See also CA 17-20R; 147; CANR 35;
DAM DRAM; DLB 13; MTCW

Bombet, Louis-Alexandre-Cesar
See Stendhal

Bomkauf
See Kaufman, Bob (Garnell)

Bonaventura . . . . NCLC 35
See also DLB 90

Bond, Edward 1934- . . . . CLC 4, 6, 13, 23
See also CA 25-28R; CANR 38;
DAM DRAM; DLB 13; MTCW

Bonham, Frank 1914-1989 . . . . CLC 12
See also AAYA 1; CA 9-12R; CANR 4, 36;
JRDA; MAICYA; SAAS 3; SATA 1, 49;
SATA-Obit 62

Bonnefoy, Yves 1923- . . . . CLC 9, 15, 58
See also CA 85-88; CANR 33; DAM MST,
POET; MTCW

Bontemps, Arna(ud Wendell)
1902-1973 . . . . CLC 1, 18; BLC
See also BW 1; CA 1-4R; 41-44R; CANR 4,
35; CLR 6; DAM MULT, NOV, POET;
DLB 48, 51; JRDA; MAICYA; MTCW;
SATA 2, 44; SATA-Obit 24

Booth, Martin 1944- . . . . CLC 13
See also CA 93-96; CAAS 2

Booth, Philip 1925- . . . . CLC 23
See also CA 5-8R; CANR 5; DLBY 82

Booth, Wayne C(layson) 1921- . . . . . CLC 24
See also CA 1-4R; CAAS 5; CANR 3, 43;
DLB 67

Borchert, Wolfgang 1921-1947 . . . . . TCLC 5
See also CA 104; DLB 69, 124

Borel, Petrus 1809-1859 . . . . NCLC 41

Borges, Jorge Luis
1899-1986 . . . CLC 1, 2, 3, 4, 6, 8, 9, 10,
13, 19, 44, 48, 83; DA; DAB; DAC;
HLC; SSC 4; WLC
See also CA 21-24R; CANR 19, 33;
DAM MST, MULT; DLB 113; DLBY 86;
HW; MTCW

Borowski, Tadeusz 1922-1951 . . . . . . TCLC 9
See also CA 106

Borrow, George (Henry)
1803-1881 . . . . NCLC 9
See also DLB 21, 55

Bosman, Herman Charles
1905-1951 . . . . TCLC 49

Bosschere, Jean de 1878(?)-1953 . . . TCLC 19
See also CA 115

Boswell, James
1740-1795 . . . . . . LC 4; DA; DAB; DAC;
WLC
See also CDBLB 1660-1789; DAM MST;
DLB 104, 142

Bottoms, David 1949-............. CLC 53
See also CA 105; CANR 22; DLB 120;
DLBY 83

Boucicault, Dion 1820-1890...... NCLC 41

Boucolon, Maryse 1937-
See Conde, Maryse
See also CA 110; CANR 30

Bourget, Paul (Charles Joseph)
1852-1935 .... TCLC 12
See also CA 107; DLB 123

Bourjaily, Vance (Nye) 1922- .... CLC 8, 62
See also CA 1-4R; CAAS 1; CANR 2;
DLB 2, 143

Bourne, Randolph S(illiman)
1886-1918 .... TCLC 16
See also CA 117; DLB 63

Bova, Ben(jamin William) 1932-.... CLC 45
See also AAYA 16; CA 5-8R; CAAS 18;
CANR 11; CLR 3; DLBY 81;
INT CANR-11; MAICYA; MTCW;
SATA 6, 68

Bowen, Elizabeth (Dorothea Cole)
1899-1973 ...... CLC 1, 3, 6, 11, 15, 22;
SSC 3
See also CA 17-18; 41-44R; CANR 35;
CAP 2; CDBLB 1945-1960; DAM NOV;
DLB 15, 162; MTCW

Bowering, George 1935-........ CLC 15, 47
See also CA 21-24R; CAAS 16; CANR 10;
DLB 53

Bowering, Marilyn R(uthe) 1949-... CLC 32
See also CA 101; CANR 49

Bowers, Edgar 1924- .... CLC 9
See also CA 5-8R; CANR 24; DLB 5

Bowie, David .... CLC 17
See also Jones, David Robert

Bowles, Jane (Sydney)
1917-1973 .... CLC 3, 68
See also CA 19-20; 41-44R, CAP 2

Bowles, Paul (Frederick)
1910- .... CLC 1, 2, 19, 53; SSC 3
See also CA 1-4R; CAAS 1; CANR 1, 19,
50; DLB 5, 6; MTCW

Box, Edgar
See Vidal, Gore

Boyd, Nancy
See Millay, Edna St. Vincent

Boyd, William 1952-........ CLC 28, 53, 70
See also CA 114; 120; CANR 51

Boyle, Kay
1902-1992 ..... CLC 1, 5, 19, 58; SSC 5
See also CA 13-16R; 140; CAAS 1;
CANR 29; DLB 4, 9, 48, 86; DLBY 93;
MTCW

Boyle, Mark
See Kienzle, William X(avier)

Boyle, Patrick 1905-1982......... CLC 19
See also CA 127

Boyle, T. C. 1948-
See Boyle, T(homas) Coraghessan

Boyle, T(homas) Coraghessan
1948- .... CLC 36, 55, 90; SSC 16
See also BEST 90:4; CA 120; CANR 44;
DAM POP; DLBY 86

Boz
See Dickens, Charles (John Huffam)

Brackenridge, Hugh Henry
1748-1816 .... NCLC 7
See also DLB 11, 37

Bradbury, Edward P.
See Moorcock, Michael (John)

Bradbury, Malcolm (Stanley)
1932- .... CLC 32, 61
See also CA 1-4R; CANR 1, 33;
DAM NOV; DLB 14; MTCW

Bradbury, Ray (Douglas)
1920- .... CLC 1, 3, 10, 15, 42; DA;
DAB; DAC; WLC
See also AAYA 15; AITN 1, 2; CA 1-4R;
CANR 2, 30; CDALB 1968-1988;
DAM MST, NOV, POP; DLB 2, 8;
INT CANR-30; MTCW; SATA 11, 64

Bradford, Gamaliel 1863-1932..... TCLC 36
See also DLB 17

Bradley, David (Henry, Jr.)
1950- .... CLC 23; BLC
See also BW 1; CA 104; CANR 26;
DAM MULT; DLB 33

Bradley, John Ed(mund, Jr.)
1958- .... CLC 55
See also CA 139

Bradley, Marion Zimmer 1930-..... CLC 30
See also AAYA 9; CA 57-60; CAAS 10;
CANR 7, 31, 51; DAM POP; DLB 8;
MTCW

Bradstreet, Anne
1612(?)-1672 ...... LC 4, 30; DA; DAC;
PC 10
See also CDALB 1640-1865; DAM MST,
POET; DLB 24

Brady, Joan 1939- .... CLC 86
See also CA 141

Bragg, Melvyn 1939- .... CLC 10
See also BEST 89:3; CA 57-60; CANR 10,
48; DLB 14

Braine, John (Gerard)
1922-1986 .... CLC 1, 3, 41
See also CA 1-4R; 120; CANR 1, 33;
CDBLB 1945-1960; DLB 15; DLBY 86;
MTCW

Brammer, William 1930(?)-1978 .... CLC 31
See also CA 77-80

Brancati, Vitaliano 1907-1954..... TCLC 12
See also CA 109

Brancato, Robin F(idler) 1936-..... CLC 35
See also AAYA 9; CA 69-72; CANR 11,
45; CLR 32; JRDA; SAAS 9; SATA 23

Brand, Max
See Faust, Frederick (Schiller)

Brand, Millen 1906-1980.......... CLC 7
See also CA 21-24R; 97-100

Branden, Barbara .... CLC 44
See also CA 148

Brandes, Georg (Morris Cohen)
1842-1927 .... TCLC 10
See also CA 105

Brandys, Kazimierz 1916- .... CLC 62

Branley, Franklyn M(ansfield)
1915- .... CLC 21
See also CA 33-36R; CANR 14, 39;
CLR 13; MAICYA; SAAS 16; SATA 4,
68

Brathwaite, Edward Kamau 1930-... CLC 11
See also BW 2; CA 25-28R; CANR 11, 26,
47; DAM POET; DLB 125

Brautigan, Richard (Gary)
1935-1984 .... CLC 1, 3, 5, 9, 12, 34, 42
See also CA 53-56; 113; CANR 34;
DAM NOV; DLB 2, 5; DLBY 80, 84;
MTCW; SATA 56

Braverman, Kate 1950- .... CLC 67
See also CA 89-92

Brecht, Bertolt
1898-1956 ...... TCLC 1, 6, 13, 35; DA;
DAB; DAC; DC 3; WLC
See also CA 104; 133; DAM DRAM, MST;
DLB 56, 124; MTCW

Brecht, Eugen Berthold Friedrich
See Brecht, Bertolt

Bremer, Fredrika 1801-1865 ..... NCLC 11

Brennan, Christopher John
1870-1932 .... TCLC 17
See also CA 117

Brennan, Maeve 1917-............. CLC 5
See also CA 81-84

Brentano, Clemens (Maria)
1778-1842 .... NCLC 1
See also DLB 90

Brent of Bin Bin
See Franklin, (Stella Maraia Sarah) Miles

Brenton, Howard 1942-............ CLC 31
See also CA 69-72; CANR 33; DLB 13;
MTCW

Breslin, James 1930-
See Breslin, Jimmy
See also CA 73-76; CANR 31; DAM NOV;
MTCW

Breslin, Jimmy .... CLC 4, 43
See also Breslin, James
See also AITN 1

Bresson, Robert 1901- .... CLC 16
See also CA 110; CANR 49

Breton, Andre
1896-1966 ..... CLC 2, 9, 15, 54; PC 15
See also CA 19-20; 25-28R; CANR 40;
CAP 2; DLB 65; MTCW

Breytenbach, Breyten 1939(?)- .. CLC 23, 37
See also CA 113; 129; DAM POET

Bridgers, Sue Ellen 1942- .... CLC 26
See also AAYA 8; CA 65-68; CANR 11,
36; CLR 18; DLB 52; JRDA; MAICYA;
SAAS 1; SATA 22

Bridges, Robert (Seymour)
1844-1930 .... TCLC 1
See also CA 104; CDBLB 1890-1914;
DAM POET; DLB 19, 98

Bridie, James.................... TCLC 3
See also Mavor, Osborne Henry
See also DLB 10

Brin, David 1950-................ CLC 34
See also CA 102; CANR 24;
INT CANR-24; SATA 65

Brink, Andre (Philippus)
    1935- . . . . **CLC 18, 36**
    See also CA 104; CANR 39; INT 103;
    MTCW

Brinsmead, H(esba) F(ay) 1922- . . . . **CLC 21**
    See also CA 21-24R; CANR 10; MAICYA;
    SAAS 5; SATA 18, 78

Brittain, Vera (Mary)
    1893(?)-1970 . . . . **CLC 23**
    See also CA 13-16; 25-28R; CAP 1; MTCW

Broch, Hermann 1886-1951 . . . . **TCLC 20**
    See also CA 117; DLB 85, 124

Brock, Rose
    See Hansen, Joseph

Brodkey, Harold 1930- . . . . **CLC 56**
    See also CA 111; DLB 130

Brodsky, Iosif Alexandrovich 1940-
    See Brodsky, Joseph
    See also AITN 1; CA 41-44R; CANR 37;
    DAM POET; MTCW

Brodsky, Joseph . . **CLC 4, 6, 13, 36, 50; PC 9**
    See also Brodsky, Iosif Alexandrovich

Brodsky, Michael Mark 1948- . . . . . **CLC 19**
    See also CA 102; CANR 18, 41

Bromell, Henry 1947- . . . . **CLC 5**
    See also CA 53-56; CANR 9

Bromfield, Louis (Brucker)
    1896-1956 . . . . **TCLC 11**
    See also CA 107; DLB 4, 9, 86

Broner, E(sther) M(asserman)
    1930- . . . . **CLC 19**
    See also CA 17-20R; CANR 8, 25; DLB 28

Bronk, William 1918- . . . . **CLC 10**
    See also CA 89-92; CANR 23

Bronstein, Lev Davidovich
    See Trotsky, Leon

Bronte, Anne 1820-1849 . . . . **NCLC 4**
    See also DLB 21

Bronte, Charlotte
    1816-1855 . . . . **NCLC 3, 8, 33; DA;
                                    DAB; DAC; WLC**
    See also AAYA 17; CDBLB 1832-1890;
    DAM MST, NOV; DLB 21, 159

Bronte, Emily (Jane)
    1818-1848 . . . . **NCLC 16, 35; DA; DAB;
                                    DAC; PC 8; WLC**
    See also AAYA 17; CDBLB 1832-1890;
    DAM MST, NOV, POET; DLB 21, 32

Brooke, Frances 1724-1789 . . . . **LC 6**
    See also DLB 39, 99

Brooke, Henry 1703(?)-1783 . . . . **LC 1**
    See also DLB 39

Brooke, Rupert (Chawner)
    1887-1915 . . . . **TCLC 2, 7; DA; DAB;
                                    DAC; WLC**
    See also CA 104; 132; CDBLB 1914-1945;
    DAM MST, POET; DLB 19; MTCW

Brooke-Haven, P.
    See Wodehouse, P(elham) G(renville)

Brooke-Rose, Christine 1926- . . . . . . **CLC 40**
    See also CA 13-16R; DLB 14

Brookner, Anita
    1928- . . . . **CLC 32, 34, 51; DAB**
    See also CA 114; 120; CANR 37;
    DAM POP; DLBY 87; MTCW

Brooks, Cleanth 1906-1994 . . . . . **CLC 24, 86**
    See also CA 17-20R; 145; CANR 33, 35;
    DLB 63; DLBY 94; INT CANR-35;
    MTCW

Brooks, George
    See Baum, L(yman) Frank

Brooks, Gwendolyn
    1917- . . . . . . **CLC 1, 2, 4, 5, 15, 49; BLC;
                                    DA; DAC; PC 7; WLC**
    See also AITN 1; BW 2; CA 1-4R;
    CANR 1, 27; CDALB 1941-1968;
    CLR 27; DAM MST, MULT, POET;
    DLB 5, 76; MTCW; SATA 6

Brooks, Mel . . . . **CLC 12**
    See also Kaminsky, Melvin
    See also AAYA 13; DLB 26

Brooks, Peter 1938- . . . . **CLC 34**
    See also CA 45-48; CANR 1

Brooks, Van Wyck 1886-1963 . . . . . . **CLC 29**
    See also CA 1-4R; CANR 6; DLB 45, 63,
    103

Brophy, Brigid (Antonia)
    1929-1995 . . . . **CLC 6, 11, 29**
    See also CA 5-8R; 149; CAAS 4; CANR 25;
    DLB 14; MTCW

Brosman, Catharine Savage 1934- . . . . **CLC 9**
    See also CA 61-64; CANR 21, 46

Brother Antoninus
    See Everson, William (Oliver)

Broughton, T(homas) Alan 1936- . . . **CLC 19**
    See also CA 45-48; CANR 2, 23, 48

Broumas, Olga 1949- . . . . **CLC 10, 73**
    See also CA 85-88; CANR 20

Brown, Charles Brockden
    1771-1810 . . . . **NCLC 22**
    See also CDALB 1640-1865; DLB 37, 59,
    73

Brown, Christy 1932-1981 . . . . **CLC 63**
    See also CA 105; 104; DLB 14

Brown, Claude 1937- . . . . **CLC 30; BLC**
    See also AAYA 7; BW 1; CA 73-76;
    DAM MULT

Brown, Dee (Alexander) 1908- . . **CLC 18, 47**
    See also CA 13-16R; CAAS 6; CANR 11,
    45; DAM POP; DLBY 80; MTCW;
    SATA 5

Brown, George
    See Wertmueller, Lina

Brown, George Douglas
    1869-1902 . . . . **TCLC 28**

Brown, George Mackay 1921- . . . . **CLC 5, 48**
    See also CA 21-24R; CAAS 6; CANR 12,
    37; DLB 14, 27, 139; MTCW; SATA 35

Brown, (William) Larry 1951- . . . . . . **CLC 73**
    See also CA 130; 134; INT 133

Brown, Moses
    See Barrett, William (Christopher)

Brown, Rita Mae 1944- . . . . . **CLC 18, 43, 79**
    See also CA 45-48; CANR 2, 11, 35;
    DAM NOV, POP; INT CANR-11;
    MTCW

Brown, Roderick (Langmere) Haig-
    See Haig-Brown, Roderick (Langmere)

Brown, Rosellen 1939- . . . . **CLC 32**
    See also CA 77-80; CAAS 10; CANR 14, 44

Brown, Sterling Allen
    1901-1989 . . . . **CLC 1, 23, 59; BLC**
    See also BW 1; CA 85-88; 127; CANR 26;
    DAM MULT, POET; DLB 48, 51, 63;
    MTCW

Brown, Will
    See Ainsworth, William Harrison

Brown, William Wells
    1813-1884 . . . . **NCLC 2; BLC; DC 1**
    See also DAM MULT; DLB 3, 50

Browne, (Clyde) Jackson 1948(?)- . . . **CLC 21**
    See also CA 120

Browning, Elizabeth Barrett
    1806-1861 . . . . . **NCLC 1, 16; DA; DAB;
                                    DAC; PC 6; WLC**
    See also CDBLB 1832-1890; DAM MST,
    POET; DLB 32

Browning, Robert
    1812-1889 . . . . **NCLC 19; DA; DAB;
                                    DAC; PC 2**
    See also CDBLB 1832-1890; DAM MST,
    POET; DLB 32, 163; YABC 1

Browning, Tod 1882-1962 . . . . **CLC 16**
    See also CA 141; 117

Brownson, Orestes (Augustus)
    1803-1876 . . . . **NCLC 50**

Bruccoli, Matthew J(oseph) 1931- . . **CLC 34**
    See also CA 9-12R; CANR 7; DLB 103

Bruce, Lenny . . . . **CLC 21**
    See also Schneider, Leonard Alfred

Bruin, John
    See Brutus, Dennis

Brulard, Henri
    See Stendhal

Brulls, Christian
    See Simenon, Georges (Jacques Christian)

Brunner, John (Kilian Houston)
    1934-1995 . . . . **CLC 8, 10**
    See also CA 1-4R; 149; CAAS 8; CANR 2,
    37; DAM POP; MTCW

Bruno, Giordano 1548-1600 . . . . **LC 27**

Brutus, Dennis 1924- . . . . **CLC 43; BLC**
    See also BW 2; CA 49-52; CAAS 14;
    CANR 2, 27, 42; DAM MULT, POET;
    DLB 117

Bryan, C(ourtlandt) D(ixon) B(arnes)
    1936- . . . . **CLC 29**
    See also CA 73-76; CANR 13;
    INT CANR-13

Bryan, Michael
    See Moore, Brian

Bryant, William Cullen
    1794-1878 . . . . . **NCLC 6, 46; DA; DAB;
                                    DAC**
    See also CDALB 1640-1865; DAM MST,
    POET; DLB 3, 43, 59

Bryusov, Valery Yakovlevich
    1873-1924 . . . . **TCLC 10**
    See also CA 107

Buchan, John 1875-1940 . . . **TCLC 41; DAB**
    See also CA 108; 145; DAM POP; DLB 34,
    70, 156; YABC 2

Buchanan, George 1506-1582 . . . . **LC 4**

Buchheim, Lothar-Guenther 1918- . . . **CLC 6**
    See also CA 85-88

Buchner, (Karl) Georg
1813-1837 .... NCLC 26

Buchwald, Art(hur) 1925-......... CLC 33
See also AITN 1; CA 5-8R; CANR 21;
MTCW; SATA 10

Buck, Pearl S(ydenstricker)
1892-1973 .... CLC 7, 11, 18; DA; DAB;
DAC
See also AITN 1; CA 1-4R; 41-44R;
CANR 1, 34; DAM MST, NOV; DLB 9,
102; MTCW; SATA 1, 25

Buckler, Ernest 1908-1984.... CLC 13; DAC
See also CA 11-12; 114; CAP 1;
DAM MST; DLB 68; SATA 47

Buckley, Vincent (Thomas)
1925-1988 .... CLC 57
See also CA 101

Buckley, William F(rank), Jr.
1925- .... CLC 7, 18, 37
See also AITN 1; CA 1-4R; CANR 1, 24;
DAM POP; DLB 137; DLBY 80;
INT CANR-24; MTCW

Buechner, (Carl) Frederick
1926- .... CLC 2, 4, 6, 9
See also CA 13-16R; CANR 11, 39;
DAM NOV; DLBY 80; INT CANR-11;
MTCW

Buell, John (Edward) 1927-........ CLC 10
See also CA 1-4R; DLB 53

Buero Vallejo, Antonio 1916- .. CLC 15, 46
See also CA 106; CANR 24, 49; HW;
MTCW

Bufalino, Gesualdo 1920(?)-........ CLC 74

Bugayev, Boris Nikolayevich 1880-1934
See Bely, Andrey
See also CA 104

Bukowski, Charles
1920-1994 .... CLC 2, 5, 9, 41, 82
See also CA 17-20R; 144; CANR 40;
DAM NOV, POET; DLB 5, 130; MTCW

Bulgakov, Mikhail (Afanas'evich)
1891-1940 .... TCLC 2, 16; SSC 18
See also CA 105; DAM DRAM, NOV

Bulgya, Alexander Alexandrovich
1901-1956 .... TCLC 53
See also Fadeyev, Alexander
See also CA 117

Bullins, Ed 1935- .. CLC 1, 5, 7; BLC; DC 6
See also BW 2; CA 49-52; CAAS 16;
CANR 24, 46; DAM DRAM, MULT;
DLB 7, 38; MTCW

Bulwer-Lytton, Edward (George Earle Lytton)
1803-1873 .... NCLC 1, 45
See also DLB 21

Bunin, Ivan Alexeyevich
1870-1953 .... TCLC 6; SSC 5
See also CA 104

Bunting, Basil 1900-1985.... CLC 10, 39, 47
See also CA 53-56; 115; CANR 7;
DAM POET; DLB 20

Bunuel, Luis 1900-1983 .. CLC 16, 80; HLC
See also CA 101; 110; CANR 32;
DAM MULT; HW

Bunyan, John
1628-1688 ...... LC 4; DA; DAB; DAC;
WLC
See also CDBLB 1660-1789; DAM MST;
DLB 39

Burckhardt, Jacob (Christoph)
1818-1897 .... NCLC 49

Burford, Eleanor
See Hibbert, Eleanor Alice Burford

Burgess, Anthony
. CLC 1, 2, 4, 5, 8, 10, 13, 15, 22, 40, 62,
81; DAB
See also Wilson, John (Anthony) Burgess
See also AITN 1; CDBLB 1960 to Present;
DLB 14

Burke, Edmund
1729(?)-1797 .... LC 7; DA; DAB; DAC;
WLC
See also DAM MST; DLB 104

Burke, Kenneth (Duva)
1897-1993 .... CLC 2, 24
See also CA 5-8R; 143; CANR 39; DLB 45,
63; MTCW

Burke, Leda
See Garnett, David

Burke, Ralph
See Silverberg, Robert

Burke, Thomas 1886-1945 .... TCLC 63
See also CA 113

Burney, Fanny 1752-1840 .... NCLC 12, 54
See also DLB 39

Burns, Robert 1759-1796........... PC 6
See also CDBLB 1789-1832; DA; DAB;
DAC; DAM MST, POET; DLB 109;
WLC

Burns, Tex
See L'Amour, Louis (Dearborn)

Burnshaw, Stanley 1906-..... CLC 3, 13, 44
See also CA 9-12R; DLB 48

Burr, Anne 1937- .... CLC 6
See also CA 25-28R

Burroughs, Edgar Rice
1875-1950 .... TCLC 2, 32
See also AAYA 11; CA 104; 132;
DAM NOV; DLB 8; MTCW; SATA 41

Burroughs, William S(eward)
1914- .... CLC 1, 2, 5, 15, 22, 42, 75;
DA; DAB; DAC; WLC
See also AITN 2; CA 9-12R; CANR 20;
DAM MST, NOV, POP; DLB 2, 8, 16,
152; DLBY 81; MTCW

Burton, Richard F. 1821-1890.... NCLC 42
See also DLB 55

Busch, Frederick 1941- .. CLC 7, 10, 18, 47
See also CA 33-36R; CAAS 1; CANR 45;
DLB 6

Bush, Ronald 1946- .... CLC 34
See also CA 136

Bustos, F(rancisco)
See Borges, Jorge Luis

Bustos Domecq, H(onorio)
See Bioy Casares, Adolfo; Borges, Jorge
Luis

Butler, Octavia E(stelle) 1947-..... CLC 38
See also BW 2; CA 73-76; CANR 12, 24,
38; DAM MULT, POP; DLB 33;
MTCW; SATA 84

Butler, Robert Olen (Jr.) 1945-..... CLC 81
See also CA 112; DAM POP; INT 112

Butler, Samuel 1612-1680 .... LC 16
See also DLB 101, 126

Butler, Samuel
1835-1902 ...... TCLC 1, 33; DA; DAB;
DAC; WLC
See also CA 143; CDBLB 1890-1914;
DAM MST, NOV; DLB 18, 57

Butler, Walter C.
See Faust, Frederick (Schiller)

Butor, Michel (Marie Francois)
1926- .... CLC 1, 3, 8, 11, 15
See also CA 9-12R; CANR 33; DLB 83;
MTCW

Buzo, Alexander (John) 1944-...... CLC 61
See also CA 97-100; CANR 17, 39

Buzzati, Dino 1906-1972 .... CLC 36
See also CA 33-36R

Byars, Betsy (Cromer) 1928-....... CLC 35
See also CA 33-36R; CANR 18, 36; CLR 1,
16; DLB 52; INT CANR-18; JRDA;
MAICYA; MTCW; SAAS 1; SATA 4,
46, 80

Byatt, A(ntonia) S(usan Drabble)
1936- .... CLC 19, 65
See also CA 13-16R; CANR 13, 33, 50;
DAM NOV, POP; DLB 14; MTCW

Byrne, David 1952-.............. CLC 26
See also CA 127

Byrne, John Keyes 1926-
See Leonard, Hugh
See also CA 102; INT 102

Byron, George Gordon (Noel)
1788-1824 ..... NCLC 2, 12; DA; DAB;
DAC; WLC
See also CDBLB 1789-1832; DAM MST,
POET; DLB 96, 110

C. 3. 3.
See Wilde, Oscar (Fingal O'Flahertie Wills)

Caballero, Fernan 1796-1877..... NCLC 10

Cabell, James Branch 1879-1958 ... TCLC 6
See also CA 105; DLB 9, 78

Cable, George Washington
1844-1925 .... TCLC 4; SSC 4
See also CA 104; DLB 12, 74; DLBD 13

Cabral de Melo Neto, Joao 1920-... CLC 76
See also DAM MULT

Cabrera Infante, G(uillermo)
1929- .... CLC 5, 25, 45; HLC
See also CA 85-88; CANR 29;
DAM MULT; DLB 113; HW; MTCW

Cade, Toni
See Bambara, Toni Cade

Cadmus and Harmonia
See Buchan, John

Caedmon fl. 658-680............. CMLC 7
See also DLB 146

Caeiro, Alberto
See Pessoa, Fernando (Antonio Nogueira)

Carver, Raymond
    1938-1988 ... **CLC 22, 36, 53, 55; SSC 8**
    See also CA 33-36R; 126; CANR 17, 34;
    DAM NOV; DLB 130; DLBY 84, 88;
    MTCW

Cary, Elizabeth, Lady Falkland
    1585-1639 .... **LC 30**

Cary, (Arthur) Joyce (Lunel)
    1888-1957 .... **TCLC 1, 29**
    See also CA 104; CDBLB 1914-1945;
    DLB 15, 100

Casanova de Seingalt, Giovanni Jacopo
    1725-1798 .... **LC 13**

Casares, Adolfo Bioy
    See Bioy Casares, Adolfo

Casely-Hayford, J(oseph) E(phraim)
    1866-1930 .... **TCLC 24; BLC**
    See also BW 2; CA 123; DAM MULT

Casey, John (Dudley) 1939-........ **CLC 59**
    See also BEST 90:2; CA 69-72; CANR 23

Casey, Michael 1947-.............. **CLC 2**
    See also CA 65-68; DLB 5

Casey, Patrick
    See Thurman, Wallace (Henry)

Casey, Warren (Peter) 1935-1988 ... **CLC 12**
    See also CA 101; 127; INT 101

Casona, Alejandro................. **CLC 49
    See also Alvarez, Alejandro Rodriguez

Cassavetes, John 1929-1989........ **CLC 20**
    See also CA 85-88; 127

Cassill, R(onald) V(erlin) 1919-... **CLC 4, 23**
    See also CA 9-12R; CAAS 1; CANR 7, 45;
    DLB 6

Cassirer, Ernst 1874-1945 .... **TCLC 61**

Cassity, (Allen) Turner 1929- .... **CLC 6, 42**
    See also CA 17-20R; CAAS 8; CANR 11;
    DLB 105

Castaneda, Carlos 1931(?)-........ **CLC 12**
    See also CA 25-28R; CANR 32; HW;
    MTCW

Castedo, Elena 1937- .... **CLC 65**
    See also CA 132

Castedo-Ellerman, Elena
    See Castedo, Elena

Castellanos, Rosario
    1925-1974 .... **CLC 66; HLC**
    See also CA 131; 53-56; DAM MULT;
    DLB 113; HW

Castelvetro, Lodovico 1505-1571..... **LC 12**

Castiglione, Baldassare 1478-1529 ... **LC 12**

Castle, Robert
    See Hamilton, Edmond

Castro, Guillen de 1569-1631........ **LC 19**

Castro, Rosalia de 1837-1885 ..... **NCLC 3**
    See also DAM MULT

Cather, Willa
    See Cather, Willa Sibert

Cather, Willa Sibert
    1873-1947 .... **TCLC 1, 11, 31; DA;**
                    DAB; DAC; SSC 2; WLC
    See also CA 104; 128; CDALB 1865-1917;
    DAM MST, NOV; DLB 9, 54, 78;
    DLBD 1; MTCW; SATA 30

Catton, (Charles) Bruce
    1899-1978 .... **CLC 35**
    See also AITN 1; CA 5-8R; 81-84;
    CANR 7; DLB 17; SATA 2;
    SATA-Obit 24

Cauldwell, Frank
    See King, Francis (Henry)

Caunitz, William J. 1933- .... **CLC 34**
    See also BEST 89:3; CA 125; 130; INT 130

Causley, Charles (Stanley) 1917-..... **CLC 7**
    See also CA 9-12R; CANR 5, 35; CLR 30;
    DLB 27; MTCW; SATA 3, 66

Caute, David 1936-............... **CLC 29**
    See also CA 1-4R; CAAS 4; CANR 1, 33;
    DAM NOV; DLB 14

Cavafy, C(onstantine) P(eter)
    1863-1933 .... **TCLC 2, 7**
    See also Kavafis, Konstantinos Petrou
    See also CA 148; DAM POET

Cavallo, Evelyn
    See Spark, Muriel (Sarah)

Cavanna, Betty .... **CLC 12**
    See also Harrison, Elizabeth Cavanna
    See also JRDA; MAICYA; SAAS 4;
    SATA 1, 30

Cavendish, Margaret Lucas
    1623-1673 .... **LC 30**
    See also DLB 131

Caxton, William 1421(?)-1491(?)..... **LC 17**

Cayrol, Jean 1911-............... **CLC 11**
    See also CA 89-92; DLB 83

Cela, Camilo Jose
    1916- .... **CLC 4, 13, 59; HLC**
    See also BEST 90:2; CA 21-24R; CAAS 10;
    CANR 21, 32; DAM MULT; DLBY 89;
    HW; MTCW

Celan, Paul ...... **CLC 10, 19, 53, 82; PC 10**
    See also Antschel, Paul
    See also DLB 69

Celine, Louis-Ferdinand
    .... **CLC 1, 3, 4, 7, 9, 15, 47**
    See also Destouches, Louis-Ferdinand
    See also DLB 72

Cellini, Benvenuto 1500-1571 .... **LC 7**

Cendrars, Blaise .... **CLC 18**
    See also Sauser-Hall, Frederic

Cernuda (y Bidon), Luis
    1902-1963 .... **CLC 54**
    See also CA 131; 89-92; DAM POET;
    DLB 134; HW

Cervantes (Saavedra), Miguel de
    1547-1616 .... **LC 6, 23; DA; DAB;**
                    DAC; SSC 12; WLC
    See also DAM MST, NOV

Cesaire, Aime (Fernand)
    1913- .... **CLC 19, 32; BLC**
    See also BW 2; CA 65-68; CANR 24, 43;
    DAM MULT, POET; MTCW

Chabon, Michael 1965(?)- .... **CLC 55**
    See also CA 139

Chabrol, Claude 1930- .... **CLC 16**
    See also CA 110

Challans, Mary 1905-1983
    See Renault, Mary
    See also CA 81-84; 111; SATA 23;
    SATA-Obit 36

Challis, George
    See Faust, Frederick (Schiller)

Chambers, Aidan 1934- .... **CLC 35**
    See also CA 25-28R; CANR 12, 31; JRDA;
    MAICYA; SAAS 12; SATA 1, 69

Chambers, James 1948-
    See Cliff, Jimmy
    See also CA 124

Chambers, Jessie
    See Lawrence, D(avid) H(erbert Richards)

Chambers, Robert W. 1865-1933... **TCLC 41**

Chandler, Raymond (Thornton)
    1888-1959 ....**TCLC 1, 7**
    See also CA 104; 129; CDALB 1929-1941;
    DLBD 6; MTCW

Chang, Jung 1952- .... **CLC 71**
    See also CA 142

Channing, William Ellery
    1780-1842 .... **NCLC 17**
    See also DLB 1, 59

Chaplin, Charles Spencer
    1889-1977 .... **CLC 16**
    See also Chaplin, Charlie
    See also CA 81-84; 73-76

Chaplin, Charlie
    See Chaplin, Charles Spencer
    See also DLB 44

Chapman, George 1559(?)-1634...... **LC 22**
    See also DAM DRAM; DLB 62, 121

Chapman, Graham 1941-1989 ...... **CLC 21**
    See also Monty Python
    See also CA 116; 129; CANR 35

Chapman, John Jay 1862-1933 ..... **TCLC 7**
    See also CA 104

Chapman, Walker
    See Silverberg, Robert

Chappell, Fred (Davis) 1936-.... **CLC 40, 78**
    See also CA 5-8R; CAAS 4; CANR 8, 33;
    DLB 6, 105

Char, Rene(-Emile)
    1907-1988 .... **CLC 9, 11, 14, 55**
    See also CA 13-16R; 124; CANR 32;
    DAM POET; MTCW

Charby, Jay
    See Ellison, Harlan (Jay)

Chardin, Pierre Teilhard de
    See Teilhard de Chardin, (Marie Joseph)
    Pierre

Charles I 1600-1649 .... **LC 13**

Charyn, Jerome 1937- .... **CLC 5, 8, 18**
    See also CA 5-8R; CAAS 1; CANR 7;
    DLBY 83; MTCW

Chase, Mary (Coyle) 1907-1981 ...... **DC 1**
    See also CA 77-80; 105; SATA 17;
    SATA-Obit 29

Chase, Mary Ellen 1887-1973....... **CLC 2**
    See also CA 13-16; 41-44R; CAP 1;
    SATA 10

Chase, Nicholas
    See Hyde, Anthony

Chateaubriand, Francois Rene de
1768-1848 . . . . **NCLC 3**
See also DLB 119

Chatterje, Sarat Chandra 1876-1936(?)
See Chatterji, Saratchandra
See also CA 109

Chatterji, Bankim Chandra
1838-1894 . . . . **NCLC 19**

Chatterji, Saratchandra . . . . **TCLC 13**
See also Chatterje, Sarat Chandra

Chatterton, Thomas 1752-1770 . . . . **LC 3**
See also DAM POET; DLB 109

Chatwin, (Charles) Bruce
1940-1989 . . . . **CLC 28, 57, 59**
See also AAYA 4; BEST 90:1; CA 85-88;
127; DAM POP

Chaucer, Daniel
See Ford, Ford Madox

Chaucer, Geoffrey
1340(?)-1400 . . . **LC 17; DA; DAB; DAC**
See also CDBLB Before 1660; DAM MST,
POET; DLB 146

Chaviaras, Strates 1935-
See Haviaras, Stratis
See also CA 105

Chayefsky, Paddy . . . . **CLC 23**
See also Chayefsky, Sidney
See also DLB 7, 44; DLBY 81

Chayefsky, Sidney 1923-1981
See Chayefsky, Paddy
See also CA 9-12R; 104; CANR 18;
DAM DRAM

Chedid, Andree 1920- . . . . **CLC 47**
See also CA 145

Cheever, John
1912-1982 . . . . . . **CLC 3, 7, 8, 11, 15, 25,**
64; DA; DAB; DAC; SSC 1; WLC
See also CA 5-8R; 106; CABS 1; CANR 5,
27; CDALB 1941-1968; DAM MST,
NOV, POP; DLB 2, 102; DLBY 80, 82;
INT CANR-5; MTCW

Cheever, Susan 1943- . . . . **CLC 18, 48**
See also CA 103; CANR 27, 51; DLBY 82;
INT CANR-27

Chekhonte, Antosha
See Chekhov, Anton (Pavlovich)

Chekhov, Anton (Pavlovich)
1860-1904 . . . . . **TCLC 3, 10, 31, 55; DA;**
DAB; DAC; SSC 2; WLC
See also CA 104; 124; DAM DRAM, MST

Chernyshevsky, Nikolay Gavrilovich
1828-1889 . . . . **NCLC 1**

Cherry, Carolyn Janice 1942-
See Cherryh, C. J.
See also CA 65-68; CANR 10

Cherryh, C. J. . . . . **CLC 35**
See also Cherry, Carolyn Janice
See also DLBY 80

Chesnutt, Charles W(addell)
1858-1932 . . . . **TCLC 5, 39; BLC; SSC 7**
See also BW 1; CA 106; 125; DAM MULT;
DLB 12, 50, 78; MTCW

Chester, Alfred 1929(?)-1971 . . . . **CLC 49**
See also CA 33-36R; DLB 130

Chesterton, G(ilbert) K(eith)
1874-1936 . . . . **TCLC 1, 6; SSC 1**
See also CA 104; 132; CDBLB 1914-1945;
DAM NOV, POET; DLB 10, 19, 34, 70,
98, 149; MTCW; SATA 27

Chiang Pin-chin 1904-1986
See Ding Ling
See also CA 118

Ch'ien Chung-shu 1910- . . . . **CLC 22**
See also CA 130; MTCW

Child, L. Maria
See Child, Lydia Maria

Child, Lydia Maria 1802-1880 . . . . **NCLC 6**
See also DLB 1, 74; SATA 67

Child, Mrs.
See Child, Lydia Maria

Child, Philip 1898-1978 . . . . **CLC 19, 68**
See also CA 13-14; CAP 1; SATA 47

Childress, Alice
1920-1994 . . **CLC 12, 15, 86; BLC; DC 4**
See also AAYA 8; BW 2; CA 45-48; 146;
CANR 3, 27, 50; CLR 14; DAM DRAM,
MULT, NOV; DLB 7, 38; JRDA;
MAICYA; MTCW; SATA 7, 48, 81

Chislett, (Margaret) Anne 1943- . . . . **CLC 34**

Chitty, Thomas Willes 1926- . . . . **CLC 11**
See also Hinde, Thomas
See also CA 5-8R

Chivers, Thomas Holley
1809-1858 . . . . **NCLC 49**
See also DLB 3

Chomette, Rene Lucien 1898-1981
See Clair, Rene
See also CA 103

Chopin, Kate
. . . . **TCLC 5, 14; DA; DAB; SSC 8**
See also Chopin, Katherine
See also CDALB 1865-1917; DLB 12, 78

Chopin, Katherine 1851-1904
See Chopin, Kate
See also CA 104; 122; DAC; DAM MST,
NOV

Chretien de Troyes
c. 12th cent. - . . . . **CMLC 10**

Christie
See Ichikawa, Kon

Christie, Agatha (Mary Clarissa)
1890-1976 . . . . . . **CLC 1, 6, 8, 12, 39, 48;**
DAB; DAC
See also AAYA 9; AITN 1, 2; CA 17-20R;
61-64; CANR 10, 37; CDBLB 1914-1945;
DAM NOV; DLB 13, 77; MTCW;
SATA 36

Christie, (Ann) Philippa
See Pearce, Philippa
See also CA 5-8R; CANR 4

Christine de Pizan 1365(?)-1431(?) . . . . **LC 9**

Chubb, Elmer
See Masters, Edgar Lee

Chulkov, Mikhail Dmitrievich
1743-1792 . . . . **LC 2**
See also DLB 150

Churchill, Caryl 1938- . . . **CLC 31, 55; DC 5**
See also CA 102; CANR 22, 46; DLB 13;
MTCW

Churchill, Charles 1731-1764 . . . . **LC 3**
See also DLB 109

Chute, Carolyn 1947- . . . . **CLC 39**
See also CA 123

Ciardi, John (Anthony)
1916-1986 . . . . **CLC 10, 40, 44**
See also CA 5-8R; 118; CAAS 2; CANR 5,
33; CLR 19; DAM POET; DLB 5;
DLBY 86; INT CANR-5; MAICYA;
MTCW; SATA 1, 65; SATA-Obit 46

Cicero, Marcus Tullius
106B.C.-43B.C. . . . . **CMLC 3**

Cimino, Michael 1943- . . . . **CLC 16**
See also CA 105

Cioran, E(mil) M. 1911-1995 . . . . . . **CLC 64**
See also CA 25-28R; 149

Cisneros, Sandra 1954- . . . . . . **CLC 69; HLC**
See also AAYA 9; CA 131; DAM MULT;
DLB 122, 152; HW

Cixous, Helene 1937- . . . . **CLC 92**
See also CA 126; DLB 83; MTCW

Clair, Rene . . . . **CLC 20**
See also Chomette, Rene Lucien

Clampitt, Amy 1920-1994 . . . . **CLC 32**
See also CA 110; 146; CANR 29; DLB 105

Clancy, Thomas L., Jr. 1947-
See Clancy, Tom
See also CA 125; 131; INT 131; MTCW

Clancy, Tom. . . . . **CLC 45**
See also Clancy, Thomas L., Jr.
See also AAYA 9; BEST 89:1, 90:1;
DAM NOV, POP

Clare, John 1793-1864 . . . . . . **NCLC 9; DAB**
See also DAM POET; DLB 55, 96

Clarin
See Alas (y Urena), Leopoldo (Enrique
Garcia)

Clark, Al C.
See Goines, Donald

Clark, (Robert) Brian 1932- . . . . **CLC 29**
See also CA 41-44R

Clark, Curt
See Westlake, Donald E(dwin)

Clark, Eleanor 1913- . . . . **CLC 5, 19**
See also CA 9-12R; CANR 41; DLB 6

Clark, J. P.
See Clark, John Pepper
See also DLB 117

Clark, John Pepper
1935- . . . . **CLC 38; BLC; DC 5**
See also Clark, J. P.
See also BW 1; CA 65-68; CANR 16;
DAM DRAM, MULT

Clark, M. R.
See Clark, Mavis Thorpe

Clark, Mavis Thorpe 1909- . . . . **CLC 12**
See also CA 57-60; CANR 8, 37; CLR 30;
MAICYA; SAAS 5; SATA 8, 74

Clark, Walter Van Tilburg
1909-1971 . . . . **CLC 28**
See also CA 9-12R; 33-36R; DLB 9;
SATA 8

Clarke, Arthur C(harles)
1917- . . . . . . **CLC 1, 4, 13, 18, 35; SSC 3**
See also AAYA 4; CA 1-4R; CANR 2, 28;
DAM POP; JRDA; MAICYA; MTCW;
SATA 13, 70

Clarke, Austin 1896-1974. . . . . **CLC 6, 9**
See also CA 29-32; 49-52; CAP 2;
DAM POET; DLB 10, 20

Clarke, Austin C(hesterfield)
1934- . . . . **CLC 8, 53; BLC; DAC**
See also BW 1; CA 25-28R; CAAS 16;
CANR 14, 32; DAM MULT; DLB 53,
125

Clarke, Gillian 1937- . . . . **CLC 61**
See also CA 106; DLB 40

Clarke, Marcus (Andrew Hislop)
1846-1881 . . . . **NCLC 19**

Clarke, Shirley 1925- . . . . **CLC 16**

Clash, The
See Headon, (Nicky) Topper; Jones, Mick;
Simonon, Paul; Strummer, Joe

Claudel, Paul (Louis Charles Marie)
1868-1955 . . . . **TCLC 2, 10**
See also CA 104

Clavell, James (duMaresq)
1925-1994 . . . . **CLC 6, 25, 87**
See also CA 25-28R; 146; CANR 26, 48;
DAM NOV, POP; MTCW

Cleaver, (Leroy) Eldridge
1935- . . . . **CLC 30; BLC**
See also BW 1; CA 21-24R; CANR 16;
DAM MULT

Cleese, John (Marwood) 1939- . . . . . **CLC 21**
See also Monty Python
See also CA 112; 116; CANR 35; MTCW

Cleishbotham, Jebediah
See Scott, Walter

Cleland, John 1710-1789 . . . . **LC 2**
See also DLB 39

Clemens, Samuel Langhorne 1835-1910
See Twain, Mark
See also CA 104; 135; CDALB 1865-1917;
DA; DAB; DAC; DAM MST, NOV;
DLB 11, 12, 23, 64, 74; JRDA;
MAICYA; YABC 2

Cleophil
See Congreve, William

Clerihew, E.
See Bentley, E(dmund) C(lerihew)

Clerk, N. W.
See Lewis, C(live) S(taples)

Cliff, Jimmy. . . . . **CLC 21**
See also Chambers, James

Clifton, (Thelma) Lucille
1936- . . . . **CLC 19, 66; BLC**
See also BW 2; CA 49-52; CANR 2, 24, 42;
CLR 5; DAM MULT, POET; DLB 5, 41;
MAICYA; MTCW; SATA 20, 69

Clinton, Dirk
See Silverberg, Robert

Clough, Arthur Hugh 1819-1861. . **NCLC 27**
See also DLB 32

Clutha, Janet Paterson Frame 1924-
See Frame, Janet
See also CA 1-4R; CANR 2, 36; MTCW

Clyne, Terence
See Blatty, William Peter

Cobalt, Martin
See Mayne, William (James Carter)

Cobbett, William 1763-1835 . . . . . **NCLC 49**
See also DLB 43, 107, 158

Coburn, D(onald) L(ee) 1938- . . . . . . **CLC 10**
See also CA 89-92

Cocteau, Jean (Maurice Eugene Clement)
1889-1963 . . . . **CLC 1, 8, 15, 16, 43; DA;**
DAB; DAC; WLC
See also CA 25-28; CANR 40; CAP 2;
DAM DRAM, MST, NOV; DLB 65;
MTCW

Codrescu, Andrei 1946- . . . . **CLC 46**
See also CA 33-36R; CAAS 19; CANR 13,
34; DAM POET

Coe, Max
See Bourne, Randolph S(illiman)

Coe, Tucker
See Westlake, Donald E(dwin)

Coetzee, J(ohn) M(ichael)
1940- . . . . **CLC 23, 33, 66**
See also CA 77-80; CANR 41; DAM NOV;
MTCW

Coffey, Brian
See Koontz, Dean R(ay)

Cohan, George M. 1878-1942 . . . . . **TCLC 60**

Cohen, Arthur A(llen)
1928-1986 . . . . **CLC 7, 31**
See also CA 1-4R; 120; CANR 1, 17, 42;
DLB 28

Cohen, Leonard (Norman)
1934- . . . . **CLC 3, 38; DAC**
See also CA 21-24R; CANR 14;
DAM MST; DLB 53; MTCW

Cohen, Matt 1942- . . . . **CLC 19; DAC**
See also CA 61-64; CAAS 18; CANR 40;
DLB 53

Cohen-Solal, Annie 19(?)- . . . . **CLC 50**

Colegate, Isabel 1931- . . . . **CLC 36**
See also CA 17-20R; CANR 8, 22; DLB 14;
INT CANR-22; MTCW

Coleman, Emmett
See Reed, Ishmael

Coleridge, Samuel Taylor
1772-1834 . . . . . **NCLC 9, 54; DA; DAB;**
DAC; PC 11; WLC
See also CDBLB 1789-1832; DAM MST,
POET; DLB 93, 107

Coleridge, Sara 1802-1852 . . . . **NCLC 31**

Coles, Don 1928- . . . . **CLC 46**
See also CA 115; CANR 38

Colette, (Sidonie-Gabrielle)
1873-1954 . . . . . . **TCLC 1, 5, 16; SSC 10**
See also CA 104; 131; DAM NOV; DLB 65;
MTCW

Collett, (Jacobine) Camilla (Wergeland)
1813-1895 . . . . **NCLC 22**

Collier, Christopher 1930- . . . . **CLC 30**
See also AAYA 13; CA 33-36R; CANR 13,
33; JRDA; MAICYA; SATA 16, 70

Collier, James L(incoln) 1928- . . . . . **CLC 30**
See also AAYA 13; CA 9-12R; CANR 4,
33; CLR 3; DAM POP; JRDA;
MAICYA; SAAS 21; SATA 8, 70

Collier, Jeremy 1650-1726. . . . . **LC 6**

Collier, John 1901-1980. . . . . **SSC 19**
See also CA 65-68; 97-100; CANR 10;
DLB 77

Collins, Hunt
See Hunter, Evan

Collins, Linda 1931- . . . . **CLC 44**
See also CA 125

Collins, (William) Wilkie
1824-1889 . . . . **NCLC 1, 18**
See also CDBLB 1832-1890; DLB 18, 70,
159

Collins, William 1721-1759 . . . . **LC 4**
See also DAM POET; DLB 109

Collodi, Carlo 1826-1890 . . . . **NCLC 54**
See also Lorenzini, Carlo
See also CLR 5

Colman, George
See Glassco, John

Colt, Winchester Remington
See Hubbard, L(afayette) Ron(ald)

Colter, Cyrus 1910- . . . . **CLC 58**
See also BW 1; CA 65-68; CANR 10;
DLB 33

Colton, James
See Hansen, Joseph

Colum, Padraic 1881-1972. . . . . **CLC 28**
See also CA 73-76; 33-36R; CANR 35;
CLR 36; MAICYA; MTCW; SATA 15

Colvin, James
See Moorcock, Michael (John)

Colwin, Laurie (E.)
1944-1992 . . . . **CLC 5, 13, 23, 84**
See also CA 89-92; 139; CANR 20, 46;
DLBY 80; MTCW

Comfort, Alex(ander) 1920- . . . . **CLC 7**
See also CA 1-4R; CANR 1, 45; DAM POP

Comfort, Montgomery
See Campbell, (John) Ramsey

Compton-Burnett, I(vy)
1884(?)-1969 . . . . . . **CLC 1, 3, 10, 15, 34**
See also CA 1-4R; 25-28R; CANR 4;
DAM NOV; DLB 36; MTCW

Comstock, Anthony 1844-1915 . . . . **TCLC 13**
See also CA 110

Comte, Auguste 1798-1857 . . . . **NCLC 54**

Conan Doyle, Arthur
See Doyle, Arthur Conan

Conde, Maryse 1937- . . . . **CLC 52, 92**
See also Boucolon, Maryse
See also BW 2; DAM MULT

Condillac, Etienne Bonnot de
1714-1780 . . . . **LC 26**

Condon, Richard (Thomas)
1915- . . . . **CLC 4, 6, 8, 10, 45**
See also BEST 90:3; CA 1-4R; CAAS 1;
CANR 2, 23; DAM NOV;
INT CANR-23; MTCW

Congreve, William
1670-1729 . . . . **LC 5, 21; DA; DAB;**
                              DAC; DC 2; WLC
See also CDBLB 1660-1789; DAM DRAM,
MST, POET; DLB 39, 84

Connell, Evan S(helby), Jr.
1924- . . . . **CLC 4, 6, 45**
See also AAYA 7; CA 1-4R; CAAS 2;
CANR 2, 39; DAM NOV; DLB 2;
DLBY 81; MTCW

Connelly, Marc(us Cook)
1890-1980 . . . . **CLC 7**
See also CA 85-88; 102; CANR 30; DLB 7;
DLBY 80; SATA-Obit 25

Connor, Ralph . . . . **TCLC 31**
See also Gordon, Charles William
See also DLB 92

Conrad, Joseph
1857-1924 . . . . **TCLC 1, 6, 13, 25, 43, 57;**
                              DA; DAB; DAC; SSC 9; WLC
See also CA 104; 131; CDBLB 1890-1914;
DAM MST, NOV; DLB 10, 34, 98, 156;
MTCW; SATA 27

Conrad, Robert Arnold
See Hart, Moss

Conroy, Pat 1945- . . . . **CLC 30, 74**
See also AAYA 8; AITN 1; CA 85-88;
CANR 24; DAM NOV, POP; DLB 6;
MTCW

Constant (de Rebecque), (Henri) Benjamin
1767-1830 . . . . **NCLC 6**
See also DLB 119

Conybeare, Charles Augustus
See Eliot, T(homas) S(tearns)

Cook, Michael 1933- . . . . **CLC 58**
See also CA 93-96; DLB 53

Cook, Robin 1940- . . . . **CLC 14**
See also BEST 90:2; CA 108; 111;
CANR 41; DAM POP; INT 111

Cook, Roy
See Silverberg, Robert

Cooke, Elizabeth 1948- . . . . **CLC 55**
See also CA 129

Cooke, John Esten 1830-1886 . . . . . **NCLC 5**
See also DLB 3

Cooke, John Estes
See Baum, L(yman) Frank

Cooke, M. E.
See Creasey, John

Cooke, Margaret
See Creasey, John

Cooney, Ray . . . . **CLC 62**

Cooper, Douglas 1960- . . . . **CLC 86**

Cooper, Henry St. John
See Creasey, John

Cooper, J. California . . . . **CLC 56**
See also AAYA 12; BW 1; CA 125;
DAM MULT

Cooper, James Fenimore
1789-1851 . . . . **NCLC 1, 27, 54**
See also CDALB 1640-1865; DLB 3;
SATA 19

Coover, Robert (Lowell)
1932- . . **CLC 3, 7, 15, 32, 46, 87; SSC 15**
See also CA 45-48; CANR 3, 37;
DAM NOV; DLB 2; DLBY 81; MTCW

Copeland, Stewart (Armstrong)
1952- . . . . **CLC 26**

Coppard, A(lfred) E(dgar)
1878-1957 . . . . **TCLC 5; SSC 21**
See also CA 114; DLB 162; YABC 1

Coppee, Francois 1842-1908 . . . . . . **TCLC 25**

Coppola, Francis Ford 1939- . . . . **CLC 16**
See also CA 77-80; CANR 40; DLB 44

Corbiere, Tristan 1845-1875 . . . . . **NCLC 43**

Corcoran, Barbara 1911- . . . . **CLC 17**
See also AAYA 14; CA 21-24R; CAAS 2;
CANR 11, 28, 48; DLB 52; JRDA;
SAAS 20; SATA 3, 77

Cordelier, Maurice
See Giraudoux, (Hippolyte) Jean

Corelli, Marie 1855-1924 . . . . **TCLC 51**
See also Mackay, Mary
See also DLB 34, 156

Corman, Cid . . . . **CLC 9**
See also Corman, Sidney
See also CAAS 2; DLB 5

Corman, Sidney 1924-
See Corman, Cid
See also CA 85-88; CANR 44; DAM POET

Cormier, Robert (Edmund)
1925- . . . . . **CLC 12, 30; DA; DAB; DAC**
See also AAYA 3; CA 1-4R; CANR 5, 23;
CDALB 1968-1988; CLR 12; DAM MST,
NOV; DLB 52; INT CANR-23; JRDA;
MAICYA; MTCW; SATA 10, 45, 83

Corn, Alfred (DeWitt III) 1943- . . . . **CLC 33**
See also CA 104; CANR 44; DLB 120;
DLBY 80

Corneille, Pierre 1606-1684 . . . . **LC 28; DAB**
See also DAM MST

Cornwell, David (John Moore)
1931- . . . . **CLC 9, 15**
See also le Carre, John
See also CA 5-8R; CANR 13, 33;
DAM POP; MTCW

Corso, (Nunzio) Gregory 1930- . . . **CLC 1, 11**
See also CA 5-8R; CANR 41; DLB 5, 16;
MTCW

Cortazar, Julio
1914-1984 . . . . . . **CLC 2, 3, 5, 10, 13, 15,**
                              33, 34, 92; HLC; SSC 7
See also CA 21-24R; CANR 12, 32;
DAM MULT, NOV; DLB 113; HW;
MTCW

CORTES, HERNAN 1484-1547 . . . . . **LC 31**

Corwin, Cecil
See Kornbluth, C(yril) M.

Cosic, Dobrica 1921- . . . . **CLC 14**
See also CA 122; 138

Costain, Thomas B(ertram)
1885-1965 . . . . **CLC 30**
See also CA 5-8R; 25-28R; DLB 9

Costantini, Humberto
1924(?)-1987 . . . . **CLC 49**
See also CA 131; 122; HW

Costello, Elvis 1955- . . . . **CLC 21**

Cotter, Joseph Seamon Sr.
1861-1949 . . . . **TCLC 28; BLC**
See also BW 1; CA 124; DAM MULT;
DLB 50

Couch, Arthur Thomas Quiller
See Quiller-Couch, Arthur Thomas

Coulton, James
See Hansen, Joseph

Couperus, Louis (Marie Anne)
1863-1923 . . . . **TCLC 15**
See also CA 115

Coupland, Douglas 1961- . . . . . **CLC 85; DAC**
See also CA 142; DAM POP

Court, Wesli
See Turco, Lewis (Putnam)

Courtenay, Bryce 1933- . . . . **CLC 59**
See also CA 138

Courtney, Robert
See Ellison, Harlan (Jay)

Cousteau, Jacques-Yves 1910- . . . . . . **CLC 30**
See also CA 65-68; CANR 15; MTCW;
SATA 38

Coward, Noel (Peirce)
1899-1973 . . . . **CLC 1, 9, 29, 51**
See also AITN 1; CA 17-18; 41-44R;
CANR 35; CAP 2; CDBLB 1914-1945;
DAM DRAM; DLB 10; MTCW

Cowley, Malcolm 1898-1989 . . . . **CLC 39**
See also CA 5-8R; 128; CANR 3; DLB 4,
48; DLBY 81, 89; MTCW

Cowper, William 1731-1800 . . . . **NCLC 8**
See also DAM POET; DLB 104, 109

Cox, William Trevor 1928- . . . **CLC 9, 14, 71**
See also Trevor, William
See also CA 9-12R; CANR 4, 37;
DAM NOV; DLB 14; INT CANR-37;
MTCW

Coyne, P. J.
See Masters, Hilary

Cozzens, James Gould
1903-1978 . . . . **CLC 1, 4, 11, 92**
See also CA 9-12R; 81-84; CANR 19;
CDALB 1941-1968; DLB 9; DLBD 2;
DLBY 84; MTCW

Crabbe, George 1754-1832 . . . . **NCLC 26**
See also DLB 93

Craddock, Charles Egbert
See Murfree, Mary Noailles

Craig, A. A.
See Anderson, Poul (William)

Craik, Dinah Maria (Mulock)
1826-1887 . . . . **NCLC 38**
See also DLB 35, 163; MAICYA; SATA 34

Cram, Ralph Adams 1863-1942 . . . . **TCLC 45**

Crane, (Harold) Hart
1899-1932 . . . . **TCLC 2, 5; DA; DAB;**
                              DAC; PC 3; WLC
See also CA 104; 127; CDALB 1917-1929;
DAM MST, POET; DLB 4, 48; MTCW

Crane, R(onald) S(almon)
1886-1967 . . . . **CLC 27**
See also CA 85-88; DLB 63

Crane, Stephen (Townley)
1871-1900 . . . . . . TCLC **11, 17, 32;** DA;
DAB; DAC; SSC **7;** WLC
See also CA 109; 140; CDALB 1865-1917;
DAM MST, NOV, POET; DLB 12, 54,
78; YABC 2

Crase, Douglas 1944- . . . . CLC **58**
See also CA 106

Crashaw, Richard 1612(?)-1649 . . . . . . LC **24**
See also DLB 126

Craven, Margaret
1901-1980 . . . . CLC **17;** DAC
See also CA 103

Crawford, F(rancis) Marion
1854-1909 . . . . TCLC **10**
See also CA 107; DLB 71

Crawford, Isabella Valancy
1850-1887 . . . . NCLC **12**
See also DLB 92

Crayon, Geoffrey
See Irving, Washington

Creasey, John 1908-1973 . . . . CLC **11**
See also CA 5-8R; 41-44R; CANR 8;
DLB 77; MTCW

Crebillon, Claude Prosper Jolyot de (fils)
1707-1777 . . . . LC **28**

Credo
See Creasey, John

Creeley, Robert (White)
1926- . . . . . CLC **1, 2, 4, 8, 11, 15, 36, 78**
See also CA 1-4R; CAAS 10; CANR 23, 43;
DAM POET; DLB 5, 16; MTCW

Crews, Harry (Eugene)
1935- . . . . CLC **6, 23, 49**
See also AITN 1; CA 25-28R; CANR 20;
DLB 6, 143; MTCW

Crichton, (John) Michael
1942- . . . . CLC **2, 6, 54, 90**
See also AAYA 10; AITN 2; CA 25-28R;
CANR 13, 40; DAM NOV, POP;
DLBY 81; INT CANR-13; JRDA;
MTCW; SATA 9

Crispin, Edmund . . . . CLC **22**
See also Montgomery, (Robert) Bruce
See also DLB 87

Cristofer, Michael 1945(?)- . . . . CLC **28**
See also CA 110; DAM DRAM; DLB 7

Croce, Benedetto 1866-1952 . . . . . . TCLC **37**
See also CA 120

Crockett, David 1786-1836 . . . . NCLC **8**
See also DLB 3, 11

Crockett, Davy
See Crockett, David

Crofts, Freeman Wills
1879-1957 . . . . TCLC **55**
See also CA 115; DLB 77

Croker, John Wilson 1780-1857 . . NCLC **10**
See also DLB 110

Crommelynck, Fernand 1885-1970 . . CLC **75**
See also CA 89-92

Cronin, A(rchibald) J(oseph)
1896-1981 . . . . CLC **32**
See also CA 1-4R; 102; CANR 5; SATA 47;
SATA-Obit 25

Cross, Amanda
See Heilbrun, Carolyn G(old)

Crothers, Rachel 1878(?)-1958 . . . . . TCLC **19**
See also CA 113; DLB 7

Croves, Hal
See Traven, B.

Crowfield, Christopher
See Stowe, Harriet (Elizabeth) Beecher

Crowley, Aleister . . . . TCLC **7**
See also Crowley, Edward Alexander

Crowley, Edward Alexander 1875-1947
See Crowley, Aleister
See also CA 104

Crowley, John 1942- . . . . CLC **57**
See also CA 61-64; CANR 43; DLBY 82;
SATA 65

Crud
See Crumb, R(obert)

Crumarums
See Crumb, R(obert)

Crumb, R(obert) 1943- . . . . CLC **17**
See also CA 106

Crumbum
See Crumb, R(obert)

Crumski
See Crumb, R(obert)

Crum the Bum
See Crumb, R(obert)

Crunk
See Crumb, R(obert)

Crustt
See Crumb, R(obert)

Cryer, Gretchen (Kiger) 1935- . . . . . . CLC **21**
See also CA 114; 123

Csath, Geza 1887-1919 . . . . TCLC **13**
See also CA 111

Cudlip, David 1933- . . . . CLC **34**

Cullen, Countee
1903-1946 . . . . . . TCLC **4, 37;** BLC; DA;
DAC
See also BW 1; CA 108; 124;
CDALB 1917-1929; DAM MST, MULT,
POET; DLB 4, 48, 51; MTCW; SATA 18

Cum, R.
See Crumb, R(obert)

Cummings, Bruce F(rederick) 1889-1919
See Barbellion, W. N. P.
See also CA 123

Cummings, E(dward) E(stlin)
1894-1962 . . . . . . CLC **1, 3, 8, 12, 15, 68;**
DA; DAB; DAC; PC **5;** WLC **2**
See also CA 73-76; CANR 31;
CDALB 1929-1941; DAM MST, POET;
DLB 4, 48; MTCW

Cunha, Euclides (Rodrigues Pimenta) da
1866-1909 . . . . TCLC **24**
See also CA 123

Cunningham, E. V.
See Fast, Howard (Melvin)

Cunningham, J(ames) V(incent)
1911-1985 . . . . CLC **3, 31**
See also CA 1-4R; 115; CANR 1; DLB 5

Cunningham, Julia (Woolfolk)
1916- . . . . CLC **12**
See also CA 9-12R; CANR 4, 19, 36;
JRDA; MAICYA; SAAS 2; SATA 1, 26

Cunningham, Michael 1952- . . . . CLC **34**
See also CA 136

Cunninghame Graham, R(obert) B(ontine)
1852-1936 . . . . TCLC **19**
See also Graham, R(obert) B(ontine)
Cunninghame
See also CA 119; DLB 98

Currie, Ellen 19(?)- . . . . CLC **44**

Curtin, Philip
See Lowndes, Marie Adelaide (Belloc)

Curtis, Price
See Ellison, Harlan (Jay)

Cutrate, Joe
See Spiegelman, Art

Czaczkes, Shmuel Yosef
See Agnon, S(hmuel) Y(osef Halevi)

Dabrowska, Maria (Szumska)
1889-1965 . . . . CLC **15**
See also CA 106

Dabydeen, David 1955- . . . . CLC **34**
See also BW 1; CA 125

Dacey, Philip 1939- . . . . CLC **51**
See also CA 37-40R; CAAS 17; CANR 14,
32; DLB 105

Dagerman, Stig (Halvard)
1923-1954 . . . . TCLC **17**
See also CA 117

Dahl, Roald
1916-1990 . . . . . . CLC **1, 6, 18, 79;** DAB;
DAC
See also AAYA 15; CA 1-4R; 133;
CANR 6, 32, 37; CLR 1, 7; DAM MST,
NOV, POP; DLB 139; JRDA; MAICYA;
MTCW; SATA 1, 26, 73; SATA-Obit 65

Dahlberg, Edward 1900-1977 . . . CLC **1, 7, 14**
See also CA 9-12R; 69-72; CANR 31;
DLB 48; MTCW

Dale, Colin . . . . TCLC **18**
See also Lawrence, T(homas) E(dward)

Dale, George E.
See Asimov, Isaac

Daly, Elizabeth 1878-1967 . . . . CLC **52**
See also CA 23-24; 25-28R; CAP 2

Daly, Maureen 1921- . . . . CLC **17**
See also AAYA 5; CANR 37; JRDA;
MAICYA; SAAS 1; SATA 2

Damas, Leon-Gontran 1912-1978 . . . CLC **84**
See also BW 1; CA 125; 73-76

Dana, Richard Henry Sr.
1787-1879 . . . . NCLC **53**

Daniel, Samuel 1562(?)-1619 . . . . LC **24**
See also DLB 62

Daniels, Brett
See Adler, Renata

Dannay, Frederic 1905-1982 . . . . CLC **11**
See also Queen, Ellery
See also CA 1-4R; 107; CANR 1, 39;
DAM POP; DLB 137; MTCW

D'Annunzio, Gabriele
1863-1938 . . . . TCLC **6, 40**
See also CA 104

Danois, N. le
See Gourmont, Remy (-Marie-Charles) de

d'Antibes, Germain
See Simenon, Georges (Jacques Christian)

Danticat, Edwidge 1969- . . . . **CLC 91**

Danvers, Dennis 1947- . . . . **CLC 70**

Danziger, Paula 1944- . . . . **CLC 21**
See also AAYA 4; CA 112; 115; CANR 37;
CLR 20; JRDA; MAICYA; SATA 36,
63; SATA-Brief 30

Da Ponte, Lorenzo 1749-1838. . . . **NCLC 50**

Dario, Ruben
1867-1916 . . . . **TCLC 4; HLC; PC 15**
See also CA 131; DAM MULT; HW;
MTCW

Darley, George 1795-1846 . . . . **NCLC 2**
See also DLB 96

Daryush, Elizabeth 1887-1977. . . . **CLC 6, 19**
See also CA 49-52; CANR 3; DLB 20

Dashwood, Edmee Elizabeth Monica de la
  Pasture 1890-1943
See Delafield, E. M.
See also CA 119

Daudet, (Louis Marie) Alphonse
1840-1897 . . . . **NCLC 1**
See also DLB 123

Daumal, Rene 1908-1944 . . . . **TCLC 14**
See also CA 114

Davenport, Guy (Mattison, Jr.)
1927- . . . . **CLC 6, 14, 38; SSC 16**
See also CA 33-36R; CANR 23; DLB 130

Davidson, Avram 1923-
See Queen, Ellery
See also CA 101; CANR 26; DLB 8

Davidson, Donald (Grady)
1893-1968 . . . . **CLC 2, 13, 19**
See also CA 5-8R; 25-28R; CANR 4;
DLB 45

Davidson, Hugh
See Hamilton, Edmond

Davidson, John 1857-1909 . . . . **TCLC 24**
See also CA 118; DLB 19

Davidson, Sara 1943- . . . . **CLC 9**
See also CA 81-84; CANR 44

Davie, Donald (Alfred)
1922-1995 . . . . **CLC 5, 8, 10, 31**
See also CA 1-4R; 149; CAAS 3; CANR 1,
44; DLB 27; MTCW

Davies, Ray(mond Douglas) 1944- . . **CLC 21**
See also CA 116; 146

Davies, Rhys 1903-1978 . . . . **CLC 23**
See also CA 9-12R; 81-84; CANR 4;
DLB 139

Davies, (William) Robertson
1913-1995 . . . . . **CLC 2, 7, 13, 25, 42, 75,**
           91; DA; DAB; DAC; WLC
See also BEST 89:2; CA 33-36R; 150;
CANR 17, 42; DAM MST, NOV, POP;
DLB 68; INT CANR-17; MTCW

Davies, W(illiam) H(enry)
1871-1940 . . . . **TCLC 5**
See also CA 104; DLB 19

Davies, Walter C.
See Kornbluth, C(yril) M.

Davis, Angela (Yvonne) 1944- . . . . . . **CLC 77**
See also BW 2; CA 57-60; CANR 10;
DAM MULT

Davis, B. Lynch
See Bioy Casares, Adolfo; Borges, Jorge
Luis

Davis, Gordon
See Hunt, E(verette) Howard, (Jr.)

Davis, Harold Lenoir 1896-1960. . . . **CLC 49**
See also CA 89-92; DLB 9

Davis, Rebecca (Blaine) Harding
1831-1910 . . . . **TCLC 6**
See also CA 104; DLB 74

Davis, Richard Harding
1864-1916 . . . . **TCLC 24**
See also CA 114; DLB 12, 23, 78, 79;
DLBD 13

Davison, Frank Dalby 1893-1970 . . . **CLC 15**
See also CA 116

Davison, Lawrence H.
See Lawrence, D(avid) H(erbert Richards)

Davison, Peter (Hubert) 1928- . . . . . **CLC 28**
See also CA 9-12R; CAAS 4; CANR 3, 43;
DLB 5

Davys, Mary 1674-1732 . . . . **LC 1**
See also DLB 39

Dawson, Fielding 1930- . . . . **CLC 6**
See also CA 85-88; DLB 130

Dawson, Peter
See Faust, Frederick (Schiller)

Day, Clarence (Shepard, Jr.)
1874-1935 . . . . **TCLC 25**
See also CA 108; DLB 11

Day, Thomas 1748-1789 . . . . **LC 1**
See also DLB 39; YABC 1

Day Lewis, C(ecil)
1904-1972 . . . . **CLC 1, 6, 10; PC 11**
See also Blake, Nicholas
See also CA 13-16; 33-36R; CANR 34;
CAP 1; DAM POET; DLB 15, 20;
MTCW

Dazai, Osamu . . . . **TCLC 11**
See also Tsushima, Shuji

de Andrade, Carlos Drummond
See Drummond de Andrade, Carlos

Deane, Norman
See Creasey, John

de Beauvoir, Simone (Lucie Ernestine Marie
  Bertrand)
See Beauvoir, Simone (Lucie Ernestine
Marie Bertrand) de

de Brissac, Malcolm
See Dickinson, Peter (Malcolm)

de Chardin, Pierre Teilhard
See Teilhard de Chardin, (Marie Joseph)
Pierre

Dee, John 1527-1608 . . . . **LC 20**

Deer, Sandra 1940- . . . . **CLC 45**

De Ferrari, Gabriella 1941- . . . . **CLC 65**
See also CA 146

Defoe, Daniel
1660(?)-1731 . . . . **LC 1; DA; DAB; DAC;**
                    WLC
See also CDBLB 1660-1789; DAM MST,
NOV; DLB 39, 95, 101; JRDA;
MAICYA; SATA 22

de Gourmont, Remy(-Marie-Charles)
See Gourmont, Remy (-Marie-Charles) de

de Hartog, Jan 1914- . . . . **CLC 19**
See also CA 1-4R; CANR 1

de Hostos, E. M.
See Hostos (y Bonilla), Eugenio Maria de

de Hostos, Eugenio M.
See Hostos (y Bonilla), Eugenio Maria de

Deighton, Len . . . . **CLC 4, 7, 22, 46**
See also Deighton, Leonard Cyril
See also AAYA 6; BEST 89:2;
CDBLB 1960 to Present; DLB 87

Deighton, Leonard Cyril 1929-
See Deighton, Len
See also CA 9-12R; CANR 19, 33;
DAM NOV, POP; MTCW

Dekker, Thomas 1572(?)-1632 . . . . **LC 22**
See also CDBLB Before 1660;
DAM DRAM; DLB 62

Delafield, E. M. 1890-1943 . . . . **TCLC 61**
See also Dashwood, Edmee Elizabeth
Monica de la Pasture
See also DLB 34

de la Mare, Walter (John)
1873-1956 . . . . **TCLC 4, 53; DAB; DAC;**
                 SSC 14; WLC
See also CDBLB 1914-1945; CLR 23;
DAM MST, POET; DLB 162; SATA 16

Delaney, Franey
See O'Hara, John (Henry)

Delaney, Shelagh 1939- . . . . **CLC 29**
See also CA 17-20R; CANR 30;
CDBLB 1960 to Present; DAM DRAM;
DLB 13; MTCW

Delany, Mary (Granville Pendarves)
1700-1788 . . . . **LC 12**

Delany, Samuel R(ay, Jr.)
1942- . . . . **CLC 8, 14, 38; BLC**
See also BW 2; CA 81-84; CANR 27, 43;
DAM MULT; DLB 8, 33; MTCW

De La Ramee, (Marie) Louise 1839-1908
See Ouida
See also SATA 20

de la Roche, Mazo 1879-1961 . . . . . . **CLC 14**
See also CA 85-88; CANR 30; DLB 68;
SATA 64

Delbanco, Nicholas (Franklin)
1942- . . . . **CLC 6, 13**
See also CA 17-20R; CAAS 2; CANR 29;
DLB 6

del Castillo, Michel 1933- . . . . **CLC 38**
See also CA 109

Deledda, Grazia (Cosima)
1875(?)-1936 . . . . **TCLC 23**
See also CA 123

Delibes, Miguel . . . . **CLC 8, 18**
See also Delibes Setien, Miguel

Delibes Setien, Miguel 1920-
 See Delibes, Miguel
 See also CA 45-48; CANR 1, 32; HW;
 MTCW

DeLillo, Don
 1936- . . . . . **CLC 8, 10, 13, 27, 39, 54, 76**
 See also BEST 89:1; CA 81-84; CANR 21;
 DAM NOV, POP; DLB 6; MTCW

de Lisser, H. G.
 See De Lisser, Herbert George
 See also DLB 117

De Lisser, Herbert George
 1878-1944 . . . . **TCLC 12**
 See also de Lisser, H. G.
 See also BW 2; CA 109

Deloria, Vine (Victor), Jr. 1933- . . . . **CLC 21**
 See also CA 53-56; CANR 5, 20, 48;
 DAM MULT; MTCW; NNAL; SATA 21

Del Vecchio, John M(ichael)
 1947- . . . . **CLC 29**
 See also CA 110; DLBD 9

de Man, Paul (Adolph Michel)
 1919-1983 . . . . **CLC 55**
 See also CA 128; 111; DLB 67; MTCW

De Marinis, Rick 1934- . . . . **CLC 54**
 See also CA 57-60; CANR 9, 25, 50

Dembry, R. Emmet
 See Murfree, Mary Noailles

Demby, William 1922- . . . . **CLC 53; BLC**
 See also BW 1; CA 81-84; DAM MULT;
 DLB 33

Demijohn, Thom
 See Disch, Thomas M(ichael)

de Montherlant, Henry (Milon)
 See Montherlant, Henry (Milon) de

Demosthenes 384B.C.-322B.C. . . . **CMLC 13**

de Natale, Francine
 See Malzberg, Barry N(athaniel)

Denby, Edwin (Orr) 1903-1983 . . . . . **CLC 48**
 See also CA 138; 110

Denis, Julio
 See Cortazar, Julio

Denmark, Harrison
 See Zelazny, Roger (Joseph)

Dennis, John 1658-1734 . . . . **LC 11**
 See also DLB 101

Dennis, Nigel (Forbes) 1912-1989 . . . . **CLC 8**
 See also CA 25-28R; 129; DLB 13, 15;
 MTCW

De Palma, Brian (Russell) 1940- . . . . **CLC 20**
 See also CA 109

De Quincey, Thomas 1785-1859 . . . **NCLC 4**
 See also CDBLB 1789-1832; DLB 110; 144

Deren, Eleanora 1908(?)-1961
 See Deren, Maya
 See also CA 111

Deren, Maya . . . . **CLC 16**
 See also Deren, Eleanora

Derleth, August (William)
 1909-1971 . . . . **CLC 31**
 See also CA 1-4R; 29-32R; CANR 4;
 DLB 9; SATA 5

Der Nister 1884-1950 . . . . **TCLC 56**

de Routisie, Albert
 See Aragon, Louis

Derrida, Jacques 1930- . . . . **CLC 24, 87**
 See also CA 124; 127

Derry Down Derry
 See Lear, Edward

Dersonnes, Jacques
 See Simenon, Georges (Jacques Christian)

Desai, Anita 1937- . . . . . . **CLC 19, 37; DAB**
 See also CA 81-84; CANR 33; DAM NOV;
 MTCW; SATA 63

de Saint-Luc, Jean
 See Glassco, John

de Saint Roman, Arnaud
 See Aragon, Louis

Descartes, Rene 1596-1650 . . . . **LC 20**

De Sica, Vittorio 1901(?)-1974 . . . . . **CLC 20**
 See also CA 117

Desnos, Robert 1900-1945 . . . . **TCLC 22**
 See also CA 121

Destouches, Louis-Ferdinand
 1894-1961 . . . . **CLC 9, 15**
 See also Celine, Louis-Ferdinand
 See also CA 85-88; CANR 28; MTCW

Deutsch, Babette 1895-1982 . . . . **CLC 18**
 See also CA 1-4R; 108; CANR 4; DLB 45;
 SATA 1; SATA-Obit 33

Devenant, William 1606-1649 . . . . . . **LC 13**

Devkota, Laxmiprasad
 1909-1959 . . . . **TCLC 23**
 See also CA 123

De Voto, Bernard (Augustine)
 1897-1955 . . . . **TCLC 29**
 See also CA 113; DLB 9

De Vries, Peter
 1910-1993 . . . . **CLC 1, 2, 3, 7, 10, 28, 46**
 See also CA 17-20R; 142; CANR 41;
 DAM NOV; DLB 6; DLBY 82; MTCW

Dexter, Martin
 See Faust, Frederick (Schiller)

Dexter, Pete 1943- . . . . **CLC 34, 55**
 See also BEST 89:2; CA 127; 131;
 DAM POP; INT 131; MTCW

Diamano, Silmang
 See Senghor, Leopold Sedar

Diamond, Neil 1941- . . . . **CLC 30**
 See also CA 108

Diaz del Castillo, Bernal 1496-1584 . . **LC 31**

di Bassetto, Corno
 See Shaw, George Bernard

Dick, Philip K(indred)
 1928-1982 . . . . **CLC 10, 30, 72**
 See also CA 49-52; 106; CANR 2, 16;
 DAM NOV, POP; DLB 8; MTCW

Dickens, Charles (John Huffam)
 1812-1870 . . . . . . **NCLC 3, 8, 18, 26, 37,
 50; DA; DAB; DAC; SSC 17; WLC**
 See also CDBLB 1832-1890; DAM MST,
 NOV; DLB 21, 55, 70, 159; JRDA;
 MAICYA; SATA 15

Dickey, James (Lafayette)
 1923- . . . . **CLC 1, 2, 4, 7, 10, 15, 47**
 See also AITN 1, 2; CA 9-12R; CABS 2;
 CANR 10, 48; CDALB 1968-1988;
 DAM NOV, POET, POP; DLB 5;
 DLBD 7; DLBY 82, 93; INT CANR-10;
 MTCW

Dickey, William 1928-1994 . . . . . . **CLC 3, 28**
 See also CA 9-12R; 145; CANR 24; DLB 5

Dickinson, Charles 1951- . . . . **CLC 49**
 See also CA 128

Dickinson, Emily (Elizabeth)
 1830-1886 . . . . **NCLC 21; DA; DAB;
 DAC; PC 1; WLC**
 See also CDALB 1865-1917; DAM MST,
 POET; DLB 1; SATA 29

Dickinson, Peter (Malcolm)
 1927- . . . . **CLC 12, 35**
 See also AAYA 9; CA 41-44R; CANR 31;
 CLR 29; DLB 87, 161; JRDA; MAICYA;
 SATA 5, 62

Dickson, Carr
 See Carr, John Dickson

Dickson, Carter
 See Carr, John Dickson

Diderot, Denis 1713-1784 . . . . **LC 26**

Didion, Joan 1934- . . . . . **CLC 1, 3, 8, 14, 32**
 See also AITN 1; CA 5-8R; CANR 14;
 CDALB 1968-1988; DAM NOV; DLB 2;
 DLBY 81, 86; MTCW

Dietrich, Robert
 See Hunt, E(verette) Howard, (Jr.)

Dillard, Annie 1945- . . . . **CLC 9, 60**
 See also AAYA 6; CA 49-52; CANR 3, 43;
 DAM NOV; DLBY 80; MTCW;
 SATA 10

Dillard, R(ichard) H(enry) W(ilde)
 1937- . . . . **CLC 5**
 See also CA 21-24R; CAAS 7; CANR 10;
 DLB 5

Dillon, Eilis 1920-1994 . . . . **CLC 17**
 See also CA 9-12R; 147; CAAS 3; CANR 4,
 38; CLR 26; MAICYA; SATA 2, 74;
 SATA-Obit 83

Dimont, Penelope
 See Mortimer, Penelope (Ruth)

Dinesen, Isak . . . . **CLC 10, 29; SSC 7**
 See also Blixen, Karen (Christentze
 Dinesen)

Ding Ling . . . . **CLC 68**
 See also Chiang Pin-chin

Disch, Thomas M(ichael) 1940- . . . **CLC 7, 36**
 See also AAYA 17; CA 21-24R; CAAS 4;
 CANR 17, 36; CLR 18; DLB 8;
 MAICYA; MTCW; SAAS 15; SATA 54

Disch, Tom
 See Disch, Thomas M(ichael)

d'Isly, Georges
 See Simenon, Georges (Jacques Christian)

Disraeli, Benjamin 1804-1881 . . **NCLC 2, 39**
 See also DLB 21, 55

Ditcum, Steve
 See Crumb, R(obert)

Dixon, Paige
 See Corcoran, Barbara

Dixon, Stephen 1936-..... **CLC 52; SSC 16**
See also CA 89-92; CANR 17, 40; DLB 130

Dobell, Sydney Thompson
1824-1874 .... **NCLC 43**
See also DLB 32

Doblin, Alfred .... **TCLC 13**
See also Doeblin, Alfred

Dobrolyubov, Nikolai Alexandrovich
1836-1861 .... **NCLC 5**

Dobyns, Stephen 1941-............ **CLC 37**
See also CA 45-48; CANR 2, 18

Doctorow, E(dgar) L(aurence)
1931- ..... **CLC 6, 11, 15, 18, 37, 44, 65**
See also AITN 2; BEST 89:3; CA 45-48;
CANR 2, 33, 51; CDALB 1968-1988;
DAM NOV, POP; DLB 2, 28; DLBY 80;
MTCW

Dodgson, Charles Lutwidge 1832-1898
See Carroll, Lewis
See also CLR 2; DA; DAB; DAC;
DAM MST, NOV, POET; MAICYA;
YABC 2

Dodson, Owen (Vincent)
1914-1983 .... **CLC 79; BLC**
See also BW 1; CA 65-68; 110; CANR 24;
DAM MULT; DLB 76

Doeblin, Alfred 1878-1957........ **TCLC 13**
See also Doblin, Alfred
See also CA 110; 141; DLB 66

Doerr, Harriet 1910- .... **CLC 34**
See also CA 117; 122; CANR 47; INT 122

Domecq, H(onorio) Bustos
See Bioy Casares, Adolfo; Borges, Jorge
Luis

Domini, Rey
See Lorde, Audre (Geraldine)

Dominique
See Proust, (Valentin-Louis-George-Eugene-)
Marcel

Don, A
See Stephen, Leslie

Donaldson, Stephen R. 1947-....... **CLC 46**
See also CA 89-92; CANR 13; DAM POP;
INT CANR-13

Donleavy, J(ames) P(atrick)
1926- .... **CLC 1, 4, 6, 10, 45**
See also AITN 2; CA 9-12R; CANR 24, 49;
DLB 6; INT CANR-24; MTCW

Donne, John
1572-1631 .... **LC 10, 24; DA; DAB;
DAC; PC 1**
See also CDBLB Before 1660; DAM MST,
POET; DLB 121, 151

Donnell, David 1939(?)-........... **CLC 34**

Donoghue, P. S.
See Hunt, E(verette) Howard, (Jr.)

Donoso (Yanez), Jose
1924- .... **CLC 4, 8, 11, 32; HLC**
See also CA 81-84; CANR 32;
DAM MULT; DLB 113; HW; MTCW

Donovan, John 1928-1992 .... **CLC 35**
See also CA 97-100; 137; CLR 3;
MAICYA; SATA 72; SATA-Brief 29

Don Roberto
See Cunninghame Graham, R(obert)
B(ontine)

Doolittle, Hilda
1886-1961 ..... **CLC 3, 8, 14, 31, 34, 73;
DA; DAC; PC 5; WLC**
See also H. D.
See also CA 97-100; CANR 35; DAM MST,
POET; DLB 4, 45; MTCW

Dorfman, Ariel 1942-.... **CLC 48, 77; HLC**
See also CA 124; 130; DAM MULT; HW;
INT 130

Dorn, Edward (Merton) 1929-... **CLC 10, 18**
See also CA 93-96; CANR 42; DLB 5;
INT 93-96

Dorsan, Luc
See Simenon, Georges (Jacques Christian)

Dorsange, Jean
See Simenon, Georges (Jacques Christian)

Dos Passos, John (Roderigo)
1896-1970 ...... **CLC 1, 4, 8, 11, 15, 25,
34, 82; DA; DAB; DAC; WLC**
See also CA 1-4R; 29-32R; CANR 3;
CDALB 1929-1941; DAM MST, NOV;
DLB 4, 9; DLBD 1; MTCW

Dossage, Jean
See Simenon, Georges (Jacques Christian)

Dostoevsky, Fedor Mikhailovich
1821-1881 ...... **NCLC 2, 7, 21, 33, 43;
DA; DAB; DAC; SSC 2; WLC**
See also DAM MST, NOV

Doughty, Charles M(ontagu)
1843-1926 .... **TCLC 27**
See also CA 115; DLB 19, 57

Douglas, Ellen .... **CLC 73**
See also Haxton, Josephine Ayres;
Williamson, Ellen Douglas

Douglas, Gavin 1475(?)-1522........ **LC 20**

Douglas, Keith 1920-1944 .... **TCLC 40**
See also DLB 27

Douglas, Leonard
See Bradbury, Ray (Douglas)

Douglas, Michael
See Crichton, (John) Michael

Douglass, Frederick
1817(?)-1895 .... **NCLC 7, 55; BLC; DA;
DAC; WLC**
See also CDALB 1640-1865; DAM MST,
MULT; DLB 1, 43, 50, 79; SATA 29

Dourado, (Waldomiro Freitas) Autran
1926- .... **CLC 23, 60**
See also CA 25-28R; CANR 34

Dourado, Waldomiro Autran
See Dourado, (Waldomiro Freitas) Autran

Dove, Rita (Frances)
1952- .... **CLC 50, 81; PC 6**
See also BW 2; CA 109; CAAS 19;
CANR 27, 42; DAM MULT, POET;
DLB 120

Dowell, Coleman 1925-1985........ **CLC 60**
See also CA 25-28R; 117; CANR 10;
DLB 130

Dowson, Ernest (Christopher)
1867-1900 .... **TCLC 4**
See also CA 105; 150; DLB 19, 135

Doyle, A. Conan
See Doyle, Arthur Conan

Doyle, Arthur Conan
1859-1930 .... **TCLC 7; DA; DAB;
DAC; SSC 12; WLC**
See also AAYA 14; CA 104; 122;
CDBLB 1890-1914; DAM MST, NOV;
DLB 18, 70, 156; MTCW; SATA 24

Doyle, Conan
See Doyle, Arthur Conan

Doyle, John
See Graves, Robert (von Ranke)

Doyle, Roddy 1958(?)-............ **CLC 81**
See also AAYA 14; CA 143

Doyle, Sir A. Conan
See Doyle, Arthur Conan

Doyle, Sir Arthur Conan
See Doyle, Arthur Conan

Dr. A
See Asimov, Isaac; Silverstein, Alvin

Drabble, Margaret
1939- .... **CLC 2, 3, 5, 8, 10, 22, 53;
DAB; DAC**
See also CA 13-16R; CANR 18, 35;
CDBLB 1960 to Present; DAM MST,
NOV, POP; DLB 14, 155; MTCW;
SATA 48

Drapier, M. B.
See Swift, Jonathan

Drayham, James
See Mencken, H(enry) L(ouis)

Drayton, Michael 1563-1631........ **LC 8**

Dreadstone, Carl
See Campbell, (John) Ramsey

Dreiser, Theodore (Herman Albert)
1871-1945 .... **TCLC 10, 18, 35; DA;
DAC; WLC**
See also CA 106; 132; CDALB 1865-1917;
DAM MST, NOV; DLB 9, 12, 102, 137;
DLBD 1; MTCW

Drexler, Rosalyn 1926- .... **CLC 2, 6**
See also CA 81-84

Dreyer, Carl Theodor 1889-1968.... **CLC 16**
See also CA 116

Drieu la Rochelle, Pierre(-Eugene)
1893-1945 .... **TCLC 21**
See also CA 117; DLB 72

Drinkwater, John 1882-1937...... **TCLC 57**
See also CA 109; 149; DLB 10, 19, 149

Drop Shot
See Cable, George Washington

Droste-Hulshoff, Annette Freiin von
1797-1848 .... **NCLC 3**
See also DLB 133

Drummond, Walter
See Silverberg, Robert

Drummond, William Henry
1854-1907 .... **TCLC 25**
See also DLB 92

Drummond de Andrade, Carlos
1902-1987 .... **CLC 18**
See also Andrade, Carlos Drummond de
See also CA 132; 123

Drury, Allen (Stuart) 1918-........ **CLC 37**
See also CA 57-60; CANR 18;
INT CANR-18

Dryden, John
1631-1700 .... **LC 3, 21; DA; DAB;**
DAC; DC 3; WLC
See also CDBLB 1660-1789; DAM DRAM,
MST, POET; DLB 80, 101, 131

Duberman, Martin 1930-.......... **CLC 8**
See also CA 1-4R; CANR 2

Dubie, Norman (Evans) 1945-...... **CLC 36**
See also CA 69-72; CANR 12; DLB 120

Du Bois, W(illiam) E(dward) B(urghardt)
1868-1963 ...... **CLC 1, 2, 13, 64; BLC;**
DA; DAC; WLC
See also BW 1; CA 85-88; CANR 34;
CDALB 1865-1917; DAM MST, MULT,
NOV; DLB 47, 50, 91; MTCW; SATA 42

Dubus, Andre 1936-... **CLC 13, 36; SSC 15**
See also CA 21-24R; CANR 17; DLB 130;
INT CANR-17

Duca Minimo
See D'Annunzio, Gabriele

Ducharme, Rejean 1941-.......... **CLC 74**
See also DLB 60

Duclos, Charles Pinot 1704-1772 ..... **LC 1**

Dudek, Louis 1918- .... **CLC 11, 19**
See also CA 45-48; CAAS 14; CANR 1;
DLB 88

Duerrenmatt, Friedrich
1921-1990 ...... **CLC 1, 4, 8, 11, 15, 43**
See also CA 17-20R; CANR 33;
DAM DRAM; DLB 69, 124; MTCW

Duffy, Bruce (?)-................ **CLC 50**

Duffy, Maureen 1933- .... **CLC 37**
See also CA 25-28R; CANR 33; DLB 14;
MTCW

Dugan, Alan 1923- .... **CLC 2, 6**
See also CA 81-84; DLB 5

du Gard, Roger Martin
See Martin du Gard, Roger

Duhamel, Georges 1884-1966 .... **CLC 8**
See also CA 81-84; 25-28R; CANR 35;
DLB 65; MTCW

Dujardin, Edouard (Emile Louis)
1861-1949 .... **TCLC 13**
See also CA 109; DLB 123

Dumas, Alexandre (Davy de la Pailleterie)
1802-1870 .... **NCLC 11; DA; DAB;**
DAC; WLC
See also DAM MST, NOV; DLB 119;
SATA 18

Dumas, Alexandre
1824-1895 .... **NCLC 9; DC 1**

Dumas, Claudine
See Malzberg, Barry N(athaniel)

Dumas, Henry L. 1934-1968 ..... **CLC 6, 62**
See also BW 1; CA 85-88; DLB 41

du Maurier, Daphne
1907-1989 .... **CLC 6, 11, 59; DAB;**
DAC; SSC 18
See also CA 5-8R; 128; CANR 6;
DAM MST, POP; MTCW; SATA 27;
SATA-Obit 60

Dunbar, Paul Laurence
1872-1906 ...... **TCLC 2, 12; BLC; DA;**
DAC; PC 5; SSC 8; WLC
See also BW 1; CA 104; 124;
CDALB 1865-1917; DAM MST, MULT,
POET; DLB 50, 54, 78; SATA 34

Dunbar, William 1460(?)-1530(?) .... **LC 20**
See also DLB 132, 146

Duncan, Lois 1934-............... **CLC 26**
See also AAYA 4; CA 1-4R; CANR 2, 23,
36; CLR 29; JRDA; MAICYA; SAAS 2;
SATA 1, 36, 75

Duncan, Robert (Edward)
1919-1988 .... **CLC 1, 2, 4, 7, 15, 41, 55;**
PC 2
See also CA 9-12R; 124; CANR 28;
DAM POET; DLB 5, 16; MTCW

Duncan, Sara Jeannette
1861-1922 .... **TCLC 60**
See also DLB 92

Dunlap, William 1766-1839 .... **NCLC 2**
See also DLB 30, 37, 59

Dunn, Douglas (Eaglesham)
1942- .... **CLC 6, 40**
See also CA 45-48; CANR 2, 33; DLB 40;
MTCW

Dunn, Katherine (Karen) 1945-..... **CLC 71**
See also CA 33-36R

Dunn, Stephen 1939- .... **CLC 36**
See also CA 33-36R; CANR 12, 48;
DLB 105

Dunne, Finley Peter 1867-1936.... **TCLC 28**
See also CA 108; DLB 11, 23

Dunne, John Gregory 1932-........ **CLC 28**
See also CA 25-28R; CANR 14, 50;
DLBY 80

Dunsany, Edward John Moreton Drax
Plunkett 1878-1957
See Dunsany, Lord
See also CA 104; 148; DLB 10

Dunsany, Lord................. **TCLC 2, 59**
See also Dunsany, Edward John Moreton
Drax Plunkett
See also DLB 77, 153, 156

du Perry, Jean
See Simenon, Georges (Jacques Christian)

Durang, Christopher (Ferdinand)
1949- .... **CLC 27, 38**
See also CA 105; CANR 50

Duras, Marguerite
1914- ...... **CLC 3, 6, 11, 20, 34, 40, 68**
See also CA 25-28R; CANR 50; DLB 83;
MTCW

Durban, (Rosa) Pam 1947-........ **CLC 39**
See also CA 123

Durcan, Paul 1944-........... **CLC 43, 70**
See also CA 134; DAM POET

Durkheim, Emile 1858-1917 ...... **TCLC 55**

Durrell, Lawrence (George)
1912-1990 .... **CLC 1, 4, 6, 8, 13, 27, 41**
See also CA 9-12R; 132; CANR 40;
CDBLB 1945-1960; DAM NOV; DLB 15,
27; DLBY 90; MTCW

Durrenmatt, Friedrich
See Duerrenmatt, Friedrich

Dutt, Toru 1856-1877.......... **NCLC 29**

Dwight, Timothy 1752-1817...... **NCLC 13**
See also DLB 37

Dworkin, Andrea 1946- .... **CLC 43**
See also CA 77-80; CAAS 21; CANR 16,
39; INT CANR-16; MTCW

Dwyer, Deanna
See Koontz, Dean R(ay)

Dwyer, K. R.
See Koontz, Dean R(ay)

Dylan, Bob 1941-...... **CLC 3, 4, 6, 12, 77**
See also CA 41-44R; DLB 16

Eagleton, Terence (Francis) 1943-
See Eagleton, Terry
See also CA 57-60; CANR 7, 23; MTCW

Eagleton, Terry.................... **CLC 63**
See also Eagleton, Terence (Francis)

Early, Jack
See Scoppettone, Sandra

East, Michael
See West, Morris L(anglo)

Eastaway, Edward
See Thomas, (Philip) Edward

Eastlake, William (Derry) 1917-..... **CLC 8**
See also CA 5-8R; CAAS 1; CANR 5;
DLB 6; INT CANR-5

Eastman, Charles A(lexander)
1858-1939 .... **TCLC 55**
See also DAM MULT; NNAL; YABC 1

Eberhart, Richard (Ghormley)
1904-............... **CLC 3, 11, 19, 56**
See also CA 1-4R; CANR 2;
CDALB 1941-1968; DAM POET;
DLB 48; MTCW

Eberstadt, Fernanda 1960-........ **CLC 39**
See also CA 136

Echegaray (y Eizaguirre), Jose (Maria Waldo)
1832-1916 .... **TCLC 4**
See also CA 104; CANR 32; HW; MTCW

Echeverria, (Jose) Esteban (Antonino)
1805-1851 .... **NCLC 18**

Echo
See Proust, (Valentin-Louis-George-Eugene-)
Marcel

Eckert, Allan W. 1931- .... **CLC 17**
See also CA 13-16R; CANR 14, 45;
INT CANR-14; SAAS 21; SATA 29;
SATA-Brief 27

Eckhart, Meister 1260(?)-1328(?) .. **CMLC 9**
See also DLB 115

Eckmar, F. R.
See de Hartog, Jan

Eco, Umberto 1932-........... **CLC 28, 60**
See also BEST 90:1; CA 77-80; CANR 12,
33; DAM NOV, POP; MTCW

Eddison, E(ric) R(ucker)
1882-1945 .... **TCLC 15**
See also CA 109

Edel, (Joseph) Leon 1907-...... **CLC 29, 34**
See also CA 1-4R; CANR 1, 22; DLB 103;
INT CANR-22

Eden, Emily 1797-1869 .... **NCLC 10**

Edgar, David 1948-............... CLC 42
See also CA 57-60; CANR 12;
DAM DRAM; DLB 13; MTCW

Edgerton, Clyde (Carlyle) 1944- .... CLC 39
See also AAYA 17; CA 118; 134; INT 134

Edgeworth, Maria 1768-1849... NCLC 1, 51
See also DLB 116, 159, 163; SATA 21

Edmonds, Paul
See Kuttner, Henry

Edmonds, Walter D(umaux) 1903- .. CLC 35
See also CA 5-8R; CANR 2; DLB 9;
MAICYA; SAAS 4; SATA 1, 27

Edmondson, Wallace
See Ellison, Harlan (Jay)

Edson, Russell.................... CLC 13
See also CA 33-36R

Edwards, Bronwen Elizabeth
See Rose, Wendy

Edwards, G(erald) B(asil)
1899-1976 .... CLC 25
See also CA 110

Edwards, Gus 1939- .... CLC 43
See also CA 108; INT 108

Edwards, Jonathan
1703-1758 .... LC 7; DA; DAC
See also DAM MST; DLB 24

Efron, Marina Ivanovna Tsvetaeva
See Tsvetaeva (Efron), Marina (Ivanovna)

Ehle, John (Marsden, Jr.) 1925- .... CLC 27
See also CA 9-12R

Ehrenbourg, Ilya (Grigoryevich)
See Ehrenburg, Ilya (Grigoryevich)

Ehrenburg, Ilya (Grigoryevich)
1891-1967 .... CLC 18, 34, 62
See also CA 102; 25-28R

Ehrenburg, Ilyo (Grigoryevich)
See Ehrenburg, Ilya (Grigoryevich)

Eich, Guenter 1907-1972 .... CLC 15
See also CA 111; 93-96; DLB 69, 124

Eichendorff, Joseph Freiherr von
1788-1857 .... NCLC 8
See also DLB 90

Eigner, Larry..................... CLC 9
See also Eigner, Laurence (Joel)
See also CAAS 23; DLB 5

Eigner, Laurence (Joel) 1927-1996
See Eigner, Larry
See also CA 9-12R; CANR 6

Eiseley, Loren Corey 1907-1977 ..... CLC 7
See also AAYA 5; CA 1-4R; 73-76;
CANR 6

Eisenstadt, Jill 1963- .... CLC 50
See also CA 140

Eisenstein, Sergei (Mikhailovich)
1898-1948 .... TCLC 57
See also CA 114; 149

Eisner, Simon
See Kornbluth, C(yril) M.

Ekeloef, (Bengt) Gunnar
1907-1968 .... CLC 27
See also CA 123; 25-28R; DAM POET

Ekelof, (Bengt) Gunnar
See Ekeloef, (Bengt) Gunnar

Ekwensi, C. O. D.
See Ekwensi, Cyprian (Odiatu Duaka)

Ekwensi, Cyprian (Odiatu Duaka)
1921- .... CLC 4; BLC
See also BW 2; CA 29-32R; CANR 18, 42;
DAM MULT; DLB 117; MTCW;
SATA 66

Elaine........................ TCLC 18
See also Leverson, Ada

El Crummo
See Crumb, R(obert)

Elia
See Lamb, Charles

Eliade, Mircea 1907-1986 .... CLC 19
See also CA 65-68; 119; CANR 30; MTCW

Eliot, A. D.
See Jewett, (Theodora) Sarah Orne

Eliot, Alice
See Jewett, (Theodora) Sarah Orne

Eliot, Dan
See Silverberg, Robert

Eliot, George
1819-1880 ..... NCLC 4, 13, 23, 41, 49;
DA; DAB; DAC; WLC
See also CDBLB 1832-1890; DAM MST,
NOV; DLB 21, 35, 55

Eliot, John 1604-1690 .... LC 5
See also DLB 24

Eliot, T(homas) S(tearns)
1888-1965 ..... CLC 1, 2, 3, 6, 9, 10, 13,
15, 24, 34, 41, 55, 57; DA; DAB; DAC;
PC 5; WLC 2
See also CA 5-8R; 25-28R; CANR 41;
CDALB 1929-1941; DAM DRAM, MST,
POET; DLB 7, 10, 45, 63; DLBY 88;
MTCW

Elizabeth 1866-1941............. TCLC 41

Elkin, Stanley L(awrence)
1930-1995 ...... CLC 4, 6, 9, 14, 27, 51,
91; SSC 12
See also CA 9-12R; 148; CANR 8, 46;
DAM NOV, POP; DLB 2, 28; DLBY 80;
INT CANR-8; MTCW

Elledge, Scott.................... CLC 34

Elliott, Don
See Silverberg, Robert

Elliott, George P(aul) 1918-1980..... CLC 2
See also CA 1-4R; 97-100; CANR 2

Elliott, Janice 1931-.............. CLC 47
See also CA 13-16R; CANR 8, 29; DLB 14

Elliott, Sumner Locke 1917-1991 ... CLC 38
See also CA 5-8R; 134; CANR 2, 21

Elliott, William
See Bradbury, Ray (Douglas)

Ellis, A. E....................... CLC 7

Ellis, Alice Thomas............... CLC 40
See also Haycraft, Anna

Ellis, Bret Easton 1964-........ CLC 39, 71
See also AAYA 2; CA 118; 123; CANR 51;
DAM POP; INT 123

Ellis, (Henry) Havelock
1859-1939 .... TCLC 14
See also CA 109

Ellis, Landon
See Ellison, Harlan (Jay)

Ellis, Trey 1962-................. CLC 55
See also CA 146

Ellison, Harlan (Jay)
1934- .... CLC 1, 13, 42; SSC 14
See also CA 5-8R; CANR 5, 46;
DAM POP; DLB 8; INT CANR-5;
MTCW

Ellison, Ralph (Waldo)
1914-1994 .... CLC 1, 3, 11, 54, 86;
BLC; DA; DAB; DAC; WLC
See also BW 1; CA 9-12R; 145; CANR 24;
CDALB 1941-1968; DAM MST, MULT,
NOV; DLB 2, 76; DLBY 94; MTCW

Ellmann, Lucy (Elizabeth) 1956-.... CLC 61
See also CA 128

Ellmann, Richard (David)
1918-1987 .... CLC 50
See also BEST 89:2; CA 1-4R; 122;
CANR 2, 28; DLB 103; DLBY 87;
MTCW

Elman, Richard 1934-............. CLC 19
See also CA 17-20R; CAAS 3; CANR 47

Elron
See Hubbard, L(afayette) Ron(ald)

Eluard, Paul................. TCLC 7, 41
See also Grindel, Eugene

Elyot, Sir Thomas 1490(?)-1546 ..... LC 11

Elytis, Odysseus 1911-......... CLC 15, 49
See also CA 102; DAM POET; MTCW

Emecheta, (Florence Onye) Buchi
1944- .... CLC 14, 48; BLC
See also BW 2; CA 81-84; CANR 27;
DAM MULT; DLB 117; MTCW;
SATA 66

Emerson, Ralph Waldo
1803-1882 ..... NCLC 1, 38; DA; DAB;
DAC; WLC
See also CDALB 1640-1865; DAM MST,
POET; DLB 1, 59, 73

Eminescu, Mihail 1850-1889 ..... NCLC 33

Empson, William
1906-1984 .... CLC 3, 8, 19, 33, 34
See also CA 17-20R; 112; CANR 31;
DLB 20; MTCW

Enchi Fumiko (Ueda) 1905-1986.... CLC 31
See also CA 129; 121

Ende, Michael (Andreas Helmuth)
1929-1995 .... CLC 31
See also CA 118; 124; 149; CANR 36;
CLR 14; DLB 75; MAICYA; SATA 61;
SATA-Brief 42; SATA-Obit 86

Endo, Shusaku 1923- ..... CLC 7, 14, 19, 54
See also CA 29-32R; CANR 21;
DAM NOV; MTCW

Engel, Marian 1933-1985.......... CLC 36
See also CA 25-28R; CANR 12; DLB 53;
INT CANR-12

Engelhardt, Frederick
See Hubbard, L(afayette) Ron(ald)

Enright, D(ennis) J(oseph)
1920- .... CLC 4, 8, 31
See also CA 1-4R; CANR 1, 42; DLB 27;
SATA 25

Enzensberger, Hans Magnus
1929- . . . . **CLC 43**
See also CA 116; 119

Ephron, Nora 1941- . . . . **CLC 17, 31**
See also AITN 2; CA 65-68; CANR 12, 39

Epsilon
See Betjeman, John

Epstein, Daniel Mark 1948- . . . . **CLC 7**
See also CA 49-52; CANR 2

Epstein, Jacob 1956- . . . . **CLC 19**
See also CA 114

Epstein, Joseph 1937- . . . . **CLC 39**
See also CA 112; 119; CANR 50

Epstein, Leslie 1938- . . . . **CLC 27**
See also CA 73-76; CAAS 12; CANR 23

Equiano, Olaudah
1745(?)-1797 . . . . **LC 16; BLC**
See also DAM MULT; DLB 37, 50

Erasmus, Desiderius 1469(?)-1536. . . . **LC 16**

Erdman, Paul E(mil) 1932- . . . . **CLC 25**
See also AITN 1; CA 61-64; CANR 13, 43

Erdrich, Louise 1954- . . . . **CLC 39, 54**
See also AAYA 10; BEST 89:1; CA 114;
CANR 41; DAM MULT, NOV, POP;
DLB 152; MTCW; NNAL

Erenburg, Ilya (Grigoryevich)
See Ehrenburg, Ilya (Grigoryevich)

Erickson, Stephen Michael 1950-
See Erickson, Steve
See also CA 129

Erickson, Steve . . . . **CLC 64**
See also Erickson, Stephen Michael

Ericson, Walter
See Fast, Howard (Melvin)

Eriksson, Buntel
See Bergman, (Ernst) Ingmar

Ernaux, Annie 1940- . . . . **CLC 88**
See also CA 147

Eschenbach, Wolfram von
See Wolfram von Eschenbach

Eseki, Bruno
See Mphahlele, Ezekiel

Esenin, Sergei (Alexandrovich)
1895-1925 . . . . **TCLC 4**
See also CA 104

Eshleman, Clayton 1935- . . . . **CLC 7**
See also CA 33-36R; CAAS 6; DLB 5

Espriella, Don Manuel Alvarez
See Southey, Robert

Espriu, Salvador 1913-1985 . . . . **CLC 9**
See also CA 115; DLB 134

Espronceda, Jose de 1808-1842 . . . **NCLC 39**

Esse, James
See Stephens, James

Esterbrook, Tom
See Hubbard, L(afayette) Ron(ald)

Estleman, Loren D. 1952- . . . . **CLC 48**
See also CA 85-88; CANR 27; DAM NOV,
POP; INT CANR-27; MTCW

Eugenides, Jeffrey 1960(?)- . . . . **CLC 81**
See also CA 144

Euripides c. 485B.C.-406B.C. . . . . **DC 4**
See also DA; DAB; DAC; DAM DRAM,
MST

Evan, Evin
See Faust, Frederick (Schiller)

Evans, Evan
See Faust, Frederick (Schiller)

Evans, Marian
See Eliot, George

Evans, Mary Ann
See Eliot, George

Evarts, Esther
See Benson, Sally

Everett, Percival L. 1956- . . . . **CLC 57**
See also BW 2; CA 129

Everson, R(onald) G(ilmour)
1903- . . . . **CLC 27**
See also CA 17-20R; DLB 88

Everson, William (Oliver)
1912-1994 . . . . **CLC 1, 5, 14**
See also CA 9-12R; 145; CANR 20; DLB 5,
16; MTCW

Evtushenko, Evgenii Aleksandrovich
See Yevtushenko, Yevgeny (Alexandrovich)

Ewart, Gavin (Buchanan)
1916-1995 . . . . **CLC 13, 46**
See also CA 89-92; 150; CANR 17, 46;
DLB 40; MTCW

Ewers, Hanns Heinz 1871-1943 . . . **TCLC 12**
See also CA 109; 149

Ewing, Frederick R.
See Sturgeon, Theodore (Hamilton)

Exley, Frederick (Earl)
1929-1992 . . . . **CLC 6, 11**
See also AITN 2; CA 81-84; 138; DLB 143;
DLBY 81

Eynhardt, Guillermo
See Quiroga, Horacio (Sylvestre)

Ezekiel, Nissim 1924- . . . . **CLC 61**
See also CA 61-64

Ezekiel, Tish O'Dowd 1943- . . . . **CLC 34**
See also CA 129

Fadeyev, A.
See Bulgya, Alexander Alexandrovich

Fadeyev, Alexander . . . . **TCLC 53**
See also Bulgya, Alexander Alexandrovich

Fagen, Donald 1948- . . . . **CLC 26**

Fainzilberg, Ilya Arnoldovich 1897-1937
See Ilf, Ilya
See also CA 120

Fair, Ronald L. 1932- . . . . **CLC 18**
See also BW 1; CA 69-72; CANR 25;
DLB 33

Fairbairns, Zoe (Ann) 1948- . . . . **CLC 32**
See also CA 103; CANR 21

Falco, Gian
See Papini, Giovanni

Falconer, James
See Kirkup, James

Falconer, Kenneth
See Kornbluth, C(yril) M.

Falkland, Samuel
See Heijermans, Herman

Fallaci, Oriana 1930- . . . . **CLC 11**
See also CA 77-80; CANR 15; MTCW

Faludy, George 1913- . . . . **CLC 42**
See also CA 21-24R

Faludy, Gyoergy
See Faludy, George

Fanon, Frantz 1925-1961 . . . . . **CLC 74; BLC**
See also BW 1; CA 116; 89-92;
DAM MULT

Fanshawe, Ann 1625-1680 . . . . **LC 11**

Fante, John (Thomas) 1911-1983 . . . **CLC 60**
See also CA 69-72; 109; CANR 23;
DLB 130; DLBY 83

Farah, Nuruddin 1945- . . . . **CLC 53; BLC**
See also BW 2; CA 106; DAM MULT;
DLB 125

Fargue, Leon-Paul 1876(?)-1947 . . . **TCLC 11**
See also CA 109

Farigoule, Louis
See Romains, Jules

Farina, Richard 1936(?)-1966 . . . . **CLC 9**
See also CA 81-84; 25-28R

Farley, Walter (Lorimer)
1915-1989 . . . . **CLC 17**
See also CA 17-20R; CANR 8, 29; DLB 22;
JRDA; MAICYA; SATA 2, 43

Farmer, Philip Jose 1918- . . . . **CLC 1, 19**
See also CA 1-4R; CANR 4, 35; DLB 8;
MTCW

Farquhar, George 1677-1707 . . . . **LC 21**
See also DAM DRAM; DLB 84

Farrell, J(ames) G(ordon)
1935-1979 . . . . **CLC 6**
See also CA 73-76; 89-92; CANR 36;
DLB 14; MTCW

Farrell, James T(homas)
1904-1979 . . . . **CLC 1, 4, 8, 11, 66**
See also CA 5-8R; 89-92; CANR 9; DLB 4,
9, 86; DLBD 2; MTCW

Farren, Richard J.
See Betjeman, John

Farren, Richard M.
See Betjeman, John

Fassbinder, Rainer Werner
1946-1982 . . . . **CLC 20**
See also CA 93-96; 106; CANR 31

Fast, Howard (Melvin) 1914- . . . . . . **CLC 23**
See also AAYA 16; CA 1-4R; CAAS 18;
CANR 1, 33; DAM NOV; DLB 9;
INT CANR-33; SATA 7

Faulcon, Robert
See Holdstock, Robert P.

Faulkner, William (Cuthbert)
1897-1962 . . . . . **CLC 1, 3, 6, 8, 9, 11, 14,
18, 28, 52, 68; DA; DAB; DAC; SSC 1;
WLC**
See also AAYA 7; CA 81-84; CANR 33;
CDALB 1929-1941; DAM MST, NOV;
DLB 9, 11, 44, 102; DLBD 2; DLBY 86;
MTCW

Fauset, Jessie Redmon
1884(?)-1961 . . . . **CLC 19, 54; BLC**
See also BW 1; CA 109; DAM MULT;
DLB 51

Follett, Ken(neth Martin) 1949- .... **CLC 18**
See also AAYA 6; BEST 89:4; CA 81-84;
CANR 13, 33; DAM NOV, POP;
DLB 87; DLBY 81; INT CANR-33;
MTCW

Fontane, Theodor 1819-1898 .... **NCLC 26**
See also DLB 129

Foote, Horton 1916- .... **CLC 51, 91**
See also CA 73-76; CANR 34, 51;
DAM DRAM; DLB 26; INT CANR-34

Foote, Shelby 1916- .... **CLC 75**
See also CA 5-8R; CANR 3, 45;
DAM NOV, POP; DLB 2, 17

Forbes, Esther 1891-1967 .... **CLC 12**
See also AAYA 17; CA 13-14; 25-28R;
CAP 1; CLR 27; DLB 22; JRDA;
MAICYA; SATA 2

Forche, Carolyn (Louise)
1950- .... **CLC 25, 83, 86; PC 10**
See also CA 109; 117; CANR 50;
DAM POET; DLB 5; INT 117

Ford, Elbur
See Hibbert, Eleanor Alice Burford

Ford, Ford Madox
1873-1939 .... **TCLC 1, 15, 39, 57**
See also CA 104; 132; CDBLB 1914-1945;
DAM NOV; DLB 162; MTCW

Ford, John 1895-1973 .... **CLC 16**
See also CA 45-48

Ford, Richard 1944- .... **CLC 46**
See also CA 69-72; CANR 11, 47

Ford, Webster
See Masters, Edgar Lee

Foreman, Richard 1937- .... **CLC 50**
See also CA 65-68; CANR 32

Forester, C(ecil) S(cott)
1899-1966 .... **CLC 35**
See also CA 73-76; 25-28R; SATA 13

Forez
See Mauriac, Francois (Charles)

Forman, James Douglas 1932- ...... **CLC 21**
See also AAYA 17; CA 9-12R; CANR 4,
19, 42; JRDA; MAICYA; SATA 8, 70

Fornes, Maria Irene 1930- ..... **CLC 39, 61**
See also CA 25-28R; CANR 28; DLB 7;
HW; INT CANR-28; MTCW

Forrest, Leon 1937- .... **CLC 4**
See also BW 2; CA 89-92; CAAS 7;
CANR 25; DLB 33

Forster, E(dward) M(organ)
1879-1970 ..... **CLC 1, 2, 3, 4, 9, 10, 13,
15, 22, 45, 77; DA; DAB; DAC; WLC**
See also AAYA 2; CA 13-14; 25-28R;
CANR 45; CAP 1; CDBLB 1914-1945;
DAM MST; DLB 34, 98, 162;
DLBD 10; MTCW; SATA 57

Forster, John 1812-1876 .... **NCLC 11**
See also DLB 144

Forsyth, Frederick 1938- ...... **CLC 2, 5, 36**
See also BEST 89:4; CA 85-88; CANR 38;
DAM NOV, POP; DLB 87; MTCW

Forten, Charlotte L. .... **TCLC 16; BLC**
See also Grimke, Charlotte L(ottie) Forten
See also DLB 50

Foscolo, Ugo 1778-1827 .... **NCLC 8**

Fosse, Bob .... **CLC 20**
See also Fosse, Robert Louis

Fosse, Robert Louis 1927-1987
See Fosse, Bob
See also CA 110; 123

Foster, Stephen Collins
1826-1864 .... **NCLC 26**

Foucault, Michel
1926-1984 .... **CLC 31, 34, 69**
See also CA 105; 113; CANR 34; MTCW

Fouque, Friedrich (Heinrich Karl) de la Motte
1777-1843 .... **NCLC 2**
See also DLB 90

Fourier, Charles 1772-1837 ...... **NCLC 51**

Fournier, Henri Alban 1886-1914
See Alain-Fournier
See also CA 104

Fournier, Pierre 1916- .... **CLC 11**
See also Gascar, Pierre
See also CA 89-92; CANR 16, 40

Fowles, John
1926- ...... **CLC 1, 2, 3, 4, 6, 9, 10, 15,
33, 87; DAB; DAC**
See also CA 5-8R; CANR 25; CDBLB 1960
to Present; DAM MST; DLB 14, 139;
MTCW; SATA 22

Fox, Paula 1923- .... **CLC 2, 8**
See also AAYA 3; CA 73-76; CANR 20,
36; CLR 1; DLB 52; JRDA; MAICYA;
MTCW; SATA 17, 60

Fox, William Price (Jr.) 1926- ..... **CLC 22**
See also CA 17-20R; CAAS 19; CANR 11;
DLB 2; DLBY 81

Foxe, John 1516(?)-1587 .... **LC 14**

Frame, Janet .... **CLC 2, 3, 6, 22, 66**
See also Clutha, Janet Paterson Frame

Francc, Anatole .... **TCLC 9**
See also Thibault, Jacques Anatole Francois
See also DLB 123

Francis, Claude 19(?)- .... **CLC 50**

Francis, Dick 1920- .... **CLC 2, 22, 42**
See also AAYA 5; BEST 89:3; CA 5-8R;
CANR 9, 42; CDBLB 1960 to Present;
DAM POP; DLB 87; INT CANR-9;
MTCW

Francis, Robert (Churchill)
1901-1987 .... **CLC 15**
See also CA 1-4R; 123; CANR 1

Frank, Anne(lies Marie)
1929-1945 .... **TCLC 17; DA; DAB;
DAC; WLC**
See also AAYA 12; CA 113; 133;
DAM MST; MTCW; SATA 87;
SATA-Brief 42

Frank, Elizabeth 1945- .... **CLC 39**
See also CA 121; 126; INT 126

Franklin, Benjamin
See Hasek, Jaroslav (Matej Frantisek)

Franklin, Benjamin
1706-1790 ..... **LC 25; DA; DAB; DAC**
See also CDALB 1640-1865; DAM MST;
DLB 24, 43, 73

Franklin, (Stella Maraia Sarah) Miles
1879-1954 .... **TCLC 7**
See also CA 104

Fraser, (Lady) Antonia (Pakenham)
1932- .... **CLC 32**
See also CA 85-88; CANR 44; MTCW;
SATA-Brief 32

Fraser, George MacDonald 1925- .... **CLC 7**
See also CA 45-48; CANR 2, 48

Fraser, Sylvia 1935- .... **CLC 64**
See also CA 45-48; CANR 1, 16

Frayn, Michael 1933- ...... **CLC 3, 7, 31, 47**
See also CA 5-8R; CANR 30;
DAM DRAM, NOV; DLB 13, 14;
MTCW

Fraze, Candida (Merrill) 1945- ..... **CLC 50**
See also CA 126

Frazer, J(ames) G(eorge)
1854-1941 .... **TCLC 32**
See also CA 118

Frazer, Robert Caine
See Creasey, John

Frazer, Sir James George
See Frazer, J(ames) G(eorge)

Frazier, Ian 1951- .... **CLC 46**
See also CA 130

Frederic, Harold 1856-1898 ...... **NCLC 10**
See also DLB 12, 23; DLBD 13

Frederick, John
See Faust, Frederick (Schiller)

Frederick the Great 1712-1786 ...... **LC 14**

Fredro, Aleksander 1793-1876 ..... **NCLC 8**

Freeling, Nicolas 1927- .... **CLC 38**
See also CA 49-52; CAAS 12; CANR 1, 17,
50; DLB 87

Freeman, Douglas Southall
1886-1953 .... **TCLC 11**
See also CA 109; DLB 17

Freeman, Judith 1946- .... **CLC 55**
See also CA 148

Freeman, Mary Eleanor Wilkins
1852-1930 .... **TCLC 9; SSC 1**
See also CA 106; DLB 12, 78

Freeman, R(ichard) Austin
1862-1943 .... **TCLC 21**
See also CA 113; DLB 70

French, Albert 1943- .... **CLC 86**

French, Marilyn 1929- ...... **CLC 10, 18, 60**
See also CA 69-72; CANR 3, 31;
DAM DRAM, NOV, POP;
INT CANR-31; MTCW

French, Paul
See Asimov, Isaac

Freneau, Philip Morin 1752-1832 .. **NCLC 1**
See also DLB 37, 43

Freud, Sigmund 1856-1939 .... **TCLC 52**
See also CA 115; 133; MTCW

Friedan, Betty (Naomi) 1921- ...... **CLC 74**
See also CA 65-68; CANR 18, 45; MTCW

Friedlaender, Saul 1932- .... **CLC 90**
See also CA 117; 130

Friedman, B(ernard) H(arper)
1926- .... **CLC 7**
See also CA 1-4R; CANR 3, 48

Friedman, Bruce Jay 1930- .... **CLC 3, 5, 56**
See also CA 9-12R; CANR 25; DLB 2, 28;
INT CANR-25

Friel, Brian 1929-. . . . . CLC 5, 42, 59
See also CA 21-24R; CANR 33; DLB 13;
MTCW

Friis-Baastad, Babbis Ellinor
1921-1970 . . . . CLC 12
See also CA 17-20R; 134; SATA 7

Frisch, Max (Rudolf)
1911-1991 . . . . . CLC 3, 9, 14, 18, 32, 44
See also CA 85-88; 134; CANR 32;
DAM DRAM, NOV; DLB 69, 124;
MTCW

Fromentin, Eugene (Samuel Auguste)
1820-1876 . . . . NCLC 10
See also DLB 123

Frost, Frederick
See Faust, Frederick (Schiller)

Frost, Robert (Lee)
1874-1963 . . . . CLC 1, 3, 4, 9, 10, 13, 15,
26, 34, 44; DA; DAB; DAC; PC 1; WLC
See also CA 89-92; CANR 33;
CDALB 1917-1929; DAM MST, POET;
DLB 54; DLBD 7; MTCW; SATA 14

Froude, James Anthony
1818-1894 . . . . NCLC 43
See also DLB 18, 57, 144

Froy, Herald
See Waterhouse, Keith (Spencer)

Fry, Christopher 1907-. . . . . . . CLC 2, 10, 14
See also CA 17-20R; CAAS 23; CANR 9,
30; DAM DRAM; DLB 13; MTCW;
SATA 66

Frye, (Herman) Northrop
1912-1991 . . . . CLC 24, 70
See also CA 5-8R; 133; CANR 8, 37;
DLB 67, 68; MTCW

Fuchs, Daniel 1909-1993 . . . . CLC 8, 22
See also CA 81-84; 142; CAAS 5;
CANR 40; DLB 9, 26, 28; DLBY 93

Fuchs, Daniel 1934-. . . . . CLC 34
See also CA 37-40R; CANR 14, 48

Fuentes, Carlos
1928-. . . . . . CLC 3, 8, 10, 13, 22, 41, 60;
DA; DAB; DAC; HLC; WLC
See also AAYA 4; AITN 2; CA 69-72;
CANR 10, 32; DAM MST, MULT,
NOV; DLB 113; HW; MTCW

Fuentes, Gregorio Lopez y
See Lopez y Fuentes, Gregorio

Fugard, (Harold) Athol
1932-. . . . CLC 5, 9, 14, 25, 40, 80; DC 3
See also AAYA 17; CA 85-88; CANR 32;
DAM DRAM; MTCW

Fugard, Sheila 1932- . . . . CLC 48
See also CA 125

Fuller, Charles (H., Jr.)
1939-. . . . . CLC 25; BLC; DC 1
See also BW 2; CA 108; 112;
DAM DRAM, MULT; DLB 38;
INT 112; MTCW

Fuller, John (Leopold) 1937-. . . . . . . CLC 62
See also CA 21-24R; CANR 9, 44; DLB 40

Fuller, Margaret . . . . NCLC 5, 50
See also Ossoli, Sarah Margaret (Fuller
marchesa d')

Fuller, Roy (Broadbent)
1912-1991 . . . . CLC 4, 28
See also CA 5-8R; 135; CAAS 10; DLB 15,
20; SATA 87

Fulton, Alice 1952-. . . . . CLC 52
See also CA 116

Furphy, Joseph 1843-1912. . . . . . . TCLC 25

Fussell, Paul 1924-. . . . . CLC 74
See also BEST 90:1; CA 17-20R; CANR 8,
21, 35; INT CANR-21; MTCW

Futabatei, Shimei 1864-1909. . . . . . TCLC 44

Futrelle, Jacques 1875-1912 . . . . . TCLC 19
See also CA 113

Gaboriau, Emile 1835-1873 . . . . . . NCLC 14

Gadda, Carlo Emilio 1893-1973 . . . . CLC 11
See also CA 89-92

Gaddis, William
1922- . . . . . CLC 1, 3, 6, 8, 10, 19, 43, 86
See also CA 17-20R; CANR 21, 48; DLB 2;
MTCW

Gaines, Ernest J(ames)
1933-. . . . . CLC 3, 11, 18, 86; BLC
See also AITN 1; BW 2; CA 9-12R;
CANR 6, 24, 42; CDALB 1968-1988;
DAM MULT; DLB 2, 33, 152; DLBY 80;
MTCW; SATA 86

Gaitskill, Mary 1954-. . . . . CLC 69
See also CA 128

Galdos, Benito Perez
See Perez Galdos, Benito

Gale, Zona 1874-1938 . . . . TCLC 7
See also CA 105; DAM DRAM; DLB 9, 78

Galeano, Eduardo (Hughes) 1940-. . . CLC 72
See also CA 29-32R; CANR 13, 32; HW

Galiano, Juan Valera y Alcala
See Valera y Alcala-Galiano, Juan

Gallagher, Tess 1943-. . . . CLC 18, 63; PC 9
See also CA 106; DAM POET; DLB 120

Gallant, Mavis
1922- . . . . . . CLC 7, 18, 38; DAC; SSC 5
See also CA 69-72; CANR 29; DAM MST;
DLB 53; MTCW

Gallant, Roy A(rthur) 1924- . . . . CLC 17
See also CA 5-8R; CANR 4, 29; CLR 30;
MAICYA; SATA 4, 68

Gallico, Paul (William) 1897-1976 . . . CLC 2
See also AITN 1; CA 5-8R; 69-72;
CANR 23; DLB 9; MAICYA; SATA 13

Gallup, Ralph
See Whitemore, Hugh (John)

Galsworthy, John
1867-1933 . . . . . TCLC 1, 45; DA; DAB;
DAC; SSC 22; WLC 2
See also CA 104; 141; CDBLB 1890-1914;
DAM DRAM, MST, NOV; DLB 10, 34,
98, 162

Galt, John 1779-1839. . . . . NCLC 1
See also DLB 99, 116, 159

Galvin, James 1951-. . . . . CLC 38
See also CA 108; CANR 26

Gamboa, Federico 1864-1939. . . . . . TCLC 36

Gandhi, M. K.
See Gandhi, Mohandas Karamchand

Gandhi, Mahatma
See Gandhi, Mohandas Karamchand

Gandhi, Mohandas Karamchand
1869-1948 . . . . TCLC 59
See also CA 121; 132; DAM MULT;
MTCW

Gann, Ernest Kellogg 1910-1991. . . . CLC 23
See also AITN 1; CA 1-4R; 136; CANR 1

Garcia, Cristina 1958- . . . . CLC 76
See also CA 141

Garcia Lorca, Federico
1898-1936 . . . TCLC 1, 7, 49; DA; DAB;
DAC; DC 2; HLC; PC 3; WLC
See also CA 104; 131; DAM DRAM, MST,
MULT, POET; DLB 108; HW; MTCW

Garcia Marquez, Gabriel (Jose)
1928-. . . . CLC 2, 3, 8, 10, 15, 27, 47, 55,
68; DA; DAB; DAC; HLC; SSC 8; WLC
See also AAYA 3; BEST 89:1, 90:4;
CA 33-36R; CANR 10, 28, 50;
DAM MST, MULT, NOV, POP;
DLB 113; HW; MTCW

Gard, Janice
See Latham, Jean Lee

Gard, Roger Martin du
See Martin du Gard, Roger

Gardam, Jane 1928-. . . . . CLC 43
See also CA 49-52; CANR 2, 18, 33;
CLR 12; DLB 14, 161; MAICYA;
MTCW; SAAS 9; SATA 39, 76;
SATA-Brief 28

Gardner, Herb(ert) 1934-. . . . . CLC 44
See also CA 149

Gardner, John (Champlin), Jr.
1933-1982 . . . . . CLC 2, 3, 5, 7, 8, 10, 18,
28, 34; SSC 7
See also AITN 1; CA 65-68; 107;
CANR 33; DAM NOV, POP; DLB 2;
DLBY 82; MTCW; SATA 40;
SATA-Obit 31

Gardner, John (Edmund) 1926-. . . . . CLC 30
See also CA 103; CANR 15; DAM POP;
MTCW

Gardner, Noel
See Kuttner, Henry

Gardons, S. S.
See Snodgrass, W(illiam) D(e Witt)

Garfield, Leon 1921-. . . . . CLC 12
See also AAYA 8; CA 17-20R; CANR 38,
41; CLR 21; DLB 161; JRDA; MAICYA;
SATA 1, 32, 76

Garland, (Hannibal) Hamlin
1860-1940 . . . . TCLC 3; SSC 18
See also CA 104; DLB 12, 71, 78

Garneau, (Hector de) Saint-Denys
1912-1943 . . . . TCLC 13
See also CA 111; DLB 88

Garner, Alan 1934-. . . . . CLC 17; DAB
See also CA 73-76; CANR 15; CLR 20;
DAM POP; DLB 161; MAICYA;
MTCW; SATA 18, 69

Garner, Hugh 1913-1979 . . . . CLC 13
See also CA 69-72; CANR 31; DLB 68

Garnett, David 1892-1981 . . . . CLC 3
See also CA 5-8R; 103; CANR 17; DLB 34

Garos, Stephanie
See Katz, Steve

Garrett, George (Palmer)
1929- .... **CLC 3, 11, 51**
See also CA 1-4R; CAAS 5; CANR 1, 42;
DLB 2, 5, 130, 152; DLBY 83

Garrick, David 1717-1779 .... **LC 15**
See also DAM DRAM; DLB 84

Garrigue, Jean 1914-1972 .... **CLC 2, 8**
See also CA 5-8R; 37-40R; CANR 20

Garrison, Frederick
See Sinclair, Upton (Beall)

Garth, Will
See Hamilton, Edmond; Kuttner, Henry

Garvey, Marcus (Moziah, Jr.)
1887-1940 .... **TCLC 41; BLC**
See also BW 1; CA 120; 124; DAM MULT

Gary, Romain .... **CLC 25**
See also Kacew, Romain
See also DLB 83

Gascar, Pierre .... **CLC 11**
See also Fournier, Pierre

Gascoyne, David (Emery) 1916- .... **CLC 45**
See also CA 65-68; CANR 10, 28; DLB 20;
MTCW

Gaskell, Elizabeth Cleghorn
1810-1865 .... **NCLC 5; DAB**
See also CDBLB 1832-1890; DAM MST;
DLB 21, 144, 159

Gass, William H(oward)
1924- ... **CLC 1, 2, 8, 11, 15, 39; SSC 12**
See also CA 17-20R; CANR 30; DLB 2;
MTCW

Gasset, Jose Ortega y
See Ortega y Gasset, Jose

Gates, Henry Louis, Jr. 1950- ...... **CLC 65**
See also BW 2; CA 109; CANR 25;
DAM MULT; DLB 67

Gautier, Theophile
1811-1872 .... **NCLC 1; SSC 20**
See also DAM POET; DLB 119

Gawsworth, John
See Bates, H(erbert) E(rnest)

Gay, Oliver
See Gogarty, Oliver St. John

Gaye, Marvin (Penze) 1939-1984 ... **CLC 26**
See also CA 112

Gebler, Carlo (Ernest) 1954- .... **CLC 39**
See also CA 119; 133

Gee, Maggie (Mary) 1948- .... **CLC 57**
See also CA 130

Gee, Maurice (Gough) 1931- .... **CLC 29**
See also CA 97-100; SATA 46

Gelbart, Larry (Simon) 1923- ... **CLC 21, 61**
See also CA 73-76; CANR 45

Gelber, Jack 1932- .... **CLC 1, 6, 14, 79**
See also CA 1-4R; CANR 2; DLB 7

Gellhorn, Martha (Ellis) 1908- .. **CLC 14, 60**
See also CA 77-80; CANR 44; DLBY 82

Genet, Jean
1910-1986 ... **CLC 1, 2, 5, 10, 14, 44, 46**
See also CA 13-16R; CANR 18;
DAM DRAM; DLB 72; DLBY 86;
MTCW

Gent, Peter 1942- .... **CLC 29**
See also AITN 1; CA 89-92; DLBY 82

Gentlewoman in New England, A
See Bradstreet, Anne

Gentlewoman in Those Parts, A
See Bradstreet, Anne

George, Jean Craighead 1919- ...... **CLC 35**
See also AAYA 8; CA 5-8R; CANR 25;
CLR 1; DLB 52; JRDA; MAICYA;
SATA 2, 68

George, Stefan (Anton)
1868-1933 .... **TCLC 2, 14**
See also CA 104

Georges, Georges Martin
See Simenon, Georges (Jacques Christian)

Gerhardi, William Alexander
See Gerhardie, William Alexander

Gerhardie, William Alexander
1895-1977 .... **CLC 5**
See also CA 25-28R; 73-76; CANR 18;
DLB 36

Gerstler, Amy 1956- .... **CLC 70**
See also CA 146

Gertler, T. .... **CLC 34**
See also CA 116; 121; INT 121

Ghalib .... **NCLC 39**
See also Ghalib, Hsadullah Khan

Ghalib, Hsadullah Khan 1797-1869
See Ghalib
See also DAM POET

Ghelderode, Michel de
1898-1962 .... **CLC 6, 11**
See also CA 85-88; CANR 40;
DAM DRAM

Ghiselin, Brewster 1903- .... **CLC 23**
See also CA 13-16R; CAAS 10; CANR 13

Ghose, Zulfikar 1935- .... **CLC 42**
See also CA 65-68

Ghosh, Amitav 1956- .... **CLC 44**
See also CA 147

Giacosa, Giuseppe 1847-1906 ...... **TCLC 7**
See also CA 104

Gibb, Lee
See Waterhouse, Keith (Spencer)

Gibbon, Lewis Grassic .... **TCLC 4**
See also Mitchell, James Leslie

Gibbons, Kaye 1960- .... **CLC 50, 88**
See also DAM POP

Gibran, Kahlil
1883-1931 .... **TCLC 1, 9; PC 9**
See also CA 104; 150; DAM POET, POP

Gibran, Khalil
See Gibran, Kahlil

Gibson, William
1914- .... **CLC 23; DA; DAB; DAC**
See also CA 9-12R; CANR 9, 42;
DAM DRAM, MST; DLB 7; SATA 66

Gibson, William (Ford) 1948- ... **CLC 39, 63**
See also AAYA 12; CA 126; 133;
DAM POP

Gide, Andre (Paul Guillaume)
1869-1951 .... **TCLC 5, 12, 36; DA;**
DAB; DAC; SSC 13; WLC
See also CA 104; 124; DAM MST, NOV;
DLB 65; MTCW

Gifford, Barry (Colby) 1946- .... **CLC 34**
See also CA 65-68; CANR 9, 30, 40

Gilbert, W(illiam) S(chwenck)
1836-1911 .... **TCLC 3**
See also CA 104; DAM DRAM, POET;
SATA 36

Gilbreth, Frank B., Jr. 1911- .... **CLC 17**
See also CA 9-12R; SATA 2

Gilchrist, Ellen 1935- .. **CLC 34, 48; SSC 14**
See also CA 113; 116; CANR 41;
DAM POP; DLB 130; MTCW

Giles, Molly 1942- .... **CLC 39**
See also CA 126

Gill, Patrick
See Creasey, John

Gilliam, Terry (Vance) 1940- .... **CLC 21**
See also Monty Python
See also CA 108; 113; CANR 35; INT 113

Gillian, Jerry
See Gilliam, Terry (Vance)

Gilliatt, Penelope (Ann Douglass)
1932-1993 .... **CLC 2, 10, 13, 53**
See also AITN 2; CA 13-16R; 141;
CANR 49; DLB 14

Gilman, Charlotte (Anna) Perkins (Stetson)
1860-1935 .... **TCLC 9, 37; SSC 13**
See also CA 106; 150

Gilmour, David 1949- .... **CLC 35**
See also CA 138, 147

Gilpin, William 1724-1804 .... **NCLC 30**

Gilray, J. D.
See Mencken, H(enry) L(ouis)

Gilroy, Frank D(aniel) 1925- .... **CLC 2**
See also CA 81-84; CANR 32; DLB 7

Ginsberg, Allen
1926- ...... **CLC 1, 2, 3, 4, 6, 13, 36, 69;**
DA; DAB; DAC; PC 4; WLC 3
See also AITN 1; CA 1-4R; CANR 2, 41;
CDALB 1941-1968; DAM MST, POET;
DLB 5, 16; MTCW

Ginzburg, Natalia
1916-1991 .... **CLC 5, 11, 54, 70**
See also CA 85-88; 135; CANR 33; MTCW

Giono, Jean 1895-1970 .... **CLC 4, 11**
See also CA 45-48; 29-32R; CANR 2, 35;
DLB 72; MTCW

Giovanni, Nikki
1943- ...... **CLC 2, 4, 19, 64; BLC; DA;**
DAB; DAC
See also AITN 1; BW 2; CA 29-32R;
CAAS 6; CANR 18, 41; CLR 6;
DAM MST, MULT, POET; DLB 5, 41;
INT CANR-18; MAICYA; MTCW;
SATA 24

Giovene, Andrea 1904- .... **CLC 7**
See also CA 85-88

Gippius, Zinaida (Nikolayevna) 1869-1945
See Hippius, Zinaida
See also CA 106

Giraudoux, (Hippolyte) Jean
  1882-1944 ....TCLC 2, 7
  See also CA 104; DAM DRAM; DLB 65

Gironella, Jose Maria 1917- ....CLC 11
  See also CA 101

Gissing, George (Robert)
  1857-1903 ....TCLC 3, 24, 47
  See also CA 105; DLB 18, 135

Giurlani, Aldo
  See Palazzeschi, Aldo

Gladkov, Fyodor (Vasilyevich)
  1883-1958 ....TCLC 27

Glanville, Brian (Lester) 1931- ......CLC 6
  See also CA 5-8R; CAAS 9; CANR 3;
  DLB 15, 139; SATA 42

Glasgow, Ellen (Anderson Gholson)
  1873(?)-1945 ....TCLC 2, 7
  See also CA 104; DLB 9, 12

Glaspell, Susan (Keating)
  1882(?)-1948 ....TCLC 55
  See also CA 110; DLB 7, 9, 78; YABC 2

Glassco, John 1909-1981 ....CLC 9
  See also CA 13-16R; 102; CANR 15;
  DLB 68

Glasscock, Amnesia
  See Steinbeck, John (Ernst)

Glasser, Ronald J. 1940(?)- ....CLC 37

Glassman, Joyce
  See Johnson, Joyce

Glendinning, Victoria 1937- ....CLC 50
  See also CA 120; 127; DLB 155

Glissant, Edouard 1928- ....CLC 10, 68
  See also DAM MULT

Gloag, Julian 1930- ....CLC 40
  See also AITN 1; CA 65-68; CANR 10

Glowacki, Aleksander
  See Prus, Boleslaw

Glueck, Louise (Elisabeth)
  1943- ....CLC 7, 22, 44, 81
  See also CA 33-36R; CANR 40;
  DAM POET; DLB 5

Gobineau, Joseph Arthur (Comte) de
  1816-1882 ....NCLC 17
  See also DLB 123

Godard, Jean-Luc 1930- ....CLC 20
  See also CA 93-96

Godden, (Margaret) Rumer 1907- ...CLC 53
  See also AAYA 6; CA 5-8R; CANR 4, 27,
  36; CLR 20; DLB 161; MAICYA;
  SAAS 12; SATA 3, 36

Godoy Alcayaga, Lucila 1889-1957
  See Mistral, Gabriela
  See also BW 2; CA 104; 131; DAM MULT;
  HW; MTCW

Godwin, Gail (Kathleen)
  1937- ....CLC 5, 8, 22, 31, 69
  See also CA 29-32R; CANR 15, 43;
  DAM POP; DLB 6; INT CANR-15;
  MTCW

Godwin, William 1756-1836......NCLC 14
  See also CDBLB 1789-1832; DLB 39, 104,
  142, 158, 163

Goethe, Johann Wolfgang von
  1749-1832 ....NCLC 4, 22, 34; DA;
                    DAB; DAC; PC 5; WLC 3
  See also DAM DRAM, MST, POET;
  DLB 94

Gogarty, Oliver St. John
  1878-1957 ....TCLC 15
  See also CA 109; 150; DLB 15, 19

Gogol, Nikolai (Vasilyevich)
  1809-1852 ....NCLC 5, 15, 31; DA;
                    DAB; DAC; DC 1; SSC 4; WLC
  See also DAM DRAM, MST

Goines, Donald
  1937(?)-1974 ....CLC 80; BLC
  See also AITN 1; BW 1; CA 124; 114;
  DAM MULT, POP; DLB 33

Gold, Herbert 1924- ....CLC 4, 7, 14, 42
  See also CA 9-12R; CANR 17, 45; DLB 2;
  DLBY 81

Goldbarth, Albert 1948- ....CLC 5, 38
  See also CA 53-56; CANR 6, 40; DLB 120

Goldberg, Anatol 1910-1982 ....CLC 34
  See also CA 131; 117

Goldemberg, Isaac 1945- ....CLC 52
  See also CA 69-72; CAAS 12; CANR 11,
  32; HW

Golding, William (Gerald)
  1911-1993 ....CLC 1, 2, 3, 8, 10, 17, 27,
                58, 81; DA; DAB; DAC; WLC
  See also AAYA 5; CA 5-8R; 141;
  CANR 13, 33; CDBLB 1945-1960;
  DAM MST, NOV; DLB 15, 100; MTCW

Goldman, Emma 1869-1940......TCLC 13
  See also CA 110; 150

Goldman, Francisco 1955- ....CLC 76

Goldman, William (W.) 1931- ....CLC 1, 48
  See also CA 9-12R; CANR 29; DLB 44

Goldmann, Lucien 1913-1970 ......CLC 24
  See also CA 25-28; CAP 2

Goldoni, Carlo 1707-1793 ....LC 4
  See also DAM DRAM

Goldsberry, Steven 1949- ....CLC 34
  See also CA 131

Goldsmith, Oliver
  1728-1774 ......LC 2; DA; DAB; DAC;
                                        WLC
  See also CDBLB 1660-1789; DAM DRAM,
  MST, NOV, POET; DLB 39, 89, 104,
  109, 142; SATA 26

Goldsmith, Peter
  See Priestley, J(ohn) B(oynton)

Gombrowicz, Witold
  1904-1969 ....CLC 4, 7, 11, 49
  See also CA 19-20; 25-28R; CAP 2;
  DAM DRAM

Gomez de la Serna, Ramon
  1888-1963 ....CLC 9
  See also CA 116; HW

Goncharov, Ivan Alexandrovich
  1812-1891 ....NCLC 1

Goncourt, Edmond (Louis Antoine Huot) de
  1822-1896 ....NCLC 7
  See also DLB 123

Goncourt, Jules (Alfred Huot) de
  1830-1870 ....NCLC 7
  See also DLB 123

Gontier, Fernande 19(?)- ....CLC 50

Goodman, Paul 1911-1972....CLC 1, 2, 4, 7
  See also CA 19-20; 37-40R; CANR 34;
  CAP 2; DLB 130; MTCW

Gordimer, Nadine
  1923- ....CLC 3, 5, 7, 10, 18, 33, 51, 70;
                    DA; DAB; DAC; SSC 17
  See also CA 5-8R; CANR 3, 28;
  DAM MST, NOV; INT CANR-28;
  MTCW

Gordon, Adam Lindsay
  1833-1870 ....NCLC 21

Gordon, Caroline
  1895-1981 ...CLC 6, 13, 29, 83; SSC 15
  See also CA 11-12; 103; CANR 36; CAP 1;
  DLB 4, 9, 102; DLBY 81; MTCW

Gordon, Charles William 1860-1937
  See Connor, Ralph
  See also CA 109

Gordon, Mary (Catherine)
  1949- ....CLC 13, 22
  See also CA 102; CANR 44; DLB 6;
  DLBY 81; INT 102; MTCW

Gordon, Sol 1923- ....CLC 26
  See also CA 53-56; CANR 4; SATA 11

Gordone, Charles 1925-1995 ......CLC 1, 4
  See also BW 1; CA 93-96; 150;
  DAM DRAM; DLB 7; INT 93-96;
  MTCW

Gorenko, Anna Andreevna
  See Akhmatova, Anna

Gorky, Maxim.........TCLC 8; DAB; WLC
  See also Peshkov, Alexei Maximovich

Goryan, Sirak
  See Saroyan, William

Gosse, Edmund (William)
  1849-1928 ....TCLC 28
  See also CA 117; DLB 57, 144

Gotlieb, Phyllis Fay (Bloom)
  1926- ....CLC 18
  See also CA 13-16R; CANR 7; DLB 88

Gottesman, S. D.
  See Kornbluth, C(yril) M.; Pohl, Frederik

Gottfried von Strassburg
  fl. c. 1210- ....CMLC 10
  See also DLB 138

Gould, Lois ....CLC 4, 10
  See also CA 77-80; CANR 29; MTCW

Gourmont, Remy (-Marie-Charles) de
  1858-1915 ....TCLC 17
  See also CA 109; 150

Govier, Katherine 1948- ....CLC 51
  See also CA 101; CANR 18, 40

Goyen, (Charles) William
  1915-1983 ....CLC 5, 8, 14, 40
  See also AITN 2; CA 5-8R; 110; CANR 6;
  DLB 2; DLBY 83; INT CANR-6

Goytisolo, Juan
  1931- ....CLC 5, 10, 23; HLC
  See also CA 85-88; CANR 32;
  DAM MULT; HW; MTCW

Gozzano, Guido 1883-1916 .... **PC 10**
See also DLB 114

Gozzi, (Conte) Carlo 1720-1806 .. **NCLC 23**

Grabbe, Christian Dietrich
1801-1836 .... **NCLC 2**
See also DLB 133

Grace, Patricia 1937-............. **CLC 56**

Gracian y Morales, Baltasar
1601-1658 .... **LC 15**

Gracq, Julien................. **CLC 11, 48**
See also Poirier, Louis
See also DLB 83

Grade, Chaim 1910-1982 .... **CLC 10**
See also CA 93-96; 107

Graduate of Oxford, A
See Ruskin, John

Graham, John
See Phillips, David Graham

Graham, Jorie 1951-............. **CLC 48**
See also CA 111; DLB 120

Graham, R(obert) B(ontine) Cunninghame
See Cunninghame Graham, R(obert)
B(ontine)
See also DLB 98, 135

Graham, Robert
See Haldeman, Joe (William)

Graham, Tom
See Lewis, (Harry) Sinclair

Graham, W(illiam) S(ydney)
1918-1986 .... **CLC 29**
See also CA 73-76; 118; DLB 20

Graham, Winston (Mawdsley)
1910- .... **CLC 23**
See also CA 49-52; CANR 2, 22, 45;
DLB 77

Grant, Skeeter
See Spiegelman, Art

Granville-Barker, Harley
1877-1946 .... **TCLC 2**
See also Barker, Harley Granville
See also CA 104; DAM DRAM

Grass, Guenter (Wilhelm)
1927- ..... **CLC 1, 2, 4, 6, 11, 15, 22, 32,
49, 88; DA; DAB; DAC; WLC**
See also CA 13-16R; CANR 20;
DAM MST, NOV; DLB 75, 124; MTCW

Gratton, Thomas
See Hulme, T(homas) E(rnest)

Grau, Shirley Ann
1929- .... **CLC 4, 9; SSC 15**
See also CA 89-92; CANR 22; DLB 2;
INT CANR-22; MTCW

Gravel, Fern
See Hall, James Norman

Graver, Elizabeth 1964-.......... **CLC 70**
See also CA 135

Graves, Richard Perceval 1945- .... **CLC 44**
See also CA 65-68; CANR 9, 26, 51

Graves, Robert (von Ranke)
1895-1985 ...... **CLC 1, 2, 6, 11, 39, 44,
45; DAB; DAC; PC 6**
See also CA 5-8R; 117; CANR 5, 36;
CDBLB 1914-1945; DAM MST, POET;
DLB 20, 100; DLBY 85; MTCW;
SATA 45

Gray, Alasdair (James) 1934- ...... **CLC 41**
See also CA 126; CANR 47; INT 126;
MTCW

Gray, Amlin 1946- .... **CLC 29**
See also CA 138

Gray, Francine du Plessix 1930-.... **CLC 22**
See also BEST 90:3; CA 61-64; CAAS 2;
CANR 11, 33; DAM NOV;
INT CANR-11; MTCW

Gray, John (Henry) 1866-1934 .... **TCLC 19**
See also CA 119

Gray, Simon (James Holliday)
1936- .... **CLC 9, 14, 36**
See also AITN 1; CA 21-24R; CAAS 3;
CANR 32; DLB 13; MTCW

Gray, Spalding 1941-............. **CLC 49**
See also CA 128; DAM POP

Gray, Thomas
1716-1771 ...... **LC 4; DA; DAB; DAC;
PC 2; WLC**
See also CDBLB 1660-1789; DAM MST;
DLB 109

Grayson, David
See Baker, Ray Stannard

Grayson, Richard (A.) 1951-....... **CLC 38**
See also CA 85-88; CANR 14, 31

Greeley, Andrew M(oran) 1928-.... **CLC 28**
See also CA 5-8R; CAAS 7; CANR 7, 43;
DAM POP; MTCW

Green, Anna Katharine
1846-1935 .... **TCLC 63**
See also CA 112

Green, Brian
See Card, Orson Scott

Green, Hannah
See Greenberg, Joanne (Goldenberg)

Green, Hannah .... **CLC 3**
See also CA 73-76

Green, Henry................... **CLC 2, 13**
See also Yorke, Henry Vincent
See also DLB 15

Green, Julian (Hartridge) 1900-
See Green, Julien
See also CA 21-24R; CANR 33; DLB 4, 72;
MTCW

Green, Julien................ **CLC 3, 11, 77**
See also Green, Julian (Hartridge)

Green, Paul (Eliot) 1894-1981...... **CLC 25**
See also AITN 1; CA 5-8R; 103; CANR 3;
DAM DRAM; DLB 7, 9; DLBY 81

Greenberg, Ivan 1908-1973
See Rahv, Philip
See also CA 85-88

Greenberg, Joanne (Goldenberg)
1932- .... **CLC 7, 30**
See also AAYA 12; CA 5-8R; CANR 14,
32; SATA 25

Greenberg, Richard 1959(?)-....... **CLC 57**
See also CA 138

Greene, Bette 1934-.............. **CLC 30**
See also AAYA 7; CA 53-56; CANR 4;
CLR 2; JRDA; MAICYA; SAAS 16;
SATA 8

Greene, Gael .... **CLC 8**
See also CA 13-16R; CANR 10

Greene, Graham
1904-1991 .... **CLC 1, 3, 6, 9, 14, 18, 27,
37, 70, 72; DA; DAB; DAC; WLC**
See also CA 13-16R; 133;
CANR 35; CDBLB 1945-1960;
DAM MST, NOV; DLB 13, 15, 77, 100,
162; DLBY 91; MTCW; SATA 20

Greer, Richard
See Silverberg, Robert

Gregor, Arthur 1923-.............. **CLC 9**
See also CA 25-28R; CAAS 10; CANR 11;
SATA 36

Gregor, Lee
See Pohl, Frederik

Gregory, Isabella Augusta (Persse)
1852-1932 .... **TCLC 1**
See also CA 104; DLB 10

Gregory, J. Dennis
See Williams, John A(lfred)

Grendon, Stephen
See Derleth, August (William)

Grenville, Kate 1950-............. **CLC 61**
See also CA 118

Grenville, Pelham
See Wodehouse, P(elham) G(renville)

Greve, Felix Paul (Berthold Friedrich)
1879-1948
See Grove, Frederick Philip
See also CA 104; 141; DAC; DAM MST

Grey, Zane 1872-1939 .... **TCLC 6**
See also CA 104; 132; DAM POP; DLB 9;
MTCW

Grieg, (Johan) Nordahl (Brun)
1902-1943 .... **TCLC 10**
See also CA 107

Grieve, C(hristopher) M(urray)
1892-1978 .... **CLC 11, 19**
See also MacDiarmid, Hugh; Pteleon
See also CA 5-8R; 85-88; CANR 33;
DAM POET; MTCW

Griffin, Gerald 1803-1840 .... **NCLC 7**
See also DLB 159

Griffin, John Howard 1920-1980.... **CLC 68**
See also AITN 1; CA 1-4R; 101; CANR 2

Griffin, Peter 1942- .... **CLC 39**
See also CA 136

Griffiths, Trevor 1935-.......... **CLC 13, 52**
See also CA 97-100; CANR 45; DLB 13

Grigson, Geoffrey (Edward Harvey)
1905-1985 .... **CLC 7, 39**
See also CA 25-28R; 118; CANR 20, 33;
DLB 27; MTCW

Grillparzer, Franz 1791-1872...... **NCLC 1**
See also DLB 133

Grimble, Reverend Charles James
See Eliot, T(homas) S(tearns)

Grimke, Charlotte L(ottie) Forten
1837(?)-1914
See Forten, Charlotte L.
See also BW 1; CA 117; 124; DAM MULT,
POET

Grimm, Jacob Ludwig Karl
1785-1863 .... **NCLC 3**
See also DLB 90; MAICYA; SATA 22

Grimm, Wilhelm Karl 1786-1859 . . **NCLC 3**
See also DLB 90; MAICYA; SATA 22

**Grimmelshausen, Johann Jakob Christoffel
      von** 1621-1676 . . . . **LC 6**

Grindel, Eugene 1895-1952
See Eluard, Paul
See also CA 104

Grisham, John 1955- . . . . **CLC 84**
See also AAYA 14; CA 138; CANR 47;
DAM POP

Grossman, David 1954- . . . . **CLC 67**
See also CA 138

Grossman, Vasily (Semenovich)
      1905-1964 . . . . **CLC 41**
See also CA 124; 130; MTCW

Grove, Frederick Philip . . . . **TCLC 4**
See also Greve, Felix Paul (Berthold
Friedrich)
See also DLB 92

Grubb
See Crumb, R(obert)

Grumbach, Doris (Isaac)
      1918- . . . . **CLC 13, 22, 64**
See also CA 5-8R; CAAS 2; CANR 9, 42;
INT CANR-9

Grundtvig, Nicolai Frederik Severin
      1783-1872 . . . . **NCLC 1**

Grunge
See Crumb, R(obert)

Grunwald, Lisa 1959- . . . . **CLC 44**
See also CA 120

Guare, John 1938- . . . . **CLC 8, 14, 29, 67**
See also CA 73-76; CANR 21;
DAM DRAM; DLB 7; MTCW

Gudjonsson, Halldor Kiljan 1902-
See Laxness, Halldor
See also CA 103

Guenter, Erich
See Eich, Guenter

Guest, Barbara 1920- . . . . **CLC 34**
See also CA 25-28R; CANR 11, 44; DLB 5

Guest, Judith (Ann) 1936- . . . . **CLC 8, 30**
See also AAYA 7; CA 77-80; CANR 15;
DAM NOV, POP; INT CANR-15;
MTCW

Guevara, Che . . . . **CLC 87; HLC**
See also Guevara (Serna), Ernesto

Guevara (Serna), Ernesto 1928-1967
See Guevara, Che
See also CA 127; 111; DAM MULT; HW

Guild, Nicholas M. 1944- . . . . **CLC 33**
See also CA 93-96

Guillemin, Jacques
See Sartre, Jean-Paul

Guillen, Jorge 1893-1984 . . . . **CLC 11**
See also CA 89-92; 112; DAM MULT,
POET; DLB 108; HW

Guillen (y Batista), Nicolas (Cristobal)
      1902-1989 . . . . . **CLC 48, 79; BLC; HLC**
See also BW 2; CA 116; 125; 129;
DAM MST, MULT, POET; HW

Guillevic, (Eugene) 1907- . . . . **CLC 33**
See also CA 93-96

Guillois
See Desnos, Robert

Guiney, Louise Imogen
      1861-1920 . . . . **TCLC 41**
See also DLB 54

Guiraldes, Ricardo (Guillermo)
      1886-1927 . . . . **TCLC 39**
See also CA 131; HW; MTCW

Gumilev, Nikolai Stephanovich
      1886-1921 . . . . **TCLC 60**

Gunesekera, Romesh . . . . **CLC 91**

Gunn, Bill . . . . **CLC 5**
See also Gunn, William Harrison
See also DLB 38

Gunn, Thom(son William)
      1929- . . . . **CLC 3, 6, 18, 32, 81**
See also CA 17-20R; CANR 9, 33;
CDBLB 1960 to Present; DAM POET;
DLB 27; INT CANR-33; MTCW

Gunn, William Harrison 1934(?)-1989
See Gunn, Bill
See also AITN 1; BW 1; CA 13-16R; 128;
CANR 12, 25

Gunnars, Kristjana 1948- . . . . **CLC 69**
See also CA 113; DLB 60

Gurganus, Allan 1947- . . . . **CLC 70**
See also BEST 90:1; CA 135; DAM POP

Gurney, A(lbert) R(amsdell), Jr.
      1930- . . . . **CLC 32, 50, 54**
See also CA 77-80; CANR 32;
DAM DRAM

Gurney, Ivor (Bertie) 1890-1937 . . . **TCLC 33**

Gurney, Peter
See Gurney, A(lbert) R(amsdell), Jr.

Guro, Elena 1877-1913 . . . . **TCLC 56**

Gustafson, Ralph (Barker) 1909- . . . . **CLC 36**
See also CA 21-24R; CANR 8, 45; DLB 88

Gut, Gom
See Simenon, Georges (Jacques Christian)

Guterson, David 1956- . . . . **CLC 91**
See also CA 132

Guthrie, A(lfred) B(ertram), Jr.
      1901-1991 . . . . **CLC 23**
See also CA 57-60; 134; CANR 24; DLB 6;
SATA 62; SATA-Obit 67

Guthrie, Isobel
See Grieve, C(hristopher) M(urray)

Guthrie, Woodrow Wilson 1912-1967
See Guthrie, Woody
See also CA 113; 93-96

Guthrie, Woody . . . . **CLC 35**
See also Guthrie, Woodrow Wilson

Guy, Rosa (Cuthbert) 1928- . . . . **CLC 26**
See also AAYA 4; BW 2; CA 17-20R;
CANR 14, 34; CLR 13; DLB 33; JRDA;
MAICYA; SATA 14, 62

Gwendolyn
See Bennett, (Enoch) Arnold

H. D. . . . . **CLC 3, 8, 14, 31, 34, 73; PC 5**
See also Doolittle, Hilda

H. de V.
See Buchan, John

Haavikko, Paavo Juhani
      1931- . . . . **CLC 18, 34**
See also CA 106

Habbema, Koos
See Heijermans, Herman

Hacker, Marilyn
      1942- . . . . **CLC 5, 9, 23, 72, 91**
See also CA 77-80; DAM POET; DLB 120

Haggard, H(enry) Rider
      1856-1925 . . . . **TCLC 11**
See also CA 108; 148; DLB 70, 156;
SATA 16

Hagiwara Sakutaro 1886-1942 . . . . **TCLC 60**

Haig, Fenil
See Ford, Ford Madox

Haig-Brown, Roderick (Langmere)
      1908-1976 . . . . **CLC 21**
See also CA 5-8R; 69-72; CANR 4, 38;
CLR 31; DLB 88; MAICYA; SATA 12

Hailey, Arthur 1920- . . . . **CLC 5**
See also AITN 2; BEST 90:3; CA 1-4R;
CANR 2, 36; DAM NOV, POP; DLB 88;
DLBY 82; MTCW

Hailey, Elizabeth Forsythe 1938- . . . **CLC 40**
See also CA 93-96; CAAS 1; CANR 15, 48;
INT CANR-15

Haines, John (Meade) 1924- . . . . **CLC 58**
See also CA 17-20R; CANR 13, 34; DLB 5

Hakluyt, Richard 1552-1616 . . . . **LC 31**

Haldeman, Joe (William) 1943- . . . . . **CLC 61**
See also CA 53-56; CANR 6; DLB 8;
INT CANR-6

Haley, Alex(ander Murray Palmer)
      1921-1992 . . . . **CLC 8, 12, 76; BLC; DA;
                                          DAB; DAC**
See also BW 2; CA 77-80; 136; DAM MST,
MULT, POP; DLB 38; MTCW

Haliburton, Thomas Chandler
      1796-1865 . . . . **NCLC 15**
See also DLB 11, 99

Hall, Donald (Andrew, Jr.)
      1928- . . . . **CLC 1, 13, 37, 59**
See also CA 5-8R; CAAS 7; CANR 2, 44;
DAM POET; DLB 5; SATA 23

Hall, Frederic Sauser
See Sauser-Hall, Frederic

Hall, James
See Kuttner, Henry

Hall, James Norman 1887-1951 . . . **TCLC 23**
See also CA 123; SATA 21

Hall, (Marguerite) Radclyffe
      1886-1943 . . . . **TCLC 12**
See also CA 110; 150

Hall, Rodney 1935- . . . . **CLC 51**
See also CA 109

Halleck, Fitz-Greene 1790-1867 . . **NCLC 47**
See also DLB 3

Halliday, Michael
See Creasey, John

Halpern, Daniel 1945- . . . . **CLC 14**
See also CA 33-36R

Hamburger, Michael (Peter Leopold)
      1924- . . . . **CLC 5, 14**
See also CA 5-8R; CAAS 4; CANR 2, 47;
DLB 27

Hamill, Pete 1935-.............. **CLC 10**
See also CA 25-28R; CANR 18

Hamilton, Alexander
1755(?)-1804 .... **NCLC 49**
See also DLB 37

Hamilton, Clive
See Lewis, C(live) S(taples)

Hamilton, Edmond 1904-1977....... **CLC 1**
See also CA 1-4R; CANR 3; DLB 8

Hamilton, Eugene (Jacob) Lee
See Lee-Hamilton, Eugene (Jacob)

Hamilton, Franklin
See Silverberg, Robert

Hamilton, Gail
See Corcoran, Barbara

Hamilton, Mollie
See Kaye, M(ary) M(argaret)

Hamilton, (Anthony Walter) Patrick
1904-1962 .... **CLC 51**
See also CA 113; DLB 10

Hamilton, Virginia 1936-.......... **CLC 26**
See also AAYA 2; BW 2; CA 25-28R;
CANR 20, 37; CLR 1, 11, 40;
DAM MULT; DLB 33, 52;
INT CANR-20; JRDA; MAICYA;
MTCW; SATA 4, 56, 79

Hammett, (Samuel) Dashiell
1894-1961 .... **CLC 3, 5, 10, 19, 47;**
SSC 17
See also AITN 1; CA 81-84; CANR 42;
CDALB 1929-1941; DLBD 6; MTCW

Hammon, Jupiter
1711(?)-1800(?) .... **NCLC 5; BLC**
See also DAM MULT, POET; DLB 31, 50

Hammond, Keith
See Kuttner, Henry

Hamner, Earl (Henry), Jr. 1923- ... **CLC 12**
See also AITN 2; CA 73-76; DLB 6

Hampton, Christopher (James)
1946-...................... **CLC 4**
See also CA 25-28R; DLB 13; MTCW

Hamsun, Knut .... **TCLC 2, 14, 49**
See also Pedersen, Knut

Handke, Peter 1942-.. **CLC 5, 8, 10, 15, 38**
See also CA 77-80; CANR 33;
DAM DRAM, NOV; DLB 85, 124;
MTCW

Hanley, James 1901-1985 ... **CLC 3, 5, 8, 13**
See also CA 73-76; 117; CANR 36; MTCW

Hannah, Barry 1942-....... **CLC 23, 38, 90**
See also CA 108; 110; CANR 43; DLB 6;
INT 110; MTCW

Hannon, Ezra
See Hunter, Evan

Hansberry, Lorraine (Vivian)
1930-1965 ...... **CLC 17, 62; BLC; DA;**
DAB; DAC; DC 2
See also BW 1; CA 109; 25-28R; CABS 3;
CDALB 1941-1968; DAM DRAM, MST,
MULT; DLB 7, 38; MTCW

Hansen, Joseph 1923-............ **CLC 38**
See also CA 29-32R; CAAS 17; CANR 16,
44; INT CANR-16

Hansen, Martin A. 1909-1955..... **TCLC 32**

Hanson, Kenneth O(stlin) 1922-.... **CLC 13**
See also CA 53-56; CANR 7

Hardwick, Elizabeth 1916- .... **CLC 13**
See also CA 5-8R; CANR 3, 32;
DAM NOV; DLB 6; MTCW

Hardy, Thomas
1840-1928 ...... **TCLC 4, 10, 18, 32, 48,**
53; DA; DAB; DAC; PC 8; SSC 2; WLC
See also CA 104; 123; CDBLB 1890-1914;
DAM MST, NOV, POET; DLB 18, 19,
135; MTCW

Hare, David 1947- .... **CLC 29, 58**
See also CA 97-100; CANR 39; DLB 13;
MTCW

Harford, Henry
See Hudson, W(illiam) H(enry)

Hargrave, Leonie
See Disch, Thomas M(ichael)

Harjo, Joy 1951- .... **CLC 83**
See also CA 114; CANR 35; DAM MULT;
DLB 120; NNAL

Harlan, Louis R(udolph) 1922-..... **CLC 34**
See also CA 21-24R; CANR 25

Harling, Robert 1951(?)- .... **CLC 53**
See also CA 147

Harmon, William (Ruth) 1938-..... **CLC 38**
See also CA 33-36R; CANR 14, 32, 35;
SATA 65

Harper, F. E. W.
See Harper, Frances Ellen Watkins

Harper, Frances E. W.
See Harper, Frances Ellen Watkins

Harper, Frances E. Watkins
See Harper, Frances Ellen Watkins

Harper, Frances Ellen
See Harper, Frances Ellen Watkins

Harper, Frances Ellen Watkins
1825-1911 .... **TCLC 14; BLC**
See also BW 1; CA 111; 125; DAM MULT,
POET; DLB 50

Harper, Michael S(teven) 1938- .. **CLC 7, 22**
See also BW 1; CA 33-36R; CANR 24;
DLB 41

Harper, Mrs. F. E. W.
See Harper, Frances Ellen Watkins

Harris, Christie (Lucy) Irwin
1907- .... **CLC 12**
See also CA 5-8R; CANR 6; DLB 88;
JRDA; MAICYA; SAAS 10; SATA 6, 74

Harris, Frank 1856-1931 .... **TCLC 24**
See also CA 109; 150; DLB 156

Harris, George Washington
1814-1869 .... **NCLC 23**
See also DLB 3, 11

Harris, Joel Chandler
1848-1908 .... **TCLC 2; SSC 19**
See also CA 104; 137; DLB 11, 23, 42, 78,
91; MAICYA; YABC 1

Harris, John (Wyndham Parkes Lucas)
Beynon 1903-1969
See Wyndham, John
See also CA 102; 89-92

Harris, MacDonald................ CLC 9
See also Heiney, Donald (William)

Harris, Mark 1922-.............. **CLC 19**
See also CA 5-8R; CAAS 3; CANR 2;
DLB 2; DLBY 80

Harris, (Theodore) Wilson 1921-.... **CLC 25**
See also BW 2; CA 65-68; CAAS 16;
CANR 11, 27; DLB 117; MTCW

Harrison, Elizabeth Cavanna 1909-
See Cavanna, Betty
See also CA 9-12R; CANR 6, 27

Harrison, Harry (Max) 1925-...... **CLC 42**
See also CA 1-4R; CANR 5, 21; DLB 8;
SATA 4

Harrison, James (Thomas)
1937- .... **CLC 6, 14, 33, 66; SSC 19**
See also CA 13-16R; CANR 8, 51;
DLBY 82; INT CANR-8

Harrison, Jim
See Harrison, James (Thomas)

Harrison, Kathryn 1961-.......... **CLC 70**
See also CA 144

Harrison, Tony 1937-............. **CLC 43**
See also CA 65-68; CANR 44; DLB 40;
MTCW

Harriss, Will(ard Irvin) 1922-...... **CLC 34**
See also CA 111

Harson, Sley
See Ellison, Harlan (Jay)

Hart, Ellis
See Ellison, Harlan (Jay)

Hart, Josephine 1942(?)-.......... **CLC 70**
See also CA 138; DAM POP

Hart, Moss 1904-1961 .... **CLC 66**
See also CA 109; 89-92; DAM DRAM;
DLB 7

Harte, (Francis) Bret(t)
1836(?)-1902 ..... **TCLC 1, 25; DA; DAC;**
SSC 8; WLC
See also CA 104; 140; CDALB 1865-1917;
DAM MST; DLB 12, 64, 74, 79;
SATA 26

Hartley, L(eslie) P(oles)
1895-1972 .... **CLC 2, 22**
See also CA 45-48; 37-40R; CANR 33;
DLB 15, 139; MTCW

Hartman, Geoffrey H. 1929-....... **CLC 27**
See also CA 117; 125; DLB 67

Hartmann von Aue
c. 1160-c. 1205 .... **CMLC 15**
See also DLB 138

Hartmann von Aue 1170-1210.... **CMLC 15**

Haruf, Kent 1943- .... **CLC 34**
See also CA 149

Harwood, Ronald 1934-........... **CLC 32**
See also CA 1-4R; CANR 4; DAM DRAM,
MST; DLB 13

Hasek, Jaroslav (Matej Frantisek)
1883-1923 .... **TCLC 4**
See also CA 104; 129; MTCW

Hass, Robert 1941-............ **CLC 18, 39**
See also CA 111; CANR 30, 50; DLB 105

Hastings, Hudson
See Kuttner, Henry

Hastings, Selina.............. **CLC 44**

Hatteras, Amelia
See Mencken, H(enry) L(ouis)

Hatteras, Owen .... TCLC 18
See also Mencken, H(enry) L(ouis); Nathan, George Jean

Hauptmann, Gerhart (Johann Robert)
1862-1946 .... TCLC 4
See also CA 104; DAM DRAM; DLB 66, 118

Havel, Vaclav
1936- .... CLC 25, 58, 65; DC 6
See also CA 104; CANR 36; DAM DRAM; MTCW

Haviaras, Stratis .... CLC 33
See also Chaviaras, Strates

Hawes, Stephen 1475(?)-1523(?) ..... LC 17

Hawkes, John (Clendennin Burne, Jr.)
1925- ...... CLC 1, 2, 3, 4, 7, 9, 14, 15, 27, 49
See also CA 1-4R; CANR 2, 47; DLB 2, 7; DLBY 80; MTCW

Hawking, S. W.
See Hawking, Stephen W(illiam)

Hawking, Stephen W(illiam)
1942- .... CLC 63
See also AAYA 13; BEST 89:1; CA 126; 129; CANR 48

Hawthorne, Julian 1846-1934 ..... TCLC 25

Hawthorne, Nathaniel
1804-1864 .... NCLC 39; DA; DAB; DAC; SSC 3; WLC
See also CDALB 1640-1865; DAM MST, NOV; DLB 1, 74; YABC 2

Haxton, Josephine Ayres 1921-
See Douglas, Ellen
See also CA 115; CANR 41

Hayaseca y Eizaguirre, Jorge
See Echegaray (y Eizaguirre), Jose (Maria Waldo)

Hayashi Fumiko 1904-1951 ...... TCLC 27

Haycraft, Anna
See Ellis, Alice Thomas
See also CA 122

Hayden, Robert E(arl)
1913-1980 ...... CLC 5, 9, 14, 37; BLC; DA; DAC; PC 6
See also BW 1; CA 69-72; 97-100; CABS 2; CANR 24; CDALB 1941-1968; DAM MST, MULT, POET; DLB 5, 76; MTCW; SATA 19; SATA-Obit 26

Hayford, J(oseph) E(phraim) Casely
See Casely-Hayford, J(oseph) E(phraim)

Hayman, Ronald 1932- .... CLC 44
See also CA 25-28R; CANR 18, 50; DLB 155

Haywood, Eliza (Fowler)
1693(?)-1756 .... LC 1

Hazlitt, William 1778-1830 ...... NCLC 29
See also DLB 110, 158

Hazzard, Shirley 1931- .... CLC 18
See also CA 9-12R; CANR 4; DLBY 82; MTCW

Head, Bessie 1937-1986 ... CLC 25, 67; BLC
See also BW 2; CA 29-32R; 119; CANR 25; DAM MULT; DLB 117; MTCW

Headon, (Nicky) Topper 1956(?)- ... CLC 30

Heaney, Seamus (Justin)
1939- ...... CLC 5, 7, 14, 25, 37, 74, 91; DAB
See also CA 85-88; CANR 25, 48; CDBLB 1960 to Present; DAM POET; DLB 40; MTCW

Hearn, (Patricio) Lafcadio (Tessima Carlos)
1850-1904 .... TCLC 9
See also CA 105; DLB 12, 78

Hearne, Vicki 1946- .... CLC 56
See also CA 139

Hearon, Shelby 1931- .... CLC 63
See also AITN 2; CA 25-28R; CANR 18, 48

Heat-Moon, William Least .... CLC 29
See also Trogdon, William (Lewis)
See also AAYA 9

Hebbel, Friedrich 1813-1863 ..... NCLC 43
See also DAM DRAM; DLB 129

Hebert, Anne 1916- ... CLC 4, 13, 29; DAC
See also CA 85-88; DAM MST, POET; DLB 68; MTCW

Hecht, Anthony (Evan)
1923- .... CLC 8, 13, 19
See also CA 9-12R; CANR 6; DAM POET; DLB 5

Hecht, Ben 1894-1964 .... CLC 8
See also CA 85-88; DLB 7, 9, 25, 26, 28, 86

Hedayat, Sadeq 1903-1951 .... TCLC 21
See also CA 120

Hegel, Georg Wilhelm Friedrich
1770-1831 .... NCLC 46
See also DLB 90

Heidegger, Martin 1889-1976 ...... CLC 24
See also CA 81-84; 65-68; CANR 34; MTCW

Heidenstam, (Carl Gustaf) Verner von
1859-1940 .... TCLC 5
See also CA 104

Heifner, Jack 1946- .... CLC 11
See also CA 105; CANR 47

Heijermans, Herman 1864-1924 ... TCLC 24
See also CA 123

Heilbrun, Carolyn G(old) 1926- ..... CLC 25
See also CA 45-48; CANR 1, 28

Heine, Heinrich 1797-1856 .... NCLC 4, 54
See also DLB 90

Heinemann, Larry (Curtiss) 1944- .. CLC 50
See also CA 110; CAAS 21; CANR 31; DLBD 9; INT CANR-31

Heiney, Donald (William) 1921-1993
See Harris, MacDonald
See also CA 1-4R; 142; CANR 3

Heinlein, Robert A(nson)
1907-1988 ...... CLC 1, 3, 8, 14, 26, 55
See also AAYA 17; CA 1-4R; 125; CANR 1, 20; DAM POP; DLB 8; JRDA; MAICYA; MTCW; SATA 9, 69; SATA-Obit 56

Helforth, John
See Doolittle, Hilda

Hellenhofferu, Vojtech Kapristian z
See Hasek, Jaroslav (Matej Frantisek)

Heller, Joseph
1923- .... CLC 1, 3, 5, 8, 11, 36, 63; DA; DAB; DAC; WLC
See also AITN 1; CA 5-8R; CABS 1; CANR 8, 42; DAM MST, NOV, POP; DLB 2, 28; DLBY 80; INT CANR-8; MTCW

Hellman, Lillian (Florence)
1906-1984 ...... CLC 2, 4, 8, 14, 18, 34, 44, 52; DC 1
See also AITN 1, 2; CA 13-16R; 112; CANR 33; DAM DRAM; DLB 7; DLBY 84; MTCW

Helprin, Mark 1947- ..... CLC 7, 10, 22, 32
See also CA 81-84; CANR 47; DAM NOV, POP; DLBY 85; MTCW

Helvetius, Claude-Adrien
1715-1771 .... LC 26

Helyar, Jane Penelope Josephine 1933-
See Poole, Josephine
See also CA 21-24R; CANR 10, 26; SATA 82

Hemans, Felicia 1793-1835 ...... NCLC 29
See also DLB 96

Hemingway, Ernest (Miller)
1899-1961 .... CLC 1, 3, 6, 8, 10, 13, 19, 30, 34, 39, 41, 44, 50, 61, 80; DA; DAB; DAC; SSC 1; WLC
See also CA 77-80; CANR 34; CDALB 1917-1929; DAM MST, NOV; DLB 4, 9, 102; DLBD 1; DLBY 81, 87; MTCW

Hempel, Amy 1951- .... CLC 39
See also CA 118; 137

Henderson, F. C.
See Mencken, H(enry) L(ouis)

Henderson, Sylvia
See Ashton-Warner, Sylvia (Constance)

Henley, Beth .... CLC 23; DC 6
See also Henley, Elizabeth Becker
See also CABS 3; DLBY 86

Henley, Elizabeth Becker 1952-
See Henley, Beth
See also CA 107; CANR 32; DAM DRAM, MST; MTCW

Henley, William Ernest
1849-1903 .... TCLC 8
See also CA 105; DLB 19

Hennissart, Martha
See Lathen, Emma
See also CA 85-88

Henry, O. .... TCLC 1, 19; SSC 5; WLC
See also Porter, William Sydney

Henry, Patrick 1736-1799 .... LC 25

Henryson, Robert 1430(?)-1506(?).... LC 20
See also DLB 146

Henry VIII 1491-1547 .... LC 10

Henschke, Alfred
See Klabund

Hentoff, Nat(han Irving) 1925- ..... CLC 26
See also AAYA 4; CA 1-4R; CAAS 6; CANR 5, 25; CLR 1; INT CANR-25; JRDA; MAICYA; SATA 42, 69; SATA-Brief 27

Heppenstall, (John) Rayner
1911-1981 .... **CLC 10**
See also CA 1-4R; 103; CANR 29

Herbert, Frank (Patrick)
1920-1986 ...... **CLC 12, 23, 35, 44, 85**
See also CA 53-56; 118; CANR 5, 43;
DAM POP; DLB 8; INT CANR-5;
MTCW; SATA 9, 37; SATA-Obit 47

Herbert, George
1593-1633 .... **LC 24; DAB; PC 4**
See also CDBLB Before 1660; DAM POET;
DLB 126

Herbert, Zbigniew 1924- .... **CLC 9, 43**
See also CA 89-92; CANR 36;
DAM POET; MTCW

Herbst, Josephine (Frey)
1897-1969 .... **CLC 34**
See also CA 5-8R; 25-28R; DLB 9

Hergesheimer, Joseph
1880-1954 .... **TCLC 11**
See also CA 109; DLB 102, 9

Herlihy, James Leo 1927-1993 ...... **CLC 6**
See also CA 1-4R; 143; CANR 2

Hermogenes fl. c. 175- .... **CMLC 6**

Hernandez, Jose 1834-1886 ..... **NCLC 17**

Herodotus c. 484B.C.-429B.C. .... **CMLC 17**

Herrick, Robert
1591-1674 ..... **LC 13; DA; DAB; DAC;
PC 9**
See also DAM MST, POP; DLB 126

Herring, Guilles
See Somerville, Edith

Herriot, James 1916-1995 .... **CLC 12**
See also Wight, James Alfred
See also AAYA 1; CA 148; CANR 40;
DAM POP; SATA 86

Herrmann, Dorothy 1941- .... **CLC 44**
See also CA 107

Herrmann, Taffy
See Herrmann, Dorothy

Hersey, John (Richard)
1914-1993 .... **CLC 1, 2, 7, 9, 40, 81**
See also CA 17-20R; 140; CANR 33;
DAM POP; DLB 6; MTCW; SATA 25;
SATA-Obit 76

Herzen, Aleksandr Ivanovich
1812-1870 .... **NCLC 10**

Herzl, Theodor 1860-1904 .... **TCLC 36**

Herzog, Werner 1942- .... **CLC 16**
See also CA 89-92

Hesiod c. 8th cent. B.C.- .... **CMLC 5**

Hesse, Hermann
1877-1962 .... **CLC 1, 2, 3, 6, 11, 17, 25,
69; DA; DAB; DAC; SSC 9; WLC**
See also CA 17-18; CAP 2; DAM MST,
NOV; DLB 66; MTCW; SATA 50

Hewes, Cady
See De Voto, Bernard (Augustine)

Heyen, William 1940- .... **CLC 13, 18**
See also CA 33-36R; CAAS 9; DLB 5

Heyerdahl, Thor 1914- .... **CLC 26**
See also CA 5-8R; CANR 5, 22; MTCW;
SATA 2, 52

Heym, Georg (Theodor Franz Arthur)
1887-1912 .... **TCLC 9**
See also CA 106

Heym, Stefan 1913- .... **CLC 41**
See also CA 9-12R; CANR 4; DLB 69

Heyse, Paul (Johann Ludwig von)
1830-1914 .... **TCLC 8**
See also CA 104; DLB 129

Heyward, (Edwin) DuBose
1885-1940 .... **TCLC 59**
See also CA 108; DLB 7, 9, 45; SATA 21

Hibbert, Eleanor Alice Burford
1906-1993 .... **CLC 7**
See also BEST 90:4; CA 17-20R; 140;
CANR 9, 28; DAM POP; SATA 2;
SATA-Obit 74

Higgins, George V(incent)
1939- .... **CLC 4, 7, 10, 18**
See also CA 77-80; CAAS 5; CANR 17, 51;
DLB 2; DLBY 81; INT CANR-17;
MTCW

Higginson, Thomas Wentworth
1823-1911 .... **TCLC 36**
See also DLB 1, 64

Highet, Helen
See MacInnes, Helen (Clark)

Highsmith, (Mary) Patricia
1921-1995 .... **CLC 2, 4, 14, 42**
See also CA 1-4R; 147; CANR 1, 20, 48;
DAM NOV, POP; MTCW

Highwater, Jamake (Mamake)
1942(?)- .... **CLC 12**
See also AAYA 7; CA 65-68; CAAS 7;
CANR 10, 34; CLR 17; DLB 52;
DLBY 85; JRDA; MAICYA; SATA 32,
69; SATA-Brief 30

Highway, Tomson 1951- ...... **CLC 92; DAC**
See also DAM MULT; NNAL

Higuchi, Ichiyo 1872-1896 .... **NCLC 49**

Hijuelos, Oscar 1951- ...... **CLC 65; HLC**
See also BEST 90:1; CA 123; CANR 50;
DAM MULT, POP; DLB 145; HW

Hikmet, Nazim 1902(?)-1963 .... **CLC 40**
See also CA 141; 93-96

Hildesheimer, Wolfgang
1916-1991 .... **CLC 49**
See also CA 101; 135; DLB 69, 124

Hill, Geoffrey (William)
1932- .... **CLC 5, 8, 18, 45**
See also CA 81-84; CANR 21;
CDBLB 1960 to Present; DAM POET;
DLB 40; MTCW

Hill, George Roy 1921- .... **CLC 26**
See also CA 110; 122

Hill, John
See Koontz, Dean R(ay)

Hill, Susan (Elizabeth)
1942- .... **CLC 4; DAB**
See also CA 33-36R; CANR 29;
DAM MST, NOV; DLB 14, 139; MTCW

Hillerman, Tony 1925- .... **CLC 62**
See also AAYA 6; BEST 89:1; CA 29-32R;
CANR 21, 42; DAM POP; SATA 6

Hillesum, Etty 1914-1943 .... **TCLC 49**
See also CA 137

Hilliard, Noel (Harvey) 1929- ...... **CLC 15**
See also CA 9-12R; CANR 7

Hillis, Rick 1956- .... **CLC 66**
See also CA 134

Hilton, James 1900-1954 .... **TCLC 21**
See also CA 108; DLB 34, 77; SATA 34

Himes, Chester (Bomar)
1909-1984 .... **CLC 2, 4, 7, 18, 58; BLC**
See also BW 2; CA 25-28R; 114; CANR 22;
DAM MULT; DLB 2, 76, 143; MTCW

Hinde, Thomas .... **CLC 6, 11**
See also Chitty, Thomas Willes

Hindin, Nathan
See Bloch, Robert (Albert)

Hine, (William) Daryl 1936- .... **CLC 15**
See also CA 1-4R; CAAS 15; CANR 1, 20;
DLB 60

Hinkson, Katharine Tynan
See Tynan, Katharine

Hinton, S(usan) E(loise)
1950- .... **CLC 30; DA; DAB; DAC**
See also AAYA 2; CA 81-84; CANR 32;
CLR 3, 23; DAM MST, NOV; JRDA;
MAICYA; MTCW; SATA 19, 58

Hippius, Zinaida .... **TCLC 9**
See also Gippius, Zinaida (Nikolayevna)

Hiraoka, Kimitake 1925-1970
See Mishima, Yukio
See also CA 97-100; 29-32R; DAM DRAM;
MTCW

Hirsch, E(ric) D(onald), Jr. 1928- ... **CLC 79**
See also CA 25-28R; CANR 27, 51;
DLB 67; INT CANR-27; MTCW

Hirsch, Edward 1950- .... **CLC 31, 50**
See also CA 104; CANR 20, 42; DLB 120

Hitchcock, Alfred (Joseph)
1899-1980 .... **CLC 16**
See also CA 97-100; SATA 27;
SATA-Obit 24

Hitler, Adolf 1889-1945 .... **TCLC 53**
See also CA 117; 147

Hoagland, Edward 1932- .... **CLC 28**
See also CA 1-4R; CANR 2, 31; DLB 6;
SATA 51

Hoban, Russell (Conwell) 1925- .. **CLC 7, 25**
See also CA 5-8R; CANR 23, 37; CLR 3;
DAM NOV; DLB 52; MAICYA;
MTCW; SATA 1, 40, 78

Hobbs, Perry
See Blackmur, R(ichard) P(almer)

Hobson, Laura Z(ametkin)
1900-1986 .... **CLC 7, 25**
See also CA 17-20R; 118; DLB 28;
SATA 52

Hochhuth, Rolf 1931- .... **CLC 4, 11, 18**
See also CA 5-8R; CANR 33;
DAM DRAM; DLB 124; MTCW

Hochman, Sandra 1936- .... **CLC 3, 8**
See also CA 5-8R; DLB 5

Hochwaelder, Fritz 1911-1986 ...... **CLC 36**
See also CA 29-32R; 120; CANR 42;
DAM DRAM; MTCW

Hochwalder, Fritz
See Hochwaelder, Fritz

Hocking, Mary (Eunice) 1921- ..... **CLC 13**
See also CA 101; CANR 18, 40

Hodgins, Jack 1938- .... **CLC 23**
See also CA 93-96; DLB 60

Hodgson, William Hope
1877(?)-1918 .... **TCLC 13**
See also CA 111; DLB 70, 153, 156

Hoffman, Alice 1952- .... **CLC 51**
See also CA 77-80; CANR 34; DAM NOV;
MTCW

Hoffman, Daniel (Gerard)
1923- .... **CLC 6, 13, 23**
See also CA 1-4R; CANR 4; DLB 5

Hoffman, Stanley 1944- .... **CLC 5**
See also CA 77-80

Hoffman, William M(oses) 1939- ... **CLC 40**
See also CA 57-60; CANR 11

Hoffmann, E(rnst) T(heodor) A(madeus)
1776-1822 .... **NCLC 2; SSC 13**
See also DLB 90; SATA 27

Hofmann, Gert 1931- .... **CLC 54**
See also CA 128

Hofmannsthal, Hugo von
1874-1929 .... **TCLC 11; DC 4**
See also CA 106; DAM DRAM; DLB 81,
118

Hogan, Linda 1947- .... **CLC 73**
See also CA 120; CANR 45; DAM MULT;
NNAL

Hogarth, Charles
See Creasey, John

Hogarth, Emmett
See Polonsky, Abraham (Lincoln)

Hogg, James 1770-1835 .... **NCLC 4**
See also DLB 93, 116, 159

Holbach, Paul Henri Thiry Baron
1723-1789 .... **LC 14**

Holberg, Ludvig 1684-1754 .... **LC 6**

Holden, Ursula 1921- .... **CLC 18**
See also CA 101; CAAS 8; CANR 22

Holderlin, (Johann Christian) Friedrich
1770-1843 .... **NCLC 16; PC 4**

Holdstock, Robert
See Holdstock, Robert P.

Holdstock, Robert P. 1948- .... **CLC 39**
See also CA 131

Holland, Isabelle 1920- .... **CLC 21**
See also AAYA 11; CA 21-24R; CANR 10,
25, 47; JRDA; MAICYA; SATA 8, 70

Holland, Marcus
See Caldwell, (Janet Miriam) Taylor
(Holland)

Hollander, John 1929- ...... **CLC 2, 5, 8, 14**
See also CA 1-4R; CANR 1; DLB 5;
SATA 13

Hollander, Paul
See Silverberg, Robert

Holleran, Andrew 1943(?)- .... **CLC 38**
See also CA 144

Hollinghurst, Alan 1954- .... **CLC 55, 91**
See also CA 114

Hollis, Jim
See Summers, Hollis (Spurgeon, Jr.)

Holmes, John
See Souster, (Holmes) Raymond

Holmes, John Clellon 1926-1988.... **CLC 56**
See also CA 9-12R; 125; CANR 4; DLB 16

Holmes, Oliver Wendell
1809-1894 .... **NCLC 14**
See also CDALB 1640-1865; DLB 1;
SATA 34

Holmes, Raymond
See Souster, (Holmes) Raymond

Holt, Victoria
See Hibbert, Eleanor Alice Burford

Holub, Miroslav 1923- .... **CLC 4**
See also CA 21-24R; CANR 10

Homer
c. 8th cent. B.C.- ..... **CMLC 1, 16; DA;
DAB; DAC**
See also DAM MST, POET

Honig, Edwin 1919- .... **CLC 33**
See also CA 5-8R; CAAS 8; CANR 4, 45;
DLB 5

Hood, Hugh (John Blagdon)
1928- .... **CLC 15, 28**
See also CA 49-52; CAAS 17; CANR 1, 33;
DLB 53

Hood, Thomas 1799-1845........ **NCLC 16**
See also DLB 96

Hooker, (Peter) Jeremy 1941-...... **CLC 43**
See also CA 77-80; CANR 22; DLB 40

Hope, A(lec) D(erwent) 1907- .... **CLC 3, 51**
See also CA 21-24R; CANR 33; MTCW

Hope, Brian
See Creasey, John

Hope, Christopher (David Tully)
1944- .... **CLC 52**
See also CA 106; CANR 47; SATA 62

Hopkins, Gerard Manley
1844-1889 .... **NCLC 17; DA; DAB;
DAC; PC 15; WLC**
See also CDBLB 1890-1914; DAM MST,
POET; DLB 35, 57

Hopkins, John (Richard) 1931-...... **CLC 4**
See also CA 85-88

Hopkins, Pauline Elizabeth
1859-1930 .... **TCLC 28; BLC**
See also BW 2; CA 141; DAM MULT;
DLB 50

Hopkinson, Francis 1737-1791 ...... **LC 25**
See also DLB 31

Hopley-Woolrich, Cornell George 1903-1968
See Woolrich, Cornell
See also CA 13-14; CAP 1

Horatio
See Proust, (Valentin-Louis-George-Eugene-)
Marcel

Horgan, Paul (George Vincent O'Shaughnessy)
1903-1995 .... **CLC 9, 53**
See also CA 13-16R; 147; CANR 9, 35;
DAM NOV; DLB 102; DLBY 85;
INT CANR-9; MTCW; SATA 13;
SATA-Obit 84

Horn, Peter
See Kuttner, Henry

Hornem, Horace Esq.
See Byron, George Gordon (Noel)

Hornung, E(rnest) W(illiam)
1866-1921 .... **TCLC 59**
See also CA 108; DLB 70

Horovitz, Israel (Arthur) 1939-..... **CLC 56**
See also CA 33-36R; CANR 46;
DAM DRAM; DLB 7

Horvath, Odon von
See Horvath, Oedoen von
See also DLB 85, 124

Horvath, Oedoen von 1901-1938... **TCLC 45**
See also Horvath, Odon von
See also CA 118

Horwitz, Julius 1920-1986........ **CLC 14**
See also CA 9-12R; 119; CANR 12

Hospital, Janette Turner 1942-..... **CLC 42**
See also CA 108; CANR 48

Hostos, E. M. de
See Hostos (y Bonilla), Eugenio Maria de

Hostos, Eugenio M. de
See Hostos (y Bonilla), Eugenio Maria de

Hostos, Eugenio Maria
See Hostos (y Bonilla), Eugenio Maria de

Hostos (y Bonilla), Eugenio Maria de
1839-1903 .... **TCLC 24**
See also CA 123; 131; HW

Houdini
See Lovecraft, H(oward) P(hillips)

Hougan, Carolyn 1943- .... **CLC 34**
See also CA 139

Household, Geoffrey (Edward West)
1900-1988 .... **CLC 11**
See also CA 77-80; 126; DLB 87; SATA 14;
SATA-Obit 59

Housman, A(lfred) E(dward)
1859-1936 ...... **TCLC 1, 10; DA; DAB;
DAC; PC 2**
See also CA 104; 125; DAM MST, POET;
DLB 19; MTCW

Housman, Laurence 1865-1959 ..... **TCLC 7**
See also CA 106; DLB 10; SATA 25

Howard, Elizabeth Jane 1923- ... **CLC 7, 29**
See also CA 5-8R; CANR 8

Howard, Maureen 1930- ..... **CLC 5, 14, 46**
See also CA 53-56; CANR 31; DLBY 83;
INT CANR-31; MTCW

Howard, Richard 1929- ...... **CLC 7, 10, 47**
See also AITN 1; CA 85-88; CANR 25;
DLB 5; INT CANR-25

Howard, Robert Ervin 1906-1936... **TCLC 8**
See also CA 105

Howard, Warren F.
See Pohl, Frederik

Howe, Fanny 1940- .... **CLC 47**
See also CA 117; SATA-Brief 52

Howe, Irving 1920-1993.......... **CLC 85**
See also CA 9-12R; 141; CANR 21, 50;
DLB 67; MTCW

Howe, Julia Ward 1819-1910 ..... **TCLC 21**
See also CA 117; DLB 1

Howe, Susan 1937- .... **CLC 72**
See also DLB 120

Howe, Tina 1937- .... **CLC 48**
See also CA 109

Jensen, Laura (Linnea) 1948- . . . . . . **CLC 37**
See also CA 103

Jerome, Jerome K(lapka)
1859-1927 . . . . **TCLC 23**
See also CA 119; DLB 10, 34, 135

Jerrold, Douglas William
1803-1857 . . . . **NCLC 2**
See also DLB 158, 159

Jewett, (Theodora) Sarah Orne
1849-1909 . . . . **TCLC 1, 22; SSC 6**
See also CA 108; 127; DLB 12, 74;
SATA 15

Jewsbury, Geraldine (Endsor)
1812-1880 . . . . **NCLC 22**
See also DLB 21

Jhabvala, Ruth Prawer
1927- . . . . **CLC 4, 8, 29; DAB**
See also CA 1-4R; CANR 2, 29, 51;
DAM NOV; DLB 139; INT CANR-29;
MTCW

Jibran, Kahlil
See Gibran, Kahlil

Jibran, Khalil
See Gibran, Kahlil

Jiles, Paulette 1943- . . . . **CLC 13, 58**
See also CA 101

Jimenez (Mantecon), Juan Ramon
1881-1958 . . . . **TCLC 4; HLC; PC 7**
See also CA 104; 131; DAM MULT,
POET; DLB 134; HW; MTCW

Jimenez, Ramon
See Jimenez (Mantecon), Juan Ramon

Jimenez Mantecon, Juan
See Jimenez (Mantecon), Juan Ramon

Joel, Billy . . . . **CLC 26**
See also Joel, William Martin

Joel, William Martin 1949-
See Joel, Billy
See also CA 108

John of the Cross, St. 1542-1591 . . . . **LC 18**

Johnson, B(ryan) S(tanley William)
1933-1973 . . . . **CLC 6, 9**
See also CA 9-12R; 53-56; CANR 9;
DLB 14, 40

Johnson, Benj. F. of Boo
See Riley, James Whitcomb

Johnson, Benjamin F. of Boo
See Riley, James Whitcomb

Johnson, Charles (Richard)
1948- . . . . **CLC 7, 51, 65; BLC**
See also BW 2; CA 116; CAAS 18;
CANR 42; DAM MULT; DLB 33

Johnson, Denis 1949- . . . . **CLC 52**
See also CA 117; 121; DLB 120

Johnson, Diane 1934- . . . . **CLC 5, 13, 48**
See also CA 41-44R; CANR 17, 40;
DLBY 80; INT CANR-17; MTCW

Johnson, Eyvind (Olof Verner)
1900-1976 . . . . **CLC 14**
See also CA 73-76; 69-72; CANR 34

Johnson, J. R.
See James, C(yril) L(ionel) R(obert)

Johnson, James Weldon
1871-1938 . . . . **TCLC 3, 19; BLC**
See also BW 1; CA 104; 125;
CDALB 1917-1929; CLR 32;
DAM MULT, POET; DLB 51; MTCW;
SATA 31

Johnson, Joyce 1935- . . . . **CLC 58**
See also CA 125; 129

Johnson, Lionel (Pigot)
1867-1902 . . . . **TCLC 19**
See also CA 117; DLB 19

Johnson, Mel
See Malzberg, Barry N(athaniel)

Johnson, Pamela Hansford
1912-1981 . . . . **CLC 1, 7, 27**
See also CA 1-4R; 104; CANR 2, 28;
DLB 15; MTCW

Johnson, Samuel
1709-1784 . . . . . **LC 15; DA; DAB; DAC;
WLC**
See also CDBLB 1660-1789; DAM MST;
DLB 39, 95, 104, 142

Johnson, Uwe
1934-1984 . . . . **CLC 5, 10, 15, 40**
See also CA 1-4R; 112; CANR 1, 39;
DLB 75; MTCW

Johnston, George (Benson) 1913- . . . **CLC 51**
See also CA 1-4R; CANR 5, 20; DLB 88

Johnston, Jennifer 1930- . . . . **CLC 7**
See also CA 85-88; DLB 14

Jolley, (Monica) Elizabeth
1923- . . . . **CLC 46; SSC 19**
See also CA 127; CAAS 13

Jones, Arthur Llewellyn 1863-1947
See Machen, Arthur
See also CA 104

Jones, D(ouglas) G(ordon) 1929- . . . . **CLC 10**
See also CA 29-32R; CANR 13; DLB 53

Jones, David (Michael)
1895-1974 . . . . **CLC 2, 4, 7, 13, 42**
See also CA 9-12R; 53-56; CANR 28;
CDBLB 1945-1960; DLB 20, 100; MTCW

Jones, David Robert 1947-
See Bowie, David
See also CA 103

Jones, Diana Wynne 1934- . . . . **CLC 26**
See also AAYA 12; CA 49-52; CANR 4,
26; CLR 23; DLB 161; JRDA; MAICYA;
SAAS 7; SATA 9, 70

Jones, Edward P. 1950- . . . . **CLC 76**
See also BW 2; CA 142

Jones, Gayl 1949- . . . . **CLC 6, 9; BLC**
See also BW 2; CA 77-80; CANR 27;
DAM MULT; DLB 33; MTCW

Jones, James 1921-1977 . . . . **CLC 1, 3, 10, 39**
See also AITN 1, 2; CA 1-4R; 69-72;
CANR 6; DLB 2, 143; MTCW

Jones, John J.
See Lovecraft, H(oward) P(hillips)

Jones, LeRoi . . . . **CLC 1, 2, 3, 5, 10, 14**
See also Baraka, Amiri

Jones, Louis B. . . . . **CLC 65**
See also CA 141

Jones, Madison (Percy, Jr.) 1925- . . . **CLC 4**
See also CA 13-16R; CAAS 11; CANR 7;
DLB 152

Jones, Mervyn 1922- . . . . **CLC 10, 52**
See also CA 45-48; CAAS 5; CANR 1;
MTCW

Jones, Mick 1956(?)- . . . . **CLC 30**

Jones, Nettie (Pearl) 1941- . . . . **CLC 34**
See also BW 2; CA 137; CAAS 20

Jones, Preston 1936-1979 . . . . **CLC 10**
See also CA 73-76; 89-92; DLB 7

Jones, Robert F(rancis) 1934- . . . . **CLC 7**
See also CA 49-52; CANR 2

Jones, Rod 1953- . . . . **CLC 50**
See also CA 128

Jones, Terence Graham Parry
1942- . . . . **CLC 21**
See also Jones, Terry; Monty Python
See also CA 112; 116; CANR 35; INT 116

Jones, Terry
See Jones, Terence Graham Parry
See also SATA 67; SATA-Brief 51

Jones, Thom 1945(?)- . . . . **CLC 81**

Jong, Erica 1942- . . . . . . **CLC 4, 6, 8, 18, 83**
See also AITN 1; BEST 90:2; CA 73-76;
CANR 26; DAM NOV, POP; DLB 2, 5,
28, 152; INT CANR-26; MTCW

Jonson, Ben(jamin)
1572(?)-1637 . . . . **LC 6; DA; DAB; DAC;
DC 4; WLC**
See also CDBLB Before 1660;
DAM DRAM, MST, POET; DLB 62,
121

Jordan, June 1936- . . . . **CLC 5, 11, 23**
See also AAYA 2; BW 2; CA 33-36R;
CANR 25; CLR 10; DAM MULT,
POET; DLB 38; MAICYA; MTCW;
SATA 4

Jordan, Pat(rick M.) 1941- . . . . **CLC 37**
See also CA 33-36R

Jorgensen, Ivar
See Ellison, Harlan (Jay)

Jorgenson, Ivar
See Silverberg, Robert

Josephus, Flavius c. 37-100 . . . . . . **CMLC 13**

Josipovici, Gabriel 1940- . . . . **CLC 6, 43**
See also CA 37-40R; CAAS 8; CANR 47;
DLB 14

Joubert, Joseph 1754-1824 . . . . **NCLC 9**

Jouve, Pierre Jean 1887-1976 . . . . . . **CLC 47**
See also CA 65-68

Joyce, James (Augustine Aloysius)
1882-1941 . . . . . . **TCLC 3, 8, 16, 35, 52;
DA; DAB; DAC; SSC 3; WLC**
See also CA 104; 126; CDBLB 1914-1945;
DAM MST, NOV, POET; DLB 10, 19,
36, 162; MTCW

Jozsef, Attila 1905-1937 . . . . **TCLC 22**
See also CA 116

Juana Ines de la Cruz 1651(?)-1695 . . . **LC 5**

Judd, Cyril
See Kornbluth, C(yril) M.; Pohl, Frederik

Julian of Norwich 1342(?)-1416(?) . . . . **LC 6**
See also DLB 146

Kennedy, Joseph Charles 1929-
See Kennedy, X. J.
See also CA 1-4R; CANR 4, 30, 40;
SATA 14, 86

Kennedy, William 1928-... **CLC 6, 28, 34, 53**
See also AAYA 1; CA 85-88; CANR 14,
31; DAM NOV; DLB 143; DLBY 85;
INT CANR-31; MTCW; SATA 57

Kennedy, X. J. .... **CLC 8, 42**
See also Kennedy, Joseph Charles
See also CAAS 9; CLR 27; DLB 5;
SAAS 22

Kenny, Maurice (Francis) 1929-.... **CLC 87**
See also CA 144; CAAS 22; DAM MULT;
NNAL

Kent, Kelvin
See Kuttner, Henry

Kenton, Maxwell
See Southern, Terry

Kenyon, Robert O.
See Kuttner, Henry

Kerouac, Jack ..... **CLC 1, 2, 3, 5, 14, 29, 61**
See also Kerouac, Jean-Louis Lebris de
See also CDALB 1941-1968; DLB 2, 16;
DLBD 3

Kerouac, Jean-Louis Lebris de 1922-1969
See Kerouac, Jack
See also AITN 1; CA 5-8R; 25-28R;
CANR 26; DA; DAB; DAC; DAM MST,
NOV, POET, POP; MTCW; WLC

Kerr, Jean 1923-................. **CLC 22**
See also CA 5-8R; CANR 7; INT CANR-7

Kerr, M. E. .... **CLC 12, 35**
See also Meaker, Marijane (Agnes)
See also AAYA 2; CLR 29; SAAS 1

Kerr, Robert .... **CLC 55**

Kerrigan, (Thomas) Anthony
1918- .... **CLC 4, 6**
See also CA 49-52; CAAS 11; CANR 4

Kerry, Lois
See Duncan, Lois

Kesey, Ken (Elton)
1935- ...... **CLC 1, 3, 6, 11, 46, 64; DA;
DAB; DAC; WLC**
See also CA 1-4R; CANR 22, 38;
CDALB 1968-1988; DAM MST, NOV,
POP; DLB 2, 16; MTCW; SATA 66

Kesselring, Joseph (Otto)
1902-1967 .... **CLC 45**
See also CA 150; DAM DRAM, MST

Kessler, Jascha (Frederick) 1929-.... **CLC 4**
See also CA 17-20R; CANR 8, 48

Kettelkamp, Larry (Dale) 1933- .... **CLC 12**
See also CA 29-32R; CANR 16; SAAS 3;
SATA 2

Keyber, Conny
See Fielding, Henry

Keyes, Daniel 1927-.... **CLC 80; DA; DAC**
See also CA 17-20R; CANR 10, 26;
DAM MST, NOV; SATA 37

Khanshendel, Chiron
See Rose, Wendy

Khayyam, Omar
1048-1131 .... **CMLC 11; PC 8**
See also DAM POET

Kherdian, David 1931-........... **CLC 6, 9**
See also CA 21-24R; CAAS 2; CANR 39;
CLR 24; JRDA; MAICYA; SATA 16, 74

Khlebnikov, Velimir .... **TCLC 20**
See also Khlebnikov, Viktor Vladimirovich

Khlebnikov, Viktor Vladimirovich 1885-1922
See Khlebnikov, Velimir
See also CA 117

Khodasevich, Vladislav (Felitsianovich)
1886-1939 .... **TCLC 15**
See also CA 115

Kielland, Alexander Lange
1849-1906 .... **TCLC 5**
See also CA 104

Kiely, Benedict 1919-.......... **CLC 23, 43**
See also CA 1-4R; CANR 2; DLB 15

Kienzle, William X(avier) 1928- .... **CLC 25**
See also CA 93-96; CAAS 1; CANR 9, 31;
DAM POP; INT CANR-31; MTCW

Kierkegaard, Soren 1813-1855.... **NCLC 34**

Killens, John Oliver 1916-1987..... **CLC 10**
See also BW 2; CA 77-80; 123; CAAS 2;
CANR 26; DLB 33

Killigrew, Anne 1660-1685........... **LC 4**
See also DLB 131

Kim
See Simenon, Georges (Jacques Christian)

Kincaid, Jamaica 1949- ... **CLC 43, 68; BLC**
See also AAYA 13; BW 2; CA 125;
CANR 47; DAM MULT, NOV;
DLB 157

King, Francis (Henry) 1923-..... **CLC 8, 53**
See also CA 1-4R; CANR 1, 33;
DAM NOV; DLB 15, 139; MTCW

King, Martin Luther, Jr.
1929-1968 .... **CLC 83; BLC; DA; DAB;
DAC**
See also BW 2; CA 25-28; CANR 27, 44;
CAP 2; DAM MST, MULT; MTCW;
SATA 14

King, Stephen (Edwin)
1947- ...... **CLC 12, 26, 37, 61; SSC 17**
See also AAYA 1, 17; BEST 90:1;
CA 61-64; CANR 1, 30; DAM NOV,
POP; DLB 143; DLBY 80; JRDA;
MTCW; SATA 9, 55

King, Steve
See King, Stephen (Edwin)

King, Thomas 1943-......... **CLC 89; DAC**
See also CA 144; DAM MULT; NNAL

Kingman, Lee.................... **CLC 17**
See also Natti, (Mary) Lee
See also SAAS 3; SATA 1, 67

Kingsley, Charles 1819-1875..... **NCLC 35**
See also DLB 21, 32, 163; YABC 2

Kingsley, Sidney 1906-1995........ **CLC 44**
See also CA 85-88; 147; DLB 7

Kingsolver, Barbara 1955-...... **CLC 55, 81**
See also AAYA 15; CA 129; 134;
DAM POP; INT 134

Kingston, Maxine (Ting Ting) Hong
1940- .... **CLC 12, 19, 58**
See also AAYA 8; CA 69-72; CANR 13,
38; DAM MULT, NOV; DLBY 80;
INT CANR-13; MTCW; SATA 53

Kinnell, Galway
1927- .... **CLC 1, 2, 3, 5, 13, 29**
See also CA 9-12R; CANR 10, 34; DLB 5;
DLBY 87; INT CANR-34; MTCW

Kinsella, Thomas 1928-......... **CLC 4, 19**
See also CA 17-20R; CANR 15; DLB 27;
MTCW

Kinsella, W(illiam) P(atrick)
1935- .... **CLC 27, 43; DAC**
See also AAYA 7; CA 97-100; CAAS 7;
CANR 21, 35; DAM NOV, POP;
INT CANR-21; MTCW

Kipling, (Joseph) Rudyard
1865-1936 ...... **TCLC 8, 17; DA; DAB;
DAC; PC 3; SSC 5; WLC**
See also CA 105; 120; CANR 33;
CDBLB 1890-1914; CLR 39; DAM MST,
POET; DLB 19, 34, 141, 156; MAICYA;
MTCW; YABC 2

Kirkup, James 1918- .... **CLC 1**
See also CA 1-4R; CAAS 4; CANR 2;
DLB 27; SATA 12

Kirkwood, James 1930(?)-1989 ...... **CLC 9**
See also AITN 2; CA 1-4R; 128; CANR 6,
40

Kirshner, Sidney
See Kingsley, Sidney

Kis, Danilo 1935-1989 .... **CLC 57**
See also CA 109; 118; 129; MTCW

Kivi, Aleksis 1834-1872 .... **NCLC 30**

Kizer, Carolyn (Ashley)
1925- .... **CLC 15, 39, 80**
See also CA 65-68; CAAS 5; CANR 24;
DAM POET; DLB 5

Klabund 1890-1928.............. **TCLC 44**
See also DLB 66

Klappert, Peter 1942-............. **CLC 57**
See also CA 33-36R; DLB 5

Klein, A(braham) M(oses)
1909-1972 .... **CLC 19; DAB; DAC**
See also CA 101; 37-40R; DAM MST;
DLB 68

Klein, Norma 1938-1989 .... **CLC 30**
See also AAYA 2; CA 41-44R; 128;
CANR 15, 37; CLR 2, 19;
INT CANR-15; JRDA; MAICYA;
SAAS 1; SATA 7, 57

Klein, T(heodore) E(ibon) D(onald)
1947- .... **CLC 34**
See also CA 119; CANR 44

Kleist, Heinrich von
1777-1811 .... **NCLC 2, 37; SSC 22**
See also DAM DRAM; DLB 90

Klima, Ivan 1931-................ **CLC 56**
See also CA 25-28R; CANR 17, 50;
DAM NOV

Klimentov, Andrei Platonovich 1899-1951
See Platonov, Andrei
See also CA 108

Klinger, Friedrich Maximilian von
1752-1831 .... **NCLC 1**
See also DLB 94

Klopstock, Friedrich Gottlieb
1724-1803 .... **NCLC 11**
See also DLB 97

Kyprianos, Iossif
See Samarakis, Antonis

La Bruyere, Jean de 1645-1696...... **LC 17**

Lacan, Jacques (Marie Emile)
1901-1981 .... **CLC 75**
See also CA 121; 104

Laclos, Pierre Ambroise Francois Choderlos
de 1741-1803 .... **NCLC 4**

Lacolere, Francois
See Aragon, Louis

La Colere, Francois
See Aragon, Louis

La Deshabilleuse
See Simenon, Georges (Jacques Christian)

Lady Gregory
See Gregory, Isabella Augusta (Persse)

Lady of Quality, A
See Bagnold, Enid

La Fayette, Marie (Madelaine Pioche de la
Vergne Comtes 1634-1693...... **LC 2**

Lafayette, Rene
See Hubbard, L(afayette) Ron(ald)

Laforgue, Jules
1860-1887 .... **NCLC 5, 53; PC 14;**
SSC 20

Lagerkvist, Paer (Fabian)
1891-1974 .... **CLC 7, 10, 13, 54**
See also Lagerkvist, Par
See also CA 85-88; 49-52; DAM DRAM,
NOV; MTCW

Lagerkvist, Par .... **SSC 12**
See also Lagerkvist, Paer (Fabian)

Lagerloef, Selma (Ottiliana Lovisa)
1858-1940 .... **TCLC 4, 36**
See also Lagerlof, Selma (Ottiliana Lovisa)
See also CA 108; SATA 15

Lagerlof, Selma (Ottiliana Lovisa)
See Lagerloef, Selma (Ottiliana Lovisa)
See also CLR 7; SATA 15

La Guma, (Justin) Alex(ander)
1925-1985 .... **CLC 19**
See also BW 1; CA 49-52; 118; CANR 25;
DAM NOV; DLB 117; MTCW

Laidlaw, A. K.
See Grieve, C(hristopher) M(urray)

Lainez, Manuel Mujica
See Mujica Lainez, Manuel
See also HW

Lamartine, Alphonse (Marie Louis Prat) de
1790-1869 .... **NCLC 11; PC 15**
See also DAM POET

Lamb, Charles
1775-1834 .... **NCLC 10; DA; DAB;**
DAC; WLC
See also CDBLB 1789-1832; DAM MST;
DLB 93, 107, 163; SATA 17

Lamb, Lady Caroline 1785-1828.. **NCLC 38**
See also DLB 116

Lamming, George (William)
1927- .... **CLC 2, 4, 66; BLC**
See also BW 2; CA 85-88; CANR 26;
DAM MULT; DLB 125; MTCW

L'Amour, Louis (Dearborn)
1908-1988 .... **CLC 25, 55**
See also AAYA 16; AITN 2; BEST 89:2;
CA 1-4R; 125; CANR 3, 25, 40;
DAM NOV, POP; DLBY 80; MTCW

Lampedusa, Giuseppe (Tomasi) di ... **TCLC 13**
See also Tomasi di Lampedusa, Giuseppe

Lampman, Archibald 1861-1899 .. **NCLC 25**
See also DLB 92

Lancaster, Bruce 1896-1963........ **CLC 36**
See also CA 9-10; CAP 1; SATA 9

Landau, Mark Alexandrovich
See Aldanov, Mark (Alexandrovich)

Landau-Aldanov, Mark Alexandrovich
See Aldanov, Mark (Alexandrovich)

Landis, John 1950-.............. **CLC 26**
See also CA 112; 122

Landolfi, Tommaso 1908-1979... **CLC 11, 49**
See also CA 127; 117

Landon, Letitia Elizabeth
1802-1838 .... **NCLC 15**
See also DLB 96

Landor, Walter Savage
1775-1864 .... **NCLC 14**
See also DLB 93, 107

Landwirth, Heinz 1927-
See Lind, Jakov
See also CA 9-12R; CANR 7

Lane, Patrick 1939- .... **CLC 25**
See also CA 97-100; DAM POET; DLB 53;
INT 97-100

Lang, Andrew 1844-1912........ **TCLC 16**
See also CA 114; 137; DLB 98, 141;
MAICYA; SATA 16

Lang, Fritz 1890-1976 .... **CLC 20**
See also CA 77-80; 69-72; CANR 30

Lange, John
See Crichton, (John) Michael

Langer, Elinor 1939- .... **CLC 34**
See also CA 121

Langland, William
1330(?)-1400(?) ...... **LC 19; DA; DAB;**
DAC
See also DAM MST, POET; DLB 146

Langstaff, Launcelot
See Irving, Washington

Lanier, Sidney 1842-1881 .... **NCLC 6**
See also DAM POET; DLB 64; DLBD 13;
MAICYA; SATA 18

Lanyer, Aemilia 1569-1645 ...... **LC 10, 30**
See also DLB 121

Lao Tzu .... **CMLC 7**

Lapine, James (Elliot) 1949-....... **CLC 39**
See also CA 123; 130; INT 130

Larbaud, Valery (Nicolas)
1881-1957 .... **TCLC 9**
See also CA 106

Lardner, Ring
See Lardner, Ring(gold) W(ilmer)

Lardner, Ring W., Jr.
See Lardner, Ring(gold) W(ilmer)

Lardner, Ring(gold) W(ilmer)
1885-1933 .... **TCLC 2, 14**
See also CA 104; 131; CDALB 1917-1929;
DLB 11, 25, 86; MTCW

Laredo, Betty
See Codrescu, Andrei

Larkin, Maia
See Wojciechowska, Maia (Teresa)

Larkin, Philip (Arthur)
1922-1985 .... **CLC 3, 5, 8, 9, 13, 18, 33,**
39, 64; DAB
See also CA 5-8R; 117; CANR 24;
CDBLB 1960 to Present; DAM MST,
POET; DLB 27; MTCW

Larra (y Sanchez de Castro), Mariano Jose de
1809-1837 .... **NCLC 17**

Larsen, Eric 1941-................ **CLC 55**
See also CA 132

Larsen, Nella 1891-1964 ..... **CLC 37; BLC**
See also BW 1; CA 125; DAM MULT;
DLB 51

Larson, Charles R(aymond) 1938-... **CLC 31**
See also CA 53-56; CANR 4

Las Casas, Bartolome de 1474-1566.. **LC 31**

Lasker-Schueler, Else 1869-1945 .. **TCLC 57**
See also DLB 66, 124

Latham, Jean Lee 1902-.......... **CLC 12**
See also AITN 1; CA 5-8R; CANR 7;
MAICYA; SATA 2, 68

Latham, Mavis
See Clark, Mavis Thorpe

Lathen, Emma .... **CLC 2**
See also Hennissart, Martha; Latsis, Mary
J(ane)

Lathrop, Francis
See Leiber, Fritz (Reuter, Jr.)

Latsis, Mary J(ane)
See Lathen, Emma
See also CA 85-88

Lattimore, Richmond (Alexander)
1906-1984 .... **CLC 3**
See also CA 1-4R; 112; CANR 1

Laughlin, James 1914-............ **CLC 49**
See also CA 21-24R; CAAS 22; CANR 9,
47; DLB 48

Laurence, (Jean) Margaret (Wemyss)
1926-1987 .... **CLC 3, 6, 13, 50, 62;**
DAC; SSC 7
See also CA 5-8R; 121; CANR 33;
DAM MST; DLB 53; MTCW;
SATA-Obit 50

Laurent, Antoine 1952- .... **CLC 50**

Lauscher, Hermann
See Hesse, Hermann

Lautreamont, Comte de
1846-1870 .... **NCLC 12; SSC 14**

Laverty, Donald
See Blish, James (Benjamin)

Lavin, Mary 1912-...... **CLC 4, 18; SSC 4**
See also CA 9-12R; CANR 33; DLB 15;
MTCW

Lavond, Paul Dennis
See Kornbluth, C(yril) M.; Pohl, Frederik

Lawler, Raymond Evenor 1922- .... **CLC 58**
See also CA 103

Lawrence, D(avid) H(erbert Richards)
1885-1930 .... **TCLC 2, 9, 16, 33, 48, 61;**
DA; DAB; DAC; SSC 4, 19; WLC
See also CA 104; 121; CDBLB 1914-1945;
DAM MST, NOV, POET; DLB 10, 19,
36, 98, 162; MTCW

Lawrence, T(homas) E(dward)
1888-1935 .... **TCLC 18**
See also Dale, Colin
See also CA 115

Lawrence of Arabia
See Lawrence, T(homas) E(dward)

Lawson, Henry (Archibald Hertzberg)
1867-1922 .... **TCLC 27; SSC 18**
See also CA 120

Lawton, Dennis
See Faust, Frederick (Schiller)

Laxness, Halldor .... **CLC 25**
See also Gudjonsson, Halldor Kiljan

Layamon fl. c. 1200- .... **CMLC 10**
See also DLB 146

Laye, Camara 1928-1980 ... **CLC 4, 38; BLC**
See also BW 1; CA 85-88; 97-100;
CANR 25; DAM MULT; MTCW

Layton, Irving (Peter)
1912- .... **CLC 2, 15; DAC**
See also CA 1-4R; CANR 2, 33, 43;
DAM MST, POET; DLB 88; MTCW

Lazarus, Emma 1849-1887 .... **NCLC 8**

Lazarus, Felix
See Cable, George Washington

Lazarus, Henry
See Slavitt, David R(ytman)

Lea, Joan
See Neufeld, John (Arthur)

Leacock, Stephen (Butler)
1869-1944 .... **TCLC 2; DAC**
See also CA 104; 141; DAM MST; DLB 92

Lear, Edward 1812-1888 .... **NCLC 3**
See also CLR 1; DLB 32, 163; MAICYA;
SATA 18

Lear, Norman (Milton) 1922- ...... **CLC 12**
See also CA 73-76

Leavis, F(rank) R(aymond)
1895-1978 .... **CLC 24**
See also CA 21-24R; 77-80; CANR 44;
MTCW

Leavitt, David 1961- .... **CLC 34**
See also CA 116; 122; CANR 50;
DAM POP; DLB 130; INT 122

Leblanc, Maurice (Marie Emile)
1864-1941 .... **TCLC 49**
See also CA 110

Lebowitz, Fran(ces Ann)
1951(?)- .... **CLC 11, 36**
See also CA 81-84; CANR 14;
INT CANR-14; MTCW

Lebrecht, Peter
See Tieck, (Johann) Ludwig

le Carre, John .... **CLC 3, 5, 9, 15, 28**
See also Cornwell, David (John Moore)
See also BEST 89:4; CDBLB 1960 to
Present; DLB 87

Le Clezio, J(ean) M(arie) G(ustave)
1940- .... **CLC 31**
See also CA 116; 128; DLB 83

Leconte de Lisle, Charles-Marie-Rene
1818-1894 .... **NCLC 29**

Le Coq, Monsieur
See Simenon, Georges (Jacques Christian)

Leduc, Violette 1907-1972 .... **CLC 22**
See also CA 13-14; 33-36R; CAP 1

Ledwidge, Francis 1887(?)-1917 ... **TCLC 23**
See also CA 123; DLB 20

Lee, Andrea 1953- .... **CLC 36; BLC**
See also BW 1; CA 125; DAM MULT

Lee, Andrew
See Auchincloss, Louis (Stanton)

Lee, Chang-rae 1965- .... **CLC 91**
See also CA 148

Lee, Don L. .... **CLC 2**
See also Madhubuti, Haki R.

Lee, George W(ashington)
1894-1976 .... **CLC 52; BLC**
See also BW 1; CA 125; DAM MULT;
DLB 51

Lee, (Nelle) Harper
1926- .... **CLC 12, 60; DA; DAB; DAC;**
WLC
See also AAYA 13; CA 13-16R; CANR 51;
CDALB 1941-1968; DAM MST, NOV;
DLB 6; MTCW; SATA 11

Lee, Helen Elaine 1959(?)- .... **CLC 86**
See also CA 148

Lee, Julian
See Latham, Jean Lee

Lee, Larry
See Lee, Lawrence

Lee, Laurie 1914- .... **CLC 90; DAB**
See also CA 77-80; CANR 33; DAM POP;
DLB 27; MTCW

Lee, Lawrence 1941-1990 .... **CLC 34**
See also CA 131; CANR 43

Lee, Manfred B(ennington)
1905-1971 .... **CLC 11**
See also Queen, Ellery
See also CA 1-4R; 29-32R; CANR 2;
DLB 137

Lee, Stan 1922- .... **CLC 17**
See also AAYA 5; CA 108; 111; INT 111

Lee, Tanith 1947- .... **CLC 46**
See also AAYA 15; CA 37-40R; SATA 8

Lee, Vernon .... **TCLC 5**
See also Paget, Violet
See also DLB 57, 153, 156

Lee, William
See Burroughs, William S(eward)

Lee, Willy
See Burroughs, William S(eward)

Lee-Hamilton, Eugene (Jacob)
1845-1907 .... **TCLC 22**
See also CA 117

Leet, Judith 1935- .... **CLC 11**

Le Fanu, Joseph Sheridan
1814-1873 .... **NCLC 9; SSC 14**
See also DAM POP; DLB 21, 70, 159

Leffland, Ella 1931- .... **CLC 19**
See also CA 29-32R; CANR 35; DLBY 84;
INT CANR-35; SATA 65

Leger, Alexis
See Leger, (Marie-Rene Auguste) Alexis
Saint-Leger

Leger, (Marie-Rene Auguste) Alexis
Saint-Leger 1887-1975 .... **CLC 11**
See also Perse, St.-John
See also CA 13-16R; 61-64; CANR 43;
DAM POET; MTCW

Leger, Saintleger
See Leger, (Marie-Rene Auguste) Alexis
Saint-Leger

Le Guin, Ursula K(roeber)
1929- ...... **CLC 8, 13, 22, 45, 71; DAB;**
DAC; SSC 12
See also AAYA 9; AITN 1; CA 21-24R;
CANR 9, 32; CDALB 1968-1988; CLR 3,
28; DAM MST, POP; DLB 8, 52;
INT CANR-32; JRDA; MAICYA;
MTCW; SATA 4, 52

Lehmann, Rosamond (Nina)
1901-1990 .... **CLC 5**
See also CA 77-80; 131; CANR 8; DLB 15

Leiber, Fritz (Reuter, Jr.)
1910-1992 .... **CLC 25**
See also CA 45-48; 139; CANR 2, 40;
DLB 8; MTCW; SATA 45;
SATA-Obit 73

Leimbach, Martha 1963-
See Leimbach, Marti
See also CA 130

Leimbach, Marti .... **CLC 65**
See also Leimbach, Martha

Leino, Eino .... **TCLC 24**
See also Loennbohm, Armas Eino Leopold

Leiris, Michel (Julien) 1901-1990 ... **CLC 61**
See also CA 119; 128; 132

Leithauser, Brad 1953- .... **CLC 27**
See also CA 107; CANR 27; DLB 120

Lelchuk, Alan 1938- .... **CLC 5**
See also CA 45-48; CAAS 20; CANR 1

Lem, Stanislaw 1921- .... **CLC 8, 15, 40**
See also CA 105; CAAS 1; CANR 32;
MTCW

Lemann, Nancy 1956- .... **CLC 39**
See also CA 118; 136

Lemonnier, (Antoine Louis) Camille
1844-1913 .... **TCLC 22**
See also CA 121

Lenau, Nikolaus 1802-1850 ...... **NCLC 16**

L'Engle, Madeleine (Camp Franklin)
1918- .... **CLC 12**
See also AAYA 1; AITN 2; CA 1-4R;
CANR 3, 21, 39; CLR 1, 14; DAM POP;
DLB 52; JRDA; MAICYA; MTCW;
SAAS 15; SATA 1, 27, 75

Lengyel, Jozsef 1896-1975 .... **CLC 7**
See also CA 85-88; 57-60

Lennon, John (Ono)
1940-1980 .... **CLC 12, 35**
See also CA 102

Lennox, Charlotte Ramsay
1729(?)-1804 .... **NCLC 23**
See also DLB 39

Lugones, Leopoldo 1874-1938 . . . . . **TCLC 15**
See also CA 116; 131; HW

Lu Hsun 1881-1936 . . . . . . **TCLC 3; SSC 20**
See also Shu-Jen, Chou

Lukacs, George . . . . **CLC 24**
See also Lukacs, Gyorgy (Szegeny von)

Lukacs, Gyorgy (Szegeny von) 1885-1971
See Lukacs, George
See also CA 101; 29-32R

Luke, Peter (Ambrose Cyprian)
1919-1995 . . . . **CLC 38**
See also CA 81-84; 147; DLB 13

Lunar, Dennis
See Mungo, Raymond

Lurie, Alison 1926- . . . . **CLC 4, 5, 18, 39**
See also CA 1-4R; CANR 2, 17, 50; DLB 2;
MTCW; SATA 46

Lustig, Arnost 1926- . . . . **CLC 56**
See also AAYA 3; CA 69-72; CANR 47;
SATA 56

Luther, Martin 1483-1546 . . . . **LC 9**

Luxemburg, Rosa 1870(?)-1919 . . . . **TCLC 63**
See also CA 118

Luzi, Mario 1914- . . . . **CLC 13**
See also CA 61-64; CANR 9; DLB 128

L'Ymagier
See Gourmont, Remy (-Marie-Charles) de

Lynch, B. Suarez
See Bioy Casares, Adolfo; Borges, Jorge
Luis

Lynch, David (K.) 1946- . . . . **CLC 66**
See also CA 124; 129

Lynch, James
See Andreyev, Leonid (Nikolaevich)

Lynch Davis, B.
See Bioy Casares, Adolfo; Borges, Jorge
Luis

Lyndsay, Sir David 1490-1555 . . . . . . **LC 20**

Lynn, Kenneth S(chuyler) 1923- . . . . **CLC 50**
See also CA 1-4R; CANR 3, 27

Lynx
See West, Rebecca

Lyons, Marcus
See Blish, James (Benjamin)

Lyre, Pinchbeck
See Sassoon, Siegfried (Lorraine)

Lytle, Andrew (Nelson) 1902-1995 . . **CLC 22**
See also CA 9-12R; 150; DLB 6

Lyttelton, George 1709-1773 . . . . **LC 10**

Maas, Peter 1929- . . . . **CLC 29**
See also CA 93-96; INT 93-96

Macaulay, Rose 1881-1958 . . . . . **TCLC 7, 44**
See also CA 104; DLB 36

Macaulay, Thomas Babington
1800-1859 . . . . **NCLC 42**
See also CDBLB 1832-1890; DLB 32, 55

MacBeth, George (Mann)
1932-1992 . . . . **CLC 2, 5, 9**
See also CA 25-28R; 136; DLB 40; MTCW;
SATA 4; SATA-Obit 70

MacCaig, Norman (Alexander)
1910- . . . . **CLC 36; DAB**
See also CA 9-12R; CANR 3, 34;
DAM POET; DLB 27

MacCarthy, (Sir Charles Otto) Desmond
1877-1952 . . . . **TCLC 36**

MacDiarmid, Hugh
. . . . **CLC 2, 4, 11, 19, 63; PC 9**
See also Grieve, C(hristopher) M(urray)
See also CDBLB 1945-1960; DLB 20

MacDonald, Anson
See Heinlein, Robert A(nson)

Macdonald, Cynthia 1928- . . . . . . **CLC 13, 19**
See also CA 49-52; CANR 4, 44; DLB 105

MacDonald, George 1824-1905 . . . . . **TCLC 9**
See also CA 106; 137; DLB 18, 163;
MAICYA; SATA 33

Macdonald, John
See Millar, Kenneth

MacDonald, John D(ann)
1916-1986 . . . . **CLC 3, 27, 44**
See also CA 1-4R; 121; CANR 1, 19;
DAM NOV, POP; DLB 8; DLBY 86;
MTCW

Macdonald, John Ross
See Millar, Kenneth

Macdonald, Ross . . . . . **CLC 1, 2, 3, 14, 34, 41**
See also Millar, Kenneth
See also DLBD 6

MacDougal, John
See Blish, James (Benjamin)

MacEwen, Gwendolyn (Margaret)
1941-1987 . . . . **CLC 13, 55**
See also CA 9-12R; 124; CANR 7, 22;
DLB 53; SATA 50; SATA-Obit 55

Macha, Karel Hynek 1810-1846 . . **NCLC 46**

Machado (y Ruiz), Antonio
1875-1939 . . . . **TCLC 3**
See also CA 104; DLB 108

Machado de Assis, Joaquim Maria
1839-1908 . . . . **TCLC 10; BLC**
See also CA 107

Machen, Arthur . . . . **TCLC 4; SSC 20**
See also Jones, Arthur Llewellyn
See also DLB 36, 156

Machiavelli, Niccolo
1469-1527 . . . . . . **LC 8; DA; DAB; DAC**
See also DAM MST

MacInnes, Colin 1914-1976 . . . . . . **CLC 4, 23**
See also CA 69-72; 65-68; CANR 21;
DLB 14; MTCW

MacInnes, Helen (Clark)
1907-1985 . . . . **CLC 27, 39**
See also CA 1-4R; 117; CANR 1, 28;
DAM POP; DLB 87; MTCW; SATA 22;
SATA-Obit 44

Mackay, Mary 1855-1924
See Corelli, Marie
See also CA 118

Mackenzie, Compton (Edward Montague)
1883-1972 . . . . **CLC 18**
See also CA 21-22; 37-40R; CAP 2;
DLB 34, 100

Mackenzie, Henry 1745-1831 . . . . **NCLC 41**
See also DLB 39

Mackintosh, Elizabeth 1896(?)-1952
See Tey, Josephine
See also CA 110

MacLaren, James
See Grieve, C(hristopher) M(urray)

Mac Laverty, Bernard 1942- . . . . **CLC 31**
See also CA 116; 118; CANR 43; INT 118

MacLean, Alistair (Stuart)
1922-1987 . . . . **CLC 3, 13, 50, 63**
See also CA 57-60; 121; CANR 28;
DAM POP; MTCW; SATA 23;
SATA-Obit 50

Maclean, Norman (Fitzroy)
1902-1990 . . . . **CLC 78; SSC 13**
See also CA 102; 132; CANR 49;
DAM POP

MacLeish, Archibald
1892-1982 . . . . **CLC 3, 8, 14, 68**
See also CA 9-12R; 106; CANR 33;
DAM POET; DLB 4, 7, 45; DLBY 82;
MTCW

MacLennan, (John) Hugh
1907-1990 . . . . **CLC 2, 14, 92; DAC**
See also CA 5-8R; 142; CANR 33;
DAM MST; DLB 68; MTCW

MacLeod, Alistair 1936- . . . . . **CLC 56; DAC**
See also CA 123; DAM MST; DLB 60

MacNeice, (Frederick) Louis
1907-1963 . . . . . . **CLC 1, 4, 10, 53; DAB**
See also CA 85-88; DAM POET; DLB 10,
20; MTCW

MacNeill, Dand
See Fraser, George MacDonald

Macpherson, James 1736-1796 . . . . . . **LC 29**
See also DLB 109

Macpherson, (Jean) Jay 1931- . . . . . . **CLC 14**
See also CA 5-8R; DLB 53

MacShane, Frank 1927- . . . . **CLC 39**
See also CA 9-12R; CANR 3, 33; DLB 111

Macumber, Mari
See Sandoz, Mari(e Susette)

Madach, Imre 1823-1864 . . . . **NCLC 19**

Madden, (Jerry) David 1933- . . . . **CLC 5, 15**
See also CA 1-4R; CAAS 3; CANR 4, 45;
DLB 6; MTCW

Maddern, Al(an)
See Ellison, Harlan (Jay)

Madhubuti, Haki R.
1942- . . . . **CLC 6, 73; BLC; PC 5**
See also Lee, Don L.
See also BW 2; CA 73-76; CANR 24, 51;
DAM MULT, POET; DLB 5, 41;
DLBD 8

Maepenn, Hugh
See Kuttner, Henry

Maepenn, K. H.
See Kuttner, Henry

Maeterlinck, Maurice 1862-1949 . . . **TCLC 3**
See also CA 104; 136; DAM DRAM;
SATA 66

Maginn, William 1794-1842 . . . . **NCLC 8**
See also DLB 110, 159

Mahapatra, Jayanta 1928- . . . . **CLC 33**
See also CA 73-76; CAAS 9; CANR 15, 33;
DAM MULT

Marquand, John P(hillips)
    1893-1960 . . . . CLC 2, 10
    See also CA 85-88; DLB 9, 102

Marquez, Gabriel (Jose) Garcia
    See Garcia Marquez, Gabriel (Jose)

Marquis, Don(ald Robert Perry)
    1878-1937 . . . . TCLC 7
    See also CA 104; DLB 11, 25

Marric, J. J.
    See Creasey, John

Marrow, Bernard
    See Moore, Brian

Marryat, Frederick 1792-1848 . . . . NCLC 3
    See also DLB 21, 163

Marsden, James
    See Creasey, John

Marsh, (Edith) Ngaio
    1899-1982 . . . . CLC 7, 53
    See also CA 9-12R; CANR 6; DAM POP;
    DLB 77; MTCW

Marshall, Garry 1934- . . . . CLC 17
    See also AAYA 3; CA 111; SATA 60

Marshall, Paule
    1929- . . . . CLC 27, 72; BLC; SSC 3
    See also BW 2; CA 77-80; CANR 25;
    DAM MULT; DLB 157; MTCW

Marsten, Richard
    See Hunter, Evan

Martha, Henry
    See Harris, Mark

Martial c. 40-c. 104 . . . . PC 10

Martin, Ken
    See Hubbard, L(afayette) Ron(ald)

Martin, Richard
    See Creasey, John

Martin, Steve 1945- . . . . CLC 30
    See also CA 97-100; CANR 30; MTCW

Martin, Valerie 1948- . . . . CLC 89
    See also BEST 90:2; CA 85-88; CANR 49

Martin, Violet Florence
    1862-1915 . . . . TCLC 51

Martin, Webber
    See Silverberg, Robert

Martindale, Patrick Victor
    See White, Patrick (Victor Martindale)

Martin du Gard, Roger
    1881-1958 . . . . TCLC 24
    See also CA 118; DLB 65

Martineau, Harriet 1802-1876. . . . NCLC 26
    See also DLB 21, 55, 159, 163; YABC 2

Martines, Julia
    See O'Faolain, Julia

Martinez, Jacinto Benavente y
    See Benavente (y Martinez), Jacinto

Martinez Ruiz, Jose 1873-1967
    See Azorin; Ruiz, Jose Martinez
    See also CA 93-96; HW

Martinez Sierra, Gregorio
    1881-1947 . . . . TCLC 6
    See also CA 115

Martinez Sierra, Maria (de la O'LeJarraga)
    1874-1974 . . . . TCLC 6
    See also CA 115

Martinsen, Martin
    See Follett, Ken(neth Martin)

Martinson, Harry (Edmund)
    1904-1978 . . . . CLC 14
    See also CA 77-80; CANR 34

Marut, Ret
    See Traven, B.

Marut, Robert
    See Traven, B.

Marvell, Andrew
    1621-1678 . . . . . . LC 4; DA; DAB; DAC;
                                      PC 10; WLC
    See also CDBLB 1660-1789; DAM MST,
    POET; DLB 131

Marx, Karl (Heinrich)
    1818-1883 . . . . NCLC 17
    See also DLB 129

Masaoka Shiki. . . . . TCLC 18
    See also Masaoka Tsunenori

Masaoka Tsunenori 1867-1902
    See Masaoka Shiki
    See also CA 117

Masefield, John (Edward)
    1878-1967 . . . . CLC 11, 47
    See also CA 19-20; 25-28R; CANR 33;
    CAP 2; CDBLB 1890-1914; DAM POET;
    DLB 10, 19, 153, 160; MTCW; SATA 19

Maso, Carole 19(?)- . . . . CLC 44

Mason, Bobbie Ann
    1940- . . . . CLC 28, 43, 82; SSC 4
    See also AAYA 5; CA 53-56; CANR 11,
    31; DLBY 87; INT CANR-31; MTCW

Mason, Ernst
    See Pohl, Frederik

Mason, Lee W.
    See Malzberg, Barry N(athaniel)

Mason, Nick 1945- . . . . CLC 35

Mason, Tally
    See Derleth, August (William)

Mass, William
    See Gibson, William

Masters, Edgar Lee
    1868-1950 . . . . . . TCLC 2, 25; DA; DAC;
                                      PC 1
    See also CA 104; 133; CDALB 1865-1917;
    DAM MST, POET; DLB 54; MTCW

Masters, Hilary 1928- . . . . CLC 48
    See also CA 25-28R; CANR 13, 47

Mastrosimone, William 19(?)- . . . . . CLC 36

Mathe, Albert
    See Camus, Albert

Matheson, Richard Burton 1926- . . CLC 37
    See also CA 97-100; DLB 8, 44; INT 97-100

Mathews, Harry 1930- . . . . CLC 6, 52
    See also CA 21-24R; CAAS 6; CANR 18,
    40

Mathews, John Joseph 1894-1979. . . CLC 84
    See also CA 19-20; 142; CANR 45; CAP 2;
    DAM MULT; NNAL

Mathias, Roland (Glyn) 1915- . . . . . CLC 45
    See also CA 97-100; CANR 19, 41; DLB 27

Matsuo Basho 1644-1694. . . . . PC 3
    See also DAM POET

Mattheson, Rodney
    See Creasey, John

Matthews, Greg 1949- . . . . CLC 45
    See also CA 135

Matthews, William 1942- . . . . CLC 40
    See also CA 29-32R; CAAS 18; CANR 12;
    DLB 5

Matthias, John (Edward) 1941- . . . . . CLC 9
    See also CA 33-36R

Matthiessen, Peter
    1927- . . . . CLC 5, 7, 11, 32, 64
    See also AAYA 6; BEST 90:4; CA 9-12R;
    CANR 21, 50; DAM NOV; DLB 6;
    MTCW; SATA 27

Maturin, Charles Robert
    1780(?)-1824 . . . . NCLC 6

Matute (Ausejo), Ana Maria
    1925- . . . . CLC 11
    See also CA 89-92; MTCW

Maugham, W. S.
    See Maugham, W(illiam) Somerset

Maugham, W(illiam) Somerset
    1874-1965 . . . . . . CLC 1, 11, 15, 67; DA;
                               DAB; DAC; SSC 8; WLC
    See also CA 5-8R; 25-28R; CANR 40;
    CDBLB 1914-1945; DAM DRAM, MST,
    NOV; DLB 10, 36, 77, 100, 162; MTCW;
    SATA 54

Maugham, William Somerset
    See Maugham, W(illiam) Somerset

Maupassant, (Henri Rene Albert) Guy de
    1850-1893 . . . . . NCLC 1, 42; DA; DAB;
                               DAC; SSC 1; WLC
    See also DAM MST; DLB 123

Maurhut, Richard
    See Traven, B.

Mauriac, Claude 1914- . . . . CLC 9
    See also CA 89-92; DLB 83

Mauriac, Francois (Charles)
    1885-1970 . . . . CLC 4, 9, 56
    See also CA 25-28; CAP 2; DLB 65;
    MTCW

Mavor, Osborne Henry 1888-1951
    See Bridie, James
    See also CA 104

Maxwell, William (Keepers, Jr.)
    1908- . . . . CLC 19
    See also CA 93-96; DLBY 80; INT 93-96

May, Elaine 1932- . . . . CLC 16
    See also CA 124; 142; DLB 44

Mayakovski, Vladimir (Vladimirovich)
    1893-1930 . . . . TCLC 4, 18
    See also CA 104

Mayhew, Henry 1812-1887 . . . . . . NCLC 31
    See also DLB 18, 55

Mayle, Peter 1939(?)- . . . . CLC 89
    See also CA 139

Maynard, Joyce 1953- . . . . CLC 23
    See also CA 111; 129

Mayne, William (James Carter)
    1928- . . . . CLC 12
    See also CA 9-12R; CANR 37; CLR 25;
    JRDA; MAICYA; SAAS 11; SATA 6, 68

Mayo, Jim
    See L'Amour, Louis (Dearborn)

Maysles, Albert 1926- . . . . CLC 16
See also CA 29-32R

Maysles, David 1932- . . . . CLC 16

Mazer, Norma Fox 1931- . . . . CLC 26
See also AAYA 5; CA 69-72; CANR 12,
32; CLR 23; JRDA; MAICYA; SAAS 1;
SATA 24, 67

Mazzini, Guiseppe 1805-1872 . . . . NCLC 34

McAuley, James Phillip
1917-1976 . . . . CLC 45
See also CA 97-100

McBain, Ed
See Hunter, Evan

McBrien, William Augustine
1930- . . . . CLC 44
See also CA 107

McCaffrey, Anne (Inez) 1926- . . . . . . CLC 17
See also AAYA 6; AITN 2; BEST 89:2;
CA 25-28R; CANR 15, 35; DAM NOV,
POP; DLB 8; JRDA; MAICYA; MTCW;
SAAS 11; SATA 8, 70

McCall, Nathan 1955(?)- . . . . CLC 86
See also CA 146

McCann, Arthur
See Campbell, John W(ood, Jr.)

McCann, Edson
See Pohl, Frederik

McCarthy, Charles, Jr. 1933-
See McCarthy, Cormac
See also CANR 42; DAM POP

McCarthy, Cormac 1933- . . . . . CLC 4, 57, 59
See also McCarthy, Charles, Jr.
See also DLB 6, 143

McCarthy, Mary (Therese)
1912-1989 . . . CLC 1, 3, 5, 14, 24, 39, 59
See also CA 5-8R; 129; CANR 16, 50;
DLB 2; DLBY 81; INT CANR-16;
MTCW

McCartney, (James) Paul
1942- . . . . CLC 12, 35
See also CA 146

McCauley, Stephen (D.) 1955- . . . . . CLC 50
See also CA 141

McClure, Michael (Thomas)
1932- . . . . CLC 6, 10
See also CA 21-24R; CANR 17, 46;
DLB 16

McCorkle, Jill (Collins) 1958- . . . . . . CLC 51
See also CA 121; DLBY 87

McCourt, James 1941- . . . . CLC 5
See also CA 57-60

McCoy, Horace (Stanley)
1897-1955 . . . . TCLC 28
See also CA 108; DLB 9

McCrae, John 1872-1918 . . . . TCLC 12
See also CA 109; DLB 92

McCreigh, James
See Pohl, Frederik

McCullers, (Lula) Carson (Smith)
1917-1967 . . . . CLC 1, 4, 10, 12, 48; DA;
DAB; DAC; SSC 9; WLC
See also CA 5-8R; 25-28R; CABS 1, 3;
CANR 18; CDALB 1941-1968;
DAM MST, NOV; DLB 2, 7; MTCW;
SATA 27

McCulloch, John Tyler
See Burroughs, Edgar Rice

McCullough, Colleen 1938(?)- . . . . . . CLC 27
See also CA 81-84; CANR 17, 46;
DAM NOV, POP; MTCW

McDermott, Alice 1953- . . . . CLC 90
See also CA 109; CANR 40

McElroy, Joseph 1930- . . . . CLC 5, 47
See also CA 17-20R

McEwan, Ian (Russell) 1948- . . . CLC 13, 66
See also BEST 90:4; CA 61-64; CANR 14,
41; DAM NOV; DLB 14; MTCW

McFadden, David 1940- . . . . CLC 48
See also CA 104; DLB 60; INT 104

McFarland, Dennis 1950- . . . . CLC 65

McGahern, John
1934- . . . . CLC 5, 9, 48; SSC 17
See also CA 17-20R; CANR 29; DLB 14;
MTCW

McGinley, Patrick (Anthony)
1937- . . . . CLC 41
See also CA 120; 127; INT 127

McGinley, Phyllis 1905-1978 . . . . . . CLC 14
See also CA 9-12R; 77-80; CANR 19;
DLB 11, 48; SATA 2, 44; SATA-Obit 24

McGinniss, Joe 1942- . . . . CLC 32
See also AITN 2; BEST 89:2; CA 25-28R;
CANR 26; INT CANR-26

McGivern, Maureen Daly
See Daly, Maureen

McGrath, Patrick 1950- . . . . CLC 55
See also CA 136

McGrath, Thomas (Matthew)
1916-1990 . . . . CLC 28, 59
See also CA 9-12R; 132; CANR 6, 33;
DAM POET; MTCW; SATA 41;
SATA-Obit 66

McGuane, Thomas (Francis III)
1939- . . . . CLC 3, 7, 18, 45
See also AITN 2; CA 49-52; CANR 5, 24,
49; DLB 2; DLBY 80; INT CANR-24;
MTCW

McGuckian, Medbh 1950- . . . . CLC 48
See also CA 143; DAM POET; DLB 40

McHale, Tom 1942(?)-1982 . . . . . . CLC 3, 5
See also AITN 1; CA 77-80; 106

McIlvanney, William 1936- . . . . CLC 42
See also CA 25-28R; DLB 14

McIlwraith, Maureen Mollie Hunter
See Hunter, Mollie
See also SATA 2

McInerney, Jay 1955- . . . . CLC 34
See also CA 116; 123; CANR 45;
DAM POP; INT 123

McIntyre, Vonda N(eel) 1948- . . . . . CLC 18
See also CA 81-84; CANR 17, 34; MTCW

McKay, Claude
. . . . TCLC 7, 41; BLC; DAB; PC 2
See also McKay, Festus Claudius
See also DLB 4, 45, 51, 117

McKay, Festus Claudius 1889-1948
See McKay, Claude
See also BW 1; CA 104; 124; DA; DAC;
DAM MST, MULT, NOV, POET;
MTCW; WLC

McKuen, Rod 1933- . . . . CLC 1, 3
See also AITN 1; CA 41-44R; CANR 40

McLoughlin, R. B.
See Mencken, H(enry) L(ouis)

McLuhan, (Herbert) Marshall
1911-1980 . . . . CLC 37, 83
See also CA 9-12R; 102; CANR 12, 34;
DLB 88; INT CANR-12; MTCW

McMillan, Terry (L.) 1951- . . . . . CLC 50, 61
See also BW 2; CA 140; DAM MULT,
NOV, POP

McMurtry, Larry (Jeff)
1936- . . . . CLC 2, 3, 7, 11, 27, 44
See also AAYA 15; AITN 2; BEST 89:2;
CA 5-8R; CANR 19, 43;
CDALB 1968-1988; DAM NOV, POP;
DLB 2, 143; DLBY 80, 87; MTCW

McNally, T. M. 1961- . . . . CLC 82

McNally, Terrence 1939- . . . CLC 4, 7, 41, 91
See also CA 45-48; CANR 2;
DAM DRAM; DLB 7

McNamer, Deirdre 1950- . . . . CLC 70

McNeile, Herman Cyril 1888-1937
See Sapper
See also DLB 77

McNickle, (William) D'Arcy
1904-1977 . . . . CLC 89
See also CA 9-12R; 85-88; CANR 5, 45;
DAM MULT; NNAL; SATA-Obit 22

McPhee, John (Angus) 1931- . . . . . . CLC 36
See also BEST 90:1; CA 65-68; CANR 20,
46; MTCW

McPherson, James Alan
1943- . . . . CLC 19, 77
See also BW 1; CA 25-28R; CAAS 17;
CANR 24; DLB 38; MTCW

McPherson, William (Alexander)
1933- . . . . CLC 34
See also CA 69-72; CANR 28;
INT CANR-28

Mead, Margaret 1901-1978 . . . . CLC 37
See also AITN 1; CA 1-4R; 81-84;
CANR 4; MTCW; SATA-Obit 20

Meaker, Marijane (Agnes) 1927-
See Kerr, M. E.
See also CA 107; CANR 37; INT 107;
JRDA; MAICYA; MTCW; SATA 20, 61

Medoff, Mark (Howard) 1940- . . . CLC 6, 23
See also AITN 1; CA 53-56; CANR 5;
DAM DRAM; DLB 7; INT CANR-5

Medvedev, P. N.
See Bakhtin, Mikhail Mikhailovich

Meged, Aharon
See Megged, Aharon

Meged, Aron
See Megged, Aharon

Megged, Aharon 1920- . . . . CLC 9
See also CA 49-52; CAAS 13; CANR 1

Mehta, Ved (Parkash) 1934- . . . . CLC 37
See also CA 1-4R; CANR 2, 23; MTCW

Melanter
See Blackmore, R(ichard) D(oddridge)

Melikow, Loris
See Hofmannsthal, Hugo von

Melmoth, Sebastian
See Wilde, Oscar (Fingal O'Flahertie Wills)

Meltzer, Milton 1915- . . . . **CLC 26**
See also AAYA 8; CA 13-16R; CANR 38;
CLR 13; DLB 61; JRDA; MAICYA;
SAAS 1; SATA 1, 50, 80

Melville, Herman
1819-1891 . . . . . **NCLC 3, 12, 29, 45, 49;**
DA; DAB; DAC; SSC 1, 17; WLC
See also CDALB 1640-1865; DAM MST,
NOV; DLB 3, 74; SATA 59

Menander
c. 342B.C.-c. 292B.C. . . . . **CMLC 9; DC 3**
See also DAM DRAM

Mencken, H(enry) L(ouis)
1880-1956 . . . . **TCLC 13**
See also CA 105; 125; CDALB 1917-1929;
DLB 11, 29, 63, 137; MTCW

Mercer, David 1928-1980 . . . . **CLC 5**
See also CA 9-12R; 102; CANR 23;
DAM DRAM; DLB 13; MTCW

Merchant, Paul
See Ellison, Harlan (Jay)

Meredith, George 1828-1909 . . . **TCLC 17, 43**
See also CA 117; CDBLB 1832-1890;
DAM POET; DLB 18, 35, 57, 159

Meredith, William (Morris)
1919- . . . . **CLC 4, 13, 22, 55**
See also CA 9-12R; CAAS 14; CANR 6, 40;
DAM POET; DLB 5

Merezhkovsky, Dmitry Sergeyevich
1865-1941 . . . . **TCLC 29**

Merimee, Prosper
1803-1870 . . . . **NCLC 6; SSC 7**
See also DLB 119

Merkin, Daphne 1954- . . . . **CLC 44**
See also CA 123

Merlin, Arthur
See Blish, James (Benjamin)

Merrill, James (Ingram)
1926-1995 . . . . **CLC 2, 3, 6, 8, 13, 18, 34,**
91
See also CA 13-16R; 147; CANR 10, 49;
DAM POET; DLB 5; DLBY 85;
INT CANR-10; MTCW

Merriman, Alex
See Silverberg, Robert

Merritt, E. B.
See Waddington, Miriam

Merton, Thomas
1915-1968 . . **CLC 1, 3, 11, 34, 83; PC 10**
See also CA 5-8R; 25-28R; CANR 22;
DLB 48; DLBY 81; MTCW

Merwin, W(illiam) S(tanley)
1927- . . . **CLC 1, 2, 3, 5, 8, 13, 18, 45, 88**
See also CA 13-16R; CANR 15, 51;
DAM POET; DLB 5; INT CANR-15;
MTCW

Metcalf, John 1938- . . . . **CLC 37**
See also CA 113; DLB 60

Metcalf, Suzanne
See Baum, L(yman) Frank

Mew, Charlotte (Mary)
1870-1928 . . . . **TCLC 8**
See also CA 105; DLB 19, 135

Mewshaw, Michael 1943- . . . . **CLC 9**
See also CA 53-56; CANR 7, 47; DLBY 80

Meyer, June
See Jordan, June

Meyer, Lynn
See Slavitt, David R(ytman)

Meyer-Meyrink, Gustav 1868-1932
See Meyrink, Gustav
See also CA 117

Meyers, Jeffrey 1939- . . . . **CLC 39**
See also CA 73-76; DLB 111

Meynell, Alice (Christina Gertrude Thompson)
1847-1922 . . . . **TCLC 6**
See also CA 104; DLB 19, 98

Meyrink, Gustav . . . . **TCLC 21**
See also Meyer-Meyrink, Gustav
See also DLB 81

Michaels, Leonard
1933- . . . . **CLC 6, 25; SSC 16**
See also CA 61-64; CANR 21; DLB 130;
MTCW

Michaux, Henri 1899-1984 . . . . . . **CLC 8, 19**
See also CA 85-88; 114

Michelangelo 1475-1564 . . . . **LC 12**

Michelet, Jules 1798-1874 . . . . . . **NCLC 31**

Michener, James A(lbert)
1907(?)- . . . . **CLC 1, 5, 11, 29, 60**
See also AITN 1; BEST 90:1; CA 5-8R;
CANR 21, 45; DAM NOV, POP; DLB 6;
MTCW

Mickiewicz, Adam 1798-1855 . . . . . **NCLC 3**

Middleton, Christopher 1926- . . . . . . **CLC 13**
See also CA 13-16R; CANR 29; DLB 40

Middleton, Richard (Barham)
1882-1911 . . . . **TCLC 56**
See also DLB 156

Middleton, Stanley 1919- . . . . **CLC 7, 38**
See also CA 25-28R; CAAS 23; CANR 21,
46; DLB 14

Middleton, Thomas 1580-1627 . . . . **DC 5**
See also DAM DRAM, MST; DLB 58

Migueis, Jose Rodrigues 1901- . . . . . **CLC 10**

Mikszath, Kalman 1847-1910 . . . . . **TCLC 31**

Miles, Josephine
1911-1985 . . . . **CLC 1, 2, 14, 34, 39**
See also CA 1-4R; 116; CANR 2;
DAM POET; DLB 48

Militant
See Sandburg, Carl (August)

Mill, John Stuart 1806-1873 . . . . . **NCLC 11**
See also CDBLB 1832-1890; DLB 55

Millar, Kenneth 1915-1983 . . . . **CLC 14**
See also Macdonald, Ross
See also CA 9-12R; 110; CANR 16;
DAM POP; DLB 2; DLBD 6; DLBY 83;
MTCW

Millay, E. Vincent
See Millay, Edna St. Vincent

Millay, Edna St. Vincent
1892-1950 . . . . . . **TCLC 4, 49; DA; DAB;**
DAC; PC 6
See also CA 104; 130; CDALB 1917-1929;
DAM MST, POET; DLB 45; MTCW

Miller, Arthur
1915- . . . . **CLC 1, 2, 6, 10, 15, 26, 47, 78;**
DA; DAB; DAC; DC 1; WLC
See also AAYA 15; AITN 1; CA 1-4R;
CABS 3; CANR 2, 30;
CDALB 1941-1968; DAM DRAM, MST;
DLB 7; MTCW

Miller, Henry (Valentine)
1891-1980 . . . . **CLC 1, 2, 4, 9, 14, 43, 84;**
DA; DAB; DAC; WLC
See also CA 9-12R; 97-100; CANR 33;
CDALB 1929-1941; DAM MST, NOV;
DLB 4, 9; DLBY 80; MTCW

Miller, Jason 1939(?)- . . . . **CLC 2**
See also AITN 1; CA 73-76; DLB 7

Miller, Sue 1943- . . . . **CLC 44**
See also BEST 90:3; CA 139; DAM POP;
DLB 143

Miller, Walter M(ichael, Jr.)
1923- . . . . **CLC 4, 30**
See also CA 85-88; DLB 8

Millett, Kate 1934- . . . . **CLC 67**
See also AITN 1; CA 73-76; CANR 32;
MTCW

Millhauser, Steven 1943- . . . . **CLC 21, 54**
See also CA 110; 111; DLB 2; INT 111

Millin, Sarah Gertrude 1889-1968 . . **CLC 49**
See also CA 102; 93-96

Milne, A(lan) A(lexander)
1882-1956 . . . . **TCLC 6; DAB; DAC**
See also CA 104; 133; CLR 1, 26;
DAM MST; DLB 10, 77, 100, 160;
MAICYA; MTCW; YABC 1

Milner, Ron(ald) 1938- . . . . **CLC 56; BLC**
See also AITN 1; BW 1; CA 73-76;
CANR 24; DAM MULT; DLB 38;
MTCW

Milosz, Czeslaw
1911- . . . **CLC 5, 11, 22, 31, 56, 82; PC 8**
See also CA 81-84; CANR 23, 51;
DAM MST, POET; MTCW

Milton, John
1608-1674 . . . . . . **LC 9; DA; DAB; DAC;**
WLC
See also CDBLB 1660-1789; DAM MST,
POET; DLB 131, 151

Min, Anchee 1957- . . . . **CLC 86**
See also CA 146

Minehaha, Cornelius
See Wedekind, (Benjamin) Frank(lin)

Miner, Valerie 1947- . . . . **CLC 40**
See also CA 97-100

Minimo, Duca
See D'Annunzio, Gabriele

Minot, Susan 1956- . . . . **CLC 44**
See also CA 134

Minus, Ed 1938- . . . . **CLC 39**

Miranda, Javier
See Bioy Casares, Adolfo

Mirbeau, Octave 1848-1917 . . . . **TCLC 55**
See also DLB 123

Miro (Ferrer), Gabriel (Francisco Victor)
1879-1930 . . . . **TCLC 5**
See also CA 104

Mishima, Yukio
...... **CLC 2, 4, 6, 9, 27; DC 1; SSC 4**
See also Hiraoka, Kimitake

Mistral, Frederic 1830-1914 ...... **TCLC 51**
See also CA 122

Mistral, Gabriela........... **TCLC 2; HLC**
See also Godoy Alcayaga, Lucila

Mistry, Rohinton 1952- ...... **CLC 71; DAC**
See also CA 141

Mitchell, Clyde
See Ellison, Harlan (Jay); Silverberg, Robert

Mitchell, James Leslie 1901-1935
See Gibbon, Lewis Grassic
See also CA 104; DLB 15

Mitchell, Joni 1943-.............. **CLC 12**
See also CA 112

Mitchell, Margaret (Munnerlyn)
1900-1949 .... **TCLC 11**
See also CA 109; 125; DAM NOV, POP;
DLB 9; MTCW

Mitchell, Peggy
See Mitchell, Margaret (Munnerlyn)

Mitchell, S(ilas) Weir 1829-1914 .. **TCLC 36**

Mitchell, W(illiam) O(rmond)
1914- .... **CLC 25; DAC**
See also CA 77-80; CANR 15, 43;
DAM MST; DLB 88

Mitford, Mary Russell 1787-1855.. **NCLC 4**
See also DLB 110, 116

Mitford, Nancy 1904-1973........ **CLC 44**
See also CA 9-12R

Miyamoto, Yuriko 1899-1951 ..... **TCLC 37**

Mo, Timothy (Peter) 1950(?)-...... **CLC 46**
See also CA 117; MTCW

Modarressi, Taghi (M.) 1931-...... **CLC 44**
See also CA 121; 134; INT 134

Modiano, Patrick (Jean) 1945-..... **CLC 18**
See also CA 85-88; CANR 17, 40; DLB 83

Moerck, Paal
See Roelvaag, O(le) E(dvart)

Mofolo, Thomas (Mokopu)
1875(?)-1948 .... **TCLC 22; BLC**
See also CA 121; DAM MULT

Mohr, Nicholasa 1935-...... **CLC 12; HLC**
See also AAYA 8; CA 49-52; CANR 1, 32;
CLR 22; DAM MULT; DLB 145; HW;
JRDA; SAAS 8; SATA 8

Mojtabai, A(nn) G(race)
1938- .... **CLC 5, 9, 15, 29**
See also CA 85-88

Moliere
1622-1673 ..... **LC 28; DA; DAB; DAC;**
WLC
See also DAM DRAM, MST

Molin, Charles
See Mayne, William (James Carter)

Molnar, Ferenc 1878-1952........ **TCLC 20**
See also CA 109; DAM DRAM

Momaday, N(avarre) Scott
1934- ... **CLC 2, 19, 85; DA; DAB; DAC**
See also AAYA 11; CA 25-28R; CANR 14,
34; DAM MST, MULT, NOV, POP;
DLB 143; INT CANR-14; MTCW;
NNAL; SATA 48; SATA-Brief 30

Monette, Paul 1945-1995......... **CLC 82**
See also CA 139; 147

Monroe, Harriet 1860-1936....... **TCLC 12**
See also CA 109; DLB 54, 91

Monroe, Lyle
See Heinlein, Robert A(nson)

Montagu, Elizabeth 1917-........ **NCLC 7**
See also CA 9-12R

Montagu, Mary (Pierrepont) Wortley
1689-1762 .... **LC 9**
See also DLB 95, 101

Montagu, W. H.
See Coleridge, Samuel Taylor

Montague, John (Patrick)
1929- .... **CLC 13, 46**
See also CA 9-12R; CANR 9; DLB 40;
MTCW

Montaigne, Michel (Eyquem) de
1533-1592 ...... **LC 8; DA; DAB; DAC;**
WLC
See also DAM MST

Montale, Eugenio
1896-1981 .... **CLC 7, 9, 18; PC 13**
See also CA 17-20R; 104; CANR 30;
DLB 114; MTCW

Montesquieu, Charles-Louis de Secondat
1689-1755 .... **LC 7**

Montgomery, (Robert) Bruce 1921-1978
See Crispin, Edmund
See also CA 104

Montgomery, L(ucy) M(aud)
1874-1942 .... **TCLC 51; DAC**
See also AAYA 12; CA 108; 137; CLR 8;
DAM MST; DLB 92; JRDA; MAICYA;
YABC 1

Montgomery, Marion H., Jr. 1925- .. **CLC 7**
See also AITN 1; CA 1-4R; CANR 3, 48;
DLB 6

Montgomery, Max
See Davenport, Guy (Mattison, Jr.)

Montherlant, Henry (Milon) de
1896-1972 .... **CLC 8, 19**
See also CA 85-88; 37-40R; DAM DRAM;
DLB 72; MTCW

Monty Python
See Chapman, Graham; Cleese, John
(Marwood); Gilliam, Terry (Vance); Idle,
Eric; Jones, Terence Graham Parry; Palin,
Michael (Edward)
See also AAYA 7

Moodie, Susanna (Strickland)
1803-1885 .... **NCLC 14**
See also DLB 99

Mooney, Edward 1951-
See Mooney, Ted
See also CA 130

Mooney, Ted .... **CLC 25**
See also Mooney, Edward

Moorcock, Michael (John)
1939- .... **CLC 5, 27, 58**
See also CA 45-48; CAAS 5; CANR 2, 17,
38; DLB 14; MTCW

Moore, Brian
1921- ...... **CLC 1, 3, 5, 7, 8, 19, 32, 90;**
DAB; DAC
See also CA 1-4R; CANR 1, 25, 42;
DAM MST; MTCW

Moore, Edward
See Muir, Edwin

Moore, George Augustus
1852-1933 .... **TCLC 7; SSC 19**
See also CA 104; DLB 10, 18, 57, 135

Moore, Lorrie .... **CLC 39, 45, 68**
See also Moore, Marie Lorena

Moore, Marianne (Craig)
1887-1972 .... **CLC 1, 2, 4, 8, 10, 13, 19,**
47; DA; DAB; DAC; PC 4
See also CA 1-4R; 33-36R; CANR 3;
CDALB 1929-1941; DAM MST, POET;
DLB 45; DLBD 7; MTCW; SATA 20

Moore, Marie Lorena 1957-
See Moore, Lorrie
See also CA 116; CANR 39

Moore, Thomas 1779-1852........ **NCLC 6**
See also DLB 96, 144

Morand, Paul 1888-1976 .. **CLC 41; SSC 22**
See also CA 69-72; DLB 65

Morante, Elsa 1918-1985........ **CLC 8, 47**
See also CA 85-88; 117; CANR 35; MTCW

Moravia, Alberto .... **CLC 2, 7, 11, 27, 46**
See also Pincherle, Alberto

More, Hannah 1745-1833 .... **NCLC 27**
See also DLB 107, 109, 116, 158

More, Henry 1614-1687............. **LC 9**
See also DLB 126

More, Sir Thomas 1478-1535 .... **LC 10, 32**

Moreas, Jean .... **TCLC 18**
See also Papadiamantopoulos, Johannes

Morgan, Berry 1919-.............. **CLC 6**
See also CA 49-52; DLB 6

Morgan, Claire
See Highsmith, (Mary) Patricia

Morgan, Edwin (George) 1920-..... **CLC 31**
See also CA 5-8R; CANR 3, 43; DLB 27

Morgan, (George) Frederick
1922- .... **CLC 23**
See also CA 17-20R; CANR 21

Morgan, Harriet
See Mencken, H(enry) L(ouis)

Morgan, Jane
See Cooper, James Fenimore

Morgan, Janet 1945- .... **CLC 39**
See also CA 65-68

Morgan, Lady 1776(?)-1859...... **NCLC 29**
See also DLB 116, 158

Morgan, Robin 1941-.............. **CLC 2**
See also CA 69-72; CANR 29; MTCW;
SATA 80

Morgan, Scott
See Kuttner, Henry

Morgan, Seth 1949(?)-1990 .... **CLC 65**
See also CA 132

Morgenstern, Christian
1871-1914 .... **TCLC 8**
See also CA 105

Morgenstern, S.
  See Goldman, William (W.)

Moricz, Zsigmond   1879-1942 ..... **TCLC 33**

Morike, Eduard (Friedrich)
  1804-1875 .... **NCLC 10**
  See also DLB 133

Mori Ogai .... **TCLC 14**
  See also Mori Rintaro

Mori Rintaro   1862-1922
  See Mori Ogai
  See also CA 110

Moritz, Karl Philipp   1756-1793 ...... **LC 2**
  See also DLB 94

Morland, Peter Henry
  See Faust, Frederick (Schiller)

Morren, Theophil
  See Hofmannsthal, Hugo von

Morris, Bill   1952-............... **CLC 76**

Morris, Julian
  See West, Morris L(anglo)

Morris, Steveland Judkins   1950(?)-
  See Wonder, Stevie
  See also CA 111

Morris, William   1834-1896 .... **NCLC 4**
  See also CDBLB 1832-1890; DLB 18, 35,
  57, 156

Morris, Wright   1910-... **CLC 1, 3, 7, 18, 37**
  See also CA 9-12R; CANR 21; DLB 2;
  DLBY 81; MTCW

Morrison, Chloe Anthony Wofford
  See Morrison, Toni

Morrison, James Douglas   1943-1971
  See Morrison, Jim
  See also CA 73-76; CANR 40

Morrison, Jim .... **CLC 17**
  See also Morrison, James Douglas

Morrison, Toni
  1931-........ **CLC 4, 10, 22, 55, 81, 87;**
  BLC; DA; DAB; DAC
  See also AAYA 1; BW 2; CA 29-32R;
  CANR 27, 42; CDALB 1968-1988;
  DAM MST, MULT, NOV, POP; DLB 6,
  33, 143; DLBY 81; MTCW; SATA 57

Morrison, Van   1945-.............. **CLC 21**
  See also CA 116

Mortimer, John (Clifford)
  1923-................... **CLC 28, 43**
  See also CA 13-16R; CANR 21;
  CDBLB 1960 to Present; DAM DRAM,
  POP; DLB 13; INT CANR-21; MTCW

Mortimer, Penelope (Ruth)   1918-.... **CLC 5**
  See also CA 57-60; CANR 45

Morton, Anthony
  See Creasey, John

Mosher, Howard Frank   1943-...... **CLC 62**
  See also CA 139

Mosley, Nicholas   1923-........ **CLC 43, 70**
  See also CA 69-72; CANR 41; DLB 14

Moss, Howard
  1922-1987 .... **CLC 7, 14, 45, 50**
  See also CA 1-4R; 123; CANR 1, 44;
  DAM POET; DLB 5

Mossgiel, Rab
  See Burns, Robert

Motion, Andrew (Peter)   1952-...... **CLC 47**
  See also CA 146; DLB 40

Motley, Willard (Francis)
  1909-1965 .... **CLC 18**
  See also BW 1; CA 117; 106; DLB 76, 143

Motoori, Norinaga   1730-1801 .... **NCLC 45**

Mott, Michael (Charles Alston)
  1930-.................... **CLC 15, 34**
  See also CA 5-8R; CAAS 7; CANR 7, 29

Mountain Wolf Woman
  1884-1960 .... **CLC 92**
  See also CA 144; NNAL

Moure, Erin   1955-.............. **CLC 88**
  See also CA 113; DLB 60

Mowat, Farley (McGill)
  1921-................. **CLC 26; DAC**
  See also AAYA 1; CA 1-4R; CANR 4, 24,
  42; CLR 20; DAM MST; DLB 68;
  INT CANR-24; JRDA; MAICYA;
  MTCW; SATA 3, 55

Moyers, Bill   1934-.............. **CLC 74**
  See also AITN 2; CA 61-64; CANR 31

Mphahlele, Es'kia
  See Mphahlele, Ezekiel
  See also DLB 125

Mphahlele, Ezekiel   1919-..... **CLC 25; BLC**
  See also Mphahlele, Es'kia
  See also BW 2; CA 81-84; CANR 26;
  DAM MULT

Mqhayi, S(amuel) E(dward) K(rune Loliwe)
  1875-1945 .... **TCLC 25; BLC**
  See also DAM MULT

Mr. Martin
  See Burroughs, William S(eward)

Mrozek, Slawomir   1930-........ **CLC 3, 13**
  See also CA 13-16R; CAAS 10; CANR 29;
  MTCW

Mrs. Belloc-Lowndes
  See Lowndes, Marie Adelaide (Belloc)

Mtwa, Percy   (?)-................. **CLC 47**

Mueller, Lisel   1924-.......... **CLC 13, 51**
  See also CA 93-96; DLB 105

Muir, Edwin   1887-1959 .... **TCLC 2**
  See also CA 104; DLB 20, 100

Muir, John   1838-1914 .... **TCLC 28**

Mujica Lainez, Manuel
  1910-1984 .... **CLC 31**
  See also Lainez, Manuel Mujica
  See also CA 81-84; 112; CANR 32; HW

Mukherjee, Bharati   1940-......... **CLC 53**
  See also BEST 89:2; CA 107; CANR 45;
  DAM NOV; DLB 60; MTCW

Muldoon, Paul   1951-.......... **CLC 32, 72**
  See also CA 113; 129; DAM POET;
  DLB 40; INT 129

Mulisch, Harry   1927-............. **CLC 42**
  See also CA 9-12R; CANR 6, 26

Mull, Martin   1943-.............. **CLC 17**
  See also CA 105

Mulock, Dinah Maria
  See Craik, Dinah Maria (Mulock)

Munford, Robert   1737(?)-1783 .... **LC 5**
  See also DLB 31

Mungo, Raymond   1946-.......... **CLC 72**
  See also CA 49-52; CANR 2

Munro, Alice
  1931- ... **CLC 6, 10, 19, 50; DAC; SSC 3**
  See also AITN 2; CA 33-36R; CANR 33;
  DAM MST, NOV; DLB 53; MTCW;
  SATA 29

Munro, H(ector) H(ugh)   1870-1916
  See Saki
  See also CA 104; 130; CDBLB 1890-1914;
  DA; DAB; DAC; DAM MST, NOV;
  DLB 34, 162; MTCW; WLC

Murasaki, Lady.................. **CMLC 1**

Murdoch, (Jean) Iris
  1919-...... **CLC 1, 2, 3, 4, 6, 8, 11, 15,**
  22, 31, 51; DAB; DAC
  See also CA 13-16R; CANR 8, 43;
  CDBLB 1960 to Present; DAM MST,
  NOV; DLB 14; INT CANR-8; MTCW

Murfree, Mary Noailles
  1850-1922 .... **SSC 22**
  See also CA 122; DLB 12, 74

Murnau, Friedrich Wilhelm
  See Plumpe, Friedrich Wilhelm

Murphy, Richard   1927-........... **CLC 41**
  See also CA 29-32R; DLB 40

Murphy, Sylvia   1937-............. **CLC 34**
  See also CA 121

Murphy, Thomas (Bernard)   1935-... **CLC 51**
  See also CA 101

Murray, Albert L.   1916- .... **CLC 73**
  See also BW 2; CA 49-52; CANR 26;
  DLB 38

Murray, Les(lie) A(llan)   1938- ..... **CLC 40**
  See also CA 21-24R; CANR 11, 27;
  DAM POET

Murry, J. Middleton
  See Murry, John Middleton

Murry, John Middleton
  1889-1957 .... **TCLC 16**
  See also CA 118; DLB 149

Musgrave, Susan   1951- .... **CLC 13, 54**
  See also CA 69-72; CANR 45

Musil, Robert (Edler von)
  1880-1942 .... **TCLC 12; SSC 18**
  See also CA 109; DLB 81, 124

Muske, Carol   1945-.............. **CLC 90**
  See also Muske-Dukes, Carol (Anne)

Muske-Dukes, Carol (Anne)   1945-
  See Muske, Carol
  See also CA 65-68; CANR 32

Musset, (Louis Charles) Alfred de
  1810-1857 .... **NCLC 7**

My Brother's Brother
  See Chekhov, Anton (Pavlovich)

Myers, L. H.   1881-1944......... **TCLC 59**
  See also DLB 15

Myers, Walter Dean   1937- ... **CLC 35; BLC**
  See also AAYA 4; BW 2; CA 33-36R;
  CANR 20, 42; CLR 4, 16, 35;
  DAM MULT, NOV; DLB 33;
  INT CANR-20; JRDA; MAICYA;
  SAAS 2; SATA 41, 71; SATA-Brief 27

Myers, Walter M.
  See Myers, Walter Dean

Myles, Symon
See Follett, Ken(neth Martin)

Nabokov, Vladimir (Vladimirovich)
1899-1977 ..... **CLC 1, 2, 3, 6, 8, 11, 15, 23, 44, 46, 64; DA; DAB; DAC; SSC 11; WLC**
See also CA 5-8R; 69-72; CANR 20; CDALB 1941-1968; DAM MST, NOV; DLB 2; DLBD 3; DLBY 80, 91; MTCW

Nagai Kafu..................... **TCLC 51**
See also Nagai Sokichi

Nagai Sokichi 1879-1959
See Nagai Kafu
See also CA 117

Nagy, Laszlo 1925-1978........... **CLC 7**
See also CA 129; 112

Naipaul, Shiva(dhar Srinivasa)
1945-1985 .... **CLC 32, 39**
See also CA 110; 112; 116; CANR 33; DAM NOV; DLB 157; DLBY 85; MTCW

Naipaul, V(idiadhar) S(urajprasad)
1932- .... **CLC 4, 7, 9, 13, 18, 37; DAB; DAC**
See also CA 1-4R; CANR 1, 33, 51; CDBLB 1960 to Present; DAM MST, NOV; DLB 125; DLBY 85; MTCW

Nakos, Lilika 1899(?)- .... **CLC 29**

Narayan, R(asipuram) K(rishnaswami)
1906- .... **CLC 7, 28, 47**
See also CA 81-84; CANR 33; DAM NOV; MTCW; SATA 62

Nash, (Fredric) Ogden 1902-1971 .. **CLC 23**
See also CA 13-14; 29-32R; CANR 34; CAP 1; DAM POET; DLB 11; MAICYA; MTCW; SATA 2, 46

Nathan, Daniel
See Dannay, Frederic

Nathan, George Jean 1882-1958 ... **TCLC 18**
See also Hatteras, Owen
See also CA 114; DLB 137

Natsume, Kinnosuke 1867-1916
See Natsume, Soseki
See also CA 104

Natsume, Soseki .... **TCLC 2, 10**
See also Natsume, Kinnosuke

Natti, (Mary) Lee 1919-
See Kingman, Lee
See also CA 5-8R; CANR 2

Naylor, Gloria
1950- ..... **CLC 28, 52; BLC; DA; DAC**
See also AAYA 6; BW 2; CA 107; CANR 27, 51; DAM MST, MULT, NOV, POP; MTCW

Neihardt, John Gneisenau
1881-1973 .... **CLC 32**
See also CA 13-14; CAP 1; DLB 9, 54

Nekrasov, Nikolai Alekseevich
1821-1878 .... **NCLC 11**

Nelligan, Emile 1879-1941....... **TCLC 14**
See also CA 114; DLB 92

Nelson, Willie 1933-............. **CLC 17**
See also CA 107

Nemerov, Howard (Stanley)
1920-1991 .... **CLC 2, 6, 9, 36**
See also CA 1-4R; 134; CABS 2; CANR 1, 27; DAM POET; DLB 5, 6; DLBY 83; INT CANR-27; MTCW

Neruda, Pablo
1904-1973 ..... **CLC 1, 2, 5, 7, 9, 28, 62; DA; DAB; DAC; HLC; PC 4; WLC**
See also CA 19-20; 45-48; CAP 2; DAM MST, MULT, POET; HW; MTCW

Nerval, Gerard de
1808-1855 ..... **NCLC 1; PC 13; SSC 18**

Nervo, (Jose) Amado (Ruiz de)
1870-1919 .... **TCLC 11**
See also CA 109; 131; HW

Nessi, Pio Baroja y
See Baroja (y Nessi), Pio

Nestroy, Johann 1801-1862...... **NCLC 42**
See also DLB 133

Neufeld, John (Arthur) 1938- ...... **CLC 17**
See also AAYA 11; CA 25-28R; CANR 11, 37; MAICYA; SAAS 3; SATA 6, 81

Neville, Emily Cheney 1919-....... **CLC 12**
See also CA 5-8R; CANR 3, 37; JRDA; MAICYA; SAAS 2; SATA 1

Newbound, Bernard Slade 1930-
See Slade, Bernard
See also CA 81-84; CANR 49; DAM DRAM

Newby, P(ercy) H(oward)
1918- .... **CLC 2, 13**
See also CA 5-8R; CANR 32; DAM NOV; DLB 15; MTCW

Newlove, Donald 1928- .... **CLC 6**
See also CA 29-32R; CANR 25

Newlove, John (Herbert) 1938-..... **CLC 14**
See also CA 21-24R; CANR 9, 25

Newman, Charles 1938-.......... **CLC 2, 8**
See also CA 21-24R

Newman, Edwin (Harold) 1919- .... **CLC 14**
See also AITN 1; CA 69-72; CANR 5

Newman, John Henry
1801-1890 .... **NCLC 38**
See also DLB 18, 32, 55

Newton, Suzanne 1936-........... **CLC 35**
See also CA 41-44R; CANR 14; JRDA; SATA 5, 77

Nexo, Martin Andersen
1869-1954 .... **TCLC 43**

Nezval, Vitezslav 1900-1958 ...... **TCLC 44**
See also CA 123

Ng, Fae Myenne 1957(?)-.......... **CLC 81**
See also CA 146

Ngema, Mbongeni 1955- .... **CLC 57**
See also BW 2; CA 143

Ngugi, James T(hiong'o)........ **CLC 3, 7, 13**
See also Ngugi wa Thiong'o

Ngugi wa Thiong'o 1938-...... **CLC 36; BLC**
See also Ngugi, James T(hiong'o)
See also BW 2; CA 81-84; CANR 27; DAM MULT, NOV; DLB 125; MTCW

Nichol, B(arrie) P(hillip)
1944-1988 .... **CLC 18**
See also CA 53-56; DLB 53; SATA 66

Nichols, John (Treadwell) 1940- .... **CLC 38**
See also CA 9-12R; CAAS 2; CANR 6; DLBY 82

Nichols, Leigh
See Koontz, Dean R(ay)

Nichols, Peter (Richard)
1927- .... **CLC 5, 36, 65**
See also CA 104; CANR 33; DLB 13; MTCW

Nicolas, F. R. E.
See Freeling, Nicolas

Niedecker, Lorine 1903-1970.... **CLC 10, 42**
See also CA 25-28; CAP 2; DAM POET; DLB 48

Nietzsche, Friedrich (Wilhelm)
1844-1900 .... **TCLC 10, 18, 55**
See also CA 107; 121; DLB 129

Nievo, Ippolito 1831-1861 .... **NCLC 22**

Nightingale, Anne Redmon 1943-
See Redmon, Anne
See also CA 103

Nik. T. O.
See Annensky, Innokenty Fyodorovich

Nin, Anais
1903-1977 ...... **CLC 1, 4, 8, 11, 14, 60; SSC 10**
See also AITN 2; CA 13-16R; 69-72; CANR 22; DAM NOV, POP; DLB 2, 4, 152; MTCW

Nishiwaki, Junzaburo 1894-1982 .... **PC 15**
See also CA 107

Nissenson, Hugh 1933-........... **CLC 4, 9**
See also CA 17-20R; CANR 27; DLB 28

Niven, Larry .... **CLC 8**
See also Niven, Laurence Van Cott
See also DLB 8

Niven, Laurence Van Cott 1938-
See Niven, Larry
See also CA 21-24R; CAAS 12; CANR 14, 44; DAM POP; MTCW

Nixon, Agnes Eckhardt 1927-...... **CLC 21**
See also CA 110

Nizan, Paul 1905-1940........... **TCLC 40**
See also DLB 72

Nkosi, Lewis 1936-.......... **CLC 45; BLC**
See also BW 1; CA 65-68; CANR 27; DAM MULT; DLB 157

Nodier, (Jean) Charles (Emmanuel)
1780-1844 .... **NCLC 19**
See also DLB 119

Nolan, Christopher 1965-.......... **CLC 58**
See also CA 111

Noon, Jeff 1957-................. **CLC 91**
See also CA 148

Norden, Charles
See Durrell, Lawrence (George)

Nordhoff, Charles (Bernard)
1887-1947 .... **TCLC 23**
See also CA 108; DLB 9; SATA 23

Norfolk, Lawrence 1963-.......... **CLC 76**
See also CA 144

Norman, Marsha 1947- .... **CLC 28**
See also CA 105; CABS 3; CANR 41; DAM DRAM; DLBY 84

Norris, Benjamin Franklin, Jr.
1870-1902 .... TCLC **24**
See also Norris, Frank
See also CA 110

Norris, Frank
See Norris, Benjamin Franklin, Jr.
See also CDALB 1865-1917; DLB 12, 71

Norris, Leslie 1921- .... CLC **14**
See also CA 11-12; CANR 14; CAP 1;
DLB 27

North, Andrew
See Norton, Andre

North, Anthony
See Koontz, Dean R(ay)

North, Captain George
See Stevenson, Robert Louis (Balfour)

North, Milou
See Erdrich, Louise

Northrup, B. A.
See Hubbard, L(afayette) Ron(ald)

North Staffs
See Hulme, T(homas) E(rnest)

Norton, Alice Mary
See Norton, Andre
See also MAICYA; SATA 1, 43

Norton, Andre 1912- .... CLC **12**
See also Norton, Alice Mary
See also AAYA 14; CA 1-4R; CANR 2, 31;
DLB 8, 52; JRDA; MTCW

Norton, Caroline 1808-1877 ...... NCLC **47**
See also DLB 21, 159

Norway, Nevil Shute 1899-1960
See Shute, Nevil
See also CA 102; 93-96

Norwid, Cyprian Kamil
1821-1883 .... NCLC **17**

Nosille, Nabrah
See Ellison, Harlan (Jay)

Nossack, Hans Erich 1901-1978 ..... CLC **6**
See also CA 93-96; 85-88; DLB 69

Nostradamus 1503-1566 .... LC **27**

Nosu, Chuji
See Ozu, Yasujiro

Notenburg, Eleanora (Genrikhovna) von
See Guro, Elena

Nova, Craig 1945- .... CLC **7, 31**
See also CA 45-48; CANR 2

Novak, Joseph
See Kosinski, Jerzy (Nikodem)

Novalis 1772-1801 .... NCLC **13**
See also DLB 90

Nowlan, Alden (Albert)
1933-1983 .... CLC **15; DAC**
See also CA 9-12R; CANR 5; DAM MST;
DLB 53

Noyes, Alfred 1880-1958 .... TCLC **7**
See also CA 104; DLB 20

Nunn, Kem 19(?)- .... CLC **34**

Nye, Robert 1939- .... CLC **13, 42**
See also CA 33-36R; CANR 29;
DAM NOV; DLB 14; MTCW; SATA 6

Nyro, Laura 1947- .... CLC **17**

Oates, Joyce Carol
1938- ...... CLC **1, 2, 3, 6, 9, 11, 15, 19,
33, 52; DA; DAB; DAC; SSC 6; WLC**
See also AAYA 15; AITN 1; BEST 89:2;
CA 5-8R; CANR 25, 45;
CDALB 1968-1988; DAM MST, NOV,
POP; DLB 2, 5, 130; DLBY 81;
INT CANR-25; MTCW

O'Brien, Darcy 1939- .... CLC **11**
See also CA 21-24R; CANR 8

O'Brien, E. G.
See Clarke, Arthur C(harles)

O'Brien, Edna
1936- ... CLC **3, 5, 8, 13, 36, 65; SSC 10**
See also CA 1-4R; CANR 6, 41;
CDBLB 1960 to Present; DAM NOV;
DLB 14; MTCW

O'Brien, Fitz-James 1828-1862 ... NCLC **21**
See also DLB 74

O'Brien, Flann .... CLC **1, 4, 5, 7, 10, 47**
See also O Nuallain, Brian

O'Brien, Richard 1942- .... CLC **17**
See also CA 124

O'Brien, Tim 1946- .... CLC **7, 19, 40**
See also AAYA 16; CA 85-88; CANR 40;
DAM POP; DLB 152; DLBD 9;
DLBY 80

Obstfelder, Sigbjoern 1866-1900 ... TCLC **23**
See also CA 123

O'Casey, Sean
1880-1964 ...... CLC **1, 5, 9, 11, 15, 88;
DAB; DAC**
See also CA 89-92; CDBLB 1914-1945;
DAM DRAM, MST; DLB 10; MTCW

O'Cathasaigh, Sean
See O'Casey, Sean

Ochs, Phil 1940-1976 .... CLC **17**
See also CA 65-68

O'Connor, Edwin (Greene)
1918-1968 .... CLC **14**
See also CA 93-96; 25-28R

O'Connor, (Mary) Flannery
1925-1964 .... CLC **1, 2, 3, 6, 10, 13, 15,
21, 66; DA; DAB; DAC; SSC 1; WLC**
See also AAYA 7; CA 1-4R; CANR 3, 41;
CDALB 1941-1968; DAM MST, NOV;
DLB 2, 152; DLBD 12; DLBY 80;
MTCW

O'Connor, Frank .... CLC **23; SSC 5**
See also O'Donovan, Michael John
See also DLB 162

O'Dell, Scott 1898-1989 .... CLC **30**
See also AAYA 3; CA 61-64; 129;
CANR 12, 30; CLR 1, 16; DLB 52;
JRDA; MAICYA; SATA 12, 60

Odets, Clifford
1906-1963 .... CLC **2, 28; DC 6**
See also CA 85-88; DAM DRAM; DLB 7,
26; MTCW

O'Doherty, Brian 1934- .... CLC **76**
See also CA 105

O'Donnell, K. M.
See Malzberg, Barry N(athaniel)

O'Donnell, Lawrence
See Kuttner, Henry

O'Donovan, Michael John
1903-1966 .... CLC **14**
See also O'Connor, Frank
See also CA 93-96

Oe, Kenzaburo
1935- .... CLC **10, 36, 86; SSC 20**
See also CA 97-100; CANR 36, 50;
DAM NOV; DLBY 94; MTCW

O'Faolain, Julia 1932- .... CLC **6, 19, 47**
See also CA 81-84; CAAS 2; CANR 12;
DLB 14; MTCW

O'Faolain, Sean
1900-1991 .... CLC **1, 7, 14, 32, 70;
SSC 13**
See also CA 61-64; 134; CANR 12;
DLB 15, 162; MTCW

O'Flaherty, Liam
1896-1984 .... CLC **5, 34; SSC 6**
See also CA 101; 113; CANR 35; DLB 36,
162; DLBY 84; MTCW

Ogilvy, Gavin
See Barrie, J(ames) M(atthew)

O'Grady, Standish James
1846-1928 .... TCLC **5**
See also CA 104

O'Grady, Timothy 1951- .... CLC **59**
See also CA 138

O'Hara, Frank
1926-1966 .... CLC **2, 5, 13, 78**
See also CA 9-12R; 25-28R; CANR 33;
DAM POET; DLB 5, 16; MTCW

O'Hara, John (Henry)
1905-1970 .... CLC **1, 2, 3, 6, 11, 42;
SSC 15**
See also CA 5-8R; 25-28R; CANR 31;
CDALB 1929-1941; DAM NOV; DLB 9,
86; DLBD 2; MTCW

O Hehir, Diana 1922- .... CLC **41**
See also CA 93-96

Okigbo, Christopher (Ifenayichukwu)
1932-1967 ..... CLC **25, 84; BLC; PC 7**
See also BW 1; CA 77-80; DAM MULT,
POET; DLB 125; MTCW

Okri, Ben 1959- .... CLC **87**
See also BW 2; CA 130; 138; DLB 157;
INT 138

Olds, Sharon 1942- .... CLC **32, 39, 85**
See also CA 101; CANR 18, 41;
DAM POET; DLB 120

Oldstyle, Jonathan
See Irving, Washington

Olesha, Yuri (Karlovich)
1899-1960 .... CLC **8**
See also CA 85-88

Oliphant, Laurence
1829(?)-1888 .... NCLC **47**
See also DLB 18

Oliphant, Margaret (Oliphant Wilson)
1828-1897 .... NCLC **11**
See also DLB 18, 159

Oliver, Mary 1935- .... CLC **19, 34**
See also CA 21-24R; CANR 9, 43; DLB 5

Olivier, Laurence (Kerr)
1907-1989 .... CLC **20**
See also CA 111; 150; 129

Parker, Robert B(rown) 1932-...... **CLC 27**
See also BEST 89:4; CA 49-52; CANR 1,
26; DAM NOV, POP; INT CANR-26;
MTCW

Parkin, Frank 1940-............. **CLC 43**
See also CA 147

Parkman, Francis, Jr.
1823-1893 .... **NCLC 12**
See also DLB 1, 30

Parks, Gordon (Alexander Buchanan)
1912- .... **CLC 1, 16; BLC**
See also AITN 2; BW 2; CA 41-44R;
CANR 26; DAM MULT; DLB 33;
SATA 8

Parnell, Thomas 1679-1718 .... **LC 3**
See also DLB 94

Parra, Nicanor 1914-........ **CLC 2; HLC**
See also CA 85-88; CANR 32;
DAM MULT; HW; MTCW

Parrish, Mary Frances
See Fisher, M(ary) F(rances) K(ennedy)

Parson
See Colcridge, Samuel Taylor

Parson Lot
See Kingsley, Charles

Partridge, Anthony
See Oppenheim, E(dward) Phillips

Pascoli, Giovanni 1855-1912 ...... **TCLC 45**

Pasolini, Pier Paolo
1922-1975 .... **CLC 20, 37**
See also CA 93-96; 61-64; DLB 128;
MTCW

Pasquini
See Silone, Ignazio

Pastan, Linda (Olenik) 1932- ...... **CLC 27**
See also CA 61-64; CANR 18, 40;
DAM POET; DLB 5

Pasternak, Boris (Leonidovich)
1890-1960 ...... **CLC 7, 10, 18, 63; DA;
DAB; DAC; PC 6; WLC**
See also CA 127; 116; DAM MST, NOV,
POET; MTCW

Patchen, Kenneth 1911-1972 ... **CLC 1, 2, 18**
See also CA 1-4R; 33-36R; CANR 3, 35;
DAM POET; DLB 16, 48; MTCW

Pater, Walter (Horatio)
1839-1894 .... **NCLC 7**
See also CDBLB 1832-1890; DLB 57, 156

Paterson, A(ndrew) B(arton)
1864-1941 .... **TCLC 32**

Paterson, Katherine (Womeldorf)
1932- .... **CLC 12, 30**
See also AAYA 1; CA 21-24R; CANR 28;
CLR 7; DLB 52; JRDA; MAICYA;
MTCW; SATA 13, 53

Patmore, Coventry Kersey Dighton
1823-1896 .... **NCLC 9**
See also DLB 35, 98

Paton, Alan (Stewart)
1903-1988 ...... **CLC 4, 10, 25, 55; DA;
DAB; DAC; WLC**
See also CA 13-16; 125; CANR 22; CAP 1;
DAM MST, NOV; MTCW; SATA 11;
SATA-Obit 56

Paton Walsh, Gillian 1937-
See Walsh, Jill Paton
See also CANR 38; JRDA; MAICYA;
SAAS 3; SATA 4, 72

Paulding, James Kirke 1778-1860.. **NCLC 2**
See also DLB 3, 59, 74

Paulin, Thomas Neilson 1949-
See Paulin, Tom
See also CA 123; 128

Paulin, Tom.................... **CLC 37**
See also Paulin, Thomas Neilson
See also DLB 40

Paustovsky, Konstantin (Georgievich)
1892-1968 .... **CLC 40**
See also CA 93-96; 25-28R

Pavese, Cesare
1908-1950 ..... **TCLC 3; PC 13; SSC 19**
See also CA 104; DLB 128

Pavic, Milorad 1929- .... **CLC 60**
See also CA 136

Payne, Alan
See Jakes, John (William)

Paz, Gil
See Lugones, Leopoldo

Paz, Octavio
1914- .... **CLC 3, 4, 6, 10, 19, 51, 65;
DA; DAB; DAC; HLC; PC 1; WLC**
See also CA 73-76; CANR 32; DAM MST,
MULT, POET; DLBY 90; HW; MTCW

Peacock, Molly 1947-.............. **CLC 60**
See also CA 103; CAAS 21; DLB 120

Peacock, Thomas Love
1785-1866 .... **NCLC 22**
See also DLB 96, 116

Peake, Mervyn 1911-1968....... **CLC 7, 54**
See also CA 5-8R; 25-28R; CANR 3;
DLB 15, 160; MTCW; SATA 23

Pearce, Philippa.................. **CLC 21**
See also Christie, (Ann) Philippa
See also CLR 9; DLB 161; MAICYA;
SATA 1, 67

Pearl, Eric
See Elman, Richard

Pearson, T(homas) R(eid) 1956- .... **CLC 39**
See also CA 120; 130; INT 130

Peck, Dale 1967- .... **CLC 81**
See also CA 146

Peck, John 1941- .... **CLC 3**
See also CA 49-52; CANR 3

Peck, Richard (Wayne) 1934-...... **CLC 21**
See also AAYA 1; CA 85-88; CANR 19,
38; CLR 15; INT CANR-19; JRDA;
MAICYA; SAAS 2; SATA 18, 55

Peck, Robert Newton
1928- .... **CLC 17; DA; DAC**
See also AAYA 3; CA 81-84; CANR 31;
DAM MST; JRDA; MAICYA; SAAS 1;
SATA 21, 62

Peckinpah, (David) Sam(uel)
1925-1984 .... **CLC 20**
See also CA 109; 114

Pedersen, Knut 1859-1952
See Hamsun, Knut
See also CA 104; 119; MTCW

Peeslake, Gaffer
See Durrell, Lawrence (George)

Peguy, Charles Pierre
1873-1914 .... **TCLC 10**
See also CA 107

Pena, Ramon del Valle y
See Valle-Inclan, Ramon (Maria) del

Pendennis, Arthur Esquir
See Thackeray, William Makepeace

Penn, William 1644-1718........... **LC 25**
See also DLB 24

Pepys, Samuel
1633-1703 ..... **LC 11; DA; DAB; DAC;
WLC**
See also CDBLB 1660-1789; DAM MST;
DLB 101

Percy, Walker
1916-1990 .... **CLC 2, 3, 6, 8, 14, 18, 47,
65**
See also CA 1-4R; 131; CANR 1, 23;
DAM NOV, POP; DLB 2; DLBY 80, 90;
MTCW

Perec, Georges 1936-1982 .... **CLC 56**
See also CA 141; DLB 83

Pereda (y Sanchez de Porrua), Jose Maria de
1833-1906 .... **TCLC 16**
See also CA 117

Pereda y Porrua, Jose Maria de
See Pereda (y Sanchez de Porrua), Jose
Maria de

Peregoy, George Weems
See Mencken, H(enry) L(ouis)

Perelman, S(idney) J(oseph)
1904-1979 ... **CLC 3, 5, 9, 15, 23, 44, 49**
See also AITN 1, 2; CA 73-76; 89-92;
CANR 18; DAM DRAM; DLB 11, 44;
MTCW

Peret, Benjamin 1899-1959 .... **TCLC 20**
See also CA 117

Perctz, Isaac Loeb 1851(?)-1915... **TCLC 16**
See also CA 109

Peretz, Yitzhok Leibush
See Peretz, Isaac Loeb

Perez Galdos, Benito 1843-1920 ... **TCLC 27**
See also CA 125; HW

Perrault, Charles 1628-1703 .... **LC 2**
See also MAICYA; SATA 25

Perry, Brighton
See Sherwood, Robert E(mmet)

Perse, St.-John .... **CLC 4, 11, 46**
See also Leger, (Marie-Rene Auguste) Alexis
Saint-Leger

Perutz, Leo 1882-1957.......... **TCLC 60**
See also DLB 81

Peseenz, Tulio F.
See Lopez y Fuentes, Gregorio

Pesetsky, Bette 1932-............. **CLC 28**
See also CA 133; DLB 130

Peshkov, Alexei Maximovich 1868-1936
See Gorky, Maxim
See also CA 105; 141; DA; DAC;
DAM DRAM, MST, NOV

Pessoa, Fernando (Antonio Nogueira)
1888-1935 .... **TCLC 27; HLC**
See also CA 125

Peterkin, Julia Mood 1880-1961.... **CLC 31**
See also CA 102; DLB 9

Peters, Joan K. 1945-............ **CLC 39**

Peters, Robert L(ouis) 1924-........ **CLC 7**
See also CA 13-16R; CAAS 8; DLB 105

Petofi, Sandor 1823-1849....... **NCLC 21**

Petrakis, Harry Mark 1923-........ **CLC 3**
See also CA 9-12R; CANR 4, 30

Petrarch 1304-1374................ **PC 8**
See also DAM POET

Petrov, Evgeny .... **TCLC 21**
See also Kataev, Evgeny Petrovich

Petry, Ann (Lane) 1908- ...... **CLC 1, 7, 18**
See also BW 1; CA 5-8R; CAAS 6;
CANR 4, 46; CLR 12; DLB 76; JRDA;
MAICYA; MTCW; SATA 5

Petursson, Halligrimur 1614-1674 .... **LC 8**

Philips, Katherine 1632-1664....... **LC 30**
See also DLB 131

Philipson, Morris H. 1926- .... **CLC 53**
See also CA 1-4R; CANR 4

Phillips, David Graham
1867-1911 .... **TCLC 44**
See also CA 108; DLB 9, 12

Phillips, Jack
See Sandburg, Carl (August)

Phillips, Jayne Anne
1952- .... **CLC 15, 33; SSC 16**
See also CA 101; CANR 24, 50; DLBY 80;
INT CANR-24; MTCW

Phillips, Richard
See Dick, Philip K(indred)

Phillips, Robert (Schaeffer) 1938-... **CLC 28**
See also CA 17-20R; CAAS 13; CANR 8;
DLB 105

Phillips, Ward
See Lovecraft, H(oward) P(hillips)

Piccolo, Lucio 1901-1969......... **CLC 13**
See also CA 97-100; DLB 114

Pickthall, Marjorie L(owry) C(hristie)
1883-1922 .... **TCLC 21**
See also CA 107; DLB 92

Pico della Mirandola, Giovanni
1463-1494 .... **LC 15**

Piercy, Marge
1936- .... **CLC 3, 6, 14, 18, 27, 62**
See also CA 21-24R; CAAS 1; CANR 13,
43; DLB 120; MTCW

Piers, Robert
See Anthony, Piers

Pieyre de Mandiargues, Andre 1909-1991
See Mandiargues, Andre Pieyre de
See also CA 103; 136; CANR 22

Pilnyak, Boris .... **TCLC 23**
See also Vogau, Boris Andreyevich

Pincherle, Alberto 1907-1990 ... **CLC 11, 18**
See also Moravia, Alberto
See also CA 25-28R; 132; CANR 33;
DAM NOV; MTCW

Pinckney, Darryl 1953- .... **CLC 76**
See also BW 2; CA 143

Pindar 518B.C.-446B.C......... **CMLC 12**

Pineda, Cecile 1942-............. **CLC 39**
See also CA 118

Pinero, Arthur Wing 1855-1934 ... **TCLC 32**
See also CA 110; DAM DRAM; DLB 10

Pinero, Miguel (Antonio Gomez)
1946-1988 .... **CLC 4, 55**
See also CA 61-64; 125; CANR 29; HW

Pinget, Robert 1919- .... **CLC 7, 13, 37**
See also CA 85-88; DLB 83

Pink Floyd
See Barrett, (Roger) Syd; Gilmour, David;
Mason, Nick; Waters, Roger; Wright,
Rick

Pinkney, Edward 1802-1828 ..... **NCLC 31**

Pinkwater, Daniel Manus 1941-.... **CLC 35**
See also Pinkwater, Manus
See also AAYA 1; CA 29-32R; CANR 12,
38; CLR 4; JRDA; MAICYA; SAAS 3;
SATA 46, 76

Pinkwater, Manus
See Pinkwater, Daniel Manus
See also SATA 8

Pinsky, Robert 1940-..... **CLC 9, 19, 38, 91**
See also CA 29-32R; CAAS 4;
DAM POET; DLBY 82

Pinta, Harold
See Pinter, Harold

Pinter, Harold
1930- ..... **CLC 1, 3, 6, 9, 11, 15, 27, 58,
73; DA; DAB; DAC; WLC**
See also CA 5-8R; CANR 33; CDBLB 1960
to Present; DAM DRAM, MST; DLB 13;
MTCW

Pirandello, Luigi
1867-1936 ...... **TCLC 4, 29; DA; DAB;
DAC; DC 5; SSC 22; WLC**
See also CA 104; DAM DRAM, MST

Pirsig, Robert M(aynard)
1928- .... **CLC 4, 6, 73**
See also CA 53-56; CANR 42; DAM POP;
MTCW; SATA 39

Pisarev, Dmitry Ivanovich
1840-1868 .... **NCLC 25**

Pix, Mary (Griffith) 1666-1709....... **LC 8**
See also DLB 80

Pixerecourt, Guilbert de
1773-1844 .... **NCLC 39**

Plaidy, Jean
See Hibbert, Eleanor Alice Burford

Planche, James Robinson
1796-1880 .... **NCLC 42**

Plant, Robert 1948- .... **CLC 12**

Plante, David (Robert)
1940-.................. **CLC 7, 23, 38**
See also CA 37-40R; CANR 12, 36;
DAM NOV; DLBY 83; INT CANR-12;
MTCW

Plath, Sylvia
1932-1963 ..... **CLC 1, 2, 3, 5, 9, 11, 14,
17, 50, 51, 62; DA; DAB; DAC; PC 1;
WLC**
See also AAYA 13; CA 19-20; CANR 34;
CAP 2; CDALB 1941-1968; DAM MST,
POET; DLB 5, 6, 152; MTCW

Plato
428(?)B.C.-348(?)B.C..... **CMLC 8; DA;
DAB; DAC**
See also DAM MST

Platonov, Andrei .... **TCLC 14**
See also Klimentov, Andrei Platonovich

Platt, Kin 1911- .... **CLC 26**
See also AAYA 11; CA 17-20R; CANR 11;
JRDA; SAAS 17; SATA 21, 86

Plautus c. 251B.C.-184B.C.......... **DC 6**

Plick et Plock
See Simenon, Georges (Jacques Christian)

Plimpton, George (Ames) 1927-..... **CLC 36**
See also AITN 1; CA 21-24R; CANR 32;
MTCW; SATA 10

Plomer, William Charles Franklin
1903-1973 .... **CLC 4, 8**
See also CA 21-22; CANR 34; CAP 2;
DLB 20, 162; MTCW; SATA 24

Plowman, Piers
See Kavanagh, Patrick (Joseph)

Plum, J.
See Wodehouse, P(elham) G(renville)

Plumly, Stanley (Ross) 1939- ...... **CLC 33**
See also CA 108; 110; DLB 5; INT 110

Plumpe, Friedrich Wilhelm
1888-1931 .... **TCLC 53**
See also CA 112

Poe, Edgar Allan
1809-1849 .... **NCLC 1, 16, 55; DA;
DAB; DAC; PC 1; SSC 1, 22; WLC**
See also AAYA 14; CDALB 1640-1865;
DAM MST, POET; DLB 3, 59, 73, 74;
SATA 23

Poet of Titchfield Street, The
See Pound, Ezra (Weston Loomis)

Pohl, Frederik 1919- .... **CLC 18**
See also CA 61-64; CAAS 1; CANR 11, 37;
DLB 8; INT CANR-11; MTCW;
SATA 24

Poirier, Louis 1910-
See Gracq, Julien
See also CA 122; 126

Poitier, Sidney 1927-.............. **CLC 26**
See also BW 1; CA 117

Polanski, Roman 1933- .... **CLC 16**
See also CA 77-80

Poliakoff, Stephen 1952- .... **CLC 38**
See also CA 106; DLB 13

Police, The
See Copeland, Stewart (Armstrong);
Summers, Andrew James; Sumner,
Gordon Matthew

Polidori, John William
1795-1821 .... **NCLC 51**
See also DLB 116

Pollitt, Katha 1949- .... **CLC 28**
See also CA 120; 122; MTCW

Pollock, (Mary) Sharon
1936- .... **CLC 50; DAC**
See also CA 141; DAM DRAM, MST;
DLB 60

Polo, Marco 1254-1324 .... **CMLC 15**

Polonsky, Abraham (Lincoln)
1910- .... **CLC 92**
See also CA 104; DLB 26; INT 104

Polybius c. 200B.C.-c. 118B.C. .... **CMLC 17**

Pomerance, Bernard 1940- .... **CLC 13**
See also CA 101; CANR 49; DAM DRAM

Ponge, Francis (Jean Gaston Alfred)
1899-1988 .... **CLC 6, 18**
See also CA 85-88; 126; CANR 40;
DAM POET

Pontoppidan, Henrik 1857-1943 ... **TCLC 29**

Poole, Josephine .... **CLC 17**
See also Helyar, Jane Penelope Josephine
See also SAAS 2; SATA 5

Popa, Vasko 1922-1991 .... **CLC 19**
See also CA 112; 148

Pope, Alexander
1688-1744 ...... **LC 3; DA; DAB; DAC;**
WLC
See also CDBLB 1660-1789; DAM MST,
POET; DLB 95, 101

Porter, Connie (Rose) 1959(?)- ..... **CLC 70**
See also BW 2; CA 142; SATA 81

Porter, Gene(va Grace) Stratton
1863(?)-1924 .... **TCLC 21**
See also CA 112

Porter, Katherine Anne
1890-1980 ...... **CLC 1, 3, 7, 10, 13, 15,**
27; DA; DAB; DAC; SSC 4
See also AITN 2; CA 1-4R; 101; CANR 1;
DAM MST, NOV; DLB 4, 9, 102;
DLBD 12; DLBY 80; MTCW; SATA 39;
SATA-Obit 23

Porter, Peter (Neville Frederick)
1929- .... **CLC 5, 13, 33**
See also CA 85-88; DLB 40

Porter, William Sydney 1862-1910
See Henry, O.
See also CA 104; 131; CDALB 1865-1917;
DA; DAB; DAC; DAM MST; DLB 12,
78, 79; MTCW; YABC 2

Portillo (y Pacheco), Jose Lopez
See Lopez Portillo (y Pacheco), Jose

Post, Melville Davisson
1869-1930 .... **TCLC 39**
See also CA 110

Potok, Chaim 1929- .... **CLC 2, 7, 14, 26**
See also AAYA 15; AITN 1, 2; CA 17-20R;
CANR 19, 35; DAM NOV; DLB 28, 152;
INT CANR-19; MTCW; SATA 33

Potter, Beatrice
See Webb, (Martha) Beatrice (Potter)
See also MAICYA

Potter, Dennis (Christopher George)
1935-1994 .... **CLC 58, 86**
See also CA 107; 145; CANR 33; MTCW

Pound, Ezra (Weston Loomis)
1885-1972 ...... **CLC 1, 2, 3, 4, 5, 7, 10,**
13, 18, 34, 48, 50; DA; DAB; DAC; PC 4;
WLC
See also CA 5-8R; 37-40R; CANR 40;
CDALB 1917-1929; DAM MST, POET;
DLB 4, 45, 63; MTCW

Povod, Reinaldo 1959-1994 .... **CLC 44**
See also CA 136; 146

Powell, Adam Clayton, Jr.
1908-1972 .... **CLC 89; BLC**
See also BW 1; CA 102; 33-36R;
DAM MULT

Powell, Anthony (Dymoke)
1905- .... **CLC 1, 3, 7, 9, 10, 31**
See also CA 1-4R; CANR 1, 32;
CDBLB 1945-1960; DLB 15; MTCW

Powell, Dawn 1897-1965 .... **CLC 66**
See also CA 5-8R

Powell, Padgett 1952- .... **CLC 34**
See also CA 126

Power, Susan .... **CLC 91**

Powers, J(ames) F(arl)
1917- .... **CLC 1, 4, 8, 57; SSC 4**
See also CA 1-4R; CANR 2; DLB 130;
MTCW

Powers, John J(ames) 1945-
See Powers, John R.
See also CA 69-72

Powers, John R. .... **CLC 66**
See also Powers, John J(ames)

Pownall, David 1938- .... **CLC 10**
See also CA 89-92; CAAS 18; CANR 49;
DLB 14

Powys, John Cowper
1872-1963 .... **CLC 7, 9, 15, 46**
See also CA 85-88; DLB 15; MTCW

Powys, T(heodore) F(rancis)
1875-1953 .... **TCLC 9**
See also CA 106; DLB 36, 162

Prager, Emily 1952- .... **CLC 56**

Pratt, E(dwin) J(ohn)
1883(?)-1964 .... **CLC 19; DAC**
See also CA 141; 93-96; DAM POET;
DLB 92

Premchand .... **TCLC 21**
See also Srivastava, Dhanpat Rai

Preussler, Otfried 1923- .... **CLC 17**
See also CA 77-80; SATA 24

Prevert, Jacques (Henri Marie)
1900-1977 .... **CLC 15**
See also CA 77-80; 69-72; CANR 29;
MTCW; SATA-Obit 30

Prevost, Abbe (Antoine Francois)
1697-1763 .... **LC 1**

Price, (Edward) Reynolds
1933- .. **CLC 3, 6, 13, 43, 50, 63; SSC 22**
See also CA 1-4R; CANR 1, 37;
DAM NOV; DLB 2; INT CANR-37

Price, Richard 1949- .... **CLC 6, 12**
See also CA 49-52; CANR 3; DLBY 81

Prichard, Katharine Susannah
1883-1969 .... **CLC 46**
See also CA 11-12; CANR 33; CAP 1;
MTCW; SATA 66

Priestley, J(ohn) B(oynton)
1894-1984 .... **CLC 2, 5, 9, 34**
See also CA 9-12R; 113; CANR 33;
CDBLB 1914-1945; DAM DRAM, NOV;
DLB 10, 34, 77, 100, 139; DLBY 84;
MTCW

Prince 1958(?)- .... **CLC 35**

Prince, F(rank) T(empleton) 1912- .. **CLC 22**
See also CA 101; CANR 43; DLB 20

Prince Kropotkin
See Kropotkin, Peter (Aleksieevich)

Prior, Matthew 1664-1721 .... **LC 4**
See also DLB 95

Pritchard, William H(arrison)
1932- .... **CLC 34**
See also CA 65-68; CANR 23; DLB 111

Pritchett, V(ictor) S(awdon)
1900- .... **CLC 5, 13, 15, 41; SSC 14**
See also CA 61-64; CANR 31; DAM NOV;
DLB 15, 139; MTCW

Private 19022
See Manning, Frederic

Probst, Mark 1925- .... **CLC 59**
See also CA 130

Prokosch, Frederic 1908-1989 .... **CLC 4, 48**
See also CA 73-76; 128; DLB 48

Prophet, The
See Dreiser, Theodore (Herman Albert)

Prose, Francine 1947- .... **CLC 45**
See also CA 109; 112; CANR 46

Proudhon
See Cunha, Euclides (Rodrigues Pimenta) da

Proulx, E. Annie 1935- .... **CLC 81**

Proust, (Valentin-Louis-George-Eugene-)
Marcel
1871-1922 .... **TCLC 7, 13, 33; DA;**
DAB; DAC; WLC
See also CA 104; 120; DAM MST, NOV;
DLB 65; MTCW

Prowler, Harley
See Masters, Edgar Lee

Prus, Boleslaw 1845-1912 .... **TCLC 48**

Pryor, Richard (Franklin Lenox Thomas)
1940- .... **CLC 26**
See also CA 122

Przybyszewski, Stanislaw
1868-1927 .... **TCLC 36**
See also DLB 66

Pteleon
See Grieve, C(hristopher) M(urray)
See also DAM POET

Puckett, Lute
See Masters, Edgar Lee

Puig, Manuel
1932-1990 ... **CLC 3, 5, 10, 28, 65; HLC**
See also CA 45-48; CANR 2, 32;
DAM MULT; DLB 113; HW; MTCW

Purdy, Al(fred Wellington)
1918- .... **CLC 3, 6, 14, 50; DAC**
See also CA 81-84; CAAS 17; CANR 42;
DAM MST, POET; DLB 88

Purdy, James (Amos)
1923- .... **CLC 2, 4, 10, 28, 52**
See also CA 33-36R; CAAS 1; CANR 19,
51; DLB 2; INT CANR-19; MTCW

Pure, Simon
See Swinnerton, Frank Arthur

Pushkin, Alexander (Sergeyevich)
1799-1837 ..... **NCLC 3, 27; DA; DAB;**
DAC; PC 10; WLC
See also DAM DRAM, MST, POET;
SATA 61

P'u Sung-ling 1640-1715 .... **LC 3**

Putnam, Arthur Lee
See Alger, Horatio, Jr.

Puzo, Mario 1920- .... **CLC 1, 2, 6, 36**
See also CA 65-68; CANR 4, 42;
DAM NOV, POP; DLB 6; MTCW

Pym, Barbara (Mary Crampton)
1913-1980 .... **CLC 13, 19, 37**
See also CA 13-14; 97-100; CANR 13, 34;
CAP 1; DLB 14; DLBY 87; MTCW

Pynchon, Thomas (Ruggles, Jr.)
1937- ..... **CLC 2, 3, 6, 9, 11, 18, 33, 62,
72; DA; DAB; DAC; SSC 14; WLC**
See also BEST 90:2; CA 17-20R; CANR 22,
46; DAM MST, NOV, POP; DLB 2;
MTCW

Qian Zhongshu
See Ch'ien Chung-shu

Qroll
See Dagerman, Stig (Halvard)

Quarrington, Paul (Lewis) 1953-.... **CLC 65**
See also CA 129

Quasimodo, Salvatore 1901-1968 ... **CLC 10**
See also CA 13-16; 25-28R; CAP 1;
DLB 114; MTCW

Queen, Ellery.................... **CLC 3, 11**
See also Dannay, Frederic; Davidson,
Avram; Lee, Manfred B(ennington);
Sturgeon, Theodore (Hamilton); Vance,
John Holbrook

Queen, Ellery, Jr.
See Dannay, Frederic; Lee, Manfred
B(ennington)

Queneau, Raymond
1903-1976 .... **CLC 2, 5, 10, 42**
See also CA 77-80; 69-72; CANR 32;
DLB 72; MTCW

Quevedo, Francisco de 1580-1645.... **LC 23**

Quiller-Couch, Arthur Thomas
1863-1944 .... **TCLC 53**
See also CA 118; DLB 135, 153

Quin, Ann (Marie) 1936-1973 .... **CLC 6**
See also CA 9-12R; 45-48; DLB 14

Quinn, Martin
See Smith, Martin Cruz

Quinn, Peter 1947-............... **CLC 91**

Quinn, Simon
See Smith, Martin Cruz

Quiroga, Horacio (Sylvestre)
1878-1937 .... **TCLC 20; HLC**
See also CA 117; 131; DAM MULT; HW;
MTCW

Quoirez, Francoise 1935-........... **CLC 9**
See also Sagan, Francoise
See also CA 49-52; CANR 6, 39; MTCW

Raabe, Wilhelm 1831-1910 .... **TCLC 45**
See also DLB 129

Rabe, David (William) 1940-... **CLC 4, 8, 33**
See also CA 85-88; CABS 3; DAM DRAM;
DLB 7

Rabelais, Francois
1483-1553 ..... **LC 5; DA; DAB; DAC;
WLC**
See also DAM MST

Rabinovitch, Sholem 1859-1916
See Aleichem, Sholom
See also CA 104

Racine, Jean 1639-1699 ...... **LC 28; DAB**
See also DAM MST

Radcliffe, Ann (Ward)
1764-1823 .... **NCLC 6, 55**
See also DLB 39

Radiguet, Raymond 1903-1923 .... **TCLC 29**
See also DLB 65

Radnoti, Miklos 1909-1944 .... **TCLC 16**
See also CA 118

Rado, James 1939-.............. **CLC 17**
See also CA 105

Radvanyi, Netty 1900-1983
See Seghers, Anna
See also CA 85-88; 110

Rae, Ben
See Griffiths, Trevor

Raeburn, John (Hay) 1941-........ **CLC 34**
See also CA 57-60

Ragni, Gerome 1942-1991 .... **CLC 17**
See also CA 105; 134

Rahv, Philip 1908-1973 .... **CLC 24**
See also Greenberg, Ivan
See also DLB 137

Raine, Craig 1944-............... **CLC 32**
See also CA 108; CANR 29, 51; DLB 40

Raine, Kathleen (Jessie) 1908- .. **CLC 7, 45**
See also CA 85-88; CANR 46; DLB 20;
MTCW

Rainis, Janis 1865-1929 .... **TCLC 29**

Rakosi, Carl..................... **CLC 47**
See also Rawley, Callman
See also CAAS 5

Raleigh, Richard
See Lovecraft, H(oward) P(hillips)

Raleigh, Sir Walter 1554(?)-1618 .... **LC 31**
See also CDBLB Before 1660

Rallentando, H. P.
See Sayers, Dorothy L(eigh)

Ramal, Walter
See de la Mare, Walter (John)

Ramon, Juan
See Jimenez (Mantecon), Juan Ramon

Ramos, Graciliano 1892-1953 ..... **TCLC 32**

Rampersad, Arnold 1941-.......... **CLC 44**
See also BW 2; CA 127; 133; DLB 111;
INT 133

Rampling, Anne
See Rice, Anne

Ramsay, Allan 1684(?)-1758 .... **LC 29**
See also DLB 95

Ramuz, Charles-Ferdinand
1878-1947 .... **TCLC 33**

Rand, Ayn
1905-1982 ...... **CLC 3, 30, 44, 79; DA;
DAC; WLC**
See also AAYA 10; CA 13-16R; 105;
CANR 27; DAM MST, NOV, POP;
MTCW

Randall, Dudley (Felker)
1914- .... **CLC 1; BLC**
See also BW 1; CA 25-28R; CANR 23;
DAM MULT; DLB 41

Randall, Robert
See Silverberg, Robert

Ranger, Ken
See Creasey, John

Ransom, John Crowe
1888-1974 .... **CLC 2, 4, 5, 11, 24**
See also CA 5-8R; 49-52; CANR 6, 34;
DAM POET; DLB 45, 63; MTCW

Rao, Raja 1909-.............. **CLC 25, 56**
See also CA 73-76; CANR 51; DAM NOV;
MTCW

Raphael, Frederic (Michael)
1931- .... **CLC 2, 14**
See also CA 1-4R; CANR 1; DLB 14

Ratcliffe, James P.
See Mencken, H(enry) L(ouis)

Rathbone, Julian 1935- .... **CLC 41**
See also CA 101; CANR 34

Rattigan, Terence (Mervyn)
1911-1977 .... **CLC 7**
See also CA 85-88; 73-76;
CDBLB 1945-1960; DAM DRAM;
DLB 13; MTCW

Ratushinskaya, Irina 1954-........ **CLC 54**
See also CA 129

Raven, Simon (Arthur Noel)
1927- .... **CLC 14**
See also CA 81-84

Rawley, Callman 1903-
See Rakosi, Carl
See also CA 21-24R; CANR 12, 32

Rawlings, Marjorie Kinnan
1896-1953 .... **TCLC 4**
See also CA 104; 137; DLB 9, 22, 102;
JRDA; MAICYA; YABC 1

Ray, Satyajit 1921-1992........ **CLC 16, 76**
See also CA 114; 137; DAM MULT

Read, Herbert Edward 1893-1968.... **CLC 4**
See also CA 85-88; 25-28R; DLB 20, 149

Read, Piers Paul 1941- ...... **CLC 4, 10, 25**
See also CA 21-24R; CANR 38; DLB 14;
SATA 21

Reade, Charles 1814-1884 .... **NCLC 2**
See also DLB 21

Reade, Hamish
See Gray, Simon (James Holliday)

Reading, Peter 1946-............. **CLC 47**
See also CA 103; CANR 46; DLB 40

Reaney, James 1926-........ **CLC 13; DAC**
See also CA 41-44R; CAAS 15; CANR 42;
DAM MST; DLB 68; SATA 43

Rebreanu, Liviu 1885-1944 .... **TCLC 28**

Rechy, John (Francisco)
1934- .... **CLC 1, 7, 14, 18; HLC**
See also CA 5-8R; CAAS 4; CANR 6, 32;
DAM MULT; DLB 122; DLBY 82; HW;
INT CANR-6

Redcam, Tom 1870-1933 .... **TCLC 25**

Reddin, Keith.................... **CLC 67**

Author Index

Rilke, Rainer Maria
1875-1926 . . . . **TCLC 1, 6, 19; PC 2**
See also CA 104; 132; DAM POET;
DLB 81; MTCW

Rimbaud, (Jean Nicolas) Arthur
1854-1891 . . . . . **NCLC 4, 35; DA; DAB;**
DAC; PC 3; WLC
See also DAM MST, POET

Rinehart, Mary Roberts
1876-1958 . . . . **TCLC 52**
See also CA 108

Ringmaster, The
See Mencken, H(enry) L(ouis)

Ringwood, Gwen(dolyn Margaret) Pharis
1910-1984 . . . . **CLC 48**
See also CA 148; 112; DLB 88

Rio, Michel 19(?)- . . . . **CLC 43**

Ritsos, Giannes
See Ritsos, Yannis

Ritsos, Yannis 1909-1990 . . . . . **CLC 6, 13, 31**
See also CA 77-80; 133; CANR 39; MTCW

Ritter, Erika 1948(?)- . . . . **CLC 52**

Rivera, Jose Eustasio 1889-1928 . . . **TCLC 35**
See also HW

Rivers, Conrad Kent 1933-1968 . . . . . . **CLC 1**
See also BW 1; CA 85-88; DLB 41

Rivers, Elfrida
See Bradley, Marion Zimmer

Riverside, John
See Heinlein, Robert A(nson)

Rizal, Jose 1861-1896 . . . . **NCLC 27**

Roa Bastos, Augusto (Antonio)
1917- . . . . **CLC 45; HLC**
See also CA 131; DAM MULT; DLB 113;
HW

Robbe-Grillet, Alain
1922- . . . . . . **CLC 1, 2, 4, 6, 8, 10, 14, 43**
See also CA 9-12R; CANR 33; DLB 83;
MTCW

Robbins, Harold 1916- . . . . **CLC 5**
See also CA 73-76; CANR 26; DAM NOV;
MTCW

Robbins, Thomas Eugene 1936-
See Robbins, Tom
See also CA 81-84; CANR 29; DAM NOV,
POP; MTCW

Robbins, Tom . . . . **CLC 9, 32, 64**
See also Robbins, Thomas Eugene
See also BEST 90:3; DLBY 80

Robbins, Trina 1938- . . . . **CLC 21**
See also CA 128

Roberts, Charles G(eorge) D(ouglas)
1860-1943 . . . . **TCLC 8**
See also CA 105; CLR 33; DLB 92;
SATA-Brief 29

Roberts, Kate 1891-1985 . . . . **CLC 15**
See also CA 107; 116

Roberts, Keith (John Kingston)
1935- . . . . **CLC 14**
See also CA 25-28R; CANR 46

Roberts, Kenneth (Lewis)
1885-1957 . . . . **TCLC 23**
See also CA 109; DLB 9

Roberts, Michele (B.) 1949- . . . . **CLC 48**
See also CA 115

Robertson, Ellis
See Ellison, Harlan (Jay); Silverberg, Robert

Robertson, Thomas William
1829-1871 . . . . **NCLC 35**
See also DAM DRAM

Robinson, Edwin Arlington
1869-1935 . . . . **TCLC 5; DA; DAC; PC 1**
See also CA 104; 133; CDALB 1865-1917;
DAM MST, POET; DLB 54; MTCW

Robinson, Henry Crabb
1775-1867 . . . . **NCLC 15**
See also DLB 107

Robinson, Jill 1936- . . . . **CLC 10**
See also CA 102; INT 102

Robinson, Kim Stanley 1952- . . . . . . **CLC 34**
See also CA 126

Robinson, Lloyd
See Silverberg, Robert

Robinson, Marilynne 1944- . . . . **CLC 25**
See also CA 116

Robinson, Smokey . . . . **CLC 21**
See also Robinson, William, Jr.

Robinson, William, Jr. 1940-
See Robinson, Smokey
See also CA 116

Robison, Mary 1949- . . . . **CLC 42**
See also CA 113; 116; DLB 130; INT 116

Rod, Edouard 1857-1910 . . . . **TCLC 52**

Roddenberry, Eugene Wesley 1921-1991
See Roddenberry, Gene
See also CA 110; 135; CANR 37; SATA 45;
SATA-Obit 69

Roddenberry, Gene . . . . **CLC 17**
See also Roddenberry, Eugene Wesley
See also AAYA 5; SATA-Obit 69

Rodgers, Mary 1931- . . . . **CLC 12**
See also CA 49-52; CANR 8; CLR 20;
INT CANR-8; JRDA; MAICYA;
SATA 8

Rodgers, W(illiam) R(obert)
1909-1969 . . . . **CLC 7**
See also CA 85-88; DLB 20

Rodman, Eric
See Silverberg, Robert

Rodman, Howard 1920(?)-1985 . . . . . **CLC 65**
See also CA 118

Rodman, Maia
See Wojciechowska, Maia (Teresa)

Rodriguez, Claudio 1934- . . . . **CLC 10**
See also DLB 134

Roelvaag, O(le) E(dvart)
1876-1931 . . . . **TCLC 17**
See also CA 117; DLB 9

Roethke, Theodore (Huebner)
1908-1963 . . . . . . **CLC 1, 3, 8, 11, 19, 46;**
PC 15
See also CA 81-84; CABS 2;
CDALB 1941-1968; DAM POET; DLB 5;
MTCW

Rogers, Thomas Hunton 1927- . . . . . **CLC 57**
See also CA 89-92; INT 89-92

Rogers, Will(iam Penn Adair)
1879-1935 . . . . **TCLC 8**
See also CA 105; 144; DAM MULT;
DLB 11; NNAL

Rogin, Gilbert 1929- . . . . **CLC 18**
See also CA 65-68; CANR 15

Rohan, Koda . . . . **TCLC 22**
See also Koda Shigeyuki

Rohmer, Eric . . . . **CLC 16**
See also Scherer, Jean-Marie Maurice

Rohmer, Sax . . . . **TCLC 28**
See also Ward, Arthur Henry Sarsfield
See also DLB 70

Roiphe, Anne (Richardson)
1935- . . . . **CLC 3, 9**
See also CA 89-92; CANR 45; DLBY 80;
INT 89-92

Rojas, Fernando de 1465-1541 . . . . . . **LC 23**

Rolfe, Frederick (William Serafino Austin
Lewis Mary) 1860-1913 . . . . . . **TCLC 12**
See also CA 107; DLB 34, 156

Rolland, Romain 1866-1944 . . . . . . **TCLC 23**
See also CA 118; DLB 65

Rolvaag, O(le) E(dvart)
See Roelvaag, O(le) E(dvart)

Romain Arnaud, Saint
See Aragon, Louis

Romains, Jules 1885-1972 . . . . **CLC 7**
See also CA 85-88; CANR 34; DLB 65;
MTCW

Romero, Jose Ruben 1890-1952 . . . **TCLC 14**
See also CA 114; 131; HW

Ronsard, Pierre de
1524-1585 . . . . **LC 6; PC 11**

Rooke, Leon 1934- . . . . **CLC 25, 34**
See also CA 25-28R; CANR 23; DAM POP

Roper, William 1498-1578 . . . . **LC 10**

Roquelaure, A. N.
See Rice, Anne

Rosa, Joao Guimaraes 1908-1967 . . . **CLC 23**
See also CA 89-92; DLB 113

Rose, Wendy 1948- . . . . **CLC 85; PC 13**
See also CA 53-56; CANR 5, 51;
DAM MULT; NNAL; SATA 12

Rosen, Richard (Dean) 1949- . . . . **CLC 39**
See also CA 77-80; INT CANR-30

Rosenberg, Isaac 1890-1918 . . . . . . **TCLC 12**
See also CA 107; DLB 20

Rosenblatt, Joe . . . . **CLC 15**
See also Rosenblatt, Joseph

Rosenblatt, Joseph 1933-
See Rosenblatt, Joe
See also CA 89-92; INT 89-92

Rosenfeld, Samuel 1896-1963
See Tzara, Tristan
See also CA 89-92

Rosenthal, M(acha) L(ouis) 1917- . . . **CLC 28**
See also CA 1-4R; CAAS 6; CANR 4, 51;
DLB 5; SATA 59

Ross, Barnaby
See Dannay, Frederic

Ross, Bernard L.
See Follett, Ken(neth Martin)

Ross, J. H.
See Lawrence, T(homas) E(dward)

Ross, Martin
See Martin, Violet Florence
See also DLB 135

Ross, (James) Sinclair
1908- . . . . **CLC 13; DAC**
See also CA 73-76; DAM MST; DLB 88

Rossetti, Christina (Georgina)
1830-1894 . . . . . **NCLC 2, 50; DA; DAB;**
DAC; PC 7; WLC
See also DAM MST, POET; DLB 35, 163;
MAICYA; SATA 20

Rossetti, Dante Gabriel
1828-1882 . . . . **NCLC 4; DA; DAB;**
DAC; WLC
See also CDBLB 1832-1890; DAM MST,
POET; DLB 35

Rossner, Judith (Perelman)
1935- . . . . **CLC 6, 9, 29**
See also AITN 2; BEST 90:3; CA 17-20R;
CANR 18, 51; DLB 6; INT CANR-18;
MTCW

Rostand, Edmond (Eugene Alexis)
1868-1918 . . . . . . **TCLC 6, 37; DA; DAB;**
DAC
See also CA 104; 126; DAM DRAM, MST;
MTCW

Roth, Henry 1906-1995 . . . . **CLC 2, 6, 11**
See also CA 11-12; 149; CANR 38; CAP 1;
DLB 28; MTCW

Roth, Joseph 1894-1939 . . . . **TCLC 33**
See also DLB 85

Roth, Philip (Milton)
1933- . . . . . **CLC 1, 2, 3, 4, 6, 9, 15, 22,**
31, 47, 66, 86; DA; DAB; DAC; WLC
See also BEST 90:3; CA 1-4R; CANR 1, 22,
36; CDALB 1968-1988; DAM MST,
NOV, POP; DLB 2, 28; DLBY 82;
MTCW

Rothenberg, Jerome 1931- . . . . **CLC 6, 57**
See also CA 45-48; CANR 1; DLB 5

Roumain, Jacques (Jean Baptiste)
1907-1944 . . . . **TCLC 19; BLC**
See also BW 1; CA 117; 125; DAM MULT

Rourke, Constance (Mayfield)
1885-1941 . . . . **TCLC 12**
See also CA 107; YABC 1

Rousseau, Jean-Baptiste 1671-1741 . . . **LC 9**

Rousseau, Jean-Jacques
1712-1778 . . . . . **LC 14; DA; DAB; DAC;**
WLC
See also DAM MST

Roussel, Raymond 1877-1933 . . . . . **TCLC 20**
See also CA 117

Rovit, Earl (Herbert) 1927- . . . . **CLC 7**
See also CA 5-8R; CANR 12

Rowe, Nicholas 1674-1718 . . . . **LC 8**
See also DLB 84

Rowley, Ames Dorrance
See Lovecraft, H(oward) P(hillips)

Rowson, Susanna Haswell
1762(?)-1824 . . . . **NCLC 5**
See also DLB 37

Roy, Gabrielle
1909-1983 . . . . . **CLC 10, 14; DAB; DAC**
See also CA 53-56; 110; CANR 5;
DAM MST; DLB 68; MTCW

Rozewicz, Tadeusz 1921- . . . . **CLC 9, 23**
See also CA 108; CANR 36; DAM POET;
MTCW

Ruark, Gibbons 1941- . . . . **CLC 3**
See also CA 33-36R; CAAS 23; CANR 14,
31; DLB 120

Rubens, Bernice (Ruth) 1923- . . . **CLC 19, 31**
See also CA 25-28R; CANR 33; DLB 14;
MTCW

Rudkin, (James) David 1936- . . . . . . **CLC 14**
See also CA 89-92; DLB 13

Rudnik, Raphael 1933- . . . . **CLC 7**
See also CA 29-32R

Ruffian, M.
See Hasek, Jaroslav (Matej Frantisek)

Ruiz, Jose Martinez . . . . **CLC 11**
See also Martinez Ruiz, Jose

Rukeyser, Muriel
1913-1980 . . . . **CLC 6, 10, 15, 27; PC 12**
See also CA 5-8R; 93-96; CANR 26;
DAM POET; DLB 48; MTCW;
SATA-Obit 22

Rule, Jane (Vance) 1931- . . . . **CLC 27**
See also CA 25-28R; CAAS 18; CANR 12;
DLB 60

Rulfo, Juan 1918-1986 . . . . **CLC 8, 80; HLC**
See also CA 85-88; 118; CANR 26;
DAM MULT; DLB 113; HW; MTCW

Runeberg, Johan 1804-1877 . . . . . . **NCLC 41**

Runyon, (Alfred) Damon
1884(?)-1946 . . . . **TCLC 10**
See also CA 107; DLB 11, 86

Rush, Norman 1933- . . . . **CLC 44**
See also CA 121; 126; INT 126

Rushdie, (Ahmed) Salman
1947- . . . . . . **CLC 23, 31, 55; DAB; DAC**
See also BEST 89:3; CA 108; 111;
CANR 33; DAM MST, NOV, POP;
INT 111; MTCW

Rushforth, Peter (Scott) 1945- . . . . . **CLC 19**
See also CA 101

Ruskin, John 1819-1900 . . . . **TCLC 63**
See also CA 114; 129; CDBLB 1832-1890;
DLB 55, 163; SATA 24

Russ, Joanna 1937- . . . . **CLC 15**
See also CA 25-28R; CANR 11, 31; DLB 8;
MTCW

Russell, George William 1867-1935
See A. E.
See also CA 104; CDBLB 1890-1914;
DAM POET

Russell, (Henry) Ken(neth Alfred)
1927- . . . . **CLC 16**
See also CA 105

Russell, Willy 1947- . . . . **CLC 60**

Rutherford, Mark . . . . **TCLC 25**
See also White, William Hale
See also DLB 18

Ruyslinck, Ward 1929- . . . . **CLC 14**
See also Belser, Reimond Karel Maria de

Ryan, Cornelius (John) 1920-1974 . . . **CLC 7**
See also CA 69-72; 53-56; CANR 38

Ryan, Michael 1946- . . . . **CLC 65**
See also CA 49-52; DLBY 82

Rybakov, Anatoli (Naumovich)
1911- . . . . **CLC 23, 53**
See also CA 126; 135; SATA 79

Ryder, Jonathan
See Ludlum, Robert

Ryga, George 1932-1987 . . . . . **CLC 14; DAC**
See also CA 101; 124; CANR 43;
DAM MST; DLB 60

S. S.
See Sassoon, Siegfried (Lorraine)

Saba, Umberto 1883-1957 . . . . **TCLC 33**
See also CA 144; DLB 114

Sabatini, Rafael 1875-1950 . . . . **TCLC 47**

Sabato, Ernesto (R.)
1911- . . . . **CLC 10, 23; HLC**
See also CA 97-100; CANR 32;
DAM MULT; DLB 145; HW; MTCW

Sacastru, Martin
See Bioy Casares, Adolfo

Sacher-Masoch, Leopold von
1836(?)-1895 . . . . **NCLC 31**

Sachs, Marilyn (Stickle) 1927- . . . . . **CLC 35**
See also AAYA 2; CA 17-20R; CANR 13,
47; CLR 2; JRDA; MAICYA; SAAS 2;
SATA 3, 68

Sachs, Nelly 1891-1970 . . . . **CLC 14**
See also CA 17-18; 25-28R; CAP 2

Sackler, Howard (Oliver)
1929-1982 . . . . **CLC 14**
See also CA 61-64; 108; CANR 30; DLB 7

Sacks, Oliver (Wolf) 1933- . . . . **CLC 67**
See also CA 53-56; CANR 28, 50;
INT CANR-28; MTCW

Sade, Donatien Alphonse Francois Comte
1740-1814 . . . . **NCLC 47**

Sadoff, Ira 1945- . . . . **CLC 9**
See also CA 53-56; CANR 5, 21; DLB 120

Saetone
See Camus, Albert

Safire, William 1929- . . . . **CLC 10**
See also CA 17-20R; CANR 31

Sagan, Carl (Edward) 1934- . . . . **CLC 30**
See also AAYA 2; CA 25-28R; CANR 11,
36; MTCW; SATA 58

Sagan, Francoise . . . . **CLC 3, 6, 9, 17, 36**
See also Quoirez, Francoise
See also DLB 83

Sahgal, Nayantara (Pandit) 1927- . . . **CLC 41**
See also CA 9-12R; CANR 11

Saint, H(arry) F. 1941- . . . . **CLC 50**
See also CA 127

St. Aubin de Teran, Lisa 1953-
See Teran, Lisa St. Aubin de
See also CA 118; 126; INT 126

Sainte-Beuve, Charles Augustin
1804-1869 . . . . **NCLC 5**

Shone, Patric
See Hanley, James

Shreve, Susan Richards 1939-...... **CLC 23**
See also CA 49-52; CAAS 5; CANR 5, 38;
MAICYA; SATA 46; SATA-Brief 41

Shue, Larry 1946-1985............ **CLC 52**
See also CA 145; 117; DAM DRAM

Shu-Jen, Chou 1881-1936
See Lu Hsun
See also CA 104

Shulman, Alix Kates 1932- ...... **CLC 2, 10**
See also CA 29-32R; CANR 43; SATA 7

Shuster, Joe 1914- .... **CLC 21**

Shute, Nevil...................... **CLC 30**
See also Norway, Nevil Shute

Shuttle, Penelope (Diane) 1947- ..... **CLC 7**
See also CA 93-96; CANR 39; DLB 14, 40

Sidney, Mary 1561-1621 .... **LC 19**

Sidney, Sir Philip
1554-1586 ..... **LC 19; DA; DAB; DAC**
See also CDBLB Before 1660; DAM MST,
POET

Siegel, Jerome 1914- .... **CLC 21**
See also CA 116

Siegel, Jerry
See Siegel, Jerome

Sienkiewicz, Henryk (Adam Alexander Pius)
1846-1916 .... **TCLC 3**
See also CA 104; 134

Sierra, Gregorio Martinez
See Martinez Sierra, Gregorio

Sierra, Maria (de la O'LeJarraga) Martinez
See Martinez Sierra, Maria (de la
O'LeJarraga)

Sigal, Clancy 1926-................ **CLC 7**
See also CA 1-4R

Sigourney, Lydia Howard (Huntley)
1791-1865 .... **NCLC 21**
See also DLB 1, 42, 73

Siguenza y Gongora, Carlos de
1645-1700 .... **LC 8**

Sigurjonsson, Johann 1880-1919... **TCLC 27**

Sikelianos, Angelos 1884-1951 .... **TCLC 39**

Silkin, Jon 1930- .... **CLC 2, 6, 43**
See also CA 5-8R; CAAS 5; DLB 27

Silko, Leslie (Marmon)
1948-.......... **CLC 23, 74; DA; DAC**
See also AAYA 14; CA 115; 122;
CANR 45; DAM MST, MULT, POP;
DLB 143; NNAL

Sillanpaa, Frans Eemil 1888-1964... **CLC 19**
See also CA 129; 93-96; MTCW

Sillitoe, Alan
1928-.......... **CLC 1, 3, 6, 10, 19, 57**
See also AITN 1; CA 9-12R; CAAS 2;
CANR 8, 26; CDBLB 1960 to Present;
DLB 14, 139; MTCW; SATA 61

Silone, Ignazio 1900-1978 .... **CLC 4**
See also CA 25-28; 81-84; CANR 34;
CAP 2; MTCW

Silver, Joan Micklin 1935- .... **CLC 20**
See also CA 114; 121; INT 121

Silver, Nicholas
See Faust, Frederick (Schiller)

Silverberg, Robert 1935-........... **CLC 7**
See also CA 1-4R; CAAS 3; CANR 1, 20,
36; DAM POP; DLB 8; INT CANR-20;
MAICYA; MTCW; SATA 13

Silverstein, Alvin 1933- .... **CLC 17**
See also CA 49-52; CANR 2; CLR 25;
JRDA; MAICYA; SATA 8, 69

Silverstein, Virginia B(arbara Opshelor)
1937- .... **CLC 17**
See also CA 49-52; CANR 2; CLR 25;
JRDA; MAICYA; SATA 8, 69

Sim, Georges
See Simenon, Georges (Jacques Christian)

Simak, Clifford D(onald)
1904-1988 .... **CLC 1, 55**
See also CA 1-4R; 125; CANR 1, 35;
DLB 8; MTCW; SATA-Obit 56

Simenon, Georges (Jacques Christian)
1903-1989 .... **CLC 1, 2, 3, 8, 18, 47**
See also CA 85-88; 129; CANR 35;
DAM POP; DLB 72; DLBY 89; MTCW

Simic, Charles 1938-... **CLC 6, 9, 22, 49, 68**
See also CA 29-32R; CAAS 4; CANR 12,
33; DAM POET; DLB 105

Simmons, Charles (Paul) 1924-..... **CLC 57**
See also CA 89-92; INT 89-92

Simmons, Dan 1948-............. **CLC 44**
See also AAYA 16; CA 138; DAM POP

Simmons, James (Stewart Alexander)
1933-...................... **CLC 43**
See also CA 105; CAAS 21; DLB 40

Simms, William Gilmore
1806-1870 .... **NCLC 3**
See also DLB 3, 30, 59, 73

Simon, Carly 1945-............... **CLC 26**
See also CA 105

Simon, Claude 1913-...... **CLC 4, 9, 15, 39**
See also CA 89-92; CANR 33; DAM NOV;
DLB 83; MTCW

Simon, (Marvin) Neil
1927-.......... **CLC 6, 11, 31, 39, 70**
See also AITN 1; CA 21-24R; CANR 26;
DAM DRAM; DLB 7; MTCW

Simon, Paul 1942(?)- .... **CLC 17**
See also CA 116

Simonon, Paul 1956(?)- .... **CLC 30**

Simpson, Harriette
See Arnow, Harriette (Louisa) Simpson

Simpson, Louis (Aston Marantz)
1923-.................. **CLC 4, 7, 9, 32**
See also CA 1-4R; CAAS 4; CANR 1;
DAM POET; DLB 5; MTCW

Simpson, Mona (Elizabeth) 1957-... **CLC 44**
See also CA 122; 135

Simpson, N(orman) F(rederick)
1919-...................... **CLC 29**
See also CA 13-16R; DLB 13

Sinclair, Andrew (Annandale)
1935-..................... **CLC 2, 14**
See also CA 9-12R; CAAS 5; CANR 14, 38;
DLB 14; MTCW

Sinclair, Emil
See Hesse, Hermann

Sinclair, Iain 1943-............... **CLC 76**
See also CA 132

Sinclair, Iain MacGregor
See Sinclair, Iain

Sinclair, Mary Amelia St. Clair 1865(?)-1946
See Sinclair, May
See also CA 104

Sinclair, May................... **TCLC 3, 11**
See also Sinclair, Mary Amelia St. Clair
See also DLB 36, 135

Sinclair, Upton (Beall)
1878-1968 ...... **CLC 1, 11, 15, 63; DA;
DAB; DAC; WLC**
See also CA 5-8R; 25-28R; CANR 7;
CDALB 1929-1941; DAM MST, NOV;
DLB 9; INT CANR-7; MTCW; SATA 9

Singer, Isaac
See Singer, Isaac Bashevis

Singer, Isaac Bashevis
1904-1991 .... **CLC 1, 3, 6, 9, 11, 15, 23,
38, 69; DA; DAB; DAC; SSC 3; WLC**
See also AITN 1, 2; CA 1-4R; 134;
CANR 1, 39; CDALB 1941-1968; CLR 1;
DAM MST, NOV; DLB 6, 28, 52;
DLBY 91; JRDA; MAICYA; MTCW;
SATA 3, 27; SATA-Obit 68

Singer, Israel Joshua 1893-1944... **TCLC 33**

Singh, Khushwant 1915-........... **CLC 11**
See also CA 9-12R; CAAS 9; CANR 6

Sinjohn, John
See Galsworthy, John

Sinyavsky, Andrei (Donatevich)
1925-....................... **CLC 8**
See also CA 85-88

Sirin, V.
See Nabokov, Vladimir (Vladimirovich)

Sissman, L(ouis) E(dward)
1928-1976 .... **CLC 9, 18**
See also CA 21-24R; 65-68; CANR 13;
DLB 5

Sisson, C(harles) H(ubert) 1914-..... **CLC 8**
See also CA 1-4R; CAAS 3; CANR 3, 48;
DLB 27

Sitwell, Dame Edith
1887-1964 .... **CLC 2, 9, 67; PC 3**
See also CA 9-12R; CANR 35;
CDBLB 1945-1960; DAM POET;
DLB 20; MTCW

Sjoewall, Maj 1935-............... **CLC 7**
See also CA 65-68

Sjowall, Maj
See Sjoewall, Maj

Skelton, Robin 1925-............. **CLC 13**
See also AITN 2; CA 5-8R; CAAS 5;
CANR 28; DLB 27, 53

Skolimowski, Jerzy 1938-......... **CLC 20**
See also CA 128

Skram, Amalie (Bertha)
1847-1905 .... **TCLC 25**

Skvorecky, Josef (Vaclav)
1924-.......... **CLC 15, 39, 69; DAC**
See also CA 61-64; CAAS 1; CANR 10, 34;
DAM NOV; MTCW

Slade, Bernard.................. **CLC 11, 46**
See also Newbound, Bernard Slade
See also CAAS 9; DLB 53

Slaughter, Carolyn 1946- . . . . CLC 56
See also CA 85-88

Slaughter, Frank G(ill) 1908- . . . . . . CLC 29
See also AITN 2; CA 5-8R; CANR 5;
INT CANR-5

Slavitt, David R(ytman) 1935- . . . . CLC 5, 14
See also CA 21-24R; CAAS 3; CANR 41;
DLB 5, 6

Slesinger, Tess 1905-1945 . . . . TCLC 10
See also CA 107; DLB 102

Slessor, Kenneth 1901-1971 . . . . CLC 14
See also CA 102; 89-92

Slowacki, Juliusz 1809-1849 . . . . . NCLC 15

Smart, Christopher
1722-1771 . . . . LC 3; PC 13
See also DAM POET; DLB 109

Smart, Elizabeth 1913-1986 . . . . CLC 54
See also CA 81-84; 118; DLB 88

Smiley, Jane (Graves) 1949- . . . . CLC 53, 76
See also CA 104; CANR 30, 50;
DAM POP; INT CANR-30

Smith, A(rthur) J(ames) M(arshall)
1902-1980 . . . . CLC 15; DAC
See also CA 1-4R; 102; CANR 4; DLB 88

Smith, Anna Deavere 1950- . . . . CLC 86
See also CA 133

Smith, Betty (Wehner) 1896-1972 . . . CLC 19
See also CA 5-8R; 33-36R; DLBY 82;
SATA 6

Smith, Charlotte (Turner)
1749-1806 . . . . NCLC 23
See also DLB 39, 109

Smith, Clark Ashton 1893-1961 . . . . CLC 43
See also CA 143

Smith, Dave . . . . CLC 22, 42
See also Smith, David (Jeddie)
See also CAAS 7; DLB 5

Smith, David (Jeddie) 1942-
See Smith, Dave
See also CA 49-52; CANR 1; DAM POET

Smith, Florence Margaret 1902-1971
See Smith, Stevie
See also CA 17-18; 29-32R; CANR 35;
CAP 2; DAM POET; MTCW

Smith, Iain Crichton 1928- . . . . CLC 64
See also CA 21-24R; DLB 40, 139

Smith, John 1580(?)-1631 . . . . LC 9

Smith, Johnston
See Crane, Stephen (Townley)

Smith, Joseph, Jr. 1805-1844 . . . . NCLC 53

Smith, Lee 1944- . . . . CLC 25, 73
See also CA 114; 119; CANR 46; DLB 143;
DLBY 83; INT 119

Smith, Martin
See Smith, Martin Cruz

Smith, Martin Cruz 1942- . . . . CLC 25
See also BEST 89:4; CA 85-88; CANR 6,
23, 43; DAM MULT, POP;
INT CANR-23; NNAL

Smith, Mary-Ann Tirone 1944- . . . . . CLC 39
See also CA 118; 136

Smith, Patti 1946- . . . . CLC 12
See also CA 93-96

Smith, Pauline (Urmson)
1882-1959 . . . . TCLC 25

Smith, Rosamond
See Oates, Joyce Carol

Smith, Sheila Kaye
See Kaye-Smith, Sheila

Smith, Stevie . . . . . . CLC 3, 8, 25, 44; PC 12
See also Smith, Florence Margaret
See also DLB 20

Smith, Wilbur (Addison) 1933- . . . . . CLC 33
See also CA 13-16R; CANR 7, 46; MTCW

Smith, William Jay 1918- . . . . CLC 6
See also CA 5-8R; CANR 44; DLB 5;
MAICYA; SAAS 22; SATA 2, 68

Smith, Woodrow Wilson
See Kuttner, Henry

Smolenskin, Peretz 1842-1885 . . . . NCLC 30

Smollett, Tobias (George) 1721-1771 . . LC 2
See also CDBLB 1660-1789; DLB 39, 104

Snodgrass, W(illiam) D(e Witt)
1926- . . . . CLC 2, 6, 10, 18, 68
See also CA 1-4R; CANR 6, 36;
DAM POET; DLB 5; MTCW

Snow, C(harles) P(ercy)
1905-1980 . . . . CLC 1, 4, 6, 9, 13, 19
See also CA 5-8R; 101; CANR 28;
CDBLB 1945-1960; DAM NOV; DLB 15,
77; MTCW

Snow, Frances Compton
See Adams, Henry (Brooks)

Snyder, Gary (Sherman)
1930- . . . . CLC 1, 2, 5, 9, 32
See also CA 17-20R; CANR 30;
DAM POET; DLB 5, 16

Snyder, Zilpha Keatley 1927- . . . . . . CLC 17
See also AAYA 15; CA 9-12R; CANR 38;
CLR 31; JRDA; MAICYA; SAAS 2;
SATA 1, 28, 75

Soares, Bernardo
See Pessoa, Fernando (Antonio Nogueira)

Sobh, A.
See Shamlu, Ahmad

Sobol, Joshua . . . . CLC 60

Soderberg, Hjalmar 1869-1941 . . . . TCLC 39

Sodergran, Edith (Irene)
See Soedergran, Edith (Irene)

Soedergran, Edith (Irene)
1892-1923 . . . . TCLC 31

Softly, Edgar
See Lovecraft, H(oward) P(hillips)

Softly, Edward
See Lovecraft, H(oward) P(hillips)

Sokolov, Raymond 1941- . . . . CLC 7
See also CA 85-88

Solo, Jay
See Ellison, Harlan (Jay)

Sologub, Fyodor . . . . TCLC 9
See also Teternikov, Fyodor Kuzmich

Solomons, Ikey Esquir
See Thackeray, William Makepeace

Solomos, Dionysios 1798-1857 . . . NCLC 15

Solwoska, Mara
See French, Marilyn

Solzhenitsyn, Aleksandr I(sayevich)
1918- . . . . . . CLC 1, 2, 4, 7, 9, 10, 18, 26,
34, 78; DA; DAB; DAC; WLC
See also AITN 1; CA 69-72; CANR 40;
DAM MST, NOV; MTCW

Somers, Jane
See Lessing, Doris (May)

Somerville, Edith 1858-1949 . . . . . TCLC 51
See also DLB 135

Somerville & Ross
See Martin, Violet Florence; Somerville,
Edith

Sommer, Scott 1951- . . . . CLC 25
See also CA 106

Sondheim, Stephen (Joshua)
1930- . . . . CLC 30, 39
See also AAYA 11; CA 103; CANR 47;
DAM DRAM

Sontag, Susan 1933- . . . CLC 1, 2, 10, 13, 31
See also CA 17-20R; CANR 25, 51;
DAM POP; DLB 2, 67; MTCW

Sophocles
496(?)B.C.-406(?)B.C. . . . . . CMLC 2; DA;
DAB; DAC; DC 1
See also DAM DRAM, MST

Sordello 1189-1269 . . . . CMLC 15

Sorel, Julia
See Drexler, Rosalyn

Sorrentino, Gilbert
1929- . . . . CLC 3, 7, 14, 22, 40
See also CA 77-80; CANR 14, 33; DLB 5;
DLBY 80; INT CANR-14

Soto, Gary 1952- . . . . CLC 32, 80; HLC
See also AAYA 10; CA 119; 125;
CANR 50; CLR 38; DAM MULT;
DLB 82; HW; INT 125; JRDA; SATA 80

Soupault, Philippe 1897-1990 . . . . . . CLC 68
See also CA 116; 147; 131

Souster, (Holmes) Raymond
1921- . . . . CLC 5, 14; DAC
See also CA 13-16R; CAAS 14; CANR 13,
29; DAM POET; DLB 88; SATA 63

Southern, Terry 1924(?)-1995 . . . . CLC 7
See also CA 1-4R; 150; CANR 1; DLB 2

Southey, Robert 1774-1843 . . . . NCLC 8
See also DLB 93, 107, 142; SATA 54

Southworth, Emma Dorothy Eliza Nevitte
1819-1899 . . . . NCLC 26

Souza, Ernest
See Scott, Evelyn

Soyinka, Wole
1934- . . . . CLC 3, 5, 14, 36, 44; BLC;
DA; DAB; DAC; DC 2; WLC
See also BW 2; CA 13-16R; CANR 27, 39;
DAM DRAM, MST, MULT; DLB 125;
MTCW

Spackman, W(illiam) M(ode)
1905-1990 . . . . CLC 46
See also CA 81-84; 132

Spacks, Barry 1931- . . . . CLC 14
See also CA 29-32R; CANR 33; DLB 105

Spanidou, Irini 1946- . . . . CLC 44

Spark, Muriel (Sarah)
    1918- . . . . **CLC 2, 3, 5, 8, 13, 18, 40;**
                    DAB; DAC; SSC 10
    See also CA 5-8R; CANR 12, 36;
      CDBLB 1945-1960; DAM MST, NOV;
      DLB 15, 139; INT CANR-12; MTCW

Spaulding, Douglas
    See Bradbury, Ray (Douglas)

Spaulding, Leonard
    See Bradbury, Ray (Douglas)

Spence, J. A. D.
    See Eliot, T(homas) S(tearns)

Spencer, Elizabeth 1921- . . . . **CLC 22**
    See also CA 13-16R; CANR 32; DLB 6;
      MTCW; SATA 14

Spencer, Leonard G.
    See Silverberg, Robert

Spencer, Scott 1945- . . . . **CLC 30**
    See also CA 113; CANR 51; DLBY 86

Spender, Stephen (Harold)
    1909-1995 . . . . . . **CLC 1, 2, 5, 10, 41, 91**
    See also CA 9-12R; 149; CANR 31;
      CDBLB 1945-1960; DAM POET;
      DLB 20; MTCW

Spengler, Oswald (Arnold Gottfried)
    1880-1936 . . . . **TCLC 25**
    See also CA 118

Spenser, Edmund
    1552(?)-1599 . . . . **LC 5; DA; DAB; DAC;**
                         PC 8; WLC
    See also CDBLB Before 1660; DAM MST,
      POET

Spicer, Jack 1925-1965 . . . . . . **CLC 8, 18, 72**
    See also CA 85-88; DAM POET; DLB 5, 16

Spiegelman, Art 1948- . . . . **CLC 76**
    See also AAYA 10; CA 125; CANR 41

Spielberg, Peter 1929- . . . . **CLC 6**
    See also CA 5-8R; CANR 4, 48; DLBY 81

Spielberg, Steven 1947- . . . . **CLC 20**
    See also AAYA 8; CA 77-80; CANR 32;
      SATA 32

Spillane, Frank Morrison 1918-
    See Spillane, Mickey
    See also CA 25-28R; CANR 28; MTCW;
      SATA 66

Spillane, Mickey . . . . **CLC 3, 13**
    See also Spillane, Frank Morrison

Spinoza, Benedictus de 1632-1677 . . . . **LC 9**

Spinrad, Norman (Richard) 1940- . . . **CLC 46**
    See also CA 37-40R; CAAS 19; CANR 20;
      DLB 8; INT CANR-20

Spitteler, Carl (Friedrich Georg)
    1845-1924 . . . . **TCLC 12**
    See also CA 109; DLB 129

Spivack, Kathleen (Romola Drucker)
    1938- . . . . **CLC 6**
    See also CA 49-52

Spoto, Donald 1941- . . . . **CLC 39**
    See also CA 65-68; CANR 11

Springsteen, Bruce (F.) 1949- . . . . . . **CLC 17**
    See also CA 111

Spurling, Hilary 1940- . . . . **CLC 34**
    See also CA 104; CANR 25

Spyker, John Howland
    See Elman, Richard

Squires, (James) Radcliffe
    1917-1993 . . . . **CLC 51**
    See also CA 1-4R; 140; CANR 6, 21

Srivastava, Dhanpat Rai 1880(?)-1936
    See Premchand
    See also CA 118

Stacy, Donald
    See Pohl, Frederik

Stael, Germaine de
    See Stael-Holstein, Anne Louise Germaine
      Necker Baronn
    See also DLB 119

Stael-Holstein, Anne Louise Germaine Necker
    Baronn 1766-1817 . . . . **NCLC 3**
    See also Stael, Germaine de

Stafford, Jean 1915-1979 . . . **CLC 4, 7, 19, 68**
    See also CA 1-4R; 85-88; CANR 3; DLB 2;
      MTCW; SATA-Obit 22

Stafford, William (Edgar)
    1914-1993 . . . . **CLC 4, 7, 29**
    See also CA 5-8R; 142; CAAS 3; CANR 5,
      22; DAM POET; DLB 5; INT CANR-22

Staines, Trevor
    See Brunner, John (Kilian Houston)

Stairs, Gordon
    See Austin, Mary (Hunter)

Stannard, Martin 1947- . . . . **CLC 44**
    See also CA 142; DLB 155

Stanton, Maura 1946- . . . . **CLC 9**
    See also CA 89-92; CANR 15; DLB 120

Stanton, Schuyler
    See Baum, L(yman) Frank

Stapledon, (William) Olaf
    1886-1950 . . . . **TCLC 22**
    See also CA 111; DLB 15

Starbuck, George (Edwin) 1931- . . . . **CLC 53**
    See also CA 21-24R; CANR 23;
      DAM POET

Stark, Richard
    See Westlake, Donald E(dwin)

Staunton, Schuyler
    See Baum, L(yman) Frank

Stead, Christina (Ellen)
    1902-1983 . . . . **CLC 2, 5, 8, 32, 80**
    See also CA 13-16R; 109; CANR 33, 40;
      MTCW

Stead, William Thomas
    1849-1912 . . . . **TCLC 48**

Steele, Richard 1672-1729 . . . . **LC 18**
    See also CDBLB 1660-1789; DLB 84, 101

Steele, Timothy (Reid) 1948- . . . . **CLC 45**
    See also CA 93-96; CANR 16, 50; DLB 120

Steffens, (Joseph) Lincoln
    1866-1936 . . . . **TCLC 20**
    See also CA 117

Stegner, Wallace (Earle)
    1909-1993 . . . . **CLC 9, 49, 81**
    See also AITN 1; BEST 90:3; CA 1-4R;
      141; CAAS 9; CANR 1, 21, 46;
      DAM NOV; DLB 9; DLBY 93; MTCW

Stein, Gertrude
    1874-1946 . . . . . . **TCLC 1, 6, 28, 48; DA;**
                      DAB; DAC; WLC
    See also CA 104; 132; CDALB 1917-1929;
      DAM MST, NOV, POET; DLB 4, 54, 86;
      MTCW

Steinbeck, John (Ernst)
    1902-1968 . . . . . . **CLC 1, 5, 9, 13, 21, 34,**
        45, 75; DA; DAB; DAC; SSC 11; WLC
    See also AAYA 12; CA 1-4R; 25-28R;
      CANR 1, 35; CDALB 1929-1941;
      DAM DRAM, MST, NOV; DLB 7, 9;
      DLBD 2; MTCW; SATA 9

Steinem, Gloria 1934- . . . . **CLC 63**
    See also CA 53-56; CANR 28, 51; MTCW

Steiner, George 1929- . . . . **CLC 24**
    See also CA 73-76; CANR 31; DAM NOV;
      DLB 67; MTCW; SATA 62

Steiner, K. Leslie
    See Delany, Samuel R(ay, Jr.)

Steiner, Rudolf 1861-1925 . . . . **TCLC 13**
    See also CA 107

Stendhal
    1783-1842 . . . . **NCLC 23, 46; DA; DAB;**
                        DAC; WLC
    See also DAM MST, NOV; DLB 119

Stephen, Leslie 1832-1904 . . . . **TCLC 23**
    See also CA 123; DLB 57, 144

Stephen, Sir Leslie
    See Stephen, Leslie

Stephen, Virginia
    See Woolf, (Adeline) Virginia

Stephens, James 1882(?)-1950 . . . . . . **TCLC 4**
    See also CA 104; DLB 19, 153, 162

Stephens, Reed
    See Donaldson, Stephen R.

Steptoe, Lydia
    See Barnes, Djuna

Sterchi, Beat 1949- . . . . **CLC 65**

Sterling, Brett
    See Bradbury, Ray (Douglas); Hamilton,
      Edmond

Sterling, Bruce 1954- . . . . **CLC 72**
    See also CA 119; CANR 44

Sterling, George 1869-1926 . . . . **TCLC 20**
    See also CA 117; DLB 54

Stern, Gerald 1925- . . . . **CLC 40**
    See also CA 81-84; CANR 28; DLB 105

Stern, Richard (Gustave) 1928- . . . **CLC 4, 39**
    See also CA 1-4R; CANR 1, 25; DLBY 87;
      INT CANR-25

Sternberg, Josef von 1894-1969 . . . . . **CLC 20**
    See also CA 81-84

Sterne, Laurence
    1713-1768 . . . . . . **LC 2; DA; DAB; DAC;**
                          WLC
    See also CDBLB 1660-1789; DAM MST,
      NOV; DLB 39

Sternheim, (William Adolf) Carl
    1878-1942 . . . . **TCLC 8**
    See also CA 105; DLB 56, 118

Stevens, Mark 1951- . . . . **CLC 34**
    See also CA 122

Terkel, Louis 1912-
See Terkel, Studs
See also CA 57-60; CANR 18, 45; MTCW

Terkel, Studs..................... CLC 38
See also Terkel, Louis
See also AITN 1

Terry, C. V.
See Slaughter, Frank G(ill)

Terry, Megan 1932-............. CLC 19
See also CA 77-80; CABS 3; CANR 43;
DLB 7

Tertz, Abram
See Sinyavsky, Andrei (Donatevich)

Tesich, Steve 1943(?)-......... CLC 40, 69
See also CA 105; DLBY 83

Teternikov, Fyodor Kuzmich 1863-1927
See Sologub, Fyodor
See also CA 104

Tevis, Walter 1928-1984 .... CLC 42
See also CA 113

Tey, Josephine.................. TCLC 14
See also Mackintosh, Elizabeth
See also DLB 77

Thackeray, William Makepeace
1811-1863 .... NCLC 5, 14, 22, 43; DA;
DAB; DAC; WLC
See also CDBLB 1832-1890; DAM MST,
NOV; DLB 21, 55, 159, 163; SATA 23

Thakura, Ravindranatha
See Tagore, Rabindranath

Tharoor, Shashi 1956-............ CLC 70
See also CA 141

Thelwell, Michael Miles 1939-..... CLC 22
See also BW 2; CA 101

Theobald, Lewis, Jr.
See Lovecraft, H(oward) P(hillips)

Theodorescu, Ion N. 1880-1967
See Arghezi, Tudor
See also CA 116

Theriault, Yves 1915-1983.... CLC 79; DAC
See also CA 102; DAM MST; DLB 88

Theroux, Alexander (Louis)
1939-.................... CLC 2, 25
See also CA 85-88; CANR 20

Theroux, Paul (Edward)
1941-......... CLC 5, 8, 11, 15, 28, 46
See also BEST 89:4; CA 33-36R; CANR 20,
45; DAM POP; DLB 2; MTCW;
SATA 44

Thesen, Sharon 1946-............ CLC 56

Thevenin, Denis
See Duhamel, Georges

Thibault, Jacques Anatole Francois
1844-1924
See France, Anatole
See also CA 106; 127; DAM NOV; MTCW

Thiele, Colin (Milton) 1920-....... CLC 17
See also CA 29-32R; CANR 12, 28;
CLR 27; MAICYA; SAAS 2; SATA 14,
72

Thomas, Audrey (Callahan)
1935-......... CLC 7, 13, 37; SSC 20
See also AITN 2; CA 21-24R; CAAS 19;
CANR 36; DLB 60; MTCW

Thomas, D(onald) M(ichael)
1935- .... CLC 13, 22, 31
See also CA 61-64; CAAS 11; CANR 17,
45; CDBLB 1960 to Present; DLB 40;
INT CANR-17; MTCW

Thomas, Dylan (Marlais)
1914-1953 ... TCLC 1, 8, 45; DA; DAB;
DAC; PC 2; SSC 3; WLC
See also CA 104; 120; CDBLB 1945-1960;
DAM DRAM, MST, POET; DLB 13, 20,
139; MTCW; SATA 60

Thomas, (Philip) Edward
1878-1917 .... TCLC 10
See also CA 106; DAM POET; DLB 19

Thomas, Joyce Carol 1938-........ CLC 35
See also AAYA 12; BW 2; CA 113; 116;
CANR 48; CLR 19; DLB 33; INT 116;
JRDA; MAICYA; MTCW; SAAS 7;
SATA 40, 78

Thomas, Lewis 1913-1993 .... CLC 35
See also CA 85-88; 143; CANR 38; MTCW

Thomas, Paul
See Mann, (Paul) Thomas

Thomas, Piri 1928-............... CLC 17
See also CA 73-76; HW

Thomas, R(onald) S(tuart)
1913- .... CLC 6, 13, 48; DAB
See also CA 89-92; CAAS 4; CANR 30;
CDBLB 1960 to Present; DAM POET;
DLB 27; MTCW

Thomas, Ross (Elmore) 1926-1995 .. CLC 39
See also CA 33-36R; 150; CANR 22

Thompson, Francis Clegg
See Mencken, H(enry) L(ouis)

Thompson, Francis Joseph
1859-1907 .... TCLC 4
See also CA 104; CDBLB 1890-1914;
DLB 19

Thompson, Hunter S(tockton)
1939- .... CLC 9, 17, 40
See also BEST 89:1; CA 17-20R; CANR 23,
46; DAM POP; MTCW

Thompson, James Myers
See Thompson, Jim (Myers)

Thompson, Jim (Myers)
1906-1977(?) .... CLC 69
See also CA 140

Thompson, Judith .... CLC 39

Thomson, James 1700-1748...... LC 16, 29
See also DAM POET; DLB 95

Thomson, James 1834-1882...... NCLC 18
See also DAM POET; DLB 35

Thoreau, Henry David
1817-1862 ..... NCLC 7, 21; DA; DAB;
DAC; WLC
See also CDALB 1640-1865; DAM MST;
DLB 1

Thornton, Hall
See Silverberg, Robert

Thucydides c. 455B.C.-399B.C.... CMLC 17

Thurber, James (Grover)
1894-1961 .... CLC 5, 11, 25; DA; DAB;
DAC; SSC 1
See also CA 73-76; CANR 17, 39;
CDALB 1929-1941; DAM DRAM, MST,
NOV; DLB 4, 11, 22, 102; MAICYA;
MTCW; SATA 13

Thurman, Wallace (Henry)
1902-1934 .... TCLC 6; BLC
See also BW 1; CA 104; 124; DAM MULT;
DLB 51

Ticheburn, Cheviot
See Ainsworth, William Harrison

Tieck, (Johann) Ludwig
1773-1853 .... NCLC 5, 46
See also DLB 90

Tiger, Derry
See Ellison, Harlan (Jay)

Tilghman, Christopher 1948(?)-..... CLC 65

Tillinghast, Richard (Williford)
1940-...................... CLC 29
See also CA 29-32R; CAAS 23; CANR 26,
51

Timrod, Henry 1828-1867 .... NCLC 25
See also DLB 3

Tindall, Gillian 1938-.............. CLC 7
See also CA 21-24R; CANR 11

Tiptree, James, Jr. .... CLC 48, 50
See also Sheldon, Alice Hastings Bradley
See also DLB 8

Titmarsh, Michael Angelo
See Thackeray, William Makepeace

Tocqueville, Alexis (Charles Henri Maurice
Clerel Comte) 1805-1859..... NCLC 7

Tolkien, J(ohn) R(onald) R(euel)
1892-1973 .... CLC 1, 2, 3, 8, 12, 38;
DA; DAB; DAC; WLC
See also AAYA 10; AITN 1; CA 17-18;
45-48; CANR 36; CAP 2;
CDBLB 1914-1945; DAM MST, NOV,
POP; DLB 15, 160; JRDA; MAICYA;
MTCW; SATA 2, 32; SATA-Obit 24

Toller, Ernst 1893-1939 .... TCLC 10
See also CA 107; DLB 124

Tolson, M. B.
See Tolson, Melvin B(eaunorus)

Tolson, Melvin B(eaunorus)
1898(?)-1966 .... CLC 36; BLC
See also BW 1; CA 124; 89-92;
DAM MULT, POET; DLB 48, 76

Tolstoi, Aleksei Nikolaevich
See Tolstoy, Alexey Nikolaevich

Tolstoy, Alexey Nikolaevich
1882-1945 .... TCLC 18
See also CA 107

Tolstoy, Count Leo
See Tolstoy, Leo (Nikolaevich)

Tolstoy, Leo (Nikolaevich)
1828-1910 ...... TCLC 4, 11, 17, 28, 44;
DA; DAB; DAC; SSC 9; WLC
See also CA 104; 123; DAM MST, NOV;
SATA 26

Tomasi di Lampedusa, Giuseppe 1896-1957
See Lampedusa, Giuseppe (Tomasi) di
See also CA 111

Vesaas, Tarjei 1897-1970......... **CLC 48**
See also CA 29-32R

Vialis, Gaston
See Simenon, Georges (Jacques Christian)

Vian, Boris 1920-1959 .... **TCLC 9**
See also CA 106; DLB 72

Viaud, (Louis Marie) Julien 1850-1923
See Loti, Pierre
See also CA 107

Vicar, Henry
See Felsen, Henry Gregor

Vicker, Angus
See Felsen, Henry Gregor

Vidal, Gore
1925- ..... **CLC 2, 4, 6, 8, 10, 22, 33, 72**
See also AITN 1; BEST 90:2; CA 5-8R;
CANR 13, 45; DAM NOV, POP; DLB 6,
152; INT CANR-13; MTCW

Viereck, Peter (Robert Edwin)
1916-....................... **CLC 4**
See also CA 1-4R; CANR 1, 47; DLB 5

Vigny, Alfred (Victor) de
1797-1863 .... **NCLC 7**
See also DAM POET; DLB 119

Vilakazi, Benedict Wallet
1906-1947 .... **TCLC 37**

Villiers de l'Isle Adam, Jean Marie Mathias
Philippe Auguste Comte
1838-1889 .... **NCLC 3; SSC 14**
See also DLB 123

Villon, Francois 1431-1463(?) .... **PC 13**

Vinci, Leonardo da 1452-1519...... **LC 12**

Vine, Barbara .... **CLC 50**
See also Rendell, Ruth (Barbara)
See also BEST 90:4

Vinge, Joan D(ennison)
1948-............... **CLC 30**
See also CA 93-96; SATA 36

Violis, G.
See Simenon, Georges (Jacques Christian)

Visconti, Luchino 1906-1976...... **CLC 16**
See also CA 81-84; 65-68; CANR 39

Vittorini, Elio 1908-1966..... **CLC 6, 9, 14**
See also CA 133; 25-28R

Vizinczey, Stephen 1933-......... **CLC 40**
See also CA 128; INT 128

Vliet, R(ussell) G(ordon)
1929-1984 .... **CLC 22**
See also CA 37-40R; 112; CANR 18

Vogau, Boris Andreyevich 1894-1937(?)
See Pilnyak, Boris
See also CA 123

Vogel, Paula A(nne) 1951-......... **CLC 76**
See also CA 108

Voight, Ellen Bryant 1943-........ **CLC 54**
See also CA 69-72; CANR 11, 29; DLB 120

Voigt, Cynthia 1942- .... **CLC 30**
See also AAYA 3; CA 106; CANR 18, 37,
40; CLR 13; INT CANR-18; JRDA;
MAICYA; SATA 48, 79; SATA-Brief 33

Voinovich, Vladimir (Nikolaevich)
1932-.................... **CLC 10, 49**
See also CA 81-84; CAAS 12; CANR 33;
MTCW

Vollmann, William T. 1959-........ **CLC 89**
See also CA 134; DAM NOV, POP

Voloshinov, V. N.
See Bakhtin, Mikhail Mikhailovich

Voltaire
1694-1778 ..... **LC 14; DA; DAB; DAC;
SSC 12; WLC**
See also DAM DRAM, MST

von Daeniken, Erich 1935- .... **CLC 30**
See also AITN 1; CA 37-40R; CANR 17,
44

von Daniken, Erich
See von Daeniken, Erich

von Heidenstam, (Carl Gustaf) Verner
See Heidenstam, (Carl Gustaf) Verner von

von Heyse, Paul (Johann Ludwig)
See Heyse, Paul (Johann Ludwig von)

von Hofmannsthal, Hugo
See Hofmannsthal, Hugo von

von Horvath, Odon
See Horvath, Oedoen von

von Horvath, Oedoen
See Horvath, Oedoen von

von Liliencron, (Friedrich Adolf Axel) Detlev
See Liliencron, (Friedrich Adolf Axel)
Detlev von

Vonnegut, Kurt, Jr.
1922- ...... **CLC 1, 2, 3, 4, 5, 8, 12, 22,
40, 60; DA; DAB; DAC; SSC 8; WLC**
See also AAYA 6; AITN 1; BEST 90:4;
CA 1-4R; CANR 1, 25, 49;
CDALB 1968-1988; DAM MST, NOV,
POP; DLB 2, 8, 152; DLBD 3; DLBY 80;
MTCW

Von Rachen, Kurt
See Hubbard, L(afayette) Ron(ald)

von Rezzori (d'Arezzo), Gregor
See Rezzori (d'Arezzo), Gregor von

von Sternberg, Josef
See Sternberg, Josef von

Vorster, Gordon 1924-............ **CLC 34**
See also CA 133

Vosce, Trudie
See Ozick, Cynthia

Voznesensky, Andrei (Andreievich)
1933-................. **CLC 1, 15, 57**
See also CA 89-92; CANR 37;
DAM POET; MTCW

Waddington, Miriam 1917-........ **CLC 28**
See also CA 21-24R; CANR 12, 30;
DLB 68

Wagman, Fredrica 1937-.......... **CLC 7**
See also CA 97-100; INT 97-100

Wagner, Richard 1813-1883....... **NCLC 9**
See also DLB 129

Wagner-Martin, Linda 1936-....... **CLC 50**

Wagoner, David (Russell)
1926-................... **CLC 3, 5, 15**
See also CA 1-4R; CAAS 3; CANR 2;
DLB 5; SATA 14

Wah, Fred(erick James) 1939-...... **CLC 44**
See also CA 107; 141; DLB 60

Wahloo, Per 1926-1975 .... **CLC 7**
See also CA 61-64

Wahloo, Peter
See Wahloo, Per

Wain, John (Barrington)
1925-1994 .... **CLC 2, 11, 15, 46**
See also CA 5-8R; 145; CAAS 4; CANR 23;
CDBLB 1960 to Present; DLB 15, 27,
139, 155; MTCW

Wajda, Andrzej 1926-............. **CLC 16**
See also CA 102

Wakefield, Dan 1932-............. **CLC 7**
See also CA 21-24R; CAAS 7

Wakoski, Diane
1937-..... **CLC 2, 4, 7, 9, 11, 40; PC 15**
See also CA 13-16R; CAAS 1; CANR 9;
DAM POET; DLB 5; INT CANR-9

Wakoski-Sherbell, Diane
See Wakoski, Diane

Walcott, Derek (Alton)
1930- .... **CLC 2, 4, 9, 14, 25, 42, 67, 76;
BLC; DAB; DAC**
See also BW 2; CA 89-92; CANR 26, 47;
DAM MST, MULT, POET; DLB 117;
DLBY 81; MTCW

Waldman, Anne 1945- .... **CLC 7**
See also CA 37-40R; CAAS 17; CANR 34;
DLB 16

Waldo, E. Hunter
See Sturgeon, Theodore (Hamilton)

Waldo, Edward Hamilton
See Sturgeon, Theodore (Hamilton)

Walker, Alice (Malsenior)
1944-....... **CLC 5, 6, 9, 19, 27, 46, 58;
BLC; DA; DAB; DAC; SSC 5**
See also AAYA 3; BEST 89:4; BW 2;
CA 37-40R; CANR 9, 27, 49;
CDALB 1968-1988; DAM MST, MULT,
NOV, POET, POP; DLB 6, 33, 143;
INT CANR-27; MTCW; SATA 31

Walker, David Harry 1911-1992.... **CLC 14**
See also CA 1-4R; 137; CANR 1; SATA 8;
SATA-Obit 71

Walker, Edward Joseph 1934-
See Walker, Ted
See also CA 21-24R; CANR 12, 28

Walker, George F.
1947-......... **CLC 44, 61; DAB; DAC**
See also CA 103; CANR 21, 43;
DAM MST; DLB 60

Walker, Joseph A. 1935-.......... **CLC 19**
See also BW 1; CA 89-92; CANR 26;
DAM DRAM, MST; DLB 38

Walker, Margaret (Abigail)
1915-................. **CLC 1, 6; BLC**
See also BW 2; CA 73-76; CANR 26;
DAM MULT; DLB 76, 152; MTCW

Walker, Ted..................... **CLC 13**
See also Walker, Edward Joseph
See also DLB 40

Wallace, David Foster 1962-....... **CLC 50**
See also CA 132

Wallace, Dexter
See Masters, Edgar Lee

Wallace, (Richard Horatio) Edgar
1875-1932 .... **TCLC 57**
See also CA 115; DLB 70

Wallace, Irving 1916-1990 . . . . . . CLC **7, 13**
See also AITN 1; CA 1-4R; 132; CAAS 1;
CANR 1, 27; DAM NOV, POP;
INT CANR-27; MTCW

Wallant, Edward Lewis
1926-1962 . . . . CLC **5, 10**
See also CA 1-4R; CANR 22; DLB 2, 28,
143; MTCW

Walley, Byron
See Card, Orson Scott

Walpole, Horace 1717-1797 . . . . LC **2**
See also DLB 39, 104

Walpole, Hugh (Seymour)
1884-1941 . . . . TCLC **5**
See also CA 104; DLB 34

Walser, Martin 1927- . . . . CLC **27**
See also CA 57-60; CANR 8, 46; DLB 75,
124

Walser, Robert
1878-1956 . . . . TCLC **18**; SSC **20**
See also CA 118; DLB 66

Walsh, Jill Paton . . . . CLC **35**
See also Paton Walsh, Gillian
See also AAYA 11; CLR 2; DLB 161;
SAAS 3

Walter, Villiam Christian
See Andersen, Hans Christian

Wambaugh, Joseph (Aloysius, Jr.)
1937- . . . . CLC **3, 18**
See also AITN 1; BEST 89:3; CA 33-36R;
CANR 42; DAM NOV, POP; DLB 6;
DLBY 83; MTCW

Ward, Arthur Henry Sarsfield 1883-1959
See Rohmer, Sax
See also CA 108

Ward, Douglas Turner 1930- . . . . CLC **19**
See also BW 1; CA 81-84; CANR 27;
DLB 7, 38

Ward, Mary Augusta
See Ward, Mrs. Humphry

Ward, Mrs. Humphry
1851-1920 . . . . TCLC **55**
See also DLB 18

Ward, Peter
See Faust, Frederick (Schiller)

Warhol, Andy 1928(?)-1987 . . . . CLC **20**
See also AAYA 12; BEST 89:4; CA 89-92;
121; CANR 34

Warner, Francis (Robert le Plastrier)
1937- . . . . CLC **14**
See also CA 53-56; CANR 11

Warner, Marina 1946- . . . . CLC **59**
See also CA 65-68; CANR 21

Warner, Rex (Ernest) 1905-1986 . . . . CLC **45**
See also CA 89-92; 119; DLB 15

Warner, Susan (Bogert)
1819-1885 . . . . NCLC **31**
See also DLB 3, 42

Warner, Sylvia (Constance) Ashton
See Ashton-Warner, Sylvia (Constance)

Warner, Sylvia Townsend
1893-1978 . . . . CLC **7, 19**
See also CA 61-64; 77-80; CANR 16;
DLB 34, 139; MTCW

Warren, Mercy Otis 1728-1814 . . . NCLC **13**
See also DLB 31

Warren, Robert Penn
1905-1989 . . . . CLC **1, 4, 6, 8, 10, 13, 18,
39, 53, 59; DA; DAB; DAC; SSC 4; WLC**
See also AITN 1; CA 13-16R; 129;
CANR 10, 47; CDALB 1968-1988;
DAM MST, NOV, POET; DLB 2, 48,
152; DLBY 80, 89; INT CANR-10;
MTCW; SATA 46; SATA-Obit 63

Warshofsky, Isaac
See Singer, Isaac Bashevis

Warton, Thomas 1728-1790 . . . . LC **15**
See also DAM POET; DLB 104, 109

Waruk, Kona
See Harris, (Theodore) Wilson

Warung, Price 1855-1911 . . . . TCLC **45**

Warwick, Jarvis
See Garner, Hugh

Washington, Alex
See Harris, Mark

Washington, Booker T(aliaferro)
1856-1915 . . . . TCLC **10**; BLC
See also BW 1; CA 114; 125; DAM MULT;
SATA 28

Washington, George 1732-1799 . . . . . . LC **25**
See also DLB 31

Wassermann, (Karl) Jakob
1873-1934 . . . . TCLC **6**
See also CA 104; DLB 66

Wasserstein, Wendy
1950- . . . . CLC **32, 59, 90; DC 4**
See also CA 121; 129; CABS 3;
DAM DRAM; INT 129

Waterhouse, Keith (Spencer)
1929- . . . . CLC **47**
See also CA 5-8R; CANR 38; DLB 13, 15;
MTCW

Waters, Frank (Joseph)
1902-1995 . . . . CLC **88**
See also CA 5-8R; 149; CAAS 13; CANR 3,
18; DLBY 86

Waters, Roger 1944- . . . . CLC **35**

Watkins, Frances Ellen
See Harper, Frances Ellen Watkins

Watkins, Gerrold
See Malzberg, Barry N(athaniel)

Watkins, Paul 1964- . . . . CLC **55**
See also CA 132

Watkins, Vernon Phillips
1906-1967 . . . . CLC **43**
See also CA 9-10; 25-28R; CAP 1; DLB 20

Watson, Irving S.
See Mencken, H(enry) L(ouis)

Watson, John H.
See Farmer, Philip Jose

Watson, Richard F.
See Silverberg, Robert

Waugh, Auberon (Alexander) 1939- . . CLC **7**
See also CA 45-48; CANR 6, 22; DLB 14

Waugh, Evelyn (Arthur St. John)
1903-1966 . . . . . . CLC **1, 3, 8, 13, 19, 27,
44; DA; DAB; DAC; WLC**
See also CA 85-88; 25-28R; CANR 22;
CDBLB 1914-1945; DAM MST, NOV,
POP; DLB 15, 162; MTCW

Waugh, Harriet 1944- . . . . CLC **6**
See also CA 85-88; CANR 22

Ways, C. R.
See Blount, Roy (Alton), Jr.

Waystaff, Simon
See Swift, Jonathan

Webb, (Martha) Beatrice (Potter)
1858-1943 . . . . TCLC **22**
See also Potter, Beatrice
See also CA 117

Webb, Charles (Richard) 1939- . . . . . . CLC **7**
See also CA 25-28R

Webb, James H(enry), Jr. 1946- . . . . CLC **22**
See also CA 81-84

Webb, Mary (Gladys Meredith)
1881-1927 . . . . TCLC **24**
See also CA 123; DLB 34

Webb, Mrs. Sidney
See Webb, (Martha) Beatrice (Potter)

Webb, Phyllis 1927- . . . . CLC **18**
See also CA 104; CANR 23; DLB 53

Webb, Sidney (James)
1859-1947 . . . . TCLC **22**
See also CA 117

Webber, Andrew Lloyd . . . . CLC **21**
See also Lloyd Webber, Andrew

Weber, Lenora Mattingly
1895-1971 . . . . CLC **12**
See also CA 19-20; 29-32R; CAP 1;
SATA 2; SATA-Obit 26

Webster, John 1579(?)-1634(?) . . . . DC **2**
See also CDBLB Before 1660; DA; DAB;
DAC; DAM DRAM, MST; DLB 58;
WLC

Webster, Noah 1758-1843 . . . . NCLC **30**

Wedekind, (Benjamin) Frank(lin)
1864-1918 . . . . TCLC **7**
See also CA 104; DAM DRAM; DLB 118

Weidman, Jerome 1913- . . . . CLC **7**
See also AITN 2; CA 1-4R; CANR 1;
DLB 28

Weil, Simone (Adolphine)
1909-1943 . . . . TCLC **23**
See also CA 117

Weinstein, Nathan
See West, Nathanael

Weinstein, Nathan von Wallenstein
See West, Nathanael

Weir, Peter (Lindsay) 1944- . . . . CLC **20**
See also CA 113; 123

Weiss, Peter (Ulrich)
1916-1982 . . . . CLC **3, 15, 51**
See also CA 45-48; 106; CANR 3;
DAM DRAM; DLB 69, 124

Weiss, Theodore (Russell)
1916- . . . . CLC **3, 8, 14**
See also CA 9-12R; CAAS 2; CANR 46;
DLB 5

Welch, (Maurice) Denton
1915-1948 . . . . **TCLC 22**
See also CA 121; 148

Welch, James 1940- . . . . **CLC 6, 14, 52**
See also CA 85-88; CANR 42;
DAM MULT, POP; NNAL

Weldon, Fay
1933- . . . . **CLC 6, 9, 11, 19, 36, 59**
See also CA 21-24R; CANR 16, 46;
CDBLB 1960 to Present; DAM POP;
DLB 14; INT CANR-16; MTCW

Wellek, Rene 1903-1995 . . . . **CLC 28**
See also CA 5-8R; 150; CAAS 7; CANR 8;
DLB 63; INT CANR-8

Weller, Michael 1942- . . . . **CLC 10, 53**
See also CA 85-88

Weller, Paul 1958- . . . . **CLC 26**

Wellershoff, Dieter 1925- . . . . **CLC 46**
See also CA 89-92; CANR 16, 37

Welles, (George) Orson
1915-1985 . . . . **CLC 20, 80**
See also CA 93-96; 117

Wellman, Mac 1945- . . . . **CLC 65**

Wellman, Manly Wade 1903-1986 . . **CLC 49**
See also CA 1-4R; 118; CANR 6, 16, 44;
SATA 6; SATA-Obit 47

Wells, Carolyn 1869(?)-1942 . . . . . . **TCLC 35**
See also CA 113; DLB 11

Wells, H(erbert) G(eorge)
1866-1946 . . . . **TCLC 6, 12, 19; DA;**
DAB; DAC; SSC 6; WLC
See also CA 110; 121; CDBLB 1914-1945;
DAM MST, NOV; DLB 34, 70, 156;
MTCW; SATA 20

Wells, Rosemary 1943- . . . . **CLC 12**
See also AAYA 13; CA 85-88; CANR 48;
CLR 16; MAICYA; SAAS 1; SATA 18,
69

Welty, Eudora
1909- . . . . . . **CLC 1, 2, 5, 14, 22, 33; DA;**
DAB; DAC; SSC 1; WLC
See also CA 9-12R; CABS 1; CANR 32;
CDALB 1941-1968; DAM MST, NOV;
DLB 2, 102, 143; DLBD 12; DLBY 87;
MTCW

Wen I-to 1899-1946 . . . . **TCLC 28**

Wentworth, Robert
See Hamilton, Edmond

Werfel, Franz (V.) 1890-1945 . . . . . . **TCLC 8**
See also CA 104; DLB 81, 124

Wergeland, Henrik Arnold
1808-1845 . . . . **NCLC 5**

Wersba, Barbara 1932- . . . . **CLC 30**
See also AAYA 2; CA 29-32R; CANR 16,
38; CLR 3; DLB 52; JRDA; MAICYA;
SAAS 2; SATA 1, 58

Wertmueller, Lina 1928- . . . . **CLC 16**
See also CA 97-100; CANR 39

Wescott, Glenway 1901-1987 . . . . **CLC 13**
See also CA 13-16R; 121; CANR 23;
DLB 4, 9, 102

Wesker, Arnold 1932- . . **CLC 3, 5, 42; DAB**
See also CA 1-4R; CAAS 7; CANR 1, 33;
CDBLB 1960 to Present; DAM DRAM;
DLB 13; MTCW

Wesley, Richard (Errol) 1945- . . . . **CLC 7**
See also BW 1; CA 57-60; CANR 27;
DLB 38

Wessel, Johan Herman 1742-1785 . . . . **LC 7**

West, Anthony (Panther)
1914-1987 . . . . **CLC 50**
See also CA 45-48; 124; CANR 3, 19;
DLB 15

West, C. P.
See Wodehouse, P(elham) G(renville)

West, (Mary) Jessamyn
1902-1984 . . . . **CLC 7, 17**
See also CA 9-12R; 112; CANR 27; DLB 6;
DLBY 84; MTCW; SATA-Obit 37

West, Morris L(anglo) 1916- . . . . . **CLC 6, 33**
See also CA 5-8R; CANR 24, 49; MTCW

West, Nathanael
1903-1940 . . . . . **TCLC 1, 14, 44; SSC 16**
See also CA 104; 125; CDALB 1929-1941;
DLB 4, 9, 28; MTCW

West, Owen
See Koontz, Dean R(ay)

West, Paul 1930- . . . . **CLC 7, 14**
See also CA 13-16R; CAAS 7; CANR 22;
DLB 14; INT CANR-22

West, Rebecca 1892-1983 . . **CLC 7, 9, 31, 50**
See also CA 5-8R; 109; CANR 19; DLB 36;
DLBY 83; MTCW

Westall, Robert (Atkinson)
1929-1993 . . . . **CLC 17**
See also AAYA 12; CA 69-72; 141;
CANR 18; CLR 13; JRDA; MAICYA;
SAAS 2; SATA 23, 69; SATA-Obit 75

Westlake, Donald E(dwin)
1933- . . . . **CLC 7, 33**
See also CA 17-20R; CAAS 13; CANR 16,
44; DAM POP; INT CANR-16

Westmacott, Mary
See Christie, Agatha (Mary Clarissa)

Weston, Allen
See Norton, Andre

Wetcheek, J. L.
See Feuchtwanger, Lion

Wetering, Janwillem van de
See van de Wetering, Janwillem

Wetherell, Elizabeth
See Warner, Susan (Bogert)

Whale, James 1889-1957 . . . . **TCLC 63**

Whalen, Philip 1923- . . . . **CLC 6, 29**
See also CA 9-12R; CANR 5, 39; DLB 16

Wharton, Edith (Newbold Jones)
1862-1937 . . . . . . **TCLC 3, 9, 27, 53; DA;**
DAB; DAC; SSC 6; WLC
See also CA 104; 132; CDALB 1865-1917;
DAM MST, NOV; DLB 4, 9, 12, 78;
DLBD 13; MTCW

Wharton, James
See Mencken, H(enry) L(ouis)

Wharton, William (a pseudonym)
. . . . **CLC 18, 37**
See also CA 93-96; DLBY 80; INT 93-96

Wheatley (Peters), Phillis
1754(?)-1784 . . . . **LC 3; BLC; DA; DAC;**
PC 3; WLC
See also CDALB 1640-1865; DAM MST,
MULT, POET; DLB 31, 50

Wheelock, John Hall 1886-1978 . . . . **CLC 14**
See also CA 13-16R; 77-80; CANR 14;
DLB 45

White, E(lwyn) B(rooks)
1899-1985 . . . . **CLC 10, 34, 39**
See also AITN 2; CA 13-16R; 116;
CANR 16, 37; CLR 1, 21; DAM POP;
DLB 11, 22; MAICYA; MTCW;
SATA 2, 29; SATA-Obit 44

White, Edmund (Valentine III)
1940- . . . . **CLC 27**
See also AAYA 7; CA 45-48; CANR 3, 19,
36; DAM POP; MTCW

White, Patrick (Victor Martindale)
1912-1990 . . **CLC 3, 4, 5, 7, 9, 18, 65, 69**
See also CA 81-84; 132; CANR 43; MTCW

White, Phyllis Dorothy James 1920-
See James, P. D.
See also CA 21-24R; CANR 17, 43;
DAM POP; MTCW

White, T(erence) H(anbury)
1906-1964 . . . . **CLC 30**
See also CA 73-76; CANR 37; DLB 160;
JRDA; MAICYA; SATA 12

White, Terence de Vere
1912-1994 . . . . **CLC 49**
See also CA 49-52; 145; CANR 3

White, Walter F(rancis)
1893-1955 . . . . **TCLC 15**
See also White, Walter
See also BW 1; CA 115; 124; DLB 51

White, William Hale 1831-1913
See Rutherford, Mark
See also CA 121

Whitehead, E(dward) A(nthony)
1933- . . . . **CLC 5**
See also CA 65-68

Whitemore, Hugh (John) 1936- . . . . . **CLC 37**
See also CA 132; INT 132

Whitman, Sarah Helen (Power)
1803-1878 . . . . **NCLC 19**
See also DLB 1

Whitman, Walt(er)
1819-1892 . . . . . **NCLC 4, 31; DA; DAB;**
DAC; PC 3; WLC
See also CDALB 1640-1865; DAM MST,
POET; DLB 3, 64; SATA 20

Whitney, Phyllis A(yame) 1903- . . . . **CLC 42**
See also AITN 2; BEST 90:3; CA 1-4R;
CANR 3, 25, 38; DAM POP; JRDA;
MAICYA; SATA 1, 30

Whittemore, (Edward) Reed (Jr.)
1919- . . . . **CLC 4**
See also CA 9-12R; CAAS 8; CANR 4;
DLB 5

Whittier, John Greenleaf
1807-1892 . . . . **NCLC 8**
See also CDALB 1640-1865; DAM POET;
DLB 1

Whittlebot, Hernia
See Coward, Noel (Peirce)

Wicker, Thomas Grey   1926-
See Wicker, Tom
See also CA 65-68; CANR 21, 46

Wicker, Tom . . . . **CLC 7**
See also Wicker, Thomas Grey

Wideman, John Edgar
1941- . . . . **CLC 5, 34, 36, 67; BLC**
See also BW 2; CA 85-88; CANR 14, 42;
DAM MULT; DLB 33, 143

Wiebe, Rudy (Henry)
1934- . . . . **CLC 6, 11, 14; DAC**
See also CA 37-40R; CANR 42;
DAM MST; DLB 60

Wieland, Christoph Martin
1733-1813 . . . . **NCLC 17**
See also DLB 97

Wiene, Robert   1881-1938 . . . . **TCLC 56**

Wieners, John   1934- . . . . **CLC 7**
See also CA 13-16R; DLB 16

Wiesel, Elie(zer)
1928- . . . . . . **CLC 3, 5, 11, 37; DA; DAB; DAC**
See also AAYA 7; AITN 1; CA 5-8R;
CAAS 4; CANR 8, 40; DAM MST,
NOV; DLB 83; DLBY 87; INT CANR-8;
MTCW; SATA 56

Wiggins, Marianne   1947- . . . . **CLC 57**
See also BEST 89:3; CA 130

Wight, James Alfred   1916-
See Herriot, James
See also CA 77-80; SATA 55;
SATA-Brief 44

Wilbur, Richard (Purdy)
1921- . . . **CLC 3, 6, 9, 14, 53; DA; DAB; DAC**
See also CA 1-4R; CABS 2; CANR 2, 29;
DAM MST, POET; DLB 5;
INT CANR-29; MTCW; SATA 9

Wild, Peter   1940- . . . . **CLC 14**
See also CA 37-40R; DLB 5

Wilde, Oscar (Fingal O'Flahertie Wills)
1854(?)-1900 . . . . **TCLC 1, 8, 23, 41; DA; DAB; DAC; SSC 11; WLC**
See also CA 104; 119; CDBLB 1890-1914;
DAM DRAM, MST, NOV; DLB 10, 19,
34, 57, 141, 156; SATA 24

Wilder, Billy . . . . **CLC 20**
See also Wilder, Samuel
See also DLB 26

Wilder, Samuel   1906-
See Wilder, Billy
See also CA 89-92

Wilder, Thornton (Niven)
1897-1975 . . . . . . **CLC 1, 5, 6, 10, 15, 35, 82; DA; DAB; DAC; DC 1; WLC**
See also AITN 2; CA 13-16R; 61-64;
CANR 40; DAM DRAM, MST, NOV;
DLB 4, 7, 9; MTCW

Wilding, Michael   1942- . . . . **CLC 73**
See also CA 104; CANR 24, 49

Wiley, Richard   1944- . . . . **CLC 44**
See also CA 121; 129

Wilhelm, Kate . . . . **CLC 7**
See also Wilhelm, Katie Gertrude
See also CAAS 5; DLB 8; INT CANR-17

Wilhelm, Katie Gertrude   1928-
See Wilhelm, Kate
See also CA 37-40R; CANR 17, 36; MTCW

Wilkins, Mary
See Freeman, Mary Eleanor Wilkins

Willard, Nancy   1936- . . . . **CLC 7, 37**
See also CA 89-92; CANR 10, 39; CLR 5;
DLB 5, 52; MAICYA; MTCW;
SATA 37, 71; SATA-Brief 30

Williams, C(harles) K(enneth)
1936- . . . . **CLC 33, 56**
See also CA 37-40R; DAM POET; DLB 5

Williams, Charles
See Collier, James L(incoln)

Williams, Charles (Walter Stansby)
1886-1945 . . . . **TCLC 1, 11**
See also CA 104; DLB 100, 153

Williams, (George) Emlyn
1905-1987 . . . . **CLC 15**
See also CA 104; 123; CANR 36;
DAM DRAM; DLB 10, 77; MTCW

Williams, Hugo   1942- . . . . **CLC 42**
See also CA 17-20R; CANR 45; DLB 40

Williams, J. Walker
See Wodehouse, P(elham) G(renville)

Williams, John A(lfred)
1925- . . . . **CLC 5, 13; BLC**
See also BW 2; CA 53-56; CAAS 3;
CANR 6, 26, 51; DAM MULT; DLB 2,
33; INT CANR-6

Williams, Jonathan (Chamberlain)
1929- . . . . **CLC 13**
See also CA 9-12R; CAAS 12; CANR 8;
DLB 5

Williams, Joy   1944- . . . . **CLC 31**
See also CA 41-44R; CANR 22, 48

Williams, Norman   1952- . . . . **CLC 39**
See also CA 118

Williams, Sherley Anne
1944- . . . . **CLC 89; BLC**
See also BW 2; CA 73-76; CANR 25;
DAM MULT, POET; DLB 41;
INT CANR-25; SATA 78

Williams, Shirley
See Williams, Sherley Anne

Williams, Tennessee
1911-1983 . . . . . **CLC 1, 2, 5, 7, 8, 11, 15, 19, 30, 39, 45, 71; DA; DAB; DAC; DC 4; WLC**
See also AITN 1, 2; CA 5-8R; 108;
CABS 3; CANR 31; CDALB 1941-1968;
DAM DRAM, MST; DLB 7; DLBD 4;
DLBY 83; MTCW

Williams, Thomas (Alonzo)
1926-1990 . . . . **CLC 14**
See also CA 1-4R; 132; CANR 2

Williams, William C.
See Williams, William Carlos

Williams, William Carlos
1883-1963 . . . . **CLC 1, 2, 5, 9, 13, 22, 42, 67; DA; DAB; DAC; PC 7**
See also CA 89-92; CANR 34;
CDALB 1917-1929; DAM MST, POET;
DLB 4, 16, 54, 86; MTCW

Williamson, David (Keith)   1942- . . . . **CLC 56**
See also CA 103; CANR 41

Williamson, Ellen Douglas   1905-1984
See Douglas, Ellen
See also CA 17-20R; 114; CANR 39

Williamson, Jack . . . . **CLC 29**
See also Williamson, John Stewart
See also CAAS 8; DLB 8

Williamson, John Stewart   1908-
See Williamson, Jack
See also CA 17-20R; CANR 23

Willie, Frederick
See Lovecraft, H(oward) P(hillips)

Willingham, Calder (Baynard, Jr.)
1922-1995 . . . . **CLC 5, 51**
See also CA 5-8R; 147; CANR 3; DLB 2,
44; MTCW

Willis, Charles
See Clarke, Arthur C(harles)

Willy
See Colette, (Sidonie-Gabrielle)

Willy, Colette
See Colette, (Sidonie-Gabrielle)

Wilson, A(ndrew) N(orman)   1950- . . **CLC 33**
See also CA 112; 122; DLB 14, 155

Wilson, Angus (Frank Johnstone)
1913-1991 . . **CLC 2, 3, 5, 25, 34; SSC 21**
See also CA 5-8R; 134; CANR 21; DLB 15,
139, 155; MTCW

Wilson, August
1945- . . . . **CLC 39, 50, 63; BLC; DA; DAB; DAC; DC 2**
See also AAYA 16; BW 2; CA 115; 122;
CANR 42; DAM DRAM, MST, MULT;
MTCW

Wilson, Brian   1942- . . . . **CLC 12**

Wilson, Colin   1931- . . . . **CLC 3, 14**
See also CA 1-4R; CAAS 5; CANR 1, 22,
33; DLB 14; MTCW

Wilson, Dirk
See Pohl, Frederik

Wilson, Edmund
1895-1972 . . . . **CLC 1, 2, 3, 8, 24**
See also CA 1-4R; 37-40R; CANR 1, 46;
DLB 63; MTCW

Wilson, Ethel Davis (Bryant)
1888(?)-1980 . . . . **CLC 13; DAC**
See also CA 102; DAM POET; DLB 68;
MTCW

Wilson, John   1785-1854 . . . . **NCLC 5**

Wilson, John (Anthony) Burgess   1917-1993
See Burgess, Anthony
See also CA 1-4R; 143; CANR 2, 46; DAC;
DAM NOV; MTCW

Wilson, Lanford   1937- . . . . **CLC 7, 14, 36**
See also CA 17-20R; CABS 3; CANR 45;
DAM DRAM; DLB 7

Wilson, Robert M.   1944- . . . . **CLC 7, 9**
See also CA 49-52; CANR 2, 41; MTCW

Wilson, Robert McLiam   1964- . . . . . **CLC 59**
See also CA 132

Wilson, Sloan   1920- . . . . **CLC 32**
See also CA 1-4R; CANR 1, 44

Wilson, Snoo   1948- . . . . **CLC 33**
See also CA 69-72

Wilson, William S(mith)   1932- . . . . . **CLC 49**
See also CA 81-84

Winchilsea, Anne (Kingsmill) Finch Counte
　1661-1720 . . . . LC **3**

Windham, Basil
　See Wodehouse, P(elham) G(renville)

Wingrove, David (John)　1954- . . . . . . CLC **68**
　See also CA 133

Winters, Janet Lewis . . . . CLC **41**
　See also Lewis, Janet
　See also DLBY 87

Winters, (Arthur) Yvor
　1900-1968 . . . . CLC **4, 8, 32**
　See also CA 11-12; 25-28R; CAP 1;
　DLB 48; MTCW

Winterson, Jeanette　1959- . . . . CLC **64**
　See also CA 136; DAM POP

Winthrop, John　1588-1649 . . . . LC **31**
　See also DLB 24, 30

Wiseman, Frederick　1930- . . . . CLC **20**

Wister, Owen　1860-1938 . . . . TCLC **21**
　See also CA 108; DLB 9, 78; SATA 62

Witkacy
　See Witkiewicz, Stanislaw Ignacy

Witkiewicz, Stanislaw Ignacy
　1885-1939 . . . . TCLC **8**
　See also CA 105

Wittgenstein, Ludwig (Josef Johann)
　1889-1951 . . . . TCLC **59**
　See also CA 113

Wittig, Monique　1935(?)- . . . . CLC **22**
　See also CA 116; 135; DLB 83

Wittlin, Jozef　1896-1976 . . . . CLC **25**
　See also CA 49-52; 65-68; CANR 3

Wodehouse, P(elham) G(renville)
　1881-1975 . . . CLC **1, 2, 5, 10, 22; DAB;**
　　　　　　　　　　　　　　　DAC; SSC 2
　See also AITN 2; CA 45-48; 57-60;
　CANR 3, 33; CDBLB 1914-1945;
　DAM NOV; DLB 34, 162; MTCW;
　SATA 22

Woiwode, L.
　See Woiwode, Larry (Alfred)

Woiwode, Larry (Alfred)　1941- . . . CLC **6, 10**
　See also CA 73-76; CANR 16; DLB 6;
　INT CANR-16

Wojciechowska, Maia (Teresa)
　1927- . . . . CLC **26**
　See also AAYA 8; CA 9-12R; CANR 4, 41;
　CLR 1; JRDA; MAICYA; SAAS 1;
　SATA 1, 28, 83

Wolf, Christa　1929- . . . . CLC **14, 29, 58**
　See also CA 85-88; CANR 45; DLB 75;
　MTCW

Wolfe, Gene (Rodman)　1931- . . . . . . CLC **25**
　See also CA 57-60; CAAS 9; CANR 6, 32;
　DAM POP; DLB 8

Wolfe, George C.　1954- . . . . CLC **49**
　See also CA 149

Wolfe, Thomas (Clayton)
　1900-1938 . . . . . TCLC **4, 13, 29, 61; DA;**
　　　　　　　　　　　　　　　　DAB; DAC; WLC
　See also CA 104; 132; CDALB 1929-1941;
　DAM MST, NOV; DLB 9, 102; DLBD 2;
　DLBY 85; MTCW

Wolfe, Thomas Kennerly, Jr.　1931-
　See Wolfe, Tom
　See also CA 13-16R; CANR 9, 33;
　DAM POP; INT CANR-9; MTCW

Wolfe, Tom . . . . CLC **1, 2, 9, 15, 35, 51**
　See also Wolfe, Thomas Kennerly, Jr.
　See also AAYA 8; AITN 2; BEST 89:1;
　DLB 152

Wolff, Geoffrey (Ansell)　1937- . . . . . CLC **41**
　See also CA 29-32R; CANR 29, 43

Wolff, Sonia
　See Levitin, Sonia (Wolff)

Wolff, Tobias (Jonathan Ansell)
　1945- . . . . CLC **39, 64**
　See also AAYA 16; BEST 90:2; CA 114;
　117; CAAS 22; DLB 130; INT 117

Wolfram von Eschenbach
　c. 1170-c. 1220 . . . . CMLC **5**
　See also DLB 138

Wolitzer, Hilma　1930- . . . . CLC **17**
　See also CA 65-68; CANR 18, 40;
　INT CANR-18; SATA 31

Wollstonecraft, Mary　1759-1797 . . . . . . LC **5**
　See also CDBLB 1789-1832; DLB 39, 104,
　158

Wonder, Stevie . . . . CLC **12**
　See also Morris, Steveland Judkins

Wong, Jade Snow　1922- . . . . CLC **17**
　See also CA 109

Woodcott, Keith
　See Brunner, John (Kilian Houston)

Woodruff, Robert W.
　See Mencken, H(enry) L(ouis)

Woolf, (Adeline) Virginia
　1882-1941 . . . . TCLC **1, 5, 20, 43, 56;**
　　　　　　　　　　　DA; DAB; DAC; SSC 7; WLC
　See also CA 104; 130; CDBLB 1914-1945;
　DAM MST, NOV; DLB 36, 100, 162;
　DLBD 10; MTCW

Woollcott, Alexander (Humphreys)
　1887-1943 . . . . TCLC **5**
　See also CA 105; DLB 29

Woolrich, Cornell　1903-1968 . . . . CLC **77**
　See also Hopley-Woolrich, Cornell George

Wordsworth, Dorothy
　1771-1855 . . . . NCLC **25**
　See also DLB 107

Wordsworth, William
　1770-1850 . . . . NCLC **12, 38; DA; DAB;**
　　　　　　　　　　　　　　　DAC; PC 4; WLC
　See also CDBLB 1789-1832; DAM MST,
　POET; DLB 93, 107

Wouk, Herman　1915- . . . . CLC **1, 9, 38**
　See also CA 5-8R; CANR 6, 33;
　DAM NOV, POP; DLBY 82;
　INT CANR-6; MTCW

Wright, Charles (Penzel, Jr.)
　1935- . . . . CLC **6, 13, 28**
　See also CA 29-32R; CAAS 7; CANR 23,
　36; DLBY 82; MTCW

Wright, Charles Stevenson
　1932- . . . . CLC **49; BLC 3**
　See also BW 1; CA 9-12R; CANR 26;
　DAM MULT, POET; DLB 33

Wright, Jack R.
　See Harris, Mark

Wright, James (Arlington)
　1927-1980 . . . . CLC **3, 5, 10, 28**
　See also AITN 2; CA 49-52; 97-100;
　CANR 4, 34; DAM POET; DLB 5;
　MTCW

Wright, Judith (Arandell)
　1915- . . . . CLC **11, 53; PC 14**
　See also CA 13-16R; CANR 31; MTCW;
　SATA 14

Wright, L(aurali) R.　1939- . . . . CLC **44**
　See also CA 138

Wright, Richard (Nathaniel)
　1908-1960 . . . . CLC **1, 3, 4, 9, 14, 21, 48,**
　　　74; BLC; DA; DAB; DAC; SSC 2; WLC
　See also AAYA 5; BW 1; CA 108;
　CDALB 1929-1941; DAM MST, MULT,
　NOV; DLB 76, 102; DLBD 2; MTCW

Wright, Richard B(ruce)　1937- . . . . . . CLC **6**
　See also CA 85-88; DLB 53

Wright, Rick　1945- . . . . CLC **35**

Wright, Rowland
　See Wells, Carolyn

Wright, Stephen Caldwell　1946- . . . . CLC **33**
　See also BW 2

Wright, Willard Huntington　1888-1939
　See Van Dine, S. S.
　See also CA 115

Wright, William　1930- . . . . CLC **44**
　See also CA 53-56; CANR 7, 23

Wroth, LadyMary　1587-1653(?) . . . . . LC **30**
　See also DLB 121

Wu Ch'eng-en　1500(?)-1582(?) . . . . LC **7**

Wu Ching-tzu　1701-1754 . . . . LC **2**

Wurlitzer, Rudolph　1938(?)- . . . CLC **2, 4, 15**
　See also CA 85 88

Wycherley, William　1641-1715 . . . . LC **8, 21**
　See also CDBLB 1660-1789; DAM DRAM;
　DLB 80

Wylie, Elinor (Morton Hoyt)
　1885-1928 . . . . TCLC **8**
　See also CA 105; DLB 9, 45

Wylie, Philip (Gordon)　1902-1971 . . . CLC **43**
　See also CA 21-22; 33-36R; CAP 2; DLB 9

Wyndham, John . . . . CLC **19**
　See also Harris, John (Wyndham Parkes
　Lucas) Beynon

Wyss, Johann David Von
　1743-1818 . . . . NCLC **10**
　See also JRDA; MAICYA; SATA 29;
　SATA-Brief 27

Xenophon
　c. 430B.C.-c. 354B.C. . . . . CMLC **17**

Yakumo Koizumi
　See Hearn, (Patricio) Lafcadio (Tessima
　Carlos)

Yanez, Jose Donoso
　See Donoso (Yanez), Jose

Yanovsky, Basile S.
　See Yanovsky, V(assily) S(emenovich)

Yanovsky, V(assily) S(emenovich)
　1906-1989 . . . . CLC **2, 18**
　See also CA 97-100; 129

SSC Cumulative Nationality Index

SSC Cumulative Title Index

Title Index

Title Index

Title Index

Title Index

Title Index

Title Index

ISBN 0-7876-0754-1